AA

DAYS OUT
Guide

ENJOY 30% OFF LEISURE BREAKS

Choose from over 50 hotels in locations the length and breadth of the country. Whether you are planning a short romantic interlude, a family break or a few days shopping you are sure to find a Corus hotel to suit you. Corus hotels are fresh, bright and stylish with an enthusiastic approach to service and a commitment to getting the simple things right every time.

To book please call us on **0870 609 6180** to make your reservation quoting The AA Pub Guide. For a copy of our Escapes brochure please call **0870 2400 111** or visit **www.corushotels.com**

CREDITS

Produced by AA Publishing
© Automobile Association Developments Limited 2005 All rights reserved. No part of this publication may be reproduced, stored in a retrieval system, or transmitted in any form or by any means – electronic, mechanical, photocopying, recording or otherwise – unless the written permission of the publisher has been given beforehand. This book may not be lent, resold, hired out or otherwise disposed of by way of trade in any form of binding or cover other than that in which it is published, without the prior consent of the publisher. Directory generated by the AA Establishment Database, Information Research, AA Hotel Services The contents of this book are believed correct at the time of printing. Nevertheless, the Publisher cannot be held responsible for any errors or omissions, or for changes in the details given in this guide or for the consequences of any reliance on the information provided in the same. This does not affect your statutory rights. We have tried to ensure accuracy in this guide but things do change and we would be grateful if readers would advise us of any inaccuracies they may encounter.

Web Site addresses are included where they have been supplied and specified by the respective establishment. Such Web Sites are not under the control of The Automobile Association Developments Limited and as such The Automobile Association Developments Limited has no control over them and will not accept any responsibility or liability in respect of any and all matters whatsoever relating to such Web Sites including access, content, material and functionality. By including the addresses of third party Web Sites the AA does not intend to solicit business or offer any security to any person in any country, directly or indirectly.

Advertisement Sales: advertisingsales@theAA.com
Editorial: lifestyleguides@theAA.com

Cover pictures: AA Picture Library

Typeset/Repro by Servis Filmsetting Ltd Manchester, England.

Printed in Italy by Printer Trento SRL, Trento

Published by AA Publishing, which is a trading name of Automobile Association Developments Limited whose registered office is Fanum House, Basingstoke, Hampshire, RG21 4EA

CIP catalogue record for this book is available from the British Library
Registered number 1878835.

ISBN-10: 0-7495-4729-4
ISBN-13: 978-0-7495-4729-5

A02586

 Ordnance Survey® **This product includes** mapping data licensed from Ordnance Survey® with the permission of the Controller of Her Majesty's Stationery Office. © Crown copyright 2005. All rights reserved. Licence number 399221.

This product includes mapping based upon data licensed from Ordnance Survey of Northern Ireland® reproduced by permission of the Chief Executive, acting on behalf of the Controller of Her Majesty's Stationery Office. © Crown copyright 2005. Permit number 40466

Republic of Ireland mapping based on Ordnance Survey Ireland Permit number MP000105. © Ordnance Survey Ireland and Government of Ireland.

Maps prepared by the Cartography Department of The Automobile Association. Maps © Automobile Association Developments Limited 2005

CONTENTS

04 How to use the guide

07
England
Channel Islands 285

293
Scotland

346
Wales

371
Northern Ireland

384
Republic of Ireland

400 Atlas
419 Index
431 Free Days Out
435 Readers' Report Form
437 2-for-1 Vouchers
440 Classified Advertising

How to use the Guide

1

BEDFORD Map 04 TL04 — 1

BEDFORD MUSEUM `2 for 1` — 4
Castle Ln MK40 3XD
2 — ➲ (close to town bridge and Embankment)
3 — ☎ 01234 353323 🖷 01234 273401
e-mail: bmuseum@bedford.gov.uk
Embark on a fascinating journey through the human and natural history of north Bedfordshire, pausing briefly to glimpse
at wonders from more distant lands. The courtyard and galleries provide an excellent setting for the varied collections.
5 — **Times:** Open all year, Tue-Sat 11-5, Sun 2-5. (Closed Mon ex BH Mon
afternoon, Good Fri & Xmas). **Fee:** ✱ £2.20 (ch, pen & con free). Fri — 6
free for everyone. Annual ticket £8.80. **Facilities:** P (50mtrs) 🍴 — 7
8 — ♿ (lift available on request, subject to staff availability) toilets for
disabled shop ✖ (ex guide dogs) 💳 ——————— 9

The Directory
The directory is arranged in countries, counties, then in
alphabetical location order within each county. Each county
has an introductory panel that gives general information on
selected events and festivals.

1 Map References and Atlas Map references for attractions are based
on the National Grid, and can be used with the Atlas at the back of
this book.. First comes the map page number, followed by the
National Grid reference. To find the location, read the first figure
horizontally and the second figure vertically within the lettered
square.

2 Directions may be given after the address of each attraction and
where shown have been provided by the places of interest themselves.

3 Telephone Numbers have the STD code shown before the telephone number. (If dialling Northern Ireland from England use the
STD code, but for the Republic you need to prefix the number
with 00353, and drop the first zero from the Irish area code).

4 2-FOR-1 Voucher Scheme `2 for 1`
This symbol indicates which attractions have chosen to
participate in our 2-for-1 voucher scheme. Visitors
using one of the vouchers from the front of this guide
will be able to buy 2 tickets for the price of one, with certain
restrictions that are detailed on the voucher itself. Some attractions
also have individual restrictions, which are detailed in their entries.

5 Opening Times quoted in the guide are inclusive - for instance,
where you see Apr-Oct, that place will be open from the beginning of April to the end of October.

6 Fees quoted for the majority of entries are current. If no price is
quoted, you should check with the attraction concerned before
you visit. Places which are open 'at all reasonable times' are
usually free, and many places which do not charge admission at
all may ask for a voluntary donation. Remember that prices can
go up, and those provided to us by the attractions are provisional.

Free Entry `FREE`
These attractions do not charge a
fee for entry, although they may charge for
use of audio equipment, for example. We
have not included attractions that expect a
donation in this category.

7 Facilities This section includes parking, dogs
allowed, refreshments, worksheets etc. See
page 5 for a key to Symbols and
Abbreviations used in this guide.

8 Visitors with Mobility Disabilities should
look for the wheelchair symbol showing
where all or most of the establishment is
accessible to the wheelchair-bound visitor.
We strongly recommend that you telephone in advance of your visit to check the
exact details, particularly regarding access
to toilets and refreshment facilities.
Assistance dogs are usually accepted where
the attractions show the 'No Dogs' symbol
✖ unless stated otherwise. For the hard of
hearing induction loops are indicated by a
symbol at the attraction itself.

9 Credit & Charge cards are taken by a
number of attractions for admission charges.
To indicate which accept credit cards we
have used this symbol at the end of the
entry. 💳

PHOTOGRAPHY is restricted in some
places and there are many where it
is only allowed in specific areas.
Visitors are advised to check with
places of interest on the rules for
taking photographs and the use of
video cameras.

SPECIAL EVENTS are held at many of
these attractions, and although we
have listed a few of the more
important ones on the county
introduction pages, we cannot hope
to give details of them all, so please
ring the places of interest for details
of exhibitions, themed days, talks,
guided walks and more.

ATTRACTIONS with Italic headings
These are entries that were unable
to provide the relevant information
in time for publication.

...AND FINALLY Opening times and
admission prices can be subject to
change. Please check with the
attraction before making your
journey.

Key to Symbols

☎ Telephone number

♿ Suitable for visitors in wheelchairs

🅿 Parking at Establishment

🅿 Parking nearby

🍴 Refreshments

📄 Worksheets

✗ Restaurant

🐕 No Dogs

🚌 No Coaches

✱ Admission prices relate to 2005

♦ Cadw (Welsh Mouments)

✚ English Heritage

❖ National Trust

❧ National Trust for Scotland

⚑ Historic Scotland

ABBREVIATIONS

BH Bank Hoildays

PH Public Holidays

Etr Easter

ex except

Free Admission free

£1 Admission £1

ch 50p Children 50p

ch 15 50p Children under 15 50p

Pen Senior Citizens

Party Special or reduced rates for parties booked in advance

Party 30+ Special or reduced rates for parties of 30 or more booked in advance

Happy Visiting!

The AA Days Out Guide provides useful information about a large number of museums, art galleries, theme parks, national parks, visitor centres and stately homes across Britain and Ireland. Entries include contact details for each attraction, along with a short description and details of opening times, prices and special facilities. Each county has a list of events and festivals. We hope that this guide will help you and your family get the most out of your time.

Public Holidays
- **New Year's Day** 2 January
- **New Year's Holiday** 3 January (Scotland only)
- **St Patrick's Day** 17 March (N.I & R.O.I)
- **Good Friday** 14 April
- **Easter Monday** 17 April
- **May Day Bank Holiday** 1 May
- **Spring Bank Holiday** 29 May (excluding R.O.I)
- **Battle of the Boyne** 12 July (Orangemen's Day) (N.I)
- **Summer Bank Holiday** 7 August (Scotland & R.O.I only)
- **Summer Bank Holiday** 28 August (excluding R.O.I)
- **Bank Holiday** 25 October (R.O.I)
- **Christmas Day** 25 December
- **Boxing Day** 26 December (St Stephen's Day in R.O.I)

✱ Admission prices

followed by an asterisk relate to 2005. It should be noted that in some entries the opening dates and times may also have been supplied as 2005. Please check with the establishment before making your journey.

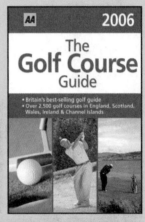
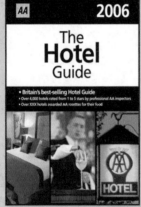
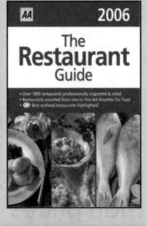

ENGLAND

BEDFORDSHIRE

EVENTS & FESTIVALS

March
4th-11th Bedfordshire Festival of Music,
Speech & Drama, various venues in Bedford

May
1st Ickwell May Festival,
The Maypole, Ickwell Green
tbc Bedfordshire Classic Motor Show,
Shuttleworth
tbc Luton Carnival, Britain's
multi-cultural showcase

June
tbc Bedford International Kite Festival

July
15th-16th Bedford River Festival
(entertainment, parade, fete, raft races)
tbc International Air Rally & Exhibition,
Cranfield Airfield, Cranfield (provisional)

August
5th Proms in the Park, Bedford Park
(provisional)
September
4th-7th Bedford Beer Festival, Bedford Corn
Exchange (provisional)
16th-17th Bedfordshire Steam & Country
Fayre, Old Warden Park, near Biggleswade
(provisional)
October
tbc National Apple Day at Bromham Mill,
apples, cider, apple bobbing, farmers
market and entertainment (provisional)
December
tbc Bedford Victorian Christmas Fayre,
Bedford town centre

Above: Bears at Whipsnade Wild Animal Park

AMPTHILL   Map 04 TL03

HOUGHTON HOUSE
➲ (1m NE off A421)   **FREE**
Now a ruin, the mansion was built for Mary Countess of
Pembroke, the sister of Sir Philip Sidney. Inigo Jones is
thought to have been involved in work on the house, which
may have been the original 'House Beautiful' in Bunyan's
Pilgrim's Progress.
Times: Open at all reasonable times. **Facilities:** 🅿 & ♯

BEDFORD   Map 04 TL04

BEDFORD MUSEUM
Castle Ln MK40 3XD
➲ (close to town bridge and Embankment)
☎ 01234 353323   **FREE**
e-mail: bmuseum@bedford.gov.uk
web: www.bedfordmuseum.org
Embark on a fascinating journey through the human and
natural history of north Bedfordshire, pausing briefly to
glimpse at wonders from more distant lands. Go back in
time and visit the delightful rural room sets and the Old
School Museum, where Blackbeard's Sword, 'Old Billy' the
record breaking longest-living horse, and numerous other
treasures and curiosities can be found. Housed in the former
Higgins and Sons Brewery, Bedford Museum is situated
within the gardens of what was once Bedford Castle, beside
the Great Ouse embankment. The courtyard and galleries
provide an excellent setting for the varied collections.
Times: Open all year, Tue-Sat 11-5, Sun 2-5. (Closed Mon ex BH Mon
afternoon, Good Fri & Xmas). **Facilities:** 🅿 (50mtrs) 🍴 & (lift
available on request, subject to staff availability) toilets for disabled
shop ✖ (ex guide dogs) 🍴

CECIL HIGGINS ART GALLERY & MUSEUM
Castle Ln MK40 3RP
➲ (in town centre close to Embankment)
☎ 01234 211222
e-mail: chag@bedford.gov.uk   **FREE**
web: www.cecilhigginsartgallery.org
A recreated Victorian mansion, with the rooms arranged as
though the house is still lived in. Includes a bedroom with
furniture designed by Victorian architect William Burges, and
the adjoining gallery has an outstanding collection of ceramics,
glass and changing exhibition of prints, drawings and
watercolours. Also includes the Thomas Lester lace collection.
Times: Open all year, Tue-Sat 11-5, Sun & BH Mon 2-5. (Closed Mon,
Good Fri, 25-26 Dec & 1 Jan). **Facilities:** 🅿 (100yds) (pay & display)
(free on Sun) 🍴 & (wheelchair available) toilets for disabled shop
✖ (ex guide dogs) 🍴

LEIGHTON BUZZARD   Map 04 SP92

LEIGHTON BUZZARD RAILWAY
Pages Park Station, Billington Rd LU7 4TN   **2 for 1**
➲ (0.75m SE on A4146 signposted in and around
Leighton Buzzard, near rdbt junct with A505)
☎ 01525 373888
The Leighton Buzzard Railway offers a 70 minute journey
into the vanished world of the English light railway, with its
sharp curves, steep gradients, level crossings and unique
roadside running. Built in 1919 to serve the local sand
industry, the railway has carried a steam passenger service,
operated by volunteers, since 1968.
Times: Open Mar-Oct, Sun & BH wknds; Jan-Jul, Wed; Aug, Tue-Thu,
Sat & BH wknds. **Fee:** ✱ Return ticket £6 (ch 2-15 £3, pen £5 & ch
under 2 free). Party 10+. **Facilities:** 🅿 🍴 🎁 & (platform & train
access for wheelchairs) toilets for disabled shop 🍴

LUTON   Map 04 TL02

JOHN DONY FIELD CENTRE
Hancock Dr, Bushmead LU2 7SF
➲ (signposted from rdbt on A6, at Barnfield
College on New Bedford Rd)
☎ 01582 486983   FREE
e-mail: donyj@luton.gov.uk
web: www.luton.gov.uk/museums
This is a purpose built study centre for exploring the
landscapes, plants and animals of the Luton area. Featuring
permanent displays on local archaeology, natural history and
the management of the local nature reserve, it explains how
ancient grasslands and hedgerows are conserved and
follows 4000 years of history from Bronze Age to modern
times.
Times: Open all year, Mon-Fri 9.30-4.45. Closed BHs.
Facilities: 🅿 ♿ toilets for disabled ✈ (ex assist dogs)

STOCKWOOD CRAFT MUSEUM & GARDENS
Stockwood Country Park, Farley Hill LU1 4BH
➲ (signposted from M1 junct 10 and from Hitchin,
Dunstable, Bedford and from Luton town centre)
☎ 01582 738714 & 546739   FREE
e-mail: museum.gallery@luton.gov.uk
web: www.luton.gov.uk/museums
The Museum is set in period gardens which incorporate the
Ian Hamilton Finlay Sculpture Gardens. The Mossman
collection of horse-drawn vehicles traces the history of
transport from Roman times to the 1940s. Craft
demonstrations are held at weekends in the summer. Please
telephone for details of special events.
Times: Open all year; Mar-Oct, Tue-Sun 10-5; Nov-Mar, wknds 10-4.
(closed Xmas & 1 Jan) **Facilities:** 🅿 💷 🃏 ♿ (stair lift, parking,
induction loop, automatic door) toilets for disabled shop ✈ (ex guide
& hearing dogs)

WARDOWN PARK MUSEUM
Wardown Park, Old Bedford Rd LU2 7HA
➲ (Follow brown signs from the town centre
north.Turn off A6 towards Bedford)
☎ 01582 546722 & 546739   FREE
e-mail: museum.gallery@luton.gov.uk
web: www.luton.gov.uk/museums
A Victorian mansion, with displays illustrating the natural
and cultural history, archaeology and industries of the area,
including the development of Luton's hat industry, and the
Bedfordshire and Hertfordshire Regimental Collections. New
'Luton Life' displays tell the story of the town and its
residents over the past 200 years. Exhibitions and events
throughout the year.
Times: Open all year, Tue-Sat 10-5, Sun 1-5 (Closed Xmas, 1 Jan &
Mon ex BH Mons). **Facilities:** 🅿 💷 🃏 ♿ (parking adjacent to
entrance, lift to 1st floor) toilets for disabled shop ✈ (ex guide dogs &
hearing dogs)

OLD WARDEN   Map 04 TL14

THE SHUTTLEWORTH COLLECTION
Old Warden Park SG18 9EA
➲ (2m W from rdbt on A1, Biggleswade by-pass)
☎ 01767 627288
web: www.shuttleworth.org
Housed in eight hangars on a classic grass aerodrome, 40
working historic aeroplanes span the progress of aviation
with exhibits ranging from a 1909 Bleriot to a 1941 Spitfire.
continued

A garage of roadworthy motor vehicles explores the eras of
the 1898 Panhard Levassor to the Railton sports car of 1937.
The 19th-century coach house displays horse-drawn vehicles
from 1880 to 1914.
Times: ✱ Open Apr-Oct 10-5 (last admission 4), Nov-Mar 10-4 (last
admission 3). Closed Xmas-New Year. **Facilities:** 🅿 💷 ✗ licensed
🃏 ♿ toilets for disabled shop ✈ (ex guide dogs) ⛴

SANDY   Map 04 TL14

RSPB NATURE RESERVE
The Lodge Shop SG19 2DL
➲ (1m E, on B1042 Potton road)
☎ 01767 680541
e-mail: claire.wallace@rspb.org.uk
web: www.rspb.org.uk
The headquarters of the Royal Society for the Protection of
Birds. The house and buildings are not open to the public,
but there are waymarked paths and formal gardens, and two
species of woodpecker, nuthatches and woodland birds may
be seen, as may muntjac deer. Another feature is the
specialist wildlife garden created in conjunction with the
Henry Doubleday Association.
Times: ✱ Open all year, Mon-Fri 9-5, Sat, Sun & BHs 10-5. Closed
25-26 Dec. **Facilities:** 🅿 🃏 ♿ (partial access) toilets for disabled
shop ✈ (ex in restricted areas) ⛴

SILSOE   Map 04 TL03

WREST PARK GARDENS
MK45 4HS
➲ (0.75m E off A6)
☎ 01525 860152
Audio tour through a century and a half of gardening styles
as you explore the 90 acres of formal gardens that make up
Wrest Park.
Times: Open 26 Mar-Sep, Sat, Sun & BH 10-6; Oct, Sat, Sun 10-5.
Fee: £4.30 (ch £2.20, concessions £3.20, family £10.80). Opening times
and prices are subject to change, for further details please phone 0870
333 1181 **Facilities:** 🅿 ✈ (ex on lead in certain areas) ⛟

WHIPSNADE   Map 04 TL01

WHIPSNADE WILD ANIMAL PARK
LU6 2LF
➲ (signposted from M1 junct 9 & 12)
☎ 01582 872171
web: www.whipsnade.co.uk
Located in beautiful Bedfordshire countryside, Whipsnade is
home to more than 2,500 rare and exotic animals and is one
of the largest conservation centres in Europe. Hop aboard
the Safari Bus or take a ride on the Great Whipsnade Railway
and get the chance to see tigers, elephants, hippos, giraffes,
rhinos and more, out and about in their huge outdoor
enclosures. And don't be surprised to find a wallaby or one
of the strange-looking mara wandering idly by as you make
your way through the park. With lovely picnic areas, free
daily keeper talks, animal shows, exciting events and
exhibitions, there are plenty of reasons to bring your family
to Whipsnade for a day out of discovery and fun. 2006 is the
75th anniversary of the opening of Whipsnade.
Times: Open all year, daily. (Closed 25 Dec). **Fee:** ✱ £14.50 (ch 3-15
£11, concessions £12.50). Family ticket (2ad + 2ch) £46. Car entry £11
Facilities: 🅿 (charged) 💷 🃏 ♿ (1 carer free per registered disabled
visitor) toilets for disabled shop ✈ ⛴

WOBURN   Map 04 SP93

WOBURN ABBEY

MK17 9WA
➲ (Just off M1 junct 12/13)
☎ 01525 290333
e-mail: admissions@woburnabbey.co.uk
web: www.woburnabbey.co.uk

Standing in 3000 acres of parkland, this palatial 18th-century mansion was originally a Cistercian Abbey, and the Dukes of Bedford have lived here since 1547. The art collection includes works by Canaletto, Rembrandt, Van Dyck, and Gainsborough. 14 state apartments are on view, and the private apartments are shown when not in use. Special events are held during the year, including the De-Havilland Tiger Moth Fly-In and a garden show.

Times: 24 Mar-2 Oct, 11am-4pm (last entry) closes 5.30pm (5 Nov-24 Dec wknds only) **Fee:** ✱ Deer Park only car & passengers £3. Motorcycles & passengers £3. Abbey adult £9.50, 5-15yrs £5, Senior citizens £8.50, under 5 yrs free. **Facilities:** 🅿 (charged) ▱ ✗ licensed ▤ ♿ (wheelchairs accommodated by prior arrangement) toilets for disabled shop ✈ ▰

WOBURN SAFARI PARK

Woburn Park MK17 9QN
➲ (Signposted from M1 junct 13)
☎ 01525 290407
e-mail: info@woburnsafari.co.uk
web: www.woburnsafari.co.uk

Set in the 3000 acres of parkland belonging to Woburn Abbey, Woburn Safari Park has an extensive collection of many species. The safari road passes through an African plains area stocked with eland, zebra, hippo and rhino, then through well-keepered tiger and lion enclosures and on past bears and monkeys. Animal encounters, sea lion and parrot shows, and elephant displays, are all popular attractions. The large leisure complex also offers a boating lake, adventure playgrounds, railway train, walk-through aviary, squirrel monkey exhibit and 'the Australian Walkabout', with friendly wallabies. A new attraction is underwater viewing at Sealion Cove.

Times: Open daily, mid Mar-Oct, 10-5. Winter season 31 Oct-10 Mar wk ends only, 11-19 Feb daily 11-3 (closed 24-25 Dec) **Fee:** ✱ £14.50 (ch 3-15 £11, pen £11.50). Prices vary in high season.

Facilities: 🅿 ▱ ✗ licensed ♿ toilets for disabled shop ✈ ▰

HRH Queen Elizabeth II.

The British monarch was born in April 1926, and the year of her 80th birthday will see many national celebrations, as well as those that are to be staged in London.

BERKSHIRE

EVENTS & FESTIVALS

February
7th Shrove Tuesday Great
   Newbury Pancake Race

May
11th-14th Royal Windsor Horse Show
   tbc Newbury International Spring Festival
   of music and the visual arts

June
24th-25th Garden & Leisure Show, Newbury
   Showground
30th-2nd Jul Bracknell Festival (provisional)
   tbc The Garden & Leisure Show, Newbury
   Showground, Priors Court, Hermitage,
   Thatcham
   tbc Newbury International Orchid Show
   tbc Royal Ascot, Ascot Race Course

July
   tbc Cartier International Polo, Smiths Lawn,
   Windsor Great Park (provisional)
   tbc De Beers Diamond Day, Ascot Race Course
   tbc Kennet Valley Kite Festival, Thatcham
   (provisional)
   tbc WOMAD World Music & Arts Festival,
   Rivermead, Reading

August
25th-27th Carling Reading Festival, Richfield
   Avenue, Reading (provisional)
   tbc Cookham Regatta
   tbc Shergar Cup (team competition), Ascot
   Race Course

September
16th-17th Newbury & Royal County of
   Berkshire Show, Newbury Showground
   (provisional)
   tbc Ascot Festival of Racing
   tbc Windsor Festival, music and arts, various
   venues

October
14th The Ploughing Match, Newbury &
   District Agricultural Society

Above: Eton College

BRACKNELL — Map 04 SU86

THE LOOK OUT DISCOVERY CENTRE
Nine Mile Ride RG12 7QW
➲ (3m S of town centre. From M3 junct 3, take A322 to Bracknell and from M4 junct 10, take A329M to Bracknell. Follow brown tourist signs)
☎ 01344 354400
e-mail: thelookout@bracknell-forest.gov.uk
web: www.bracknell-forest.gov.uk/lookout

A hands-on, interactive science and nature exhibition where budding scientists can spend many hours exploring and discovering over 70 fun filled exhibits within five themed zones, the topics covered are linked to the National Curriculum. Zones include Light and Colour, Forces and Movement and the Body and Perception. A new exciting zone, Woodland and Water; with a vortex, stream, ant colony and many more interactive exhibits. Climb the 88 steps to the Look Out tower and look towards Bracknell and beyond or enjoy a nature walk in the surrounding 2,600 acres of Crown Estate woodland. Interactive shows for the public and schools running throughout the year. Please note the tower is closed when wet.

Times: Open all year. Christmas period may alter, please check for details(Closed 24-26 Dec). **Fee:** £4.95 (ch & concessions £3.30). Family (2 adults + 2 ch or 1 adult + 3 ch) £13.20. **Facilities:** 🅿 ♨ 🍴 ♿ lift to first floor toilets for disabled shop 🐾 (ex in grounds) 🎫

ETON — Map 04 SU97

DORNEY COURT
Dorney SL4 6QP
➲ (signposted from M4 junct 7, via B3026)
☎ 01628 604638 **2 for 1**
e-mail: palmer@dorneycourt.co.uk
web: www.dorneycourt.co.uk

An enchanting brick and timber manor house (c1440) in a tranquil setting. With tall Tudor chimneys and a splendid great hall, it has been the home of the present family since 1510.

Times: Open BH Sun & Mon in May 1.30-4.30. Aug every afternoon ex Sat 1.30-4.30. **Fee:** ✱ £6 (ch £4, under 10's free). **Facilities:** 🅿 ♨ 🍴 ♿ (ramps) toilets for disabled garden centre 🐾 (ex guide dogs)

HAMPSTEAD NORREYS — Map 04 SU57

THE LIVING RAINFOREST
RG18 OTN
➲ (follow brown tourist signs from M4/A34)
☎ 01635 202444 **2 for 1**
e-mail: enquiries@livingrainforest.org
web: www.livingrainforest.org

By providing education and supporting research into the relationship between humanity and the rainforests, this wonderful attraction hopes to promote a more sustainable future. Visitors to the Living Rainforest will see plants and wildlife that are under threat in their natural habitat, and be encouraged to take part in a large variety of activities, workshops and exhibitions.

Times: Open all year daily 10-5.15. (Closed from 1pm 24 Dec & 25-26 Dec) **Fee:** ✱ £5.95 (concessions £5.35, ch 5-14 £3.95 & ch 3-4 £2.95) **Facilities:** 🅿 ♨ 🍴 ♿ toilets for disabled shop 🐾 (ex guide dogs) 🎫

LOWER BASILDON — Map 04 SU67

BASILDON PARK
RG8 9NR
➲ (7m NW of Reading on W side of A329 between Reading & Wallingford)
☎ 0118 984 3040 **2 for 1**
e-mail: basildonpark@nationaltrust.org.uk
web: www.nationaltrust.org.uk/basildonpark

This 18th-century house, built of Bath stone, fell into decay in the 20th century, but has been beautifully restored by Lord and Lady Iliffe. The classical front has a splendid central portico and pavilions, and inside there are delicate plasterwork decorations on the walls and ceilings. The Octagon drawing room has fine pictures and furniture, and there is a small formal garden. The 2-for-1 voucher is only valid during normal visiting hours and cannot be used for any ticketed events.

Times: House open Apr-end Oct, Wed-Sun & BH Mon 1-5.30. Park & garden Apr-end Oct, Wed-Sun & BH Mon 11-5.30. **Fee:** ✱ House & grounds £5 (ch £2.50), family ticket £12.50; Grounds only £2.40 (ch £1.20), family ticket £6. **Facilities:** 🅿 ✗ licensed 🍴 ♿ (driven buggy, ltd access to main show rooms) toilets for disabled shop 🐾

BEALE PARK
Lower Basildon RG8 9NH
➲ (M4 junct 12, follow brown tourist signs to Pangbourne, A329 towards Oxford)
☎ 0118 984 5172
e-mail: bealepark@bun.com
web: www.bealepark.co.uk
Beale Park is home to an extraordinary bird collection including peacocks, swans, owls and parrots. It also offers a steam railway, rare breeds of farm animals, a great pet corner, meerkats, wallabies, a deer park, two splash pools, a huge adventure playground, acres of gardens, sculptures, trails and environmental education in a traditional, family park, beside the Thames. There are summer riverboat trips and excellent lake and river fishing.
Times: ✽ Open Mar-Dec. Facilities: 🅿 💻 📁 ⅊ (wheelchair available, parking) toilets for disabled shop ✖ (ex guide dogs)

NEWBURY   Map 04 SU46
WEST BERKSHIRE MUSEUM
The Wharf RG14 5AS
➲ (from London take M4 junct 13, then southbound on A34, follow signs for town centre)
☎ 01635 30511   FREE
e-mail: heritage@westberks.gov.uk
web: westberkshiremuseum.org.uk
Occupying two adjoining buildings in the centre of Newbury; the Cloth Hall built in 1627 and the Granary built in 1720. The museum includes displays of fine and decorative art, costume, local history and archaeology.
Times: Open all year Apr-Sep, Tue-Sat 10-5: Oct-Mar, Tue-Sat 10-4. Open BH. Facilities: 🅿 (15yds) 📁 ⅊ shop ✖ (ex guide dogs)

OLD WINDSOR   Map 04 SU97
RUNNYMEDE
North Lodge, Windsor Rd SL4 2JL
➲ (From M25 junct 13. On the Thames, 2m W of Runnymede Bridge on S side of A308. 6m E of Windsor)
☎ 01784 432891
e-mail: runnymede@nationaltrust.org.uk
web: www.nationaltrust.org.uk/runnymede
Partly designated as a Site of Special Scientific Interest, Runnymede is an area of meadows, grassland, and woodland that sits alongside the Thames. Best known as the site where King John signed the Magna Carta in 1215, this momentous event was commemorated by the American Bar Association, who built a monument here in 1957. There is also a memorial to American President, John F Kennedy. Also the Fairhaven Lodges, designed by Edward Lutyens.
Times: Car parks; Oct-Mar 9-5, Apr-Sep 9-7 Fee: ✽ Car parks; 0-2hrs £1.50, 2-4hrs £2.50, all day £3.80 Facilities: 🅿 (charged) 💻 ✖ ⅊ (Braille guide, audio tour) toilets for disabled shop

READING   Map 04 SU77
MUSEUM OF ENGLISH RURAL LIFE
University of Reading, Redlands Rd RG1 5EX
➲ (close to the Royal Berkshire Hospital)
☎ 0118 378 8660   FREE
e-mail: merl@reading.ac.uk
web: www.merl.org.uk
Recently moved to larger premises, this museum houses a national collection of agricultural, domestic and crafts exhibits, including wagons, tools and a wide range of other equipment used in the English countryside over the last 150 years. Special facilities are available for school parties. The museum also contains extensive documentary and photographic archives, which can be studied by appointment. There is a regular programme of events and activities, please see website for details.
Times: Open all year, Tue-Fri, 10-4.30, Sat & Sun 2-4.30 (Closed BH's & Xmas-New Year). Facilities: 🅿 ⅊ Chair lifts, hearing loop toilets for disabled shop ✖

RISELEY   Map 04 SU76
WELLINGTON COUNTRY PARK
RG7 1SP
➲ (signposted off A33, between Reading & Basingstoke)
☎ 0118 932 6444   2 for 1
e-mail: info@wellington-country-park.co.uk
web: www.wellington-country-park.co.uk

350 acres of woodland walks and parkland provided for a family outing. Attractions appealing to younger and older children include; miniature railway, animal farm, adventure playground, crazy golf and 'in season' rowing boat hire.
Times: Open Mar-Oct, daily 10-5.30. Fee: ✽ £6 (ch £4, under 3's free, pen £5) Facilities: 🅿 💻 ⅊ (fishing platform & nature trail for disabled) toilets for disabled shop 🍴

WINDSOR
Map 04 SU97

FROGMORE HOUSE
Home Park SL4 1NJ
⮕ (entrance from B3021 between Datchet & Old Windsor)
☎ 020 7766 7305
e-mail: windsorcastle@royalcollection.org.uk
web: www.royalcollection.org.uk

Frogmore House, set in the private Home Park, is renowned for its beautiful landscaped garden and lake. Queen Victoria loved Frogmore so much that she broke with royal tradition and chose to build a mausoleum for herself and Prince Albert there. The house is no longer a royal residence but is frequently used by the Royal Family for entertaining. The former library is the setting for furniture and paintings from the Royal Yacht Britannia.

Times: ✱ Open 3 days May, 10-5.30 (last admission 4). Aug BH, 10-5.30 (last admission 4). Prebooked guided tours for groups Aug-Sep.
Facilities: P shop ✕ ▬

LEGOLAND WINDSOR
Winkfield Rd SL4 4AY
⮕ (on B3022 Windsor to Ascot road well signposted from M3 junct 3 & M4 junct 6)
☎ 01753 626111
e-mail: customer.services@legoland.co.uk
web: www.legoland.co.uk

With over 50 interactive rides, live shows, building workshops, driving schools and attractions. Set in 150 acres of beautiful parkland, LEGOLAND Windsor is a different sort of family theme park. An atmospheric and unique experience for the whole family, a visit to LEGOLAND Windsor is more than a day out, it's a lifetime of memories. 2006 is LEGOLAND'S 10th anniversary.

Times: Open daily 12 Mar-5 Nov **Fee:** ✱ £24 (ch £22)
Facilities: P (charged) ▬ ✕ ▤ ⛁ (signing staff, wheelchair hire, parking) toilets for disabled shop ✕ (ex guide dogs) ▬

See advertisement on page 11

ST GEORGE'S CHAPEL
SL4 1NJ
⮕ (M4 junct 6 & M3 junct 3)
☎ 01753 865538

St George's Chapel, within the precincts of Windsor Castle, is one of the most beautiful ecclesiastical buildings in England. Founded by Edward IV in 1475, it is the burial place of ten monarchs, including Henry VIII and his favourite wife Jane Seymour. The Chapel is the spiritual home of the Order of the Garter, the oldest and most senior order of British Chivalry.

Times: Open Mar-Oct (9.45-17.15) Nov-Feb (9.45-16.15). May close at short notice - 24hr info line - 01753 831118. (Closed Sun, worshippers very welcome) **Facilities:** P 400 yds ⛁ shop ✕ (ex guide dogs)

SAVILL GARDEN (WINDSOR GREAT PARK)
Wick Ln, Englefield Green TW20 0UU
⮕ (M25 junct 13, signposted off A30 between Egham & Virginia Water)
☎ 01753 847518
e-mail: savillgarden@crownestate.co.uk
web: www.savillgarden.co.uk

The magnificent 35-acre garden lies within Windsor Great Park. It has spectacular woodland displays in spring, sweeping herbaceous borders in summer, fiery autumn colours and misty winter vistas. The garden's temperate house is a year-round delight.

Times: Open all year, daily 10-6 (10-4 Nov-Feb). (Closed 25-26 Dec).
Facilities: P ▬ ✕ licensed ▤ ⛁ (wheelchairs available) toilets for disabled shop garden centre ✕ (ex guide dogs) ▬

WINDSOR CASTLE
SL4 1NJ
⮕ (M4 junct 6 & M3 junct 3)
☎ 020 7766 7304
e-mail: windsorcastle@royalcollection.org.uk
web: www.royal.gov.uk

Covering 13 acres, this is the official residence of HM The Queen and the largest inhabited castle in the world. Begun as a wooden fort by William the Conqueror, it has been added to by almost every monarch since. The Upper Ward includes the State Apartments, magnificently restored following the fire of 1992, and the Lower Ward where St George's Chapel is situated. The Doll's House designed for Queen Mary in the 1920s by Lutyens, is also on display.

Times: ✱ Open all year, daily except Good Fri & 25-26 Dec. Nov-Feb, 9.45-4.15 (last admission 3), Mar-Oct 9.45-5.15 (last admission 4). As Windsor Castle is a royal residence the opening arrangements may be subject to change at short notice - 24hr info line - 01753 831118
Fee: ✱ £12.50 (ch 5-16 £6.50, under 5's free, concessions £10.50). Family ticket £31.50 (2ad + 3ch) **Facilities:** P (400yds) ⛁ (ramps) toilets for disabled shop ✕ (ex guide dogs) ▬

BRISTOL

EVENTS & FESTIVALS

Commemorating the 200th anniversary of the birth of Isambard Kingdom Brunel, there will be a number of public events, projects and competitions for both locals and visitors to Bristol during 2006

February
tbc Bristol Beer Festival

April
tbc Animated Encounters, Animation Festival, Watershed Media Centre, Bristol

June
8th-12th bristolive! International festival for amateur ensembles, various venues
tbc Bristol Bike Fest, Ashton Court Estate, Long Ashton
tbc Bristol Motor & Classic Car Show, The Downs

July
15th-16th Ashton Court Festival, Ashton Court Estate, Long Ashton
tbc Bristol Children's Festival, The Downs
tbc Bristol Harbour Festival

August
10th-13th Bristol Balloon Fiesta, Ashton Court Estate, Long Ashton
23rd-25th Bristol Flower Show, The Downs (provisional)

September
2nd-3rd Organic Food Fair, Bristol Harbourside
tbc International Kite Festival, Ashton Court Estate, Long Ashton

October
10th-15th Wildscreen Festival, the world's largest festival of moving images from the natural world, Watershed Media Centre, Bristol
tbc Poetry Festival, various venues in Bristol

November
tbc Brief Encounters, Short Film Festival, Watershed, Bristol

Above: Bristol Docks, S.S. Great Britain

BRISTOL   Map 03 ST57

AT-BRISTOL
Anchor Rd, Harbourside BS1 5DB
⊃ (from city centre, A4 to Anchor Rd. Located on left opposite Cathedral)
☎ 0845 345 1235
e-mail: information@at-bristol.org.uk
web: www.at-bristol.org.uk

For the interactive adventure of a lifetime head for At-Bristol's three attractions on the city's habourside. A clever fusion of sci-fi architecture and historic buildings are home to 'Wildwalk', a breathtaking journey through the plant and animal kingdoms; Explore, the UK's most exciting hands-on science centre; and the IMAX theatre, the largest cinema screen in the West of England. At-Bristol will be participating in the city wide Brunel 200 anniversary, with many events from April 2006.

Times: Open all year, term-time wkdays 10-5, wknds & school hols 10-6. Closed 25 Dec. **Fee:** ✱ Ticket for 3 attractions £17 (ch £12, concessions £14). Family ticket £54. **Facilities:** 🄿 (charged) 💷 ✗ licensed 🎫 ⅙ (induction loop & mini com 0117 914 3475) toilets for disabled shop 🐾 (ex guide dogs) ◤

BLAISE CASTLE HOUSE MUSEUM
Henbury Rd, Henbury BS10 7QS
⊃ (4m NW of city, off B4057)   FREE
☎ 0117 903 9818
e-mail: general_museum@bristol-city.gov.uk
web: www.bristol-city.gov.uk/museums

Built in the 18th century for a Quaker banker, this mansion is now Bristol's Museum of Social History. Nearby Blaise Hamlet is a picturesque estate village, designed by John Nash.

Times: Open all year, Sat-Wed, 10-5. **Facilities:** 🄿 ⅙ shop 🐾 (ex guide dogs)

BRISTOL INDUSTRIAL MUSEUM
Prince's Wharf, Prince St, City Docks BS1 4RN   FREE
⊃ (within walking distance of the city centre)
☎ 0117 925 1470
e-mail: general_museum@bristol-city.gov.uk
web: www.bristol-city.gov.uk/museums

The museum is housed in a converted dockside transit shed. Motor and horse-drawn vehicles from the Bristol area are shown, with locally built aircraft and aero-engines. Railway exhibits include the industrial locomotive *Henbury*. At weekends from April to October there are trips around the harbour in either the tug *John King* or the steam tug *Mayflower* or the fire boat *Pyronant*; or trips around the dockside on the Bristol Harbour Railway. On certain weekends visitors can watch the steam crane and electric crane at work.

Times: Open all year Sat-Wed 10-5. Closing for refurbishment towards the end of 2006. **Fee:** *Prices not confirmed for 2006* **Facilities:** 🄿 (charged) 🎫 ⅙ toilets for disabled shop 🐾 (ex guide dogs)

BRISTOL'S CITY MUSEUM & ART GALLERY

Queen's Rd, Clifton BS8 1RL
➲ (follow signs to City Centre, then follow tourist board signs to City Museum & Art Gallery)
☎ 0117 922 3571   FREE
e-mail: general_museum@bristol-city.gov.uk
web: www.bristol-city.gov.uk/museums

Regional and international collections representing ancient history, natural sciences, and fine and applied arts. Displays include dinosaurs, Bristol ceramics, silver, Chinese and Japanese ceramics. A full programme of Special Exhibitions take place throughout the year. Ring for details.
Times: Open all year, daily 10-5. (Closed 25-26 Dec).
Facilities: P (NCP 400yds) ⭑ ⭑ (lift) toilets for disabled shop ✕ (ex guide dogs)

BRISTOL'S GEORGIAN HOUSE

7 Great George St, off Park St BS1 5RR
➲ (5 mins walk from Bristol City Centre)
☎ 0117 921 1362   FREE
e-mail: general_museum@bristol-city.gov.uk
web: www.bristol-city.gov.uk/museums

A carefully preserved example of a late 18th-century merchant's town house, with many original features and furnished to illustrate life both above and below stairs. A bedroom is now open, featuring a four-poster bed plus a small display recounting Bristol's involvement in the slave trade.
Times: Open Sat-Wed, 10-5. **Facilities:** P (pay & display street parking) ✕ (ex guide dogs)

BRISTOL'S RED LODGE

Park Row BS1 5LJ
➲ (5 mins walk from Bristol City Centre)
☎ 0117 921 1360   FREE
e-mail: general_museum@bristol-city.gov.uk
web: www.bristol-city.gov.uk/museums

The house was built in 1590 and then altered in 1730. It has fine oak panelling and carved stone chimney pieces and is furnished in the style of both periods. The garden has now been laid out in Elizabethan style.
Times: Open all year Sat-Wed 10-5. **Facilities:** P (NCP, adjacent) ✕ (ex guide dogs)

BRISTOL ZOO GARDENS

Clifton BS8 3HA
➲ (M5 junct 17, take A4018 then follow brown elephant signs. Also signed from city centre)
☎ 0117 974 7399
e-mail: information@bristolzoo.org.uk
web: www.bristolzoo.org.uk

Enjoy a whole day filled with excitement and discovery at Bristol Zoo Gardens. From the smallest and rarest tortoise in the world to the largest ape, there are 300 exotic and endangered species to explore. The Zoo is dedicated to conservation and involved in international breeding programmes. In Zona Brazil, visitors can experience first hand the stunning and diverse species found in the threatened coastal rainforests of Brazil. A winding wooden walkway will lead you past stunning birds, dainty agouti, grazing tapirs, and the world's largest living rodent -the capybara. Award-winning Seal & Penguin Coasts enable visitors to come face to face with penguins and seals in their natural element - beneath the waves - through transparent

underwater walkways. Other favourites include Bug World, Twilight World, and the Reptile House.
Times: Open all year, daily (ex 25 Dec) from 9. Closing times approx 5.30 (summer) 5 (winter) **Fee:** ✱ £9.70 (ch £6.20, concessions £8.50). Family ticket (2ad + 2 ch) £28.50 **Facilities:** P (charged) ⭑ ✕ licensed ⭑ ⭑ (wheelchairs/electric scooters for use in zoo grounds) toilets for disabled shop ✕ (kennels for service dogs) ⭑

BRITISH EMPIRE & COMMONWEALTH MUSEUM

Station Approach, Temple Meads BS1 6QH
➲ (in city centre, near Temple Meads station)
☎ 0117 925 4980   2 for 1
e-mail: admin@empiremuseum.co.uk
web: www.empiremuseum.co.uk

Exploring the dramatic 500-year history of the rise and fall of the British Empire and the emergence of the modern Commonwealth, this internationally acclaimed museum uses video stations, interactive exhibits, and computer games, as well as more traditional techniques. Visitors have the opportunity to dress in period costume, learn Morse code or sample exotic spices. The museum is divided into three sections: Britain's first empire 1500-1790, the British Empire at its height 1790-1914, and Independence and Beyond, and is housed in a restored railway terminus built by Brunel. 2006 is the 200th anniversary of the birth of Isambard Kingdom Brunel.
Times: Open all year, daily 10-5. Closed 25-26 Dec **Fee:** ✱ £6.50 (ch & pen £3.95, students £5.50) **Facilities:** P (charged) ⭑ ⭑ toilets for disabled shop ✕ (ex guide dogs) ⭑

HORSEWORLD

Staunton Manor Farm, Staunton Ln,
Whitchurch BS14 0QJ
➲ (A37 Bristol to Wells road, follow brown signs from Maes Knoll traffic lights)
☎ 01275 540173
e-mail: visitor.centre@horseworld.org.uk
web: www.horseworld.org.uk

One of the largest horse rescue centres in Britain, set in Mendip-stone farm buildings on the edge of Bristol. Meet the friendly horses, ponies and donkeys. Enjoy the miniature farm, 'touch and groom' areas, pony rides, daily presentations, nature trail, educational displays, video theatre and adventure playground.
Times: Open all year daily 10-5 (Winter; closed Mon) **Fee:** ✱ £5.50 (ch £4.25, concessions £5) **Facilities:** P ⭑ ✕ ⭑ ⭑ toilets for disabled shop ⭑

JOHN WESLEY'S CHAPEL (THE NEW ROOM)

36 The Horsefair, Broadmead BS1 3JE
➲ (M32 towards Broadmead. In the centre of Broadmead Shopping Centre. Entrance opposite Boots the Chemist)
☎ 0117 926 4740
e-mail: wesleynewroom@surefish.co.uk
web: www.newroombristol.org.uk

The oldest Methodist chapel in the world, built in 1739 and extended in 1748. Above the chapel are the preacher's rooms where John Wesley, Charles Wesley and the early Methodist preachers stayed.
Times: Open all year, Mon-Sat 10-4. **Fee:** Donation requested. £4 per person for pre-arranged group tours **Facilities:** P (250yds) main entrance in pedestrian precinct ⭑ ⭑ ⭑ shop ✕ (ex guide dogs) ⭑

continued

MARITIME HERITAGE CENTRE
Gas Ferry Rd BS1 6UN
➲ (M5 junct 18, follow brown signs 'Anchor')
☎ 0117 926 0680
e-mail: commerical@ss-great-britain.com
web: www.ss-great-britain.com

Exploring 200 years of Bristol shipbuilding, with special reference to Charles Hill & Son, and their predecessor, James Hillhouse. At the Great Western Dock the museum forms part of the *SS Great Britain* and John Cabot's *Matthew* experience.

Times: ✱ Open all year, daily 10-5.30, 4.30 in winter. (Closed 24 & 25 Dec). **Facilities:** 🅿 (charged) 🍴 ♿ toilets for disabled shop ✖ (ex guide dogs) 🍴

SS GREAT BRITAIN
Great Western Dock, Gas Ferry Rd BS1 6TY
➲ (off Cumberland Rd)
☎ 0117 926 0680

Built and launched in Bristol in 1843, the *SS Great Britain*, designed by Isambard Kingdom Brunel, was the first ocean-going, propeller-driven, iron ship. After a life as a passenger liner, troop transport and cargo carrier, she was abandoned in the Falkland Islands in 1886. But in 1970 she was towed back to Bristol and is now being conserved in the Great Western Dock where she was built.

Times: ✱ Open all year daily 10-5.30, 4.30 in winter. (Closed 24 & 25 Dec). **Facilities:** 🅿 (charged) 🍴 ♿ shop ✖ 🍴

Clifton Suspension Bridge

BUCKINGHAMSHIRE

EVENTS & FESTIVALS

February
7th Shrove Tuesday Olney Pancake Day Race

May
1st Marlow Spring Regatta,
  Higginson Park, Marlow
29th Marlow May Fayre,
  Higginson Park, Marlow

June
4th Coombe Hill Run, Wendover
10th-11th Marlow Town Regatta & Festival,
  Higginson Park, Marlow (provisional)
11th Folk on the Green, Horsefair Green,
  Stony Stratford (now part of
  Milton Keynes)
17th Marlow Regatta (Dorney Reach)
25th Milton Keynes Carnival,
  central Milton Keynes

July
1st-8th Buckingham Summer Festival, musical
  events, various venues

August
31st Bucks County Show, Weedon Park,
  Aylesbury

September
10th Thames Valley Grand Prix Raft Race,
  Higginson Park, Marlow
16th Marlow Carnival,
  Higginson Park, Marlow

November
tbc Marlow Music Festival, various venues

December
tbc Haddenham Festival, Haddenham Village,
  between Thame & Aylesbury

Above: Statue of John Hampden, whose defiance of King Charles I started the English Civil War

AYLESBURY   Map 04 SP81

BOARSTALL DUCK DECOY NEW
Boarstall HP18 9UX
➲ (A41/B4011, towards Long Crendon. Turn right to Boarstall & follow brown sign - decoy 200yds on right, through Manor Farm)
☎ 01280 822850
e-mail: stowegarden@nationaltrust.org.uk
web: www.nationaltrust.org.uk
A rare survival of a 17th century decoy in working order. Working decoy demonstration on Saturday and Sunday 11am to 3pm.
Times: Open Wed 3.30-6.30, Sat-Sun 10-4, mid Mar-Aug
Fee: ✱ £2.30 (ch £1.10) Family £5.50 **Facilities:** 🅿 📕 ♿ ✈ (ex assist dogs) 🦴

KING'S HEAD NEW
King's Head Passage, Market Square HP20 2RW
➲ (A41 follow signs for Aylesbury)
☎ 01296 381501
e-mail: emily.hirons@nationaltrust.org.uk
web: www.nationaltrust.org.uk
This historic coaching inn was established in 1455 and is still trading today. It has many notable architectural features, including a medieval stained glass window, extensive timber framing and an ancient cobbled courtyard. Once a base for Oliver Cromwell it now houses among other features a history centre.
Times: Open all year NT office 9-6. (Inn Mon-Sat 11am-11pm & Sun 11am-10.30pm) **Fee:** ✱ £2 (ch £1) **Facilities:** 💷 📕 ✈ (ex assist dogs) 🦴

BEACONSFIELD   Map 04 SU99

BEKONSCOT MODEL VILLAGE AND RAILWAY
Warwick Rd HP9 2PL
➲ (M40 junct 2, 4m M25 junct 16)
☎ 01494 672919
e-mail: info@bekonscot.co.uk
web: www.bekonscot.com

A miniature world, depicting rural England in the 1930s. A Gauge 1 model railway meanders through six little villages, each with their own tiny population. Rides on the sit-on miniature railway take place weekends and school holidays.
Times: Open mid Feb-Oct, 10-5. **Fee:** ✱ £5.80 (ch £3.50, concessions £4). **Facilities:** 🅿 💷 📕 ♿ (wheelchair loan) toilets for disabled shop ✈ (ex guide dogs) 🍴

BLETCHLEY   Map 04 SP93

BLETCHLEY PARK
The Mansion, Bletchley Park MK3 6EB
➲ (Approach Bletchley from V7 Saxon St. At rdbt, southern end of Saxon St. go under railway bridge towards Buckingham & follow signs to Bletchley Park)
☎ 01908 640404
e-mail: info@bletchleypark.org.uk
web: www.bletchleypark.org.uk

Known as 'Station X' during World War II, this was the home of the secret scientific team that worked to decipher German military messages sent using the Enigma code machine. Visitors can find out more about the Enigma machine; the 'bombes', computers used to crack the code; Alan Turing, one of the leading mathematicians of his day, who worked on the project; as well as see a number of other displays including the use of pigeons during the war, wartime vehicles, and a Churchill collection.
Times: Open daily 9.30-5.30 (Tours at 11 & 2). Weekends open 10.30-5. Closed 25 & 26 Dec. **Fee:** ✱ £10 (ch & concessions £8) Family £25 under 8's free. **Facilities:** 🅿 (charged) 💷 ✈ licensed ♿ toilets for disabled shop 🍴

CHALFONT ST GILES   Map 04 SU99

CHILTERN OPEN AIR MUSEUM
Newland Park, Gorelands Ln HP8 4AB
➲ (M25 junct 17, M40 junct 2. Follow brown signs)
☎ 01494 871117
e-mail: coamuseum@netscape.net
web: www.coam.org.uk
Saved from demolition and moved brick by brick to Newland Park, this collection of old buildings includes barns, granaries and even a tin chapel. Step back in time and get a feel of the 1940s in a fully furnished Prefab, or experience 50AD at the Iron Age House. Demonstrations including brick making, rug making, black smithing and storytelling. Regular living history re-enactments.
Times: ✱ Open 31 Mar-Oct, daily 10-5. **Facilities:** 🅿 💷 📕 ♿ (Braille guide books & taped guides available, wheelchairs) toilets for disabled shop ✈ (ex on lead) 🍴

MILTON'S COTTAGE

Dean Way HP8 4JH

➲ (0.5m W of A413. 3m N of M40 junct 2)

☎ 01494 872313

e-mail: info@miltonscottage.org

web: www.miltonscottage.org

A timber-framed, 16th-century cottage, with a charming garden, the only surviving home in which John Milton lived and worked. He completed *Paradise Lost* and started *Paradise Regained* here. First editions of these works are among the many rare books and artefacts on display.
Times: Open Mar-Oct, Tue-Sun 10-1 & 2-6. Also open Spring & Summer BH. **Fee:** ✱ £3 (ch 15 £1). Party 20+ £2 each.
Facilities: 🅿 ✖ licensed 🗐 ♿ (special parking area closer to cottage) shop ✖ (ex guide dogs)

CLIVEDEN   Map 04 SU98

CLIVEDEN

SL6 0JA

➲ (2m N of Taplow, follow brown signs on A4)

☎ 01628 605069   **2 for 1**

e-mail: cliveden@nationaltrust.org.uk

web: www.nationaltrust.org.uk

The 375 acres of garden and woodland overlook the River Thames, and include a magnificent parterre, topiary, lawns with box hedges, and water gardens. The palatial house, former home of the Astors, is now a hotel - The Great Hall and French Dining Room can be visited on certain afternoons. The 2-for-1 voucher is only valid during normal visiting hours and cannot be used for any ticketed events.
Times: Open Grounds 15 Mar-Oct daily 11-6, Nov-22 Dec daily 11-4 (Woodlands open all year). House Apr-Oct, Thu & Sun 3-5.30 by timed ticket. **Fee:** ✱ Grounds: £7 (ch £3.50). House: £1 extra (ch 50p extra). Family ticket £17.50. Group £6 each. Woodlands £3 (ch £1.50) Family £7.50 **Facilities:** 🅿 ✖ licensed ♿ (powered vehicle & wheelchairs available, parking) toilets for disabled shop ✖ Dogs allowed in woodland 🐾

GREAT MISSENDEN   Map 06 SP80

THE ROALD DAHL MUSEUM & STORY CENTRE NEW

81-83 High St HP16 0AL

☎ 01494 892192

e-mail: info@roalddahlmuseum.org

web: roalddahlmuseum.org

Roald Dahl's life and displays of unique archive in the village where he lived for over 70 years. Discover more of the world famous writer and some of his contemporaries. Unearth secrets about the people and places which inspired Dahl's tales, in our interactive galleries, discover how he wrote. Use the touch-screens to read his hand written notes and visit a replica of his writing hut. Check out top tips from today's leading authors - use your own Ideas Book just as Dahl did and you too could be a writer! Rolling programme of workshops and events.
Times: Open all year, Tue-Fri & BH Mon 10-5. Closed 25-26 Dec
Fee: £4.50 (ch 3-18 & concessions £3.50). Family ticket £15.
Facilities: 🅿 💻 ♿ (audioloops, tactile maps) toilets for disabled shop ✖ (ex assist dogs)

HIGH WYCOMBE   Map 04 SU89

WYCOMBE LOCAL HISTORY & CHAIR MUSEUM

Castle Hill House, Priory Av HP13 6PX

➲ (signposted by brown tourism sign from A404 (Amersham Hill) N of High Wycombe town centre just past railway station)

☎ 01494 421895   **FREE**

e-mail: museum@wycombe.gov.uk

web: www.wycombe.gov.uk/museum

High Wycombe is famous for chair making and the museum has an extensive collection of chairs and artefacts from the furniture industry. There is also a gallery featuring local scenes and artists. Other aspects of Wycombe's history are also represented along with changing exhibitions.
Times: Open all year, Mon-Sat 10-5, Sun 2-5. Closed on BHs except special events - ring for details. **Facilities:** 🅿 💻 🗐 ♿ (special parking & drop off point) toilets for disabled shop ✖ (ex guide dogs)

HUGHENDEN   Map 04 SU89

HUGHENDEN MANOR

HP14 4LA

➲ (1.5m N of High Wycombe, on W side of A4128)

☎ 01494 755573

e-mail: hughenden@nationaltrust.org.uk

web: www.nationaltrust.org.uk

Fascinating Victorian Manor, home of Prime Minister Benjamin Disraeli from 1847-1881. Many of his possessions are still on display, along with beautiful gardens designed by his wife Mary-Anne. Other facilities include circular woodland walks, family tracker packs, I-spy sheets in the Manor and an exhibition revealing Hughenden's role in WWII.
Times: House open 5-27 Mar, Sat & Sun only. Apr-Oct, Wed-Sun & BH Mon 1-5. Last admission 4.30. Gardens same dates as house 12-5. Park open all year. Also open Good Fri. **Fee:** ✱ £5 (ch £2.50). Family ticket £12.50. Garden only £1.80 (ch 90p). Park free.
Facilities: 🅿 ✖ licensed 🗐 ♿ (Braille leaflet, wheelchairs, ramp to house) toilets for disabled shop ✖ (ex guide dogs; in grounds) 🐾

LONG CRENDON   Map 04 SP60

COURTHOUSE

HP18 9AN

➲ (2m N of Thame, via B4011 when entering village turn right into the High St. Courthouse on left at end of High St)

☎ 01280 822850

e-mail: richard.pearce@nationaltrust.org.uk

web: www.nationaltrust.org.uk

One of the finest examples of early timber framed building in the area. Probably built as a wool store in the early 1400s, but also used as a manorial courthouse until the late 19th century, this timber-framed building stands out, even in this picturesque village. Although the windows and doors have been altered and the chimney stack is Tudor, the magnificent timber roof is original.
Times: Open, Upper storey Apr-Sep, Wed 2-6, Sat, Sun & BH Mons 11-6. **Fee:** *Prices not confirmed for 2006* **Facilities:** 🅿 (street) (not suitable for large vehicles) ✖ 🐾

MIDDLE CLAYDON   Map 04 SP72
CLAYDON HOUSE
MK18 2EY
➲ (off A413 in Padbury, follow National Trust signs. Entrance by north drive only)
☎ 01296 730349
2 for 1
e-mail: claydon@nationaltrust.org.uk
web: www.nationaltrust.org.uk

The rather sober exterior of this 18th-century house gives no clue to the extravagances that lie inside, in the form of fantastic rococo carvings. Ceilings, cornices, walls and overmantels are adorned with delicately carved fruits, birds, beasts and flowers by Luke Lightfoot. The Chinese room is particularly splendid. There is also a spectacular parquetry staircase. The 2-for-1 voucher is valid only during normal visiting hours, and cannot be used for any ticketed events.
Times: House open 26 Mar-30 Oct, Sat-Wed 1-5, 25-31 Oct 1-4.30 (Closed Thu & Fri). Grounds open 1-5. (Last admission 4.30). Closed Good Fri. **Fee:** ✱ £5 (ch £2.50). Family ticket £12.50. Group £4.20 each. Grounds £1.10 **Facilities:** 🅿 💷 ✕ licensed 🎞 ♿ (Braille guide, photograph albums) toilets for disabled ✖ (ex guide dogs or in park) ♨

QUAINTON   Map 04 SP72
BUCKINGHAMSHIRE RAILWAY CENTRE
Quainton Rd Station HP22 4BY
➲ (Signed off A41 Aylesbury-Bicester road at Waddesdon, 7m NW of Aylesbury)
☎ 01296 655720
2 for 1
e-mail: bucksrailcentre@btopenworld.com
web: www.bucksrailcentre.org

Housed in a former Grade II listed building, the Centre features an interesting and varied collection of about 20 locomotives with 40 carriages and wagons from places as far afield as South Africa, Egypt and America. Items date from the 1800s up to the 1960s. Visitors can take a ride on full-size and miniature steam trains, and stroll around the 20-acre site to see locomotives and rolling stock. The Centre runs locomotive driving courses for visitors. Regular 'Days out with Thomas' events take place throughout the year. 2-for-1 not valid for Thomas or Santa events.
Times: Open with engines in steam Apr-Oct, Sun & BH Mon; School hol Wed; 10.30-5.30. Dec Sat & Sun Santa's Magical Steamings-advanced booking essential. Also open for static viewing Wed-Sat. **Fee:** Steaming Days; £6 (ch & pen £4). Family ticket £18. BH wknds £7 (ch & pen £5). Family ticket £20. Static viewing £3 (ch & pen £2). **Facilities:** 🅿 💷 ♿ (ramped bridge with wheelchair lift) toilets for disabled ▰

STOWE   Map 04 SP63
STOWE HOUSE
MK18 5EH
➲ (3m NW Buckingham)
☎ 01280 818282
e-mail: sses@stowe.co.uk
web: www.stowe.co.uk

Set in the National Trust's landscaped gardens, Stowe is a splendid 18th-century mansion. The leading designers of the day were called in to lay out the gardens, and leading architects - Vanbrugh, Gibbs, Kent and Leoni - commissioned to decorate them with garden temples. The house is now a major public school.
Times: Open 19-20 Feb & 12-13 Mar, Sat-Sun guided tours only; 25 Mar-17 Apr, Wed-Sun & Etr Mon noon-5, (last admission 4pm) guided
continued

tour at 2pm; 30 May-3 Jun, Wed-Sun & BH Mon guided tour only 2pm; 3 Jul-25 Aug, Wed-Sun & BH Mon noon-5pm (last admission 4pm) guided tour at 2pm; 31 Aug-16 Oct Wed-Sun for guided tour only 2pm; 19-20 Nov & 17-18 Dec Sat-Sun guided tour at 2pm **Fee:** ✱ £2 (ch £1). Guided tours £3 (ch £1.50). **Facilities:** 🅿 🎞 ♿ toilets for disabled shop ✖ (ex guide dogs)

STOWE LANDSCAPE GARDENS
MK18 5EH
➲ (3m NW of Buckingham via Stoke Ave, off A422)
☎ 01280 822850
e-mail: stowegarden@nationaltrust.org.uk
web: www.nationaltrust.org.uk

Stowe is a breathtaking 18th-century creation, an idealised version of nature, and is one of the first and foremost of the great English landscape gardens. Hidden amongst spectacular views and vast open spaces there are over 40 monuments, temples and secret corners to be discovered.
Times: Open all year early Mar-Oct, Wed-Sun, 10-5.30, (last admission 4); Nov-Feb, Sat-Sun 10-4 **Fee:** ✱ £5.80 (ch £2.90). Family ticket £14.50 **Facilities:** 🅿 ✕ licensed 🎞 ♿ (manual wheelchairs unsuitable, powered batricars available) toilets for disabled shop ♨ ▰

WADDESDON   Map 04 SP71
WADDESDON MANOR
HP18 0JH
➲ (entrance off A41, 6m NW of Aylesbury)
☎ 01296 653211, 653226 & 653203
e-mail: suzy.barron@nationaltrust.org.uk
web: www.waddesdon.org.uk

Built in the 19th century, this 16th-century French style chateau is home to a fine collection of French decorative arts. Its Victorian gardens are known for their parterre, seasonal displays, walks, views, fountains and statues. The aviary is stocked with species that were once part of Baron Ferdinand's collection and the wine cellar contains Rothschild wines dating back to 1868. Special Events: Please telephone 01296 653226 for details of events running throughout the year.
Times: Open, Grounds & Aviary, until 23 Dec, Wed-Sun & BH Mon 10-5. House until 30 Oct, Wed-Sun & BH Mon 11-4. East Wing 16 Nov-23 Dec Wed-Sun 12-4. Entrance by timed ticket. **Fee:** ✱ Grounds £4 (ch £2, pre-Xams free). House and grounds £11 (ch £8), pre-Xmas £8 (ch £2). Bachelors Wing £3. NT members free. Please telephone for details of group rates. **Facilities:** 🅿 ✕ licensed ♿ (wheelchairs, Braille guide, parking, scented plants) toilets for disabled shop ✖ (ex guide dogs) ♨ ▰

WEST WYCOMBE   Map 04 SU89
THE HELL-FIRE CAVES
HP14 3AJ
➲ (on A40 in West Wycombe)
☎ 01494 524411 (office) & 533739 (caves)
e-mail: mary@west-wycombe-estate.co.uk
web: www.hellfirecaves.co.uk

The entrance to West Wycombe caves is halfway up the hill that dominates the village. On the summit stands the parish church and the mausoleum of the Dashwood family. The caves are not natural but were dug on the orders of Sir Francis Dashwood between 1748 and 1752. Sir Francis, the Chancellor of the Exchequer, was also the founder of the Hell Fire Club, whose members were reputed to have held outrageous and blasphemous parties in the caves, which extend approximately half a mile underground. The
continued

entrance, from a large forecourt, is a brick tunnel that leads into the caves, where tableaux and curiosities are exhibited.
Times: Open all year, Mar-Oct, daily 11-6; Nov-Feb, Sat & Sun 1-5.
Facilities: 🅿 💻 📶 ♿ toilets for disabled shop
✈ (ex guide dogs) 🍴

WEST WYCOMBE PARK
HP14 3AJ
➲ (S of A40, at W end of West Wycombe)
☎ 01494 755573   **2 for 1**
e-mail: hughenden@nationaltrust.org.uk
web: www.nationaltrust.org.uk
Set in 300 acres of beautiful parkland, the house was rebuilt in the Palladian style, between 1745 and 1771, for Sir Francis Dashwood. Of particular note are the painted ceilings by Borgnis. The park was laid out in the 18th century and given an artificial lake and classical temples. The 2-for-1 voucher is valid only during normal visiting hours, and cannot be used for any ticketed events.
Times: Open, House & grounds Jun-Aug, Sun-Thu 2-6. Grounds only Apr-May, Sun-Thu 2-6 & Etr, May Day & Spring BH Sun & Mon 2-6. (Last admission 5.15). Entry by timed tickets. Parties must book in advance. **Fee:** ✱ House & grounds £5.40 (ch £2.70) Family £13.50. Group £4.60. Grounds only £2.80 (ch £1.40). **Facilities:** 🅿 ♿ (partial access to ground floor & gardens) ✈ (assist dogs allowed) 🐾

WING   Map 04 SP82
ASCOTT
LU7 0PS
➲ (0.5m E of Wing, 3m SW of Leighton Buzzard on S side of A418)
☎ 01296 688242
e-mail: info@ascottestate.co.uk
web: www.ascottestate.com
A National Trust property since 1949, Ascott holds an exceptional collection of paintings, Chinese porcelain and English and French furniture. The 30-acre garden is a fine example of Victorian gardening and the grounds are stunning at any time of the year.
Times: House & Gardens: mid Mar-Apr daily 2-6 (ex Mon), 3 May-28 Jul Tue-Thu 2-6, 2-31 Aug daily 2-6 (ex Mon). **Fee:** ✱ House & Garden £6.50 (ch £3.25). Gardens only: £4 (ch £2). National Trust members free ex 2 May & 29 Aug. **Facilities:** 🅿 ♿ (w/chairs avail, assistance required, large print guide) toilets for disabled ✈ 🐾

> ## Isambard Kingdom Brunel (1806-1859).
> 2006 is the 200th anniversary of the birth of one of Britain's most important engineers. His bicentenary will be celebrated by many attractions both directly and indirectly connected with Brunel.

CAMBRIDGESHIRE

EVENTS & FESTIVALS

January
   13th-15th Whittlesea Straw Bear Festival
   tbc Cambridge Winter Ale Festival, venue tbc
March
   18th-19th National Shire Horse Spring Show, East of England Showground, Peterborough
   tbc Daffodil Weekend, Thriplow (village festival)
May
   1st Stilton Cheese Rolling, Stilton
   5th-7th St Neots Folk Festival, The Priory Centre, St Neots
   28th-1st Jun Wisbech Rose Fair, SS Peter & Paul Church, Wisbech
   tbc Cambridge Beer Festival, Jesus Green, Cambridge
June
   2nd-4th East of England Garden Show, Wood Green Animal Shelter, Godmanchester
   16th-18th East of England Country Show, East of England Showground, Peterborough
   24th-26th Hemingford Abbots Open Gardens & Flower Festival Weekend
   tbc Strawberry Fair, free festival of music and entertainment, Midsummer Common, Cambridge
July
   7th-9th Ely Folk Weekend, Ely Outdoor Sports Association, Downham Road
   8th World Pea Shooting Championships & Village Fair, Village Green, Witcham, Ely (provisional)
   tbc Cambridge Folk Festival, Cherry Hinton Hall Grounds, Cherry Hinton Road, Cambridge
   tbc Cambridge Summer Music Festival, various venues, mid July-mid August
August
   22nd-27th Peterborough Beer Festival, biggest locally organised real ale festival in the UK

Above: Roses at Elton Hall

CAMBRIDGE Map 05 TL45

CAMBRIDGE & COUNTY FOLK MUSEUM
2/3 Castle St CB3 0AQ
⮕ (off A14 onto A3019, museum NW of town)
☎ 01223 355159
e-mail: info@folkmuseum.org.uk
web: www.folkmuseum.org.uk
This timber-framed inn houses items covering the everyday life of the people of Cambridgeshire from the early times to the present day. There are also temporary exhibitions. Special exhibitions and children's activity days take place throughout the year. Please telephone for details.
Times: Open all year, Apr-Sep, Mon-Sat 10.30-5, Sun 2-5. Oct-Mar, Tue-Sat 10.30-5, Sun 2-5. (Last admissions 30 mins before closing). Closed 1 Jan, Good Fri, 24-31 Dec **Fee:** £3 (ch 5-12 £1, concessions £2) one free ch with every full paying adult. **Facilities:** P (300yds) (pay and display on street parking) & (Braille touch tables, tape guides & large print guides) toilets for disabled shop ✺ (ex guide dogs)

CAMBRIDGE UNIVERSITY BOTANIC GARDEN
Cory Lodge, Bateman St CB2 1JF
⮕ (1m S of city centre)
☎ 01223 336265
e-mail: enquiries@botanic.cam.ac.uk
web: www.botanic.cam.ac.uk
The Cambridge University Botanic Garden is a 40-acre oasis of beautifully landscaped gardens and glasshouses close to the heart of the historic city. Opened on its present site in 1846, the garden showcases a collection of some 8000 plant species. This Grade II heritage landscape features the Rock Garden, displaying alpine plants, the Winter and Autumn Gardens, tropical rainforest and seasonal displays in the Glasshouses, the historic Systematic Beds, the Scented Garden, Herbaceous Beds and the finest collection of trees in the east of England.
Times: Open all year daily 10-6 (Apr-Sep); 10-5 (Feb-Mar, Oct), 10-4 (Nov-Jan). Glasshouses close 30mins before garden. Please call to check Christmas closure. Entry by Bateman St & Station Rd gates on wkdays & by Bateman St gate only at wknds & BH. **Fee:** ✻ £3 (conc £2.50). **Facilities:** P (on street parking or park & ride) � & (guiding service, manual & motorised wheelchairs-prebooked) toilets for disabled shop (open Mar-Oct) ✺ (ex guide dogs)

FITZWILLIAM MUSEUM
Trumpington St CB2 1RB
⮕ (M11 junct 11, 12 or 13. Near city centre) FREE
☎ 01223 332900
e-mail: fitzmuseum-enquiries@lists.cam.ac.uk
web: www.fitzmuseum.cam.ac.uk
The Fitzwilliam is the art museum of the University of Cambridge and one of the oldest public museums in Britain. It contains magnificent collections spanning centuries and civilisations including antiquities from Ancient Egypt, Greece and Rome; sculpture, furniture, armour, ceramics; manuscripts, coins and medals, paintings, drawings and prints.
Times: Open all year Tue-Sat 10-5, Sun 12-5. (Closed Mon ex BH, & 24-26, 31 Dec & 1 Jan). **Facilities:** P (400yds) (2hr max, metered) ▮ & (induction loop) toilets for disabled shop ✺ (ex assist dogs)

SCOTT POLAR RESEARCH INSTITUTE MUSEUM
Lensfield Rd CB2 1ER
⮕ (1km S of City Centre)
☎ 01223 336540 FREE
e-mail: rkh10@cam.ac.uk
An international centre for polar studies, including a museum featuring displays of Arctic and Antarctic expeditions, with special emphasis on those of Captain Scott and the exploration of the Northwest Passage. Other exhibits include Eskimo work and other arts of the polar regions, as well as displays on current scientific exploration. Public lectures run from October to December and February to April.
Times: Open all year, Tue-Sat 2.30-4. Closed some BHs wknds, public & university hols. **Facilities:** P (400mtrs) & shop ✺ (ex guide dogs)

UNIVERSITY MUSEUM OF ARCHAEOLOGY & ANTHROPOLOGY
Downing St CB2 3DZ
⮕ (located opposite Crowne Plaza Hotel in city centre)
☎ 01223 333516 FREE
e-mail: cumaa@hermes.cam.ac.uk
web: cumaa.archanth.cam.ac.uk
The museum is part of the Faculty of Archaeology and Anthropology of the University of Cambridge. It was established in 1884 and is still housed in its 1916 building on the Downing Site in the city centre. It has three floors displaying renowned archaeological and anthropological collections from around the world. Programme of changing special exhibitions.
Times: Open all year Tue-Sat 2-4.30. (Closed 1wk Etr & 1wk Xmas). Telephone for extended summer hours. **Facilities:** P (100yds) & (lift available) shop ✺ (ex guide dogs)

DUXFORD Map 05 TL44

IMPERIAL WAR MUSEUM DUXFORD
CB2 4QR
⮕ (off M11 junct 10, on A505)
☎ 01223 835000
e-mail: duxford@iwm.org.uk
web: www.iwm.org.uk
Duxford is one of the world's most spectacular aviation heritage complexes with a collection of nearly 200 aircraft, the American Air Museum and a fine collection of military vehicles plus special exhibitions including The Battle of Britain, Normandy Experience and Monty. The Museum holds four Air Shows throughout the summer plus other special events such as the Military Vehicle Show and Flying Proms.
Times: Open all year, mid Mar-mid Oct daily 10-6; mid Oct-mid Mar daily 10-4. (Closed 24-26 Dec) **Fee:** ✻ £12 (pen £9 & concessions £7). Ch under 16yrs free. Different rates apply for air shows.
Facilities: P ▮ ✗ licensed & (w/chair available-phone in advance, ramps) toilets for disabled shop ✺ (ex guide dogs) ◀

ELY Map 05 TL58

ELY CATHEDRAL
CB7 4DL
⮕ (A10 or A142, 15m from Cambridge)
☎ 01353 667735
e-mail: receptionist@cathedral.ely.anglican.org
web: www.cathedral.ely.anglican.org
The Octagon Tower of Ely Cathedral can be seen for miles as it rises above the surrounding flat fenland. A monastery was
continued

founded on the site by St Etheldreda in 673, but the present cathedral church dates from 1083 and is a magnificent example of Romanesque architecture.
Times: Open daily, Summer 7-7, Winter 7.30-6 (5pm Sun).
Fee: ✱ £4.80 (concessions £4.20). Ch free in family group. Group reductions (15+) **Facilities:** P (walking distance) ▰ ✗ licensed ▤ ♿ (touch tour for blind/partially sighted) toilets for disabled shop ✖ (ex assist dogs) ▰

OLIVER CROMWELL'S HOUSE
29 St Mary's St CB7 4HF
➲ (follow brown tourist signs from main roads. Adjacent to Saint Mary's Church)
☎ 01353 662062
e-mail: tic@eastcambs.gov.uk
web: www.eastcambs.gov.uk
Cromwell inherited the house and local estates from a maternal uncle and moved here in 1636, along with his mother, sisters, wife and eight children. There are displays and period rooms dealing with Cromwell's life, the Civil War and domestic life in the 17th century, as well as the history of The Fens and the house itself, from its medieval origins to its role as an inn in the 19th century.
Times: Open all year: Apr-Oct, daily 10-5.30; Nov-Mar, Mon-Fri 11-4, Sat 10-5. Sun, 11.15-4. **Fee:** £3.75 (concessions £3.25). Family ticket £10. **Facilities:** P (100yds) ♿ shop ✖ (ex guide dogs) ▰

THE STAINED GLASS MUSEUM
The Cathedral CB7 4DN
➲ (15m N of Cambridge via A10)
☎ 01353 660347
e-mail: curator@stainedglassmuseum.com
web: www.stainedglassmuseum.com
Situated in the cathedral, this museum is the only one of its kind in the country. Case exhibits show how stained-glass windows are designed and made, and there is an exhibition of approximately 100 panels dating from the 13th century to the present day, displayed at eye level in back-lit cases. The museum has recently reopened after a total refurbishment, with new loans from the Victoria & Albert Museum.
Times: ✱ Open daily, Mon-Fri 10.30-4.30, Sat & BH 10.30-5 & Sun 12-6. **Facilities:** P (400yds) ▰ ✗ licensed ▤ ♿ (Inter-active video visit) toilets for disabled shop ✖ (ex guide dogs) ▰

HAMERTON   Map 04 TL17
HAMERTON ZOO PARK
PE28 5RE
➲ (off A1 junct 15, signed Sawtry)
☎ 01832 293362
e-mail: office@hamertonzoopark.com
web: www.hamertonzoopark.com
A wildlife breeding centre, dedicated to the practical conservation of endangered species including gibbons, marmosets, lemurs, wildcats, meerkats, sloths and many more. There is also a large and varied bird collection, with several species unique to Hamerton. Over 120 species in all. Other attractions include a children's play area, and new "creature contact" sessions.
Times: Open Summer daily 10.30-6; Winter daily 10.30-4. Closed 25 Dec **Fee:** Prices on application **Facilities:** P ▰ ♿ toilets for disabled shop ✖ ▰

LINTON   Map 05 TL54
CHILFORD HALL VINEYARD
Chilford Hall, Balsham Rd CB1 6LE
➲ (signposted from A1307 and A11)
☎ 01223 892641
e-mail: simonalper@chilfordhall.co.uk
web: www.chilfordhall.co.uk
Taste and buy award-winning wines from the largest vineyard in Cambridgeshire. See the grapes growing in the 18-acre vineyard and take a winery tour to learn how English wine is made and appreciate the subtle difference between each of the Chilford quality wines. Telephone for details of special events.
Times: Open Mar-Oct , Fri-Sun & BHs **Facilities:** P ▰ ♿ toilets for disabled shop ▰

LINTON ZOOLOGICAL GARDENS
Hadstock Rd CB1 6NT
➲ (M11 junct 9/10, on B1052 off A1307 between Cambridge & Haverhill, signposted)
☎ 01223 891308
web: www.lintonzoo.co.uk
Linton Zoo places emphasis on conservation and education where visitors can see a combination of beautiful gardens and a wealth of wildlife from all over the world. There are many rare and exotic creatures to see including tapirs, snow leopards, tigers, lions, Grevy's zebra, tamarin monkeys, lemurs, owls, parrots, giant tortoises, snakes, tarantula spiders and many others. The zoo is set in 16-acres of gardens with plenty of picnic areas, children's play area and bouncy castle.
Times: Open all year, daily 10.30-4, last admission 3. Hours extended during summer. Closed 25-26 Dec. **Fee:** £7 (pen £6.50, ch 2-13 £4.50) **Facilities:** P ▰ ♿ toilets for disabled shop ✖ ▰

LODE   Map 05 TL56
ANGLESEY ABBEY
CB5 9EJ
➲ (6m NE of Cambridge on B1102, signposted from A14)
☎ 01223 810080
e-mail: angleseyabbey@ntrust.org.uk
web: www.nationaltrust.org.uk/angleseyabbey
A medieval undercroft has survived from the priory founded here in 1135, but the house dates mainly from 1600. Thomas Hobson of *Hobson's Choice* was one of the owners. A later owner was Lord Fairhaven, who amassed the huge collection of pictures, and laid out the beautiful gardens.
Times: Open House & Mill: 24 Mar-7 Nov, Wed-Sun & BH Mon's, 1-5. Gardens open 10.30-5.30 and also open in winter 10 Nov-20 Mar, daily, 10.30-4.30. Closed 24-28 Dec. **Fee:** House and garden £8. Garden only £4.50 (£4 in winter). Family & party discounts available.
Facilities: P ✗ licensed ▤ ♿ (electric buggy, wheelchairs, large print & braille guides) toilets for disabled shop garden centre ✖ (ex guide dogs) ▨ ▰

PETERBOROUGH   Map 04 TL19
FLAG FEN BRONZE AGE CENTRE
The Droveway, Northey Rd PE6 7QJ
☎ 01733 313414
e-mail: office@flagfen.freeserve.co.uk   **2 for 1**
web: www.flagfen.com
Although visitors enter this site through a 21st-century roundhouse, the rest of their day will be spent in the Bronze
continued

Age, some 3,000 years ago. Flag Fen is one of Europe's most important Bronze Age sites, and contains reconstructions of Iron Age as well as Bronze Age roundhouses. There is also a museum of artefacts found on the site over the last 20 years, as well as a Preservation Hall that contains a 60ft mural depicting the fens in ancient times.
Times: Open daily 10-4 (last admission). Site closes 5pm. (Closed 24 Dec-2 Jan) **Fee:** £4.25 (pen £3.75, ch & students £3)
Facilities: P ⬛ 🖼 ♿ toilets for disabled shop ✗ (ex assistance dogs)◀

LONGTHORPE TOWER
Thorpe Rd, Longthorpe PE1 1HA
☎ 01733 268482
See the finest domestic wall paintings in northern Europe hidden in the tower for centuries until revealed by a World War II bomb.
Times: Open Jul-Aug, Sat 12-5. All other days pre-booked tours only.
Fee: £2.30 (ch £1.20, concessions £1.70). Opening times and prices are subject to change, for further details please phone 0870 333 1181
Facilities: P ✗ ⬛

PETERBOROUGH CATHEDRAL
PE1 1XS
➲ (access from A1 juncts with A605 or A47, follow signs)
☎ 01733 343342
e-mail: a.watson@peterborough-cathedral.org.uk
web: www.peterborough-cathedral.org.uk
With one of the most dramatic West fronts in the country, its three arches an extraordinary creation of medieval architecture, it would be easy for the interior to be an anticlimax, but it is not. The dramatic Romanesque interior is little altered since its completion 800 years ago. Particular highlights of a visit include the unique painted nave ceiling, the elaborate fan vaulting of the 'new' building, Saxon carvings from an earlier church and the burial place of two Queens. An exhibition in the North aisle tells the story of the cathedral. A range of tours can be booked in advance: please contact the Chapter office for details.
Times: Open all year, daily 9-5. Closed 25-26 Dec. **Fee:** Free - donations towards the cost of upkeep are requested but £3.50 charge for group tours (£2.50 for concessions). **Facilities:** P (300yds) (no parking within cathedral precincts) ⬛ ✗ licensed 🖼 ♿ (touch & hearing centre, Braille guide, ramps) toilets for disabled shop ✗ (ex guide dogs or in grounds)

RAILWORLD
Oundle Rd PE2 9NR
➲ (from A1(M) Peterborough, turn onto A1139 then off at junct 5 to city centre. At 1st rdbt, follow "Little Puffer" tourist signs. Entrance for Railworld is off Oundle Rd at City end through car park)
☎ 01733 344240 `2 for 1`
e-mail: railworld@aol.com
web: www.railworld.net
An exhibition centre and museum dedicated to all things rail related, especially the environment. Attractions include model railways, hands-on exhibits, a rail industry showcase, hover-trains, local rail history gallery and a car. Special events during 2006 include National Science week 10-19 March and Brunel Bicentenary mini-display May to August.
Times: Mar-Oct daily 11-4, Nov-Feb Mon-Fri 11-4 **Fee:** £5 (ch £2.50, concessions £4) Family £12 **Facilities:** P ⬛ 🖼 ♿ (reasonable access) toilets for disabled shop (ex guide dogs)

RAMSEY Map 04 TL28
RAMSEY ABBEY GATEHOUSE
Abbey School PE17 1DH
➲ (SE edge of Ramsey, where Chatteris Road joins B1096)
☎ 0870 609 5388 `FREE`
web: www.nationaltrust.org.uk/regions/eastanglia
The ruins of this 15th-century gatehouse, together with the 13th-century Lady Chapel, are all that remain of the abbey. Half of the gatehouse was taken away after the Dissolution. Built in ornate late-Gothic style, it has panelled buttresses and friezes.
Times: Open Apr-Oct, daily 10-5. **Facilities:** ✗ 🌿

WANSFORD Map 04 TL09
NENE VALLEY RAILWAY
Wansford Station, Stibbington PE8 6LR
➲ (A1 at Stibbington, W of Peterborough, 1m south of the A47 junct)
☎ 01780 784444
e-mail: nvrorg@aol.com
web: www.nvr.org.uk
Visit Britain's International Steam Railway and see steam and diesel engines, carriages and wagons from Europe including the UK. All the sights and sounds of the golden age of steam come alive here. Travelling between Yarwell Junction, Wansford and Peterborough the 7.5 miles of track pass through the heart of the 500-acre Ferry Meadows Country Park. Nene Valley Railway is also the home of 'Thomas'- children's favourite engine.
Times: Train services operate on Sun from Jan; wknds from Apr-Oct; Wed from May, plus other mid-week services in summer. **Fee:** ✱ £10 (ch 3-15 £5, concessions £7.50). Family ticket £25. **Facilities:** P ⬛ ♿ (disabled access to trains) toilets for disabled shop ◀

WATERBEACH Map 05 TL46
THE FARMLAND MUSEUM AND DENNY ABBEY
Ely Rd CB5 9PQ
➲ (on A10 between Cambridge and Ely)
☎ 01223 860988 `2 for 1`
e-mail: f.m.denny@tesco.net
web: www.dennyfarmlandmuseum.org.uk
Explore two areas of rural life at this fascinating museum. The Abbey tells the story of those who have lived there, including Benedictine monks, Franciscan nuns, and the mysterious Knights Templar. The farm museum features the craft workshops of a wheelwright, a basketmaker, and a blacksmith. There is also a 1940s farmworker's cottage and a village shop.
Times: Open daily Apr-Oct, noon-5pm **Fee:** ✱ £3.80 (concessions £3, ch £1.60) **Facilities:** P ⬛ 🖼 ♿ (wheelchairs) toilets for disabled shop ◀

WIMPOLE Map 05 TL35
WIMPOLE HALL
SG8 0BW
➲ (M11 junct 12, 8m SW of Cambridge off A603)
☎ 01223 206000
e-mail: wimpolehall@nationaltrust.org.uk
web: www.wimpole.org
Wimpole Hall is one of the grandest mansions in East Anglia, and has 360 acres of parkland devised and planted by no less than four celebrated landscape designers, Charles Bridgeman, 'Capability' Brown, Sanderson Miller and
continued

Humphrey Repton. The house dates back to 1640, but was altered into a large 18th-century mansion with a Georgian façade. The chapel has a trompe l'oeil ceiling.
Times: Open Mar-Oct, Sat-Wed, BH Mon & Good Fri, 1-5; Aug Sat-Thu, BH Mon 11-5; Nov, Sun only 1-4. **Fee:** ✱ £6.90 (ch £3.40).
Facilities: 🅿 💻 ✗ licensed 📷 🚻 (Braille & large print guide, buggies, stairlift, w/chair) toilets for disabled shop ✈ (ex park only) 🐾 🍴

WIMPOLE HOME FARM
SG8 0BW
➲ (M11 junct 12 8m SW of Cambridge off A603)
☎ 01223 206000
e-mail: wimpolehall@nationaltrust.org.uk
web: www.wimpole.org
When built in 1794, the Home Farm was one of the most advanced agricultural enterprises in the country. The Great Barn, now restored, holds a display of farm machinery and implements of the kind used at Wimpole over the past two centuries. On the farm there are rare breeds of domestic animals. Please ring for details of special events.
Times: Open Mar-Oct, Sat-Wed, Good Fri & BH Mon's 10.30-5; Aug, Sat-Thu 10.30-5; Nov-Mar, Sat & Sun 11-4. (open everyday Cambridge Etr hols & Oct/Feb half terms) **Fee:** ✱ £5.40 (ch £3.40). NT members £2.80 (ch £1.80). **Facilities:** 🅿 💻 ✗ licensed 📷 🚻 (braille guide, wheelchairs, electric buggies) toilets for disabled shop ✈ (ex guide dogs) 🐾 🍴

WISBECH   Map 09 TF40
PECKOVER HOUSE & GARDEN
North Brink PE13 1JR
➲ (Leave A47 & take town centre signs, then follow brown signs)
☎ 01945 583463
e-mail: ian.grafton@nationaltrust.org.uk
web: www.peckoverhouse.co.uk
Dating from 1722, Peckover House is a beautiful Georgian brick townhouse with a two-acre walled town garden, one of the finest such gardens in Britain and home to over 70 types of rose. The Victorian glasshouses include a fern house, and an orangery with 300-year-old trees that still bear fruit.
Times: Open, mid Mar-mid Nov, Sat-Sun & Tue-Wed, noon-5
Fee: House & garden £5 (ch £2.50). **Facilities:** 🅿 (400yds) 💻
✗ licensed 📷 🚻 (Batricar, induction loops, large print & Braille guides) toilets for disabled shop ✈ (ex guide dogs) 🐾 🍴

WOODHURST   Map 05 TL37
THE RAPTOR FOUNDATION
The Heath, St Ives Rd PE28 3BT
➲ (B1040 to Somersham, follow brown signs, 2m on left)
☎ 01487 741140   **2 for 1**
e-mail: heleowl@aol.com
web: www.raptorfoundation.org.uk
Permanent home to over 250 birds of which there are 40 different varieties. This is a unique opportunity to meet and learn about birds of prey. Depending on weather and time of year flying demonstrations are held, usually three times a day and audiences have the chance to participate in displays. There are nearly 60 birds in the flying team, so each display has a different set of birds. Educational trail linking to new education room. 2006 is the tenth anniversary of The Raptor Foundation.
Times: Open all year, daily 10-5. Closed 25-26 Dec & 1 Jan.
Fee: ✱ £3.75 (ch £2.25, pen £2.75) **Facilities:** 🅿 💻 ✗ 🚻 (ramped areas) toilets for disabled shop ✈ 🍴

CHESHIRE

EVENTS & FESTIVALS

March
   tbc North of England Head
      of the River Race, Chester
April
   tbc The Cheshire Run, Historic Vehicle Road
      Run, Lymm
May
   6th Knutsford Royal May Day
   17th-20th Alderley Edge Music Festival,
      Festival Theatre, Alderley Edge
   26th-29th Chester Folk Festival, Kelsall
June
   16th-17th International Church Music
      Festival, Chester Cathedral
   16th-18th Folk & Boat Festival, Middlewich
   20th-21st Cheshire County Show, The
      Showground, Tabley, nr Knutsford
   tbc World Worm Charming Championship,
      Willaston Primary School, Willaston
July
   14th-22nd Chester Summer Music Festival
   15th-16th Halton Show, Spike Island, Halton
   15th-30th Chester Fringe Festival (drama,
      dance and music), various venues
   19th-23rd Royal Horticultural Society Flower
      Show, Tatton Park, Knutsford
   tbc Halton Show, Spike Island, Halton
August
   20th Family Fun Day, West Park, Macclesfield
   26th Poynton Horticultural & Agricultural
      Show, Poynton Park, Poynton
   tbc Chester Regatta
      (oldest regatta in the country)
   tbc Tatton Park Country Show, Knutsford
September
   9th-10th Yesteryear Steam Rally, Malpas
      (provisional)
   30th-1st Oct Vintage Fair Organ & Steam
      Rally, Victoria Park, Widnes
October
   7th-28th Chester Literature Festival,
November
   tbc Festival of Trees, Chester

Above: Bridge Street, Chester

BEESTON Map 07 SJ55

BEESTON CASTLE

Tarporley CW6 9TX

➲ (on minor road off A49 or A41)

☎ 01829 260464

Legend tells of a vast treasure hidden here by Richard II, but the real treasure at Beeston lies in its 4,000 years of history waiting to be discovered. Breathtaking views extend from the Pennines to the mountains of Wales.

Times: Open all year, Apr-Sep, daily 10-6; Oct-Mar, daily 10-4. Closed 24-26 Dec & 1 Jan. **Fee:** £3.60 (ch £1.80, concessions £2.70, family £9.00). Opening times and prices are subject to change, for further details please phone 0870 333 1181 **Facilities:** P shop ✈ (in certain areas) ⛭

CAPESTHORNE Map 07 SJ87

CAPESTHORNE HALL

SK11 9JY

➲ (On A34 between Congleton and Wilmslow)

☎ 01625 861221

e-mail: info@capesthorne.com

web: www.capesthorne.com

Capesthorne has been the home of the Bromley-Davenport family and their ancestors since Domesday times. The present house dates from 1719 and was designed by the Smiths of Warwick. It was subsequently altered by Edward Blore in 1837 and after a disastrous fire in 1861 the whole of the centre portion was rebuilt by Anthony Salvin.

Capesthorne contains a great variety of sculptures, paintings and other items including a collection of American Colonial furnishings.

Times: Open Apr-Oct, Wed, Sun & BH's (Closed Xmas & New Year). Park & Garden 12-5.30, Hall 1.30-3.30. **Fee:** ✱ Park, Garden & Chapel £4 (ch £2). Park, Gardens, Chapel & Hall £6 (ch £3 & pen £5). Family ticket £15. Special deal on Wed's £10 per car (up to 4 persons).

Facilities: P ꙮ ✗ licensed 🏠 ♿ (ramp access to ground floor of hall & gardens) toilets for disabled ✈ (ex guide dogs & in gardens)

CHESTER Map 07 SJ46

CHESHIRE MILITARY MUSEUM

The Castle CH1 2DN

➲ (follow signs to Military Museum from town centre)

☎ 01244 327617

web: www.chester.ac.uk/militarymuseum

This military museum boasts exhibits from the history of the Cheshire Regiment, Cheshire Yeomanry, 5th Royal Inniskilling Dragoon Guards, and 3rd Carabiniers. Display of the work of George Jones, Victorian battle artist, and an exhibition of life in barracks in the 1950s. Research available by written appointment and donation. There are special events throughtout the year, please phone for details.

Times: Open all year, daily 10-5 (last entry 4pm). (Closed 22 Dec-2 Jan). **Fee:** ✱ £2 (concessions £1). **Facilities:** P (400yds) 🏠 ♿ all of museum accessible by wheelchairs toilets for disabled shop ✈ (ex guide dogs)

CHESTER CATHEDRAL

Saint Werburgh St CH1 2HU

➲ (opposite the town hall)

☎ 01244 324756

e-mail: office@chestercathedral.com

web: www.chestercathedral.com

Founded as a Benedictine monastery in 1092 on the sites of earlier churches, in 1541 it became the cathedral of the newly created Diocese of Chester and is a good example of a medieval monastic complex. Restored in the 19th century, the building contains work by Gilbert Scott, Clayton, Pugin and Kempe. There are daily services and visitors are welcome to join in. A summer music festival is held in July.

Times: Mon-Sat, 9-5, Sun 1-5, Please telephone to check. **Fee:** £4 (pen, student & groups 10+ £3, ch 5-16 £1.50). Family ticket £10 **Facilities:** P (200yds) (multi-storey) ꙮ ✗ licensed ♿ (induction loop, tactile model, wide doors) toilets for disabled shop ✈ (ex guide dogs) ◀

CHESTER VISITOR CENTRE

Vicars Ln CH1 1QX

➲ (opposite St Johns Church Roman Amphitheatre on Vicars Lane.)

☎ 01244 351609 **FREE**

e-mail: tis@chestercc.gov.uk

web: www.chestertourism.com

Among the attractions at this large visitor information centre are guided walks of Chester; World of Names, which explores the history of family and first names; displays on the history of Chester; a café and a gift shop. Chester is the most complete walled city in Britain, and was originally settled by the Romans in the first century AD. The city also played its part in battles with the Vikings, the Norman invasion, and the Civil War.

Times: Open all year, Mon-Sat 10-5, Sun 10-4 **Facilities:** P (200mtrs) (short stay visitor parking) ꙮ ♿ (ramped access from Vicars Lane) toilets for disabled shop ✈ (ex guide dogs)

CHESTER ZOO
Upton-by-Chester CH2 1LH
➲ (2m N of city centre off A41& M53 junct 10 southbound, junct 12 all other directions)
☎ 01244 380280
e-mail: marketing@chesterzoo.co.uk
web: www.chesterzoo.org

The largest zoological gardens in the UK, with more than 7000 animals of more than 500 species. Catch feeding time on Sealion Beach, visit Islands in Danger with the Komodo Dragons, feel the Spirit of the Jaguar and the awesome Tsavo-the Black Rhino Experience. Take to the treetops in the Zoofari overhead railway.
Times: Open all year, daily from 10. Last admission varies with season from 5.30pm high summer to 3.30pm winter. (Closed 25-26 Dec).
Fee: ✱ £9.50, ch £7.50 (£8.50 concessions). Family ticket £32 (2+2)
Facilities: 🅿 💷 ✗ licensed 🍴 ♿ (electric scooters, audio guide, induction loop, Braille) toilets for disabled shop ✖ (ex guide & sensory dogs) ◢

DEVA ROMAN EXPERIENCE
Pierpoint Ln, (off Bridge St) CH1 1NL
➲ (city centre)
☎ 01244 343407

Stroll along reconstructed streets experiencing the sights, sounds and smells of Roman Chester. From the streets of Deva (the Roman name for Chester) you return to the present day on an extensive archeological 'dig', where you can discover the substantial Roman, Saxon and medieval remains beneath modern Chester.
Times: Open all year, daily Feb-Nov 9-5, Dec-Jan 10-4 . (Closed 25-26 Dec). **Fee:** £4.25 (ch £2.50, under 5's free, pen & student £3.75). Family ticket £12. Party. **Facilities:** 🅿 (200yds) 🍴 ♿ shop ✖ (ex guide dogs)

CHOLMONDELEY   Map 07 SJ55
CHOLMONDELEY CASTLE GARDENS
SY14 8AH
➲ (off A49 Tarporley to Whitchurch road)
☎ 01829 720383
e-mail: pennypritchard@btconnect.com

Dominated by a romantic Gothic Castle built in 1801 of local sandstone, the gardens are laid out with fine trees and water gardens, and have been replanted with rhododendrons, azaleas, cornus, and acer. There is also a rose and lavender garden, lakeside and woodland walks, and rare breeds of farm animals.
Times: ✱ Open Apr-Sep, Wed-Thu, Sun & BHs 11.30-5. **Fee:** Adult £4, children £1.50 **Facilities:** 🅿 💷 ♿ (disabled car park, part of garden accessible) toilets for disabled shop garden centre

CONGLETON   Map 07 SJ86
LITTLE MORETON HALL
CW12 4SD
➲ (4m SW of Congleton, on E side of A34)
☎ 01260 272018
e-mail: littlemoretonhall@nationaltrust.org.uk
web: www.nationaltrust.org.uk

One of the best examples of half-timbered architecture in England. By 1580 the house was much as it is today, and the long gallery, chapel and the great hall are very impressive. The garden has a knot garden, orchard and herbaceous borders. Ring for details of special events.
Times: Open 5 Mar-6 Nov, Wed-Sun 11.30-5 or dusk if earlier; 12 Nov-18 Dec, wknds 11.30-4. BH Mon 11.30-5 **Fee:** ✱ £5.25 (ch £2.50). Family ticket £12.50, Groups £4.50, Special Openings £10
Facilities: 🅿 (charged) ✗ licensed ♿ (wheelchair, electric vehicle, Braille & large print guides) toilets for disabled shop ✖ (ex guide & assistance dogs) ◢

DISLEY   Map 07 SJ98
LYME PARK
SK12 2NX
➲ (off A6, 6.5m SE of Stockport. 12m NW of Buxton. House & car park 1m from entrance)
☎ 01663 762023
e-mail: lymepark@nationaltrust.org.uk
web: www.nationaltrust.org.uk

Home of the Legh family for 600 years and the largest house in Cheshire, Lyme Park featured as Pemberley in the BBC's production of *Pride and Prejudice*. It also featured in Granada's production of the *Forsyte Saga*. Parts of the original Elizabethan house remain, with 18th and 19th century additions. Set in extensive historic gardens with a lake and also a 1,400 acre park, home to red and fallow deer.
Times: Open daily Park: Apr-Oct, 8am-8.30pm; Nov-30 Mar, 8-6. Gardens: 31 Mar-30 Oct, Fri-Tue 11-5, Wed-Thu 1-5; 6 Nov-18 Dec, wknds 12-3. House: 21 Mar-30 Oct, Fri-Tue 1-5 (last admission 4.30). BH Mon 11-5. Cage: Apr-Oct, 2nd & 4th wknd of each month 12-4. Paddock Cottage Apr-Oct, 1st & 3rd wknd of each month, 1-4.
Fee: ✱ Park £3.80 per car (refundable on purchase of house & garden ticket). Garden £3 (ch £1.50), House only £4.50 (ch £2.30), House and Garden £6.20 (ch £3.10). Family ticket £15. NT members free, ch under 5 free. **Facilities:** 🅿 (charged) 💷 ✗ licensed 🍴 ♿ (Braille guide, courtesy minibus from parking) toilets for disabled shop ✖ (ex park on lead) ◢

ELLESMERE PORT　　　Map 07 SJ47

BLUE PLANET AQUARIUM
Cheshire Oaks CH65 9LF
➲ (off M53 junct 10 at Cheshire Oaks. Follow signs for aquarium).
☎ 0151 357 8804
e-mail: info@blueplanetaquarium.co.uk
web: www.blueplanetaquarium.com

A voyage of discovery on the longest moving walkway in the world. Beneath the waters of the Carribean Reef, see giant rays and menacing sharks pass inches from your face and stroke some favourite fish in the special rock pools or pay a visit to the incredible world of poisonous frogs. Divers hand feed the fish and sharks throughout the day and they can answer questions via state of the art communication systems.

Times: Open all year, daily from 10. (Closed Xmas). Seasonal variations in closing times, please call to confirm. **Fee:** £9.45 (ch (3-15) £7, under 3's free, concessions £7). Family ticket from £32.
Facilities: 🅿 ✕ licensed 🗊 ⌖ (wheelchair hire, lifts) toilets for disabled shop ✖ (ex guide dogs) ◼

BOAT MUSEUM
South Pier Rd CH65 4FW
➲ (M53 junct 9)
☎ 0151 355 5017　　　**2 for 1**
e-mail: bookings@thewaterwaystrust.org
web: www.boatmuseum.org.uk

Occupying a historic dock complex at the junction of the Shropshire Union and Manchester Ship Canals, this museum has the world's largest collection of floating canal craft, from a small weedcutter to a 300-ton coaster. Boat trips are also available. There are indoor exhibitions on canal life and local history, together with period worker's cottages, a blacksmith's forge and working engines.

Times: Open Summer daily 10-5. Winter daily (ex Thu & Fri) 11-4. (Closed 25 & 26 Dec). **Fee:** £5.95 (ch £4.25, concessions £4.75). Family ticket £18.50, senior family ticket £17.25. **Facilities:** 🅿 🖭 🗊 ⌖ (tactile map for blind, wheelchairs) toilets for disabled shop ✖ ex guide dogs ◼

GAWSWORTH　　　Map 07 SJ86

GAWSWORTH HALL
SK11 9RN
➲ (2.5m S of Macclesfield on A536)
☎ 01260 223456
e-mail: enquiries@gawsworthhall.com
web: www.gawsworthhall.com

This fine Tudor black-and-white manor house was the birthplace of Mary Fitton, thought by some to be the 'Dark Lady' of Shakespeare's sonnets. Pictures and armour can be seen in the house, which also has a tilting ground - now thought to be a rare example of an Elizabethan pleasure garden.

Times: Open daily, Etr-Sep. Flower Festival in Dec **Fee:** ✱ £5 (ch £2.50). Party 20+ £4 each. **Facilities:** 🅿 🖭 🗊 ⌖ (disabled parking in front of house) toilets for disabled shop ✖ (guide dogs in garden only) ◼

JODRELL BANK VISITOR　　　Map 07 SJ77
CENTRE & ARBORETUM

JODRELL BANK VISITOR CENTRE & ARBORETUM
SK11 9DL
➲ (M6 junct 18, A535 Holmes Chapel to Chelford road)
☎ 01477 571339
web: www.manchester.ac.uk/jodrellbank

At Jodrell Bank, a scientific and engineering wonder awaits you - the magnificent Lovell telescope, one of the largest radio telescopes in the world. A pathway leads you 180 degrees around the telescope as it towers above you surveying and exploring the Universe. Then, the visitor can wander along pathways amongst the trees of the extensive arboretum. The Centre is currently under a redevelopment, which will take 2-3 years to complete. The 2-for-1 voucher can only be used for the 3D theatre in the small Visitor Centre.

Times: Open daily Nov-mid Mar 10.30-3, wknds 11-4; mid Mar-end Oct 10.30-5.30 **Fee:** £1.50 (ch 4-16yrs £1) 3D theatre £1
Facilities: 🅿 🖭 🗊 ⌖ (wheelchair loan) toilets for disabled shop ✖ (ex guide dogs) ◼

KNUTSFORD　　　Map 07 SJ77

TABLEY HOUSE
WA16 0HB
➲ (leave M6 junct 19 onto A556 S towards Chester. Entrance for cars off A5033, 2m W of Knutsford)
☎ 01565 750151
e-mail: enquiries@tableyhouse.co.uk
web: www.tableyhouse.co.uk

This finest Palladian House in the North West, holds the first great collection of English pictures ever made, furniture by Chippendale, Gillow and Bullock, and fascinating Leicester family memorabilia. Friendly stewards are available to talk about the Leicester's 700 years at Tabley.

Times: ✱ Open Apr-end Oct, Thu-Sun & BHs, 2-5 (last entry 4.30).
Facilities: 🅿 🖭 ⌖ (phone administrator in advance for help) toilets for disabled shop ✖ (ex guide dogs)

If an attraction name appears in *italics*, details have not been confirmed for 2006.

TATTON PARK
WA16 6QN
➲ (5m from M6 junct 19, or M56 junct 7. Signed on A556, 4m S of Altrincham. Entrance to Tatton Park on Ashley Rd, 1.5m NE of junct A5034 with A50)
☎ 01625 534400
e-mail: tatton@cheshire.gov.uk

Tatton is one of England's most complete historic estates, with gardens and a 1000-acre country park. The centrepiece is the Georgian mansion, with gardens laid out by Humphry Repton and Sir Joseph Paxton. More recently, a Japanese garden with a Shinto temple was created. The Tudor Old Hall is the original manor house, where a guided tour is available. Special events most weekends include the RHS flower show and open air concerts.
Times: Open mid Mar-early Oct, Tue-Sun & BH 1-5; Gardens & parkland all year Tue-Sun & BH. **Fee:** ✱ Mansion, £3 (ch £2), family £8, groups 12+ £2.40 (ch £1.60) Saver tickets available
Facilities: ▣ (charged) ▣ ✕ licensed ▦ ⅋ (old hall & areas of farm not accessible, Braille guides) toilets for disabled shop garden centre ✖ (ex in parkland) ⅋ ▬

MACCLESFIELD   Map 07 SJ97
HARE HILL
Over Alderley SK10 4QB
➲ (Between Alderley Edge and Macclesfield (B5087). Turn off onto Prestbury Road, continue 0.75m. Hare Hill entrance on left.)
☎ 01625 584412
web: www.nationaltrust.org.uk
The beautiful parkland at Hare Hill also features a pretty walled garden and pergola. There are woodland paths and ponds, and, in late spring, a brilliant display of rhododendrons and azaleas.
Times: Open Apr-8 May, Wed-Thu, Sat-Sun 10-5. Daily 9-29 May, 10-5. Jun-30 Oct, Wed-Thur, Sat-Sun 10-5. (Last admission 1 hr before closing). **Fee:** ✱ £2.70 (ch £1.25). £1.50 per car (refundable on entry to garden). **Facilities:** ▣ (charged) ⅋ (Braille guides) ✖ (ex guide dogs) ⅋

> Directions are provided by the attractions.

MACCLESFIELD SILK MUSEUM
Heritage Centre, Roe St SK11 6UT
➲ (Turn off A523 & follow brown signs. Museum in town centre)
☎ 01625 613210
e-mail: info@macclesfield.silk.museum
web: www.macclesfield.silk.museum
The story of silk in Macclesfield, told through a colourful audio-visual programme, exhibitions, textiles, garments, models and room settings. The Silk Museum is part of the Heritage centre, a restored Georgian Sunday school, which runs a full programme of musical and artistic events throughout the year.
Times: Open all year, Mon-Sat 11-5, Sun & BH Mon 12-5. Closed 25-26 Dec, 1 Jan & Good Fri. Please ring for winter opening times.
Fee: ✱ £3.45 (concessions £2.70). Joint ticket with Paradise Mill £6.95 (concessions £5.50). Accompanied ch free **Facilities:** ▣ (50mtrs) ▣ ✕ licensed ▦ ⅋ (ramps, chairlift, audio guides, induction loop) toilets for disabled shop ✖ (ex guide dogs) ▬

PARADISE MILL & SILK INDUSTRY MUSEUM
Park Ln SK11 6TJ
➲ (turn off A523 'The Silk Rd' & follow brown signs)
☎ 01625 612045
e-mail: info@macclesfield.silk.museum
web: www.macclesfield.silk.museum
A working silk mill until 1981, with restored jacquard hand looms in their original location. Knowledgeable guides, many of them former silk mill workers, illustrate the silk production process with the help of demonstrations from weavers. Exhibitions and room settings give an impression of working conditions at the mill during the 1930s. Adjacent Silk Industry Museum opened in 2001 and focuses on design and manufacturing processes.
Times: Open all year, BH Mon & Mon-Sat from 11-5 (Closed Sundays, 25-26 Dec & 1 Jan, Good Fri). Ring for winter opening **Fee:** ✱ £3.95 (conc £3.80), family £10.80, joint ticket with Silk Museum £6.95 (conc £5.50) **Facilities:** ▣ (100yds) ▦ ⅋ (care needed on uneven floors) ✖ (ex guide dogs) ▬

MOULDSWORTH   Map 07 SJ57
MOULDSWORTH MOTOR MUSEUM
Smithy Ln CH3 8AR
➲ (6m E of Chester, off B5393, close to Delamere Forest & Oulton Park Racing Circuit, signposted. Or M56 junct 12 into Frodsham then B5393 into Mouldsworth, follow brown heritage signs in village)
☎ 01928 731781
web: www.mouldsworthmotormuseum.com
Housed in an 1937 large Art Deco building close to Delamere Forest, this is a superb collection of over 60 motor cars, motorcycles and bicycles. There is also a massive collection of automobilia - old signs, pumps, tools, mascots and badges, as well as old motoring toys, Dinky cars and pedal cars all complemented by a motoring art gallery, that has posters and advertising material. School parties are encouraged for a guided tour and structured talk. Motoring clubs visit on Sundays. There is also a Harry Potter car for children to sit in. Also holds a collection of early teapots, many from 1920s and 30s.
Times: Open Feb-Nov (Sun only), Etr wknd, early May BH Mon, Spring BH Sun-Mon & Aug BH wknd; Sun, Feb-Nov; also Wed, Jul-Aug, noon-5. **Fee:** ✱ £3 (ch £1.50) **Facilities:** ▣ ▦ ⅋ (hands on items) shop

NANTWICH   Map 07 SJ65

HACK GREEN SECRET NUCLEAR BUNKER
French Ln, Hack Green CW5 8AP
⮑ (from Nantwich take A530 towards Whitchurch, follow brown signs)
☎ 01270 629219
e-mail: coldwar@hackgreen.co.uk
web: www.hackgreen.co.uk

One of the nations most secret defence sites. Declassified in 1993, this underground bunker would have been the centre of regional government had nuclear war broken out. Observe the preparations the government made for nuclear war and step into the lives of people who worked here. View the Minister of State's office, life support, communication centre, decontamination facilities, telephone exchange and much more.

Times: Open 20 Apr-30 Oct, daily 10.30-5.30; Nov, Jan, Feb wknds, 11-4. Closed Dec. **Fee:** ✱ £5.80 (ch £4, pen £5.50) **Facilities:** 🅿 💻 ✕ 🍴 ♿ (facilities for blind & hard of hearing) toilets for disabled shop ✈ (ex guide dogs) 🎦

STAPELEY WATER GARDENS
London Rd, Stapeley CW5 7LH
⮑ (off M6 junct 16, 1m S of Nantwich on A51)
☎ 01270 623868 & 628628
e-mail: info@stapeleywg.com
web: www.stapeleywg.com

2 for 1

Stapeley Water Gardens consists of three main areas. The Palms Tropical Oasis is a glass pavilion which is home to Koi carp, giant Amazon water-lilies, sharks, piranhas, parrots and exotic flowers. The two-acre Water Garden Centre houses the national collection of water-lilies, and there is also a garden centre with a children's play area.

Times: Open Summer: Mon-Sat 9-6, BHs 10-6, Sun 10-4, Wed 9-8; Winter: Mon-Sat 9-5, BHs 10-5, Sun 10-4, (Wed 9-8 Angling dept only). The Palms Tropical Oasis open from 10am. **Fee:** The Palms Tropical Oasis £4.45 (ch £2.60, pen £3.95). Family ticket (2 ad & 2 ch) £12.10 (2 ad & 3 ch) £14.30. **Facilities:** 🅿 💻 ✕ licensed 🍴 ♿ (free wheelchair loan service) toilets for disabled shop garden centre ✈ (ex guide dogs) 🎦

NESTON   Map 07 SJ27

LIVERPOOL UNIVERSITY BOTANIC GARDENS (NESS GARDENS)
Ness Gardens CH64 4AY
⮑ (off A540 near Ness-on-Wirral, follow signs)
☎ 0151 353 0123
e-mail: nessgdns@liv.ac.uk
web: www.nessgardens.org.uk

A long association with plant collectors ensures a wide range of plants, providing interest for academics, horticulturists and amateurs alike. There are tree and shrub collections, water and rock gardens, herbaceous borders and glasshouses. A regular programme of lectures, courses and special events take place throughout the year for which tickets must be obtained in advance. A new visitor centre should be complete by the time this guide is published.

Times: Open all year, Nov-Feb, daily 9.30-4; Mar-Oct, daily 9.30-5. (Closed 25 Dec). **Fee:** ✱ £4.70 (ch free admission when accompanied with an adult, concessions £4.30) **Facilities:** 🅿 💻 ♿ (wheelchair route, induction loop in lecture theatre) toilets for disabled shop garden centre ✈ (ex guide dogs) 🎦

NETHER ALDERLEY   Map 07 SJ87

NETHER ALDERLEY MILL
Congleton Rd SK10 4TW
⮑ (1.5m S of Alderley Edge on E side of A34)
☎ 01625 584412
e-mail: netheralderleymill@nationaltrust.org.uk
web: www.nationaltrust.org.uk

Built in the 15th century, this water-mill is much larger inside than it looks. Inside there are tandem overshot water-wheels, original Elizabethan timber work, and Victorian machinery which was restored to full working order in the 1960s after being derelict for 30 years. Wheat is ground regularly for demonstration purposes.

Times: Open Apr-Oct, Wed-Fri, Sun & BH Mon 1-5. Parties by arrangement. **Fee:** ✱ £2.50 (ch £1.20) family ticket £8 **Facilities:** 🅿 ✈ 🐂

NORTHWICH   Map 07 SJ67

ARLEY HALL & GARDENS
CW9 6NA
⮑ (5m N of Northwich on B5075. 5m NW of Knutsford A556)
☎ 01565 777353 & 777284
e-mail: enquiries@arleyhallandgardens.com
web: www.arleyhallandgardens.com

Owned by the same family since medieval times, the present Arley Hall is a good example of the early Victorian Jacobean style and contains fine furniture, plasterwork, panelling and family portraits. The gardens include a walled garden, unique clipped Ilex avenue, herb garden, scented garden and a woodland garden with rhododendrons, azaleas and exotic trees as well as the double herbaceous borders, one of the earliest to be established in England (1846).

Times: Gardens: Open Etr-end Sep & wknds in Oct 11-5; Hall: 27 Mar-2 Oct Tue, Sun & BHs 12-5. **Fee:** ✱ Gardens, Grounds & Chapel £4.70 (ch 6-16 £2, pen £4.20) Family ticket £11.80 Hall £2.50 (ch 6-16 £1, pen £2). Party 15+. **Facilities:** 🅿 💻 ✕ licensed 🍴 ♿ (ramps, parking by entrance) toilets for disabled shop garden centre ✈ (ex in gardens on lead) 🎦

SALT MUSEUM
162 London Rd CW9 8AB
➲ (on A533 0.5m S of town centre and 0.5m N of A556. Well signposted from A556)
2 for 1
☎ 01606 41331
e-mail: cheshiremuseums@cheshire.gov.uk
web: www.saltmuseum.org.uk
Britain's only Salt Museum tells the fascinating story of Cheshire's oldest industry. Models, reconstructions, original artefacts and audio-visual programmes throw new light on something we all take for granted.
Times: Open Tue-Fri 10-5, wknds 2-5 (Sun 12-5 in Aug). Open BH & Mons in Aug 10-5. **Fee:** ✱ £2.40 (ch £1.20, concessions £2) Family ticket (2 adults + 2 ch) £6 **Facilities:** 🅿 💷 🗐 ও (inductory video with induction loop facilities) toilets for disabled shop garden centre ✕ (ex guide dogs) 🖾

RUNCORN   Map 07 SJ58

NORTON PRIORY MUSEUM & GARDENS
Tudor Rd, Manor Park WA7 1SX
➲ (from M56 junct 11 in direction of Warrington, follow brown signs)
☎ 01928 569895
e-mail: info@nortonpriory.org
web: www.nortonpriory.org

Thirty-eight acres of peaceful woodland gardens are the setting for the medieval priory remains, museum and Walled Garden. Displays tell the story of the transformation of the priory into a Tudor manor house and then into an elegant Georgian mansion. Please telephone for details of special events.
Times: Open all year, Apr-Oct, Mon-Fri 12-5; Sat, Sun & BHs 12-6; Nov-Mar daily 12-4. Closed 24-26 Dec & 1 Jan. Walled Garden open Apr-Oct, daily 1.30-4.30 **Fee:** ✱ £4.50 (ch 5-16, concessions £3.25). Family ticket £12.(2ad & 3ch) **Facilities:** 🅿 💷 🗐 ও (wheelchairs, large print & audio guides, induction loop) toilets for disabled shop garden centre ✕ (only wall garden)

STYAL   Map 07 SJ88

QUARRY BANK MILL & STYAL ESTATE
SK9 4LA
➲ (1.5m N of Wilmslow off B5166, 2.5m from M56 junct 5, 10m S of Manchester. Heritage signs from A34 and M56)
☎ 01625 527468
e-mail: quarrybankmill.reception@nationaltrust.org.uk
web: www.nationaltrust.org.uk
Quarry Bank Mill is a working water and steam powered cotton mill. Spinning and weaving from throughout the industrial revolution are demonstrated every day and items made from the cloth are sold in the shop. Quarry Bank Mill and its colony village is set in the beautiful Styal Estate beside the River Bollin. Lots of practical 'hands-on' activities plus a new children's playground and railway. The Apprentice House and its Victorian vegetable garden show how life was for the mill apprentices.
Times: Mill open all year, Apr-Sep daily 10.30-5.30 (last admission 4); Oct-19 Mar, daily 10.30-5 (closed Mon in term time). Last admission 3.30. Apprentice House & Garden, Tue-Fri from 11 (2-3.30 term time), Sat-Sun & Aug from 11. Closed Mon (ex school hols). **Fee:** ✱ Mill & Apprentice House £8 (ch £4.70). Family ticket £18. Mill only £5.50 (ch £3.70). Family ticket £15. **Facilities:** 🅿 (charged) 💷 ✕ licensed 🗐 ও (wheelchairs, chairlift, ramps, Braille & large print guide) toilets for disabled shop ✕ (ex in park) 🐾 🖾

WIDNES   Map 07 SJ58

CATALYST SCIENCE DISCOVERY CENTRE
Mersey Rd WA8 0DF
➲ (signed from M62 junct 7 and M56 junct 12)
☎ 0151 420 1121
e-mail: info@catalyst.org.uk
web: www.catalyst.org.uk
Discover a world where science and technology come alive, with over 100 interactive exhibits and hands-on displays which guarantee a fun-filled day out for all the family. Take a trip in an all-glass lift to the Observatory, 100 feet above the River Mersey. A range of special events is planned throughout the year. Please ring for details.
Times: ✱ Open all year, Tue-Fri daily & BH Mon 10-5, wknds 11-5. (Closed Mon ex BH's, 24-26 Dec & 1 Jan). **Facilities:** 🅿 💷 🗐 ও toilets for disabled shop ✕ (ex guide dogs) 🖾

CORNWALL & THE ISLES OF SCILLY

EVENTS & FESTIVALS

March
18th-19th Falmouth Spring Flower Show, Princess Pavilion, Falmouth (provisional)

April
28th-29th May Day Festival, St Ives
29th Trevithick Day, Camborne (festival celebrating engineer Richard Threvithick)
30th Giant Bolster Festival, St Agnes, lantern procession with bonfire (provisional)

May
1st Padstow 'Obby 'Oss celebrations, Padstow
6th Helston Flora Day (pre-Christian festival)
13th-14th Re-enactment of the Battle of Stamford Hill, Bude (provisional)
tbc Daphne du Maurier Festival of Arts & Literature, Fowey

June
8th-10th Royal Cornwall Show, Wadebridge
17th-18th Murdoch Weekend, Redruth
tbc Golowan Festival incorporating Mazey Eve and Mazey Day, Penzance

July
17th Stithians Show, Stithians Showground, Truro (provisional)
tbs RNAS Culdrose Air Day

August
4th-6th Re-enactment of Arthurian Battle of Camlann, Tintagel (provisional)
6th-12th Falmouth Regatta Week, sailing regatta with on shore entertainment
25th-28th Cornwall Folk Festival, Wadebridge
26th-28th Morval Vintage Steam Rally, Bray Farm, Nomansland, Looe
26th-2nd Sep Bude Jazz Festival (provisional)
28th Newlyn Fish Festival (provisional)
tbc Dartmouth Royal Regatta
tbc Fowey Royal Regatta

September
2nd Cornish Gorsedd, Redruth (provisional)
tbc Falmouth Festival of Literature & Arts

October
tbc Lowender Peran, Perranporth

December
23rd Tom Bawcock's Eve, Mousehole

Above: Falmouth

BODMIN   Map 02 SX06

MILITARY MUSEUM
The Keep PL31 1EG
➲ (on B3268, Lostwithiel Rd, beside steam railway station)
☎ 01208 269516   **2 for 1**
e-mail: dclimus@talk21.com

The history of a famous County Regiment with fascinating displays of uniforms, weapons, medals, badges and much more. Please telephone for details of events planned throughout the year. Special Event: 150th Anniversary of 'Seige of Lucknow' in 2007.
Times: Open all year Mon-Fri 9-5, Sun during Jul & Aug 10-5. (Closed Xmas). **Fee:** £2.50 (ch 50p). Parties 10+ £2 each. **Facilities:** 🅿 ⑆ & shop

PENCARROW
Washaway PL30 3AG
➲ (4m NW of Bodmin, signposted off A389 & B3266)
☎ 01208 841369   **2 for 1**
e-mail: pencarrow@aol.com
web: www.pencarrow.co.uk

Still a family home, this Georgian house has a superb collection of pictures, furniture and porcelain. The 50 acres of formal and woodland gardens include a Victorian rockery, a lake, 700 different rhododendrons and an acclaimed conifer collection. There is also a craft centre and a children's play area. Special Events: Snowdrop Sunday 5 Feb, Bluebell Sunday 30 Apr, Summer Concert 18 Jun, Jazz in the Garden 11 Aug, Crafts for Christmas 2-3 Dec.
Times: House: 2 Apr-26 Oct, Sun-Thu 11-5 (last house tour 4pm). Gardens: Daily Mar-3 Oct 9.30-5.30. **Fee:** House & Garden £8. Gardens only £4 (ch £1). Family ticket £22. Party 20-30 £7 each, Party 31+ £6 each. **Facilities:** 🅿 💷 ⑆ & (1 wheelchairs, disabled parking at house) toilets for disabled shop ✖ (gardens only) ▬

CALSTOCK   Map 02 SX46

COTEHELE
St Dominick PL12 6TA
➲ (between Tavistock & Callington. Turn off A390 at St. Anne's Chapel, signed 2.5m S of junct)
☎ 01579 351346 & 352739 (info)
e-mail: cotehele@ntrust.org.uk
web: www.nationaltrust.org.uk

A 15th-century house that contains tapestries, embroideries, furniture and armour; and outside, a beautiful garden on different levels, including a formal Italian-style garden, medieval stewpond, dovecote, and an 18th-century tower with lovely views. There is a restored water mill in the valley below, and at the Victorian riverside quay a Maritime Museum.
Times: Open 19 Mar-30 Oct daily ex Fri (open Good Fri), 11-5 (11-4.30 Oct). Garden open all year, daily 10.30-dusk. Limited opening from 1 Nov to 23 Dec. **Fee:** ✱ House, Garden & Mill £7.40. Garden & Mill £4.40 (ch 1/2 price, under 5's & NT members free). Family ticket £18.50 for House, Garden and Mill, £11 for Garden and Mill only. Party £6 each. **Facilities:** 🅿 💷 ✖ licensed ⑆ & (garden limited access,Braille guide,audio loop,wheelchairs) toilets for disabled shop garden centre ✖ (except guide dogs) ⚘ ▬

CAMELFORD   Map 02 SX18

BRITISH CYCLING MUSEUM

The Old Station PL32 9TZ

➲ (1m N of Camelford on B3266 at junct with B3314)

☎ 01840 212811   **2 for 1**

web: www.chycor.co.uk/britishcyclingmuseum

This is the nation's foremost museum of cycling history from 1818 to the present day, with over 400 cycles; more than 1000 cycling medals, fobs and badges; an extensive library; displays of gas, candle, battery and oil lighting; and many ad posters and enamel signs.

Times: Open all year, Sun-Thu 10-5. **Fee:** ✱ £2.90 (ch 5-17 £1.90). **Facilities:** 🅿 ♿ shop ✖ (ex guide dogs)

CHYSAUSTER ANCIENT VILLAGE   Map 02 SW43

CHYSAUSTER ANCIENT VILLAGE

TR20 8XA

➲ (2.5m NW of Gulval, off B3311)

☎ 07831 757934

This unique Celtic settlement includes probably the oldest known 'Village Street' in the country. Explore the remains of 2,000-year-old stone houses.

Times: Open 24 Mar-Jun & Sep, daily 10-5; Jul-Aug, daily 10-6; Oct, daily 10-4. **Fee:** £2.30 (ch £1.20, concessions £1.70). Opening times and prices are subject to change, for further details please phone 0870 333 1181 **Facilities:** 🅿 ✖ ✿

DOBWALLS   Map 02 SX26

DOBWALLS FAMILY ADVENTURE PARK

PL14 6HB

➲ (turn off A38 in centre of Dobwalls and follow the brown signs for approx 0.5m)

☎ 01579 320325 & 321129

e-mail: dobwallsadventurepark@hotmail.com

web: www.dobwallsadventurepark.co.uk

Plenty to do here, with stretches of miniature American railroads to ride -there are steam and diesel locos, and visitors can take the Rio Grande ride through the forests or the Union Pacific route over the prairies. Also Adventureland - action-packed areas filled with both indoor and outdoor adventure play equipment.

Times: Open Etr to Oct, daily 10.30-5 (10-5.30 high season). Closed some days in Apr, May & Oct **Facilities:** 🅿 💻 ♿ (manual wheelchairs subject to availability) toilets for disabled shop 🍴

FALMOUTH   Map 02 SW83

NATIONAL MARITIME MUSEUM CORNWALL

Discovery Quay TR11 3QY

➲ (follow signs from A39 for park/float ride and museum)

☎ 01326 313388

e-mail: enquiries@nmmc.co.uk

web: www.nmmc.co.uk

This award winning Museum has achieved wide national and international acclaim for its architecture, hands-on displays, world renowned boats and associated video footage, maritime heritage and interactive entertainment. With only one of three natural underwater viewing locations in the world, breathtaking views from the 29m high tower,

continued

and a new Endurance and Survival exhibition, the National Maritime Museum Cornwall is a great family day out.

National Maritime Museum Cornwall

Times: Open daily 10-5. Closed 25 & 26 Dec **Fee:** ✱ £6.50 (ch, pen & students £4.30). Family ticket (2ad&3ch) £17. **Facilities:** 🅿 (charged) 💻 ✖ licensed 🗐 ♿ (wheelchairs provided on arrival) toilets for disabled shop ✖ (ex guide dogs) 🍴

PENDENNIS CASTLE

TR11 4LP

➲ (1m SE)

☎ 01326 316594

Together with St Mawes Castle, Pendennis forms the end of a chain of castles built by Henry VIII along the south coast as protection from attack from France. Journey through 450 years of history and discover the castle's wartime secrets.

Times: Open all year, 24 Mar-Jun & Sep, daily 10-5 (Sat 10-4); Jul-Aug, daily 10-6 (Sat 10-4); Oct-Mar, daily 10-4. Closed 24-26 Dec & 1 Jan). **Fee:** £4.60 (ch £2.30, concessions £3.50). Family £11.50. Opening times and prices are subject to change, for further details please phone 0870 333 1181 **Facilities:** 🅿 💻 ♿ shop ✖ (ex on lead in certain areas) ✿

FOWEY   Map 02 SX15

ST CATHERINE'S CASTLE

➲ (0.75m SW of Fowey along footpath off A3082)   **FREE**

A small sixteenth-century fort built by Henry VIII to defend Fowey Harbour. It has two storeys with gun ports at ground level.

Times: Open at any reasonable time. **Facilities:** 🅿 (0.5m) ✖ (ex dogs on leads) ✿

GODOLPHIN CROSS   Map 02 SW63

GODOLPHIN HOUSE

TR13 9RE

➲ (situated on a minor road from Godolphin Cross to Townsend)

☎ 01736 763194

e-mail: godo@euphony.net

web: www.godolphinhouse.com

A romantic Tudor and Stuart mansion, begun in 1475 and considerably extended over the centuries. The Godolphin family's taste is evident throughout the mansion, and of particular note are examples of 16th and 17th-century English oak furniture and Wootton's 1731 painting, *Godolphin Arabian*, one of the three Arab stallion ancestors

continued

of all British bloodstock. The gardens are Tudor, with some areas even earlier. Major repair programme on the mansion funded by English Heritage.

Godolphin House

Times: ✱ National Trust Estate open all year. House open May-Sep, Thu & Fri 11-5 & Sun 2-5 (also Tue 11-5 in Jul & Aug). Open BH Mon 11-5. Phone for Etr opening details. **Facilities:** 🅿 ♨ ✗ 📷 ♿ (telephone prior to visit, lift to first floor) toilets for disabled shop garden centre ✖ (ex guide dogs) 🍴

GOONHAVERN   Map 02 SW75

WORLD IN MINIATURE
Bodmin Rd TR4 9QE
⮑ (turn off A30 at Boxheater junct onto B3285)
☎ 0870 458 4433
e-mail: info@worldinminiature.co.uk
web: www.worldinminiature.co.uk

There are six major attractions for the price of one at this theme park. Visitors can stroll amongst famous landmarks such as the Taj Mahal and the Statue of Liberty, all in miniature scale, set in spectacular gardens. Then there is Tombstone, a wild-west town complete with saloon, bank, shops, livery stable and jail. The Adventure Dome is the original super cinema 180 direct from the USA, which shows two exciting films. The 12-acre gardens are beautifully landscaped with over 70,000 plants and shrubs. See Jurassic Adventure World, Super X Simulator and children's fairground rides.

Times: ✱ Open Etr-Oct, daily from 10am. **Facilities:** 🅿 ♨ ♿ toilets for disabled shop garden centre 🍴

GORRAN   Map 02 SW94

CAERHAYS CASTLE GARDENS
PL26 6LY
⮑ (off A390 onto B3287. Right at T-junct, left at next T-junct, next left and continue to Porthluney Beach car park)
☎ 01872 501144 & 501310   **2 for 1**
e-mail: estateoffice@caerhays.co.uk
web: www.caerhays.co.uk

For centuries this magnolia filled garden was a deer park, and it was not until the late 19th century that John Charles Williams ("JCW") inherited Caerhays and not until the early 20th that new and exotic plants were introduced here. Now the gardens are a blaze of plants from Chile, China, New Zealand, the Himalayas, and many other distant lands. Magnolias, Rhododendrons, Camellia, and Japonicas can all be seen on marked walks, and the house can be visited in small groups during the spring.

Times: Gardens open mid Feb-Jun 10-5.30. House open mid Mar-Jun.
Fee: ✱ £5.50 house or garden; £9.50 combined ticket
Facilities: 🅿 ♨ 📷 ♿ toilets for disabled garden centre plant sales and advice on lead only 🍴

GWEEK   Map 02 SW72

NATIONAL SEAL SANCTUARY
TR12 6UG
⮑ (pass RNAS Culdrose & take A3293 & then B3291 to Gweek, the sanctuary is signed from village)
☎ 01326 221361 & 221874   **2 for 1**
e-mail: slcgweek@merlin-entertainments.com
web: www.sealsanctuary.co.uk

Britain's largest seal rescue facility - offering a unique opportunity to learn more about these beautiful creatures. Every year it rescues, rehabilitates and releases around 30 sick or abandoned seal pups.

Times: Open all year, daily from 10. Closed 25 Dec. **Fee:** Please call for admission prices. **Facilities:** 🅿 ♨ 📷 ♿ toilets for disabled shop 🍴

HELSTON   Map 02 SW62

THE FLAMBARDS EXPERIENCE
Culdrose Manor TR13 0QA
⮑ (0.5m SE of Helston on A3083, Lizard road)
☎ 01326 573404   **2 for 1**
e-mail: info@flambards.co.uk
web: www.flambards.co.uk

Three award-winning, all-weather attractions can be visited on one site here. Flambards Victorian Village is a recreation of streets, shops and houses from 1830-1910. Britain in the Blitz is a life-size wartime street featuring shops, a pub and a living room with Morrison shelter. The Science Centre is a science playground that brings physics alive for the whole family. Along with the Thunderbolt and Extreme Force, we also offer the Hornet Rollercoaster, the Family Log Flume, Go-Kart circuit, and rides and play areas for the very young. The Wildlife Experience show features lizards, snakes, large spiders and birds of prey. Special Event: 30th Anniversary Jun 2006.

Times: Open winter Feb-early Apr 11-4. Open summer early Apr.
Fee: ✱ £11.50 (ch 5-14 £9.25 over 55's £6.25). Family of 3 £29.55, of 4 £39, of 5 £47.75 of 6 £56.40 **Facilities:** 🅿 ♨ 📷 ♿ (95% accessible, free loan of wheelchairs, route guides) toilets for disabled shop garden centre ✖ (ex guide dogs) 🍴

GOONHILLY SATELLITE EARTH STATION EXPERIENCE

Goonhilly Downs TR12 6LQ

➲ (7m from Helston on B3293, Helston to St Keverne road)

☎ 0800 679593

2 for 1

e-mail: goonhilly.visitorscentre@bt.com
web: www.goonhilly.bt.com

Making a dramatic impression on the Lizard Peninsula landscape, this is the largest earth station in the world, with over 60 dishes. Opened in 1962 with only one dish, Goonhilly now handles millions of e-mails, phone calls, and TV broadcasts. In the fully interactive visitors centre, explore the world of communications, experience tomorrow's technology today, and see your own animated 3D virtual head.
Times: Open all year, daily 10-6 (last entry 5pm). After 1 Nov please call 0800 679593 for opening details. **Fee:** ✱ £6 (ch5-16 £4, under 4's free; concessions £4.50) **Facilities:** 🅿 💻 ✗ licensed 🏠 ♿ induction loop, wheelchair height terminals toilets for disabled shop ➤ (ex guide dogs) 🍴

TREVARNO ESTATE GARDEN & MUSEUM OF GARDENING

Trevarno Manor, Crowntown TR13 0RU

➲ (E of Crowntown. Leave Helston on the Penzance road signed B3302)

☎ 01326 574274

2 for 1

e-mail: enquiry@trevarno.co.uk
web: www.trevarno.co.uk

Victorian gardens with the splendid fountain garden conservatory, unique range of crafts and the National Museum of Gardening. In the tranquil gardens and grounds, follow the progress of restoration projects, visit craft areas including handmade soap workshop, explore Britain's largest and most comprehensive collection of antique tools, implements, memorabilia and ephemera, creatively displayed to illustrate how gardens and gardening influences most peoples lives.
Times: Open daily 10.30-5. Closed 25-26 Dec **Fee:** ✱ £4.95 (ch 5-14 £1.95, pen £4.25, disabled £2.50). Group 12+ **Facilities:** 🅿 💻 ♿ parking, disabled route toilets for disabled shop garden centre 🍴

LANHYDROCK   Map 02 SX06

LANHYDROCK

PL30 5AD

➲ (2.5m SE of Bodmin, signed from A30, A38 & B3268)

☎ 01208 265950

e-mail: lanhydrock@nationaltrust.org.uk
web: www.nationaltrust.org.uk

Part-Jacobean, part-Victorian building that gives a vivid picture of life in Victorian times. The 'below stairs' sections have a huge kitchen, larders, dairy, bakehouse, cellars, and servants' quarters. The long gallery has a moulded ceiling showing Old Testament scenes, and overlooks the formal gardens with their clipped yews and bronze urns. The higher garden, famed for its magnolias and rhododendrons, climbs the hillside behind the house.
Times: Open mid Mar-Oct: House daily (ex Mon), 11-5.30 (11-5 in Oct), open BH Mon. Gardens daily from mid Feb, (last admission half hour before closing). Winter: Gardens, Nov-Feb during daylight hours.
Fee: House & Grounds £7.90 (ch £3.95). Grounds £4.40 (ch £2.20). Family ticket £19.75 one adult £11.95. Pre-booked group £6.90 each (ch £3.45 each) **Facilities:** 🅿 💻 ✗ licensed 🏠 ♿ (lift, self drive buggy (pre-book), wheelchairs) toilets for disabled shop garden centre ➤ (ex on lead in park) 🥤 🍴

LAUNCESTON   Map 02 SX38

LAUNCESTON CASTLE

Castle Lodge PL15 7DR

☎ 01566 772365

Commanding the town and surrounding countryside, this castle controlled the route onto Cornwall.
Times: Open 24 Mar-Jun & Sep, daily 10-5; Jul-Aug, daily 10-6; Oct, daily 10-4. Closed Nov-Mar. **Fee:** £2.30 (ch £1.20, concessions £1.70). Prices & opening times relate to 2004, for further details phone or log onto www.english-heritage.org.uk/visits **Facilities:** ♿ (outer bailey only) shop ➤ 🏠

LAUNCESTON STEAM RAILWAY

St Thomas Rd PL15 8DA

➲ (turn off A30 Launceston, well signed)

☎ 01566 775665

The Launceston Steam Railway links the historic town of Launceston with the hamlet of New Mills. Tickets are valid for unlimited travel on the day of issue and you can break your journey at various points along the track. Launceston Station houses railway workshops, a transport museum, gift shop and book shop.
Times: Open Good Fri for 8 days inclusive; Spring, BH Sun for 6 days; Jun, Sun-Wed; Jul-Sep, daily ex Sat; Oct half-term week. **Fee:** ✱ £6.75 (ch £4.40, pen £5). Family ticket £20 (2 ad & up to 4 ch). Dogs 50p. **Facilities:** 🅿 💻 🏠 ♿ shop

THE TAMAR OTTER SANCTUARY

North Petherwin PL15 8GW

➲ (5m NW off B3254 Bude road)

☎ 01566 785646

web: www.ottertrust.org.uk/Tamar_Home.html

The Tamar Otter Sanctuary has a breeding programme for the British otter and has to date bred and released over 100 otters into the wild. Visitors to the sanctuary can see otters in large natural enclosures, as well as fallow and muntjac deer, waterfowl, and wallabies.
Times: Open Apr-Oct, daily 10.30-6 **Fee:** ✱ £6 (ch £3.50) **Facilities:** 🅿 💻 ♿ shop ➤ (ex guide dogs)

LOOE   Map 02 SX25

THE MONKEY SANCTUARY TRUST

St Martins PL13 1NZ

➲ (signposted on B3253 at No Man's Land between East Looe & Hessenford)

☎ 01503 262532

e-mail: info@monkeysanctuary.org
web: www.monkeysanctuary.org

Visitors can see a colony of Amazonian woolly monkeys in extensive indoor and outdoor territory. There are also conservation gardens, children's play area, activity room, a display room and vegetarian cafe. In addition a bat cave is on site where visitors can watch a colony of rare 'horseshoe' bats.
Times: Open Sun-Thu 11-4.30 from the Sun before Etr-end Sep. Also open Autumn Half Term. **Fee:** ✱ £5 (under 5's free, ch £3 & concession £4). Family ticket (2 ad + 2 ch) £15. **Facilities:** 🅿 💻 ♿ toilets for disabled shop ➤ 🍴

MARAZION · Map 02 SW53

St Michael's Mount
TR17 0HT
➲ (access is by Causeway on foot at low tide.
0.5m S of A394 at Marazion)
☎ 01736 710507 & 710265
e-mail: godolphin@manor-office.co.uk
web: www.nationaltrust.org.uk
Reached on foot by causeway at low tide, or by ferry at high tide in the summer only, St Michael's Mount rises dramatically from the sea, a medieval castle to which a magnificent east wing was added in the 1870s. It is home to Lord St Leven, whose ancestor John St Aubyn acquired it in the 17th century.
Times: ✱ Open 31 Mar-Oct, Mon-Fri 10.30-5.30. Last admission 4.45; Nov-Mar, telephone for details. The Castle and grounds are open most wknds during the summer season. Special charity open days, NT members are also asked to pay. Group bookings 01736 710507.
Facilities: P (on mainland) ♨ ✗ licensed 🗐 (Braille guide) shop ✈ (ex guide dogs) ♨ ➡

MAWNAN SMITH · Map 02 SW72

Glendurgan
TR11 5JZ
➲ (4m SW of Falmouth. 0.5m SW of Mawnan
Smith on road to Helford Passage)   **2 for 1**
☎ 01872 862090
e-mail: glendurgan@nationaltrust.org.uk
web: www.nationaltrust.org.uk
This delightful garden, set in a valley above the River Helford, was started by Alfred Fox in 1820. The informal landscape contains trees and shrubs from all over the world, including the Japanese loquat and tree ferns from New Zealand. There is a laurel maze, and a Giant's Stride which is popular with children. The house is not open. The 2-for-1 voucher is valid only during normal visiting hours and cannot be used for any ticketed events.
Times: Open mid Feb-Oct, Tue-Sat & BH Mon. Last admission 4.30 (Closed Good Fri). **Fee:** ✱ £4.50 (ch £2.20). Family ticket £11.20
Facilities: P ♨ 🗐 & (Braille guide, limited access to gardens/ground floor) toilets for disabled shop garden centre ✈ (ex guide dogs) ♨ ➡

Trebah Garden
TR11 5JZ
➲ (signed at Treliever Cross rdbt at junct of A39/A394 & follow brown tourist signs)
☎ 01326 250448
e-mail: mail@trebah-garden.co.uk
web: www.trebah-garden.co.uk
A 25-acre wooded ravine garden, descending 200 feet from the 18th-century house down to a private cove on the Helford River. The cascading Water Garden has pools of giant koi and exotic water plants, winding through two acres of blue and white hydrangeas to the beach. There are glades of sub-tropical tree ferns and palms, as well as rhododendrons and many other trees and shrubs. The beach is open to visitors and there are children's trails and activities all year.
Times: Open daily 10.30-5 (last admission). In winter 10.30 til dusk.
Fee: ✱ Mar-Oct £5.50 (ch & disabled £3, pen £5, ch under 5 free); Nov-Feb 1/2 price **Facilities:** P ♨ ✗ licensed 🗐 & (2 powered wheelchairs & wheelchair route) toilets for disabled shop garden centre plant sales ➡

NEWQUAY · Map 02 SW86

Blue Reef Aquarium
Towan Promenade TR7 1DU   **2 for 1**
➲ (from A30 follow signs to Newquay, follow Blue Reef Aquarium signs to car park in town centre)
☎ 01637 878134
e-mail: newquay@bluereefaquarium.co.uk
web: www.bluereefaquarium.co.uk
Take the ultimate undersea safari at the Blue Reef Aquarium. Discover Cornish marine life from native sharks and rays to the incredibly intelligent and playful octopus. From here journey through warmer waters to watch the magical seahorses, unusual shape shifting, jet-propelled cuttlefish and the vibrant, swaying tentacles of living sponges and anemones. Continue your safari through the underwater tunnel below a tropical sea. Here you will encounter the activities of a coral reef alive with shoals of brightly coloured fish and the graceful, black tip reef sharks which glide silently overhead. Daily talks and regular feeding demonstrations bring the experience to life.
Times: Open all year, daily 10-5. (Closed 25 Dec). Open until 6 during summer holidays. **Fee:** £6.50 (ch £4.50, pen & student £5.50). Family ticket £18.99 (2 ad & up to 3 ch) **Facilities:** P (5mins walk) (prior contact for disabled parking) ♨ 🗐 & (lifts, wheelchair, ramps) toilets for disabled shop ✈ (ex guide dogs & service dogs) ➡

Dairy Land Farm World
Summercourt TR8 5AA
➲ (Signed from A30 at exit for Mitchell/Summercourt)
☎ 01872 510246
e-mail: info@dairylandfarmworld.co.uk
web: www.dairylandfarmworld.com
Visitors can watch while the cows are milked to music on a spectacular merry-go-round milking machine. The life of a Victorian farmer and his neighbours is explored in the Heritage Centre, and a Farm Nature Trail features informative displays along pleasant walks. Children will have fun getting to know the farm animals in the Farm Park. They will also enjoy the playground, assault course and indoor play areas.
Times: Open daily, late Mar-Oct 10-5. (Bull pen additional winter openings Thu-Sun & school hols, please telephone for more information) **Fee:** £7.25 (ch £6.25, under 3s free, pen £5.25). Family Supersaver £25 (2 ad & up to 3 ch). Telephone for info about parties & groups. **Facilities:** P ♨ 🗐 & (wheelchairs for loan; disabled viewing gallery - milking) toilets for disabled shop ✈ ➡

Newquay Zoo
Trenance Gardens TR7 2LZ
➲ (off A3075 and follow signs to Zoo)
☎ 01637 873342
e-mail: info@newquayzoo.org.uk
web: www.newquayzoo.org.uk
There's always something new at Newquay Zoo. Explore the rainforest exhibit in the tropical house where you'll discover a world of exotic animals. Water cascades down the ancient temple walls to pools filled with tropical fish. Spot the iguanas, sloths and flying foxbats, and explore the mini-beasts room complete with Arrow Poison Frog enclosure. Among the sub-tropical lakeside gardens live hundreds of animals from around the world ranging from small monkeys to shy red pandas. Look out for meerkats on sentry duty, penguins splashing in their pool, or glimpse the endangered lemurs and fossa. The zoo gardens feature a Tarzan trail,

continued

children's play area, dragon maze, as well as picnic areas, snack bar and gift shop.
Times: ✷ Open Apr-Oct, daily 9.30-6; Nov-Mar 10-dusk. (Closed 25 Dec) **Facilities:** 🅿 (charged) 💻 ✕ 🗂 ♿ (85% free wheelchairs, guided tours & sensory sculptures) toilets for disabled shop ✖ (ex guide dogs) 🍴

PADSTOW   Map 02 SW97

PRIDEAUX PLACE
PL28 8RP
➲ (off B3276 Padstow to Newquay road. Follow brown heritage signs)
☎ 01841 532411
e-mail: office@prideauxplace.fsnet.co.uk
web: www.prideauxplace.co.uk
Built by Sir Nicholas Prideaux in 1592, this impressive country house has been inhabited by his family for fourteen generations, and is still in use by them today. Visitors can see relics of the English Civil War, including a pardon from Charles II and a double-sided brooch of Cromwell and the King, as well as fascinating rooms filled with antique furniture, paintings and a 16th-century ceiling depicting the biblical story of Susannah. The house was used as a location for Trevor Nunn's film version of *Twelfth Night* and has been used in the making of many *Rosamunde Pilcher* films and television productions.
Times: Open early May-early Oct, Sun-Thu 1.30-4 (house tours). Grounds 12.30-5. Open all year to pre-booked groups (15+)
Fee: ✷ House & grounds £6.50 (ch £2), Grounds only £2 (ch £1)
Facilities: 🅿 💻 🗂 ♿ ramps to main entrance and tea room toilets for disabled shop ✖ (ex on leads in grounds) 🍴

PENDEEN   Map 02 SW33

GEEVOR TIN MINE
TR19 7EW
➲ (Geevor is beside the B3306 Lands End to St Ives coast road. From Penzance take A3071 towards St Just, then the B3318 towards Pendeen. From St Ives follow B3306 to Pendeen)
☎ 01736 788662   **2 for 1**
e-mail: info@geevor.com
web: www.geevor.com
A preserved tin mine and museum provide an insight into the methods and equipment used in the industry that was once so important in the area. The Geevor Tin Mine only actually stopped operation in 1990. Guided tours let visitors see the tin treatment plant, and a video illustrates the techniques employed. The underground tour is well worth the trip.
Times: Open daily except Sat 9-5, closes at 4pm Nov-Mar. Closed 19-27 Dec & 1 Jan. **Fee:** ✷ £7 (ch & students £4.30, pen £6.50) Family £19 **Facilities:** 🅿 💻 ✕ 🗂 ♿ wheelchair, lift, ramps toilets for disabled shop (not underground) 🍴

PENTEWAN   Map 02 SX04

THE LOST GARDENS OF HELIGAN
PL26 6EN
➲ (signposted from A390 & B3273)
☎ 01726 845100
e-mail: info@heligan.com
web: www.heligan.com
Heligan, seat of the Tremayne family for more than 400 years, is one of the most mysterious estates in England. At the end of the 19th-century its thousand acres were at their zenith, but only a few years after the Great War, bramble and
continued

ivy were already drawing a green veil over this sleeping beauty. Today the garden offers 200 acres for exploration, which include productive gardens, pleasure grounds, sustainably-managed farmland, wetlands, and ancient woodlands. Please telephone for details of spring-time and harvest-time events and for summer evening theatre.
Times: Open daily 10-6 (last admission 4.30pm): winter 10-dusk. Closed 24-25 Dec. **Fee:** ✷ £7.50. Please telephone to confirm concessions prices. **Facilities:** 🅿 💻 ✕ licensed 🗂 ♿ (free loan of wheelchairs and trained access advisors) toilets for disabled shop garden centre Nov-Feb only, assist all year 🍴

PENZANCE   Map 02 SW43

TRENGWAINTON GARDEN
TR20 8RZ
➲ (2m NW Penzance, 0.5m W of Heamoor off Penzance - Morvah road (B3312), 0.5m off St Just road, A3071)
☎ 01736 363148   **2 for 1**
e-mail: trengwainton@nationaltrust.org.uk
web: www.nationaltrust.org.uk
Unusual plants from four continents fill a range of secluded walled gardens, along with many plants that are difficult to grow in Britain. The mild climate means that seed collected on expeditions to the Far East and southern hemisphere have flourished to produce a magnificent display in this 20th-century garden. The 2-for-1 voucher is valid only during normal visiting hours and cannot be used for any ticketed events.
Times: Open 16 Feb-Oct, daily 10-5.30 (closed Fri-Sat) but open Good Fri 10-5.30 (Feb, Mar & Oct 10-5). Last admission 30mins before closing. **Fee:** ✷ £4.40. Family ticket £11(2 adults), £6.70 (1 adult). Party £3.80 each. **Facilities:** 🅿 💻 🗂 ♿ (special route, 2 wheelchairs) toilets for disabled shop garden centre 🐾 🍴

POOL   Map 02 SW64

CORNISH MINES & ENGINES
TR15 3NP
➲ (2m W of Redruth on A3047, signposted from A30, Pool exit)
☎ 01209 315027 & 210900
e-mail: jane.affleck@nationaltrust.org.uk
Impressive relics of the tin mining industry, these great beam engines were used for pumping water from 2000ft down and for lifting men and ore from the workings below ground. The mine at East Pool has been converted into the Cornwall Industrial Heritage Centre which includes audio visual theatre giving background to all aspects of Cornwall's industrial heritage.
Times: Open Apr-Jun & Oct, Mon,Wed, Thu & Sun 11-5. Jun-Sep Sun-Fri 11-5. **Fee:** £5 (ch 2.50, under 5's free, 2 adult family £12.50, 1 adult family £7.50) Groups 15+ £4.30 each. **Facilities:** 🅿 🗂 ♿ (lift to all levels, parking by arrangement, Braille guide) toilets for disabled shop ✖ (ex guide dogs) 🐾 🍴

PROBUS   Map 02 SW84

TREWITHEN GARDENS
Grampound Rd TR2 4DD
➲ (on A390 between Truro & St Austell)
☎ 01726 883647
e-mail: gardens@trewithen-estate.demon.co.uk
web: www.trewithengardens.co.uk
The Hawkins family has lived in this charming, intimate country house since it was built in 1720. The internationally
continued

renowned landscaped garden covers some 30 acres and grows camellias, magnolias and rhododendrons as well as many rare trees and shrubs seldom seen elsewhere. The nurseries are open all year.
Times: Open Mar-Sep, Mon-Sat 10-4.30; daily Feb-May.
Fee: ✱ Feb-Jun: £4.75 (group 20+ £4.25), Jul-Sep: £4.25 (group 20+ £4) **Facilities:** 🅿 💺 📷 ﴾ toilets for disabled garden centre on leads only ◼

RESTORMEL   Map 02 SX16
RESTORMEL CASTLE
PL22 0BD
➲ (1.5m N of Lostwithiel off A390)
☎ 01208 872687
High on a moated mound, this splendid Norman stronghold offers spectacular views across the Cornish countryside.
Times: Open 24 Mar-Jun & Sep, daily 10-5; Jul-Aug, daily 10-6; Oct, daily 10-4. **Fee:** £2.30 (ch £1.20, concessions £1.70). Opening times and prices are subject to change, for further details please phone 0870 333 1181 **Facilities:** 🅿 ﴾ shop ✖ (ex dogs on leads) ❀

ST AUSTELL   Map 02 SX05
CHARLESTOWN SHIPWRECK & HERITAGE CENTRE
Quay Rd, Charlestown PL25 3NJ
➲ (signed off A390 from St. Austell close to Eden Project)
☎ 01726 69897
e-mail: admin@shipwreckcharlestown.com
web: www.shipwreckcharlestown.com
Charlestown is a small and unspoilt village with a unique sea-lock, china-clay port, purpose built in the 18th century. The Shipwreck and Heritage Centre houses the largest display of shipwreck artefacts in the UK, along with local heritage and diving exhibits, and also a Titanic display.
Times: Open Mar-Oct, daily 10-5 (later in high season). (Last admission 1 hour before closing) **Fee:** £5.95 (ch under 10 free if accompanied by paying adult, ch under 16 £2.50, concessions £3.95) group prices on request. **Facilities:** 🅿 (charged) 💺 ✖ licensed 📷 ﴾ (ramps in place) toilets for disabled shop maritime gifts and collectables not in restaurant ◼

THE CHINA CLAY MUSEUM - WHEAL MARTYN
Carthew PL26 8XG
➲ (2m N on B3274, follow brown signs 'China Clay Museum')
☎ 01726 850362
e-mail: info@chinaclaycountry.co.uk
web: www.chinaclaycountry.co.uk
This museum tells the story of Cornwall's most important present-day industry: china clay production. The open-air site includes a complete 19th-century clayworks, with huge granite-walled settling tanks, working water-wheels and a wooden slurry pump. There is a short audio-visual programme, nature trails and a children's adventure trail. New exhibition halls and interactive displays depict the life of claypit workers from 1800 to the present.
Times: (last admission 5pm) phone for winter opening times.
Fee: ✱ £6 (ch & concessions £4.50). **Facilities:** 🅿 💺 ﴾ toilets for disabled shop ◼

EDEN PROJECT
Bodelva PL24 2SG
➲ (overlooking St Austell Bay signposted from A390/A30/A391)
☎ 01726 811911
e-mail: information@edenproject.com
web: www.edenproject.com
An unforgettable experience in a breathtaking location, the Eden Project is a gateway into the fascinating world of plants and human society. Space age technology meets the lost world in the biggest greenhouse ever built. Located in a 50 metre deep crater the size of 30 football pitches are two gigantic geodesic conservatories: the Humid Tropics Biome and the Warm Temperate Biome. This is a startling and unique day out.
Times: Open daily Mar-Oct 10-6 (last admission 4.30pm), Nov-Feb 10-4.30 (last admission 3pm). Closed 24-25 Dec. See local press or website for details of evening opening. **Fee:** £12.50 (ch 5-15 £5, student £6, pen £9.50). Family ticket £30. Annual membership available for additional £3pp or £6 family. **Facilities:** 🅿 💺 ✖ licensed 📷 ﴾ (wheelchairs, car shuttle to visitor centre/biomes) toilets for disabled shop garden centre ✖ (ex guide dogs) ◼

ST IVES   Map 02 SW54
(Park your car at Lelant Station and take advantage of the park and ride service. The fee includes parking and journeys on the train between Lelant and St Ives during the day.)

BARBARA HEPWORTH MUSEUM & SCULPTURE GARDEN
Barnoon Hill TR26 1AD
➲ (M5 to Exeter, A30 onto Penzance & St Ives, in town centre)
☎ 01736 796226
e-mail: tatestivesinfo@tate.org.uk
web: www.tate.org.uk/stives
Visiting the museum and garden is a unique experience, which offers a remarkable insight into the work and outlook of one of Britain's most important twentieth-century artists, Dame Barbara Hepworth.
Times: Open Mar-Oct, daily 10-5.30 (last admission 5); Nov-Feb, Tue-Sun 10-4.30 (last admission 4). Closed 25 Dec **Fee:** £4.50. (concessions £2.25). **Facilities:** 🅿 (880yds) 📷 ﴾ (accessible with assistance, please call) toilets for disabled ✖ (ex guide dogs)

TATE ST IVES
Porthmeor Beach TR26 1TG
➲ (M5 to Exeter, then A30 onto Penzance & St Ives. Located on Porthmeor Beach)
☎ 01736 796226
e-mail: tatestivesinfo@tate.org.uk
web: www.tate.org.uk/stives
Home of post-war British Modernism, St Ives provides the artistic foundations for Tate St Ives. Built in 1993, the gallery celebrates the surroundings and atmosphere that inspired the Modernists, and its unique architecture recalls the 'White Relief' work of Ben Nicholson as well as the unexpected twists and turns of the town itself. The gallery presents a varied programme of both Cornish and international artists, from the past and present, including displays on loan from Tate Modern.
Times: Open Mar-Oct, daily 10-5.30; Nov-Feb, Tue-Sun 10-4.30. Closed 24-26 Dec **Fee:** £5.50 (concessions £2.75). **Facilities:** 🅿 (800yds) 💺 ✖ licensed 📷 ﴾ (access ramp, lift, wheelchairs) toilets for disabled shop ✖ (ex guide dogs) ◼

ST MARY'S — Map 02

ISLES OF SCILLY MUSEUM
Church St, Hugh Town TR21 0LP
➲ (Located in the centre of Hugh Town)
☎ 01720 422337
e-mail: info@iosmuseum.org
web: www.iosmuseum.org

A small, independent museum, which seeks to safeguard and promote the islands' history and traditions, and reflect every aspect of island life. 2005 will see an exhibition of material from the HMS Colossus, a 72-gun frigate that sank within the Isles of Scilly in 1798.
Times: Etr-Sep, Mon-Sat 10-4.30. Oct-Etr, Mon-Sat 10-12 **Fee:** ✱ £2.50 (ch 50p sen & students £1.50) **Facilities:** ⬛ ♿

ST MAWES — Map 02 SW83

ST MAWES CASTLE
TR2 3AA
➲ (on A3078)
☎ 01326 270526

Wonderful location alongside the pretty fishing village of St Mawes, this castle is Henry VIII's most picturesque fort.
Times: Open all year, 24 Mar-Jun & Sep, daily 10-5; Jul-Aug, daily 10-6; Oct, daily 10-4; Nov-Mar, Fri-Mon 10-4. Closed between 24-26 Dec & 1 Jan. **Fee:** £3.60 (ch £1.80, concessions £2.70). Opening times and prices are subject to change, for further details please phone 0870 333 1181 **Facilities:** ⬛ ♿ shop ✘ (ex dogs on leads in grounds) ⚫

SANCREED — Map 02 SW42

CARN EUNY ANCIENT VILLAGE
➲ (1.25m SW of Sancreed, off A30) **FREE**

The remains of an Iron-Age settlement. Surviving features include the foundations of stone huts and an intriguing curved underground passage or 'fogou'.
Times: Open at any reasonable time. **Facilities:** ℗ (600mtrs) ⚫

TINTAGEL — Map 02 SX08

TINTAGEL CASTLE
PL34 0HE
➲ (on Tintagel Head, 0.5m along uneven track from Tintagel, no vehicles)
☎ 01840 770328

Overlooking the wild Cornish coast, Tintagel is one of the most spectacular spots in the country associated with King Arthur and Merlin. Recent excavations revealed Dark Age connections between Spain and Cornwall, alongside the discovery of 'Arthnou' stone suggesting that this was a royal place for the Dark Age rulers of Cornwall.
Times: Open all year, 24 Mar-Sep, daily 10-6; Oct, daily 10-5; Nov-Mar, daily 10-4. Closed 24-26 Dec & 1 Jan. **Fee:** £3.90 (ch £2.00, concessions £2.90). Opening times and prices are subject to change, for further details please phone 0870 333 1181 **Facilities:** ℗ (in village) shop ✘ (ex dogs on leads) ⚫

TORPOINT — Map 02 SX45

ANTONY HOUSE
PL11 2QA
➲ (2m NW, off A374 from Trerulefoot rdbt, 2m from Torpoint Ferry)
☎ 01752 812191
e-mail: philip.brunsdon@nationaltrust.org.uk
web: www.nationaltrust.org.uk/antony

A fine, largely unaltered mansion, built in brick and

continued

Pentewan stone for Sir William Carew between 1711 and 1721. The stable block and outhouses remain from an earlier 17th-century building. The house contains contemporary furniture and family portraits. The grounds include a dovecote and the Bath Pond House.
Times: ✱ Open Apr-Oct, Tue-Thu & BH Mon 1.30-5.30 (last admission 4.45). Also open Sun in Jun-Sep. **Facilities:** ⬛ ⬛♿ (braille guide, recommended route in garden) toilets for disabled shop ✘ (ex guide dogs) ⚫ ◄

MOUNT EDGCUMBE HOUSE & COUNTRY PARK
Cremyll PL10 1HZ
➲ (from Plymouth via Cremyll Foot Ferry, Torpoint ferry or Saltash Bridge. Via Liskeard to A374, B3247 follow brown heritage signs)
☎ 01752 822236
e-mail: mt.edgcumbe@plymouth.gov.uk
web: www.mountedgcumbe.gov.uk

Covering some 800 acres, the country park surrounding Mount Edgcumbe contains a deer park, an amphitheatre, formal gardens, sculpture, the 18th-century Earl's Garden, and woodlands containing California redwoods. The coastal footpath runs along the shores of the Park from Cremyll to Whitsand Bay. Sir Richard Edgcumbe of Cotehele built Mount Edgcumbe between 1547 and 1553. It survived a direct hit by bombs in 1941, and was restored in the 1950s. It now contains antique paintings and furniture, 16th-century tapestries, and 18th-century porcelain. Events and exhibitions held each year.
Times: Open: House & Earl's Garden Apr-Sep, Sun-Thu & BH Mon, 11-4.30. (Closed Fri & Sat). Country Park open all year. **Fee:** House & Earl's Garden £4.50 (ch 5-15 £2.25, concessions £3.50) Family ticket (2ad +2ch or 1ad+3 ch) £10. Country Park free.
Facilities: ⬛ (charged) ⬛ ✘ licensed ♿ toilets for disabled shop ✘ (ex guide dogs & in park) ◄

TREDINNICK — Map 02 SW97

CORNWALL'S CREALY GREAT ADVENTURE PARK
Trelow Farm PL27 7RA
➲ (signposted off A39)
☎ 01841 541215
e-mail: shirespark@tiscali.co.uk

Cornwall's best kept Park is once again even more fun this year with 'The Haunted Castle', full of demons, skeletons and ghosts. Enter the 'Dragon Kingdom', the Country's largest indoor adventure zone consisting of two floors of slides, climbs, ropes, balls and towers. Take a walk through the Enchanted Forest to Greengate Meadow and meet fully

continued

animated moles, Mr Badger and their woodland friends. New attractions include Thunder Falls, double log flume ride, plus Raging River Watercoaster and Viking Warrior Pirate Ship. Acres of outdoor adventure play with the highest aerial bridges and the longest, steepest slides in Cornwall. Plus train rides around the lakes and the majestic Shire Houses including new born foals with farmyard friends.
Times: ✱ Open Good Fri-end Oct, daily 10-5. **Facilities:** 🅿 🖭
✖ licensed ♿ (most areas are ramped) toilets for disabled shop
See advertisement on this page

TRELISSICK GARDEN Map 02 SW83
TRELISSICK GARDEN
TR3 6QL
➲ (Trelissick is located 4m S of Truro on both sides of B3289, King Harry Ferry Road)
☎ 01872 862090 `2 for 1`
e-mail: trelissick@nationaltrust.org.uk
web: www.nationaltrust.org.uk
Set amidst more than 500 acres of park and farmland, with panoramic views down the Carrick Roads to Falmouth and the sea. The garden is well known for its large collection of hydrangeas, camellias, rhododendrons and exotic and tender plants. The Cornish Apple Orchard contains the definitive collection of Cornish apple varieties and is particularly lovely in the spring. Two galleries on the property display Cornish Arts and Crafts. Special Event: 50 years Trust ownership to be celebrated in 2005-06. The 2-for-1 voucher is valid only during normal visiting hours and cannot be used for any ticketed events.
Times: Open mid Feb-Oct, daily 10.30-5.30. Phone for winter opening hours. Park & woodland walks open all year. **Fee:** ✱ £5 (Family ticket £12.50). Party rate 15+ £4.30 each. Car park charge £3 (refundable on admission). **Facilities:** 🅿 (charged) 🖭 ✖ licensed 🍴 ♿ (audio guide, wheelchairs, batricar, induction loops) toilets for disabled shop garden centre ✈ assist dogs 🐕 🍴

TRERICE Map 02 SW85
TRERICE
TR8 4PG
➲ (3m SE of Newquay off A3058 at Kestle Mill)
☎ 01637 875404
e-mail: trerice@nationaltrust.org.uk
web: www.nationaltrust.org.uk
The Trerice you see today was built in 1571 by Sir John Arundell IV and, having suffered no major changes since then due to a succession of absentee landlords, it is still somehow caught in the spirit of its age. The plaster ceilings in the Great Hall and Great Chamber are of particular merit and the façade of the building is now thought to be the oldest such example of Dutch influenced architecture still extant in the country. The house contains many fine pieces of furniture and a large collection of clocks. A barn houses a fascinating display of lawnmowers. The garden is planted so as to provide colour and interest throughout the year and features an orchard containing many varieties of Cornish apple trees.
Times: Open end Mar-Nov, daily (ex Tue & Sat) 11-5.30 (11-5 Oct-Nov). Open Sun-Fri from end Jul-Sep. **Fee:** ✱ House: £5.50 Family ticket (2 ad & 3 ch) 2 adult family ticket £13.75, 1 adult family ticket £8.25. Groups £4.70 each. **Facilities:** 🅿 ✖ licensed 🍴 ♿ (Braille/large print guide, tape tour, 2 wheelchairs) toilets for disabled shop ✈ (car park only, ex guide dogs) 🐕 🍴

TRURO Map 02 SW84
ROYAL CORNWALL MUSEUM
River St TR1 2SJ
➲ (follow A390 towards town centre)
☎ 01872 272205 `FREE`
e-mail: enquiries@royalcornwallmuseum.org.uk
web: www.royalcornwallmuseum.org.uk
Cornwall's oldest and most prestigious museum, famed for its internationally important collections. Visitors can see large collections of minerals, a naked mummy, and many aspects of Cornwall's unique culture. The art gallery has a fine collection of Newlyn School paintings, while the museum has a range of exhibitions throughout the year together with an extensive programme for all the family. Contact the museum for details of events and activities.
Times: Open all year, Mon-Sat 10-5. Library closes 1-2. (Closed BHs).
Facilities: 🅿 (200yds) (disabled parking on street) 🖭 ✖ licensed 🍴 ♿ (lift, ramps to main entrances) toilets for disabled shop ✈ (ex guide dogs) 🍴

An asterisk * indicates that opening times and prices are for 2005. Please contact the attraction for up-to-date information.

WENDRON Map 02 SW63

POLDARK MINE AND HERITAGE COMPLEX

TR13 0ER
➲ (3m from Helston on B3297 Redruth road, follow brown signs)
☎ 01326 573173
e-mail: info@poldark-mine.com
web: www.poldark-mine.com

The centre of this attraction is the 18th-century tin mine where visitors can join a guided tour of workings which retain much of their original character. The site's Museum explains the history of tin production in Cornwall from 1800BC through to the 19th century and the fascinating story of the Cornish overseas. In addition to the Museum, the audio-visual presentation gives more insight into Cornwall's mining heritage.

Times: ✱ Open Etr-1st wk Nov, 10-5.30 (last tour 4pm).
Facilities: 🅿 💷 🗐 ♿ (newly refurbished museum allowing disabled access) shop ▰

ZENNOR Map 02 SW43

WAYSIDE FOLK MUSEUM

TR26 3DA
➲ (4m W of St Ives, on B3306)
☎ 01736 796945

Founded in 1937, this museum covers every aspect of life in Zennor and surrounding district from 3000BC to the 1930s. Over 5000 items are displayed in 12 workshops and rooms covering wheelwrights, blacksmiths, agriculture, fishing, wrecks, mining, domestic and archaeological artefacts. A photographic exhibition entitled People of the Past tells the story of the village.

Times: Open Etr-end Oct, daily 10.30-5.30. **Fee:** ✱ £3 (ch £1.75, over 60's £2.75). Party rates 10+. **Facilities:** 🅿 (50yds) 🗐 ♿ (not suitable for wheelchair users) shop ▰

> ## Are there any excellent Days Out that we've missed? Use the Readers' Report form at the back of the book to tell us about them.

CUMBRIA

EVENTS & FESTIVALS

April
30th-1st May Carlisle & Borders Spring Flower Show, Carlisle

May
11th-14th Jennings Keswick Jazz Festival,

June
2nd-3rd Keswick Beer Festival, Davidson Park, Keswick
2nd-4th Holker Garden Festival, Holker Hall
2nd-4th La'al Cumbrian Beer Festival, Wasdale Head
8th-14th Appleby Horse Fair, Roman Road, Appleby-in-Westmorland

July
8th-9th Lakeland Rose Show, Westmorland County Showfield
14th-16th Furness Tradition Festival, Ulverston
15th Cumberland County Show, Carlisle
23rd Coniston County Fair, Coniston Hall
28th-30th Maryport Blues Festival, various venues
29th-30th The Cumbria Steam Gathering, Cark Airfield, Flookburgh

August
2nd Cartmel Show, Cartmel Park, Grange-Over-Sands
16th Gosforth Agricultural Show, The Showfield, Gosforth
27th Grasmere Lakeland Sports & Show, The Show Field, Grasmere

September
7th Westmorland County Show, Lane Farm, Crooklands, Milnthorpe
16th Egremont Crab Fair & Sports (including world renowned gurning competition)

October
14th Wasdale Head Show & Shepherds Meet, Wasdale Head

November
16th Biggest Liar in the World Competition, Santon Bridge (provisional)
12th-20th Kendal Mountain Film Festival, Highgate, Kendal

Above: Catbells and Derwent Water seen from Keswick

ALSTON   Map 12 NY74

NENT VALLEY
Nenthead Mines Heritage Centre, Nenthead CA9 3PD
➲ (5m E of Alston, on A689)
☎ 01434 382726
e-mail: administration.office@virgin.net
web: www.npht.com

Set in 200 acres in the North Pennines, this hands-on heritage centre contains exhibitions and displays on geology, local wildlife, and social history. Visitors can operate three enormous water wheels, gaze down a 328ft deep brewery shaft, and take an underground trip through the Nenthead mines, last worked for lead in 1915. Special events take place throughout the year.
Times: Open Etr-Oct, daily during school hols & BH's 10.30-5 (last entry to mine 3.30). Closed Mon & Tue in term time. **Fee:** ✱ £4-£6.50 (pen £3.25-5.50, ch site free, mine £2). Family ticket £15.50
Facilities: 🅿 💷 🗐 ᬳ (ramps & motorised scooter) toilets for disabled shop ⬛

SOUTH TYNEDALE RAILWAY
The Railway Station, Hexham Rd CA9 3JB
➲ (0.25m N, on A686)
☎ 01434 381696
web: www.strps.org.uk   `2 for 1`

Running along the beautiful South Tyne valley, this narrow-gauge railway follows the route of the former Alston to Haltwhistle branch. At present the line runs between Alston and Kirkhaugh.
Times: Open Apr-Oct & Dec, wknds and BHs; 20 Jul-Aug, daily. Also open school hols & some wknds in Dec. Please enquire for times of trains. **Fee:** ✱ Return £5 (ch 3-15 £2). Single £3 (ch 3-15 £1.50). All day £12.50 (ch 3-15 £5). **Facilities:** 🅿 💷 🗐 ᬳ (railway carriage for wheelchairs, pre-booking required) toilets for disabled shop ⬛

AMBLESIDE   Map 07 NY30

THE ARMITT
Rydal Rd LA22 9BL
➲ (On the main Kendal-Keswick A591 road, opposite Rydal Rd car park in Ambleside. Next to St Martins College)
☎ 015394 31212
e-mail: info@armitt.com
web: www.armitt.com   `2 for 1`

A fascinating and entertaining place that celebrates over 2000 years of Lake District history, from the time of

Ambleside's Roman occupation to the 20th century. Facts, artefacts, historic photographs and renowned works of art by not only the area's better known former inhabitants such as Beatrix Potter, Kurt Schwitters and John Ruskin, but also displays about the daily lives of its hard-working townspeople in past times. Over 11,000 books are contained within a reference library and a changing programme of exhibitions. Special events: Tools of the Trade from June to October.
Times: Open all year, daily 10-5 (last entrance 4.30). Closed 25-26 Dec. **Fee:** ✱ £2.50 (ch, students, pen £1.80) Family ticket £5.60.
Facilities: 🅿 (50yds) 🗐 ᬳ (chairlift to upstairs library, parking at establishment) toilets for disabled shop ✖ (ex guide dogs) ⬛

BARROW-IN-FURNESS   Map 07 SD26

THE DOCK MUSEUM
North Rd LA14 2PW
➲ (A590 to Barrow-in-Furness. Follow brown tourist signs)
☎ 01229 894444   `FREE`
e-mail: dockmuseum@barrowbc.gov.uk
web: www.dockmuseum.org.uk

Explore this museum and relive the fascinating history of Barrow-in-Furness. Discover how the industrial revolution prompted the growth of the town from a small hamlet into a major industrial power through models, graphics and computer kiosks.
Times: Open mid Mar-Nov (Tue-Fri 10-5, Sat-Sun 11-5); Nov-Feb (Wed-Fri 10.30-4, Sat-Sun 11-4.30) **Facilities:** 🅿 💷 🗐 ᬳ (hearing & induction loops, 2 w/chairs for loan) toilets for disabled shop ✖ (ex assist dogs) ⬛

FURNESS ABBEY
LH13 0TJ
➲ (1.5m NE on unclass road)
☎ 01229 823420

Located in a peaceful valley, the majestic red sandstone remains of this beautiful abbey once housed a wealthy monastic order. View the fine stone carvings and visit the exhibition to find out more about the powerful religious community that was once based here.
Times: Open all year, Apr-Sep, daily 10-6; Oct-Mar, Thu-Mon 10-4. Closed 24-26 Dec & 1Jan. **Fee:** £3.30 (ch £1.70, concessions £2.50). Opening times and prices are subject to change, for further details please phone 0870 333 1181 **Facilities:** 🅿 ᬳ shop ✖ (ex on lead in certain areas) ✿

BASSENTHWAITE   Map 11 NY23

TROTTERS WORLD OF ANIMALS
Coalbeck Farm CA12 4RD
☎ 017687 76239
e-mail: info@trottersworld.com
web: www.trottersworld.com

Home to hundreds of friendly creatures including lemurs, wallabies, zebras, red pandas, otters and other exotic animals along with reptiles and birds of prey and a family of gibbons which will keep families amused for hours. Informative, amusing demonstrations daily bring visitors closer to the animals. "Clown About" is an indoor play centre with soft play area and ballpools for toddlers upwards.
Times: Open all year, except 25 Dec & 1 Jan. Summer 10-5.30, Winter 11-4.30 **Fee:** £5.95 (ch £4.50, under 3 free). **Facilities:** 🅿 💷 🗐 ᬳ toilets for disabled shop ✖ (ex guide dogs) ⬛

continued

BIRDOSWALD   Map 12 NY66

BIRDOSWALD ROMAN FORT

CA8 7DD

⮑ (signposted off A69 between Brampton & Hexham)

☎ 016977 47602

e-mail: birdoswald@dial.pipex.com

web: www.birdoswaldromanfort.org

A visitor centre introduces you to Hadrian's Wall and the Roman Fort. This unique section of Hadrian's Wall overlooks the Irthing Gorge, and is the only point along the Wall where all the components of the Roman frontier system can be found together. Birdoswald isn't just about the Romans, though, it's also about border raids in the Middle Ages, and recent archaeological discoveries.

Times: Open Mar-9 Nov, daily 10-5.30. Winter season exterior only **Fee:** £3.60 (ch £1.80, concessions £2.70, Family £9.00) **Facilities:** 🅿 💷 🗐 ♿ (ramp outside, disabled parking, lift) toilets for disabled shop 🗑

BORROWDALE   Map 11 NY21

HONISTER SLATE MINE

Honister Pass CA12 5XN

⮑ (from Keswick take B5289 through Borrowdale & Rosthwaite, follow road to top of pass. From Cockermouth take B5292 towards Keswick for 4m, turn right onto B5289 to Low Larton & Buttermere. Follow road to top of pass)

☎ 01768 777230

e-mail: info@honister.com

web: www.honister.com

The last working slate mine in England. Fully guided tours allow you to explore the caverns hacked out by Victorian miners. Learn the history of the famous Honister green slate, see local skills in action, and how to river slates.

Times: Open Mon-Fri 9-5; wknds 10-5. Closed 23 Dec-11 Jan. Telephone for details as may be open during Xmas hols. **Fee:** ✱ Free entry to Visitor Centre. Tours £9.50 (ch £4.50) Family £26 **Facilities:** 🅿 💷 ✕ licensed 🗐 ♿ toilets for disabled shop garden centre

BOWNESS-ON-WINDERMERE   Map 07 SD49

BLACKWELL THE ARTS & CRAFTS HOUSE

LA23 3JR

⮑ (M6 junct 36. 1.5m S of Bowness on B5360, off A5074)

☎ 015394 46139

e-mail: info@blackwell.org.uk

web: www.blackwell.org.uk

Blackwell was designed by architect M H Baillie Scott (1865-1945) and completed in 1900. Part of the late 19th-century Arts and Crafts Movement it houses changing exhibitions of high quality applied arts and crafts, as well as original design features including stained glass, stonework, carved oak panelling, and plasterwork.

Times: Open 7 Feb-23 Dec daily 10.30-5; (Nov-Dec, Feb-Mar 10.30-4). **Fee:** ✱ £5 (ch & students £2.75) Family ticket £13, groups £4.25 per person. Combined ticket with Abbot Hall £6.95. **Facilities:** 🅿 💷 ♿ (lift to upper floor, photos for inaccessible rooms) toilets for disabled shop 🗑 (ex assist dogs) 🗑

BRAMPTON   Map 12 NY56

LANERCOST PRIORY

CA8 2HQ

⮑ (2.5m NE)

☎ 01697 73030

Close to Hadrian's Wall are the atmospheric ruins of this Augustinian priory founded in the 12th-century.

Times: Open Apr-Sep, daily 10-6; Oct, Thu-Mon, 10-4. **Fee:** £2.60 (ch £1.30, concessions £2.00). Opening times and prices are subject to change, for further details please phone 0870 333 1181 **Facilities:** 🅿 shop

BROUGH   Map 12 NY71

BROUGH CASTLE

CA17 4EJ

⮑ (8m SE of Appleby, S of A66)   **FREE**

☎ 0191 261 1585

Dating from Roman times the twelfth-century keep at this site replaced an earlier stronghold destroyed by the Scots in 1174. It was restored by Lady Anne Clifford in the seventeenth century. You can still see the outline of her kitchen gardens.

Times: Open at any reasonable time. **Facilities:** 🅿 🐕 (ex dogs on leads) 🏚

BROUGHAM   Map 12 NY52

BROUGHAM CASTLE

CA10 2AA

⮑ (1.5m SE of Penrith on minor road off A66)

☎ 01768 862488

Explore the maze of stairs and passages in the ruins of this once glorious 11th-century castle on the banks of the River Eamont. Enjoy the lively exhibition where you'll see relics from the nearby Roman Fort.

Times: Open all year, 24 Mar-Sep, daily 10-6; Oct, Thu-Mon, 10-4. **Fee:** £2.60 (ch £1.30, concessions £2.00).Opening times and prices are subject to change, for further details please phone 0870 333 1181 **Facilities:** 🅿 ♿ (ex keep) shop 🏚

CARLISLE   Map 11 NY35

CARLISLE CASTLE

CA3 8UR

⮑ (north side of city centre, close to station)

☎ 01228 591992

Discover a thrilling and bloody past and enjoy panoramic views over the city and hills of the Lake District and Southern Scotland. Uncover an exciting history through lively exhibitions, which tell of William Rufus, Mary Queen of Scots and Bonnie Prince Charlie.

Times: Open all year, Apr-Sep, daily 9.30-6; Oct-Mar, daily 10-4. Closed 24-26 Dec & 1 Jan. **Fee:** £4.00 (ch £2.00, concessions £3.00). Opening times and prices are subject to change, for further details please phone 0870 333 1181 **Facilities:** 🅿 (400yds) ♿ (parking for disabled at Castle) shop 🐕 (ex on lead in certain areas) 🏚

CARLISLE CATHEDRAL

Castle St CA3 8TZ

⮑ (M6 junct 42,43 or 44, located in City Centre)

☎ 01228 535169 & 548151

e-mail: office@carlislecathedral.org.uk

web: www.carlislecathedral.org.uk

The Cathedral, founded in 1122 as a Norman Priory for Augustinian canons has had services conducted for nearly

continued

900 years. Items of special interest include the East Window, with its tracery containing some very fine 14th-century stained glass and the Brougham Triptych, a magnificent 16th-century carved Flemish altarpiece in St. Wilfrid's Chapel. There is an interesting 14th-century barrel vaulted painted ceiling in the Choir and in the north and south aisles medieval paintings depict the Life of St. Cuthbert and St. Anthony and the figures of the 12 Apostles.
Times: Open daily throughout the year, Mon-Sat 7.30-6.15, Sun 7.30-5, summer BHs 9.45-6.15, winter BHs, Xmas & New Year 9.45-4.
Fee: Suggested donation of £2 per adult. **Facilities:** P (5 mins walk) (2 disabled spaces only) ✖ licensed ▥ ♿ (parking, ramps, loop system, large print books, chairlifts) toilets for disabled shop ✖ (ex guide dogs)

GUILDHALL MUSEUM
Green Market CA3 8JE
⮑ (town centre, opposite The Crown & Mitre Hotel)
☎ 01228 534781
e-mail: barbaral@carlisle-city.gov.uk
web: www.tulliehouse.co.uk

`FREE`

One of Carlisle's oldest buildings, c.1405 and Grade I listed. The Guildhall was once the meeting place of Carlisle's eight trade guilds, few of which still meet today. Experience the cabin-like atmosphere of the shoemaker's room and the 'modernised' butcher's room with its Victorian features. There are amazing objects such as the medieval town chest, dating from around 1400, two small silver balls (one dated 1599)- reputed to be the earliest surviving horse racing prizes in the country.
Times: Open Apr-Oct, 12-4.30 **Facilities:** P (500yds) (disc parking on street, 1 hr limit) ▥ shop ✖ (ex guide dogs)

TULLIE HOUSE MUSEUM & ART GALLERY
Castle St CA3 8TP
⮑ (M6 junct 42, 43 or 44 follow signs to city centre. Car park in Devonshire Walk)
☎ 01228 534781
e-mail: barbaral@carlisle.gov.uk
web: www.tulliehouse.co.uk

Dramatic audio-visual displays, striking recreations of long vanished scenes and imaginative hands-on displays. There is something for everyone, no matter what age - the stunning underground millennium gallery or Border River pathway linking to Carlisle Castle. This unique project combines the museum's own collections with the cutting edge of

continued

contemporary art. The new multi-media room features touch sensitive computer screens and a short film.
Times: Open: Nov-Mar, Mon-Sat 10-4, Sun 12-4; Apr-Jun & Sep-Oct, Mon-Sat 10-5, Sun 12-5; Jul-Aug, Mon-Sat 10-5, Sun 11-5. Closed 25-26 Dec & 1 Jan. **Fee:** ✱ Ground floor (including Art Gallery & Old Tullie House) - Free. Upper floors & New Millennium Gallery - £5.20 (ch £2.60 concessions £3.60) Family ticket (2ad+3ch) £14.50 **Facilities:** P (5mins walk) (disabled parking on site by request) ✖ licensed ▥ ♿ (chair lift) toilets for disabled shop ✖ (ex guide dogs) ◀

COCKERMOUTH   Map 11 NY13
JENNINGS BREWERY TOUR AND SHOP
The Castle Brewery CA13 9NE
⮑ (A66 to Cockermouth, follow tourist signs to brewery)
☎ 0845 129 7190
e-mail: tourandshop@jenningsbrewery.co.uk
web: www.jenningsbrewery.co.uk
Jennings Brewery was originally established as a family business in 1828 and moved to its current location in 1874. It is a traditional brewer, using Lakeland water drawn from the Brewery's own well, malt made from Maris Otter barley and hops from Kent and Herefordshire.
Times: Tours: Jan-Feb & Nov- Dec, Mon-Sat at 2; Mar-Jun & Sep-Oct, Mon-Sat, at 11 & 2; Jul-Aug, daily, at 11 & 2. **Fee:** ✱ £4.95 (ch over 12 £2). **Facilities:** P (250mtrs) ▥ ♿ toilets for disabled shop ✖ (ex assist dogs) ◀

LAKELAND SHEEP & WOOL CENTRE
Egremont Rd CA13 0QX
⮑ (M6 junct 40, W on A66 to rdbt at Cockermouth on A66/A586 junct)
☎ 01900 822673
e-mail: reception@sheep-woolcentre.co.uk
web: www.sheep-woolcentre.co.uk
Come face to face with 19 different breeds of live sheep. Stage show with 'One Man and his Dog' demonstration and our Jersey cow. Shows four times daily, March-end Oct. All indoors.
Times: Open all year, daily 9.30-5.30 (Closed 25 Dec & 5-16 Jan). **Fee:** £4.25 (ch £3.25) for sheep shows **Facilities:** P ▣ ✖ licensed ♿ (hearing loop system) toilets for disabled shop ✖ (ex assist dogs) ◀

WORDSWORTH HOUSE
Main St CA13 9RX
⮑ (W end of Main Street)
☎ 01900 820882
e-mail: wordsworthhouse@nationaltrust.org.uk
web: www.wordsworthhouse.org.uk
William Wordsworth was born here on 7th April 1770, and happy memories of the house had a great effect on his work. The house is imaginatively presented for the first time as the home of the Wordsworth family in the 1770s. It offers a lively and interactive visit with hands-on activities and costumed living history.
Times: Open 21 Mar-29 Oct, Mon-Sat 11-4.30 Shop open; 9 Mar-24 Dec, Mon-Sat 10-5, 4-28 Jan, Wed-Sat 10-4 **Fee:** ✱ £4.50 (ch £2.50). Family ticket £13. Groups 15+ £3.50 Ask for details of discount with Dove Cottage and Rydal Mount. **Facilities:** P (300yds) ♿ (Braille guide, touch list, computer) toilets for disabled shop ✖ (ex assist dogs) ⛟ ◀

CONISTON   Map 07 SD39

BRANTWOOD
LA21 8AD
➲ (2.5m SE off B5285, unclass road. Regular ferry services from Coniston Pier)
☎ 015394 41396
e-mail: enquiries@brantwood.org.uk
web: www.brantwood.org.uk

Brantwood, home of John Ruskin, is a beautifully situated house with fine views across Coniston Water. Inside, there is a large collection of Ruskin paintings and memorabilia, and visitors can enjoy delightful nature walks through the Brantwood Estate.

Times: Open mid Mar-mid Nov, daily 11-5.30. Winter, Wed-Sun 11-4.30. (Closed 25-26 Dec). **Fee:** ✱ House & Estate £5.50 (ch £1, student £4). Family ticket £11.50. Estate only £3.75 **Facilities:** 🅿 💷 ✗ licensed 🗐 ᓚ (wheelchairs, photos of inaccessible areas, Braille guides) toilets for disabled shop ✖ (ex guide dogs & in grounds) 🍴

RUSKIN MUSEUM
The Institute, Yewdale Rd LA21 8DU
➲ (In village centre opposite fire station, accessed from A593, A595 & B5285)
☎ 015394 41164
e-mail: vmj@ruskinmuseum.com   2 for 1
web: www.ruskinmuseum.com

John Ruskin (1819-1900) was one of Britain's most versatile and important political thinkers and artists. The museum contains many of his watercolours, drawings, letters, sketchbooks and other relics. The geology, mines and quarries of the area, Arthur Ransome's *Swallows and Amazons* country, and Donald Campbell's *Bluebird* are also explored in the Museum.

Times: Open all year, mid Mar-mid Nov, daily 10-5.30; Winter opening, mid Nov-mid Feb, 10.30-3.30, mid Feb-mid Mar, 10.30-4.30 **Fee:** £3.75 (ch £1.75). Family ticket £9.50. Ruskin passport gives exclusive discount for cruise on S.Y. Gondola. **Facilities:** 🅿 🗐 ᓚ (audio guide, handling specimens) toilets for disabled shop ✖ (ex guide dogs) 🍴

> If an attraction name appears in *italics*, details have not been confirmed for 2006.

STEAM YACHT GONDOLA
Coniston Pier LA22 8AN
➲ (A593 to Coniston, follow signs near garage 'to boats' & S Y Gondola. Coniston Pier is at end of Lake Road.)
☎ 015394 41288
e-mail: gondola@nationaltrust.org.uk
web: www.nationaltrust.org.uk/gondola

Originally launched in 1859, the graceful Gondola worked on Coniston Water until 1936. Beautifully rebuilt, she came back into service in 1980, and visitors can once again enjoy her silent progress and old-fashioned comfort.

Times: Open Apr-Oct to scheduled daily timetable. Trips commence from 11 at Coniston Pier. Piers at Coniston & Brantwood.
Fee: ✱ Round trip £5.80 (ch £2.80). Family ticket (2 ad+2 ch) £14 **Facilities:** 🅿 (charged) shop ᓚ 🍴

DALEMAIN   Map 12 NY42

DALEMAIN
CA11 0HB
➲ (M6 junct 40, between Penrith & Ullswater on A592)
☎ 017684 86450   2 for 1
e-mail: admin@dalemain.com
web: www.dalemain.com

Originally a mediaeval pele tower, Dalemain was added to in Tudor times, and the imposing Georgian façade was completed in 1745. It has oak panelling, Chinese wallpaper, Tudor plasterwork and fine period furniture. The tower contains the Westmorland and Cumberland Yeomanry Museum, and there is a countryside collection in the 16th-century Great Barn. The gardens include a collection of old fashioned roses, and in early summer a magnificent display of blue Himalayan poppies.

Times: Open Gardens, Mediaeval Hall and agricultural & countryside collections: 20 Mar-30 Oct , Sun-Thu 10.30-5. House open 11-4.
Fee: ✱ House £6 (ch £3.50) Family ticket £14.50. Gardens £4. (ch free when accompanied). Party. **Facilities:** 🅿 💷 ✗ licensed ᓚ (ramp access at entrance, electric scooter) toilets for disabled shop garden centre ✖ (ex guide dogs) 🍴

DALTON-IN-FURNESS   Map 07 SD27

SOUTH LAKES WILD ANIMAL PARK
Crossgates LA15 8JR
➲ (M6 junct 36, A590 to Dalton-in-Furness, follow tourist signs)
☎ 01229 466086
e-mail: office@wildanimalpark.co.uk
web: www.wildanimalpark.co.uk

The North's leading zoo park is a unique safari on foot with many animals wandering free. Visitors can walk with kangaroos and emus in the bush, and watch parrots fly free in the trees. Hand feed (supervised at 2pm) families of nine different species of lemur, wonder at the amazing skills of gibbons, macaques and spider monkeys, and see the lions and tigers climb high into trees to catch their food. See both Amur and Sumatran tigers, and spectacled bears. An African plain is approximated by keeping four rhino, six giraffes and a family of baboons in the same field. Also see cheetah, red panda, and over 100 other species. This is an active conservation park with partnerships all over the world to save animals and their habitats.

Times: Open all year, daily 10-5 (last admission 4.15); Nov-Feb 10-4.30 (last admission 3.45). (Closed 25 Dec). **Fee:** ✱ £9.50 (ch, pen, wheelchair users & registered blind £6). Reduced prices Nov-Mar.
Facilities: 🅿 💷 🗐 ᓚ (wheelchair users may need help) toilets for disabled shop ✖ 🍴

EGREMONT   Map 11 NY01

FLORENCE MINE HERITAGE CENTRE

Florence Mine CA22 2NR

➲ (on A595 Egremont by-pass. Turn off at Wilton/Haile, follow signs)

☎ 01946 825830

e-mail: info@florencemine.co.uk

web: www.florencemine.co.uk

Based in the last deep working, iron ore mine in Western Europe, the centre offers a mining museum, geology and mineral room, a reconstructed drift (or tunnel) and a research facility. Underground tours are also available all year, including weekdays, by prior arrangement. Please phone the mine for details. Suitable footwear and old clothes are advised for underground tours.

Times: Open Apr-Oct, daily, 10-4. Nov-Mar, Mon-Fri 9.30-3.30

Fee: ✱ Centre: £2 (ch £1); Mine Tour: £6.50 (ch £4.50)

Facilities: P ➲ & (hands-on display) toilets for disabled shop ✖ (ex guide dogs)

GRASMERE   Map 11 NY30

DOVE COTTAGE & THE WORDSWORTH MUSEUM

LA22 9SH

➲ (S, off A591, immediately before Grasmere village)

☎ 015394 35544

e-mail: enquiries@wordsworth.org.uk

web: www.wordsworth.org.uk

Dove Cottage was the inspirational home of William Wordsworth for over eight years (1799-1808), and it was here that he wrote some of his best-known poetry. The cottage has been open to the public since 1891, and is kept in its original condition. The museum displays manuscripts, works of art and items that belonged to the poet.

Times: Open daily 9.30-5.30, last admission 5pm. (Closed early Jan-early Feb & 24-26 Dec). **Fee:** ✱ Admission charge, discount and concessions available. Reciprocal discount offer with Rydal Mount, Ambleside & Wordsworth House, Cockermouth. **Facilities:** P ➲ ✖ licensed ▥ & (ramps, induction loop, virtual tour) toilets for disabled shop ✖ (ex guide dogs) ▬

HARDKNOTT CASTLE ROMAN FORT   Map 07 NY20

HARDKNOTT CASTLE ROMAN FORT

➲ (9m NE of Ravenglass, at W end of Hardknott Pass)   `FREE`

One of the most dramatic Roman sites in Britain, with stunning views of the Lakeland falls. The fort built between AD120 and AD138, controlled the road from Ravenglass to Ambleside. The remains include the headquarters building and Commandant's house, with a bath house and parade ground outside the fort.

Times: Open any reasonable time. Access may be hazardous in winter.

Facilities: ✖ (ex dogs on leads) ▭ ▮

> Directions are provided
> by the attractions.

HAWKSHEAD   Map 07 SD39

BEATRIX POTTER GALLERY

Main St LA22 0NS

➲ (situated on main street in village centre)

☎ 015394 36355

e-mail: beatrixpottergallery@nationaltrust.org.uk

web: www.nationaltrust.org.uk

An annually changing exhibition of Beatrix Potter's original illustrations from her children's storybooks, housed in the former office of her husband, solicitor William Heelis.

Times: Open 3 Apr-Oct & Good Fri, Sat-Wed 10.30-4.30 (last admission 4). Admission is by timed ticket including NT members.

Fee: ✱ £3.50 (ch £1.70) Family ticket £8.70 (2ad+3ch)

Facilities: P (300mtrs) (Braille guide) shop ✖ ▬ ▮

HOLKER   Map 07 SD37

HOLKER HALL & GARDENS

Cark in Cartmel, Grange over Sands LA11 7PL

➲ (from M6 junct 36, follow A590, signposted)

☎ 015395 58328

e-mail: publicopening@holker.co.uk

web: www.holker-hall.co.uk

Dating from the 16th century, the new wing of the Hall was rebuilt in 1871, after a fire. It has a notable woodcarving and many fine pieces of furniture which mix happily with family photographs from the present day. There are magnificent gardens, both formal and woodland and the Lakeland Motor Museum, exhibitions, deer park and adventure playground are further attractions.

Times: Open 20 Mar-30 Oct, Sun-Fri 10.30-5.30. Hall open 10.30-4.45. (Closed Sat). **Fee:** ✱ Gardens & Grounds £4.50 (ch 6-15 £2.75) Family ticket £13.75. All 3 attractions £9.25 (ch £5.50) Family ticket £27.75. **Facilities:** P ➲ ✖ licensed ▥ & (ramps, wheelchairs & scooters available for hire) toilets for disabled shop (on lead, not in garden)

KENDAL   Map 07 SD59

ABBOT HALL ART GALLERY

LA9 5AL

➲ (M6 junct 36, follow signs to Kendal. Located at south end of town centre beside parish church)

☎ 01539 722464

e-mail: info@abbothall.org.uk

web: www.abbothall.org.uk

The ground floor rooms of this splendid house have been restored to their former glory, with original carvings and fine panelling. The walls are hung with paintings by Romney, Gardner, Turner and Ruskin. The gallery has notable temporary exhibitions and a fine permanent collection of 18th- and 19th-century watercolours of the Lake District, and 20th-century British art, including works by Hepworth, Frink, Nicholson, Sutherland, Riley and Freud.

Times: Open 18 Jan-16 Dec, Mon-Sat 10.30-5 (Jan-Mar & Nov-Dec closes at 4). **Fee:** ✱ £3.75 (ch & students £2.75). Family ticket £11. Groups £3.75 per person. Abbot Hall/Blackwell combined group ticket £6.95. Exhibition & Collection £4.75 (ch & students £3.75). Family ticket £14 **Facilities:** P ➲ & (chair lifts in split level galleries, large print labels) toilets for disabled shop ✖ (ex assist dogs) ▬

KENDAL MUSEUM
Station Rd LA9 6BT
⮑ (opposite railway station)
☎ 01539 721374
e-mail: info@kendalmuseum.org.uk
web: www.kendalmuseum.org.uk
The archaeology and natural history of the Lakes is explored in this popular museum which also features a world wildlife exhibition and a display devoted to author Alfred Wainwright, who was honorary clerk to the museum.
Times: ✱ Open mid Feb-end Dec, Mon-Sat 10.30-5. Reduced hours Feb-Mar; Nov & Dec, 10.30-4. Closed Sun. **Facilities:** 🅿 🗐 🚻 toilets for disabled shop 🗙 (ex guide dogs) 🍴

MUSEUM OF LAKELAND LIFE
Abbot Hall LA9 5AL
⮑ (M6 junct 36, follow signs to Kendal. Located at south end of Kendal beside Abbot Hall Art Gallery)
☎ 01539 722464
e-mail: info@lakelandmuseum.org.uk
web: www.lakelandmuseum.org.uk
The life and history of the Lake District is captured by the displays in this museum, housed in Abbot Hall's stable block. The working and social life of the area are well illustrated by a variety of exhibits including period rooms, a Victorian Cumbrian street scene and a farming display. Two of the rooms are devoted to the memory of Arthur Ransome.
Times: Open 20 Jan-mid Dec, Mon-Sat 10.30-5. (Closing at 4pm Jan, Feb, Mar, Nov, Dec) **Fee:** ✱ £3.76 (ch & students £2.75). Family ticket £11. Combined ticket with Abbot Hall & Lakeland Life (same day), £5.95. **Facilities:** 🅿 🍴 🗐 🚻 (listening posts, large print labels) toilets for disabled shop 🗙 (ex service dogs) 🍴

KESWICK   Map 11 NY22
CUMBERLAND PENCIL MUSEUM
Southey Works, Greta Bridge CA12 5NG
⮑ (M6 N onto A66 at Penrith. Left at 2nd Keswick exit, left at T-Junct, left over Greta Bridge)
☎ 017687 73626
e-mail: museum@acco-uk.co.uk
web: www.pencils.co.uk
Investigating the history and technology of an object most of us take utterly for granted, this interesting museum includes a replica of the Borrowdale mine where graphite was first discovered, the world's largest pencil, and displays on brass-rubbing and various artistic techniques that use pencils.
Times: Open daily 9.30-4 (hours may be extended during peak season). (Closed 25-26 Dec & 1 Jan) **Fee:** ✱ £2.50 (ch & pen £1.25, students £1.75). Family ticket (2 ad + 3 ch) £6.25 **Facilities:** 🅿 🗐 🚻 toilets for disabled shop 🍴

KESWICK MUSEUM & GALLERY
Fitz Park, Station Rd CA12 4NF
⮑ (M6 junct 40, A66 to Keswick, then follow tourist signs for Museum & Art Gallery)
☎ 017687 73263
e-mail: keswick.museum@allerdale.gov.uk
web: www.allerdale.gov.uk/keswick-museum
Keswick's surprising past, from industrial mining centre to peaceful tourist town, is revealed in this fine example of a late Victorian museum. Set in the beautiful Fitz Park, the collections cover local and natural history, famous inhabitants and visitors, including the Lake Poets, and houses the work of many artists who have been captivated

continued

by the local landscape and history. The art gallery hosts a variety of special exhibitions, which change monthly.
Times: Open Good Fri-Oct, Tue-Sat 10-4 **Fee:** Free. Donations welcome **Facilities:** 🅿 (on road outside) (2 hour limit) 🗐 🚻 (ramp at front entrance, with handrails) shop 🗙 (ex guide & hearing dogs)

MIREHOUSE
CA12 4QE
⮑ (3m N of Keswick on A591)
☎ 017687 72287
e-mail: info@mirehouse.com
web: www.mirehouse.com
Visitors return to Mirehouse for many reasons: close links to Tennyson and Wordsworth, the spectacular setting of mountain and lake, the varied gardens, changing displays on the Poetry Walk, free children's nature notes, four woodland playgrounds, live classical piano music in the house, generous Cumbrian cooking in the tearoom, and a relaxed, friendly welcome.
Times: Open Apr-Oct. Grounds: daily 10.30-5.30 House: Wed, Sun, (also Fri in Aug) 2-last entry 4.30. Parties by arrangement.
Fee: ✱ House & grounds £4.60 (ch £2.30). Grounds only £2.20 (ch £1.10). Family ticket £13.80 (2 ad & up to 4 ch) **Facilities:** 🅿 🍵 🗐 🚻 toilets for disabled 🗙 (ex on leads & guide dogs)

LAKESIDE   Map 07 SD38
AQUARIUM OF THE LAKES
LA12 8AS
⮑ (M6, junct 36, take A590 to Newby Bridge. Turn right over bridge, follow Hawkshead Rd to Lakeside. Well signed)
☎ 015395 30153
e-mail: aquariumofthelakes@reallive.co.uk
web: www.aquariumofthelakes.co.uk
Featuring the UK's largest collection of freshwater fish in naturally themed habitats of the Lake District, see giant carp and diving ducks from an underwater tunnel. Visitors can learn about the mysterious life of a river after dark and encounter a variety of British mammals including harvest mice, bank voles and brown rats. Also on display, otters, British sharks and rays. An all-weather attraction.
Times: Open all year, daily from 9. Closed 25 Dec. **Fee:** ✱ £6.25 (ch £3.95, pen £5.50). Family ticket (2ad+2ch £21.45, 2ad+4ch £24.90). **Facilities:** 🅿 (charged) 🍵 🗐 🚻 (lift to first floor, wheelchairs) toilets for disabled shop 🗙 (ex guide dogs) 🍴

LEVENS   Map 07 SD48
LEVENS HALL
LA8 0PD
⮑ (M6 junct 36. 5m S of Kendal, on A6)
☎ 015395 60321
e-mail: houseopening@levenshall.co.uk
web: www.levenshall.co.uk
An Elizabethan mansion, built onto a 13th-century pele tower, with fine plasterwork and panelling. The topiary garden, laid out in 1694, has been little changed.
Times: Open: House & gardens mid Apr-mid Oct, Sun-Thu. Gardens 10-5. House 12-5. Last admission 4.30. **Fee:** ✱ House & garden £7.50 (ch £3.70), garden only £5.80 (ch £2.60). **Facilities:** 🅿 🍵 🗐 🚻 (ramps within garden) toilets for disabled shop garden centre 🗙 (ex guide dogs) 🍴

NEAR SAWREY Map 07 SD39

HILL TOP
LA22 0LF

➲ (2m S of Hawkshead. Behind The Tower Bank Arms)

☎ 015394 36269

e-mail: hilltop@nationaltrust.org.uk

web: www.nationaltrust.org.uk

This small 17th-century house is where Beatrix Potter wrote many of her famous children's stories. It remains as she left it, and in each room can be found something that appears in one of her books.

Times: Open 18 Mar-Oct, Sat-Wed 10.30-4.30, last admission 4. Garden only: 19 Mar-30 Oct, Thu-Fri 11-4. Shop 3 Apr-Oct, Sat-Wed 10.30-5; 8 Apr-29 Oct, Thu-Fri 11-4. **Fee:** ✱ £5 (ch £2) Family ticket £12 (2ad+3ch) **Facilities:** P (200mtrs) (no parking for coaches) ♿ (Braille guide,handling items,accessibility by arrangement) shop ✈ (ex guide dogs) 🐾🍴

PENRITH Map 12 NY53

RHEGED - THE VILLAGE IN THE HILL
Redhills CA11 0DQ

➲ (M6 junct 40, on A66 towards Keswick)

☎ 01768 868000

e-mail: enquiries@rheged.com

web: www.rheged.com

A cinema screen as big as six double decker buses shows four family movies daily, including *Rheged - the Movie*. A spectacular birds eye view of Cumbria, The Lake District and Everest. The National Mountaineering Exhibition at the village is Britain's only permanent celebration of mountaineering.

Times: Open daily 10-5.30. (Closed 25 Dec) **Fee:** Each attraction £5.95 (ch £4 & pen £4.95). Family ticket £17 **Facilities:** P 🍴 ✗ licensed ♿ toilets for disabled shop ✈ (ex guide dogs) 🍴

WETHERIGGS COUNTRY POTTERY
Clifton Dykes CA10 2DH

➲ (approx 2m off A6, S from Penrith, signed)

☎ 01768 892733   FREE

e-mail: info@wetheriggs-pottery.co.uk

web: www.wetheriggs-pottery.co.uk

The only steam-powered pottery in Britain, with 7.5 acres of things to do, including the Pots of Fun Studio, where you can throw or paint a pot, Designer-Makers at work, Café, Bistro, shops. Newt pond, play areas and pottery museum.

Times: Open daily, Etr-Oct 10-5.30; Nov-Etr 10-4.30 **Facilities:** P 🍴 ✗ licensed ♿ toilets for disabled shop ✈ (ex guide dogs) 🍴

RAVENGLASS Map 06 SD09

RAVENGLASS & ESKDALE RAILWAY
CA18 1SW

➲ (close to A595, Barrow to Carlisle road)

☎ 01229 717171

e-mail: steam@ravenglass-railway.co.uk

web: www.ravenglass-railway.co.uk

From the Lake District National Park's only coastal village of Ravenglass, small steam engines haul trains through 7 miles of outstanding, unspoilt beauty to the foot of England's highest mountains in Eskdale. Enjoy the freedom of open or cosy covered carriages. Children learn about steam with 'La'al Ratty', the Water-vole Stationmaster.

Times: Open: trains operate daily mid Mar-early Nov. Most winter wknds, plus daily in Feb Half term. **Fee:** ✱ Return fare £8.60 (ch 5-15 £4.30). Family tickets available **Facilities:** P (charged) 🍴✗♿ (special coaches - prior notice advisable) toilets for disabled shop 🍴

RYDAL Map 11 NY30

RYDAL MOUNT AND GARDENS
LA22 9LU

➲ (1.5m from Ambleside on A591 to Grasmere)

☎ 015394 33002

e-mail: rydalmount@aol.com

web: www.rydalmount.co.uk

The family home of William Wordsworth from 1813 until his death in 1850. The house contains important family portraits, furniture, and many of the poet's personal possessions, together with first editions of his work. In a lovely setting overlooking Windermere and Rydal Water, the gardens were designed by Wordsworth himself. Evening visits for groups can be organised.

Times: Open Mar-Oct daily 9.30-5; Nov-Feb daily (ex Tue) 10-4 (Closed 8 Jan-1 Feb). **Facilities:** P 🍴 ♿ shop ✈ (ex guide dogs & garden) 🍴

SHAP Map 12 NY51

SHAP ABBEY   FREE
CA10 3NB

➲ (1.5m W of Shap on bank of River Lowther)

Dedicated to St Mary Magdalene, the abbey was founded by the Premonstratensian order in 1199, but most of the ruins are of 13th-century date. The most impressive feature is the 16th-century west tower of the church.

Times: Open at any reasonable time. **Facilities:** P ♿ ✈ (ex dogs on leads)

SIZERGH Map 07 SD48

SIZERGH CASTLE & GARDEN
LA8 8AE

➲ (3.5m S of Kendal, signed from A590)

☎ 015395 60951

e-mail: sizergh@nationaltrust.org.uk

web: www.nationaltrust.org.uk

The castle has a 60-foot high tower, built in the 14th century, but most of the castle dates from the 15th to the 18th centuries. There are panelled rooms with fine carved overmantles and adze-hewn floors, and the gardens, laid out in the 18th century, contain the National Trust's largest limestone rock garden.

Times: Open Apr-Oct, Sun-Thu 1.30-5.30; Garden open Apr-Oct, from 12.30. (Last admission 5pm). **Fee:** ✱ House & Garden £5.80 (ch £2.90). Family ticket £14.50. Group rate £4.80 each. Garden only £3.50 (ch £1.70). **Facilities:** P 🍴♿ (ramps, Braille guide, wheelchair, powered buggy) toilets for disabled shop ✈ (ex guide & hearing dogs) 🐾🍴

SKELTON   Map 12 NY43

HUTTON-IN-THE-FOREST
CA11 9TH
➲ (6m NW of Penrith on B5305 to Wigton, 2.5m from M6 junct 41)
☎ 017684 84449
e-mail: info@hutton-in-the-forest.co.uk
web: www.hutton-in-the-forest.co.uk

A beautiful house, set in woods which were once part of the medieval forest of Inglewood. The house consists of a 14th-century pele tower with later additions, and contains a fine collection of furniture, portraits, tapestries and china, a 17th-century gallery and cupid staircase. The walled garden has a large collection of herbaceous plants, and there are 19th-century topiary terraces, a 17th-century dovecote and a woodland walk with impressive specimen trees.
Times: Open, House; 25 Mar-3 Apr & May-2 Oct Thu, Fri, Sun & BH 12.30-4; Gardens daily (ex Sat) Good Fri-Oct 11-5. **Facilities:** ⊇ ▣ ⓖ shop ✖ (ex in grounds on leads)

TEMPLE SOWERBY   Map 12 NY62

ACORN BANK GARDEN AND WATERMILL
CA10 1SP
➲ (6m E of Penrith on A66)
☎ 017683 61893
e-mail: acornbank@nationaltrust.org.uk
web: www.nationaltrust.org.uk
A delightful garden of some two and a half acres, where an extensive collection of over 180 varieties of medicinal and culinary herbs is grown. Scented plants are grown in the small greenhouse, and a circular walk runs beside the Crowdundle Beck to the partially restored watermill. Please ring for details of special events.
Times: Open late Mar-Oct, daily (ex Mon & Tue) 10-5 (last admission 4.30pm). **Fee:** ✱ £3 (ch £1.50). Family ticket £7.50. Party 15+ £2.50.
Facilities: ⊇ ▣ ⓖ (Braille guide, wheelchairs available) toilets for disabled shop ✖ (ex on lead on woodland walk) ⫚ ◗

TROUTBECK   Map 07 NY40

TOWNEND
LA23 1LB
➲ (3m SE of Ambleside at S end of village)
☎ 015394 32628
e-mail: townend@nationaltrust.org.uk
web: www.nationaltrust.org.uk
The house is one of the finest examples of a 'statesman' (wealthy yeoman) farmer's house in Cumbria, built in 1626 for George Browne, whose descendents lived here until 1943. Inside is the original home-made carved furniture, with domestic utensils, letters and papers of the farm.
Times: Open Apr-Oct, Tue-Fri, Sun & BH Mon 1-5 or dusk if earlier. Last admission 4.30pm. **Fee:** ✱ £3.40 (ch £1.70). Family ticket £8.50 **Facilities:** ⊇ (Braille guide) ✖ ◗

WHITEHAVEN   Map 11 NX91

THE BEACON
West Strand CA28 7LY
➲ (A595, after Parton right onto New Rd. Follow one way system & town museum tourist signs to The Beacon on harbourside)
☎ 01946 592302   `2 for 1`
e-mail: thebeacon@copelandbc.gov.uk
web: www.thebeacon-whitehaven.co.uk
Home to the town's museum collection, The Beacon traces the social, industrial and maritime heritage of the area using local characters, audio-visual displays and museum pieces. Enjoy panoramic views of the town and coast from the Met Office Weather Gallery. Regular displays in Habour gallery.
Times: Open Tue-Sun, Etr-Oct 10-5.30, Nov-Mar 10-4.30. Open school & BH Mons. Closed 25 Dec. **Fee:** ✱ £4.50 (ch £2.90, pen £3.60) Family £13.50. Art gallery free. **Facilities:** ⊇ (charged) ▣ ⓖ (chair/stair lift, Braille signs) toilets for disabled shop ✖ ◗

THE RUM STORY
27 Lowther St CA28 7DN
➲ (A595, follow town centre signs)
☎ 01946 592933
e-mail: dutymanagers@rumstory.co.uk
web: www.rumstory.co.uk
Set in the original shop, courtyards, cellars and bonded warehouses of the Jefferson family, - the oldest rum trading family in the UK - this fascinating story takes the visitor back in time to the days of the rum trade, its links with the slave trade, sugar plantations, the Royal Navy, barrel-making and more.
Times: Open daily, Apr-Sep 10-5, Oct-Mar 10-4. Closed 25 Dec & 1 Jan.
Facilities: ⊇ (various in area) (disc zones up to 1hr) ▣ ✖ licensed ⫚ ⓖ (wheelchairs, wide doors, lifts) toilets for disabled ◗

WINDERMERE   Map 07 SD49

LAKE DISTRICT VISITOR CENTRE AT BROCKHOLE

LA23 1LJ

➲ (on A591, between Windermere and Ambleside, follow brown tourist signs)

☎ 015394 46601

e-mail: infodesk@lake-district.gov.uk

web: www.lake-district.gov.uk

Set in 32 acres of landscaped gardens and grounds, on the shore of Lake Windermere, this house became England's first National Park Visitor Centre in 1969. It offers exhibitions, audio-visual programmes, lake cruises, an adventure playground and an extensive events programme.
Times: Open mid Mar-Oct, daily, 10-5. Grounds & gardens open all year. **Fee:** ✱ Free admission but pay & display parking.
Facilities: 🅿 (charged) 💻 ✗ licensed 📖 ♿ (manual & electric wheelchairs, lifts, induction loops) toilets for disabled shop 🛍

WINDERMERE STEAMBOAT CENTRE

Rayrigg Rd LA23 1BN

➲ (0.5m N of Bowness-on-Windermere on A592)

☎ 015394 45565

e-mail: steamboat@ecosse.net

web: www.steamboat.co.uk

A unique collection of Victorian and Edwardian steamboats and vintage motorboats, including the oldest steamboat in the world - the *S L Dolly* of 1850. Displays tell the social and commercial history of England's largest lake, and there are steamboat trips daily, weather permitting.
Times: ✱ Open 17 Mar-7 Nov daily, 10-5. Steamboat trips subject to availability & weather. **Facilities:** 🅿 💻 📖 ♿ toilets for disabled shop 🛍

Helvellyn Mountain rising above Thirlmere

DERBYSHIRE

EVENTS & FESTIVALS

February
3rd-4th Chesterfield Beer & Cider Festival, Winding Wheel, Chesterfield
7th Shrove Tuesday Winster Pancake Races, Main Street, Winster

April
18th Flagg Races, point-to-point steeplechases, Flagg Moor
29th-1st May Derbyshire Steam Fair, Hartington Moor Showground

May
13th-14th Chatsworth International Horse Trials, Chatsworth
29th Castleton Garland Ceremony

June
25th Derbyshire County Show, Showground, Elvaston
30th-2nd Jul Dove Beer & Jazz Festival, Dove Holes, Buxton

July
7th-23rd Buxton Festival, opera, music and literature, Buxton Opera House, Water Street, Buxton (provisional)
15th-16th Derby Caribbean Carnival, Market Square
16th Ashbourne Highland Gathering (provisional)
25th Medieval Market, Chesterfield

August
2nd-3rd Bakewell Show, The Showground, Bakewell
28th Chesterfield Evening Fireworks

September
2nd-3rd Chatsworth Country Fair, Chatsworth Park
16th-17th Buxton Country Music Festival, Palace Hotel, Buxton

October
18th-20th Ilkeston Charter Fair, fun fair throughout the streets of Ilkeston

November
5th Dovedale Dash, fun run at Thorpe Pastures, Thorpe

Above: Longdendale Valley

BOLSOVER   Map 08 SK47
BOLSOVER CASTLE
Castle St S44 6PR
➲ (on A632)
☎ 01246 822844

This award winning property has the air of a romantic storybook castle, with its turrets and battlements rising from a wooded hilltop. See the stunning Venus garden with its beautiful statuary and fountain. State of the art audio tours are available.
Times: Open all year, Apr, Sep-Oct, Thu-Mon 10-5 (4 on Sat); May-Aug, daily 10-6 (4 on Sat); Aug, daily 10-7; Nov-Mar, Thu-Mon 10-4. (Closed 24-26 Dec & 1 Jan). **Fee:** £6.60 (ch £3.30, concessions £5.00). Family £16.50. Opening times and prices are subject to change, for further details please call 0870 333 1181 **Facilities:** 🅿 ⬛ & (keep not accessible) shop ✖ ♯

BUXTON   Map 07 SK07
POOLE'S CAVERN (BUXTON COUNTRY PARK)
Green Ln SK17 9DH
➲ (1m from Buxton town centre, off A6 and A515)
☎ 01298 26978
e-mail: info@poolescavern.co.uk
web: www.poolescavern.co.uk

Limestone rock, water, and millions of years created this natural cavern containing thousands of crystal formations. A 45-minute guided tour leads the visitor through chambers used as a shelter by Bronze-Age cave dwellers, Roman metal workers and as a hideout by the infamous robber Poole. Attractions include the underground source of the River Wye, the 'Poached Egg Chamber', Mary, Queen of Scots' Pillar, the Grand Cascade and underground sculpture formations.
Times: Open Mar-Oct, daily 10-5. (Open in winter for groups only).
Fee: £5.80 (ch £3.20, pen & students £4.60). Family ticket £16.
Facilities: 🅿 🍴 & audio loops, wheelchair ramps, underwater cameras toilets for disabled shop ✖ (ex guide dogs or in park) 🍴
See advertisement on opposite page

CALKE   Map 08 SK32
CALKE ABBEY
DE73 1LE
➲ (9m S of Derby, on A514)
☎ 01332 863822
e-mail: calkeabbey@nationaltrust.org.uk
web: www.nationaltrust.org.uk

This fine baroque mansion dating from the early 18th century was built for Sir John Harpur. Among its treasures
continued

are an extensive natural history collection, a magnificent Chinese silk state bed, and a spectacular red and white drawing room. The house stands in extensive wooded parkland and also has walled flower gardens.

Times: Open 26 Mar-30 Oct, Sat-Wed & BH Mon; House 1-5.30; Gardens & Church 11-5.30; Restaurant 10.30-5; Shop 10.30-5.30.

Fee: *Prices not confirmed for 2006* **Facilities:** ▣ ✕ licensed ♿ (Braille guide, hearing system, buggy/wheelchair available) toilets for disabled shop ✖ (ex guide dogs) ♨

CASTLETON   Map 07 SK18

BLUE-JOHN CAVERN & MINE
Buxton Rd S33 8WP
➲ (follow brown "Blue-John Cavern" signs from Castleton)
☎ 01433 620638 & 620642
e-mail: lesley@bluejohn.gemsoft.co.uk
web: www.bluejohn.gemsoft.co.uk

A remarkable example of a water-worn cave, over a third of a mile long, with chambers 200ft high. It contains 8 of the 14 veins of Blue John stone, and has been the major source of this unique form of fluorspar for nearly 300 years.

Times: ✱ Open all year, daily, 9.30-5 (or dusk). Guided tours of approx 1hr every 10 mins tour. **Facilities:** ▣ ▣ 🖼 (not suitable for disabled visitors) shop ◥

PEAK CAVERN
S33 8WS
➲ (on A6187, in centre of Castleton)
☎ 01433 620285
e-mail: info@peakcavern.co.uk
web: www.devilsarse.com

`2 for 1`

One of the most spectacular natural limestone caves in the Peak District, with an electrically-lit underground walk of about half a mile. Ropes have been made for over 500 years in the 'Grand Entrance Hall', and traces of a row of cottages can be seen. Rope-making demonstrations are included on every tour.

Times: Open all year, daily 10-5. Closed 25 Dec **Fee:** ✱ £6 (ch £4, other concessions £5). Family ticket £17.50. **Facilities:** ▣ (charged) 🖼 shop ◥

A Magical Underworld Journey

Poole's Cavern

& Buxton Country Park

Magnificent Natural Cavern
01298 26978
Great Family Day Out
www.poolescavern.co.uk

PEVERIL CASTLE
Market Place S33 8WQ
➲ (on S side of Castleton)
☎ 01433 620613

The romantic ruins of this Norman fortress are situated high on a rocky crag and the views from the great square tower of the surrounding Peak District are breathtaking. Sir Walter Scott glamourised the castle in his novel, *Peveril of the Peak*.

Times: Open 24 Mar-30 Apr, daily 10-5; 1 May-31 Aug, daily 10-6.

Fee: £3.00 (ch £1.50, concessions £2.30). Family £7.50. Opening times and prices are subject to change, for further details please phone 0870 333 1181 **Facilities:** shop ✪

SPEEDWELL CAVERN
Winnats Pass S33 8WA
➲ (A625 becomes A6187 at Hathersage. 0.5m W of Castleton)
☎ 01433 620512
e-mail: info@speedwellcavern.co.uk
web: www.speedwellcavern.co.uk

Descend 105 steps to a boat that takes you on a one-mile underground exploration of the floodlit cavern.
Times: Open all year, Etr-Oct daily 9.30-5.30, Nov-Etr 10-5. (Closed 25 Dec). Phone to check Winter opening times due to weather. Last boat 1hr before closing. **Fee:** £6.50 (ch £4.50). **Facilities:** 🅿 (charged) 🍴 shop 🛍

TREAK CLIFF CAVERN
S33 8WP
➲ (0.75m W of Castleton on A6187)
☎ 01433 620571
e-mail: treakcliff@bluejohnstone.com
web: www.bluejohnstone.com

An underground world of stalactites, stalagmites, flowstone, rock and cave formations, minerals and fossils. There are rich deposits of the rare and beautiful Blue John Stone, and the show caves include the Witch's Cave, Aladdin's Cave and Fairyland Grotto and some of the finest stalactites in the Peak District.
Times: ✱ Open all year, Mar-Oct, daily 10-last tour 4.20, Aug only, last tour 4.45; Nov-Feb daily 10-last tour at 3.20. Enquire for last tour of day & possible closures.
Facilities: 🅿 🍴 (establishment can only cater for walking disabled) shop 🛍

CHATSWORTH   Map 08 SK27
CHATSWORTH
DE45 1PP
➲ (8m N of Matlock off B6012. 16m from M1 junct 29, signposted via Chesterfield, follow brown signs)
☎ 01246 582204
e-mail: visit@chatsworth.org
web: www.chatsworth.org
Home of the Duke and Duchess of Devonshire, Chatsworth contains a massive private collection of fine and decorative arts. There is a splendid painted hall, and a great staircase leads to the chapel, decorated with statues and paintings. There are pictures, furniture and porcelain, and a trompe l'oeil painting of a violin on the music room door. The park was laid out by 'Capability' Brown, but is most famous as the work of Joseph Paxton, head gardener in the 19th century.
Times: ✱ Open 17 Mar-19 Dec, House & Garden 11-5.30, Farmyard 10.30-5.30. **Facilities:** 🅿 (charged) 🍴 ✗ licensed 🍴 & (3 electric wheelchairs available for garden) toilets for disabled shop garden centre ✗ (ex park & gardens on lead) 🛍

CRESWELL   Map 08 SK57
CRESWELL CRAGS MUSEUM AND EDUCATION CENTRE
Crags Rd, Welbeck S80 3LH
➲ (on the B6042, Crags Road, between A616 and A60, 1m E of Creswell village)
☎ 01909 720378
e-mail: info@creswell-crags.org.uk
web: www.creswell-crags.org.uk
Creswell Crags, a picturesque limestone gorge with lakes and caves, is one of Britain's most important archaeological sites. The many caves on the site have yielded Ice Age remains, including bones of woolly mammoth, reindeer, hyena and bison, stone tools of Ice Age hunters from over 10,000 years ago and new research has revealed the only Ice Age rock art in Britain (about 13000 years old). Visit the Museum and Education Centre to learn more about your Ice Age ancestors through an exhibition, touchscreen computers and video. Join a 'Virtually the Ice Age' cave tour, picnic in Crags Meadow, or try the new activity trail.
Times: Open all year, Feb-Oct, daily, 10.30-4.30; Nov-Jan, Sun only 10.30-4.30. **Fee:** ✱ Museum & site free. Cave & site tour £3.90 (ch £2.50, no under 5's). £2 parking donation requested.
Facilities: 🅿 🍴 & (mobility scooter, tour may be unsuitable due to steps) toilets for disabled shop (only assist dogs in museum) 🛍

CRICH   Map 08 SK35
CRICH TRAMWAY VILLAGE
DE4 5DP
➲ (off B5035, 8m from M1 junct 28)
☎ 0870 758 7267
e-mail: enquiry@tramway.co.uk
web: www.tramway.co.uk
A mile-long scenic journey through a period street to open countryside with panoramic views. You can enjoy unlimited vintage tram rides, and the exhibition hall houses the largest

continued

collection of vintage electric trams in Britain. Ring for details of special events.

Crich Tramway Village

Times: ✱ Open Apr-Oct, daily 10-5.30 (6.30 wknds Jun-Aug & BH wknds). Nov-Dec wknds 10.30-4 **Facilities:** 🅿 💻 ✗ licensed 🗑 ♿ (Braille guidebooks, converted tram, talktype facility) toilets for disabled shop 🛍

CROMFORD   Map 08 SK25

ARKWRIGHT'S CROMFORD MILL
Mill Ln DE4 3RQ
➲ (off A6, 3m S of Matlock)
☎ 01629 824297
e-mail: info@cromfordmill.co.uk   **2 for 1**
web: www.cromfordmill.co.uk

Sir Richard Arkwright established the world's first successful water-powered cotton spinning mill at Cromford in 1771. The Arkwright Society are involved in a major restoration to create a lasting monument to an extraordinary genius. Guided tours are available, and there is a programme of lectures and visits - ring for details. The Mill site is part of the Derwent Valley Mill World Heritage site.
Times: Open all year, daily 9-5 (Closed 25 Dec). **Fee:** Guided tour & exhibitions £2 (ch & pen £1.50). Mill site Free.
Facilities: 🅿 ✗ ♿ ramps toilets for disabled shop 🛍

DENBY   Map 08 SK34

DENBY POTTERY VISITOR CENTRE
Derby Rd DE5 8NX
➲ (8m N of Derby off A38, on B6179, 2m S of Ripley)
☎ 01773 740799
e-mail: visitor.centre@denby.co.uk   **2 for 1**
web: www.denbyvisitorcentre.co.uk

Situated around a cobbled courtyard with shops and a restaurant. Pottery tours are available daily including hands on activities such as paint-a-plate and make a clay souvenir. Extensive cookshop with free half hour demonstrations daily. There are lots of bargains on Denby seconds in the factory shop, hand-made blown glass from the Glass Studio,
continued

Dartington Crystal Shop, local artists gallery and hand painted Denby. (2-for-1 Voucher applies to factory tour only.)

Denby Pottery Visitor Centre

Times: Open all year. Factory tours, Mon-Thu 10.30 & 1. Craftroom tour, daily 11-3. Visitor Centre Mon-Sat 9.30-5, Sun 10-5. Closed 25-26 Dec. **Fee: ✱** Free. Factory tour £4.95 (ch £3.95). Craftroom tour £3.50 (ch £2.50) **Facilities:** 🅿 💻 ✗ licensed ♿ (lift) toilets for disabled shop garden centre 🐕 (outside only, ex guide dogs) 🛍

DERBY   Map 08 SK33

DERBY MUSEUM & ART GALLERY
The Strand DE1 1BS
➲ (follow directions to city centre)
☎ 01332 716659
e-mail: david.fraser@derby.gov.uk   **FREE**
web: www.derby.gov.uk/museums

The museum has a wide range of displays, notably of Derby porcelain, and paintings by the local artist Joseph Wright (1734-97). Also antiquities, natural history and militaria, as well as many temporary exhibitions.
Times: Open all year, Mon 11-5, Tue-Sat 10-5, Sun & BHs 1-4. Closed Xmas & New Year, telephone for details. **Facilities:** 🅿 (50yds) ♿ (lift to all floors, portable mini-loop, large print labels) toilets for disabled shop 🐕 (ex guide dogs)

THE SILK MILL DERBY'S MUSEUM OF INDUSTRY AND HISTORY
Silk Mill Ln, off Full St DE1 3AR
➲ (From Derby inner ring road, head for Cathedral & Assembly Rooms car park. 5 mins walk from here)
☎ 01332 255308
e-mail: roger.shelley@derby.gov.uk   **FREE**
web: www.derby.gov.uk/museums

The museum is set in an early 18th-century silk mill and adjacent flour mill on the site of the worlds first modern factory. Displays cover local mining, quarrying and industries, and include a major collection of Rolls Royce aero-engines from 1915 to the present. There is also a section covering the history of railway engineering in Derby. The building is now part of the Derwent Valley Mills World Heritage Site.
Times: Open all year, Mon 11-5, Tue-Sat 10-5, Sun & BHs 1-4. (Closed Xmas & New Year, telephone for details). **Facilities:** 🅿 5 min walk (museum parking restricted to disabled) ♿ (lift to all floors) toilets for disabled shop 🐕 (ex guide dogs)

PICKFORD'S HOUSE MUSEUM OF GEORGIAN LIFE & COSTUME

41 Friar Gate DE1 1DA

➲ (from A38 into Derby, follow signs to city centre)

☎ 01332 255363

e-mail: elizabeth.spencer@derby.gov.uk

web: www.derby.gov.uk/museums

FREE

The house was built in 1770 by the architect Joseph Pickford as a combined workplace and family home. It now shows domestic life at different periods, with Georgian reception rooms and service areas and a 1930s bathroom. Other galleries are devoted to temporary exhibitions. There is also a display on the growth of Georgian Derby, and on Pickford's contribution to Midlands architecture.

Times: Open all year, Mon 11-5, Tue-Sat 10-5, Sun & BHs 1-4. (Closed Xmas & New Year, telephone for details). **Facilities:** 🅿 ♿ (tape guides, video with sign language subtitles) shop 🐾 (ex guide dogs)

ROYAL CROWN DERBY VISITOR CENTRE

194 Osmaston Rd DE23 8JZ

➲ (on A514, opposite Derby Royal Infirmary)

☎ 01332 712800

2 for 1

e-mail: enquiries@royal-crown-derby.co.uk

web: www.royal-crown-derby.co.uk

This museum traces the history of the company from 1750 to the present day, while the factory tour demonstrates the making of Royal Crown Derby in detail from clay through to the finished product. A demonstration studio gives you the opportunity to watch craftspeople at close quarters and try out a variety of different skills.

Times: Open all year, daily, Mon-Sat 9-5 & Sun 10-4 (shop, Sun 10.30-4.30). **Fee:** ✱ Visitor centre £2.95 (concessions £2.75). Factory tour £4.95 (concessions £4.75). **Facilities:** 🅿 💻 ✗ licensed ♿ (ramps) toilets for disabled shop 🐾 (ex guide dogs) 🏴

EYAM   Map 08 SK27

EYAM HALL

S32 5QW

➲ (Turn off A623 just after Calver Crossroads & village of Stoney Middleton. Turn left at the top of the hill. Eyam Hall in centre of village opposite the stocks).

☎ 01433 631976

2 for 1

e-mail: nicola@eyamhall.com

web: www.eyamhall.com

An intimate 17th-century manor house in the heart of the famous "plague village". Home to the Wright family since 1671, the Hall offers a glimpse of domestic history through the eyes of one family, in portraits, furniture, tapestries, costumes and memorabilia. Converted farm buildings house the Eyam Hall Craft Centre. Please telephone for details of musical and theatrical events throughout the season.

Times: Open House: Etr wk, Jul-Aug, Wed-Thu, Sun & BH Mon 11-4. Craft Centre open all year Tue-Sun 11-5. **Fee:** House £5 (ch £3.50, concessions £4.50). Family ticket £15.50. Craft centre free admission. **Facilities:** 🅿 💻 ✗ licensed ♿ (disabled entrance via special gate, ramps) toilets for disabled shop 🐾 (ex guide & dogs in grounds) 🏴

HADDON HALL   Map 08 SK26

HADDON HALL

DE45 1LA

➲ (1.5m S of Bakewell off A6)

☎ 01629 812855

e-mail: info@haddonhall.co.uk

web: www.haddonhall.co.uk

Originally held by the illegitimate son of William the Conqueror, Haddon has been owned by the Manners family since the 16th century. Little has been added since the reign of Henry VIII, and, despite its time-worn steps, few medieval houses have so successfully withstood the ravages of time.

Times: ✱ Open Apr-Sep, daily 10.30-4.30; Oct, Thu-Sun 10.30-4. **Facilities:** 🅿 (charged) ✗ licensed 📷 ♿ (access is impossible for those in wheelchairs) toilets for disabled shop 🐾 (ex guide dogs) 🏴

HARDWICK HALL   Map 08 SK46

HARDWICK HALL

Doe Lea S44 5QJ

➲ (2m S M1 junct 29)

☎ 01246 850430

e-mail: hardwickhall@nationaltrust.org.uk

web: www.nationaltrust.org.uk

The romantic ruins of this impressive Elizabethan mansion have spectacular views over the country park and New Hall.

Times: Open 23 Mar-30 Oct, Wed-Thu, Sat-Sun, BH Mon & Good Fri, 12-4.30. (Last admission 30mins before closing). Garden Wed-Sun, 11-5.30. Old Hall Mon, Wed, Thur, Sat & Sun 11-6. Parkland gates all year 8-6 (5.30 in winter). **Fee:** Prices not confirmed for 2006 **Facilities:** 🅿 ✗ licensed ♿ (large print & Braille guide, wheelchair (pre-book)) toilets for disabled shop 🐾 (ex in park on leads) 🐕

ILKESTON   Map 08 SK44

AMERICAN ADVENTURE THEME PARK

DE7 5SX

➲ (off M1 junct 26, signed, take A610 to A608 then A6007)

☎ 0845 330 2929

e-mail: sales@americanadventure.co.uk

web: www.americanadventure.co.uk

This is one of Britain's few fully themed parks, based on the legend of a whole continent. A major facelift will be taking place in the next two years, so some rides or attractions may be unavailable, but there's still plenty to do. Ride the Runaway Train, visit JCB World, or hold on tight at the Buffalo Stampede. New rides include the Rascal Rocket, the

continued

Bronco Buggies and more. There's a lake with boats, and the Aztec Kingdom indoor play area will be open every weekend until the Christmas holidays.
Times: Open 19 Mar-6 Sep & 22-30 Oct, daily from 10am; 10 Sep-16 Oct wknds only from 10am **Fee:** ✱ £14.99 (ch under 1mtr free, ch 12yrs & under £11.99, pen £4.99). **Facilities:** P ▣ ✗ licensed ♿ (free wheelchair hire, must pre book, call 0845 330 2929) toilets for disabled shop ✖ (ex guide dogs) ◀

KEDLESTON HALL — Map 08 SK34
KEDLESTON HALL
DE22 5JH
➲ (5m NW of Derby)
☎ 01332 842191
e-mail: kedlestonhall@nationaltrust.org.uk
web: www.nationaltrust.org.uk
Kedleston has been the Derbyshire home of the Curzon family for over eight centuries. The original house was demolished at the end of the 17th century. In 1760 Robert Adam built the south front and designed most of the interior including the marble hall. There are pictures, furniture and china displayed in the house together with an Indian Museum containing the collection accumulated by Lord Curzon, Viceroy of India.
Times: ✱ Open all year: House; 22 Mar-2 Nov, Sat-Wed 12-4.30. Last admission 4. Garden; same as house but open 10-6. Park open daily, Mar-Oct 10-6, Nov-Feb 10-4. **Fee:** *Prices not confirmed for 2006*
Facilities: P ✗ licensed ▣ ♿ (braille guide, w/chair, self-drive vehicle) toilets for disabled shop ✖ (ex in park, must be on leads) ♨

MATLOCK BATH — Map 08 SK25
THE HEIGHTS OF ABRAHAM CABLE CARS, CAVERNS & HILLTOP PARK
DE4 3PD
➲ (on A6, signposted from M1 junct 28 & A6. Base station next to Matlock Bath railway station)
☎ 01629 582365
e-mail: enquiries@h-of-a.co.uk
web: www.heights-of-abraham.co.uk

The visit begins with a spectacular cable car journey across the Derwent Valley to the summit of the hill top country park. The most famous aspects of the Heights of Abraham are the two spectacular show caverns, which provide exciting tours to the underground world within the hillside. There's the 'miners tale', in the Great Rutland Cavern-Nestus Mine and the 'story of the rock' at the Masson Cavern

continued

Pavilion. There is also an Explorer's Challenge, woodland walks and the Victoria Prospect Tower.
Times: ✱ Open daily 14-22 Feb & Etr-Oct 10-5 (later in high season), 28 Feb-26 Mar wknds only, for Autumn & Winter opening telephone for details. **Facilities:** P (300mtrs) ▣ ✗ licensed ▣ ♿ (please ring for details) toilets for disabled shop ✖ (ex in grounds & cable car) ◀

PEAK DISTRICT MINING MUSEUM
The Pavilion DE4 3NR
➲ (On A6 alongside River Derwent)
☎ 01629 583834
e-mail: mail@peakmines.co.uk
web: www.peakmines.co.uk
A large display explains the history of the Derbyshire lead industry from Roman times to the present day. The geology of the area, mining and smelting processes, the quarrying and the people who worked in the industry, are illustrated by a series of static and moving exhibits. The museum also features an early 19th-century water pressure pumping engine. There is a new recycling display in the Pump Room.
Times: Open all year, daily 11-4 (later in summer season). Closed 25 Dec. **Fee:** ✱ Museum & Mine: £4 (ch, students, disabled & pen £2.50). Family £9. Museum only or mine only £2.50 (ch, students, disabled £1.50). Family £6. Party rates. **Facilities:** P (charged) ▣ ♿ (chair lift to mezzanine) shop ✖ (ex guide dogs)

TEMPLE MINE
Temple Rd DE4 3NR
➲ (off A6. Telephone for directions.)
☎ 01629 583834
e-mail: mail@peakmines.co.uk
web: www.peakmines.co.uk
A typical Derbyshire mine which was worked from the early 1920s until the mid 1950s for fluorspar and associated minerals and shows examples of mining methods which give an insight into working conditions underground.
Times: Open all year, Summer 10-5, Winter timed visits during afternoon. **Fee:** ✱ Museum & Mine: £5 (conc £4.50, ch £3), Family ticket £11.50. Museum only or mine only: £3 (conc £2.50, ch £2), Family £8.50. **Facilities:** P (100mtrs) ▣ ✖ (ex guide dogs)

MELBOURNE — Map 08 SK32
MELBOURNE HALL & GARDENS
DE73 1EN
➲ (9m S of Derby on A514, in Melbourne take turn by bus shelter in the Market Place, follow road to Church Sq)
☎ 01332 862502
e-mail: gillweston@globalnet.co.uk
web: www.melbournehall.com
Sir John Coke (Charles I's Secretary of State) bought the lease of Melbourne Hall in 1628 and the house has been home to two Prime Ministers: Lord Melbourne and Lord Palmerston. The glorious formal gardens are among the finest in Britain.
Times: Open, house daily throughout Aug only (ex first three Mons) 2-5 (last admission 4.15). Prebooked parties by appointment in Aug. Gardens Apr-Sep, Wed, Sat, Sun & BH Mon 1.30-5.30. Upstairs rooms available by appointment. **Fee:** ✱ House Tue-Sat (guided tour) £3.50 (ch £2, pen £3), Sun & BH Mon (no guided tour) £3 (ch £1.50, pen £2.50). House & Garden (Aug only) £5.50 (ch £3.50, pen £4.50). Garden only £3 (pen £2). Family £8. **Facilities:** P (200yds) (no parking in visitor centre courtyard) ▣ ▣ ♿ (ramp at garden entrance) shop ✖ (ex guide dogs)

MIDDLETON BY WIRKSWORTH   Map 08 SK25

MIDDLETON TOP ENGINE HOUSE
Middleton Top Visitor Centre DE4 4LS
➲ (Signed off A6 in Cromford then, 0.5m S from B5036 Cromford/Wirksworth road)
☎ 01629 823204
e-mail: middletontop@derbyshire.gov.uk
web: www.derbyshire.gov.uk/countryside

A beam engine built in 1829 for the Cromford and High Peak Railway, and its octagonal engine house. The engine's job was to haul wagons up the Middleton Incline, and its last trip was in 1963 after 134 years' work. The visitor centre tells the story of this historic railway.

Times: Open: Information Centre, daily, wknds only winter. Engine House Etr-Oct 1st wknd in month (engine in motion). **Fee:** ✱ Static Engine 70p (ch 40p). Working Engine £1.30 (ch 70p).
Facilities: ⯒ (charged) ♿ toilets for disabled shop

OLD WHITTINGTON   Map 08 SK37

REVOLUTION HOUSE
High St S41 9LA
➲ (3m N of Chesterfield town centre, on B6052 off A61, signposted)
☎ 01246 345727   FREE
e-mail: museum@chesterfieldbc.gov.uk
web: www.visitchesterfield.info

Originally the Cock and Pynot alehouse, this 17th-century cottage was the scene of a meeting between local noblemen to plan their part in the Revolution of 1688. The house is now furnished in 17th-century style. A video relates the story of the Revolution and there is a small exhibition room.

Times: Open Good Fri-Sep, daily 11-4 (ex Tue). 17-24 & 28-31 Dec, daily 11-4 **Facilities:** ⯒ (100yds) ♿ (signing available by prior arrangement) shop ✖ (ex guide dogs)

RIPLEY   Map 08 SK35

MIDLAND RAILWAY BUTTERLEY
Butterley Station DE5 3QZ
➲ (1m N of Ripley on B6179, signposted from A38)
☎ 01773 747674 & 749788   2 for 1
e-mail: mrc@rapidial.co.uk
web: www.midlandrailwaycentre.co.uk

A regular steam-train passenger service runs here, to the centre where the aim is to depict every aspect of the golden days of the Midland Railway and its successors. Exhibits range from the steam locomotives of 1866 to an electric locomotive, with a large section of rolling stock spanning the last 100 years. Also a farm and country park, along with narrow gauge, miniature and model railways.

Times: Open all year, trains run wknds Feb-Dec & most school holidays **Fee:** ✱ £8.95 (ch 5-16 £4.50, pen £7.95) children under 5 free. Party 15+. **Facilities:** ⯒ ▣ ▥ ♿ (special accommodation on trains) toilets for disabled shop ◾

SUDBURY   Map 07 SK13

SUDBURY HALL
DE6 5HT
➲ (6m E of Uttoxeter)
☎ 01283 585305
e-mail: sudburyhall@nationaltrust.org.uk
web: www.nationaltrust.org.uk

This country house was started in 1664 by Lord George Vernon. It has unusual diapered brickwork, a carved two-storey stone frontispiece, a cupola and tall chimneys. The interior features work by craftsmen including Edward Pierce and Grinling Gibbons. The Museum of Childhood contains a Victorian schoolroom, collections of toys, and displays.

Times: Open House & Museum 6 Mar-30 Oct, Wed-Sun 1-5 (open BH Mons). Last admissions 30 mins before closing. Gardens open 11-6.
Fee: *Prices not confirmed for 2006* **Facilities:** ⯒ ▣ ♿ (w/chair available, large print/Braille guide & touch list) toilets for disabled shop ✖ (ex in grounds) ⯒

WIRKSWORTH   Map 08 SK25

WIRKSWORTH HERITAGE CENTRE
Crown Yard DE4 4ET
➲ (on B5023 off A6 in centre of Wirksworth)
☎ 01629 825225
e-mail: heritage@crownyard.fsnet.co.uk
web: www.gilkin.demon.co.uk

The Centre has been created in an old silk and velvet mill. The three floors of the mill have interpretative displays of the town's past history as a prosperous lead-mining centre. Each floor offers many features of interest including a computer game called 'Rescue the injured lead-miner', a mock-up of a natural cavern, and a Quarryman's House. During the Spring Bank Holiday you can also see the famous Well Dressings. A new exhibition has opened, honouring the achievements of local girl, Ellen MacArthur, together with a gallery exhibiting and selling paintings, photographs, sculptures and ceramics by local artists.

Times: Open Etr-Sep, Wed-Sun & BHs 10.30-4.30 **Fee:** ✱ £3 (ch £1, pen £2). Party 20+ 10% discount **Facilities:** ⯒ (80yds) (pay & display) ▣ ✖ licensed shop ✖ (ex guide dogs)

English Heritage
Find out more about English Heritage sites, their policies and the work they do, at their website:
www.english-heritage.org.uk

DEVON

EVENTS & FESTIVALS

February
13th-25th Animated Exeter (films, workshops, exhibitions, events), various venues

March
3rd-19th Vibraphonic, various venues in Exeter (jazz, soul, funk, blues, hip hop)
31st-2nd Apr Exeter Festival of South West England Food & Drink and South West Beer Festival, Northernhay Gardens, Exeter

May
18th-20th Devon County Show, Westpoint, Clyst St Mary
tbc Blackawton International Festival of Worm Charming, Normandy Arms, Blackawton
tbc Brixham Heritage Festival (music, dance, street theatre & fireworks)

June
16th-2nd Jul Exeter Summer Festival (music, entertainment, jazz, comedy & dance), various venues
30th-1st Jul Plymouth Beer Festival, Plymouth Pavilions

July
tbc Okehampton Balloon Fiesta, Simmons Park, Okehampton
tbc Port of Plymouth Regatta

August
10th Okehampton Agricultural Show
11th-13th Dartmoor Folk Festival, South Zeal, Okehampton
17th Chagford Agricultural Show
24th-26th Port of Dartmouth Royal Regatta
tbc Sidmouth International Festival (folk music, dance & song), various venues
tbc West Country Balloon Fiesta, Tavistock College, Crowndale Road, Tavistock

September
14th Widecombe Fair, Old Field, Widecombe-in-the-Moor
tbc Plymouth International Music Festival, Royal William Yard

Above: The Merry Maidens, St Buryan

ARLINGTON Map 02 SS64

ARLINGTON COURT
EX31 4LP
➲ (7m NE of Barnstaple, on A39)
☎ 01271 850296
e-mail: arlingtoncourt@nationaltrust.org.uk
web: www.nationaltrust.org.uk

Arlington Court was built in 1822 and is situated in the thickly wooded Yeo Valley. The centrepiece is the Victorian mansion, surrounded by formal and informal gardens. Also open to visitors is the working stable yard, housing a collection of carriages and horse-drawn vehicles. The extensive parkland around the house is grazed by Jacob sheep and Red Devon cattle. Please telephone for details of events running throughout the year.
Times: Open 20 Mar-30 Oct, daily (ex Sat) 10.30-5. Last admission 4.30. Grounds open Nov-Mar during daylight hours. **Fee:** ✱ House & grounds £6.50 (ch £3.20), Family £16.20. Grounds only £4.20 (ch £2.10). Parties 15+ pre-booked 15% discount. **Facilities:** 🅿 ▆
🍴 ♿ (wheelchairs, ramps at house, batricar, Braille guide) toilets for disabled shop garden centre ✖ (ex in grounds on lead) ♨ ▆

BARNSTAPLE Map 02 SS53

MARWOOD HILL GARDENS
Marwood EX31 4EB
➲ (signed off A361 Barnstaple to Braunton road, follow brown tourist signs)
☎ 01271 342528
web: www.marwoodhillgarden.co.uk

The 18-acre gardens with their three small lakes contain many rare trees and shrubs. There is a large bog garden and a walled garden, collections of clematis, camellias and eucalyptus. Alpine plants are also a feature, and there are plants for sale.
Times: Open daily (ex 25 Dec), dawn to dusk. **Facilities:** 🅿 ▆
♿ garden centre ▆

BEER Map 03 SY28

PECORAMA PLEASURE GARDENS
Underleys EX12 3NA
➲ (from A3052 take B3174, Beer road, signed)
☎ 01297 21542
web: www.peco-uk.com

The gardens are high on a hillside, overlooking Beer. A miniature steam and diesel passenger line offers visitors a stunning view of Lyme Bay as it runs through the Pleasure Gardens. Attractions include an aviary, crazy golf, children's
continued

activity area and the Peco Millennium Garden. The main building houses an exhibition of railway modelling in various small gauges. There are souvenir and railway model shops, plus full catering facilities. Please telephone for details of events running throughout the year.
Times: Open Etr-Oct , Mon-Fri 10-5.30, Sat 10-1. Open Sun Etr & Whitsun-early Sep. **Fee:** ✱ £5.50 (ch 4-14 £3.65, pen £5, over 80 & under 4 free) **Facilities:** 🅿 💻 ✕ licensed ♿ (access with helper, wheelchair. Garden steep in places) toilets for disabled shop Includes Dartington Glass products ✖ (ex guide dogs) ◾

BICTON Map 03 SY08

BICTON PARK BOTANICAL GARDENS
East Budleigh EX9 7BJ
➲ (2m N of Budleigh Salterton on B3178, leave M5 at junct 30 & follow brown tourist signs)
☎ 01395 568465
e-mail: info@bictongardens.co.uk
web: www.bictongardens.co.uk

Unique Grade 1-listed 18th-century historic gardens with palm house, orangery, plant collections, extensive countryside museum, indoor and outdoor activity play areas, pinetum, arboretum, nature trail, woodland railway garden centre and restaurant. All this set in 63 acres of beautiful parkland that has been cherished for 300 years.
Times: Open Winter 10-5, Summer 10-6. Closed 25 & 26 Dec.
Fee: £5.95 (ch & concessions £4.95). Family ticket (2 adults, 2 ch) £19.95.
Facilities: 🅿 💻 ✕ licensed 🍴 ♿ (adapted carriage on woodland railway, wheelchairs) toilets for disabled shop garden centre ◾

BLACKMOOR GATE Map 03 SS64

EXMOOR ZOOLOGICAL PARK
South Stowford, Bratton Fleming EX31 4SG
➲ (off A361 link road onto A399, follow brown tourist signs)
☎ 01598 763352   **2 for 1**
e-mail: exmoorzoo@fsbdial.co.uk
web: www.exmoorzoo.co.uk
Exmoor Zoo is both personal and friendly. Open since 1982 it is an ideal family venue, catering particularly for the younger generation. The zoo specialises in smaller animals, many endangered, such as the golden headed lion tamarins. Over 14 species of this type of primate are exhibited. Contact pens are provided throughout and children are encouraged to participate. Twice daily guided tours at feeding times along with handling sessions.
Times: Open daily, Apr-Oct 10-6; Nov-Mar 10-4. **Fee:** ✱ £6.95 (ch £4.95, concessions £5.95). **Facilities:** 🅿 💻 ✕ ♿ toilets for disabled shop ✖ (ex guide dogs) ◾

BUCKFASTLEIGH Map 03 SX76

BUCKFAST ABBEY
TQ11 0EE
➲ (0.5m from A38, midway between Exeter and Plymouth. Turn off at 'Dart Bridge' junct and follow brown tourist signs)
☎ 01364 645500   **FREE**
e-mail: enquiries@buckfast.org.uk
web: www.buckfast.org
The Abbey, founded in 1018, was dissolved by Henry VIII in the 16th century. Restoration began in 1907, when four monks with little building experience began the work. The church was built on the old foundations, using local blue limestone and Ham Hill stone. The precinct contains several medieval monastic buildings, including the 14th-century guest hall which contains an exhibition of the history of the Abbey.
Times: Open all year daily. Closed Good Fri, 24-26 Dec.
Facilities: 🅿 💻 🍴 ♿ (Braille & audio information) toilets for disabled shop ✖ (ex guide dogs) ◾

BUCKFAST BUTTERFLY FARM & DARTMOOR OTTER SANCTUARY
TQ11 0DZ
➲ (off A38, at Dart Bridge junct, follow tourist signs)
☎ 01364 642916
e-mail: info@ottersandbutterflies.co.uk
web: www.ottersandbutterflies.co.uk
Visitors can wander around a specially designed, undercover tropical garden, where free-flying butterflies and moths from around the world can be seen. The otter sanctuary has large enclosures with underwater viewing areas. Three types of otters can be seen - the native British otter along with Asian and North American otters.
Times: Open Good Fri-end Oct, daily 10-5.30 or dusk (if earlier).
Fee: ✱ £5.95 (ch £4.50, pen £5.50). Family ticket £16.95.
Facilities: 🅿 💻 ♿ (wheelchair ramps) shop ✖ (ex guide dogs) ◾

BUCKLAND ABBEY Map 02 SX46

BUCKLAND ABBEY
PL20 6EY
➲ (off A386 0.25m S of Yelverton, signed)
☎ 01822 853607
e-mail: bucklandabbey@nationaltrust.org.uk
web: www.nationaltrust.org.uk
Originally a prosperous 13th-century Cistercian Abbey, and then home of the Grenville family, Buckland Abbey was sold to Sir Francis Drake in 1581, who lived there until his death in 1596. Several restored buildings house a fascinating exhibition about the abbey's history. Among the exhibits is Drake's drum, which is said to give warning of danger to England. A recently created Elizabethan garden is also open.
Times: Open end Mar-Nov, daily (ex Thu) 10.30-5.30. Nov-end Mar, Sat -Sun. Closed Xmas to mid-Feb. (Last admissions 45mins before closing). **Fee:** ✱ Abbey & grounds £6. Grounds only £3. Party 15+ £4.60 each. **Facilities:** 🅿 ✕ licensed 🍴 ♿ (wheelchairs & motorised buggy available) toilets for disabled shop ✖ (ex assist dogs) 🐾

Directions are provided
by the attractions.

CHITTLEHAMPTON Map 03 SS62

COBBATON COMBAT COLLECTION

Cobbaton EX37 9RZ

➲ (signed from A361 & A377)

☎ 01769 540740

2 for 1

e-mail: info@cobbatoncombat.co.uk

web: www.cobbatoncombat.co.uk

World War II British and Canadian military vehicles, war documents and military equipment can be seen in this private collection. There are over 50 vehicles including tanks, one a Gulf War Centurian, and a recently added Warsaw Pact section. There is also a section on 'Mum's War' and the Home Front. The Home Front section is now in a new purpose-built building.

Times: Open Apr-Oct, daily (ex Sat) 10-5; Jul-Aug daily. Winter most wkdays, phone for details. **Fee:** ✱ £5 (ch £3.50, pen £4.50).

Facilities: 🅿 ♨ 🍴 ♿ (most areas accessible) toilets for disabled shop ✈ (ex guide dogs, outside) 🍴

CHUDLEIGH Map 03 SX87

CANONTEIGN FALLS

EX6 7NT

➲ (off A38 at Chudleigh/Teign Valley junct onto B3193 and follow tourist signs for 3m)

☎ 01647 252434

e-mail: info@canonteignfalls.com

web: www.canonteignfalls.com

A magical combination of waterfalls, woodlands and lakes.

Times: Open all year, summer 10-6, winter 10-dusk. Last admission 1 hour before closing **Fee:** ✱ £5.50 (ch £3.50, pen £4.75). Family ticket £16. **Facilities:** 🅿 ♨ ✗ licensed 🍴 ♿ (grounds partly accessible) shop garden centre 🍴

CHURSTON FERRERS Map 03 SX95

GREENWAY GARDEN

TQ5 0ES

➲ (off A3022 into Galmpton. Follow Manor Vale Rd into village then brown signs for Greenway Garden, establishment signed)

☎ 01803 842382

e-mail: greenway@nationaltrust.org.uk

web: www.nationaltrust.org.uk/devoncornwall

Greenway is a beautiful woodland garden set on the banks of the River Dart which time seems to have passed by. A garden held on the edge of wilderness, renowned for rare half-hardy trees and shrubs, underplanted by native wild flowers, Devon's best kept secret. The surrounding estate has many walks which give stunning views over the estuary. Travel by river to enjoy this peaceful haven. Greenway is not easily accessible, having some steep and slippery paths and all visitors are asked to wear walking shoes and to follow routes and directions according to their fitness on the day.

Times: Open Mar-8 Oct, Wed-Sat. **Fee:** £4.80 (ch £2.40) Groups £4.00

Facilities: 🅿 ♨ 🍴 ♿ (part access to garden, Braille guide, large print, T Loop) toilets for disabled shop ✈ (ex guide dogs & in Parkland) 🎈🍴

> If an attraction name appears in *italics*, details have not been confirmed for 2006.

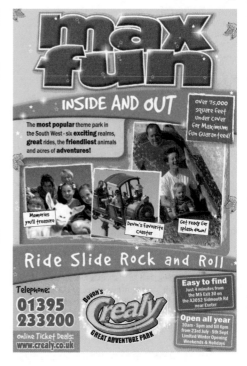

CLOVELLY Map 02 SS32

THE MILKY WAY ADVENTURE PARK

EX39 5RY

➲ (on A39, 2m from Clovelly)

☎ 01237 431255

e-mail: info@themilkyway.co.uk

web: www.themilkyway.co.uk

One of the West Country's leading attractions for the biggest rides and the best shows. Attractions include Clone Zone - Europe's first interactive adventure ride featuring a suspended roller coaster; Time Warp-indoor adventure play area; daily displays from the North Devon Bird of Prey Centre; archery centre; golf driving nets; railway; pets corner and more. A new attraction 'Droid Destroyers' has been added which invites pilots to save the Earth from the Vega Asteroid.

Times: Open Etr-Oct, daily 10.30-6. Telephone for winter opening times. **Fee:** £8 (ch £7). Family ticket £25.50 extra ch £5.50 each.

Facilities: 🅿 ♨ ♿ (ramps) toilets for disabled shop 🍴

CLYST ST MARY Map 03 SX99

CREALY ADVENTURE PARK

Sidmouth Rd EX5 1DR

➲ (M5 junct 30 onto A3052 Exeter to Sidmouth road)

☎ 01395 233200

e-mail: fun@crealy.co.uk

web: www.crealy.co.uk

Crealy Adventure Park offers an unforgettable day for all the family with Tidal Wave log flume, El Pastil Loco Coaster, Queen Bess Pirate Ship, Techno Race Karts, Bumper Boats,

continued

Victorian Carousel, Funosaurus show and all weather play area. Visit the Animal Realm to ride, feed, milk, groom or cuddle the animals. Relax on the Prairie Train tour around the worlds 1st Sunflower Maze.

Crealy Adventure Park

Times: Open all year, Jan-mid July & 6 Sep-Dec, daily 10-5. Closed winter term time Mon-Tue; mid Jul-5 Sep, daily 10-6.
Fee: ✱ £8.95-£9.95 (ch under 92cm free, pen £6.20-£7.20). Party 4+ £8.65-£9.65. Lower rates during winter months **Facilities:** 🅿 💻 ✗ licensed 🗐 ♿ (carers admitted free, rollercoaster has disabled facility) toilets for disabled shop ⬛

See advertisement on page 59

COMBE MARTIN   Map 02 SS54

COMBE MARTIN WILDLIFE PARK & DINOSAUR PARK
EX34 0NG
➲ (M5 junct 27 then A361 towards Barnstaple, turn right onto A399)
☎ 01271 882486
e-mail: info@dinosaur-park.com
web: www.dinosaur-park.com

The land that time forgot. A subtropical paradise with hundreds of birds and animals and animatronic dinosaurs, so real they're alive! Fantastic sealion shows, falconry displays and animal handling sessions. Snow leopards, meerkats, timber wolves, apes & monkeys. Host to the UK's only World Education and Research Centre. Also featuring 'Tomb of the Pharaohs' exhibition. A spectacular lightshow,
continued

Destination Mars, and Earthquake Canyon, the most unique train ride in the UK.
Times: Open 19 Mar-30 Oct, daily 10-4 (last admission 3).
Fee: ✱ £12 (ch 3-15 £7, ch under 3 free, pen £8). Family (2ad+2ch) £34. **Facilities:** 🅿 💻 🗐 shop ✖ (ex guide dogs) ⬛

See advertisement on opposite page

COMPTON   Map 03 SX86

COMPTON CASTLE
TQ3 1TA
➲ (off A381 Newton Abbot to Totnes road at Ipplepen. Or, off A380 Torquay, Pakinton ring road at Marldon (no coaches on this road)
☎ 01803 875740
e-mail: greenway@nationaltrust.org.uk
web: www.nationaltrust.org.uk/devoncornwall

Within an eight metre high curtain wall, which was built after there were French raids in the area, lies this impressive house built and extended during the 14th to 16th centuries. Compton has been the home of the Gilbert family for 600 years, and visitors can find out about their part in the exploration of the New World. The Great Kitchen still has its spiral staircase, bread ovens and knife-sharpening marks, and the withdrawing room has squints through which occupants could watch services in the chapel.
Times: Open Apr-Oct, Mon, Wed & Thu 11-4.30 **Fee:** Castle & garden £3.70 (ch £1.85) Party 15+ £3.20 (ch £1.60) **Facilities:** 🅿 🗐 ✖ (ex guide dogs) 🐾

CULLOMPTON   Map 03 ST00

DIGGERLAND
Verbeer Manor EX15 2PE
➲ (M5 junct 27. E on A38 & at rdbt turn right onto A3181. Diggerland is 3m on left)
☎ 08700 344437
e-mail: mail@diggerland
web: www.diggerland.com

[2 for 1]

An adventure park with a difference, where kids of all ages can experience the thrills of driving real earth moving equipment. Choose from various types of diggers and dumpers ranging from 1 ton to 8 and a half tons. Supervised by an instructor complete the Dumper Truck Challenge or dig for buried treasure. New rides include JCB Robots, the Supertrack, Landrover Safari and Spin Dizzy. Even under 5's can join in, with mum or dad's help. Please telephone for details of events during school and Bank Holidays.
Times: Open mid Feb-Nov, BHs & school hols. **Fee:** ✱ £2.50 (pen £1.25, under 2's free). Additional charge to drive/ride machinery.
Facilities: 🅿 💻 ♿ shop ✖ (ex guide dogs) ⬛

DARTMOUTH   Map 03 SX85

BAYARD'S COVE FORT
TQ6 9AT
➲ (in Dartmouth on riverfront)

[FREE]

Built by the townspeople to protect the harbour, the remains of the circular stronghold still stand at the southern end of the harbour.
Times: Open at any reasonable times. **Facilities:** ✖ ⚑

DARTMOUTH CASTLE

Castle Rd TQ6 0JN

⮞ (1m SE off B3205, narrow approach road)

☎ **01803 833588**

Built at the water's edge in a superb scenic setting, the castle's military history spans well over 500 years.

Times: Open all year, 24 Mar-Jun & Sep, daily 10-5; Jul-Aug, daily 10-6; Oct, daily 10-4; Nov-Mar, Sat-Sun, 10-4. Closed 24-26 Dec & 1 Jan.

Fee: £3.60 (ch £1.80, concessions £2.70). Prices & opening times relate subject to change, for further details phone or log onto www.english-heritage.org.uk/visits **Facilities:** 🅿 (charged) shop ✈ ⛺

WOODLANDS LEISURE PARK

Blackawton TQ9 7DQ

⮞ (W, off A3122)

☎ **01803 712598**

e-mail: fun@woodlandspark.com

web: www.woodlandspark.com

An all weather park, with 60 acres of attractions for all ages. The park features; 15 palyzones, 3 Watercoasters, 500m Toboggan Run, Arctic Gliders, centres for pre-schoolers and the new Avalanche Ride. The large indoor fun houses contain action challenges and interactive play, including; 2 rides, a train, Trauma Tower with 50ft sheer drop and Master Blaster game. The Falconry Centre and Animal Funtime host a vast selection of animals and birds. Special Event: Woodlands Firework Festival 4 Nov 2006.

Times: Open daily 18 Mar-5 Nov, 6 Nov-19 Mar wknds and school holidays only. **Fee:** ✱ £8.25. Family ticket £31.20 (2ad+2ch). **Facilities:** 🅿 💷 🍴 ♿ (ramps) toilets for disabled shop ✈ (ex guide dogs) 🍴

DREWSTEIGNTON　　　Map 03 SX79

CASTLE DROGO

EX6 6PB

⮞ (5m S of A30 Exeter-Okehampton. Coaches turn off A382 at Sandy Park)

☎ **01647 433306**

e-mail: castledrogo@nationaltrust.org.uk

web: www.nationaltrust.org.uk

India tea baron Julius Drewe's dream house. This granite castle, built between 1910 and 1930, is one of the most remarkable works of Sir Edward Lutyens, and combines the grandeur of a medieval castle with the comfort of the 20th century. A great country house with terraced formal garden, woodland spring garden, huge circular croquet lawn and colourful herbaceous borders. Standing at more than 900ft

continued

overlooking the wooded gorge of the River Teign with stunning views of Dartmoor, and delightful walks.
Times: Castle open 18 Mar-5 Nov, daily (ex Tue) 10.30-5.30 (or dusk if earlier). Garden open all year, daily 10.30-5.30 (or dusk if earlier).
Fee: House & garden £6.80 (ch £3.30). Family £16.50. Garden only £4.50 (ch £2.50) **Facilities:** 🅿 🔌 ᴝ (Braille & large print guide, touch list) toilets for disabled shop garden centre ✖ (ex guide/hearing dogs) �️ ➡

EXETER   Map 03 SX99

EXETER CATHEDRAL NEW
1 The Cloisters EX1 1HS
☎ 01392 285983
e-mail: visitors@exeter-cathedral.org.uk
web: www.exeter-cathedral.org.uk
A fine example of a medieval cathedral, famous for its two Norman towers, impressive West Front carvings and the longest unbroken stretch of Gothic vaulting in the world. It has been the seat of the bishops of Exeter for over one thousand years and remains a vibrant worshipping community. The Cathedral has an on-going programme of concerts and recitals throughout the year.
Times: Open all year, Mon-Fri 9.30-6.30, Sat 9.30-5, Sun 7.30-6.30. Times may vary according to special services. **Fee:** ✱ £3.50 (students £2) **Facilities:** 🅿 🔌 🛍 ᴝ toilets for disabled ✖ (ex assist dogs)

GUILDHALL
High St EX4 3EB
➲ (city centre)
☎ 01392 665500   FREE
e-mail: guildhall@exeter.gov.uk
web: www.exeter.gov.uk
This is one of the oldest municipal buildings still in use. It was built in 1330 and then altered in 1446, and the arches and façade were added in 1592-5. The roof timbers rest on bosses of bears holding staves, and there are portraits of Exeter dignitaries, guild crests, civic silver and regalia.
Times: Open when there are no mayoral functions. Times are posted outside weekly. Special opening by arrangement.
Facilities: 🅿 (200yds) ᴝ toilets for disabled ✖ (ex guide dogs)

KILLERTON HOUSE & GARDEN
EX5 3LE
☎ 01392 881345
(For full entry see Killerton House & Garden)

QUAY HOUSE VISITOR CENTRE NEW
46 The Quay EX2 4AN
☎ 01392 271611   FREE
Two thousand years of Exeter history in an audio-visual presentation of the city from Roman times to present day. Learn about the cities quayside history from the small museum.
Times: Open all year, Apr-Oct, daily 10-5; Nov-Mar, Sat-Sun 11-4.
Facilities: 🅿 🛍 shop ✖ (ex guide dogs)

If an attraction name appears in *italics*, details have not been confirmed for 2006.

ROYAL ALBERT MEMORIAL MUSEUM
Queen St EX4 3RX
➲ (in city centre)
☎ 01392 665858   FREE
e-mail: ramm@exeter.gov.uk
web: www.exeter.gov.uk/museums
Situated in the heart of Exeter and home to 16 galleries of displays and a lively programme of events and exhibitions. Travel in time from pre-history to the present day and take a voyage of discovery from Exeter all around the world. Also home to the city's largest gallery and exhibition space.
Times: Open Mon-Sat 10-5. **Facilities:** 🅿 (200yds) 🔌 🛍 ᴝ (parking, ramp, entrance lift) toilets for disabled shop ✖ (ex guide dogs)

EXMOUTH   Map 03 SY08

THE WORLD OF COUNTRY LIFE
Sandy Bay EX8 5BU
➲ (M5 junct 30, take A376 to Exmouth. Follow signs to Sandy Bay)
☎ 01395 274533
All-weather family attraction including owl displays, and a safari train that rides through a forty acre deer park. Kids will enjoy the friendly farm animals, pets centre and animal nursery. There are also a Victorian street, working models and thousands of exhibits from a bygone age, including steam and vintage vehicles.
Times: ✱ Open Etr-Oct, daily 10-5. **Facilities:** 🅿 🔌 ✖ ᴝ (all parts accessible ex 'safari train') toilets for disabled shop ✖ (ex guide dogs) ➡

GREAT TORRINGTON   Map 02 SS41

DARTINGTON CRYSTAL
EX38 7AN
➲ (Turn off A386 in centre of Great Torrington down School Lane (opposite church). Dartington Crystal is 200mtrs on left)
☎ 01805 626242   2 for 1
e-mail: sfrench@dartington.co.uk
web: www.dartington.co.uk
Dartington Crystal has won many international design awards in recognition of its excellence. The factory tour allows visitors to watch the glassware being crafted, from the safety of elevated viewing galleries. All age groups are encouraged to have fun in the glass activity area and to discover the fascinating story of glass and the history of Dartington in the Visitor Centre.
Times: Open all year. Visitor centre, Factory tour, Pavilion Cafe and Shops Mon-Fri 9-5 (last tour 3.15), Sat 10-5, Sun 10-4 (tours closed wknds). For Xmas, New Year and BH opening please telephone for details. **Fee:** ✱ £4.50 (ch under 16 free, pen £3.50). Max 5 ch with every full paying adult. **Facilities:** 🅿 🔌 ✖ licensed 🛍 ᴝ (wheelchairs available) toilets for disabled shop ✖ (ex guide dogs) ➡

RHS GARDEN ROSEMOOR
EX38 8PH
➲ (1m SE of Great Torrington on A3124)
☎ 01805 624067   2 for 1
e-mail: rosemooradmin@rhs.org.uk
web: www.rhs.org.uk/rosemoor
RHS Garden Rosemoor is situated in the beautiful Torridge Valley, set within extensive woodlands. Rich in variety, the Formal Garden includes 200 varieties of roses, and there is a

continued

herb garden, potager, cottage garden, winter garden, alpine terrace and extensive herbaceous borders. Please telephone for details of events running throughout the year.

RHS Garden Rosemoor

Times: Open: Gardens all year; Apr-Sep 10-6, Oct-Mar 10-5. Closed 25 Dec; Visitor Centre as for Gardens but closed 24-26 Dec. **Fee:** £5.50 (ch 6-16 £1.50, under 6 free). Party 10+ £4.50. RHS memebers 1 guest free. **Facilities:** 🅿 💺 ✗ licensed 🍴 ♿ (herb garden for disabled, wheelchairs) toilets for disabled shop garden centre ✖ (ex guide dogs) 🔊

HALWILL JUNCTION   Map 02 SS40

WINSFORD WALLED GARDEN NEW
EX21 3XT
➲ (Leave A30 at Okehampton, take A3079 to Bude. At Halwill Junction follow brown signs to garden)
☎ **01409 221477**
e-mail: muddywellies@winsfordwalledgarden.co.uk
web: www.winsfordwalledgarden.co.uk
Modern summer garden containing over three thousand varieties of plants in tropical temperate and alpine houses. A covered exhibition highlights the work so far and details the extensive Victorian history.
Times: Open mid Apr-Oct, daily 9.30-5.30 **Fee:** £4 **Facilities:** 🅿 🍴 ♿ (Some beds at wheelchair height) toilets for disabled

HONITON   Map 03 ST10

ALLHALLOWS MUSEUM
High St EX14 1PG
➲ (next to parish church of St Paul in High Street)
☎ **01404 44966 & 42996**
e-mail: info@honitonmuseum.co.uk
web: www.honitonmuseum.co.uk
The museum, housed in a chapel dating back to around 1200, has a wonderful display of Honiton lace, and there are lace demonstrations from June to August. The town's history is also illustrated. Special Event: Diamond Anniversary Nov 2005-Nov 2006.
Times: Open Mon before Etr-Sep; Mon-Fri 9.30-4.30 & Sat 9.30-1; Oct, Mon-Fri 9.30-3.30, Sat 9.30-12.30. **Fee:** £2 (pen £1.50, accompanied ch free). **Facilities:** 🅿 (400yds) 🍴 ♿ (stair lift, wheelchair, hearing loop) shop ✖ (ex guide dogs)

ILFRACOMBE   Map 02 SS54

ILFRACOMBE MUSEUM
Runnymede Gardens, Wilder Rd EX34 8AF
➲ (next to Landmark Theatre & TIC on seafront)
☎ **01271 863541**   **2 for 1**
e-mail: ilfracombe@devonmuseums.net
web: www.devonmuseums.net
Ilfracombe was an important trading port from the 14th to the 16th centuries and during the Napoleonic Wars became a popular resort. The history, archaeology, geology, natural history and maritime traditions of the area are illustrated here, along with Victoriana, costumes, photographs and china.
Times: Open all year, Easter-Oct, daily 10-5; Nov-Mar, Mon-Fri 10-1.
Fee: £2 (accompanied ch free, concessions £1.50). Booked disabled nad school groups free. **Facilities:** 🅿 (10yds) 🍴 ♿ (ramp to front door, wide aisles) shop ✖ (ex guide dogs)

WATERMOUTH CASTLE & FAMILY THEME PARK
EX34 9SL
➲ (3m NE off A399, midway between Ilfracombe & Combe Martin)
☎ **01271 863879**
e-mail: enquiries@watermouthcastle.com
web: www.watermouthcastle.com
A popular family attraction including mechanical music demonstrations, musical water show, dungeon labyrinths, Victorian displays, bygone pier machines, animated fairy tale scenes, tube slide, mini golf, children's carousel, swingboats, aeroplane ride, water fountains, river ride, gardens and a maze.
Times: Open Apr-end Oct, closed Sat. (Also closed some Mon & Fri off season). Ring for further details. **Fee:** £9.75 (ch 3-13 £8.25 & pen £7)
Facilities: 🅿 💺 ♿ (special wheelchair route) toilets for disabled shop ✖ (ex guide dogs) 🔊

KILLERTON HOUSE & GARDEN   Map 03 SS90

KILLERTON HOUSE & GARDEN
EX5 3LE
➲ (off B3181 Exeter to Culhampton road)
☎ **01392 881345**

Elegant 18th-century house set in an 18-acre garden with sloping lawns and herbaceous borders. A majestic avenue of beech trees runs up the hillside, past an arboretum of rhododendrons and conifers. The garden has an ice house and rustic summer house where the family's pet bear was

continued

once kept. Inside the house are displays from the Killerton Dress Collection, and a Victorian kitchen. Please telephone for details of annual events.

Times: Open: House, daily (ex Tue), Mar & Oct, Wed-Sun, Aug daily 11-5. Gardens open all year, daily from 10.30. **Fee:** House & grounds £6.50. Grounds only £5. **Facilities:** 🅿 💷 ✗ licensed ⑪ ♿ (wheelchairs & motorised buggy available) toilets for disabled shop garden centre ✖ (ex in park & guide dogs) 🐾

KINGSBRIDGE   Map 03 SX74

COOKWORTHY MUSEUM OF RURAL LIFE

The Old Grammar School, 108 Fore St TQ7 1AW
➲ (A38 onto A384, then A381 to Kingsbridge, museum at top of town)
☎ 01548 853235
e-mail: wcookworthy@talk21.com
web: www.devonmuseums.net

The 17th-century schoolrooms of this former grammar school are now the setting for another kind of education. Reconstructed room-sets of a Victorian kitchen, an Edwardian pharmacy, a costume room and extensive collection of local historical items are gathered to illustrate South Devon life. A walled garden and farm gallery are also features of this museum, founded to commemorate William Cookworthy, 'father' of the English china clay industry. The Local Heritage Resource Centre with public access databases, microfilm of local newspapers since 1855 and Devon record service point are available to visitors. Please ring for details of special events. "The South Hams at War" is a display showing life in the area during World War II, and a viewing gallery where you can take a virtual museum tour.

Times: Open all year, Apr-Sep, Mon-Sat 10.30-5; Oct 10.30-4. Nov-Mar groups by arrangement. Local Heritage Resource Centre open all year, Mon-Thu 10-12 & Wed also 2-4, other times by appointment. **Fee:** £2 (ch £1, pen & student £1.50). Family ticket £5 (2ad+4ch). **Facilities:** 🅿 (100mtrs) (max 3hrs) ⑪ ♿ (Braille labels on selected exhibits) toilets for disabled shop ✖ (ex guide dogs)

KINGSWEAR   Map 03 SX85

COLETON FISHACRE HOUSE & GARDEN

Brownstone Rd TQ6 0EQ
➲ (3m from Kingswear. Take Ferry Rd and turn off at Toll House, follow brown tourist signs)
☎ 01803 752466
e-mail: coletonfishacre@nationaltrust.org.uk
web: www.nationaltrust.org.uk

The house, set in a stream-fed valley on a beautiful stretch of south Devon coastline, was designed in the 1920s for Rupert and Lady D'Oyly Carte (of Gilbert & Sullivan fame) reflecting the Arts & Crafts tradition, but with art deco-influenced interiors. A luxuriant garden was created around it, and has year-round interest with a wide variety of rare and exotic plants. Please telephone for details of music events throughout the year.

Times: Garden open 1-30 Mar, Sat & Sun only 11-5; 31 29 Mar-29 Oct, Wed-Sun & BH Mon 10.30-5.30. House open 29 Mar-29 Oct, Wed-Sun & BH Mon 11-4.30. **Fee:** ✱ House & garden £5.50 (ch £2.75). Family ticket £13.75. 1 ad family ticket £8.25 Party £4.70 (ch £2.35). Garden only £4.40 (ch £2.10) Party £3.70. **Facilities:** 🅿 💷 ⑪ ♿ (wheelchairs available, Braille guides, mobile T loop) toilets for disabled shop garden centre ✖ (ex assist dogs) 🐾 ▰

KNIGHTSHAYES COURT   Map 03 SS91

KNIGHTSHAYES COURT

EX16 7RQ
➲ (M5 junct 27, 2m N of Tiverton off A396)
☎ 01884 254665 & 257381
e-mail: knightshayes@nationaltrust.org.uk
web: www.nationaltrust.org.uk

This fine Victorian mansion, a rare example of William Burges' work, offers much of interest to all ages. The garden is one of the most beautiful in Devon, with formal terraces, amusing topiary, a pool garden and woodland walks.

Times: House & garden open 23 Mar-30 Oct, daily (House closed Fri) 11-5.30, 11-5 in Oct. **Fee:** ✱ House & garden £6.50 (ch £3.20). Party rates available. **Facilities:** 🅿 💷 ✗ licensed ⑪ ♿ (wheelchairs available, lift, braille & audio guide) toilets for disabled shop garden centre ✖ (ex guide dogs in house) 🐾 ▰

LYDFORD   Map 02 SX58

LYDFORD CASTLE AND SAXON TOWN

EX20 4BH
➲ (in Lydford off A386)   [FREE]

Standing above the gorge of the River Lyd, this tower, dating back to the twelfth century, was notorious as a prison. The earthworks of the original Norman fort lie to the south.

Times: Open at any reasonable times. **Facilities:** 🅿 🐾

LYDFORD GORGE

EX20 4BH
➲ (off A386, between Okehampton & Tavistock)
☎ 01822 820320 & 820441
e-mail: lydfordgorge@nationaltrust.org.uk
web: www.nationaltrust.org.uk

The spectacular gorge has been formed by the River Lyd, which has cut into the rock and caused swirling boulders to scoop out potholes in the stream bed. This has created some dramatic features, notably the Devil's Cauldron close to Lydford Bridge. At the end of the gorge is the 90ft-high White Lady Waterfall.

Times: Open Apr-Sep, daily 10-5.30; Oct, daily 10-4. (Nov-Mar, waterfall entrance only, daily 10.30-3). **Fee:** ✱ £4.50 (ch 5-16 £2.20, under 5 free) Party £3.40 (ch £1.70). **Facilities:** 🅿 💷 ♿ (easy access path above gorge, audio tapes) toilets for disabled shop 🐾 ▰

MORWELLHAM   Map 02 SX47

MORWELLHAM QUAY

PL19 8JL
➲ (4m W of Tavistock, off A390. Midway between Gunnislake & Tavisock. Signed)
☎ 01822 832766 & 833808   [2 for 1]
e-mail: enquiries@morwellham-quay.co.uk
web: www.morwellham-quay.co.uk

A unique, open-air museum based around the ancient port and copper mine workings in the heart of the Tamar Valley. Journey back into another time as costumed interpreters help you re-live the daily life of a 19th-century mining village and shipping quay. A tramway takes you deep into the workings of the George and Charlotte mine. Special events include

continued

music festivals, classic car shows, and a Victorian food festival.

Morwellham Quay

Times: Open all year (ex Xmas wk) 10-6 (4.30 Nov-Etr). Last admission 3.30 (2.30 Nov-Etr). **Fee:** £8.90 (ch 5-16 £6, pen & students £7.80). Family ticket (2ad + 2ch) £26 **Facilities:** 🅿 💷 ✗ licensed ⊞ ₺ (smooth paths, but difficult areas in Victorian village) toilets for disabled shop ➡

NEWTON ABBOT   Map 03 SX87

BRADLEY MANOR
TQ12 6BN
➲ (SW of Newton Abbot on A381 Totnes road. 1m from town centre)
☎ 01626 354513
e-mail: greenway@nationaltrust.org
web: www.nationaltrust.org.uk/devoncornwall
A National Trust property of 70 acres, the 15th-century house and chapel are surrounded by woodland. The River Lemon and a millstream flow through the estate.
Times: Open Apr-Sep, Tue-Thu, 2-5; Oct by appointment **Fee:** £3.70 (ch £1.85) **Facilities:** 🅿 ⊞ ₺ T loop, large print guide ✗ 🚐 ⛟

HEDGEHOG HOSPITAL AT PRICKLY BALL FARM
Denbury Rd, East Ogwell TQ12 6BZ
➲ (1.5m from Newton Abbot on A381 towards Totnes, follow brown heritage signs)
☎ 01626 362319 & 330685
e-mail: hedgehog@hedgehog.org.uk
web: www.hedgehog.org.uk
See, touch and learn about this wild animal. In mid-season see baby hogs bottle feeding. Find out how to encourage hedgehogs into your garden and how they are put back into the wild. Talks on hedgehogs throughout the day, short basic video information about hedgehogs available.
Times: Open wk before Etr-end Oct, 10.30-5. (Last admission 1hr before closing) **Facilities:** 🅿 💷 ⊞ ₺ (large print menu, use of wheelchair, Braille menu) toilets for disabled shop garden centre ✗ (ex guide dogs) ➡

> **Directions are provided by the attractions.**

TUCKERS MALTINGS
Teign Rd TQ12 4AA
➲ (follow brown tourist signs from Newton Abbot railway station)
☎ 01626 334734
e-mail: info@tuckersmaltings.com
web: www.tuckersmaltings.com
The only working Malthouse in England open to the public, producing malt from barley for over 30 West Country breweries. Learn all about the process of malting - and taste the end product at the in-house brewery. Guided tours last an hour.
Times: Open Good Fri-end Oct, Mon-Sat (Closed Sun). Speciality bottled beer shop open throughout the year. Phone to check winter opening. **Fee:** ✱ £5.45 (ch 5-15 £3.45, 16-17 £3.95, pen £4.95). Family ticket £15.45. **Facilities:** 🅿 (100yds) (pay & display car park) ₺ toilets for disabled shop ➡

OKEHAMPTON   Map 02 SX59

MUSEUM OF DARTMOOR LIFE
3 West St EX20 1HQ
➲ (follow brown signs off all major roads into Okehampton. Museum on main road next to White Hart Hotel)
☎ 01837 52295   **2 for 1**
e-mail: dartmoormuseum@eclipse.co.uk
web: museumofdartmoorlife.eclipse.co.uk
Housed on three floors in an early 19th-century mill, the museum tells the story of how people have lived, worked and played on and around Dartmoor through the centuries. It shows how the moorland has shaped their lives just as their work has shaped the moorland. In the Cranmere Gallery, temporary exhibitions feature local history, art and crafts.
Times: Open Etr-Nov, Mon-Sat 10-5. Winter opening times, telephone for details. **Fee:** ✱ £2.50 (students £1). Family ticket £6.25. Party 10+.
Facilities: 🅿 💷 ⊞ ₺ Braille, desk loop, lift toilets for disabled shop

OKEHAMPTON CASTLE
Castle Lodge EX20 1JB
➲ (1m SW of town centre)
☎ 01837 52844
Once the largest castle in Devon set amongst the stunning Dartmoor foothills. A free audio tour brings this romantic ruin to life.
Times: Open Apr-Jun & Sep, daily 10-5; Jul-Aug, daily 10-6. Closed Oct-Mar. **Fee:** £3.00 (ch £1.50, concessions £2.30). Opening times and prices are subject to change, for further details please phone 0870 333 1181 **Facilities:** 🅿 shop ⌗

OTTERTON   Map 03 SY08

OTTERTON MILL CENTRE
EX9 7HG
➲ (on the B3178 between Budleigh Salterton and Newton Poppleford)
☎ 01392 568521   **FREE**
e-mail: escape@ottertonmill.com
web: www.ottertonmill.com
Set beside the River Otter in one of Devon's loveliest valleys, Otterton Mill is a centuries-old working watermill, a famous bakery and shop full of local produce, a restaurant, and a gallery of arts and crafts from local artists. Please see website for details of music nights and art events
Times: Open every day from 10. **Facilities:** 🅿 ✗ licensed ⊞ ₺ (free entry to ground floor) toilets for disabled shop ➡

PAIGNTON   Map 03 SX86

PAIGNTON & DARTMOUTH STEAM RAILWAY
Queens Park Station, Torbay Rd TQ4 6AF
➲ (from Paignton follow brown tourist signs)
☎ 01803 555872
e-mail: mail@pdsr.eclipse.co.uk
web: www.paignton-steamrailway.co.uk
Steam trains run for seven miles from Paignton to Kingswear on the former Great Western line, stopping at Goodrington Sands, Churston, and Kingswear, connecting with the ferry crossing to Dartmouth. Combined river excursions available. Ring for details of special events.
Times: Open Jun-Sep, daily 9-5.30 & selected days Oct & Apr-May.
Fee: ✱ Paignton to Kingswear £7 (ch £5, pen £6.50). Family £22. Paignton to Dartmouth (including ferry) £8.50 (ch £5.80, pen £8). Family £26. **Facilities:** P (5mins walk) ◢█ & (wheelchair ramp for boarding train) toilets for disabled shop ◼

PAIGNTON ZOO ENVIRONMENTAL PARK
Totnes Rd TQ4 7EU
➲ (1m from Paignton town centre on A3022 Totnes road)
☎ 01803 697500
e-mail: info@paigntonzoo.org.uk
web: www.paigntonzoo.org.uk

Paignton is one of Britain's biggest zoos, set in a beautiful and secluded woodland valley, where new enclosures are spacious and naturalistic. A tour will take you through some of the world's threatened habitats - Forest, Savannah, Wetland and Desert, with hundreds of species, many of them endangered and part of conservation breeding programmes. There are regular keeper talks, a children's play area, and special events include an annual Easter Egg Safari.
Times: Open all year, daily 10-6 (5 in winter). Last admission 5 (4 in winter). Closed 25 Dec. **Fee:** ✱ £10 (ch 3-15 £6.70, students £8.25). Family ticket £30 **Facilities:** P ◢█ ✕ licensed & (some steep hills, wheelchair loan-booking essential) toilets for disabled shop ◼ (ex guide dogs) ◼

PLYMOUTH   Map 02 SX45

CITY MUSEUM & ART GALLERY
Drake Circus PL4 8AJ
➲ (off A38 onto A374, museum on NW of city centre, opposite university)
☎ 01752 304774   [FREE]
e-mail: enquiry@plymouth.gov.uk
web: www.plymouthmuseum.gov.uk
The City Museum and Art Gallery is home to a Fine and Decorative Art Collection of paintings, prints and Reynolds family portraits, silver and Plymouth China, and the Cottonian Collection of drawings, sculpture and books. There is a lively programme of art exhibitions, as well as archaeology, local and natural history displays, and the Discovery Centre with a 'hands-on' section for children.
Times: Open all year, Tue-Fri 10-5.30, Sat 10-5, BH Mon 10-5. Closed Good Fri & 25-26 Dec. **Facilities:** P (200yds) & (wheelchair available) toilets for disabled shop ◼ (ex guide dogs)

THE GREEN HOUSE VISITOR CENTRE
The Ride PL9 7JA
➲ (2 miles E of Plymouth City Centre on A379 Kingsbridge road. Follow signs for Chelson Meadow)
☎ 01752 482392
e-mail: nowaste@the greenhouseplymouth.org.uk
web: www.thegreenhouseplymouth.org.uk
The UK's first leisure-based, sustainable waste, education exhibition. A responsible attitude to waste is promoted via informal, yet informative, interactive exhibitions. These include a giant energy-generating hamster wheel; underground caves where the whole family can learn about waste separation and the machinery used to do it, helped along by Colin the Can and Betty the Bottle; waste disposal challenges, and more.
Times: ✱ Open Tue-Sat 10-5. \9Last entry at 4) **Facilities:** P ◢█ ▦ & toilets for disabled shop ◼ (ex guide dogs)

MERCHANT'S HOUSE MUSEUM
33 St Andrews St PL1 2AX
➲ (Turn off A38 onto A374, follow signs to city centre, house located behind St Andrew's Church).
☎ 01752 304774
e-mail: enquiry@plymouth.gov.uk
web: www.plymouthmuseum.gov.uk
The largest and finest 16th-century house surviving in Plymouth. Inside visitors can discover various aspects of Plymouth's past, including a reconstructed Victorian pharmacy, life during World War II, and a Victorian schoolroom which is available for group bookings.
Times: Open Apr-Sep, Tue-Fri 10-5.30, Sat 10-5, BH Mon 10-5 during summer (closed 1-2). **Fee:** ✱ £1.30 (ch 80p). **Facilities:** P (400yds) & shop ◼

NATIONAL MARINE AQUARIUM NEW
Rope Walk, Coxside PL4 0LF
⊃ (A38 to Marsh Mills (Sainsbury's) then head for
city centre & follow brown signs for Barbican &
Coxside car park)
☎ 01752 600301
e-mail: enquiries@national-aquarium.co.uk
web: www.national-aquarium.co.uk
Over 3000 fish at Britain's biggest and Europe's deepest
aquarium. Discover an exciting world where science and
conservation come to life in the ocean experience. Events
through spring, summer and autumn.
Times: Open all year daily, mid Mar-Oct 10-6; Nov-mid Mar 10-5
Fee: ✱ £8.75 (ch £5.25, concessions £7.25). Family £25 (2+2)
Facilities: P ⬛ ⬛ ♿ toilets for disabled shop
✖ (ex guide dogs) ⬛

PLYMOUTH DOME
The Hoe PL1 2NZ
☎ 01752 603300 & 600608 (recorded
message)
web: www.plymouthdome.info
This high-tech visitor centre lets you explore the sounds and
smells of an Elizabethan street, walk the gun-deck of a
galleon, dodge the press gang, stroll with film stars on an
ocean liner, and witness the devastation of the Blitz.
Examine satellite weather pictures as they arrive from space,
keep up to date with shipping movements and monitor the
busy harbour on radar. An excellent introduction to
Plymouth and a colourful interpretation of the past. Ring for
details of special events.
Times: Open Apr-Oct, daily 10-5; Nov-Mar, Tue-Sat 10-4 **Fee:** ✱ £4.75
(ch £3.25 ch under 5 free, pen & students £3.75). Family (2 ad+2 ch)
£13. **Facilities:** P (200yds) ⬛ ♿ (audio descriptions, induction
loop, wheelchairs available) toilets for disabled shop
✖ (ex guide dogs) ⬛

ROYAL CITADEL
PL1 2PD
⊃ (at the end of Plymouth Hoe)
☎ 01752 775841
e-mail: plymouthbbg@hotmail.com
A dramatic 17th-century fortress built to defend the coastline
from the Dutch. It is still in use today.
Times: Open May-Sep, Tue-Thu 2.30pm by guided tour only
Fee: £3.50 (EH Members £3.00). Opening times and prices are subject
to change, for further details please phone 0870 333 1181
Facilities: ✖ ⚷

PLYMPTON — Map 02 SX55

SALTRAM
PL7 1UH
⊃ (3.5m E of Plymouth, between A38 & A379.
Take Plympton turn at Marsh Mill rdbt, turn right
at 4th traffic lights to Cot Hill. At t-junct right into
Merafield Rd, Saltram 0.25m on right)
☎ 01752 333500 & 01752 333503
e-mail: saltram@nationaltrust.org.uk
web: www.nationaltrust.org.uk
This magnificent George II house still has its original
contents. The collection of paintings was begun at the
suggestion of Reynolds and includes many of his portraits.
The saloon and dining room were designed by Robert Adam
and have superb decorative plasterwork and period
continued

furniture. The extensive gardens include a working Orangery
and several follies.
Times: Open House: Mar-Sep, 12-4.30, Oct 11.30-3.30. Garden open
all year, 11-5. Park open all year, dawn to dusk. **Fee:** ✱ House and
garden £7. Garden only £3.50. NT members free. **Facilities:** P ⬛
✖ licensed ⬛ ♿ (wheelchairs available, lift, Braille & audio guides)
toilets for disabled shop ✖ (ex in park on leads) ⬛ ⬛

POWDERHAM — Map 03 SX98

POWDERHAM CASTLE
EX6 8JQ
⊃ (signed off A379 Exeter/Dawlish road)
☎ 01626 890243 `2 for 1`
e-mail: castle@powderham.co.uk
web: www.powderham.co.uk
Built between 1390 and 1420, this ancestral home of the
Earls of Devon was damaged in the Civil War. The house
was restored and altered in later times and is set in beautiful
rose gardens with views over the deer park to the Exe
Estuary. Please telephone for details of special events.
Times: Open Etr-end Oct, 10-5.30 (last admission 5). Closed Sat.
Fee: ✱ £7.45 (ch £4.15, pen £4.25). Family ticket £19.90 concessions
£5.65 **Facilities:** P ⬛ ✖ licensed ♿ (ramps) toilets for disabled
shop garden centre ⬛

SALCOMBE — Map 03 SX73

OVERBECKS MUSEUM & GARDEN
Sharpitor TQ8 8LW
⊃ (1.5m SW of Salcombe, signed from
Malborough & Salcombe, narrow approach road)
☎ 01548 842893
e-mail: vicki.pepper@nationaltrust.org.uk
The garden is on the most southerly tip of Devon, and allows
many exotic plants to flourish. The Edwardian house
displays toys, dolls and a natural history collection, and there
is a secret room for children where they can search for 'Fred'
the friendly ghost.
Times: Open Apr-Jul, Sun-Fri 11-5.30; Aug, daily 11-5.30; Sep, Sun-Fri
11-5.30; Oct, Sun-Thu 11-5. Gardens open all year, 10-6 (or sunset if
earlier). **Fee:** ✱ Museum & gardens £4.60 (ch £2.30). Gardens only
£3.40 (ch £1.70). Family ticket £11.50. **Facilities:** P ⬛ ⬛ ♿ (ramp
from garden, Braille guide, hearing loop) shop ✖ (ex guide dogs)
🚌 small parties only ⬛ ⬛

SOUTH MOLTON — Map 03 SS72

QUINCE HONEY FARM
EX36 3AZ
⊃ (3.5m W of A361, on N edge of South Molton)
☎ 01769 572401 `2 for 1`
e-mail: info@quincehoney.co.uk
web: www.quincehoney.com
Follow the story of honey and beeswax from flower to table.
The exhibition allows you to see the world of bees close up
in complete safety; hives open at the press of a button
revealing the honeybees' secret life. After viewing the bees
at work, sample the fruits of their labour in the café or shop.
Times: Open daily, Apr-Sep 9-6; Oct 9-5; Shop only Nov-Etr 9-5.
Closed 25 Dec-4 Jan. **Fee:** ✱ £3.50 (ch 5-16 £2, pen £2.80)
Facilities: P ⬛ ⬛ ♿ toilets for disabled shop
✖ (ex guide dogs) ⬛

STICKLEPATH   Map 03 SX69
FINCH FOUNDRY
EX20 2NW
➲ (off A30 at Okehampton junct, follow brown
signs to Finch Foundry. Located in main street of
village)
☎ 01837 840046
Finch Foundry was, in the 19th century, a water-powered
factory for making sickles, scythes, shovels and other hand
tools. Although no longer in production, three waterwheels
can still be seen driving huge hammers, shears, grindstone
and other machinery, with daily working demonstrations.
These demonstrations explain the key role the foundry
played in the local community. Special Event: St. Clements
Day (St. Clements is the patron saint of blacksmiths) 3rd Sat
in Nov.
Times: Open Apr-Nov, daily (ex Tue), 11-5.30 (Last entry 5).
Fee: ✱ £3.50 (ch £1.75). **Facilities:** 🅿 ▄▆ 🗊 ᵫ (access to shop/tea
room, view main foundry via shop) shop ⅛ ▅

TAVISTOCK
See Morwellham

TIVERTON   Map 03 SS91
TIVERTON CASTLE
EX16 6RP
➲ (M5 junct 27, then 7m on A361 towards
Tiverton to rdbt where Castle is signposted)
☎ 01884 253200 & 255200   2 for 1
e-mail: tiverton.castle@ukf.net
web: www.tivertoncastle.com
The original castle, built in 1106 by order of Henry I, was
rebuilt in the late 13th-14th centuries. It resisted General
Fairfax during the Civil War but fell to him when a lucky shot
hit the drawbridge chain. Now a private house, the gardens
are lovely and there's a fine Civil War armoury. Special
Event: 2006 is the 900th anniversary of original castle
building.
Times: Open Etr Sun-end Oct, Sun,Thu & BH Mon only 2.30-5.30. Last
admission 5. **Fee:** £4 (ch 7-16 £2, under 7 free). Disabled half price if
accessing ground floor only. **Facilities:** 🅿 ᵫ toilets for disabled shop
✺ (ex guide dogs)

TIVERTON MUSEUM OF MID DEVON LIFE
Beck's Square EX16 6PJ
➲ (in centre of town next to Beck's Square car
park)
☎ 01884 256295
e-mail: curator@tivertonmuseum.org.uk
web: www.tivertonmuseum.org.uk
This large and comprehensive museum now with 15
galleries, re-opened after extensive rebuilding and
redisplayed throughout. It is housed in a 19th-century school
and the exhibits include a Heathcote Lace Gallery featuring
items from the local lace-making industry. There is also an
agricultural section with a collection of farm wagons and
implements. Other large exhibits include two waterwheels
and a railway locomotive with many GWR items.
Times: Open Feb-mid Dec, Mon-Fri 10.30-4.30, Sat 10-1. Railway
Gallery undergoing major structural work during 2005. **Fee:** ✱ £3.50
(ch £1, pen £2.50) **Facilities:** 🅿 (100yds) ᵫ (lift, induction loop)
toilets for disabled shop ✺ (ex guide dogs)

TORQUAY   Map 03 SX96
BABBACOMBE MODEL VILLAGE
Hampton Av, Babbacombe TQ1 3LA
➲ (follow brown tourist signs from outskirts of
town)
☎ 01803 328669 & 315315
e-mail: ss@babbacombemodelvillage.co.uk
web: www.babbacombemodelvillage.co.uk
Set in four acres of beautifully maintained, miniature
landscaped garden, the village contains over 400 models and
1200ft of model railway. City Lights, an evening illuminations
feature, depicts Piccadilly Circus in miniature. At the end of
your visit, enjoy a new facility that offers breathtaking views
over the model village. Vintage model railway layout, the
Aquaviva, an evening water, light and sound spectacular and
the new 'Silvers Model Circus'.
Times: May-Sep, Sun, Tue & Thu 10-9. Mon, Wed, Fri-Sat 10-5. Jun,
Sun-Thu 10-9.30, Fri-Sat 10-5. Jul-Aug, 10-9.30. Winter 10-4. **Fee:** £6.90
(ch £4.20, pen £5.90). Family ticket £20 Price includes free return
voucher valid for 7 days April-Sep. **Facilities:** 🅿 (charged) ▄▆ ✗ 🗊
ᵫ (push button audio information) toilets for disabled shop garden
centre ▅

'BYGONES'
Fore St, St Marychurch TQ1 4PR
➲ (follow tourist signs into Torquay and St
Marychurch)
☎ 01803 326108
web: www.bygones.co.uk
Step back in time in this life-size Victorian exhibition street
of over 20 shops including a forge, pub and period display
rooms, housed in a former cinema. Exhibits include a large
model railway layout, illuminated fantasyland, railwayana
and military exhibits including a walk-through World War I
trench. At Christmas the street is turned into a winter
wonderland. A new set piece features Babbacombe's John
Lee ('the man they couldn't hang') in his cell. There is
something here for all the family.
Times: ✱ Open all year, Summer 10-9.30, (Fri-Sun 10-6); Spring &
Autumn 10-6; Winter 10-4, wknds & school hols 10-5. (Last entry 1hr
before closing). **Facilities:** 🅿 (50yds) ▄▆ 🗊 (ramp) shop
✺ (ex guide dogs)

KENTS CAVERN
Cavern House, 91 Ilsham Rd, Wellswood TQ1 2JF
➲ (1.25m NE off B3199, follow brown tourist
signs. 1m from Torquay Harbour)
☎ 01803 215136
e-mail: caves@kents-cavern.co.uk
web: www.kents-cavern.co.uk
Probably the most important Palaeolithic site in Britain and
recognised as one of the most significant archaeological
areas. This is not only a world of spectacular natural beauty,
but also a priceless record of past times, where a multitude
of secrets of mankind, animals and nature have become
trapped and preserved over the last 500,000 years. 170 years
after the first excavations and with over 80,000 remains
already unearthed, modern research is still discovering new
clues to our past. Please visit website for details of special
events.
Times: Open all year daily from 10am, last tour 3.30pm Nov-Feb, 4pm
Mar-Jun & Sep-Oct, 4.30pm Jul-Aug. **Fee:** ✱ Daytime: £6.50 (ch 4-15
£5) Family £21. Ghost evening tour: £5.50. **Facilities:** 🅿 ▄▆
✗ licensed ᵫ toilets for disabled shop ✺ (ex guide dogs) ▅

LIVING COASTS

Beacon Quay TQ1 2BG
➲ (once in Torquay follow A379 and brown tourist signs to Torquay harbour)
☎ 01803 202470
e-mail: info@livingcoasts.org.uk
web: www.livingcoasts.org.uk

Living Coasts is an unusual and ambitious attraction that allows visitors to take a trip around the coastlines of the world without leaving Torquay. Specially designed environments are home to fur seals, puffins, penguins, ducks, rats, and waders among others. All the animals can be seen above and below the water, while the huge meshed aviary allows the birds to fly free over your head. Visitors can obtain special joint tickets which will allow them to visit nearby Paignton Zoo.
Times: Open daily from 10. Closed 25 Dec. **Fee:** ✱ £5.90 (ch over 3 £4.10, pen £4.60). Family ticket (2ad+2ch) £18 **Facilities:** P 10-15 min walk ➤ ✗ licensed 🎫 ᴊ (pre-booked wheelchair hire) toilets for disabled shop ✖ (ex assist dogs) ◼

TOTNES   Map 03 SX86

GUILDHALL

Rampart Walk, off High St TQ9 5QH
➲ (behind St Mary's Church on the main street)
☎ 01803 862147
e-mail: office@totnestowncouncil.gov.uk
web: www.totnestowncouncil.gov.uk
Originally the refectory, kitchens, brewery and bakery for the Benedictine Priory of Totnes (1088-1536), the building was established as the Guildhall in 1553 during the reign of Edward VI. A magistrates' court and a prison opened in 1624, and the council chamber is still used today.
Times: Open Apr-Sep, Mon-Wed 10-3; Other times by appointment.
Fee: ✱ £1 (ch 25p). **Facilities:** P (50yds) 🎫

TOTNES CASTLE

TQ9 5NU
➲ (on hill overlooking town)
☎ 01803 864406
One of the best surviving examples of a Norman motte and bailey castle with spectacular views. The once great ditch that surrounded the keep is today filled with the cottages and gardens of the town.
Times: Open 24 Mar-Jun & Sep, daily 10-5; Jul-Aug, daily 10-6; Oct, daily 10-4. **Fee:** £2.30 (ch £1.20, concessions £1.70). Opening times and prices are subject to change, for further details please phone 0870 333 1181 **Facilities:** P (70yds) (payment required) shop ⊞

TOTNES MUSEUM

70 Fore St TQ9 5RU
➲ (from bottom of Totnes Town, turn into Fore St, museum on left of main street, just before East Gate Arch Clock Tower)
☎ 01803 863821
e-mail: totnesmuseum@btconnect.com
web: www.devonmuseums.net/totnes
An Elizabethan merchant's house, dating from 1575, said to have been built for Sir Walter Kelland, a wealthy merchant. The building houses archaeological and social history collection and room dedicated to Charles Babbage, inventor of the first computer. Study centre archives located at the rear of the museum.
Times: Open 13 Mar-27 Oct, Mon-Fri 10.30-5 (last entry 4.30)
Fee: £1.50 (ch 5-16 50p, students & pen £1). **Facilities:** P (440yds) (restricted parking on main street) 🎫 ᴊ (personal guided tours available) shop

UFFCULME   Map 03 ST01

COLDHARBOUR MILL WORKING WOOL MUSEUM

Coldharbour Mill EX15 3EE
➲ (2m from M5 junct 27, off B3181. Follow signs to Willand, then brown signs to museum)
☎ 01884 840960
e-mail: info@coldharbourmill.org.uk
web: www.coldharbourmill.org.uk
The Picturesque Coldharbour Mill is set in idyllic Devon countryside. It has been producing textiles since 1799 and is now a working museum, still making knitting wools and fabrics on period machinery. The Fox Gallery exhibits a variety of temporary exhibitions including textiles, photography, mixed media and craft. With machine demonstrations, a water wheel and steam engines, Coldharbour Mill is a wonderful and very different family day out.
Times: Mar-Sep 10.30-5, Oct-Feb 11-4 **Fee:** ✱ £5.95 (ch 5-16 £2.95, pen £5.50). Family ticket £16. **Facilities:** P ➤ ✗ licensed 🎫 ᴊ (helpful guides & lift, indoor restaurant not accessible) toilets for disabled shop ✖ (ex guide dogs or in grounds) ◼

YELVERTON   Map 02 SX56

YELVERTON PAPERWEIGHT CENTRE

4 Buckland Ter, Leg O'Mutton Corner PL20 6AD
➲ (at Yelverton off A386, Plymouth to Tavistock road)   **FREE**
☎ 01822 854250
e-mail: paperweightcentre@btinternet.com
web: www.paperweightcentre.co.uk
This unusual centre is the home of the Broughton Collection - a glittering permanent collection of glass paperweights of all sizes and designs. The centre also has an extensive range of modern glass paperweights for sale. Prices range from a few pounds to over £1000. There is also a series of oil and watercolour paintings by talented local artists.
Times: Open Apr-Oct, daily 10.30-5; 10-24 Dec, daily; Nov & Jan-Mar by appointment. **Facilities:** P (100yds) ᴊ (ramp on request) shop ◼

DORSET

EVENTS & FESTIVALS

January
1st Annual Bath Race, Poole Quay, Poole

April
tbc Dorchester Festival

May
5th-7th Dorset Garden Show, Canford Park Arena, Wimborne
5th-7th Weymouth Folk Festival, various venues
tbc Old Harbour Oyster Festival, Brewers Quay, Weymouth
tbc Trawler Race & Water Carnival, Weymouth Old Harbour, Weymouth
tbc Weymouth International Beach Kite Festival, Weymouth Beach

June
9th-11th Wimborne Folk Festival, town centre, Wimborne
tbc Bournemouth Live Music Festival

July
14th-16th Tolpuddle Martyrs Memorial Rally & Festival, Tolpuddle
22nd-30th Lyme Regis Lifeboat Week, The Cobb, Lyme Regis
tbc Lyme Regis Jazz Festival
tbc Portland Steam & Vintage Show

August
30th-3rd Sep Great Dorset Steam Fair, South Down Farm, Tarrant Hinton
tbc Bournemouth Regatta
tbc Victorian Festival, Nothe Fort, Weymouth

September
2nd-3rd Dorchester Show, Cokers Frome Showground, Dorchester
tbc Dorset Town Criers competition, venue to be confirmed

December
25th Christmas Day harbour swim, Weymouth

Above: Dorset's rugged coastline

ABBOTSBURY   Map 03 SY58

ABBOTSBURY SWANNERY
New Barn Rd DT3 4JG
➜ (turn off A35 at Winterborne Steepleton near Dorchester. Abbotsbury on B3157 coastal road, between Weymouth and Bridport)
☎ 01305 871858   **2 for 1**
e-mail: info@abbotsbury-tourism.co.uk
web: www.abbotsbury-tourism.co.uk
Abbotsbury is the breeding ground of the only managed colony of mute swans. The swans can be seen safely at close quarters, and the site is also home or stopping point for many wild birds. The highlight of the year is the cygnet season, end of May to the end of June, when there may be over 100 nests on site. Visitors can often take pictures of cygnets emerging from eggs at close quarters. There is an audio-visual show, as well as mass feeding at noon and 4pm daily, and an ugly duckling trail.
Times: Open 19 Mar-30 Oct, daily 10-6 (last admission 5).
Fee: ✱ £6.80 (ch £4 & pen £6). **Facilities:** 🅿 ▣ ✗ licensed ▤ ♿ (free wheelchair loan, herb garden for blind) toilets for disabled shop ✖ ◗

ATHELHAMPTON   Map 03 SY79

ATHELHAMPTON HOUSE & GARDENS
DT2 7LG
➜ (off A35 Northbrook junct, follow brown tourist signs towards Puddletown. Left at traffic lights, attraction approx 1m on left)
☎ 01305 848363   **2 for 1**
e-mail: pcooke@athelhampton.co.uk
web: www.athelhampton.co.uk
Athelhampton, one of the finest 15th-century houses in England, contains magnificently furnished rooms including The Great Hall of 1485 and the library. The glorious Grade I gardens contain the world-famous topiary pyramids, fountains, and collections of tulips, magnolias, roses, clematis and lilies in season.
Times: Open Mar-Oct, daily 10.30-5. Also Sun in Winter (ex Xmas). (Closed Fri & Sat). **Fee:** ✱ House & Garden £8 (ch free, pen £7.25, student & disabled £5.75). Garden only £5.75 (ch free).
Facilities: 🅿 ▣ ✗ licensed ♿ (wheelchairs available) toilets for disabled shop ✖ (ex assistance dogs) ◗

BEAMINSTER   Map 03 ST40

MAPPERTON
DT8 3NR
➜ (2m SE off A356 & B3163)
☎ 01308 862645
e-mail: office@mapperton.com
web: www.mapperton.com
Several acres of terraced valley gardens with specimen trees and shrubs, and formal borders surround a manor house that dates back to the 16th century. There are also fountains, grottoes, stone sculpture fishponds and an orangery, and the garden offers good views and walks. A plant fair is held annually, usually in April.
Times: Open Gardens: Mar-Oct, daily (exc Sat) 11-5. House open 26 Jun-4 Aug, 29 May, 28 Aug, BHs, wkday afternoons 2-4.30.
Fee: Gardens £4 (ch 5-18 £2, under 5 free). House £3.50.
Facilities: 🅿 ▣ ▤ ♿ (ramp from parking area to garden) toilets for disabled shop ✖ (ex guide dogs) ◗

BLANDFORD FORUM   Map 03 ST80
ROYAL SIGNALS MUSEUM
Blandford Camp DT11 8RH
➲ (signposted off the B3082 Blandford/Wimborne road & A354 Salisbury road. Follow brown signs for the Royal Signals Museum.)
☎ 01258 482248
e-mail: info@royalsignalsmuseum.com
web: www.royalsignalsmuseum.com

The Royal Signals Museum depicts the history of military communications, science and technology from the Crimea to current day. As well as displays on all major conflicts involving British forces, there are the stories of the ATS, the Long Range Desert Group, Air Support, Airborne, Para and SAS Signals. For children there are trails and interactive exhibits.

Times: Open Mon-Fri 10-5, Mar-Oct Sat-Sun 10-4. Closed 10 days over Xmas & New Year **Facilities:** 🅿 💻 🗐 ♿ (ramps & lifts) toilets for disabled shop ✖ (ex guide dogs) 🍴

BOURNEMOUTH   Map 04 SZ09
OCEANARIUM
Pier Approach, West Beach BH2 5AA
➲ (from A338 Wessex Way, follow Oceanarium tourist signs)
☎ 01202 311993
e-mail: oceanarium@reallive.co.uk
web: www.oceanarium.co.uk

Explore the secrets of the ocean in an adventure that will take you to some of the world's most amazing waters. The Oceanarium Bournemouth brings you face to face with a vast array of creatures from piranhas and clownfish to tiny freshwater turtles. Take a walk through our amazing underwater tunnel to get even closer to sharks, sea turtles, stingrays and eels.

Times: Open all year, daily from 10. Late night opening during school summer hols. Closed 25 Dec. **Fee:** Telephone for admission charges. **Facilities:** 🅿 (100mtrs) 💻 🗐 ♿ (wheelchair for hire) toilets for disabled shop ✖ (ex guide dogs) 🍴

BOVINGTON CAMP   Map 03 SY88
CLOUDS HILL
BH20 7NQ
➲ (1m N of Bovington Camp & Tank Museum)
☎ 01929 405616
web: www.nationaltrust.org.uk

T E Lawrence ('Lawrence of Arabia') bought this cottage in 1925 when he was a private in the Tank Corps at Bovington. He would escape here to play records and entertain friends to feasts of baked beans and China tea. The furniture and contents were Lawrence's own and a new display tells the story of Lawrence's life.

Times: Open 18 Mar-Oct, Thu-Sun. 12-5 **Fee:** ✱ £3.50.
Facilities: 🅿 ♿ (Braille guide) shop ✖ 🚌 🐾

THE TANK MUSEUM
BH20 6JG
➲ (off A352 or A35, follow brown tank signs from Bere Regis & Wool)
☎ 01929 405096
e-mail: info@tankmuseum.co.uk
web: www.tankmuseum.co.uk

The Tank Museum houses the world's finest international collection of Armoured Fighting Vehicles. Tanks in Action

continued

displays are held every Thursday at noon during July-September and every Tuesday from end July to August Bank Holiday. Armoured vehicle rides are available throughout the summer, and various special events take place - please telephone for details.

Times: Open all year, daily 10-5. Closed 23-29 Dec. **Fee:** £8 (ch £6, pen £7.50). Family saver £23 (2ad+2ch); £22 (1ad+3ch). Group rates available. **Facilities:** 🅿 💻 ✖ licensed 🗐 ♿ (wheelchairs available & audio tours) toilets for disabled shop ✖ (ex in grounds) 🍴

BROWNSEA ISLAND   Map 03 SZ08
BROWNSEA ISLAND
BH13 7EE
➲ (located in Poole Harbour)
☎ 01202 707744
e-mail: brownseaisland@nationaltrust.org.uk
web: www.nationaltrust.org.uk

This is a 250-acre nature reserve partly managed by the Dorset Trust for Nature Conservation. The island is most famous as the site of the first scout camp, held by Lord Baden-Powell in 1907. Scouts and Guides are still the only people allowed to stay here overnight. It is a haven for red squirrels and seabirds.

Times: Open 12 Mar -22 Jul, 10-5 all week; 23 Jul -2 Sep, 10-6 all week; 3-30 Sep 10-5 all week; 1-30 Oct, 10-4 all week **Fee:** ✱ £4.20 (ch £2). Family ticket £10.40. Party £3.60 (ch £1.70) **Facilities:** 💻 ✖ ♿ (Braille/Audio guide, 2 selfdrive vehicles- booking advised) toilets for disabled shop ✖ 🐾

CANFORD CLIFFS   Map 04 SZ08
COMPTON ACRES GARDENS
Canford Cliffs Rd BH13 7ES
➲ (on B3065, follow brown tourist signs)
☎ 01202 700778
e-mail: sales@comptonacres.co.uk
web: www.comptonacres.co.uk

2 for 1

The ten acres of Compton Acres incorporate Japanese and Italian gardens, rock and water gardens, and heather gardens. There are fine views over Poole Harbour and the Purbeck Hills. The beautiful wooded valley is an amazing place to explore the wide range of plants.

Times: Open Apr-Oct 9-6, Nov-Mar 9-4 (last entry 1hr before close). Closed 25 & 26 Dec. **Fee:** ✱ £5.95 (ch £3.95, pen £5.45). Party 15+ £5.45 (ch £3.95, pen £4.95) **Facilities:** 🅿 💻 ✖ licensed 🗐 ♿ (level paths and ramps into shops and cafe) toilets for disabled shop garden centre ✖ (ex guide & hearing dogs) 🍴

CHRISTCHURCH   Map 04 SZ19
CHRISTCHURCH CASTLE & NORMAN HOUSE
➲ (near Christchurch Priory)   **FREE**

Set on the river bank, the ruins of this Norman keep and constable's house date back to the twelfth century.
Times: Open at any reasonable time. **Facilities:** ⌗

RED HOUSE MUSEUM & GARDENS
Quay Rd BH23 1BU
➲ (follow brown tourist signs from Christchurch, Red House is on corner of Quay Rd)
☎ 01202 482860
web: www.hants.gov.uk/museum/redhouse

A museum with plenty of variety, featuring local history, archaeology, and natural history, displayed in a beautiful Georgian house. There's an excellent costume collection,

continued

some Arthur Romney-Green furniture and gardens with a woodland walk and herb garden. Regularly changing temporary exhibitions include contemporary art and crafts, plus historical displays.
Times: Open Tues-Sat 10-5, Sun 2-5 (last admission 4.30). Open BHs (spring&summer) Closed 25 Dec-1 Jan & Good Fri. **Fee:** Free until end Mar 2006 then charges may apply **Facilities:** P (200yds) 🅿 🌐 👜 ♿ (hearing aid and loop in reception only) toilets for disabled shop ✖ (ex guide & hearing dogs)

CORFE CASTLE   Map 03 SY98

CORFE CASTLE
BH20 5EZ
➲ (follow A351 from Wareham to Swanage. Corfe Castle approx 5m along this road)
☎ 01929 481294
e-mail: corfecastle@nationaltrust.org.uk
web: www.nationaltrust.org.uk

Built in Norman times, the castle was added to by King John. It was defended during the Civil War by Lady Bankes, who surrendered after a stout resistance. Parliament ordered the demolition of the castle, and today it is one of the most impressive ruins in England. Ring for details of special events.
Times: Shop & Castle open daily, Mar 10-5; Apr-end Sep 10-6; Oct 10-5; Nov-Feb 10-4. (Last admission 30 mins before closing). Closed 25-26 Dec. Tearoom open daily Mar 10-5, Apr-Sep 10-5.30, Oct 10-5, Nov-Feb 10-4. **Fee:** ✱ £5 (ch £2.50). Family ticket (2ad+3ch) £12.50 or (1ad+3ch) £7.50. NT members free. Groups £4.30 (ch £2.10) **Facilities:** P 🅿 ✖ licensed (Braille/large print guide & menu) shop 🍴 👜

CORFE CASTLE MUSEUM
West St BH20 5HE
➲ (to side of church on left of West St upon leaving village square)
☎ 01929 480974
e-mail: kenwollaston@tesco.net
The tiny, rectangular building was partly rebuilt in brick after a fire in 1780, and is the smallest town hall building in England. It has old village relics, and dinosaur footprints 130 million years old. A council chamber on the first floor is reached by a staircase at one end. The Ancient Order of Marblers meets here each Shrove Tuesday.
Times: ✱ Open all year, Apr-Oct, daily 9.30-6; Nov-Mar, wknds and Xmas holidays 10-5. **Facilities:** P (200yds) ♿ ✖

DORCHESTER   Map 03 SY69

DINOSAUR MUSEUM
Icen Way DT1 1EW
➲ (off A35 into Dorchester, museum in town centre just off High East St)
☎ 01305 269880
e-mail: info@thedinosaurmuseum.com
web: www.thedinosaurmuseum.com
Britain's award-winning museum devoted to dinosaurs has an appealing mixture of fossils, skeletons, life-size reconstructions and interactive displays such as the 'feelies'. There are audio-visual presentations and computer displays providing an all-round family attraction with new displays each year. It is part of the Jurassic Coast experience.
Times: Open all year, daily 9.30-5.30 (10-4.30 Nov-Mar). Closed 24-26 Dec. **Fee:** ✱ £6 (ch £4.50, pen & student £5.25, under 4's free). Family ticket £18.50 **Facilities:** P (50yds) 👜 ♿ (many low level displays) shop 👜

DORSET COUNTY MUSEUM
High West St DT1 1XA
➲ (off A354 signed Dorchester, attraction on right half way up main street)
☎ 01305 262735
e-mail: dorsetcountymuseum@dor-mus.demon.co.uk
web: www.dorsetcountymuseum.org
Displays cover prehistoric and Roman times, including sites such as Maiden Castle, and there's a gallery on Dorset writers with sections on the poet William Barnes, Thomas Hardy (with a reconstruction of his study), and 20th-century writers. Also geology, local wildlife and social history are explored in the museum.
Times: Open all year, Mon-Sat, 10-5. Also open Sun, Jul-Sep. Closed 24-26 Dec **Fee:** ✱ £5 (ch free, concessions £4)
Facilities: P (600yds) (nearby parking charged) ♿ (free entry for disabled visitors, ramp, audio commentary) shop ✖ (ex guide dogs) 👜

DORSET TEDDY BEAR MUSEUM
Antelope Walk, Cornhill DT1 1BE
➲ (off A35, museum in town centre near Tourist Information Centre)
☎ 01305 263200
e-mail: info@teddybearmuseum.co.uk
web: www.teddybearmuseum.co.uk
A visit to the museum begins with the home of Edward Bear and his extended family of human-sized teddy bears. Then, in a more traditional museum setting, view hundreds of teddy bears from throughout the last century in atmospheric and evocative displays.
Times: Open daily, Mon-Sat 9.30-5, Sun 10-4.30. Closed 25-26 Dec.
Facilities: P (500mtrs) 👜 shop ✖ (ex guide dogs) 👜

HARDY'S COTTAGE
Higher Bockhampton DT2 8QJ
➲ (3m NE of Dorchester, 0.5m S of A35. Turn off A35 at Kingston Maurward rdbt towards Stinsford and Bockhampton. Left onto Bockhampton Ln, signed to Hardy's Cottage)
☎ 01305 262366
web: www.nationaltrust.org.uk
The small cob and thatch cottage where novelist and poet Thomas Hardy was born in 1840 and from where he would

continued

walk 6 miles to school in Dorchester every day. It was built by his great-grandfather and is little altered since. The interior has been furnished by the Trust. It was here that he wrote his early novels 'Under the Greenwood Tree' and 'Far from the Madding Crowds'. It has a charming cottage garden.

Times: Open 18 Mar-Oct, Thurs-Mon, 11-5 **Fee:** ✱ £3
Facilities: 🅿 (10 min walk) (no coach parking) ♿ (parking by arrangement, large print/Braille guide) ✖ ⚘

MAIDEN CASTLE

DT1 9PR
⊃ (2m S of Dorchester, access off A354, N of bypass) **FREE**

The Iron Age fort ranks among the finest in Britain. It covers 47 acres, and has daunting earthworks, with a complicated defensive system around the entrances. One of its main purposes may well have been to protect grain from marauding bands. The first single-rampart fort dates from around 700BC, and by 100BC the earthworks covered the whole plateau. It was finally overrun by Roman troops in AD43.

Times: Open at any reasonable time. **Facilities:** 🅿 ⚏

THE MILITARY MUSEUM OF DEVON & DORSET

The Keep, Bridport Rd DT1 1RN
⊃ (situated near the top of High West St leading out of town towards Bridport)
☎ 01305 264066 **2 for 1**
e-mail: keep.museum@talk21.com
web: www.keepmilitarymuseum.org

Three hundred years of military history, with displays on the Devon Regiment, Dorset Regiment, Dorset Militia and Volunteers, the Queen's Own Dorset Yeomanry, and Devonshire and Dorset Regiment (from 1958). The Museum uses modern technology, interactive and creative displays to tell the stories of the Infantry, Cavalry and Artillerymen.

Times: Open Apr-Sep, Mon-Sat 9-5; Oct-Mar, Tue-Sat 9-5; (also Jul & Aug, Sun 10-4). Closed Xmas & New Year. **Fee:** ✱ £3.50 (ch, student & pen £2.50). Family ticket £10 **Facilities:** 🅿 ♿ (lift availble to 3 floors) toilets for disabled shop ✖ (ex guide dogs) ◼

TUTANKHAMUN EXHIBITION

High West St DT1 1UW
⊃ (off A35 into Dorchester town centre)
☎ 01305 269571
e-mail: info@tutankhamun-exhibition.co.uk
web: www.tutankhamun-exhibition.co.uk

The exhibition recreates the excitement of one of the world's greatest discoveries of ancient treasure. A reconstruction of the tomb and recreations of its treasures are displayed. The superbly preserved mummified body of the boy king can be seen, wonderfully recreated in every detail. Facsimiles of some of the most famous treasures, including the golden funerary mask and the harpooner can be seen in the final gallery.

Times: Open all year daily, Apr-Oct, 9.30-5.30; Nov-Mar wkdays 9.30-5, wknds 10-4.30. Closed 24-26 Dec. **Fee:** ✱ £6 (ch £4.50, pen & student £5.25, under 5's free). Family ticket £18.50 **Facilities:** 🅿 (200yds) ♿ shop ✖ (ex guide dogs) ◼

> **Directions are provided by the attractions.**

MINTERNE MAGNA Map 03 ST60

MINTERNE GARDENS

DT2 7AU
⊃ (2m N of Cerne Abbas on A352 Dorchester-Sherborne road)
☎ 01300 341370

Wander through 20 acres of wild woodland, where magnolias, rhododendrons, eucryphias, hydrangeas, water plants and water lillies provide a new vista at each turn. This was the home of the Churchill and Digby families for 350 years, and contains small lakes and cascades landscaped in the 18th century.

Times: Open Mar-10 Nov, daily 10-7. **Fee:** ✱ £4 (accompanied ch free). **Facilities:** 🅿

POOLE Map 03 SZ09

WATERFRONT MUSEUM

4 High St BH15 1BW
⊃ (off Poole Quay)
☎ 01202 262600 **FREE**
e-mail: museums@poole.gov.uk
web: www.boroughofpoole.com/museums

The museum tells the story of Poole's history, including the Studland Bay wreck and trade with Newfoundland with displays and hands-on activities. A local history centre with research facilities on local and family history can also be found. Scaplen's Court, just a few yards from the museum, is a beautifully restored domestic building dating from the medieval period. Although it is only open to the public in August, Scaplen's Court is not to be missed, with a Victorian school room, a kitchen and scullery.

Times: Museum: open Apr-Oct, Mon-Sat 10-5, Sun noon-5; Nov-Mar (phone for details). Scaplen's Court: open Aug, Mon-Sat 10-5, Sun noon-5. **Facilities:** 🅿 (250mtrs) 🍴 ♿ (Scaplen's Court not accessible) toilets for disabled shop ✖ (ex guide dogs) ◼

PORTLAND Map 03 SY67

PORTLAND CASTLE

Castleton DT5 1AZ
⊃ (overlooking Portland harbour)
☎ 01305 820539

Visit one of Henry VIII's finest coastal forts in use right up to the Second World War. Home to the Wrens and scene of the US troops' embarkation for the D-Day invasion in 1944. Explore the Captain's House and Gardens.

Times: Open, 24 Mar-June & Sep, daily 10-5; Jul-Aug, daily 10-6; Oct, daily 10-4. Closed Nov-Mar. **Fee:** £3.60 (ch £1.80, concessions £2.70). Opening times and prices are subject to change, for further details please phone 0870 333 1181 **Facilities:** 🅿 🍴 ♿ shop ✖ ⚏

PORTLAND MUSEUM

217 Wakeham DT5 1HS
⊃ (A354, through Fortuneswell to Portland Heights Hotel, then English Heritage signs)
☎ 01305 821804
e-mail: tourism@weymouth.gov.uk
web: www.weymouth.gov.uk

Avice's cottage in Thomas Hardy's book *The Well-Beloved*, this building is now a museum of local and historical interest, with varied displays. Regular temporary exhibitions are held. The adjoining Marie Stopes cottage houses the shop and a display of maritime history.

Times: Open Good Fri-Oct, Fri-Tue (ex school hols open daily), 10.30-5 (Closed 1-1.30 daily) **Fee:** ✱ £2 (accompanied ch free, pen £1) **Facilities:** 🅿 (50yds) (coach parking on roadside) ♿ shop ✖ (ex guide dogs)

SHAFTESBURY   Map 03 ST82

SHAFTESBURY ABBEY MUSEUM & GARDEN

Park Walk SP7 8JR

➲ (follow signs to Shaftesbury town centre.
Shaftesbury Abbey is signed from opposite
Wharf's Restaurant)

☎ 01747 852910

e-mail: user@shaftesburyabbey.fsnet.co.uk

web: www.shaftesburyabbey.co.uk

The Abbey at Shaftesbury was part of a nunnery founded by
King Alfred in 888. Patronage and pilgrims to the shrine of St
Edward helped to make the abbey both rich and famous. It
became one of the wealthiest in the country but was
destroyed during the Dissolution in 1539. The excavated
ruins show the foundations of the abbey church. The story is
told through the use of carved stone and medieval floor tiles
and illustrations from ancient manuscripts.

Times: Open Apr-Oct, daily, 10-5. **Fee:** ✱ £2 (ch 60p, concessions
£1.50). **Facilities:** P (250yds) (2hr restriction on nearest car park) 🗐
🕭 (large print guides, audio tour, interactive display) toilets for
disabled shop

SHERBORNE   Map 03 ST61

SHERBORNE CASTLE

New Rd DT9 5NR

➲ (off A30/A352, 0.5m SE of Sherborne)

☎ 01935 813182 & 812072 (castle)

e-mail: enquiries@sherbornecastle.com

web: www.sherbornecastle.com

Built by Sir Walter Raleigh in 1594, Sherborne Castle has
been the home of the Digby family since 1617. Prince
William of Orange was entertained here in 1688, and George
III visited in 1789. Splendid collections of art, furniture and
porcelain are on show in the Castle. Lancelot 'Capability'
Brown created the lake in 1753 and 30 acres beautiful
gardens and grounds surround it.

Times: Open Apr-Oct, Tue-Thu, Sat-Sun & BH Mon 11-4.30. (Last
admission 4.30). Castle open from 2.30 on Sat. **Fee:** ✱ £7.50 (pen
£7). Gardens only £3.50 (ch under 15 free, max 4 ch per adult). Party
15+ £6.50 **Facilities:** P 🍴 🕭 (Braille guide book) toilets for
disabled shop 🍴

SHERBORNE MUSEUM

Abbey Gate House, Church Ln DT9 3BP

➲ (From the bottom of Cheap St (main shopping
street), walk through Church Ln towards the
Abbey, museum on left)

☎ 01935 812252

e-mail: admin@shermus.fsnet.co.uk

The museum features a model of Sherborne's original
Norman castle, as well as a fine Victorian doll's house and
other domestic and agricultural bygones. There are also
items of local geological, natural history and archaeological
interest, including Roman material. The Sherborne Missal,
one of the greatest medieval manuscripts, has returned
home this year thanks to the latest digital technology which
enables the visitor to 'turn the pages' of the manuscript with
the sweep of a hand - with touch, zoom and audio facilities.

Times: Open Apr-Oct, Tue-Sat 10.30-4.30, some Sun 2.30-4.30, BH
Mon 2.30-4.30 **Fee:** £1 (ch & concessions free)

Facilities: P (200yds) 🕭 (video of upper floor displays) toilets for
disabled shop 🍴 (ex guide dogs) 🍴

SHERBORNE OLD CASTLE

Castleton D19 3SA

➲ (0.5m E off B3145)

☎ 01935 812730

The ruins of this early 12th-century castle are a testament to
the 16 days Oliver Cromwell's army took capture of it during
the Civil War.

Times: Open 24 Mar-Jun & Sep, Tue-Thu & Sat-Sun 10-5; Jul-Aug,
Tue-Thu & Sat-Sun 10-6; Oct, Tue-Thu & Sat-Sun 10-4. Open BH 24
Mar-31 Aug. Closed Nov-Mar. **Fee:** £2.30 (ch £1.20, concessions
£1.70). Opening times and prices are subject to change, for further
details please phone 0870 333 1181 **Facilities:** P 🍴 shop 🍴 🕭

SWANAGE   Map 03 SZ07

SWANAGE RAILWAY

Station House BH19 1HB

➲ (signed from A351)

☎ 01929 425800

e-mail: general@swanrail.freeserve.co.uk

web: www.swanagerailway.co.uk

The railway from Swanage to Wareham was closed in 1972,
and in 1976 the Swanage Railway took possession and have
gradually restored the line, which now runs for 6 miles,
passing the ruins of Corfe Castle. Ring for details of special
events.

Times: ✱ Open every wknd throughout year, daily Apr-Oct.

Facilities: P 🍴 ✗ licensed 🗐 🕭 (special disabled persons coach)
toilets for disabled shop (shop at Swanage Station) 🍴

TOLPUDDLE   Map 03 SY79

TOLPUDDLE MARTYRS MUSEUM

DT2 7EH

➲ (off A35 from Dorchester, Tolpuddle is signed at
Troytown turn off. Continue on old A35, Museum
has brown heritage sign giving clear directions)

☎ 01305 848237   **FREE**

e-mail: jpickering@tuc.org.uk

web: www.tolpuddlemartyrs.org.uk

One dawn, in the bitter February of 1834, six Tolpuddle farm
labourers were arrested after forming a trade union. A
frightened squire's trumped up charge triggered one of the
most celebrated stories in the history of human rights. That
dawn arrest created the Tolpuddle Martyrs, who were
punished with transportation as convicts to Australia. Packed
with illustrative displays, this new state-of-the-art,
interactive exhibition tells the Tolpuddle Martyrs story. Every
summer the weekend of the third Sunday in July, the
museum holds the Tolpuddle Martyrs Festival. The weekend
combines celebration with tradition offering traditional and
contemporary music as well as many other attractions.

Times: Open all year, Apr-Oct, Tue-Sat 10-5.30, Sun 11-5.30; Nov-Mar,
Tue-Sat 10-4, Sun 11-4. Open BH Mon. Closed 20 Dec-2 Jan.

Facilities: P (outside museum) 🗐 🕭 (parking, interactive computers
at wheelchair height) toilets for disabled shop 🍴 (ex guide dogs) 🍴

**If an attraction name
appears in *italics*, details
have not been confirmed
for 2006.**

WEST LULWORTH Map 03 SY88
LULWORTH CASTLE & PARK
BH20 5QS
➲ (from Wareham, W on A352 for 1m, left onto B3070 to E Lulworth, follow tourist signs)
☎ 01929 400352 **2 for 1**
e-mail: estate.office@lulworth.com
web: www.lulworth.com
Glimpse life below stairs in the restored kitchen, and enjoy beautiful views from the top of the tower of this historic castle set in beautiful parkland. The 18th-century chapel is the first Catholic chapel built in England after the Reformation. Children will enjoy the animal farm, play area, indoor activity room and pitch and putt.
Times: Open 25 Mar-Sep, Sun-Fri 10.30-6; 2 Oct-Dec, Sun-Fri 10.30-4; 2-7 Jan, Sun-Fri 10.30-4; 23 an-24 Mar, Sun-Fri 10.30-4. Closed 24-25 Dec, 7-21 Jan. **Fee:** £7.00 (ch £4.00, concessions £5.00) non-jousting season. £8.50 (ch £4.50, concessions £7.00) jousting season. Family £21.00 (2 ad + 3 ch), £15 (1 ad + 3 ch). **Facilities:** 🅿 ➟ 🎑 ♿ (limited in castle due to grade one listing) toilets for disabled shop ➟

WEYMOUTH Map 03 SY67
DEEP SEA ADVENTURE & SHARKY'S PLAY & PARTY
9 Custom House Quay, Old Harbour North DT4 8BG
➲ (A35 to Weymouth, then Old Harbour North. Attraction between pavillion & town bridge. Follow brown tourist signs.)
☎ 0871 222 5760
e-mail: enquiries@deepsea-adventure.co.uk
web: www.deepsea-adventure.co.uk
A fascinating attraction telling the story of underwater exploration and marine exploits. Discover the history of Weymouth's Old Harbour, compelling tales of shipwreck survival, explore the Black Hole and search for Ollie the Oyster. Also a unique display telling the gripping tale of the *Titanic* disaster. Sharky's Play Area is four floors of fun-packed adventure. Separate toddler area for the under fives. 'Paint your own Pottery' studio can also be found on site. Laser shoot out evenings now available.
Times: Open all year, daily from 9.30. Closed 25-26 Dec & 1 Jan. **Fee:** Sharky's Play Zone: Adults free (ch £3.50). Deep Sea Adventure: £3.95 (ch 5-15 £2.95, concessions £3.50). **Facilities:** 🅿 (100yds) ✗ licensed 🎑 ♿ (lift & sign language for deaf) toilets for disabled shop ➟ (ex guide dogs) ➟

RSPB NATURE RESERVE RADIPOLE LAKE
The Swannery Car Park DT4 7TZ
➲ (close to seafront & railway station)
☎ 01305 778313
web: www.rspb.org.uk
Covering 222 acres, the Reserve offers firm paths, hide and a visitor centre. Several types of warblers, mute swans, gadwalls, teals and great crested grebes may be seen, and the visitor centre has viewing windows overlooking the lake. Phone for details of special events.
Times: Open daily 9-5 **Facilities:** 🅿 (charged) 🎑 ♿ toilets for disabled shop ➟

SEA LIFE PARK & MARINE SANCTUARY
Lodmoor Country Park DT4 7SX
➲ (on A353)
☎ 01305 788255 **2 for 1**
e-mail: slcweymouth@merlinentertainments.biz
web: www.sealifeeurope.com
A unique mix of indoor and outdoor attractions set in 7 acres. The park offers a day of fun, bringing you face to face with penguins, otters, seals and much more.
Times: Open all year, daily from 10. (Closed 25 Dec). **Fee:** ✱ £10.50 (ch £7.50, concessions £7.95) **Facilities:** 🅿 (charged) ➟ ✗ ♿ toilets for disabled shop ➟ (ex guide dogs) ➟

WIMBORNE Map 03 SZ09
KINGSTON LACY HOUSE, GARDEN & PARK
BH21 4EA
➲ (1.5m W of Wimborne, B3082)
☎ 01202 883402 (Mon-Fri) & 880413 (infoline)
e-mail: kingstonlacy@nationaltrust.org.uk
web: www.nationaltrust.org.uk
Kingston Lacy House was the home of the Bankes family for over 300 years. The original house is 17th century, but in the 1830s was given a stone façade. The Italian marble staircase, Venetian ceiling, treasures from Spain and an Egyptian obelisk were also added. There are outstanding pictures by Titian, Rubens, Velasquez, Reynolds and Van Dyck. No photography is allowed in the house.
Times: Open: House 20 Mar-Oct, 11-5, Wed-Sun. Garden & Park 10.30-6, all week 5 Nov-19 Dec, 10.30-4, Fri-Sun 5 Feb-20 Mar, 10.30-4, Sat-Sun. **Fee:** ✱ House, Garden & Park £8 (ch £4) Family £20. Park & Gardens only £4 (ch £2) Family £10. **Facilities:** 🅿 ➟ ✗ licensed ♿ (4 manual wheelchairs, Braille guides, parking) toilets for disabled shop ➟ (ex on leads in park & wood) ➟

KNOLL GARDENS & NURSERY
Stapehill Rd, Hampreston BH21 7ND
➲ (3m E between Wimborne and Ferndown off A31, at Canford Bottom rdbt, into B3073 signed Ham Lane. Follow brown signs)
☎ 01202 873931
e-mail: enquiries@knollgardens.co.uk
web: www.knollgardens.co.uk
Over 6000 plant species from all over the world thrive here, within a six-acre site. There are water gardens with waterfalls, pools and a stream, herbaceous borders, and many other features. There is also a 'Dragon' formal garden and a Mediterranean-style gravel garden. The nursery offers a wide range of plants; best known for its range of Ornamental Grasses and 'plants for the modern lifestyle'.
Times: Open all year, Wed-Sun, 10-5 (or dusk if earlier). Closed 18 Dec-1 Feb. **Fee:** £4 (ch 5-15 £2.50, concessions £3.50). Family £9.50 Party 15+ £3. **Facilities:** 🅿 ➟ ♿ (wheelchairs available) toilets for disabled garden centre ➟ (ex guide dogs) ➟

PRIEST'S HOUSE MUSEUM AND GARDEN
23-27 High St BH21 1HR
➲ (located on High Street, opposite The Minster)
☎ 01202 882533
e-mail: priesthouse@eastdorset.gov.uk
web: www.priest-house.co.uk
An award-winning local history museum, set in an historic house. The 17th-century hall, Georgian parlour and working Victorian kitchen reveal the history of the building and its inhabitants. The museum houses exhibitions on East Dorset

continued

from prehistoric to modern times. There are regular special exhibitions and a walled garden to explore.

Times: Open Apr-Oct, Mon-Sat, 10-4.30. **Fee:** ✱ £3 (ch £1, concesssions £2). Family & season ticket £7.50 **Facilities:** P (200yds) 🍽 📖 ⅃ (hands on archaeology gallery) shop ✾ (ex guide dogs)

STAPEHILL ABBEY

Wimborne Rd West BH21 2EB   `2 for 1`
➲ (2.5m E off A31 at Canford Bottom rdbt)
☎ 01202 861686

This early 19th-century abbey, home for nearly 200 years to Cistercian nuns, is now a busy working crafts centre with many attractions under cover. There are award-winning landscaped gardens, parkland and picnic spots, and the Power to the Land exhibition. Telephone for details of special events.

Times: Open Etr-Sep, daily 10-5; Oct-Etr, Wed-Sun 10-4. Closed 22 Dec-Feb. **Fee:** £7.50 (ch 4-16 £4.50, students & pen £7). Family ticket (2ad+2ch) £19.50. **Facilities:** P 🍽 ⅃ toilets for disabled shop garden centre ✾ (ex guide dogs) 🍴

WOOL   Map 03 SY88

MONKEY WORLD

Longthorns BH20 6HH
➲ (1m N of Wool on Bere Regis road)
☎ 01929 462537 & 0800 456600
e-mail: apes@monkeyworld.org
web: www.monkeyworld.org

Set up in order to rescue monkeys and apes from abuse and illegal smuggling, Monkey World houses over 160 primates in 65 acres of Dorset woodland. There are 58 chimps, the largest grouping outside Africa, as well as orang-utans, gibbons, woolly monkeys, lemurs, macaques and marmosets. Those wishing to help the centre continue in its quest to rescue primates from lives of misery may like to take part in the adoption scheme which includes free admission to the park for one year. There are keeper talks every half hour, and a Great Ape Play Area for the kids.

Times: Open daily 10-5 (Jul-Aug 10-6). (Last admission 1 hour before closing) **Fee:** ✱ £9 (ch & concessions £6.50). Family ticket (1ad+2ch) £20, (2ad+2ch) £27. Group 15+ £8 (£5.50). **Facilities:** P 🍽 ✗ 📖 ⅃ toilets for disabled shop ✾ (ex guide dogs) 🍴

COUNTY DURHAM

EVENTS & FESTIVALS

April
tbc Teesdale Thrash, concerts, ceilidhs, music sessions and morris dancing in Bernard Castle

June
24th-25th Weardale Steam Transport Festival, Bondisle Field, Stanhope
tbc Durham Regatta, River Wear, Durham (provisional)

July
1st-2nd Summer Festival, various venues, Durham city centre
8th Durham Miners Gala, colourful miners' banners paraded through the city of Durham (provisional)
tbc Chester-le-Street Traction Engine Rally, South Burn Grange
tbc Durham County Show, New Herrington Country Park, Penshaw

August
26th-27th Weardale Agricultural Show, Showfield, St John's Chapel (provisional)
27th-28th Durham Light Infantry Vehicle Rally, DLI Museum and Durham Art Gallery (provisional)
tbc Billingham International Folklore Festival, Billingham, Stockton-on-Tees

September
2nd-3rd Wolsingham & Wear Valley Agricultural Show, Wolsingham (provisional)
9th-10th Stanhope Agricultural Show & Country Fair, Stanhope (provisional)

December
2nd-3rd Victorian Christmas Festival, Durham city centre (provisional)

Above: The small Church of St Mary, Seaham

BARNARD CASTLE · Map 12 NZ01

BARNARD CASTLE
DL12 9AT
☎ 01833 638212
Imposing remains of one of England's largest medieval castles perched high on a rugged escarpment above the banks of the River Tees.
Times: Open all year, Apr-Sep, daily 10-6; Oct, daily 10-4; Nov-Mar, Thur-Mon 10-4. Closed 24-26 Dec & 1 Jan. **Fee:** £3.30 (ch £1.70, concessions £2.50). Opening times and prices are subject to change, for further details please phone 0870 333 1181 **Facilities:** ♿ shop ⌗

THE BOWES MUSEUM
DL12 8NP
➲ (located in Barnard Castle, just off A66)
☎ 01833 690606
e-mail: info@bowesmuseum.org.uk
web: www.bowesmuseum.org.uk

John and Joséphine Bowes founded the Bowes Museum over 100 years ago. The magnificent building houses a collection of treasures from fine and decorative art to major temporary exhibitions of international quality and interest. The icon of the collection is The Silver Swan, a unique life-size, musical automaton which plays everyday. A continuous, rolling programme of major exhibitions is also in place.
Times: Open daily 11-5. Closed 25-26 Dec & 1 Jan. **Fee:** £7 (ch under 16 free, concessions £6) **Facilities:** 🅿 💷 📱 ♿ (lift, ramped entrance, reserved parking, audio guide/loop) toilets for disabled shop 🐕 (ex guide dogs & in park) 🍴

EGGLESTONE ABBEY
DL12 8QN · FREE
➲ (1m S of Barnard Castle on minor road off B6277)
The scant, but charming remains of a small medieval monastery. The picturesque ruins of Egglestone are located above a bend in the River Tees. A large part of the church can be seen, as can remnants of monastic buildings.
Times: Open daily, 10-6. **Facilities:** 🅿 ♿ ⌗

Directions are provided by the attractions.

BEAMISH · Map 12 NZ25

BEAMISH, THE NORTH OF ENGLAND OPEN-AIR MUSEUM
DH9 0RG
➲ (off A693 & A6076. Signed from A1M junct 63.)
☎ 0191 370 4000
e-mail: museum@beamish.org.uk
web: www.beamish.org.uk

Set in 200 acres of countryside, award winning Beamish recreates life in the early 1800s and 1900s. Costumed staff welcome visitors to a 1913 town street, colliery village, farm and railway station; a re-creation of how people lived and worked. Ride on early electric tramcars, take a ride on a replica of an 1825 steam railway and visit Pockerley Manor where a yeoman farmer and his family would have lived.
Times: Open 19 Mar-30 Oct daily, 10-5; 31 Oct-Mar 10-4, closed Mon & Fri & 12 Dec-2 Jan. (Last admission 3) **Fee:** ✱ Summer £15 (ch £9, pen £12). Winter £6 (ch & pen £6). Winter visit is centered on town & tramway only, other areas are closed. **Facilities:** 🅿 💷 📱 ♿ (not ideal for wheelchairs, assistance recommended) toilets for disabled shop 🍴

BISHOP AUCKLAND · Map 08 NZ22

AUCKLAND CASTLE
DL14 7NR
➲ (follow signs to Market Place then brown tourist sign for Castle)
☎ 01388 601627
e-mail: auckland.castle@zetnet.co.uk
web: www.auckland-castle.co.uk
Serving as the principal county residence of the Prince Bishops since the 12th century, Auckland Castle is the home of the Bishop of Durham. Built on a promontory overlooking the River Wear and the Roman Fort of Binchester, the Castle has been added to and adapted over the centuries. St Peter's Chapel houses many of the treasures of past Bishops.
Times: Open Etr Mon-Sep, Sun & Mon 2-5; Aug also Wed.
Facilities: 🅿 💷 📱 ♿ (chair walker available by prior arrangement) toilets for disabled shop 🐕 (ex guide dogs) 🍴

BOWES · Map 12 NY91

BOWES CASTLE
DL12 9LD
➲ (in Bowes village, just off A66) · FREE
Massive ruins of Henry II's tower keep, three storeys high, set within the earthworks of a Roman fort and overlooking the valley of the River Greta.
Times: Open at any reasonable time. **Facilities:** ♿ 🚗 ⌗

The Otter Trust's North Pennines Reserve

Vale House Farm DL12 9RH
➲ (S side of A66 Scotch Corner to Penrith Rd, 2m W of Bowes)
☎ 01833 628339
web: www.ottertrust.org.uk/Pennines_Home.html

Set in 230 acres of upland farmland, the Otter Trust reserve isn't just about otters, although there is an ongoing release programme that aims to protect the otter from extinction. Visitors can also see red and fallow deer, mouflon sheep, and a wide range of birds including curlew, oystercatchers, snipe, and black grouse. The visitor centre contains exhibits on some of the animals as well as local history, and overlooks the charming River Greta.

Times: Open Apr-Oct, daily 10.30-6 **Fee:** ✱ £5 (ch £3)
Facilities: 🅿 💻 📖 ♿ toilets for disabled shop ✖ (ex guide dogs)

COWSHILL   Map 12 NY84

Killhope The North of England Lead Mining Museum

DL13 1AR
➲ (beside A689 midway between Stanhope & Alston)
☎ 01388 537505   **2 for 1**
e-mail: killhope@durham.gov.uk
web: www.durham.gov.uk/killhope

Equipped with hard hats and lamps, you can explore the working conditions of lead miners. The lead mine and 19th-century crushing mill have been restored to look as they would have done in the 1870s, and the 34ft water wheel has been restored to working order. There is also a visitor centre and mineral exhibition, a woodland walk, children's play area and a red squirrel and bird hide.

Times: Open Apr-Oct, daily 10.30-5 (BHs & summer school hols open until 5.30) **Fee:** ✱ Mine & Site: £6 (ch £3, concessions £5.50). Family £17. Site: £4.50 (ch £1.70, concessions £4). Family £11
Facilities: 🅿 💻 📖 ♿ (electric scooter, sympathetic hearing scheme) toilets for disabled shop 🍴

DARLINGTON   Map 08 NZ21

Darlington Railway Centre & Museum

North Rd Station DL3 6ST
➲ (0.75m N, off A167)
☎ 01325 460532   **2 for 1**
e-mail: museum@darlington.gov.uk

Housed in the carefully restored North Road Station, this museum's prize exhibit is *Locomotion*, which pulled the first passenger train on the Stockton to Darlington railway and was built by Robert Stephenson & Co in 1825. Several other steam locomotives are also shown, together with models and other exhibits relating to the Stockton and Darlington and the North Eastern Railway companies. Recently arrived at the museum for a two year period is an A2 Pacific No60532 'Blue Peter'. Refreshments are available.

Times: Open daily 10-5. Closed 25-26 Dec & 1 Jan. **Fee:** ✱ £2.50 (ch £1.50, pen £1.50). **Facilities:** 🅿 💻 📖 ♿ toilets for disabled shop ✖ (ex guide dogs) 🍴

DURHAM   Map 12 NZ24

Durham Cathedral

DH1 3EH
➲ (A690 into city, follow signs to car parks)
☎ 0191 386 4266
e-mail: enquiries@durhamcathedral.co.uk
web: www.durhamcathedral.co.uk

Founded in 1093 as a shrine to St Cuthbert, the cathedral is a remarkable example of Norman architecture, set in an impressive position high above the River Wear. A full programme of concerts throughout the year. St Cuthbert's Day Procession (phone for details).

Times: ✱ Open all year, daily 9.30-6.15; 21 Jun-8 Sep 9.30-8. (Sun 12.30-5). Cathedral is closed to visitors during evening recitals & concerts. **Facilities:** 🅿 (in city centre) ✖ licensed 📖 ♿ (Braille guide, touch/hearing centre, stairclimber) toilets for disabled shop ✖ (ex guide dogs)

Durham Light Infantry Museum & Durham Art Gallery

Aykley Heads DH1 5TU
➲ (0.5m NW, turn right off A691)
☎ 0191 384 2214
e-mail: dli@durham.gov.uk
web: www.durham.gov.uk/dli

The history of the Regiment is told in displays of artefacts, medals, uniforms and vehicles. The Art Gallery has a continuous programme of temporary exhibitions, and holds regular lectures and concerts.

Times: ✱ Open all year, Apr-Oct, daily 10-5; Nov-Mar, daily 10-4. Closed 25 Dec. **Facilities:** 🅿 💻 📖 ♿ (wheelchair available, lift, ramps) toilets for disabled shop ✖ (ex guide dogs) 🍴

Finchale Priory

Brasside, Newton Hall DH1 5SH
➲ (3m NE)
☎ 0191 386 3828

Dating from the 13th-century, these beautiful priory ruins are in a wooded setting beside the River Wear.

Times: Open 24 Mar-Sep, Sat, Sun & BHs, 10-6. **Fee:** £2.30 (ch £1.20, concessions £1.70). Opening times and prices are subject to change, for further details please phone 0870 333 1181 **Facilities:** 🅿 (charged) 💻 shop ⌗

Oriental Museum

University of Durham, Elvet Hill DH1 3TH
➲ (signed from A167 & A177)
☎ 0191 334 5694
e-mail: oriental.museum@durham.ac.uk
web: www.dur.ac.uk/oriental.museum

The Marvels of China gallery opened in 2000 and introduces the visitor to contemporary China, its history and decorative arts. Other displays cover the Islamic World, Buddhism, Chinese archaeology, the story of writing, a Javanese Gamelan Orchestra and an Egyptian Gallery containing everything from mummies to magic amulets.

Times: Open Mon-Fri 10-5, wknds 12-5. Closed Xmas-New Year.
Facilities: 🅿 💻 📖 ♿ (lifts to all floors) toilets for disabled shop ✖🍴

HARTLEPOOL   Map 08 NZ53

Hartlepool's Maritime Experience NEW

Maritime Av TS24 0XZ

➲ (from A19 take A179 and follow signs for marina then historic quay)

☎ 01429 860077

e-mail: info@
hartlepoolsmaritimeexperience.com

web: www.hartlepoolsmaritimeexperience.com

Britain's maritime heritage is brought to life, with the sights, sounds and smells of an 1800s quayside. Learn about the birth of the Royal Navy, and visit the Quayside shops, the admiral's house, the oldest warship afloat *HMS Trincomalee* or the naval prison. Other features include children's maritime adventure centre, regular demonstrations of sword fighting, and canon firing. There's a full programme of events, for further details see website.

Times: Open all year daily 10-5 . Closed 25-26 Dec & 1 Jan.
Fee: ✱ £6.25 (ch £3.75, concessions £4.75). Family ticket £16.50.
Museum is free **Facilities:** 🅿 💻 ✗ licensed ♿ (all areas ramped or lift access) toilets for disabled shop ✈ (ex assist dogs) 📶

HMS Trincomalee

Jackson Dock TS24 0SQ

➲ (From A19 take A689 or A179, follow signs for Hartlepool Historic Quay)

☎ 01429 223193

e-mail: office@hms-trincomalee.co.uk

web: www.hms-trincomalee.co.uk

HMS Trincomalee, is the oldest ship afloat in the UK and the last of the commissioned frigates of the Nelson era. Now fully restored in an award-winning maritime heritage project. Come aboard for a unique experience of navy life two centuries ago.

Times: ✱ Open all year, Summer: 10-5, Winter: 10.30-4. Closed Xmas & New Year. **Facilities:** 🅿 ♿ (3 out of the 4 decks are accessible by lift) shop ✈ (ex guide dogs) 📶

Museum of Hartlepool

Jackson Dock, Maritime Av TS24 0XZ

➲ (Historic Quay & Museum towards Marina)

☎ 01429 860077

This museum tells the story of Hartlepool from prehistory to the present day and includes many original artefacts, models, computer interactives and hands-on exhibits. See how iron and steel ships were built and climb aboard the

continued

Humber ferry *Wingfield Castle*, a paddle steamer built in Hartlepool in 1934.

Times: ✱ Open all year, daily. Closed 25-26 Dec & 1 Jan.
Facilities: 🅿 💻 ♿ toilets for disabled shop ✈ (ex guide dogs)

LANGLEY PARK   Map 12 NZ24

Diggerland

DH7 9TT

➲ (A1(M) junct 62. Head W following signs to Consett. After 6m left at rdbt, signed Langley Park, then right into Riverside Ind Est)

☎ 08700 344437   **2 for 1**

e-mail: mail@diggerland.com

web: www.diggerland.com

An adventure park with a difference, where kids of all ages can experience the thrills of driving real earth moving equipment. Choose from various types of diggers and dumpers ranging from 1 ton to 8 and a half tons. Supervised by an instructor complete the Dumper Truck Challenge or dig for buried treasure. New rides include JCB Robots, the Supertrack, Landrover Safari and Spin Dizzy. Even under 5s can join in, with mum or dad's help.

Times: Open mid Feb-Nov, 10-5, wknds BHs & school hols only
Fee: ✱ £2.50 (pen £1.25, under 2's free). Additional charge to drive/ride machinery. **Facilities:** 🅿 💻 ♿ toilets for disabled shop ✈ (ex guide dogs) 📶

SHILDON   Map 08 NZ22

Locomotion: The National Railway Museum at Shildon

DL4 1PQ

➲ (A1(M) junct 68, take A68 & A6072 to Shildon, attraction is 0.25m SE of town centre)

☎ 01388 777999   **FREE**

e-mail: gill@hamer-loco.fsnet.co.uk

web: www.locomotion.uk.com

Timothy Hackwood (1786-1850) was an important figure in the development of steam travel. He constructed *Puffing Billy* for William Hedley, ran Stephenson's Newcastle Works, and also became the first superintendent of the Stockton & Darlington Railway. The museum and house detail Hackwood's life and the steam transport revolution, as well as displaying working models and locomotives from various periods. Steam train rides are available throughout the year, on event days. The Collections building contains 60 vehicles from the National Collection.

Times: Telephone for details **Facilities:** 🅿 💻 🎞 ♿ (bus available to transport guests, please contact) toilets for disabled shop ✈ (ex guide dogs) 📶

STAINDROP   Map 12 NZ12
RABY CASTLE
DL2 3AH
➲ (on A688, Barnard Castle to Bishop Auckland road, 1m N of Staindrop)
☎ 01833 660202
e-mail: admin@rabycastle.com
web: www.rabycastle.com

This dramatic 14th-century castle, built by the Nevills has been home to Lord Barnard's family since 1626. It has an impressive gateway, nine towers, a vast hall and an octagonal Victorian drawing room that has re-emerged as one of the most striking interiors from the 19th century. Rooms contain fine furniture, impressive artworks and elaborate architecture. In the grounds are a deer park, large walled gardens, coach and carriage collections, a woodland adventure playground, a picnic area and gift shop.

Times: Open May, Jun & Sep, Wed & Sun only. Jul-Aug, Sun-Fri. Castle open 1-5. Park & gardens 11-5.30, (5. Sep) (last admission 4.30). Open BH wknds. **Fees:** Castle, park & gardens £9 (ch £4, concessions £8). Family ticket £25 (2+3) Park & gardens £4 (ch £2.50. Concessions £3.50). Family ticket £12.50 (2+3). Party 12+. **Facilities:** 🅿 💺 🎁 & (most of ground floor accessible) toilets for disabled shop ✈ (ex guide dogs & on lead) 🔊

TANFIELD   Map 12 NZ15
TANFIELD RAILWAY
Old Marley Hill NE16 5ET
➲ (on A6076 1m S of Sunniside)
☎ 0191 388 7545
e-mail: tanfield@ingsoc.demon.co.uk
web: www.tanfield_railway.co.uk

A 3-mile working steam railway and the oldest existing railway in the world. The Causey Arch, the first large railway bridge of its era, is the centrepiece of a deep wooded valley, with picturesque walks. You can ride in carriages that first saw use in Victorian times, and visit Marley Hill shed, the home of 35 engines; inside the shed you can see the stationary steam engine at work driving some of the vintage machine tools. The blacksmith is also often at work forging new parts for the restoration work. Special events are held throughout the year, please telephone for details.

Times: ✱ Open all year, Summer daily 10-5; Winter daily 10-4. Trains: Sun & Summer BHs wknds; also Thu & Sat mid Jul-Aug. Santa's Specials Sat & Sun in Dec (booking essential). Mince pie specials Boxing Day. **Facilities:** 🅿 💺 & (all trains carry ramps for wheelchair access) toilets for disabled shop

ESSEX

EVENTS & FESTIVALS

January
tbc Maldon Mud Race (around 500 competitors racing 400 metres on the river bed at low tide)

April
29th-1st May, Southend Garden Show, Garons Park, Southend-on-Sea

May
19th-21st Essex Garden Show, Brentwood Centre, Brentwood
21st Essex Young Farmers Show, Essex County Showground, Great Leighs
28th-29th Southend Air Show, Europe's largest free show (provisional)
tbc Tour de Tendring Cycle Ride, Tendring area

June
3rd-4th Thaxted Morris Ring Meet, various venues, annual meeting of morris men
16th-18th South East Essex Garden Show, Barleylands, Billericay
30th-9th Jul Harwich Festival, various venues

July
8th Tendring Hundred Show, Lawford House Park, Manningtree – agricultural show
tbc Classic Car Rally London-Southend

August
24th-28th Clacton Jazz Festival (provisional)
26th-28th Southend Garden Show, Garon Park, Southend-on-Sea
tbc Clacton Air Show, Clacton Seafront
tbc Southend Jazz Festival, various venues

September
1st-3rd Walton Folk Festival
9th-10th Colchester Festival, in Colchester Town centre and The Castle Park (provisional)

Above: Audley End House

AUDLEY END   Map 05 TL53
AUDLEY END HOUSE & GARDENS
CB11 4JF
➲ (1m W of Saffron Walden on B1383)
☎ 01799 522399

One of the most significant Jacobean houses in England with 31 opulent rooms on view. Set in 'Capability' Brown landscaped park, with walled Victorian kitchen garden. **Times:** House; 3 21 Mar, Thur-Mon, 10-4 (Tours Only); 23 Mar-3 Oct, Wed-Mon, 12-5 tours available; 6-31 Oct, Thu-Mon, 10-4 (Tours only); Garden: 3-21 Mar Thu-Mon, 10-5; 23 Mar-3 Oct, Wed-Mon 10-6; 6-31 Oct, Thu-Mon 10-5. Some rooms will not be open throughout the season. **Fee:** House & Gardens: £8.95 (ch £4.50, concessions £6.70, family £22.40). Grounds only £4.60 (ch £2.30, concessions £3.50, family £11.50). Opening times and prices are subject to change, for further details please phone 0870 333 1181 **Facilities:** 🅿 (charged) 🅿 ♿ shop ⛆

BRENTWOOD   Map 05 TQ69
KELVEDON HATCH SECRET NUCLEAR BUNKER
CM14 5TL
➲ (on A128 Brentwood to Chipping Ongar road at Kelvedon Hotel
☎ 01277 364883
e-mail: bunker@japer.demon.co.uk   **2 for 1**
web: www.secretnuclearbunker.co.uk

Witness the three phases of the bunker's life. From its role with the RAF where the overall tactical controller would react to a nuclear attack from Britain's enemies, through to its role as Regional Government HQ. When there could have been up too 600 personnel, possibly including the Prime Minister, organising the survival of the civilian population in the aftermath of nuclear war. See for yourself the equipment and rooms needed to support the plotting of nuclear fall out patterns. **Times:** Mar-Oct, wkdays 10-4 wknds 10-5; Nov-Feb, Thu-Sun 10-4. **Fee:** ✱ £5 (ch£3). Family ticket (2ad+2ch) £12 **Facilities:** 🅿 🅿 ✗ ♿ toilets for disabled shop 🐾 guide dogs only

CASTLE HEDINGHAM   Map 05 TL73
COLNE VALLEY RAILWAY & MUSEUM
Castle Hedingham Station CO9 3DZ
➲ (4m NW of Halstead on A1017)
☎ 01787 461174
web: www.colnevalleyrailway.co.uk

Many former Colne Valley and Halstead railway buildings have been rebuilt here. Stock includes seven steam locomotives plus 80 other engines, carriages and wagons. Visitors can dine in style in restored Pullman carriages while travelling along the line. Please telephone for a free timetable and details of the many special events. **Times:** Open all year, daily 10-dusk. Steam days, rides from 12-4. Closed 23 Dec-1 Feb. Steam days every Sun and BH from Mothering Sunday to end Oct, Wed of school summer hols & special events. Railway Farm Park open May-Sep. Phone 01787 461174 for timetable information or visit website. Please phone or see website for 2006 details. **Fee:** ✱ Steam days: £6 (ch £3, pen £5) Family ticket £18. Diesel days £5 (ch £2.50); Family ticket £15. Prices are provisional **Facilities:** 🅿 🅿 ✗ licensed 📷 ♿ (ramps for wheelchairs to get onto carriages) toilets for disabled shop 🐾 (ex guide dogs) ⛆

HEDINGHAM CASTLE
CO9 3DJ
➲ (on B1508, 1m off A1017 Colchester/Cambridge. Follow brown heritage signs to Hedingham Castle)
☎ 01787 460261
e-mail: hedinghamcastle@aspects.net
web: www.hedinghamcastle.co.uk

This impressive Norman castle was built in 1140. It was besieged by King John, and visited by Henry VII, Henry VIII and Elizabeth I, and was home to the de Veres, Earls of Oxford, for over 500 years. During the summer months Hedingham's colourful heritage comes to life with a full programme of special events. There are medieval jousts and sieges with authentic living history displays and encampments. Please telephone for details. **Times:** ✱ Open Etr-Oct, Thu, Fri & Sun, 11-4. **Facilities:** 🅿 🅿 📷 shop 🐾 (ex in grounds) ⛆

CHELMSFORD   Map 05 TL70
RHS GARDEN HYDE HALL
Buckhatch Ln, Rettendon CM3 8ET
➲ (from M25 junct 28 (signed A12) or 29 (signed A127). SE of Chelmsford signed from A130. Exit Rettendon Turnpike, N through Rettendon Village, follow brown tourist signs)
☎ 01245 400256
e-mail: hydehall@rhs.org.uk   **2 for 1**
web: www.rhs.org.uk

Calling itself "A garden of inspirational beauty", RHS Garden Hyde Hall is a great day out for plant-lovers, and includes highlights such as the Dry Garden, a modern rose garden designed by Robin Williams, colour themed herbaceous borders, a farmhouse garden, and the NCCPG National Collection(tm)of Viburnum. New areas include The Queen Mother's Garden and a model Garden for Wildlife. **Times:** Open all year, Apr-Sep, daily 10-6; Jan-Mar & Oct-Dec, daily 10-dusk. Last admission 1hr before closing. **Fee:** ✱ £4.50 (ch 6-16 £1, ch under 6 free, disabled carer/companion free). Groups 10+ £3.50 each. **Facilities:** 🅿 ✗ licensed ♿ (ramps and easy access to visitor centre) toilets for disabled shop garden centre 🐾 (ex guide dogs)

COGGESHALL   Map 05 TL82
PAYCOCKE'S
West St CO6 1NS
➲ (Signposted from A120, on S side of West Street)
☎ 01376 561305

This timber-framed house is a fine example of a medieval merchant's home. It was completed in about 1505 and has interesting carvings on the outside timbers, including the Paycocke trade sign. Inside there are further elaborate carvings and linenfold panelling. Behind the house is a pretty garden. **Times:** Open 27 Mar-9 Oct Tue, Thu, Sun & BH Mon 2-5.30. **Fee:** ✱ £2.40, joint ticket with Coggeshall Grange Barn £3.50. **Facilities:** 🅿 (400yds) ♿ 🐾 (ex guide dogs) ⛆

COLCHESTER   Map 05 TL92

BETH CHATTO GARDENS
Elmstead Market CO7 7DB
➲ (5m E of Colchester on A133)
☎ 01206 822007
e-mail: info@bethchatto.fsnet.co.uk
web: www.bethchatto.co.uk

Begun almost 40 years ago, when Beth Chatto and her late husband began working on acres of wasteland. Now an area of landscaped gardens with many unusual plants grown in a variety of conditions.

Times: Open all year, Mar-Oct, Mon-Sat 9-5; Nov-Feb, Mon-Fri 9-4. (Closed Sun). **Fee:** £4 (accompanied ch under 14 free)
Facilities: ☐ ☐ ☐ & (parts of garden may be awkward, parking, large print guide) toilets for disabled garden centre
✈ (ex guide dogs) ◀

COLCHESTER CASTLE MUSEUM
Castle Park, High St CO1 1TJ
➲ (at E end of High St)
☎ 01206 282939
web: www.colchestermuseums.org.uk

The largest Norman castle keep in Europe - built over the remains of the magnificent Roman Temple of Claudius which was destroyed by Boudicca in AD60. Colchester was the first capital of Roman Britain, and the archaeological collections are among the finest in the country. Please telephone for details of a range of events held throughout the year.

Times: ✱ Open all year, Mon-Sat 10-5, Sun 11-5. Closed Xmas/New Year **Facilities:** ☐ (town centre) ☐ & (all parts accessible except vaults/roof tour) toilets for disabled shop ✈ (ex guide dogs) ◀

COLCHESTER ZOO
Stanway, Maldon Rd CO3 0SL
➲ (turn off A12 onto A1124 and follow elephant signs)
☎ 01206 331292
e-mail: enquiries@colchester-zoo.co.uk
web: www.colchester-zoo.co.uk

One of England's finest zoos, Colchester Zoo has over 200 types of animals. Visitors can meet the elephants, handle a snake, and see parrots, seals, penguins and birds of prey all appearing in informative daily displays. New enclosures include Spirit of Africa, Elephant Kingdom, Penguin Shores, the Wilds of Asia for orangutans, and Chimp World. There is also an undercover soft play complex, road train, four adventure play areas, eating places and gift shops, all set in 40 acres of gardens. The new Play Patagonia Sealion experience features a 24m under water tunnel.

Times: Open all year, daily from 9.30. Last admission 5.30 (1hr before dusk out of season). Closed 25 Dec. **Fee:** ✱ £12.99 (ch 3-14 £6.99, disabled £4.99, pen £ 8.99). Prices are seasonal. **Facilities:** ☐ ☐
✈ licensed ☐ & (easy route developed, but zoo has hills, electric scooters) toilets for disabled shop garden centre ✈ (ex guide dogs) ◀

HADLEIGH   Map 05 TQ88

HADLEIGH CASTLE
➲ (0.75m S of A13)
☎ 01760 755161   [FREE]

The subject of several of Constable's paintings, the castle has fine views of the Thames estuary. It is defended by ditches on three sides, and the north-east and south-east towers are still impressive.

Times: Open at any reasonable time. **Facilities:** (limited access due to hilly surroundings) ▦

HARWICH   Map 05 TM23

HARWICH REDOUBT FORT
CO12 3TE
➲ (behind 29 Main Rd)
☎ 01255 503429   [2 for 1]
e-mail: theharwichsociety@quista.net
web: www.harwich-society.com

The 180ft-diameter circular fort was built in 1808 in case of invasion by Napoleon. It has a dry moat and 8ft-thick walls, with 18 rooms for stores, ammunition and quarters for 300 men. The Redoubt is being restored by the Harwich Society, and contains three small museums. Ten guns can be seen on the battlements.

Times: Open May-Aug, daily 10-4.30; Sep-Apr, Sun only 10-4.
Fee: ✱ £1 (accompanied ch free). **Facilities:** ☐ (200yds) ☐ shop

HEDINGHAM
See **Castle Hedingham**

LAYER MARNEY   Map 05 TL91

LAYER MARNEY TOWER
CO5 9US
➲ (off B1022 Colchester to Maldon road, signposted)
☎ 01206 330784
e-mail: info@layermarneytower.co.uk
web: www.layermarneytower.co.uk

The tallest Tudor gatehouse in the country, intended to be the entrance to a courtyard which would have rivalled Hampton Court Palace. The death of Henry, 1st Lord Marney in 1523, and of his son in 1525, meant that the building work ceased before completion. The beautiful parish church lies within the grounds and a wildlife walk offers the chance to see a range of livestock.

Times: Open Apr-Sep, Sun-Thu 12-5, & BHs (Sun & Mon) 11-5.
Fee: £4 (ch £2.50). Family ticket (2ad + 2ch) £12. Guided tour £5.
Facilities: ☐ ☐ ✈ licensed & (ramps in garden and farm) toilets for disabled shop ✈ (ex guide dogs & dogs on lead) ◀

MISTLEY   Map 05 TM13

MISTLEY TOWERS
CO11 1NJ
➲ (on B1352, 1.5m E of A137 at Lawford)   [FREE]
☎ 01206 393884

All that remains of the grand hall and church, designed by Robert Adam, are the lodges built in 1782 for the hall, and two square towers, topped with drums and domes which came from an earlier church.

Times: Open all reasonable times. Key available from Mistley Quay Workshops-01206 393884 **Facilities:** &

NEWPORT   Map 05 TL53

MOLE HALL WILDLIFE PARK
Widdington CB11 3SS
➲ (M11 junct 8. Situated between Stansted & Saffron Walden, off B1383)
☎ 01799 540400 & 541359   [2 for 1]
e-mail: enquiries@molehall.co.uk
web: www.molehall.co.uk

The Park covers 20 acres and has been lovingly developed by the Johnstone family for over 40 years. The wide variety of animals range from South American Lama Guanaco to Red squirrels, Leopard-like Serval Cat and the Formosan Sika Deer, which is extinct in the wild. Mole Hall is also

continued

home to 2 species of otter, being the first regular breeders in the UK of the North American Otter. Other residents include chimpanzees, capuchins, lemurs and much more. In the tropical butterfly pavilion, see butterflies on the wing and free flying small birds. Tarantulas, snakes, leaf-eating ants, pools of aquatic life, small monkeys, tortoises and lovebirds.

Mole Hall Wildlife Park

Times: Open all year, daily 10.30-6 (or dusk). Closed 25 Dec. Butterfly House and Water Maze open mid Mar-Oct. **Fee:** ✽ £5 (ch £3.50 under 3's free, pen, student & disabled £4). **Facilities:** 🅿 🖳 📶 ♿ (Difficult in wet weather for wheelchairs) toilets for disabled shop garden centre 🐕 (ex guide dogs) 🍴

SAFFRON WALDEN   Map 05 TL53

SAFFRON WALDEN MUSEUM
Museum St CB10 1JL
➲ (Close to M11, take B184/B1052 & follow signs to Saffron Walden)
☎ 01799 510333
e-mail: museum@uttesford.gov.uk   2 for 1
Opened in 1835, this friendly, family-size museum lies near the castle ruins in the centre of town. Its collections include local history and archaeology, natural history, ceramics, glass, costume, furniture, toys, an ancient Egyptian room, a natural history gallery, Discovery Centre and important ethnography collections. This museum has won the Museum of the Year award for being the best museum of social history and awards for disabled access. There is a regular programme of special exhibitions, events and family holiday activities.
Times: Open all year, Mar-Oct, Mon-Sat 10-5, Sun & BHs 2-5; Nov-Feb, Mon-Sat, 10-4.30, Sun & BHs 2-4.30. Closed 24 & 25 Dec. **Fee:** £1 (concessions 50p, ch free). **Facilities:** 🅿 ♿ (ramps, wheelchairs available, stairlifts, hearing loop) toilets for disabled shop 🐕 (ex guide & hearing dogs)

SOUTHEND-ON-SEA   Map 05 TQ88

SOUTHEND MUSEUM, PLANETARIUM & DISCOVERY CENTRE
Victoria Av SS2 6ES
➲ (take A127 or A13 towards town centre. Museum is adjacent to Southend Victoria Railway Station)
☎ 01702 434449
e-mail: southendmuseum@hotmail.com
web: www.southendmuseums.co.uk
A fine Edwardian building housing displays of archaeology, natural history and local history, telling the story of man in
continued

the south-east Essex area. Also the only planetarium in the South East outside London. Ring for details of special events.
Times: Open Central Museum: Tue-Sat 10-5 (Closed Sun-Mon & BH); Planetarium: Wed-Sat, shows at 11, 2 & 4. **Fee:** ✽ Central Museum free. Planetarium £2.50 (ch & pen £1.80). Family tickets £7.90 Party rates on request. **Facilities:** 🅿 (50mtrs) (disabled only behind museum) ♿ (planetarium not accessible, disabled access to centre) shop 🐕 (ex guide dogs)

SOUTHEND PIER MUSEUM
Western Esplanade SS1 2EL
➲ (A127 follow signs to seafront and pier, attraction is at shore end of pier, access from shore train station)
☎ 01702 611214 & 614553
Southend Pier is one and a third miles long and was built in 1830. This living museum portrays the history of the pier, its railway, its disasters, and the people who have lived and worked there. Exhibits include ex-pier rolling stock, a reconstructed signal box with working levers, and antique slot machines.
Times: ✽ Open May-Oct. Tue, Wed, Sat, Sun & BHs 11-5 (during school hols 5.30) **Facilities:** 🅿 (50yds) 📶 ♿ (Access to museum through fire door at Adventure Island) shop 🐕 (ex guide dogs)

STANSTED   Map 05 TL52

HOUSE ON THE HILL MUSEUM ADVENTURE
CM24 8SP
➲ (off B1383 in the centre of Stansted Mountfitchet)
☎ 01279 813567
e-mail: mountfitchetcastle1066@btinternet.com
web: www.mountfitchetcastle.com
A large, privately-owned toy museum, housed on two floors covering 7,000 sq. ft. A huge variety of toys, books and games from the late Victorian period up to the 1970s. There is a space display, Teddy Bears' picnic, Action Man, Sindy, Barbie, military displays and much more. Additional displays of film, theatre, rock n roll and television memorabilia are on show, plus end of the pier slot machines.
Times: Open daily, 10-5; (closed for a few days over the Xmas period & Mon in Jan & Feb) **Fee:** £4 (ch under 14 £3.20, pen £3.50). Party 15+. **Facilities:** 🅿 (charged) shop 🐕 (ex guide dogs) 🍴

MOUNTFITCHET CASTLE & NORMAN VILLAGE
CM24 8SP
➲ (off B1383, in centre of village. 5 min from M11 junct 8)
☎ 01279 813237
e-mail: mountfitchetcastle1066@btinternet.com
web: www.mountfitchetcastle.com
Norman motte and bailey castle and village reconstructed as it was in Norman England of 1066, on its original historic site. A vivid illustration of village life in Domesday England, complete with houses, church, seige tower, seige weapons, and many types of animals roaming freely. Animated wax figures in all the buildings give historical information to visitors.
Times: Open daily, mid Mar-mid Nov, 10-5. **Fee:** ✽ £6 (ch under 2 free, ch 2-14 £5, pen £5.50). **Facilities:** 🅿 (charged) 🖳 📶 ♿ (laser commentaries) toilets for disabled shop 🐕 (ex guide dogs) 🍴

TILBURY   Map 05 TQ67

TILBURY FORT
No 2 Office Block, The Fort RM18 7NR
➲ (0.5 mile E off A126)
☎ 01375 858489
View the finest example of 17th-century military engineering, a
spectacular sight on the River Thames. View the World War I
and II gun emplacements and even fire a real anti-aircraft gun.
Times: Open all year, Apr-Sep, daily 10-6; Oct, daily 10-5; Nov-Mar,
Thu-Mon 10-4. **Fee:** £3.30 (ch £1.70, concessions £2.50, family £8.30).
£1.30 to fire anti-aircraft gun. Opening times and prices are subject to
change, for further details please phone 0870 333 1181
Facilities: ﾭ shop ✖ (ex on lead in certain areas) ﾭ

WALTHAM ABBEY   Map 05 TL30

LEE VALLEY PARK FARMS
Stubbins Hall Ln, Crooked Mile EN9 2EG
➲ (M25 junct 26, follow to Waltham Abbey. 2m
from Waltham Abbey on B914)
☎ 01992 892781 & 702200
e-mail: hayeshill@leevalleypark.org.uk
web: www.leevalleypark.org.uk
Set in the heart of Lee Valley Country Park, Hayes Hill Farm
offers young and old the chance to view many types of farm
animals. Meet a variety of rare breeds in the traditional-style
farmyard. In the pet centre, see many creatures from
meerkats to chipmunks. During summer, there are tractor
and trailor rides to Holyfield Hall, a 700-acre working dairy
and arable farm.
Times: Open all year, Mon-Fri 10-4.30, wknds & BHs 10-5.30.
Fee: ✱ £4.10 (ch 3+ £3.10, concessions £3.60). Family (2ad+3ch)
£16.50 **Facilities:** 🅿 💷 🛢 ﾭ (graded concrete paths, signed
routes) toilets for disabled shop ▰

ROYAL GUNPOWDER MILLS
Beaulieu Dr EN9 1JY
➲ (M25 junct 26. Follow signs for A121 to
Waltham Abbey at rdbt, entrance in Beaulieu
Drive)
☎ 01992 707370
e-mail: info@royalgunpowdermills.com
web: www.royalgunpowdermills.com
Set in 175 acres of parkland, this amazing scientific complex
has 21 buildings of historical importance. Before it closed in
1991 this was the site of major scientific research and
development, including work on Congreve's Rocket in the
early 19th century, up to more recent work on ejector seats
and fuel for rocket motors. Explosives were made in many of
the buildings on the site which are connected by five miles
of navigational canals.
Times: Open 30 Apr-25 Sep, 11-5, last entry at 3.30. (Wknds and BHs
only) **Fee:** ✱ £5.50 (ch £3, concessions £4.70, under 5's free) Family
£17 **Facilities:** 🅿 💷 🛢 ﾭ (ramps, lift, tactile with audio tour) toilets
for disabled shop ✖ (ex guide dogs) ▰

WALTHAM ABBEY GATEHOUSE, BRIDGE & ENTRANCE TO CLOISTERS
➲ (in Waltham Abbey off A112)
☎ 01992 702200   FREE
Beside the great Norman church at Waltham are the slight
remains of the abbey buildings - bridge, gatehouse and part
of the north cloister. The bridge is named after King Harold,
founder of the abbey.
Times: Open at any reasonable time. **Facilities:** ﾭ (sensory trail
guide)

GLOUCESTERSHIRE

EVENTS & FESTIVALS

January
   27th-29th Cajun Music Festival, Gloucester
February
   tbc Cheltenham Folk Festival
March
   14th-17th National Hunt Festival (Gold Cup
   Week), Prestbury Park, Cheltenham
April
   26th-1st May Cheltenham International Jazz
   Festival, various venues
May
   1st Cheese Roll, A46 nr Brockworth
   3rd-14th Cheltenham Competitive Festival, a
   showcase of local talent (provisional)
   4th-7th Badminton Horse Trials, Badminton
June
   2nd Robert Dover's Cotswold Olimpick
   Games, Dover's Hill, Chipping Coopers Hill
   7th-11th Cheltenham Festival of Science,
   Cheltenham Town Hall
   30th-16th Jul Cheltenham International
   Festival of Music
   30th-16th Jul Cheltenham Fringe Festival
July
   8th-9th Tewkesbury Medieval Festival,
   Cupshill Fields, Tewkesbury (provisional)
   14th-16th Tewkesbury Water Festival
   15th-16th Royal International Air Tattoo, RAF
   Fairford
   22nd-23rd International Kite Festival,
   Tewkesbury, (provisional)
   tbc The Cotswold Show & Country Fair,
   Cirencester Park, Cirencester
   tbc Gloucester Festival, multicultural event
   with carnival, street theatre, music & dance
   tbc Longborough Festival Opera, (provisional)
   tbc Musica Deo Sacra, Tewkesbury Abbey
August
   tbc Gloucester International Blues Festival
   tbc Twyning to Tewkesbury Raft Race
October
   tbc Cheltenham Festival of Literature
   tbc Tewkesbury Mop Fair (street fair)

Above: The Cotswold Way

ALDSWORTH Map 04 SP11
LODGE PARK & SHERBORNE ESTATE
GL54 3PP
➲ (approach from A40 only, between Northleach & Burford rdbts)
☎ 01451 844130 01451 844257
e-mail: lodgepark@nationaltrust.org.uk
web: www.nationaltrust.org.uk
Situated on the picturesque Sherborne Estate in the Cotswolds, Lodge Park was created in 1634 by John 'Crump' Dutton. Inspired by his passion for gambling and banqueting it is a unique survival of what would have been called a grandstand, with its deer course and park.
Times: Open Grandstand: 18 Mar-30 Oct, Mon, Fri & Sun 11-4, Sat 11-3; Estate: daily all year. **Fee:** ✱ Grandstand: £4.50 (ch £2.20). Family £11. Estate: free. **Facilities:** P ▦ ⅙ (Braille guide, manual wheelchair, drop off point) toilets for disabled under close control ⅗

BERKELEY Map 03 ST69
BERKELEY CASTLE
GL13 9BQ
➲ (just off A38 midway between Bristol & Gloucester. From M5 take junct 14 or 15)
☎ 01453 810332
e-mail: info@berkeley-castle.com
web: www.berkeley-castle.com
2 for 1
Berkeley Castle is the amazing fortress home of the Berkeley family, who have lived in the building since the Keep was completed in 1153. The castle is still intact, from dungeon to elegant drawing rooms, and reflects nearly a thousand years of English history: a king's murder, the American Colonies, London's Berkeley Square. Rose-clad terraces surround this most romantic castle.
Times: Open Apr-2 Oct, Tue-Sat & BH Mon 11-4, Sun 2-5; Oct, Sun only 2-5. **Fee:** ✱ Castle & Gardens & Butterfly House: £7.50 (ch 5-15 £4.50, pen £6). Family ticket (2ad+2ch) £21. **Facilities:** P ▦ ▦ ⅙ Special tours can be arranged shop garden centre ✖ (ex guide dogs) ▦

JENNER MUSEUM
Church Ln, High St GL13 9BN
➲ (follow tourist signs from A38 to town centre, turn left into High Street & left again into Church Lane)
☎ 01453 810631
e-mail: manager@jennermuseum.com
web: www.jennermuseum.com
2 for 1
This beautiful Georgian house was the home of Edward Jenner, the discoverer of vaccination against smallpox. The house and the garden, with its Temple of Vaccinia, are much as they were in Jenner's day. The displays record Jenner's life as an 18th-century country doctor, his work on vaccination and his interest in natural history.
Times: Open Apr-Sep, Tue-Sat 12.30-5.30, Sun 1-5.30. Oct, Sun 1-5.30. (Closed Mon, ex BH Mon 12.30-5.30). **Fee:** ✱ £3.50 (ch £2, students & pen £2.80). Family ticket £9. Party 20+. **Facilities:** P ▦ ⅙ toilets for disabled shop ✖ (ex guide dogs) ▦

BOURTON-ON-THE-HILL Map 04 SP13
BOURTON HOUSE GARDEN
GL56 9AE
➲ (1.75m W of Moreton-in-Marsh on A44)
☎ 01386 700754
e-mail: cd@bourtonhouse.com
web: www.bourtonhouse.com
Since 1983 a dedicated team has been working to restore this 18th-century house and its large gardens. The result is an impressive landscape full of hedges, water features, paths and plants.
Times: Open end May-Aug, Wed-Fri, end Sep-Oct Thu-Fri, 10-5
Fee: £5 (ch free) **Facilities:** P ▦ ⅙ (garden is 70% accessible) toilets for disabled shop garden centre plants, garden tools ✖

BOURTON-ON-THE-WATER Map 04 SP12
BIRDLAND
Rissington Rd GL54 2BN
➲ (on A429)
☎ 01451 820480
e-mail: simon@birdland.co.uk
web: www.birdland.co.uk

Birdland is a natural setting of woodland, river and gardens, which is inhabited by over 500 birds; flamingos, pelicans, penguins, cranes, storks, cassowary and waterfowl can be seen on various aspects of the water habitat. Over 50 aviaries of parrots, falcons, pheasants, hornbills, touracos, pigeons, ibis and many more. Tropical, Toucan and Desert Houses are home to the more delicate species.
Times: Open all year, Apr-Oct, daily 10-6; Nov-Mar, daily 10-4. (Last admission 1hr before closing). Closed 25 Dec. **Fee:** ✱ £4.95 (ch 4-14 £3, pen £4). Family ticket (2ad+2ch) £14.50. Party 10+.
Facilities: P (adjacent) ▦ ▦ ⅙ toilets for disabled shop on a lead ▦

MODEL VILLAGE
Old New Inn GL54 2AF
☎ 01451 820467
e-mail: reception@theoldnewinn.co.uk
web: www.theoldnewinn.co.uk
The model is built of Cotswold stone to a scale of one-ninth, and is a perfect replica of the village. It includes a miniature River Windrush, a working model waterwheel, churches and shops, with tiny trees, shrubs and alpine plants.
Times: Open all year 10-5.45 (summer), 10-dusk (winter). Closed 25 Dec. **Fee:** ✱ £2.75 (ch £2.25, pen £2.50). **Facilities:** P (500yds) ▦ ✖ licensed shop ✖ (ex guide dogs) ▦

CHEDWORTH Map 04 SP01
CHEDWORTH ROMAN VILLA
Yanworth GL54 3LJ
➲ (3m NW of Fossebridge on A429)
☎ 01242 890256
e-mail: chedworth@nationaltrust.org.uk
web: www.nationaltrust.org.uk
The remains of a Romano-British villa, excavated 1864-66 'Britains oldest county house'. Set in a beautiful wooded combe, there are fine 4th-century mosaics, two bath houses, and a temple with spring. The museum houses the smaller finds and there is a 9-minute video programme. Telephone for further details of special events.
Times: Open 8 Feb-26 Mar, daily 11-4; 27 Mar-24 Oct, daily 10-5; 26 Oct-14 Nov, daily 11-4. (Closed Mons ex BH Mon). **Fee:** ✱ £5 (ch £2.50). Family ticket £12.50. **Facilities:** P ⅙ (audio tour, induction loop, Braille guide) toilets for disabled shop ✖ ⅗ ▦

CHELTENHAM Map 03 SO92

Cheltenham Art Gallery & Museum

Clarence St GL50 3JT
➲ (close to town centre and bus station, 2 min walk from promenade)
☎ **01242 237431**
e-mail: artgallery@cheltenham.gov.uk
web: www.cheltenham.artgallery.museum

The museum has an outstanding collection relating to the Arts and Crafts Movement, including fine furniture and exquisite metalwork. The Art Gallery contains Dutch and British paintings from the 17th century to the present day. The Oriental Gallery features pottery, costumes and treasures from the Ming Dynasty to the reign of the last Chinese Emperor. There is also a display about Edward Wilson who journeyed with Captain Scott in 1911-12, together with the history of Britain's most complete Regency town and archaeological treasures from the neighbouring Cotswolds. Special exhibitions are held throughout the year.

Times: Open all year, Mon-Sat 10-5.20 (first Thu in month, 11-5.20). Closed BHs and Good Fri **Fee:** Free, donations welcome. **Facilities:** P (500 mtrs) disabled parking on site ♿ (handling tables; speech reinforcement system) toilets for disabled shop (ex guide dogs)

Holst Birthplace Museum

4 Clarence Rd GL52 2AY
➲ (opposite gateway of Pittville Park. 10 min walk from town centre)
☎ **01242 524846**
2 for 1
e-mail: holstmuseum@btconnect.com
web: www.holstmuseum.org.uk

Gustav Holst, composer of *The Planets* was born at this Regency house in 1874. The museum contains unique displays on Holst's life, including his original piano. The rooms of the house have been carefully restored, each area evoking a different period in the history of the house from Regency to Edwardian times.

Times: Open Tue-Sat 10-4 (Closed Mon & Dec-Jan, ex pre-booked groups) **Fee:** £3.50 (ch & concessions £3). Family ticket (2ad+3ch) £8. **Facilities:** P (250yds) (large print & Braille guide, special hands-on tours) shop Specialist cds/books, and victorian toys (ex guide dogs)

CIRENCESTER Map 04 SP00

Corinium Museum

Park St GL7 2BX
➲ (in town centre)
☎ **01285 655611**
e-mail: museums@cotswold.gov.uk
web: www.cotswold.gov.uk

Discover the treasures of the Cotswolds at the new Corinium Museum. Two years and over £5 million in the making, it has been transformed into a must-see attraction. Featuring archaeological and historical material from Cirencester and the Cotswolds, from prehistoric times to the 19th century. The museum is known for its Roman mosaic sculpture and other material from one of Britain's largest Roman towns. New on display are Anglo-Saxon treasures from Lechlade bringing to life this little known period. The museum also houses Medieval, Tudor, Civil War and 18th-19th century displays.

Times: Open Mon-Sat 10-5, Sun 2-5. Closed 25-26 Dec & 1 Jan. **Fee:** *Prices not confirmed for 2006* **Facilities:** P (2mins walk) ♿ Large print + Braille guides toilets for disabled shop assisst dogs

CLEARWELL Map 03 SO50

Clearwell Caves Ancient Iron Mines

GL16 8JR
➲ (1.5m S of Coleford town centre, off B4228 follow brown tourist signs)
☎ **01594 832535**
e-mail: jw@clearwellcaves.com
web: www.clearwellcaves.com

These impressive natural caves have also been mined since the earliest times for paint pigment and iron ore. Today visitors explore nine large caverns with displays of local mining and geology. Colour room where ochre pigments are still produced and blacksmith shop. Deep level excursions available for more adventurous visitors, must be pre booked. Christmas fantasy event when the caverns are transformed into a world of light and sound.

Times: Open Mar-Oct daily 10-5; Jan-Feb Sat-Sun 10-5; Christmas Fantasy 1-24 Dec, daily 10-5. **Fee:** £4.50 (ch £2.80, concessions £4) Family ticket £12.90 **Facilities:** P ♿ (hands-on exhibits, Braille guide book, contact in advance) toilets for disabled shop (ex guide & hearing dogs)

CRANHAM Map 03 SO81

Prinknash Abbey and Pottery

GL4 8EX
➲ (on A46 between Cheltenham & Stroud)
☎ **01452 812066**
e-mail: shop@prinknash135.fsnet.co.uk
web: www.prinknashabbey.org.uk

Set in a large park, the old priory building is a 12th to 16th-century house, used by Benedictine monks and guests of Gloucester Abbey until 1539. It became an abbey for Benedictine monks from Caldey in 1928. Home to the reconstruction of the Great Orpheus Pavement. It is the largest mosaic in Britain. as mentioned in the Guinness Book of Records. Also visit the bird and deer park.

Times: Open all year. Abbey Church: April-end Oct 9-5.30, Nov-end Mar 10-4.30. Closed Good Friday, 25-26 Dec. **Facilities:** P ♿ (Radar approved) toilets for disabled shop

If an attraction name appears in *italics*, details have not been confirmed for 2006.

PRINKNASH BIRD & DEER PARK

GL4 8EU

➲ (M5 junct 11a, A417 Cirencester. Take 1st exit signed A46 Stroud. Follow brown tourist signs)

☎ 01452 812727

web: www.prinknash-bird-and-deerpark.com

Nine acres of parkland and lakes make a beautiful home for black swans, geese and other water birds. There are also exotic birds such as white and Indian blue peacocks and crown cranes, as well as tame fallow deer and pygmy goats. The Golden Wood is stocked with ornamental pheasants, and leads to the reputedly haunted monks' fishpond, which contains trout. An 80-year old, free-standing, 16ft tall Wendy House in the style of a Tudor house has recently been erected near the picnic area.

Times: Open all year, daily 10-5 (4 in winter). Closed 26 Dec & Good Fri. **Fee:** ✱ £4.50 (ch £3, pen £4). Party 10+ £4 (ch £2.50, pen £3.50). **Facilities:** 🅿 🅿 📗 shop ✗

DEERHURST — Map 03 SO82

ODDA'S CHAPEL

➲ (off B4213 near River Severn at Abbots Court SW of parish church) FREE

This rare Saxon chapel was built by Earl Odda and dedicated in 1056. When it was discovered, it had been incorporated into a farmhouse. It has now been carefully restored.

Times: Open Apr-Oct, daily 10-6; Nov-Mar, daily 10-4. Closed 24-26 Dec & 1 Jan. **Facilities:** 🅿 (charged) ✗

DYRHAM — Map 03 ST77

DYRHAM PARK

SN14 8ER

➲ (8m N of Bath, 2m from M4 junct 18)

☎ 0117 937 2501

e-mail: dyrhampark@nationaltrust.org.uk

web: www.nationaltrust.org.uk

Dyrham Park is a splendid Baroque Country house, with interiors that have hardly altered since the late 17th century. It has contemporary Dutch-style furnishings, Dutch pictures and blue-and-white Delft ware. Around the house is an ancient park with fallow deer, where Dyrham derives its name. In the beautiful gardens, famous for the tulip festival in April, is a medieval Church.

Times: House 18 Mar-30 Oct, 12-4.45, Fri-Tue. Garden 18 Mar-30 Oct, 11-5, Fri-Tue. Park all year, 11-5, all week. Shop 18 Mar-30 Oct, 11-5, Fri-Tue. Tea room, 18 Mar-30 Oct, 11-5, Fri-Tue. **Fee:** ✱ House £8.80 (ch £4.35). Family £21.75. Ground only £3.40 (ch £1.70). Family £7.75). Park only £2.25 (ch £1.10). **Facilities:** 🅿 🅿 ✗ licensed 📗 � (Braille/audio guides, stairclimber, free bus from car park) toilets for disabled shop ✗ (ex in dog walk area) 🐾

GLOUCESTER — Map 03 SO81

GLOUCESTER CITY MUSEUM & ART GALLERY

Brunswick Rd GL1 1HP

➲ (centre of Gloucester)

☎ 01452 396131 FREE

e-mail: city.museum@gloucester.gov.uk

web: www.gloucester.gov.uk

An impressive range of Roman artefacts including the Rufus Sita tombstone; the amazing Iron Age Birdlip Mirror; one of the earliest backgammon sets in the world; dinosaur fossils; and paintings by famous artists such as Turner and Gainsborough. There is something for everyone, full-sized dinosaurs; wildlife from the City and the Gloucestershire countryside; beautiful antique furniture, glass, ceramics and

continued

silver; hands-on displays, computer quizzes and activity workstations throughout the galleries. There is an exciting range of temporary exhibitions from contemporary art and textiles to dinosaurs and local history; children's holiday activities and regular special events.

Gloucester City Museum & Art Gallery

Times: Open all year, Tue-Sat 10-5. **Facilities:** 🅿 (500yds) 📗 ⅗ lift to 1st floor galleries, induction loops toilets for disabled shop ✗ (ex guide dogs) 🍽

GLOUCESTER FOLK MUSEUM

99-103 Westgate St GL1 2PG

➲ (from W - A40 & A48; from N - A38 & M5, from E - A40 & B4073; from S - A4173 & A38)

☎ 01452 396868 396869 FREE

e-mail: folk.museum@gloucester.gov.uk

web: www.gloucester.gov.uk

Three floors of splendid Tudor and Jacobean timber-framed buildings dating from the 16th and 17th centuries along with new buildings housing the Dairy, Ironmonger's shop and Wheelwright and Carpenter workshops. Local history, domestic life, crafts, trades and industries from 1500 to the present, including Toys and Childhood gallery with hands-on toys and a puppet theatre, the Siege of Gloucester, a Victorian Class Room, Victorian Kitchen and laundry equipment. A wide range of exhibitions, hands-on activities, events, demonstrations and role play sessions are held throughout the year. There is an attractive cottage garden and courtyard for events, often with live animals, and outside games.

Times: Tue-Sat, 10-5 **Facilities:** 🅿 (500yds) 📗 ⅗ (virtual tour in Protal gallery, induction loops) shop ✗ (ex guide dogs) 🍽

THE NATIONAL WATERWAYS MUSEUM
Llanthony Warehouse, The Docks GL1 2EH
➲ (From M5, A40 and within the city follow brown signs for historic docks)
☎ 01452 318200
e-mail: bookingsnwm@thewaterwaystrust.org
web: www.nwm.org.uk

Based in Gloucester Docks, this museum takes up three floors of a seven-storey Victorian warehouse, and documents the 200-year history of Britain's water-based transport. The emphasis is on hands-on experience, including working models and engines, interactive displays, actual craft, computer interactions and the national collection of inland waterways. Boat trips are also available between Easter and October.

Times: Open all year, daily 10-5. (Last admission 4). Closed 25 Dec. **Fee:** ✱ £5.50 (under 5's free, concessions £4.25). Family ticket £17.50 **Facilities:** 🅿 (charged) 🍴 🛍 ♿ (wheelchair, lifts, limited access to floating exhibits) toilets for disabled shop ✖ (ex guide dogs) 🎫

NATURE IN ART
Wallsworth Hall, Tewkesbury Rd, Twigworth GL2 9PA
➲ (0.5m off main A38 between Gloucester and Tenkesbury, 2m N of Gloucester. Follow brown tourist signs Tewkesbury)
☎ 01452 731422 0845 4500233
e-mail: ninart@globalnet.co.uk
web: www.nature-in-art.org.uk

Nature is the theme at this museum and art gallery set in a Georgian Mansion, where there are many outstanding exhibits including sculpture, tapestries and ceramics. There is an 'artist in residence' programme Feb-Nov, and events include regular monthly talks, film showings and a full programme of temporary exhibitions and art courses. See website for full details. Work from over 60 countries spanning 1500 years is included in the collection, which has been specially commended twice in the National Heritage Museum of the Year Awards. From Picasso to David Shepherd, Flemish masters to ethnic art, contemporary sculpture to Japanese prints - there is something for everyone.

Times: Open all year, Tue-Sun & BHs 10-5. Closed 24-26 Dec. **Fee:** ✱ £3.60 (ch, pen & students £3.00, ch under 8 free). Family ticket £11. Party 15+. **Facilities:** 🅿 🍴 ✖ licensed ♿ (lift & ramps at entrance) toilets for disabled shop full range of paints and art materials ✖ (ex guide dogs)

GUITING POWER   Map 04 SP02

COTSWOLD FARM PARK
GL54 5UG
➲ (signed off B4077 from M5 junct 9)
☎ 01451 850307
e-mail: info@cotswoldfarmpark.co.uk
web: www.cotswoldfarmpark.co.uk

At the Cotswold Farm Park there are nearly 50 breeding herds and flocks of the rarest British breeds of sheep, cattle, pigs, goats, horses, and poultry. Lots of activities for children including rabbits and guinea pigs to cuddle, lambs and calves to bottle feed, tractor and trailer rides, battery powered tractors and safe rustic-themed play areas indoors and outdoors. Lambing occurs in early May, followed by shearing and then milking demonstrations later in the season.

Times: Open 19 Mar-4 Sep, daily 10.30-5 (then open wknds only until end Oct & Autumn half term 10.30-4). **Fee:** ✱ £5.10 (ch £4 pen £4.70). Family ticket £16 **Facilities:** 🅿 🍴 🛍 ♿ (ramps) toilets for disabled shop ✖ (ex guide dogs) 🎫

HAILES   Map 04 SP02

HAILES ABBEY
GL54 5PB
➲ (2m NE of Winchcombe off B4632)
☎ 01242 602398

Explore the atmospheric ruins of this great medieval pilgrimage abbey, in the midst of the Cotswolds. Built in the 13th-century Hailes become famous when presented with a phial that was said to contain the blood of Christ.

Times: Open 24 Mar-Jun & Sep, daily 10-5; Jul-Aug, daily 10-6; Oct, daily 10-4. **Fee:** £3.30 (ch £1.70, concessions £2.50). **Facilities:** 🅿 ♿ shop 👺

LYDNEY   Map 03 SO60

DEAN FOREST RAILWAY
Norchard Railway Centre, New Mills, Forest Rd GL15 4ET
➲ (At Lydney, turn off the Gloucester to Chepstow (A48) road and follow brown tourist signs to Norchard Railway Centre, on B4234 Lydney-Parkend road)
☎ 01594 843423 (info)
e-mail: commercial@deanforestrailway.co.uk
web: www.deanforestrailway.co.uk

Just north of Lydney lies the headquarters of the Dean Forest Railway where a number of steam locomotives, plus lots of coaches, wagons and railway equipment are on show and

continued

guided tours are available by prior arrangement. Standard gauge passenger service on steam haulage runs from Norchard to Lydney Junction and back to Norchard, the diesel train runs from Lydney Junction to Tufts and back to Lydney Junction.

Dean Forest Railway

Times: Open Apr-Oct, Sun; Jun-Sep, Wed, Sat, Sun; also Thu in Aug and BH's; Dec wknds (Santa Specials) **Fee:** £7 (under 5's free, ch £5, pen £6.50). Family ticket (2ad+2ch) £23 **Facilities:** 🅿 💻 ✗ ♿ (specially adapted coach for wheelchairs, phone for details) toilets for disabled shop ⊠

MICKLETON   Map 04 SP14

HIDCOTE MANOR GARDEN

Chipping Campden GL55 6LR
➲ (1m E of B4632, near village of Mickleton)
☎ 01386 438333
e-mail: hidcote@nationaltrust.org.uk
web: www.nationaltrust.org.uk/hidcote

One of the most delightful arts and crafts gardens in England, created by the horticulturist Major Laurence Johnston and comprising a series of small gardens within the whole, separated by walls and hedges of different species. It is famous for its rare shrubs and trees, outstanding herbaceous borders and unusual worldwide plant species.
Times: Garden: 19 Mar-2 Oct, 10.30-6, Sat-Wed, 3-30 Oct 10.30-5 Sat-Wed **Fee:** ✱ £6.60 (ch £3.30). Family £16.10. Groups £5.90 (ch £2.65) **Facilities:** 🅿 💻 ✗ licensed ♿ (partial access, ltd due to stone paths, w/chair available) toilets for disabled shop garden centre ✗ (ex guide dogs) ♨

KIFTSGATE COURT GARDEN

Mickleton GL55 6LN
➲ (0.5m S off A46, adjacent Hidcote NT garden)
☎ 01386 438777
e-mail: kiftsgte@aol.com
web: www.kiftsgate.co.uk

Kiftsgate Garden is spectacularly set on the edge of the Cotswold Escarpment, with views over the Vale of Evesham. It contains many rare plants collected by three generations of women gardeners, including the largest rose in England, the R. Filipes Kiftsgate.
Times: Open Apr-May & Aug-Sep; Wed, Thu, Sun & BH Mon 2-6. Jun-Jul Mon, Wed, Thu, Sat & Sun 12-6. **Fee:** ✱ £5 (ch £1.50).
Facilities: 🅿 💻 📱 garden centre ✗ (ex guide dogs)

MORETON-IN-MARSH   Map 04 SP23

BATSFORD ARBORETUM

Admissions Centre, Batsford Park GL56 9QB
➲ (1.5m NW, off A44 from Moreton-in-Marsh)
☎ 01386 701441
e-mail: mail@batsarb.co.uk
web: www.batsarb.co.uk

Batsford Arboretum has one of the largest private collections of trees in Great Britain and wonderful views across the Vale of Evenlode. Visitors can stroll amongst the spring flowers that cascade down the hillside, and see many rare and unusual trees. There is an impressive display of colour during autumn, and the garden is very peaceful. View the Buddha and cave and try and negotiate the waterfall without getting too wet. Sheer Cotswold magic.
Times: ✱ Open Feb-mid Nov, daily 10-5; mid Nov-Jan, wknds only 10-4. **Facilities:** 🅿 💻 📱 ♿ (some steep, slippery paths, wheelchair available) toilets for disabled shop garden centre ⊠

COTSWOLD FALCONRY CENTRE

Batsford Park GL56 9QB
➲ (1m W of Moreton-in-Marsh on A44)
☎ 01386 701043   **`2 for 1`**
e-mail: geoffdalton@yahoo.co.uk
web: www.cotswold-falconry.co.uk

Conveniently located by the Batsford Park Arboretum, the Cotswold Falconry gives daily demonstrations in the art of falconry. The emphasis here is on breeding and conservation, and eagles, hawks, owls and falcons can be seen.
Times: Open mid Feb-mid Nov, 10.30-5.30. (Last admission 5pm).
Fee: ✱ £5 (ch 4-15 £2.50, concession £4). Joint ticket with Batsford Arboretum £8.50 (ch 4-15 £3, concession £8). **Facilities:** 🅿 ♿ (no steps, wide doorways) toilets for disabled shop garden centre ✗ (ex on leads in arboretum) ⊠

SEZINCOTE

GL56 9AW
➲ (1.5m out of Moreton-in-Marsh on A44, Evesham road)
☎ 01386 700444

The Indian-style house at Sezincote was the inspiration for Brighton Pavilion; its charming water garden adds to its exotic aura and features trees of unusual size.
Times: Open: House, May-Jul & Sep, Thu & Fri 2.30-6. Garden only, all year (ex Dec) Thu, Fri & BH Mon 2-6 or dusk if earlier. **Fee:** ✱ House & garden £6 Garden only £4 (ch £1.50 under 5 free). Children not allowed in the House. Groups by appointment only.
Facilities: 🅿 ♿ toilets for disabled ✗ (ex guide dogs)

NEWENT   Map 03 SO72

THE NATIONAL BIRDS OF PREY CENTRE

GL18 1JJ
➲ (follow A40, right onto B4219 towards Newent. Follow brown tourist signs from Newent town)
☎ 0870 9901992
e-mail: katherine@nbpc.co.uk
web: www.nbpc.co.uk

Trained birds can be seen at close quarters in the Hawk Walk and the Owl Courtyard and there are also breeding aviaries, a gift shop, bookshop, picnic areas, coffee shop and children's play area. Birds are flown three times daily in summer and winter, giving an exciting and educational display. There are over 80 aviaries on view with 40 species.
Times: Open Feb-Oct, daily 10.30-5.30. **Facilities:** 🅿 💻 📱 ♿ (special tours available, pre-booking required) toilets for disabled shop ✗ ⊠

THE SHAMBLES
Church St GL18 1PP
⮑ (close to town centre near church)
☎ 01531 822144
web: www.shamblesnewent.co.uk

Cobbled streets, alleyways, cottages and houses set in over an acre with display shops and trades, even a tin chapel and cottage garden all helping to recreate the feel and atmosphere of a small Victorian town.

Times: Open mid Mar-end Oct, Tue-Sun & BHs 10-5 (or dusk); Nov-Dec wknds only. **Fee:** ✱ £4.35 (ch £2.75, pen £3.75).
Facilities: P (100yds) 🍴 & toilets for disabled shop 🖼

NORTHLEACH   Map 04 SP11

KEITH HARDING'S WORLD OF MECHANICAL MUSIC
The Oak House, High St GL54 3ET
⮑ (at crossroads of A40 & A429)
☎ 01451 860181
e-mail: keith@mechanicalmusic.co.uk
web: www.mechanicalmusic.co.uk

A fascinating collection of antique clocks, musical boxes, automata and mechanical musical instruments, restored and maintained in the world-famous workshops, displayed in a period setting, and played during regular tours. There is an exhibition of coin operated instruments which visitors can play.

Times: Open all year, daily 10-6. Last tour 5. Closed 25-26 Dec.
Fee: ✱ £6 (ch £3, pen & students £5). Discounts for families & groups.
Facilities: P & (Safety rails, non-slip floor) toilets for disabled shop 🐕 (ex guide dogs) 🖼

OWLPEN   Map 03 ST79

OWLPEN MANOR
GL11 5BZ
⮑ (3m E of Dursley, ssignted at village green in Uley off B4066)
☎ 01453 860261
e-mail: sales@owlpen.com
web: www.owlpen.com

A romantic Tudor manor house, with unique 17th-century painted cloth wallhangings, furniture, pictures and textiles. The house is set in formal terraced gardens, and is part of a picturesque Cotswold manorial group including a Jacobean Court House, a Victorian church and medieval tithe barn.

Times: Open May-Sep, Tue, Thur & Sun 2-5 **Fee:** ✱ £4.80 (ch £2).
Facilities: P 🍴 ✗ licensed 🗐 🐕 🖼

PAINSWICK   Map 03 SO80

PAINSWICK ROCOCO GARDEN
GL6 6TH
⮑ (on B4073 0.5m NW of Painswick)
☎ 01452 813204
e-mail: info@rococogarden.co.uk
web: www.rococogarden.co.uk

This beautiful Rococo garden (a compromise between formality and informality) is the only one of its period to survive complete. There are ponds, woodland walks, a maze, kitchen garden and herbacious borders, all set in a Cotswold valley famous for snowdrops in the early spring. Ring for details of special events.

Times: Open 10 Jan-Oct, daily 11-5. **Fee:** £5 (ch £2.50, pen £4)
Facilities: P 🍴 ✗ licensed 🗐 shop garden centre plants and pots 🖼

SLIMBRIDGE   Map 03 SO70

WWT SLIMBRIDGE
GL2 7BT
⮑ (off A38, signed from M5 junct 13 & 14)
☎ 0870 33 44 000   **2 for 1**
e-mail: slimbridge@wwt.org.uk
web: www.wwt.org.uk

Slimbridge is home to the world's largest collection of exotic wildfowl - and the only place in Europe where all six types of flamingo can be seen. Up to 8,000 wild birds winter on the 800-acre reserve of flat fields, marsh and mudflats on the River Severn. Facilities include a tropical house, discovery centre, shop and restaurant. 2006 marks the 60th anniversary of the foundation of the Wildfowl and Wetlands Trust.

Times: Open all year, daily from 9.30-5 (winter 4). Closed 25 Dec.
Fee: ✱ £6.75 (ch £4, pen £5.50). Family ticket £17.50.
Facilities: P 🍴 ✗ licensed & (wheelchair loan, tapes for blind, hearing pads & loops) toilets for disabled shop 🐕 (ex guide & hearing dogs) 🖼

SNOWSHILL   Map 04 SP03

SNOWSHILL MANOR
WR12 7JU
⮑ (3m SW of Broadway, off A44)
☎ 01386 852410
e-mail: snowshillmanor@nationaltrust.org.uk
web: www.nationaltrust.org.uk

Arts and crafts garden designed by its owner Charles Paget Wade in collaboration with M.H. Baillie Scott, as a series of outdoor rooms to compliment his traditional Cotswold manor house filled with his unique collection of craftsmanship including musical instruments, clocks, toys, bicycles and Japanese armour. This was the first National Trust garden to be managed following organic principles. It is a lively mix of cottage flowers, bright colours and delightful scents with stunning views across Cotswold countryside.

Times: House: 25 Mar-2 May, 12-5, Thu-Sun, 4 May-30 Oct, 12-5, Wed-Sun; Garden: 25 Mar-2 May, 11-5.30, Thu-Sun, 4 May-30 Oct, 11-5.30, Wed-Sun; Shop: As garden, also 5 Nov-11Dec, 12-4, Sat & Sun; Restaurant: As shop **Fee:** ✱ House & Garden: £7, (ch £3.50). Family £17.80. Garden, Restaurant & Shop: £4, (ch £2). Family £10
Facilities: P ✗ licensed & (Braille guides, audio tapes, 2 manual wheelchairs) toilets for disabled shop 🐕 (ex guide dogs) 🎗 🖼

SOUDLEY — Map 03 SO61
DEAN HERITAGE CENTRE
Camp Mill GL14 2UB
➲ (on B4227, in Forest of Dean)
☎ 01594 822170   **2 for 1**
e-mail: deanmuse@btinternet.com
web: www.deanheritagemuseum.com
The Centre tells the story of this unique area, and its people, from pre-historic times to present day. Displays include a reconstructed cottage, a working beam engine from Lightmore Colliery, charcoal burners camp and art gallery. There are also nature trails with animals. There is an adventure playground that includes a maze and swing bridge. Library and research facilities are available by appointment. Annual events include the Sheep Fair in April and a Herb Day in July.
Times: Open all year, daily, British Winter 10-4, British Summer 10-5.30. Closed 24-26 Dec & 1 Jan. **Fee:** ✱ £4.50 (ch £2.50, under 5's free, pen & concessions £3.50). Family ticket £13. **Facilities:** 🅿 🅿 ⓰ (lift, ramps, help from establishment staff) toilets for disabled shop ✖ (ex guide dogs) ⬛

TETBURY — Map 03 ST89
CHAVENAGE HOUSE
GL8 8XP
➲ (2m NW of Tetbury signed off B4014. 7m SE of Stroud, signed off A46)
☎ 01666 502329 & 01453 832700   **2 for 1**
e-mail: info@chavenage.com
web: www.chavenage.com
Built in 1576, this unspoilt Elizabethan house contains stained glass from the 16th-century and earlier with some good furniture and tapestries. The owner during the Civil War was a Parliamentarian, and the house contains Cromwellian relics. In more recent years, the house has been the location for *Grace and Favour*, *Poirot*, *The House of Elliot*, *Berkeley Square*, *Casualty* and *Cider with Rosie*. Tours of the house are enlivened by ghost stories.
Times: Open May-Sep, Thu, Sun & BHs 2-5. Also Etr Sun & Mon. Other days by appointment only. **Fee:** £6 (ch £3).
Facilities: 🅿 ⓰ ✖ (ex guide dogs)

ULEY — Map 03 ST79
ULEY LONG BARROW (HETTY PEGLER'S TUMP)
➲ (3.5m NE of Dursley on B4066)   **FREE**
This 180ft Neolithic long barrow is popularly known as Hetty Pegler's Tump. The mound, surrounded by a wall, is about 85ft wide. It contains a stone central passage, and three burial chambers.
Times: Open at any reasonable time.

> An asterisk * indicates that opening times and prices are for 2005. Please contact the attraction for up-to-date information.

WESTBURY ON SEVERN — Map 03 SO71
WESTBURY COURT GARDEN
GL14 1PD
➲ (9m SW of Gloucester on A48)
☎ 01452 760461
e-mail: westburycourt@nationaltrust.org.uk
web: www.nationaltrust.org.uk
This formal water garden with canals and yew hedges was laid out between 1696 and 1705. It is the earliest of its kind remaining in England and was restored in 1971 and planted with species dated pre-1700, including apple, pear and plum trees.
Times: ✱ Open 10-5, Mar-Jun Wed-Sun, Jul-Aug daily, Sep-Oct Wed-Sun. Nov-Feb by appointment. **Fee:** ✱ £3.75 (ch £1.85)
Facilities: 🅿 ⓰ (Braille guide, w/chair available) toilets for disabled shop ✖ (ex guide dogs) ⬛

WESTONBIRT — Map 03 ST88
WESTONBIRT THE NATIONAL ARBORETUM
GL8 8QS
➲ (3m S Tetbury on A433)
☎ 01666 880220
web: www.westonbirtarboretum.com
Begun in 1829, this arboretum contains one of the finest and most important collections of trees and shrubs in the world. There are 18,000 specimens, planted from 1829 to the present day, covering 600 acres of landscaped Cotswold countryside. Magnificent displays of Rhododendrons, Azaleas, Magnolias and wild flowers, and ablaze with colour in the autumn from the national collection of Japanese Maples.
Times: Open all year, daily 10-8 or sunset. Visitor centre & shop all year. Closed Xmas & New Year. **Fee:** ✱ Mar-Nov £6.50 Family ticket £15. Nov-Mar £5 (pen £4) Family ticket £11. Apr-Jun £6 (pen £5) Family ticket £12 **Facilities:** 🅿 🅿 ✖ licensed ⓰ (electric & manual wheelchair for loan, telephone to book) toilets for disabled shop garden centre ⬛

WINCHCOMBE — Map 04 SP02
SUDELEY CASTLE & GARDENS
GL54 5JD
➲ (B4632 to Winchcombe, Castle is signed from town)
☎ 01242 602308
e-mail: enquiries@sudeley.org.uk
web: www.sudeleycastle.co.uk
Sudeley Castle was home to Katherine Parr, who is buried in the Chapel. Henry VIII, Anne Boleyn, Lady Jane Grey and Elizabeth I all stayed or visited here; and it was the headquarters of Prince Rupert during the Civil War. The Queen's Garden is famous for its rose collection, there are exhibitions and a children's adventure playground.
Times: Open daily Mar-Oct, Grounds, Gardens, Exhibitions, Shop & Plant Centre 10.30-5.30. **Fee:** ✱ £7.20 (conc £6.20, ch 5-15 £4.20). Group 20+ £6.20 (conc £5.20, ch £4.20). Seasonal pricing on Sun & BHs between 2 May-31 Aug **Facilities:** 🅿 ✖ licensed 📷 ⓰ (limited access to gardens only, parking) toilets for disabled shop garden centre ✖ (by request on arrival) ⬛

GREATER MANCHESTER

EVENTS & FESTIVALS

January
29th Chinese New Year Celebrations, parade from Town Hall to Chinatown

June
2nd-4th Garden of Delights, magical environment, Platt Fields Park, Fallowfield
tbc Greater Manchester Youth Games, Robin Park Stadium, Wigan (provisional)

July
1st Unity Festival, Chorlton Park, Manchester, celebrating diversity
22nd-23rd Chadkirk Festival, Stockport, music and entertainment (provisional)
21st-29th Manchester Jazz Festival, various venues including outdoors (provisional)
tbc Manchester Mega Mela, Platt Fields Park, Rusholme, Manchester, celebration of Asian Culture
tbc Manchester Theatre Festival, various venues
tbc Quays Festival, a celebration of all things aquatic, Salford Quays

August
18th-28th Manchester Pride, city centre
tbc Bolton Festival, a wide range of activities and performances
tbc Caribbean Carnival, Alexandra Park, Manchester
tbc Salford Show, horticultural show and fairground at Buile Hill Park, Salford

September
tbc In the City, international music convention, various venues

October
tbc Manchester International Literary Festival

Above: A stained glass window inside the Church of St Michael in Ashton-under-Lyne

ALTRINCHAM   Map 07 SJ78

DUNHAM MASSEY
WA14 4SJ
➲ (3m SW of Altrincham (off A56), off M6 junct 19 or off M56 junct 7, then follow brown signs)
☎ 0161 941 1025
e-mail: dunhammassey@nationaltrust.org.uk
web: www.nationaltrust.org.uk

A fine 18th-century house, garden and park, home of the Earls of Stamford until 1976. The house contains fine furniture and silverware, and some thirty rooms, including the library, billiard room, fully-equipped kitchen, butler's pantry and laundry. The garden is on an ancient site with waterside plantings, mixed borders and fine lawns. There is also a 300 acre deer park. Telephone for details of special events.

Times: Open: Park, restaurant & shop open all year. House open 19 Mar-30 Oct, 12-5 (11 Sun & BH Mon, closes at 4 during late Oct). Garden, 11-5.30 (closes 4.30 in late Oct). Last entry to house 30mins before closing time. **Fee:** ✱ House & Garden £6.50 (ch £3.25). House only £4.50 (ch £2.25). Garden only £4.50 (ch £2.25). Family ticket £16.25. Park only, £3.80 per car. £1 per motorbike

Facilities: ◘ (charged) ✗ licensed ⓑ (wheelchairs, lift, Braille & large print guide, parking) toilets for disabled shop ✖ (ex on lead in park) ⓧ ◀

ASHTON-UNDER-LYNE   Map 07 SJ99

CENTRAL ART GALLERY
Central Library Building, Old St OL6 7SG
☎ 0161 342 2650   `FREE`
e-mail: central.artgallery@tameside.gov.uk
web: www.tameside.gov.uk

Set in a fine Victorian Gothic building, the Central Art Gallery has three areas, each of which offers a varied programme of temporary exhibitions. A range of tastes and styles are covered, with group and solo shows of work by artists from the region including paintings, sculpture, installation and textiles.

Times: ✱ Open all year, Tue, Wed & Fri 10-12.30 & 1-5; Thu 1-7.30 & Sat 9-12.30 & 1-4. **Facilities:** ◘ (100mtrs) (pay and display) ▦ ⓑ (induction loop) toilets for disabled shop ✖ (ex guide dogs)

MUSEUM OF THE MANCHESTER REGIMENT
The Town Hall, Market Place OL6 6DL
➲ (in town centre, on market square, follow signs for museum)
☎ 0161 342 3078 & 0161 342 3710   `FREE`
e-mail: portland.basin@tameside.gov.uk
web: www.tameside.gov.uk

The social and regimental history of the Manchesters is explored at this museum, tracing the story back to its origins in the 18th century. The Manchesters fought in both World Wars, the Boer War, and the Crimea.

Times: Open all year, Mon-Sat, 10-4. (Closed Sun).
Facilities: ◘ (50yds) (pay & display) ⓑ toilets for disabled shop ✖ (ex guide dogs)

PORTLAND BASIN MUSEUM

Portland Place OL7 0QA

➲ (M60 junct 23 into Ashton town centre. Museum is near Cross Hill Street & car park)

☎ 0161 343 2878 **FREE**

e-mail: portland.basin@tameside.gov.uk

web: www.tameside.gov.uk

Exploring the social and industrial history of Tameside, this museum is part of the recently rebuilt Ashton Canal Warehouse, built in 1834. Visitors can walk around a 1920s street, dress up in old hats and gloves, steer a virtual canal boat, and see the original canal powered waterwheel that once drove the warehouse machinery. Portland Basin Museum also features changing exhibitions and event programme- so there's always something new to see!

Times: Open all year, Tue-Sun 10-5. (Closed Mon, ex BHs)

Facilities: 🅿 ☕ 🗎 ♿ (wheelchair, lift, loop system) toilets for disabled shop ✖ (ex guide dogs) 🛝

BRAMHALL   Map 07 SJ88

BRAMALL HALL & PARK

SK7 3NX

➲ (from A6 right at Blossoms public house through Davenport village then right - signed)

☎ 0161 485 3708 **2 for 1**

e-mail: bramall.hall@stockport.gov.uk

web: www.bramallhall.org.uk

This large timber-framed hall dates from the 14th century, and is one of the finest black-and-white houses in the North West. It has rare 16th-century wall paintings and period furniture, and was the home of the Davenport family for 500 years. Much of the house is open to the public and available for hire. Open air concerts and plays are a feature in summer.

Times: Open all year, Good Fri-Sep, daily 1-5 & BHs 11-5; Oct-1 Jan, Tue-Sun 1-4 & BHs 11-4; 2 Jan-Good Fri Sat & Sun 12-4. Closed 25-26 Dec. **Fee:** ✱ £3.95 (concessions £2.50). Family ticket £11.

Facilities: 🅿 (charged) ☕ 🗎 ♿ (access for wheelchair users) toilets for disabled shop ✖ (ex guide dogs) 🛝

MANCHESTER   Map 07 SJ89

GALLERY OF COSTUME

Platt Hall, Rusholme M14 5LL

➲ (situated in Platt Fields Park, Rusholme, access from Wilmslow Rd. 2m S of city centre)

☎ 0161 224 5217 **FREE**

e-mail: a.jarvis@notes.manchester.gov.uk

With one of the most comprehensive costume collections in Great Britain, this gallery makes captivating viewing. Housed in a fine Georgian mansion, the displays focus on the changing styles of everyday fashion and accessories over the last 400 years. Contemporary fashion is also illustrated. Because of the vast amount of material in the collection, no one period is permanently illustrated.

Times: Open to public on last Sat of month. Mon-Fri by appointment, please ring 0161 224 5217 **Facilities:** 🅿 ♿ shop ✖ (ex guide dogs)

Directions are provided by the attractions.

IMPERIAL WAR MUSEUM NORTH

The Quays, Trafford Wharf Rd, Trafford Park M17 1TZ

➲ (M60 junct 9, join Parkway (A5081) towards Trafford Park. At 1st island take 3rd exit onto Village Way. At next island take 2nd exit onto Warren Bruce Rd. Right at T-junct onto Trafford Wharf Rd. Alternatively, leave M602 junct 2 and follow signs)

☎ 0161 836 4000 **FREE**

e-mail: info@iwmnorth.org.uk

web: www.iwm.org.uk

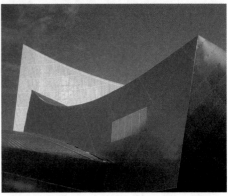

This recently-opened war museum is built to resemble three shards of a shattered globe, representing conflict on land, sea, and in the air. Inside are thousands of exhibits, interactive sessions, performances, and recreations that explore the way that 20th and 21st century conflict has shaped our lives.

Times: Open daily Mar-Oct 10-6, Nov-Feb 10-5. Closed 24-26 Dec. **Facilities:** 🅿 (charged) ✖ licensed ♿ (lifts, parking, wheelchairs, Braille sign in lift) toilets for disabled shop ✖ (ex guide dogs)

MANCHESTER ART GALLERY

Mosley St/Princess St M2 3JL

➲ (from M60 follow signs to city centre)

☎ 0161 235 8888 **FREE**

web: www.manchestergalleries.org

Manchester Art Gallery houses the city's magnificent art collection and a lively programme of exhibitions and events in stunning Victorian surroundings.

Times: Open Tue-Sun, 10-5 (closed Mon except BH). Closed Good Fri, 24-26 & 31 Dec & 1 Jan. **Facilities:** 🅿 (NCP-5 mins walk) ☕ ✖ 🗎 ♿ toilets for disabled shop ✖ (ex guide dogs)

MANCHESTER MUSEUM

The University, Oxford Rd M13 9PL

➲ (S of city centre on B5117)

☎ 0161 275 2634 0161 275 2643 **FREE**

e-mail: anna.j.davey@man.ac.uk

web: www.museum.man.ac.uk

The Manchester Museum has leading research facilities and collections in archaeology, botany, Egyptology, ethnology, mineralogy, numismatics, and zoology, among others. There are large galleries devoted to most of these departments, but the Egyptology collection is particularly impressive, and includes mummies excavated by Sir William Flinders Petrie.

Times: Open all year, Mon-Sat 10-5, Sun & BHs 11-4.

Facilities: 🅿 (charged) ☕ 🗎 ♿ (lift access, hearing loop, accessible parking) toilets for disabled shop ✖ (ex guide dogs) 🛝

MANCHESTER UNITED MUSEUM & TOUR CENTRE

Sir Matt Busby Way, Old Trafford M16 0RA
➲ (2m from city centre, off A56)
☎ 0870 442 1994
e-mail: tours@manutd.co.uk
web: www.manutd.com

This museum was opened in 1986 and is the first purpose-built British football museum. It covers the history of Manchester United in words, pictures, sound and vision, from its inception in 1878 to the present day.
Times: Open daily 9.30-5 (open until 30mins before kick off on match days). Closed some days over Xmas & New Year. **Fee:** ✱ Stadium tour & Museum: £9 (ch & pen £6) Family ticket £25. Museum only: £5.50 (ch & pen £3.75) Family ticket £15.50. **Facilities:** 🅿 ✕ licensed 🗐 ⓓ (w/chair, audio visual scripts) toilets for disabled shop ✈ (ex guide dogs) 🍴

THE MUSEUM OF SCIENCE AND INDUSTRY IN MANCHESTER

Liverpool Rd, Castlefield M3 4FP
➲ (follow brown tourist signs from city centre)
☎ 0161 832 2244 & 832 1830
e-mail: marketing@msim.org.uk
web: www.msim.org.uk

FREE

This museum is housed in the buildings of the world's oldest passenger railway station. Colourful galleries packed full of fascinating facts and amazing artefacts bring the past to life. Walk away from your own shadow in Xperiment! The mind bending science centre, see wheels of industry turning in the

continued

Power Hall, and the planes that made flying history in the Air and Space Hall. A programme of changing exhibitions.
Times: Open all year, daily 10-5. Last admission 4.30. Closed 24-26 Dec. (Extended hrs for some special events) **Facilities:** 🅿 (charged) 🍽 ✕ licensed ⓓ (lifts, wheelchair loan service) toilets for disabled shop ✈ (ex guide dogs) 🍴

MUSEUM OF TRANSPORT

Boyle St, Cheetham M8 8UW
➲ (museum adjacent to Queens Rd bus depot. 1.25m N of city centre on Boyle St)
☎ 0161 205 2122
e-mail: Gmts.enquire@btinternet.com
web: www.gmts.co.uk

2 for 1

This museum is a must-see for fans of public transport! Among the many interesting exhibits are more than 80 beautifully restored buses and coaches from the region - the biggest collection in the UK. Displays of old photographs, tickets and other memorabilia complement the vehicles, some of which date back to 1890. Please telephone for details of special events.
Times: Open all year Mar-Oct, 10-5; Nov-Feb, 10-4; Wed, Sat, Sun & BH ex Xmas **Fee:** £4 (ch u5 free, ch 5-15 & concessions £2, registered disabled, UB40 free). Family ticket £10 (2ad+3ch). **Facilities:** 🅿 🍽 🗐 ⓓ toilets for disabled shop 🍴

See advertisement on opposite page

URBIS

Cathedral Gardens M4 3BG
➲ (next to Victoria Railway Station)
☎ 0161 907 9099
e-mail: info@urbis.org.uk
web: www.urbis.org.uk

FREE

Urbis explores the dynamic culture of the modern city. The top three floors of interactive exhibits explore cities around the world from Tokyo to Paris, revealing how different cities work, how they change and how they affect others.
Times: Open Tues-Sun 10-6 & BHs **Facilities:** 🅿 (200yds) 🍽 ✕ licensed 🗐 ⓓ toilets for disabled shop ✈ (ex guide dogs) 🍴

> If an attraction name appears in *italics*, details have not been confirmed for 2006.

THE WHITWORTH ART GALLERY

The University of Manchester, Oxford Rd M15 6ER
➲ (follow brown tourist signs, on Oxford Rd
(B5117) to S of city centre. Gallery in Whitworth
Park, opp Manchester Royal Infirmary)
☎ 0161 275 7450   FREE
e-mail: whitworth@manchester.ac.uk
web: www.manchester.ac.uk/whitworth

The gallery houses an impressive range of modern and
historic drawings, prints, paintings and sculpture, as well as
the largest collection of textiles and wallpapers outside
London and an internationally famous collection of British
watercolours. The gallery hosts an innovative programme of
touring exhibitions. A selection of tour lectures, workshops
and concerts complement the exhibition programme.
Times: Open Mon-Sat 10-5, Sun 2-5. Closed Good Fri & Xmas-New
Year. **Facilities:** ⯃ 💺 ♿ (wheelchair available, induction loop,
Braille lift buttons) toilets for disabled shop ✖ (ex guide dogs)

PRESTWICH   Map 07 SD80

HEATON HALL

Heaton Park M25 2SW
☎ 0161 773 1231 or 0161 234 1456   FREE
Designed by James Wyatt for Sir Thomas Egerton in 1772,
the house has magnificent period interiors decorated with
fine plasterwork, paintings and furniture. Other attractions
include a unique circular room with Pompeian-style
paintings, and the original Samuel Green organ still in
working order.
Times: Open Etr-end Oct, but phone for time details on 0161-234
1456. **Facilities:** ⯃ (charged) ♿ (occasional 'touch tours'. Phone for
details) toilets for disabled shop ✖ (ex guide dogs)

SALFORD   Map 07 SJ89

THE LOWRY

Pier Eight, Salford Quays M50 3AZ
➲ (M60 junct 12 for M602. Salford Quays is 0.25m
from junct 3 of M602, follow brown Lowry signs)
☎ 0870 787 5774
e-mail: info@thelowry.com
web: www.thelowry.com

The Lowry is an award-winning building housing galleries,
shops, cafés and a restaurant, plus two theatres showing
everything from West End plays and musicals, comedians,
ballet and live bands. With regular family activity too, you
can make a whole day of your visit.
Times: ✱ Open daily from 10. Galleries, Sun-Fri from 11, Sat from 10.
Closed 25 Dec. **Facilities:** ⯃ (charged) 💺 ✖ licensed 🗐
♿ (Sennheiser System) toilets for disabled shop
✖ (ex guide dogs) 🍴

SALFORD MUSEUM & ART GALLERY

Peel Park, Crescent M5 4WU
➲ (from N leave M60 junct 13, A666. From S
follow signs from end of M602. Museum on A6)
☎ 0161 736 2649   FREE
e-mail: salford.museum@salford.gov.uk
web: www.salfordmuseum.org

The museum features a reconstruction of a 19th-20th
century northern street with original shop fronts. Upstairs in
the galleries there are temporary exhibitions and a gallery
displaying paintings, sculptures and ceramics. Recent
additions include the lifetimes gallery, featuring audio, IT
continued

MUSEUM of TRANSPORT

Boyle Street, Cheetham, Manchester M8 8UW
Tel: 0161 205 2122   Fax: 0161 202 1110
web: www.manchester.bus.museum

A trip down memory lane

Over 80 buses, coaches and trams representing
over a century of road public transport in
Greater Manchester.

Special events including a Vintage vehicle rally,
themed displays, a weekend for people with
disabilities and participation in the National
Heritage Weekend.

The Museum has tearooms, shop, facilities for
the disabled. A small exhibits area and archive.

zones, temporary exhibitions, a spectacular Pilkington's
display and lots of hands-on activities and dressing up areas
Times: Open all year Mon-Fri 10-4.45, Sat & Sun 1-5. Closed Good Fri,
Etr Sat, 25 & 26 Dec, 1 Jan. **Facilities:** ⯃ 💺 🗐 ♿ (Braille & large
print labels & visitor packs, hearing loop) toilets for disabled shop
✖ (ex guide dogs) 🍴

STALYBRIDGE   Map 07 SJ99

ASTLEY CHEETHAM ART GALLERY

Trinity St GK15 2BN
☎ 0161 338 6767   FREE
e-mail: astley.cheetham@tameside.gov.uk
web: www.tameside.gov.uk

Built as a gift to the town in 1901 by mill owner John
Frederick Cheetham, this one-time lecture hall has been an
art gallery since 1932 when Cheetham left his collection to
the town. Among the works are Italian paintings from the
Renaissance, British masters such as Cox and Burne-Jones,
and more recent gifts such as works by Turner and local
artist Harry Rutherford. The gallery hosts a programme of
temporary exhibitions of the collection and regional artists,
and a variety of workshops are run for families throughout
the year.
Times: ✱ Open all year, Mon-Wed & Fri 10-12.30, 1-5; Sat 9-12.30,
1-4. **Facilities:** ⯃ (2hrs on street parking) 🗐 (induction loop) shop
✖ (ex guide dogs)

STOCKPORT   Map 07 SJ89

HAT WORKS MUSEUM

Wellington Mill, Wellington Rd South SK3 0EU

➲ (M60 junct 1, follow signs for town centre.
Museum opp bus station)

☎ 0161 355 7770/6

e-mail: bookings.hatworks@stockport.gov.uk

web: www.hatworks.org.uk

Hat Works is the UK's only museum of the hatting industry,
hats and headwear, offering an insight into a once
flourishing industry. See how hats are made with a unique
working collection of Victorian millinery machinery and take
a tour with expert guides who will give visitors an insight
into the Hatter's World. Browse an extensive collection of
hats before relaxing in the Level 2 café.

Times: Open daily Mon-Fri 10-5, Sat, Sun & BHs 1-5. (Telephone for
Xmas opening times) **Fee:** ✱ (charges apply for guided tours,
organised group visits and special events) **Facilities:** P 5min walk
(limited pay & display parking) 🅿 📱 ♿ toilets for disabled shop
✈ (ex guide dogs) 🍴

UPPERMILL   Map 07 SD90

SADDLEWORTH MUSEUM & ART GALLERY

High St OL3 6HS

➲ (M62 E junct 22 or M62 W junct 21. On A670)

☎ 01457 874093

e-mail: curator@saddleworthmuseum.co.uk

web: www.saddleworthmuseum.co.uk

Based in an old mill building next to the Huddersfield canal,
the museum explores the history of the Saddleworth area.
Wool weaving is the traditional industry, displayed in the
18th-century Weaver's Cottage and the Victoria Mill Gallery.
The textile machinery is run regularly by arrangement. The
Art Gallery has regular exhibitions.

Times: Open all year, Nov-late Mar, daily 1-4; late Mar-Oct, Mon-Sat
10-5, Sun 12-5. Closed 24-25 Dec & 31 Dec-1 Jan. **Fee:** Museum - £2
(concessions £1) Family ticket £4. Art gallery - free **Facilities:** P 📱
♿ (stairlift, ramps, Braille & large print guides, wheelchair) toilets for
disabled shop ✈ (ex guide dogs)

WIGAN   Map 07 SD50

WIGAN PIER

Wallgate WN3 4EU

➲ (follow brown tourist signs from M6 junct 25-
27/M61 junct 6-8)

☎ 01942 323666

e-mail: wiganpier@wlct.org

web: www.wiganpier.net

2 for 1

Wigan Pier is a journey never to be forgotten. Part museum,
part theatre, Wigan Pier is a mixture of entertainment and
education. Step back in time at 'The Way We Were' heritage
centre, visit the world's largest original mill steam engine, or
enjoy trips along the Leeds-Liverpool canal, walks in the
grounds, or events from a regular programme.

Times: Open all year, Mon-Thu 10-5; Sun 11-5. Closed every Fri & Sat,
25-26 Dec & 1 Jan. **Fee:** £5.25 (concessions £4.25) **Facilities:** P 📱
♿ (Braille guide, audio tape, large text leaflet, minicom) toilets for
disabled shop ✈ (ex guide dogs) 🍴

HAMPSHIRE

EVENTS & FESTIVALS

April
8th-9th Brunel Celebrations,
    Portsmouth Historic Dockyard
13th-17th Gosport & Fareham Easter Folk
    Festival, Fareham

May
1st-3rd Heavy Horse Show, Castle Field and
    Southsea Common

June
tbc Power in the Park, pop concert,
    Southampton Common
tbc Southampton Beer Festival

July
15th Sport Relief Mile Race, Southampton
17th-23rd Farnborough International Airshow,
    Farnborough Airfield
21st-23rd Netley Marsh Steam Engine Rally,
    Netley Marsh, Southampton (provisional)
tbc Hat Fair, Winchester, the oldest street
    theatre fair in England
tbc New Forest Show
tbc Southampton Balloon & Flower Festival,
    The Common, Southampton
tbc Winchester Festival (multi-arts festival)

August
4th-6th Portsmouth & Southsea Show,
    Southsea Common
5th Bournemouth Regatta (provisional)
26th-28th Kite Festival, Southsea Common
tbc Eastleigh Festival, Fleming Park, Eastleigh

September
9th Romsey Show, Broadlands Park, Romsey
15th-24th Southampton International Boat
    Show, Mayflower Park, Southampton

October
7th Mini & Junior Great South Run,
    Portsmouth
8th Great South Run, Southsea Seafront

November
24th-27th A Festival of Christmas, Naval Base
    Heritage Area, Portsmouth

*Above: A sailing lesson under the Itchen Bridge,
Southampton*

ALDERSHOT　　　　Map 04 SU85

AIRBORNE FORCES MUSEUM

Browning Barracks, Queens Av GU11 2BU

➲ (M3 take A325 to Aldershot then next left)

☎ 01252 349619

The museum traces the history of the Parachute Regiment and British Airborne Forces since 1940. Using weapons, equipment, dioramas and briefing models it depicts the story of airborne actions such as the early raids, D-Day, Arnhem, the Rhine Crossing, and post-war campaigns such as Suez, the Falklands and Kosovo.

Times: Open all year, Mon-Fri 10-4.30 (last admission 3.45), Sat-Sun & BH 10-4. Closed Xmas. **Fee:** £3 (ch, pen & former members of the Regiment £1, under 5's free) **Facilities:** 🅿 ♿ (wheelchair ramps) shop 🗙 (ex guide dogs)

ALDERSHOT MILITARY MUSEUM

Evelyn Woods Rd, Queens Av GU11 2LG

➲ (A331 exit for 'Aldershot Military Town (North)', attraction near to North Camp)

☎ 01252 314598

e-mail: sally.l.day@hants.gov.uk

web: www.hants.gov.uk/museum/aldershot

2 for 1

Follow the development of the 'Home of the British army' and the 'Birthplace of British aviation' through brand new displays. Also discover the fascinating local history of Aldershot and Farnborough including British first powered flight.

Times: Open Mar-Oct, daily 10-5; Nov-Feb, daily 10-5. **Fee:** ✱ £2 (ch & unemployed £1, pen £1.50) **Facilities:** 🅿 🗊 ♿ shop 🗙 (ex guide dogs)

AMPFIELD　　　　Map 04 SU42

THE SIR HAROLD HILLIER GARDENS

Jermyns Ln SO51 OQA

➲ (3m NE of Romsey, signed off A3090 & A3057)

☎ 01794 368787

e-mail: info@hilliergardens.org.uk

web: www.hilliergardens.org.uk

2 for 1

Established in 1953, this 180-acre public garden comprises the greatest collection of hardy trees and shrubs in the world. A garden for all seasons with stunning range of seasonal colour and interest and featuring eleven national plant collections. Champion trees, the Gurkha Memorial Garden and the largest Winter Garden in Europe.

Times: Open all year, daily, 10.30-6 (or dusk if earlier). Closed 25-26 Dec. **Fee:** £7 (ch under 16 free, concessions £6).

Facilities: 🅿 🗙 licensed ♿ (all ability path) toilets for disabled shop garden centre 🗙 (ex guide dogs)

ANDOVER　　　　Map 04 SU34

FINKLEY DOWN FARM PARK

SP11 6NF

➲ (signed from A303 & A343, 1.5m N of A303 & 2m E of Andover)

☎ 01264 352195

e-mail: admin@finkleydownfarm.co.uk

web: www.finkleydownfarm.co.uk

This fun family farm park is jam packed with things to do. You can join in with feeding time, groom a pony, cuddle a rabbit, or collect duck eggs. Lots of activities are scheduled throughout the day, or kids can just let off steam in the playground or on the trampolines. From chipmunks to

continued

chinchillas, pygmy goats to peacocks, and lambs to llamas, Finkley Down Farm has something for everyone!

Times: Open mid Mar-Oct, daily 10-6. Last admission 5. **Fee:** ✱ £5.50 (ch £4.50, pen £5). Family ticket £19 (2ad+2ch). **Facilities:** 🅿 🔌 ♿ toilets for disabled shop 🗙 (ex guide dogs)

ASHURST　　　　Map 04 SU31

LONGDOWN DAIRY FARM

Longdown SO40 7EH

➲ (off A35 between Lyndhurst & Southampton)

☎ 023 8029 3326

e-mail: enquiries@longdownfarm.co.uk

web: www.longdownfarm.co.uk

Fun for all the family with a variety of hands-on activities every day, including small animal handling and bottle feeding calves and goat kids. Indoor and outdoor play areas, with trampolines and ball pools. Land Rover driving for adults, pedal tractors for children. Tearoom, picnic area and excellent gift shop.

Times: Open Feb-Dec, daily 10-5. **Fee:** ✱ £5.50 (ch 3-14 & pen £4.50). Saver ticket £19 (2ad+2ch). **Facilities:** 🅿 🔌 ♿ (concrete path for wheelchairs) toilets for disabled shop 🗙 (kennels provided) 🔌

AVINGTON　　　　Map 04 SU53

AVINGTON PARK

SO21 1DB

➲ (off B3047 at Itchen Abbas between Winchester and Alresford. 4m from both on River Itchen)

☎ 01962 779260

e-mail: enquiries@avingtonpark.co.uk

web: www.avingtonpark.co.uk

Avington is a charming hamlet in the Itchen Valley, and Avington Park is its great house, a 17th-century Palladian mansion built largely of red brick. Standing in wooded parkland with a lake, with interior paintings and gildings, and two very unusual 19th-century wrought iron conservatories.

Times: Open May-Sep, Sun, BHs 2.30-5.30 & Mon in Aug **Fee:** ✱ £4 **Facilities:** 🅿 🔌 ♿ toilets for disabled (on leads)

BASINGSTOKE   Map 04 SU65

MILESTONES - HAMPSHIRE'S LIVING HISTORY MUSEUM

Basingstoke Leisure Park, Churchill Way West RG21 6YR
➲ (M3 junct 6, take ringway road (West) and follow brown signs for Leisure Park)
☎ 01256 477766
e-mail: jane.holmes@hants.gov.uk
web: www.milestones-museum.com

Milestones brings Hampshire's recent past to life through stunning period street scenes and exciting interactive areas, all under one roof. Nationally important collections of transport, technology and everyday life are presented in an entertaining way. Staff in period costumes, mannequins and sounds all bring the streets to life.
Times: Open Tue-Fri & BHs 10-5, Sat-Sun 11-5. Closed 25-26 Dec & 1 Jan. **Facilities:** 🅿 💺 📖 ♿ (induction loops, subtitles screens, scooters, wheelchairs) toilets for disabled shop ✖ (ex guide dogs) ▬

BEAULIEU   Map 04 SU30

BEAULIEU : NATIONAL MOTOR MUSEUM

SO42 7ZN
➲ (M27 junct 2, A326, B3054, then follow tourist signs)
☎ 01590 612345
e-mail: info@beaulieu.co.uk
web: www.beaulieu.co.uk
Set in the heart of William the Conqueror's New Forest, on the banks of the Beaulieu River, stands this 16th-century house. It has become most famous as the home of the National Motor Museum. The site also contains the picturesque abbey building ruins, which have an exhibition on life in the middle ages, and various family treasures and memorabilia. The new Secret Army Exhibition tells the story of the secret agents trained at the Beaulieu 'Finishing School' during WWII.
Times: Open all year - Palace House & Gardens, National Motor Museum, Beaulieu Abbey & Exhibition of Monastic Life, May-Sep 10-6; Oct-Apr 10-5. Closed 25 Dec. **Fee:** Please contact for current prices.
Facilities: 🅿 💺 📖 ♿ (ramp access, lift to upper level, induction loop) toilets for disabled shop ▬

BISHOP'S WALTHAM   Map 04 SU51

BISHOP'S WALTHAM PALACE

SO32 1DH
➲ (on A333)
☎ 01489 892460
Discover the medieval seat of the Bishops of Winchester. Enjoy the wonderful moated grounds and an exhibition about the powerful Winchester Bishops.
Times: Grounds only: May-Sep, 10-5, Mon-Fri. Farmhouse and Grounds, May-Sep, 10-5, Sun & BHs **Fee:** £2.60 (ch £1.30, concessions £2.00). Opening times and prices are subject to change, for further details please phone 0870 333 1181 **Facilities:** 🅿 ♿ shop ✖ (ex on lead in certain areas) ▤

BOLDRE   Map 04 SZ39

SPINNERS GARDEN AND NURSERY

School Ln SO41 5QE
➲ (off A337, between Brockenhurst & Lymington)
☎ 01590 673347
The garden has been entirely created by the owners since 1960. It has azaleas, rhododendrons, camellias, magnolias and Japanese Maples interspersed with a huge range of woodland and bog plants. The nursery is well known for its rare trees, shrubs and plants.
Times: Open Apr-mid Sep, daily 10-5. Other times on application. Mid Sep-Mar Nursery & part of garden open **Fee:** £2.50 (ch under 6 free). Nursery & part of garden, free (mid Sep-Mar) **Facilities:** 🅿 (help provided where possible) garden centre ✖ (ex guide dogs)

BREAMORE   Map 04 SU11

BREAMORE HOUSE & COUNTRYSIDE

SP6 2DF
➲ (turn off A338, between Salisbury & Fordingbridge and follow signs for 1m)
☎ 01725 512468   `2 for 1`
e-mail: breamore@ukonline.co.uk
web: www.breamorehouse.com
The handsome manor house was completed in around 1583 and has a fine collection of paintings, china and tapestries. The museum has good examples of steam engines, and uses reconstructed workshops and other displays to show how people lived and worked a century or so ago. There is also a children's playground.
Times: Open Apr, Tue, Sun & Etr, May-Jul & Sep, Tue-Thu & Sat, Sun & all BH; Aug, daily (ex Mon) 2-5.30 (Countryside Museum 1pm).
Fee: ✱ £6 (ch £4). Party £5 each. **Facilities:** 🅿 💺 📖 ♿ (ramps, parking, recorded message & book about 1st floor) toilets for disabled shop ✖ (ex guide dogs)

BUCKLER'S HARD   Map 04 SU40

BUCKLER'S HARD VILLAGE & MARITIME MUSEUM

SO42 7XB
➲ (M27 junct 2, A326, B3054 then follow tourist signs to Beaulieu & Buckler's Hard)
☎ 01590 616203
e-mail: info@bucklershard.co.uk
web: www.bucklershard.co.uk
An enticing port of call, the historic and picturesque shipbuilding village of Buckler's Hard is where ships from Nelson's fleet were built. After setting a course for the Buckler's Hard Story and authentically reconstructed 18th-century Historic Cottages savour the sight and sounds of the countryside on a ramble along the Riverside Walk or enjoy a *continued*

cruise on the Beaulieu River on 'Swiftsure' during the summer months.

Times: Open all year, Etr-Sep 10.30-5, winter 11-4. Closed 25 Dec.
Fee: Please contact for current prices. **Facilities:** 🅿 💺 ✘ licensed 🍴 ♿ toilets for disabled shop 🛍

BURGHCLERE   Map 04 SU46

SANDHAM MEMORIAL CHAPEL

RG20 9JT
➲ (4m S Newbury, 0.5m E of A34. Follow signs to Highclere/Burghclere, then brown signs to Sandham Memorial Chapel)
☎ 01635 278394
e-mail: sandham@nationaltrust.org.uk
web: www.nationaltrust.org.uk/sandham

This red brick chapel was built in the 1920s for the artist Stanley Spencer to fill with paintings inspired by his experiences in WWI. Influenced by Giotto's Arena Chapel in Padua, Spencer took 5 years to complete what is arguably his finest achievement. The chapel is set amongst lawns and orchards with views over Watership Down.

Times: Open 23 Mar-Oct, Wed-Sun, & BH Mon. Wknds in early Mar & Nov open 11-4, Dec-Feb by arrangement. **Fee:** ✱ £3 (ch £1.50). **Facilities:** 🅿 (20yds) 🍴 ♿ (Braille guide, large print guide, hearing loop, ramps) ✘ (ex assist dogs) 🐾

CHAWTON   Map 04 SU73

JANE AUSTEN'S HOUSE

GU34 1SD
➲ (1m SW of Alton, in centre of village)
☎ 01420 83262
e-mail: enquiries@
jane-austens-house-museum.org.uk
web: www.jane-austens-house-museum.org.uk

Jane Austen lived and wrote here from 1809 to 1817. Restored to look as it would have done in the early 1800s, with items such as the author's donkey cart and writing table to be seen.

Times: ✱ Open daily Mar-Nov; Dec-Feb wknds only. Also open 27 Dec-1 Jan & Feb half term. **Facilities:** 🅿 (100yds) 🍴 ♿ (wheelchair ramp) toilets for disabled shop ✘ (ex guide dogs & service dogs) 🛍

EXBURY   Map 04 SU40

EXBURY GARDENS & RAILWAY

Exbury Estate Office SO45 1AZ
➲ (from M27 W junct 2, 3m from Beaulieu, off B3054)
☎ 023 8089 1203
e-mail: nigel.philpott@exbury.co.uk   **2 for 1**
web: www.exbury.co.uk

A 200-acre landscaped woodland garden on the east bank of the Beaulieu River, with one of the finest collections of rhododendrons, azaleas, camellias and magnolias in the world - as well as many rare and beautiful shrubs and trees. A labyrinth of tracks and paths enable you to explore the beautiful gardens and walks. Year round interest is ensured in various parts of the gardens and a steam railway has several features. 2-for-1 voucher does not apply during April and May.

Times: Open 26 Feb-6 Nov, daily 10-5.30; Santa Steam Specials 10-11,17-20 Dec **Fee:** ✱ £5-£7 (ch under 3 free, ch 3-15 £1-£1.50, pen £4.50-£6.50, £6 Tue-Thu). Railway £2.50-£3. **Facilities:** 🅿 ✘ licensed ♿ (free wheelchair loans & access maps, buggy tours £3.50) toilets for disabled shop garden centre 🛍

FAREHAM   Map 04 SU50

ROYAL ARMOURIES FORT NELSON

Portsdown Hill Rd PO17 6AN
➲ (from M27 junct 11, follow brown tourist signs for Royal Armouries).
☎ 01329 233734   **FREE**
e-mail: fnenquiries@armouries.org.uk
web: www.royalarmouries.org

Home to the Royal Armouries' collection of big guns, this superbly restored Victorian fort overlooks Portsmouth Harbour. Built in the 1860s to deter a threatened French invasion, there are secret tunnels, underground chambers and grass ramparts to explore with daily guided tours.

Times: Open Apr-Oct, daily 10-5 (Tue 11-5); Nov-Mar, daily 10.30-4 (Tue 11.30-4) **Facilities:** 🅿 💺 ♿ (access & audio guide, ramps, induction loop, wheelchair) toilets for disabled shop ✘ (ex guide & hearing dogs) 🛍

GOSPORT   Map 04 SZ69

EXPLOSION! MUSEUM OF NAVAL FIREPOWER

Priddy's Hard PO12 4LE
➲ (A32 and follow signs)
☎ 023 9250 5600   **2 for 1**
e-mail: info@explosion.org.uk
web: www.explosion.org.uk

Explosion! The Museum of Naval Firepower set in the green Heritage Area of Priddy's Hard in Gosport on the shores of Portsmouth Harbour, telling the story of naval firepower from the days of gunpowder to modern missiles. Come face to face with the atom bomb, the Exocet missile and the Gatling Gun and take a trip into the fascinating story of the men and women who supplied the Royal Navy. Walk around the buildings that were a state secret for 200 years and discover the Grand Magazine, an amazing vault once packed full with gunpowder, now a stunning multimedia film show.

Times: Open all year, Apr-Oct & all school hols, daily 10-5.30; Nov-Mar, Thu, Sat & Sun 10-4.30. Closed 24-26 Dec. **Fee:** ✱ £5 (ch £3.50, pen £4.50). Family ticket £15 **Facilities:** 🅿 💺 🍴 ♿ toilets for disabled shop ✘ (ex guide dogs) 🛍

Are there any excellent Days Out that we've missed? Use the Readers' Report form at the back of the book to tell us about them.

We endeavour to be as accurate as possible, but changes to times and other information can occur after the guide has gone to press.

ROYAL NAVY SUBMARINE MUSEUM & HMS ALLIANCE

Haslar Jetty Rd PO12 2AS

➲ (M27 junct 11, follow signs for Submarine Museum)

☎ 023 9252 9217 & 9251 0354

e-mail: rnsubs@rnsubmus.co.uk

web: www.rnsubs.co.uk

The great attraction of this museum is the chance to see inside a submarine, and there are guided tours of *HMS Alliance*, as well as displays exploring the development of submarines. Two periscopes from *HMS Conqueror* can be seen in the reconstruction of a nuclear submarine control room, giving panoramic views of Portsmouth Harbour. A new gallery shows the development of submarine weapons from the tiny torpedo to the huge polaris nuclear missile. The Navy's first submarine is back on display in a new gallery and exhibition space.

Times: ✱ Open all year, Apr-Oct 10-5.30; Nov-Mar 10-4.30. Closed 24 Dec-1 Jan. (Allow 3 hrs for visit. Last tour 1 hour before closing).
Facilities: ▣ ➟ ♿ (information in Braille, lift to upper gallery) toilets for disabled shop ✖ (ex guide dogs) ◼

HARTLEY WINTNEY   Map 04 SU75

WEST GREEN HOUSE GARDENS

West Green RG27 8JB

➲ (off A30, at Phoenix Green take sign to West Green, along Thackhams Lane. House last left)

☎ 01252 844611

The gardens are now considered to be one of the top 50 gardens in England and were the subject of a BBC television programme. Today the Queen Anne house is surrounded by four walled gardens, lakes, follies, the green theatre, nymphaeum, mixed border and potager. The owner is a noted garden writer and lecturer.

Times: Open Etr-Aug, Wed-Sun 11-4.30 & wknds in Sep **Fee:** £5 (ch 5yrs £2.50) **Facilities:** ▣ ✖ ♿ (most areas accessible) shop garden centre ✖ (ex guide dogs)

HAVANT   Map 04 SU70

STAUNTON COUNTRY PARK

Middle Park Way PO9 5HB

➲ (off B2149, between Havant & Horndean)

☎ 023 9245 3405   **2 for 1**

e-mail: amanda.fallbrown@hants.gov.uk

web: www.hants.gov.uk/staunton

This colourful Victorian Park offers a wonderful range of attractions for all age groups. Meet and feed the friendly

continued

animals at the Ornamental Farm where there is a broad range of animals from llama and shire horses to pigs and pigmy goats. Explore the Victorian tropical glasshouses with exotic flowers from around the world, including the giant Amazonian waterlily (summer months only). 1000 acres of parkland. With hidden follies to explore and an ornamental lake available for angling.

Times: Open 10-5 (4 winter). **Fees:** £4.60 (ch £3.50, concessions £4).
Facilities: ▣ ➟ ✖ ▤ ♿ (wheelchair for visitors, most areas accessible) toilets for disabled shop ✖ (dogs in parkland only) ◼

HIGHCLERE   Map 04 SU45

HIGHCLERE CASTLE & GARDENS

RG20 9RN

➲ (4.5m S of Newbury, off A34)

☎ 01635 253210   **2 for 1**

e-mail: theoffice@highclerecastle.co.uk

web: www.highclerecastle.co.uk

This splendid early Victorian mansion stands in beautiful parkland. It has sumptuous interiors and numerous Old Master pictures. Also shown are early finds by the 5th Earl of Carnarvon, one of the discoverers of Tutankhamun's tomb.

Times: Open early Jun-early Sep Mon-Fri; 2 BHs wknds in May, wknd mid Jun, Aug BH Mon 11-4 (last entry 3). Telephone 01635 253210 before travelling as Highclere Castle reserves the right to close at other times. **Fee:** ✱ £7.50 (ch 4-15 £4, concessions £6). Family ticket (2ad + 2ch or 1ad + 3ch) £18 Grounds & gardens only free.
Facilities: ▣ ➟ ✖ licensed ♿ (wheelchair available) toilets for disabled shop ✖ (ex guide dogs) ◼

HINTON AMPNER   Map 04 SU62

HINTON AMPNER GARDEN

SO24 0LA

➲ (off A272, 1m W of Bramdean)

☎ 01962 771305   **2 for 1**

e-mail: hintonampner@nationaltrust.org.uk

web: www.nationaltrust.org.uk

A masterpiece of design by Ralph Dutton, 8th and last Lord Sherborne, the 12 acre garden unites a formal layout with varied and informal plantings in pastel shades. There are magnificent vistas over 80 acres of parkland and rolling Hampshire countryside. The house, which is tenanted, contains Ralph Dutton's fine collection of Regency furniture, Italian paintings and hardstone items. 2-for-1 entry vouchers are only accepted during normal visiting hours and cannot be used for any ticketed events.

Times: Open Garden: Apr-Sep, Sat-Wed 12-5. House: Apr-Sep, Tue & Wed 1.30-5 (also Aug, Sat & Sun 1.30-5). **Fee:** ✱ House and Garden £6 (ch £3). Group £5.30 each. Garden only £5 (ch £2.50)
Facilities: ▣ ➟ ▤ ♿ (Braille guides, special parking, wheelchair loan) toilets for disabled ✖ (ex guide dogs) ✤

HURST CASTLE   Map 04 SZ38

HURST CASTLE

SO4 0FF

➲ (on Pebble Spit S of Keyhaven)

☎ 01590 642344

Built by Henry VIII, Hurst Castle was the pride of Tudor England's coastal defences. Crouched menacingly on a shingle spit, the castle has a fascinating history, including involvement in the smuggling trade in the 17th and 18th centuries.

Times: Open 25 Mar-Oct, daily 10.30-5. **Fee:** £3 (ch £1.80, concessions £2.70). Opening times and prices are subject to change, for further details please phone 0870 333 1181 **Facilities:** ➟ ✖ (ex on lead in certain areas)

LIPHOOK   Map 04 SU83
HOLLYCOMBE STEAM COLLECTION
Iron Hill, Midhurst Rd GU30 7LP
➲ (1m SE Liphook on Midhurst road, follow brown tourist signs)
☎ 01428 724900
e-mail: info@hollycombe.co.uk
web: www.hollycombe.co.uk

A comprehensive collection of working steam-power, including a large Edwardian fairground, three railways, one with spectacular views of the South Downs, traction engine hauled rides, steam agricultural machinery, pets corner, sawmill and even a paddle steamer engine.
Times: Open 2 Apr-8 Oct Sun & BHs, 30 Jul-28 Aug, daily 12-5
Fee: ✱ £8.50 (ch 3-15 & pen £7). **Facilities:** 🅿 💷 ♿ toilets for disabled shop ✖ (ex assist dogs) ➠

LYNDHURST   Map 04 SU30
NEW FOREST MUSEUM & VISITOR CENTRE
Main Car Park, High St SO43 7NY
➲ (leave M27 at Cadnam & follow A337 to Lyndhurst. Museum signed)
☎ 023 8028 3444
e-mail: office@newforestmuseum.org.uk
web: www.newforestmuseum.org.uk
The story of the New Forest - history, traditions, character and wildlife, told through an audio-visual show and exhibition displays. With life-size models of Forest characters, and the famous New Forest embroidery.
Times: Open all year daily, from 10. Closed 25 & 26 Dec. **Fee:** ✱ £3 (concessions £2.50). Family ticket (2ad+4ch) £9 , under 8yrs free.
Facilities: 🅿 (charged) 📖 ♿ (lift to 1st floor) toilets for disabled shop ➠

MARWELL   Map 04 SU52
MARWELL ZOOLOGICAL PARK
Colden Common SO21 1JH
➲ (M3 junct 11 or M27 junct 5. Zoo located on B2177, follow brown tourist signs)
☎ 01962 777407
e-mail: marwell@marwell.org.uk
web: www.marwell.org.uk
Marwell has over 200 species of rare and wonderful animals including tigers, snow leopards, rhino, meerkats, hippo and zebra. Highlights include The World of Lemurs, Encounter Village with unusual domesticated animals, Tropical World with its rainforest environment, Into Africa for giraffes and monkeys, Penguin World and Desert Carnivores. Recent additions include an exciting new snow leopard enclosure. Marwell is dedicated to saving endangered species and every visit helps conservation work. With road and rail trains, holiday activities, restaurant, gift shops and adventure playgrounds Marwell provides fun and interest for all ages.
Times: Open all year, daily 10-6 (summer), 10-4 (winter). (Last admission 90 min before closing). Closed 25 Dec. **Fee:** £11 (ch £8, pen £9.50). Family ticket (2ad+2ch) £36. **Facilities:** 🅿 💷 ✖ ♿ (wheelchairs & tours for visually impaired/disabled groups) toilets for disabled shop ✖ ➠

MIDDLE WALLOP   Map 04 SU23
MUSEUM OF ARMY FLYING
SO20 8DY
➲ (on A343, between Andover & Salisbury)
☎ 01980 674421
e-mail: enquiries@flying-museum.org.uk
web: www.flying-museum.org.uk
One of the country's finest historical collections of military kites, gliders, aeroplanes and helicopters. Imaginative dioramas and displays trace the development of Army flying from before the First World War to more recent conflicts in Ireland, the Falklands and the Gulf. Sit at the controls of a real Scout helicopter and test your skills on the flight simulator, plus children's education centre and 1940s house.
Times: Open all year, daily 10-4.30. Closed week prior to Xmas. Evening visits by special arrangement. **Fee:** ✱ £5 (ch £3.50, pen & student £4) Family £15. Party 10+. **Facilities:** 🅿 💷 ✖ licensed 📖 ♿ (lifts to upper levels) toilets for disabled shop ➠

MINSTEAD   Map 04 SU21
FURZEY GARDENS
SO43 7GL
➲ (1m S of junct A31/M3 Cadnam off A31 or A337 near Lyndhurst)
☎ 023 8081 2464 & 8081 2297   2 for 1
e-mail: info@furzey-gardens.org
web: www.furzey-gardens.org
A large thatched gallery is the venue for refreshments and displays of local arts and crafts, and the eight acres of peaceful glades which surround it include winter and summer heathers, rare flowering trees and shrubs and a mass of spring bulbs. There is a 16th-century cottage, lake, and the nursery, run by the Minstead Training Project for Young People with Learning Disabilities, sells a wide range of produce.
Times: Gardens open daily, 10-5 (or dusk if earlier). Gallery open: Mar-Oct, 10-5 & wknds unitl mid Dec. Closed Xmas. **Fee:** ✱ Mar-Oct: £3.80 (ch £1.50, pen £3) Family £9. Nov-Feb: £1.50 (ch 50p, pen £1) Family £3. Party 10+. **Facilities:** 🅿 💷 📖 ♿ (garden access for wheelchair visitors with assistance) toilets for disabled shop garden centre ✖ (ex guide dogs) ➠

MOTTISFONT — Map 04 SU32

MOTTISFONT ABBEY GARDEN

SO51 0LP

➲ (4.5m NW Romsey, 1m W of A3057)
2 for 1
☎ 01794 340757

e-mail: mottisfontabbey@nationaltrust.org.uk

web: www.nationaltrust.org.uk/
mottisfontabbey

In a picturesque setting by the River Test, Mottisfont Abbey is an 18th-century house adapted from a 12th-century priory. The north front shows its medieval church origins quite clearly, and the garden has splendid old trees and a walled garden planted with the national collection of old-fashioned roses. The estate includes Mottisfont village and surrounding farmland and woods. The 2-for-1 voucher is valid only during normal visiting hours and cannot be used for any ticketed events.
Times: Open Garden 5 Feb-20 Mar 11-4. Garden & House: 21 Mar-1 Jun, Sat-Wed 11-6; 4-26 Jun daily from 11-6 (garden to 8.30); 27 Jun-Aug, Sat-Thu 11-6; Sep-Oct, Sat-Wed 11-6. (Last admission to grounds 1hr before closing). **Fee:** ✱ £7 (ch £3.50) Family ticket £17.50
Facilities: 🅿 💷 ✗ licensed 📖 ♿ (Braille guide, wheelchair available, driven buggy) toilets for disabled shop closed 5 Feb-20 Mar garden centre ✖ (ex assist dogs) 🐾 📧

NETLEY — Map 04 SU40

NETLEY ABBEY

SO31 5FB

➲ (4m SE of Southampton, facing Southampton Water)
FREE
☎ 02392 581059

A romantic ruin, set among green lawns and trees, this 13th-century Cistercian abbey was founded by Peter des Roches, tutor to Henry III. Nearby is the 19th-century Gothic Netley Castle.
Times: Open any reasonable time. **Facilities:** 🅿 ♿ ✖ ♯

NEW ALRESFORD — Map 04 SU53

WATERCRESS LINE

The Railway Station SO24 9JG

➲ (stations at Alton & Alresford signed off A31, follow brown tourist signs)

☎ 01962 733810
2 for 1
e-mail: info@watercressline.co.uk

web: www.watercressline.co.uk

The Watercress Line runs through ten miles of rolling scenic countryside between Alton and Alresford. All four stations are 'dressed' in period style, and there's a locomotive yard and picnic area at Ropley. Special events throughout the year.
Times: Open May-Sep, Tue-Thu & wknds; Jan-Apr & Oct, wknds only.
Fee: ✱ Unlimited travel for the day, £10 (ch £5, pen £9). Family ticket £25. **Facilities:** 🅿 (charged) 💷 ✗ licensed ♿ (ramp access to trains) toilets for disabled shop (at Alresford, Alton & Ropley stations) charge for dogs 📧

NEW MILTON — Map 04 SZ29

SAMMY MILLER MOTORCYCLE MUSEUM

Bashley Cross Rd BH25 5SZ

➲ (signed off A35, 15m W of Southampton, 10m E of Bournemouth, N of New Milton town centre)

☎ 01425 620777

e-mail: info@sammymiller.co.uk

web: www.sammymiller.co.uk

The museum houses over 300 rare and classic bikes and with machines dating back to 1900, some are the only surviving examples of their type. The Racing collection features World Record breaking bikes and their history, including the first bike to lap a Grand Prix Course at over 100 miles per hour. Special events include marque days.
Times: Open daily 10-4.30. (Closed 2 Jan-1 Feb for refurbishment)
Fee: ✱ £4.50 (ch £2). **Facilities:** 🅿 💷 ✗ licensed ♿ (special rates for disabled people) toilets for disabled shop ✖ (ex guide dogs) 📧

Are there any excellent Days Out that we've missed? Use the Readers' Report form at the back of the book to tell us about them.

An asterisk * indicates that opening times and prices are for 2005. Please contact the attraction for up-to-date information.

OLD BASING   Map 04 SU65
BASING HOUSE
Redbridge Ln RG24 7HB
➲ (signed from Basingstoke Ring Road)
☎ 01256 467294
The largest house of Tudor England, almost entirely
destroyed by Parliament during a two-year siege ending in
1645. Built on the site of a Norman castle in 1530, the ruins
include a 300ft long tunnel. There is a re-creation of a
garden of 1600 and exhibitions showing the history of the
house. A fine 16th-century barn stands nearby.
Times: Open Apr-Sep, Wed-Sun & BH 2-6. **Fee:** ✱ £2 (ch & pen £1).
Registered disabled free. **Facilities:** 🅿 🍴 ♿ (disabled parking by
prior arangement) toilets for disabled shop

OWER   Map 04 SU31
PAULTONS PARK
SO51 6AL
➲ (exit M27 junct 2, near junct A31 & A36)
☎ 023 8081 4442
e-mail: info@paultons.co.uk
web: www.paultonspark.co.uk
Paultons Park offers a great day out for all the family with
over 50 different attractions. Many fun activities include new
Kontiki ride, drop rides, roller coaster, 6-lane astroglide,
teacup ride, log flume, pirate ship swingboat, dragon
roundabout, and wave-runner coaster. Attractions for
younger children include Kid's Kingdom, Tiny Tots Town,
Rabbit Ride, the Magic Forest where nursery rhymes come to
life, Wonderful World of Wind in the Willows and the
Ladybird ride. In beautiful parkland setting with extensive
'Capability' Brown gardens landscaped with ponds and
aviaries for exotic birds; lake and hedge maze. There is also
the Romany Experience Museum with unique collection of
gypsy wagons and the Village Life Museum. Something for
everyone.
Times: Open mid Mar-Oct, daily 10-6; Nov & Dec, wknds only until
Xmas. **Fee:** ✱ £13.50 (ch under 14). Children under 1m tall enter for
free. Range of Family Supersavers. **Facilities:** 🅿 🍴 ✗ licensed
♿ (pre-booked wheelchair hire, some rides unsuitable) toilets for
disabled shop ✖ (ex guide dogs) ⬛

PORTCHESTER   Map 04 SU60
PORTCHESTER CASTLE
Castle St PO16 9QW
➲ (off A27)
☎ 01705 378291
Discover 2,000 years of history from its Roman beginnings to
the years of medieval splendour. Stand where Henry V
rallied his troops before setting out to the battle of Agincourt
in 1415.
Times: Open all year, 24 Mar-Sep, daily 10-6; Oct-Mar, daily 10-4.
Closed 24-26 Dec & 1 Jan. **Fee:** £3.70 (ch £1.90, concessions £2.80).
Opening times and prices are subject to change, for further details
please phone 0870 333 1181 **Facilities:** 🅿 ♿ shop ✖ (ex on lead in
certain areas) ⧓

PORTSMOUTH   Map 04 SU60
BLUE REEF AQUARIUM
Clarence Esplanade PO5 3PB
➲ (on approach to city follow brown tourist signs
to seafront or Aquarium. Located on Southsea
seafront between D-Day Museum and The
Hoverport)
☎ 023 9287 5222
e-mail: portsmouth@bluereefaquarium.co.uk
web: www.bluereefaquarium.co.uk
Spectacular underwater walkthrough tunnels offer amazing
sights of exotic coral reefs - home to sharks and shimmering
shoals of brightly-coloured fish. Mediterranean and tropical
waters are recreated in giant ocean tanks, home to a
stunning array of undersea life including seahorses, puffer
fish, coral, piranhas, and incredible crustaceans. Visit the
website for current special events.
Times: Open daily from 10. Closing times vary with season, please
telephone for details. **Fee:** ✱ £6.95 (pen £4.95, ch 3-16 £3.95)
Facilities: 🅿 (under 50mtrs) ⬛ 🍴 ♿ (all on 1 level) toilets for
disabled shop ✖ (ex assist dogs) ⬛

CHARLES DICKENS' BIRTHPLACE MUSEUM
393 Old Commercial Rd PO1 4QL
➲ (accessible from M27, 1st left at 1st rdbt)
☎ 023 9282 7261
e-mail: Christopher.Spendlove@
portsmouthcc.gov.uk
web: www.portsmouthmuseums.co.uk
A small terraced house built in 1805 which became the
birthplace and early home of the famous novelist, born in
1812. On display are items pertaining to Dickens' work,
portraits of the Dickens' family, and the couch on which he
died. Dickens readings are given in the exhibition room on
the first Sunday of each month at 3pm.
Times: Open Apr-Sep, daily 10-5.30; Oct, daily 10-5. (Last admission
5pm). **Fee:** £2.50 (ch & student £1.50, accompanied ch 13 free, pen
£1.80). Family ticket £6.50. **Facilities:** 🅿 (150mtrs) shop ✖ (ex guide
& helper dogs) ⬛

CITY MUSEUM & RECORDS OFFICE
Museum Rd PO1 2LJ
➲ (M27/M275 into Portsmouth, follow museum
symbol signs)
☎ 023 9282 7261   FREE
e-mail: Christopher.Spendlove@
portsmouthcc.gov.uk
web: www.portsmouthmuseums.co.uk.
Dedicated to local history, fine and decorative art, 'The Story
of Portsmouth' displays room settings showing life here from
the 17th century to the 1950s. The 'Portsmouth at Play'
exhibition features leisure pursuits from the Victorian period
to the 1970s. The museum has a fine and decorative art
gallery, plus a temporary exhibition gallery with regular
changing exhibitions. The Record Office contains the official
records of the City of Portsmouth from the 14th century.
Times: Open all year, Apr-Oct daily 10-5.30; Nov-Mar daily 10-5.
Closed 24-26 Dec and Record Office closed on public holidays.
Facilities: 🅿 ⬛ ♿ (induction loops, lift & wheelchairs available,
parking) toilets for disabled shop ✖ (ex guide & helper dogs)

D-DAY MUSEUM & OVERLORD EMBROIDERY

Clarence Esplanade PO5 3NT

➲ (M27/M275 into Portsmouth, follow D-Day Museum & seafront signs)

☎ 023 9282 7261

e-mail: Christopher.Spendlove@portsmouthcc.gov.uk

web: www.portsmouthmuseums.co.uk

Portsmouth's D-Day Museum tells the dramatic story of the Allied landings in Normandy in 1944. Centrepiece is the magnificent 'Overlord Embroidery', 34 individual panels and 83 metres in length. Experience the world's largest ever seaborne invasion, and step back in time to scenes of wartime Britain. Military equipment, vehicles, landing craft and personal memories complete this special story.

Times: Open all year, Apr-Sep daily 10-5.30. Oct-Mar, 10-5. **Fee:** £5.50 (ch £3.30, pen £4). Family ticket £14.30 **Facilities:** P (charged) ⬛ & (induction loops, sound aids, w/chairs available) toilets for disabled shop ✖ (ex guide & helper dogs) ▰

EASTNEY BEAM ENGINE HOUSE

Henderson Rd, Eastney PO4 9JF

➲ (accessible from A3(M), A27 & A2030, turn left at Bransbury Park traffic lights)

☎ 023 9282 7261

e-mail: christopher.spendlove@portsmouthcc.gov.uk

web: www.portsmouthmuseums.co.uk

FREE

The main attraction here is a magnificent pair of James Watt Beam Engines still housed in their original High-Victorian engine house opened in 1887. One of these engines is in steam when the museum is open. A variety of other pumping engines, many in running order are also on display.

Times: Open last wknd of month, 1-5 (last admission 30 minutes before closing). (Closed Aug & Dec). **Facilities:** P (300mtrs) shop ✖ (ex guide & helper dogs)

NATURAL HISTORY MUSEUM & BUTTERFLY HOUSE

Cumberland House, Eastern Pde PO4 9RF

➲ (accessed via A3(M), A27 or A2030, follow signs to seafront)

☎ 023 9282 7261

e-mail: Christopher.Spendlove@portsmouthcc.gov.uk

web: www.portsmouthmuseums.co.uk

FREE

Focusing on the natural history and geology of the area, with

continued

wildlife dioramas including a riverbank scene with fresh water aquarium. During the summer British and European butterflies fly free in the Butterfly House.

Times: Open all year daily, Apr-Oct 10-5.30; Nov-Mar 10-5. **Facilities:** P (200mtrs) shop ✖ (ex guide & helper dogs) ▰

PORTSMOUTH HISTORIC DOCKYARD

HM Naval Base PO1 3LJ

➲ (M27/M275 & follow brown historic waterfront and dockyard signs)

☎ 023 9283 9766

e-mail: enquiries@historicdockyard.co.uk

web: www.historicdockyard.co.uk

Portsmouth Historic Dockyard is home to the world's greatest historic ships: *Mary Rose* - King Henry VIII's favourite ship, *HMS Victory* - Lord Nelson's flagship at the Battle of Trafalgar and *HMS Warrior* - the first iron-hulled warship. In addition, the Royal Naval Museum has the most significant, permanent collections relating to Nelson and the Battle of Trafalgar, and Action Stations gives an interactive insight into the modern day Royal Navy.

Times: Open all year, Apr-Oct, daily 10-5.30; Nov-Mar, daily 10-5. Please enquire for Xmas closures. **Fee:** ✱ All inclusive ticket: £15.50 (ch & pen £12.50, under 5's free). Family £45 **Facilities:** P (charged) ⬛ ✖ licensed & (wheelchairs, facilities for visually & hearing impaired) toilets for disabled shop ✖ (ex assist dogs) ▰

THE ROYAL MARINES MUSEUM

Southsea PO4 9PX

➲ (signed from seafront)

☎ 023 9281 9385

2 for 1

e-mail: info@royalmarinesmuseum.co.uk

web: www.royalmarinesmuseum.co.uk

Telling the story of the 330-year history of the Marines through dramatic displays, exciting films and videos, state of the art interactives and there's even a live snake and scorpion. Also a world famous medal collection, portraits and silverware.

Times: Open all year, Jun-Aug, daily 10-5; Sep-May, daily 10-4.30. Closed 24-26 Dec. **Fee:** ✱ £4.75 (ch under 16 free, students £2.25, disabled £1.50, pen £3.50). **Facilities:** P ⬛ & (wheelchairs, hearing loops, special tours-prior notice) toilets for disabled shop ✖ (ex guide dogs or in grounds) ▰

SOUTHSEA CASTLE

Clarence Esplanade PO5 3PA

➲ (accessible from M27, A27, A3M, A2030, follow castle signposts)

☎ 023 9282 7261

e-mail: Christopher.Spendlove@portsmouthcc.gov.uk

web: www.portsmouthmuseums.co.uk

Part of Henry VIII's national coastal defences, this fort was built in 1544. In the 'Time Tunnel' experience, the ghost of the castle's first master gunner guides you through the dramatic scenes from the castle's eventful history. Audio-visual presentation, underground passages, Tudor military history displays, artillery, and panoramic views of the Solent and Isle of Wight.

Times: Open all year, Apr-Sep, daily 10-5.30; Oct-Mar, daily 10-5. **Fee:** £2.50 (ch & students £1.50, ch accompanied under 13 free, pen £1.80). Family ticket £6.50. **Facilities:** P & (wheelchair available) shop ✖ (ex guide & helper dogs) ▰

THE SPINNAKER TOWER
Gunwharf Quays PO1 3TT
☎ 023 9285 7520
e-mail: info@spinnakertower.co.uk
web: spinnakertower.co.uk
Elegant sculptural and inspired by Portsmouth's maritime heritage, the Spinnaker Tower is set to become a new national icon - a 'must-see' landmark for visitors worldwide. Soaring 170 metres above Portsmouth Harbour, with three viewing decks, the Spinnaker Tower is now open to view. Glide to the top in style in the panoramic lift, or take the high speed internal lift and step right out into the best view in the country. Dare you 'walk on air' on our glass floor, the largest in Europe? Watch history unfold through our unique 'Time Telescopes'. Back down to earth you can shop for souvenirs or talk about your travels over a snack in our friendly waterfront Tower Café Bar.
Times: Open all year. Mon-Wed, 10-6; Thu-Sat, 10-8; Sun 11-5.
Fee: £4.95 (ch 5-15 £4, concessions £4.50). Family (2+2) £16 🅿 💷 👂 (hearing loop) 🍴

SPITBANK FORT
P O Box 129 PO12 2XY
⤴ (Ferries depart from HM Naval Base Portsmouth, Portsmouth Hard, Gosport Ferry Pontoon, by the side of Portsmouth Harbour Railway Stn and Gunwarf Quays shopping centre)
☎ 02392 504207
e-mail: enquiries@spitbankfort.co.uk
web: www.spitbankfort.co.uk
Built in the 1860s as part of the coastal defences against the French, this massive granite and iron fortress stands a mile out to sea, with magnificent views across the Solent. The interior is a maze of passages connecting over 50 rooms on two levels.
Times: Open Etr-Sep, Wed-Sun. (Weather permitting). **Fee:** ✱ £6.50 (ch £5) includes ferry charge. Boat ride takes approx 20 mins, visitors should allow 2hr to view. Pub nights: (Wed/Thu) £16.50 (ch £10). Parties: (Fri/Sat) £25 (adult only). Sun Lunch: £16.50 (ch £10)
Facilities: 🅿 💷 ✕ licensed (many steps) 🐕 (ex guide dogs) 🍴

RINGWOOD   Map 04 SU10
MOORS VALLEY COUNTRY PARK
Horton Rd, Ashley Heath BH24 2ET
⤴ (1.5m from Ashley Heath rdbt on A31 near Three Legged Cross)
☎ 01425 470721
e-mail: moorsvalley@eastdorsetdc.gov.uk
web: www.moors-valley.co.uk
Fifteen hundred acres of forest, woodland, heathland, lakes, river and meadows provide a home for a wide variety of plants and animals, and there's a Visitor Centre, Adventure Playground, picnic area, Moors Valley Railway, Tree Top Trail and the 'Go Ape'- high ropes course (book on 0870 444 5562). Cycle hire is also available.
Times: Open all year, 8-dusk (8pm at latest). Visitor centre open 9.30-4.30 (later in summer). Closed 25 Dec. **Fee:** ✱ No admission charge but parking up to £7 per day. **Facilities:** 🅿 (charged) 💷 ✕ licensed 👍 (visitor centre/park accessible, scooter & wheelchairs) toilets for disabled shop (some areas on leads) 🍴

ROCKBOURNE   Map 04 SU11
ROCKBOURNE ROMAN VILLA
SP6 3PG
⤴ (from Salisbury exit A338 at Fordingbridge, take B3078 westwards through Sandleheath & follow signs. Or turn off A354 Salisbury to Blandford road, W of Coombe Bissett)
☎ 01725 518541   **2 for 1**
web: www.hants.gov.uk/museum/rockbourne
Discovered in 1942, the site features the remains of a 40-room Roman villa and is the largest in the area. Displays include mosaics and a very rare hypocaust system. The museum displays the many artefacts found on the site during excavations. Roman re-enactments are performed - please ring for details.
Times: Open Apr-Sep, daily 10.30-6. (Last admission 5.30)
Fee: ✱ £2.25 (concessions £1.25). **Facilities:** 🅿 💷 📷 👍 (ramps in & out of museum) toilets for disabled shop 🐕 (ex guide/hearing dogs)

ROMSEY   Map 04 SU32
BROADLANDS
SO51 9ZD
⤴ (main entrance on A3090 Romsey by-pass)
☎ 01794 505010
e-mail: admin@broadlands.net
web: www.broadlands.net
Famous as the home of the late Lord Mountbatten, Broadlands is now home to his grandson Lord Romsey. An elegant Palladian mansion in a beautiful landscaped setting on the banks of the River Test, Broadlands was also the country residence of Lord Palmerston, the great Victorian statesman.
Times: Open wkdays,30 Jun-2 Sep, 1-5.30. Last admission 4. Open BHs. **Fee:** ✱ £7 (ch 12-16 £4, concessions £6). Party 15+.
Facilities: 🅿 👍 toilets for disabled 🐕 (ex guide dogs)

ROWLAND'S CASTLE   Map 04 SU71
STANSTED PARK
PO9 6DX
⤴ (follow brown heritage signs "Stansted House" from A3 or A27)
☎ 023 9241 2265
e-mail: enquiry@stanstedpark.co.uk
web: www.stanstedpark.co.uk
Stansted Park is set in 1750 acres of park and woodland. The mansion rooms house the Beesborough family collection of furniture and paintings, and below stairs the restored servants' quarters can be found, with an extensive collection of household artefacts giving an insight into the running of the house. The ancient Chapel of St Paul was an inspiration to the poet John Keats and is open in conjunction with the house.
Times: Open Etr Sun-end Sep, Sun & Mon 1-5; Jul & Aug, Sun-Wed (last admission 4pm) **Fee:** £5.50 (ch £3.50, sen £4.50). Family £14.50 (2ad+2ch) **Facilities:** 🅿 ✕ licensed 👍 (wheelchair lift to house) toilets for disabled garden centre 🐕 (ex guide dogs)

SELBORNE — Map 04 SU73

GILBERT WHITE'S HOUSE & THE OATES MUSEUM

High St GU34 3JH
➲ (on village High St)
☎ 01420 511275

Charming 18th-century house, home of famous naturalist, the Rev. Gilbert White, author of *The Natural History and Antiquities of Selborne*. Over 25 acres of garden and parkland, shop and tea parlour serving some 18th-century fare. Special events include an unusual plants fair and concert evening in June, Gilbert White day in July and mulled wine day in December.
Times: ✱ Open daily Jan-24 Dec, 11-5. **Fee:** £5 (ch £3, concessions £4.50). **Facilities:** P ⬛ ✗ ♿ toilets for disabled shop ✖ (ex guide dogs) ◼

SHERBORNE ST JOHN — Map 04 SU65

THE VYNE

RG24 9HL
➲ (4m N of Basingstoke, off A340, signed from A33, A339 & A340)
☎ 01256 883858   **2 for 1**
e-mail: thevyne@nationaltrust.org.uk
web: www.nationaltrust.org.uk

Built in the early 16th-century for Lord Sandys, Henry VIII's Lord Chamberlain, the house acquired a classical portico in the mid-17th century (the first of its kind in England) and contains a fascinating Tudor chapel with renaissance glass, a palladian staircase and a wealth of old panelling and fine

continued

furniture. The attractive grounds feature herbaceous borders and a wild garden, with lawns, lakes and woodland walks. The 2-for-1 voucher is not valid for special events such as classical concerts in the grounds.
Times: Open House & Gardens 20 Mar-Oct daily (ex Thu & Fri) 1-5, wknds 11-5. Gardens also open wknds in Feb & Mar, 11-5. (Gardens 11-5 Mon-Wed). **Fee:** ✱ House & Grounds £7 (ch £3.50). Family £17.50, Group £5.50. Grounds & Gardens only £4 (ch £2). NT members free. **Facilities:** P ⬛ ✗ licensed 🎧 ♿ (Braille guides, hearing loop & touch tours) toilets for disabled shop ✖ (ex guide & hearing dogs) ♨ ◼

SILCHESTER — Map 04 SU66

CALLEVA MUSEUM   **FREE**

Bramley Rd RG7 2LU
➲ (between Basingstoke & Reading. Reached from A340, follow brown tourist signs)
Little remains of the Roman town of Calleva Atrebatum except the 1.5 miles of city wall, still an impressive sight, and the ampitheatre. This small museum shows what life may have been like in a Roman town, while the main artefacts from the site can be seen in the Silchester Gallery at Reading Museum.
Times: Open daily 9.30-sunset. Closed 25 Dec. **Facilities:** P ♿ (on leads)

SOUTHAMPTON — Map 04 SU41

MUSEUM OF ARCHAEOLOGY

God's House Tower, Winkle St SO14 2NY
➲ (near the waterfront close to Queen's Park and the Town Quay)
☎ 023 8063 5904 & 8083 2768   **FREE**
e-mail: museums@southampton.gov.uk
web: www.southampton.gov.uk/leisure
The museum housed in an early fortified building, dating from the 1400s and taking its name from the nearby medieval hospital. Exhibits on the Roman, Saxon and medieval towns of Southampton are displayed.
Times: Open Nov-Mar: Tue-Fri 10-4; Sat 10-12 & 1-4; Sun 1-4. Apr-Oct: Tue-Fri 10-12 & 1-5; Sat 10-12 & 1-4; Sun 2-5. Also open BH Mon.
Facilities: P (400 yds) (designated areas only, parking charges) 🎧 ♿ shop ✖ (ex guide dogs)

SOUTHAMPTON CITY ART GALLERY

Civic Centre, Commercial Rd SO14 7LP
➲ (situated on the Watts Park side of the Civic Centre, a short walk from the station, on Commercial Rd)
☎ 023 8083 2277   **FREE**
e-mail: art.gallery@southampton.gov.uk
web: www.southampton.gov.uk/art
The largest gallery in the south of England, with the finest collection of contemporary art in the country outside London. Varied displays of landscapes, portrait paintings or recent British art are always available, as well as a special display, selected by members of the public.
Times: Open all year, Tue-Sat 10-5, Sun 1-4. Closed 25-27 & 31 Dec.
Facilities: P (50yds) (nearby street parking is 1hr only) ⬛ ✗ 🎧 ♿ (free BSL signed tours by arrangement, 'touch tour') toilets for disabled shop ✖ (ex guide dogs)

SOUTHAMPTON MARITIME MUSEUM

The Wool House, Town Quay SO14 2AR
➲ (on the waterfront, near to the Town Quay)
☎ 023 8022 3941 & 8063 5904 `FREE`
e-mail: museums@southampton.gov.uk
web: www.southampton.gov.uk/leisure

The Wool House was built in the 14th century as a warehouse for wool, and now houses a maritime museum, with models and displays telling the history of the Victorian and modern port of Southampton. There are exhibitions of the *Titanic*, *The Queen Mary* and an interactive area for children.
Times: Open Nov-Mar: Tue-Fri 10-4; Sat 10-1 & 2-4; Sun 1-4. Apr-Oct: Tue-Fri 10-1 & 2-5; Sat 10-1 & 2-4; Sun 2-5. Also open BH Mon.
Facilities: P (400yds) (metered parking adjacent) 🍴 ♿ (hearing loop on Titanic presentation) shop ✈ (ex guide dogs)

TITCHFIELD   Map 04 SU50

TITCHFIELD ABBEY

Place House Studio, Mill Ln PO15 5RA
➲ (0.5m N off Titchfield, off A27)
☎ 01329 842133 `FREE`

Also known as 'Place House', in Tudor times this was the seat of the Earl of Southampton, built on the site of the abbey founded in 1232. He incorporated the gatehouse and the nave of the church into his house.
Times: Open Apr-Sep, daily 10-6; Oct, daily 10-5; Nov-Mar, daily 10-4. Closed 25 Dec. **Facilities:** P ♿

WEYHILL   Map 04 SU34

THE HAWK CONSERVANCY AND COUNTRY PARK

SP11 8DY
➲ (3m W of Andover, signed from A303)
☎ 01264 773850
e-mail: info@hawk-conservancy.org
web: www.hawk-conservancy.org

This is the largest centre in the south for birds of prey from all over the world including eagles, hawks, falcons, owls, vultures and kites. Exciting birds of prey demonstrations are held daily at noon, 2pm, and 3.30pm, including the 'Valley of the Eagles' at 2pm. Different birds are flown at these times and visitors may have the opportunity to hold a bird and adults can fly a Harris hawk.
Times: Open Feb half term-Oct half term, daily from 10.30-5.30 (last admission 4). **Fee:** £8 (ch £5, pen & student £7.25). Family ticket £25.
Facilities: P 🍴 ✕ 🍴 ♿ (wheelchair area in flying grounds, viewing areas in hides) toilets for disabled shop ✈ 🍴

WHITCHURCH   Map 04 SU44

WHITCHURCH SILK MILL

28 Winchester St RG28 7AL
➲ (halfway between Winchester & Newbury signposted clearly on the A34. Located in centre of the town)
☎ 01256 892065
e-mail: silkmill@btinternet.com
web: www.whitchurchsilkmill.org.uk

The mill is idyllically located on the River Test. Whitchurch Silk Mill is the oldest surviving textile mill in Southern England. Fine silks and ribbons are still woven for interiors and fashion. See the 19th-century waterwheel pounding and learn about winding, warping and weaving. There is a programme of exhibitions, workshops and children's activities.
Times: ✱ Open Tue-Sun & BH Mon 10.30-5 (last admission 4.15). Closed 24 Dec-1 Jan. **Facilities:** P 🍴 ♿ (disabled parking adjacent site) toilets for disabled shop ✈ (ex guide dogs) 🍴

WINCHESTER   Map 04 SU42

GURKHA MUSEUM

Peninsula Barracks, Romsey Rd SO23 8TS
➲ (M3 junct 9 to Winchester, follow round traffic circuit into High St, 1st left after Westgate)
☎ 01962 842832
e-mail: curator@thegurkhamuseum.co.uk
web: www.thegurkhamuseum.co.uk

This museum tells the fascinating story of the Gurkha's involvement with the British Army. Travel from Nepal to the North-West Frontier and beyond, with the help of life-sized dioramas, interactive exhibits and sound displays.
Times: Open all year, Mon-Sat 10-5, Sun 12-4. Closed 25-26 Dec & 1 Jan **Fee:** £2 (pen £1, ch under 16 free). **Facilities:** P 🍴 ♿ (lift & chair lift) toilets for disabled shop ✈ (ex guide dogs)

HOSPITAL OF ST CROSS

St Cross SO23 9SD
➲ (on B3335, 0.5m from M3 junct 11)
☎ 01962 851375 `2 for 1`
e-mail: visitors@stcrosshospital.co.uk
web: www.stcrosshospital.co.uk

A beautiful group of Grade I listed medieval and Tudor buildings, in a tranquil setting by the water meadows, St. Cross is home to 25 elderly brothers. In keeping with tradition, they wear gowns and trencher hats and act as visitor guides. The hospital is world-famous for its ancient and unique tradition of the Wayfarers Dole - a beaker of beer and a morsel of bread is given by the porter to all visitors who request it. Visitors can admire the medieval and Tudor architecture, explore the medieval hall, the Georgian kitchen and the Tudor cloister as well as the walled garden with many plants of American origin.
Times: Open all year, Apr-Oct, 9.30-5; Nov-Mar 10.30-3.30. (Closed Sun, Good Fri, 25 Dec) **Fee:** ✱ £2.50 (ch 50p, pen £2).
Facilities: P 🍴 🍴 ♿ toilets for disabled shop ✈ (ex guide dogs) 🍴

INTECH - FAMILY SCIENCE CENTRE

Telegraph Way, Morn Hill SO21 1HX
➲ (M3 junct 10 (S) or junct 9 (N) onto A31 then B3404 Alresford road)
☎ 01962 863791 `2 for 1`
e-mail: htct@intech-uk.com
web: www.intech-uk.com

This purpose-built, 3500 square metre family attraction houses 100 interactive exhibits, which demonstrate the

continued

science and technology of the world around us in an engaging and exciting way. The philosophy is most definitely 'hands-on', and the motto of the centre is 'Doing is Believing'. Exhibits deal with things like viscosity, tornados, and Newton's Cradle among others. Activities and science shows take place during school holidays.
Times: Open all year, daily 10-4. Closed Xmas. **Fee:** £5.95 (ch £3.90, pen £4.50) **Facilities:** 🅿 💺 📷 ♿ toilets for disabled shop ✈ (ex guide dogs) 🍽

The King's Royal Hussars Regimental Museum

Peninsula Barracks, Romsey Rd SO23 8TS
⊃ (M3 junct 9/10 follow signs for city centre, then hospital A&E red signs to Romsey road. Vehicle access is from Romsey road.
☎ 01962 828539 & 828541   `FREE`
e-mail: beresford@krhmuseum.freeserve.co.uk
web: www.hants.gov.uk/leisure/museum/royalhus
The Royal Hussars were formed by the amalgamation of two regiments raised at the time of the Jacobite Rebellion in 1715, the 10th Royal Hussars and the 11th Hussars. This museum tells their story.
Times: Due to reopen Spring 2006 after refurbishment, then open until 18 Dec, Tue-Fri 10-4, wknds, BH's & half term Mon, 12-4. (Closed daily between 12.45-1.15) **Facilities:** 🅿 💺 ♿ (lift to first floor) toilets for disabled shop ✈ (ex guide dogs)

Royal Hampshire Regiment Museum & Memorial Garden

Serle's House, Southgate St SO23 9EG
⊃ (Museum near city centre, 150mtrs from traffic lights in High St)
☎ 01962 863658   `FREE`
e-mail: serleshouse@aol.com
web: www.royalhampshireregimentmuseum.co.uk
Regimental Museum of the Royal Hampshire Regiment 1702-1992, set in an 18th-century house by the regiment's Memorial Garden. The museum tells the history of the regiment, its regulars, militia, volunteers and Territorials.
Times: Normally open all year (ex 2 wks Xmas & New Year), Mon-Fri 10-4; Apr-Oct wknds & BH 12-4. **Facilities:** 🅿 (800mtrs) ♿ shop ✈ (ex guide dogs)

The Great Hall

Castle Av SO23 8PJ
⊃ (situated at top of High St. Park & Ride recommended)
☎ 01962 846476
e-mail: the.great.hall@hants.gov.uk
web: www.hants.gov.uk/discover/places/great-hall1.html
The only surviving part of Winchester Castle, once home to the Domesday Book, this 13th-century hall was the centre of court and government life. Built between 1222-1235 during the reign of Henry III, it is one of the largest and finest five bay halls in England to have survived to present day. The Round Table based on the Arthurian Legend and built between 1230-1280 hangs in the hall. Queen Eleanor's Garden, a re-creation of a late 13th-century ornamental garden, was opened in 1986 by the Queen Mother.
Times: Open all year, Mar-Oct daily 10-5; Nov-Feb, daily 10-5, wknds 10-4. Closed 25-26 Dec. **Fee:** Free. Donations greatly appreciated.
Facilities: 🅿 (200yds) 📷 ♿ toilets for disabled shop ✈ (ex guide/hearing dogs) 🍽

Winchester Cathedral

1 The Close SO23 9LS
⊃ (in city centre - follow city heritage signs)
☎ 01962 857200 & 866854
e-mail: cathedral.office@winchester-cathedral.org.uk
web: www.winchester-cathedral.org.uk
The longest medieval church in Europe, founded in 1079 on a site where Christian worship had already been offered for over 400 years. Among its treasures are the 12th-century illuminated Winchester Bible, the font, medieval wall paintings and Triforium Gallery Museum. Items of interest include Jane Austen's tomb and the statue of the Winchester diver, William Walker, who in 1905 saved the cathedral by underpinning its foundations, working up to six hours a day over a period of six years, often in 20 feet of water. Visitors can also descend into the crypt to see a sculpture by Anthony Gormley, best known as creator of *The Angel of The North*, or ascend to the tower and bell chamber.
Times: Open all year, daily 8.30-5.30. Subject to services and special events. **Fee:** ✱ Admission free, voluntary donations: £4 (concessions £3). **Facilities:** 🅿 (500mtrs) 💺 ✕ licensed 📷 ♿ (chair lift to east end of Cathedral, touch & hearing model) toilets for disabled shop ✈ (ex guide dogs) 🍽

Winchester City Mill

Bridge St SO23 8EJ
⊃ (by the city bridge between King Alfred's statue & Chesil St)
☎ 01962 870057   `2 for 1`
e-mail: winchestercitymill@nationaltrust.org.uk
web: www.nationaltrust.org.uk
Built over the fastflowing River Itchen in 1744, the mill has a delightful small island garden and an impressive millrace. There are regular milling demonstrations and guided wildlife walks. The 2-for-1 is not valid for ticketed events.
Times: Open: Mill & Shop, 5-27 Mar, Sat-Sun 11-5, 28 Mar-10 Apr & 4 Jul-23 Dec, daily 11-5, 13 Apr-3 Jul, Wed-Sun 11-5. Last admission to Mill 4.30pm **Fee:** ✱ £3 (ch £1.50) Family £7.50. Group £2.50 each **Facilities:** 🅿 (200yds) 📷 (hearing loop, large print guide, photo album) shop ✈ (ex guide dogs) 🐾 🍽

Winchester College

College St SO23 9NA
⊃ (in Winchester City Centre S of Cathedral Close, beyond Kingsgate arch. Limited vehicle access along College St)
☎ 01962 621209
e-mail: enterprises@wincoll.ac.uk
web: www.winchestercollege.org
Founded in 1382, Winchester College is believed to be the oldest continuously running school in England. The College has greatly expanded over the years but the original buildings remain intact. Visitors can follow in the footsteps of John Keats, and see the College's many historic buildings, including a schoolhouse thought to have been designed by Christopher Wren. Also the 14th-century gothic chapel with one of the earliest examples of a fan vaulted roof constructed from wood rather than stone, the original scholars dining room and the cloister containing memorials to former members of the college including one to Mallory the Mountaineer.
Times: Open all year. Closed 24 Dec-1 Jan. Guided tours available Mon, Wed, Fri & Sat; 10.45, 12, 2.15 & 3.30. Tue & Thu 10.45 & 12. Sun 2.15 & 3.30. Groups of 10+ at times to suit by arrangement only.
Fee: £3.50 (ch, pen & students £3). **Facilities:** 🅿 (250yds) (street parking max stay 1hr) ♿ (access ramps) toilets for disabled shop ✈ (ex guide dogs) 🍽

HEREFORDSHIRE

Events & Festivals

April
30th-1st May Blossom Time Weekend,
    Putley nr Ledbury
tbc Ledbury English Festival, English food,
    drink, music and culture

May
2nd-4th Hereford May Fair, fair rides, side
    shows, stalls and ancient ceremonies, city
    centre streets (provisional)

June
23rd-25th Music Festival, Dore Abbey,
    Abbeydore
tbc Leominster Festival (mixed arts, various
    venues)

July
7th-16th Ledbury Poetry Festival

August
5th-12th Three Choirs Fringe Festival
    (provisional)
6th-11th Three Choirs Festival, Hereford
    Cathedral

September
8th-10th Bromyard Folk Festival

October
14th-15th Big Apple Weekend, Much Marcle,
    nr Ledbury
tbc Exposure, the Hereford Photography
    Festival, various venues

Above: Hereford Cathedral

ASHTON   Map 03 SO56

BERRINGTON HALL
Berrington HR6 0DW
➲ (3m N of Leominster, on A49)
☎ 01568 615721
e-mail: berrington@nationaltrust.org.uk
web: www.nationaltrust.org.uk

An elegant neo-classical house of the late 18th century,
designed by Henry Holland and set in a park landscape by
'Capability' Brown. There is a restored bedroom suite, a
nursery, a Victorian laundry and a tiled Georgian dairy.
Times: Open 5-20 Mar Sat-Sun, Sat-Wed, 21 Mar- end Oct & Good Fri
1-4.30. (Last admission 30mins before closing). Garden open 12-5
(4.30 in Oct). Park walk open Jul-end Oct, 12-5. **Fee:** ✱ £5 (ch £2.50)
Family ticket £12.50. Garden only £3.50. Joint ticket with Croft Castle
£6.50 **Facilities:** ▣ ✗ licensed ▥ ⅋ (by arrangement,
wheelchairs/batricar, steps to entrance) toilets for disabled shop
✈ (ex guide dogs) ❧▰

BROCKHAMPTON   Map 03 SO65

BROCKHAMPTON ESTATE
WR6 5TB
➲ (2m E of Bromyard on A44)
☎ 01885 482077 & 488099
e-mail: brockhampton@nationaltrust.org.uk
web: www.nationaltrust.org.uk

This traditionally formed 1700 acre estate has extensive
areas of wood and parkland, with a rich variety of wildlife
and over 5 miles of walks. At the heart of the estate lies
Lower Brockhampton House, a late 14th-century moated
manor house with a beautiful timber-framed gatehouse and
ruined chapel.
Times: Open Mar-Oct daily (ex Mon & Tue) but open BH Mons
Apr-Oct 12-5 (12-4 in Oct). Woodland walks open to dusk throughout
the year. **Fee:** ✱ Lower Brockhampton £3.60 (ch £1.80) Family £8.50
Facilities: ▣ ▰ ▥ ⅋ (special parking, ramps, Braille guide) toilets
for disabled shop (no dogs in house ex assist) ❧

CROFT   Map 03 SO46

CROFT CASTLE
HR6 9PW
➲ (off B4362)
☎ 01568 780246
e-mail: croft@nationaltrust.org.uk
web: www.nationaltrust.org.uk

Home of the Croft family since Domesday (with a break of
170 years from 1750); walls and towers date from the 14th
and 15th centuries; the interior is mainly 18th century. There
is a splendid avenue of 350-year-old Spanish chestnuts, and
an Iron Age Fort (Croft Ambrey) may be reached by footpath.
Times: Park open all year, daily. Gardens & Tea Room open 29
Mar-Jun, Wed-Sun 12-5; Jul-Aug, Tue-Sun 12-5; Sep, Wed-Sun 12-5;
Oct-2 Nov, Sat-Sun 12-5. Castle open 18 Apr-Jun & Sep, Wed-Sun 1-5;
Jul-Aug, Tue-Sun 1-5; Oct-2 Nov, Sat-Sun 1-5. **Fee:** ✱ Garden only
£3.20. Castle & Garden £4.60 (ch £2.30). Family ticket £11.50. Joint
ticket with Berrington £6.50. Car park £2.50. **Facilities:** ▣ (charged)
▰ ▥ ⅋ (parking available, Braille guide) toilets for disabled
✈ (ex guide dogs & in park) ❧▰

GOODRICH — Map 03 SO51

GOODRICH CASTLE

HR9 6HY
➲ (5m S of Ross-on-Wye, off A40)
☎ 01600 890538

A magnificent red sandstone fortress rising out of a rocky outcrop above the Wye Valley. Climb the huge towers for exhilarating views and explore a maze of small rooms and passageways.
Times: Open all year, Mar-May, Sep-Oct, daily, 10-5; Jun-Aug, daily, 10-6; Nov-Feb, Thu-Mon, 10-4. Closed 24-26 Dec & 1 Jan. **Fee:** £4.30 (ch £2.20, concessions £3.20, family £10.80). Opening times and prices are subject to change, for further details please phone 0870 333 1181
Facilities: 🅿 shop ✖ ⇌

HEREFORD — Map 03 SO53

CIDER MUSEUM & KING OFFA DISTILLERY

21 Ryelands St HR4 0LW
➲ (off A438 Hereford to Brecon road)
☎ 01432 354207 | 2 for 1 |
e-mail: info@cidermuseum.fsnet.co.uk
web: www.cidermuseum.co.uk

Explore the fascinating history of cider making - old cidermaking equipment, the cooper's workshop and vat house with hydraulic presses and bottling machinery. An annual International cider competition is held and cidermaking festival weekends take place.
Times: Open all year, Apr-Oct 10-5; Nov-Mar 12-4, closed Sun-Mon.
Fee: ✱ £3 (ch & students £2, pen £2.50). Party 15+, 50p reduction per person. **Facilities:** 🅿 💷 ✖ ♿ (audiotapes, large print guide sheets) toilets for disabled shop ✖ (ex guide dogs)

HEREFORD CATHEDRAL

HR1 2NG
➲ (A49 signed from city inner ring roads)
☎ 01432 374200 | 2 for 1 |
e-mail: office@herefordcathedral.org
web: www.herefordcathedral.org

The cathedral is mainly Norman with a 13th-century Lady Chapel. Hereford's two outstanding treasures are exhibited here - the Mappa Mundi - drawn C.1290, and the famous Chained Library - containing over 1400 chained books.
Times: Cathedral open daily for visitors 9.30-5; Mappa Mundi & Chained Library Exhibition Summer: Mon-Sat 10-4.15, Sun 11-3.15. Winter: Mon-Sat 11-3.15 (closed Sun). **Fee:** Cathedral admission free (donation invited). Mappa Mundi & Chained Library Exhibition £4.50 (concessions £3.50). Family ticket £6-£10. Party 10+.
Facilities: 🅿 (0.25m) 💷 📱 ♿ (touch facility for blind, Braille & large print info) toilets for disabled shop ✖ (ex guide dogs) ⇌

OLD HOUSE

High Town HR1 2AA
➲ (located in the centre of the High Town) | FREE |
☎ 01432 260694
e-mail: herefordmuseums@herefordshire.gov.uk
web: www.herefordshire.gov.uk

The Old House is a fine Jacobean building dating from around 1621, and was once in a row of similar houses. Its rooms are furnished in 17th-century style.
Times: Open all year, 10-5. Apr-Sep, Tue-Sat 10-5, Sun & BH Mon 10-4.
Facilities: 🅿 (400mtrs) 📱 ♿ (virtual tour, Braille guide, tactile images) shop ✖ (ex guide dogs)

KINGTON — Map 03 SO25

HERGEST CROFT GARDENS

HR5 3EG
➲ (off A44 W of Kington and follow signs)
☎ 01544 230160 | 2 for 1 |
e-mail: gardens@hergest.co.uk
web: www.hergest.co.uk

From spring bulbs to autumn colour, this is a garden for all seasons. A fine collection of trees and shrubs surrounds the Edwardian house. There's an old fashioned kitchen garden with spring and summer borders, and a hidden valley.
Times: Apr-end Oct, 12.30-5.30; May-Jun, noon-6. Open wknds in Mar 12.30-5.30 **Fee:** £5 (ch under 16 free). Party 20+ £4 (£6 with tour)
Facilities: 🅿 💷 ♿ (portable ramp & wheelchair available) toilets for disabled shop garden centre (on leads) ⇌

LEDBURY — Map 03 SO73

EASTNOR CASTLE

Eastnor HR8 1RL
➲ (the castle is 2.5m E of Ledbury on the A438)
☎ 01531 633160
e-mail: eastnorcastle@eastnorcastle.com
web: www.eastnorcastle.com

A magnificent Georgian castle in a lovely setting, with a deer park, arboretum and lake. Inside are tapestries, fine art and armour, and the Italianate and Gothic interiors have been beautifully restored. There's an adventure playground, nature trails and lakeside walks. Events take place throughout the year.
Times: Open mid Apr-1 Oct, Sun & BH Mon; Jul & Aug, Sun-Fri 11-5
Fee: Castle & grounds £7 (ch £4, pen £6) Family £18. Grounds only £5 (ch £3, pen £4). **Facilities:** 🅿 💷 📱 ♿ (please telephone for access & facilities details) shop ⇌

SWAINSHILL — Map 03 SO44

THE WEIR GARDENS

HR4 7QF
➲ (5m W of Hereford, on A438)
☎ 01981 590509 | 2 for 1 |
e-mail: theweir@nationaltrust.org.uk
web: www.nationaltrust.org.uk

A delightful riverside garden, with lovely displays of naturalised bulbs set in woodland and grassland walks. Garden walks can be taken here, with fine views of the River Wye and the Black Mountains. The 2-for-1 voucher is valid only during normal visiting hours and cannot be used for any ticketed events.
Times: Open mid Jan-Feb wknds only; Feb & Apr-Oct Wed-Sun; Mar daily, 11-4. **Fee:** ✱ £3.60 (ch £1.80) Family £8.50.
Facilities: 🅿 ♿ (access limited) toilets for disabled ✖ 🐾

HERTFORDSHIRE

EVENTS & FESTIVALS

April
tbc Hertford Theatre Week

May
6th-21st Baldock Festival, a variety of events in the community
20th-21st Herts Garden Show, Knebworth House (provisional)
27th-28th Herts County Show, Herts County Showground, Redbourn

June
17th-1st Jul Stevenage Festival of the arts, a series of events promoting amateur societies
18th Rock in the Park, Fairlands Valley Park, Stevenage (provisional)
31st-1st Jul Ware Festival, including carnival

July
1st-16th Hitchin Festival, various events and venues (provisional)
22nd-23rd Waltham Abbey Festival Week, community festival
15th-16th Rhythms of the World, largest free world music festival in UK in the streets of Hitchin
tbc St Albans Festival

August
27th-28th Knebworth Classic Motor Show, Knebworth (provisional)

September
27th-30th St Albans Beer Festival (provisional)

Above: St Mary's Church, Furneux Pelham

AYOT ST LAWRENCE   Map 04 TL11
SHAW'S CORNER
AL6 9BX
➲ (A1(M) junct 4 or M1 junct 10. Follow B653 signed Wheathampstead & follow National Trust signs to Shaw's Corner)
☎ 01438 820307   **2 for 1**
e-mail: shawscorner@nationaltrust.org.uk
web: www.nationaltrust.org.uk/shawscorner
An Edwardian arts and crafts influenced house, the home of George Bernard Shaw from 1906 until his death in 1950. The rooms remain much as he left them, with many literary and personal effects evoking the individuality and genius of this great dramatist. The kitchen and outbuildings are evocative of early 20th-century domestic life. Shaw's writing hut is hidden at the bottom of the garden, which has richly planted borders and views over the Hertfordshire countryside. A selection of plants in addition to a small collection of George Bernard Shaw plays are available to buy. 2006 marks the 150th anniversary of George Bernard Shaw's birth and 100 years since he took up residence at the house. The 2-for-1 voucher is valid only during normal visiting hours and cannot be used for any ticketed events.
Times: Open 18 Mar-29 Oct, Wed-Sun (also open BH Mons), Gardens 12-5.30, House 1-5 (last admission 4.30). **Fee:** ✱ £3.80 (ch £1.90). Family ticket £9.50. **Facilities:** 🅿 🍴 ♿ (Braille/large print guides, scented plants, items to touch) 🐕 (ex on lead in car park) 🗱

BERKHAMSTED   Map 04 SP90
ASHRIDGE ESTATE VISITOR CENTRE
Moneybury Hill, Ringshall HP4 1LX
➲ (between Northchurch & Ringshall, just off B4506)
☎ 01442 851227 & 755557
e-mail: ashridge@nationaltrust.org.uk   **2 for 1**
web: www.nationaltrust.org.uk
Miles of paths through woodland and open country with spring bluebells, ancient trees, fungi and breath-taking views. Discover more about the wildlife in the visitor centre next to the Bridgewater monument, with an interactive exhibition room. A wide range of activities and events for all the family take place through out the year. 2-for-1 entry voucher only accepted during normal visiting hours and cannot be used for any ticketed events.
Times: Open Estate; all year. Visitor Centre; 27 Mar-11 Dec, Mon-Fri 1-5, Sat & Sun 12-5 (or dusk if earlier) Tea Room; 27 Mar-12 Dec, Tue-Sun, 12-5. Bridgewater Monument; 27 Mar-Oct, Sat, Sun, BH Mon 12-5 (last entry 4.30) **Fee:** ✱ Visitor centre & estate free, Monument £1.30 (ch 60p) **Facilities:** 🅿 🍴 ♿ Disabled paprking next to visitor centre toilets for disabled shop 🗱

BERKHAMSTED CASTLE
HP4 1HF
➲ (by Berkhamsted station)   **FREE**
Roads and a railway have cut into the castle site, but its huge banks and ditches remain impressive. The original motte-and-bailey was built after the Norman Conquest, and there is a later stone keep, owned by the Black Prince, eldest son of King Edward III, where King John of France was imprisoned.
Times: Open all year, Summer, daily 10-6; Winter, daily 10-4. Closed 25 Dec & 1 Jan. 🏛

HATFIELD   Map 04 TL20

HATFIELD HOUSE, PARK AND GARDENS

AL9 5NQ

➲ (2m from junct 4 A1(M) on A1000, 7m from M25 junct 23. House is opposite Hatfield railway station)

☎ 01707 287010

e-mail: visitors@hatfield-house.co.uk

web: www.hatfield-house.co.uk

The house, built by Robert Cecil in 1611, is the home of the 7th Marquess of Salisbury and is full of exquisite tapestries, furniture and famous paintings. The 42 acres of gardens include formal, knot, scented and wilderness areas, and reflect their Jacobean history. Includes the national collection of model soldiers and children's play area. The Old Tudor Place, close by the house, is the childhood home of Elizabeth I and was where she held her first Council of State when she became Queen in 1558. Events take place throughout the year. **Times:** Open Etr Sat-Sep. House: Wed-Sun & BH's 12-4; Park & West Garden: daily 11-5.30. East Garden & guided tours of house on Thu **Fee:** House, park & West Garden: £8 (ch £4). Park only £2 (ch £1), West Garden £2.50 extra. Park & Gardens on Thu: £7, house tour £5 extra (no concesssions). **Facilities:** 🅿 ✗ licensed 🍴 ⅙ (lift to 1st floor, wheelchairs) toilets for disabled shop ◼

KNEBWORTH   Map 04 TL22

KNEBWORTH HOUSE, GARDENS & COUNTRY PARK

SG3 6PY

➲ (direct access from A1(M) junct 7 Stevenage South)

☎ 01438 812661

e-mail: info@knebworthhouse.com

web: www.knebworthhouse.com

Home of the Lytton family since 1490, the original Tudor Manor was transformed in 1843 by the spectacular high Gothic decoration of Victorian novelist Sir Edward Bulwer Lytton. The formal gardens, laid out by Edwin Lutyens in 1908, include a Gertrude Jekyll herb garden, a maze, recently restored walled garden and the dinosaur trail in the

continued

wilderness garden. The 250-acre park includes a miniature railway, an adventure playground and a deer park.

Knebworth House, Gardens & Country Park

Times: Open daily 1-17 Apr, 27 May-4 Jun, 1 Jul-3 Sep; wknds & BHs 25-26 March, 22 Apr-1 May, 6 May-21 May, 10-25 Jun, 9-24 Sep. **Fee:** ✱ Please contact for details, or visit website. **Facilities:** 🅿 💷 🍴 ⅙ (transport to door, wheelchair, carers free entry.) toilets for disabled shop (2 shops) garden centre ✗ (ex guide dogs & in park) ◼

See advertisement on opposite page

LETCHWORTH   Map 04 TL23

MUSEUM & ART GALLERY

Broadway SG6 3PF

➲ (situated next door to Public Library, in town centre, near Broadway Cinema)

☎ 01462 685647   `FREE`

e-mail: letchworth.museum@north-herts.gov.uk

web: www.north-herts.gov.uk

Opened in 1914 to house the collections of the Letchworth Naturalists' Society, this friendly town-centre museum has exhibits on local wildlife, geology, arts and crafts, and archaeology. There is also a museum shop and a regular programme of art exhibitions and workshops. **Times:** Open all year Mon-Tue, Thu-Sat (Closed BHs), 10-5. **Facilities:** 🅿 (100yds) 🍴 ⅙ (ramp, touch screeen computer) shop ✗ (ex guide dogs)

LONDON COLNEY   Map 04 TL10

DE HAVILLAND AIRCRAFT HERITAGE CENTRE

Salisbury Hall AL2 1EX

➲ (M25 junct 22. Follow signs for 'Mosquito Aircraft Museum' onto B556)

☎ 01727 826400 & 822051(info)   `2 for 1`

e-mail: w4050.dhamt@fsmail.net

web: www.dehavillandmuseum.co.uk

The oldest aircraft museum in Britain, opened in 1959 to preserve and display the de Havilland Mosquito prototype on the site of its conception. A working museum with displays of 20 de Havilland aircraft and sections together with a comprehensive collection of de Havilland engines and

continued

memorabilia. Selective cockpits are open to enter. Education storyboard 'maze style' now open.

de Havilland Aircraft Heritage Centre

Times: Open first Sun Mar-last Sun Oct, Sun & BHs 10.30-5.30, Tue, Thu & Sat 2-5.30. **Fee:** ✱ £5 (ch under 5 free, ch & pen £3) Family ticket £13 (2ad+2ch) **Facilities:** 🅿 💻 📖 ♿ (w/chairs available) toilets for disabled shop ✖ (ex assist dogs) ▰

ST ALBANS   Map 04 TL10

CLOCK TOWER
Market Place AL3 3DR
➲ (city centre, junct of High St (A1081) & Market Place)
☎ 01727 819340
e-mail: museum@stalbans.gov.uk
web: www.stalbansmuseums.org.uk
This early 15th-century curfew tower, which faces the High Street, provides fine views over the city (especially of the abbey) and the surrounding countryside. This is one of the only two medieval curfew towers in the country. It has a bell, older than the tower itself, which strikes on the hour.
Times: Open Etr-Oct, Sat, Sun & BH 10.30-5. **Fee:** ✱ 50p (ch 5-11 20p, accompanied ch under 5 free) **Facilities:** 🅿 (400yds) shop ✖

GORHAMBURY
AL3 6AH
➲ (entry via lodge gates on A414)
☎ 01727 855000
This house was built by Sir Robert Taylor between 1774 and 1784 to house an extensive picture collection of 17th-century portraits of the Grimston and Bacon families and their contemporaries. Also of note is the 16th-century enamelled glass collection and an early English pile carpet.
Times: Open May-Sep, Thu 2-5. **Facilities:** 🅿 ✖

MUSEUM OF ST ALBANS
Hatfield Rd AL1 3RR
➲ (city centre on A1057 Hatfield road)
☎ 01727 819340   FREE
e-mail: museum@stalbans.gov.uk
web: www.stalbansmuseums.org.uk
Exhibits include the Salaman collection of craft tools, and reconstructed workshops. The history of St Albans is traced from the departure of the Romans up to the present day. There is a special exhibition gallery with a surprising variety of exhibitions and a wildlife garden with picnic area.
Times: Open all year, daily 10-5, Sun 2-5. Closed 25-26 Dec.
Facilities: 🅿 ♿ toilets for disabled shop ✖ (ex guide dogs) ▰

ROMAN THEATRE OF VERULAMIUM
St Michaels AL3 6AH
➲ (Gorhambury Drive off Bluehouse Hill A4147)
☎ 01727 835035
The theatre was first found in 1847, was fully excavated by 1935. It is semicircular in shape with a stage area. The seating would have accommodated over 2000 spectators.
Times: Open all year, daily 10-5 (4 in winter). Closed 25-26 Dec. 1 Jan by appointment only. **Fee:** ✱ £1.50 (ch 50p, students & pen £1). (Ch under 5yrs & disabled free). **Facilities:** 🅿 ♿ (limited access to viewing path) shop

ST ALBANS CATHEDRAL
Sumpter Yard AL1 1BY
➲ (M25 junct 22a, in the centre of St Albans)
☎ 01727 860780
e-mail: mail@stalbanscathedral.org.uk
web: www.stalbanscathedral.org.uk
An imposing Norman abbey church built on the site of the execution of St Alban, Britain's first martyr (c250AD). The cathedral is constructed from recycled Roman brick taken from nearby Verulamium.
Times: Open daily, 9-5.45. Closed 25 Dec (pm) **Fee:** Admission free. Suggested donation £2.50 per adult. **Facilities:** 🅿 (200mtrs) 💻 📖 ♿ (touch & hearing centre, Braille guides) toilets for disabled shop

VERULAMIUM MUSEUM
St Michaels AL3 4SW
➲ (follow signs for St Albans, museum signed)
☎ 01727 751810   2 for 1
e-mail: a.coles@stalbans.gov.uk
web: www.stalbansmuseums.org.uk
Verulamium was one of the largest and most important

continued

Roman towns in Britain - by the lst century AD it was declared a 'municipium', giving its inhabitants the rights of Roman citizenship, the only British city granted this honour. A mosaic and underfloor heating system can be seen, and the museum has wall paintings, jewellery, pottery and other domestic items. On the second weekend of every month legionaries occupy the galleries and describe the tactics and equipment of the Roman Imperial Army and the life of a legionary.

Times: Open all year wkdys 10-5.30, Sun 2-5.30. Closed 25-26 Dec.
Fee: £3.30 (ch, pen & students £2). Family ticket £8. Subject to change.
Facilities: P (charged) 🍴 & (ramp access to main entrance) toilets for disabled shop ✖ (ex guide dogs) 🍴

TRING   Map 04 SP91

THE WALTER ROTHSCHILD ZOOLOGICAL MUSEUM
Akeman St HP23 6AP
➲ (signed from A41)
☎ 020 7942 6171
e-mail: tring-enquiries@nhm.ac.uk
web: www.nhm.ac.uk/museum/tring

An unusual museum, founded in the 1890s by Lionel Walter, 2nd Baron Rothschild, scientist, eccentric and natural history enthusiast. Now part of the Natural History Museum, it houses more than 4000 specimens from whales to fleas, and humming birds to tigers.
Times: Open all year, Mon-Sat 10-5, Sun 2-5. Closed 24-26 Dec.
Facilities: P 🍴 🍴 & (ramps to shop & cafe, disabled parking space) toilets for disabled shop ✖ (ex guide dogs)

WARE   Map 05 TL31

SCOTT'S GROTTO
Scott's Rd SG12 9JQ
➲ (off A119)
☎ 01920 464131
e-mail: jg@ware-herts.org.uk
web: www.scotts-grotto.org

Scott's Grotto, built in the 1760s by the Quaker poet John Scott, has been described by English Heritage as 'one of the finest in England'. Recently restored by the Ware Society, it consists of underground passages and chambers decorated with flints, shells, minerals and stones, and extends 67ft into the side of the hill. Please wear flat shoes and bring a torch, the grotto is not lit.
Times: Open Apr-Sep, Sat & BH Mon 2-4.30. Other times by appointment only. **Fee:** Donations welcome **Facilities:** P on street restucted at times ✖ 🚎

KENT

EVENTS & FESTIVALS

May
    27th-29th Kent Garden Show,
        Kent County Showground, Detling,
        Maidstone (provisional)
    27th-29th Sellindge Steam Festival, Ashford

June
    1st-14th Whitstable Biennale Arts Festival
    tbc Broadstairs Dickens Festival

July
    1st-15th Deal Summer Music Festival
    14th-16th Kent County Show, Maidstone
    22nd-30th Whitstable Oyster Festival
        (provisional)
    23rd-29th Deal Regatta Week (provisional)
    tbc Kent Beer Festival, Merton Farm,
        Canterbury

August
    5th-13th Herne Bay Festival
    11th-18th Broadstairs Folk Week
    20th-28th Sandwich Festival, a variety of
        events around Sandwich (provisional)
    28th Sedan Chair Race, The Pantiles,
        Tunbridge Wells

September
    2nd-3rd Biggin Hill International Air Fair,
        London Biggin Hill Airport
    8th-10th Deal Maritime Folk Festival, various
        venues in Deal

October
    14th-28th Canterbury Festival, classical
        concerts, theatre, dance, opera, jazz, blues,
        folk, children's events, exhibitions and
        walks

Above: The Romney, Hythe, and Dymchurch Railway

AYLESFORD
Map 05 TQ75

AYLESFORD PRIORY
The Friars ME20 7BX
➲ (M20 junct 6 onto A229, M2 junct 3 onto A229, signposted)
☎ 01622 717272
e-mail: friarsevents@hotmail.com
web: www.thefriars.org.uk

Built in the 13th and 14th centuries, the Priory has been restored and is now a house of prayer, guesthouse, conference centre and a place of pilgrimage and retreat. It has fine cloisters, and displays sculpture and ceramics by modern artists.
Times: Open all year, daily 9-dusk. Gift, book shop & tea rooms May-Sep, 10-5; Oct-Apr, 10-4 (Sun 11am). Guided tours of the priory by arrangement. **Fee:** Free, donations welcome. **Facilities:** ⓟ 🍽 ♿ (wheelchairs available, ramps) toilets for disabled shop ✖ (ex guide & hearing dogs)

BEKESBOURNE
Map 05 TR15

HOWLETTS WILD ANIMAL PARK
CT4 5EL
➲ (off A2, 3m S of Canterbury, follow brown tourist signs)
☎ 0870 750 4647
e-mail: info@totallywild.net
web: www.totallywild.net

`2 for 1`

Set in 90 acres of parkland, Howletts is home to some of the world's most rare and endangered animals. Howletts boasts the UK's largest group of African elephants, Indian and Siberian tigers, many small cats and rare monkeys and the world's largest group of Western Lowland gorillas. Glass fronted tiger enclosures, children's adventure playground and the new Jurassic Mine with ice and gem cave are not to be missed. Visit the new Natureworks Arts and Craft Studio for painting, pottery, arts and crafts and the new opentopped Javan Langur enclosure where the endangered monkeys can be seen in a natural environment.
Times: Open all year, daily 10-6 during summer (last admission 4.30), 10-dusk during winter (last admission 3). Closed 25 Dec.
Fee: ✱ £12.95 (ch 4-14 £9.95, pen £8.95). Family ticket (2 ad & 2 ch) £38, (2 ad & 3 ch) £44. **Facilities:** ⓟ 🍽 ✖ licensed ♿ (wheelchairs for hire, book in advance) toilets for disabled shop ✖ 🍴

BELTRING
Map 05 TQ64

HOP FARM & COUNTRY PARK
TN12 6PY
➲ (on A228 at Paddock Wood)
☎ 01622 872068
e-mail: enquiry@thehopfarm.co.uk
web: www.thehopfarm.co.uk

The Hop Farm is a popular South East family visitor attraction and event location. Set among the largest collection of Victorian Oast houses, attractions include museums and exhibitions, indoor and outdoor play areas, animal farm and shire horses, and restaurant and gift shop. Special events throughout the year include craft shows,
continued

motor shows, food and drink festivals and themed holiday weeks.

Hop Farm & Country Park

Times: ✱ Open from 10. Closed 24-26 Dec, 23 May & 20 June
Facilities: ⓟ 🍽 ✖ licensed 🍴 ♿ toilets for disabled shop 🍴

BIDDENDEN
Map 05 TQ83

BIDDENDEN VINEYARDS & CIDER WORKS
Little Whatmans, Gribble Bridge Ln TN27 8DF
➲ (0.5m S off A262, 0.5m from Biddenden Village. Bear right at Woolpack Corner)
☎ 01580 291726
e-mail: info@biddendenvineyards.co.uk
web: www.biddendenvineyards.com

The present vineyard was established in 1969 and now covers 22 acres. Visitors are welcome to stroll around the vineyard and to taste wines, ciders and apple juice available at the shop.
Times: Open all year, Shop: Mon-Fri 10-5, Sat 10-5, Sun & BH 11-5. Closed noon 24 Dec-2 Jan & Sun in Jan & Feb. **Fee:** Non-guided groups and individuals free. Pre-booked guided tours (minimum 15 adults) £3.80 (ch 10-18 £1.50, ch under 10 free) Evening guided tour max 35c people £6. **Facilities:** ⓟ 🍽 ♿ shop 🍴

BIRCHINGTON
Map 05 TR36

POWELL-COTTON MUSEUM, QUEX HOUSE & GARDENS
Quex Park CT7 0BH
➲ (W of Margate on A28. In Birchington right into Park Lane before rdbt in town centre. Entrance 600yds on left)
☎ 01843 842168
e-mail: powell-cotton.museum@virgin.net
web: www.powell-cottonmuseum.co.uk

Major Powell-Cotton spent much of his life on the study of African animals and many different cultures. This museum, founded in 1895, is his legacy, consisting of animal dioramas, photographs, extensive notes, and artefacts from around the world. Also on display in Quex House, the family home, are collections of Eastern and Asian furniture, Kashmir walnut wall carvings, Chinese silk embroidery, and English period furniture. All set within 15 acres of mature gardens, including a Victorian walled garden. Various events throughout the summer.
Times: Open Apr-Oct, Tue-Thu, Sun & BH 11-5, Quex House 2-4.30; Mar, Sun 11-4, Quex House closed, Closed Nov-Feb. **Fee:** ✱ Summer £5 (ch & pen £4, under 5's free), Family ticket (2ad+3ch) £14. Winter £4 (ch & pen £3), Family ticket (2ad+3ch) £10. Garden only £1.50 (ch & pen £1). **Facilities:** ⓟ 🍽 ✖ licensed 🍴 ♿ (two wheelchairs available) toilets for disabled shop ✖ (ex assistance dogs) 🍴

BOROUGH GREEN   Map 05 TQ65

GREAT COMP GARDEN
TN15 8QS
➲ (2m E off B2016)
☎ 01732 882669 886154
e-mail: greatcompgarden@aol.com
web: www.greatcomp.co.uk

A beautiful seven-acre garden created since 1957 by Mr and Mrs R Cameron for low maintenance and year-round interest. There is a plantsmans' collection of trees, shrubs, heathers and herbaceous plants in a setting of fine lawns and grass paths. The 17th-century house is not open. Chamber music, classical concerts and other events are organised by the Great Comp Society, details from the Secretary, Great Comp Society at the above address.
Times: Open Apr-Oct, daily 11-5.30. **Facilities:** 🅿 💺 ✕ 🗑
🚹 (wheelchair for hire) toilets for disabled garden centre
🐕 (ex guide dogs)

BRASTED   Map 05 TQ45

EMMETTS GARDEN
Ide Hill TN14 6AY
➲ (1m S of A25, Sundridge-Ide Hill road)
☎ 01732 750367
e-mail: emmetts@nationaltrust.org.uk
web: www.nationaltrust.org.uk/emmettsgarden

Emmetts is a charming hillside shrub garden, with bluebells, azaleas and rhododendrons in spring and fine autumn colours. It has magnificent views over Bough Beech Reservoir and the Weald.
Times: ✱ Open 20 Mar-27 Jun, Wed-Sun & BH 11-5 (last admission 4.15); 30 Jun-Oct Wed, Sat & Sun **Facilities:** 🅿 💺 🗑
🚹 (wheelchairs, buggy service, Braille/large print guide) toilets for disabled shop 🐕

BROADSTAIRS   Map 05 TR36

DICKENS HOUSE MUSEUM
2 Victoria Pde CT10 1QS
➲ (on the seafront)
☎ 01843 863453
e-mail: leeault@tiscali.co.uk
web: www.dickenshouse.co.uk

The house was immortalised by Charles Dickens in *David Copperfield* as the home of the hero's aunt, Betsy Trotwood, whom Dickens based on owner Miss Mary Pearson Strong. Dickens' letters and possessions are shown, with local and Dickensian prints, costumes and general Victoriana.
Times: Open Etr-Oct, daily 2-5, also Sat-Sun mid Jun-Aug 10.30-5.
Fee: ✱ £2 (ch & student £1). Family ticket (2 ad & 2 ch) £5.
Facilities: 🅿 (400yds) (pay & display) 🗑 shop 🐕 (ex guide dogs)

CANTERBURY   Map 05 TR15

CANTERBURY ROMAN MUSEUM
Butchery Ln, Longmarket CT1 2RA
➲ (in centre close to cathedral and city centre car parks)
☎ 01227 785575
e-mail: museums@canterbury.gov.uk
web: www.canterbury-museum.co.uk

Step below today's Canterbury to discover an exciting part of the Roman town including the real remains of a house with fine mosaics. Experience everyday life in the reconstructed market place and see exquisite silver and glass. Try your
continued

skills on the touch screen computer, and in the hands-on area with actual finds. Use the computer animation of Roman Canterbury to join the search for the lost temple.
Times: Open all year, Mon-Sat 10-5 & Sun (Jun-Oct) 1.30-5. (Last admission 4). Closed Good Fri & Xmas period. **Fee:** ✱ £2.90 (ch 5-18, disabled, pen & students £1.80). Family ticket £7.40
Facilities: 🅿 (walking distance) 🚹 (lift) toilets for disabled shop
🐕 (ex guide dogs)

THE CANTERBURY TALES
St. Margaret's St CT1 2TG
➲ (In heart of city centre, located in St Margaret's St)
☎ 01227 479227   **2 for 1**
e-mail: info@canterburytales.org.uk
web: www.canterburytales.org.uk

Step back in time to experience the sights sounds and smells of the Middle Ages in this reconstruction of 14th century England. Travel from the Tabard Inn, in London, to St. Thomas Becket's Shrine in Canterbury with Chaucer's colourful pilgrims. Their tales of chivalry, romance and intrigue are vividly brought to life for you along your journey.
Times: Open all year, Mar-Jun 10-5, Jul-Aug 9.30-5, Sep-Oct 10-5 & Nov-Feb 10-4.30. Closed 25 Dec **Fee:** £6.95 (ch £5.25, concessions £5.95) Family ticket (2 ad & 2 ch) £22.50 **Facilities:** 🅿 (200mtrs) 💺 🗑 🚹 (notice required for wheelchairs, hearing loop facility) toilets for disabled shop 🐕 (ex guide dogs) 🍴

CANTERBURY WEST GATE MUSEUM
St. Peter's St CT1 2RA
➲ (at end of main street beside river. Entrance under main arch)
☎ 01227 789576
e-mail: museums@canterbury.gov.uk
web: www.canterbury-museum.co.uk

The last of the city's fortified gatehouses sits astride the London road with the river as a moat. Rebuilt in around 1380 by Archbishop Sudbury, it was used as a prison for many years. The battlements give a splendid panoramic view of the city and are a good vantage point for photographs. Arms and armour can be seen in the guardroom, and there are cells in the towers. Brass rubbings can be made and children can try on replica armour.
Times: Open all year (ex Good Fri & Xmas period), Mon-Sat; 11-12.30 & 1.30-3.30. Last admission 15 mins before closure. **Fee:** ✱ £1.10 (ch, disabled, pen, students & UB40 70p). Family ticket £2.60.
Facilities: 🅿 (100yds) shop 🐕 (ex guide dogs)

DRUIDSTONE PARK

Honey Hill, Blean CT2 9JR

➲ (3m NW on A290 from Canterbury)

☎ 01227 765168

2 for 1

web: www.druidstone.net

Idyllic garden setting with enchanted woodland walks where dwells the sleeping dragon. See the mystical Oak circle with the old man of the oaks. Children's farmyard, play areas, gift shop and cafeteria.

Times: Open Etr-Nov, daily, 10-5.30. **Fee:** ✱ £4.80 (ch £3.50 & pen £4). Family ticket £14.50 **Facilities:** 🅿 ⬛ ♿ toilets for disabled shop ✕ (ex guide dogs) 🍴

MUSEUM OF CANTERBURY

Stour St CT1 2RA

➲ (in the Medieval Poor Priests' Hospital, just off St Margaret's St or High St)

☎ 01227 475202

e-mail: museums@canterbury.gov.uk

web: www.canterbury-museum.co.uk

Discover the story of Canterbury in new interactive displays for all the family. See the city's treasures including the famous Canterbury Cross. Try the fun activities in the Medieval Discovery Gallery, find out about the mysteries surrounding Christopher Marlowe's life and death and spot friend or foe planes in the WW2 Blitz gallery. Meet favourite children's TV character Bagpuss and friends and enjoy the Rupert Bear Museum - full of adventure and surprises.

Times: Open all year, Mon-Sat 10.30-5 & Sun (Jun-Sep) 1.30-5 (last admission 4pm). (Closed Good Fri & Xmas period). **Fee:** ✱ £3.10 (concessions £2.10). Family ticket £8.20 (2 Adults + 3 ch) **Facilities:** 🅿 walking ♿ toilets for disabled shop ✕ (ex guide dogs)

ROYAL MUSEUM & ART GALLERY WITH BUFFS MUSEUM

High St CT1 2RA

➲ (in Beaney Institute (1st floor) in High St)

☎ 01227 452747

FREE

e-mail: museums@canterbury.gov.uk

web: www.canterbury-artgallery.co.uk

A splendid Victorian building, houses decorative arts and the city's picture collections- including a gallery for T.S. Cooper, England finest cattle painter. The art gallery is the major space in the area for the visual arts with a varied exhibition programme. Here too is the Buffs Museum, which tells the story of one of England's oldest infantry regiments and its worldwide service.

Times: Open all year, Mon-Sat 10-5. Closed Good Fri and Xmas period. (Last admission 4.45) **Facilities:** 🅿 (500mtrs) shop ✕ (ex guide dogs)

ST AUGUSTINE'S ABBEY

CT1 1TF

➲ (off A28)

☎ 01227 767345

Part of the Canterbury World Heritage site, this is considered by many as the birthplace of Christianity in England. Visit the fascinating museum and take the free interactive audio tour.

Times: Open all year, 24 Mar-Sep, daily, 10-6; Oct-Mar, Wed-Sun, 10-4. Closed 24-26 Dec & 1 Jan. **Fee:** £3.70 (ch £1.90, concessions £2.80). Opening times and prices are subject to change, for further details please phone 0870 333 1181 **Facilities:** 🅿 ♿ shop ♿

CHARTWELL

Map 05 TQ45

CHARTWELL

TN16 1PS

➲ (off A25 onto B2026 at Westerham, Chartwell 2m S of village)

☎ 01732 866368 (info line) & 868381

e-mail: chartwell@nationaltrust.org.uk

web: www.nationaltrust.org.uk/chartwell

The former home of Sir Winston Churchill is filled with reminders of the great statesman, from his hats and uniforms to gifts presented by Stalin, Roosevelt, de Gaulle and many other State leaders. There are portraits of Churchill and other works by notable artists, and also many paintings by Churchill himself.

Times: ✱ Open House, Garden & Studio 20 Mar-7 Nov, Wed-Sun 11-5. Open BH Mon & Tue in Jul & Aug. (Last admission 4.15; 5.30 BH) **Facilities:** 🅿 ✕ licensed 🎫 ♿ (2 steps to lift, parking, guides, sensory facilities) toilets for disabled shop 🐾 🍴

CHATHAM

Map 05 TQ76

FORT AMHERST

Dock Rd ME4 4UB

➲ (adjacent to A231 dock road, 0.5m from Chatham Dockyard)

☎ 01634 847747

e-mail: info@fortamherst.com

web: www.fortamherst.com

A fine Georgian fortress set in over 15 acres of attractive parkland. A fascinating collection of caves, tunnels, gun-batteries and barracks gives visitors an insight into the life of the Napoleonic soldier. Please telephone for details of special events, including historic re-enactments.

Times: Open Sat-Sun Mar-Sep and every day during school holidays. 10.30-4 **Fee:** ✱ £6 (concessions £4) Family ticket £16. **Facilities:** 🅿 ⬛ ♿ (road access up to fort) toilets for disabled shop ✕ (ex guide dogs) 🍴

THE HISTORIC DOCKYARD CHATHAM

ME4 4TZ

➲ (M20 & M2 junct 3, follow signs for Chatham on A229. Then A230 and A231, following brown tourist signs. Brown anchor signs lead to visitors entrance)

☎ 01634 823807

2 for 1

e-mail: info@chdt.org.uk

web: www.thedockyard.co.uk

The Historic Dockyard celebrates over 400 years of naval history in one 80-acre site. Exhibits include Battle Ships with WWII destroyer *HMS Cavalier* and the spy sub *Ocelot*. Lifeboat with a display of 15 full size boats, archive film and artefacts; and Wooden Walls which looks at the life of a carpenter's apprentice in the 18th century. The naval architecture is spectacular.

Times: Open mid Feb-early Nov, daily 10-6. Last entry 4. **Fee:** £10 (ch 5-15 £6.50, concessions £7.50). Family ticket (2ad+2ch) £26.50, additional child £3.25 **Facilities:** 🅿 ⬛ ✕ licensed 🎫 ♿ (wheelchair available, virtual tours) toilets for disabled shop 🍴

CHIDDINGSTONE   Map 05 TQ54
CHIDDINGSTONE CASTLE
TN8 7AD
➲ (off B2027, at Bough Beech)
☎ 01892 870347
The 'castle' is a 17th-century house, almost completely rebuilt in the castle style c1800 by William Atkinson. It contains Stewart and Jacobite paintings and other relics, Egyptian and Oriental antiquities, and a fine collection of Japanese lacquer and swords. The interior has recently been refurbished with extra rooms open to visitors.
Times: ✱ Open Apr-May, Oct, Etr & Public Hols, Jun-Sep, Wed-Fri & Sun. Wkdays 2-5.30; Sun & BH 11.30-5.30. **Facilities:** 🅿 💻 📖 ⅏ shop ✖ (ex guide dogs on lead)

DEAL   Map 05 TR35
DEAL CASTLE
Victoria Rd CT14 7BA
➲ (SW of Deal town centre)
☎ 01304 372762
Discover the history of this formidable fortress as you explore the long, dark passages that once linked a garrison of 119 guns.
Times: Open 24 Mar-Sep, daily 10-6 **Fee:** £3.70 (ch £1.90, concessions £2.80). Opening times and prices are subject to change, for further details please phone 0870 333 1181 **Facilities:** ⅏ (parking available) shop ✖ ⅏

WALMER CASTLE
Kingsdown Rd CT14 7LJ
➲ (1m S on coast, off A258)
☎ 01304 364288
Originally built by Henry VIII as a formidable and austere fortress, the castle has since been transformed into an elegant stately home, formerly used by HM The Queen Mother. Many of her rooms are open to view, but the special highlight is the magnificent gardens.
Times: Open Apr-Sep, daily 10-6 (closes 4pm Sat); Oct, Wed-Sun 10-4; Mar, daily, 10-4. Closed when Lord Warden in residence. **Fee:** £5.95 (ch £3.00, concessions £4.50). Family ticket £14.90. Opening times and prices are subject to change, for further detals please phone 0870 333 1181 **Facilities:** 🅿 💻 ⅏ (parking available) shop ✖ ⅏

DOVER   Map 05 TR34
CRABBLE CORN MILL
Lower Rd, River CT17 0UY
➲ (A2 to Whitfield rdbt then 2nd turning down Whitfield Hill, left. At traffic lights right into River Crabble, under railway bridge and 1st right. Mill 500mtrs on left)
☎ 01304 823292
e-mail: miller@ccmt.org.uk
web: www.ccmt.org.uk
Visit this beautifully restored working Kentish water mill dating from 1812. Regular demonstrations of waterwheel working and making stoneground wholemeal flour from Kentish organic wheat. Flour for sale, also home-baked produce in café. Exhibition space displays work of local artists and craftspeople.
Times: ✱ Open all year, Mar-Sep, daily 11-5; Winter, Sun only (except by appointment). Open all year for groups by arrangement. Closed Xmas & Jan. **Facilities:** 🅿 💻 📖 ⅏ shop ✖ (ex guide dogs)

DOVER CASTLE & SECRET WARTIME TUNNELS
CT16 1HU
☎ 01304 211067
Various exhibitions demonstrate how Dover Castle has served as a vital strategic centre for the Iron Age onwards. In May 1940 the tunnels under the castle became the nerve centre for 'Operation Dynamo' - the evacuation of Dunkirk. These wartime secrets are now revealed for all to see.
Times: 24 Mar-Jun, 10-6, daily. Jul-Aug, 9.30-6.30, daily. Sep, 10-6, daily. Oct, 10-5, daily. Nov-Jan, 10-4, Thu-Mon. Feb-Mar, 10-4 daily. Closed 24-26 Dec & 1 Jan. Keep closes at 5 on days of hospitality events. Site open from noon on 12 Apr for the installation of the new Lord Warden. **Fee:** £8.95 (ch £4.50, concessions £6.70). Family £22.40 (2ad+2ch). Opening times and prices are subject to change, for further details please phne 0870 333 1181 **Facilities:** 🅿 ✖ ⅏ shop ✖ (ex on lead in certain areas) ⅏

ROMAN PAINTED HOUSE
New St CT17 9AJ
➲ (follow A20 to York St bypass, located in town centre)
☎ 01304 203279
Visit five rooms of a Roman hotel built 1800 years ago, famous for its unique, well-preserved Bacchic frescos. The Roman underfloor heating system and part of a late-Roman defensive wall are also on view. There are extensive displays on Roman Dover.
Times: Open Apr-Sep, Tue-Sun 10-5, also BH Mon & Mon Jul & Aug. **Fee:** ✱ £2 (ch & pen 80p) **Facilities:** 🅿 📖 ⅏ (touch table, glass panels on gallery for wheelchairs) shop ✖ (ex assist dogs)

DYMCHURCH   Map 05 TR12
DYMCHURCH MARTELLO TOWER
High St CT16 1HU
➲ (access from High St not seafront)
☎ 01304 211067
This artillery tower formed part of a chain of strongholds intended to resist invasion by Napoleon.
Times: Opening Aug Bank Holiday and Heritage Open Days **Fee:** £2.00 (ch £1.00, concessions £1.50). Opening times and prices are subject to change **Facilities:** ✖ ⅏

EDENBRIDGE
See **Hever**

EYNSFORD   Map 05 TQ56
EAGLE HEIGHTS
Lullingstone Ln DA4 0JB
➲ (M25 junct 3/A20 towards West Kingsdown. Right after 2 rdbts onto A225. Follow brown signs)
☎ 01322 866466
e-mail: office@eagleheights.co.uk
web: www.eagleheights.co.uk
Eagle Heights is an impressive display of birds of prey from all over the world. Many are flown out across the Darenth valley twice daily. Meet the owls, pygmy goat and rabbits in the paddock.
Times: Mar-Nov daily 10.30-5. Nov, Jan-Feb wknd only 11-4. Dec closed. **Fee:** ✱ £6.70 (ch £4.70 4-14yrs, concessions £5.70) **Facilities:** 🅿 💻 ⅏ toilets for disabled shop ✖ 🍴

EYNSFORD CASTLE

➲ (in Eynsford, off A225)　　FREE

One of the first stone castles to be built by the Normans. The moat and remains of the curtain wall and hall can still be seen.
Times: 24 Mar-Sep, 10-6, daily. Oct-Nov, 10-4, daily. Dec-Jan, 10-4, Wed-Sun. Feb-Mar, 10-4, daily. Closed 24-26 Dec and 1 Jan
Facilities: P & ♯

LULLINGSTONE CASTLE

DA4 0JA
➲ (1m SW of Eynsford via A225 & Lullingstone Roman Villa)
☎ 01322 862114

The house was altered extensively in Queen Anne's time, and has fine state rooms and beautiful grounds. The 15th-century gate tower was one of the first gatehouses in England to be made entirely of bricks, and there is a church with family monuments. Please telephone for details of special events.
Times: House & Garden Apr-Oct, Fri-Sat 12-5, Sun & BH 2-6. Parties by arrangement. **Fee:** ✱ House & Gardens £5.50 (ch £2.50 & pen £5) Family £12.50. **Facilities:** P 🍽 & shop ✖ (ex guide dogs)

LULLINGSTONE ROMAN VILLA

Lullingstone Ln DA4 0JA
➲ (0.5m SW off A225)
☎ 01322 863467

One of the most exciting finds with wonderful mosaic floors, wall paintings and skeletal remains. Audio tours offer a fascinating insight into the life of a well-to-do Roman family.
Times: Open 24 Mar-Sep, 10-6, daily. Oct-Nov, 10-4, daily. Dec-Jan, 10-4, Wed-Sun. Feb-Mar, 10-4, daily. Closed 24-26 Dec & 1 Jan
Fee: £3.70 (ch £1.90, concessions £2.80). Opening times and prices are subject to change, for further details please phone 0870 333 1181
Facilities: P ✖ ♯

FAVERSHAM　　　　　　Map 05 TR06

FLEUR DE LIS HERITAGE CENTRE

10-13 Preston St ME13 8NS
➲ (3 minutes drive from M2 junct 6)
☎ 01795 534542　　　　2 for 1
e-mail: faversham@btinternet.com
web: www.faversham.org

Recently expanded and updated, and housed in 16th-century premises, the Centre features colourful displays and room settings that vividly evoke the 2000 year history of Faversham. Special features include the 'Gunpowder Experience' and a working old-style village telephone exchange, one of only two remaining in Britain. In July, during the Faversham Open House Scheme, over 20 historic properties in the town are opened to the public.
Times: Open all year, Mon-Sat, 10-4; Sun 10-1. **Fee:** ✱ £2 (ch & pen £1) **Facilities:** P (200yds) & DVD show of parts that are inaccessible toilets for disabled shop ◼

GILLINGHAM　　　　　　Map 05 TQ76

ROYAL ENGINEERS MUSEUM

Prince Arthur Rd ME4 4UG
➲ (follow brown signs from Gillingham & Chatham town centres)
☎ 01634 822839　　　　2 for 1
e-mail: mail@re-museum.co.uk
web: www.royalengineers.org.uk

The museum covers the diverse and sometimes surprising work of the Royal Engineers. Learn about the first military
continued

divers, photographers, aviators and surveyors; see memorabilia relating to General Gordon and Field Marshal Lord Kitchener, Wellington's battle map from Waterloo and a Harrier jump-jet. The superb medal displays include 26 Victoria Crosses.
Times: Open all year, Tue-Fri 9-5, Sat-Sun & BH Mon 11.30-5. Closed Good Fri, Xmas week & 1 Jan. **Fee:** £5.75 (concessions £3).
Facilities: P 🍽 & (help available if required, chair lift to upper level) toilets for disabled shop ✖ (ex guide dogs) ◼

GOUDHURST　　　　　　Map 05 TQ73

FINCHCOCKS

TN17 1HH
➲ (off A262)
☎ 01580 211702
e-mail: katrina@finchcocks.co.uk
web: www.finchcocks.co.uk

This fine early Georgian house stands in a spacious park with a beautiful garden, and contains an outstanding collection of keyboard instruments from the 17th century onwards. They have been restored to playing condition, and there are musical tours on all open days and private visits. Visually handicapped visitors may touch the instruments as well as hear them.
Times: Open Etr-Sep, Sun & BH Mon 2-6; Aug, Wed, Thu & Sun only 2-6. Private groups on other days by appointment Apr-Oct & Dec.
Facilities: P 🍽 ✖ licensed & (wheelchair available, Braille signs) toilets for disabled shop garden centre ✖ (ex guide dogs)

GROOMBRIDGE PLACE　　Map 05 TQ53

GROOMBRIDGE PLACE GARDENS & ENCHANTED FOREST

TN3 9QG
➲ (M25 junct 5, follow A21 S, exit at A26 (signed Tunbridge Wells), then take A264 - follow signs to Groombridge village and Groombridge Place Gardens)
☎ 01892 861444
e-mail: office@groombridge.co.uk
web: www.groombridge.co.uk

This award-winning attraction, set in 200 acres, features a series of magnificent walled gardens set against the backdrop of a romantic 17th-century moated manor. Explore the herbaceous border, the white rose garden, the 'Drunken Topiary', the 'Secret Garden' and the peacock walk. By way of contrast in the ancient woodland of the 'Enchanted Forest', the imagination is stimulated by mysterious features such as the 'Dark Walk', 'Dinosaur and Dragon Valley' and
continued

'Groms' Village'. There are also bird of prey flying displays, canal boat cruises, and a full programme of special events. **Times:** Open Apr-5 Nov, daily 10-5.30 **Fee:** £8.70 (ch 3-12 & pen £7.20). Family ticket (2ad+2ch) £29.50. Groups 20+ available on request. **Facilities:** 🅿 ✗ ⅱ ♿ toilets for disabled shop ✖ (ex guide/hearing dogs) ◼

See advertisement on opposite page

HAWKINGE — Map 05 TR23

KENT BATTLE OF BRITAIN MUSEUM
Aerodrome Rd CT18 7AG
⮑ (off A260, 1m along Aerodrome road)
☎ 01303 893140
e-mail: kentbattleofbritainmuseum@
btinternet.com
web: www.kbobm.org

Once a Battle of Britain Station, today it houses the largest collection of relics and related memorabilia of British and German aircraft involved in the fighting. Also shown, full-size replicas of the Hurricane, Spitfire and Me109 used in Battle of Britain films. The year 2000 was the 60th anniversary of the Battle of Britain and a new memorial was dedicated. Artefacts on show, recovered from over 600 battle of Britain aircraft, all form a lasting memorial to all those involved in the conflict.
Times: ✱ Open Etr-Sep, daily 10-5; Oct, daily 11-4. (Last admission 1 hour before closing). **Facilities:** 🅿 ◼ ♿ shop ✖ (ex guide dogs)

HEVER — Map 05 TQ44

HEVER CASTLE & GARDENS
TN8 7NG
⮑ (M25 junct 5 or 6, 3m SE of Edenbridge, off B2026)
☎ 01732 865224
e-mail: mail@hevercastle.co.uk
web: www.hevercastle.co.uk

This enchanting, double-moated, 13th-century castle was the childhood home of Anne Boleyn. Restored by the American millionaire William Waldorf Astor at the beginning of the 20th century, it shows superb Edwardian craftsmanship. Astor also transformed the grounds, creating topiary, a yew maze, 35 acre lake and Italian gardens filled with antique sculptures. There is also a 100 metre herbaceous border, 'splashing' water maze on the Sixteen Acre Island, as well as a woodland walk known as Sunday Walk. Adventure play area with the Henry VIII Tower Maze.
Times: Open Mar-Nov, daily. Castle 12-6, Gardens 11-6. (Last admission 5). (Closes 4pm Mar & Nov). **Fee:** ✱ Castle & Gardens

continued

£9.20 (ch 5-14 £5, pen £7.70). Family ticket £23.40. Gardens only £7.30 (ch 5-14 £4.80, pen £6.30). Family ticket £19.40. . **Facilities:** 🅿 ◼ ✗ licensed ♿ (wheelchairs available, book in advance) toilets for disabled shop garden centre ✖ (ex in garden on leads) ◼

HYTHE — Map 05 TR13

ROMNEY, HYTHE & DYMCHURCH RAILWAY
TN28 8PL
⮑ (M20 junct 11, off A259 signed New Romney)
☎ 01797 362353 & 363256
e-mail: rhdr@romneyrail.fsnet.co.uk
web: www.rhdr.demon.co.uk

The world's smallest public railway has its headquarters here. The concept of two enthusiasts coincided with Southern Railway's plans for expansion, and so the thirteen-and-a-half mile stretch of 15 inch gauge railway came into being, running from Hythe through New Romney and Dymchurch to Dungeness Lighthouse.
Times: ✱ Open daily Etr-Sep, also wknds in Mar & Oct. For times apply to: The Manager, RH & DR, New Romney, Kent.
Facilities: 🅿 (charged) ◼ ⅱ ♿ (stairlift to Toy & Model Museum) toilets for disabled shop (Dymchurch & Dungeness high season only) ◼

IGHTHAM — Map 05 TQ55

IGHTHAM MOTE
TN15 0NT
⮑ (2.5m S off A227, 6m E of Sevenoaks)
☎ 01732 810378 & 811145 (info line)
e-mail: ighthammote@nationaltrust.org.uk
web: www.nationaltrust.org.uk

This moated manor house, nestling in a sunken valley, dates from 1330. The main features of the house span many centuries and include the Great Hall, old chapel and crypt, Tudor chapel with painted ceiling, drawing room with Jacobean fireplace, frieze and 18th-century handpainted Chinese wallpaper and the billiards room. There is an extensive garden as well as interesting walks in the surrounding woodland. Following completion of all conservation work visitors can enjoy the most extensive visitor route to date, including the bedroom of Charles Henry Robinson who bequeathed Ightham Mote to the National Trust.
Times: Open 12 Mar-29 Oct, daily ex Tue & Sat, 10-5.30. Open Good Fri. (Last admission 5). **Fee:** £8.50 (ch £4). Family ticket £21.
Facilities: 🅿 ◼ ✗ licensed ⅱ ♿ (wheelchairs,special parking ask at office, virtual tour) toilets for disabled shop ✖ (ex hearing & guide dogs) ◼◼

GROOMBRIDGE PLACE GARDENS
& ENCHANTED FOREST

These award winning gardens, set in 200 acres of wooded parkland, feature a series of magnificent walled gardens set against the romantic backdrop of a 17th century moated manor house, including -

- Secret Garden
- Paradise Walk
- Knot Garden
- Herbaceous borders
- White Rose Garden

In complete contrast, in the ancient woodland of the 'Enchanted Forest' there's mystery, magic and excitement to challenge the imagination of young and old alike. Children love the -

- Giant Swings Walk
- Tree Fern Valley
- Village of the Groms
- Mystic Pool
- Canal Boat Rides
- Birds of Prey Flying Displays

RESTAURANT, PICNIC AREA & GIFT SHOP. SPECIAL EVENTS PROGRAMME
Open daily: 10.00am–5.30pm, 1st April to 5th November, 2006.
Groombridge Place, Groombridge, Nr. Tunbridge Wells, Kent TN3 9QG. Only 25 minutes south of the M25 Junction 5.

Info Hotline: Call 01892 861444 or visit the website www.groombridge.co.uk

---

LAMBERHURST · Map 05 TQ63

BAYHAM ABBEY
TN3 8DE
➲ (off B2169, 2m W in East Sussex)
☎ 01892 890381
Explore the romantic ruins of this 13th-century abbey built by French monks in an 18th-century landscaped setting.
Times: Open 24 Mar-Sep, daily 11-5. Closed Oct-Mar. **Fee:** £3.30 (ch £1.70, concessions £2.50). Opening times and prices are subject to change, for further details please phone 0870 333 1181
Facilities: 🅿 ♿ ✿

SCOTNEY CASTLE GARDEN
TN3 8JN
➲ (1m S, of Lamberhurst on A21)
☎ 01892 891081
e-mail: scotneycastle@nationaltrust.org.uk
web: www.nationaltrust.org.uk
The beautiful gardens at Scotney were planned in the 19th century around the remains of the old, moated Scotney Castle. There is something to see at every time of year, with spring flowers followed by rhododendrons, azaleas and a mass of roses, and then superb autumn colours. Estate walks all year through 770 acres of woodlands and meadows, walker's guide available.
Times: Garden: Apr-end Oct. Old Castle: May-mid Sep, Wed-Sun, 11-6 or sunset if earlier. BH Mon 11-6. Closed Good Fri. (Last admission 1hr before closing). **Fee:** ✱ Telephone for details. **Facilities:** 🅿 📷 ♿ (wheelchair hire, Braille/large print guidebook, audio tape) toilets for disabled shop garden centre small plants ✖ (ex guide & hearing dogs) 🐾 🍴

LYDD · Map 05 TR02

RSPB NATURE RESERVE
Boulderwall Farm, Dungeness Rd TN29 9PN
➲ (off Lydd to Dungeness road, 1m SE of Lydd, follow tourist signs)
☎ 01797 320588
e-mail: dungeness@rspb.org.uk
web: www.rspb.org.uk
This coastal reserve comprises 2106 acres of shingle beach and flooded pits. An excellent place to watch breeding terns, gulls and other water birds. Wheatears, great crested and little grebes also nest here, and outside the breeding season there are large flocks of teals, shovelers, and goldeneyes, goosanders, smews and both Slavonian and red-necked grebes. 2006 marks the 75th anniversary of the reserve.
Times: Open: Visitor Centre all year, daily 10-5 (10-4 Nov-Feb). Reserve open all year, daily 9am-9pm (or sunset if earlier). Closed 25-26 Dec.
Fee: £3 (ch £1, concessions £2). **Facilities:** 🅿 📷 ♿ (access by car to some hides) toilets for disabled shop ✖ (ex guide dogs) 🍴

LYMPNE · Map 05 TR13

PORT LYMPNE WILD ANIMAL PARK, MANSION & GARDEN
CT21 4PD
➲ (M20 junct 11, follow brown tourist signs)
☎ 0870 750 4647
e-mail: info@totallywild.net
web: www.totallywild.net

2 for 1

A 400-acre wild animal park that houses hundreds of rare animals: Indian elephants, rhinos, wolves, bison, snow leopards, Siberian and Indian tigers, gorillas and monkeys. New features include a glass-fronted lion enclosure and an

continued

open-topped woodland home for the Colobus monkeys. The mansion designed by Sir Herbert Baker is surrounded by 15 acres of spectacular gardens. Inside, notable features include the restored Rex Whistler Tent Room, a Moroccan patio, and the hexagonal library where the Treaty of Paris was signed after World War I. Visit the Spencer Roberts mural room and the Martin Jordan animal mural room. Various events through 2006, a year that also marks Port Lympne's 30th anniversary.

Times: Open all year, daily 10-6 (closes at dusk in summer). (Last admission 4.30 summer, 3 winter. Closed 25 Dec. **Fee:** £12.95 (ch 4-14 & pen £9.95). Family ticket £38 (2ad+2ch) £44 (2ad+3ch).

Facilities: P ▣ ✗ licensed ঙ (very limited access for disabled, special route available) toilets for disabled shop garden centre (in season) ✖ ▄

MAIDSTONE   Map 05 TQ75

LEEDS CASTLE

ME17 1PL

➲ (7m E of Maidstone at junct 8 of M20/A20, clearly signed)

☎ 01622 765400

e-mail: enquiries@leeds-castle.co.uk
web: www.leeds-castle.com

Set on two islands in the centre of a lake, Leeds Castle has been called the 'loveliest castle in the world', and was home to six medieval Queens of England, as well as being Henry VIII's Royal Palace. Among the treasures inside are many paintings, tapestries and furnishings. Attractions in the grounds include formal gardens, exotic aviary, dog collar museum, vineyard, woodland walks, toddlers play area, yew maze with secret underground grotto and daily falconry displays.

Times: Open daily, Mar-Oct 10-5 (Castle 11-5.30). Nov-Mar 10-3 (Castle 10-3). Closed 26 Jun; 3 Jul; 5 Nov; 25 Dec **Fee:** ✱ Fully incl ticket £13 (ch & disabled £9, conc £11). Family (2ad+3ch) £39. Grounds, aviary & dog collar museum £10.50 (ch & disabled £6.50, conc £8.50). Family (2ad + 3ch) £33. **Facilities:** P ✗ licensed ▦ ঙ (Braille information, induction loops & wheelchair, lift) toilets for disabled shop garden centre ✖ (ex guide dogs) ▄

MAIDSTONE MUSEUM & BENTLIF ART GALLERY

Saint Faith's St ME14 1LH

➲ (close to County Hall & Maidstone E train stn)

☎ 01622 602838   FREE

e-mail: museum@maidstone.gov.uk
web: www.museum.maidstone.gov.uk

Set in an Elizabethan manor house which has been much extended over the years, this museum houses an outstanding collection of fine and applied arts, including watercolours, furniture, ceramics, and a collection of Japanese art and artefacts. The museum of the Queen's Own Royal West Kent Regiment is also housed here. Please apply for details of temporary exhibitions, workshops etc.

Times: Open all year, Mon-Sat 10-5.15, Sun & BH Mon 11-4. Closed 25-26 Dec. **Facilities:** P (150 mtrs) ▣ ▦ ঙ shop ✖ (ex guide dogs) ▄

MUSEUM OF KENT LIFE

Lock Ln, Sandling ME14 3AU

➲ (from M20 junct 6 onto A229 Maidstone road, follow signs for Aylesford)   2 for 1

☎ 01622 763936

e-mail: enquiries@museum-kentlife.co.uk
web: www.museum-kentlife.co.uk

Kent's award-winning open air museum is home to an outstanding collection of historic buildings which house exhibitions on life in Kent over the last 100 years. An early 20th-century village hall and reconstruction of cottages from the 17th & 20th-centuries are more recent buildings to be viewed.

Times: Open Feb-Nov, daily 10-5, in winter open every wknd 10-3. **Fee:** ✱ £6.50 (ch 4-15 £4.50, under 4's free, pen £5). Family ticket £20. **Facilities:** P ▣ ✗ ▦ ঙ (wheelchairs available, ramps, transport available) toilets for disabled shop on leads only ▄

TYRWHITT DRAKE MUSEUM OF CARRIAGES

The Archbishop's Stables, Mill St ME15 6YE

➲ (close to River Medway & Archbishops Palace, just off A229 in town centre)

☎ 01622 602838   FREE

e-mail: museuminfo@maidstone.gov.uk
web: www.museum.maidstone.gov.uk

The museum is home to a unique collection of horse-drawn vehicles and transport curiosities. More than 60 vehicles are on display, from grand carriages and ornate sleighs to antique sedan chairs and Victorian cabs, there is even an original ice-cream cart.

Times: Open Jun-mid Sep, 10.30-4.30 **Facilities:** P (50yds) ▦ ঙ shop ✖ (ex guide dogs)

PENSHURST   Map 05 TQ54

PENSHURST PLACE & GARDENS

TN11 8DG

➲ (M25 junct 5 take A21 Hastings road then exit at Hildenborough & follow signs)

☎ 01892 870307

e-mail: enquiries@penshurstplace.com
web: www.penshurstplace.com

Built between 1340 and 1345, the original house is perfectly preserved. Enlarged by successive owners during the 15th, 16th and 17th centuries, the great variety of architectural styles creates a dramatic backdrop for the extensive collections of English, French and Italian furniture, tapestries and paintings. The chestnut-beamed Baron's Hall is the oldest and finest in the country, and the house is set in .

continued

Directions are provided by the attractions.

magnificent formal gardens. There is a toy museum, venture playground, woodland trail and 10 acres of walled formal gardens.
Times: Open: wknds from early Mar, daily from late Mar-late Oct. Grounds open 10.30-6. House open noon-4. **Fee:** ✱ House & Grounds £7 (ch 5-16 £5, pen & students £6.50). Family £20. Grounds only £5.50 (ch 5-16 £4.50, pen & students £5) Family £17. Party 20+. Garden season ticket £35. **Facilities:** 🅿 ✗ licensed ⅊ (ramp into Barons Hall, Braille & large print guides) toilets for disabled shop ✖ (ex guide dogs) ▰

RAMSGATE   Map 05 TR36
RAMSGATE MARITIME MUSEUM
Clock House, Pier Yard, Royal Harbour CT11 8LS
➲ (follow Harbour signs)
☎ 01843 587765 & 570622
e-mail: museum@ekmt.fsnet.co.uk
web: www.ekmt.fsnet.co.uk

2 for 1

The Maritime Museum Ramsgate is housed in the early 19th-century Clock House, and contains four galleries depicting various aspects of the maritime heritage of the East Kent area. A temporary gallery/conservation room is due to open in summer 2005, featuring a 17th Century naval gun. The 'Dunkirk Little Ship' motor yacht 'Sundower' may also be visited by prior arrangement.
Times: Open Etr-Sep, Tue-Sun 10-5. Oct-Etr Thu-Sun 10-4.30.
Fee: ✱ Combined ticket for museum £1.50. (ch & pen 75p). Family £4.
Facilities: 🅿 (charged) 🍽 ⅊ (restricted) shop ✖

RECULVER   Map 05 TR26
RECULVER TOWERS & ROMAN FORT
CT6 6SU
➲ (3m E of Herne Bay)
☎ 01227 740676

FREE

An imposing 12th-century landmark: twin towers and the walls of a Roman fort.
Times: Open any reasonable time, external viewing only.
Facilities: 🅿 ⅊ (long slope from car park to fort) ♿

RICHBOROUGH   Map 05 TR36
RICHBOROUGH CASTLE
CT13 9JW
➲ (1.5m N of Sandwich off A257)
☎ 01304 612013

Explore the site of the first Roman landing in Britain and visit the museum with its collection of artefacts uncovered on site. See the remains of the huge triumphal arch, once 25 metres high.
Times: Open 24 Mar-Sep, daily 10-6. **Fee:** £3.70 (ch £1.90, concessions £2.80). Opening hours and prices are subject to change, for further details please phone 0870 333 1181
Facilities: 🅿 ⅊ shop ♿

ROCHESTER   Map 05 TQ76
GUILDHALL MUSEUM
High St ME1 1PY
➲ (follow signs from A2 to Rochester city centre, museum is at N end of High St)
☎ 01634 848717

FREE

e-mail: guildhall.museum@medway.gov.uk
web: www.medway.gov.uk
Housed in two adjacent buildings, one dating from 1687 and the other from 1909. The collections are arranged chronologically from Prehistory to the Victorian and

continued

Edwardian periods. They cover local history and archaeology, fine and decorative art. There is a gallery devoted to the prison hulks of the River Medway. The museum stages a regular programme of temporary exhibitions.
Times: Open all year, daily 10-4.30. (Last admission 4). Closed Xmas & New Year. **Facilities:** 🅿 (250 yds) ⅊ shop ✖ (ex guide & hearing dogs)

ROCHESTER CASTLE
ME1 1SX
➲ (M2 junct 1 & M25 junct 2, A2, by Rochester Bridge)
☎ 01634 402276

Built on the Roman City Wall, this Norman bishop's castle was a vital royal stronghold.
Times: Open all year, Apr-Sep, daily 10-6; Oct-Mar, daily 10-4. Closed 24-26 Dec & 1 Jan. **Fee:** £4 (ch & concessions £3). Family £11.
Facilities: shop ✖

ROLVENDEN   Map 05 TQ83
C M BOOTH COLLECTION OF HISTORIC VEHICLES
Falstaff Antiques, 63 High St TN17 4LP
➲ (on A28, 3m from Tenterden)
☎ 01580 241234
e-mail: info@morganmuseum.co.uk
web: www.morganmuseum.co.uk

2 for 1

Not just vehicles, but various other items of interest connected with transport. There is a unique collection of three-wheel Morgan cars, dating from 1913, and the only known Humber tri-car of 1904, as well as a 1929 Morris van, a 1936 Bampton caravan, motorcycles and bicycles. There is also a toy and model car display.
Times: Open all year, Mon-Sat 10-5.30. Closed 25-26 Dec. **Fee:** ✱ £2 (ch £1) **Facilities:** 🅿 (roadside) shop Antiques ▰

SEVENOAKS   Map 05 TQ55
KNOLE
TN15 0RP
➲ (From town centre, off A225 Tonbridge road)
☎ 01732 462100 & 450608 (info line)
e-mail: knole@nationaltrust.org.uk
web: www.nationaltrust.org.uk/knole

Knole's historic links with kings, queens and the nobility, as well as literary connections with Vita Sackville-West and Virginia Woolf, make this one of the most intriguing houses

continued

in England. Thirteen staterooms are laid out much the same as they were in the 17th century, to impress visitors with the wealth and standing of those who lived there. The house includes rare furniture, paintings by Gainsborough, Van Dyck and Reynolds, as well as many 17th-century tapestries. Knole is set at the heart of the only remaining medieval deer park in Kent.

Times: House open end Mar-end Oct, Wed-Sun & BH Mon 12-4 (last entry 3.30). Garden restricted opening, telephone for details.
Fee: £7.50 (ch £3.75). Family ticket £18.75. Parking £2.50 per car. Groups 15+ £6.50. **Facilities:** 🅿 (charged) 💷 ♿ (audio loop, Braille guide, virtual tour) toilets for disabled shop ✖ (ex assist dogs & in park) 🐾 🍴

SISSINGHURST   Map 05 TQ73

SISSINGHURST CASTLE GARDEN
TN17 2AB
➲ (1m E of Sissinghurst village on A262)
☎ 01580 710700
e-mail: sissinghurst@nationaltrust.org.uk
web: www.nationaltrust.org.uk

Made in the ruins of a large Elizabethan house and set in unspoilt countryside, Sissinghurst Castle Garden is one of the most celebrated gardens created by Vita Sackville-West and her husband Sir Harold Nicolson. Phone for details of special events.

Times: Open: Gardens mid Mar-end Oct, Mon, Tue & Fri 11-6.30, Sat, Sun & BH's 10-6.30. (Last admission 5.30). Closed Wed & Thu. (Peace & Tranquillity after 3) **Fee:** £7.50 (ch £3.50) Family £18.50
Facilities: 🅿 ✖ licensed ♿ (admission restricted to 2 wheelchairs at any one time) toilets for disabled shop ✖ (ex guide dogs) 🐾 🍴

SITTINGBOURNE   Map 05 TQ96

DOLPHIN SAILING BARGE MUSEUM
Crown Quay Ln ME10 3SN
➲ (N on A2, signed)
☎ 01795 421549 & 424132
web: www.kentaccess.org.uk/artmuse/dolphin

The museum presents the history of the Thames spritsail sailing barge, many of which were built along the banks of Milton Creek. Tools of the trade, photographs and associated artefacts can be seen at the barge yard along with the sailing barge Cambria. Privately owned barges are repaired - there's a forge, shipwright's shop and sail loft. There are many fine models.

Times: ✱ Open Etr-Oct, Sun & BHs 11-5. May only, Sat 1-4. Other times by arrangement. **Facilities:** 🅿 📷 ♿ toilets for disabled

SMALLHYTHE   Map 05 TQ83

SMALLHYTHE PLACE
TN30 7NG
➲ (2m S of Tenterden, on E side of the Rye Road on B2082)
☎ 01580 762334
e-mail: smallytheplace.ntrust.org.uk
web: www.nationaltrust.org.uk

Once a Tudor harbour master's house, this half-timbered, 16th-century building was Dame Ellen Terry's last home, and is now a museum of Ellen Terry memorabilia. The Barn Theatre houses a display and the cottage garden contains roses, an orchard and spring garden.

Times: Open 4-19 Mar, Sat & Sun only; 25 Mar-29 Oct, Sat-Wed 11-5 (last admission 4.30pm) **Fee:** £4.50 (ch £2). Family £11
Facilities: 🅿 📷 ♿ (album of descriptions & photos of upstairs, Braille guide) ✖ (ex guide dogs & on a lead) 🐾

STROOD   Map 05 TQ76

DIGGERLAND
Medway Valley Leisure Park, Roman Way ME2 2NU
➲ (M2 junct 2, follow A228 towards Rochester. At rdbt turn right. Diggerland on right)
☎ 08700 344437   **2 for 1**
e-mail: mail@diggerland.com
web: www.diggerland.com

An adventure park with a difference. Experience the thrills of driving real earth moving equipment. Choose from various types of diggers and dumpers ranging from 1 ton to 8.5 tons. Complete the Dumper Truck Challenge or dig for buried treasure supervised by an instructor. New rides include JCB Robots, the Supertrack, Landrover Safari, Spin Dizzy and the Diggerland Tractors.

Times: Open all year, 10-5, wknds, BHs & school hols only
Fee: ✱ £2.50 for all over 2yrs (pen £1.25) Additional charges to ride/drive real machinery **Facilities:** 🅿 💷 ♿ toilets for disabled shop ✖ (ex guide dogs) 🍴

SWINGFIELD MINNIS   Map 05 TR24

THE BUTTERFLY CENTRE
MacFarlanes Garden Centre CT15 7HX
➲ (on A260 by junction with Elham-Lydden road)
☎ 01303 844244   **2 for 1**
e-mail: macfarlanes@
gardensandtress.fsnet.co.uk

A tropical greenhouse garden with scores of colourful free-flying butterflies from all over the world among exotic plants such as bougainvillea, oleander and banana. The temperate section houses British butterflies, with many favourite species and some rarer varieties.

Times: Open Apr-1 Oct, daily 10-5. Closed Etr Sun. **Fee:** £3 (ch £2 & concessions £2.50). Family ticket (2ad+2ch) £8.50. **Facilities:** 🅿 💷 ✖ 📷 ♿ toilets for disabled shop garden centre ✖ (ex guide dogs) 🍴

TENTERDEN   Map 05 TQ83

KENT & EAST SUSSEX RAILWAY NEW
Tenterden Town Station, Station Rd TN30 6HE
➲ (A28 turn into Station Rd beside The Vine Public House, station 200yds on right)
☎ 0870 6006074
e-mail: enquiries@kesr.org.uk
web: www.kesr.org.uk

Less than an hour from the M25 lies an area of hills, woods and marshland. The railway line joins together the Weald, Tenterden Town and Bodiam Castle, brushing past the Sussex village of Northiam on the way. The railway has featured many times in both films and television.

Times: Open Etr-Sep weekdays & wknds. Other times of the year wknds & school holidays. See web site for details. Five trains per day
Fee: ✱ £10 (ch £5, senior £9) Family £26 **Facilities:** 🅿 💷 ✖ licensed ♿ (Converted coach for w/chairs) toilets for disabled shop 🍴

> ## If an attraction name appears in *italics*, details have not been confirmed for 2006.

TUNBRIDGE WELLS (ROYAL)   Map 05 TQ53

TUNBRIDGE WELLS MUSEUM AND ART GALLERY

Civic Centre, Mount Pleasant TN1 1JN
➲ (adjacent to Town Hall, off A264)
☎ 01892 554171 & 526121   **FREE**
web: www.tunbridgewells.gov.uk/museum

The museum displays local history, along with Tunbridge ware, archaeology, toys and dolls, and domestic and agricultural bygones. The art gallery has regularly changing art and craft exhibitions and touring displays from British and European museums.

Times: Open all year, daily 9.30-5. Sun 10-4. Closed BHs & Etr Sat.
Facilities: P (200 yds) ⬗ & (parking adjacent to building) shop ✈ (ex guide dogs)

UPNOR   Map 05 TQ77

UPNOR CASTLE

ME2 4XG
➲ (on unclass road off A228)
☎ 01634 718742 & 338110

16th-century gun fort built to protect Elizabeth I's warships. It saw action in 1667, when the Dutch navy sailed up the Medway to attack the dockyard at Chatham.

Times: Open 25-31 Mar, 10-4, daily; Apr-Sep, daily 10-6; Oct, daily 10-4. **Fee:** Adult £4.00 (ch & concessions £3.00). Family ticket £11.00
Facilities: P &

WESTERHAM   Map 05 TQ45

QUEBEC HOUSE

TN16 1TD
➲ (at E end of village on N side of A25 facing junct with B2026 Edenbridge Road)
☎ 01892 890651
e-mail: chartwell@nationaltrust.org.uk
web: www.nationaltrust.org.uk

Westerham was the birthplace of General Wolfe, who spent his childhood in this multi-gabled, square brick house, now renamed Quebec House. The house probably dates from the 16th century and was extended and altered in the 17th century. It contains a Wolfe museum and an exhibition on Wolfe and the Quebec campaign.

Times: ✱ Open Apr-Oct, Tue & Sun only 2-5.30. (Last admission 5.00). Parties by written arrangement. **Facilities:** P (150m) ⬗ & (tactile items) toilets for disabled ✈ (ex guide dogs) ⬥

SQUERRYES COURT MANOR HOUSE & GARDENS

TN16 1SJ   **2 for 1**
➲ (0.5m W of town centre, signed off A25)
☎ 01959 562345 & 563118
e-mail: squerryes.court@squerryes.co.uk
web: www.squerryes.co.uk

This beautiful manor house, built in 1681, has been the home of the Wardes since 1731. It contains a fine collection of pictures, furniture, porcelain and tapestries. The lovely garden was landscaped in the 18th century and has a lake, restored formal garden, and woodland walks.

Times: Open Apr-Sep, Wed, Thu, Sun & BH Mon. Garden open 11.30-5, House 1-5 (last entry 5) **Fee:** ✱ House & grounds £5.50 (ch 16 £3 & pen £5). Family ticket £13. Grounds £3.60 (ch 16 £2 & pen £3.30)
Facilities: P ⬗ ⬗ & (telephone in advance, part of grounds accessible) toilets for disabled shop ✈ (ex on leads in grounds)

WEST MALLING   Map 05 TQ65

ST LEONARD'S TOWER

ME19 6PE
➲ (on unclass road W of A228)
☎ 01732 870872   **FREE**

Early example of a Norman tower keep, built c.1080 by Gundulf, Bishop of Rochester. The tower stands almost to its original height and takes its name from a chapel dedicated to St Leonard that once stood nearby.

Times: Open any reasonable time for exterior viewing. Contact West Malling Parish Council for interior viewing - 01732 870872.
Facilities: & ⬕

YALDING   Map 05 TQ75

YALDING ORGANIC GARDENS

Benover Rd ME18 6EX
➲ (on B2162, 0.5m S of Yalding.)
☎ 01622 814650   **2 for 1**
e-mail: enquiry@hdra.org.uk
web: www.hdra.org.uk

Fourteen gardens tell the history of gardening in an imaginatively landscaped setting. Travel through representations of ancient woodlands, medieval physic, knot and paradise gardens and a 19th-century artisan's plot, borders inspired by Gertrude Jekyll's ideas before reaching a 1950s 'Dig for Victory' allotment. The remainder of the garden is devoted to the vision of the 'organic' future of horticulture - including one of Britains largest pergolas, constructed of discarded hop poles.

Times: Open Apr & Oct wknds only; May-Sep, Wed-Sun & BHs 10-5
Fee: ✱ £3.50 (ch free, concessions £3) **Facilities:** P ⬗ & shop garden centre ✈ (ex guide dogs)

LANCASHIRE

EVENTS & FESTIVALS

January
21st-22nd Pigeon Racing: British Homing World Show of the Year, Winter Gardens, Blackpool

April
10th-13th Wasted Festival, punk music, Winter Gardens, Blackpool
14th-17th Burnley National Blues Festival, various venues
14th-17th Easter Maritime Festival, Lancaster
22nd-1st May Wray Scarecrow Festival, school field, Wray Village

June
3rd-11th Forest of Bowland Festival, celebrating the area of outstanding natural beauty
tbc Blackpool Marathon
tbc Chorley Folk Festival
tbc Clitheroe Great Days Festival, music to suit all tastes

July
tbc Glasson Festival, Glasson Docks, folk and traditional
tbc Saddleworth Folk Festival, Uppermill, Oldham

August
25th-28th Great British R&B Festival, Colne

September
1st-3rd Fylde 2006 (folk festival), Fleetwood
tbc Heritage Gala, Morecambe
tbc Jazz Festival Lancaster (provisional)

December
tbc Annual Lancaster Festival of Christmas Trees

Above: The Old Salt Road on Croasdale Fell

BLACKPOOL   Map 07 SD33

BLACKPOOL ZOO PARK
East Park Dr FY3 8PP
➲ (M55 junct 4, follow brown tourist signs)
☎ 01253 830830
e-mail: contact@blackpoolzoo.org.uk
web: www.blackpoolzoo.org.uk

This modern zoo, built in 1972, houses over 1500 animals within its 32 acres of landscaped gardens. There is a miniature railway, lots of close encounters and animals in action, a children's play area, animal feeding times and keeper talks throughout the day.

Times: Open all year daily, summer 10-6; winter 10-5 or dusk. Closed 25 Dec. **Fee:** £9 (ch £6.50). Family (2ad+2ch) £27, (2ad+3 ch) £33. Seniors £7.50, disabled & carers £4.50, concessions for groups

Facilities: 🅿 💺 ✕ licensed 🍴 ♿ (wheelchair loan, Braille factsheets, sensory experiences) toilets for disabled shop 🐕 📷

CHARNOCK RICHARD   Map 07 SD51

CAMELOT THEME PARK
PR7 5LP
➲ (from M6 junct 27/28, or M61 junct 8 follow brown tourist signs)
☎ 01257 452100
2 for 1
e-mail: kingarthur@camelotthemepark.co.uk
web: www.camelotthemepark.co.uk

Join Merlin, King Arthur and the Knights of the Round Table at the magical kingdom of Camelot. Explore five magic lands filled with thrilling rides, spectacular shows, and many more attractions. From white-knuckle thrills on The Whirlwind spinning rollercoaster, to wet-knuckle thrills on Pendragon's Plunge, there's something for everyone.

Times: Open 8 Apr-29 Oct. Telephone for further details. **Fee:** ✱ £16 (ch under 1 metre, free). Family ticket £55 **Facilities:** 🅿 💺 🍴 ♿ (disabled car parking) toilets for disabled shop 🐕 (ex assist dogs) 📷

CHORLEY Map 07 SD51

Astley Hall Museum & Art Gallery

Astley Park PR7 1NP

➲ (M61 junct 8, signed Botany Bay. Follow brown signs)

☎ 01257 515555

`FREE`

e-mail: astley.hall@chorley.gov.uk

web: www.astleyhall.co.uk

A charming Tudor/Stuart building set in beautiful parkland, this lovely Hall retains a comfortable 'lived-in' atmosphere. There are pictures and pottery to see, as well as fine furniture and rare plasterwork ceilings. Special events throughout the year.

Times: Open Apr (or Etr)-Oct, Sat-Sun & BH Mon 12-5; By appointment only during the week **Facilities:** 🅿 🗌 🕭 (video of upper floors, print/Braille guide, CD audio guide) shop ✈ (ex guide dogs) 🖃

CLITHEROE Map 07 SD74

Clitheroe Castle Museum

Castle House, Castle Gate, Castle St BB7 1BA

➲ (follow Clitheroe signs from A59 Preston-Skipton by-pass. Museum located in castle grounds near town centre)

☎ 01200 424635

`2 for 1`

e-mail: museum@ribblevalley.gov.uk

web: www.ribblevalley.gov.uk/castlemuseum

The museum has a good collection of carboniferous fossils, and items of local interest. Displays include local history and the industrial archaeology of the Ribble Valley, while special features include the restored Hacking ferry boat believed to be the inspiration for "Buckleberry Ferry" featured in JRR Tolkien's *Fellowship of the Ring*, printer's and clogger's shops and Edwardian kitchen. The area is renowned for its early 17th-century witches, and the museum has a small display on witchcraft.

Times: Open late Feb-Etr, Mon-Sat 11.15-4.30, Sun 1-4.30; Etr-Oct, daily inc BH; Nov, Dec & Feb, wknds & school half terms. Closed Jan **Fee:** £2 (ch 50p, pen £1). Family ticket £4.50 **Facilities:** 🅿 (500yds) (disabled only parking at establishment) 🖳 🕭 shop ✈ (ex guide dogs)

LANCASTER Map 07 SD46

City Museum (also 15 Castle Hill)

Market Sq LA1 1HT

➲ (in city centre just off A6)

☎ 01524 64637

e-mail: paul.thompson@mus.lancscc.gov.uk

web: www.lancsmuseums.gov.uk

The fine Georgian town hall is the setting for the museum, which explores the history and archaeology of the city from prehistoric and Roman times onwards. Also housed here is the museum of the King's Own Royal Lancaster Regiment. The Cottage Museum, furnished in the style of an artisan's house of around 1820, faces Lancaster Castle.

Times: Open all year, Mon-Sat, 10-5. Closed 25 Dec-1 Jan. 15 Castle Hill, Etr-Sep, daily 2-5. **Fee:** ✱ City Museum free. 15 Castle Hill £1 (concessions 25p). Accompanied children free **Facilities:** 🅿 (5 mins walk) 🕭 (ramp to entrance/ground floor, 2 stairlifts) shop ✈ (ex guide dogs)

Lancaster Maritime Museum

St George's Quay LA1 1RB

➲ (close to M6, junct 33 & 34. From A6 follow signs to Lancaster town centre)

☎ 01524 64637

`2 for 1`

e-mail: paul.thompson@mus.lancscc.gov.uk

web: www.lancsmuseums.gov.uk

Graceful Ionic columns adorn the front of the Custom House, built in 1764. Inside, the histories of the 18th-century transatlantic maritime trade of Lancaster, the Lancaster Canal and the fishing industry of Morecambe Bay are well illustrated.

Times: Open all year, daily, Etr-Oct 11-5; Nov-Etr 12.30-4. **Fee:** £2 (concessions £1). Free to accompanied children and residents of Lancaster district **Facilities:** 🅿 🖳 🗌 🕭 (ramped access, lift to all floors, ground floor entry) toilets for disabled shop ✈ (ex guide dogs)

Shire Hall

Lancaster Castle, Castle Pde LA1 1YJ

➲ (follow brown tourist signs from M6 junct 33/34)

☎ 01524 64998

e-mail: christine.goodier@mus.lancscc.gov.uk

web: www.lancastercastle.com

Founded on the site of three Roman forts, Lancaster Castle dominates Castle Hill, above the River Lune. The Norman keep was built in about 1170 and King John added a curtain wall and Hadrian's Tower. The Shire Hall, noted for its Gothic revival design, contains a splendid display of heraldry. The Crown Court was notorious as having handed out the greatest number of death sentences of any court in the land. Various events through the year.

Times: Open daily 10.30 (1st tour)-4 (last tour). Court sittings permitting - it is advisable to telephone before visiting. Closed Xmas & New Year. **Fee:** ✱ £4 (ch, pen & students £2.50). Family ticket £11. **Facilities:** 🅿 (100mtrs) (voucher system) 🕭 shop ✈ (ex guide dogs) 🖃

LEIGHTON HALL · Map 07 SD47

LEIGHTON HALL
LA5 9ST
➲ (M6 junct 35 onto A6 & follow signs)
☎ 01524 734474
e-mail: info@leightonhall.co.uk
web: www.leightonhall.co.uk

2 for 1

Early Gillow furniture is displayed among other treasures in the fine interior of this neo-Gothic mansion. Outside, a large collection of birds of prey can be seen, and flying displays are given each afternoon. There are also fine gardens, a maze and a woodland walk. A programme of events takes place throughout the year, including craft fairs.
Times: Open May-Sep, Tue-Fri & BH Sun/Mon; Aug, Tue-Fri, Sun & BH Mon 12.30-5. Groups all year by arrangement **Fee:** £5.50 (ch 5-12 £4, pen & student £5). Family ticket £17. **Facilities:** 🅿 🍴 ⛽ ♿ shop garden centre ✗ (ex guide dogs & in park)

LEYLAND · Map 07 SD52

BRITISH COMMERCIAL VEHICLE MUSEUM
King St PR25 2LE
➲ (0.75m from M6 junct 28 in town centre)
☎ 01772 451011
web: www.commercialvehiclemuseum.co.uk

A unique line-up of historic commercial vehicles and buses spanning a century of truck and bus building. There are more than 50 exhibits on permanent display.
Times: Open Apr-Sep, Sun, Tue-Thu & BH Mon (Oct open Sun only).
Fee: £4 (ch & pen £2). Family ticket (2ad+3ch) £10. **Facilities:** 🅿 🍴 ♿ (ramps to decked viewing area) toilets for disabled shop ✗ (ex guide dogs)

MARTIN MERE · Map 07 SD41

WWT MARTIN MERE
L40 0TA
➲ (signed from M61, M58 & M6, 6m from Ormskirk, off A59)
☎ 01704 895181
e-mail: info@martinmere.co.uk
web: www.martinmere.co.uk

2 for 1

One of Britain's most important wetland sites, where you can get really close to a variety of ducks, geese and swans from all over the world as well as two flocks of flamingos. Thousands of wildfowl, including pink-footed geese, Bewick's and Whooper swans, winter here. Other features include a children's adventure playground, exhibition gallery, craft area and an educational centre. The Annual North West Bird Fair takes place during November and wild swans by floodlight from 1st November to 31st January.
Times: Open all year, daily 9.30-5.30 (5 in winter). Closed 25 Dec.
Fee: ✱ £5.95 (ch £3.75, concessions £4.75). Family ticket £15.50
Facilities: 🅿 🍴 ♿ (wheelchair loan, Braille trail, heated hide, audio tours) toilets for disabled shop ✗ (ex guide dogs) 🍴

PADIHAM · Map 07 SD73

GAWTHORPE HALL
BB12 8UA
➲ (on E outskirts of Padiham, 0.75m on A671)
☎ 01282 771004
e-mail: gawthorpe@nationaltrust.org.uk
web: www.nationaltrust.org.uk

An early 17th-century manor house, built around Britain's most southerly pele tower, restored in 1850. A collection of portraits from the National Portrait Gallery and the Kay

Shuttleworth Collections of costume, embroidery and lace are on show in the expanded exhibition areas.
Times: Open Apr-2 Nov, Garden: daily 10-6. Hall: Tue-Thu, Sat & Sun 1-5. Also open BH Mon & Good Fri. (Last admission 4.30).
Fee: ✱ House: £3 (ch & concessions £1.50). Garden free.
Facilities: 🅿 🍴 ♿ (level entrance to shop, photo album) toilets for disabled shop ✗ (ex in grounds) 🌿

PRESTON · Map 07 SD52

HARRIS MUSEUM & ART GALLERY
Market Square PR1 2PP
➲ (M6 junct 31, follow signs for city centre, park at bus stn car park)
☎ 01772 258248
e-mail: harris.museum@preston.gov.uk
web: www.visitpreston.com

FREE

An impressive grade I listed Greek Revival building containing extensive collections of fine and decorative art including a gallery of Clothes and Fashion. The Story of Preston covers the city's history and the lively exhibition programmes of contemporary art and social history are accompanied by events and activities throughout the year.
Times: Open all year, Mon-Sat 10-5, Sun 11-4. Closed BHs.
Facilities: 🅿 (5 mins walk) (blue badge disabled parking only) 🍴 ♿ (wheelchair available, chair lift to mezzanine galleries) toilets for disabled shop ✗ (ex guide & assist dogs) 🍴

THE NATIONAL FOOTBALL MUSEUM
Sir Tom Finney Way, Deepdale PR1 6RY
➲ (2m from M6 juncts 31, 31A or 32. Follow brown tourist signs)
☎ 01772 908442
e-mail: enquiries@nationalfootballmuseum.com
web: www.nationalfootballmuseum.com

FREE

What location could be more fitting for a National Football Museum than Deepdale Stadium, the home of Preston North End, first winners of the professional football league in 1888-9? This fascinating trip through football past and present includes the FIFA Museum Collection, a fine display of memorabilia and artefacts; interactive displays that allow visitors to commentate on matches, and take virtual trips to every League ground in the country; and an art gallery dedicated to the Beautiful Game.
Times: Open Tue-Sat 10-5, Sun 11-5. Closed Mon ex BHs. Contact for opening times on match days. **Facilities:** 🅿 🍴 ♿ (lifts, multi-sensory exhibitions) toilets for disabled shop ✗ (ex guide dogs) 🍴

ROSSENDALE · Map 07 SD72

WHITAKER PARK & ROSSENDALE MUSEUM
Whitaker Park, Haslingden Rd, Rawtenstall BB4 6RE
➲ (off A681, 0.25m W of Rawtenstall centre)
☎ 01706 244682
e-mail: rossendalemuseum@btconnect.com

FREE

Former mill owner's house, built in 1840 and set in the delightful Whitaker Park. Displays include fine and decorative arts, a Victorian drawing room, natural history, costume, local and social history and regular temporary exhibitions.
Times: Open Apr-Oct, Tue-Thu, Sat-Sun & BHs, 1-4.30 Nov-Mar, 1-4.
Facilities: 🅿 ♿ (large print, audio guides, induction loop, lift) toilets for disabled shop ✗ (ex guide dogs)

continued

RUFFORD Map 07 SD41

RUFFORD OLD HALL
L40 1SG
➲ (M6 junct 27 & follow signs to Rufford. Hall on E side of A59)
☎ 01704 821254
e-mail: ruffordoldhall@nationaltrust.org.uk
web: www.nationaltrust.org.uk

There is a story that William Shakespeare performed here for the owner Sir Thomas Hesketh in the magnificent Great Hall. Built in 1530, Rufford remained in the Hesketh family for over 400 years. The Carolean Wing, altered in 1821, features fine collections of 16th and 17th century oak furniture, arms, armour and tapestries.

Times: Open mid Mar-Oct, Sat-Wed. Hall 1-5 (last admission 4.30). Garden, restaurant & shop 11-5. **Fee:** ✱ House and garden: £4.70 (ch £2.20). Family ticket £11.50. Groups £2.90 each (ch £1). Garden only £2.60 (ch £1.20). No groups Sun and BH Mon.
Facilities: 🅿 ✕ licensed ♿ (Braille guide, wheelchairs, large print guide) toilets for disabled shop ✖ (ex in grounds & on a lead) 🐾

SAMLESBURY Map 07 SD53

SAMLESBURY HALL
Preston New Rd PR5 0UP
➲ (M6 junct 31/A677 for 3m, as indicated by brown tourist signs)
☎ 01254 812010 & 812229 **2 for 1**
e-mail: samlesburyhall@btconnect.co.uk
web: www.samlesburyhall.co.uk

A well restored half-timbered manor house, built during the 14th and 15th centuries, and set in 5 acres of beautiful grounds. Sales of antiques and collector's items, craft shows and temporary exhibitions are held all year round. Live theatre productions and seasonal events throughout the year.

Times: Open all year, Sun-Fri 11-4.30. Closed 25-26 Dec & 1 Jan and Sat for weddings **Fee:** £3 (ch 4-16 £1). **Facilities:** 🅿 ➍ ✕ licensed ▤ ♿ toilets for disabled shop garden centre ✖ (ex guide dogs)

SILVERDALE Map 07 SD47

RSPB *NATURE RESERVE*
Myers Farm LA5 0SW
➲ (M6 junct 35, west on A501(M) for 0.5m. Turn right and head N on A6. Follow brown tourist signs)
☎ 01524 701601
e-mail: leighton.moss@rspb.org.uk
web: www.rspb.org.uk

A large reed swamp with meres with willow and alder scrub in a valley with woodland on its limestone slopes. The reserve covers 321 acres, and is home to the North West's largest concentration of bitterns, together with bearded tits, reed, sedge and grasshopper warblers, shovelers, pochards, tufted ducks and marsh harriers. Black terns and ospreys regularly pass through in spring and greenshanks and various sandpipers in the autumn. Wintering wildfowl include large flocks of mallards, teals, wigeons, and shovelers.

Times: Reserve: open daily 9-dusk (or sunset if earlier). Visitor Centre daily 9.30-5. Feb-Oct 9.30-4.30 Nov-Jan. Closed 25 Dec.
Facilities: 🅿 ➍ ✕ ▤ ♿ (stairlift available to tea room) toilets for disabled shop ✖ (ex guide dogs) 🚩

WATERSLACK FARM SHOP, CAFE & GARDEN CENTRE
Ford Ln LA5 0UH
➲ (M6 junct 35, follow A6 towards Milnthorpe. Turn off A6 at Nineteen Acre Lane & follow signs for Leighton Moss Nature Reserve. Pass Reserve, turn right at T-junct & follow signs)
☎ 01524 701255 **FREE**
e-mail: waterslackfarm@aol.com

With a beautiful plant section, unique Vesage arts and crafts collection, freshly made foods and stunning surroundings, Waterslack offers everything for your perfect day out. Come and see the sheep, geese, chickens, ducks and many other animals or enjoy a walk through one of the nature reserves around Waterslack.

Times: Open Mar-Oct, Mon-Sat 9-6 & Sun 10-5; Nov-Feb, Mon-Sat 9-5
Facilities: 🅿 ➍ ▤ ♿ shop garden centre 🚩

TURTON BOTTOMS — Map 07 SD71

TURTON TOWER
BL7 OHG
➲ (on B6391, off A666 or A676)
☎ 01204 852203
e-mail: turton.tower@mus.lanscc.gov.uk

A historic house incorporating a 15th-century tower house and Elizabethan half-timbered buildings, and displaying a major collection of carved wood furniture. During the 19th century, the house became associated with the Gothic revival and later typified the idealism of the Arts and Crafts movement. The gardens are being restored in late-Victorian style.
Times: Open May-Sep, Mon-Thu 11-5, wknds 1-5; Mar-Oct, Mon-Wed 1-5, wknds 1-4; Apr Sat-Wed 1-5; Nov & Feb, Sun 1-4. Other times by prior arrangement. **Fee:** ✱ £3 (concessions £1.50). Guided tour with supper/lunch, prices vary. **Facilities:** 🅿 🍴 ♿ toilets for disabled shop ✖ (ex in grounds) 🍴

WHALLEY — Map 07 SD73

WHALLEY ABBEY
BB7 9SS
➲ (off A59 4m S of Clitheroe)
☎ 01254 828400
e-mail: office@whalleyabbey.org

The ruins of a 14th-century Cistercian abbey, set in the delightful gardens of the Blackburn Diocesan Retreat and Conference House, a 17th-century manor house with gardens reaching down to the River Calder. The remains include two gateways, a chapter house and the abbot's lodgings and kitchen.
Times: Open 4 Jan daily, 10-5. Closed Xmas & New Year. **Fee:** ✱ £2 (ch 50p, pen £1.25) Family (2ad+ch) £4.50 **Facilities:** 🅿 🍴 ✖ licensed 🍴 ♿ (chair lifts, ramps) toilets for disabled shop ✖ (ex guide dogs)

2-for-1 This symbol indicates attractions which have chosen to participate in our 2-for-1 voucher scheme

English Heritage
Find out more about English Heritage sites, their policies and the work they do, at their website:
www.english-heritage.org.uk

LEICESTERSHIRE

EVENTS & FESTIVALS

February
10th-19th Comedy Festival, Leicester
April
29th Beltane May Fayre, Castle Gardens, Leicester
30th-1st May Leicestershire County Show, Dishley Grange, Loughborough
May
16th-18th The Big Session Folk Festival, De Montfort Hall & Gardens, Leicester
20th-10th Jun Leicester Early Music Festival
29th-11th Jun Spark Children's Arts Festival, various venues in Leicester city and county
June
17th-26th International Music Festival, New Walk Museum, Leicester
July
8th Belgrave Mela, Abbey Park, Leicester (provisional)
August
3rd-6th Leicestershire Country Music Festival, Victoria Caravan & Rally Park, Claybrook Magna, Leicester
11th-13th Summer Sundae Weekender Festival, De Montfort Hall & Gardens, Leicester
21st-28th Castle Park Festival, various venues in Leicester's old town
tbc Caribbean Carnival, Victoria Park, Leicester
tbc City of Leicester Horticultural Show
tbc Leicester Pride, events, city centre parade and park site festival
September
tbc Riverside Festival, Bede Park, boat trips, live music, stalls & events
October
tbc Diwali Celebrations, Leicester

Above: Belvoir Castle, overlooking the Vale of Belvoir

ASHBY-DE-LA-ZOUCH Map 08 SK31

ASHBY-DE-LA-ZOUCH CASTLE

South St LE65 1BR

☎ 01530 413343

Impressive ruins of a late medieval castle. The magnificent 24 metre Hastings Tower offers panoramic views of the surrounding countryside. Ashby was the setting for the famous jousting scene in Sir Walter Scott's classic romance *Ivanhoe*.

Times: Open Apr-Jun & Sep-Oct, Thu-Mon 10-5; Jul-Aug, daily 10-6; Nov-Mar, Thu-Mon 10-4. Closed 24-26 Dec & 1 Jan. **Fee:** £3.30 (ch £1.70, concessions £2.50, Family £8.30). Opening times and prices are subject to change, for further details please phone 0870 333 1181
Facilities: 🅿 ♿ shop ♯

BELVOIR Map 08 SK83

BELVOIR CASTLE

NG32 1PD

➲ (between A52 & A607, follow the brown heritage signs from A1, A52, A607 & A46)

☎ 01476 871002

e-mail: info@belvoircastle.com
web: www.belvoircastle.com

Although Belvoir Castle has been the home of the Dukes of Rutland for many centuries, the turrets, battlements, towers and pinnacles of the house are a 19th-century fantasy. Amongst the many treasures to be seen inside are paintings by Murillo, Holbein and other famous artists. Also here is the museum of the Queens Royal Lancers. Lovingly restored gardens are also open to visitors. Special events planned every weekend throughout the season, phone for details.
Times: Open Apr-Sep, closed Mon & Fri **Fee:** £10 (ch £5, pen £9).
Facilities: 🅿 🖵 ✗ licensed 🎞 ♿ (permitted to be driven/drive right up to castle entrance) toilets for disabled shop ✈ (ex guide dogs) ◼

CASTLE DONINGTON Map 08 SK42

DONINGTON GRAND PRIX COLLECTION

Donington Park DE74 2RP

➲ (2m from M1 junct 23a/24 and M42/A42 close to Nottingham, Derby and Leicester)

☎ 01332 811027

e-mail: enquiries@doningtoncollection.co.uk
web: www.doningtoncollection.com

From the turn of the twentieth century to the new millennium, it's all here. The largest collection of McLaren racing cars on public display. The world's only complete collection of the famous Racing Green Vanwalls, every William F1 car from 1983 to 1999, a superb BRM display, more rare four wheel drive racing cars than you'll see anywhere else, Ferraris driven by Asvar; and Ickx, Senna's winning McLaren from the 1993 European Grand Prix at Donington, Stirling Moss's Lotus which defeated the might of the works Ferraris at Monaco in 1961, Jim Clark's beautiful Lotus 25, Ronnie Peterson's Unique six wheel Tyrell, together with several other examples of his famous marque-including Jacky Stewart's Tyrell 001,they're all here, and many, many more.
Times: ✱ Open daily 10-5 (last admission 4). Open later on race days. Closed over Xmas period - telephone to confirm opening times.
Facilities: 🅿 🖵 ✗ licensed ♿ shop ✈ (ex guide dogs) ◼

COALVILLE Map 08 SK41

SNIBSTON DISCOVERY PARK

Ashby Rd LE67 3LN

➲ (4.5m from M1 junct 22/2m or from A42/M42 junct 13 on A511 on W side of Coalville)

☎ 01530 278444 **2 for 1**

e-mail: snibston@leics.gov.uk
web: www.leics.gov.uk/museums

At Leicestershire's all-weather science and industry museum, visitors can try over 50 hands-on experiments, or explore our rich heritage in the Transport, Extractive, Engineering and Textile and Fashion Galleries. Ex-miners give tours of Snibston's colliery buildings, and kids can let off steam in the outdoor science and water playgrounds or in the Toybox play area. New for 2005 - The Fashion Gallery comprising displays of historic and contemporary clothes.
Times: Open daily, Apr-Oct 10-5; Nov-Mar 10-3. Closed 1 week in Jan & Xmas period. **Fee:** ✱ £5.70 (ch £3.60, concessions £3.90). Family ticket £17.50. Party. **Facilities:** 🅿 🖵 ♿ (Braille labels, touch tables, parking available) toilets for disabled shop ✈ (ex guide dogs) ◼

DONINGTON-LE-HEATH Map 05 SK41

DONINGTON-LE-HEATH MANOR HOUSE

Manor Rd LE67 2FW

➲ (S of Coalville)

☎ 01530 831259 **FREE**

e-mail: museum@leics.gov.uk
web: www.leics.gov.uk/museums

This is a rare example of a medieval manor house, tracing its history back to about 1280. It has now been restored as a period house, with fine oak furnishings. The surrounding grounds include period gardens, and the adjoining stone barn houses a restaurant.
Times: Open Apr-Sep, 11-5; Oct, Nov & Mar 11-3. Dec-Feb wknds only
Facilities: 🅿 🖵 ✗ licensed ♿ toilets for disabled shop ✈ (ex guide dogs)

LEICESTER   Map 04 SK50

ABBEY PUMPING STATION
Corporation Rd, Abbey Ln LE4 5PX
➲ (off A6, 1m N from city centre)
☎ 0116 299 5111   **FREE**
web: www.leicester.gov.uk/museums
Built as a sewage pumping station in 1891, this fascinating museum features some of the largest steam beam engines in the country, and an exhibition on the history and technology of toilets, water and hygiene. There are also a steam shovel and a passenger carrying narrow gauge railway.
Times: ✱ Open Apr-Sep, Mon-Sat 10-5, Sun 1-5; Oct-Mar, Mon-Sat 10-4, Sun 1-4. Closed 24-26 & 31 Dec-1 Jan. **Facilities:** 🅿 📳 🍴 ♿ (loan of wheelchairs, wheelchair lift) toilets for disabled shop ✖ (ex guide dogs) 🖼

BELGRAVE HALL & GARDENS
Church Rd, off Thurcaston Rd, Belgrave LE4 5PE
➲ (off Belgrave/Loughborough road, 1m from city centre)
☎ 0116 266 6590
web: www.leicester.gov.uk/museums
A delightful three-storey Queen Anne house dating from 1709 with beautiful period and botanic gardens. Authentic room settings contrast Georgian elegance with Victorian cosiness and include the kitchen, drawing room, music room and nursery.
Times: ✱ Open all year, Apr-Sep, Mon-Sat 10-5, Sun 1-5; Oct-Mar, Mon-Sat 10-4, Sun 1-4. Closed 24-26 Dec & 31 Dec-1 Jan.
Facilities: 🅿 🍴 ♿ (loan of wheelchair) toilets for disabled shop ✖ (ex guide dogs)

THE GUILDHALL
Guildhall Ln LE1 5FQ
➲ (next to Leicester Cathedral)
☎ 0116 253 2569
web: www.leicester.gov.uk/museums
A preserved medieval building dating back to the 14th century, the Guildhall is the city's oldest building still in use. Over the centuries it has served as the Hall of the Guild of Corpus Christi, the Civic Centre and Town Hall, a judicial centre for court sessions and home to Leicester's first police force. The Guildhall now houses one of the oldest libraries in the country, as well as hosting events, activities and performances.
Times: ✱ Open all year: Apr-Sep, Mon-Sat 10-5, Sun 1-5; Oct-Mar, Mon-Sat 10-4, Sun 1-4. Closed 24-26 Dec & 1 Jan.
Facilities: 🅿 (100yds) 📳 🍴 ♿ (wheelchair loan, induction loop, voice minicom) toilets for disabled shop ✖ (ex guide dogs) 🖼

JEWRY WALL MUSEUM & SITE
St Nicholas Circle LE1 4LB
➲ (opposite The Holiday Inn)
☎ 0116 225 4971
web: www.leicester.gov.uk/museums
Behind the massive fragment of the Roman Jewry wall and a Roman Baths site of the 2nd century AD is the Museum of Leicestershire Archaeology, which covers finds from the earliest times to the Middle Ages.
Times: ✱ Open Apr-Sep, Mon-Sat 10-5, Sun 1-5; Oct-Mar, Mon-Sat 10-4, Sun 1-4. Closed 24-26 & 31 Dec & 1 Jan. **Facilities:** 🅿 (300yds) (limited on-street parking) 🍴 ♿ toilets for disabled shop ✖ (ex guide dogs)

LEICESTERSHIRE MUSEUM & ART GALLERY
53 New Walk LE1 7EA
➲ (situated on New Walk. Access by car from A6 onto Waterloo Way at Railway Stn. Right into Regent Rd, right onto West St, right onto Princess Rd which leads to car park)
☎ 0116 225 4900
web: www.leicester.gov.uk/museums
This major regional venue houses local and national collections. There's an internationally famous collection of German Expressionism and other displays include the Rutland Dinosaur and the Egyptian Gallery. An Extensive Natural History collection augmented by art from the renaissance to contemporary.
Times: ✱ Open all year, Apr-Sep, Mon-Sat 10-5, Sun 1-5. Oct-Mar, Mon-Sat 10-4, Sun 1-4. Closed 24-26 & 31 Dec & 1 Jan)
Facilities: 🅿 📳 🍴 ♿ (wheelchairs for loan, minicom, induction loop) toilets for disabled shop ✖ (ex guide dogs) 🖼

NATIONAL SPACE CENTRE
Exploration Dr LE4 5NS
➲ (off A6, 2m N of city centre midway between Leicester's central & outer ring roads. Follow brown rocket signs from M1 (junct 21, 21a or 22) & all arterial routes around Leicester)
☎ 0870 607 7223   **2 for 1**
e-mail: info@spacecentre.co.uk
web: www.spacecentre.co.uk
A great day out for all the family that is out of this world, but not out of reach. The National Space Centre is the UK's largest attraction dedicated to space. From the minute you catch sight of the futuristic 42-metre tall rocket tower you'll be treated to hours of discovery and inter-active fun. Special events may include Robot Wars, Star Wars and astronaut visits. Check the website or call the centre for details.
Times: Open during school term: Tue-Sun, 10-5 (last entry 3.30). During school holidays: daily, 10-5 (last entry 3.30) **Fee:** £9.95 (ch 4-16yrs & concessions £7.95). Family of 4 £30, of 5 £36
Facilities: 🅿 📳 ✖ licensed 🍴 ♿ (induction loop, large text, wheelchairs, lifts) toilets for disabled shop ✖ (ex guide dogs) 🖼

NEWARKE HOUSES
The Newarke LE2 7BY
➲ (opposite De Montfort University)
☎ 0116 225 4980
web: www.leicester.gov.uk/museums
This museum follows Leicestershire's social history from the 15th century to the present, showing everyday life and social change throughout the county. Clocks, toys, domestic objects, greetings cards and Asian arts are among the many collections. A reconstructed street scene gives a glimpse of Victorian life and the fascinating story of Daniel Lambert, the famous 52-stone gaoler of the 18th century, is also told.
Times: ✱ Open Apr-Sep, Mon-Sat 10-5, Sun 1-5; Oct-Mar, Mon-Sat 10-4, Sun 1-4. Closed 24-26 & 31 Dec & 1 Jan. **Facilities:** 🅿 (200yds) 🍴 ♿ (car parking can be arranged) shop ✖ (ex guide dogs)

> If an attraction name appears in *italics*, details have not been confirmed for 2006.

THE RECORD OFFICE FOR LEICESTERSHIRE & RUTLAND

Long St, Wigston Magna LE18 2AH
➲ (old A50, S of Leicester City)
☎ 0116 257 1080 `FREE`
e-mail: recordoffice@leics.gov.uk
web: www.leics.gov.uk/museums

Housed in a converted 19th-century school in Wigston, the Record Office holds photographs, electoral registers and archive film, files of local newspapers, history tapes and sound recordings, all of which can be studied. **Times:** Open all year, Mon, Tue & Thu 9.15-5, Wed 9.15-7.30, Fri 9.15-4.45, Sat 9.15-12.15. Closed Sun & BH wknds Sat-Tue. **Facilities:** P & toilets for disabled ✖ (ex guide dogs) 🚌

UNIVERSITY OF LEICESTER HAROLD MARTIN BOTANIC GARDEN

Beaumont Hall, Stoughton Dr South, Oadby LE2 2NA
➲ (3m SE A6, entrance at 'The Knoll', Glebe Rd, Oadby)
☎ 0116 271 7725 & 271 2933 (tours)

The grounds of four houses, now used as student residences and not open to the public, make up this 16-acre garden. A great variety of plants in different settings provide a delightful place to walk, including rock, water and sunken gardens, trees, borders, glasshouses and national collections of hardy fuchsias, aubrieta, skimmia and Lauren cypress. **Times:** Open Mon-Fri 10-4, Sat & Sun 10-4 (from 3rd wknd in Mar to 2nd wknd in Nov inclusive). Closed 25-26 Dec & 1 Jan. **Fee:** Free except charity 'Open Days'. **Facilities:** P (adjacent) & toilets for disabled ✖ (ex guide dogs)

LOUGHBOROUGH Map 08 SK51

GREAT CENTRAL RAILWAY

Great Central Rd LE11 1RW
➲ (signed from A6)
☎ 01509 230726 `2 for 1`
e-mail: booking_office@gcrailway.co.uk
web: www.gcrailway.co.uk

This private steam railway runs over eight miles from Loughborough Central to Leicester North, with all trains calling at Quorn & Woodhouse and Rothley. The locomotive *continued*

depot and museum are at Loughborough Central. A buffet car runs on most trains. **Times:** Open all year daily, trains run daily Jun-Aug & sch hols; Sep-May, Sat, Sun & BHs **Fee:** ✱ Runabout (all day unlimited travel) £12 (ch & pen £8). Family ticket (2ad+3ch) £30 (1ad+3ch) £20 **Facilities:** P 🍴 ✖ licensed & (disabled coach available on most trains, check beforehand) toilets for disabled shop 🛒

MARKET BOSWORTH Map 04 SK40

THE BATTLEFIELD LINE

Shackerstone Station, Shackerstone,
Nuneaton CV13 6NW
➲ (from A444/A447 take B585 to Market Bosworth and follow signs for Congerstone/Shackerstone)
☎ 01827 880754
web: www.battlefield-line-railway.co.uk

Together with a regular railway service (mainly steam) from Shackerstone to Shenton, there is an extensive railway museum featuring a collection of rolling stock and many other relics from the age of steam **Times:** ✱ Open all year, Passenger steam train service operates Apr-Oct, Sat, Sun & BH Mon. Heritage Railcar Wed Jul-Aug **Facilities:** P 🍴 ✖ & toilets for disabled shop 🛒

BOSWORTH BATTLEFIELD VISITOR CENTRE & COUNTRY PARK

Ambion Hill, Sutton Cheney CV13 0AD
➲ (follow brown tourist signs from A447, A444 & A5)
☎ 01455 290429
e-mail: bosworth@leics.gov.uk
web: www.leics.gov.uk

The Battle of Bosworth Field was fought in 1485 between the armies of Richard III and the future Henry VII. The visitor centre offers a comprehensive interpretation of the battle, with exhibitions, models and a film theatre. Special medieval attractions are held in the summer months. **Times:** Open: Country Park and Battle Trails all year. Visitor Centre open Apr-Oct, daily, 11-5; Nov-Dec, Sun 11-4; Mar, wknds 11-5. Parties all year by arrangement. **Fee:** ✱ Visitor Centre £3 (concessions £2). Family ticket £8.50. Special charges apply on event days. Subject to review. **Facilities:** P (charged) 🍴 ✖ licensed 🍴 & (wheelchair & electric scooter hire, tactile exhibits) toilets for disabled shop 🛒

MOIRA Map 08 SK31

CONKERS

Millennium Av, Rawdon Rd DE12 6GA
➲ (on B5003 in Moira, signed from A444 and M42)
☎ 01283 216633 `2 for 1`
e-mail: info@visitconkers.com
web: www.visitconkers.com

Explore over one hundred indoor interactive exhibits, together with 120 acres that contain lakeside walks and trails, habitats, an assault course, adventure play areas, a miniature train, and bike hire facilities. There are also events in the covered amphitheatre, and many other opportunities for you and your family to be entertained and educated. **Times:** Open daily, summer 10-6, winter 10-5. Closed 25 Dec. **Fee:** ✱ £6.25 (ch 3-15yrs £4.25, ch under 3 free, concessions £5.25). Family ticket (2ad+2ch) £17.95 **Facilities:** P 🍴 ✖ licensed & (multi access walks & trails accessible to wheelchairs) toilets for disabled shop ✖ (ex guide dogs) 🛒

SHACKERSTONE — Map 04 SK30

BATTLEFIELD LINE RAILWAY
Shackerstone Station, CV13 6NW
➲ (Follow brown signs from major routes onto B585, through Congerstone & Shackerstone)
☎ 01827 880754
web: www.battlefield-line-railway.co.uk
Last remaining part of Ashby and Nuneaton Joint Railway. Opened in 1873.
Times: ✱ Station open all year, Sat noon-5, Sun & BH Mon 10.30-5.30
Fee: £7 (ch £4, pen £5). Family ticket £20 (2A+2ch) **Facilities:** 🅿 🍴 🛢 ♿ toilets for disabled shop 🛍

SWINFORD — Map 04 SP57

STANFORD HALL
LE17 6DH
➲ (7.5m NE of Rugby, 1.5m from Swinford. 2m from the M1, M6, A14 junct)
☎ 01788 860250
e-mail: enquiries@stanfordhall.co.uk
web: www.stanfordhall.co.uk
A beautiful William and Mary house, built in 1697 by Sir Roger Cave. The house contains antique furniture, paintings and family costumes. Special events include car and motorcycle owners' club rallies.
Times: Open Etr Sun-end Sep, Sun & BH Mon 1.30-5; grounds open noon on BH & earlier on Event Days. Open any day or evening (ex Sat) during season for pre-booked parties of 20+. **Fee:** ✱ House & Grounds £5 (ch £2); Grounds only £3 (ch £1); Party 20+ £4.75 each. **Facilities:** 🅿 🍴 ♿ (please contact for details) toilets for disabled shop 🐕 (ex guide dogs & in park)

TWYCROSS — Map 04 SK30

TWYCROSS ZOO PARK
CV9 3PX
➲ (on A444 Burton to Nuneaton road, directly off M42 junct 11)
☎ 01827 880250
web: www.twycrosszoo.com

Set in 50 acres of parkland, the zoo is home to around 1000 animals, most of which are endangered species. Twycross is the only zoo in Britain to house Bonobos - humans' 'closest living relative'. There are also various other animals such as lions, elephants and giraffes, and a pets' corner for younger children.
Times: ✱ Open all year, daily 10-6 (4 in winter). Closed 25 Dec.
Facilities: 🅿 (charged) 🍴 🛢 ♿ toilets for disabled shop 🐕 (ex guide dogs) 🛍

LINCOLNSHIRE

EVENTS & FESTIVALS

January
    29th The Great Australian Breakfast (celebrating Australia Day), Lawn Visitor Centre, Lincoln (provisional)

April
    2nd Lincoln 10k Run (provisional)
    29th Spalding Flower Parade & Springfields Country Fair

May
    7th Lincoln Grand Prix Cycle Race
    26th-29th Cleethorpes Folk Festival, Winter Gardens, Cleethorpes

June
    21st-22nd Lincolnshire Show, Lincolnshire Showground, Grange-de-Lings, Lincoln

July
    1st Riverside Festival, Stamford Meadows, Stamford
    1st-2nd Royal Air Force Waddington International Air Show, RAF Waddington
    29th-30th Heckington Show, Estate Showground, Heckington (provisional)
    tbc Lincoln Waterfront Festival, Brayford Pool

August
    19th-20th Lincolnshire Steam & Vintage Rally, Lincolnshire Showground, Grange-de-Lings, Lincoln

September
    tbc Cleethorpes Jazz Festival, The Beachcomber Cleethorpes

December
    tbc Lincoln Christmas Market, Up-Hill, Lincoln

Above: A signpost at Melholme near Alvingham

BELTON Map 08 SK93

Belton House Park & Gardens

NG32 2LS

➲ (3m NE Grantham on A607)

☎ 01476 566116

e-mail: belton@nationaltrust.org.uk

web: www.nationaltrust.org.uk

The ground floor of the house has a succession of state rooms, with the Marble Hall as its centrepiece. Splendid furnishings and decorations throughout the house include tapestries and hangings, family portraits, porcelain and fine furniture.

Times: Open 23 Mar-30 Oct, Wed-Sun. House open 12.30-5 (last admission 4.30). Garden & Park open 11-5.30. Garden open 4 Nov-18 Dec, Fri-Sun 12-4. **Facilities:** �ℙ ✕ licensed ⅁ (Braille guide, hearing scheme, audio guide) toilets for disabled shop ✖ (ex in grounds) 🐾

CLEETHORPES Map 08 TA30

Pleasure Island Family Theme Park

Kings Rd DN35 0PL

➲ (Follow signs to Pleasure Island from A180)

☎ 01472 211511

e-mail: pleasureisland@btinternet.com

web: www.pleasure-island.co.uk

Pleasure Island is packed with over seventy rides and attractions. Hold on tight as the colossal wheel of steel rockets you into the sky at a G-force of 2.5, then hurtles you around 360 degrees, sending riders into orbit and giving the sensation of complete weightlessness. It's not just grown ups and thrill seekers who are catered for at Pleasure Island. For youngsters there's hours of fun in Tinkaboo Town, an indoor themed area full of rides and attractions.

Times: ✱ Open 6 Apr-7 Sep, daily from 10. Plus wknds during Sep-Oct & daily during half term (25 Oct-2 Nov). **Facilities:** ℙ 💺 ✕ licensed ⅁ toilets for disabled shop 🍴

CONINGSBY Map 08 TF25

Battle of Britain Memorial Flight Visitor Centre

LN4 4SY

➲ (on A153 in Coningsby village - follow heritage signs)

☎ 01526 344041

e-mail: bbmf@lincolnshire.gov.uk

web: www.lincolnshire.gov.uk/bbmf

2 for 1

View the aircraft of the Battle of Britain Memorial Flight, comprising the only flying Lancaster in Europe, five Spitfires, two Hurricanes, a Dakota and two Chipmunks. Because of operational commitments, specific aircraft may not be available. Ring for information before planning a visit.

Times: Open Mon-Fri, conducted tours 10.30-3.30; 4-5 Jun & 23-24 Jul, Sat-Sun; 28-29 Aug, Sun-Mon. (Closed 2 wks Xmas). **Fee:** ✱ £3.70 (concessions £2.15) Family £9.60 **Facilities:** ℙ 💺 📋 ⅁ (electric wheelchairs not allowed in hangar) toilets for disabled shop ✖ (ex guide dogs) 🍴

If an attraction name appears in *italics*, details have not been confirmed for 2006.

EPWORTH Map 08 SE70

Old Rectory

1 Rectory St DN9 1HX

➲ (on A161, 3m S of M180 junct 2. Follow brown signs)

☎ 01427 872268

e-mail: curator@epwortholdrectory.org.uk

web: www.epwortholdrectory.org.uk

John and Charles Wesley were brought up in this handsome rectory, built in 1709. Maintained by the World Methodist Council as 'The Home of the Wesleys', the house displays items which belonged to John and Charles Wesley and their parents Samuel and Susanna. The house is a registered museum.

Times: Open daily Mar-Oct, Mon-Sat, 10-12 & 2-4, Sun 2-4 (only in Mar, Apr & Oct); May-Sep Mon-Sat 10-4.30, Sun 2-4.30. Other times by prior arrangement. **Fee:** ✱ £3.50 (ch £1, concessions £3, students £2). Family £7.50. **Facilities:** ℙ ⅁ toilets for disabled shop ✖ (ex guide dogs) 🍴

GAINSBOROUGH Map 08 SK88

Gainsborough Old Hall

Parnell St DN21 2NB

➲ (turn off A1 onto A57 to Gainsborough. Follow brown heritage signs in city centre. Old Hall is adjacent to town centre.)

☎ 01427 612669

e-mail: gainsborougholdhall@lincolnshire.gov.uk

A complete medieval manor house dating back to 1460-80 and containing a remarkable Great Hall and original kitchen with a variety of room settings. Richard III, Henry VIII, the Mayflower Pilgrims and John Wesley all visited the Old Hall.

Times: Open 24-26 Mar, Mon-Sat 10-5; 27 Mar-Oct, Mon-Sat 10-5, Sun 1-4.30. **Fee:** £3.25 (ch £2.50, concessions £2.50). Family ticket (2ad+3ch) £9.00. Opening times and prices are subject to change, for further details please call 0870 333 1181 **Facilities:** ℙ (100yds) (unrestricted parking 100yds from Hall) 💺 📋 ⅁ (audio tour, induction loop, wheelchair for visitors use) shop ✖ (ex guide dogs)

GRIMSBY Map 08 TA20

National Fishing Heritage Centre

Alexandra Dock DN31 1UZ

➲ (follow signs off M180)

☎ 01472 323345

Sign on as a crew member for a journey of discovery, and experience the harsh reality of life on board a deep sea trawler built inside the Centre. Through interactive games and displays, your challenge is to navigate the icy waters of the Arctic in search of the catch.

Times: ✱ Open Apr-Sep, Mon-Thu 10-4, Sat-Sun 11-5 (10.30-5.30 Jul-Sep). **Facilities:** ℙ 💺 ⅁ (easy access route) toilets for disabled shop ✖ (ex guide dogs) 🍴

GRIMSTHORPE Map 08 TF02

Grimsthorpe Castle

PE10 0LY

➲ (on A151, 8m E of Colsterworth rbt on A1)

☎ 01778 591205

e-mail: ray@grimsthorpe.co.uk

web: www.grimsthorpe.co.uk

2 for 1

Seat of the Willoughby de Eresby family since 1516, the castle has a medieval tower and a Tudor quadrangular house with a Baroque north front by Vanbrugh. There are eight

continued

state rooms and two picture galleries, and an important collection of furniture, pictures and tapestries.

Times: Open early Apr-late Sep, Sun, Thu & BH Mon. Daily in Aug ex Fri & Sat. Park & Gardens also open daily Jun-Aug ex Fri & Sat; 12-6. Castle 1-5 (last admission 4.30). **Fee:** ✱ Park & Gardens £3 (ch £2, concessions £2.50). Combined ticket £7 with castle (ch £3.50, concessions £6). **Facilities:** 🅿 💻 ✗ licensed 🔥 (virtual castle tour via laptop) toilets for disabled shop ▄

LINCOLN   Map 08 SK97

THE COLLECTION: ART & ARCHAEOLOGY IN LINCOLNSHIRE

Danes Ter LN2 1LP

➲ (located on the lower part of Lincoln, between Central Library and St Swithins close to the Waterside Shopping Centre)

☎ 01522 550990

e-mail: thecollection@lincolnshire.gov.uk
web: www.thecollection.lincoln.museum

The county's main archaeology museum, housed in a magnificent medieval building, forms part of Greyfriars.

Times: Open all year, daily, 10-5 **Fee:** Small charge to visit temporary exhibitions **Facilities:** 🅿 300mtrs (Broadgate multi storey car park) 💻 ✗ licensed 📠 🔥 (Parking for disabled) toilets for disabled shop ✗ (ex guide dogs) ▄

LINCOLN CASTLE

Castle Hill LN1 3AA

➲ (off A46 Lincoln Ring Road in heart of historic city)

☎ 01522 511068

e-mail: lincoln_castle@lincolnshire.gov.uk
web: www.lincolnshire.gov.uk/lincolncastle

Situated in the centre of Lincoln, the Castle, built in 1068 by William the Conqueror, dominates the Bailgate area alongside the great Cathedral. In addition to its many medieval features, Lincoln Castle has strong 19th-century connections and the unique Victorian prison chapel is perhaps the most awe-inspiring. The beautiful surroundings are ideal for historical adventures, picnics and special events that include jousting, Roman re-enactments, and Vintage vehicle rallies. The Castle is the home of the Magna Carta and there is an exhibition interpreting and displaying this important document.

Times: Open: Summer, Mon-Sat 9.30-5.30, Sun 11-5.30. Winter, Mon-Sat 9.30-4.30, Sun 11-4.30. Closed 24-26 & 31 Dec & 1 Jan. **Facilities:** 🅿 (100yds) 💻 📠 🔥 (hearing loop, audio visual tour) toilets for disabled shop ✗ (ex guide dogs) ▄

See advertisement on opposite page

MUSEUM OF LINCOLNSHIRE LIFE

Burton Rd LN1 3LY

➲ (100mtr walk from Lincoln Castle)

☎ 01522 528448   **2 for 1**

e-mail: lincolnshirelife.museum@
lincolnshire.gov.uk
web: www.lincolnshire.gov.uk/museum of
lincolnshirelife

A large and varied social history museum, where two centuries of Lincolnshire life are illustrated by enthralling displays of domestic implements, industrial machinery, agricultural tools and a collection of horse-drawn vehicles. The exciting and interactive Royal Lincolnshire Regiment Museum contains videos, an audio tour, and touch screen computers.

Times: Open all year, May-Sep, daily 10-5; Oct-Mar, Mon-Sat 10-5 (last admission 4). Closed 24-26 & 31 Dec, 1 Jan. **Fee:** ✱ £2.10 (concessions £1.30). Family (2ad+3ch) £5.50. **Facilities:** 🅿 💻 🔥 (wheelchair available, parking space) toilets for disabled shop ✗ (ex assist dogs)

USHER GALLERY

Lindum Rd LN2 1NN

➲ (in city centre, signed)

☎ 01522 527980   **FREE**

e-mail: usher.gallery@lincolnshire.gov.uk
web: www.lincolnshire.gov.uk/usher

Built as the result of a bequest by Lincoln jeweller James Ward Usher, the Gallery houses his magnificent collection of watches, porcelain and miniatures, as well as topographical works, watercolours by Peter de Wint, Tennyson memorabilia and coins. The gallery has a popular and changing display of contemporary visual arts and crafts. There is a lively lecture programme and children's activity diary.

Times: Open all year, Tue-Sat 10-5 (last entry 4.30), Sun 1-5 (last entry 4.30), from 1 Jun daily 10-5. Open BHs. Closed 24-26 Dec & 1 Jan. **Facilities:** 🅿 💻 📠 🔥 (large print guides, induction loop, parking) toilets for disabled shop ✗ (ex guide dogs) ▄

SCUNTHORPE   Map 08 SE81

NORMANBY HALL COUNTRY PARK

Normanby DN15 9HU

➲ (4m N of Scunthorpe off B1430)

☎ 01724 720588

e-mail: normanby-hall@northlincs.gov.uk
web: www.northlincs.gov.uk

A whole host of activities and attractions are offered in the 300 acres of grounds that surround Normanby Hall, including riding, nature trails and a farming museum. Inside the Regency mansion the fine rooms are decorated and furnished in period style. Fully restored and working Victorian kitchen garden. There is also a Victorian walled garden selling a wide range of Victorian and other unusual plants from barrows located at the gift shop and Farming Museum.

Times: Open: Park all year, daily, 9-dusk. Walled garden, daily 10.30-5 (4 in winter). Hall & Farming Museum, Apr-Sep, daily 1-5. **Fee:** ✱ Mar-Sep £4.20 (ch £2.10, under 5s free, concessions £3.80). Family season ticket £15. **Facilities:** 🅿 (charged) 💻 ✗ licensed 📠 🔥 (audio tour, sensory bed in garden, wheelchair/scooter) toilets for disabled shop garden centre ✗ (ex guide dogs, & on leads) ▄

SKEGNESS Map 09 TF56
CHURCH FARM MUSEUM
Church Rd South PE25 2HF
➲ (follow brown museum signs on entering Skegness)
☎ 01754 766658
e-mail: churchfarmmuseum@lincolnshire.gov.uk

A farmhouse and outbuildings, restored to show the way of life on a Lincolnshire farm at the end of the 19th century, with farm implements and machinery plus household equipment on display. Temporary exhibitions are held in the barn with special events throughout the season. A timber framed mud and stud cottage is restored on site.
Times: Open Apr-Oct, daily 10-5 (last entry 4.30) **Fee:** Free admission apart from special events **Facilities:** P ▣ 🗐 ♿ (wheelchair available, grounds accessible with care) toilets for disabled shop ✖ (ex guide dogs)

SKEGNESS NATURELAND SEAL SANCTUARY
North Pde PE25 1DB
➲ (N end of seafront)
☎ 01754 764345
e-mail: natureland@fsbdial.co.uk
web: www.skegnessnatureland.co.uk

Natureland houses seals, penguins, tropical birds, aquarium, reptiles, pets' corner etc. Also free-flight tropical butterflies (May-Oct). Natureland is well known for its rescue of abandoned seal pups, and has successfully reared and returned to the wild a large number of them. The hospital unit incorporates a public viewing area, and a large seascape seal pool (with underwater viewing).
Times: Open all year, daily at 10. Closing times vary according to season. Closed 25-26 Dec & 1 Jan. **Fee:** ✱ £5.20 (ch under 3 free, ch £3.40, pen £4.15). Family ticket £15.50. **Facilities:** P (100yds) ▣ ♿ (low windows on seal pools) toilets for disabled shop ◧

SPALDING Map 08 TF22
BUTTERFLY & WILDLIFE PARK
Long Sutton PE12 9LE
➲ (off A17 at Long Sutton)
☎ 01406 363833 & 363209
e-mail: butterflypark@hotmail.com
web: www.butterflyandwildlifepark.co.uk

The Park contains one of Britain's largest walk-through tropical houses, in which hundreds of butterflies and birds from all over the world fly freely. Outside are 15 acres of butterfly and bee gardens, wildflower meadows, nature trail, farm animals, a pets' corner and a large adventure playground. At The Lincolnshire Birds of Prey Centre, there are daily birds of prey displays. See an ant room where visitors can observe leaf-cutting ants in their natural working habitat, and Reptile Land, home to crocodiles and snakes.
Times: Open 20 Mar-end Oct, daily 10-5. (Sep & Oct 10-4). **Fee:** £5.50 (ch 3-16 £4, pen £5). Family ticket £17-£20. Party rates on application. **Facilities:** P ✖ licensed ♿ (wheelchairs available) toilets for disabled shop ✖ (ex guide dogs) ◧

STAMFORD Map 04 TF00
BURGHLEY HOUSE
PE9 3JY
➲ (1.5m off A1 at Stamford)
☎ 01780 752451
e-mail: burghley@burghley.co.uk
web: www.burghley.co.uk

This great Elizabethan palace, built by William Cecil, has all the hallmarks of that ostentatious period. The vast house is three storeys high and the roof is a riot of pinnacles, cupolas and paired chimneys in classic Tudor style. However, the interior was restyled in the 17th century, and the state rooms are now Baroque, with silver fireplaces, elaborate plasterwork and painted ceilings. These were painted by Antonio Verrio, whose Heaven Room is quite awe-inspiring.
Times: Open end Mar-Oct, daily (ex Fri). Please telephone for details. **Fee:** ✱ £8.20 (ch 5-15 £3.70, pen £7.20) Family £21 **Facilities:** P ▣ ✖ licensed ♿ (chairlift access, some mobility required) toilets for disabled shop garden centre ✖ (ex in park & on lead) ◧

We endeavour to be as accurate as possible, but changes to times and other information can occur after the guide has gone to press.

STAMFORD MUSEUM

Broad St PE9 1PJ

➲ (from A1 follow town centre signs from any Stamford exit)

☎ 01780 766317 `FREE`

e-mail: stamford_museum@lincolnshire.gov.uk

web: www.lincolnshire.gov.uk/stamfordmuseum

Displays illustrate the history of this fine stone town and include Stamford Ware pottery, the visit of Daniel Lambert and the Town's more recent industrial past. The new Stamford Tapestry depicts the history of the town in wool.

Times: Open all year, Apr-Sep, Mon-Sat 10-5, Sun 1-4; Oct-Mar Mon-Sat 10-5. Closed 24-26 & 31 Dec & 1 Jan. **Facilities:** P (200yds) (on street parking is limited waiting) 🔊 ♿ (audio loop at reception, Braille leaflets) shop ✖ (ex guide dogs)

TATTERSHALL Map 08 TF25

TATTERSHALL CASTLE

LN4 4LR

➲ (S of A153, 15m NE of Sleaford)

☎ 01526 342543

e-mail: tattershallcastle@nationaltrust.org.uk

web: www.nationaltrust.org.uk

This large fortified house was built in 1440 by Ralph Cromwell, Treasurer of England, and has a keep 100ft high. Restored in 1911-14, it contains four great chambers with large Gothic fireplaces, tapestries and brick vaulting. Spectacular views from battlements and museum room in guardhouse.

Times: Open 5 Mar-11 Dec, Mar, Sat & Sun 12-4, Apr-Oct, Sat-Wed 11-5.30 (Oct 4pm), 5 Nov-11 Dec, Sat & Sun 12-4. **Facilities:** P ♿ (Braille guide) toilets for disabled shop ✖ (ex guide dogs)

THORNTON Map 08 TA11

THORNTON ABBEY AND GATEHOUSE

DN39 6TU `FREE`

➲ (7m SE of Humber Bridge, on road E of A1077)

This abbey, founded in 1139 for a community of Augustinian cannons, was reconstructed from the 1260s as its prestige and riches grew. The remains of a beautiful octagonal chapter-house are notably fine. Most impressive is the fourteenth-century gatehouse, recognised as one of the grandest in England.

Times: Open Abbey Grounds: Daily 10-6. Gatehouse: Apr-Sep, 1st & 3rd Sun of month, 12-6; Oct-Mar, 3rd Sun of month 12-4. **Facilities:** P ♿ (mostly accessible apart from gatehouse) ♯

WOOLSTHORPE Map 08 SK92

WOOLSTHORPE MANOR

23 Newton Way NG33 5NR

➲ (7m S of Grantham, 1m W of A1)

☎ 01476 860338

e-mail: woolsthorpemanor@nationaltrust.org.uk

web: www.nationaltrust.org.uk

A fine stone-built, 17th-century farmhouse which was the birthplace of the scientist and philosopher Sir Isaac Newton. He also lived at the house from 1665-67 during the Plague. An early edition of his Principia Mathematica (1687) is in the house. Science Discovery Centre and exhibition.

Times: Open Apr-Sep, Wed-Sun 1-5; Oct, Sat & Sun 1-5, BH Mon **Facilities:** P ♿ (Braille & large print guide, wheelchair available) toilets for disabled ✖ (ex guide dogs) 🌿

LONDON

EVENTS & FESTIVALS

January
1st New Year's Day Parade, Parliament Square, SW1, to Berkeley Square
5th-15th London Boat Show, Docklands
tbc Chinese New Year Celebrations, Gerrard Street and Leicester Square

March
25th Head of the River Race, River Thames, Mortlake to Putney (provisional)

April
2nd Oxford & Cambridge Boat Race
23rd London Marathon

May
1st Unity Festival (Love Music Hate Racism) Trafalgar Square
23rd-27th Chelsea Flower Show, Royal Chelsea Hospital

June
11th London to Brighton Classic Car Run
17th Trooping the Colour for the Queen's Birthday, Horse Guards Parade
tbc Beating Retreat by the Household Division Massed Bands, Horse Guards Parade

July
4th-9th Hampton Court Palace Flower Show, (provisional)

August
27th-28th Notting Hill Carnival
tbc Great British Beer Festival, Olympia

September
16th-17th Mayor's Thames Festival,

October
1st Pearly Harvest Festival, St Martin in the Fields
22nd Trafalgar Day Parade, Trafalgar Square

November
5th London to Brighton Veteran Car Run, Hyde Park
11th Lord Mayor's Show, City of London
12th Remembrance Day Service & Parade, Cenotaph, Whitehall

December
tbc Christmas Tree, Trafalgar Square

Above: The Royal Courts of Justice in the Strand

E2

GEFFRYE MUSEUM

136 Kingsland Rd, Shoreditch E2 8EA
➲ (S end of Kingsland Rd A10 in Shoreditch between Cremer St & Pearson St)
☎ 020 7739 9893
e-mail: info@geffrye-museum.org.uk
web: www.geffrye-museum.org.uk

FREE

The only museum in the UK to specialise in the domestic interiors and furniture of the urban middle classes. Displays span the 400 years from 1600 to the present day, forming a sequence of period rooms which capture the nature of English interior style. The museum is set in elegant, 18th-century buildings, surrounded by delightful gardens including an award-winning walled herb garden and a series of historical gardens which highlight changes in urban middle-class gardens from the 17th to 20th centuries. One of the museum's historic almshouses has recently been fully restored to its original condition and is open on selected days (ring for details).
Times: Open all year, Tue-Sat 10-5, Sun & BH Mon 12-5. Closed Mon, Good Fri, 24-26 Dec & New Year. **Facilities:** P (150yds) (meter parking, very restricted) ✗ licensed 🍴 ♿ (ramps, lift, wheelchair available) toilets for disabled shop ✕ (ex guide dogs)

E9

SUTTON HOUSE

2 & 4 Homerton High St E9 6JQ
➲ (10 min walk from Hackney Central train station)
☎ 020 8986 2264
e-mail: suttonhouse@nationaltrust.org.uk
web: www.nationaltrust.org.uk

2 for 1

In London's East End, the building is a rare example of a Tudor red-brick house. Built in 1535 by Sir Ralph Sadleir, Principal Secretary of State for Henry VIII, the house has 18th-century alterations and later additions. The 2-for-1 voucher is valid only during normal visiting hours, and cannot be used for any ticketed events.
Times: Open 21 Jan-18 Dec, Fri & Sat 1-5; Sun & BH Mon 11.30-5. Closed Good Fri **Fee:** ✱ £2.50 (ch 50p) Family ticket £5.50. Group £2 each **Facilities:** P (on street parking) (meters) 🍴 ✗ licensed 🍴 ♿ (induction loop, Braille/large print guide) toilets for disabled shop ✕ (ex assist dogs) 🐾

E14

MUSEUM IN DOCKLANDS NEW

West India Quay E14 4AL
➲ (Signposted from West India Quay DLR)
☎ 0870 444 3855/56
e-mail: info@museumdocklands.org.uk
web: www.museumdocklands.org.uk

Housed in a converted 18th-century warehouse the museum explores the 2000 year history of London's river, port and people. Four floors of interactive displays and a unique collection that journeys through the history of the Thames, from the first Roman settlements to the massive regeneration that brought the Docklands into the 21st century. A changing programme of activities for all ages, includes re-enactments by old sailors, talks by history experts, films and guided walks through Docklands. A soft play gallery, Mudlarks is for children under eleven, and offers an opportunity to learn how to winch and weigh cargo or to take a diver's eye view of work under water. Discover archaeological finds on the foreshore, or even reconstruct a simple model of Canary Wharf.
Times: Open all year, daily 10-6 (last admission 5.30) **Fee:** £5 (ch16 free, concessions £3) **Facilities:** P (opp rear museum) Disabled parking at rear 🍴 ✗ licensed 🍴 ♿ (w/chairs, power scooters & various aids) shop ✕ (ex guide dogs)

E17

WILLIAM MORRIS GALLERY

Lloyd Park, Forest Rd E17 4PP
➲ (Underground - Blackhorse Rd, take bus no. 123 along Forest Rd, get off at the Lloyd Park stop)
☎ 020 8527 3782
e-mail: wmg.enquiries@lbwf.gov.uk
web: www.lbwf.gov.uk/wmg

Victorian artist, craftsman, poet and free thinker William Morris lived here from 1848 to 1856, and the gallery houses displays illustrating his life and work. Exhibits include fabrics, stained glass, wallpaper and furniture, as well as Pre-Raphaelite paintings, ceramics and a collection of pictures by Frank Brangwyn, who worked briefly for Morris.
Times: Open all year, Tue-Sat and 1st Sun in each month 10-1 & 2-5. Closed Mon & BHs. Telephone for Xmas/New Year opening times.
Fee: ✱ Free admission, guided tours charged for. **Facilities:** P 🍴 ♿ shop ✕ (ex guide dogs) 🍴

EC1

MUSEUM OF THE ORDER OF ST JOHN

St John's Gate, St John's Ln, Clerkenwell EC1M 4DA
➲ (Underground - Farringdon, Barbican)
☎ 020 7324 4070
e-mail: museum@nhq.sja.org.uk
web: www.sja.org.uk/museum

The Priory of Clerkenwell was built in 1140s by the Crusading Hospitaller and it is their remarkable story which lies behind the modern work of St John Ambulance. The Knights' surprising tale is revealed in the ground floor galleries housed in the Tudor gatehouse and includes furniture, paintings, silver, armour, stained glass and an interactive, multimedia gallery 'Time to Care' which explores the work of St John Ambulance from 1877 to the present day.
Times: Open all year, Mon-Sat 10-5, Sat 10-4. Closed Etr, Xmas wk & BH wknds. Guided tours 11 & 2.30 Tue, Fri & Sat. **Fee:** ✱ Museum free. For tours of St John's Gate & Grand Priory Church a donation of £5 (concessions £4). **Facilities:** P (meters/NCP 300yds) 🍴 ♿ toilets for disabled shop ✕ (ex guide dogs) 🍴

WESLEY'S CHAPEL, HOUSE & MUSEUM OF METHODISM

49 City Rd EC1Y 1AU

➲ (Underground - Old Street - exit number 4)

☎ 020 7253 2262   `FREE`

e-mail: museum@wesleyschapel.org.uk

web: www.wesleyschapel.org.uk

Wesley's Chapel has been the Mother Church of World Methodism since its construction in 1778. The crypt houses a museum which traces the development of Methodism from the 18th century to the present day. Wesley's house - built by him in 1779 - was his home when not touring and preaching. Special events are held on May 24th (the anniversary of Wesley's conversion), and November 1st (the anniversary of the Chapel's opening).

Times: Open all year, Mon-Sat , 10-4, Sun 12-2. Closed Thu 12.45-1.30, Xmas & New Year, BHs, except Good Fri. (Last entry 30mins before closing). **Facilities:** P (5min) (NCP at Finsbury Square) 🍴 ㅎ (lift to the crypt of the chapel) toilets for disabled shop ✖ (ex guide dogs) ◼

EC2

BANK OF ENGLAND MUSEUM

Threadneedle St EC2R 8AH

➲ (museum housed in Bank of London, entrance in Bartholomew Lane)

☎ 020 7601 5545   `FREE`

e-mail: museum@bankofengland.co.uk

web: www.bankofengland.co.uk/museum

The museum tells the story of the Bank of England from its foundation in 1694 to its role in today's economy. Interactive programmes with graphics and video help explain its many and varied roles. Popular exhibits include a unique collection of banknotes and a genuine gold bar, which may be handled. **Times:** Open all year, Mon-Fri 10-5. Closed wknds & BHs. Open on day of Lord Mayor's Show. **Facilities:** P (10 mins walk) 🍴 ㅎ (special need presentation, advance notice helpful) toilets for disabled shop ✖ (ex assist dogs)

THE GUILDHALL

Gresham St EC2V 5AE

➲ (Underground - Bank, St Paul's)

☎ 020 7606 3030   `FREE`

e-mail: pro@corpoflondon.gov.uk

web: www.cityoflondon.gov.uk

The Court of Common Council (presided over by the Lord Mayor) administers the City of London and meets in the Guildhall. Dating from 1411, the building was badly damaged in the Great Fire and again in the Blitz. The great hall, traditionally used for the Lord Mayor's Banquet and other important civic functions, is impressively decorated with the banners and shields of the livery companies, of which there are more than 90. The Clock Museum, which has a collection of 700 exhibits, charts the history of 500 years of time-keeping.

Times: ✱ Open all year, May-Sep, daily 10-5; Oct-Apr, Mon-Sat 10-5. Closed Xmas, New Year, Good Fri, Etr Mon & infrequently for Civic occasions. Please contact 020 7606 3030 ext 1463 before visit to be certain of access. **Facilities:** P (NCP parking nearby) 🍴 ㅎ (lift for east and west crypts) toilets for disabled shop ✖

MUSEUM OF LONDON

150 London Wall EC2Y 5HN

➲ (Underground - St Paul's, Barbican. N of St Paul's Cathedral at the end of St Martins le Grand and S of the Barbican. S of Aldersgate St)

☎ 0870 444 3851   `FREE`

e-mail: info@museumoflondon.org.uk

web: www.museumoflondon.org.uk

Dedicated to the story of London and its people, the Museum of London exists to inspire a passion for London in all who visit it. As well as the permanent collection, the Museum has a varied exhibition programme with major temporary exhibitions and topical displays each year. There are also smaller exhibitions in the foyer gallery. A wide programme of lectures and events explore London's history and its evolution to the city we know today.

Times: Open all year, Mon-Sat 10-5.50, Sun 12-5.50. Last admission 5.30. **Facilities:** P 🍴 🍴 ㅎ (w/chairs & power scooters, lifts & induction loops) toilets for disabled shop ✖ (ex guide dogs) ◼

EC3

THE MONUMENT

Monument St EC3R 8AH

➲ (Underground - Monument)

☎ 020 7626 2717

e-mail: enquiries@towerbridge.org.uk

web: www.towerbridge.org.uk

Designed by Wren and Hooke and erected in 1671-7, the Monument commemorates the Great Fire of 1666 which is reputed to have started in nearby Pudding Lane. The fire destroyed nearly 90 churches and about 13,000 houses. This fluted Doric column stands 202ft high (Pudding Lane is exactly 202ft from its base) and you can climb the 311 steps to a platform at the summit, and receive a certificate as proof of your athletic abilities.

Times: Open all year, daily, 9.30-5. **Fee:** £2 (ch £1). **Facilities:** ✖

TOWER OF LONDON

Tower Hill EC3N 4AB

➲ (Underground - Tower Hill)

☎ 0870 756 6060

web: www.hrp.org.uk

Perhaps the most famous castle in the world, the Tower of London has played a central part in British history. The White Tower, built by William the Conqueror as a show of strength to the people of London, remains one of the most outstanding examples of Norman military architecture in Europe. For hundreds of years the Tower was used, among

continued

other things, as the State Prison. It was here that Henry VIII had two of his wives executed, here that Lady Jane Grey died and here that Sir Walter Raleigh was imprisoned. The Yeoman Warders, or 'Beefeaters' play an important role in the protection of the Tower - home of the Crown Jewels - and are informative and entertaining. Look out for the ravens, whose continued existence is said to ensure that the Kingdom does not fall. The Crowns and Diamonds exhibition features a number of crowns never displayed to the public before and more than 12,000 rough and polished diamonds. Also open to the public are the Royal Armouries, which received their first recorded visitor as long ago as 1489. The displays include an extensive range of arms and armour dating from the Norman ages, a collection of Spanish arms and the Line of Kings.

Times: ✱ Open all year, Mar-Oct, Mon-Sat 9-6, Sun 10-6 (last admission 5); Nov-Feb, Tue-Sat 9-5, Sun 10-5 (last admission 4). Closed 24-26 Dec & 1 Jan. **Facilities:** P (100yds) (NCP Lower Thames St) 🍽 ✗ licensed 🎁 & (access guide can be obtained in advance call 020 7488 5694) toilets for disabled shop ✖ (ex guide dogs) ▰

EC4

DR JOHNSON'S HOUSE
17 Gough Square EC4A 3DE
➲ (Underground - Temple, Blackfriars, Chancery Lane)
☎ 020 7353 3745
e-mail: curator@drjohnsonshouse.org
web: www.drjohnsonshouse.org

The celebrated literary figure, Dr Samuel Johnson, lived here between 1748 and 1759. He wrote his English Dictionary here, and a facsimile third edition is on display at the house. The dictionary took nine and a half years to complete and contained 40,000 words. Johnson then undertook the formidable task of editing the complete works of Shakespeare. The house is a handsome example of early 18th-century architecture, and includes a collection of prints, letters and other Johnson memorabilia.

Times: ✱ Open all year, May-Sep, daily 11-5.30; Oct-Apr 11-5. Closed Sun, BHs, Good Fri & 24 Dec. **Facilities:** P (500yds) (limited meters) (large print info sheets, handrails, seating) shop ✖ (ex guide dogs)

MIDDLE TEMPLE HALL
The Temple EC4Y 9AT
➲ (Underground - Temple, Blackfriars. Turn left at the embankment & left into Middle Temple Lane. Hall half way up on left)   `FREE`
☎ 020 7427 4800
e-mail: banqueting@middletemple.org.uk
web: www.middletemple.org.uk

Between Fleet Street and the Thames are the Middle and Inner Temples, separate Inns of Court, so named after the Knights Templar who occupied the site from about 1160. Middle Temple Hall is a fine example of Tudor architecture and was completed in about 1570. The hall has a double hammerbeam roof and beautiful stained glass. The 29ft-long high table was made from a single oak tree from Windsor Forest. Sir Francis Drake was a visitor to and friend of the Middle Temple, and a table made from timbers from the *Golden Hind* - the ship in which he sailed around the world - is shown.

Times: Open all year, Mon-Fri 10-12 & 3-4. Closed BH & legal vacations. **Facilities:** 🍽 & shop ✖ (ex assist dogs) 🚌

ST PAUL'S CATHEDRAL
St Pauls Courtyard EC4M 8AD
☎ 020 7246 8348
e-mail: chapterhouse@stpaulscathedral.org.uk
web: www.stpauls.co.uk

Completed in 1710, Sir Christopher Wren's architectural masterpiece is the cathedral church of the Bishop of London, and arose, like so much of this area of London, from the ashes of the Great Fire of London in 1666. Among the worthies buried here are Nelson and the Duke of Wellington, while Holman Hunt's masterpiece, *Light of the World* hangs in the nave. Impressive views of London can be seen from the Golden Gallery.

Times: ✱ Open Cathedral, Crypt, Ambulatory, Mon-Sat 8.30. Galleries 9.30. (Last admission 4). Cathedral may close for special services. **Facilities:** P (400mtrs) (meter parking in area) 🍽 ✗ licensed 🎁 & toilets for disabled shop ✖ (ex guide dogs) ▰

N1

THE LONDON CANAL MUSEUM
12/13 New Wharf Rd N1 9RT
➲ (Underground - Kings Cross. Follow York Way along East side of King's Cross Stn, turn right at Wharfdale Rd, then left into New Wharf Rd).
☎ 020 7713 0836
e-mail: info@canalmuseum.org.uk
web: www.canalmuseum.org.uk

The museum covers the development of London's canals (particularly Regent's Canal), canal vessels and trade, and the way of life of the canal people. Housed in a former ice warehouse and stables, it also illustrates horse transport and the unusual trade of importing ice from Norway; there are two large ice wells under the floor. Facilities include temporary moorings, so you can arrive by boat if you want. There are regular special exhibitions.

Times: Open all year, Tue-Sun & BH Mon 10-4.30 (last admission 3.45). Closed 24-26 & 31 Dec. **Fee:** £3 (ch £1.50, students, pen & UB40s £2, under 8's free). Groups 10+ **Facilities:** P (0.25m) (parking Mon-Fri before 6.30pm,Sat 1.30) 🎁 & (large print guides, induction loop, Braille signs) toilets for disabled shop ✖ (ex guide dogs) ▰

N3   Map 03 TQ29

THE JEWISH MUSEUM
The Sternberg Centre, 80 East End Rd, Finchley N3 2SY
➲ (Underground - Finchley Central, 10 mins walk via Station Rd & Manor View)
☎ 020 8349 1143   `2 for 1`
e-mail: enquiries@jewishmuseum.org.uk
web: www.jewishmuseum.org.uk

The Jewish Museum traces the story of Jewish immigration and settlement in London, including a reconstruction of an East End tailoring workshop. It also has a Holocaust Education Gallery with an exhibition on Leon Greenman - British Citizen and Auschwitz survivor. There is a regular programme of changing exhibitions and events.

Times: Open all year, Sun 10.30-4.30, Mon-Thu 10.30-5. Closed Jewish festivals, public holidays & 24 Dec-4 Jan. Also closed Sun in Aug & BH wknds. **Fee:** £2 (ch free, concessions £1) **Facilities:** P (50mtrs) (on street parking) 🍽 🎁 & toilets for disabled shop ✖

N6

HIGHGATE CEMETERY

Swains Ln N6 6PJ

➲ (Underground - Archway, see directions posted at exit)

☎ 020 8340 1834

web: www.highgate-cemetery.org.uk

Highgate Cemetery is the most impressive of a series of large, formally arranged and landscaped cemeteries which were established around the perimeter of London in the mid-19th century. There's a wealth of fine sculpture and architecture amongst the tombstones, monuments and mausoleums as well as the graves of such notables as the Rossetti family, George Eliot, Michael Faraday and Karl Marx. It is also a Grade II listed park.

Times: Open all year. Eastern Cemetery: daily 10 (11 wknds)-5 (4 in winter). Western Cemetery by guided tour only: Sat & Sun 11-4 (3 in winter); midweek tours at 2, advisable to book. Closed 25-26 Dec & during funerals. **Fee:** East cemetery £2. Tour of West cemetery £3 (ch 8-16 £1, no ch under 8 on tours). Donations encouraged to assist restoration. Camera permits for private use £1 on each side (no video or flash). **Facilities:** ▥ ✕ (ex guide dogs)

N7

FREIGHTLINERS CITY FARM

Sheringham Rd, Islington N7 8PF

➲ (off Liverpool Rd)

☎ 020 7609 0467   **FREE**

e-mail: robert@freightlinersfarm.org.uk

web: www.freightlinersfarm.org.uk

A city farm bringing rural life into an urban setting. A variety of animals can be seen at the farm, including cows, pigs, goats, sheep and poultry. Some interesting building projects are taking place at the farm, including a strawbale building, solar dome, an outside bread oven and a continental beehive.

Times: Winter: 10-4. Summer: 10-4.45 **Facilities:** ℙ (charged) ▥ ▤ ♿ toilets for disabled shop garden centre ✕ (ex guide dogs)

NW1

THE JEWISH MUSEUM

Raymond Burton House, 129-131 Albert St, Camden Town NW1 7NB

➲ (Underground - Camden Town, 3 mins walk from station)

☎ 020 7284 1997   **2 for 1**

e-mail: marketing@jmus.org.uk

web: www.jewishmuseum.org.uk

Attractive galleries illustrating Jewish history and religious life in Britain and beyond. One of the world's finest collections of Jewish ceremonial art. There are constantly-changing temporary exhibitions, events and workshops. Early 2006 sees an exhibition on Einstein, and the whole

continued

An asterisk * indicates that opening times and prices are for 2005. Please contact the attraction for up-to-date information.

year is the anniversary of the re-admission of Jews into Britain in 1656.

The Jewish Museum

Times: Open Mon-Thu, 10-4, Sun 10-5. Closed Jewish Festivals. **Fee:** £3.50 (ch, students, disabled & UB40 £1.50, pen £2.50) Family ticket £8. **Facilities:** ℙ (outside museum) (pay & display parking) ▥ ♿ (induction loop in lecture room linked to audio-visual unit) toilets for disabled shop ✕ (ex guide dogs) ▤

LONDON ZOO

Regents Park NW1 4RY

➲ (Underground - Camden Town or Regents Park)

☎ 020 7449 6235

e-mail: marketing@zsl.org

web: www.londonzoo.co.uk

London Zoo is home to over 12,000 animals, insects, reptiles and fish. First opened in 1828, the Zoo can claim the world's first aquarium, insect and reptile house. There's lots to do, plenty to see and so much to learn. Visit the cheeky, the deadly and the wild. Meet the world's largest lizards in the new Komodo dragon exhibit. Get closer to your favourite animals, learn about them at the keeper talks and watch them show off their skills at special events. By visiting London Zoo, visitors help protect endangered species, conserve natural habitats and bring learning to life for all ages.

Times: Open all year, daily from 10. Closed 25 Dec. **Fee:** £14 (ch 3-15 £10.75, concessions £12). Family £45. **Facilities:** ℙ (charged) ▥ ✕ licensed ♿ (wheelchairs & booster scooter available) toilets for disabled shop ✕ ▤

MADAME TUSSAUD'S & THE LONDON PLANETARIUM

Marylebone Rd NW1 5LR

➲ (Underground - Baker Street)

☎ 020 7935 6861

e-mail: csc@madame-tussauds.com

web: www.madame-tussauds.com

Madame Tussaud's world-famous waxwork collection was founded in Paris in 1770. It moved to England in 1802 and found a permanent home in London's Marylebone Road in 1884. The 21st century has brought new innovations and new levels of interactivity. Listen to Kylie Minogue whisper in your ear, become an A-list celeb in the 'Blush' nightclub, and take your chances in a high security prison populated by dangerous serial killers. Madame Tussaud's has recently been combined with the equally memorable London

continued

Planetarium, where visitors can interact with characters from Disney's *Treasure Planet*.

Times: ✱ Open all year 10-5.30 (9.30 wknds, 9 summer) **Facilities:** P (200mtrs) ✗ licensed ♿ (all parts accessible except Spirit of London ride) toilets for disabled shop ✈ (ex guide dogs) 🚃

NW3

FENTON HOUSE
Windmill Hill NW3 6RT

➲ (Underground - Hampstead, right out of station. Cross Heath St, up Holly Hill. Take right fork at top of hill into Hampstead Grove. Entrance on left)
☎ 020 7435 3471
e-mail: fentonhouse@nationaltrust.org.uk
web: www.nationaltrust.org.uk

A William and Mary merchants house built about 1686 and set in a walled garden, Fenton House is now owned by the National Trust. It contains outstanding displays of Oriental and European porcelain, 17th-century needlework pictures and Georgian furniture as well as the Benton Fletcher collection of early keyboard instruments. 2 for 1 entry vouchers are only accepted during normal visiting hours and cannot be used for any ticketed events.

Times: Open Mar, Sat & Sun 2-5; Apr-Oct, Sat-Sun & BH Mon 11-5, Wed-Fri 2-5. (Last admission 4.30). **Fee:** ✱ £4.80 (ch £2.40). Family ticket £12. Group 15+ £4. **Facilities:** 📷 ♿ (photographs of areas which are not accessible) ✈ (ex assist dogs) ⚘

FREUD MUSEUM
20 Maresfield Gardens, Hampstead NW3 5SX
➲ (Underground - Finchley Road, follow blue signs to museum)
☎ 020 7435 2002 & 7435 5167
e-mail: info@freud.org.uk
web: www.freud.org.uk

In 1938, Sigmund Freud left Vienna as a refugee from the Nazi occupation and chose exile in England, transferring his entire domestic and working environment to this house. He worked here until his death a year later. His extraordinary collection of Egyptian, Greek, Roman and Oriental antiquities, his working library and papers, and his fine furniture including the famous desk and couch are all here.

Times: Open all year, Wed-Sun 12-5. Closed BHs, telephone for Xmas Holiday times. **Fee:** £5 (ch 12-18, students, UB40 & pen £2, ch under 12 free). **Facilities:** P (100yds) (metered parking) 📷 ♿ (personal tours can be arranged if booked in advance) shop ✈ (ex guide dogs) 🚃

KEATS HOUSE
Keats Grove, Hampstead NW3 2RR
➲ (Underground - Hampstead, about 15 mins walk from station)
☎ 020 7435 2062
e-mail: keatshouse@corpoflondon.gov.uk
web: www.cityoflondon.gov.uk

The poet John Keats lived in this house from 1818-1820 and wrote some of his most famous poems, including *Ode to a Nightingale* here. His fiancee, Fanny Brawne, lived next door, and they often walked together on nearby Hampstead Heath. The house contains many of his personal items including inkstand, engagement ring, paintings, jewellery and manuscripts.

Times: Open 23 Apr-10 Dec, Tue-Sun 1-5. Tue-Sat between 10-12 guided tours, schools & visits by appointment take place. **Fee:** £3.50 (under 16's free, concessions £1.75) Party 10+. Garden free. **Facilities:** P (500yds) (residents parking in operation) 📷 ♿ shop ✈ (ex assist dogs) 🚃

KENWOOD HOUSE
Hampstead Ln NW3 7JR
➲ (Underground - Hampstead)
☎ 020 8348 1286
FREE

In splendid grounds beside Hampstead Heath, this outstanding neo-classical house contains one of the most important collections of paintings ever given to the nation. Works by Rembrandt, Vermeer, Turner, Gainsborough and Reynolds are all set against a backdrop of sumptuous rooms. Scenes from *Notting Hill* and *Mansfield Park* were both filmed here.

Times: Open all year, 24 Mar-Oct, daily 11-5; Nov-Mar, daily 11-4 (park stays open later, see notices). Closed 24-26 Dec & 1 Jan. **Facilities:** P 🍴 ✗ licensed ♿ toilets for disabled shop ♯

2 WILLOW ROAD
2 Willow Rd, Hampstead NW3 1TH

2 for 1

➲ (Hampstead tube (Northern Line), along High Street, left Flask Walk, right at end into Willow Rd)
☎ 020 7435 6166
e-mail: 2willowroad@nationaltrust.org.uk
web: www.nationaltrust.org.uk

Discover the 1939 home built by the architect Erno Goldfinger for himself and his family. On display is his modern art collection including works by Henry Moore, Bridget Riley, Max Ernst and Marcel Duchamp as well as an extensive collection of original furniture designed by the architect. 2 for 1 entry vouchers are only accepted during normal visiting hours and cannot be used for any ticketed events.

Times: Open Mar & Nov, Sat only (open Good Fri). Apr-end Oct, Thu, Fri & Sat: guided tours 12,1 & 2; Free flow 3-5 except 1st Thu of each month open 5-9, tours at 5 & 6; Free flow 7-9. **Fee:** £4.60 (ch £2.30). Joint admission with Fenton House £6.60. **Facilities:** P (100mtrs) (very limited, car park closes often) 📷 (video tour of house in cinema) ✈

NW8

LORD'S TOUR & M.C.C. MUSEUM
Lord's Ground NW8 8QN
➲ (Underground - St John's Wood)
☎ 020 7616 8595 & 7616 8596
e-mail: tours@mcc.org.uk
web: www.lords.org

Established in 1787, Lord's is the home of the MCC and cricket. Guided tours take you behind the scenes, and highlights include the Long Room and the MCC Museum, where the Ashes and a large collection of paintings and memorabilia are displayed. The Museum is open on match days for spectators. 2-for-1 Voucher applies to public guided tours only, not match day admission to museum

Times: Open all year, Oct-Mar tours at 12 & 2. Apr-Sep 10, 12 & 2 (restrictions on some match days). Telephone for details & bookings. **Fee:** ✱ Guided tour £8 (ch £5, concessions £6). Family ticket (2ad+2ch) £22. Party 25+. Museum only £2.50 (concessions £1) plus ground admission (match days only). **Facilities:** P ✗ licensed ♿ (by arrangement) toilets for disabled shop ✈ (ex guide dogs) 🚃

> If an attraction name appears in *italics*, details have not been confirmed for 2006.

NW9

ROYAL AIR FORCE MUSEUM
Grahame Park Way, Hendon NW9 5LL
➲ (within easy reach of the A5, A41, M1 and North Circular A406 roads. Tube on Northern Line to Colindale. Rail to Mill Hill Broadway station. Bus route 303 passes the door)
☎ 020 8205 2266
e-mail: groups@rafmuseum.org **FREE**
web: www.rafmuseum.org

Take off to the Royal Air Force Museum and soar through the history of aviation from the earliest balloon flights to the latest Eurofighter. Gaze at a world-class collection of over 100 aircraft, aviation/wartime memorabilia and artefacts together with a sound and light show that takes you back in time to the Battle of Britain. The Aeronauts Interactive Centre offers hands-on entertainment and education for all ages and includes cockpit controls, co-ordination tests, engine lifting, air speed, drop zone and pilot testing.

Times: Open daily 10-6. (Last admission 5.30). Closed 24-26 Dec & 1 Jan **Facilities:** 🅿 🍴 ✗ licensed & (lifts, ramps & wheelchairs available) toilets for disabled shop ✖ (ex guide dogs) ◄

SE1

BANKSIDE GALLERY
48 Hopton St SE1 9JH
➲ (E of Blackfriars Bridge, South Bank of the Thames, adjacent to Tate Modern and the Millennium Bridge)
☎ 020 7928 7521
e-mail: info@banksidegallery.com **FREE**
web: www.banksidegallery.com

Bankside Gallery is the home of the Royal Watercolour Society (RWS) and the Royal Society of Painter-Printmakers (RE). A series of regularly changing exhibitions throughout the year displays the work of both societies.

Times: Open daily during exhibitions, 11-6. **Facilities:** 🅿 🍴 & shop ✖ (ex assist dogs) ◄

BRITISH AIRWAYS LONDON EYE
Riverside Building, County Hall, Westminster Bridge Rd SE1 7PB
➲ (Underground - Waterloo/Westminster)
☎ 0870 500 0600
e-mail: customer.services@ba-londoneye.com
web: www.ba-londoneye.com

British Airways London Eye is one of the most inspiring and visually dramatic additions to the London skyline. At 135m/443ft high, it is the world's tallest observation wheel, allowing you to see one of the world's most exciting cities from a completely new perspective. The London Eye takes you on a gradual, 30 minute, 360 degree rotation, revealing parts of the city, which are simply not visible from the ground. For Londoners and visitors alike, it is the best way to see London and its many celebrated landmarks. The London Eye provides the perfect location for private parties and entertaining and offers a wide variety of in-flight hospitality packages, like champagne and canapés, which are available to enjoy from the privacy of a private capsule.

Times: Open daily Oct-Apr 9.30-8; May-Jun & Sep 9.30-9; Jul-Aug 9.30am-10pm. **Fee:** ✱ £12.50 (ch under 5 free, ch £6.50, disabled visitors £10, pen £10). Fast track entry £25. **Facilities:** 🅿 (500yds) 🍴 & (Braille guidebooks, w/chair hire, T-loop, carer ticket) toilets for disabled shop ✖ (ex guide & hearing dogs) ◄

DALI UNIVERSE
County Hall Gallery, Riverside Building, South Bank SE1 7PB
➲ (Waterloo Station - follow signs to South Bank and County Hall, attraction next to London Eye. Westminster Underground - cross Westminster Bridge, County Hall on left).
☎ 0870 744 7485
e-mail: info@countyhallgallery.com
web: www.countyhallgallery.com

Set in County Hall Gallery, the Dali Universe is host to the worlds largest exhibit of surreal and anthropomorphic sculpture by Salvador Dali, including the *Profile of Time* and *Alice in Wonderland*. The exhibition also features a multiplicity of gold ornaments and works in crystal, an unrivalled collection of rare graphics and surreal furniture - including the Mae West Lips Sofa - and the monumental *Spellbound* canvas commissioned for the 1945 Hitchcock film of the same name.

Times: Open daily 10-6.30 (last entry 5.30). Closed 25 Dec. Check website for late summer openings. **Facilities:** 🅿 (5 mins) 🍴 & (elevator, ramp access) toilets for disabled shop ✖ (ex guide dogs) ◄

DESIGN MUSEUM
Shad Thames SE1 2YD
➲ (Turn off Tooley St onto Shad Thames. Underground - London Bridge or Tower Hill)
☎ 0870 909 9009
e-mail: info@designmuseum.org **2 for 1**
web: www.designmuseum.org

The Design Museum is the first museum in the world to be dedicated to 20th and 21st century design. Since opening in 1989, it has become one of London's most inspiring attractions and has won international acclaim for its ground-breaking exhibition and education programmes. As one of the leading museums of design, fashion and architecture, the Design Museum has a changing programme of exhibitions, combining compelling insights into design history with innovative contemporary design.

Times: Open all year, daily 10-5.45 (last entry 5.15). Late opening on Fri, during summer months only 9pm (last entry 8.30pm). Closed 25 Dec. **Fee:** ✱ £6 (ch under 12 free, concessions £4) **Facilities:** 🅿 (3 mins) (Gainsford St car park is chargeable) 🍴 🍴 & (ramped entrance, wheelchair & lift) toilets for disabled shop ✖ (ex guide dogs) ◄

THE FASHION & TEXTILE MUSEUM
83 Bermondsey St SE1 3XF
☎ 020 7403 0222
e-mail: info@ftmlondon.org
web: www.ftmlondon.org

Set on the South Bank, and opened in 2002, the FTM is the first exhibition space in London to dedicate itself to the global fashion industry. The Museum will hold two or three major exhibitions a year, manage an education and outreach programme, and host an extensive digital fashion and textile archive.

Times: ✱ Open Tue-Sun 11-5.45 (last admission 5.15) **Facilities:** 🅿 & toilets for disabled shop ✖ ◄

FLORENCE NIGHTINGALE MUSEUM

St Thomas' Hospital, Gassiot House, 2 Lambeth Palace Rd SE1 7EW

➲ (Underground - Westminster, Waterloo. On the site of St Thomas' Hospital)

☎ 020 7620 0374

e-mail: info@florence-nightingale.co.uk

web: www.florence-nightingale.co.uk

Florence Nightingale needs no introduction, but this museum shows clearly that she was more than 'The Lady with the Lamp'. Beautifully designed, the museum creates a personal setting in which a large collection of Florence's personal items including childhood souvenirs, her dress, furniture from her houses and honours awarded to her in old age are displayed. There is a small military history collection of souvenirs from the Crimean War, including military medals and a military nursing uniform.

Times: Open Mon-Fri 10-5; wknds & BHs 10-4.30. (Last admission 1hr before closing). Closed Good Fri, Etr Sat&Sun & 22 Dec-2 Jan.

Fee: £5.80 (ch & concessions £4.20). Family ticket (2ad+ up to 5ch) £13. Discounted rates for pre-booked groups of 15+.

Facilities: P (20mtrs) (hospital parking limited and charged) 🗐 ♿ toilets for disabled shop 🛪 (ex guide dogs) ◥

GOLDEN HINDE EDUCATIONAL TRUST

6A Horseshoe Wharf, Clink St SE1 9FE

➲ (On the Thames path between Southwark Cathedral and the new Globe Theatre)

☎ 020 7403 0123

e-mail: info@goldenhinde.co.uk

web: www.goldenhinde.co.uk

2 for 1

A full size replica of Sir Francis Drake's famous 16th-century galleon. Just like the original, this *Golden Hinde* has circumnavigated the globe. You can explore the five decks, and replica furnishings add to the atmosphere. Special events include Living History re-enactments. There are holiday workshops for children and the ship is also available for private hire.

Times: Open all year, 9.30-5.30. Visitors are advised to check opening times as they may vary due to closures for functions. **Fee:** £3.50 (ch £2.50, concessions £3). Family (2ad+3ch) £10 **Facilities:** P (on street parking) 🗐 shop 🛪 (ex guide dogs) ◥

HMS *BELFAST*

Morgans Ln, Tooley St SE1 2JH

➲ (Underground - London Bridge/Tower Hill/Monument. Rail: London Bridge)

☎ 020 7940 6300

e-mail: hmsbelfast@iwm.org.uk

web: www.iwm.org.uk

Europe's last surviving big gun armoured warship from the Second World War, *HMS Belfast* was launched in 1938 and served in the North Atlantic and Arctic with the Home Fleet. She led the Allied naval bombardment of German positions on D-Day, and was saved for the nation in 1971. A tour of the ship will take you from the Captain's Bridge through nine decks to the massive Boiler and Engine Rooms. You can visit the cramped Mess decks, Officers' Cabins, Galley, Sick Bay, Dentist and Laundry.

Times: ✱ Open all year, daily. Mar-Oct 10-6 (last admission 5.15); Nov-Feb 10-5 (last admission 4.15). Closed 24-26 Dec. **Facilities:** 💷 🗐 ♿ (wheelchair lift for access on board) toilets for disabled shop 🛪 (ex guide dogs) ◥

IMPERIAL WAR MUSEUM

Lambeth Rd SE1 6HZ

➲ (Underground - Lambeth North, Elephant & Castle or Waterloo)

☎ 020 7416 5000

e-mail: mail@iwm.org.uk

web: www.iwm.org.uk

Founded in 1917, this museum illustrates and records all aspects of the two World Wars and other military operations involving Britain and the Commonwealth since 1914. There are always special exhibitions and the programme of special and family events include film shows and lectures. The museum also has a wealth of military reference material, although some reference departments are open to the public by appointment only.

Times: Open all year, daily 10-6. Closed 24-26 Dec. **Fee:** Free admission (charges apply for some temporary exhibitions).

Facilities: P (on street, 100mtrs) (metered Mon-Fri) 💷 ✗ licensed ♿ (parking & w/chair hire book in advance, study room, T-Loop) toilets for disabled shop 🛪 (ex guide dogs) ◥

LONDON AQUARIUM

County Hall, Riverside Building, Westminster Bridge Rd SE1 7PB

➲ (Underground-Waterloo & Westminster. On south bank next to Westminster Bridge, nr Big Ben & London Eye)

☎ 020 7967 8000

e-mail: info@londonaquarium.co.uk

web: www.londonaquarium.co.uk

The London Aquarium is one of Europe's largest displays of global aquatic life with over 350 species in over 50 displays, ranging from the mystical seahorse to the deadly stonefish. The huge Pacific display is home to a variety of jacks, stingrays and seven sharks. Come and witness the spectacular Atlantic feed where our team of divers hand feed rays and native British sharks. The rainforest feed incorporates a frenzied piranha attack with the amazing marksmanship of the archerfish. There is also a range of education tours and literature to enhance any visit.

Times: Open all year, daily 10-6. (Last admission 1hr before closing). Closed 25 Dec. Late opening over summer months see website for details. **Fee:** ✱ Peak - £9.75 (ch 3-14 £6.25, ch under 3 free, concessions & registered disabled £7.50) Family ticket (2ad+2ch) £29. Off peak - £8.75 (ch 3-14 £5.25, ch under 3 free, concessions & registered disabled £6.50). Family ticket (2ad+2ch) £25.

Facilities: P (300mtrs) 💷 🗐 ♿ (wheelchairs available) toilets for disabled shop 🛪 (ex guide & hearing dogs) ◥

LONDON DUNGEON

28-34 Tooley St SE1 2SZ

➲ (Next to London Bridge Station)

☎ 020 7403 7221

e-mail: london.dungeon@merlinentertainments.biz

web: www.thedungeons.com

Blood and guts, torture and terror, in re-enactments of some of the most gruesome events in British history. Brave the Great Fire of London, sail down the Thames towards Traitor's Gate, or visit Executioners corner. You can also meet some especially Wicked Women. Step back to 1665 to dodge the rats inhabiting London's newest feature, 'The Great Plague'.

Times: Open all year, daily, Apr-Sep 10-5.30; Oct-Mar 10.30-5. Late night opening in the Summer. Telephone for exact times.

Fee: ✱ £12.95 (ch 14 £8.25, concessions £11.25). Group 20+ **Facilities:** P (NCP 200yds) 💷 🗐 ♿ (cards for deaf visitors) toilets for disabled shop 🛪 (ex guide dogs) ◥

MUSEUM OF GARDEN HISTORY
Lambeth Palace Rd SE1 7LB
⮕ (Underground - Waterloo, Westminster, Vauxhall. Next to Lambeth Palace, near Lambeth Bridge)
☎ 020 7401 8865
e-mail: info@museumgardenhistory.org
web: www.museumgardenhistory.org
Situated in the restored church of St. Mary-At-Lambeth, adjacent to Lambeth Palace, the Museum of Garden History provides an insight into the history and development of gardens and gardening in the UK. It houses a fine public display of tools and artefacts. In addition, there is a replica 17th-century knot garden filled with flowers and shrubs of the period, created around the tombs of the famous plant hunters, the John Tradescants, father and son, and Captain William Bligh of the 'Bounty'.
Times: Daily, 10.30-5. Closed 18 Dec-2 Jan **Fee:** ✱ Donations appreciated. Suggested donations: £3 (concessions £2.50)
Facilities: P (100yds) (metered) 💷 📖 👍 toilets for disabled shop ✈ (ex guide dogs)

SHAKESPEARE'S GLOBE EXHIBITION AND THEATRE TOUR
21 New Globe Walk, Bankside SE1 9DT
⮕ (Underground - London Bridge, walk along Bankside. Mansion House, walk across Southwark Bridge. St Pauls, walk across Millennium Bridge)
☎ 020 7902 1500
e-mail: info@shakespearesglobe.com
web: www.shakespeares-globe.org
Guides help to bring England's theatrical heritage to life at the 'unparalleled and astonishing' recreation of this famous theatre. Discover what an Elizabethan audience would have been like, find out about the rivalry between the Bankside theatres, the bear baiting and the stews, hear about the penny stinkards and find out what a bodger is.
Times: ✱ Open all year, May-Sep, daily 9-12 (12-5 Rose Theatre tour); Oct-Apr 10-5. **Facilities:** P (0.5m) (very limited on-street parking) 💷 ✗ licensed 👍 (parking spaces, 'touch tours' available by appointment) toilets for disabled shop ✈ (ex guide & hearing dogs) 🔌

SOUTHWARK CATHEDRAL
London Bridge SE1 9DA
⮕ (adjacent to London Bridge (Rd & Station), off Borough High St)
☎ 020 7367 6700
e-mail: cathedral@southwark.anglican.org
web: www.southwark.anglican.org/cathedral
Originally an Augustinian priory, this is London's oldest gothic church building, and has been a place of worship for more than 1,000 years. It became a cathedral for the Diocese of Southwark in 1905, and has links with Chaucer, Dickens and Shakespeare. John Gower and Shakespeare's brother Edmund are buried here. John Harvard of US university fame was baptised here in 1607, and there is a chapel to his memory. Visitors can view part of a Roman road, 14th-century cloister work, and kilns used for Southwark delftware in the 17th/18th centuries.
Times: Open daily: Cathedral 9-6. No tourism permitted on Good Fri & 25 Dec. **Fee:** ✱ Free, suggested donation £4. Mandatory charge for groups, which should pre-book on 020 7367 6734
Facilities: P (10min walk) ✗ licensed 📖 👍 (induction loop, wheelchair available) toilets for disabled shop ✈ (ex service dogs)

TATE MODERN
Bankside SE1 9TG
⮕ (Underground - Southwark, Blackfriars)
☎ 020 7887 8008 (info) & 020 7887 8888
e-mail: information@tate.org.uk
web: www.tate.org.uk
This is the UK's largest museum of modern art and is housed in the impressive Bankside power station. Entrance to the permanent collection, which includes works from artists like Picasso, Warhol and Dalí, is free. Tate Modern also holds world-acclaimed temporary exhibitions as well as education programmes, events and activities.
Times: Open all year, Sun-Thu 10-6, Fri & Sat 10am-10pm. Closed 24-26 Dec. **Fee:** ✱ Free. A charge is made for special exhibitions.
Facilities: P (very limited) 💷 ✗ licensed 📖 👍 (parking & wheelchairs available call 020 7887 8888) toilets for disabled shop ✈ (ex guide dogs) 🔌

THE TOWER BRIDGE EXHIBITION
Tower Bridge Rd SE1 2UP
⮕ (Underground - Tower Hill or London Bridge)
☎ 020 7940 3985
e-mail: enquiries@towerbridge.org.uk
web: www.towerbridge.co.uk
One of the capital's most famous landmarks, its glass-covered walkways stand 142ft above the Thames, affording panoramic views of the river. Much of the original machinery for working the bridge can be seen in the engine rooms. The Tower Bridge Exhibition uses state-of-the-art effects to present the story of the bridge in a dramatic and exciting fashion.
Times: Open all year, Apr-Sep 10-6.30 (last ticket 5.30); Oct-Mar 9.30-6 (last ticket 5) **Fee:** ✱ £5.50 (ch £3, concessions £4.25) Family tickets from £14. **Facilities:** P (100yds) 📖 👍 toilets for disabled shop ✈ (ex guide dogs) 🔌

VINOPOLIS, CITY OF WINE
1 Bank End SE1 9BU
⮕ (Underground-London Bridge. Borough High St West exit, right into Stoney St, then left into Park St & follow road round to Vinopolis main entrance)
☎ 0870 241 4040
e-mail: sales@vinopolis.co.uk
web: www.vinopolis.co.uk
Vinopolis is London's premiere wine attraction, situated on a 2.5 acre site on the vibrant South Bank. It offers an imaginative, interactive tour around the world of wine as well as great tastings. The setting is delightful, with Victorian vaulted ceilings and intricate, almost rustic red brickwork. The 2-for-1 voucher is not valid on Saturdays and is valid only for the classic Vinopolis Package.
Times: Open all year, Mon, Fri & Sat 12-9, Tue-Thu & Sun 12-6, (last admission 2 hrs before closing). Please call for opening hours in Dec and BHs. **Fee:** Classic - Mon, Fri-Sun, £12.50, (ch u16 free, pen £11.50), Tue-Thu £11, (ch u16 free, pen £10). Premium £15. Ultimate £20. **Facilities:** P (5-10 min walk) (NCP parking) 💷 ✗ licensed 👍 (lifts & ramps) toilets for disabled shop ✈ (ex guide dogs) 🔌

WINSTON CHURCHILL'S BRITAIN AT WAR EXPERIENCE

64/66 Tooley St SE1 2TF

➲ (mid way down Tooley St, between London Bridge & Tower Bridge. 2min walk from London Bridge Stn)

☎ 020 7403 3171

e-mail: info@britainatwar.org.uk

web: www.britainatwar.co.uk

A realistic adventure back to the home front to experience life in war-torn Britain during World War II. Take the lift to the underground, where many spent sleepless nights. Explore evacuation, weddings, rationing, air-raids, gas masks, the blackout and walk through the London blitz. **Times:** Open all year, Apr-Sep 10-5; Oct-Mar 10-4 (last entry 1hr before closing). Closed 24-26 Dec. **Fee:** ✱ £8.50 (ch 5-16 £4.50, student & pen £5.50). Family ticket (2ad+2ch) £20. **Facilities:** P (400mtrs) 📷 🅳 (wheelchair for loan) toilets for disabled shop ✖ (ex guide dogs) 🍴

SE5

SOUTH LONDON GALLERY

65 Peckham Rd SE5 8UH

➲ (from Vauxhall take A202 to Camberwell Green. Gallery halfway between Camberwell Green and Peckham).

☎ 020 7703 6120 & 7703 9799-info   FREE

e-mail: mail@southlondongallery.org

web: www.southlondongallery.org

The gallery presents a programme of up to eight exhibitions a year of cutting-edge contemporary art, and has established itself as South East London's premier venue for contemporary visual arts. The Gallery also aims to bring contemporary art of the highest standards to audiences in South London and to assist in the regeneration of the area by attracting audiences from across Britain and abroad. **Times:** Open Tue-Sun, 12-6. Closed Mon **Facilities:** P (on-street parking) 🍴 📷 🅳 (disabled access, induction loop) toilets for disabled ✖ (ex guide dogs)

SE9

ELTHAM PALACE HOUSE & GARDENS

Court Yard SE9 5QE

☎ 020 8294 2548

Stephen and Virginia Courtauld's stunning country house shows the glamour and allure of 1930s Art Deco style and is a feast of luxurious design ideas. The house incorporates the medieval Great Hall and stunning moated gardens. **Times:** Open Apr-Oct, Sun-Wed & BHs 10-5; Oct, Nov-21 Dec & 1 Feb-Mar, Sun-Wed 10-4. Closed 22 Dec-Jan and 18 Jul **Fee:** House & Gardens: £7.30 (ch £3.70, concessions £5.50). Gardens only: £4.60 (ch £2.30, concessions £3.50). Family £18.30. Opening times and prices are subject to change, for further details please phone 0870 333 1181 **Facilities:** P 🅳 shop ✖ 🚐 ⚃

SE10

CUTTY SARK CLIPPER SHIP

King William Walk, Greenwich SE10 9HT

➲ (situated in dry dock beside Greenwich Pier)

☎ 020 8858 2698   2 for 1

e-mail: enquiries@cuttysark.org.uk

web: www.cuttysark.org.uk

The fastest tea clipper ever, built in 1869, she once sailed 363 miles in a single day. Preserved in dry dock since 1957, her graceful lines dominate the riverside at Greenwich. The world's only surviving tea clipper with an amazing history is the highpoint of the age of sail. *Cutty Sark* contains the largest collection of merchant figureheads in the world and fascinating and historic crew quarters. **Times:** Open daily 10-4.30 (Closed Oct-Dec for refit, please phone for details). **Fee:** ✱ £4.50 (ch £3.25, concessions £3.75). Family ticket £12. **Facilities:** P (50mtrs) 📷 🅳 shop ✖ (ex guide dogs) 🍴

NATIONAL MARITIME MUSEUM

Romney Rd SE10 9NF
➲ (central Greenwich)
☎ 020 8312 6565
e-mail: bookings@nmm.ac.uk
web: www.nmm.ac.uk

Britain's seafaring history displayed in an impressive modern museum. Themes include exploration and discovery, Nelson, trade and empire, passenger shipping and luxury liners, maritime London, costume, art and the sea, and the future of the sea. There are interactive displays for children.
Times: Open all year, daily 10-5 (10-6 Jul-Aug). Closed Xmas/New Year. **Facilities:** P (50 yds) (parking in Greenwich limited) 🍽 ✕ licensed 🎫 ♿ (wheelchairs, advisory service for hearing/sight impaired) toilets for disabled shop ✖ (assist dogs) 🔁

OLD ROYAL NAVAL COLLEGE

2 Cutty Sark Gardens, Greenwich SE10 9LW
➲ (In centre of Greenwich, off the one way system, (college approach), located on the Thames next to the Cutty Sark and Greenwich Pier)
☎ 020 8269 4791
e-mail: info@greenwichfoundation.org.uk
web: www.greenwichfoundation.org.uk
The grade one listed Old Royal Naval College buildings are now in the care of the Greenwich Foundation. They occupy the site of the Tudor palace where Henry VIII and Elizabeth I were born. The former Greenwich Hospital buildings incorporate the magnificent Painted Hall by Thornhill and a Chapel by James Stuart. Also open to the public are the beautiful grounds of the estate, and a visitor centre featuring an exhibition on the World Heritage Site of maritime Greenwich and the history of the site.
Times: Open all year (Painted Hall, Chapel and Visitor Centre), daily 10-5 (last admission 4.15). Chapel open to visitors from 12.30pm on Sun, public worship from 11am. **Fee:** Admission free, guided tours £4. **Facilities:** P (200mtrs) (all local streets, yellow line roads) 🍽 ✕ licensed 🎫 ♿ (parking, wheelchair, staircrawler, access, all with notice) toilets for disabled shop ✖ (ex guide dogs) 🔁

Directions are provided
by the attractions.

THE QUEENS HOUSE

Romney Rd, Greenwich SE10 9NF
➲ (central Greenwich)
☎ 020 8312 6565
e-mail: bookings@nmm.ac.uk
web: www.nmm.ac.uk
The first Palladian-style villa in England, designed by Inigo Jones for Anne of Denmark and completed for Queen Henrietta Maria, wife of Charles I. The Great Hall, the State Rooms and a Loggia overlooking Greenwich Park are notable features. Also displays the extensive art collection of the National Maritime Museum including Tudor and Stuart royalty.
Times: Open daily 10-5. Please telephone for closed dates. **Fee:** Free, except special exhibitions **Facilities:** P (50 yds) (parking Sat-Sun only) ✕ licensed ♿ (blind kit/stairclimber/wheelchairs) toilets for disabled shop ✖ (ex assist dogs) 🔁

ROYAL OBSERVATORY GREENWICH

Greenwich Park, Greenwich SE10 9NF
➲ (off A2, Greenwich Park)
☎ 020 8312 6565
e-mail: bookings@nmm.ac.uk
web: www.nmm.ac.uk
Charles II founded the Royal Observatory in 1675 'for perfecting navigation and astronomy'. It stands at zero meridian longitude and is the original home of Greenwich Mean Time. It houses an extensive collection of historic timekeeping, astronomical and navigational instruments. Planetarium shows throughout the year. Events are planned for the school holidays. Some galleries may be closed for restoration July-Dec 2005.
Times: Open all year, daily 10-5 (10-6 Jul-Aug). Partial closures 31 Dec, 1 Jan and Marathon day. **Facilities:** P (charged) ♿ toilets for disabled shop ✖ 🔁

THE WERNHER COLLECTION AT RANGER'S HOUSE

Chesterfield Walk, Blackheath SE10 8QY
☎ 020 8853 0035
Handsome 18th-century house with lovely views over London, Greenwich Park, Blackheath and the Thames. View the 'Wernher Collection' of self-made millionaire Julius Wernher, who made his fortune in the diamond mines of South Africa.
Times: Open Apr-Sep, Wed-Sun & BHs 10-5; Oct-21 Dec & Mar, pre-booked appointments only. Closed 22 Dec-28 Feb **Fee:** £5.30 (ch £2.70, concessions £4.00). Opening times and prices are subject to change, for further details please phone 0870 333 1181
Facilities: P ♿ toilets for disabled shop ⚏

SE18

FIREPOWER

Royal Arsenal, Woolwich SE18 6ST
➲ (A205, right at Woolwich ferry onto A206, attraction signed)
☎ 020 8855 7755
e-mail: info@firepower.org.uk
web: www.firepower.org.uk
Firepower is the Royal Artillery Museum in the historic Royal Arsenal. It spans 2000 years of artillery and shows the development from Roman catapult to guided missile to self-propelled gun. Put science into action with touchscreen displays and be awed by the big guns.
Times: ✱ Open Wed-Sun & BHs 11-5.30. Phone for winter opening times. **Facilities:** P (charged) 🎫 ♿ (wheelchairs available) toilets for disabled shop ✖ (ex guide dogs) 🔁

THAMES BARRIER INFORMATION & LEARNING CENTRE

1 Unity Way SE18 5NJ
➲ (Turn off A102(M) onto A206, turn onto Eastmoor St and follow signs)
☎ 020 8305 4188
e-mail: learningcentre@environment-agency.gov.uk
web: www.environment-agency.gov.uk

Spanning a third of a mile, the Thames Barrier is the world's largest movable flood barrier. The visitors' centre and exhibition on the South Bank explains the flood threat and the construction of this £535 million project, now valued at £1 billion. Each month a test closure of all ten gates, lasting over 2 hours, is carried out and the annual full day closure of all ten gates takes place in the autumn.

Times: Open 31 Mar-29 Sep, 10.30-4.30. 30 Sep-30 Mar 11-3.30. Closed 25 Dec-3 Jan **Fee:** £1.50 (ch 75p, pen £1). Car park £1.50. Coach park £10 **Facilities:** P (charged) ▣ 🎫 ⅙ (lift from river pier approach) toilets for disabled shop ✘ (ex guide dogs) ◀

SE21

DULWICH PICTURE GALLERY

Gallery Rd, Dulwich SE21 7AD
➲ (off South Circular A205, follow signs to Dulwich village)
☎ 020 8693 5254   **2 for 1**
e-mail: info@dulwichpicturegallery.org.uk
web: www.dulwichpicturegallery.org.uk

This is the oldest public picture gallery in England, housing a magnificent collection of Old Masters, including works by Poussin, Claude, Rubens, Murillo, Van Dyck, Rembrandt, Watteau and Gainsborough. The gallery was designed by Sir John Soane in 1811. The collection, the building and the critically acclaimed loan exhibitions make the gallery a must see for art lovers.

Times: Open all year Tue-Fri 10-5, wknds & BH Mon 11-5. Closed 24-26 Dec, 1 Jan & Good Fri. **Fee:** £4 (pen £3, ch, students, UB40 & disabled free). **Facilities:** P ✘ licensed 🎫 ⅙ (wheelchairs available, hearing loop) toilets for disabled shop ✘ (ex guide dogs) ◀

> If an attraction name appears in *italics*, details have not been confirmed for 2006.

SE23

THE HORNIMAN MUSEUM & GARDENS

London Rd, Forest Hill SE23 3PQ
➲ (situated on A205)
☎ 020 8699 1872   **FREE**
e-mail: enquiry@horniman.ac.uk
web: www.horniman.ac.uk

Founder Frederick Horniman, a tea merchant, gave the museum to the people of London in 1901. The collection covers the natural and cultural world including Natural History with displays on Vanishing Birds and African Worlds, The Music Gallery, which displays Britain's largest collection of musical instruments and the Centenary Gallery which showcases world cultures. There are 16 acres of gardens, and the museum hosts a variety of workshops and activities for all ages.

Times: Open all year, daily 10.30-5.30. Closed 24-26 Dec. Gardens close at sunset. **Facilities:** P (opposite museum) ▣ 🎫 ⅙ (large print leaflets, induction loop) toilets for disabled shop ✘ (ex guide dogs or in gardens)

SW1

BANQUETING HOUSE AT WHITEHALL PALACE

Whitehall SW1A 2ER
➲ (Underground - Westminster, Charing Cross or Embankment)
☎ 020 7930 4179
web: www.hrp.org.uk

Designed by Inigo Jones, this is the only surviving building of the vast Whitehall Palace, destroyed by fire 300 years ago. The Palace has seen many significant royal events, including the execution of Charles I in 1649. The Banqueting House's Rubens ceiling paintings are stunning examples of the larger works of the Flemish Master and its classical Palladian style set the fashion for much of London's later architecture.

Times: Open all year, Mon-Sat 10-5. Closed Good Fri, 24 Dec-1 Jan & BHs. Liable to close at short notice for Government functions.
Fee: ✱ £4 (ch 5-16 £2.60, under 5 free, concessions £3).
Facilities: P (5 mins) (no parking in Whitehall) ⅙ toilets for disabled shop ✘ (ex guide/hearing dogs) ◀

BUCKINGHAM PALACE

Buckingham Palace Rd SW1 1AA
➲ (Underground - Victoria, Green Park, St James' Park)
☎ 020 7766 7300
e-mail: buckinghampalace@royalcollection.org.uk
web: www.royalcollection.org.uk

Buckingham Palace has been the official London residence of Britain's sovereigns since 1837. Today it serves as both the home and office of Her Majesty the Queen. Its nineteen State Rooms, which open for eight weeks a year, form the heart of the working palace and more than 50,000 people visit each year as guests at State, ceremonial and official occasions and garden parties. After visiting the State Rooms, visitors can enjoy a walk along the south side of the garden, which offers superb views of the west front of the Palace and the 19th-century lake.

Times: Open Aug-Sep 9.30-6.30 (last admission 4.15). Entry by timed-ticket. **Fee:** ✱ £13.50 (ch under 17 £7, concessions £11.50). Family ticket (2ad + 3 ch) £34. Tickets bought in advance £1 booking fee. **Facilities:** P (200yds) (very limited, driving not recommended) ⅙ (ex gardens, pre-booking essential. Please call 020 7766 7324) toilets for disabled shop ✘ (ex guide dogs) ◀

CHURCHILL MUSEUM & CABINET WAR ROOMS

Clive Steps, King Charles St SW1A 2AQ
⊃ (Underground - Westminster (exit 6) or St James Park)
☎ **020 7930 6961**
e-mail: cwr@iwm.org.uk
web: www.iwm.org.uk

Learn more about the man who inspired Britain's finest hour at the interactive and innovative Churchill Museum, the world's first major museum dedicated to the life of the 'Greatest Briton'. Step back in tome and discover the secret underground headquarters that were the nerve centre of Britain's war effort. Located in the heart of Westminster, visitors can view this complex of historic rooms left as they were in 1945, while at the same time taking in the new Churchill Museum.

Times: Open all year, daily 9.30-6. ((last admission 5). Closed 24-26 Dec. **Fee:** ✱ £10 (ch under 16 free, concessions £8). Party 10+ £8 (concessions £7) **Facilities:** P (2 mins walk) (meter parking) ♿ (education service, object handling session, induction loop) toilets for disabled shop (ex guide dogs)

HOUSES OF PARLIAMENT

Westminster SW1A 0AA
⊃ (Underground - Westminster)
☎ **020 7219 4272**
web: www.parliament.uk

The Houses of Parliament occupy the Palace of Westminster, a royal palace for nearly 1000 years. Visitors will see the Queen's Robing Room, the Royal Gallery, the Chambers of both the House of Lords and House of Commons, the voting lobbies, historic Westminster Hall (c.1097) where Charles I and Guy Fawkes were put on trial, plus other areas normally hidden from public view.

Times: Open 24 Jul-4 Sep, Mon, Tue, Fri & Sat, 9.15-4.30, Wed & Thu, 1.15-4.30; 18 Sep-2 Oct, Mon, Fri & Sat, 9.15-4.30, Tue, Wed & Thu 1.15-4.30. Times are for 1st and last tours of the day. **Fee:** ✱ £7 (ch 5-16 £5, concessions £5) Family ticket £22. Foreign language tours £7.50-£9. Group rates on application. **Facilities:** P (50mtrs) (limited parking, metered) ♿ (touch & sound model for visually impaired) toilets for disabled shop (ex guide dogs)

MALL GALLERIES

The Mall SW1Y 5BD
⊃ (Underground - Charing Cross, situated on the Mall, near Trafalgar Square and Admiralty Arch)
☎ **020 7930 6844** **2 for 1**
e-mail: info@mallgalleries.com
web: www.mallgalleries.org.uk

The venue for the annual open exhibitions of nine national art societies. There is also a wide range of individual and group shows. The galleries display work which is both traditional and contemporary by a large number of prominent international artists. A variety of subjects are displayed in a number of mediums, including oil, watercolour, drawings and sculpture. Phone for details of special events.

Times: Open all year, daily 10-5. Closed between exhibitions and at Christmas. Some late night opening, please phone for details
Fee: £2.50 (ch & concessions £1.50). Groups 10+ £1.50 each (Special exhibitions may have different prices - phone for details)
Facilities: P (50 yds) (no parking on the Mall) ♿ (chairlift to galleries) toilets for disabled (ex guide dogs)

THE QUEEN'S GALLERY

Buckingham Palace, Buckingham Palace Rd SW1A 1AA
⊃ (Underground - Victoria, Green Park & St. James' Park)
☎ **020 7766 7301**
e-mail: buckinghampalace@royalcollection.org.uk
web: www.royalcollection.org.uk

The Gallery hosts changing exhibitions of works of art from the Royal Collection. The collection has largely been formed since the restoration of the Monarchy in 1660 and includes paintings, drawings and watercolours, furniture, ceramics, clocks, silver, sculpture, jewellery, books, manuscripts, prints and maps, arms and armour, fans, and textiles. Works of art from the Royal Collection are also on display at the principal royal residences. Exhibitions for 2006 include - Canaletto in Venice (until 23 Apr 06), Watercolours and Drawings from the Collection of Queen Elizabeth the Queen Mother (19 May-5 Nov 06).

Times: ✱ Open all year, daily, 10-5.30. Last admission 4.30. Closed Good Fri, 25 & 26 Dec and between exhibitions. Entry by timed ticket.
Fee: ✱ £7.50 (ch under 5 free, ch under 17 £4, pen £6). Family ticket (2ad + 3 ch) £19. **Facilities:** P (200yds) ♿ Please call 020 7766 7324 toilets for disabled shop (ex guide dogs)

THE ROYAL MEWS

Buckingham Palace, Buckingham Palace Rd SW1W 0QH
⊃ (Underground - Victoria, Green Park, St. James Park)
☎ **020 7766 7302**
e-mail: buckinghampalace@royalcollection.org.uk
web: www.royalcollection.org.uk

Designed by John Nash and completed in 1825, the Royal Mews houses the State Coaches, horse drawn carriages and motor cars used for coronations, state visits, royal weddings and the State Opening of Parliament. These include the Gold State Coach, made in 1762, with panels painted by the Florentine artist Cipriani. As one of the finest working stables in existence, the Royal Mews provides a unique opportunity for you to see a working department of the Royal Household.

Times: Open Mar-Oct, 11-4; Aug-Sep, daily, 10-5. (Last admission 3.15; Aug-Sep 4.15). Closed Fri. **Fee:** ✱ £6 (ch under 5 free, ch 5-16 £3.50, concessions £5). Family ticket (2ad + 3 ch) £15.50.
Facilities: P (200yds) ♿ (telephone for access information) toilets for disabled shop (ex guide dogs)

TATE BRITAIN

Millbank SW1P 4RG
➲ (Underground - Pimlico)
☎ 020 7887 8000 & rec info 7887 8008
e-mail: information@tate.org.uk
web: www.tate.org.uk

Tate Britain is the national gallery of British art from 1500 to the present day, from Tudors to the Turner Prize. Tate holds the greatest collection of British art in the world, including works by Blake, Constable, Epstein, Gainsborough, Gilbert and George, Hatoum, Hirst, Hockney, Hodgkin, Hogarth, Moore, Rossetti, Sickert, Spencer, Stubbs and Turner. The gallery is the world centre for the understanding and enjoyment of British art. The opening of the Tate Centenary provides Tate Britain with ten new and five refurbished galleries used for special exhibitions and the permanent collection.

Times: Open daily 10-5.50. Closed 24-26 Dec. **Fee:** ✱ Free. Donations welcomed. Prices vary for special exhibitions.
Facilities: P (100mtrs) metered parking ☕ ✗ licensed 🍴 ♿ (wheelchairs on request, parking by prior arrangement) toilets for disabled shop ✖ (ex guide & hearing dogs) 📷

WESTMINSTER ABBEY

Broad Sanctuary SW1P 3PA
➲ (Underground - Westminster, St James's Park. Next to Parliament Square and opposite the Houses of Parliament)
☎ 020 7222 5152 & 7654 4900
e-mail: press@westminster-abbey.org
web: www.westminster-abbey.org

Westminster Abbey was originally a Benedictine monastery. In the 11th century, it was re-founded by St. Edward the Confessor. The great Romanesque abbey Edward built next to his royal palace became his burial place shortly after it was completed. Over the centuries that followed, many more kings and queens have been buried, and many great figures commemorated, in the abbey. The abbey has been the setting for nearly every coronation since that of William the Conqueror in 1066, and for numerous other royal occasions. The present building, begun by Henry III in 1245, is one of the most visited churches in the world.

Times: Abbey: Mon-Fri 9.30-3.45, Sat 9-1.45. Wed late night til 7. (Last admission 1hr before closing). No tourist visiting on Sun, however visitors are welcome at services. The Abbey may at short notice be closed for special services & other events. **Fee:** ✱ £8 (ch & concessions £6). Family ticket (2ad+2ch) £18. **Facilities:** ☕ ♿ (areas accessible induction loop) shop ✖ (ex guide dogs) 📷

WESTMINSTER CATHEDRAL

Victoria St SW1P 1QW
➲ (300 yds from Victoria Station)
☎ 020 7798 9055
e-mail: barrypalmer@rcdow.org.uk
web: www.westminstercathedral.org.uk

Westminster Cathedral is a fascinating example of Victorian architecture. Designed in the Early Christian Byzantine style by John Francis Bentley, its strongly oriental appearance makes it very distinctive. The foundation stone was laid in 1895 but the interior decorations are not fully completed. The Campanile Bell Tower is 273ft high and has a four-sided viewing gallery with magnificent views over London. The lift is open daily 9am-5pm Mar-Nov but shut Mon-Wed from Dec-Feb.

Times: Open all year, daily 7am-7pm. **Facilities:** P (0.25m) (2hr metered parking) ☕ 🍴 ♿ (all parts accessible except side chapels, loop system) shop ✖ (ex guide dogs)

WESTMINSTER HALL

Houses of Parliament, Westminster SW1A 0AA
➲ (Underground - Westminster Tube)
☎ 020 7219 4272
web: www.parliament.uk

Visitors to the home of the British Parliament are guided by a qualified Blue Badge Guide. They follow the route taken by the Queen when she performs the State Opening of Parliament, which includes the Queen's Robing Room, the Royal Gallery, and the Prince's Chamber. The route goes from the House of Lords, through the various lobbies and into the chamber of the House of Commons. After this, visitors go through Westminster Hall, with its magnificent 14th-century hammerbeam roof, and on to the gift shop and café.

Times: Summer opening: Aug-Sep, open to all. At other times by application to MP. (UK constituents only) **Fee:** £7 (concessions £5, tours in English), (£9 foreign language tours, £7 concessions). Tours via MP free. **Facilities:** P (limited 50yds) ☕ ♿ toilets for disabled shop ✖ (ex guide dogs) 📷

SW3

CARLYLE'S HOUSE

24 Cheyne Row SW3 5HL
➲ (Underground - Sloane Square. Off Cheyne Walk between Battersea & Albert Bridges)
☎ 020 7352 7087
e-mail: carlyleshouse@nationaltrust.org.uk
web: www.nationaltrust.org.uk/carlyleshouse

'The Sage of Chelsea' - distinguished essayist and writer of historical works, Thomas Carlyle - lived here, with his wife Jane, from 1834 until his death in 1881. Such literary notables as Tennyson, Thackeray, Browning, George Eliot and Dickens were frequent visitors. The 2-for-1 voucher is valid only during normal visiting hours, and cannot be used for any ticketed events.

Times: Open Apr-Oct, Wed-Fri 2-5, Sat-Sun & BH Mon, 11-5. (Last admission 4.30). Closed Mon-Tue. **Fee:** £4 (ch 5-16, £2). **Facilities:** P (street metered) (residents parking Mon-Sat) (not suitable for wheelchair users) ✖ (ex guide & hearing dogs) 🚐 🐾

CHELSEA PHYSIC GARDEN

66 Royal Hospital Rd,
(entrance in Swan Walk) SW3 4HS
➲ (Underground - Sloane Square)
☎ 020 7352 5646
e-mail: enquiries@chelseaphysicgarden.co.uk
web: www.chelseaphysicgarden.co.uk
Begun in 1673 for the study of plants used by the Society of
Apothecaries, this garden is one of Europe's oldest botanic
gardens and is the only one to retain the title 'Physic' after
the old name for the healing arts. The garden is still used for
botanical and medicinal research, and offers displays of
many fascinating plants in lovely surroundings.
Times: Open Apr-Oct, Wed 12-5, Sun 2-6. Additional opening during
Chelsea Flower Show week, late May & Chelsea Festival week late Jun.
Groups at other times by appointment. **Fee:** £6 (ch 5-15, students &
UB40 £3.50, ch under 5 free) **Facilities:** P (0.5m) (west end of
Battersea Park) ⬛ 🍴 ♿ (disabled parking, wheelchair access) toilets
for disabled shop ✖ (ex guide dogs)

NATIONAL ARMY MUSEUM

Royal Hospital Rd, Chelsea SW3 4HT
➲ (Underground - Sloane Square)
☎ 020 7730 0717   FREE
e-mail: info@national-army-museum.ac.uk
web: www.national-army-museum.ac.uk
The museum offers a unique insight into the lives of Britain's
soldiers, with displays including weapons, paintings,
equipment, models, medals, and uniforms.
Times: Open all year, daily 10-5.30. Closed Good Fri, May Day, 24-26
Dec & 1 Jan. **Facilities:** P ⬛ 🍴 ♿ (wheelchair lift to access lower
ground floor) toilets for disabled shop ✖ (ex guide dogs)

ROYAL HOSPITAL CHELSEA

Royal Hospital Rd SW3 4SR
➲ (near Sloane Square, off A3216 & A3031)
☎ 020 7881 5204   FREE
e-mail: info@chelsea-pensioners.org.uk
web: www.chelsea-pensioners.org.uk
Founded in 1682 by Charles II as a retreat for army veterans
who had become unfit for duty, through injury or long
service. The Royal Hospital Chelsea was built on the site of a
theological college founded by James I in 1610. The buildings
were designed and built by Sir Christopher Wren, and then
added to by Robert Adam and Sir John Soane. The hospital
houses some 330 'In-Pensioners', some of whom do
voluntary work as tour guides, clerical assistants and ground
staff. Visitors can stroll around the grounds, gain admission
to the Chapel, Great Hall and visit the Museum.
Times: Open Mon-Sat, 10-12 & 2-4, Sun 2-4. (Museum closed
Oct-Mar) **Facilities:** P (limited) ♿ (induction loop in post office)
toilets for disabled shop ✖ (ex staff & guide dogs) ◀

SW7

THE NATURAL HISTORY MUSEUM

Cromwell Rd SW7 5BD
➲ (Underground - South Kensington)
☎ 020 7942 5000
e-mail: marketing@nhm.ac.uk
web: www.nhm.ac.uk
This vast and elaborate Romanesque-style building, with its
terracotta facing showing relief mouldings of animals, birds
and fishes, covers an area of four acres. Holding over 70
million specimens from all over the globe, from dinosaurs to
diamonds and earthquakes to ants, the museum provides a
continued

journey into Earth's past, present and future. Discover more
about the work of the museum in the Darwin Centre, where
you can go behind the scenes and talk to some of the
scientists.
Times: Open Mon-Sat 10-5.50, Sun 11-5.50 (last admission 5.30).
Closed 24-26 Dec. **Fee:** ✱ Free. Charge made for some special
exhibitions. **Facilities:** P (180yds) (limited parking, use public
transport) ⬛ ✖ licensed 🍴 ♿ (top floor/one gallery not accessible,
wheelchair hire) toilets for disabled shop ✖ (ex guide dogs) ◀

SCIENCE MUSEUM

Exhibition Rd, South Kensington SW7 2DD
➲ (Underground - South Kensington, signed from
tube stn)
☎ 0870 870 4868
e-mail: sciencemuseum@nmsi.ac.uk
web: www.sciencemuseum.org.uk
See iconic objects from the history of science, from
Stephenson' *Rocket* to the *Apollo 10* command module; be
amazed by a 2D or 3D IMAX movie; take a ride in a
simulator; visit an exhibition; and generally encounter the
past, present and future of technology in seven floors of free
galleries, including the famous hands-on section where
children can have fun investigating science with the
Museum's dedicated Explainers. The Museum is free, but
charges apply to the IMAX cinema, special exhibitions and
simulators.
Times: Open all year, daily 10-6. Closed 24-26 Dec.
Fee: ✱ Admission free. Charges apply for IMAX cinema, simulators &
some special exhibitions. **Facilities:** P (metered 0.5m away) ⬛
✖ licensed 🍴 ♿ (personal 2hr tour of museum) toilets for disabled
shop ✖ (ex guide dogs) ◀

VICTORIA AND ALBERT MUSEUM

Cromwell Rd, South Kensington SW7 2RL
➲ (Underground - South Kensington, Museum
situated on A4, Buses C1,14,74,414 stop outside
the Cromwell Road entrance)
☎ 020 7942 2000
e-mail: vanda@vam.ac.uk
web: www.vam.ac.uk
The world's finest museum of art and design, with
collections spanning 3000 years, and comprising sculpture,
furniture, fashion and textiles, paintings, silver, glass,
ceramics, jewellery, books, prints, and photographs from
Britain and all over the world. Highlights include the national
collection of paintings by John Constable, the Dress Court
showing fashion from 1500 to the present day, a superb
Asian collection, the Jewellery Gallery including the Russian
Crown Jewels, and the 20th Century Gallery, devoted to
contemporary art and design. The stunning British Galleries
1500-1900 tell the story of British design from the Tudor age
to the Victorian era.
Times: Open all year, Mon-Sun 10-5.45. Wed & last Fri of month open
late, 10am-10pm. Closed 24-26 Dec. **Fee:** ✱ Free admission but some
exhibitions may carry an extra charge. **Facilities:** P (500yds) (limited,
charged parking) ⬛ ✖ licensed ♿ (Facilities available. Call for details
020 7942 2211) toilets for disabled shop ✖ (ex guide dogs) ◀

SW13

London Wetland Centre

Queen Elizabeth Walk SW13 9WT
➲ (underground - Hammersmith).
☎ **020 8409 4400** **2 for 1**
e-mail: info@wetlandcentre.org.uk
web: www.wwt.org.uk

An inspiring wetland landscape that stretches over 105 acres, almost in the heart of London, in Barnes SW13. 30 wild wetland habitats have been created from reservoir lagoon to ponds, lakes and reedbeds and all are home to a wealth of wildlife.

Times: Winter 9.30-4, Summer 9.30-5. **Fee:** ✱ £6.75 (ch £4 & pen £5.50). Family ticket £17.50. Groups 10+. Car park £2 charge on Sun & BH's per vehicle. **Facilities:** 🅿 (charged) ☕ 🍴 licensed ♿ (ramps, lifts) toilets for disabled shop 🚫 (ex guide dogs)

SW19

Wimbledon Lawn Tennis Museum

Centre Court, The All England Club,
Church Rd SW19 5AE
➲ (Underground - Southfields, 15mins walk)
☎ **020 8946 6131**
e-mail: museum@aeltc.com
web: www.wimbledon.org/museum

Pictures, displays and memorabilia trace the development of the game over the last century. See the world famous Championship's trophies, as well as film and video footage of great players in action from the 1920s to the present day. There is also the chance to go for a behind-the-scenes guided tour of Centre Court, No. 1 Court, and the press interview room.

Times: Open daily all year, 10.30-5. Closed middle Sun of Championships, Mon immediately following the Championships, 24-26 Dec & 1 Jan. **Fee:** £6 (ch £3.75, ch under 5 free, concessions £5). Party 15+. **Facilities:** 🅿 ☕ 🍴 licensed ♿ (lift, stairlift to cafe) toilets for disabled shop 🚫 (ex guide dogs) 💳

W1

Apsley House, The Wellington Museum

149 Piccadilly, Hyde Park Corner WIJ 7NT
➲ (Underground - Hyde Park Corner, exit 1 overlooking rdbt)
☎ **020 7499 5676**
web: www.english-heritage.org.uk

Number One, London, is the popular name for one of the Capital's finest private residences, 19th-century home of the first Duke of Wellington. Built in the 1770s, its rich interiors have been returned to their former glory, and house the Duke's magnificent collection of paintings, silver, porcelain, sculpture and furniture.

Times: Open all year Apr-Oct, Tue-Sun 10-5. Nov-Mar, Tue-Sun 10-4. Closed Mon ex BH Mon, 24-26 Dec & 1 Jan. **Fee:** £4.95 (ch £2.50, concessions £3.70). Joint ticket to House & Wellington Arch: £6.30 (ch £3.20, concessions £4.70). Opening times and prices are subject to change, for further details please phone 0870 333 1181 **Facilities:** 🅿 (NCP 10mins walk) 📋 ♿ (lift) shop 🚫 (ex guide dogs) # 💳

Handel House Museum

25 Brook St W1K 4HB
➲ (off Park Lane into Brook Gate, then Upper Brook Street. Pass Claridge's Hotel on right. The entrance is in Lancashire Court)
☎ **020 7495 1685**
e-mail: mail@handelhouse.org
web: www.handelhouse.org

Home to George Frideric Handel from 1723 until his death in 1759, the Handel House Museum celebrates Handel's career and times. It was here that Handel composed, *Messiah, Zadok the Priest* and *Fireworks Music*. Over 200 years later, live music, educational projects and public events still bring Handel's former home to life.

Times: Open Tue, Wed, Fri & Sat 10-6, Thu 10-8, Sun 12-6. Closed Mon & BHs, 25-26 Dec & 1-2 Jan. **Fee:** ✱ £5 (ch £2, concessions £4.50) **Facilities:** 🅿 📋 ♿ (lift) toilets for disabled shop 🚫 (ex guide dogs) 💳

Pollock's Toy Museum

1 Scala St W1T 2HL
➲ (Underground - Goodge St)
☎ **020 7636 3452** **2 for 1**
e-mail: pollocks@btconnect.com
web: www.pollockstoymuseum.com

Teddy bears, wax and china dolls, dolls' houses, board games, toy theatres, tin toys, mechanical and optical toys, folk toys and nursery furniture, are among the attractions to be seen in this appealing museum. Items from all over the world and from all periods are displayed in two small, interconnecting houses with winding staircases and charming little rooms.

Times: Open all year, Mon-Sat 10-5. Closed BH, Sun & Xmas. **Fee:** ✱ £3 (ch 3-18 £1.50) **Facilities:** 🅿 (100yds) (Central London restrictions) ♿ shop 💳

Royal Academy Of Arts

Burlington House, Piccadilly W1J 0BD
➲ (Underground - Piccadilly Circus, head towards Green Park)
☎ **020 7300 8000 & 7300 5760**
e-mail: traveltrade@royalacademy.org.uk
web: www.royalacademy.org.uk

Known principally for its exhibitions, the Royal Academy of Arts was founded in 1768 and is Britain's oldest Fine Arts institution. Two of its founding principles were to provide a free school and to mount 'an annual exhibition open to all artists of distinguished merit', now known as the Summer Exhibition. Both continue today. The Royal Academy's most prized possession, Michelangelo's Tondo, *'The Virgin and Child with the Infant St John'*, one of only four marble sculptures by the artist outside Italy, is on permanent display in the Sackler Wing. The recently opened John Madejski Fine Rooms are a suite of six rooms displaying the highlights from the RA collection. Many exhibitions planned for 2006.

Times: Open daily 10-6. Late night opening Fri 10am-10pm. Closed 25 Dec **Fee:** £7-£11 (ch, students, pen & group visitors reduced price). Prices vary for each exhibition. Free entry to permanent collection. **Facilities:** 🅿 (400yds) (disabled parking call in advance) ☕ 🍴 licensed 📋 ♿ (large-print guides/labels, sign language) toilets for disabled shop 🚫 (ex guide dogs) 💳

WALLACE COLLECTION

Hertford House, Manchester Square W1U 3BN

➲ (Underground - Bond St, Baker St, Oxford Circus)

☎ 020 7563 9500

e-mail: enquiries@wallacecollection.org

web: www.wallacecollection.org

FREE

An elegant 18th-century town house is an appropriate gallery for this outstanding collection of art. Founded by the 1st Marquis of Hertford, it was bequeathed to the nation in 1897 and came on public display three years later. As well as an unrivalled representation of 18th-century French art with paintings by Boucher, Watteau and Fragonard, Hertford House is the home of Frans Hals' *Laughing Cavalier* and of paintings by Gainsborough, Rubens, Delacroix and Titian. It also houses the largest collection of arms and armour outside the Tower of London.

Times: ✱ Open all year, Mon-Sat 10-5, Sun 12-5. Closed Good Fri, May BH, 24-26 Dec & 1 Jan. **Facilities:** P (NCP & meters) (meters free on Sun) ⬛ ✗ licensed 🚻 ♿ (lift, ramp, wheelchair available upon request) toilets for disabled shop ✖ (ex guide dogs) ▰

W2

SERPENTINE GALLERY

Kensington Gardens W2 3XA

➲ (Underground - Knightsbridge, Lancaster Gate, South Kensington. Bus 9, 10, 12, 52, 94)

☎ 020 7402 6075

e-mail: varind@serpentinegallery.org

web: www.serpentinegallery.org

FREE

The Serpentine Gallery, named after the lake in Hyde Park, is situated in the heart of Kensington Gardens in a 1934 tea pavilion, and was founded in 1970 by the Arts Council of Great Britain. Today the Gallery attracts over 400,000 visitors a year and is one the best places in London for modern and contemporary art and architecture.

Times: ✱ Open daily 10-6. **Facilities:** P (charged) 🚻 ♿ toilets for disabled shop ✖ (ex guide dogs) ▰

W4

CHISWICK HOUSE

Burlington Ln, Chiswick W4 2RD

➲ (Underground - Gunnersbury)

☎ 020 8995 0508

Discover the story of this celebrated Palladian villa, a fine example of 18th-century English architecture with lavish interiors and classical landscaping.

Times: Open Apr-Oct, Wed-Sun & BHs 10-5 (closes 2 Sat). Closed Nov-Mar but pre-booked are available, please telephone for details. **Fee:** £4.00 (ch £2.00, concessions £3.00). Opening times and prices are subject to change, for further details please phone 0870 333 1181 **Facilities:** P ⬛ ♿ (telephone in advance for wheelchair facilities) shop ⌗

HOGARTH HOUSE

Hogarth Ln, Great West Rd W4 2QN

➲ (50yds W of Hogarth rdbt on Great West Road A4)

☎ 020 8994 6757

e-mail: info@cip.org.uk

web: www.hounslow.info

FREE

This 18th-century house was the country home of artist William Hogarth (1697-1764) during the last 15 years of his life. The house contains displays on the artist's life, and
continued

many of his satirical engravings. The gardens contain Hogarth's famous mulberry tree.

Times: Open Apr-Oct, Tue-Fri 1-5, Sat-Sun 1-6; Nov-Mar, Tue-Fri 1-4, Sat-Sun 1-5. Closed Mon (ex BHs), Jan, Good Fri & 25-26 Dec. **Facilities:** P (25 & 50yds) (spaces marked in Axis Centre car park) ♿ (telephone in advance to confirm) toilets for disabled shop ✖ (ex guide dogs)

W8

KENSINGTON PALACE STATE APARTMENTS & ROYAL CEREMONIAL DRESS COLLECTION

Kensington Gardens W8 4PX

➲ (Underground - High Street Kensington or Notting Hill Gate)

☎ 0870 751 5170

web: www.hrp.org.uk

Highlights of a visit to Kensington include the recently restored Kings Apartments with a fine collection of Old Masters; Tintoretto and Van Dyke amongst them. The Royal Ceremonial Dress Collection includes a selection of HM The Queen's dresses, representations of tailor's and dressmaker's workshops, and a display of dresses belonging to Diana, Princess of Wales.

Times: Open Mar-Oct 10-6 (last admission 5); Nov-end Feb 10-5 (last admission 4). Closed 24-26 Dec. **Fee:** ✱ £10 (ch 5-16 £6.50, under 5's free, students & pens £7.50). Family ticket (2ad+3ch) £30. **Facilities:** P (500yds) ⬛ ♿ (cafeteria has wheelchair access ramp) toilets for disabled shop ✖ (ex guide dogs) ▰

LINLEY SAMBOURNE HOUSE

18 Stafford Ter W8 7BH

➲ (Underground - High Street Kensington)

☎ 020 7602 3316 ext 305

e-mail: museums@rbkc.gov.uk

web: www.rbkc.gov.uk/linleysambournehouse

The home of Linley Sambourne (1844-1910), chief political cartoonist at *Punch* magazine, has had its magnificent artistic interior preserved, almost untouched, since the late 19th century. Also displayed are many of Sambourne's own drawings and photographs. Tours are lead by costumed actors with scripts developed from the Sambourne family archive.

Times: all access by guided tour. 5 Mar-11 Dec. Sat & Sun tours 10, 11.15, 1, 2.15, 3.30. Wkdays book in advance **Facilities:** P (2 min walk) (metered parking) shop ✖ ▰

W12

BBC TELEVISION CENTRE TOURS

BBC Television Centre, Wood Ln W12 7RJ

➲ (Underground - Central Line/White City)

☎ 0870 603 0304

e-mail: bbctours@bbc.co.uk

web: www.bbc.co.uk/tours

Take a look behind the scenes at the world's most famous TV centre. As the BBC TV Centre is a working building, no guarantees can be made as to what visitors will see, although dressing rooms, the News Centre, the Weather Centre, and various studios are all possible. The uncertain nature of the visit means that no two are the same, and that only pre-booked guided tours are available. For children 7 years and over find out what goes on behind the scenes of CBBC's television programmes.

Times: Open Mon-Sat. Tours at 10, 10.20, 10.40, 1.15, 1.30, 1.45, 3.30, 3.45 & 4. Closed Xmas & BH's. All tours must be pre-booked. **Fee:** ✱ £8.95 (concessions £7.95, student £6.50). Family ticket £25 **Facilities:** P (10min walk) (no site disabled parking only) ♿ (wheelchair & sign language available) toilets for disabled shop ✖ (ex guide/hearing dogs) ▰

W14

LEIGHTON HOUSE MUSEUM & ART GALLERY
12 Holland Park Rd W14 8LZ
➲ (Underground - High St Kensington. Museum is N of Kensington High St, off Melbury Rd)
☎ 020 7602 3316
e-mail: museums@rbkc.gov.uk
web: www.rbkc.gov.uk/leightonhousemuseum
An opulent and exotic example of high Victorian taste, Leighton House was built for the President of the Royal Academy, Frederic Lord Leighton. The main body of the house was built in 1866 but the fabulous Arab Hall, an arresting 'Arabian Nights' creation, was not completed until 13 years later.
Times: ✱ Open all year, daily 11-5. Closed Tue.
Facilities: P (100mtrs) (metered) 🍴 shop 🚫 🎧

WC1

BRITISH MUSEUM
Great Russell St WC1B 3DG
➲ (Underground - Russell Sq, Tottenham Court Rd, Holborn)
☎ 020 7323 8000   FREE
e-mail: information@thebritishmuseum.ac.uk
web: www.thebritishmuseum.ac.uk
Of the world and for the world, the British Museum brings together astounding examples of universal heritage. Enter through the largest covered square in Europe. Discover the world through objects like the Aztec mosaics, the Rosetta Stone, El Anatsui's African textiles or the clossal Ramesses II.
Times: ✱ Open all year, Gallery: Sat-Wed 10-5.30 & Thu-Fri 10-8.30. Great Court: Sun-Wed 9-6, Thu-Sat 9am-11pm. Closed Good Fri, 24-26 Dec & 1 Jan. **Fee:** Free except for special exhibitions. **Facilities:** P (5 mins walk) 🍽 ✖ licensed 🍴 ♿ (parking by arrangement) toilets for disabled shop 🚫 (ex guide/companion dogs) 🎧

THE CHARLES DICKENS MUSEUM
48 Doughty St WC1N 2LX
➲ (Underground - Russell Square or Chancery Lane)
☎ 020 7405 2127
e-mail: info@dickensmuseum.com
web: www.dickensmuseum.com

Charles Dickens lived in Doughty Street in his twenties and it was here he worked on his first full-length novel, *The Pickwick Papers*, and later *Oliver Twist* and *Nicholas Nickleby*. Pages of the original manuscripts are on display, together
continued

with valuable first editions, his marriage licence and many other personal mementoes.
Times: ✱ Open all year, Mon-Sat 10-5, Sun 11-5. **Facilities:** P (in street) (metered, 2 hrs max) 🍴 ♿ shop 🚫 🎧

PETRIE MUSEUM OF EGYPTIAN ARCHAEOLOGY
Malet Place, Univerity College London WC1E 6BT
➲ (on 1st floor of the D M S Watson building, in Malet Place, off Torrington Place)
☎ 020 7679 2884   FREE
e-mail: petrie.museum@ucl.ac.uk
web: www.petrie.ucl.ac.uk
One of the largest and most inspiring collections of Egyptian archaeology anywhere in the world. The displays illustrate life in the Nile Valley from prehistory, through the era of the Pharoahs to Roman and Islamic times. Especially noted for its collection of the personal items that illustrate life and death in Ancient Egypt, including the world's earliest surviving dress (c 2800BC).
Times: Open all year, Tue-Fri 1-5, Sat 10-1. Closed for 1 wk at Xmas/Etr.
Facilities: 🍴 ♿ (wheelchair lift) toilets for disabled shop 🚫 (ex guide dogs)

WC2

COURTAULD GALLERY
Somerset House, Strand WC2R 0RN
➲ (Underground - Temple, Embankment, & Covent Garden)
☎ 020 7848 2526
e-mail: galleryinfo@courtauld.ac.uk
web: www.courtauld.ac.uk
The Galleries contain the superb collection of paintings begun by Samuel Courtauld in the 1920s and 1930s and presented to the University of London in memory of his wife. This is the most important collection of Impressionist and post-Impressionist works in Britain and includes major works by Cezanne, Renoir, Degas, van Gogh, Monet, Manet, Seurat and others. A programme of temporary exhibitions regularly includes works from the prints and drawings collection, while the long-term loan or early 20th-century paintings have added to the depth and range of the displays. Contact the gallery for current exhibition schedule.
Times: Open daily 10-6. (Last admission 5.15). **Facilities:** P (NCP Drury Lane) 🍽 🍴 ♿ (parking by arrangement only, call 020 7836 8686, lift) toilets for disabled shop 🚫 (ex guide dogs) 🎧

GILBERT COLLECTION
Somerset House, Strand WC2R 1LA
➲ (Underground - Temple, Covent Garden)
☎ 020 7420 9400
e-mail: info@gilbert-collection.org.uk
web: www.gilbert-collection.org.uk
An outstanding collection of decorative arts and an important bequest to the nation. The Gilbert Collection is the gift of Sir Arthur Gilbert and is on permanent display at Somerset House. The museum includes European silver, gold snuff boxes and Italian mosaics, the displays also include furniture, clocks and portrait miniatures. Temporary exhibitions run throughout the year.
Times: ✱ Open daily 10-6, last admission 5.15.
Facilities: P (400mtrs) 🍽 ✖ licensed 🍴 ♿ (lifts, hearing loop, wheelchair hire, disabled parking) toilets for disabled shop 🚫 (ex guide dogs) 🎧

HUNTERIAN MUSEUM

The Royal College of Surgeons, 35-43 Lincoln's Inn Fields WC2A 3PE

⮌ (Underground - Holborn)

☎ 020 7869 6560

e-mail: museums@rcseng.ac.uk

web: www.rcseng.ac.uk

`FREE`

The Hunterian Museum at the Royal College of Surgeons houses over 3000 anatomical and pathological preparations collected by the surgeon John Hunter (1728-1793). New interpretive displays explore Hunter's life and work, the history of the Hunterian Museum and the College, and the development of surgery from the 18th century to the present. The MacRae Gallery provides a dedicated space for learning based on the museum's reserve collections. The museum also stages a changing programme of temporary exhibitions, lectures and other public events on themes related to the history and current practice of surgery.

Times: Open all year Tues-Sat 10-5. Closed 24 Dec-2 Jan, Good Fri & Etr Sat. **Facilities:** P (15mtrs) (pay & display 8.30-6.30pm) 🛈 ᴌ (Descriptive tours by arrangement) toilets for disabled shop ✖ (ex guide dogs)

NATIONAL GALLERY

Trafalgar Square WC2N 5DN

⮌ (Underground - Charing Cross, Leicester Square, Embankment & Piccadilly Circus. Rail: Charing Cross. Located on N side of Trafalgar Sq)

☎ 020 7747 2885

e-mail: information@ng-london.org.uk

web: www.nationalgallery.org.uk

All the great periods of Western European painting from 1260-1900 are represented here. The Gallery's particular treasures include Velázquez's *Toilet of Venus*, Leonardo da Vinci's Cartoon (*The Virgin and Child with Saints Anne and John the Baptist*), Rembrandt's *Belshazzar's Feast*, Van Gogh's *Sunflowers*, and Titian's *Bacchus and Ariadne*. The British paintings include Gainsborough's *Mr and Mrs Andrews* and Constable's *Haywain*. Free guided tours everyday.

Times: Open all year, daily 10-6, (Wed until 9). Special major charging exhibitions open normal gallery times. Closed 24-26 Dec & 1 Jan. **Fee:** Free. Admission charged for some major exhibitions.

Facilities: P (100yds) 🍽 ✖ licensed 🛈 ᴌ (wheelchair, induction loop, lift, deaf/blind visitor tours) toilets for disabled shop ✖ (ex guide & hearing dogs)

NATIONAL PORTRAIT GALLERY

St Martin's Place WC2H 0HE

⮌ (Underground - Charing Cross, Leicester Square. Buses to Trafalgar Square)

☎ 020 7306 0055

web: www.npg.org.uk

The National Portrait Gallery is home to the largest collection of portraiture in the world featuring famous British men and woman who have created history from the Middle Ages until the present day. Over 1000 portraits are on display across three floors form Henry VIII and Florence Nightingale to The Beatles and The Queen. And, if you want to rest those weary feet, visit the fabulous Portrait Restaurant on the top floor with roof-top views across London. The gallery will be celebrating its 150th anniversary in 2006, with special events throughout the year.

Times: Open all year, Mon-Wed & Sat-Sun 10-6, Thu-Fri 10-9. Closed Good Fri, 24-26 Dec & 1 Jan. (Gallery closure commences 10mins prior to stated time). **Fee:** Free (ex special exhibitions)

Facilities: P (200yds) 🍽 ✖ licensed 🛈 ᴌ (stair climber,touch tours,audio guide,large print captions) toilets for disabled shop ✖ (ex guide dogs)

SIR JOHN SOANE'S MUSEUM

13 Lincoln's Inn Fields WC2A 3BP

⮌ (Underground - Holborn)

☎ 020 7405 2107

e-mail: jbrock@soane.org.uk

web: www.soane.org

Sir John Soane was responsible for some of the most splendid architecture in London, and his house, built in 1812, contains his collections of antiquities, sculpture, paintings, drawings and books. Amongst his treasures are the *Rake's Progess* and *Election* series of paintings by Hogarth.

Times: Open all year, Tue-Sat 10-5. Also first Tue of month 6-9pm. (Closed BH, Good Fri & 24 Dec). Lecture tour Sat 2.30 (limited no of tickets sold from 2pm) **Fee:** ✱ Donations welcome.

Facilities: P (200yds) (metered parking) 🛈 ᴌ (wheelchair available, phone for details of accessibility) shop ✖ (ex guide dogs)

THEATRE MUSEUM

Russell St, Covent Garden WC2E 7PR

⮌ (Underground - Covent Garden, Leicester Sq)

☎ 020 7943 4700

e-mail: tmenquiries@vam.ac.uk

web: www.theatremuseum.org

Major developments, events and personalities from the performing arts, including stage models, costumes, prints, drawings, posters, puppets, props and a variety of other theatre memorabilia. There are guided tours, demonstrations on the art of stage make-up, and you can dress up in costumes from National Theatre companies. Groups are advised to book in advance. Theatre and walking tours 2pm Saturdays.

Times: Open all year, Tue-Sun 10-6. Closed 24-26 Dec & 1 Jan. **Fee:** ✱ Free (ex pre-booked groups which are charged for)

Facilities: P (meters, NCP 250yds) 🛈 ᴌ (Braille guides, audio tours, workshops) toilets for disabled shop ✖ (ex guide dogs)

BARNET   Map 04 TQ29
MUSEUM OF DOMESTIC DESIGN & ARCHITECTURE
Middlesex University, Cat Hill EN4 8HT
➲ (from M25, junct 24 signed A111 Cockfosters to Cat Hill rdbt, straight over onto Chase side. Entrance 1st right opposite Chicken Shed Theatre on Cat Hill Campus)
☎ 020 8411 5244
e-mail: moda@mdx.ac.uk
web: www.moda.mdx.ac.uk

MoDA is a museum of the history of the home. It holds one of the world's most comprehensive collections of decorative design for the period 1870 to 1960, and is a rich source of information on how people decorated and lived in their homes. MoDA has two galleries, a lecture theatre for study days, a seminar room with practical workshops for both adults and children, and a study room which gives visitors access to the collections.
Times: Open Tue-Sat 10-5, Sun 2-5. Closed Mon, Etr, Xmas & New Year. **Fee:** Free entrance. Charges for study days, workshop & group tours **Facilities:** 🅿 🍴 ᕫ (induction loop fitted in lecture theatre) toilets for disabled shop ✖ (ex guide dogs)

BEXLEY   Map 05 TQ47
HALL PLACE
Bourne Rd DA5 1PQ
➲ (near junct of A2 & A233)
☎ 01322 526574   **FREE**
web: www.hallplace.com

Hall Place is an attractive Grade I listed mansion of chequered flint and brick, with wonderful gardens. There is topiary in the form of the 'Queen's Beasts'; rose, rock, peat and water gardens; and a herb garden with a fascinating range of plants (labelled in braille) for medicine and cooking. There is also a conservatory, a local studies centre and museum. Please telephone for details of the programme of temporary exhibitions, lectures and concerts in the museum and Great Hall.
Times: Open all year, House: Mon-Sat 10-5, Sun & BHs 11-5 (Apr-Oct); Tue-Sat 10-4.15 (Nov-Mar). Gardens: Mon-Fri 7.30-dusk, Sat & Sun 9-dusk. **Facilities:** 🅿 💺 ✖ licensed 🍴 ᕫ toilets for disabled shop garden centre (award winning Greenflag) ✖ (ex guide/hearing dogs)

BEXLEYHEATH   Map 05 TQ47
RED HOUSE NEW
Red House Ln DA6 8JF
➲ (off A221 Bexleyheath. At 1st rdbt take 2nd exit then 3rd exit at next rdbt, then 1st left into Danson Rd)
☎ 01494 755588

Commissioned by William Morris in 1859 and designed by Philip Webb, Red House is of enormous international significance in the history of domestic architecture and garden design. The building is constructed of warm red brick, under a steep red-tiled roof, with an emphasis on natural materials and a strong gothic influence. The garden was designed to 'clothe' the house with a series of subdivided areas which still exist. Inside, the house retains many of the original features and fixed items of furniture designed by Morris and Webb.
Times: 16-27 Feb & Oct-Dec, 11-4.15; 2 Mar-Sep, 11-5. Open BH Mons. Closed 25-26 Dec & Jan-14 Feb 06. **Fee:** ✱ £6 (ch £3). Family ticket £15. NT members free **Facilities:** 🅿 20 min walk 💺 ᕫ shop ✖ (ex assist dogs) 🐾 🍴

BRENTFORD   Map 04 TQ17
KEW BRIDGE STEAM MUSEUM
Green Dragon Ln TW8 0EN
➲ (Underground - Kew Gardens, District line then 391 bus. Museum 100yds from N side of Kew Bridge. From M4 junct 2 follow A4 to Chiswick rdbt, take A315 to Kew Bridge, Green Dragon Ln 1st right after lights)
☎ 020 8568 4757
e-mail: info@kbsm.org
web: www.kbsm.org

This Victorian pumping station has steam engines and six beam engines, of which five are working and one is the largest in the world. A diesel house and waterwheel can also be seen along with London's only steam narrow-gauge railway, which operates every Sunday (Mar-Nov). The Water for Life Gallery tells the story of London's water supply from Pre-Roman times. The newest exhibit is a water pump, once powered by horses.
Times: Open all year, daily 11-5. Engines in steam, wknds & BHs. Closed Good Fri, Xmas wk & New Year. **Fee:** ✱ Wkdays £4.25, wknds £5.75 (ch free, concessions available) **Facilities:** 🅿 💺 🍴 ᕫ (wheelchairs, large print guide) toilets for disabled shop 🍴

MUSICAL MUSEUM
400 High St TW8 0BD
➲ (Underground - Gunnersbury, nr Kew Bridge)
☎ 020 8560 8108
web: www.musicalmuseum.co.uk

This museum will take you back to a bygone age to hear and see a marvellous working collection of automatic musical instruments from small music boxes to a mighty Wurlitzer theatre organ. Working demonstrations.
Times: Apr-Oct, Sat-Sun 2-5. **Fee:** £5 (ch free). **Facilities:** 🅿 💺 🍴 ᕫ toilets for disabled shop ✖ (guide dogs)

CHESSINGTON   Map 04 TQ16
CHESSINGTON WORLD OF ADVENTURES
Leatherhead Rd KT9 2NE
➲ (M25 junct 9/10, on A243)
☎ 0870 444 7777
web: www.chessington.com

Feel the fantasy of Hocus Pocus Hall - the magical 4-D experience home to a wacky wizard and mischievous goblins and where magical mayhem is literally brought to life in front of your eyes! Plus don't miss the fang-tastic Vampire, quick fire challenge of Tomb Blaster or fun-filled Dennis's Madhouse in Beanoland. Take a safari trip down Trail of the Kings then journey into Toytown with Toadie's Crazy Cars, Berry Bouncers and Tiny Truckers. Or, for the more daring, face a power of the mighty Samurai, or find Rameses waiting to seek his Revenge. There's so much to feed the imagination and excite the senses!
Times: ✱ Open 10 Apr-2 Nov (excluding some off peak days) either 10-5, 10-6 or 10-7 (telephone for details). Open until 7.30 during Halloween Hocus Pocus. **Facilities:** 🅿 💺 ✖ licensed 🍴 ᕫ (some rides not accessible, disabled guide available) toilets for disabled shop ✖ (ex guide dogs & hearing dogs) 🍴

CHISLEHURST   Map 05 TQ47

CHISLEHURST CAVES
Old Hill BR7 5NB

⮑ (off A222 near Chislehurst railway stn. Turn into station approach, then right & right again into Caveside Close)

☎ 020 8467 3264   **2 for 1**

e-mail: enquiries@chislehurstcaves.co.uk
web: www.chislehurstcaves.co.uk

Miles of mystery and history beneath your feet. Grab a lantern and get ready for an amazing adventure! Visit the caves and your whole family can travel back in time as you explore the maze of passageways dug through the chalk deep beneath Chislehurst. Accompanied by an experienced guide on a 45 minute tour you'll see the tunnels made famous as a shelter during the Second World War, visit the cave's church, druid altar, the haunted pool and much more!
Times: Open all year, Wed-Sun, 10-4. Daily during local school hols (incl half terms). Closed Xmas. **Fee:** £4 (ch & pen £2).
Facilities: 🅿 🖵 ✗ licensed 🗐 shop ✖ (ex guide dogs) ◀

DOWNE   Map 05 TQ46

DOWN HOUSE - HOME OF CHARLES DARWIN
BR6 7JT

⮑ (off A233, signed)
☎ 01689 859119

Charles Darwin, perhaps the most influential scientist of the 19th-century, lived at Down House for over 40 years. He wrote the revolutionary book, *On the Origin of Species* here. Explore the exhibition on the first floor and visit the ground floor study, which was the centre of his life.
Times: Open Apr-Sep, Wed-Sun & BHs 10-6; Oct, Wed-Sun 10-5; Nov-Mar, Wed-Sun 10-4.Closed 19 Dec-2 Feb. **Fee:** £6.60 (ch £3.30, concessions £5.00). Family £16.50. Opening times and prices are subject to change, for further details please phone 0870 333 1181
Facilities: 🅿 ⅘ shop ✖

ESHER   Map 04 TQ16

CLAREMONT LANDSCAPE GARDEN
Portsmouth Rd KT10 9JG

⮑ (1m S of Esher on A307)
☎ 01372 467806

e-mail: claremont@nationaltrust.org.uk
web: www.nationaltrust.org.uk/claremont

Laid out by Vanbrugh and Bridgeman before 1720, extended and naturalised by Kent, this is one of the earliest surviving example of an English landscaped garden. Its 50 acres include a lake with an island pavilion, a grotto and a turf amphitheatre.
Times: Open all year Apr-Oct daily, Mon-Fri 10-6, Sat-Sun & BH Mon 10-7, Nov-Mar daily (ex Mon) 10-5 or sunset if earlier. (Closed all day 19-22 & 26 Jul, closed 2pm 23-24 Jul). Closed 25 Dec & 1 Jan. House not National Trust. **Fee:** ✱ £5 (ch £2.50). Family ticket £12.50
Facilities: 🅿 🖵 🗐 ⅘ (wheelchairs available, Braille guide) toilets for disabled shop ✖ (ex on leads, Nov-Mar only) ◀

HAM   Map 04 TQ17

HAM HOUSE
Ham St TW10 7RS

⮑ (W of A307, between Kingston & Richmond)
☎ 020 8940 1950

e-mail: hamhouse@nationaltrust.org.uk
web: www.nationaltrust.org.uk/hamhouse

Ham House is a fine example of 17th-century fashion and power. Built in 1610, the house was enlarged in the 1670s

continued

when it was at the heart of Restoration court life and intrigue. It was then occupied by the same family until 1948. The formal garden is significant for its survival in an area known as the cradle of the English Landscape Movement. The outbuildings include an orangery, an ice house, a still house, and a dairy.
Times: Open Gardens: all year, Sat-Wed 11-6 or dusk if earlier. Closed 25-26 Dec & 1 Jan. House: 19 Mar-30 Oct, Sat-Wed 1-5. (Last admission 4.30). **Fee:** ✱ House & Garden £7.50 (ch £3.75). Family ticket £18.75. Garden only £3.50 (ch £1.75). Family ticket £8.75.
Facilities: 🅿 🖵 🗐 ⅘ (Braille guide, wheelchairs, stairclimber, lift, parking) toilets for disabled shop ✖ (ex assist dogs) ◀

HAMPTON COURT   Map 04 TQ16

HAMPTON COURT PALACE
KT8 9AU

⮑ (A3 to Hook underpass then A309. Train from Waterloo - Hampton Court, 2mins walk from station)

☎ 0870 752 7777

e-mail: hamptoncourt@hrp.org.uk
web: www.hrp.org.uk

With over 500 years of royal history Hampton Court Palace has something to offer everyone, from the magnificent State Apartments to the domestic reality of the Tudor Kitchens. Costumed guides and audio tours bring the palace to life and provide an insight into how life in the palace would have been in the time of Henry VIII and William III. There is also an exhibition that explores community life after the departure of the monarchy from the Palace, along with a fascinating new audio installation in the world famous maze.
Times: Open all year from 10, closes 6 mid Mar-mid Oct, 4.30 mid Oct-mid Mar. Closed 24-26 Dec. **Fee:** ✱ £12 (ch £7.80, concessions £9). Family £35. **Facilities:** 🅿 (charged) 🖵 ✗ licensed ⅘ (lifts, buggies for gardens, wheelchairs, wardens to assist) toilets for disabled shop (4 shops on site) ✖ (ex guide/hearing dogs) ◀

ISLEWORTH   Map 04 TQ17

SYON HOUSE
TW8 8JF

⮑ (A310 Twickenham road into Park Rd)
☎ 020 8560 0882 020 8560 0883   **2 for 1**
e-mail: info@syonpark.co.uk
web: www.syonpark.co.uk

Set in 200 acres of parkland, Syon House is the London home of the Duke of Northumberland, whose family have lived here since the late 16th century. During the second half of the 18th century the first Duke of Northumberland engaged Robert Adam to remodel the interior and 'Capability' Brown to landscape the grounds. Adam was also responsible for the furniture and decorations, and the result is particularly spectacular in the superbly coloured Ante-Room and Long Gallery.
Times: ✱ Open 24 Mar-Oct, Wed-Thu, Sun & BH 11-5 (last ticket 4.15). **Facilities:** 🅿 🖵 ⅘ (stairclimer available) toilets for disabled shop garden centre ✖ ◀

SYON PARK
TW8 8JF

⮑ (A310 Twickenham road into Park Rd)
☎ 020 8560 0882   **2 for 1**
e-mail: info@syonpark.co.uk
web: www.syonpark.co.uk

Contained within the 40 acres that make up Syon Park Gardens is one of the inspirations for the Crystal Palace at

continued

the Great Exhibition of 1851: a vast crescent of metal and glass, the first construction of its kind in the world and known as the Great Conservatory. Although the horticultural reputation of Syon Park goes back to the 16th century, its beauty today is thanks to the master of landscape design, 'Capability' Brown.

Times: Open all year, Apr-Oct daily, 10.30-5.30; (4pm Nov-Mar) **Fee:** ✱ £3.50 (concessions £2.50). Combined ticket for house & gardens £7.25 (ch & concessions £5.95). Family ticket £9. **Facilities:** P ⬛ ᪲ (stair lift for show house) toilets for disabled shop garden centre ✖ (ex guide dogs) ▬

KEW   Map 04 TQ17

Kew Gardens (Royal Botanic Gardens)
TW9 3AB
⮑ (Underground - Kew Gdns)
☎ 020 8332 5655
e-mail: info@kew.org
web: www.kew.org

Kew Gardens is a paradise throughout the seasons. Lose yourself in the magnificent conservatories and discover plants from the world's deserts, mountains and oceans. Wide-open spaces, stunning vistas, listed buildings and wildlife contribute to the Garden's unique atmosphere. As well as being famous for its beautiful gardens, Kew is world renowned for its contribution to botanical and horticultural science.

Times: Open all year, Gardens daily 9.30. Closing times vary (seasonal, visit website or phone to verify). Closed 24&25 Dec. **Fee:** £10 (concessions £7, ch under 17 free). **Facilities:** P (charged) ⬛ ✖ licensed ▤ ᪲ (16 seat bus tour: enquiries ring 020 8332 5643) toilets for disabled shop ✖ (ex guide dogs) ▬

Kew Palace
Royal Botanic Gardens TW9 3AB
⮑ (Underground - Kew Bridge)
☎ 020 8781 9540
web: www.hrp.org.uk

A favourite country residence during the reign of the first three Hanoverian Kings, Kew was the site of several royal houses. A fairly modest red-brick building, built in the Dutch style with gables, Kew Palace was built in 1631 and used until 1818 when Queen Charlotte died. A major renovation project means that the palace should re-open around Easter 2006. Visitors will be able to see artefacts that belonged to George III and his family, and gain access to the second floor, which has never before been open to the public.

Times: Palace is due to reopen to public Etr 2006. For further info and details of the work visit www.hrp.org.uk **Fee:** Visit www.hrp.org.uk for price info. **Facilities:** P (charged) ᪲ toilets for disabled ✖

The National Archives
Ruskin Av TW9 4DU
⮑ (Underground - Kew Gardens)
☎ 020 8392 5202 & 020 8487 9202   FREE
e-mail: events@pro.gov.uk
web: www.pro.gov.uk/

The National Archives houses one of the finest, most complete archives in Europe, comprising the records of the central government and law courts from the Norman Conquest to the present century. It is a mine of information and some of the most interesting material including Domesday Book.

Times: ✱ Open Mon, Wed & Fri, 9-4.45; Tue, 10-7; Thu, 9-7. Closed 1st wk in Dec, Sun & public holiday wknds. **Facilities:** P ⬛ ᪲ (hearing loops & large print text in museum) toilets for disabled shop ✖ (ex guide dogs)

Queen Charlotte's Cottage
Royal Botanic Gardens TW9 3AB
⮑ (Underground - Kew Gardens)
☎ 020 8332 5189
web: www.hrp.org.uk

Typical of the fashionable rustic style popular with the gentry in the 18th century, the cottage was built for George III and Queen Charlotte as a home for their menagerie of exotic pets, as well as a picnic spot and summer house.

Times: Open wknds Jul & Aug. **Fee:** Free with entry to Botanical gardens. **Facilities:** P shop ✖

MORDEN   Map 05 TQ26

Morden Hall Park
Morden Hall Rd SM4 5JD
⮑ (A298 (Bushey Rd), right at 2nd lights into Martin Way. Morden Hall signed)   FREE
☎ 020 8545 6850
e-mail: mordenhallpark@nationaltrust.org.uk
web: www.nationaltrust.org.uk

A green oasis in the heart of South West London. A former deer park, with a network of waterways including meadow, wetland and woodland habitats. Also discover the picturesque rose garden with over 2000 roses, fragrant from May to September.

Times: Open daily, 8-6. **Facilities:** P ⬛ ✖ licensed ▤ ᪲ (wheelchair, Braille guides, large handled cutlery) toilets for disabled shop (open 10-5) garden centre ⚘

OSTERLEY   Map 04 TQ17

Osterley Park and House
Jersey Rd TW7 4RB
⮑ (signed from A4. Underground - Osterley)
☎ 020 8232 5050   2 for 1
e-mail: osterley@nationaltrust.org.uk
web: www.nationaltrust.org.uk/osterley

In 1761, the founders of Child's Bank commissioned Robert Adam to transform a crumbling Tudor mansion into an elegant, neo-classical villa. This was their house in the country, created to entertain and impress friends and business associates. Today the spectacular interiors contain one of Britain's most complete examples of Adam's work. The house is set in over 350 acres of park and farm land, complete with Pleasure Grounds, ornamental lakes and garden buildings. The 2-for-1 voucher is valid only during normal visiting hours and cannot be used for any ticketed events.

Times: Open all year: Park & pleasure grounds, daily 9-7.30 or sunset if earlier. House: Mar Sat & Sun 1-4.30, Apr-Oct, Wed-Sun 1-4.30, BH Sun & Mon 1-4.30. Closed 25-26 Dec. **Fee:** ✱ £4.90. (ch £2.40) Family ticket £12.20. Group 15+(booked in advance) £4 each **Facilities:** P (charged) ⬛ ▤ ᪲ (Braille guide, wheelchairs, electric carts, stair climber) toilets for disabled shop ✖ (ex assist dogs in house) ⚘

TWICKENHAM   Map 04 TQ17

Marble Hill House
Richmond Rd TW1 2NL
☎ 020 8892 5115

A magnificent Thames-side Palladian villa built for Henrietta Howard, mistress of King George II, set in 66 acres of riverside parklands.

Times: Open 24 Mar-Oct, Sat 10-2, Sun & BHs 10-5. Closed Nov-Mar but pre-booked groups by arrangement. **Fee:** £4.00 (ch £2, concessions £3). Opening times and prices are subject to change, for further details please phone 0870 333 1181 **Facilities:** P ⬛ ✖ licensed ᪲ toilets for disabled shop ✖ (ex on lead in certain areas) ♯

MUSEUM OF RUGBY & TWICKENHAM STADIUM TOURS

Rugby Football Union, Rugby Rd TW1 1DZ
⮑ (A316, follow signs to museum)
☎ 0870 405 2021
e-mail: museum@rfu.com
web: www.rfu.com/microsites/museum/

Combine a behind the scenes guided tour of the world's most famous rugby stadium with a visit to The Museum of Rugby. The tour includes breathtaking views from the top of
continued

the North Stand, a visit to the England dressing room and ends by walking through the players tunnel to pitch side. The multi-media museum appeals to enthusiasts of all ages and charts the history and world-wide growth of rugby. You can also test your skills on the scrum machine

Times: Open, Tue-Sat 10-5 (last museum admission 4.30), Sun 11-5 (last admission 4.30). Closed post Twickenham match days, Etr Sun, 24-26 Dec & 1 Jan. **Fee:** Museum & Tour £9 (concessions £6). Family £30. **Facilities:** 🅿 💺 ✕ licensed ♿ toilets for disabled shop ✖ (ex guide dogs) 🎒

ORLEANS HOUSE GALLERY

Riverside TW1 3DJ
⮑ (Richmond road (A305), Orleans Rd is on right just past Orleans Park School)
☎ 020 8831 6000   FREE
e-mail: m.denovellis@richmond.gov.uk
web: www.richmond.gov.uk

Stroll beside the Thames and through the woodland gardens of Orleans House, where you will find stunning 18th-century interior design and an excellent public art gallery. Visitors of all ages can try out their own artistic talents in pre-booked workshops, and wide-ranging temporary exhibitions are held throughout the year - please telephone for details.

Times: Open Oct-Mar, Tue-Sat 1-4.30, Sun & BH 2-4.30; Apr-Sep Tue-Sat 1-5.30, Sun & BH 2-5.30. **Facilities:** 🅿 📖 ♿ (handling objects & large print labels for some exhibitions) toilets for disabled shop ✖ (ex guide dogs)

Gargoyles at Hampton Court

MERSEYSIDE

EVENTS & FESTIVALS

January
tbc Chinese New Year celebrations, in and around Chinatown, Liverpool

April
6th-8th Grand National Festival, Aintree Racecourse, Liverpool

May
tbc Liverpool Women's 10k Run

June
tbc Mersey International Shanty Festival, Albert Dock, Pier Head and Birkenhead
tbc The Mersey River Festival, River Mersey and Albert Dock, Liverpool

July
2nd Liverpool-Chester-Liverpool Bike Ride
28th-30th St Helens Show, Sherdley Park, St Helens
tbc Aintree Show, Aintree Racecourse
tbc Liverpool Corporate Cup Run, 5km course in the city centre
tbc Merseyside International Street Festival

August
5th-6th Wirral Show, Promenade, New Brighton, Wirral (provisional)
12th-13th Motor Show North West, Haydock Park Racecourse (provisional)
24th-29th International Beatles Week (provisional)
tbc Creamfields Festival, Old Liverpool Airfield, Speke Boulevard
tbc Southport Flower Show, Victoria Park, Rotten Row, Southport

September
tbc The Southport Airshow, The Promenade, Southport

Above: Southport Arts Centre, dating from the 1870s

BIRKENHEAD   Map 07 SJ38

HISTORIC WARSHIPS
East Float, Dock Rd CH41 1DJ
➲ (end of M53 all docks turn off follow tourist signs. From Liverpool Wallasey tunnel 1st exit after toll & follow brown heritage signs)
☎ 0151 650 1573
e-mail: manager@historicwarships.org
web: www.historicwarships.org

HMS Onyx served in the Falklands and is the only submarine afloat in the UK that visitors can explore. *HMS Plymouth*, an anti-submarine frigate also served in the Falklands. The U534 is the only WWII German U-Boat to be raised from the sea bed. Pre-booking required, only adults and children over 12 years (2 per adult) admitted to U-Boat.

Times: Open all year, Sep-Mar daily 10-4, Apr-Aug daily 10-5. Closed 24-26 Dec, only open wknds for first 6 wks of year. **Fee:** ✱ £6.50 (ch £4.50, pen £5.50). Family ticket £19. Combined ships £15.50, U-Boat £9.
Facilities: 🅿 💷 🍴 ♿ (museum, ltd access to HMS Plymouth,multimedia tour of U534) toilets for disabled shop ✖ (ex guide dogs) 🍽

LIVERPOOL   Map 07 SJ39

THE BEATLES STORY
Britannia Pavilion, Albert Dock L3 4AD
➲ (follow signs to Albert Dock. Located outside Britannia Pavilion, next to Premier Lodge Hotel)
☎ 0151 709 1963   **2 for 1**
e-mail: info@beatlesstory.com
web: www.beatlesstory.com

Relive the story of the four lads from Liverpool who took the world by storm and changed the face of popular music for ever.

Times: Open all year 10-6 (last admission 5). Closed 25-26 Dec.
Fee: £8.99 (ch 5-16yrs £4.99 & concessions £5.99). Family ticket (2ad+3ch) £25. **Facilities:** 🅿 (charged) 🍴 ♿ (hearing loop) shop ✖ (ex guide dogs) 🍽

CENTRAL LIBRARY
William Brown St L3 8EW
➲ (located between museum and art gallery)
☎ 0151 233 5858   **FREE**
e-mail: refhum.central.library@liverpool.gov.uk
web: www.liverpool.gov.uk

The Picton, Hornby and Brown buildings, situated in the Victorian grandeur of William Brown Street, house Liverpool's collection of over one million books, forming one of Britain's largest and oldest public libraries. The Liverpool Record Office is one of the country's largest and most significant County Record offices. Regular exhibitions of treasures from the collections are held, please telephone for details. Special Event: Centenary of the Hornby Library in 2006.

Times: Open all year, Mon-Fri 9-6, Sat 10-4 & Sun 12-4. Closed BHs.
Facilities: 🅿 (50 yds) (pay & display parking only) ♿ (lift, text magnification, reading machine) toilets for disabled ✖ (ex guide dogs)

> If an attraction name appears in *italics*, details have not been confirmed for 2006.

CONSERVATION CENTRE

White Chapel L1 6HZ

➲ (follow brown tourist signs to Whitechapel)

☎ 0151 478 4999   **FREE**

web: www.nmgm.org.uk

Award winning centre, the only one of its kind, gives the public an insight into the world of museum and gallery conservation. **Times:** Mon-Sat 10-5, Sun 12-5. Closed 23-26 Dec & 1 Jan. **Facilities:** 🅿 (charged) 💻 📶 ♿ toilets for disabled shop ✈ (ex guide dogs) ◀

THE GRAND NATIONAL EXPERIENCE

Aintree Racecourse, Ormskirk Rd L9 5AS

➲ (Aintree Racecourse on A59 (Liverpool to Preston road), clearly signed)

☎ 0151 522 2921

e-mail: aintree@rht.net

web: www.aintree.co.uk

A fascinating look at Britain's most famous horserace, the Grand National. Visitors can sit in the jockeys' weighing-in chair, walk around the dressing rooms, watch video presentations, and view a gallery of paintings and photography depicting the race. **Times:** Please telephone for details. **Fee:** Please telephone for details. **Facilities:** 🅿 ✕ licensed ♿ toilets for disabled ✈ (ex guide dogs) ◀

HM CUSTOMS & EXCISE NATIONAL MUSEUM

Merseyside Maritime Museum, Albert Dock L3 4AQ

➲ (Albert Dock - follow brown signs)

☎ 0151 478 4999   **FREE**

web: www.nmgm.org.uk

Enter the exciting world of smuggle busting where everyday items reveal their hidden secrets. Find a fake, rummage for hidden goods and spot a suspect traveller. Look into the illustrious history of HM Customs & Excise, it's the longest battle in history and it's still going on today! **Times:** Open daily 10-5. Closed 23-26 Dec & 1 Jan. **Facilities:** 🅿 💻 ✕ licensed 📶 ♿ (restricted wheelchair access, no access to basement) toilets for disabled shop ✈ (ex guide dogs) ◀

LIVERPOOL CATHEDRAL

St James' Mount L1 7AZ

➲ (follow city centre signs 'Cathedrals'. St James' Mount is off Upper Duke St in S side of city centre, adjacent to 'Chinatown')

☎ 0151 709 6271

e-mail: lew.eccleshall@ liverpoolcathedral.org.uk

web: www.liverpoolcathedral.org.uk

Although it appears at first sight to be as old as any other monumental cathedral in Britain, Liverpool Cathedral is in fact a 20th-century structure that was only completed in 1978. Its foundation stone was laid in 1904, and through two World Wars the building continued. It is the largest Anglican Cathedral in Europe, and has the largest pipe organ and the heaviest ringing peal of bells in the world. Numerous events taking place throughout the year, please telephone or see website for details. **Times:** Open daily 8-6, 25 Dec 8-3. **Fee:** Free. £3 donation per person recommended. Tower £4.25 (concessions £2) Family ticket (2ad+3ch) £10. **Facilities:** 🅿 (charged) 💻 ✕ licensed 📶 ♿ (Braille leaflets, handrails, lift) toilets for disabled shop ✈ (ex assist dogs) ◀

LIVERPOOL FOOTBALL CLUB VISITORS CENTRE TOUR

Anfield Rd L4 0TH

☎ 0151 260 6677

e-mail: Museum1@liverpoolfc.tv

web: www.liverpoolfc.tv

Touch the famous "This is Anfield" sign as you walk down the tunnel to the sound of the crowd at the LFC museum and tour centre. Celebrate all things Liverpool, past and present. Bright displays and videos chart the history of England's most successful football club and more recent glories are recalled, as the 2001 "Treble" is on display, as well as the "Fab Four" European cups. **Times:** Open all year: Museum daily 10-5 last admission 4. Closed 25-26 Dec. Match days 9 until last admission - 1hr before kick off. Museum & Tour - tours are run subject to daily demand. Advance booking is essential to avoid disappointment. **Facilities:** 🅿 💻 ✕ licensed ♿ (lifts, ramps to all areas for wheelchairs) toilets for disabled shop ✈ (ex guide dogs) ◀

LIVERPOOL MUSEUM

William Brown St L3 8EN

➲ (in city centre next to St George's Hall and Lime St, follow brown signs)

☎ 0151 478 4393   **FREE**

e-mail: themuseum@liverpoolmuseums.org.uk

web: www.liverpoolmuseum.org.uk

One of Britain's most interesting museums, the Liverpool Museum has diverse collections ranging from the Amazonian rain forests to the mysteries of outer space. Special attractions include the award-winning hands-on Natural History Centre and the Planetarium. The museum is currently undergoing extensive building improvements and refurbishment, and many new features are due in 2005. Please note that during construction work some galleries may be closed. **Times:** Open Mon-Sat 10-5, Sun noon-5. Closed 23-26 Dec & 1 Jan. **Facilities:** 🅿 💻 📶 ♿ toilets for disabled shop ✈ (ex guide dogs)

MERSEYSIDE MARITIME MUSEUM

Albert Dock L3 4AQ

➲ (entry into Dock from The Strand)

☎ 0151 478 4499   FREE

web: www.liverpoolmuseums.org.uk

Set in the heart of Liverpool's magnificent waterfront, the Merseyside Maritime Museum offers a unique insight into the history of the great port of Liverpool, its ships and its people.

Times: Open daily 10-5. Closed 23-26 Dec & 1 Jan.
Facilities: P ✗ licensed 🔌 ♿ (lifts, wheelchairs, ramps, ex pilot boat & basement) toilets for disabled shop ✖ (ex guide dogs) ⛽

METROPOLITAN CATHEDRAL OF CHRIST THE KING

Mount Pleasant L3 5TQ

➲ (10 mins walk from either Liverpool Lime St or Liverpool Central Railway Station. 'Smart' buses stop outside. Cathedral well signed from Liverpool city centre)

☎ 0151 709 9222

e-mail: met.cathedral@boltblue.com

web: www.liverpoolmetrocathedral.org.uk

A modern Roman Catholic cathedral which provides a focal point on the Liverpool skyline. The imposing structure of curving concrete ribs and stained glass was designed by Sir Frederick Gibberd and consecrated in 1967. Monumental crypt of brick and granite by Sir Edwin Lutyens 1933. Numerous modern works of art.

Times: Open daily 8-6 (Sun 5 in winter). **Fee:** Free admission, although donations welcome. **Facilities:** P (charged) 🔌 🔌 ♿ (lift, loop system, no access to Crypt) toilets for disabled shop ✖ (ex guide dogs) ⛽

NATIONAL WILDFLOWER CENTRE

Court Hey Park L16 3NA

➲ (M62 junct 5, take A5080 to rdbt. Exit into Roby Rd, entrance 0.5m on left)

☎ 0151 738 1913

e-mail: info@nwc.org.uk

web: www.nwc.org.uk

Set in a public park on the outskirts of Liverpool, the National Wildflower Centre promotes the creation of wildflower habitats around the country and provides educational materials, wildflower seeds and interactive facilities. The Centre has demonstration areas, children's activities, a working nursery, compost display and rooftop walk. The centre has a comprehensive programme of events

continued

through the summer. Special Events: Annual Winter Celebration Dec 2005, Annual Green Fayre and Farmers Market Jun 2006, Annual Knowsley Flower Show Aug 2006.
Times: Open Apr-Sep, daily 10-5. **Fee:** ✱ £3 (ch 5-16, pen, students & unemployed £1.50). Family ticket (2ad+2ch) £7.50. Season tickets & group discount tickets available. **Facilities:** P 🔌 🔌 ♿ (electric buggy & wheelchair available) toilets for disabled shop garden centre ✖ (ex guide dogs & in park) ⛽

TATE LIVERPOOL

Albert Dock L3 4BB

➲ (within walking distance of Liverpool Lime Street train station)

☎ 0151 702 7400 & 0151 702 7402

e-mail: liverpoolinfo@tate.org.uk

web: www.tate.org.uk/liverpool/

A converted Victorian warehouse with stunning views across the River Mersey, Tate Liverpool displays the best of the National Collection of 20th-Century Art. A changing programme of exhibitions draws on works from public and private collections across the world.

Times: Open Tue-Sun, 10-5.50. Closed Mon ex BH Mon, 24-26 Dec, 1 Jan & Good Fri. **Fee:** Admission free. £4 (concessions £3) for special exhibitions, phone for details. **Facilities:** P 🔌 ♿ (wheelchairs available, leaflets in Braille, hearing loop) toilets for disabled shop ✖ (ex assist dogs) ⛽

WALKER ART GALLERY

William Brown St L3 8EL

➲ (follow brown and white signs)

☎ 0151 478 4199   FREE

web: www.nmgm.org.uk

For over 120 years, visitors have been surprised, charmed & moved by The Walker's world-famous collection including masterpieces by Rembrandt, Poussin, Rubens and Murillo. Newly refurbished galleries will display an exciting and varied programme of must see exhibitions.

Times: Open Mon-Sat 10-5, Sun 12-5. Closed 23-26 Dec & 1 Jan.
Facilities: P (charged) 🔌 ✗ 🔌 ♿ (prior notice appreciated, wheelchair on request) toilets for disabled shop ✖ (ex guide dogs)

We endeavour to be as accurate as possible, but changes to times and other information can occur after the guide has gone to press.

This symbol indicates attractions which have chosen to participate in our 2-for-1 voucher scheme

PORT SUNLIGHT   Map 07 SJ38

LADY LEVER ART GALLERY
CH62 5EQ
➲ (Follow brown heritage signs)
☎ 0151 478 4136
e-mail: ladyleverartgallery@nmgm.org
web: www.nmgm.org.uk

The Lady Lever Art Gallery houses many world famous works of art, including Pre-Raphaelite masterpieces by Millais, Burne-Jones and Rossetti. Dramatic landscapes by the great British painters, Turner and Constable are also displayed alongside portraits by Gainsborough, Romney and Reynolds.

Times: Open all year, Mon-Sat 10-5, Sun 12-5. Closed 23-26 Dec & 1 Jan. **Facilities:** 🅿 (charged) 💷 🗐 ⛽ (prior notice appreciated, wheelchair on request) toilets for disabled ✖ (ex guide dogs)

PRESCOT   Map 07 SJ49

KNOWSLEY SAFARI PARK
L34 4AN
➲ (M62 junct 6 onto M57 junct 2. Follow 'safari park' signs)
☎ 0151 430 9009
e-mail: safari.park@knowsley.com
web: www.knowsley.com

A five-mile drive through the reserves enables visitors to see lions, tigers, elephants, rhinos, monkeys and many other animals in spacious, natural surroundings. Also a children's amusement park, reptile house, pets' corner plus sealion shows. Other attractions include an amusement park and a miniature railway.

Times: Open all year, Mar-Oct, daily 10-4. Winter Nov-Feb, 11-3. **Fee:** ✱ £9.50 (ch & pen £6.50). **Facilities:** 🅿 💷 ⛽ toilets for disabled shop ✖ (kennels provided) 🍴

PRESCOT MUSEUM
34 Church St L34 3LA
➲ (situated on corner of High St (A57) & Church St. Follow brown heritage signs)
☎ 0151 430 7787   FREE
e-mail: prescot.museum.dlcs@knowsley.gov.uk
web: www.knowsley.gov.uk/leisure/museum

Permanent exhibitions reflecting the local history of the area, including its important clock and watch making heritage. There is a programme of special exhibitions, events and holiday activities, telephone for details.

Times: Open all year, Tue-Sat 10-5 (closed 1-2), Sun 2-5. Closed BHs. **Facilities:** 🅿 (100 yds) 🗐 ⛽ (ramp to ground floor) shop ✖ (ex guide dogs)

ST HELENS   Map 07 SJ59

WORLD OF GLASS
Chalon Way East WA10 1BT
➲ (5mins from M62 junct 7)
☎ 08700 114466   2 for 1
e-mail: info@worldofglass.com
web: www.worldofglass.com

Ideal for all the family, this fascinating attraction is in the heart of St Helens, a town shaped by glass-making. Features include the world's first continuous glass-making furnace, and two museum galleries that show glass in the ancient world and Victorian life in St Helens. There is also a Mirror Maze where Wizard Filligrano works, a newly refurbished café and a gift shop.

Times: Open Tue-Sun & BH, 10-5. Closed 25-26 Dec & 1 Jan. **Fee:** ✱ £5.30 (ch £3.80, pen £3.80) Family & group discounts. **Facilities:** 🅿 💷 🗐 ⛽ toilets for disabled shop ✖ (ex guide dogs) 🍴

SOUTHPORT   Map 07 SD31

ATKINSON ART GALLERY
Lord St PR8 1DH
➲ (located in centre of Lord St, next to Town Hall)   FREE
☎ 01704 533133 ext 2110
e-mail: atkinson.gallery@leisure.sefton.gov.uk
web: www.seftonarts.co.uk

The gallery specialises in 19th-and 20th-century oil paintings, watercolours, drawings and prints, as well as 20th-century sculpture. Temporary exhibitions are shown regularly at the art gallery.

Times: Open all year, Mon-Wed & Fri 10-5, Thu & Sat 10-1. Closed 25-26 Dec & 1 Jan. Closed BHs. **Facilities:** 🅿 (next street) (pay & display) ✖ licensed ⛽ shop ✖ (ex guide dogs)

THE BRITISH LAWNMOWER MUSEUM
106-114 Shakespeare St PR8 5AJ
⮑ (From M6, M58 or M57 follow signs towards town centre, then brown heritage signs to museum)
☎ 01704 501336   **2 for 1**
e-mail: info@lawnmowerworld.com
web: www.lawnmowerworld.com
This award-winning museum houses a private collection of over 250 rare exhibits of garden machinery of special interest dating from 1799. There is also the largest collection of vintage toy lawnmowers and games in the world. See the lawnmowers of the rich and famous as well as machines made by Rolls Royce, Royal Enfield, Hawker Sidley and many more. A tribute to the garden machine industry over the last 200 years.
Times: Open daily, 9-5.30, ex Sun & BH Mon. **Fee:** £1 (ch 50p). Guided tour £4. **Facilities:** 🅿 🍴 shop ✘ (ex guide dogs) ⬛

PLEASURELAND
Marine Dr PR8 1RX
⮑ (signed from Southport Town Centre)
☎ 0870 220 0204   **2 for 1**
e-mail: mail@pleasurelandltd.freeserve.co.uk
web: www.pleasureland.uk.com
Pleasureland is home to over 100 rides and attractions, including the; TRAUMAtizer suspended rollercoaster, the Lucazade Space Shot, the Cyclone rollercoaster, Ghost Train and Lost Dinosaurs of the Sahara.
Times: Open Mar-Nov opening times vary please call for information. **Fee:** ✱ £18 all day (juniors £12). Entry for 4 (adults and/or children) £60. **Facilities:** 🅿 (charged) 💻 ✘ licensed 🍴 ♿ (access on some rides) toilets for disabled shop ✘ (ex guide dogs) ⬛

SPEKE   Map 07 SJ48

SPEKE HALL
The Walk L24 1XD
⮑ (on N bank of Mersey, 1m off A561 on W side of Liverpool Airport. Follow airport signs from M62 junct 6, A5300; M56 junct 12, follow brown signs)
☎ 0151 427 7231
e-mail: spekehall@nationaltrust.org.uk
web: www.nationaltrust.org.uk
A remarkable timber-framed manor house set in tranquil gardens and grounds. The house has a Tudor Great Hall, Stuart plasterwork, and William Morris wallpapers. Outside are varied grounds, including a rose garden, bluebell woods and woodland walks. Also, a live interpretation by costumed guides.
Times: House open: 19 Mar-30 Oct, Wed-Sun (open BH Mon) 1-5.30; 5 Nov-4 Dec, Sat & Sun 1-4.30. Garden open daily 11-5.30 or dusk. Closed Mon (ex BH), 24-26 & 31 Dec, 1 Jan & Good Fri. **Fee:** ✱ Hall & Gardens: £6.25 (ch £3.50). Gardens only: £3.25 (ch £1.75). Family ticket £19. Gardens Family ticket £10. Reduced rate when arriving by public transport, cycle or on foot. **Facilities:** 🅿 (charged) 💻 ✘ ♿ (wheelchairs, electric car, Braille guide) toilets for disabled shop ♻ ⬛

Interior of Cathedral of Christ the King

NORFOLK

EVENTS & FESTIVALS

May
1st King's Lynn May Garland Procession, town centre, King's Lynn
3rd-14th Norfolk & Norwich Festival (music and the arts)
12th-14th Norfolk Garden Show, Norfolk Showground, Norwich

June
28th-29th Royal Norfolk Show, Royal Norfolk Showground
30th-8th Jul Wymondham Music Festival, a whole range of musical styles
tbc Deepdale Jazz Festival, venue to be confirmed, Burnham Deepdale

July
13th-16th Lord Mayor's Celebrations, Norwich city centre
15th-16th Weeting Steam Engine Rally & country Show (provisional)
29th Langham Street Fayre, old English fayre on the high street
tbc Morris & Folk Festival, Sheringham
tbc Norwich Music Festival
tbc Sandringham Flower Show, Sandringham Estate
tbc Worstead Village Festival

August
6th-12th Mundesley Festival
26th-31st Kid Zone, outdoor activities, sports, crafts, music, arts in open spaces around Norwich
28th Aylsham Agricultural Show, Blickling Park

September
8th-10th Norfolk Garden Show, Norfolk Showground, Norwich
tbc Great Yarmouth Maritime Festival, South Quay, Great Yarmouth

November
27th-29th Great Yarmouth Norwegian Christmas Fayre

Above: The lakeside of Horsey Mare, Norfolk Broads National Park

BACONSTHORPE   Map 09 TG13

BACONSTHORPE CASTLE
NR25 6LN
➲ (0.75m N of Baconsthorpe off unclass road, 3m E of Holt)
☎ 01799 322399   **FREE**

The remains of a fifteenth-century castle, built by Sir John Heydon during the Wars of the Roses. The exact date when the building was started is not known, since Sir John did not apply for the statutory royal licence necessary to construct a fortified house. In the 1560s, Sir John's grandson added the outer gatehouse, which was inhabited until the 1920s, when one of the turrets fell down. The remains of red brick and knapped flint are reflected in the lake, which partly embraces the castle as a moat.

Times: Open at any reasonable time. **Facilities:** 🅿 🚻

BANHAM   Map 05 TM08

BANHAM ZOO
The Grove NR16 2HE
➲ (on B1113, signed off A11 and A140. Follow brown tourist signs)
☎ 01953 887771 & 887773
e-mail: info@banhamzoo.co.uk
web: www.banhamzoo.co.uk

Set in 35 acres of magnificent parkland, see hundreds of animals ranging from big cats to birds of prey and siamangs to shire horses. Tiger Territory is a purpose-built enclosure for Siberian tigers, including a rock pool and woodland setting. See also Lemur Island and Tamarin and Marmoset Islands. The Heritage Farm Stables & Falconry displays Norfolk's rural heritage with majestic shire horses and birds of prey. Other attractions include Children's Farmyard Barn and Adventure Play Area.

Times: Open all year, daily from 10. (Last admission 1 hour before closing). Closed 25 & 26 Dec. **Fee:** ✱ Please phone Zoo for details **Facilities:** 🅿 ♨ ✕ licensed ᕆ (3 wheelchairs for hire, special parking) toilets for disabled shop ✖ 🍴

BLICKLING   Map 09 TG12

BLICKLING HALL
NR11 6NF
➲ (on B1354, 1.5m NW of Aylsham, signposted off A140 Norwich to Cromer road)
☎ 01263 738030   **2 for 1**
e-mail: blickling@nationaltrust.org.uk
web: www.nationaltrust.org.uk/blickling

Flanked by dark yew hedges and topped by pinnacles, the warm red brick front of Blickling is a memorable sight. The grounds include woodland and a lake, a formal parterre, and a dry moat filled with roses, camellias and other plants. The 2-for-1 voucher is valid only during normal visiting hours and cannot be used for any ticketed events.

Times: Hall open 19 Mar-30 Oct, Wed-Sun & BH, 1-4.30 (1-3.30 Oct). Garden, shop & restaurant same days as hall 10.15-5.15 & also Tue in Aug. **Fee:** ✱ £7.30 (ch £3.65). **Facilities:** 🅿 ♨ ✕ licensed 🗊 ᕆ (wheelchairs & batricars, Braille guide, lift, parking) toilets for disabled shop garden centre ✖ (ex guide dogs) 🧷 🍴

BRESSINGHAM Map 05 TM08

BRESSINGHAM STEAM MUSEUM & GARDENS

IP22 2AB

➲ (on A1066 2.5m W of Diss, between Thetford & Diss)

☎ 01379 686900 & 687386

e-mail: info@bressingham.co.uk

web: www.bressingham.co.uk

Alan Bloom is an internationally recognised nurseryman and a steam enthusiast, and has combined his interests to great effect at Bressingham. There are three miniature steam-hauled trains, including a 15in gauge running through two and a half miles of the wooded Waveney Valley. The Dell Garden has 5000 species of perennials and alpines; Foggy Bottom has wide vistas, pathways, trees, shrubs, conifers and winter colour (restricted opening). A steam roundabout is another attraction, and the Norfolk fire museum is housed here. Various events are held, including Friends of Thomas the Tank Engine, please telephone for details.

Times: Open: Steam Museum, Dad's Army collection, Foggy Bottom & Dell Garden Apr-Sep, daily 10.30-5.30 (Mar & Oct 10.30-4.30). (Last admission 1 hour before closing time). **Fee:** ✱ £7-£10 (ch 3-16 £5-£8, pen £6-£8). Family £21-£30. Season tickets available.

Facilities: 🅿 💷 ✗ licensed 🔗 (wheelchairs can be taken onto Nursery & Waveney lines) toilets for disabled shop garden centre ✗ (ex guide dogs)

BURGH CASTLE Map 05 TG40

BERNEY ARMS WINDMILL

NR30 1SB

☎ 01493 700605

One of the largest and best-preserved Victorian windmills in Norfolk, with seven floors to explore. Built to grind cement, its superb machinery is still fully operational.

Times: Open 24 Mar-Sep; pre-booked groups only. **Fee:** £2.30 (ch £1.20, concessions £1.70). Opening times and prices are subject to change, for further details please phone 0870 333 1181

Facilities: shop ✗ ⛟

BURGH CASTLE

NR31 9PZ 　　　　　　　　　　　　FREE

➲ (at far W end of Breydon Water on unclass road, 3m W of Great Yarmouth)

Burgh Castle was built in the third century AD by the Romans, as one of a chain of forts along the Saxon Shore - the coast where Saxon invaders landed. Sections of the massive walls still stand.

Times: Open at any reasonable time. **Facilities:** ✗

CAISTER-ON-SEA Map 09 TG51

CAISTER ROMAN SITE 　　　　　　　FREE

➲ (3m N of Great Yarmouth)

The name Caister has Roman origins, and this was in fact a Roman naval base. The remains include the south gateway, a town wall built of flint with brick courses and part of what may have been a seamen's hostel.

Times: Open at any reasonable time. **Facilities:** ✗

CASTLE ACRE Map 09 TF81

CASTLE ACRE PRIORY AND CASTLE

Stocks Green PE32 2XD

☎ 01760 755394

Britain's best-preserved Cluniac priory with walled herb garden where visitors can find out about the medieval uses of herbs. Nearby Castle Acre Castle is also well worth a visit.

Times: Prior: Open all year 24 Mar-Sep, daily 10-6; Oct-Mar, Wed-Sun 10-4. Closed 24-26 Dec & 1 Jan. Castle open at any reasonble time. **Fee:** Castle; Free entry; Priory; £4.30 (ch £2.20, concessions £3.20, family £10.80). Opening times and prices are subject to change, for further details please phone 0870 333 1181 **Facilities:** 🅿 🔗 shop ⛟

CASTLE RISING Map 09 TF62

CASTLE RISING CASTLE

PE31 6AH

➲ (off A149)

☎ 01553 631330

A fine twelfth-century domestic keep, set amid huge defensive earthworks, once the palace and home to Isabella, the 'She Wolf' of France, dowager Queen of England. The keep walls stand to their original height.

Times: Open all year, 19 Mar-Nov, daily 10-6; 2 Nov-31 Mar, Wed-Sun 10-4. Closed 24-26 Dec. **Fee:** £3.85 (ch £2.20, concessions £3.10, family £11.50). Opening times and prices are subject to change, for further details please phone 0870 333 1181 **Facilities:** 🅿 🔗 (exterior only) toilets for disabled shop ⛟

CROMER Map 09 TG24

HENRY BLOGG MUSEUM

No 2 Boathouse, The Promenade NR27 9HE

➲ (located at the bottom of East Gangway)

☎ 01263 511294

e-mail: jumbo@csma-netlink.co.uk

A lifeboat has been stationed at the Cromer since 1804, and the museum at the bottom of The Gangway covers local lifeboat history and the RNLI in general. The main exhibit is the WWII Watson Class lifeboat *H F Bailey*, the boat Henry Blogg coxed. In ten years he helped to save over 500 lives. The new building to open in November 2005 hosts a number of new features including; interactive displays and radio/navigation instruction.

Times: Open from Nov 2005 daily 10-4 **Fee:** ✱ Donations welcome. **Facilities:** 🅿 under 1m 🗐 🔗 full disabled access built into new building toilets for disabled shop

ERPINGHAM Map 09 TG13

WOLTERTON PARK

NR11 7LY

➲ (signed from A140 Norwich to Cromer)

☎ 01263 584175

web: www.manningtongardens.co.uk

Covering some 800 hectares this estate contains managed conservation areas, 18th-century landscaped gardens, and Wolterton Hall, built in the 1720s. Special events include gardening demonstrations, concerts, plays, opera, craft fairs, guided walks and history lectures.

Times: Open: Park daily; Hall, late Apr-end Oct, Fri 2-5 (last entry 4). **Fee:** ✱ Hall £5. Car park £2 (free for hall visitors) **Facilities:** 🅿 (charged) 🔗 (partly accessible) toilets for disabled shop ✗ (ex guide dogs)

FAKENHAM · Map 09 TF93

See also **Thursford Green**

PENSTHORPE WATERFOWL PARK & NATURE RESERVE

Pensthorpe NR21 0LN
➲ (just outside Fakenham on the A1067 to Norwich)
☎ 01328 851465
e-mail: info@pensthorpe.com
web: www.pensthorpe.co.uk

Covering 500 acres of beautiful Wensum Valley countryside, with five lakes which are home to one of the largest collections of waterfowl and waders in Europe. Spacious walk-through enclosures and a network of hardsurfaced pathways ensures close contact with birds at the water's edge. Gardens by acclaimed designers Piet Dudolf and Julie Toll.
Times: Open Jan-Mar, daily 10-4. Apr-Dec, 10-5 **Fee:** ✱ £7 (ch £3.50, pen £6) **Facilities:** 🅿 ♨ ♿ (network of hard surfaced pathways ensures access) toilets for disabled shop ✖ (ex guide dogs) ▰

FELBRIGG · Map 09 TG23

FELBRIGG HALL

NR11 8PR
➲ (off B1436 betweeen A148 Cromer to Kings Lynn & A140 Cromer to Norwich)
☎ 01263 837444
e-mail: felbrigg@nationaltrust.org.uk
web: www.nationaltrust.org.uk   **2 for 1**

Felbrigg is a 17th-century house built on the site of an existing medieval hall. It contains a superb collection of 18th-century furniture and pictures and an outstanding library. A 550-acre wood shelters the house from the North Sea and contains waymarked walks and a working dovecot. The 2-for-1 voucher is valid only during normal visiting hours and cannot be used for any ticketed events.
Times: Open house and garden: 19 Mar-30 Oct, Sat-Wed, house 1-5, garden 11-5. Park walks available daily dawn-dusk. **Fee:** ✱ House & garden £6.60 (ch £3.10). Garden only £2.70 (ch £1) **Facilities:** 🅿 ♨ ✖ licensed ♿ (electric wheelchair for garden, Braille guide) toilets for disabled shop ✖ (ex guide dogs) ♨ ▰

FILBY · Map 09 TG41

THRIGBY HALL WILDLIFE GARDENS

NR29 3DR
➲ (on unclass road off A1064, between Acle & Caister-on-Sea)
☎ 01493 369477
web: www.thrigbyhall.co.uk

The 250-year-old park of Thrigby Hall is now the home of animals and birds from Asia, and the lake has ornamental wildfowl. There are tropical bird houses, a unique blue willow pattern garden and tree walk and a summer house as old as the park. The enormous jungled swamp hall has special features such as underwater viewing of large crocodiles.
Times: Open all year, daily from 10. **Fee:** £7.50 (ch 4-14 £5.50, pen £6.50). **Facilities:** 🅿 ♨ ♨ ♿ (wheelchairs available, ramps, parking) toilets for disabled shop ✖ (ex guide dogs) ▰

GREAT BIRCHAM · Map 09 TF73

BIRCHAM WINDMILL   **2 for 1**

PE31 6SJ
➲ (0.5m W off unclassified Snettisham road).
☎ 01485 578393
e-mail: birchamwindmill@btinternet.com
web: www.birchamwindmill.co.uk

This windmill is one of the last remaining in Norfolk. Sails turn on windy days, and the adjacent tea room serves home-made cakes, light lunches and cream teas. There is also a bakery shop and cycle hire. In addition, crafts people feature on a number of weekends throughout the year.
Times: Open Etr-Sep, 10-5. **Fee:** ✱ £3 (ch £1.75, pen £2.75)
Facilities: 🅿 ♨ ♨ ♿ toilets for disabled shop ▰

GREAT YARMOUTH · Map 05 TG50

ELIZABETHAN HOUSE MUSEUM

4 South Quay NR30 2SH
➲ (from A12 & A47 follow town centre signs, then Historic South Quay signs, leading onto South Quay)
☎ 01493 855746
e-mail: yarmouth.museums@norfolk.gov.uk
web: www.museums.norfolk.gov.uk

Experience the lives of families who lived in this splendid quayside house from Tudor to Victorian times. Decide for yourself if the death of Charles I was plotted in the Conspiracy Room. Dress the family in Tudor costumes. Discover Victorian life, upstairs and downstairs, and what it was like to work in the kitchen and scullery. Children can play in the toy room, while parents relax in the small but delightful walled garden.
Times: Open 21 Mar-30 Oct, Mon-Fri 10-5; Sat & Sun 1.15-5.
Fee: ✱ £2.90 (ch £1.50, concessions £2.40). Adult in a family group £2.30 **Facilities:** 🅿 (250yds) ♨ ♿ (Braille guide) shop ✖ (ex guide dogs)

MERRIVALE MODEL VILLAGE

Marine Pde NR30 3JG
➲ (Marine parade seafront, next to Wellington Pier)
☎ 01493 842097   **2 for 1**

Set in more than an acre of attractive landscaped gardens, this comprehensive miniature village is built on a scale of 1:12, and features streams, a lake and waterfalls. Among the models are a working fairground, a stone quarry, houses, shops, and a garden railway. There are even illuminations at dusk! The Penny Arcade gives you the chance to play old amusements.
Times: Open daily Etr-end Oct **Fee:** Please telephone for details.
Facilities: 🅿 (opposite) ♨ ♨ ♿ toilets for disabled shop ✖ (ex on lead)

ROW 111 HOUSES/OLD MERCHANT'S HOUSE AND GREYFRIARS CLOISTERS

South Quay NR30 2RQ
➲ (follow signs to dock and south quay)
☎ 01493 857900

Visit these 17th-century houses unique to Great Yarmouth, and the remains of a Franciscan friary with rare early wall paintings. Guided tours explain how the rich and poor lived in these properties over various time periods.
Times: ✱ Open Apr-Oct, daily 10-5. Guided tours depart from Row 11 House at 10, 12, 2 & 5. All tours include Old Merchant's House and Greyfriar's Cloisters. **Facilities:** shop ✖ ♨

TIME AND TIDE MUSEUM OF GREAT YARMOUTH LIFE NEW
Tower Curing Works, Blackfriar's Rd NR30 3BX
➲ (from A12 & A47 follow AA signs to museum)
☎ 01493 743930
e-mail: yarmouth.museums@norfolk.gov.uk
web: www.museums.norfolk.gov.uk
Set in one of the UK's best preserved Victorian herring curing works, Time and Tide tells the story of Great Yarmouth from its Ice Age origins to the present day.
Times: Open 21 Mar-30 Oct daily, 10-5 inc BH's. **Fee:** ✱ £5.45 (ch £3.50, concessions £4.90. Adult in family group £4.80)
Facilities: P 🍴 🎫 ᕊ (lift) toilets for disabled shop ✈ (ex guide dogs) 🍴

TOLHOUSE MUSEUM
Tolhouse St NR30 2SH
➲ (from A12 & A47 follow AA signs to town centre, then signs to South Quay. Museum attached to Central Library.)
☎ 01493 858900
e-mail: yarmouth.museums@norfolk.gov.uk
web: www.museums.norfolk.gov.uk
Visit one of the oldest prisons in the country and explore Great Yarmouth's story of crime and punishment. With the free audio guide you can hear the gaoler and his prisoners describe their experiences. Discover the fate of the thieves, smugglers, witches, pirates and murderers at a time when punishments included transportation or execution. Other exhibits detail the history of this 12th-century former merchant's house that went on to become one of the town's most important civic buildings.
Times: Open 21 Mar-30 Oct, Mon-Fri 10-5; Sat & Sun 1.15-5.
Fee: ✱ £2.90 (ch £1.50, concessions £2.40). Adult in family group £2.30 **Facilities:** P (500yds) 🎫 (lift to ground & 2nd floor, notice preferable) shop ✈ (ex guide dogs)

GRESSENHALL   Map 09 TF91
ROOTS OF NORFOLK
NR20 4DR
➲ (on B1146 3m NW of Dereham, follow brown signs from A47 or Dereham town centre)
☎ 01362 860563
e-mail: gressenhall.museum@norfolk.gov.uk
web: www.museums.norfolk.gov.uk
Set among 50 acres of beautiful Norfolk countryside, this museum looks at the folkways, history and traditions of the area. Visit a workhouse and hear stories of the people who lived there. Explore traditional cottages and village shops. Take a free cart ride round the farm and get up close with rare breed animals. Relax in the tranquil gardens, or let off steam in the adventure playground. Extra family activities during school holidays.
Times: Open 13-20 Feb, 11-4. 23 Mar-30 Oct, 10-5. **Fee:** ✱ £6.60 (ch £4.40, under 4's free, concessions £5.50) **Facilities:** P 🍴 🎫 ᕊ (sound guide, wheelchair loan, induction loops) toilets for disabled shop ✈ 🍴

GRIMES GRAVES   Map 05 TL88
GRIMES GRAVES
IP26 5DE
➲ (7m NW of Thetford off A134)
☎ 01842 810656
These unique and remarkable Neolithic flint mines are the earliest major industrial site in Europe.
Times: Open 3-31 Mar; Thu-Mon, 10-5; Apr-Sep, daily 10-6; 6-31 Oct, Thu-Mon 10-5. **Fee:** £2.60 (ch £1.30, concessions £2, family £6.50). Opening times and prices are subject to change, for further details please phone 0870 333 1181 **Facilities:** P ᕊ (exhibition area, grounds only, access track rough) shop 🎫

HEACHAM   Map 09 TF63
NORFOLK LAVENDER
Caley Mill PE31 7JE
➲ (follow signs on A149 & A148. Car park entrance on B1454, 100yds E of junct with A149)
☎ 01485 570384   [2 for 1]
e-mail: admin@norfolk-lavender.co.uk
web: www.norfolk-lavender.co.uk
This is the largest lavender-growing and distilling operation in Britain. Different coloured lavenders are grown in strips and harvested in July and August. There are also herb gardens and a fragrant Plant Centre, as well as guided tours of the distillery and gardens. The 2-for-1 voucher is valid for garden tours, available from May to September.
Times: Open all year, daily, Apr-Oct 9.30-5; Nov-Mar 9.30-4. (Closed 25-26 Dec & 1 Jan). **Fee:** ✱ Admission to grounds free. Guided tours £2.25 (May-Sep). Trip to Lavender Field £4.50, mid Jun-mid Aug.
Facilities: P 🍴 ✗ licensed ᕊ (2 wheelchairs for loan) toilets for disabled shop garden centre 🍴

HOLKHAM   Map 09 TF84
HOLKHAM HALL & BYGONES MUSEUM
NR23 1AB
➲ (off A149, 2m W of Wells-next-the-Sea)
☎ 01328 710227
e-mail: enquiries@holkham.co.uk
web: www.holkham.co.uk
This classic Palladian mansion was built between 1734 and 1764 by Thomas Coke, 1st Earl of Leicester, and is home to his descendants. It has a magnificent alabaster entrance hall and the sumptuous state rooms house Roman statuary, fine furniture and paintings by Rubens, Van Dyck, Gainsborough and others. The Bygones Museum, housed in the stable block, has over 5,000 items of domestic and agricultural display - from gramophones to fire engines.
Times: Open June-Sep, Thu-Mon 1-5; Etr, May & Summer BHs also open Sat-Mon 12-5. **Fee:** ✱ Hall £6.50 (ch £3.25). Bygones £5 (ch £2.50). Combined ticket Hall & Bygones: £10 (ch £5). Family ticket £25. **Facilities:** P 🍴 🎫 ᕊ (wheelchair ramps at all entrances) toilets for disabled shop garden centre ✈ (ex guide dogs) 🍴

HORSEY   Map 09 TG42
HORSEY WINDPUMP
NR29 4EF
➲ (15m N of Great Yarmouth, on the B1159 4m NE of Martham)
☎ 01493 393904   [2 for 1]
web: www.nationaltrust.co.uk
Set in a remote part of the Norfolk Broads, the windpump mill was built 200 years ago to drain the area, and then

continued

rebuilt in 1912 by Dan England, a noted Norfolk millwright. It has been restored since being struck by lightning in 1943, and overlooks Horsey Mere and marshes, noted for their wild birds and insects, as a site of International Importance for Nature Conservation. The 2-for-1 voucher is valid only during normal visiting hours and cannot be used for any ticketed events.

Times: Open Mar; Sat-Sun 10-4.30, Apr-Oct; Wed-Sun 10-4.30, BH Mon 10.30-4. **Fee:** £2 (ch £1). NT members free entry & parking. Mooring fees payable to the Horsey Estate (inc NT members).

Facilities: ▯ (charged) �__ ♿ (parking, ramps to ground floor) toilets for disabled shop ⚐

HORSHAM ST FAITH   Map 09 TG21

CITY OF NORWICH AVIATION MUSEUM
Old Norwich Rd NR10 3JF

➲ (follow brown tourist signs from A140 Norwich to Cromer Road)

☎ 01603 893080

e-mail: norwichairmuseum@hotmail.com

web: www.cnam.co.uk

A massive Avro Vulcan bomber, veteran of the Falklands War, dominates the collection of military and civilian aircraft at this museum. There are several displays relating to the aeronautical history of Norfolk, including some on the role played by Norfolk-based RAF and USAAF planes during World War II, and a section dedicated to the operations of RAF Bomber Command's 100 group.

Times: Open all year, Apr-Oct Tue-Sat, 10-5. Sun & BH Mons 12-5 (Mons during school hols). Nov-Mar, Wed & Sat 10-4. Sun 12-4.

Fee: ✱ £2.50 (ch & concessions £1.50, pen £2.50) Family ticket £8.50.

Facilities: ▯ �__ ♿ (assistance available) shop ✈ (ex guide dogs) ◧

HOUGHTON   Map 09 TF72

HOUGHTON HALL
PE31 6UE

➲ (1.25m off A148. 13m E of King's Lynn & 10m W of Fakenham on A148)

☎ 01485 528569   **2 for 1**

e-mail: administrator@houghtonhall.com

web: www.houghtonhall.com

Houghton Hall built in the 1720s by Sir Robert Walpole, Britain's first Prime Minister, is one of the grandest surviving Palladian Houses in England. Now owned by the 7th Marquess of Cholmondeley. The spectacular 5-acre walled garden, restored by Lord Cholmondeley, has been divided into areas for fruit and vegetables, spacious herbaceous

continued

borders, and formal rose gardens with over 150 varieties. A collection of Model Soldiers contains over 20,000 models laid out in various battle formations.

Times: House open 1.30-5 (last entry 4.30). Grounds and Soldier Museum open 11-5.30. **Fee:** ✱ £7 (ch £3). Family ticket £16. Grounds only £4.50 (ch £2). **Facilities:** ▯ �__ ✗ licensed ▥ ♿ (lift, motorised buggies) toilets for disabled shop ✈ (ex guide dogs) ◧

HUNSTANTON   Map 09 TF64

HUNSTANTON SEA LIFE SANCTUARY
Southern Promenade PE36 5BH

☎ 01485 533576

With over 30 fascinating displays of marine life, this fascinating aquarium offers close encounters with starfish, sharks, octopus, eels and many other underwater wonders. Feeding demonstrations, talks and special presentations. Latest addition: Otters.

Times: ✱ Open all year, daily from 10. (Closed 25 Dec)

Facilities: ▯ (charged) �__ ✗ ♿ toilets for disabled shop ✈ (ex guide dogs) ◧

KING'S LYNN   Map 09 TF62

AFRICAN VIOLET CENTRE
Terrington St Clement PE34 4PL

➲ (situated beside A17 5m from Kings Lynn and 3m from A47/A17 junct)

☎ 01553 828374   **FREE**

e-mail: info@africanvioletcentre.ltd.uk

web: www.africanvioletcentre.ltd.uk

A warm and friendly welcome awaits you at the African Violet Centre. As a major plant specialist the centre offers a wide variety of plants for any enthusiast. Best known for their vast selection and display of African violets. The African Violet Centre is a winner of many Chelsea Gold Medals.

Times: Open daily Mon-Sat 9-5, Sun 10-5. Closed Xmas & New Year.

Facilities: ▯ �__ ♿ (ramps & wide doors) toilets for disabled shop garden centre ✈ (ex guide dogs) ◧

KING'S LYNN ARTS CENTRE
27-29 King St PE30 1HA

➲ (located just off Tuesday Market Place in King Street, next to Globe Hotel)

☎ 01553 764864   **FREE**

e-mail: entertainment_admin@west-norfolk.gov.uk

web: www.kingslynnarts.co.uk

Although it has been used for many purposes, the theatrical associations of this 15th-century Guildhall are strongest: Shakespeare himself is said to have performed here. A year round programme of film, performing and visual arts takes place. Contact box office for details.

Times: Open Mon-Sat, 10-2. Closed show days, Sun, BHs, Good Fri & 24 Dec-1st Mon in Jan. **Facilities:** ▯ (50yds) (pay & display) �__ ✗ licensed ▥ ♿ (hearing loop, ramp) ✈ ⚐

TOWN HOUSE MUSEUM
46 Queen St PE30 5DQ

➲ (in town centre close to historic South Quay)

☎ 01553 773450

e-mail: lynn.museum@norfolk.gov.uk

web: www.museums.norfolk.gov.uk

A charming museum set in a 19th-century town house. Explore everyday life in King's Lynn through the ages in a series of carefully re-constructed rooms, from medieval

continued

times to the 1950s. Enjoy collections of historic toys and costumes, and take the air in the delightful garden. Dotted around the displays are colourful games and activities that will keep the children amused.

Times: Open May-Sep, Mon-Sat 10-5. Oct-Apr, Mon-Sat 10-4.
Fee: ✱ £2.60 (ch £1.50, concessions £2.20). **Facilities:** P (100yds) & shop ✖ ■

LENWADE   Map 09 TG01

DINOSAUR ADVENTURE PARK
Weston Park NR9 5JW
⊃ (9m from Norwich. From A47 or A1067 follow brown signs to Park)
☎ 01603 876310
e-mail: info@dinosaurpark.co.uk
web: www.dinosaurpark.co.uk

Children will have great fun coming face to face with lots of friendly farm animals (real), and giant dinosaurs (thankfully not real). Alongside the animals there are adventure play areas, a fossil workshop, raptor racers, Jurassic putt, a Victorian walled garden, and the Neanderthal walk.

Times: Open daily until 11 Sep & Oct half term; 12 Sep-23 Oct, Fri-Sun.
Fee: ✱ £7.25 (ch & pen £6.50, under 3's free) **Facilities:** P ■ ■
& (Swing) toilets for disabled shop ✖ (ex guide dogs) ■

LITTLE WALSINGHAM   Map 09 TF93

WALSINGHAM ABBEY GROUNDS & SHIREHALL MUSEUM
NR22 6BP
⊃ (follow B1105 from Fakenham. Entrance to museum through tourist info centre in village)
☎ 01328 820510 & 820259
e-mail: walsingham.museum@farmline.com

In the grounds of the Abbey are the ruins of the original Augustinian priory built in the 1100s. The priory was built over the shrine of Our Lady of Walsingham which had been established in 1061. Shirehall Museum consists of an original Georgian Courthouse, displays on the history of Walsingham and local artefacts. The museum is situated in 20 acres of tranquil and picturesque gardens with access to woodland and river walks across the historic parkland.

Times: Open Feb daily 10-4. 19 Mar-30 Oct, daily 10-4.30; Nov-Dec, wknds only 10-4; **Fee:** ✱ £3 (concessions £1.50)
Facilities: P (100yds) ■ & toilets for disabled shop garden centre ✖ ■

NORTH CREAKE   Map 09 TF83

CREAKE ABBEY
NR21 9LF
⊃ (off B1355)   FREE
The ruins of the church of an Augustinian almshouse, later converted to an abbey.
Times: Open at any reasonable time. **Facilities:** ✖ (ex dogs on leads) ⌗

NORWICH   Map 05 TG20

AIR DEFENCE RADAR MUSEUM
RAF Neatishead NR12 8YB
⊃ (follow brown signs from A1062 at Horning)
☎ 01692 633309   2 for 1
e-mail: curator@radarmuseum.co.uk
web: www.radarmuseum.co.uk

This multi-award winning Museum, housed in the original 1942 Radar Operations building, features the Battle of Britain
continued

Room, 1942 Ground Controlled Interception Room, Radar Engineering, Military Communications Systems, Cold War Operations Room, Royal Observer Corps, Space Defence, Bloodhound Missiles and Original Mobile Radar Vehicles.

Times: Open year round 2nd Sat each month; Apr-Oct Tue & Thu & BH Mons 10-5 **Fee:** ✱ £4 (ch £3, under 13 free, concessions £3.50)
Facilities: P ■ ■ & (video tour for inaccessible areas) shop ✖ (ex guide dogs)

BRIDEWELL MUSEUM
Bridewell Alley NR2 1AQ
⊃ (in city centre)
☎ 01603 629127
e-mail: museums@norfolk.gov.uk
web: www.museums.norfolk.gov.uk

Built in the late 14th century, this flint-faced merchant's house was used as a prison from 1583 to 1828. It now houses displays illustrating the trades and industries of Norwich during the past 200 years, including a large collection of locally made boots and shoes. There are also a reconstructed 1930s pharmacy, pawnbrokers shop and a blacksmith's smithy.

Times: Open Apr-Oct, Tue-Fri 10-4.30; Sat 10-5. School hols, Mon-Sat 10-5. **Fee:** £2.90 (ch £1.50, concessions £2.40) Family ticket £6.50.
Facilities: P (5 min walk) ■ shop ✖ (ex guide dogs)

NORWICH CASTLE MUSEUM
Castle Meadow NR1 3JU
⊃ (in city centre)
☎ 01603 493625
e-mail: museums@norfolk.gov.uk
web: www.museums.norfolk.gov.uk

The Castle keep was built in the 12th century, and the museum houses displays of art, archaeology, natural history, Lowestoft porcelain, Norwich silver, a large collection of paintings (with special emphasis on the Norwich School of Painters) and 18th century ceramic teapots. There are also guided tours of the dungeons and battlements. A programme of exhibitions, children's events, gallery and evening talks takes place throughout the year. Please ring for details.

Times: Open all year, Mon-Fri 10-4.30, Sat 10-5, Sun 1-5; School hols, Mon-Sat 10-5.30, Sun 1-5. **Fee:** All zones £5.95 (ch 4-16 £4.45, concessions £4.95). Castle & History Zone £3.95 (ch £2.95, concessions £3.35). Art & Exhibitions Zone £3.45 (ch £2.60, concessions £2.95)
Facilities: P (200mtrs) ■ ■ & (lift to first floor, disabled parking, virtual tour) toilets for disabled shop ✖ (ex guide dogs) ■

NORWICH CATHEDRAL
The Close NR1 4DH
⊃ (A47, A11 to city centre, inner ring road to Barrack St rdbt, take road towards city centre to Tombland)
☎ 01603 218321
e-mail: vis-profficer@cathedral.org.uk
web: www.cathedral.org.uk

The splendour and tranquillity of Norwich Cathedral have attracted visitors and pilgrims for nearly 1000 years. Norwich has the second highest spire, and the largest monastic cloister in England, and the 1,000 carved medieval roof bosses are amazing. The building remains a place of quiet reflection and prayer as well as for participation in daily worship or the rich pageantry of the Church's festivals.

Times: Open daily, 7.30-7 (6 mid Sep-mid May). **Fee:** ✱ Donations welcomed £4 (ch £1). Guided tours £4 (ch £1).
Facilities: P (440yds) ✖ licensed ■ & (lift, touch & hearing centre, audio-induction loop) toilets for disabled shop ■

ROYAL NORFOLK REGIMENTAL MUSEUM
Shirehall, Market Av NR1 3JQ
➲ (adjacent to Norwich Castle Museum)
☎ 01603 493649
e-mail: regimental.museum@norfolk.gov.uk
web: www.norfolk.gov.uk
Museum displays deal with the social as well as military history of the county regiment from 1685, including the daily life of a soldier. Audio-visual displays and graphics complement the collection and there's a programme of temporary exhibitions.
Times: Open all year, Tue-Fri 10-4.30; Sat 10-5. School Hols Mon-Sat 10-5. Closed Xmas period & 1 Jan. **Fee:** ✱ £2.90 (ch £1.50, concessions £2.40). Family £6.50 **Facilities:** P (400yds) & (stair lift available, ring for details) shop ✖ (ex guide dogs)

OXBOROUGH   Map 05 TF70
OXBURGH HALL
PE33 9PS
➲ (7m SW of Swaffham. Signed from A134 at Stoke ferry & Swaffham)
☎ 01366 328258   **2 for 1**
e-mail: oxburghhall@nationaltrust.org.uk
web: www.nationaltrust.org.uk
The outstanding feature of this 15th-century moated building is the 80ft high Tudor gatehouse which has remained unaltered throughout the centuries. Henry VII lodged in the King's Room in 1487. A parterre garden of French design stands outside the moat. Rare needlework by Mary Queen of Scots and Bess of Hardwick is on display. A particular attraction is a genuine 16th-century priests hole, which is accessible to members of the public. Please telephone for details of special events running throughout the year. The 2-for-1 voucher is valid only during normal visiting hours and cannot be used for any ticketed events.
Times: Open House: 22 Mar-2 Nov, daily (ex Thu & Fri) 1-5, BH Mon 11-5, (last admission 4.30). Garden: 1-16 Mar, wknds, 11-4; 23 Mar-3 Nov daily (ex Thu & Fri) 11-5.30; Aug daily 11-5.30. **Fee:** ✱ House & Gardens £6 (ch £3), Family ticket £15.50. Gardens only £3 (ch £1.50). Party 15+ £5. **Facilities:** P ▣ ✖ licensed 🍴 & (Braille guide, wheelchairs available, touch tour) toilets for disabled shop ✖ (ex guide dogs) ♨ ▅

REEDHAM   Map 05 TG40
PETTITTS ANIMAL ADVENTURE PARK
NR13 3UA
➲ (off A47 at Acle then follow brown signs)
☎ 01493 700094 & 701403
e-mail: pettittsreedham@aol.com
web: www.pettittsadventurepark.co.uk
Three parks in one, aimed at the younger child. Rides include a railway and roller coaster; the adventure play area has a golf course, ball pond and tearoom; and entertainment is provided by clowns, puppets and live musicians. Among the animals that can be seen are small horses, wallabies, birds of prey, goats, chickens and ducks.
Times: Open daily 19 Mar-30 Oct, 10-5/5.30. **Fee:** ✱ £7.95, (ch £7.95, under 3's free, concessions £5.85) **Facilities:** P ▣ & (ramps to all areas) toilets for disabled shop ✖ ▅

ST OLAVES   Map 05 TM49
ST OLAVE'S PRIORY
➲ (5.5m SW of Great Yarmouth on A143)   **FREE**
Remains of an Augustinian priory founded nearly 200 years after the death in 1030 of the patron saint of Norway, after whom it was named.
Times: Open at any reasonable time. **Facilities:** ✿

SANDRINGHAM   Map 09 TF62
SANDRINGHAM HOUSE, GROUNDS, MUSEUM & COUNTRY
PE35 6EN
➲ (off A148)
☎ 01485 612908
e-mail: visits@sandringhamestate.co.uk
web: www.sandringhamestate.co.uk
The private country retreat of Her Majesty The Queen, this neo-Jacobean house was built in 1870 for King Edward VII. The main rooms used by the Royal Family when in residence are all open to the public. Sixty acres of glorious grounds surround the House and offer beauty and colour throughout the season. Sandringham Museum contains fascinating displays of Royal memorabilia.
Times: Open Etr Sat-mid Jul & early Aug-Oct. House open 11-4.45, Museum 11-5 & Grounds 10.30-5. **Fee:** ✱ House, Museum & Grounds: £7.50 (ch £4.50, pen £6). Family ticket £19.50.
Facilities: P ▣ ✖ licensed 🍴 & (wheelchair loan, free transport in grounds, Braille guide) toilets for disabled shop garden centre ✖ (ex guide dogs) ▅

SAXTHORPE   Map 09 TG13
MANNINGTON GARDENS & COUNTRYSIDE
Mannington Hall NR11 7BB
➲ (signed from Corpusty/Saxthorpe on B1149 Norwich-Holt road. Follow brown signs)
☎ 01263 584175   **2 for 1**
e-mail: laurelwalpole@
manningtongardens.co.uk
web: www.manningtongardens.co.uk
The moated manor house, built in 1460 and still a family home, forms a centre-piece for the pretty gardens which surround it. Visitors can take in the Heritage rose garden, lakes, a scented garden, a ruined church, and horse graves.
Times: Open: Gardens Jun-Aug, Wed-Fri 11-5; also Sun noon-5; 30 Apr-1 Oct. Walks open every day from 9. Hall open by prior appointment only. **Fee:** ✱ Garden £3 (accompanied ch 16 free, students & pen £2.50). Walks free (car park for walkers £2).
Facilities: P ▣ & (boardwalk across meadow, wheelchair entrance) toilets for disabled shop ✖ (ex guide dogs) ▅

SHERINGHAM   Map 09 TG14
NORTH NORFOLK RAILWAY
Sheringham Station NR26 8RA
➲ (from A148 take A1082. Next to large car park by rdbt in town centre)
☎ 01263 820800
e-mail: enquiries@nnrailway.com
web: www.nnr.co.uk
A full size heritage railway running between Sheringham and Holt, with an intermediate station at Weybourne. The route runs for 5.5m along the coast, through the heathland
continued

and features genuine Victorian stations. The William Marriott Railway Museum at Holt, is due to open in 2006.

North Norfolk Railway

Times: Open mid Feb-Oct and wknds in Dec; daily steam trains mid Mar-end Oct, Santa specials. Please telephone or see website for details
Fee: £9 (ch £5.50, pen £8). Family ticket £26, cycles & dogs £1.
Facilities: 🅿 (charged) 🍺 🍴 ♿ (ramps to trains, carriage converted for wheelchair access) toilets for disabled shop 🛍
See advertisement on this page

SOUTH WALSHAM   Map 09 TG31
FAIRHAVEN WOODLAND & WATER GARDEN
School Rd NR13 6DZ
➲ (follow brown heritage signs from A47 onto B1140 to South Walsham. Through village towards Gt Yarmouth. Left into School Rd, 100yds past South Walsham Hall)
☎ 01603 270449   **2 for 1**
e-mail: fairhavengardens@norfolkbroads.com
web: www.norfolkbroads.com/fairhaven

These delightful woodland and water gardens offer a combination of cultivated and wild flowers. In spring there are masses of primroses and bluebells, with azaleas and rhododendrons in several areas. Candelabra primulas and some unusual plants grow near the waterways, and in summer the wild flowers provide a habitat for butterflies, bees and dragonflies. Summer flowers include Day Lilies, Ligularia, Hostas, Hydrangeas and flowering shrubs,

continued

including Viburnum Mariesii (Wedding Cake Viburnum), Cornus Kousa Chinensis and Cornus Florida Rubra.
Times: Open daily 10-5, May-Aug extended opening Wed & Thu 10-9. Closed 25 Dec. **Fee:** £4 (ch £1.50, under 5 free, pen & concessions £3.50). Single membership tickets £15. Family membership ticket £35. Dog membership £2.50. Wildlife Sanctuary £1.50. Subject to change.
Facilities: 🅿 🍺 🍴 ♿ (ramp, grab rail) toilets for disabled shop garden centre 🐕 (ex on lead) 🛍

THETFORD   Map 05 TL88
THETFORD PRIORY   **FREE**
➲ (on W side of Thetford near station)
A glimpse of medieval religious life before the dissolution of the monasteries. The Priory of Our Lady of Thetford belonged to the Order of Cluny, and was founded in 1103 by Roger Bigod, an old soldier and friend of William the Conqueror.
Times: Open all year at any reasonable time. **Facilities:** ♿

THETFORD WARREN LODGE   **FREE**
➲ (2m W of Thetford, off B1107)
The remains of a two-storey hunting lodge, built in the 15th-century of flint with stone dressings.
Times: Open at any reasonable time. **Facilities:** ♿

THURSFORD GREEN   Map 09 TF93
THURSFORD COLLECTION
NR21 0AS
➲ (1m off A148. Halfway between Fakenham and Holt)
☎ 01328 878477
e-mail: admin@thursfordcollection.co.uk
web: www.thursford.com

This exciting collection specialises in organs, with a Wurlitzer cinema organ, fairground organs, barrel organs and street organs among its treasures. There are live musical shows every day. The collection also includes showmen's engines, ploughing engines and farm machinery. There is a children's play area and a breathtaking 'Venetian gondola' switchback ride.

Times: Open Good Fri-last Sun in Sep, daily, 12-5. Closed Sat.
Fee: ✱ £5.50 (ch under 4 free, ch 4-14 £3, students £4.75 pen £5.20). Party 15+ £4.75 each. **Facilities:** 🅿 💷 ✕ licensed ♿ toilets for disabled shop (five different giftshops) ✘ (ex guide dogs) ▇

TITCHWELL   Map 09 TF74
RSPB NATURE RESERVE
PE31 8BB
➲ (6m E of Hunstanton on A149, signed entrance)
☎ 01485 210779   FREE
e-mail: titchwell@rspb.org.uk
web: rspb@org.uk

On the Norfolk coast, Titchwell Marsh is the RSPB's most visited reserve. Hundreds and thousands of migrating birds pass through in spring and autumn and many stay during winter, providing an opportunity to see many species of ducks, waders, seabirds and geese and also the RSPB emblem bird, the Avocet.

Times: Open at all times. Visitor Centre daily 9.30-5 (4 Nov-Mar).
Facilities: 🅿 (charged) 💷 📶 ♿ (ramps to hides, wheelchair bays in hides) toilets for disabled shop (not in visitor centre) ▇

WEETING   Map 05 TL78
WEETING CASTLE
IP27 0RQ
➲ (2m N of Brandon off B1106)   FREE
This ruined 11th-century fortified manor house stands in a moated enclosure. There are interesting but slight remains of a three-storey cross-wing.

Times: Open at any reasonable time. **Facilities:** ♿

WELLS-NEXT-THE-SEA   Map 09 TF94
WELLS & WALSINGHAM LIGHT RAILWAY
NR23 1QB
➲ (A149 Cromer road)
☎ 01328 711630

The railway covers the four miles between Wells and Walsingham, and is the longest ten and a quarter inch gauge track in the world. The line passes through some very attractive countryside, particularly noted for its wild flowers and butterflies. This is the home of the unique Garratt Steam Locomotive specially built for this line.

Times: Open daily Good Fri-end Oct. **Fee:** ✱ £6.50 return (ch £5 return). **Facilities:** 🅿 💷 ♿ shop

WELNEY   Map 05 TL59
WWT WELNEY
Hundred Foot Bank PE14 9TN
➲ (off A1101, N of Ely)
☎ 01353 860711   **2 for 1**
e-mail: welney@wwt.org.uk
web: www.wwt.org.uk

This important wetland site on the beautiful Ouse Washes is famed for the breathtaking spectacle of wild ducks, geese and swans which spend the winter here. Impressive observation facilities, including hides, towers and an observatory, offer outstanding views of the huge numbers of wildfowl which include Bewicks and whooper swans, wigeon, teal and shoveler. Floodlit evening swan feeds take place between November and February. There are two hides for wheelchair users.

Times: Open all year, daily 10-5. Closed 25 Dec. **Fee:** ✱ £3.90 (ch £2.30, pen £3.20). Family ticket £10.50. **Facilities:** 🅿 💷 ♿ toilets for disabled shop ✘ (ex guide/hearing dogs) ▇

WEST RUNTON   Map 09 TG14
NORFOLK SHIRE HORSE CENTRE
West Runton Stables NR27 9QH
➲ (off A149 in village of West Ranton half-way between Cromer & Sheringham, follow brown signs)
☎ 01263 837339
e-mail: bakewell@norfolkshirehorse.fsnet.co.uk
web: www.norfolk-shirehorse-centre.co.uk

The Shire Horse Centre has a collection of draught horses and some breeds of mountain and moorland ponies. There are also exhibits of horse-drawn machinery, waggons and carts, and harnessing and working demonstrations are given twice every day. Other attractions include a children's farm, a photographic display of draught horses past and present, talks and a video show. There is a riding school on the premises as well. Please telephone for details of special events.

Times: Open 4 Apr-29 Oct, Sun-Fri; also Sat BHs. (Last admission 3.45) **Fee:** ✱ £5.50 (ch £3.50, pen £4.50). **Facilities:** 🅿 💷 ♿ (video room, concrete yards all ramped) toilets for disabled shop ✘ (ex on lead) ▇

WEYBOURNE   Map 09 TG14
THE MUCKLEBURGH COLLECTION
Weybourne Military Camp NR25 7EG
➲ (on A149, coast road, 3m W of Sheringham)
☎ 01263 588210 & 588608
e-mail: info@muckleburgh.co.uk
web: www.muckleburgh.co.uk

The largest privately-owned military collection of its kind in the country, which incorporates the Museum of the Suffolk and Norfolk Yeomanry. Exhibits include restored and working tanks, armoured cars, trucks and artillery of WWII, and equipment and weapons from the Falklands and the Gulf War. Live tank demonstrations are run daily (except Sat) during school holidays.

Times: check website or phone for details **Fee:** ✱ £5.50 (ch £3 & pen £4.50). Family ticket £13.50. **Facilities:** 🅿 💷 ✕ ♿ (ramped access, wheelchairs available) toilets for disabled shop ✘ (ex guide, kennels provided) ▇

NORTHAMPTONSHIRE

Events & Festivals

May

19th-21st Moulton Village Festival, folk song, music and dance (Sat main day of event)
tbc British Waterways Annual Boat Show, Crick (provisional)

June

tbc Northampton Music & Arts Festival

July

1st-2nd Hollowell Steam & Heavy Horse Show, Hollowell nr Northampton
tbc Northampton Rotary Dragon Boat Race (provisional)
tbc Northampton Town Show, Abington Park, Northampton

August

tbc Northampton Balloon Festival, Northampton Racecourse, Northampton

October

8th World Conker Championship, Village Green, Ashton, near Oundle

Above: The Triangular Lodge built by Sir Thomas Tresham

We endeavour to be as accurate as possible, but changes to times and other information can occur after the guide has gone to press.

ALTHORP — Map 04 SP66

Althorp

NN7 4HQ
➲ (from S, exit M1 junct 16, & N junct 18, follow signs towards Northampton until directed by brown signs)
☎ 01604 770107 0870 167 9000
e-mail: mail@althorp.com
web: www.althorp.com

Althorp House has been the home of the Spencer family since 1508. The house was built in the 16th century, but has been changed since, most notably by Henry Holland in the 18th century. Recently restored by the present Earl, the house is carefully maintained and in immaculate condition. The award-winning exhibition 'Diana, A Celebration' is located in the 18th century stable block and depicts the life and work of Diana, Princess of Wales. Set in the heart of the park is the Round Oval, where Diana, Princess of Wales is laid to rest.

Times: Open Jul-Sep, daily 11-5. Closed 31 Aug. **Facilities:** P ☕ ♿ (disabled parking, wheelchairs, audio tour, shuttle) toilets for disabled shop ✖ (ex guide dogs)

CANONS ASHBY — Map 04 SP55

Canons Ashby House

NN11 3SD
➲ (easy access from either M40, junct 11 or M1, junct 16)
☎ 01327 861900
e-mail: canonsashby@nationaltrust.org.uk
web: www.nationaltrust.org.uk

Home of the Dryden family since the 16th century, this is an exceptional small manor house, with Elizabethan wall paintings and Jacobean plasterwork. It has restored gardens, a small park and a church - part of the original 13th-century Augustinian priory.

Times: Open 23 Mar-2 Nov, Sat-Wed & BH Mon 1-5.30 (12-4.30 Oct & Nov) or dusk if earlier. Gardens,shop, tearoom open 5 Nov-18 Dec, wknds 12-4. Closed Good Fri. **Facilities:** P ☕ ♿ (Braille/large print guide, taped guide, w/chair available) toilets for disabled shop

DEENE — Map 04 SP99

Deene Park

NN17 3EW
➲ (0.5m off A43, between Kettering & Stamford)
☎ 01780 450278 & 450223
e-mail: admin@deenepark.com
web: www.deenepark.com

A mainly 16th-century house of great architectural importance, and home of the Brudenell family since 1514 (including the 7th Earl of Cardigan who led the Charge of the Light Brigade). There's a large lake and park, and extensive gardens with old-fashioned roses, rare trees and shrubs. Phone for details of garden openings and any other special events.

Times: Open 2-5 BHs (Sun & Mon) Etr, May, Spring & Aug; Jun-Aug, Sun. Party 20+ by prior arrangement with House Keeper.
Fee: * House & Gardens: £6 (ch 10-14 £2.50, concessions £5.50). Gardens only: £3.50 (ch £1.50). Children under 10 free admission with accompanying adult. **Facilities:** P ☕ ♿ (ramps to cafeteria and gardens) toilets for disabled shop ✖ (ex guide dogs in garden only)

KIRBY HALL

NN17 5EN

⮑ (on unclass road off A43, 4m NE of Corby)

☎ 01536 203230

An outstanding Elizabethan mansion with unusually strict symmetry and amazing Renaissance detail. The beautiful formal gardens gained a reputation in the 17th-century as being the finest in England.

Times: Open all year, Apr-Jun & Sep-Oct, Thu-Mon 10-5; Jul-Aug, daily 10-6; Nov-Mar, Thu-Mon 10-4. Closed 24-26 Dec & 1 Jan. **Fee:** £4.30 (ch £2.20, concessions £3.20, Family £10.80).Opening times and prices are subject to change, for further details please phone 0870 333 1181

Facilities: 🅿 ♿ shop

KETTERING   Map 04 SP87

ALFRED EAST GALLERY

Sheep St NN16 OAN

⮑ (A43/A6, located in town centre)

☎ 01536 534274

e-mail: museum@kettering.gov.uk   `FREE`

web: www.kettering.gov.uk

The Gallery has a permanent exhibition space showing work by Sir Alfred East, Thomas Cooper Gotch and other local artists, as well as selections from the Gallery's contemporary collection. Two further display spaces are dedicated to monthly changing exhibitions of art, craft and photography by local artists. There is also a monthly lunchtime talks programme.

Times: Open all year, Tue-Sat 9.30-5 (closed BHs)

Facilities: 🅿 (300yds) 🍴 ♿ shop 🐕 (ex guide dogs)

LYVEDEN NEW BIELD   Map 04 SP98

LYVEDEN NEW BIELD

PE8 5AT

⮑ (4m SW Oundle via A427)

☎ 01832 205358

e-mail: lyvedennewbield@nationaltrust.org.uk

web: www.nationaltrust.org.uk

An incomplete Elizabethan garden house and moated garden. Building began in 1595 by Sir Thomas Tresham, to symbolise his Catholic faith, and Lyveden remains virtually unaltered since work stopped when he died in 1605. The house has fascinating Elizabethan detail and in the grounds is one of the oldest garden layouts in Britain.

Times: House, Elizabethan Water Garden & Visitor Information Room open 31 Mar-Oct, Wed-Sun 10.30-5, 5-27 Nov & 4 Feb-27 Mar, Sat & Sun 10.30-4. **Facilities:** 🅿 (0.5 m along track) 🐾

Are there any excellent Days Out that we've missed? Use the Readers' Report form at the back of the book to tell us about them.

NASSINGTON   Map 04 TL09

PREBENDAL MANOR HOUSE

PE8 6QG

⮑ (off A605 Warmington rdbt and follow brown heritage signs, manor is opposite church)

☎ 01780 782575

e-mail: info@prebendal-manor.co.uk

web: www.prebendal-manor.co.uk

Dating from the early 13th-century, this is the oldest manor in Northamptonshire. There's a 15th-century dovecote and tithe barn museum, and the largest re-created medieval garden in Europe, boasting fishponds, herbers, arbours, turf seats, trellised herbers, medieval vegetable garden and vineyard. The gardens and the manor have been featured in BBC2's *Royal Gardeners* and Channel 4's *Time Team* respectively. Special events every month throughout the summer.

Times: Open Etr Mon-Sep, Wed & Sun & BH Mon 1-5.30.

Fee: ✱ House & garden £5.50 (ch £2.50) pen £5. Garden only £4.

Facilities: 🅿 🍴 🍴 ♿ (ramps, video of house and garden) shop 🐕 (ex guide dogs)

NORTHAMPTON   Map 04 SP76

NORTHAMPTON MUSEUM & ART GALLERY

Guildhall Rd NN1 1DP

⮑ (situated in town centre, in Guildhall Rd)

☎ 01604 838111

e-mail: museums@northampton.gov.uk   `FREE`

web: www.northampton.gov.uk/museums

Reflecting Northampton's proud standing as Britain's boot and shoe capital, the museum houses a collection of boots and shoes in two new galleries. 'Life and Sole' focuses on the industrial, commercial and health aspects of footwear and includes interactives and an audio-visual display. 'Followers of Fashion' looks at shoe fashion and design. There are galleries and displays with changing programmes. Workshops for children during school holidays.

Times: Open all year, Mon-Sat 10-5, Sun 2-5. **Facilities:** 🅿 (200 yds) 🍴 ♿ (wheelchairs available, large print catalogues) toilets for disabled shop 🐕 (ex guide/assistance dogs)

ROCKINGHAM   Map 04 SP89

ROCKINGHAM CASTLE

LE16 8TH

⮑ (2m N of Corby, off A6003)

☎ 01536 770240   `2 for 1`

e-mail: a.norman@rockinghamcastle.com

web: www.rockinghamcastle.com

Set on a hill overlooking five counties, the castle was built by William the Conqueror. The site of the original keep is now a rose garden, but the outline of the curtain wall remains as do the foundations of the Norman hall, and the twin towers of the gatehouse. A royal residence for 450 years, the castle was granted to Edward Watson in the 16th century, and the Watson family have lived there ever since.

Times: Open May-Sep, Sun & BH Mon. Grounds open from 12. Castle open from 1. **Fee:** £7.50 (ch 5-16yrs £4.50 & pen £6.50). Family ticket (2ad+2ch) £19.50. **Facilities:** 🅿 🍴 🍴 ♿ (ramps, audio tour, parking adjacent to Castle) toilets for disabled shop 🍴

RUSHTON   Map 04 SP88

TRIANGULAR LODGE
NN14 1RP
☎ **01536 710761**
A delightful Elizabethan folly designed to symbolise the Holy
Trinity, with its three sides, three floors, trefoil windows and
three triangular gables on each side. Designed and built by
Sir Thomas Gresham.
Times: ✱ Open Apr-Sep, daily 10-6; Oct, daily 10-5.
Facilities: P shop ♯

STOKE BRUERNE   Map 04 SP74

CANAL MUSEUM
NN12 7SE
⊃ (A508, 4m S of M1 junct 15. 5m from Towcester
A43/A5 junct)
☎ **01604 862229**
e-mail: **canal.museum@**
thewaterwaystrust.co.uk
web: **www.thewaterwaystrust.co.uk**
Housed on three floors of an old cornmill, the colourful
collection vividly portrays the many aspects of inland
waterways from their origins to the present day,
complementing the flight of locks and long canal tunnel
outside.
Times: ✱ Open Etr-Oct daily, 10-5; Nov-Etr Tue-Sun, 10-4. Closed
25-26 Dec. (Last admission 30 mins before closing time).
Facilities: P (charged) 🍴 ♿ toilets for disabled shop
✕ (ex guide dogs) 🔲

SULGRAVE   Map 04 SP54

SULGRAVE MANOR
Manor Rd OX17 2SD
⊃ (off B4525 Banbury to Northampton road. 6m
from M40 junct 11, 15m from M1 junct 15a)
☎ **01295 760205**
e-mail: **sulgrave-manor@talk21.com**
web: **www.sulgravemanor.org.uk**

Home to George Washington's ancestors until 1656 when his
great grandfather, John, emigrated to Virginia. Inside the
house there are many relics of George Washington. Though
much of the house is a 20th-century restoration, original
parts include the porch (with a carving of the original
American flag), a screens passage, the great hall and the
great Chamber.
Times: Open Apr-Oct 2-5.30. Closed Mon & Fri ex BHs. Other times by
appointment **Facilities:** P 🍷 🍴 ♿ toilets for disabled shop
✕ (ex guide dogs) 🔲

Harlestone Heath

NORTHUMBERLAND

EVENTS & FESTIVALS

April
21st-23rd Morpeth Northumbrian Gathering, Morpeth Town Hall

May
1st Riding the Bounds, Berwick-upon-Tweed (traditional horseback ride)
29th Northumberland County Show, Tynedale Park, Corbridge

June
10th-11th Annual Steam & Vintage Rally, Tynedale Rugby Club, Corbridge
17th Ovingham Goose Fair, Ovingham Village Green
28th-2nd Jul Alnwick Medieval Fair (provisional)

July
1st-2nd Amble Sea Fair, Amble (provisional)
29th-5th Aug Alnwick International Music Festival, traditional music and dance from around the world (provisional)
30th Alnwick Castle Tournament, Alnwick
tbc Brinkburn Music Summer Festival, Brinkburn Priory
tbc Rothbury Traditional Music Festival, Rothbury

August
5th Powburn Show & Sheepdog Trials
12th Slaley Show, Townhead Field, Slaley
tbc Military Tattoo, Barracks, Berwick-upon-Tweed

September
15th-23rd Hexham Abbey Festival (music and arts), Hexham Abbey

November
tbc Alnwick Northumbrian Gathering, celebration of traditional Northumbrian music, dance and song, Alnwick Playhouse

Above: The 13th-century keep of Warkworth Castle

ALNWICK   Map 12 NU11

ALNWICK CASTLE
NE66 1NQ
➲ (off A1 on outskirts of town, follow signs for The Alnwick Garden & Castle)
☎ 01665 510777
e-mail: enquiries@alnwickcastle.com
web: www.alnwickcastle.com

Alnwick Castle is the main seat of the Duke of Northumberland whose family have lived here since 1309. The stern, medieval exterior belies the treasure house within, furnished in Renaissance style, with paintings by Titian, Van Dyck and Canaletto, and an exquisite collection of Meissen china. The Regiment Museum of Royal Northumberland Fusiliers is housed in the Abbot's Tower of the Castle. Recently refurbished towers include museums of local archaeology and the Percy Tenantry volunteers.
Times: ✱ Open 28 Mar-25 Oct, daily 11-5 (last admission 4.15).
Facilities: 🅿 💷 & (Castle lift for those able to walk a little) toilets for disabled shop ✖ (ex guide dogs) 🍴

BAMBURGH   Map 12 NU13

BAMBURGH CASTLE
NE69 7DF
➲ (A1 Belford by-pass, E on B1342 to Bamburgh)
☎ 01668 214515 & 214208
e-mail: bamburghcastle@aol.com
web: www.bamburghcastle.com

Rising dramatically from a rocky outcrop, Bamburgh Castle is a huge, square Norman castle. Last restored in the 19th century, it has an impressive hall and an armoury with a large collection of armour from the Tower of London. Guide services are available.
Times: Open 11 Mar-Oct, daily 11-5 (last admission 4.30). Other times by prior arrangement. **Fee:** £6 (ch £2.50, pen £5)
Facilities: 🅿 (charged) 💷 & shop ✖ (ex guide dogs) toilets for disabled

BARDON MILL   Map 12 NY76

VINDOLANDA (CHESTERHOLM)
Vindolanda Trust NE47 7JN
➲ (signed from A69 or B6318)
☎ 01434 344277
e-mail: info@vindolanda.com
web: www.vindolanda.com

Vindolanda was a Roman fort and frontier town. It was started well before Hadrian's Wall, and became a base for 500 soldiers. The civilian settlement lay just west of the fort and has been excavated. The excellent museum in the country house of Chesterholm nearby has displays and reconstructions. There are also formal gardens and an open-air museum with Roman Temple, shop, house and Northumbrian croft.
Times: Open Feb-Mar, daily 10-5. Apr-Sep 10-6, Oct & Nov 10-5.
Fee: £4.50 (ch £2.90, student & pen £3.80, free admission for disabled). Saver ticket for joint admission to sister site - The Roman Army Museum £6.50 (ch £4.30, pen £5.50) Party. Family ticket £13, joint site family ticket £20. **Facilities:** 🅿 💷 📷 & (please contact for further info) toilets for disabled shop ✖ (ex guide dogs) 🍴

BELSAY   Map 12 NZ07

BELSAY HALL, CASTLE AND GARDENS
NE20 0DX
➲ (on A696)
☎ 01661 881636
Beautiful neo-classical hall, built from its own quarries with a spectacular garden deservedly listed Grade I in the Register of Gardens. It is slightly unclear who built the 'Grecian-style hall', however it was designed by Sir Charles in 1807, in Greek Revival style. The magnificent 30 acres of grounds contain the ruins of a 14th-century castle.
Times: Open all year, Apr-Sep, daily 10-6; Oct, daily 10-4; Nov-Mar, Thurs-Mon 10-4. Closed 24-26 Dec & 1 Jan. **Fee:** £5.30 (ch £2.70, concessions £4.00, Family £13.30). Opening times and prices are subject to change, for further details please phone 0870 333 1181
Facilities: 🅿 💻 ♿ toilets for disabled shop ♯

BERWICK-UPON-TWEED   Map 12 NT95

BERWICK-UPON-TWEED BARRACKS
TD15 1DF
➲ (on the Parade, off Church St, Berwick town centre)
☎ 01289 304493
Take an informative journey into our military past at the famous border town's barracks.
Times: Open Apr-Sep, daily 10-6; Oct daily 10-4; Nov-Mar, call site for details. Closed between 24-26 Dec & 1 Jan and during Tattoo events. **Fee:** £3.30 (ch £1.70, concessions £2.50). Opening times and prices are subject to change, for further details please phone 0870 333 1181
Facilities: 🅿 (town centre) shop ♯

PAXTON HOUSE
TD15 1SZ
➲ (3m from A1 Berwick-upon-Tweed bypass on B6461 Kelso road)
☎ 01289 386291
e-mail: info@paxtonhouse.com
web: www.paxtonhouse.com
Built in 1758 for the Laird of Wedderburn, the house is a fine example of neo-Palladian architecture. Much of the house is furnished by Chippendale and there is a large picture gallery. The house is set in 80 acres beside the River Tweed, and the grounds include an adventure playground.
Times: Open daily from Apr-Oct, House & gallery 11-5 (last tour of house 4.15). Grounds 10-sunset. **Facilities:** 🅿 💻 ✕ licensed 🍴 ♿ (lifts to main areas of house, parking close to reception) toilets for disabled shop ➡

CAMBO   Map 12 NZ08

WALLINGTON HOUSE WALLED GARDEN & GROUNDS
NE61 4AR
➲ (6m NW of Belsay)
☎ 01670 773600
e-mail: wallington@nationaltrust.org.uk
web: www.nationaltrust.org.uk
Wallington is the largest country estate protected by the National Trust. With 13,000 acres that include the entire village of Cambo, the main attraction is the country house set among woods and gardens. There is a Pre-Raphaelite central hall, and a Cabinet of Curiosities that includes dolls houses. There are plenty of walks exploring the historic

continued

landscape, and a walled garden created by the Trevelyan family in the 1920s.
Times: Open: House daily (ex Tue) Mar-Sep 1-5.30; Sep & Oct 1-4.30. Walled garden open daily Apr-Sep 10-7; Oct 10-6; Nov-Mar 10-4
Fee: House, walled garden & grounds: £7.30 (ch £3.65). Family £18.25; Garden & grounds only £5.20 (ch 2.60). Family £13. **Facilities:** 🅿 💻 ✕ ♿ (Vessa Ventura scooter, Braille guide) toilets for disabled shop garden centre 🌿 ➡

CARRAWBROUGH   Map 12 NY87

TEMPLE OF MITHRAS (HADRIAN'S WALL)   FREE
➲ (3.75m W of Chollerford on B6318)
This fascinating Mithraic temple was uncovered by a farmer in 1949. Its three altars to the war god Mithras, date from the third century AD, and are now in the Museum of Antiquities in Newcastle, but there are copies on site.
Times: Open at any reasonable time. **Facilities:** 🅿 ♯

CHILLINGHAM   Map 12 NU02

CHILLINGHAM CASTLE
NE66 5NJ
➲ (signed from A1 & A697)
☎ 01668 215359
e-mail: enquiries@chillingham.castle.com
web: www.chillingham-castle.com
This remarkable castle with its alarming dungeons and torture chamber is now undergoing restoration. Romantic grounds laid out by Sir Jeffry Wyatville command views over the Cheviots and include topiary gardens and woodland walks. Weddings, private functions and meals can be arranged, and fishing is available. Please ring for details of special events.
Times: Open Etr wknd & May-Sep, Sun-Fri (last admission 4.30). Other times by prior arrangement. Castle 1-5, grounds & tearoom 12-5.
Fee: ✱ £6 (ch £3, pen £5.50). Party 10+ £5.30 **Facilities:** 🅿 💻 🍴 ♿ shop ✕ (ex guide dogs) ➡

CHILLINGHAM WILD CATTLE PARK
NE66 5NP
➲ (off B6348, follow brown tourist signs off A1 and A697)   2 for 1
☎ 01668 215250
web: www.chillingham-wildcattle.org.uk
The park, a registered charity, at Chillingham boasts an extraordinary survival: a herd of wild white cattle descended from animals trapped in the park when the wall was built in the 13th century; they are the sole surviving pure-bred examples of their breed in the world. Binoculars are recommended for a close view. Visitors are accompanied into the park by the Warden.
Times: Open Apr-Oct, daily 10-12 & 2-5, Sun 2-5. (Closed Tue). **Fee:** ✱ £4.50 (ch £1.50 & pen £3). Family ticket £10 (2ad + 2ch) **Facilities:** 🅿 🍴 shop ✕

An asterisk * indicates that opening times and prices are for 2005. Please contact the attraction for up-to-date information.

CORBRIDGE Map 12 NY96

CORBRIDGE ROMAN SITE AND MUSEUM
NE45 5NT
➲ (0.5m NW of Corbridge on minor road - signed)
☎ 01434 632349

Originally a fort, which evolved into a prosperous town during the Roman era. An excellent starting point to explore Hadrian's Wall. The museum houses a fascinating collection of finds.

Times: Open all year, Apr-Sep, daily 10-6; Oct, daily 10-4; Nov-Mar, Sat-Sun 10-4. Closed 24-26 Dec & 1 Jan. **Fee:** £3.60 (ch £1.80, concessions £2.70). Opening times and prices are subject to change, for further details please phone 0870 333 1181 **Facilities:** 🅿 ⅁ toilets for disabled ♯

EMBLETON Map 12 NU22

DUNSTANBURGH CASTLE
Craster NE66 2RD
➲ (1.5m E on footpaths from Craster or Embleton)
☎ 01665 576231

An easy 12 mile coastal walk leads to the eerie skeleton of this wonderful 14th-century castle situated on a basalt crag more than 30 metres high with breathtaking views. The castle was built by Thomas Earl of Lancaster, nephew to King Edward II.

Times: Open all year, Apr-Sep, daily 10-6; Oct, daily 10-4; Nov-Mar, Thu-Mon 10-4. **Fee:** £2.60 (ch £1.30, concessions £2.00). Opening times and prices are subject to change, for further details please phone 0870 333 1181 **Facilities:** 🅿 (charged)

GREENHEAD Map 12 NY66

ROMAN ARMY MUSEUM
Carvoran CA8 7JB
➲ (follow brown tourist signs from A69 or B6318)
☎ 016977 47485
e-mail: info@vindolanda.com
web: www.vindolanda.com

Situated alongside the Walltown Grags Section of Hadrians Wall, the museum is a great introduction to the Roman Army. Find out about Roman weapons, training, pay, off-duty activities and much more. See if you can be persuaded to join up by watching the recruitment film, or view the Eagle's Eye film and soar with the eagle over Hadrian's Wall.

Times: Open Feb-Mar & Oct-Nov, 10-5; Apr-Sep 10-6 **Fee:** ✱ £3.50 (ch £2.20, concessions £3) Family £10. Saver tickets available.
Facilities: 🅿 💺 🛏 ⅁ ramps, subtitles on main film toilets for disabled shop ♥ (ex guide dogs) ◼

HOLY ISLAND (LINDISFARNE) Map 12 NU14

LINDISFARNE CASTLE
TD15 2SH
➲ (8m S Berwick from A1 on Holy Island)
☎ 01289 389244
e-mail: lindisfarne@nationaltrust.org.uk

This 16th-century fort was restored by Sir Edwin Lutyens in 1903. The austere outside walls belie the Edwardian comfort within, which includes antique Flemish and English furniture, porcelain and polished brass. A small walled garden designed by Gertrude Jekyll is set on the southward facing slope, some 500 metres to the north of the castle. Spectatular views from the ramparts to the Farne Islands, Bamburgh Castle and beyond.

Times: Open mid Mar-Oct, daily (closed Mon ex BHs). As Lindisfarne is a tidal island, the Castle will open 4.5 hrs which will always include 12-3 and then either earlier opening or later closing as the tide allows.
Fee: Castle & garden £5 (ch £2.50) Family ticket £12.50. Garden only £1 (ch free) **Facilities:** 🅿 (1m in village) ♥ ⚘

Staple Island, one of the Farne islands

LINDISFARNE PRIORY

TD15 2RX

➲ (can only be reached at low tide across a causeway. Tide tables posted at each end of the causeway)

☎ 01289 389200

One of the holiest Anglo-Saxon sites in England, renowned for the original burial place of St Cuthbert whose corpse was discovered 11 years after his burial and found to be mysteriously undecayed. An award-winning museum.

Times: Open all year, Apr-Sep, daily 9.30-5; Oct, daily 9.30-4; Nov-Mar, Sat-Mon 10-2. Closed 24-26 Dec & 1 Jan. **Fee:** £3.60 (ch £1.80, concessions £2.70). Opening times and prices are subject to change, for further details please phone 0870 333 1181 **Facilities:** shop 🎫

HOUSESTEADS   Map 12 NY76

HOUSESTEADS ROMAN FORT

Haydon Bridge NE47 6NN

➲ (2.5m NE of Bardon Mill on B6318)

☎ 01434 344363

The jewel in the crown of Hadrian's Wall and the most complete Roman fort in Britain. These superb remains offer a fascinating glimpse into the past glories of one of the world's greatest empires.

Times: ✱ Open all year, Apr-Sep, daily 10-6; Oct-Mar, daily 10-4. Closed 24-26 Dec & 1 Jan. **Fee:** £3.60 (ch £1.80, concessions £2.70, family £9.00). Opening times and prices are subject to change, for further details please phone 0870 333 1181 **Facilities:** 🅿 (0.25m from fort) (charge payable) (disabled parking) shop

LONGFRAMLINGTON   Map 12 NU10

BRINKBURN PRIORY

NE65 8AF

➲ (off B6344)

☎ 01665 570628

This late 12th-century church is a fine example of early gothic architecture set in beautiful riverside surroundings. Look out for some unusual modern sculptures.

Times: Open 24 Mar-Sep, daily, 10-6. **Fee:** £2.30 (ch £1.20, concessions £1.70). Opening times and prices are subject to change, for further details please phone 0870 333 1181 **Facilities:** 🅿 shop 🎫

MORPETH   Map 12 NZ28

MORPETH CHANTRY BAGPIPE MUSEUM

Bridge St NE61 1PD

➲ (off A1)

☎ 01670 500717   FREE

e-mail: anne@castlemorpeth.gov.uk

This unusual museum specialises in the history and development of Northumbrian small pipes and their music. They are set in the context of bagpipes from around the world, from India to Inverness.

Times: Open all year, Mon-Sat, 10-5, open Sun in Aug & Dec. Closed 25-26 Dec, 1 Jan & Etr Mon. **Facilities:** 🅿 (100mtrs) 🎞 ♿ (induction loop, large print text) shop ▄

NORHAM   Map 12 NT94

NORHAM CASTLE

TD15 2JY

☎ 01289 382329

A mighty border fortress built in 1160, was one of the strongest of the border castles. Take an audio tour conjuring up four centuries of sieges and war with the Scots.

Times: Open 24 Mar-Sep, Sun-Mon & BHs, 10-6. **Fee:** £2.60 (ch £1.30, concessions £2.00). Opening times and prices are subject to change, for further details please phone 0870 333 1181 **Facilities:** 🅿 ♿ ✈ 🎫

PRUDHOE   Map 12 NZ06

PRUDHOE CASTLE

NE42 6NA

➲ (on minor road off A695)

☎ 01661 833459

Explore the romantic remains of this 13th-century fortress perched on a steep wooded spur rising above the Tyne and set in lovely grounds.

Times: Open 24 Mar-Sep, daily 10-6. **Fee:** £3.30 (ch £1.70, concessions £2.50). Opening times and prices are subject to change, for further details please phone 0870 333 1181 **Facilities:** 🅿 shop 🎫

ROTHBURY   Map 12 NU00

CRAGSIDE

NE65 7PX

➲ (1m NW of Morpeth on A697, left onto B6341, entrance 1m N of Rothbury)

☎ 01669 620333 & 620150

e-mail: cragside@nationaltrust.org.uk

web: www.nationaltrust.org.uk

The aptly named Cragside was the home of Victorian inventor and landscape genius, Lord Armstrong, and sits on a rocky crag high above the Debden Burn. Crammed with ingenious gadgets it was the first house in the world to be lit by water-powered electricity. In the 1880s it also had hot and cold running water, central heating, fire alarms, telephones, and a passenger lift. In the grounds there are forty miles of footpaths to explore.

Times: Open, Estate & Gardens: 22 Mar-Oct, Tue-Sun & BH Mons 10.30-7; Nov-mid Dec Wed-Sun 11-4 (or dusk if earlier); House: 22 Mar-Sep 1-5.30. (Last admission 1hr before closing). **Fee:** House, Estate & Gardens £8.50 (ch £4) Family £20 (2ad+3ch). Estate & Gardens £5.70 (ch £2.60) Family £14. Winter opening £2.80 (ch £1.30) Family £7 **Facilities:** 🅿 ✕ licensed ♿ (ltd access, Braille guide, wheelchair path, lift) toilets for disabled shop ▥

WALWICK   Map 12 NY97

CHESTERS ROMAN FORT & MUSEUM

Chollerford NE46 4EP

➲ (0.5m W of Chollerford on B6318)

☎ 01434 681379

The best-preserved Roman cavalry fort in Britain. The museum holds displays of carved stones, altars and sculptures from all along Hadrian's Wall.

Times: Open all year, Apr-Sep, daily 9.30-6; Oct-Mar, daily 10-4. Closed 24-26 Dec & 1 Jan **Fee:** £3.60 (ch £1.80, concessions £2.70). Opening times and prices are subject to change, for further details please phone 0870 333 1181 **Facilities:** 🅿 ▆ ♿ (wheelchair access limited) shop 🎫

WARKWORTH   Map 12 NU20

WARKWORTH CASTLE & HERMITAGE

NE66 0UJ

☎ 01665 711423

The magnificent eight-towered keep of Warkworth Castle stands on a hill high above the River Coquet, dominating all around it. A complex stronghold, it was home to the Percy family, which at times wielded more power in the North than the King himself.

Times: Open all year. Castle; Apr-Sep, daily 10-6; Oct, daily 10-4; Nov-Mar, Sat-Mon 10-4. Hermitage; 24 Mar-Sep, Wed, Sun & Bank Hols 11-5. Closed 24-26 Dec & 1 Jan. **Fee:** Castle; £3.30 (ch £1.70, concessions £2.50, Family £8.30). Hermitage; £2.30 (ch £1.20, concessions £1.70). Opening times and prices are subject to change, for further details please phone 0870 333 1181 **Facilities:** 🅿 ♿ (limited access) shop 🎫

NOTTINGHAMSHIRE

EVENTS & FESTIVALS

March
17th St Patrick's Day Parade, Nottingham

April
21st-23rd Newark & Notts Garden Show, Newark & Nottinghamshire Showground, Winthorpe, Newark

May
13th-14th Newark & Nottingham County Show, Newark & Nottingham Showground, Winthorpe

June
tbc Newark on Water Festival, Riverside Park, Newark

July
2nd Mansfield Fun Run
6th-9th Americana International Festival, Newark Showground, Winthorpe, Newark
31st-6th Aug Annual Robin Hood Festival, Sherwood Forest Country Park & Visitor Centre, Edwinstowe
tbc Nottingham Mela, Asian festival with music, dance and children's activities

August
tbc Caribbean Carnival, Forest Recreation Ground, Nottingham (and parade through city)
tbc Riverside Festival, Victoria Embankment, Nottingham (world and roots music, street theatre, children's entertainers)

September
24th Robin Hood Marathon, Nottingham, from War Memorial, Victoria Embankment (provisional)

October
4th-7th Goose Fair, Forest Recreation Ground, Nottingham (Europe's largest travelling fair)

November
tbc Robin Hood Pageant, Nottingham Castle

Above: Statue of Robin Hood and Little John fighting each other at Sherwood Forest Visitor Centre

---

EASTWOOD   Map 08 SK44

D. H. LAWRENCE HERITAGE
Durban House Heritage Centre, Mansfield Rd NG16 3DZ
⮞ (M1 junct 26, then A610, follow brown tourist signs for D. H. Lawrence Heritage. From M1 junct 27 take A608 through Brinsley towards Eastwood)
☎ **01773 717353**
e-mail: culture@broxtowe.gov.uk
web: www.broxtowe.gov.uk

D H Lawrence Heritage brings to life the world of the famous novelist, poet and artist David Herbert Lawrence, best known as the writer of *Lady Chatterley's Lover*, *Women in Love* and *The Rainbow*. Discover how his home town of Eastwood, near Nottingham, shaped his creative and often controversial works. The site includes the museum and heritage centre, an art gallery, two gift shops, and a teashop.
Times: Open all year, Apr-Oct, daily 10-5; Nov-Mar, daily 10-4. Closed 24 Dec-3 Jan. **Fee:** Free Mon-Fri. Single site £2 (concessions £1.20). Both sites £3.50 (concessions £1.80). Family Ticket (2ad+2ch) Joint Site £8; Single Site £5.80 **Facilities:** 🅿 💻 ✗ licensed ♿ (lift to exhibition, wheelchair available) toilets for disabled shop ✈ (ex guide dogs) 🍴

EDWINSTOWE   Map 08 SK66

SHERWOOD FOREST COUNTRY PARK & VISITOR CENTRE
NG21 9HN
⮞ (on B6034 N of Edwinstowe between A6075 and A616)
☎ **01623 823202 & 824490**   FREE
e-mail: sherwood.forest@nottscc.gov.uk
web: www.nottinghamshire.gov.uk/countryparks

At the heart of the Robin Hood legend is Sherwood Forest. Today it is a country park and visitor centre with 450 acres of ancient oaks and shimmering silver birches. Waymarked pathways guide you through the forest. A year round programme of events includes the spectacular Robin Hood Festival. 31 Jul-6 Aug 2006.
Times: Open all year. Country Park: open daily dawn to dusk. Visitor Centre: open daily 10-5 (4.30 Nov-Mar) **Facilities:** 🅿 (charged) ✗ licensed 🍴 ♿ (wheelchair loan) toilets for disabled shop 🍴
See advertisement on opposite page

FARNSFIELD Map 08 SK65

WHITE POST FARM CENTRE
NG22 8HL
➲ (12m N of Nottingham on A614)
☎ 01623 882977 & 882026
e-mail: tim@whitepostfarmcentre.co.uk
web: www.whitepostfarmcentre.co.uk

This award-winning working farm gives an introduction to a variety of modern farming methods. It explains how farms work, with exhibits such as llamas, deer, pigs, cows, snails, quails, snakes and fish. There's a lot to see indoors, including the incubator room, mousetown and a reptile house. There is also a large indoor play area including a sledge run, trampoline and a large bouncy slide.
Times: Open daily from 10 **Facilities:** 🅿 💷 ♿ (free hire wheelchairs, book if more than 6) toilets for disabled shop 🐕 (ex guide dogs) ▰

NEWARK-ON-TRENT Map 08 SK75

MILLGATE MUSEUM
48 Millgate NG24 4TS
➲ (easy access from A1 & A46)
☎ 01636 655730
e-mail: museums@nsdc.info   **FREE**
web: www.newark-sherwooddc.gov.uk
The museum is home to diverse social collections and features fascinating exhibitions - recreated streets, shops and houses in period settings. There are also children's activities. The mezzanine gallery, home to a number of temporary exhibitions shows the work of local artists, designers and photographers.
Times: Open all year. Apr-Sep Tue-Sun 10.30-4.30. Oct-Mar 10.30-4.
Facilities: 🅿 (250yds) 💷 📖 ♿ toilets for disabled shop 🐕 (ex assistance dogs)

NEWARK AIR MUSEUM
The Airfield, Winthorpe NG24 2NY
➲ (easy access from A1, A46, A17 & Newark relief road, follow tourist signs, next to county showground.)
☎ 01636 707170   **2 for 1**
e-mail: newarkair@onetel.com
web: www.newarkairmuseum.co.uk
A diverse collection of transport, training and reconnaissance aircraft, jet fighters, bombers and helicopters, now numbering more than seventy. Two Undercover Aircraft Display Halls and an Engine Hall make

continued

the museum an all-weather attraction. Everything is displayed around a WWII airfield.
Times: Open all year, Mar-Sep daily 10-5; Oct-Feb, daily 10-4. Closed 24-26 Dec & 1 Jan. Other times by appointment. **Fee:** £6 (ch £3.50, pen £5.50). Family ticket (2ad+2ch) £16.50. Party 15+.
Facilities: 🅿 💷 📖 ♿ toilets for disabled shop ▰

VINA COOKE MUSEUM OF DOLLS & BYGONE CHILDHOOD
The Old Rectory, Cromwell NG23 6JE
➲ (5m N of Newark off A1)
☎ 01636 821364   **2 for 1**
All kinds of childhood memorabilia are displayed in this 17th-century house: prams, toys, dolls' houses, costumes and a large collection of Victorian and Edwardian dolls including Vina Cooke hand-made character dolls.
Times: Open Apr-Sep, Tue, Thu, Sat-Sun & BH 10.30-4.30. Mon,Wed, Fri and Oct-Mar by appointment, please telephone. **Fee:** ✱ £3 (ch £1.50, pen £2.50). **Facilities:** 🅿 shop 🐕 may wait outside

NEWSTEAD Map 09 SK55

NEWSTEAD ABBEY
Newstead Abbey Park NG15 8NA
➲ (off A60, between Nottingham & Mansfield, at Ravenshead)
☎ 01623 455900
web: www.newsteadabbey.org.uk
This beautiful house is best known as the home of poet Lord Byron. Visitors can see Byron's own rooms, mementoes of the poet and other splendidly decorated rooms. The grounds of over 300 acres include waterfalls, ponds, water gardens and Japanese gardens. Special events include outdoor

continued

theatre and opera, Christmas events and Ghost Tours. Special Events: Please telephone for details of events running throughout the year. **Times:** Open: Grounds all year, daily 9-dusk or 6pm whichever is earliest (ex last Fri in Nov & 25 Dec); House Apr-Sep, daily 12-5. (Last admission 4). **Fee:** House & Grounds £6 (ch £1.50, concessions £2.50) Family ticket £16. Grounds only £3 (concessions £2.50) Family ticket £8.50. Subject to change. **Facilities:** P ⬛ 🍴 ♿ (audio tour & wheelchair for loan Apr-Sep) toilets for disabled shop (open Apr-Sep) 🐕 (ex guide dogs) 🍴

NOTTINGHAM   Map 08 SK53

GALLERIES OF JUSTICE

The Shire Hall, High Pavement, Lace Market NG1 1HN
➲ (follow signs to city centre, brown heritage signs to Lace Market & Galleries of Justice)
☎ 0115 952 0555
e-mail: info@nccl.org.uk   **2 for 1**
web: www.nccl.org.uk

The Galleries of Justice are located on the site of an original Court and County Gaol. New developments include the arrival of the HM Prison Service Collection, which will now be permanently housed in the 1833 wing. Never before seen artefacts from prisons across the country offer visitors the chance to experience some of Britain's most gruesome, yet often touching, reminders of what prison life would have been for inmates and prison staff over the last three centuries. **Times:** Open all year, Tue-Sun & BH Mon 10-5 (also open Mon in school hols). (Last admission one hour before closing). Contact for Xmas opening times. **Fee:** £7.95 (concessions £5.95). Family ticket £22.95 (2ad+2ch). **Facilities:** P (5 mins walk) ⬛ ♿ (Braille control lifts, induction loop, large print lables) toilets for disabled shop 🐕 (ex guide dogs) 🍴

GREEN'S WINDMILL

Windmill Ln, Sneinton NG2 4QB
➲ (off B686, 500yds from Ice Centre)
☎ 0115 915 6878
e-mail: info@greensmill.org.uk   **FREE**
web: www.greensmill.org.uk

Restored to working order, take a look around the mill and see how grain is turned into flour by harnessing the power of the wind. Find out about the "mathematician miller" George Green and his theories, and test your mind with hands on puzzles and experiments. There's also a guinea pig piggery. **Times:** Open all year Wed-Sun, 10-4, also BHs. Phone for Xmas & New Year closing. **Facilities:** P 🍴 ♿ parking in Millyard toilets for disabled shop 🐕 Assist dogs only 🍴

THE LACE CENTRE

Severns Building, Castle Rd NG1 6AA
➲ (follow signs for Castle, situated opposite Robin Hood statue)   **FREE**
☎ 0115 941 3539

Exquisite Nottingham lace fills this small 14th-century building to capacity, with panels also hanging from the beamed ceiling. There are weekly demonstrations of lace-making on Thursday afternoons from Easter to October. Telephone for details. **Times:** Open all year. Jan-Mar, daily 10-4; Apr-Nov, 10-5. Every Sun 11-4. Closed Xmas & New Year **Facilities:** P (100yds) (metered street parking) shop 🍴

THE LACE MARKET CENTRE

3-5 High Pavement, The Lace Market NG1 1HF
➲ (follow signs for Lace Market. Parking in city centre)
☎ 0115 988 1849   **FREE**
e-mail: info@nottinghamlace.org
web: www.nottinghamlace.org

'Nottingham Lace and its People' is a free exhibition that includes a photographic story, hand-lace and machine-lace demonstrations. The Lace Market Trail, which takes about an hour, guides you to all the points of interest around this historical part of the city.
Times: ✱ Open Mon-Sat, 10-5: Sun 10.30-4. Closed Xmas. **Facilities:** P (100yds) 🍴 ♿ (counters at lower level, lift, audio & written tour) shop 🐕 (ex guide dogs) 🍴

THE MUSEUM OF NOTTINGHAM LIFE

Brewhouse Yard, Castle Boulevard NG7 1FB
➲ (follow signs to city centre)
☎ 0115 915 3640

Nestled in the rock below Nottingham Castle and housed in a row of 17th-century cottages, the museum presents a realistic glimpse of life in Nottingham over the last 300 years. Discover the caves behind the museum and peer through 1920s shop windows. **Times:** Open daily, 10-4.30. Last admission 4. Closed 24-26 Dec, 1 Jan. **Fee:** Joint ticket with castle £3 (conc £1.50) Family ticket £7. **Facilities:** P (100yds) 🍴 ♿ (call 0115 915 3700 for info on access) toilets for disabled shop 🐕 (ex guide dogs)

NOTTINGHAM CASTLE

NG1 6EL
☎ 0115 915 3700

This 17th-century building is both museum and art gallery, with major temporary exhibitions, by historical and contemporary artists, as well as the permanent collections. There is a 'Story of Nottingham' exhibition and a gallery designed especially to entertain young children. Guided tours of the underground passages take place on most days. **Times:** ✱ Open all year, daily 10-5. Grounds 8-dusk. Closed 25-26 Dec. **Facilities:** P (400yds) ⬛ 🍴 ♿ (parking at castle, for more info call 0115 915 3700) toilets for disabled shop 🐕 (ex guide dogs)

NOTTINGHAM INDUSTRIAL MUSEUM

Courtyard Buildings, Wollaton Park NG8 2AE
➲ (4m from city centre off A6514)
☎ 0115 915 3900
e-mail: carol@ncmg.demon.co.uk
web: www.nottinghamcity.gov.uk

Nottingham's industrial history is on display in this 18th-century stable block. Lace, hosiery, pharmaceuticals (Nottingham was the home of the founder of Boots the Chemists), tobacco and much else are among the exhibits. There is a beam engine and other steam engines, regularly in steam. **Times:** Open daily 11-5 **Facilities:** P (charged) ⬛ ♿ (hand & powered wheelchairs available) toilets for disabled shop 🐕 (ex guide dogs)

TALES OF ROBIN HOOD

30-38 Maid Marian Way NG1 6GF
↪ (in city centre, follow brown & white signs)
☎ 0115 948 3284
e-mail: robinhoodcentre@mail.com
web: www.robinhood.uk.com

Special effects and adventure cars transport the visitor back to medieval Nottingham and Sherwood Forest, legendary home of Robin Hood. There is commentary in seven languages via portable CD players. Medieval banquets and other events take place throughout the year.

Times: Open all year, daily 10-5.30. Last admission 4. Closed 25-26 Dec. **Fee:** £7 (ch £5.95, concessions £6.95) Family ticket from £24.95. **Facilities:** P (NCP 200 yds) 🖼 📷 & (specially adapted 'car', lift) toilets for disabled shop ✕ (ex guide dogs) 🍴

WOLLATON HALL & PARK

Wollaton NG8 2AE
↪ (M1 junct 25 signed from A52, A609, A6154, A60 and city centre)
☎ 0115 915 3900
e-mail: info@wollatonhall.org.uk
web: www.wollatonhall.org.uk

Built in the late 16th century, and extended in the 19th, Wollaton Hall and Park holds Nottingham's Natural History Museum, Nottingham's Industrial Museum, the Wollaton Park Visitor Centre, and the Yard Gallery, which has changing exhibitions exploring art and the environment. The Hall itself is set in 500 acres of deer park, with herds of red and fallow deer roaming wild. There are also formal gardens, a lake, nature trails, adventure playgrounds and a sensory garden. The many events throughout the year include pop concerts, and twilight bat walks.

Times: Due to ongoing refurbishment please ring 0115 915 3900 for details. **Fee:** ✱ Free wkdays. Ticket for both Hall & Museum £2.50 (ch & concessions £1.50). Family ticket £6. Charge made at wknds & BHs only. Group rate 1 free for every 10 tickets. **Facilities:** P (charged) 🖼 📷 & (call 0115 915 3700 for info on access) toilets for disabled shop ✕ (ex guide dogs) 🍴

OLLERTON   Map 08 SK66

RUFFORD ABBEY AND COUNTRY PARK

NG22 9DF
↪ (2m S of Ollerton, adjacent to A614)
☎ 01623 822944
e-mail: marilyn.louden@nottscc.gov.uk
web: ruffordcraftcentre.org.uk

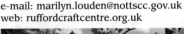

At the heart of the wooded country park stand the remains

continued

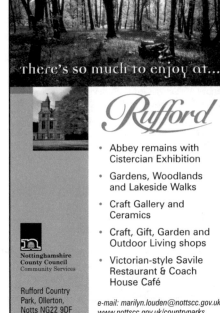
of a 12th-century Cistercian Abbey, housing an exhibition on the life of a Cistercian Monk at Rufford. Many species of wildlife can be seen on the lake, and there are lovely formal gardens, with sculptures and Britain's first centre for studio ceramics.

Times: Open all year 10.30-5 (craft centre closes 3pm Jan & Feb). For further details of opening times telephone establishment.

Facilities: P (charged) 🖼 ✕ licensed 📷 & (lift to craft centre gallery, free parking, wheelchair loan) toilets for disabled shop garden centre 🍴

See advertisement on this page

SOUTHWELL   Map 08 SK65

THE WORKHOUSE

Upton Rd NG25 0PT
☎ 01636 817250
e-mail: theworkhouse@nationaltrust.org.uk
web: www.nationaltrust.org.uk

Enter this 19th-century brick institution and discover the thought-provoking story of the 'welfare' system of the New Poor Law. The least altered workhouse in existence today, it survives from hundreds that once covered the country. Explore the segregated stairs and rooms, use the audio guide, based on archive records, to bring the 19th-century inhabitants to life in the empty rooms, then try the interactive displays exploring poverty through the years and across the country.

Times: Open 28 Mar-Oct, Thu-Mon noon-5 (Aug 11-5). (Last admission 1hr before closing). **Facilities:** P & (virtual tour, photo album, wheelchairs available) toilets for disabled ✕ (ex guide dogs) 🐾

SUTTON-CUM-LOUND　　Map 08 SK68

WETLANDS WATERFOWL RESERVE & EXOTIC BIRD PARK

Off Loundlow Rd DN22 8SB
⊃ (signed on A638)
☎ 01777 818099

The Reserve is a 32-acre site for both wild and exotic waterfowl. Visitors can see a collection of birds of prey, parrots, geese, ducks, and wigeon among others. There are also many small mammals and farm and wild animals, including llamas, wallabies, emus, monkeys, red squirrels, deer and goats.

Times: ✱ Open all year, daily 10-5.30 (or dusk - whichever is earlier). Closed 25 Dec. **Facilities:** 🅿 ➔ & (wheelchair available) shop ✗ (ex guide dogs)

WORKSOP　　Map 08 SK57

CLUMBER PARK

The Estate Office, Clumber Park S80 3AZ
⊃ (4.5m SE of Worksop, signed from A1)
☎ 01909 476592
e-mail: clumberpark@nationaltrust.org.uk
web: www.nationaltrust.org.uk

An impressive, landscaped park, laid out by 'Capability Brown'. An outstanding feature is the lake running through the park, a haven for wildfowl, covering an area of 80 acres. The park is a mixture of woodland, open grass and heathland.

Times: Open: park daily, all year during daylight hours
Facilities: 🅿 (charged) ➔ ✗ licensed & (powered self-drive vehicle available if booked) toilets for disabled shop garden centre ♨

HRH Queen Elizabeth II.

The British monarch was born in April 1926, and the year of her 80th birthday will see many national celebrations, as well as those that are to be staged in London.

OXFORDSHIRE

EVENTS & FESTIVALS

March
25th-2nd Apr Oxford Literary Festival, The Oxford Union, Oxford
26th Poohsticks World Championships, Little Wittenham

May
1st 6am Choir singing from Magdalen Tower, Magdalen College, Oxford
29th Lord Mayor's Parade, Oxford
tbc Oxford Annual Balloon Fiesta, Cutterslowe Park

June
21st Encaenia, Oxford University graduation event with gowned procession through the city (provisional)
28th-2nd Jul Henley Royal Regatta, Henley-on-Thames

July
5th-9th Henley Festival of Music & the Arts, various venues, Family Fiesta on 9th
17th-21st Swan Upping, River Thames, Sunbury-Abingdon (provisional)
23rd Sheepdog Trials at Greenlands Farm, Hambleden, Henley

September
4th-5th St Giles Fair, the southeast's largest and longest running fun fair, Oxford
9th Henley & District Agricultural Association Show, Greenlands Farm, Hambleden, Henley
21st Thame & Oxfordshire County Show, Thame Showground
tbc Dorchester-on-Thames Festival, music, dance, readings and children's events, various venues
tbc The Great British Cheese Festival, Blenheim Palace

October
1st Ploughing Match, Country Fair & Clay Shoot, Henley & District Agricultural Association Show, location to be confirmed (provisional)
tbc Banbury Folk & Good Music Day

Above: Radcliffe Camera stands between the Old Quad buildings of Brasenose College, and All Souls College

BANBURY — Map 04 SP44

BANBURY MUSEUM

Spiceball Park Rd OX16 2PQ

➥ (M40 junct 11 straight across at first rdbt into Hennef Way, left at next rdbt into Concord Ave, right at next rdbt & left at next rdbt, Castle Quay Shopping Centre & Museum on right) **FREE**

☎ 01295 259855

e-mail: banburymuseum@cherwell-dc.gov.uk

web: www.cherwell-dc.gov.uk/banburymuseum

Come and visit Banbury's stunning new museum! It is situated in an attractive canal-side location in the centre of Banbury. Exciting modern displays tell of Banbury's origins and historic past. The Civil War; the plush manufacturing industry; the Victorian market town; costume from the 17th century to the present day; Tooley's Boatyard and the Oxford Canal, are just some of the subjects illustrated in the new museum.

Times: Open all year, Mon-Sat, 10-5, Sun 10.30-4.30.

Facilities: P (500yds) ✗ licensed 🗐 ♿ toilets for disabled shop ✖ (ex guide dogs) ◼

BROUGHTON — Map 04 SP43

BROUGHTON CASTLE

OX15 5EB

➥ (2m W of Banbury Cross on B4035 Shipston-on-Stour in Broughton village, turn off B4035 by Saye & Sele Arms) **2 for 1**

☎ 01295 276070

e-mail: admin@broughtoncastle.demon.co.uk

web: www.broughtoncastle.demon.co.uk

Built by Sir John de Broughton, then owned by William of Wykeham, and later by the first Lord Saye and Sele, the castle is an early 14th-and mid 16th-century house with a moat and gatehouse. Period furniture, paintings and Civil War relics are displayed. There are fine borders in the walled garden, and against the castle walls.

Times: Open Etr Sun & Mon, May-15 Sep, Wed, Sun & BH Mon, 2-5 (also open Thu in Jul & Aug). **Fee:** ✳ £6 (ch 5-15 £2.50, pen & students £5). Family ticket (2ad & up to 3ch) £14. Garden £2.50. Group rates. **Facilities:** P ♿ 🗐 ♿ toilets for disabled shop ✖ (ex guide dogs)

See advertisement on this page

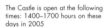

BURFORD — Map 04 SP21

COTSWOLD WILDLIFE PARK

OX18 4JW

➥ (on A361 2m S of A40 at Burford)

☎ 01993 823006

web: www.cotswoldwildlifepark.co.uk

This 160-acre landscaped zoological park, surrounds a listed Gothic-style manor house. There is a varied collection of animals from all over the world, many of which are endangered species such as Asiatic lions, leopards, white rhinos and red pandas. There's an adventure playground, a children's farmyard, and train rides during the summer. The park has also become one of the Cotswold's leading

continued

attractions for garden enthusiasts, with its exotic summer displays and varied plantings offering interest all year.
Times: Open all year, daily from 10, (last admission 4.30 Mar-Sep, 3.30 Oct-Feb). Closed 25 Dec. **Fee:** ✱ £8.50 (ch 3-16 & pen £6).
Facilities: 🅿 💻 ✕ licensed 🚹 (parking, free hire of wheelchairs) toilets for disabled shop 📺

See advertisement on opposite page

BUSCOT   Map 04 SU29

BUSCOT PARK
SN7 8BU
➲ (on A417 between Faringdon & Lechdale)
☎ 01367 240786
e-mail: estbuscot@aol.com
web: www.buscot-park.com

An 18th-century Palladian house with park and water garden. Home of the Faringdon collection of paintings and furniture. The park is landscaped with extensive water gardens designed by Harold Peto with parkland walks and a walled garden boasting seasonal herbaceous borders.
Times: Open Grounds only Good 3 Apr-26 Sep, Mon & Tue 2-6. House & Grounds open 5 Apr -29 Sep, Wed-Fri 2-6 (last entry 5) also open BHs & Sat-Sun: 8&9, 15&16 29&30 Apr, 13&14, 27&28 May, 10&11, 24&25 Jun, 8&9, 22&23 Jul, 12&13, 26&27 Aug, 9&10, 23&24 Sep.
Fee: House & Grounds £7 (ch £3.50); Grounds only £5 (ch £2.50). NT membrs free. **Facilities:** 🅿 💻 🚹 (2 motorised mobility vehicles-must pre-book) toilets for disabled 🐾 assist dogs 🐕 📺

CHASTLETON   Map 04 SP22

CHASTLETON HOUSE
GL56 0SU 6m from Stow-on-the-Wold. Approach from A436 between A44
➲ (W of Chipping Norton) and Stow.
☎ 01608 674355
e-mail: chastleton@nationaltrust.org.uk
web: www.nationaltrust.org.uk
One of England's finest and most complete Jacobean houses, Chastleton House is filled with a mixture of rare and everyday objects, furniture and textiles maintaining the atmosphere of this 400-year-old home. The gardens have a typical Elizabethan and Jacobean layout with a ring of topiary. The National Trust has focussed on conserving rather than restoring the house.
Times: Open Apr-Sep, Wed-Sat 1-5; Oct Wed-Sat, 1-4 **Fee:** ✱ £6 (ch £3) Family £15. Group £5 each **Facilities:** 🅿 📱 🚹 toilets for disabled 🐾 🐕

DEDDINGTON   Map 04 SP43

DEDDINGTON CASTLE
OX5 4TE
➲ (S of B4031 on E side of Deddington)   **FREE**
The large earthworks of the outer and inner baileys can be seen; the remains of 12th-century castle buildings have been excavated, but they are not now visible.
Times: Open any reasonable time.

DIDCOT   Map 04 SU58

DIDCOT RAILWAY CENTRE
OX11 7NJ
➲ (on A4130 at Didcot Parkway Station)
☎ 01235 817200   **2 for 1**
e-mail: didrlyc@globalnet.co.uk
web: www.didcotrailwaycentre.org.uk
Based around the original GWR engine shed, the Centre is home to the biggest collection anywhere of Great Western Railway steam locomotives, carriages and wagons. A typical GWR station has been re-created and a section of Brunel's original broad gauge track relaid, with reconstruction of 'Fire Fly' locomotive of 1840. Special Event: Brunel 200 in 2006 please telephone for details.
Times: Open all year, Sat & Sun. Daily 1-17 Apr, 27 May-3 Sep. Steamdays, Easter 14-17 Apr, 29 Apr-3 Oct, Wed 12 Jul-30 Aug. Day out with Thomas 10-12 Mar, 6-8 Oct. **Fee:** ✱ £4-£9 depending on event (ch £3-£7.50, pen £3.50-£7.50). **Facilities:** 🅿 (100yds) 💻 ✕ 📱 🚹 (advance notice recommended, awkward steps at entrance) toilets for disabled shop 📺

GREAT COXWELL   Map 04 SU29

GREAT COXWELL BARN
➲ (2m SW of Faringdon between A420 & B4019)
☎ 01793 762209
e-mail: greatcoxwellbarn@nationaltrust.org.uk
web: www.nationaltrust.org.uk
William Morris said that the barn was 'as noble as a cathedral'. It is a 13th-century stone-built tithe barn, 152ft long and 44ft wide, with a beautifully crafted framework of timbers supporting the lofty stone roof. The barn was built for the Cistercians.
Times: Open all reasonable times. For details please contact Estate Office. **Fee:** ✱ £1 **Facilities:** 🅿 🐕

HENLEY-ON-THAMES   Map 04 SU78

GREYS COURT
Rotherfield Greys RG9 4PG
➲ (A4130 take B481. Property signed 3m on left. From Henley town centre follow signs to Peppard/Greys for 3m)
☎ 01491 628529   **2 for 1**
e-mail: greyscourt@nationaltrust.org.uk
web: www.nationaltrust.org.uk
A picturesque house, originating from the 14th century but with later additions. There is a beautiful courtyard and the surviving tower which dates from 1347. The outbuildings include a Tudor wheelhouse - one supplying water to the house, walled gardens and an ornamental vegetable garden. The 2-for-1 voucher is valid only during normal visiting hours and cannot be used for any ticketed events.
Times: Open: House: part of ground floor only, Apr-24 Sep Wed-Fri & BH Mons 2-5. Closed Good Fri. Garden: Mar-Oct 2-5.30 (Mar & Oct Wed only), Apr-Sep, Tue-Sat. **Fee:** ✱ House & Garden £5.20 (ch £2.60). Family ticket £13. Garden only £3.70 (ch £1.80) Family ticket £9.20. **Facilities:** 🅿 💻 🚹 (ground floor & gardens partly accessible) shop (bookshop) 🐾 Assist dogs 🐕

RIVER & ROWING MUSEUM

Mill Meadows RG9 1BF
⊃ (off A4130, signed to Mill Meadows)
☎ 01491 415600
e-mail: museum@rrm.co.uk
web: www.rrm.co.uk

2 for 1

The award-winning River and Rowing Museum is the only museum in the world with galleries dedicated to rowing and the 'Quest for Speed', from the Greek Trireme to modern Olympic rowing boats; the River Thames from source to sea with its rich history and varied wildlife. See the boats that won gold in Sydney and the riverside town of Henley featuring the Royal Regatta. The permanent *Wind in the Willows* exhibition recreates the drawings of E. H. Shepard in a walk through attraction using models, lighting and sound to bring the classic book to life.
Times: Open Summer: May-Aug 10-5.30. Winter: Sep-Apr 10-5. Closed 24-25 & 31 Dec & 1 Jan. **Fee:** £6 (concessions £4, pens £5). Family ticket from £18. Party 10+. **Facilities:** 🅿 🍴 ✕ licensed & (lift access to upstairs galleries, ramps at entrance) toilets for disabled shop ✖ (ex guide dogs) 🍴

LONG WITTENHAM   Map 04 SU59

PENDON MUSEUM

OX14 4QD
⊃ (follow brown signs from A4130 Didcot-Wallingford or A415 Abingdon-Wallingford road)
☎ 01865 407365
web: www.pendonmuseum.com
This charming exhibition shows highly detailed and historically accurate model railway and village scenes transporting the visitor back into 1930s country landscapes. Skilled modellers can often be seen at work on the exhibits.
Times: ✱ Open Sat & Sun 2-5, BH wknds 11-5 also Wed in Jul, Aug & Oct half term. Closed Dec. **Facilities:** 🅿 🍴 📱 & (phone in advance, special seating with handrails) toilets for disabled shop ✖ (ex guide dogs) 🍴

MAPLEDURHAM   Map 04 SU67

MAPLEDURHAM HOUSE

RG4 7TR
⊃ (off A4074, follow brown heritage signs from Reading)
☎ 0118 972 3350
e-mail: mtrust1997@aol.com
web: www.mapledurham.co.uk
The small community at Mapledurham includes the house, a watermill and a church. The fine Elizabethan mansion, *continued*

surrounded by quiet parkland that runs down to the River Thames, was built by the Blount family in the 16th century. The estate has literary connections with the poet Alexander Pope, with Galsworthy's *Forsyte Saga* and Kenneth Graham's *Wind in the Willows*, and was a location for the film *The Eagle has Landed*.
Times: Open Etr-Sep, Sat, Sun & BHs 2-5.30 Picnic area 2-5.30. (Last admission 5). Group visits midweek by arrangement.
Fee: ✱ Combined house, watermill & grounds £6.50 (ch £3). House & grounds £4 (ch £2). Watermill & grounds £3 (ch £1.50).
Facilities: 🅿 🍴 & shop 🍴

MAPLEDURHAM WATERMILL

RG4 7TR
⊃ (off A4074, follow brown heritage signs from Reading)
☎ 0118 972 3350
e-mail: mtrust1997@aol.com
web: www.mapledurham.co.uk
Close to Mapledurham House stands the last working corn and grist mill on the Thames, still using traditional wooden machinery and producing flour for local bakers and shops. The watermill's products can be purchased in the shop. When Mapledurham House is open the mill can be reached by river launch.
Times: Open Etr-Sep, Sat, Sun & BHs 2-5.30. Picnic area 2-5.30. (Last admission 5). Groups midweek by arrangement. **Fee:** ✱ Watermill & grounds £3 (ch £1.50) **Facilities:** 🅿 🍴 📱 & shop 🍴

MINSTER LOVELL — Map 04 SP31

MINSTER LOVELL HALL & DOVECOT

OX8 5RN

⮕ (adjacent to Minster Lovell Church, 3m W of Witney off A40) **FREE**

Home of the ill-fated Lovell family, the ruins of the 15th-century house are steeped in history and legend. One of the main features of the estate is the medieval dovecote.
Times: Open any reasonable time. Dovecote-exterior only
Facilities: ⌗

NORTH LEIGH — Map 04 SP31

NORTH LEIGH ROMAN VILLA

OX8 6QB

⮕ (2m N of North Leigh) **FREE**

This is the remains of a large and well-build Roman courtyard villa. The most important feature is an almost complete mosaic tile floor, which is intricately patterned in reds and browns.
Times: Open, grounds all year. Viewing window for mosaic tile floor. Pedestrian access only from the main road - 600 yds. **Facilities:** P ⌗

OXFORD — Map 04 SP50

ASHMOLEAN MUSEUM OF ART & ARCHAEOLOGY

Beaumont St OX1 2PH

⮕ (city centre, opposite The Randolph Hotel)
☎ 01865 278000
web: www.ashmol.ox.ac.uk

The oldest museum in the country, opened in 1683, the Ashmolean contains Oxford University's priceless collections. Many important historical art pieces and artefacts are on display, including work from Ancient Greece through to the twentieth century.
Times: Open all year, Tue-Sat 10-5, Sun 12-5 BH Mons 10-5. Closed Etr & during St.Giles Fair in early Sep, Xmas & 1 Jan. **Fee:** ✱ Free. Guided tours by arrangement. **Facilities:** P (100-200mtrs) (pay & display) ⬛ ✗ licensed ⬛ ⬧ (entry ramp from Beaumont St. Tel. before visit) toilets for disabled shop ✖ ⬛

HARCOURT ARBORETUM

Nuneham Courtenay OX44 9PX

⮕ (400yds S of Nuneham Courtenay on A4074)
☎ 01865 343501
e-mail: piers.newth@botanic-garden.ox.ac.uk
web: www.botanic-garden.ox.ac.uk

The gardens consist of 75 acres of mixed woodland, meadow, pond, rhododendron walks and fine specimen trees.
Times: Apr-Nov, daily 10-5, Dec-Mar, Mon-Fri 10-4.30. Closed 22 Dec-4 Jan. **Fee:** ✱ £2 pay & display for car park or £5 for 1yr season ticket. **Facilities:** P (charged) ⬛ ⬧ toilets for disabled ✖ (ex guide dogs)

MUSEUM OF OXFORD

St Aldate's OX1 1DZ
☎ 01865 252761
e-mail: museum@oxford.gov.uk
web: www.oxford.gov.uk/museum

Permanent displays depict the archaeology and history of the city through the ages. There are temporary exhibitions, facilities for school parties and groups, and an audio tour.
Times: Open all year, Tue-Fri 10-4, Sat 10-5 & Sun 12-4. Closed 25-26 Dec & Good Fri. **Fee:** ✱ £2 (ch under 17 50p, concessions £1.50). Family ticket £5 **Facilities:** ⬛ shop ✖ (ex guide dogs) ⬛

MUSEUM OF THE HISTORY OF SCIENCE

Old Ashmolean Building, Broad St OX1 3AZ

⮕ (next to Sheldonian Theatre in city centre, on Broad St)
☎ 01865 277280 **FREE**
e-mail: museum@mhs.ox.ac.uk
web: www.mhs.ox.ac.uk

The first purpose built museum in Britain, containing the world's finest collection of early scientific instruments used in astronomy, navigation, surveying, physics and chemistry.
Times: Open Tue-Sat 12-4, Sun 2-5. Closed Xmas and Easter Holidays.
Facilities: P (300mtrs) (limited street parking, meters) ⬛ ⬧ (lift) toilets for disabled shop ✖ (ex guide dogs)

THE OXFORD STORY

6 Broad St OX1 3AJ

⮕ (follow signs for city centre then finger post signs to attraction, or use park & ride service)
☎ 01865 728822 **2 for 1**
e-mail: info@oxfordstory.co.uk
web: www.oxfordstory.co.uk

The Oxford Story offers the very best introduction to the city's world famous University. Climb aboard our indoor 'dark' ride to travel through 900 years of university history. In our interactive exhibition, 'Innovate' use touch-screen technology to question experts from Oxford University on modern day issues, from heart disease to climate change.
Times: Open Jan-Jun & Sep-Dec, Mon-Sat 10-4.30 & Sun 11-4.30. Jul & Aug daily 9.30-5. Closed 25 Dec. **Fee:** ✱ £6.95 (ch £5.25, concessions £5.95), Family ticket (2ad+2ch) £22.50 **Facilities:** P (300mtrs) ⬛ ⬧ (advisable to phone in advance, hearing loop facility) toilets for disabled shop ✖ (ex guide dogs) ⬛

OXFORD UNIVERSITY MUSEUM OF NATURAL HISTORY

Parks Rd OX1 3PW

⮕ (opposite Keble College)
☎ 01865 272950 **FREE**
e-mail: info@oum.ox.ac.uk
web: www.oum.ox.ac.uk

Built between 1855 and 1860, this museum of "the natural sciences" was intended to satisfy a growing interest in biology, botany, archaeology, zoology, entomology and so on. The museum reflects Oxford University's position as a 19th-century centre of learning, with displays of early dinosaur discoveries, Darwinian evolution and Elias Ashmole's collection of preserved animals. Although visitors

continued

to the Pitt-Rivers Museum must pass through the University Museum, the two should not be confused.

Times: Open daily 12-5. Times vary at Xmas & Etr.

Facilities: P (200mtrs) (meter parking) ▦ & lift access to gallery toilets for disabled shop ✈

PITT RIVERS MUSEUM

South Parks Rd OX1 3PP

➲ (10 min walk from city centre, entrance through the Univiersity Museum of Natural History)

☎ 01865 270927   `FREE`

e-mail: prm@prm.ox.ac.uk

web: www.prm.ox.ac.uk

The museum is one of the city's most popular attractions, it is part of the University of Oxford and was founded in 1884. The collections held at the museum are internationally acclaimed, and contain many objects from different cultures of the world and from various periods, all grouped by type, or purpose.

Times: Open all year. Mon-Sun 12-4.30. Closed Xmas & Etr, open BHs.

Facilities: ▦ & (audio guide, wheelchair trail and map to ground floor) toilets for disabled shop ✈ (ex guide dogs)

ST EDMUND HALL

College of Oxford University OX1 4AR

➲ (Queen's Lane Oxford at end of High St)

☎ 01865 279000   `FREE`

e-mail: bursary@seh.ox.ac.uk

web: www.seh.ox.ac.uk

This is the only surviving medieval academic hall and has a Norman crypt, 17th-century dining hall, chapel and quadrangle. Other buildings are of the 18th and 20th centuries.

Times: Open all year. Closed 24 Dec-4 Jan, 9-18 Apr & 28-31 Aug.

Facilities: ▆ & toilets for disabled ✈ (ex guide dogs)

UNIVERSITY OF OXFORD BOTANIC GARDEN

Rose Ln OX1 4AZ

➲ (E end of High St on banks of River Cherwell)

☎ 01865 286690

e-mail: postmaster@obq.ox.ac.uk

web: www.botanic-garden.ox.ac.uk

Founded in 1621, this botanic garden is the oldest in the country. There is a collection of over 8000 species of plants from all over the world. Consisting of 3 sections: the Glasshouses contain plants that need protection from the British weather. The area outside the Walled Garden contains a water garden and rock garden as well as the black border and autumn border. Within the Walled Garden plants are grouped by country of origin, botanic family or economic use.

Times: Open all year daily: 9-4.30 Jan, Feb, Nov & Dec (last admission 4.15). Mar-Apr, Sep-Oct 9-5 (last admissio 4.15) May-Aug 9-6.

Fee: ✱ £2.60 (ch free) disabled with 1 carer free, concessions £2.

Facilities: P (0.5m) (park and ride system) ▦ & toilets for disabled shop ✈ (ex guide dogs)

> **Directions are provided by the attractions.**

ROUSHAM   Map 04 SP42

ROUSHAM HOUSE

OX25 4QX

➲ (1m E of A4260. 0.5m S of B4030)

☎ 01869 347110

web: www.rousham.org

This attractive mansion was built by Sir Robert Dormer in 1635. During the Civil War it was a Royalist garrison. The house contains over 150 portraits and other pictures, and also much fine contemporary furniture. The gardens are a masterpiece by William Kent, and are his only work to survive unspoiled.

Times: Open all year, garden only, daily 10-4.30. House, May-Sep, Sun & BH Mon 2-4.30 (last entry). **Fee:** House £3, Garden £4. Groups by arrangement. No children under 15.

Facilities: P & ✈ (ex guide dogs)

RYCOTE   Map 04 SP60

RYCOTE CHAPEL

OX9 2PE

➲ (off B4013)

This small private chapel was founded in 1449 by Richard Quatremayne. It has its original font, and a particularly fine 17th-century interior. The chapel was visited by both Elizabeth I and Charles I.

Times: Open Apr-Sep, Fri-Sun, 2-6. May close at short notice for services or functions. **Fee:** Prices & opening times subject to change, for further details phone or log onto www.english-heritage.org.uk/visits

Facilities: P & (if assisted) shop ✈ ♯

STONOR   Map 04 SU78

STONOR HOUSE & PARK

RG9 6HF OnB480, approx 5m N of Henley-on-Thames

☎ 01491 638587

e-mail: jweaver@stonor.com

web: www.stonor.com

The house dates back to 1190 but features a Tudor façade. It has a medieval Catholic chapel which is still in use today, and shows some of the earliest domestic architecture in Oxfordshire. Its treasures include rare furniture, paintings, sculptures and tapestries from Britain, Europe and America. The house is set in beautiful gardens commanding views of the surrounding deer park.

Times: Open Apr-Sep, Sun 2-5.30; Jul, Aug, & Sep also Wed 2-5.30; BH Mons. Parties by appointment Tue-Thu, Apr-Sep. **Fee:** ✱ £6 (ch 14 accompanied free). Gardens only £3.50. Private guided tours £7 each.

Facilities: P ▆ ▦ shop Gardens only

UFFINGTON   Map 04 SU38

UFFINGTON CASTLE, WHITE HORSE & DRAGON HILL

➲ (S of B4507)

☎ 01793 762209   `FREE`

The 'castle' is an Iron Age fort on the ancient Ridgeway Path. It covers about eight acres and has only one gateway. On the hill below the fort is the White Horse, a 375ft prehistoric figure carved in the chalky hillside and thought to be about 3000 years old.

Times: Open at any reasonable time. **Facilities:** P ▦ (disabled car park) on lead only 🐾

WATERPERRY   Map 04 SP60

WATERPERRY GARDENS

OX33 1JZ

➲ (M40 junct 8 from London. 2.5m from A40, turn off at Wheatley)

☎ 01844 339226 & 339254

e-mail: office@waterperrygardens.fsnet.co.uk

web: www.waterperrygardens.co.uk

The manor of Waterperry is mentioned in the Domesday Book. The present house (not open) was rebuilt by Sir John Curson in 1713. The peaceful gardens and nurseries which surround the house were the home of a celebrated horticultural school between 1932 and 1971, and have fine herbaceous borders, a rock garden, riverside walk, shrub borders, lawns and trees. Please phone for details of special events.

Times: Open all year, Gardens, Apr-Oct 9-5.30, Nov-Mar 9-5 daily. Closed Xmas, New Year & during "Art in Action" 15-18 Jul.

Facilities: 🅿 💺 ✗ licensed 🛢 ♿ (grounds mostly accessible) toilets for disabled shop garden centre ✖ (ex guide dogs) ⬛

WITNEY   Map 04 SP31

COGGES MANOR FARM MUSEUM

Church Ln, Cogges OX28 3LA

➲ (0.5m SE off A4022)

☎ 01993 772602

web: www.cogges.org

The museum includes the Manor, dairy and walled garden, and has breeds of animals typical of the Victorian period. The first floor of the manor contains period rooms. Special events take place through the season.

Times: Open Apr-Oct, Tue-Fri & BH Mon 10.30-5.30, Sat & Sun 12-5.30. Early closing Oct. Closed Good Fri. **Fee:** ✱ £4.40 (ch £2.30, pen, students & UB40 £2.85). Family ticket £12.90 (2ad+2ch).

Facilities: 🅿 💺 ♿ (wheelchair available,audio tour) toilets for disabled shop ⬛

An angel in Oxford

WOODSTOCK   Map 04 SP41

BLENHEIM PALACE

OX20 1PX

➲ (M40 junct 9, follow signs to Blenheim, on A44 8m N of Oxford)

☎ 08700 602080

e-mail: admin@blenheimpalace.com

web: www.blenheimpalace.com

2 for 1

Home of the 11th Duke of Marlborough and birthplace of Sir Winston Churchill, Blenheim Palace is an English Baroque masterpiece. Fine furniture, sculpture, paintings and tapestries are set in magnificent gilded staterooms that overlook sweeping lawns and formal gardens. 'Capability' Brown landscaped the 2100-acre grounds, which are open to visitors for pleasant walks and beautiful views. Please telephone for details of events running throughout the year.

Times: Palace & Gardens mid Feb-mid Dec (ex Mon & Tue in Nov & Dec) daily 10.30-5.30 (last admission 4.45). Park daily all year 9-4.45. Closed 25 Dec. **Fee:** ✱ Palace, Park & Gardens £11.50-£13 (ch £6-£7.50, concessions £9-£10). Park & Gardens £6-£8(ch £2-£4, concessions £4-£6) **Facilities:** 🅿 💺 ✗ licensed ♿ (lift, ramps, disabled parking, buggies, wheelchairs) toilets for disabled shop ✖ assist dogs ⬛

OXFORDSHIRE MUSEUM

Fletcher's House OX20 1SN

➲ (A44 Evesham-Oxford, follow signs for Blenheim Palace. Museum opposite church)

☎ 01993 811456

e-mail: oxon.museum@oxfordshire.go.uk

web: www.oxfordshire.gov.uk/ the_oxfordshire_museum

FREE

Situated in the heart of the historic town of Woodstock, the award-winning redevelopment of Fletcher's House provides a home for the new county museum. Set in attractive gardens, the new museum celebrates Oxfordshire in all its diversity and features collections of local history, art, archaeology, landscape and wildlife as well as a gallery exploring the Country's innovative industries from nuclear power to nanotechnology. Interactive exhibits offer new learning experiences for visitors of all ages. The museum's purpose built Garden Gallery houses a variety of touring exhibitions of regional and national interest.

Times: Open all year, Tue-Sat 10-5. Closed Good Fri, 25-26 Dec & 1 Jan. Galleries closed on Mon, but open BH Mons, 2-5.

Facilities: 🅿 (outside entrance) (free parking) 💺 ✗ licensed 🛢 ♿ (chair lifts to all galleries) toilets for disabled ✖ (ex guide dogs)

RUTLAND

EVENTS & FESTIVALS

June
17th-18th Stapleford Steam, Stapleford Park

July
tbc Whissendine Feast Week, various venues and events

August
18th-20th British Birdwatching Fair, Egleton Nature Reserve, Rutland Water
27th-28th Stapleford Miniature Railway Open Weekend, Stapleford Steam Railway, Stapleford Park

Above: Fishing on Rutland Water

LYDDINGTON   Map 04 SP89

LYDDINGTON BEDE HOUSE
Blue Coat Ln LE15 9LZ
☎ 01572 822438

Once a prominent medieval palace later converted into an almshouse for the poor. Its history is bought to life in an evocative audio tour.

Times: Open 24 Mar-Oct, Thu-Mon 10-5. **Fee:** £3.30 (ch £1.70, concessions £2.50, Family £8.30). Opening times and prices are subject to change, for further details please phone 0870 333 1181

Facilities: ఈ ✖ ♿

OAKHAM   Map 04 SK80

OAKHAM CASTLE
Catmos St LE15 6HW
➲ (off Market Place)
☎ 01572 758440   FREE
e-mail: museum@rutland.gov.uk
web: www.rutnet.co.uk/rcc/rutlandmuseums

An exceptionally fine Norman Great Hall of a 12th-century fortified manor house. Earthworks, walls and remains of an earlier motte can be seen along with medieval sculptures and unique presentation horseshoes forfeited by peers of the realm and royalty to the Lord of the Manor. Licensed for Civil Marriages. Please enquire for details of the Oakham Festival.

Times: Open all year, Mon-Sat 10.30-5 (closed 1-1.30), Sun 2-4. Closed Good Fri & Xmas. **Facilities:** P (400yds) (disabled parking only by notification) 🍴 ఈ shop ✖ (ex guide dogs)

RUTLAND COUNTY MUSEUM
Catmos St LE15 6HW
➲ (on A6003, S of town centre)
☎ 01572 758440   FREE
e-mail: museum@rutland.gov.uk
web: www.rutnet.co.uk/rcc/rutlandmuseums

Rutland County Museum is the perfect introduction to England's smallest county. The 'Welcome to Rutland' gallery is a guide to its history. The museum includes a shop and study area. On show in the 18th-century Riding School are displays of archaeology, history and an extensive rural life collection.

Times: Open all year, Mon-Sat 10.30-5, Sun 2-4. Closed Good Fri, Xmas & 1 Jan. **Facilities:** P (charged) 🍴 ఈ (induction loop in meeting room) toilets for disabled shop ✖ (ex guide dogs)

Isambard Kingdom Brunel (1806-1859). 2006 is the 200th anniversary of the birth of one of Britain's most important engineers. His bicentenary will be celebrated by many attractions both directly and indirectly connected with Brunel.

SHROPSHIRE

EVENTS & FESTIVALS

April
30th-1st May British Falconry & Raptor Fair, Chetwynd Park, Newport, nr Telford

June
3rd-25th Much Wenlock Festival, various events and venues
17th Shrewsbury Carnival & Show, Quarry Park
24th-9th Jul Ludlow Festival in the ruins of Ludlow Castle
24th-25th Shropshire & West Midlands Show, Showground, Berwick Road, Shrewsbury
tbc Royal Air Force Show, Royal Air Force Museum, Cosford

July
15th-16th Wem Sweet Pea Festival, New Town Hall, High Street, Wem
tbc Festival at the Edge (storytelling), Stokes Barn, Much Wenlock

August
11th-12th Shrewsbury Flower Show
19th-20th V Festival, music festival, Weston Park, Western-under-Lizard nr Shifnel
25th-27th Bridgnorth Folk Festival (provisional)
27th-28th County of Salop Steam Rally, Onslow Park, Shrewsbury
27th-28th Shropshire Game Fair, Chetwynd Park, Newport, Telford

September
16th-17th The Midland Game & Country Sports Fair, Weston Park, Weston-under-Lizard, Nr Shifnel
tbc Shrewsbury Real Ale Festival (provisional)

Above: The bridge and the River Severn, Ironbridge

ACTON BURNELL   Map 07 SJ50

ACTON BURNELL CASTLE
SY5 7PE
➲ (in Acton Burnell on unclass road 8m S of Shrewsbury) **FREE**
The warm red sandstone shell of a fortified thirteenth-century manor house. The site of the first parliament at which the commons were fully represented.
Times: Open at all reasonable times. **Facilities:** ♿ ♨

ATCHAM   Map 07 SJ50

ATTINGHAM PARK
SY4 4TP
➲ (4m SE of Shrewsbury on B4380)
☎ **01743 708123**
e-mail: attingham@nationaltrust.org.uk **2 for 1**
Attingham Park is centred on one of Britain's finest regency mansions, set in a landscaped deer park. Close by one can meet the animals at one of Britain's only organic open farms. Please telephone for details of events running throughout the year. The 2-for-1 voucher is valid only during normal visiting hours and cannot be used for any ticketed events.
Times: House open mid Mar-end Oct, Fri-Tue 12-5, (last admission 4). BH Mon 11-5. Deer Park & Grounds daily Mar-Oct, 9-8; Nov-Feb 9-5.
Fee: ✱ House & Grounds £5.50 (ch £2.75) Family ticket £12.75. Grounds only £2.70 (ch £1.35) Family £6.75 **Facilities:** 🅿 🍴 ♿ (2 electric self drive buggies, 1 staff driven 8-seater) toilets for disabled shop (ex guide & hearing dogs) ⚘

BENTHALL   Map 07 SJ60

BENTHALL HALL
TF12 5RX
➲ (on B4375)
☎ **01952 882159**
e-mail: benthall@ntrust.org.uk **2 for 1**
The main part of the house was built around 1585. A wing at the back, which has been altered at various times, dates originally from about 1520. It is an attractive sandstone building with mullioned windows, fine oak panelling and a splendid carved staircase.
Times: Open Apr-Sep, Tue, Wed, BH Mon & Sun before BH Mons; Jul-Sep open every Sun. House 2-5.30, Garden 1.30-5.30.
Fee: ✱ House and garden £4.20 (ch £2.10). Garden only £2.60 (ch £1.30) **Facilities:** 🅿 🍴 ♿ (braille, large print guides) toilets for disabled ✗ (ex guide dogs) ⚘

BOSCOBEL   Map 07 SJ80

BOSCOBEL HOUSE AND THE ROYAL OAK
Brewood ST19 9AR
➲ (on unclass road between A41 and A5)
☎ **01902 850244**
This fully restored and refurbished lodge and famous Royal Oak tree is where King Charles II sought refuge from Cromwell's troops in 1651. The house was built around 1632.
Times: Open 24 Mar-May, Thu-Mon, 10-5; Jun-Aug, daily, 10-6; Sep-Oct, Thu-Mon, 10-5 **Fee:** £4.60 (ch £2.30, concessions £3.50) Family £11.50. Grounds only; £1.50 (ch 80p, concessions £1.10). Opening times and prices are subject to change, for further details please phone 0870 333 1181 **Facilities:** 🅿 🍴 shop ✗ ♨

WHITELADIES PRIORY

➲ (1m SW of Boscobel House, off an unclass road between A41 and A5)

Only the ruins are left of this Augustinian nunnery, which dates from 1158 and was destroyed in the Civil War. After the Battle of Worcester Charles II hid here and in the nearby woods before going on to Boscobel House.

Times: Open Apr-Oct any reasonable time. Closed Nov-Mar.
Facilities: ♿

BUILDWAS   Map 07 SJ60

BUILDWAS ABBEY
Iron Bridge TF8 7BW
➲ (on S bank of River Severn on B4378)
☎ 01952 433274

Set beside the River Severn, against a backdrop of wooded grounds, are the extensive remains of this Cistercian abbey founded in 1135.

Times: Open 24 Mar-May, Thu-Mon, 10-5; Jun-Aug, daily, 10-6; Sep, Thu-Mon, 10-5. **Fee:** £2.60 (ch £1.30, concessions £2.00). Opening times and prices are subject to change, for further information please call 0870 333 1181 **Facilities:** 🅿 ♿ shop ✖ ♿

BURFORD   Map 03 SO56

BURFORD HOUSE GARDENS
WR15 8HQ
➲ (off A456, 1m W of Tenbury Wells, 8m from Ludlow)
☎ 01584 810777   `2 for 1`
e-mail: info@burford.co.uk
web: www.burford.co.uk

Burford House and Garden Centre set within 15 acres, incorporates a Georgian mansion, which houses a shop and riverside gardens housing the National Clematis Collection.

Times: Open all year 9-6 or dusk if earlier. **Fee:** ✱ £3.95 (ch £1). Party 20+ £3 each. **Facilities:** 🅿 💷 ✖ licensed 🍴 ♿ (ramp into gardens, sloping paths, wheelchairs available) toilets for disabled shop garden centre ✖ (ex guide dogs) ⬛

COSFORD   Map 07 SJ70

ROYAL AIR FORCE MUSEUM
TF11 8UP
➲ (on A41, 1m S of M54 junct 3)
☎ 01902 376200   `FREE`
e-mail: cosford@rafmuseum.org
web: www.rafmuseum.org

This is one of the largest aviation collections in the UK. Exhibits include the Victor and Vulcan bombers, the Hastings, York and British Airways airliners, the Belfast freighter and the last airworthy Britannia. The research and development collection includes the notable TSR2, Fairey Delta, Bristol 188 and many more important aircraft.

Times: ✱ Open all year daily, 10-6 (last admission 4). Closed 24-26 Dec & 1 Jan **Facilities:** 🅿 ✖ licensed 🍴 ♿ (free loan of 3 manual wheelchairs) toilets for disabled shop ✖ (ex guide dogs)

CRAVEN ARMS   Map 07 SO48

THE SHROPSHIRE HILLS DISCOVERY CENTRE
School Rd SY7 9RS
➲ (on A49, on S edge of Craven Arms) `2 for 1`
☎ 01588 676000
e-mail: zoe.griffin@shropshire-cc.gov.uk
web: www.shropshirehillsdiscoverycentre.co.uk

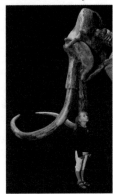

This attraction explores the history, nature and geography of the Shropshire Hills, through a series of interactive displays and simulations. These include Landscape of Contrasts, Ancient Landscape, a simulated Balloon Flight, and Land of Inspiration. The Centre has 23 acres of meadow lands sloping down to the River Onny for all visitors to explore. There is a network of cycle routes and walks and during the summer a shuttle bus service operates from the centre, at weekends, which allows visitors to explore the local landscape, hills, villages and market towns. The Centre also houses the Secret Hills Gallery which features changing displays of craft and artworks that celebrate Shropshire's creative industry. There is also a shop, restaurant and visitors information centre.

Times: Open all year, daily from 10. (Last admission 3.30 Nov-Mar, 4.30 Apr-Oct). **Fee:** £4.25 (ch £2.75 & pen £3.75, ch under 5 free). Family ticket £12.20. Groups 20+ £3.75 each, ch £2.50 each.
Facilities: 🅿 💷 ✖ licensed 🍴 ♿ (wheelchair available) toilets for disabled shop ✖ (ex guide dogs) ⬛

HAUGHMOND ABBEY   Map 07 SJ51

HAUGHMOND ABBEY
Upton Magna SY4 4RW
➲ (off B5062)
☎ 01743 709661

Absorb these extensive 12th-century Augustinian abbey ruins, and visit the small museum.

Times: Open 24 Mar-May, Sep,Thu-Mon, 10-5; Jun-Aug, daily, 10-6; **Fee:** £2.60 (ch £1.30, concessions £2.00). Opening times and prices are subject to change, for further details please call 0870 333 1181 **Facilities:** 🅿 ♿ (limited access for wheelchair users) shop ♿

HODNET
Map 07 SJ62

HODNET HALL GARDENS
TF9 3NN
➲ (M6 junct 12/15 or M54 junct 3. Hodnet is on the A442, Telford-Whitchurch road and A53 Shrewsbury-Market Drayton road).
☎ 01630 685786
e-mail: marlene@heber-percy.freeserve.co.uk
web: www.hodnethallgardens.co.uk
Over sixty acres of brilliantly coloured flowers, magnificent forest trees, sweeping lawns, and a chain of ornamental pools which run along the cultivated garden valley to provide a habitat for waterfowl and other wildlife. Big game trophies adorn the 17th-century tearooms, and plants are usually for sale in the kitchen gardens. The house, rebuilt in Victorian-Elizabethan style, is not open.
Times: Open Apr-Sep, Tue-Sun & BH Mon 12-5. Oct, Sun only 12-dusk
Fee: £4 (ch £2, pen £3.50). Party £3.50 **Facilities:** ▣ ✗ licensed ▦ ◕ (2 wheelchairs available) toilets for disabled shop garden centre

IRONBRIDGE
Map 07 SJ60

IRONBRIDGE GORGE MUSEUMS
Coach Rd TF8 7DQ
➲ (M54 junct 4, signed)
☎ 01952 884391 & 0800 590258
e-mail: tic@ironbridge.org.uk
web: www.ironbridge.org.uk
Ironbridge is the site of the world's first iron bridge. It was cast and built here in 1779, to span a narrow gorge over the River Severn. Now Ironbridge is the site of a remarkable series of museums relating the story of the bridge, recreating life in Victorian times and featuring ceramics and social history displays.
Times: Open all year, 10-5. Some small sites closed Nov-Mar. Telephone or write for exact winter details. **Fee:** ✱ £13.25 (ch £8.75, pen £11.50). Family £42. Passport to all sites, until all have been visited. It is therefore possible to return to Ironbridge on different days to ensure the whole atmosphere of the museums are captured.
Facilities: ▣ � ✗ licensed ◕ (wheelchairs, potters wheel, Braille guide, hearing loop) toilets for disabled shop ✈ (ex Blists Hill & guide dogs) ◢

LILLESHALL
Map 07 SJ71

LILLESHALL ABBEY
TF10 9HW
➲ (off A518 on unclass road)
☎ 0121 625 6820   FREE
In the beautiful grounds of Lilleshall Hall, ruined Lilleshall Abbey was founded shortly before the middle of the 12th century and from the high west front visitors can look down the entire 228ft length of the abbey church.
Times: Open 24 Mar-Sep, daily 10-5. Closed Oct-Mar ⌗

LUDLOW
Map 07 SO57

LUDLOW CASTLE
Castle Square SY8 1AY
➲ (A49 to town centre)
☎ 01584 873355
e-mail: hduce@ludlowcastle.plus.com
web: www.ludlowcastle.com
Ludlow Castle dates from about 1086. In 1473, Edward IV sent the Prince of Wales and his brother - later to become the Princes in the Tower - to live here, and Ludlow Castle became a seat of government. John Milton's *Comus* was first performed at Ludlow Castle in 1634; now contemporary performances of Shakespeare's plays, together with concerts, are put on in the castle grounds during the Ludlow Festival (end June-early July). Please telephone for details of events running throughout the year.
Times: Open all year, Jan Sat-Sun 10-4; Feb-Mar daily 10-4; Apr-Jul daily 10-5; Aug daily 10-7; Sep daily 10-5; Oct-Dec daily 10-4 (last admission 30 minutes before closing). Closed 25 Dec. **Fee:** £4 (ch under 6 free, ch £2, pen £3.50). Family ticket £11.
Facilities: ▣ (100yds) ▦ ◕ toilets for disabled shop ◢

MORETON CORBET
Map 07 SJ52

MORETON CORBET CASTLE   FREE
➲ (off B5063, in Moreton Corbet)
Inherited by the Corbets in 1235, who are thought to have remodelled the great keep, this castle may already have been standing for over 100 years. It was remodelled in the 16th century and then partially demolished to make way for a great Elizabethan mansion House. Although damaged in the civil war, the castle and mansion stand today as one of the most picturesque ruins of the Shropshire Marches.
Times: Open at any reasonable time **Facilities:** ▣ ◕ ⌗

MUCH WENLOCK
Map 07 SO69

MUCH WENLOCK PRIORY
TA3 6HS
☎ 01952 727466
Experience the ruins of this large Cluniac priory and the atmospheric remains of the 13th-century church and Norman chapter house. The audio tour offers a fascinating insight into its history. Impressive topiary figures guard the priory ruins.
Times: ✱ Open all year, Mar-May, Thu-Mon, 10-5; Jun-Aug, daily, 10-6; Sep-Oct, Thu-Mon, 10-5; Nov-Feb, Fri-Sun, 10-4. Closed 24-26 Dec & 1 Jan. **Facilities:** ▣ ⌗

OSWESTRY
Map 07 SJ22

OLD OSWESTRY HILL FORT
➲ (1m N of Oswestry, off an unclass road off A483)   FREE
An impressive Iron Age hill-fort of 68 acres, defended by a series of five ramparts, with an elaborate western entrance and unusual earthwork cisterns.
Times: Open at any reasonable time. **Facilities:** ⌗

We endeavour to be as accurate as possible, but changes to times and other information can occur after the guide has gone to press.

An asterisk * indicates that opening times and prices are for 2005. Please contact the attraction for up-to-date information.

QUATT Map 07 SO78
DUDMASTON
WV15 6QN

➲ (4m SE of Bridgnorth on A442)

☎ 01746 780866

2 for 1

e-mail: sue.pope@nationaltrust.org.uk

The 17th-century flower paintings which belonged to Francis Darby of Coalbrookdale are exhibited in this house of the same period, with modern works, botanical art and fine furniture. The house stands in an extensive parkland garden and there are dingle and lakeside walks. The 2-for-1 voucher is valid only during normal visiting hours and cannot be used for any ticketed events. **Times:** Open Apr-Sep, Tue, Wed & Sun & BH Mons, 2-5.30. Garden Mon-Wed noon-6. Closed Good Fri. **Fee:** ✻ House & Garden £4.75. Garden only £3.50. Family ticket £11. Parties 15+ £3.75 **Facilities:** 🅿 💷 📗 ♿ (Braille guides, taped tours) toilets for disabled shop ✖ (ex in grounds, & guide dogs) � ⬛

SHREWSBURY Map 07 SJ41
SHREWSBURY CASTLE AND SHROPSHIRE REGIMENTAL MUSEUM
The Castle, Castle St SY1 2AT

➲ (located in town centre, adjacent to railway station)

☎ 01743 358516

2 for 1

e-mail: shropsrm@zoom.co.uk
web: www.shrewsburymuseums.com

The museum of The King's Shropshire Light Infantry and The Shropshire Yeomanry is housed in the main surviving building of Shrewsbury Castle which once dominated the town. The grounds contain the medieval 'motte' and the romantic 'Laura's Tower'. Please telephone or visit website for details of events running throughout the year. **Times:** Open Tue-Sat 10-5, also Sun from 29 May-11 Sep & BH Mon. Closed Dec & Jan. Telephone for winter opening times. Castle grounds open Mon-Sat & Sun as above, 9-5 **Fee:** ✻ £2 (£1 concessions). All local residents, ch under 18 or in full time education free. **Facilities:** 🅿 (3 mins NCP) (metered on street parking) 📗 ♿ (please ask staff for assistance) toilets for disabled shop ✖ (ex guide dogs)

STOKESAY Map 07 SO48
STOKESAY CASTLE
SY7 9AH

➲ (1m S of Craven Arms off A49)

☎ 01588 672544

Most perfectly preserved 13th-century fortified manor house. See its superb timber-framed Jacobean gatehouse and stroll through the impressive great hall. Delightful cottage gardens. **Times:** Open all year, Mar-May, Thu-Mon, 10-5; Jun-Aug, daily, 10-6; Sep-Oct, Thu-Mon, 10-5; Nov-Feb, Fri-Sun, 10-4. Closed 24-26 Dec & 1 Jan. **Fee:** £4.60 (ch £2.30, concessions £3.50, family £11.50). Opening times and prices are subject to change, for further details please phone 0870 333 1811 **Facilities:** 🅿 ♿ (tape tour for visually handicapped, ramp for wheelchairs) toilets for disabled ✖

TELFORD Map 07 SJ60
HOO FARM ANIMAL KINGDOM
Preston-on-the-Weald Moors TF6 6DJ

➲ (M54 junct 6, follow brown tourist signs)

☎ 01952 677917

2 for 1

e-mail: info@hoofarm.com
web: www.hoofarm.com

Hoo Farm is a real children's paradise where there is always something happening. A clean, friendly farm that appeals to

continued

all ages and offers close contact with a wide variety of animals from fluffy yellow chicks and baby lambs to foxes, llamas, deer and ostriches. A daily programme of events encourages audience participation in the form of bottle feeding lambs, pig feeding and collecting the freshly laid eggs. New for this year is ferret racing! The Craft Area offers the chance to try your hand at candle dipping, glass or pottery painting or even throwing a pot on the potters wheel. There are Junior Quad Bikes and a Rifle Range, Pony Rides, powered mini tractors as well as indoor and outdoor play areas and a new games room. Please telephone for details of special events running throughout the year. **Times:** Open 19 Mar-9 Sep, daily 10-6 (last admission 5). 11 Sep-25 Nov, Tue-Sun 10-5 (last admission 4. Closed Mon ex Halloween). 26 Nov-24 Dec daily 10-5 (closes at 1pm 24 Dec). Closed 25 Dec-mid Mar. **Fee:** ✻ £4.95 (ch £4.25 & pen £4.50). Family ticket (2ad+3ch) £20. **Facilities:** 🅿 💷 📗 ♿ toilets for disabled shop ✖ (ex guide dogs) ⬛

WESTON-UNDER-REDCASTLE Map 07 SJ52
HAWKSTONE HISTORIC PARK & FOLLIES
SY4 5UY

➲ (3m from Hodnet off A53, follow brown heritage signs)

☎ 01939 200611

e-mail: info@hawkstone.co.uk
web: www.hawkstone.co.uk

Created in the 18th century by the Hill family, Hawkstone was once one of the greatest historic parklands in history. After almost one hundred years of neglect it has now been restored and designated a Grade 1 historic park. Visitors can once again experience the magical world of intricate pathways, arches and bridges, towering cliffs and follies, and an awesome grotto. The Grand Valley and woodlands have centuries-old oaks, wild rhododendrons and lofty monkey puzzles. The park covers nearly 100 acres of hilly terrain and visitors are advised to wear sensible shoes and clothing and to bring a torch. Allow 3-4 hours for the tour, which is well signposted and a route map is provided in the admission price. Attractions include 'Hear King Arthur' and meeting the Duke of Wellington in the White Tower to discuss the Battle of Waterloo. **Times:** ✻ Open from 10, Jan-Mar, Sat & Sun; Apr-May, & Sep-Oct, Wed-Sun; Jun-Aug, daily. Closed Nov & Dec. **Facilities:** 🅿 💷 ✖ licensed ♿ (no access to follies due to terrain access Valley only) toilets for disabled shop ⬛

WROXETER Map 07 SJ50
WROXETER ROMAN CITY
SY5 6PH

➲ (5m E of Shrewsbury, 1m S of A5)

☎ 01743 761330

Discover what urban life was like 2,000 years ago in the forth largest city in Roman Britain. See the remains of the impressive 2nd-century municipal baths and view the excavated treasures in the museum. **Times:** Open all year, Mar-May, daily, 10-5; Jun-Aug, daily, 10-6; Sep-Oct, daily, 10-5; Nov-Feb, daily, 10-4. Closed 24-26 Dec & 1 Jan. **Fee:** £4 (ch £2, concessions £3, family £10). Opening times and prices are subject to change, for further details please call 0870 333 1181 **Facilities:** 🅿 ♿ shop ♯

SOMERSET

EVENTS & FESTIVALS

February
4th-12th Bath Literature Festival (provisional)

March
tbc Bath Shakespeare Festival,
Theatre Royal, Bath

April
29th-1st May Bath Annual Spring Flower
Show, Royal Victoria Park

May
19th-4th Jun Bath International Music
Festival, various venues
26th-11th June Bath Fringe Festival,
various venues
31st-3rd Jun The Royal Bath & West Show,
Royal Bath & West Showground, Shepton
Mallet

July
7th-9th Priddy Folk Festival, Priddy, in the
Mendip Hills
tbc the Cheddar Challenge
Mountain Bike Racing
tbc Somerset Steam Spectacular,
Low Ham, nr Langport

August
2nd-3rd Taunton Flower Show, Vivary Park,
Taunton
tbc Glastonbury Children's Festival

September
2nd-3rd The Gorge Outdoor Festival, activities
in Cheddar and the Mendip Hills

Above: Pultney Bridge over the River Avon, Bath

AXBRIDGE   Map 03 ST45
KING JOHN'S HUNTING LODGE
The Square BS26 2AP
➲ (on corner of Axbridge High St, in the Square)
☎ 01934 732012
web: www.nationaltrust.org.uk
Nothing to do with King John or with hunting, this jettied and
timber-framed house was built around 1500. It gives a good
indication of the wealth of the merchants of that time and is
now a museum of local history, with old photographs,
paintings and items such as the town stocks and constables'
staves.
Times: Open Apr-Sep, daily 1-4. **Fee:** ✱ Donations welcome
Facilities: ᵬ shop ✖ ♨

BARRINGTON   Map 03 ST31
BARRINGTON COURT GARDEN
TA19 0NQ
➲ (5m NE of Ilminster on B3168)
☎ 01460 241938 & 242614
web: www.nationaltrust.org.uk
The house is a Tudor Manor, the interior of which is now let
out to Stuart Interiors as showrooms with antique furniture
for sale. The gardens were created in the 1920s, with the
help (through the post) of Gertrude Jekyll. They are laid out
in 'rooms' and there is a large walled kitchen garden
supplying fresh fruit and vegetables to the restaurant.
Times: Open Mar, Thu-Sun 11-4.30; Apr-Sep daily (ex Wed) 11-5.30;
Oct Thu-Sun 11-4.30. **Fee:** ✱ £6 (ch £3). Family £14.50. Groups £5.10
Facilities: 🅿 🍽 ✖ licensed ᵬ (batricars available, Braille guides,
wheelchairs) toilets for disabled shop garden centre ✖ (except guide
dogs) ♨

BATH   Map 03 ST76
AMERICAN MUSEUM
Claverton Manor BA2 7BD
➲ (2.5m SE)
☎ 01225 460503
e-mail: info@americanmuseum.org
web: www.americanmuseum.org
Claverton Manor is just two miles south east of Bath, in a
beautiful setting above the River Avon. The house was built
in 1820 by Sir Jeffrey Wyatville, and is now a museum of
American decorative arts. The gardens are well worth
seeing, and include an American arboretum and a replica of
George Washington's garden at Mount Vernon. The Folk Art
Gallery and the New Gallery are among the many exhibits in
the grounds along with seasonal exhibitions.
Times: Open mid Mar-Oct, Tue-Sun 2-5. Gardens 12-6. Open Mon in
Aug & BHs. **Fee:** ✱ £6.50 (ch £3.50, con £6). **Facilities:** 🅿 🍽 🗐
ᵬ toilets for disabled shop ◼

BATH ABBEY
Abbey Churchyard BA1 1LT
➲ (centre of Bath, next to Pump Rooms & The
Roman Baths)
☎ 01225 422462 & 446300
e-mail: office@bathabbey.org
web: www.bathabbey.org
The 15th-century abbey church was built on the site of the
Saxon abbey where King Edgar was crowned in 973. The
church is Perpendicular style with Norman arches and
superb fan-vaulting. The famous West Front carvings

continued

represent the founder-bishop's dream of angels ascending and descending from heaven.
Times: Open all year, Etr-Oct, Mon-Sat 9-6; Nov-Etr 9-4.30. Sun all year 1-2.30 & 4.30-5.30 (Etr-Oct only). **Fee:** Visitors invited to donate £2.50 each. **Facilities:** P (5 mins) (limited street parking) ⌗ & (level access, induction loop, large print leaflet) toilets for disabled shop ✖ (ex guide & hearing dogs)

BATH POSTAL MUSEUM
8 Broad St BA1 5LJ
➲ (M4 junct 18. Follow A46 to Bath, on entering city fork left at mini rdbt. After all traffic lights into Walcot St. Podium car park facing)
☎ 01225 460333
e-mail: info@bathpostalmuseum.org
web: www.bathpostalmuseum.org

Discover how 18th-century Bath influenced and developed the Postal System, including the story of the Penny Post. The first letter sent with a stamp was sent from this very building. Visitors can explore the history of written communication from Egyptian clay tablets, thousands of years ago, to the first Airmail flight from Bath to London in 1912. See the Victorian Post Office and watch three continuous video films including the in-house production entitled 'History of Writing'. Visit the children's activity room, tearoom and shop.
Times: Open all year, Mon-Sat 11-4.30. (Last admission Mar-Oct 4.30, Oct-Mar 4). Closed Sun, 25-26 Dec & 1 Jan. **Fee:** ✱ £2.90 (ch under 5 free, ch £1.50, students £1.90 & pen £2.60). Family and Party 10+ tickets available. **Facilities:** P (150yds) (no on street parking) ▆ & (films and computer games for hearing impaired) toilets for disabled shop ✖ (ex guide dogs)

THE BUILDING OF BATH MUSEUM
Countess of Huntingdons Chapel, The Vineyards, The Paragon BA1 5NA
➲ (M4 junct 18, follow A46 towards Bath city centre. Take A4, 2nd exit at mini rdbt. Along road on right)
☎ 01225 333895
e-mail: enquiries@bathmuseum.co.uk
web: www.bath-preservation-trust.org.uk

2 for 1

This new museum relates the fascinating story of how Georgian Bath was created. 17th-century Bath was a medieval market town but in the space of 100 years it was transformed into one of the most beautiful and glamorous cities in Europe. The exhibition depicts elegant society life in "Beau" Nash's spa resort and explains how the houses were

constructed. After a visit, the street scene outside seems like an extension of the exhibition. Ring for details of special events such as concerts and lectures.
Times: Open 15 Feb-Nov, Tue-Sun & BHs 10.30-5. **Fee:** £4 (ch £1.50, concessions £3). Family ticket £10. Party 10+ **Facilities:** P (500mtrs) ⌗ & shop ✖ (ex guide dogs) ▆

HOLBURNE MUSEUM OF ART
Great Pulteney St BA2 4DB
➲ (M4 junct 18 to A4 and follow brown signs)
☎ 01225 466669
e-mail: holburne@bath.ac.uk
web: www.bath.ac.uk/holburne

2 for 1

This jewel in Bath's crown was once the Georgian Sydney Hotel, whose glittering society Jane Austen watched from her house opposite. It displays the treasures collected by Sir William Holbourne: superb English and continental silver, porcelain, maiolica, glass and Renaissance bronzes. Since Sir William's time the collection has been greatly expanded and now includes landscapes by Guardi and Turner, and portraits by Stubbs, Ramsay, Raeburn, Zoffany and Bath's own artists Gainsborough, Hoare, and the Barkers of Bath.
Times: Open mid Feb-mid Dec, Tue-Sat 10-5, Sun 11-5. (Closed Mon ex group bookings by appointment). **Fee:** ✱ £4 (ch £1.50, pen £3.50, concessions available). Group rates available. **Facilities:** P ▆ ⌗ & (lift to 1st floor) shop ✖ (ex guide dogs) ▆

THE JANE AUSTEN CENTRE
40 Gay St, Queen Square BA1 2NT
➲ (in heart of Bath by Queen Square)
☎ 01225 443000
e-mail: info@janeausten.co.uk
web: www.janeausten.co.uk

2 for 1

Celebrating Bath's most famous resident, the centre offers a snapshot of life during Regency times and explores how living in this city affected Jane Austen's life and writing. Every September, Bath holds a Jane Austen festival.
Times: Open all year, daily 10-5.30. Closed 24-25 Dec & 1 Jan.
Fee: £4.95 (ch £2.50, concessions £4.15) **Facilities:** P (50mtrs) ▆ ✖ ⌗ & shop ✖ (ex guide dogs) ▆

continued

MUSEUM OF BATH AT WORK

Julian Rd BA1 2RH

➲ (from city centre, off Lansdown Rd into Julian Rd. Museum next to church on right)

☎ 01225 318348

2 for 1

e-mail: mobaw@hotmail.com

web: www.bath-at-work.org.uk

Two thousand years of Bath's commercial and industrial development are explored with exhibits on 'The Story of Bath Stone', a Bath cabinet makers workshop, a 1914 Horstmann car and a reconstruction of J B Bowllers' engineering and mineral water business. A computer info point is available.

Times: Open all year, Etr-1 Nov, daily 10.30-5; Nov-Etr, wknds 10.30-5. Closed 25-26 Dec. **Fee:** £4 (concessions £3). Family ticket £10. **Facilities:** P (0.25m) 🅿 🎞 ♿ (audio guides, ramps) shop ✖ (ex guide dogs)

MUSEUM OF COSTUME

Bennett St BA1 2QH

➲ (M4 junct 18, follow A46 into Bath. Museum near city centre)

☎ 01225 477785

e-mail: costume_bookings@bathnes.gov.uk

web: www.museumofcostume.co.uk

The Museum of Costume is one of the finest collections of fashionable dress in the world, covering the period from the late 16th-century to the present day. It is housed in Bath's famous 18th-century Assembly Rooms designed by John Wood the Younger in 1771. Entrance to the Assembly Rooms is free.

Times: Open all year, daily Jan-Feb 11-4; Mar-Oct 11-5; 11-4. Closed 25&26 Dec. **Fee:** ✱ £6.25 (ch £4.25). Family ticket £17. Combined ticket with Roman Baths, £12.50 (ch £7.30). **Facilities:** P (5 mins walk) (park & ride recommended) 🅿 🎞 ♿ (audio guides available) toilets for disabled shop ✖ (ex guide dogs) 🍴

NO 1 ROYAL CRESCENT

BA1 2LR

➲ (1st house in Royal Crescent situated above Victoria Ave & Victoria Park, Charlotte St car park)

☎ 01225 428126

e-mail: no1musuem@bptrust.org.uk

web: www.bath-preservation-trust.org.uk

Bath is very much a Georgian city, but most of its houses have naturally altered over the years to suit changing tastes and lifestyles. Built in 1768 by John Wood the Elder, No 1

continued

Royal Crescent has been restored to look as it would have done some 200 years ago. Visitors can see a grand townhouse of the late 18th-century with authentic furniture, paintings and carpets. On the ground floor are the study and dining room and on the first floor a lady's bedroom and drawing room. In the basement a period kitchen and museum shop.

Times: Open 12 Feb-29 Oct, 10.30-5; 30 Oct-27 Nov, 10.30-4. Open BH Mon. Open wknds 3-4, 10-11 Dec. Closed Good Fri. (Last admission 30 mins before closing). **Fee:** ✱ £4 (concessions £3.50). Family ticket £12. Party 10+ £3 each. Schools £2.50 each **Facilities:** P (5 mins walk) (street parking with card £1 per hour) 🎞 (virtual tour, induction loop, Braille guide) shop ✖ (ex guide dogs)

PRIOR PARK LANDSCAPE GARDEN

Ralph Allen Dr BA2 6BD

➲ (in city centre)

☎ 01225 833422 & 0900 133 5242

e-mail: priorpark@nationaltrust.org.uk

web: www.nationaltrust.org.uk

Created by local entrepreneur Ralph Allen with advice from Alexander Pope and 'Capability' Brown, this garden is set in a sweeping valley with magnificent views of the city of Bath. Many interesting features include a Palladian Bridge (250 years old in 2005), three lakes, and lovely wooded glades.

Times: Open Feb-29 Nov, Wed-Mon 11-5.30; 3 Dec-Jan, Fri-Sun 11-dusk. (BHs 11-5.30) **Fee:** ✱ £4 (ch £2). Family (2ad+2ch) £10. **Facilities:** P (park & ride) ♿ (Braille, large print guides, designated parking) toilets for disabled

ROMAN BATHS & PUMP ROOM

Abbey Church Yard BA1 1LZ

➲ (M4 junct 18, A46 into city centre)

☎ 01225 477785

e-mail: romanbaths_bookings@bathnes.gov.uk

web: www.romanbaths.co.uk

The remains of the Roman baths and temple give a vivid impression of life nearly 2000 years ago. Built next to Britain's only hot spring, the baths served the sick, and the pilgrims visiting the adjacent Temple of Sulis Minerva. Above the Temple Courtyard, the Pump Room became a popular meeting place in the 18th century. The site still flows with natural hot water and no visit is complete without a taste of the famous hot spa water.

Times: Open all year, Mar-Jun & Sep-Oct, daily 9-5; Jul & Aug daily 9am-10pm; Jan-Feb & Nov-Dec, daily 9.30-4.30. Closed 25-26 Dec. (Last exit 1hr after closing). **Fee:** ✱ £9.50 (ch £5.30). Family ticket £25. Combined ticket with Museum of Costume £12.50 (ch £7.30).

continued

Disabled visitors free admission to ground floor areas.
Facilities: P (5 mins walk) (park & ride recommended) ✕ licensed
📖 ♿ (sign language & audio tours) toilets for disabled shop
✕ (ex guide dogs) ▰

SALLY LUNN'S REFRESHMENT HOUSE & MUSEUM
4 North Pde Passage BA1 1NX
➲ (centre of Bath, follow signs, next to Bath Abbey)
☎ 01225 461634   `2 for 1`
e-mail: enquiries@sallylunns.co.uk
web: www.sallylunns.co.uk
This Tudor building is Bath's oldest house and was a popular
17th-century meeting place. The traditional 'Sally Lunn' is
similar to a brioche, and it is popularly believed to carry the
name of its first maker who came to Bath in 1680. The bun
is still served in the restaurant, and the original oven,
Georgian cooking range and a collection of baking utensils
are displayed in the museum.
Times: Open all year, Museum - Mon-Fri 10-6, Sat 10-5, Sun 11-5.
Closed 25-26 Dec & 1 Jan. **Fee:** 30p (concessions free).
Facilities: P (2-3 min walk) (cards required for street parking) 📱
✕ licensed 📖 ♿ (Braille menu available) shop

CASTLE CARY   Map 03 ST63
HADSPEN GARDEN & NURSERY
Hadspen House BA7 7NG
➲ (2m SE off A371)
☎ 01749 813707
e-mail: pope@hadspengarden.co.uk
web: www.hadspengarden.co.uk
Situated within a 17th-century curved wall, this five acre
garden has borders planted with roses and herbaceous
plants, many of which have been developed here. Plants
grown in the garden are available in the adjoining nursery.
Times: ✱ Open 4 Mar-26 Sep, Thu-Sun & BHs 10-5.
Facilities: P ✕ 📖 ♿ garden centre ✕ (ex guide dogs) ▰

CHARD   Map 03 ST30
FORDE ABBEY
TA20 4LU
➲ (5m SE of Chard, signed from A30 and A358)
☎ 01460 221290   `2 for 1`
e-mail: forde.abbey@virgin.net
web: www.fordeabbey.co.uk
As one of the top gardens in England, Forde Abbey has
much to offer keen gardeners. The 30 acres include a
colourful bog garden, a walled kitchen garden, cascades,
ponds, Ionic temple, rockery, herbaceous borders and much
more. The privately owned magnificent 12th-century house
contains outstanding Mortlake tapestries, spectacularly
decorated plaster ceilings and fine furniture and paintings.
Times: Gardens, open all year, daily 10-4.30. House Apr-Oct, Tue-Fri,
Sun & BH 12-4. **Fee:** ✱ Gardens £5.50 (under 15's free, pen £5).
House & Gardens £7.50 (ch free, pen £7). **Facilities:** P 📱
✕ licensed 📖 ♿ (large print guide, wheelchair & batricar) toilets for
disabled shop garden centre ▰

CLEVEDON   Map 03 ST47
CLEVEDON COURT
Tickenham Rd BS21 6QU
➲ (off B3130 1.5m E of Clevedon)
☎ 01275 872257
web: www.nationaltrust.org.uk
Clevedon Court is a remarkably complete manor house of
around 1320. Additions have been made in each century, so
it has a pleasing variety of styles, with an 18th-century,
terraced garden.
Times: Open 27 Mar-29 Sep, Wed-Thu, Sun & BH Mon 2-5. Car park &
Gardens will open at 1pm. **Fee:** ✱ £5 (ch £2.50). Party 20+ by
arrangement. **Facilities:** P ♿ (access via steps, Braille/large print
guide) ✕ 🐾

CRICKET ST THOMAS   Map 03 ST30
THE WILDLIFE PARK AT CRICKET ST THOMAS
TA20 4DB
➲ (3m E of Chard on A30, follow brown heritage
signs. Clearly signed from M5 junct 25)
☎ 01460 30111
e-mail: wildlifepark.cst@bourne-leisure.co.uk
web: www.wild.org.uk
The Wildlife Park offers you the chance to see more than 60
species of animals at close quarters. Visitors can learn about
what is being done to save endangered species, take a walk
through the Lemur Wood, ride on the Safari Train or visit the
Children's Farm. During peak season, park mascot Larry the
Lemur stars in his own show.
Times: Open all year, daily 10-6 last admission 4, (10-4.30, last
admission 3 in winter). Closed 25 Dec. **Fee:** £7.95 (ch 3-14 £5.95,
under 3's free, pen £6.95). Family ticket £26 (2ad+2ch).
Facilities: P 📱 ✕ licensed ♿ (some steep slopes) toilets for
disabled shop ✕ (ex guide dogs) ▰

DUNSTER   Map 03 SS94
DUNSTER CASTLE
TA24 6SL
➲ (3m SE of Minehead, approach from A39.
Approx 2m from Dunster Stn)
☎ 01643 821314 & 823004
e-mail: dunstercastle@nationaltrust.org.uk
web: www.nationaltrust.org.uk
The castle's picturesque appearance is largely due to 19th-
century work, but older features can also be seen, the superb
17th-century oak staircase for example. Sub-tropical plants
flourish in the 28-acre park and the terraced gardens are
noted for exotica such as a giant lemon tree, yuccas, mimosa
and palms as well as the National Collection of Strawberry
Trees.
Times: Castle: 20 Mar-23 Oct, Sat-Wed 11-5; 24-31Oct, Sat-Wed 11-4.
Garden & Park: Jan-19 Mar & 24 Oct-Dec, all week 11-4, 20 Mar-23 Oct,
all week, 10-5. **Fee:** ✱ Castle, Garden & Park £7.20 (ch under 16
£3.60). Family ticket £17.80. Garden & Park only £3.90 (ch under 16
£1.70). Family ticket £9.50. **Facilities:** P ♿ (Braille & audio guides,
large print guides & Batricar) toilets for disabled shop ✕ (ex in park
only) 🐾

EAST LAMBROOK   Map 03 ST41

EAST LAMBROOK MANOR GARDEN

TA13 5HH

➲ (signed off A303, at South Petherton rdbt)

☎ 01460 240328

e-mail: enquiries@eastlambrook.com

web: www.eastlambrook.com

It was the late Margery Fish who created the concept of 'cottage gardening' in the 1940s. Her wonderful Grade I listed gardens are known to garden lovers throughout the world. The gardens now house the National Collection of Geraniums, a specialist plant nursery, a tea shop and art gallery.

Times: Open Feb-Oct, daily 10-5. **Fee:** ✱ £3.95 (ch £1 & pen £3.50). Group rate available. **Facilities:** 🅿 💻 🗐 ♿ (gardens partly accessible) shop garden centre ✘ (ex guide dogs) 🍽

FARLEIGH HUNGERFORD   Map 03 ST85

FARLEIGH HUNGERFORD CASTLE

BA2 7RS

➲ (3.5m W of Trowbridge on A366)

☎ 01225 754026

Set in a picturesque valley, this castle hides many secrets and a sinister past. An audio tour reveals all.

Times: Open all year, 24 Mar-Jun & Sep, daily 10-5; Jul-Aug, daily 10-6; Oct-Mar, Sat-Sun 10-4. Closed 24-26 Dec & 1 Jan. **Fee:** £3.30 (ch £1.70, concessions £2.50). Opening times and prices are subject to change, for further details please phone 0870 333 1181

Facilities: 🅿 ♿ shop ✘ 🏕

GLASTONBURY   Map 03 ST43

GLASTONBURY ABBEY

Abbey Gatehouse, Magdalene St BA6 9EL

➲ (on A361 between Frome & Taunton. M5 junct 23 then A39 to Glastonbury)

☎ 01458 832267

e-mail: info@glastonburyabbey.com

web: glastonburyabbey.com

Few places in Britain are as rich in myth and legend as Glastonbury. Tradition maintains that the impressive ruins mark the birth place of Christianity in Britain. Joseph of Arimathea is said to have founded a chapel here in AD61, planting his staff in the ground where it flowered both at Christmas and Easter. Later, it is said, King Arthur and Guinevere were buried here, and the abbey has been a place of pilgrimage since the Middle Ages. The present abbey ruins date mostly from the 12th and 13th centuries, fell into decay

continued

after the Dissolution. The display area contains artefacts and a model of the Abbey as it might have been in 1539. During the summer months meet a character from the past, who will tell you something of this wonderful place. Thirty-six acres of grounds including two ponds, an orchard and wildlife areas.

Times: Open all year, daily, Jun-Aug 9-6; Sep-May 9.30-6 or dusk, whichever is the earliest. Dec-Feb open at 10. Closed 25 Dec. **Fee:** ✱ £4 (ch 5-15 £1.50, pen & students £3.50). Family ticket £10 (2ad+2ch) **Facilities:** 🅿 (charged) 💻 ♿ (audio tape,deaf loop,wheelchairs,lge print leaflet) toilets for disabled shop ✘ (ex on leads) 🍽

KINGSDON   Map 03 ST52

LYTES CARY MANOR

TA11 7HU

➲ (off A303, signed from Padimore rdbt at junct of A303 & A37, take A372)

☎ 01458 224471

e-mail: lytescarymanor@nationaltrust.org.uk

web: www.nationaltrust.org.uk

Fine medieval manor house and delightful 14th-century chapel, surrounded by gardens with an enchanting mixture of formality and simplicity. Much of the present house was built in the 16th century although the oldest part, the chapel, dates from 1343. The Great Hall was a 15th-century addition. Unfortunately the gardens did not survive, but the present formal gardens are being restocked with plants that were commonly grown at the time of building, according to the 'Lytes Cary Herbal'-a manuscript still on display within the property. High yew topiary hedges enclose large borders and hidden paths.

Times: Open end Mar-Oct, Mon, Wed & Fri-Sun 11-5. **Fee:** ✱ £5 (ch £2). Garden only £3, ch £1. **Facilities:** 🅿 ♿ (Braille guide, scented plants) toilets for disabled ✘ (ex guide dogs) 🐾

MONTACUTE   Map 03 ST41

MONTACUTE HOUSE

TA15 6XP

➲ (off A3088)

☎ 01935 823289

e-mail: montacute@nationaltrust.org.uk

web: www.nationaltrust.org.uk

Set amidst formal gardens, Montacute House was built by Sir Edward Phelips. He was a successful lawyer, and became Speaker of the House of Commons in 1604. Inside there are decorated ceilings, ornate fireplaces, heraldic glass and fine wood panelling. The Long Gallery displays a permanent collection of Tudor and Jacobean portraits from the National Portrait Gallery in London. Montacute has been used as the setting for successful films such as *Sense and Sensibility*.

Times: House: 19 Mar-Oct, Wed-Mon, 11-5. Garden: Jan-18 Mar & 3 Nov-Dec, Wed-Sun, 11-4, 19 Mar-Oct, Wed-Mon, 11-6. Shop: 3-18 Mar & 3 Nov-19 Dec, Wed-Sun, 11-4, 19 Mar-Oct, Wed-Mon, 11-5.30. Restaurant: 5-14 Mar & 5 Nov-19 Dec, Fri-Sun, 11-4, 19 Mar-Oct, Wed-Sun, 11-5.30. **Fee:** ✱ House, Garden & Park £7.40 (ch £3.70). Family ticket £17. Garden & Park only £3.90 (ch £1.80), 3 Nov-Mar 2006, £2 (ch £1). **Facilities:** 🅿 💻 ✘ licensed ♿ (Braille guide, 3 manual wheelchairs) toilets for disabled shop garden centre ✘ (ex in park) 🐾

MUCHELNEY   Map 03 ST42

MUCHELNEY ABBEY
TA10 0DQ
☎ 01458 250664
The monastery was first established at Muchelney by Ine, a 7th-century king of Wessex. It did not survive the Viking invasions, but the abbey was re-founded about AD950 and lasted for nearly six centuries. The present remains date largely from the 12th-century. The best preserved feature of the site today is the Abbot's lodging, which had only just been completed in 1539 when the abbey was surrendered to Henry VIII.
Times: Open 24 Mar-Jun & Sep, daily 10-5; Jul-Aug, daily 10-6; Oct, daily 10-4. **Fee:** £3.00 (ch £1.50, concessions £2.30). Opening times and prices are subject to change, for further details please phone 0870 333 1181 **Facilities:** 🅿 � shop ✈ ⚑

NETHER STOWEY   Map 03 ST13

COLERIDGE COTTAGE
35 Lime St TA5 1NQ
➲ (at W end of Nether Stowey, on S side of A39, 8m W of Bridgwater)
☎ 01278 732662
web: www.nationaltrust.org.uk
It was in this small cottage that Coleridge was most inspired as a poet and here that he wrote *The Rime of the Ancient Mariner*, part of *Christabel*, *Frost at Midnight* and "Kubla Khan". The Coleridge family moved to Nether Stowey in 1797 and became friendly with the Wordsworths who lived nearby.
Times: Open Apr-Sep, Thu-Sun & BHs 2-5. **Fee:** ✱ £3.20 (ch £1.60). **Facilities:** 🅿 (500yds) (steps to entrance, Braille & large print guides) ✈ ⚘

NUNNEY   Map 03 ST74

NUNNEY CASTLE
➲ (3.5m SW of Frome, off A361)   `FREE`
Built in 1373, and supposedly modelled on France's Bastille, this crenellated manor house has one of the deepest moats in England. It was ruined by Parliamentarian forces in the Civil War.
Times: Open at any reasonable time. **Facilities:** ⅗ ⚑

SPARKFORD   Map 03 ST62

HAYNES INTERNATIONAL MOTOR MUSEUM
BA22 7LH
➲ (from A303 follow A359 towards Castle Cary, museum clearly signed)
☎ 01963 440804
e-mail: info@haynesmotormuseum.co.uk
web: www.haynesmotormuseum.co.uk
Spectacular collection of historic cars, motorcycles and motoring memorabilia. Vehicles range from a 1903 Oldsmobile to sports cars of the 50s and 60s and modern day classics. Also at the Museum is a 70 seat video cinema, the Hall of Motorsports, a millennium hall and a picnic area and children's adventure playground. New for 2006 is a Conference, Functions and Events Centre seating up to 450 people.
Times: Open all year, Mar-Oct, daily 9.30-5.30; Nov-Feb, 10-4.30. Closed 24-26 Dec & 1 Jan. **Fee:** £6.95 (ch £3.75, concessions £5.50). Family £8.95 (1ad+1ch), £21 (2ad+3ch). **Facilities:** 🅿 ✗ licensed 🍴 ⅗ (ramps & loan wheelchairs available) toilets for disabled shop ✈ (ex guide dogs & in grounds) 🚐

The SHOE MUSEUM
Street, Somerset

opening hours
Monday - Friday
10:00am - 4:45pm

Saturday
10:00am - 5:00pm

Sunday
11:00am - 5:00pm

parties welcome-
please book in advance

Tel: 01458 842169

ADMISSION FREE

Clarks

STOKE ST GREGORY   Map 03 ST32

WILLOW & WETLANDS VISITOR CENTRE
Meare Green Court TA3 6HY
➲ (between North Curry & Stoke St Gregory, signed from A361 & A378)
☎ 01823 490249   `2 for 1`
e-mail: info@englishwillowbaskets.co.uk
web: www.englishwillowbaskets.co.uk
The centre is owned and run by Somerset Basketmakers and willow growers P H Coate & Son. The environmental exhibition gives a fascinating insight into the Somerset Levels and Moors. Guided tours of the yard and workshops are available.
Times: Open all year, Mon-Fri 9-5 (guided tours 10-4), Sat (no tours) 9-5. Closed Sun. **Fee:** ✱ Admission free, tour charge: £3.50 (ch £1.75, pen £3). Family ticket £8. Credit cards accepted if total admission price exceeds £10. **Facilities:** 🅿 🖳 🍴 ⅗ (some areas of gardens accessible) toilets for disabled shop 🚐

STOKE-SUB-HAMDON   Map 03 ST41

STOKE-SUB-HAMDON PRIORY
North St TA4 6QP
➲ (between A303 & A3088)
☎ 01985 843600   `FREE`
web: www.nationaltrust.org.uk
A complex of buildings, begun in the 14th century for the priests of the Chantry Chapel of St Nicholas (now destroyed).
Times: Open 27 Mar-Oct, daily 10-6 or dusk if earlier.
Facilities: 🅿 (Braille guides/large print guides) 🚐 (on road parking only) ⚘

STREET Map 03 ST43

The Shoe Museum

C & J Clark Ltd, High St BA16 0YA

➲ (M5 junct 23, A39 to Street, follow signs for Clarks Village)

FREE

☎ 01458 842169

The museum is in the oldest part of the shoe factory set up by Cyrus and James Clark in 1825. It contains shoes from Roman times to the present, buckles, engravings, fashion plates, machinery, hand tools and advertising material.

Times: Open all year, Mon-Fri 10-4.45, Sat 10-1.30 & 2-5, Sun 11-1.30 & 2-5. Closed 10 days over Xmas. **Facilities:** P ♿ (access wkdays only) shop (ex guide dogs)

See advertisement on page 203

TAUNTON Map 03 ST22

Hestercombe Gardens

Cheddon Fitzpaine TA2 8LG

➲ (3m N of Taunton near Cheddon Fitzpaine. Signed from all main roads)

☎ 01823 413923

e-mail: info@hestercombegardens.com

web: www.hestercombegardens.com

There are three period gardens to enjoy at Hestercombe: the 40-acre Georgian pleasure grounds with woodland walks, temples, Witch House and Great Cascade; the Victorian terrace and newly established Victorian shrubbery; and the Edwardian gardens, where the work of Gertrude Jekyll and architect Edwin Lutyens are shown off to full effect.

Times: Open daily, 10-6 (last admission 5). Closed 25 Dec.

Fee: * £5.75 (incl 2 ch, additional ch £2.50, pen £5.25)

Facilities: P ✕ licensed ♿ (gardens partially accessible) toilets for disabled shop garden centre (open Apr-Oct) (ex on lead)

TINTINHULL Map 03 ST41

Tintinhull House Garden

Farm St BA22 8PZ

➲ (0.5m S off A303. Follow signs to Tintinhull village, garden is well signed)

☎ 01935 822545

e-mail: tintinhull@nationaltrust.org.uk

web: www.nationaltrust.org.uk

An attractive, mainly 17th-century farmhouse with a Queen Anne façade, it stands in two acres of beautiful formal gardens. The gardens were largely created by Mrs Reiss, who gave the property to the National Trust in 1953.

Times: Open 24 Mar-Sep, Wed-Sun & BH Mons 11-5. Tea room: as garden, 11-4.30 **Fee:** * £4.50 (ch £2.20). **Facilities:** P (ex guide dogs)

WASHFORD Map 03 ST04

Cleeve Abbey

TA23 0PS

➲ (0.25m S of A39)

☎ 01984 640377

This 13th-century monastic site features some of the finest cloister buildings in England; medieval wall paintings, a mosaic tiled floor and an interesting exhibition.

Times: Open 24 Mar-Jun & Sep, daily 10-5; Jul-Aug, daily 10-6; Oct, daily 10-4. Closed Nov-Mar **Fee:** £3.30 (ch £1.70, concessions £2.50). Prices & opening times are subject to change for further details please phone 0870 333 1181 **Facilities:** P ♿ shop #

Tropiquaria Animal and Adventure Park

TA23 0QB

➲ (on A39, between Williton and Minehead)

☎ 01984 640688

2 for 1

e-mail: office@tropiquaria.co.uk

web: www.tropiquaria.co.uk

Housed in a 1930s BBC transmitting station, the main hall has been converted into an indoor jungle with a 15-foot waterfall, tropical plants and free-flying birds. (Snakes, lizards, iguanas, spiders, toads and terrapins are caged!) Downstairs is the submarine crypt with local and tropical marine life. Other features include landscaped gardens, the Shadowstring Puppet Theatre, and 'Wireless in the West' museum. Also two new full size pirate adventure ships are moored on the front lawn accessible to pirates of all ages! The park has an indoor playcastle for adventure and fun whatever the weather.

Times: Open Apr-Sep, daily 10-6 (last entry 4.30); Oct daily 11-5 (last entry 4); Nov-Mar wknds 11-4 (last entry 3). **Fee:** * £6.50 (ch & pen £5.50). **Facilities:** P ♿ (ramp to pirate galleon & indoor castle) toilets for disabled shop (ex guide dogs)

continued

WELLS   Map 03 ST54

THE BISHOP'S PALACE
Henderson Rooms BA5 2PD
➲ (Follow city centre signs, turn left into Market Pl and enter archway between National Trust shop and post office)
☎ 01749 678691
e-mail: info@bishopspalacewells.co.uk
web: www.bishopspalacewells.co.uk
Close to the cathedral is the moated bishop's palace. The early part of the palace, the bishop's chapel and the ruins of the banqueting hall date from the 13th century and the undercroft remains virtually unchanged from this time. There are several state rooms and a long gallery which houses portraits of former Bishops. Events include a Living History re-enactment.
Times: Open Apr-Oct, Mon-Fri 10.30-5, Sun noon-5 **Fee:** ✱ £4 (ch 12 accompanied free, 12-18 £1, students £1.50, pen & groups 10+ £3
Facilities: P (100yds) ⬛ ✕ licensed 🍴 ♿ (free use of electric wheelchair) shop

WESTON-SUPER-MARE   Map 03 ST36

THE HELICOPTER MUSEUM
The Heliport, Locking Moor Rd BS24 8PP
➲ (outskirts of town on A371, nr M5 junct 21)
☎ 01934 635227
e-mail: office@helimuseum.fsnet.co.uk
web: www.helicoptermuseum.co.uk
The world's largest rotary-wing collection and the only helicopter museum in Britain. More than 70 helicopters and autogyros are on display - including examples from France, Germany, Poland, Russia and the United States, from 1935 to the present day - with displays of models, engines and other components explaining the history and development of the rotocraft. Special events include 'Open Cockpit Days', when visitors can learn more about how the helicopter works.
Times: Open all year, Nov-Mar, Wed-Sun 10-4.30; Apr-Oct 10-5.30. Open daily during Etr & Summer school hols 10-5.30. Closed 24-26 Dec & 1 Jan. **Fee:** ✱ £4.95 (ch under 5 free, ch 5-16 £2.95, pen £3.95). Family ticket (2ad+2ch) £13, (2ad+3ch) £15. Party 12+.
Facilities: P ⬛ ♿ (large print and Braille information sheet) toilets for disabled shop ▨

NORTH SOMERSET MUSEUM
Burlington St BS23 1PR
➲ (in centre of Weston-super-Mare)
☎ 01934 621028
e-mail: museum.service@n-somerset.gov.uk
web: www.n-somerset.gov.uk/museum
This museum, housed in the former workshops of the Edwardian Gaslight Company, has displays on the seaside holiday, an old chemist's shop, a dairy and Victorian pavement mosaics. Adjoining the museum is Clara's Cottage, a Westonian home of the 1900s with period kitchen, parlour, bedroom and back yard. One of the rooms has an additional display of Peggy Nisbet dolls. Other displays include wildlife gallery, Mendip minerals, mining and local archaeology, costume, ceramics and cameras.
Times: Open all year: Mon-Sat 10-4.30. Closed 24-27 Dec & 2 Jan.
Fee: £3.75 (ch free when accompanied by an adult, pen £2.75)
Facilities: P (800yds) (some disabled parking outside museum) ⬛ ♿ toilets for disabled shop ✖ (ex guide dogs) ▨

WOOKEY HOLE   Map 03 ST54

WOOKEY HOLE CAVES & PAPERMILL
BA5 1BB
➲ (M5 junct 22 follow signs via A38 & A371, from Bristol & Bath A39 to Wells then 2m to Wookey Hole)
☎ 01749 672243   **2 for 1**
e-mail: witch@wookey.co.uk
web: www.wookey.co.uk
Britain's most spectacular caves and legendary home of the infamous Witch of Wookey. The 19th-century paper mill houses a variety of fascinating attractions including a Cave Museum, Victorian Penny Arcade, Magical Mirror Maze, Haunted Corridor of Crazy Mirrors, and the Wizard's Castle play area. Visitors can also see paper being made in Britain's only surviving handmade paper mill. Puppet theatre shows, magic lessons, an enchanted fairy garden and Dinosaur Valley round off this family day out in Wookey Gorge.
Times: Open all year, Nov-Mar, daily 10-4; Apr-Oct, daily 10-5. Closed 25 Dec. **Fee:** ✱ £9.90 (ch 4-14 & concessions £7.50, under 4's free).
Facilities: P ✕ licensed 🍴 ♿ (papermill only accessible) toilets for disabled shop ✖ (ex guide dogs) ▨

> Directions are provided
> by the attractions.

YEOVILTON
Map 03 ST52

FLEET AIR ARM MUSEUM
Royal Naval Air Station BA22 8HT
➲ (on B3151, just off A303)
☎ 01935 840565

e-mail: info@fleetairarm.com
web: www.fleetairarm.com

The Fleet Air Arm Museum has the largest collection of naval aircraft anywhere in Europe. Situated alongside Europe's largest naval air station, visitors may see Sea Harriers and helicopters going through their rigorous training procedures. Inside the museum you will have the opportunity of going on board Concorde, and being transported by a simulated helicopter flight to the replica flight deck of the aircraft carrier HMS Ark Royal, where you can experience the thrills of a working flight deck, and even see a nuclear bomb! The site includes an adventure playground, a licensed restaurant, and a shop.
Times: Open all year, daily Apr-Oct 10-5.30; Nov-Mar, Wed-Sun 10-4.30. Closed 24-26 Dec. **Fee:** £9.50 (ch under 5 free, ch 5-16 £6, concessions £7). Family ticket (2ad+3ch) £28. **Facilities:** 🅿 💷 ✖ licensed 🍴 ♿ (wheelchairs available) toilets for disabled shop ✖ (ex guide dogs) 🛥

See advertisement on page 205

Are there any excellent Days Out that we've missed? Use the Readers' Report form at the back of the book to tell us about them.

2-for-1 This symbol indicates attractions which have chosen to participate in our 2-for-1 voucher scheme

---

STAFFORDSHIRE

EVENTS & FESTIVALS

January
19th-22nd Manchester Dog Show, Staffordshire Show Ground
tbc Winter Beer & Wine Festival, Lichfield

February
2nd-4th Winter Beer & Wine Festival, Kings Head, Lichfield

April
30th-1st May The Lichfield Mysteries, cycle of 24 medieval-style plays, performed three times a day in the city.

May
31st-1st Jun Staffordshire County Show, County Showground

June
16th-18th Lichfield Folk Festival, various venues (provisional)
22nd-25th Lichfield Real Ale, Jazz & Blues Festival, Lichfield Rugby Club

July
6th-8th FUSE, the Event in a Tent, Beacon Park, Lichfield
tbc Lichfield International Arts Festival, various venues
tbc Stafford Festival, town centre and Victoria Park, Stafford

September
11th Abbots Bromley Horn Dance, throughout village
9th-10th The Early National Chrysanthemum Show, Staffordshire County Showground (provisional)

Above: The war memorial, Stoke-on-Trent

ALTON · Map 07 SK04

ALTON TOWERS
ST10 4DB
➲ (from S - M1 junct 23a or M6 junct 15. From N - M1 junct 28 or M6 junct 16)
☎ 08705 204060
e-mail: info@alton-towers.com
web: www.altontowers.com

Alton Towers is a fantastic day out for all the family. With world first rides and attractions as well as some beautiful gardens, this is more than just a theme park. Recent additions include the Spinball Whizzer, a spinner coaster, as well as The Flume, in which visitors now travel in red bath tubs, rather than rustic logs.

Times: Open daily 12 Mar-30 Oct **Facilities:** ◻ (charged) 💻
✗ licensed ♿ (disabled guest guide books) toilets for disabled shop ✈ (ex guide dogs) 🍴

BIDDULPH · Map 07 SJ85

BIDDULPH GRANGE GARDEN
Grange Rd ST8 7SD
➲ (access from A527, Tunstall-Congleton road. Entrance on Grange Rd 0.5m N of Biddulph)
☎ 01782 517999
e-mail: biddulphgrange@nationaltrust.org.uk
web: www.nationaltrust.org.uk

This exciting and rare survival of a high Victorian garden has undergone extensive restoration. Conceived by James Bateman, the fifteen acres are divided into a number of smaller gardens which were designed to house specimens from his extensive plant collection.

Times: Open mid Mar-Oct, Wed-Fri 12-5.30. Sat-Sun & BH Mon 11-5.30 (last admission 5.30 or dusk if earlier); early Nov-mid Dec, Sat-Sun 11-3 or dusk. **Fee:** ✱ Mar-Oct: £5 (ch £2.50), Family ticket £12.50; Nov-Dec: £2 (ch £1), Family ticket £5. **Facilities:** ◻ 💻 (not suitable for people with mobility problems) shop ✈ (ex guide & hearing dogs) 🐾 🍴

BURTON-UPON-TRENT · Map 08 SK22

THE BASS MUSEUM
PO Box 220, Horninglow St DE14 1YQ   [2 for 1]
➲ (off A38 at Burton-on-Trent, well signed)
☎ 0845 600 0598
e-mail: enquiries@coorsvisitorcentre.com
web: www.coorsvisitorcentre.com

Beer has been brewed in Burton upon Trent for centuries and the Museum of Brewing at the Coors Visitor Centre charts its fantastic heritage. Learn all about the history of brewing, meet the famous Coors Shire horses and explore the collection of restored vintage vehicles.

Times: Open all year, daily 10-5. (Last admission 4). Closed 25-26 Dec & 1 Jan. **Fee:** £6 (ch over 6yrs £3, concessions £4). Family ticket £16.50 (2ad+3ch); admission includes complimentary half pint of lager or beer or, tea coffee or soft drink. **Facilities:** ◻ 💻 ✗ licensed 🍴 ♿ (lift) toilets for disabled shop ✈ (ex guide dogs) 🍴

CHEDDLETON · Map 07 SJ95

CHEDDLETON FLINT MILL
Beside Caldon Canal, Leek Rd ST13 7HL
➲ (3m S of Leek on A520)   [FREE]
☎ 01782 502907
web: www.ex.ac.uk/~akoutram/cheddleton-mill

Twin water-wheels on the River Churnet drive flint-grinding pans in the two mills. Museum collection of machinery used in the preparation of materials for the ceramic industry. This includes a 100 HP Robey horizontal steam engine, model Newcomen beam engine, edge-runner mill, and the narrow boat Vienna, moored on the Caldon Canal. Display panels explain the processes of winning and treating clays, stone and flint for the pottery industry.

Times: Open all year, Sat & Sun 2-5, Mon-Fri 10-5 (by arrangement). Phone to check **Facilities:** ◻ 🃏 ♿ toilets for disabled

CHURNET VALLEY RAILWAY
The Station ST13 7EE
➲ (3m S from Leek, 3m N from Cellarhead along A520. Kingsley & Froghall Station is situated on the Stoke to Ashbourne road, A52)   [2 for 1]
☎ 01538 360522
e-mail: enquiries@churnetvalleyrailway.co.uk
web: www.churnetvalleyrailway.co.uk

The Churnet Valley Railway runs through the hidden countryside between Cheddleton, with its grade II Victorian station, Kingsley and Froghall, with the newly built station and Canal Wharf. The journey incorporates Consall, which has a sleepy rural station and nature reserve, and Leekbrook with one of the longest tunnels on a preserved railway. 2-for-1 voucher is not valid on Special Event days. Special Events: 1940's wknd Apr, Ghost Train Oct, Santa & Steam Dec, Day out with Thomas Feb and Jul.

Times: Open every Sun, Mar-Oct; all BH's Wed & Sat, Jun-Aug; Diesel trains every Tue & Thu in Aug and every Sat Mar-Oct. **Fee:** ✱ All day travel: £9 (ch £5, pen £7) **Facilities:** ◻ 💻 ♿ (ramps) toilets for disabled shop 🍴

HALFPENNY GREEN   Map 07 SO89

HALFPENNY GREEN VINEYARDS
DY7 5EP
➲ (0.5m off B4176 Dudley to Telford road)
☎ 01384 221122
e-mail: enquiries@
halfpenny-green-vineyards.co.uk `FREE`
web: www.halfpenny-green-vineyards.co.uk

Using German, French and hybrid varieties that can prosper even in the poorest British summer, this vineyard offers "The complete English wine experience." This includes a self-guided vineyard trail as well as guided tours, wine-tasting, a craft centre and a visitor centre. Visitors can purchase wines with personalised labels for special occasions. Coarse fishing is also available.
Times: ✽ Open all year, daily 10.30-5. **Facilities:** 🅿 💺 ✕ licensed 🗑 ♿ toilets for disabled shop ✈ (ex guide dogs) ◼

HIMLEY   Map 07 SO89

HIMLEY HALL & PARK
DY3 4DF
➲ (off A449, on B4176)
☎ 01384 817817
e-mail: himley.hall@dudley.gov.uk

The extensive parkland offers a range of attractions, including a nine-hole golf course and coarse fishing. The hall is open to the public when exhibitions are taking place. Permanent orienteering course, a charge is made for the maps. Guided tours at the hall available by prior arrangement. The Hall is available for private hire. There are also a large variety of outdoor events and concerts.
Times: Open Hall: early Apr-mid Sep, 2-5. Closed Mon ex BH. Park open all year. **Fee:** ✽ Free admission except for special events **Facilities:** 🅿 (charged) 💺 🗑 ♿ toilets for disabled ✈ (ex guide dogs & in park)

LEEK   Map 07 SJ95

BLACKBROOK ZOOLOGICAL PARK
Winkhill ST13 7QR
➲ (off A523 Leek to Ashbourne road)
☎ 01538 308293
e-mail: enquiries@
blackbrookzoologicalpark.co.uk
web: www.blackbrookzoologicalpark.co.uk

Blackbrook Zoological Park is a fun and educational day for all. A continually growing attraction, always with something new to see. The zoo features: rare birds, reptiles, insects and aquatics; owl flights, Pelican and Lemur feeds. Blackbrook Zoological Park is fully accessible for pushchairs and wheelchairs.
Times: Open daily 10.30-5.30; Winter 10.30-dusk **Fee:** ✽ £6.95 (ch £4.25, pen £5.75) **Facilities:** 🅿 💺 🗑 ♿ (fully accessible) toilets for disabled shop ✈ (ex guide dogs) ◼

LICHFIELD   Map 07 SK10

ERASMUS DARWIN HOUSE
Beacon St WS13 7AD
➲ (signed to Lichfield Cathedral. Access by foot through cathedral close at West End)
☎ 01543 306260 `2 for 1`
e-mail: enquiries@erasmusdarwin.org
web: www.erasmusdarwin.org

The House is dedicated to Erasmus Darwin, the grandfather of Charles Darwin, and a talented doctor, inventor, philosopher, poet and founder member of the Lunar Society. A resident of Lichfield for more than 20 years, the displays are contained within his beautiful 18th-century home, and recreate the story of Erasmus' life, ideas and inventions, through period rooms, audio visual and interactive displays.
Times: Open Apr-Sep: Tue-Sun noon-5, Oct-Mar: Sat & Sun noon-5. (Last admission 4.15). **Fee:** ✽ £2.50 (concessions £2). Family ticket (2ad+2ch) £6. **Facilities:** 🅿 (200mtrs) ♿ (audio tour) toilets for disabled shop ✈ (ex guide dogs)

LICHFIELD CATHEDRAL
WS13 7LD Take A454 and join A641 to Lichfield
➲ (signed from all major roads and within city).
☎ 01543 306240 & 306100
e-mail: enquiries@lichfield-cathedral.org
web: www.lichfield-cathedral.org

The Cathedral's three spires, known as the Ladies of the Vale, dominate the landscape. The first cathedral here was founded in AD700 to house the shrine of St Chad. The present building, with its elaborate carvings, has been much restored since it was attacked during the Civil War. Among its treasures are an 8th-century illuminated manuscript, the St Chad Gospels, a collection of modern silver and the 16th-century Flemish glass in the Lady Chapel. Many musical events take place here.
Times: Open daily 7.45-6.30. **Fee:** ✽ Suggested donation of £4 for each adult visitor. **Facilities:** 🅿 (200mtrs) (no parking ex disabled in close) 💺 ✕ licensed 🗑 ♿ (touch & hearing centre for blind) toilets for disabled shop in cathedral and opposite west front ✈ (ex guide/hearing dogs)

LICHFIELD HERITAGE CENTRE
Market Square WS13 6LG
➲ (in city centre)
☎ 01543 256611
e-mail: info@lichfieldheritage.org.uk
web: www.lichfieldheritage.org.uk

A colourful new exhibition, 'The Lichfield Story' gives a vivid account of Lichfield's rich and varied history over 2000 years. It is the home to the Staffordshire Millennium Embroideries which are displayed within their own gallery. In addition, the Exhibition houses fine examples of City, Diocesan and Regimental silver, ancient Charters and archives. Two audio visual presentations, a Family Trail and for younger children a Mouse Hole Trail provide interest and fun for all the family as they tour the Exhibition.
Times: ✽ Open all year, daily 10-5, Sun 10.30-5. (Last admission 4). Closed Xmas & New Year. **Facilities:** 🅿 (200yds) 💺 🗑 ♿ (lift to first floor) toilets for disabled shop ✈ (ex guide dogs) ◼

SAMUEL JOHNSON BIRTHPLACE MUSEUM
Breadmarket St WS13 6LG
➲ (located in city centre market place)
☎ 01543 258441   **FREE**
e-mail: sjmuseum@lichfield.gov.uk
web: www.lichfield.gov.uk/sjmuseum

Dr Samuel Johnson, author of the famous English dictionary of 1755, lexicographer, poet, critic, biographer and personality. One of England's greatest writers, Dr Johnson was born in this house in 1709. The birthplace now houses a museum dedicated to his extraordinary life, work and personality. Five floors of exhibits featuring period room settings, introductory video and personal items owned by Johnson, his family and his famous friends.

Times: Open daily Apr-Sep 10.30-4.30; Oct-Mar 12-4.30. (Last admission 4). **Facilities:** P (500yds) (large print text literature, induction loop system) shop ✖ (ex guide dogs)

SHUGBOROUGH   Map 07 SJ92
SHUGBOROUGH
ST17 0XB
➲ (6m E of Stafford off A513, signposted from M6 junct 13)
☎ 01889 881388   **2 for 1**
e-mail: shugborough.promotions@
staffordshire.gov.uk
web: www.shugborough.org.uk

Set on the edge of Cannock Chase, Shugborough is the magnificent 900-acre seat of the Earls of Lichfield. The 18th-century mansion house contains fine collections of ceramics, silver, paintings and French furniture. Part of the house is still lived in by the Lichfield family. Visitors can enjoy the Grade I listed historic garden and a unique collection of neo-classical monuments. Other attractions include the museum and the original servants' quarters, the laundry, kitchens, brewhouse and coachhouses which have all been restored and are fully operational. Shugborough Park Farm is a Georgian farmstead with an agricultural museum, working corn mill and rare breeds centre. The 2-for-1 voucher is valid only during normal visiting hours and cannot be used for any ticketed events.

Times: ✱ Open 18 Mar-28 Oct, daily 11-5. Site open all year to pre-booked parties. **Fee:** £8 (concessions £5) Family £20 Parking fee refunded on purchase of all site ticket. **Facilities:** P (charged) ⬛ ✖ licensed ▥ ♿ (step climber for wheelchairs, 2 Batricars) toilets for disabled shop ✖ (ex guide dogs & in parkland) ☘ ▰

STAFFORD   Map 07 SJ92
SHIRE HALL GALLERY
Market Square ST16 2LD
➲ (M6 junct 13, follow signs to Stafford town centre & gallery is signed from there)
☎ 01785 278345   **FREE**
e-mail: shirehallgallery@staffordshire.gov.uk
web: www.staffordshire.gov.uk/sams

A fine gallery housed in the 18th-century Shire Hall - one of Staffordshire's most magnificent buildings. It holds exhibitions of contemporary arts, contains historic courtrooms and a Crafts Council selected craft shop.

Times: Open all year Mon & Wed-Sat, 9.30-5; Tue 10-5; Sun 1-4. Gallery closes for exhibition changes and at BHs, please call for further details. **Facilities:** P (5 mins walk) ✖ ▥ ♿ toilets for disabled shop ✖ (ex guide dogs) ▰

STOKE-ON-TRENT   Map 07 SJ84
CERAMICA
Market Place, Burslem ST6 3DS
➲ (exit M6 junct 15/16 take A500 leave at A4527 (signposted Tunstall). After 0.5m right onto B5051 for Burslem. Ceramica is in Old Town Hall in centre of town.)
☎ 01782 832001
e-mail: info@ceramicauk.com
web: www.ceramicauk.com

A unique experience for all the family, Ceramica is housed in the Old Town Hall in the centre of Burslem, Mother Town of the Potteries. Explore the hands-on activities in Bizarreland, and learn how clay is transformed into china. Dig into history with the time team and take a magic carpet ride over the town. Discover the past, present and future of ceramics with the interactive displays in the Pavillions. Explore the Memory Bank and read the local news on Ceramica TV.

Times: Open Mon-Sat 9.30-5, Sun 10.30-4.30. For Xmas opening please telephone. **Facilities:** P (charged) ▥ ♿ (ramps, lift to all floors, tactile displays) toilets for disabled shop ✖ (ex guide dogs) ▰

GLADSTONE WORKING POTTERY MUSEUM
Uttoxeter Rd, Longton ST3 1PQ
➲ (M6 junct 15, follow A500 to A50 then follow brown heritage signs. From M1 follow A50 westbound then follow brown signs)
☎ 01782 319232
e-mail: gladstone@stoke.gov.uk
web: www.stoke.gov.uk/gladstone

Located at the heart of the Potteries, Gladstone Pottery Museum is the last remaining Victorian Pottery industry. Whilst touring the original factory building discover what it was like for the men, women and children to live and work in a potbank during the era of the coal firing bottle ovens. In original workshops working potters can be found demonstrating traditional pottery skills. There are also lots of opportunities for you to have a go at pottery making, throw your own pot on the potters wheel, make china flowers and decorate pottery items to take home. Also explore Flushed with Pride, dedicated to the story of the development of the toilet, and The Tile Gallery, a fine collection which traces the development of decorative tiles.

Times: Open all year, daily 10-5 (last admission 4). Limited opening Xmas & New Year. **Fee:** ✱ £4.95 (ch £3.50, students & pen £3.95). Family ticket £14 (2ad+3ch 4-16yrs). Passport ticket available annual admission to Gladstone Pottery Museum £7.50 (concessions £6.50), Family £16. **Facilities:** P ⬛ ✖ licensed ♿ (electric buggy available to loan) toilets for disabled shop ✖ (ex guide dogs) ▰

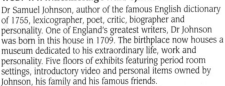

ROYAL DOULTON VISITOR CENTRE

Nile St, Burslem ST6 2AJ
⮑ (M6 junct 15 from S or 16 from N. Join A500 leaving at exit for Tunstall A527, follow tourist signs)
☎ 01782 292434
e-mail: visitor@royal-doulton.com
web: www.royal-doulton.com/visitor

The centre has extensive displays of both current products and out of production pieces together with ranges from the museum tracing the history of Royal Doulton. Live demonstrations showing the skill and craftsmanship in the creation and hand painting of figurines. Behind the scenes look at the working factory weekdays only, prior booking advised.

Times: ✱ Open all year, Mon-Sat 9.30-5, Sun 10.30-4.30. Factory tours by advance booking Mon-Fri 10.30-2 (1.30 Fri). Closed Xmas week. No tours during factory holidays. **Facilities:** 🅿 🖭 🗐 ♿ toilets for disabled shop ✖ (ex guide dogs) ◀

THE POTTERIES MUSEUM & ART GALLERY

Bethesda St, Hanley ST1 3DW
⮑ (M6 junct 15/16 take A500 to Stoke-on-Trent. Follow signs for city centre (Hanley), Cultural Quarter & The Potteries Museum)
☎ 01782 232323
e-mail: museums@stoke.gov.uk
web: www.stoke.gov.uk/museums

FREE

The history of the Potteries under one roof, including a dazzling display of the world's finest collection of Staffordshire ceramics. Other displays introduce natural, local and archaeological history from in and around The Potteries, and a Mark 16 Spitfire commemorating its locally born designer - Reginald Mitchell.

Times: Open Mar-Oct, Mon-Sat 10-5, Sun 2-5; Nov-Feb, Mon-Sat 10-4, Sun 1-4. Closed 25 Dec-1 Jan. **Facilities:** 🅿 (charged) 🖭 ♿ (lift, induction loop, 2 wheelchairs available) toilets for disabled shop ✖ (ex guide/helping dogs) ◀

> If an attraction name appears in *italics*, details have not been confirmed for 2006.

WEDGWOOD VISITOR CENTRE

Barlaston ST12 9ES
⮑ (follow tourist signs S on A34, from M6 junct 15, or N junct 14)
☎ 01782 282986
e-mail: bookings@wedgwood.com
web: www.thewedgwoodvisitorcentre.com

2 for 1

The Wedgwood Visitor Centre is situated at the home of the internationally renowned ceramic company. A variety of self-guided factory tours are available 7 days a week, together with a film theatre, two exhibition areas, demonstration/hands-on area, restaurants and shopping.

Times: Open all year, Mon-Fri 9-5, Sat & Sun 10-5. Closed 24 Dec-2 Jan. **Fee:** £7.95-£9.25 (concessions £6-£7.25). Family ticket £27.25-£31.75 **Facilities:** 🅿 ✖ licensed ♿ (fully wheelchair accessible/hearing loops) toilets for disabled shop ✖ (guide dogs only) ◀

TAMWORTH   Map 07 SK20

DRAYTON MANOR THEME PARK

B78 3TW
⮑ (M42 junct 9/10, on A4091. Exit at T2 of M6 toll)
☎ 01827 287979
e-mail: info@draytonmanor.co.uk
web: www.draytonmanor.co.uk

A popular family theme park with over 100 rides and attractions set in 280 acres of parkland and lakes. Drayton Manor features world-class rides like 'Apocalypse'- the world's first stand-up tower drop, 'Stormforce 10' - the best

continued

water ride in the country and 'Shockwave' - Europe's only stand-up rollercoaster. A new rollercoaster sensation is G-Force. Plus a host of family attractions, children's rides, zoo, museum, shops and attractions.
Times: Park open end Mar-Oct. Rides from 10.30-5 or 6. Zoo open all year. **Fee:** ✱ Please telephone or visit website for details.
Facilities: 🅿 💺 ✗ licensed 🚻 (ramps or lifts to most rides, some rides limited access) toilets for disabled shop garden centre ✖ (ex in park) 🍴

TAMWORTH CASTLE
The Holloway, Ladybank B79 7NA
➲ (M42 junct 10 & M6 junct 12, access via A5)
☎ 01827 709629 & 709626   **2 for 1**
e-mail: heritage@tamworth.gov.uk
web: www.tamworth.gov.uk

The dramatic Norman motte and bailey castle was once the home of England's Royal Champions and today is (reputedly) haunted by two lady ghosts. Quizzes, dressing-up, brass rubbing and a 'feelie' box make it a great family destination. Special Events: Tamworth Castle by candlelight Nov 18th,19th,25th,26th.
Times: Open mid Feb-Oct: Tue-Sun noon- 5.15, (last admission 4.30). Nov-mid Feb: Thu-Sun 12-5.15, (last admission 4.30). **Fee:** ✱ £4.75 (ch £2.75 & pen £3.75). Family £13. Prices subject to change.
Facilities: 🅿 (100yds & 400yds) 💺 📷 🚻 (one wheelchair for use inside the castle) shop ✖ (ex guide dogs & hearing dogs) 🍴

WALL   Map 07 SK10
WALL ROMAN SITE
Watling St WS14 0AW
➲ (off A5)
☎ 01543 480768
Explore the haunting remains of a 2,000 year old wayside staging post situated along Watling Street, the famous Kent to North Wales Roman road.
Times: Open 24 Mar-May, daily, 10-5; Jun-Aug, daily, 10-6; Sep-Oct, daily, 10-5. **Fee:** £2.90 (ch £1.50, concessions £2.20). Opening times and prices are subject to change, for further details please phone 0870 333 1811 **Facilities:** 🅿 shop ♯ ♨

WESTON PARK   Map 07 SJ81
WESTON PARK
TF11 8LE
➲ (on A5 at Weston-under-Lizard, 30min from central Birmingham 3m off M54 junct 3 and 8m off M6 junct 12).
☎ 01952 852100
e-mail: enquiries@weston-park.com
web: www.weston-park.com
Built in 1671, this fine mansion stands in elegant gardens and a vast park designed by 'Capability' Brown. Three lakes, a miniature railway, and a woodland adventure playground are to be found in the grounds, and in the house itself there is a magnificent collection of pictures, furniture and tapestries. There is also an animal centre and Deer Park.
Times: ✱ Open wknds from 19 Apr-Jul, then daily until 7 Sep.
Facilities: 🅿 💺 ✗ licensed 📷 🚻 (disabled route, access to restaurant & shop) toilets for disabled shop 🍴

WHITTINGTON   Map 07 SK10
STAFFORDSHIRE REGIMENT MUSEUM
Whittington Barracks WS14 9PY
➲ (on A51 between Lichfield/Tamworth)   **2 for 1**
☎ 01543 434390
e-mail: museum@rhqstaffords.fsnet.co.uk
Located next to Whittington Barracks, the museum tells the story of the soldiers of the Staffordshire Regiment and its predecessors. Exhibits include vehicles, uniforms, weapons, medals and memorabilia relating to three hundred years of regimental history, including distinguished service in the First and Second World Wars and the Gulf War. Visitors can experience a World War I trench system with sound effects and a World War II Anderson shelter.
Times: Open all year, Tue-Fri 10-4.30 (last admission 4); also Apr-Oct wknds and BH 12.30-4.30. Closed Xmas-New Year. Parties at other times by arrangement. **Fee:** £2.50 (concessions £1.50) Family ticket £6. Regimental Association Members & serving soldiers free.
Facilities: 🅿 📷 🚻 (ramps, lowered kerbs, graded access to attraction) toilets for disabled shop ✖ (outside only ex guide dogs)

WILLOUGHBRIDGE   Map 07 SJ74
THE DOROTHY CLIVE GARDEN
TF9 4EU
➲ (on A51 between Nantwich & Stone)
☎ 01630 647237
web: www.dorothyclivegarden.co.uk
This 200-year-old gravel quarry has been converted into a delightful woodland garden. The quarry is at the top of a small hill and the garden has fine views of the countryside and adjoining counties. There is a variety of rare trees and shrubs. The garden provides colour and interest throughout the seasons from spring to glowing autumn tints.
Times: ✱ Open Apr-Oct, daily 10-5.30. **Facilities:** 🅿 💺 🚻 (wheelchairs for use, special route) toilets for disabled

SUFFOLK

EVENTS & FESTIVALS

April
14th-16th Suffolk Spring Garden Show,
Suffolk Show Ground, Ipswich
14th-17th Easter Festival, Snape Maltings
Concert Hall, Snape
tbc East Anglian Beer Festival, Corn Exchange,
Bury St Edmunds

May
12th-28th Bury St Edmunds Festival, arts
festival, various venues
13th-14th Lowestoft Boat Show
& Maritime Festival
14th South Suffolk Show, Point-to-Point
Course, Ampton Park, Ingham
20th Hadleigh Show, Holbecks Park, Hadleigh
31st-1st Jun Suffolk Show, Suffolk
Showground, Bucklesham Road, Ipswich

June
9th-25th Aldeburgh Festival of Music & the
Arts, Snape Maltings Concert Hall, and
surrounding venues and churches

July
27th-28th Lowestoft Seafront Air Festival
tbc Southwold Festival of the Sea

August
1st-31st Snape Proms, Snape Maltings Concert
Hall, Snape

September
1st-3rd Suffolk Autumn Garden Show, Suffolk
show Ground, Ipswich

October
tbc Britten Festival, Snape Maltings Concert
Hall, Snape

BUNGAY   Map 05 TM38

OTTER TRUST
Earsham NR35 2AF
➲ (off A143, 1m W of Bungay)
☎ 01986 893470

The Otter Trust is the largest otter conservation organisation
in Britain. Covering 23 acres, British and Asian otters can be
seen under near natural conditions. There are three lakes
and walks along the banks of the River Waveney.

Times: Open Apr (or Good Fri if earlier)-Oct, daily 10.30-6. **Fee:** ✱ £6
(ch over 3 £3). Disabled person in wheelchair free. **Facilities:** 🅿 💷
🚻 toilets for disabled shop ✖ (ex guide dogs)

BURY ST EDMUNDS   Map 05 TL86

MANOR HOUSE MUSEUM
Honey Hill IP33 1RT
➲ (edge of town centre, follow signs to Police
Station, museum car park opposite)   **2 for 1**
☎ 01284 757076
e-mail: stedmundsbury@burybo.stedbc.gov.uk
web: www.stedmundsbury.gov.uk

The Georgian mansion specialises in costumes, textiles,
horology and fine and decorative art from the 17th to the
20th centuries. There is a temporary exhibition gallery as
well as workshops in textiles and horology - new features
are feely pictures and boxes.

Times: Open all year Wed-Sun, 11-4. Closed Good Fri, 25-26 Dec & 1
Jan. Other times by arrangement. **Fee:** ✱ £2.60 (ch & concessions
£2.10). Free to Borough residents. **Facilities:** 🅿 (charged) 💷 ✖ 🗒
🚻 (special tours can be arranged for disabled groups) toilets for
disabled shop garden centre Georgian herb garden
✖ (ex guide dogs) 🍴

MOYSE'S HALL MUSEUM
Cornhill IP33 1DX   **2 for 1**
➲ (take Bury central exit from A14, follow signs
for town centre, museum situated in town centre)
☎ 01284 706183
e-mail: maggie.goodger@stedsbc/gov.uk
web: www.stedmundsbury.gov.uk/moyses.htm

Moyse's Hall is a 12th-century Norman house built of flint
and stone which now serves as a local history museum, and
among the fascinating exhibits are memorabilia of the
notorious William Corder "Murder in the Red Barn". Other
collections include the history of the town, archaeology and
the Suffolk Regiment.

Times: Open all year, Mon-Fri 10.30-4.30, Sat & Sun 11-4. Closed 25-27
Dec, 1-6 Jan & Good Fri. **Fee:** £2.60 (ch & concessions £2.10). Free for
residents of St Edmondsbury. **Facilities:** 🅿 (200yds) 🗒 🚻 (stairlift,
lift, hearing loop, Braille pictures) toilets for disabled shop
✖ (ex guide dogs) 🍴

EASTON   Map 05 TM25

EASTON FARM PARK
IP13 0EQ
➲ (signed from A12 at Wickam Market, and from
A1120)
☎ 01728 746475
e-mail: easton@eastonfarmpark.co.uk
web: www.eastonfarmpark.co.uk

Award winning Farm Park on the banks of the River Deben.
There are lots of breeds of farm animals, including Suffolk
Punch horses, ponies, pigs, lambs, calves, goats, rabbits,

continued

guinea pigs & poultry. Chicks hatching and egg collecting daily. Free pat-a-pet & pony rides every day.
Times: Open Mar-end Sep, daily 10.30-6. Also open Feb & Oct half term hols. **Fee:** ✳ £5.75 (ch under 1 free, ch 1-16 £4.25 pen £5.25).
Facilities: 🅿 🖳 🍴 ♿ (special parking) toilets for disabled shop ▰

EUSTON   Map 05 TL87

EUSTON HALL
IP24 2QP
➲ (on A1088, 3m S of Thetford)
☎ 01842 766366
e-mail: lcampbell@euston-estate.co.uk
web: www.eustonhall.co.uk
Home of the Duke and Duchess of Grafton, this 18th-century house is notable for its fine collection of pictures, by Stubbs, Lely, Van Dyck and other Masters. The grounds were laid out by John Evelyn, William Kent and 'Capability' Brown, and include a 17th-century church in the style of Wren and a river walk to the newly restored watermill.
Times: Open 16 Jun-15 Sep, Thu only. Also open Sun 26 Jun, 17 Jul & 4 Sep, 2.30-5. **Fee:** £5 (ch 5-16 £2, students & pen £4). Parties 12+ £4 each. Ground only £3. **Facilities:** 🅿 🖳 ♿ toilets for disabled shop ✘ (ex guide dogs)

FLIXTON   Map 05 TM38

NORFOLK & SUFFOLK AVIATION MUSEUM
Buckeroo Way, The Street NR35 1NZ
➲ (off A143, take B1062, 2m W of Bungay)
☎ 01986 896644   **FREE**
e-mail: nsam.flixton@virgin.net
web: www.aviationmuseum.net
Situated in the Waveney Valley, the museum has over 40 historic aircraft. There is also a Bloodhound surface-to-air missile, the 446th Bomb Group Museum, RAF Bomber Command Museum, the Royal Observer Corps Museum, RAF Air-Sea Rescue and Coastal Command and a souvenir shop. Among the displays are Decoy Sites and Wartime Deception, Fallen Eagles - Wartime Luftwaffe Crashes and an ex-Ipswich airport hangar made by Norwich company Boulton and Paul Ltd.
Times: Open Apr-Oct, Sun-Thu 10-5 (last admission 4); Nov-Mar, Tue, Wed & Sun 10-4 (last admission 3). Closed late Dec-early Jan.
Facilities: 🅿 🖳 ♿ (helper advised, ramps/paths to all buildings) toilets for disabled shop

FRAMLINGHAM   Map 05 TM26

FRAMLINGHAM CASTLE
IP8 9BT
➲ (on B1116)
☎ 01728 724189
Walk the 12th-century battlements that encircle the castle site with their impressive thirteen towers. Exceptional views over the countryside and a very popular audio tour.
Times: Open all year, Apr-Sep, daily 10-6; Oct, daily 10-5; Nov-Mar, daily 10-4. Closed 24-26 Dec & 1 Jan. **Fee:** £4.30 (ch £2.20, concessions £3.20). Family ticket £10.80. Opening times and prices are subject to change, for further details please phone 0870 333 1181
Facilities: 🅿 ♿ shop ⌗

HORRINGER   Map 05 TL86

ICKWORTH HOUSE, PARK & GARDENS
IP29 5QE
➲ (2.5m SW of Bury St Edmunds in village of Horringer on A143)
☎ 01284 735270
e-mail: ickworth@ntrust.org.uk
web: www.nationaltrust.org.uk/ickworth
The eccentric Earl of Bristol created this equally eccentric house, begun in 1795, to display his collection of European art. The Georgian Silver Collection is considered the finest in private hands. 'Capability' Brown designed the parkland, and also featured are a vineyard, waymarked walks and an adventure playground. New visitor facilities are opening in the west wing of Ickworth House in 2006.
Times: Open: House 25 Mar-30 Oct, Mon, Tue, Fri, wknds & BH Mons 1-5 (4.30 in Oct). (Last admission 4.30); Garden open daily 25 Mar-30 Oct 10-5. (Last admission 4.30). 31 Oct-23 Dec wkdays, 10-4; Park daily 7-7. Gardens & park closed 25 Dec. **Fee:** ✳ House, Garden & Park £6.70 (National Trust members & ch under 5 free, ch £3) Garden & park £3.10 (ch 90p). Discount for pre-booked parties.
Facilities: 🅿 ✗ licensed 🍴 ♿ (Braille guide, batricars, hearing loop, large print guides) toilets for disabled shop ✘ (ex guide dogs & in park) 🐾

IPSWICH   Map 05 TM14

CHRISTCHURCH MANSION
Soane St IP4 2BE
➲ (S side of Christchurch Park)
☎ 01473 253246 & 213761   **FREE**
e-mail: mansion@ipswich.gov.uk
The house was built in 1548 on the site of an Augustinian priory. Set in a beautiful park, it displays period rooms and an art gallery which has changing exhibitions. The Suffolk Artists' Gallery has a collection of paintings by Constable and Gainsborough.
Times: ✳ Open all year, Tue-Sat 10-5 (dusk in winter), Sun 2.30-4.30 (dusk in winter). Closed Good Fri, 24-26 Dec & 1-2 Jan. Open BH Mon.
Facilities: 🅿 ♿ (tape guide for partially sighted) shop ✘

IPSWICH MUSEUM
High St IP1 3QH
➲ (follow tourist signs to Crown St car park. Museum 3 mins walk from here)
☎ 01473 433550   **FREE**
e-mail: museum.service@ipswich.gov.uk
The Museum has sections on Victorian Natural History, Suffolk wildlife, Suffolk geology, Roman Suffolk, Anglo-Saxon Ipswich and Peoples of the World. There is also one of the best bird collections in the country.
Times: Open all year, Tue-Sat 10-5. Closed Sun, BHs, 24-26 Dec & 1 Jan. **Facilities:** 🅿 (3 min walk) 🍴 ♿ (lift) toilets for disabled shop ✘ (ex guide dogs)

Directions are provided by the attractions.

An asterisk * indicates that opening times and prices are for 2005. Please contact the attraction for up-to-date information.

LAVENHAM   Map 05 TL94

LAVENHAM GUILDHALL
Market Place CO10 9QZ   **2 for 1**
➲ (Lavenham Market Place. A1141 & B1071)
☎ 01787 247646
e-mail: jane.gosling@nationaltrust.org.uk
web: www.nationaltrust.org.uk/regions/
eastofengland

The Guildhall of Corpus Christi is one of the finest timber framed buildings in Britain. It was built around 1530 by the prosperous Corpus Christi Guild, for religious rather than commercial reasons. The hall now houses a local history museum telling the story of Lavenham's 15th- and 16th-century cloth-trade riches. Visitors can also see the walled garden with its 19th-century lock-up and mortuary.
Times: Open Mar & Nov, Sat & Sun 11-4; Apr, Wed-Sun 11-5; May-Oct daily 11-5. (Closed Good Fri but open BH Mon) **Fee:** £3.25 (accompanied ch free). Parties £2.75 each. School parties by arrangement 60p per ch. **Facilities:** P (adjacent) ▣ & (photo album of upstairs floors, Braille guide) shop ✖ (ex guide dogs) ❧

LEISTON   Map 05 TM46

LEISTON ABBEY
IP16 4TB
➲ (N of Leiston, off B1069)
☎ 01728 831354   **FREE**
e-mail: mo@leistonabbey.fsnet.co.uk
web: www.procorda.com

For hundreds of years this 14th-century abbey was used as a farm and its church became a barn. A Georgian house, now used as a school for young musicians, was built into its fabric and remains of the choir, the church transepts and parts of the cloisters still stand.
Times: Open at any reasonable time. **Facilities:** P ▣ &

LONG SHOP MUSEUM
Main St IP16 4ES
➲ (Turn off A12, follow B1119 from Saxmundham to Leiston. Museum is in the middle of town)
☎ 01728 832189   **2 for 1**
e-mail: longshop@care4free.net
web: www.longshop.care4free.net

Discover the Magic of Steam through a visit to the world famous traction engine manufacturers. Trace the history of the factory and Richard Garrett engineering. See the traction engines and road rollers in the very place that they were built. Soak up the atmosphere of the Long Shop, built in 1852 as one of the first production line engineering halls in the world. An award-winning museum with five exhibition halls full of items from the glorious age of steam and covering 200 years of local, social and industrial history.
Times: Open Apr-Oct, Mon-Sat 10-5, Sun 11-5. **Fee:** ✱ £3.50 (ch under 5 free, ch £1, concessions £3) **Facilities:** P ▣ & (wheelchair available) toilets for disabled shop ✖ (ex guide dogs)

LINDSEY   Map 05 TL94

LINDSEY CHAPEL
Rose Green
➲ (on unclass road 0.5m E of Rose Green)   **FREE**
Built mainly in the 13th century, this small thatched, flint-and-stone chapel incorporates some earlier work.
Times: Open all year, daily 10-4. **Facilities:** & ✖ ▦

LONG MELFORD   Map 05 TL84

KENTWELL HALL
CO10 9BA
➲ (signposted off A134, between Bury St Edmunds & Sudbury)
☎ 01787 310207
e-mail: info@kentwell.co.uk
web: www.kentwell.co.uk

Kentwell Hall is a moated red brick Tudor manor with gardens, woodland walks and a rare breeds farm. Restoration started in 1971 and still continues today. The house and grounds are open to the public at certain times of the year, and recreations of Tudor and 1940s life take place at weekends. Ring for details.
Times: ✱ Open: Gardens & Farm Sun-Wed, Apr-mid Jun. House, Gardens & Farm mid Jul-early Sep daily; Mar & Oct, Sun only noon-5. Also open BH wknds & school hols. Historical recreations on selected wknds Mar-Oct. **Fee:** ✱ House, Garden & Farm £7.15 (ch £4.60, pen £6.15) Garden & Farm only £5 (ch £3.30, pen £4.30).
Facilities: P ▣ & (wheelchair ramp & 2 wheelchairs for loan) toilets for disabled shop ✖ (ex guide dogs) ◀

MELFORD HALL
CO10 9AA
➲ (off A134, 3m N of Sudbury, next to village green)
☎ 01787 379228   **2 for 1**
e-mail: melford@nationaltrust.org.uk
web: www.nationaltrust.org.uk

Set in the unspoilt village of Long Melford, the house has changed little externally since 1578 when Queen Elizabeth I was entertained here, and retains its original panelled banqueting hall. It has been the home of the Hyde Parker Family since 1786. There is a Regency library, Victorian bedrooms, good collections of furniture and porcelain and a small display of items connected with Beatrix Potter, who was related to the family. The garden contains some spectacular specimen trees and a banqueting house and there is an attractive walk through the park. The 2-for-1 voucher is valid only during normal visiting hours and cannot be used for any ticketed events.
Times: Open Apr (Sat & Sun) & 19-21; May-Sep (Wed-Sun); Oct (Sat & Sun); BH Mon. Closed Good Fri; 1.30-5pm. **Fee:** £5, (ch £2.50) National Trust Members free. **Facilities:** P ▣ & (stairlift, ramp, Braille & large print guides) toilets for disabled ✖ (ex guide dogs & dogs in park) ❧

LOWESTOFT   Map 05 TM59

EAST ANGLIA TRANSPORT MUSEUM
Chapel Rd, Carlton Colville NR33 8BL
➲ (3m SW of Lowestoft, follow brown signs from A12, A146 & B1384)
☎ 01502 518459
e-mail: enquiries@eatm.org.uk
web: www.eatm.org.uk
A particular attraction of this museum is the reconstructed 1930s street scene which is used as a setting for working vehicles: visitors can ride by tram, trolley bus and narrow gauge railway. Other motor, steam and electrical vehicles are exhibited. There is also a woodland picnic area served by trams.
Times: Open Good Fri & Etr Sat 2-4, Etr Sun-Etr Mon 11-5. May-Sep, Sun & BH's 11-5; Wed & Sat 2-5 (last entry 1 hour before closing).
Fee: £5 (ch 5-15 £3.50) pen £4. Price includes rides. Party rates available. **Facilities:** 🅿 💷 & toilets for disabled shop 🖼

MARITIME MUSEUM
Sparrow Nest Gardens, Whapload Rd NR32 1XG
➲ (on A12, 100mtrs N of Lowestoft Lighthouse, turn right down Ravine)
☎ 01502 561963   2 for 1
Models of ancient and modern fishing and commercial boats, fishing gear and shipwrights' tools are among the exhibits. There is also an exhibition of the evolution of lifeboats, and a replica of the aft cabin of a steam drifter, as well as an art gallery.
Times: Open 14 Apr-22 Apr; 29 Apr-Oct, daily 10-5. **Fee:** 75p (ch & students 25p, pen 50p). **Facilities:** 🅿 📱 & (hear for all) toilets for disabled shop 🖼 (ex guide & small dogs)

NEW PLEASUREWOOD HILLS
Leisure Way, Corton NR32 5DZ
➲ (off A12 at Lowestoft)
☎ 01502 586000 (admin) & 508200 (info)
e-mail: info@pleasurewoodhills.co.uk
web: www.pleasurewoodhills.co.uk
There are over 40 rides, shows and attractions at New Pleasurewood Hills, set in 50 acres of beautiful parkland. Old favourites such as the Tidal Wave Watercoaster and the Fairytale Fantasy Ride combine with more recent attractions such as Formula K Raceway Go-Karts, the new 100ft Drop Tower, the Crazy Coaster and the Double Decker Carousel.
Times: ✱ Open Apr-Oct & Xmas. Telephone for details.
Facilities: 🅿 💷 ✕ licensed 📱 & (all shows accessible, most ride operators able to assist) toilets for disabled shop 🖼 (ex guide dogs) 🖼

NEWMARKET   Map 05 TL66

NATIONAL HORSERACING MUSEUM AND TOURS
99 High St CB8 8JH
➲ (located in centre of High St)
☎ 01638 667333
web: www.nhrm.co.uk
This friendly award-winning museum tells the story of the people and horses involved in racing in Britain. Have a go on the horse simulator in the hands-on gallery and chat to retired jockeys and trainers about their experiences. Special mini bus tours visit the gallops, a stable and yard and horses' swimming pool.
Times: Open Etr-end Oct, Tue-Sun (also BH Mons & Mons in Jul & Aug) 11-5. 10 opening on race days. **Facilities:** 🅿 (300yds) (coach drop off in front of museum) 💷 ✕ licensed & (ramps & lift) toilets for disabled shop 🖼 (ex guide dogs) 🖼

ORFORD   Map 05 TM45

ORFORD CASTLE
IP12 2ND
➲ (on B1084)
☎ 01394 450472
A great keep of Henry II with three huge towers and commanding views over Orford Ness. Climb the spiral staircase leading to a maze of rooms and passageways.
Times: Open all year, Apr-Sep, daily 10-6; Oct-Mar, Thu-Mon, 10-4. Closed 24-26 Dec & 1 Jan. **Fee:** £4.30 (ch £2.20, concessions £3.20, family £10.80). Opening times and prices are subject to change, for further details please phone 0870 333 1181 **Facilities:** 🅿 shop 🖼 ♿

SAXTEAD GREEN   Map 05 TM26

SAXTEAD GREEN POST MILL
The Mill House IP13 9QQ
➲ (2.5m NW of Framlingham on A1120)
☎ 01728 685789
A post mill since 1287, Saxtead Green Post Mill is still in working order. Climb the wooden stairs to the various floors full of fascinating mill machinery. An audio tour explains the workings of the mill.
Times: Open 25 Mar-Sep, Fri-Sat 12-5 **Fee:** £2.60 (ch £1.30, concessions £2). Opening times and prices are subject to change, for further details please phone 0870 333 1181 **Facilities:** shop 🖼 ♿

STOWMARKET   Map 05 TM05

MUSEUM OF EAST ANGLIAN LIFE
IP14 1DL
➲ (located in centre of Stowmarket, signed from A14 & B1115)
☎ 01449 612229
e-mail: meal@meal.fsnet.co.uk
web: www.suffolkcc.gov.uk/tourism/meal
This 70-acre, all-weather museum is set in an attractive river-valley site. There are reconstructed buildings, including a water mill, a smithy and also a wind pump, and the Boby Building houses craft workshops. There are displays on Victorian domestic life, gypsies, farming and industry. These include working steam traction engines, the only surviving pair of Burrell ploughing engines of 1879, and a working Suffolk Punch horse. William Bone Building, illustrating the history of Ransomes of Ipswich.
Times: ✱ Open Apr-Oct. **Facilities:** 🅿 (adjacent) 💷 📱 & (wheelchairs available, special vehicle facilities) toilets for disabled shop 🖼

HRH Queen Elizabeth II.

The British monarch was born in April 1926, and the year of her 80th birthday will see many national celebrations, as well as those that are to be staged in London.

SUDBURY Map 05 TL84

GAINSBOROUGH'S HOUSE

46 Gainsborough St CO10 2EU

➲ (situated in centre of Sudbury. Follow pedestrian signs from town centre car parks or from train stn)

☎ 01787 372958

e-mail: mail@gainsborough.org

web: www.gainsborough.org

The birthplace of Thomas Gainsborough RA (1727-88). The Georgian-fronted town house, with an attractive walled garden, displays more of the artist's work than any other gallery, together with 18th-century furniture and memorabilia. There's a varied programme of exhibitions throughout the year including fine art, craft, photography, printmaking and sculpture.

Times: Open all year. Mon-Sat 10-5. closed Sun, Good Fri & Xmas-New Year. **Fee:** ✱ £3.50 (ch, students & disabled £1.50, pen £2.80). Party rates available. **Facilities:** P (300yds) (no parking in Gainsborough Street) ⬛ 🍴 ♿ toilets for disabled shop ✖ (ex guide dogs) 🍴

SUFFOLK WILDLIFE PARK Map 05 TM58

SUFFOLK WILDLIFE PARK

Kessingland NR33 7TF

➲ (25min S of Gt. Yarmouth, just S of Lowestoft off the A12)

☎ 01502 740291

e-mail: info@suffolkwildlifepark.co.uk

web: www.suffolkwildlifepark.co.uk

Enjoy the atmosphere and excitement of your very own African Adventure at Suffolk Wildlife Park. Spend the whole day exploring 100 acres of dramatic coastal parkland, filled with animals from the African continent and around the world. Guide your expedition to giraffe, lion, buffalo, hyena and many more exciting animals. Capture the true splendour and atmosphere of the park by going walkabout amongst the large open paddocks or join the children's favourite - the Safari Roadtrain with its live commentary of fascinating animal facts.

Times: Open all year, daily from 10. Closed 25-26 Dec. **Fee:** ✱ Please call park reception for full admission prices **Facilities:** P ⬛ ✖ ♿ (wheelchairs available for hire) toilets for disabled shop ✖ 🍴

WESTLETON Map 05 TM46

RSPB NATURE RESERVE MINSMERE

IP17 3BY

➲ (signed from A12 at Yoxford & Blythburgh and from Westleton Village)

☎ 01728 648281

e-mail: minsmere@rspb.org.uk

web: www.rspb.org.uk/reserves/minsmere

Set on the beautiful Suffolk coast, Minsmere offers an enjoyable day out for all. Nature trails take you through a variety of habitats to the excellent birdwatching hides. Spring is a time for birdsong, including nightingales and booming bitterns. In summer, you can watch breeding avocets and marsh harriers. Autumn is excellent for migrants, and in winter, hundreds of wildfowl visit the reserve. Look out for otters and red deer. The visitor centre has a well-stocked shop and licensed tearoom, and you can find out more about the reserve. There is a programme of events throughout the year, including several for children and families. Self-guided activity booklets for families.

Times: Open daily (ex Tue) 9-6 (or dusk if earlier). Visitor centre open 9-5 (Nov-Jan 9-4). **Fee:** £5 (ch £1.50, concessions £3). Family ticket £10. RSPB members free **Facilities:** P ⬛ 🍴 ♿ (batricar available for loan, booking advised) toilets for disabled shop ✖ (ex guide dogs) 🍴

WEST STOW Map 05 TL87

WEST STOW ANGLO SAXON VILLAGE

West Stow Country Park, Icklingham Rd IP28 6HG

➲ (off A1101, 7m NW of Bury St Edmunds. Follow brown heritage signs)

☎ 01284 728718   **2 for 1**

e-mail: weststow@stedsbc.gov.uk

web: www.stedmundsbury.gov.uk/weststow.htm

The village is a reconstruction of a pagan Anglo-Saxon settlement dated 420-650 AD. Seven buildings have been reconstructed on the site of the excavated settlement. There is a Visitors' Centre and a children's play area. A new Anglo-Saxon Centre houses the original objects found on the site. The village is located in the West Stow Country Park. The park is 125 acres with river, lake, woodland and heath and has many trails and paths.

Times: Open all year, daily 10-5. Last entry 4 (3.30 in Winter) Except Xmas period. **Fee:** ✱ £5 (ch £4). Family ticket £15. (Prices subject to changes for special events) **Facilities:** P ⬛ ♿ (ramps) toilets for disabled shop ✖ (ex guide dogs) 🍴

WOODBRIDGE Map 05 TM24

SUTTON HOO

IP12 3DJ

➲ (off B1083 Woodbridge to Bawdsey road. Follow signs from A12 avoiding Woodbridge itself)

☎ 01394 389700

e-mail: suttonhoo@nationaltrust.org.uk

web: www.nationaltrust.org.uk

Discovered in 1939 by an amateur archaeologist, this is the site of one of the most important archaeological finds in Britain's history: the complete 7th-century ship burial of an Anglo-Saxon king, which had been missed by grave-robbers for 1300 years. Sutton Hoo Displays reveal how Anglo-Saxon nobles lived, went to war and found a new kingdom in East Anglia. The centre-piece is a full sized replica of an Anglo-Saxon warrior king's burial chamber.

Times: Open Mar-end Sep, daily 10-5; Oct, Wed-Sun 10-5; Nov-Feb, Fri-Sun 10-4 **Facilities:** P ✖ licensed 🍴 ♿ (ramps, no stairs to main areas) toilets for disabled shop 🎃 🍴

WOODBRIDGE TIDE MILL

Tide Mill Way IP12

➲ (follow signs for Woodbridge off A12, 7m E of Ipswich - Tide Mill is on riverside)

☎ 01728 746959

e-mail: wtm@redpoll.co.uk

web: www.tidemill.org.uk

The machinery of this 18th-century mill has been completely restored. There are photographs and working models on display. Situated on a busy quayside, the unique building looks over towards the historic site of the Sutton Hoo Ship Burial. Every effort is made to run the machinery for a while whenever the mill is open and the tides are favourable.

Times: Open Etr, then daily May-Sep; Apr, Oct wknds only, 11-5. **Fee:** £2 (ch & concessions £1.50). **Facilities:** P (400yds) (no parking or turning in Tide Mill Way) 🍴 ♿ shop ✖ (ex guide dogs)

SURREY

EVENTS & FESTIVALS

May
29th Surrey County Show, Stoke Park, Guildford

June
6th-8th Wisley Flower Show, Royal Horticultural Society Garden, Wisley (provisional)

July
14th-16th Guilfest, live music festival (provisional)
tbc Guildford Summer Festival (various events throughout the month)

August
6th Cranleigh Show, Showground, Cranleigh
22nd-24th Wisley Flower Show, Royal Horticultural Society Garden, Wisley

September
24th Surrey Country Fair & Ploughing Match, Loseley Park, Guildford
30th Surbiton Festival, various events and street festival

October
tbc Guildford Book Festival, various venues in the town centre

Above: Church Lane, Farnham

ASH VALE   Map 04 SU85

ARMY MEDICAL SERVICES MUSEUM
Keogh Barracks GU12 5RQ
⮑ (M3 junct 4 on A331 to Mytchett then follow tourist signs)
☎ 01252 868612   FREE
e-mail: museum@keogh72.freeserve.co.uk
The museum traces the history of Army medicine, nursing, dentistry and veterinary science from 1660 until the present day. Medical equipment and ambulances complement displays including uniforms and medals.
Times: Open all year, Mon-Fri 10-3.30. Closed Xmas, New Year & BH. Wknds & BH by appointment only. **Facilities:** ▣ 🗐 ᵹ (hand rails, wide doors, audio guide, Braille guides) toilets for disabled shop ✖ (ex guide dogs)

CHERTSEY   Map 04 TQ06

THORPE PARK
Staines Rd KT16 8PN
⮑ (M25 junct 11 or 13 and follow signs via A320 to Thorpe Park)
☎ 0870 444 4466
web: www.thorpepark.com
Home to one of the world's most intense, disorientating, exhilarating rollercoasters - Nemesis Inferno - the legendary feet-free, suspended coaster with volcanic theming and effects, plus the wrenching Quantum. Back for a second sense-ational season, Colossus, the world's first 10-looping rollercoaster will continue to demonstrate the mighty power of Ten. Experience the trio of "must ride" thrill sensations - explosive Detonator, awesome Vortex and spinning Zodiac. Plus Tidal Wave, one of Europe's highest water drop rides, the white water thrills of Ribena Rumba Rapids, X:/No Way Out, Loggers Leap, Pirates-4D, Neptune's Beach, Thorpe farm and lots more besides.
Times: ✱ Open from 5 Apr-2 Nov (ex some off-peak days) 9/10-5/6 (times vary), 7.30 from 25 Jul-7 Sep, until 8 on fireworks night & from noon-11 on Fri nights. **Facilities:** ▣ ▣ ✖ licensed ᵹ (some rides not accessible, wheelchair hire available) toilets for disabled shop ✖ (ex guide dogs) 🍴

EAST CLANDON   Map 04 TQ05

HATCHLANDS PARK
GU4 7RT
⮑ (E of Guildford, off A246)
☎ 01483 222482
e-mail: hatchlands@nationaltrust.org.uk
web: www.nationaltrust.org.uk
Built in the 1750s for Admiral Boscawen, hero of the battle of Louisburg and set in a beautiful 430-acre Repton Park offering a variety of park and woodlands walks, Hatchlands boasts the earliest known decorative works by Robert Adam. Hatchlands is home to the Cobbe collection, the world's largest group of keyboard instruments associated with famous composers. There is also a small garden by Gertrude Jekyll, flowering from late May to early July and a beautiful bluebell wood in May.
Times: House & Gardens: Apr-Oct, Tue-Thu & Sun, 2-5.30 (also open BH & Fri in Aug). Park Walks open Apr-Oct, daily, 11-6. **Fee:** ✱ £6 (ch £3). Park walks £3 (ch £1.50). Family ticket £15. Combined ticket with Clandon Park £9 (ch £4.50). Family £22.50
Facilities: ▣ ✖ licensed 🗐 ᵹ (wheelchair available & special parking) toilets for disabled shop 🐾 🍴

FARNHAM   Map 04 SU84

BIRDWORLD & UNDERWATERWORLD
Holt Pound GU10 4LD
➲ (3m S of Farnham on A325)
☎ 01420 22140

e-mail: bookings@birdworld.co.uk
web: www.birdworld.co.uk

Birdworld is the largest bird collection in the country and includes toucans, pelicans, flamingoes, ostriches and many others. Underwater World is a tropical aquarium with brilliant lighting that shows off collections of marine and freshwater fish, as well as the swampy depths of the alligator exhibit. Visitors can also visit some beautiful gardens, the Jenny Wren farm and the Heron Theatre.
Times: Open daily, 10-6 (summer), 10-4.30 (winter). **Fee:** ✱ £9.75 (ch 3-14 £7.95, pen £7.95). Family ticket (2ad+2ch) £32.50
Facilities: 🅿 ✗ 🍴 ⚹ (wheelchairs available) toilets for disabled shop garden centre ✖ (ex guide dogs) 🍴

FARNHAM CASTLE KEEP
Castle Hill GU6 0AG
➲ (0.5m N on A287)
☎ 01252 713393
A motte and bailey castle, once one of the seats of the bishop of Winchester, has been in continuous occupation since the 12th-century.
Times: Open 24 Mar-Sep, 12-5, Fri- Sun & BHs **Fee:** £2.60 (ch £1.30, concessions £2.00). Opening times and prices are subject to change, for further details please phone 0870 333 1181 **Facilities:** 🅿 shop 🎏

GODSTONE   Map 05 TQ35

GODSTONE FARM
RH9 8LX
➲ (M25 junct 6, S of village, signed)
☎ 01883 742546
e-mail: havefun@godstonefarm.co.uk
web: www.godstonefarm.co.uk
An ideal day out for children, Godstone Farm has lots of friendly animals, big sand pits and play areas. The Indoor Play Barn costs 80p extra on rainy days.
Times: Open Mar-Oct, 10-6 (last admission 5); Nov-Feb 10-5 (last admission 4). Closed 25 & 26 Dec. **Fee:** ✱ Contact for admission prices. **Facilities:** 🅿 💷 🍴 ⚹ toilets for disabled shop ✖ (ex guide dogs) 🍴

GREAT BOOKHAM   Map 04 TQ15

POLESDEN LACEY
RH5 6BD
➲ (2m S off A246 from village of Bookham)
☎ 01372 452048
e-mail: polesdenlacey@nationaltrust.org.uk
web: www.nationaltrust.org.uk/polesdenlacey
King George VI and Queen Elizabeth (the Queen Mother) spent part of their honeymoon here, and photographs of other notable guests can be seen. The house is handsomely furnished and full of charm, and it is set in spacious grounds. There is also a summer festival, where concerts and plays are performed. Please phone 01372 452048 for details of special events.
Times: Open all year. Grounds, Garden & Landscape walks: daily 11-6. House: 23 Mar-6 Nov, Wed-Sun 11-5. Also BH Mon 11-5 (last admission 30mins before closing) **Facilities:** 🅿 💷 ✗ licensed 🍴 ⚹ (Braille guide & disabled parking by arrangement) toilets for disabled shop garden centre ✖

GUILDFORD   Map 04 SU94

DAPDUNE WHARF
Wharf Rd GU1 4RR
➲ (off Woodbridge Rd to rear of Surrey County Cricket Ground)
☎ 01483 561389
e-mail: riverwey@nationaltrust.org.uk
web: www.nationaltrust.org.uk/riverwey
The visitor centre at Dapdune Wharf is the centrepiece of one of the National Trust's most unusual properties, the River Wey Navigations. A series of interactive exhibits and displays allow you to discover the fascinating story of Surrey's secret waterway, one of the first British rivers to be made navigable. See where huge Wey barges were built and climb aboard Reliance, one of the last surviving barges. Children's trails and special events run throughout the season.
Times: Open Apr-Oct, Thu-Mon 11-5. River trips Thu-Mon 11-5 (conditions permitting) **Fee:** ✱ £2.50 (ch £1.50). Family ticket £6.50. National Trust Members free. **Facilities:** 🅿 💷 🍴 ⚹ (Braille guide) toilets for disabled shop ✖ (ex on leads) ✖

GUILDFORD HOUSE GALLERY
155 High St GU1 3AJ
➲ (N side of High St, opposite Sainsbury's)
☎ 01483 444740

e-mail: guildfordhouse@guildford.gov.uk
An impressive building in its own right, Guildford House dates from 1660 and has been Guildford's art gallery since 1959. A changing selection from the Borough's Art Collection is on display, including pastel portraits by John Russell, topographical paintings and contemporary craftwork, as well as temporary exhibitions.
Times: Open Tue-Sat 10-4.45. Closed Good Fri & Xmas
Facilities: 🅿 (100yds) 💷 ✗ 🍴 ⚹ shop ✖ (ex guide dogs) 🍴

Loseley Park

GU3 1HS
➲ (2m SW of Guildford, off A3 onto B3000)
☎ 01483 304440 & 505501
e-mail: enquiries@loseley-park.com
web: www.loseley-park.com

Magnificent Elizabethan mansion, home of the More-Molyneux family for over 450 years. Set in magnificent parkland scenery. Based on a Gertude Jekyll design. The walled garden contains five gardens each with its own theme and character. These include the award-wining Rose Garden, Vine Walk, Fruit, Flower Garden & the Serene White Fountain Garden.

Times: Open Grounds and Walled Garden: May-Sep, Tue-Sun & BH 11-5. House May-Aug, Tue-Thu, Sun & BH 1-5. **Fee:** House & Gardens £7 (ch £3.50, ch under 5 free, concessions £6.50). Gardens only £4 (ch £2, concessions £3.50). Discount for pre-booked groups. Garden season ticket £12 (admits ticket holder & guest from May-Sep)
Facilities: 🅿 💻 ✕ licensed ⅃ (wheelchair available, parking outside shop) toilets for disabled shop garden centre ✖ (ex guide dogs) ▄

HASCOMBE   Map 04 SU94

Winkworth Arboretum

Hascombe Rd GU8 4AD
➲ (2m SE of Golalming, e side of B2130, follow brown tourist signs from Godalming)
☎ 01483 208477
e-mail: winkwortharboretum@ nationaltrust.org.uk
web: www.nationaltrust.org.uk/ winkwortharboretum

This lovely woodland covers a hillside of nearly 100 acres, with fine views over the North Downs. The best times to visit are April and May, for the azaleas, bluebells and other flowers, and October for the autumn colours. A delightful Victorian boathouse is open Apr-Oct with fine views over Rowes Flashe lake. Many rare trees and shrubs in group plantings for spring and autumn colour effect.

Times: Open all year, daily during daylight hours. (Could close when weather is bad) **Fee:** ✱ £4.50 (ch £2). Family ticket £10, additional family member £1.75. **Facilities:** 🅿 💻 📷 ⅃ (suggested route, free entry for helpers) toilets for disabled shop on lead only ✖ ▄

OUTWOOD   Map 04 TQ34

Outwood Windmill

Outwood Common RH1 5PW
➲ (M25 junct 6, take A25 through Godstone towards Redhill, after 1m turn S off A25 at Bletchingly, between The Prince Albert & The White Hart. Mill 3m on left)
☎ 01342 843458 & 843644
e-mail: info@outwoodwindmill.co.uk
web: www.outwoodwindmill.co.uk

This award-winning example of a post-mill dates from 1665 and is the oldest working windmill in England and one of the best preserved in existence. Standing 400ft above sea level, it is surrounded by common land and National Trust property. Ducks and geese wander freely in the grounds.

Times: Open Etr Sun-3rd Sun in Oct, Sun & BH Mons only 2-6. Other times for parties only by arrangement. **Fee:** £2 (ch £1).
Facilities: 🅿 (10yds) 📷 ⅃ toilets for disabled shop

PAINSHILL PARK   Map 04 TQ06

Painshill Park

KT11 1JE
➲ (W of Cobham on A245)
☎ 01932 868113
e-mail: info@painshill.co.uk
web: www.painshill.co.uk

Within its 160 acres created by Charles Hamilton as a series of subtle and surprising vistas, its landscapes (The Hamilton Landscapes) include authentic 18th-century plantings, working vineyard, Gothic Temple, Chinese Bridge, Crystal Grotto, Turkish Tent, restored Hermitage and Gothic Tower. Special Events: American Roots 2006, a major horticultural exhibition. Please telephone or visit website for details.

Times: Open Mar-Oct, Tue-Sun & BH, 10.30-6. (last entry 4.30). Nov-Feb, Wed-Sun, & BH 11-4 (gates close 3). Closed 25 Dec.
Fee: ✱ £6 (ch 5-16 £3.50, concessions £5.25). Pre-booked adult groups 10+ £5. Please telephone 01932 868113 for 2006 prices. For more details check website **Facilities:** 🅿 💻 📷 ⅃ (wheelchairs & buggies available - pre-booked) toilets for disabled shop Selling Pains Hill wines on lead only ▄

REIGATE   Map 04 TQ24

Reigate Priory Museum

Bell St RH2 7RL
➲ (in Priory Park close to town centre, use Bell St car park on A217)
☎ 01737 222550
web: reigatepriorymuseum.org.uk

The Priory Museum is housed in Reigate Priory which was originally founded before 1200, this Grade I listed building was converted to a mansion in Tudor times. Notable features include the magnificent Holbein fireplace, 17th-early 18th century oak staircase and murals. The small museum has changing exhibitions on a wide range of subjects, designed to appeal to both adults and children. The collection includes domestic bygones, local history and costume.

Times: Open Etr-early Dec, Wed & Sat, 2-4.30 in term time.
Fee: Donations welcome. **Facilities:** 🅿 (50yds) 📷 ⅃ (hands on facilities) shop ✖

TILFORD
Map 04 SU84

RURAL LIFE CENTRE
Reeds Rd GU10 2DL
➲ (off A287, 3m S of Farnham, signed)
☎ 01252 795571
e-mail: rural.life@lineone.net
web: www.rural-life.org.uk

The museum covers village life from 1750 to 1960. It is set in over ten acres of garden and woodland and incorporates purpose-built and reconstructed buildings, including a chapel. Displays show village crafts and trades, such as wheelwrighting, thatching, ploughing and gardening. The historic village playground provides entertainment for children and there is an arboretum featuring over 100 trees from around the world.

Times: Open late Mar-early Oct, Wed-Sun & BH 10-5; Winter Wed & Sun only 11-4 **Fee:** £5 (ch £3 & pen £4). Family ticket £14 (2ad+2ch) **Facilities:** ℙ ⬛ ✗ licensed 🍴 ♿ (3 wheelchairs for use) toilets for disabled shop ▦

WEST CLANDON
Map 04 TQ05

CLANDON PARK
GU4 7RQ
➲ (E of Guildford on A247)
☎ 01483 222482
e-mail: clandonpark@nationaltrust.org.uk
web: www.nationaltrust.org.uk/clandonpark

A grand Palladian mansion built c.1730 by the Venetian architect Giacomo Leoni, and notable for its magnificent marble hall. The house is filled with the superb Gubbay collection of 18th-century furniture, porcelain, textiles and carpets. The attractive gardens contain a parterre, grotto, sunken Dutch garden and a Maori meetinghouse.

Times: House and Garden open Apr-Oct, Tue-Thu & Sun 11-5 (also BHs) **Fee:** ✱ House & Garden £6 (ch £3). Family ticket £15. Combined ticket with Hatchlands Park £9 (ch £4.50). Family £22.50 **Facilities:** ℙ ✗ licensed 🍴 ♿ (wheelchairs, Braille guide & disabled parking) toilets for disabled shop ✖ (ex guide dogs) 🐾 ▦

2-for-1 This symbol indicates attractions which have chosen to participate in our 2-for-1 voucher scheme

WEYBRIDGE
Map 04 TQ06

BROOKLANDS MUSEUM
Brooklands Rd KT13 0QN
➲ (M25 junct 10/11, museum off B374)
☎ 01932 857381
e-mail: info@brooklandsmuseum.com
web: www.brooklandsmuseum.com

Brooklands racing circuit was the birthplace of British motorsport and aviation. From 1907 to 1987 it was a world-renowned centre of engineering excellence. The Museum features old banked track and the 1-in-4 Test Hill. Many of the original buildings have been restored including the Clubhouse, the Shell and BP Petrol Pagodas, and the Malcolm Campbell Sheds in the Motoring Village. Many motorcycles, cars and aircraft are on display. Ring for details of special events.

Times: ✱ Open Tue-Sun & BHs 10-5 (4 in winter). **Facilities:** ℙ ⬛ ♿ toilets for disabled shop ✖ (ex guide dogs) ▦

WISLEY
Map 04 TQ05

RHS GARDEN WISLEY
GU23 6QB
➲ (on A3, close to M25 junct 10)
☎ 01483 224234
web: www.rhs.org.uk

Royal Horticultural Society

Covering over 240 acres, Wisley is the flagship of the Royal Horticultural Society demonstrating the very best in gardening practices. The gardens have a wide variety of trees, shrubs and plants, many of which are unusual in Britain. Whatever the season the garden serves as a working encyclopedia for gardeners of all levels.

Times: Open all year, Mon-Fri 10-6 (4.30 Nov-Feb), Sat-Sun, 9-6 (4.30 Nov-Feb). Closed 25 Dec. **Fee:** ✱ £7 (ch 6-16 £2) Group bookings 10+ £5.50 (ch £1.60) **Facilities:** ℙ ⬛ ✗ licensed 🍴 ♿ (free wheelchairs, electric buggies, wheelchair route) toilets for disabled shop garden centre ✖ (ex guide dogs) ▦

EAST SUSSEX

EVENTS & FESTIVALS

May
6th-28th Brighton International Festival, various venues (England's largest mixed arts festival)
19th-27th Aug Glyndebourne Festival Opera, Glyndebourne, Glynde, Lewis

June
11th London to Brighton Bike Race
tbc London to Brighton Classic Car Run

July
tbc Hastings Beer & Music Festival, Alexandra Park, Hastings
tbc Rye Medieval Festival, Rye

August
tbc Pride in Brighton & Hove, parade, Preston Park (provisional)

September
tbc Rye Festival of Music & the Arts, various venues

October
14th Hastings Borough Bonfire Celebrations (provisional)
14th-15th Battle of Hastings re-enactment, Battle Abbey
tbc Hastings Week (various venues)

November
5th London to Brighton Veteran Car Run, Hyde Park

December
21st Burning of the Clocks Parade with lanterns and fireworks, Brighton seafront

Above: The South Downs near Alfriston

ALFRISTON   Map 05 TQ50

ALFRISTON CLERGY HOUSE
The Tye BN26 5TL
➲ (4m NE of Seaford, E of B2108, next to church)
☎ 01323 870001
e-mail: alfriston@nationaltrust.org.uk
web: www.nationaltrust.org.uk
This 14th-century thatched Wealden 'hall house' was the first building to be acquired by the National Trust in 1896. It has an unusual chalk and sour milk floor, and its pretty cottage garden is in an idyllic setting beside Alfriston's parish church, with views across the meandering River Cockmere. Special Events: Please telephone for details of events running throughout the year.
Times: Open 6-21 Mar, Sat-Sun 11-4; Apr-Oct, Sat-Mon, daily (ex Tue & Fri), 10-5. 2 Nov-18 Dec daily (ex Tue & Fri) 11-4. **Fee:** ✱ £3.10 (ch £1.55). Family ticket £7.75 **Facilities:** ℗ (0.25m) 📖 (Braille/large print guides, sensory guide) shop ✕ (ex guide dogs) ♨ ⏭

DRUSILLAS PARK
BN26 5QS
➲ (off A27 near Alfriston 12m from Brighton & 7m from Eastbourne)
☎ 01323 874100
e-mail: info@drusillas.co.uk
web: www.drusillas.co.uk
Situated amidst the stunning scenery of the Cuckmere Valley at Alfriston, Drusillas is widely recognised as the Best Small Zoo in England. There are over 100 animal species in naturalistic environments, including meerkats, bats, penguins, monkeys, reptiles and creepy crawlies. The large adventure play area is paradise for anyone who needs to let off steam. There are also beautiful gardens, Panning for Gold, a Wacky Workshop, Jungle Adventure Golf, Explorers Lagoon, Mokomo's Jungle Rock, Vertical Limit, Penguin Plunge, a train that goes through the llama paddock and the Discovery Centre, Amazon Adventure, a vast indoor play area.
Times: Open all year, daily 10-6 (winter 10-5). Closed 24-26 Dec. **Fee:** ✱ Family super saver tickets: Family of 3 £30, family of 4 £40, family of 5 £50 **Facilities:** ℗ 💺 ✕ licensed 📖 ♿ (rear train carriage & sensory trails) toilets for disabled shop ✕ (ex guide dogs) ⏭

BATTLE   Map 05 TQ71

BATTLE MUSEUM OF LOCAL HISTORY
The Almonry, High St TN33 0EA
➲ (A21 towards Hastings. Right onto A2001. Museum on High St adjacent to Market Sq, N end of town)
☎ 01424 775955
e-mail: enquiries@battlemuseum.org.uk
web: www.battlemuseum.org.uk
The focal point of this museum is the only battle-axe head yet from the Battle of Hastings and a reproduction of the Bayeux Tapestry. There are also local history exhibits. There is a special exhibition displaying the wealth of finds at the Beauport Park Roman Bath House excavated just outside Battle. The museum holds two or three temporary exhibitions each year.
Times: Open Apr-Oct, daily 10.30-4.30 (Sun 2-5). **Fee:** ✱ £1 (ch 20p, ch accompanied free). **Facilities:** ℗ (20yds) 📖 ♿ (single storey building) toilets for disabled shop ✕ (ex guide dogs)

1066 BATTLE OF HASTINGS ABBEY & BATTLEFIELD

TN33 0AD

➲ (A21 onto A2100)

☎ 01424 773792

Explore the site of the Battle of Hastings, where on 14th October 1066, one of the most famous events in English history took place. Free interactive wand tour of the battlefield and atmospheric abbey ruins.

Times: Open all year, Apr-Sep, daily 10-6; Oct-Mar, daily 10-4. Closed 24-26 Dec & 1 Jan. **Fee:** £5.30 (ch £2.70, concessions £4.00). Family £13.30. Opening times and prices are subject to change, for further details please phone 0870 333 1181 **Facilities:** ▣ (charged) ♿ shop ▦

YESTERDAY'S WORLD

89-90 High St TN33 0AQ

➲ (Junct 5 off M25, A21 onto A2100 towards Battle, opposite Battle Abbey Gatehouse)

☎ 01424 775378 & 774269

e-mail: info@yesterdaysworld.co.uk

web: www.yesterdaysworld.co.uk

A fun day out for all the family, as the past is brought to life. Walk down the cobbled streets of yesteryear and meet the colourful characters in over 30 shop and room settings including a 1930s grocer's and a Victorian kitchen. The exhibition contains many rarities from the 1850s onwards, including some of Queen Victoria's personal effects and letters written by the present queen. The museum is housed in beautiful gardens with children's play village, miniature golf and summer tea rooms. Special Events: Please visit website for details of events running throughout the year.

Times: Open all year, Winter, daily 9.30-5; Summer, daily 9.30-6. Closed 25-26 Dec and 1 Jan. **Fee:** ✱ £5.95 (ch £3.95, pen £4.95). Family ticket £16.99. Discount for groups of 15+.

Facilities: ▣ (100yds) (£2.50 per day) ▣ ▦ ♿ (limited access for wheelchairs) toilets for disabled shop ▰

BODIAM   Map 05 TQ72

BODIAM CASTLE

TN32 5UA

➲ (2m E of A21 Hurst Green)

☎ 01580 830436

e-mail: bodiamcastle@nationaltrust.org.uk

web: www.nationaltrust.org.uk/places/bodiamcastle

With its tall round drum towers at each corner, Bodiam is something of a fairytale castle. It was built in 1386 by Sir Edward Dalnygrigge, for comfort and defence. The walls measure some 6ft 6in thick, and the great gatehouse was defended by gun loops and three portcullises.

Times: ✱ Open 16 Feb-Oct, daily 10-6 or dusk if earlier; Nov-15 Feb, Sat & Sun 10-4 or dusk. (Last admission 1 hour before closing). **Facilities:** ▣ (charged) ▣ ♿ (Braille/large print guides, special parking on request) toilets for disabled shop ▨ ▰

BRIGHTON   Map 04 TQ30

BOOTH MUSEUM OF NATURAL HISTORY

194 Dyke Rd BN1 5AA

➲ (from A27 Brighton by pass, 1.5m NW of town centre, opposite Dyke Rd Park)

☎ 01273 292777   `FREE`

e-mail: boothmuseum@brighton-hove.gov.uk

web: www.virtualmuseum.info

The museum was built in 1874 to house the bird collection of Edward Thomas Booth (1840-1890). His collection is still on display, but the museum has expanded considerably since Booth's day and now includes thousands of butterfly and insect specimens, geology galleries with fossils, rocks and local dinosaur bones, a magnificent collection of animal skeletons, largely collected by the Brighton solicitor F W Lucas (1842-1932), and an interactive discovery gallery.

Times: Open all year, Mon-Sat (ex Thu) 10-5, Sun 2-5. Closed Good Fri, Xmas & 1 Jan. **Facilities:** ▣ (road opposite) (2 hr limit) ▦ ♿ shop ✖ (ex guide dogs) ▰

BRIGHTON MUSEUM & ART GALLERY

Royal Pavilion Gardens BN1 1EE

➲ (A23/M23 from London. In city centre near seafront. New entrance in Royal Pavilion Gardens)

☎ 01273 290900   `FREE`

web: www.brighton.virtualmuseum.info

A £10 million redevelopment has transformed Brighton museum into a state-of-the-art visitor attraction. Dynamic and innovative new galleries, including fashion, 20th-century design and world art, featuring exciting interactive displays appealing to all ages. The museum also benefits from a spacious new entrance located in the Royal Pavilion gardens and full disabled access.

Times: ✱ Open all year, Tue 10-7, Wed-Sat 10-5 & Sun 2-5. (Closed Mon ex BHs). **Facilities:** ▣ (5 mins walk) (Church St NCP & on street) ▣ ♿ (lift,tactile exhibits,induction loops,ramps,automatic door) toilets for disabled shop ✖ (ex guide dogs)

PRESTON MANOR

Preston Drove BN1 6SD

➲ (off A23, 2m N of Brighton)

☎ 01273 292770

e-mail: visitor.services@brighton-hove.gov.uk

web: www.prestonmanor.virtualmuseum.info

This charming Edwardian manor house is beautifully furnished with notable collections of silver, furniture and paintings and presents a unique opportunity to see an Edwardian home both 'upstairs' and 'downstairs'. The servants' quarters can also be seen, featuring kitchen, butler's pantry and boot hall. The house is set in beautiful gardens, which include a pet cemetery and the 13th-century parish church of St Peter. The restored walled garden enables disabled people to explore the garden for the first time.

Times: Open Apr-Sep, Tue-Sat 10-5, Sun 2-5. Closed Mon & from Oct-Mar. **Fee:** £3.90 (ch £2.25, concessions £3.20). Family ticket £6.15-£10. Party 20+ £3.30 each. **Facilities:** ▣ ▦ ♿ (call prior to visit to discuss access requirements) shop ✖ (ex guide dogs)

ROYAL PAVILION

BN1 1EE

⮑ (M23/A23 from London. In city centre near seafront. 15 min walk from rail station)

☎ 01273 290900

e-mail: visitor.services@brighton-hove.gov.uk
web: www.royalpavilion.org.uk

Acclaimed as one of the most exotically beautiful buildings in the British Isles, the Royal Pavilion was the magnificent seaside residence of George IV. The breathtaking Regency palace is decorated in Chinese style, with a romanticised Indian exterior, and surrounded by restored Regency gardens.

Times: ✱ Open all year, Apr-Sep, daily 9.30-5.45 (last admission 5); Oct-Mar, daily 10-5.15 (last admission 4.30). **Facilities:** P (5 mins walk) (NCP & on Church St) 🍽 📖 ♿ (tours for the disabled by arrangement, wheelchairs) toilets for disabled shop ✖ (ex guide dogs) 🍴

SEA LIFE CENTRE

Marine Pde BN2 1TB

⮑ (next to Brighton Pier between Marine Parade & Madeira Drive)

☎ 01273 604234

e-mail: slcbrighton@merlinentertainments.biz
web: www.sealife.co.uk

Experience spectacular marine displays, set in the world's oldest functioning aquarium. Take a look at over 100 species in their natural habitat, including seahorses, sharks and rays. Over forty exhibits include Adventures at 20,000 Leagues complete with NASA-designed walkthrough observation tunnel. Features also include a Captain Pugwash quiz trail, a soft play area, a cafe and a giftshop.

Times: ✱ Open all year, daily 10-6. (Last admission 5). Open later on wknds in summer & school hols. Closed 25 Dec.

Facilities: P (200yds) (pay & display) 🍽 📖 ♿ toilets for disabled shop ✖ (ex guide dogs) 🍴

BURWASH Map 05 TQ62

BATEMAN'S

TN19 7DS

⮑ (0.5m SW off A265)

☎ 01435 882302

e-mail: batemans@nationaltrust.org.uk
web: www.nationaltrust.org.uk

Rudyard Kipling lived for over 34 years in this 17th-century manor house and it remains much the same as it was during *continued*

his lifetime. His 1928 Rolls Royce Phantom is on display, and the watermill at the bottom of the garden grinds wheat into flour on Saturday afternoons and Wednesdays. Special Event: 70th Anniversary of Kipling's death.

Times: Open Apr-1 Nov, Sat-Wed 11-5.30, also open Good Fri, (last admission 4.30). House closes at 5. **Fee:** ✱ £5.90 (ch £2.95). Family ticket £14.75 Party 15+ £4.90 each. **Facilities:** P 🍽 ✖ licensed 📖 ♿ (Braille guide,touch test,computerised tour of upper floors) toilets for disabled shop ✖ (ex guide/hearing dogs) 🥾 🍴

EASTBOURNE Map 05 TV69

"HOW WE LIVED THEN" MUSEUM OF SHOPS & SOCIAL HISTORY

20 Cornfield Ter BN21 4NS

⮑ (just off seafront, between town centre & theatres, signed)

☎ 01323 737143

e-mail: howwelivedthen@btconnect.com
web: www.how-we-lived-then.co.uk

Over the last 50 years, Jan and Graham Upton have collected over 100,000 items which are now displayed on four floors of authentic old shops and room-settings, transporting visitors back to their grandparents' era. Other displays, such as seaside souvenirs, wartime rationing and Royal mementoes, help to capture 100 years of social history.

Times: Open all year, daily, 10-5.30 (last entry 5). Winter times subject to change, telephone establishment. **Fee:** £4 (ch 5-15 £3, under 5's free, pen £3.50). Party 10+. **Facilities:** P (outside) 📖 ♿ (no charge for disabled) shop

WISH TOWER PUPPET MUSEUM

Martello Tower No 73, King Edward Pde BN21 4BU

⮑ (on seafront, W of pier)

☎ 01323 417776

e-mail: puppet.workshop@virgin.net
web: www.puppets.co.uk

This museum hosts a unique display of puppets from all over the world. From early shadow puppets of Asia, through over 300 years of Punch and Judy in England to television and film puppets of today. Puppet shows sometimes take place during the summer.

Times: ✱ Open May-mid Jul & Sep, wknds 11-5; mid Jul-Aug, daily 11-5. **Facilities:** P (100mtrs) shop ✖ 🍴

FIRLE Map 05 TQ40

FIRLE PLACE

BN8 6LP

⮑ (off A27, Eastbourne to Brighton road near Lewes)

☎ 01273 858307

e-mail: gage@firleplace.co.uk
web: www.firleplace.co.uk

Home of the Gage family for over 500 years, the house has a Tudor core but was remodelled in the 18th century. Its treasures include important European and English Old Master paintings, fine English and French furniture, and porcelain, including notable examples from Sèvres and English factories. There are family monuments and brasses in the church at West Firle.

Times: Open May-Sep, Sun, Wed, Thu & BHs 2-4.30. **Fee:** ✱ £5.75 (ch £3.50, concessions £5.25). Groups 25+. Connoisseurs Day £7.50 each. Private viewing 25+ by appointment only.

Facilities: P ✖ licensed ♿ (virtual tour video) toilets for disabled shop ✖ (ex in garden) 🍴

FOREST ROW   Map 05 TQ43
ASHDOWN FOREST LLAMA PARK
Wych Cross RH18 5JN
➲ (on A22 between Uckfield & East Grinstead,
250mtrs S of junct with A275)
☎ 01825 712040
e-mail: info@llamapark.co.uk
web: www.llamapark.co.uk

One of the leading llama breeding centres in the country.
Walk around three 18th-century barns and a new visitor
centre to discover over 100 llamas and alpacas. Llamas and
alpacas were first domesticated in South America more than
5,000 years ago, and visitors can learn all about their
contribution to these societies at the museum. Visitors can
also walk with llamas in the grounds, but these walks do
need to be booked and paid for in advance. Contact the park
for more details.

Times: Open daily 10-5. Closed 25 & 26 Dec   **Facilities:** 🅿 💻
⬤ (ramps, wheelchairs provided for free) toilets for disabled shop 🔚

GLYNDE   Map 05 TQ40
GLYNDE PLACE
BN8 6SX
➲ (off A27 between Lewes & Eastbourne)
☎ 01273 858224
e-mail: hampden@glyndeplace.co.uk
web: www.glyndeplace.co.uk

A lovely Elizabethan manor with 18th-century additions, in a
beautiful downland setting. Glynde Place is the family home
of Viscount and Viscountess Hampden whose forebears built
the house in 1569 using a mixture of flint and stone.
Portraits, furniture, silver, embroidery and books testify to
400 years of family life.

Times: Open May-Aug, Wed, Sun & Aug BH 2-4.45. **Fee:** ✱ £5.50
(ch £2.75). Parties 25+ £4 each. Gardens only £2.50.
Facilities: 🅿 💻 🍴 ⬤ toilets for disabled shop 🔚 (ex guide dogs)

HAILSHAM   Map 05 TQ50
MICHELHAM PRIORY
Upper Dicker BN27 3QS
➲ (off A22 & A27, 2m W of Hailsham, 8m NW of
Eastbourne, signed from A27 & A22)
☎ 01323 844224
e-mail: adminmich@sussexpast.co.uk
web: www.sussexpast.co.uk

Set on a moated island surrounded by glorious gardens,
Michelham Priory is one of the most beautiful historic houses
in Sussex. Founded in 1229 for Augustinian canons, the
Priory is approached through a 14th-century gatehouse
spanning the longest water-filled medieval moat in the
country. Most of the original priory was demolished during
the Dissolution, but the remains were incorporated into a
Tudor farm that became a country house. Outside, the
gardens are enhanced by a working watermill, physic
garden, smithy, rope museum and the dramatic Elizabethan
Great Barn.

Times: Open Mar-Oct, Tue-Sun (daily in Aug & BH Mons). Mar & Oct
10.30-4.30, Apr-Jul & Sep 10.30-5, Aug 10.30-5.30. **Fee:** £6.50 (ch 5-15
£2.90, pen & student £4.70). Family ticket (2ad+2ch) £14.30.
Disabled/carer £2.80 each. **Facilities:** 🅿 💻 ✗ licensed
⬤ (pre-booked wheelchairs, Braille guide & tactile tours) toilets for
disabled shop 🔚 (ex guide dogs) 🔚

HALLAND   Map 05 TQ51
BENTLEY WILDFOWL & MOTOR MUSEUM
BN8 5AF
➲ (7m NE of Lewes, signposted off A22, A26 &
B2192)
☎ 01825 840573
e-mail: barrysutherland@pavilion.co.uk
web: www.bentley.org.uk

Hundreds of swans, geese and ducks from all over the world
can be seen on lakes and ponds along with flamingoes and
peacocks. There is a fine array of Veteran, Edwardian and
Vintage vehicles, and the house has splendid antiques and
wildfowl paintings. The gardens specialise in old fashioned
roses. Other attractions include woodland walks, a nature
trail, education centre, adventure playground and a
miniature train.

Times: ✱ Open 17 Mar-Oct, daily 10.30-4.30. House open from noon,
Apr-Nov, Feb & part of Mar, wknds only. Estate closed Dec & Jan.
House closed all winter. **Facilities:** 🅿 💻 🍴 ⬤ (wheelchairs
available) toilets for disabled shop 🔚 (ex guide dogs) 🔚

HASTINGS   Map 05 TQ80
OLD TOWN HALL MUSEUM OF LOCAL HISTORY
Old Town Hall, High St TN34 3EW
➲ (off A259 coast road into High St in Hastings
old town. Signed)   `FREE`
☎ 01424 781166
e-mail: oldtownmuseum@hastings.gov.uk
web: www.hmag.org.uk

Situated in the heart of Hastings Old Town, the museum was
originally a Georgian Town Hall built in 1823. Refurbished
displays tell the story of Hastings Old Town as a walk back in
time, with features including a Cinque Ports ship, and
interactive displays.

Times: Winter: Oct-Mar, Mon-Fri 10-4 Sat-Sun 11-4. Summer: Apr-Sep
Mon-Sat 10-5 Sun 11-5. **Facilities:** 🅿 (150yds) (parking meters in
operation) 🍴 ⬤ (lift, evac chair, low-level displays, audio tour) toilets
for disabled shop 🔚 (ex guide dogs)

SMUGGLERS ADVENTURE
St Clements Caves, West Hill TN34 3HY
➲ (follow brown signs on A259, coast road,
through Hastings. Use seafront car park, then take
West Cliff railway or follow signed footpath)
☎ 01424 422964
e-mail: smugglers@discoverhastings.co.uk
web: www.discoverhastings.co.uk

A Smuggler's Adventure is a themed experience housed in a
labyrinth of caverns and passages deep below the West Hill.
Visitors first tour a comprehensive exhibition and museum,
followed by a video theatre, before embarking on the
Adventure Walk - a trip through several acres of caves with
life-size tableaux, push-button automated models and
dramatic scenic effects depicting life in the days of 18th-
century smuggling.

Times: Open all year daily, Etr-Sep 10-5.30; Oct-Etr 11-4.30. Closed
24-26 Dec. **Fee:** ✱ £5.95 (ch £3.95, concessions £4.95). Family ticket
£16.50. **Facilities:** 🅿 (500yds) (parking meters on some streets) 🍴
shop 🔚 (ex guide dogs) 🔚

1066 Story in Hastings Castle

Castle Hill Rd, West Hill TN34 3RG
➲ (close to A259 seafront, 2m from B2093)
☎ 01424 781111 & 781112 (info line)
e-mail: bookings@discoverhastings.co.uk
web: www.hastings.gov.uk

The ruins of the Norman castle stand on the cliffs, close to the site of William the Conqueror's first motte-and-bailey castle in England. It was excavated in 1825 and 1968, and old dungeons were discovered in 1894. An unusual approach to the castle can be made via the West Hill Cliff Railway.

Times: Open daily, Oct-26 Mar 11-3.30, 27 Mar-Sep 10-5. Closed 24-26 Dec. **Fee:** ✱ £3.40 (ch £2.25, pen & students £2.75, disabled free). Family ticket £10 (fee entitles visitor to third off Caves & Underwater World) **Facilities:** P (seafront) (time restrictions, pay & display) ♿ (concrete slope, some uneven ground) shop (ex guide dogs)

HERSTMONCEUX Map 05 TQ61

The Observatory Science Centre

BN27 1RN (0.75m N of Wartling village.)
☎ 01323 832731
e-mail: info@the-observatory.org
web: www.the-observatory.org

From the 1950s to the 1980s this was part of the Royal Greenwich Observatory, and was used by astronomers to observe and chart movements in the night sky. Visitors can learn about not only astronomy, but also other areas of science in a series of interactive and engaging displays. There are also exhibitions, a discovery park, and a collection of unusual giant exhibits.

Times: Open daily from 1Feb-30 Nov and 3-4, 10-11 Dec. Jan-Mar & Oct-Dec 10-5, Apr-Sep 10-6. **Fee:** ✱ £6.20 (ch 4-15 £4.50). Family ticket (2ad+3ch or 1ad+4ch) £18.60, Family of 5 £21.30. **Facilities:** P ♿ (ramps & disabled entrance, lift to 1st floor) toilets for disabled shop (ex guide dogs)

The Truggery

Coopers Croft BN27 1QL
➲ (from A22 at Hailsham, Boship rdbt, take A271 towards Bexhill for 4m)
☎ 01323 832314 FREE
e-mail: sarah@truggery.fsnet.co.uk
web: www.truggery.co.uk

The art of Sussex trug making can be seen through all the work processes including preparing timber, use of the draw knife and assembly of trug.

Times: Open Mon-Fri 10-5, Sat 10-1. Closed Sun. Jan-Apr opening times may vary. **Facilities:** P ♿ shop full range of Trugs

HOVE Map 04 TQ20

British Engineerium-Museum of Steam & Mechanical Antiquities

off Nevill Rd BN3 7QA
➲ (signed off A27 from Worthing & Eastbourne)
☎ 01273 559583
e-mail: info@britishengineerium.com
web: www.britishengineerium.com

This restored Victorian water pumping station has an original working beam engine of 1876, and a French Corliss horizontal engine which won first prize at the Paris International Exhibition of 1889. There are also traction engines, fire engines, and many other full-size and model engines. Also an exhibition of craftsmen's tools and domestic appliances. Boilers are fired up and in steam on special days.

Times: ✱ Open all year, daily 10-4. In steam first Sun in month & Sun & Mon of BHs. Telephone for details of days closed prior to Xmas. **Facilities:** P ♿ shop (ex guide dogs)

LEWES Map 05 TQ41

Anne of Cleves House

52 Southover High St BN7 1JA
➲ (S of town centre off A27/A26/A275)
☎ 01273 474610
e-mail: anne@sussexpast.co.uk
web: www.sussexpast.co.uk

Henry VIII gave this beautiful timber-framed house to Anne of Cleves, his fourth wife, as part of her divorce settlement. Today there are collections of early English furniture, Sussex pottery and stone from Lewes Priory, plus a local social history exhibition. The Wealden Iron Gallery tells the story of the industrial past of Sussex and contains a large collection of iron artefacts.

Times: Open Jan-Feb & Nov-Dec, Tue-Sat 10-5; Mar-Oct, Tue-Sat 10-5, Sun, Mon & BHs 11-5. Closed 24-26 Dec. **Fee:** £3.10 (ch 5-15 £1.55, pen & student £2.80). Family ticket £7.90 (2ad+2ch), £6.30 (1ad+4ch). Disabled/Carer £1.55 **Facilities:** P (25yds) (on street-2hr restriction) ♿ shop (ex guide dogs)

Lewes Castle & Barbican House Museum

169 High St BN7 1YE
➲ (N of High St off A27/A26/A275)
☎ 01273 486290
e-mail: castle@sussexpast.co.uk
web: www.sussexpast.co.uk

High above the medieval streets stands Lewes Castle, begun soon after the Norman Conquest by William de Warenne as his stronghold in Sussex and added to over the next 300 years, culminating in the magnificent Barbican. Thomas Read Kemp and his family owned and updated the ruins during Georgian times. Barbican House is next to the castle, and now houses a museum covering the area from pre-history to the late medieval period. Visitors can climb to the top of the castle, from where they are rewarded by stunning views. A 'sound and light' show in the museum below tells the story of the town of Lewes through the ages.

Times: Open daily, Tue-Sat 10-5.30, Sun, Mon & BHs 11-5.30. (Last admission 30 mins before closing). Closed Xmas & Mon in Jan. **Fee:** £4.50 (ch (5-15) £2.25, pen & student £4). Family ticket (2ad+2ch) £11.70, (1ad+4ch) £9.20. Disabled/Carer £2.25. **Facilities:** P (on street parking) shop (ex guide dogs)

NEWHAVEN — Map 05 TQ40

PARADISE PARK & GARDENS

Avis Rd BN9 0DH

➲ (signed off A26 & A259)

☎ 01273 512123

e-mail: enquiries@paradisepark.co.uk

web: www.paradisepark.co.uk

A perfect day out for plant lovers whatever the season. Discover the unusual garden designs with waterfalls, fountains and lakes, including the Caribbean garden and the tranquil Oriental garden. The Conservatory Gardens complex contains a large variety of the world's flora divided into several zones. There's also a Sussex history trail and Planet Earth with moving dinosaurs and interactive displays, plus rides and amusements for children.

Times: ✱ Open all year, daily 9-6. Closed 25-26 Dec.

Facilities: 🅿 💺 ✕ licensed 🍴 ♿ (all areas level or ramped) toilets for disabled shop garden centre ✖ (ex guide dogs) 🍴

NORTHIAM — Map 05 TQ82

GREAT DIXTER HOUSE & GARDENS

TN31 6PH

➲ (off A28, signed)

☎ 01797 252878

e-mail: office@greatdixter.co.uk

web: www.greatdixter.co.uk

Birthplace and home of Christopher Lloyd, gardening writer, Great Dixter was built in 1460 and boasts one of the largest timber-framed buildings in the country. Lutyens was employed to restore both the house and gardens in 1910. The gardens are now a combination of meadows, ponds, topiary and notably the Long Border and Exotic Garden.

Times: Open Apr-Oct, Tue-Sun & BH Mon, 2-5.30 (last admission 5); Gardens open from 11 on Sun & Mon BH wknds only. **Fee:** House & Gardens £7 (ch £2). Gardens only £5.50 (ch £1.50). Party 25+.

Facilities: 🅿 ♿ (2 wheelchairs available free of charge) toilets for disabled shop garden centre ✖ (ex guide dogs) 🍴

PEVENSEY — Map 05 TQ60

PEVENSEY CASTLE

BN24 5LE

➲ (off A259)

☎ 01323 762604

William the Conqueror landed here in 1066 and established his first stronghold. Discover the history of the Norman castle and the remains of an unusual keep through the free audio tour.

Times: Opening hours: 24 Mar-Sep, 10-6, daily. Oct-Mar, 10-4, Sat-Sun. Closed 24-26 Dec & 1 Jan **Fee:** £3.70 (ch £1.90, concessions £2.80). Opening times and prices are subject to change, for further details please phone 0870 333 1181 **Facilities:** 🅿 (charged) 💺 ♿ shop ⊞

> We endeavour to be as accurate as possible, but changes to times and other information can occur after the guide has gone to press.

RYE — Map 05 TQ92

LAMB HOUSE

West St TN31 7ES

➲ (facing W end of Church)

☎ 01732 453401

web: www.nationaltrust.org.uk

This 18th-century house was the home of novelist Henry James from 1898 until his death in 1916, and was later occupied by the writer, E F Benson. Some of James' personal posessions can be seen. There is also a charming walled garden.

Times: Open 26 Mar-29 Oct, Wed & Sat 2-6, (last admission 5.30).

Fee: ✱ £2.90 (ch £1.40). Family ticket £7.25. Groups £2.50 per person

Facilities: 🅿 (500mtrs) 🍴 (scented plants & herbs, some steps to house) ✖ (ex guide dogs) 🍴

RYE CASTLE MUSEUM

3 East St TN31 7JY

➲ (in town centre, on A259)

☎ 01797 226728

2 for 1

Part of the museum is housed in a stone tower built as a fortification in 1249. The museum's collection of ironwork, medieval pots and smuggling items are on display here, while the East Street site contains the rest of the collection, including pottery made in Rye, fashions, an eighteenth-century fire engine, toys, cinque port regalia, a special exhibition on Rye between the wars, descriptions of the changes to the harbour and shipbuilding in Rye and businesses and leisure in Rye during the 19th and 20th centuries. The museum tells the story of Rye's long and illustrious history.

Times: Open all year Nov-Mar wknds only 10.30-3; Apr-Oct Thu-Mon 10.30-5 (last entry 4.30). Closed between 1-2. **Fee:** Entrance to both sites: £2.90 (ch under 7 free, ch 7-16 £1.50, concessions £2). Family ticket £5.90. Single entry only: £1.90 (ch under 7 free, ch 7-16 £1, concessions £1.50). Family ticket £4.50. Party 8+. Subject to change.

Facilities: 🅿 (30yds) (street 1hr) (long stay 10mins away) 🍴 ♿ (only East Street accessible, part of garden) toilets for disabled shop ✖ (ex guide dogs)

SHEFFIELD PARK — Map 05 TQ42

SHEFFIELD PARK GARDEN

TN22 3QX

➲ (midway between East Grinstead & Lewes, 5m NW of Uckfield, on E side of A275, between A272 & A22)

☎ 01825 790231

e-mail: sheffieldpark@nationaltrust.org.uk

web: www.nationaltrust.org.uk/sheffieldpark

Sheffield Park was originally landscaped by 'Capability' Brown, in about 1775 to create a beautiful park with four lakes and cascades. Further extensive planting was done at the beginning of the 20th century, to give emphasis to autumn colour among the trees. In May and June masses of azaleas and rhododendrons bloom and later there are magnificent waterlilies on the lakes. Autumn brings stunning colours from the many rare trees and shrubs. Special events throughout the season.

Times: Open all year. Please phone fro details. **Fee:** ✱ £5.50 (ch £2.75, ch under 5 free). Family ticket £13.75. NT members free.

Facilities: 🅿 💺 🍴 ♿ (powered self drive cars & wheelchairs pre-book) toilets for disabled shop ✖ (ex guide/hearing dogs) 🍴 🍴

SHEFFIELD PARK STATION Map 05 TQ42

BLUEBELL RAILWAY
Sheffield Park Station TN22 3QL
➲ (4.5m E of Haywards Heath, off A275, 10m S of East Grinstead A22-A275)
☎ 01825 720800 & 722370
e-mail: info@bluebell-railway.co.uk
web: www.bluebell-railway.co.uk

A volunteer-run heritage steam railway with nine miles of track running through pretty Sussex countryside. Please note that there is no parking at Kingscote Station. If you wish to board the train here, catch the bus (service 473) which connects Kingscote and East Grinstead.
Times: Open all year, Sat & Sun, daily May-Sep & during school holidays. Santa Specials run Dec. For timetable and information regarding trains contact above. **Fee:** 3rd class return fare £9 (ch £4.50). Family ticket £25. Admission to Sheffield Park Station only £1.60 (ch 80p). Other tickets available on request. Maybe subject to change, please telephone for details. **Facilities:** 🅿 💺 ✕ licensed ♿ (special carriage for wheelchairs & carers with lift) toilets for disabled shop 🍴

TICEHURST Map 05 TQ63

PASHLEY MANOR GARDENS
TN5 7HE
➲ (on B2099 between A21 and Ticehurst village, follow brown tourist signs)
☎ 01580 200888
e-mail: info@pashleymanorgardens.com
web: www.pashleymanorgardens.com

Once belonging to the family of Anne Boleyn, Pashley Manor has a beautiful traditional English garden that has been open to the public since 1992. Visitors can wander among fine old trees, fountains, springs and large ponds, all surrounded by romantic landscaping and imaginative plantings. Statues and sculptures by Europe's leading sculptors are on display both in the gardens and in the Great Hall. A series of craft and speciality plant fairs take place throughout the year. Please telephone for details of events happening throughout the year.
Times: Open 8 Apr-Sep, Tue-Thu, Sat & BH Mon 11-5; Garden only Oct, Mon-Fri 10-4. **Fee:** £6 (pen £5.50) **Facilities:** 🅿 ✕ licensed 📋 ♿ toilets for disabled shop ✖ (ex guide dogs) 🍴

Winchelsea

WEST SUSSEX

EVENTS & FESTIVALS

April
14th British & World Marbles Championships, Greyhound pub, Radford Road, Tinsley Green, Crawley
30th-1st May Spring Garden & Leisure Show, Showground, Ardingly, Haywards Heath

May
14th Town Centre Cycle Races, Crawley
14th-15th Corpus Christi Carpet of Flowers & Floral Festival, Cathedral of Our Lady & St Philip Howard, Arundel

June
1st-3rd Flower Festival, Chichester Cathedral
8th-10th South of England Show, Showground, Ardingly, Haywards Heath
17th-18th Parham Steam Rally, Parham House, Pulborough
30th-2nd Jul Crawley Folk Festival, The Hawth, Hawth Avenue, Crawley

July
9th Crawley Fun Run, K2 Leisure Centre, Crawley
28th-30th Crawley International Mela, The Hawth, Crawley
tbc Chichester Festivities, various venues
tbc Petworth Festival (various Venues)

August
12th-13th Crawley Circus Festival, The Hawth, Crawley (provisional)
tbc Arundel Festival
tbc Bognor Birdman, attempts at self-powered flight, esplanade & seafront, Bognor Regis
tbc Crawley Irish Festival

September
9th Findon Great Sheep Fair, Nepcote Green, Findon (provisional)
30th-1st Oct South of England Autumn Show, Showground, Ardingly, Haywards Heath

Above: 11th-century Arundel Castle, completely rebuilt in the 19th century

AMBERLEY — Map 04 TQ01

AMBERLEY WORKING MUSEUM
BN18 9LT
➲ (on B2139, between Arundel and Storrington, adjacent to Amberley railway station)
☎ 01798 831370
e-mail: office@amberleymuseum.co.uk
web: www.amberleymuseum.co.uk

36 acre open-air museum dedicated to the industrial heritage of the south east of England. Traditional craftspeople on site (including a blacksmith and potter), working narrow-gauge railway and vintage bus collection, Connected Earth telecommunications display, Seeboard Electricity Hall, stationary engines, print workshop, woodturners, wheelwrights, nature trails, restaurant, shop and much more.

Times: ✱ Open 12 Mar-2 Nov, Wed-Sun & BH Mon 10-5.30 (last admission 4.30). Also open daily during school hols.
Facilities: 🅿 💷 📺 ♿ (wheelchairs available for loan & large print guides) toilets for disabled shop ■

ARDINGLY — Map 05 TQ32

WAKEHURST PLACE & MILLENNIUM SEED BANK
Royal Botanic Gardens RH17 6TN
➲ (M23 junct 10, 1.5m NW of Ardingly, on B2028, follow brown tourist signs)
☎ 01444 894066
e-mail: wakehurst@kew.org
web: www.kew.org

Woodland and lakes linked by a pretty watercourse make this large garden a beautiful place to walk, and it also has an amazing variety of interesting trees and shrubs, a winter garden, and a rock walk. It is administered and maintained by the Royal Botanic Gardens, Kew.

Times: 10-4 Jan-Feb, 10-6 Mar-Oct, Nov-Oct 10-4. Closed 24-25 Dec.
Fee: £8.50, under 17's free. **Facilities:** 🅿 💷 ✗ licensed 📺 ♿ (manual and electric wheelchairs available) toilets for disabled shop garden centre 🐕 (ex guide dogs) ■

ARUNDEL — Map 04 TQ00

ARUNDEL CASTLE
BN18 9AB
➲ (on A27 between Chichester & Worthing)
☎ 01903 883136
e-mail: info@arundelcastle.org
web: www.arundelcastle.org

Set high on a hill in West Sussex, this magnificent castle and stately home, seat of the Dukes of Norfolk for nearly 1000 years, commands stunning views across the river Arun and out to sea. Climb to the keep and battlements; marvel at a fine collection of 16th-century furniture; portraits by Van Dyke, Gainsborough, Canaletto and others; tapestries and the personal possessions of Mary, Queen of Scots; wander in the grounds and renovated Victorian flower and vegetable gardens.

Times: Open 25 Mar-Oct, Sun-Fri 11-5, Castle open 12-5. (Last admission 4). Closed Sat ex on BH. **Fee:** ✱ £11 (ch 5-16 £7.50, pen £9). Family ticket £30. Party 20+. **Facilities:** 🅿 💷 📺 ♿ toilets for disabled shop 🐕 (ex guide dogs) ■

WWT ARUNDEL

Mill Rd BN18 9PB
➲ (signed from A27 & A29)
☎ 01903 883355   **2 for 1**
e-mail: arundel@wwt.org.uk
web: www.wwt.org.uk

More than a thousand ducks, geese and swans from all over the world can be found here, many of which are so friendly that they will eat from your hand. The wild reserve attracts a variety of birds and includes a reedbed habitat considered so vital to the wetland wildlife it shelters that it has been designated a Site of Special Scientific Interest. Visitors can walk right through this reedbed on a specially designed boardwalk. There is a packed programme of events and activities throughout the year.

Times: Open all year, daily; summer 9.30-5; winter 9.30-4.30. (Last admission summer 5; winter 4). Closed 25 Dec. **Fee:** ✱ £5.95 (ch £3.75, pen £4.75). Family ticket £15.50. **Facilities:** 🅿 💷
✗ licensed 🗐 ♿ (level paths, free wheelchair loan) toilets for disabled shop ✈ (ex guide & hearing dogs) ◀

ASHINGTON   Map 04 TQ11

HOLLY GATE CACTUS GARDEN

Billingshurst Rd RH20 3BB
➲ (off A24, towards Ashington then B2133 towards Billingshurst for 0.5m)
☎ 01903 892930   **2 for 1**
e-mail: info@hollygatecactus.co.uk
web: www.hollygatecactus.co.uk

A mecca for the cactus enthusiast, with more than 30,000 succulent and cactus plants, including many rare types. They come from both arid and tropical parts of the world, and are housed in over 10,000 sq ft of greenhouses.

Times: Open all year, daily 9-5. Closed 25-26 Dec. **Fee:** ✱ £2 (ch & pen £1.50). Family ticket £6. Party 20+ 25p deduction.
Facilities: 🅿 ♿ shop garden centre Plants and pots for sale
✈ (ex guide dogs) ◀

BIGNOR   Map 04 SU91

BIGNOR ROMAN VILLA & MUSEUM

RH20 1PH
➲ (6m S of Pulborough & 6m N of Arundel on A29, signed. 8m S of Petworth on A285, signed)
☎ 01798 869259   **2 for 1**
e-mail: bignorromanvilla@care4free.net
web: www.pyrrha.demon.co.uk

Rediscovered in 1811, this Roman house was built on a grand scale. It is one of the largest known, and has spectacular mosaics. The heating system can also be seen, and various finds from excavations are on show. The longest mosaic in Britain (82ft) is on display here in its original position.

Times: Open Mar-Apr, Tue-Sun & BH 10-5; May daily 10-5; Jun-Sep daily 10-6, Oct daily 10-5 **Fee:** ✱ £4.20 (ch 5-15 £1.80, pen £3). Party 10+ 20% discount. Guided tours by arrangement. **Facilities:** 🅿 💷
🗐 ♿ (most areas accessible) shop ✈ (ex guide dogs) ◀

BRAMBER   Map 04 TQ11

BRAMBER CASTLE

BN4 3FB
➲ (on W side of village off A283)   **FREE**

The remains of a Norman motte and bailey castle. The gatehouse, still standing almost to its original height, and walls are still visible.

Times: Open any reasonable time. **Facilities:** 🅿 🜨

CHICHESTER   Map 04 SU80

CHICHESTER CATHEDRAL

West St PO19 1PX
➲ (in city centre)
☎ 01243 782595   **FREE**
e-mail: visitors@chichestercathedral.org.uk
web: www.chichestercathedral.org.uk

The beauty of the 900-year-old cathedral, site of the shrine of St Richard, is enhanced by many art treasures, ancient and modern.

Times: Open end Mar-end Sep daily 7.15-7; end Sep-end Mar 7.15-6.
Facilities: 🅿 (within city walls) 💷 ✗ 🗐 ♿ (touch & hearing centre, loop system) toilets for disabled shop ✈ (ex guide dogs)

MECHANICAL MUSIC & DOLL COLLECTION

Church Rd, Portfield PO19 4HN
➲ (1m E of Chichester, signed off A27)
☎ 01243 372646

A unique opportunity to see and hear barrel organs, polyphons, musical boxes, fair organs etc - all fully restored and playing. A magical musical tour to fascinate and entertain all ages. The doll collection contains fine examples of Victorian china and wax dolls, and felt and velvet dolls of the 1920s.

Times: Open Jun-Sep, Wed 1-4; Group bookings anytime in the year by prior arrangement. **Fee:** £2.50 (ch £1.25). **Facilities:** 🅿 ♿ shop
✈ (ex guide dogs)

PALLANT HOUSE GALLERY

9 North Pallant PO19 1TJ
➲ (from city centre (the Cross) take East St turning right at Superdrug. Gallery at end of North Pallant on left)
☎ 01243 774557
e-mail: info@pallant.org.uk
web: www.pallant.org.uk

A Queen Anne townhouse and a modern building have been combined to house a fine collection of 20th-century British art. The permanent collection includes pieces by: Auerbach, Blake, Bomberg, Caulfield, Freud, Hamilton, Hitchens, Leger, Moore, Nash, Nicholson, Piper, Richards, Severini, Sickert and Sutherland. Telephone or visit website for details of temporary exhibitions.

Times: Closed until Mar 2006 for refurbishment **Fee:** ✱ tbc
Facilities: 🅿 (100 yds) 💷 ✗ licensed 🗐 ♿ 2 toilets providing left and right hand access. toilets for disabled shop ✈ (ex guide dogs) ◀

EAST GRINSTEAD Map 05 TQ33

STANDEN

RH19 4NE

➲ (2m S of East Grinstead, signed from B2110)

☎ 01342 323029

e-mail: standen@nationaltrust.org.uk

web: www.nationaltrust.org.uk/standen

Standen is a showpiece of the 19th-century Arts and Crafts Movement. It was designed by Philip Webb for the Beale family, and is decorated throughout with William Morris wallpapers and fabrics. The interior has been carefully preserved. Webb also designed some of the furniture and details. There is a hillside garden and two woodland walks. Telephone for details of special events.

Times: House open Apr-Nov, Wed-Sun & BH 11-5. Garden open same dates as house 11-6 & Nov-mid Dec, Sat-Sun 11-3. (Last entry to house 4.30) **Fee:** ✱ House & garden £6.50. Garden only £3.90 (ch half price). Family ticket £15. Joint ticket which includes same day entry to Nymans garden £10, available Wed-Fri. **Facilities:** 🅿 ✕ licensed 🎟 ⅆ (Braille guide & touch list & large print guide) toilets for disabled shop ✖ (ex guide dogs & on wood walk) ⅋ 🢒

FISHBOURNE Map 04 SU80

FISHBOURNE ROMAN PALACE

Salthill Rd PO19 3QR

➲ (off A27 onto A259 into Fishbourne. Turn right into Salthill Rd & right into Roman Way)

☎ 01243 785859

e-mail: adminfish@sussexpast.co.uk

web: www.sussexpast.co.uk

This is the largest known Roman residence in Britain. It was occupied from the 1st to the 3rd centuries AD, and has mosaic floors and painted walls. 25 of these mosaic floors can still be seen in varying states of completeness, including others rescued from elsewhere in the area. Outside, part of the garden has been replanted to its original 1st-century plan. The museum displays a collection of finds from the excavations and tells the story of the site's discovery. An audio-visual presentation helps bring the site back to life, as it would have been many centuries ago.

Times: Open all year, daily Feb-15 Dec. Feb, Nov-Dec 10-4; Mar-Jul & Sep-Oct 10-5; Aug 10-6. Winter wknds 10-4. **Fee:** £6.50 (ch 5-15 £3.40, pen & students £5.50, registered disabled £4.90). Family ticket £16.60 (2ad+2ch). **Facilities:** 🅿 ⅇ 🎟 ⅆ (self guiding tapes & tactile objects for the blind) toilets for disabled shop garden centre ✖ (ex guide dogs) 🢒

FONTWELL Map 04 SU90

DENMANS GARDEN

Denmans Ln BN18 0SU

➲ (5m E of Chichester off A27 W between Chichester and Arundel, adjacent to Fontwell racecourse)   **2 for 1**

☎ 01243 542808

e-mail: denmans@denmans-garden.co.uk

web: www.denmans-garden.co.uk

A garden designed for year round interest, through the use of forms, colour and texture. It is nearly 4 acres in size and the home of renowned garden designer and writer, John Brookes MBE. The garden features; a dry gravel 'stream',

continued

natural look pond, walled garden, a refurbished conservatory and a grass area for tender plants.

Times: Open all year daily 9-5. Closed 24-26 Dec & 1 Jan **Fee:** ✱ £3.70 (ch £1.95, ch under 4 free, pen £3.25). Family ticket £10 Party 15+ £3 each. **Facilities:** 🅿 ⅇ 🎟 ⅆ shop garden centre ✖ (ex guide dogs) 🢒

GOODWOOD Map 04 SU81

GOODWOOD HOUSE

PO18 0PX

➲ (3m NE of Chichester)

☎ 01243 755048

e-mail: curator@goodwood.co.uk

web: www.goodwood.co.uk

Set within 12,000 acres of a working country estate, Goodwood House has been the ancestral home of the Dukes of Richmond for over 300 years. A tour of the State Apartments offers the visitor an insight into the House's history, the luxurious yellow drawing room and Egyptian dining room. The art collection includes paintings by Canaletto and Stubbs.

Times: Open end Mar-end Sep, Sun & Mon 1-5; Aug, Sun-Thu 1-5. **Fee:** £7 (ch under 12 free, ch & student £3, pen £6). Family ticket £15. Groups 25+ £6 each. **Facilities:** 🅿 ⅇ ⅆ (ramp at front of house, disabled parking area) toilets for disabled shop ✖ 🢒

HANDCROSS Map 04 TQ22

NYMANS GARDEN

Staplefield Rd RH17 6EB

➲ (on B2114 at Handcross, 4.5m S of Crawley)

☎ 01444 400321

e-mail: nymans@nationaltrust.org.uk

web: www.nationaltrust.org.uk/nymans

Nymans is one of the great gardens of the Sussex Weald. It has a fascinating and exotic plant collection, with romantic ruins and woodland walks. There are great opportunities to enjoy Nymans and the surrounding estate in any season.

Times: Open Garden: 16 Feb-30 Oct, Wed-Sun & BH. Nov-Mar, wknds 11-4 (restricted access due to ground conditions). House open end 16 Mar-30 Oct, 11.30-5. Closed 25-26 Dec & 1-2 Jan. **Fee:** ✱ £6.70 (ch £3.30), Family ticket £16.70; Winter: £3.30 (ch £1.60), Family ticket £8 **Facilities:** 🅿 ⅇ 🎟 ⅆ (wheelchair route, Batricar, Braille guide) toilets for disabled shop garden centre ✖ (ex guide dogs & hearing dogs) ⅋ 🢒

HAYWARDS HEATH Map 05 TQ32

BORDE HILL GARDEN

Balcombe Rd RH16 1XP

➲ (0.5m N of Haywards Heath on Balcombe Rd, 3m from A23)

☎ 01444 450326

e-mail: info@bordehill.co.uk

web: www.bordehill.co.uk

This glorious garden flows into linked *garden rooms,* boasting their own distinctive character and style. Year-round colour and interest with spring flowering rhododendrons, azaleas, camellias, magnolias and the many *champion* trees. The Rose and Italian Gardens with the herbaceous borders provide colour for summer and into autumn. Set in 200 acres of parkland with panoramic views, woodland and lakeside walks.

Times: Open all year, daily 10-6 or dusk if earlier. **Fee:** £6 (ch £3.50, pen & group £5). **Facilities:** 🅿 ⅇ ✕ licensed ⅆ (wheelchairs available, audio/Braille guides) toilets for disabled shop garden centre 🢒

HIGHDOWN
Map 04 SU91

HIGHDOWN
Highdown Gardens BN12 6PE
➲ (N off A259 between Worthing & Littlehampton. Access off dual carriageway, when coming from E proceed to rdbt)
☎ 01903 501054
e-mail: chris.beardsley@worthing.gov.uk
web: www.worthing.gov.uk/wbc

FREE

Set on downland countryside this unique garden overlooks the sea, and has been deemed a National collection due to the unique assortment of rare plants and trees. The garden was the achievement of Sir Frederick and Lady Stern, who worked for fifty years to prove that plants could grow on chalk. Many of the original plants were collected in China and the Himalayas.
Times: Open all year: Apr-Sep, Mon-Fri 10-6. Winter: Oct-Nov & Feb-Mar, Mon-Fri, 10-4.30; Dec-Jan, 10-4. **Facilities:** P & toilets for disabled ✱ (ex guide dogs)

LITTLEHAMPTON
Map 04 TQ00

LOOK & SEA! VISITOR CENTRE
63-65 Surrey St BN17 5AW
➲ (on harbour front 10 mins walk from Littlehampton Station)
☎ 01903 718984
e-mail: info@lookandsea.co.uk
web: www.lookandsea.co.uk

An interactive museum exploring the history and geography of Littlehampton and the surrounding area. Inside the modern waterfront building you can meet the 500,000 year old Boxgrove Man, become a ship's captain in an interactive computer game, and enjoy spectacular panoramic views of the Sussex coast from the circular glass tower.
Times: Open all year, daily 9-5 **Fee:** ✱ £2.95 (ch £2.50, pen & student £2.50). **Facilities:** P 20 mtrs ✱ licensed ▤ & toilets for disabled shop ✱ (ex guide dogs) ▦

LOWER BEEDING
Map 04 TQ22

LEONARDSLEE LAKES & GARDENS
RH13 6PP
➲ (4m SW from Handcross, at junct of B2110 & A281)
☎ 01403 891212
e-mail: gardens@leonardslee.com
web: www.leonardslee.com

This Grade I listed garden is set in a peaceful valley with walks around seven beautiful lakes. It is a paradise in spring, with banks of rhododendrons and azaleas along paths lined with bluebells. Wallabies live in parts of the valley, deer in the parks and wildfowl on the lakes. Enjoy the Rock Garden, the fascinating Bonsai, the new 'Behind the Doll's House' exhibition and the collection of Victorian Motorcars (1889-1900).
Times: Open Apr-Oct, daily 9.30-6 **Fee:** ✱ Apr & Jun-Oct £6, May (Mon-Fri) £8, (wknds & BH) £9 (ch £4 anytime). **Facilities:** P ✱ X licensed shop garden centre ✱ ▦

PETWORTH
Map 04 SU92

PETWORTH HOUSE & PARK
GU28 0AE
➲ (in town centre, A272/283)
☎ 01798 342207 & 343929
e-mail: petworth@nationaltrust.org.uk
web: www.nationaltrust.org.uk/petworth

Petworth house is an impressive 17th-century mansion set in a 700 acre Deer Park, landscaped by 'Capability' Brown, and immortalised in Turner's paintings. At Petworth you will find the National Trust's finest art collection including work by Van Dyck, Titian, and Turner, as well as sculpture, ceramics and fine furniture. Fascinating Servants' Quarters show the domestic side of life of this great estate.
Times: Mar-Oct 11-5 last entry 4.30. (closed Thu-Fri) **Fee:** £7.50 (ch £4). Family ticket £19. Party 15+ £6.50 each. NT members free. Pleasure Ground £2 (ch £1). **Facilities:** P ✱ X licensed ▤ & (wheelchairs available, Braille guide, virtual tour) toilets for disabled shop ✱ (ex guide/hearing dogs) ✿ ▦

An asterisk * indicates that opening times and prices are for 2005. Please contact the attraction for up-to-date information.

If an attraction name appears in *italics*, details have not been confirmed for 2006.

PULBOROUGH   Map 04 TQ01

PARHAM HOUSE & GARDENS

Parham Park, Storrington RH20 4HS
➲ (midway between A29 & A24, off A283
between Pulborough & Storrington)
☎ 01903 744888 & 742021
e-mail: enquiries@parhaminsussex.co.uk
web: www.parhaminsussex.co.uk

Surrounded by a deer park, fine gardens and 18th-century pleasure grounds in a beautiful downland setting, this Elizabethan family home contains an important collection of paintings, furniture, carpets and rare needlework. A brick and turf maze has been created in the grounds - designed with children in mind, it is called 'Veronica's Maze'.

Times: Open Etr Sun-Sep, Wed, Thu, Sun & BH Mons (also open Tue & Fri in Aug). Gardens open 12-6; House 2-6 (last entry 5).
Fee: ✱ House & Gardens £6.50 (ch 5-15 £2.50, pen & disabled visitors £5.50). Family ticket £15.50. Gardens only £5 (ch £1). Party rates available. **Facilities:** 🅿 💷 ⚒ ♿ (wheelchairs, ramps, recorded tour tape, parking) toilets for disabled shop garden centre ✖ (ex guide dogs & in grounds) 🍴

See advertisement on opposite page

RSPB PULBOROUGH BROOKS NATURE RESERVE

Uppertons Barn Visitor Centre, Wiggonholt RH20 2EL
➲ (signed on A283, 2m SE of Pulborough & 2m NW of Storrington)
☎ 01798 875851
e-mail: pulborough.brooks@rspb.org.uk
web: www.rspb.org.uk

Set in the scenic Arun Valley and easily reached via the visitor centre at Wiggonholt, this is an excellent reserve for year-round family visits. A nature trail through hedgerow-lined lanes to viewing hides overlooking water-meadows. Breeding summer birds include nightingales and warblers, ducks and wading birds, and nightjars and hobbies on nearby heathland. Unusual wading birds and hedgerow birds regularly pass through on spring and autumn migration.

Times: Open daily, Reserve: 9-9, (or sunset if earlier). Visitor centre: 10-5. Reserve closed 25 Dec, Visitor Centre closed 25-26 Dec.
Fee: ✱ £3.50 (ch £1, concessions £2.50). Family ticket £7.
Facilities: 🅿 💷 ⚒ ♿ (free hire electric buggy and wheelchair) toilets for disabled shop ✖ (ex guide dogs) 🍴

SINGLETON   Map 04 SU81

WEALD & DOWNLAND OPEN AIR MUSEUM

PO18 0EU
➲ (6m N of Chichester on A286)
☎ 01243 811348
e-mail: office@wealddown.co.uk
web: www.wealddown.co.uk

A showcase of English architectural heritage, where historic buildings have been rescued from destruction and rebuilt in a parkland setting. Vividly demonstrating the evolution of building techniques and use of local materials, these fascinating buildings bring to life the homes, farms and rural industries of the south east of the past 500 years.

Times: Open all year, Mar-Oct, daily 10.30-6. Call or see website for winter opening. **Fee:** ✱ £7.70 (ch £4.10, pen £6.70). Family ticket (2ad+3ch) £21. **Facilities:** 🅿 💷 ⚒ ♿ (separate entrance and ramps available for some buildings) toilets for disabled shop Country crafts, local produce 🍴

SOUTH HARTING   Map 04 SU71

UPPARK

GU31 5QR
➲ (A3 take A272, B2146 to South Harting, follow signs to Uppark)
☎ 01730 825415 825857
e-mail: uppark@nationaltrust.org.uk
web: www.nationaltrust.org.uk/uppark

A late 17th-century house set high on the South Downs with magnificent sweeping views to the sea. An extensive exhibition tells the dramatic story of the 1989 fire and subsequent restoration of the house and its collections. The elegant Georgian interior houses a famous Grand Tour collection that includes paintings, furniture and ceramics. An 18th-century dolls' house with original features is one of the more impressive items. The servants' quarters appear as they did in Victorian days, when H G Wells' mother was housekeeper, while the garden is restored in the early 19th-century 'Picturesque' style.

Times: Open end Mar-end Oct, Sun-Thu. House 1-5 (12-5 on Sun in Aug & 11-5 on BH Mon). Car park, woodland walk, garden & exhibition. (Last admission to house 4.15). Closes at 4.30 in Oct. **Fee:** ✱ House, garden & exhibition £6. Family ticket £15. **Facilities:** 🅿 💷 ✖ licensed ⚒ ♿ (ramps, lift to basement, chair lift in exhibition) toilets for disabled shop ✖ (ex woodland walk & car park) 🐕 🍴

TANGMERE
Map 04 SU90

TANGMERE MILITARY AVIATION MUSEUM TRUST
PO20 2ES
➲ (off A27, 3m E of Chichester towards Arundel)
☎ 01243 775223
e-mail: tangmeretrust@aol.com
web: www.tangmere-museum.org.uk

Based at an airfield that played an important role during the World Wars, this museum spans 80 years of military aviation. There are photographs, documents, aircraft and aircraft parts on display along with a Hurricane replica, Spitfire replica and cockpit simulator. A hangar houses a Supermarine Swift and the record-breaking aircraft Meteor and Hunter. Aircraft outside include; Lockheed T33, English Electric Lightning, De Havilland Sea Vixen, McDonnell Douglas Phantom F4, Gloster Meteor and a Westland Whirlwind helicopter.
Times: Open Mar-Oct, daily 10-5.30; Feb & Nov, daily 10-4.30.
Fee: ✱ £5 (ch £1.50 & pen £4) Family £11.50 (2ad+2ch).
Facilities: 🅿 💻 📵 ♿ (wheelchairs available) toilets for disabled shop 🐕 (ex guide dogs)

WEST DEAN
Map 04 SU81

WEST DEAN GARDENS
PO18 0QZ
➲ (on A286, 6m N of Chichester)
☎ 01243 818210 & 811301
e-mail: gardens@westdean.org.uk
web: www.westdean.org.uk
Award winning historic garden of 35 acres in a tranquil downland setting. Noted for its 300ft long Harold Peto pergola, mixed and herbaceous borders, rustic summerhouses and specimen trees. Walled kitchen garden with magnificent collection of 16 Victorian glasshouses and frames. The visitors' centre provides a high level of facilities with a beautiful prospect of the River Lavant and West Dean Park.
Times: Open Mar, Apr & Oct, daily 11-5; May-Sep 10.30-5. (Last ticket 4.30) **Fee:** ✱ £5.50 (ch £2.50, pen £5). Family ticket £13, adult season ticket £20. **Facilities:** 🅿 ✖ licensed 📵 ♿ (reserved parking, 2 wheelchairs available) toilets for disabled shop 🐕 (ex guide dogs on a lead) 📷

TYNE & WEAR

EVENTS & FESTIVALS

April
8th-9th Gateshead Spring Flower Show, Gateshead Central Nursery (provisional)
29th-30th Green Festival, Leazes Park, Newcastle

July
1st-2nd Sunderland International Festival, kites, music and dance, Stephenson, Washington (provisional)
29th-30th Sunderland International Air Show, Promenade, Seaburn, Sunderland (provisional)

August
4th-6th Gateshead Summer Flower Show, Central Nursery, Lobley Hill, Gateshead
5th-6th Motor Show North East, Herrington Country Park, Sunderland
27th-28th Newcastle Mela (free Asian festival), Exhibition Park, Newcastle-upon-Tyne

September/October
tbc Junior Great North Run, Gateshead International Stadium, Gateshead
tbc Great North Run (Newcastle-upon-Tyne to South Shields)

October
tbc Houghton Feast, traditional local event with various activities and events

Above: Ornate ceiling decorations in the 14th-century Percy Chapel at Tynemouth Priory

---

GATESHEAD Map 12 NZ26

BALTIC CENTRE FOR CONTEMPORARY ART
South Shore Rd NE8 3BA
➲ (follow signs for Quayside, Millennium Bridge. (15 mins' walk from Gateshead Metro & Newcastle Central Station)
☎ 0191 478 1810 0191 440 4944   FREE
e-mail: info@balticmill.com
web: www.balticmill.com
Once a 1950s grain warehouse, part of the old Baltic Flour Mills, the Baltic Centre for Contemporary Art is an international centre presenting a dynamic and ambitious programme of complementary exhibitions and events. It consists of five art spaces, cinema, auditorium, library and archive, eating and drinking areas and a shop. Check website for current events information.
Times: ✱ Please see website for details (www.balticmill.com)
Facilities: 🅿 (charged) 💻 ✗ licensed 📖 ♿ (wheelchairs/scooters, Braille/large-print guides toilets for disabled shop ✖ (ex guide dogs & hearing dogs)

JARROW Map 12 NZ36

BEDES WORLD & ST PAUL'S CHURCH
Church Bank NE32 3DY
➲ (off A185 near S end of Tyne tunnel)
☎ 0191 489 2106   2 for 1
e-mail: visitor.info@bedesworld.co.uk
web: www.bedesworld.co.uk

The Venerable Bede lived over 1300 years ago and was one of early Britain's greatest scholars, author of the "Historia Ecclesiastica Gentis Anglorum" - the definitive history of the early medieval period. As well as exhibits detailing Bede's monastic life and work, the museum re-creates an Anglo-Saxon farm and incorporates the ruins of the medieval monastery.
Times: Open all year, Apr-Oct, Mon-Sat 10-5.30, Sun noon-5.30; Nov-Mar, Mon-Sat 10-4.30 & Sun 12-4.30; Xmas-New Year opening times vary. Church open Mon-Sat 10-4 & Sun 2.30-4 **Fee:** £4.50 (ch & concessions £3). Family ticket £10. Concession Family ticket £7. Party rates 15+. **Facilities:** 🅿 💻 ✗ licensed 📖 ♿ (wheelchair & elec. wheelchair on request, disabled parking) toilets for disabled shop ✖ (ex guide dogs) 🍴

NEWCASTLE UPON TYNE Map 12 NZ26

HANCOCK MUSEUM
Barras Bridge NE2 4PT
➲ (follow exit signs for city centre A167, off A1)
☎ 0191 222 7418
e-mail: hancock@twmuseums.org.uk
web: www.twmuseums.org.uk/hancock
Newcastle's premier Natural History museum unravels the natural world, through sensational galleries and close encounters with resident reptiles and insects. For more than 100 years the Hancock Museum has provided visitors with a glimpse of the animal kingdom and the powerful and often destructive forces of nature. From the Dinosaurs to live animals, the Hancock is home to creatures past and present and the odd Egyptian mummy or two.
Times: ✱ Open all year, Mon-Sat, 10-5, Sun 2-5. Closed 25-26 Dec & 1 Jan. **Facilities:** 🅿 🍴 📋 ♿ (stair lift, audio & Braille guide, sign language) toilets for disabled shop 🐕 (ex guide dogs) ◼

LIFE SCIENCE CENTRE
Times Square NE1 4EP
➲ (A1M, A69, A184, A1058 & A167, follow signs to Life Science Centre or Central Station)
☎ 0191 243 8210
The Life Science Centre is an interactive, action-packed day out that takes the visitor to the beginning of life and back again. From single-celled organisms to dinosaurs, from 4 billion years ago to today, this is a fascinating attraction that deals with perhaps the most fundamental subject of all: Life Itself.
Times: Open Mon-Sat 10-6, Sun 11-6 . Closed 25 Dec & 1 Jan. (Last entry subject to seasonal demand). **Fee:** £6.95 (ch £4.50, concessions £5.50). Family ticket £19.95. **Facilities:** 🅿 (200mtrs) 🍴 ✗ licensed ♿ (ramps, wheelchairs, induction loops) toilets for disabled shop 🐕 (ex guide dogs) ◼

MUSEUM OF ANTIQUITIES
The University NE1 7RU
➲ (Situated on main campus of Newcastle University between The Haymarket & Queen Victoria Rd)
☎ 0191 222 7849   **FREE**
e-mail: m.o.antiquities@ncl.ac.uk
web: www.ncl.ac.uk/antiquities
Artefacts from north east England from prehistoric times to AD 1600 are on display here. The principal museum for Hadrian's Wall, this collection includes models of the wall, life-size Roman soldiers and a newly refurbished reconstruction of the Temple of Mithras.
Times: Open all year, daily (ex Sun), 10-5. Closed Good Fri, 24-26 Dec & 1 Jan. **Facilities:** 🅿 (400yds) 📋 ♿ (large print guide) shop 🐕 (ex guide dogs) ◼

ROWLANDS GILL Map 12 NZ15

GIBSIDE
NE16 6BG
➲ (turn off A1 western Bypass following brown tourist signs from Gibside & Gibside Chapel, 3m W of Metro Centre & 6m SW of Gateshead, on B6314)
☎ 01207 542255
e-mail: gibside@nationaltrust.org.uk
web: www.thenationaltrust.co.uk
This 18th-century landscaped garden is the former home of the Bowes-Lyon family, with miles of walks through the
continued

wooded slopes and riverside of the Derwent valley. Discover hidden vistas, wildlife or wild flowers, or just enjoy a Georgian style lunch in the tea room. Lots of events and activities for children and families, and those interested can hold an Anglican wedding in the unique Palladian Chapel.
Times: Open all year daily 7 Mar-23 Oct 10-6 (last entry 4.30); 24 Oct-5 Mar 10-4 (last entry 3.30) closed 20-26 Dec, 30 Dec-1 Jan; Chapel open 7 Mar-23 Oct 11-4.30; Shop & tea room open 23 Mar-3 Nov 10-5; 4 Nov-end Mar 10-4 **Fee:** £3.50 (ch £2). Discounts for families **Facilities:** 🅿 🍴 ♿ (Braille guide, wheelchairs & wheelchair carrier) toilets for disabled shop 🐄 ◼

SOUTH SHIELDS Map 12 NZ36

ARBEIA ROMAN FORT & MUSEUM
Baring St NE33 2BB
➲ (5 mins' walk from town centre)
☎ 0191 456 1369
web: www.twmuseums.org.uk
In South Shields town are the extensive remains of Arbeia, a Roman fort in use from the 2nd to 4th century. It was the supply base for the Roman army's campaign against Scotland. On site there are full size reconstructions of a fort gateway, a barrack block and part of the commanding officer's house. Archaeological evacuations are in progress throughout the summer.
Times: Open all year, Apr-Oct, Mon-Sat 10-5.30, Sun 1-5; Nov-Mar, Mon-Sat 10-3.30. Closed 25-26 Dec & 1 Jan **Fee:** Fort & Museum free of charge ex for 'Timequest' Archaeological Interpretation Gallery £1.50 (ch & concessions 80p). **Facilities:** 🅿 ♿ (Minicom system, portable induction loop) toilets for disabled shop ◼

SUNDERLAND Map 12 NZ35

NATIONAL GLASS CENTRE
Liberty Way SR6 0GL
➲ (A19 onto A1231, signposted from all major roads)
☎ 0191 515 5555
e-mail: info@nationalglasscentre.com
web: www.nationalglasscentre.com
Housed in a striking modern building, the National Glass Centre celebrates the unique material and explains its history. Visitors can see the changing exhibitions of glass art, featuring pieces by leading artists. There is also the opportunity to witness the glass-making process and learn more about the substance and how it impacts on our lives. The brave can even walk on the glass roof 30 feet above the riverside.
Times: ✱ Open daily 10-5 (last admission to glass tour 4). Closed 25 Dec & 1 Jan. **Facilities:** 🅿 ✗ licensed ♿ (lifts, ramps, parking facilites) toilets for disabled shop 🐕 (ex guide dogs) ◼

SUNDERLAND MUSEUM & WINTER GARDENS
Burdon Rd SR1 1PP
➲ (in city centre on Burden Rd)
☎ 0191 553 2323   **FREE**
e-mail: sunderland@twmuseums.org.uk
web: www.twmuseums.org.uk/sunderland
An award-winning attraction with wide-ranging displays and many hands-on exhibits that cover the archaeology and geology of Sunderland, the coal mines and shipyards of the area and the spectacular glass and pottery made on Wearside. Other galleries show the changes in the lifestyles of Sunderland women over the past century, works by LS Lowry and wildlife from all corners of the globe. The Winter Gardens are a horticultural wonderland where the exotic
continued

plants from around the world can be seen growing to their full natural height in a spectacular glass and steel rotunda.
Times: Open all year, Mon-Sat 10-4, Sun 2-5. **Facilities:** P (150 yds) 🍽 ✕ licensed 🛍 ⅋ (lifts to all floors, induction loops) toilets for disabled shop ✈ (ex guide dogs) 🍴

TYNEMOUTH   Map 12 NZ36
BLUE REEF AQUARIUM
Grand Pde NE30 4JF
➲ (follow A19, taking A1058 (coast road), signed Tynemouth. Situated on seafront)
☎ 0191 258 1031
e-mail: tynemouth@bluereefaquarium.co.uk
web: www.bluereefaquarium.co.uk
From its position overlooking one of the North East's prettiest beaches, Blue Reef is home to a dazzling variety of creatures including seahorses, puffer fish, octopi, and even the deadly piranha. Visitors can walk through an underwater tunnel in a 250,000 litre tropical ocean tank. This offers close encounters with all manner of undersea wonders like sharks and stingrays.
Times: Open all year, daily from 10. Closed 25 Dec **Fee:** £5.50 (ch 3-16 £3.75, pen & students £4.95). Family ticket (2ad+2ch) £16.95, (2ad+3ch) £19.99 **Facilities:** P (charged) 🍽 🛍 ⅋ (wheelchair available) toilets for disabled shop ✈ (ex guide dogs) 🍴

TYNEMOUTH PRIORY AND CASTLE
NE30 4BZ
➲ (near North Pier)
☎ 0191 257 1090
Discover a rich and varied history as you explore the priory, castle and underground chambers beneath a World War I gun battery.
Times: Open all year, Apr-Sep, daily 10-6; Oct, daily 10-4; Nov-Mar, Thu-Mon 10-4. Gun Battery: Jun-Aug, Sat, Sun & Bank Hols, 10-6. Closed 24-26 Dec & 1 Jan. **Fee:** £3.30 (ch £1.70, concessions £2.50, family £8.30). Opening times and prices are subject to change, for further details please phone 0870 333 1181 **Facilities:** ⅋ (wheelchair access to priory) shop 🎌

WALLSEND   Map 12 NZ26
SEGEDUNUM ROMAN FORT, BATHS & MUSEUM
Buddle St NE28 6HR
➲ (A187 from Tyne Tunnel, signposted)   2 for 1
☎ 0191 236 9347
e-mail: segedunum@twmuseums.org.uk
web: www.twmuseums.org.uk
Hadrian's Wall was built by the Roman Emperor, Hadrian in 122AD, Segedunum was built as part of the Wall, serving as a garrison for 600 soldiers until the collapse of Roman rule around 410AD. This major historical venture shows what life would have been like then, using artefacts, audio-visuals, reconstructed buildings and a 34m high viewing tower.
Times: Open all year, Apr-Aug 9.30-5.30, Sep-Oct 10-5, Nov-Apr 10-3.30 **Fee:** £3.50 (ch, pen & concessions £1.95). Family ticket £9 **Facilities:** P 🍽 🛍 ⅋ (lifts) toilets for disabled shop ✈ (ex guide dogs) 🍴

WASHINGTON   Map 12 NZ35
WASHINGTON OLD HALL
The Avenue, Washington Village NE38 7LE
➲ (from A1 and A19 follow signs to Washington, then District 4. The Avenue, next to Holy Trinity Church)
☎ 0191 416 6879
e-mail: washington.oldhall@nationaltrust.org.uk
web: www.nationaltrust.org.uk
Sitting next to Washington's Holy Trinity church, the Old Hall was the home of George Washington's ancestors from 1183 to 1613, and was originally a medieval manor, but was rebuilt in the 17th century. The house has been restored and filled with period furniture, and contains displays on George Washington and the history of American Independence. Enjoy a peaceful walk in the formal Jacobean garden.
Times: Open and Mar-Oct, Sun-Wed & Good Fri 11-5. **Fee:** £3.80 (ch £2.30). Family ticket £10. **Facilities:** P 🍽 ⅋ (Braille guide, sensory scented gardens, handrails, ramps) toilets for disabled shop ✈ (ex guide dogs) 🐾

WWT WASHINGTON
District 15 NE38 8LE
➲ (signposted off A195, A1231 & A182)
☎ 0191 416 5454   2 for 1
e-mail: washington@wwt.org.uk
web: www.wwt.org.uk
In a parkland setting, on the north bank of the River Wear, WWT Washington is the home of a wonderful collection of exotic wildfowl from all over the world. There is also a heronry where visitors can watch a colony of wild Grey Herons on CCTV. The 100-acre site includes an area for wintering wildfowl which can be observed from hides, and a flock of Chilean Flamingos. Other features include a discovery centre, waterfowl nursery, picture windows and a viewing gallery from which to observe the birds.
Times: Open all year, daily 9.30-5 (summer) or 9.30-4 (winter). Closed 25 Dec. **Fee:** £5.95 (ch £3.75, concessions £4.75). Family £15.50 **Facilities:** P 🍽 ✕ licensed ⅋ (lowered windows in certain hides, wheelchairs to hire free) toilets for disabled shop ✈ (ex guide/hearing dogs) 🍴

WHITBURN   Map 12 NZ46
SOUTER LIGHTHOUSE
Coast Rd SR6 7NH
➲ (on A183 coast road, 2m S of South Shields, 3m N of Sunderland)
☎ 0191 529 3161 & 01670 773966
e-mail: souter@nationaltrust.org.uk
web: www.nationaltrust.org.uk
When it opened in 1871, Souter was the most advanced lighthouse in the world, and warned shipping off the notorious rocks in the river approaches of the Tyne and Wear. Painted red and white and standing at 150ft high, it is a dramatic building and hands-on displays and volunteers help bring it to life. Visitors can explore the whole building with its engine room and lighthouse keeper's cottage. You can take part in hands-on activities concerning shipwrecks and the workings of the lighthouse, and see coastal creatures in the Rockpool Fishtank. Climb to the top of the lighthouse, or walk along the Leas, a 2.5 mile stretch of spectacular coastline.
Times: Open 19 Mar-6 Nov daily ex Fri (open Good Fri) 11-5 (last entry 30mins before closing). **Fee:** £3.80 (ch £2.30) Family ticket £10. **Facilities:** P ✕ 🛍 ⅋ (Braille guide, induction loops, tactile exhibits) toilets for disabled shop ✈ (ex guide dogs) 🐾 🍴

WARWICKSHIRE

EVENTS & FESTIVALS

April
22nd Shakespeare Birthday Celebrations, Stratford-Upon-Avon
28th-7th May Leamington Festival

June
30th-9th Jul Warwick Festival, various venues

July
2nd-5th The Royal Show, National Agricultural Centre, Stoneleigh Park
21st-23rd Warwick Folk Festival (various venues)

August
19th-20th Warwickshire & West Midlands Game & Country Fair, Ragley Hall, Alcester (provisional)
26th-28th Town & Country Festival, NAC Stoneleigh

October
13th-21st Stratford-Upon-Avon Music Festival, various venues

Above: View of Castle ruins at Kenilworth

HRH Queen Elizabeth II.

The British monarch was born in April 1926, and the year of her 80th birthday will see many national celebrations, as well as those that are to be staged in London.

ALCESTER Map 04 SP05

RAGLEY HALL
B49 5NJ
➲ (8m SW of Stratford-upon-Avon, off A46/A435, follow brown tourist signs)
☎ 01789 762090
e-mail: info@ragleyhall.com
web: www.ragleyhall.com

Built in 1680, Ragley is the family home of the Marquess and Marchioness of Hertford and houses a superb collection of 18th century paintings, porcelain and furniture. Set in 27 acres of gardens and 400 acres of parkland, The house contains a stunning mural by Graham Rust "The Temptation" and England's finest Baroque plasterwork dated 1750. Ticket includes the house, Terrace Tea rooms overlooking the rose garden, gift shop, adventure playground, unique 3D maze, lakeside picnic area, woodland walk and stables containing equestrian memorabilia. Location for BBC production of *Scarlet Pimpernel.*

Times: ✱ Open mid Apr-end Sep, Thu-Sun & BH Mon. Park & Garden open daily, mid Jul-end Aug. **Facilities:** 🅿 ♨ ♿ (lift to first floor) toilets for disabled shop

BADDESLEY CLINTON Map 04 SP27

BADDESLEY CLINTON HALL
B93 0DQ
[2 for 1]
➲ (0.75m W off A4141, 7.5m NW of Warwick)
☎ 01564 783294
e-mail: baddesleyclinton@nationaltrust.org.uk
web: www.nationaltrust.org.uk

A romantically-sited medieval moated house, dating from the 14th century, that has changed very little since 1634. With family portraits, priest's holes, chapel, garden, ponds, nature trail and lake walk.

Times: Open Garden, Restaurant & Shop: 2 Mar-30 Apr & Oct-6 Nov, Wed-Sun 12-5; May-Sep, Wed-Sun 12-5.30; 9 Nov-11 Dec, Wed-Sun 12-4.30. House: 2 Mar-30 Apr & Oct-6 Nov, Wed-Sun 1.30-5; May-Sep, Wed-Sun 1.30-5.30. BH Mon Good Fri. **Fee:** ✱ Garden only £3.30 (ch £1.65). House & Garden £6.60 (ch £3.30). Family ticket £16.50. Joint ticket with Packwood House £9.60 (ch £4.80). Family ticket £24. Joint ticket for gardens only £4.80 (ch £2.40). National Trust members and children under 5 free. **Facilities:** 🅿 ✗ licensed 🍴 ♿ (4 wheelchairs for hire, Braille guides, tactile route) toilets for disabled shop ✖ (ex guide dogs) ♨ ▬

CHARLECOTE Map 04 SP25

CHARLECOTE PARK
CV35 9ER
➲ (5m E of Stratford, 1m W of Wellesbourne, off B4086)
☎ 01789 470277 Events-07788 658495
e-mail: charlecote.park@nationaltrust.org.uk
web: www.nationaltrust.org.uk

Queen Elizabeth I and William Shakespeare knew Charlecote Park well. Follow in their footsteps at this impressive Warwickshire house and ancient deer park. Special events held every week, from outdoor picnic concerts to family events, outdoor theatre and specialist tours. Call for event details.

Times: Open 6 Mar-2 Nov, Fri-Tue (Fri-Wed Jul & Aug); Grounds 10.30-5.30, (Park until 6), House noon-5. Open wkends Nov & Dec
Fee: ✱ House & Grounds; £6.40 (ch £3.20), Family £26, Groups £5.40. Grounds only; £3 (ch £1.50). NT members free. **Facilities:** 🅿 ♨ ✗ licensed 🍴 ♿ (Braille guides, induction loop) toilets for disabled shop ✖ (ex assist dogs) ♨

COMPTON VERNEY   Map 04 SP35

COMPTON VERNEY NEW
CV35 9HZ
➲ (7m E of Stratford on B4085 between
Wellesbourne & Kineton)
☎ 01926 645500
e-mail: info@comptonverney.org.uk
web: www.comptonverney.org.uk

Warwickshire largest gallery, housed in an 18th-century
Grade I Robert Adam mansion house, set in 120 acres of
'Capability' parkland. Six permanent collections include;
Naples 1600-1800, German 1450-1650, British portraits,
China, British Folk Art and the Marx-Lambert collection.
There is also a programme of changing exhibitions, special
events, tours and workshops. An exhibition of Van Gogh's
work will be opening in March 2006.
Times: Open Etr-Oct, Tue-Sun 11-5 & Thu until 8pm. Closed Mon
except BH **Fee:** ✱ £6 (ch under 5's free, 5-16 £2, concessions £4)
Family £14 (2+up to 4 ch). Tue half price **Facilities:** 🅿 💻 📱
♿ (w/chairs, large print guides, hearing loop) toilets for disabled shop
✖ (ex assist dogs) 📷

COUGHTON   Map 04 SP06

COUGHTON COURT
B49 5JA
➲ (2m N of Alcester on E side of A435)
☎ 01789 762435 400702
web: www.coughtoncourt.co.uk
Home of the Throckmorton family since the 15th century, the
house contains a collection of family portraits, whilst the
gardens created over the last 10 years feature one of
Britain's finest walled gardens.
Times: Open 5 Mar-31 Mar wknds only. Daily Apr-Jun, Wed-Sun;
Jul-Aug, Tue-Sun; Sep, Wed-Sun; Oct wknds only. Also open BH Mons.
(Closed 21 Jun). **Fee:** ✱ £8.60 (ch £4.30). Family ticket £24.80-£28.75.
Garden only £5.90 (ch £2.95). Family ticket £17-£19.50.
Facilities: 🅿 (charged) ✖ licensed 📱 ♿ (Braille guide, parking,
wheelchair available) toilets for disabled shop garden centre
✖ (ex guide dogs) 📷

FARNBOROUGH   Map 04 SP44

FARNBOROUGH HALL
OX17 1DU
➲ (6m N of Banbury, 0.5m W of A423)
☎ 01295 690002   **2 for 1**
web: www.nationaltrust.org.uk
A classical mid 18th-century stone house with notable
plasterwork; the entrance hall, staircase and two principal
rooms are shown. The grounds contain charming 18th-
century temples, a 0.75-mile terrace walk and an obelisk.
Times: House, grounds & terrace walk open Apr-Sep, Wed & Sat, 5 & 6
May 2-6. Terrace walk Thu & Fri by appointment only, 2-6. (Last
admission 5.30). Closed Good Fri **Fee:** ✱ House, Garden & Terrace
walk £3.60 (ch £1.80), Family £9. Terrace walk £1.80. Terrace walk only
(Thu & Fri) £1. **Facilities:** 🅿 📱 ♿ ✖ (ex guide dogs) 📷

GAYDON   Map 04 SP35

HERITAGE MOTOR CENTRE
Banbury Rd CV35 0BJ
➲ (M40 junct 12 and take B4100. Attraction
signed)
☎ 01926 641188
e-mail: enquiries@heritage-motor-centre.co.uk
web: www.heritage-motor-centre.co.uk

Home to the largest collection of historic British cars in the
world, the Heritage Motor Centre is set in 65 acres of
grounds. Attractions at the Centre include the Time Road, a
fascinating journey through Britain's motoring and social
history, the motoring cinema, and the 'Get Behind the Wheel'
zone, where visitors get the chance to sit in a variety of cars
from the collection. Outside features include; Land Rover 4x4
off-roading, go-karting, and children's miniature roadway.
Times: Open daily 10-5. (Closed 24-26 Dec). **Fee:** ✱ £8 (ch 5-16 £6,
under 5 free, & pen £7). Family ticket £25. Additional charges apply to
outdoor activities **Facilities:** 🅿 💻 📱 ♿ (lift to all floors, limited
number of manual wheelchairs) toilets for disabled shop ✖ (ex
guide/hearing dogs) 📷

KENILWORTH   Map 04 SP27

KENILWORTH CASTLE

CV8 1NE

☎ 01926 852078

Explore the largest and most extensive castle ruin in England, with a past rich in famous names and events in history. Its massive red sandstone towers, keep and wall glow brightly in the sunlight. Discover the history of Kenilworth through the interactive model in Leicester's Barn.

Times: Open all year, Mar-May, Sep-Oct daily, 10-5; Jun-Aug, daily, 10-6; Nov-Feb, daily, 10-4. Closed 24-26 Dec & 1 Jan **Fee:** £4.95 (ch £2.50, concessions £3.70, family £12.40). Opening times and prices are subject to change, for further details please phone 0870 333 1181 **Facilities:** 🅿 💻 🕭 shop ♯

STONELEIGH ABBEY

CV8 2LF

➲ (entrance off B4115 close to junct of A46 and A452)

☎ 01926 858535 & 858585

e-mail: enquire@stoneleighabbey.org

web: www.stoneleighabbey.org

Stoneleigh Abbey is one of the finest country house estates in the Midlands and has seen the subject of considerable restoration work. The abbey, founded in the reign of Henry II, is now managed by a charitable trust. Visitors will experience a wealth of architectural styles spanning more than 800 years. The magnificent state rooms and chapel, the medieval Gatehouse and the Regency stables are some of the major areas to be admired. Set in 690 acres of parkland.

Times: Open Good Fri-Oct, Tue-Thu, Sun & BHs for guided tours at 11, 1 & 3. Grounds open 10-5. **Fee:** Grounds only, £2. Guided tour of house, £6 (1ch 5-12 free, additional ch £2.50) pen £4.

Facilities: 🅿 💻 🔲 🕭 (Lift acces to state rooms) toilets for disabled shop grounds only (ex assist dogs)

MIDDLETON   Map 07 SP19

ASH END HOUSE CHILDRENS FARM

Middleton Ln B78 2BL

➲ (signed from A4091)

☎ 0121 329 3240

e-mail: contact@thechildrensfarm.co.uk

web: www.thechildrensfarm.co.uk

Ideal for young children, this is a small family-owned farm with many friendly animals to feed and stroke, including some rare breeds. Cafe, shop, gift shop, play areas, picnic barns and lots of undercover activities. Special Events: 25th Anniversary in 2006

Times: Open daily 10-5 or dusk in winter. Closed 25 Dec-1 Jan and wkdays in Jan. **Fee:** ✱ £3.90 (ch £4.90 includes animal feed, farm badge & all activities). **Facilities:** 🅿 💻 🔲 🕭 toilets for disabled shop ✾ (ex guide dogs) 🍴

MIDDLETON HALL

B78 2AE

➲ (M42 junct 9, on A4091 midway between Belfry & Drayton Manor, follow brown heritage signs)

☎ 01827 283095

e-mail: middletonhall@btconnect.com

web: www.middletonhalltrust.co.uk

Once the home of two great 17th-century naturalists, Francis Willughby and John Ray, the Hall shows several architectural styles, from c1300 to a Georgian west wing. The grounds include a nature reserve, lake, meadow, orchard and

continued

woodland, all Sites of Special Scientific Interest. Please telephone or visit website for details of events running throughout the year.

Times: Open Apr-13 Oct, Sun 2-5, BH 11-5. **Fee:** ✱ £2.50 (ch free, pen £1.50). BH & some Sun £4 (ch 50p, pen £3) **Facilities:** 🅿 💻 🔲 🕭 (wheelchair available) toilets for disabled shop

NUNEATON   Map 04 SP39

ARBURY HALL

CV10 7PT

➲ (2m SW of Nuneaton, off B4102 Meriden road)

☎ 024 7638 2804

e-mail: brenda.newell@arburyhall.net

The 16th-century Elizabethan house, Gothicised in the 18th century, has been the home of the Newdegate family for over 450 years. It is the finest complete example of Gothic revival architecture in existence, and contains pictures, furniture, and beautiful plasterwork ceilings. The 17th-century stable block, with a central doorway by Wren, houses the tearooms and lovely gardens with lakes and wooded walks.

Times: Open Etr-Sep 2-5.30 (last admission 5). Hall & Gardens: Sun & Mon of BH wknds only. For other opening days & times, contact Administrator. **Fee:** ✱ £6.50 (ch £4) Gardens only £4.50 (ch £3) **Facilities:** 🅿 💻 🕭 toilets for disabled shop ✾ (ex guide dogs & in grounds)

PACKWOOD HOUSE   Map 07 SP17

PACKWOOD HOUSE

B94 6AT

➲ (on unclass road off A34)

☎ 01564 782024   `2 for 1`

e-mail: packwood@nationaltrust.org.uk

web: nationaltrust.org.uk

Dating from the 16th century, Packwood House has been extended and much changed over the years. An important collection of tapestries and textiles is displayed. Equally important are the stunning gardens with renowned herbaceous borders, attracting many visitors, and the almost surreal topiary garden based on the Sermon on the Mount.

Times: Open Gardens: 2 Mar-6 Nov Wed-Sun, BH Mon, Good Fri. Mar/Oct/Nov 11-4.30. May-Sep 11-5.30; House Mar-Nov 12-4.30 **Fee:** ✱ House & Garden £6 (ch £3). Family ticket £15. Garden only £3 (ch £1.50). Joint ticket with other establishments available.

Facilities: 🅿 🔲 🕭 (2 w/chairs available, tactile tour, Braille guide) toilets for disabled shop ✾ (ex guide dogs) 🧺 🍴

RUGBY   Map 04 SP57

THE WEBB ELLIS RUGBY FOOTBALL MUSEUM

5 Saint Matthew's St CV21 3BY

➲ (on A428 opposite Rugby School)

☎ 01788 567777   `FREE`

e-mail: service@webb-ellis.co.uk

web: www.webb-ellis.co.uk

An intriguing collection of Rugby football memorabilia is housed in the shop in which rugby balls have been made since 1842. Visitors can watch a craftsman at work, hand-stitching the footballs. Situated near to Rugby School and its famous playing field.

Times: ✱ Open all year, Mon-Sat 9-5. Phone for holiday opening times. **Facilities:** 🅿 (500yds) 🕭 shop ✾ (ex guide dogs)

RYTON-ON-DUNSMORE   Map 04 SP37

RYTON ORGANIC GARDENS

CV8 3LG

⮑ (5m SE of Coventry signed off A45, on road to village of Wolston)

☎ 024 7630 3517

e-mail: enquiry@hdra.org.uk

web: www.hdra.org.uk

2 for 1

Ten acres of glorious gardens show how you can grow flowers, fruit and vegetables nature's way without added chemicals. More than thirty individual gardens to look at and enjoy, plus 'The Vegetable Kingdom' - learn all about vegetables, their history, varieties, and how they help to keep us healthy, in a fully interactive visitor centre. Ryton Organic Gardens is the home of HDRA, the organic organisation. Special events, tours, restaurant and coffee shop.

Times: Open daily 9-5. Closed Xmas. **Fee:** ✱ £4.50 (ch £2, concessions £4). **Facilities:** 🅿 💷 ✗ licensed 🗐 ⅂ (wheelchairs available & scooter) toilets for disabled shop garden centre ✖ (ex guide dogs) 🖾

SHOTTERY   Map 04 SP15

ANNE HATHAWAY'S COTTAGE

Cottage Ln CV37 9HH

⮑ (House in Shottery Village, 1m from Stratford)

☎ 01789 292100

e-mail: info@shakespeare.org.uk

web: www.shakespeare.org.uk

Before her marriage to William Shakespeare, Anne Hathaway lived in this substantial 12-roomed thatched Tudor farmhouse with her prosperous yeoman family. The house now shows many aspects of domestic life in 16th-century England, and has a lovely traditional cottage garden, Shakespeare tree and sculpture gardens, maze, gardening history exhibition and romantic willow cabin.

Times: ✱ Open Nov-Mar, daily 10-4; Apr-May & Oct-Nov, Mon-Sat 9.30-5, Sun 10-5; Jun-Aug, Mon-Sat 9-5, Sun 9.30-5. **Facilities:** 🅿 💷 ⅂ (access room with virtual reality tours of cottage) toilets for disabled shop ✖ (ex assist dogs) 🖾

> If an attraction name appears in *italics*, details have not been confirmed for 2006.

STRATFORD-UPON-AVON   Map 04 SP25

HALL'S CROFT

Old Town CV37 6EP

⮑ (located in the centre of Stratford upon Avon)

☎ 01789 292107

e-mail: info@shakespeare.org.uk

web: www.shakespeare.org.uk

A Tudor house with outstanding furniture and paintings where Shakespeare's daughter Susanna and her husband, Dr John Hall, lived before moving to New Place on the dramatist's death. There is an exhibition on Tudor medicine, and fine walled gardens can also be seen.

Times: ✱ Open Nov-Mar, daily 11-4; Apr-May and Sep-Oct, daily 11-5; Jun-Aug, Mon-Sat 9.30-5, Sun 10-5. **Facilities:** 🅿 💷 ⅂ toilets for disabled shop ✖ (ex assist dogs) 🖾

NEW PLACE / NASH'S HOUSE

Chapel St CV37 6EP

⮑ (located in centre of Stratford upon Avon)

☎ 01789 292325

e-mail: info@shakespeare.org.uk

web: www.shakespeare.org.uk

The elegant home of Shakespeare's granddaughter, Elizabeth Hall's first husband Thomas Nash. The adjacent site of New Place, where Shakespeare retired and subsequently died in 1616, is now preserved as a picturesque garden space with an attractive Elizabethan knot garden.

Times: ✱ Open Nov-Mar, daily 11-4; Apr-May & Sep-Oct, daily 11-5; Jun-Aug, Mon-Sat 9.30-5, Sun 10-5.30. **Facilities:** 🅿 (250yds) ⅂ toilets for disabled ✖ (ex assist dogs) 🖾

ROYAL SHAKESPEARE COMPANY COLLECTION

Royal Shakespeare Theatre, Waterside CV37 6BB

⮑ (M40 junct 14 take A46 S. At 1st rdbt take 1st exit (A439). Park in town centre, follow RSC signs)

☎ 01789 262870

e-mail: info@rsc.org.uk

web: www.rsc.org.uk

The RSC gallery opened in 1881, and was part of the first Shakespeare Memorial Theatre. In 1926 fire destroyed the theatre leaving only a semi circular wall and the gallery. The exhibition space now displays costumes from past RSC productions, paintings and other Theatre Memorabilia.

Times: Open all year, Mon-Fri 1.30-6.30, Sat 10.30-6.30 & Sun 11.30-4.30. Closed 24-25 Dec.Theatre tours usually Mon-Fri (ex matinee days), 1.30 & 5.30, Sun 12, 1, 2 & 3. **Fee:** ✱ Exhibition £2 (ch, pen & students £1). Family ticket £4. **Facilities:** 🅿 (charged) 💷 ✗ licensed 🗐 ⅂ (services for hearing impaired, Braille books/reading room) toilets for disabled shop ✖ (ex guide dogs)

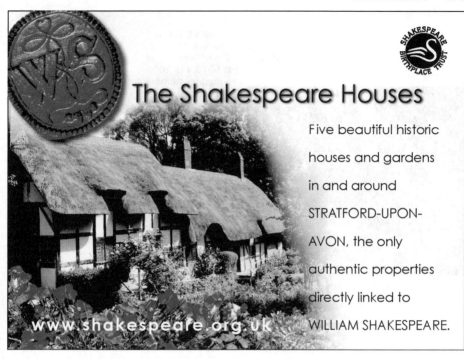

The Shakespeare Houses

Five beautiful historic houses and gardens in and around STRATFORD-UPON-AVON, the only authentic properties directly linked to WILLIAM SHAKESPEARE.

www.shakespeare.org.uk

SHAKESPEARE'S BIRTHPLACE
Henley St CV37 6QW
➲ (in town centre)
☎ 01789 204016
e-mail: info@shakespeare.org.uk
web: www.shakespeare.org.uk

Shakespeare was born in the half-timbered house in 1564. It is now presented as it may have been when he was a boy. The ticket price includes entrance to an exhibition of the author's life, including a first edition of his complete works.
Times: ✱ Open Nov-Mar, Mon-Sat 10-4, Sun 10.30-4; Apr-May & Sep-Oct, Mon-Sat 10-5, Sun 10.30-5; Jun-Aug, Mon-Sat 9-5, Sun 9.30-5.
Facilities: P & (computer based virtual reality tour of upper floor) toilets for disabled shop ✈ (ex assist dogs) ◼
See advertisement on this page

STRATFORD BUTTERFLY FARM
Tramway Walk, Swan's Nest Ln CV37 7LS
➲ (south bank of River Avon opposite RSC)
☎ 01789 299288
e-mail: sales@butterflyfarm.co.uk
web: www.butterflyfarm.co.uk
Europe's largest live Butterfly and Insect Exhibit. Hundreds of the world's most spectacular and colourful butterflies, in the unique setting of a lush tropical landscape, with splashing waterfalls and fish-filled pools. See also the strange and fascinating Insect City, a bustling metropolis of ants, bees, stick insects, beetles and other remarkable insects. See the dangerous and deadly in Arachnoland!
Times: Open daily 10-6 (winter 10-dusk). Closed 25 Dec.
Fee: ✱ £4.75 (ch £3.75) concessions £4.25. Family £13.95
Facilities: P (opposite entrance) (site parking orange badge holders only) ◼ & shop ✈ ◼

THE TEDDY BEAR MUSEUM

19 Greenhill St CV37 6LF
➲ (M40 junct 15, follow signs to town centre)
☎ 01789 293160
e-mail: info@theteddybearmuseum.com **2 for 1**
web: www.theteddybearmuseum.com

Collection of some of the oldest and rarest teddy bears in the world, displayed in a house once owned by Henry VIII. Lots of modern teddy bear stars too, including the original Fozzie Bear, Paddington Bear from the earliest television series, Mr Bean's bear, and many more.
Times: Open all year, daily 9.30-5.30 (ex Jan & Feb 10-4.30). Closed 25-26 Dec. **Fee:** £2.95 (ch £1.95, concessions £2.45). Family ticket £9.50 (2ad+3ch or 1ad+4ch) **Facilities:** P (30yds & 200yds) 🗐 (access to ground floor shop only) shop ✖ (ex guide dogs) 🚌

UPTON HOUSE   Map 04 SP34

UPTON HOUSE

OX15 6HT
➲ (M40 junct 12, on A422, 7m NW of Banbury, 12m SE of Stratford)
☎ 01295 670266
e-mail: uptonhouse@nationaltrust.org.uk
web: www.nationaltrust.org.uk
The house, built of mellow local stone, dates from 1695, and contains an outstanding collection of paintings by English and Continental Old Masters, Brussels tapestries, Sévres porcelain, Chelsea figures, 18th-century furniture, and a collection of original artwork used to advertise Shell oil during the 1920s and 30s. Viscount Bearsted, the donor of Upton, was chairman of Shell and the son of its founder.
Times: Open 5 Nov-18 Dec, Sat & Sun 12-4. 19 Mar-2 Nov, Sat-Wed; House 1-5, Garden 12-5, (Sat & Sun 11-5 garden) **Fee:** ✱ £6.80 (ch £4) Family £16. Garden only £4 (ch £2, under 5's free) Party 15+
Facilities: P 💻 ✖ 🗐 ᕒ (Braille guide, parking nr house, buggy for lower garden) toilets for disabled shop ✖ (ex assist dogs) 🐾 🚌

WARWICK   Map 04 SP26

WARWICK CASTLE

CV34 4QU
➲ (2m from M40 junct 15)
☎ 0870 442 2000
e-mail: customer.information@warwick-castle.com
web: www.warwick-castle.co.uk
From the days of William the Conqueror to the reign of Queen Victoria, Warwick Castle has provided a backdrop for many turbulent times. Attractions include the gloomy Dungeon and Torture Chamber, the grand State Rooms, the Great Hall, and a reconstruction of a Victorian Party. Please telephone for details of events running throughout the year.
Times: Open all year, daily 10-6 (5pm Nov-Mar). Closed 25 Dec.
Fee: ✱ £12.95-£16.95 (ch 4-16 £7.95-£9.95, pen £9.25-£11.75, students £9.95-£11.95). Family ticket (2ad+2ch) £34-£45. Wheelchair bound visitors free. Group discounts are available if pre-booked.
Facilities: P (charged) 💻 ✖ licensed 🗐 ᕒ (hearing loop, large print guides, DVD) toilets for disabled shop ✖ (ex assistance dogs) 🚌

WARWICKSHIRE YEOMANRY MUSEUM

The Court House Vaults, Jury St CV34 4EW
➲ (situated on corner of Jury St & Castle St, 2m E of M40 junct 15)
☎ 01926 492212
The vaults of the courthouse display militaria from the county Yeomanry, dating from 1794 to 1945. It includes regimental silver, paintings, uniforms and weapons. A small room in the cellars now houses the HUJ Gun project, a field gun captured by the Yeomanry in 1917.
Times: Open Etr-Oct, Sat-Sun & BHs, 10-1 & 2-4. Other times by prior arrangement. **Fee:** ✱ Donations welcome. **Facilities:** P (300yds) (2hr max in nearby streets) shop ✖

WILMCOTE   Map 04 SP15

MARY ARDEN'S HOUSE AND THE SHAKESPEARE COUNTRYSIDE MUSEUM

Station Rd CV37 9UN
➲ (3m NW of Stratford-upon-Avon off A3400)
☎ 01789 293455
e-mail: info@shakespeare.org.uk
web: www.shakespeare.org.uk
This picturesque, half-timbered Tudor house was the childhood home of Shakespeare's mother, Mary Arden. The site also includes Palmers Farm - a working farm with rare breed farm animals, including Gloucester Old Spot Pigs, Cotswold Sheep and Longhorn cattle. Falconry displays take place and there is a children's adventure playground.
Times: ✱ Open Nov-Mar, Mon-Sat 10-4, Sun 10.30-4; Apr-May & Sep-Oct, Mon-Sat 10-5, Sun 10.30-5; Jun-Aug, Mon-Sat 9.30-5, Sun 10-5. **Facilities:** P 💻 ᕒ toilets for disabled shop ✖ (ex assist dogs) 🚌

WEST MIDLANDS

EVENTS & FESTIVALS

January
tbc Chinese New Year Celebrations,
Birmingham

March
9th-12th Crufts Dog Show, National
Exhibition Centre, Birmingham
17th St Patrick's Day Pageant, Coventry

May
25th-29th Coventry Jazz Festival, various
venues in the city centre

June
14th-18th BBC Gardeners' World Live, NEC,
Birmingham

July
8th-9th City of Wolverhampton Show
(provisional)
22nd-23rd Wolvestock Music Festival,
Hickman Park, Bilston (provisional)
tbc Birmingham International Jazz Festival, 70
venues citywide
tbc Godiva Festival, free festival with three
stages, War Memorial Park, Coventry
tbc Lord Mayor's Show, Birmingham, weekend
of free family entertainment

September
2nd-3rd Coventry Festival of Motoring,
Millennium Place, and Memorial Park,
Coventry
tbc Birmingham Artsfest, UK's largest free arts
festival, city centre

Above: Walsall Arboretum

BIRMINGHAM — Map 07 SP08

ASTON HALL
Trinity Rd, Aston B6 6JD
➲ (M6 junct 6 follow A38(M) Aston Expressway
towards city centre. Leave at Aston Waterlinks
and follow brown signs to Aston Hall) **FREE**
☎ 0121 327 0062
e-mail: bmag-enquiries@birmingham.gov.uk
web: www.bmag.org.uk

Built by Sir Thomas Holte, Aston Hall is a fine Jacobean
mansion complete with a panelled Long Gallery, balustraded
staircase and magnificent plaster friezes and ceilings. King
Charles I spent a night here during the Civil War and the
house was damaged by Parliamentary troops. It was also
leased to James Watt Junior, the son of the great industrial
pioneer.

Times: ✱ Open Etr-Oct, Tue-Sun 11.30-4. Closed Mon ex BHs.
Facilities: ⓟ 🖭 ⬤ (ground floor only partially accessible) shop
✖ (ex guide dogs)

BIRMINGHAM BOTANICAL GARDENS & GLASSHOUSES
Westbourne Rd, Edgbaston B15 3TR
➲ (2m W of city centre, follow signs for
Edgbaston, then brown heritage signs)
☎ 0121 454 1860
e-mail: admin@
birminghambotanicalgardens.org.uk
web: www.birminghambotanicalgardens.org.uk

Originally opened in 1832, the gardens include the Tropical
House, which has a 24ft-wide lily pool and lush vegetation.
The Mediterranean house features a wide variety of citrus
fruits and the Arid House has a desert scene with its giant
agaves and opuntias. Outside, a tour of the gardens includes
rhododendrons and azalea borders and a collection of over
200 trees. Young children's discovery garden and a sculpture
trail.

Times: Open daily all year, wkdays 9-7 or dusk, Sun 10-7 or dusk
whichever is earlier. Closed 25 Dec. **Fee:** ✱ £5.90 (concessions
£3.50); £6.20 summer Sun & BHs. Family £17 (£18 summer & BHs)
Groups 10+ £4.80 (concessions £3.10) **Facilities:** ⓟ 🖭 ✖ licensed
🍴 ⬤ (3 wheelchairs, 2 electric scooters & Braille guides) toilets for
disabled shop garden centre ✖ (ex guide dogs) 🖼

See advertisement on page 245

BIRMINGHAM MUSEUM & ART GALLERY
Chamberlain Sq B3 3DH
☎ 0121 303 2834   FREE
e-mail: bmag-enquiries@birmingham.gov.uk
web: www.bmag.org.uk

One of the world's best collections of Pre-Raphaelite paintings can be seen here, including important works by Burne-Jones, a native of Birmingham. Also on display are fine silver, ceramics and glass. The archaeology section has prehistoric Egyptian, Greek and Roman antiquities, and also objects from the Near East, Mexico and Peru.
Times: ✳ Open all year, Mon-Thu & Sat 10-5, Fri 10.30-5 and Sun 12.30-5. **Facilities:** P ⬛ ✗ licensed ♿ (lift) toilets for disabled shop ✕ ◼

BLAKESLEY HALL
FREE
Blakesley Rd, Yardley B25 8RN
⮑ (A4040 onto Blakesley Rd, Hall 100yds on right)
☎ 0121 783 2193

Blakesley Hall is a fine Yeoman farmers residence, built by Richard Smalbroke in 1590. It has a half-timbered exterior and a Stuart interior, with a wonderful herb garden. The visitor centre has a varied exhibition programme, tea room and gift shop. Regular weekend events take place throughout the summer holidays.
Times: ✳ Open Apr-Oct, Tue-Sun & BHs, 11.30-4 **Facilities:** P ⬛ ◻ shop ✕

MUSEUM OF THE JEWELLERY QUARTER
75-79 Vyse St, Hockley B18 6HA
⮑ (off A41 into Vyse St, museum on left after 1st side street)   FREE
☎ 0121 554 3598
e-mail: bmag-enquiries@birmingham.gov.uk
web: www.bmag.org.uk

The Museum tells the story of jewellery making in Birmingham from its origins in the Middle Ages right through to the present day. Discover the skill of the jeweller's craft and enjoy a unique tour of an original jewellery factory frozen in time. For over eighty years the family firm of Smith and Pepper produced jewellery from the factory. This perfectly preserved 'time capsule' workshop has changed little since the beginning of the century. The Jewellery Quarter is still very much at the forefront of jewellery manufacture in Britain and the Museum showcases the work of the city's most exciting new designers.
Times: ✳ Open Etr-Oct, Tue-Sun 11.30-4. (Closed Mon ex BH Mon) **Facilities:** P (limited 2hr stay/pay & display) ⬛ ♿ (tours for hearing/visually impaired booked in advance) toilets for disabled shop ✕ (ex guide dogs) ◼

RSPB SANDWELL VALLEY NATURE RESERVE
20 Tanhouse Av, Great Barr B43 5AG
⮑ (off B4167 Hamstead Rd into Tanhouse Ave)
☎ 0121 357 7395
web: www.rspb.org.uk   FREE

Opened in 1983 on the site of an old colliery, Sandwell Valley is home to hundreds of bird, animal and insect species in five different habitats. Summer is the best time to see the yellow wagtail or reed warblers, while wintertime attracts goosanders, snipe, and redshanks. There are guided walks and bug hunts for the kids in summer, and a shop and visitor centre all year round.
Times: ✳ Open Tue-Fri 9-5, Sat & Sun 10-5 (closes at dusk in winter). Closed Mon, 24 Dec-2 Jan **Facilities:** P ◻ ♿ toilets for disabled shop

SAREHOLE MILL
Cole Bank Rd, Hall Green B13 0BD
⮑ (M42 junct 4. Take A34 towards Birmingham. After 5m turn left on B4146, attraction on left)
☎ 0121 777 6612   FREE
web: www.bmag.org.uk

Home to Birmingham's only working watermill; Sarehole Mill was built in the 1760s. Used for both flour production and metal rolling up to the last century, the Mill can still be seen in action during the summer months. Restored with financial backing from JRR Tolkien, who grew up in the area and cites Sarehole as an influence for writing The Hobbit and Lord of the Rings.
Times: ✳ Open Etr-Oct, Tue-Sun 11.30-4. (Closed Mon, ex BH Mon)
Facilities: P ✕ (ex guide dogs)

SELLY MANOR MUSEUM
Maple Rd, Bournville B30 2AE
⮑ (off A38)
☎ 0121 472 0199
e-mail: gillianellis@bvt.org.uk

These two timber-framed manor houses date from the 13th and early 14th centuries, and have been re-erected in the 'garden suburb' of Bournville. There is a herb garden and events are held all year.
Times: Open mid Jan-mid Dec, Tue-Fri 10-5; Apr-Sep & BH, Sat-Sun 2-5. **Facilities:** P ♿ toilets for disabled shop

SOHO HOUSE
Soho Av, Handsworth B18 5LB
⮑ (from city centre follow A41 to Soho Rd, follow brown heritage signs to Soho Ave)   FREE
☎ 0121 554 9122
e-mail: bmag-enquiries@birmingham.gov.uk
web: www.bmag.org.uk

Soho House was the elegant home of industrial pioneer Matthew Boulton between 1766 and 1809. Here, he met with some of the most important thinkers and scientists of his day. The house has been carefully restored and contains many of Boulton's possessions including furniture, clocks, silverware and the original dining table where the Lunar Society met.
Times: ✳ Open Etr-Oct, Tue-Sun 11.30-4. (Closed Mon ex BH Mons) **Facilities:** P ⬛ ♿ (induction loop) toilets for disabled shop ✕ (ex guide dogs) ◼

THINKTANK AT MILLENNIUM POINT
Millennium Point, Curzon St B4 7XG
☎ 0121 202 2222
e-mail: findout@thinktank.ac
web: www.thinktank.ac

Thinktank is the award winning, Birmingham Museum of Science and Discovery. Four floors with ten themed galleries are packed with interactive exhibits that explore everything from locomotives and aircraft to intestines and taste buds to emotional robots! Themed events, exhibitions, talks and tours run throughout the year. Special Event: Digital Planetarium from Dec 2005, 'Alien Lab' Apr-Sep 2006.
Times: Open daily 10-5 (last entry 4). Closed 24-26 Dec **Fee:** ✳ £6.95 (ch £4.95). Family ticket (2ad+2ch) £20, concessions £5 (peak) £3.50 (off peak) **Facilities:** P (charged) ⬛ ♿ induction loop, wheelchair loan, BSL events, parking toilets for disabled shop science kits, talking clocks, puzzles ✕ (ex guide dogs) ◼

BOURNVILLE Map 07 SP08

CADBURY WORLD
Linden Rd B30 2LD
➲ (1m S of A38 Bristol Rd, on A4040 Ring Rd.
Follow brown signs from M5 junct 2 and junct 4)
☎ 0121 451 4159
e-mail: cadbury.world@csplc.com
web: www.cadburyworld.co.uk

Lots of recent changes have meant Cadbury World now has much more to see, do and taste. There is the chance to get involved in the chocolate making process, and to find out how the chocolate is used to make famous confectionery. Visitors can learn about the early struggles and triumphs of the Cadbury business, and follow the history of Cadbury television advertising. Besides all this, visitors can relax on the gentle Cadabra ride, and be a big kid in CadburyLand, the Fantasy Factory, and in the Happiness Room.
Times: Contact information line 0121 451 4180 for opening times.
Fee: ✱ £10.50 (ch £7.90, concessions £8.30) **Facilities:** Ⓟ ➡
✕ licensed 🍴 ＆ (adapted ride & lift to 2nd floor, subtitles) toilets for disabled shop ✽ (ex guide dogs) 🖃

CASTLE BROMWICH Map 07 SP18

CASTLE BROMWICH HALL GARDENS
Chester Rd B36 9BT
➲ (M6 junct 5, follow brown tourist signs)
☎ 0121 749 4100
e-mail: admin@cbhgt.colebridge.net
web: www.cbhgt.colebridge.net
This recently-restored 17th-century formal garden illustrates a period of history in an unusual and fascinating way. Although the garden is an accurate reconstruction of the garden as it was around 1680-1740, there is an addition: the holly maze, which was created in the 19th century, based on 17th-century plans.
Times: Open: Apr-Oct, Wed-Fri 12-4; Sat, Sun & BH Mon 1-5
Fee: ✱ £3.50 (ch £1.50, pen £2.50) **Facilities:** Ⓟ ➡ 🍴
＆ (wheelchairs available for free) toilets for disabled shop garden centre

---

Directions are provided by the attractions.

COVENTRY Map 04 SP37

COVENTRY CATHEDRAL & VISITOR CENTRE
7 Priory Row CV1 5ES
➲ (signposted on all approaches to the city)
☎ 024 7622 7597
e-mail: information@coventrycathedral.org
web: www.coventrycathedral.org
Coventry's old cathedral was bombed during an air raid of November 1940 which devastated the city. The remains have been carefully preserved. The new cathedral was designed by Sir Basil Spence and consecrated in May 1962. It contains outstanding modern works of art, including a huge tapestry designed by Graham Sutherland, the west screen (a wall of glass engraved by John Hutton with saints and angels), bronzes by Epstein, and the great baptistry window by John Piper.
Times: ✱ Open all year, daily, Etr-Oct 8.30-6, Oct-Etr 8.30-5.30.
Facilities: Ⓟ (250yds) ➡ ＆ (lift, touch and hearing centre, paved wheelchair access) toilets for disabled shop ✽ (ex guide dogs)

COVENTRY TRANSPORT MUSEUM
Millennium Place, Hales St CV1 1PN
➲ (just off junct 1, Coventry ring road, Tower St in city centre)
☎ 024 7623 4270   FREE
e-mail: enquiries@transport-museum.com
web: www.transport-museum.com
Coventry is the traditional home of the motor industry, and the museum's world-renowned collection displays over 150 years of its history. You can design your own car, feel what

continued

its like to break the sound barrier at 763mph and even travel into the future.

Times: Open all year, daily 10-5. Closed 24-26 Dec.
Facilities: P (adjacent) (pay & display) 🎧 ⴲ (audio tour, tactile floor & models, wheelchairs for hire) toilets for disabled shop ✈ (ex guide dogs) 🛒

HERBERT ART GALLERY & MUSEUM

Jordan Well CV1 5QP
➲ (in city centre near Cathedral)
☎ 024 7683 2381 & 7683 2565   FREE
e-mail: artsandheritage@coventry.gov.uk
web: www.coventrymuseum.org.uk
'Godiva City', tells Coventry's story over 1,000 years, through interactive exhibits, objects, pictures and words. Changing displays of art, craft, social and industrial history. It is Coventry's premier museum hosting a range of exhibitions and events.
Times: ✱ Open all year, Mon-Sat 10-5.30, Sun 12-5. Closed 24-26, 31 Dec & 1 Jan **Facilities:** P (500yds) 🎧 🗐 ⴲ (disabled parking, automatic doors, tactile/audio displays) toilets for disabled shop ✈ (ex guide/assistance dogs)

JAGUAR DAIMLER HERITAGE CENTRE

Browns Ln, Allesley CV5 9DR
➲ (on A45, follow signs for Browns Lane Plant)
☎ 024 7620 3322   FREE
e-mail: jagtrust@jaguar.com
web: www.jdht.com
Established in 1983, the Jaguar-Daimler Heritage Trust maintains a unique collection of motor vehicles and artefacts manufactured by Jaguar Cars Ltd, and the many other renowned marques associated with the company.
Times: Open Mon-Thu 9-4, Fri 9-3 & last Sun of month 10-4.
Facilities: P 🎧 🗐 ⴲ toilets for disabled shop ✈ (ex guide dogs)

LUNT ROMAN FORT

Coventry Rd, Baginton CV8 3AJ
➲ (S side of city, off Stonebridge highway, A45)
☎ 024 7683 2381 & 7683 2565
e-mail: artsandheritage@coventry.co.uk
web: www.coventrymuseum.org
The turf and timber Roman fort from around the end of the 1st century has been faithfully reconstructed. An Interpretation Centre is housed in the granary.
Times: ✱ Open 27 Mar-Oct, Sat-Sun & BH Mon 10-5; mid Jul-end Aug, Thu-Tue 10-5; Spring BH wk, Thu-Tue 10-5.
Facilities: P ⴲ (ramp to Granary Interpretation Centre) toilets for disabled shop ✈ (ex guide/assistance dogs)

PRIORY VISITOR CENTRE

Priory Row CV1 5EX
➲ (in city centre near Cathedral)
☎ 024 7683 2381   FREE
e-mail: artsandheritage@coventry.gov.uk
web: www.coventrymuseum.org.uk
Earl Leofric and his wife Lady Godiva founded a monastery in Coventry in the 11th century. This priory disappeared somewhere beneath the cathedral that was built on the site, until this cathedral was in turn demolished by Henry VIII in the 16th century. Soon after that most of the buildings on the site had been reduced to ground level, leaving modern archaeologists to discover the outlines of history. This visitor centre displays finds from the site as well as telling the story of Coventry's first cathedral.
Times: ✱ Open Mon-Sat 10-5.30, Sun noon-4 **Facilities:** P (500yds) 🗐 ⴲ toilets for disabled shop ✈ (ex guide/assistance dogs)

ST MARY'S GUILDHALL

Bayley Ln CV1 5QP
➲ (in city centre near ruined Cathedral)
☎ 024 7683 2381   FREE
e-mail: artsandheritage@coventry.gov.uk
web: www.coventrymuseum.org.uk
This impressive medieval Guildhall has stood in the heart of Coventry for over 650 years, and has played its part in the history of the area. It served as Henry VI's court during the War of the Roses, was a prison to Mary Queen of Scots, and was used as a setting by George Eliot in her novel *Adam Bede*. The Great Hall contains a Tournai tapestry commissioned for the visit of Henry VII and Queen Elizabeth in 1500.
Times: ✱ Open Etr Sun-Sep, Sun-Thu 10-4 **Facilities:** P (600yds) ⴲ shop ✈ (ex guide/assistance dogs)

DUDLEY   Map 07 SO99

BLACK COUNTRY LIVING MUSEUM

Tipton Rd DY1 4SQ
➲ (on A4037, near Showcase cinema)
☎ 0121 557 9643 & 0121 520 8054
e-mail: info@bclm.co.uk
web: www.bclm.co.uk
On the 26-acre site is a recreated canal-side village, with shops, houses and workplaces. Meet the costumed guides and find out what life was like around 1900. Ride on a tramcar, take a trip down the underground mine, venture into the limestone caverns or visit the olde tyme fairground (additional charge). There are also demonstrations of chainmaking, glass engraving and sweet-making. Watch a silent movie in the Limelight cinema, taste fish and chips cooked on a 1930s range, and finish your visit with a glass of real ale in the Bottle and Glass Inn.
Times: Open all year, Mar-Oct daily 10-5; Nov-Feb, Wed-Sun 10-4. (Telephone for Xmas closing) **Fee:** ✱ £9.95 (ch 5-18 £5.75, pen £8.75). Family ticket (2ad+3ch) £28. **Facilities:** P (charged) 🎧 ✗ licensed ⴲ (ramps available) toilets for disabled shop ✈ (ex guide dogs) 🛒

DUDLEY ZOOLOGICAL GARDENS

2 The Broadway DY1 4QB
➲ (M5 junct 2 towards Wolverhampton/Dudley, signed)
☎ 01384 215313
e-mail: marketing@dudleyzoo.org.uk
web: www.dudleyzoo.org.uk
From lions and tigers to snakes and spiders, enjoy animal encounters and feeds. Get closer to some furry, and some not so furry creatures, and have fun on the fair rides, land train, and the adventure playground. Step back in time and see history come to life in the castle.
Times: Open all year, Etr-mid Sep, daily 10-4; mid Sep-Etr, daily 10-3. Closed 25 Dec. **Fee:** ✱ £8.95 (ch 4-15 £5.75, concessions £6.25). Family ticket £31 (2ad+3ch) **Facilities:** P (charged) 🎧 ✗ licensed 🗐 ⴲ (land train from gates-castle, wheelchair hire) toilets for disabled shop ✈ (ex guide dogs) 🛒

> If an attraction name appears in *italics*, details have not been confirmed for 2006.

MUSEUM & ART GALLERY

St James's Rd DY1 1HU

➲ (M5 N junct 2. Take A4123 signed to Dudley)

☎ 01384 815575

e-mail: museum.pls@mbc.dudley.gov.uk

web: www.dudley.gov.uk

FREE

The museum houses the Brooke Robinson collection of 17th, 18th- and 19th-century European painting, furniture, ceramics and enamels. A fine geological gallery, 'The Time Trail' has spectacular displays of fossils from the local Wenlock limestone and coal measures.

Times: ✱ Open all year, Mon-Sat 10-4. Closed BHs.
Facilities: 🅿 (25mtrs) 🍴 ⅙ (Braille & large print text. Tactile objects) shop ✖ (ex guide dogs)

KINGSWINFORD   Map 07 SO88

BROADFIELD HOUSE GLASS MUSEUM

Compton Dr DY6 9NS

➲ (Off A491 Stourbridge to Wolverhampton road, just S of Kingswinford Village Centre)

☎ 01384 812745

e-mail: glass.museum@dudley.gov.uk

web: www.glassmuseum.org.uk

FREE

This magnificent collection of 19th-and 20th-century glass focuses on the cut, etched, engraved and coloured glass made in nearby Stourbridge during the last century. Highlights include cameo glass by Alphonse Lechevrel and George Woodall, and rock crystal engraving by William Fritsche. Also on display are the Michael Parkington collection of 18th-, 19th-and 20th-century British glass, the Hulbert of Dudley collection, and the Notley/Lerpiniere collection of Carnival Glass.

Times: Open all year, Tue-Sun & BHs 12-4. Please phone for Xmas/Etr openings **Facilities:** 🅿 ⅙ toilets for disabled shop ✖ (ex guide dogs)

SOLIHULL   Map 07 SP17

NATIONAL MOTORCYCLE MUSEUM

Coventry Rd, Bickenhill B92 0EJ

➲ (M42 junct 6, off A45 near NEC)

☎ 01675 443311

web: www.nationalmotorcyclemuseum.co.uk

Five exhibition halls showing British motorcycles built during the Golden Age of motorcycling. Spanning 90 years, the immaculately restored machines are the products of around 150 different factories. Over 700 machines are on show, most are owned by the museum, while others are from collections or private owners. Restoration work is carried out by enthusiasts, and new motorcycles are acquired from all over the world.

Times: Open all year, daily 10-6. Closed 24-26 Dec. **Fee:** ✱ £6.95 (ch 12 & pen £4.95). Party 20+ £5.95 **Facilities:** 🅿 ✖ licensed ⅙ toilets for disabled shop ✖ (ex guide dogs)

STOURBRIDGE   Map 07 SO88

THE FALCONRY CENTRE

Hurrans Garden Centre, Kidderminster Rd South, Hagley DY9 0JB

➲ (off A456)

☎ 01562 700014

e-mail: info@thefalconrycentre.co.uk

web: www.thefalconrycentre.co.uk

2 for 1

The centre houses some 70 birds of prey including owls, hawks and falcons and is also a rehabilitation centre for sick and injured birds of prey. Spectacular flying displays are put

continued

on daily from midday. There are picnic areas, special fun days and training courses available.

Times: Open all year, daily 10-5 & Sun 11-5. Closed 25, 26 Dec & Etr Sun. **Fee:** £3.50 (ch, pen & disabled £2.50). Party 25+ 10% discount.
Facilities: 🅿 ⅙ Ramps in most places toilets for disabled shop garden centre ✖ (ex guide dogs)

WALSALL   Map 07 SP09

NEW ART GALLERY WALSALL

Gallery Square WS2 8LG

➲ (signed from all major routes into town centre)

☎ 01922 654400

e-mail: info@artatwalsall.org.uk

web: www.artatwalsall.org.uk

FREE

Opened in 2000, this exciting new art gallery has at its core the Garman Ryan Collection, and a Children's Discovery Gallery that offers access to the very best in contemporary art in the only interactive art gallery designed especially for young people.

Times: Open all year, Tue-Sat 10-5, Sun noon-5. Closed Mon ex BH Mon, 25-28 Dec & 1 Jan. Please telephone to confirm.
Facilities: 🅿 🛒 🍴 ⅙ (lift access to facilties, induction loop, large print) toilets for disabled shop ✖ (ex guide dogs)

WALSALL LEATHER MUSEUM

Littleton St West WS2 8EQ

➲ (On Walsall ring-road A4148 on N side of town)

☎ 01922 721153

e-mail: leathermuseum@walsall.gov.uk

web: www.walsall.gov.uk/leathermuseum

FREE

Award winning working museum in the saddlery and leathergoods 'capital' of Britain. Watch skilled craftsmen and women at work in this restored Victorian leather factory. Displays tell the story of Walsall's leatherworkers past and present. Large shop stocks range of Walsall made leathergoods, many at bargain prices. Saddle Room Café serves delicious home-cooked cakes and light lunches. Groups very welcome, guided tours available.

Times: Open all year, Tue-Sat 10-5 (Nov-Mar 4), Sun noon-5 (Nov-Mar 4). Open BH Mon. Closed 24-26 Dec, 1 Jan, Good Fri, Etr Sun & May Day. **Facilities:** 🅿 (10mtrs) 🛒 ⅙ (staff with sign language skills,tactile activities, parking) toilets for disabled shop ✖ (ex guide dogs)

WOLVERHAMPTON   Map 07 SO99

BANTOCK HOUSE AND PARK

Finchfield Rd WV3 9LQ

➲ (follow signs for Wolverhampton. Bantock House 1m out of city & well signed from ring road)

☎ 01902 552195

e-mail: bantockhouse@dial.pipex.com

web: www.wolverhampton.gov.uk

FREE

A rare survival of a Georgian farmhouse that was extended in the early 19th century to double its size. The current interior represents the Edwardian era, when the décor was radically altered. The ground floor is set out as the family home, while upstairs visitors can discover Wolverhampton's history. The gardens have been restored to their Edwardian designs and include a rose garden, Dutch garden and woodland pond.

Times: Open early Apr-end Oct, 11-5; Nov-end Mar, 12-4. Closed Mon
Facilities: 🅿 🛒 🍴 ⅙ (wheelchair, induction loop, Braille guide) toilets for disabled shop ✖ (ex assist dogs)

MOSELEY OLD HALL

2 for 1

Fordhouses WV10 7HY

➲ (4m N of Wolverhampton, off A460 and A449)

☎ 01902 782808

e-mail: moseleyoldhall@nationaltrust.org.uk

web: www.nationaltrust.org

Charles II sheltered in Moseley Old Hall after the Battle of Worcester in 1651. There are numerous pictures and other reminders of the king. The house itself is an Elizabethan timber-framed building which was encased in brick in the 19th century. The small garden has a nut walk, period herbs and plants, and a formal knot garden. For details of special events please send a 9" x 4" envelope.

Times: Open 19 Mar-30 Oct, Sat, Sun & Wed 1-5; 6 Nov-18 Dec, Sun 1-4. **Fee:** ✱ £4.80 (ch £2.40). Family ticket £12 **Facilities:** 🅿 💻 🗐 ♿ (Braille & large print, 1 wheelchair, thick handled cutlery) toilets for disabled shop ✖

WIGHTWICK MANOR

WV6 8EE

➲ (3m W, beside Mermaid Inn off A454 Bridgnorth)

☎ 01902 761400

2 for 1

e-mail: wightwickmanor@nationaltrust.org.uk

web: www.nationaltrust.org.uk

This house was begun in 1887 and is one of the finest examples of 19th-century decorative style. All aspects of William Morris's talents are shown in the house - wallpapers, textiles, carpets, tiles, embroidery and even books. The garden reflects late Victorian and Edwardian design. The 2-for-1 voucher is valid only during normal visiting hours and cannot be used for any ticketed events.

Times: Open Mar-23 Dec, Thu, Sat & BH Sun & Mon 1.30-5. (Last admission 4.30). Garden & servant tours throughout the year, please phone for details. **Fee:** £6 (accompanied ch & students £3.20). Gardens only £3.20 (ch free in garden) **Facilities:** 🅿 💻 ♿ (car parking call 01902 761400 for details) shop ✖ (ex assist dogs & in gardens) ✖

WORDSLEY   Map 07 SO88

THE RED HOUSE GLASS CONE NEW

High St DY8 4AZ

➲ (A491 just N of Stourbridge)

☎ 01384 812750

2 for 1

e-mail: redhouse.cone@dudley.gov.uk

web: www.redhousecone.co.uk

One of only four cones left in the UK and one of the most complete glass cone sites in Europe, over one hundred feet tall. Explore the fascinating history, watch glassblowers in action and discover the underground tunnels. 2-for-1 voucher may be used for audio guides.

Times: Open all year, summer Mon-Sat 10-5,Sun 10-4; winter daily 10-5. **Fee:** ✱ Admission free. Audio guides charged £2.50 (ch £1.50, concessions £2) see description **Facilities:** 🅿 💻 ♿ toilets for disabled shop ✖ (ex guide dogs) 📼

> An asterisk * indicates that opening times and prices are for 2005. Please contact the attraction for up-to-date information.

ISLE OF WIGHT

EVENTS & FESTIVALS

April
14th-16th Easter Challenge yacht racing, start of the yachting season, in Cowes

May
21st Isle of Wight Marathon, 50th anniversary
tbc Schneider Trophy Air Races, Bembridge Airport

June
3rd Round the Island Yacht Race
25th-2nd Jul Commodore's Cup, international ocean racing team event, Cowes
tbc Isle of Wight Festival, Seaclose Park, Newport
tbc Old Gaffers Festival, Yarmouth, festival of gaff-rigged vessels, entertainment and stalls

July
22nd-23rd Isle of Wight County Show, Showground, Northwood, nr Newport
tbc Annual Regatta, Royal Solent Yacht Club, Yarmouth
tbc Cowes Week, international yachting regatta, music and street theatre

August
5th-6th Chale Summer Show, horticultural show with arena events
25th-28th The Island Steam Show, Havenstreet
tbc Isle of Wight Garlic Festival, Newchurch

October
21st-29th White Air Extreme Sports Festival, Yaverland Beach

Above: Sunset over Compton Bay

ALUM BAY   Map 04 SZ38

THE NEEDLES OLD BATTERY

West High Down PO30 0JH

➲ (at Needles Headland, W of Freshwater Bay and Alum Bay, B3322)

☎ 01983 754772   `2 for 1`

e-mail: isleofwight@nationaltrust.org.uk

web: www.nationaltrust.org.uk/isleofwight

The threat of a French invasion prompted the construction in 1862 of this spectacularly sited fort, which still retains its original gun barrels. The laboratory, searchlight position-finding cells have all been restored and a 65m tunnel leads to stunning views of the Hampshire and Dorset coastline. Special Event. 50th year of rocket testing. 2-for-1 voucher is valid only during normal visiting hours, and cannot be used for any ticketed events.

Times: Open 27 Mar-29 Oct Sat-Thu 10.30-5. Jul-Aug daily. **Fee:** £3.90 (ch £1.95). Family ticket £8.90. Group £3.30 each. May be subject to change. **Facilities:** P (0.5m) ⬛ 🍴 ⬛ & (ramp & audio tours, hearing loops) toilets for disabled shop 🐾 🎴

THE NEEDLES PARK

PO39 0JD

➲ (signed on B3322)

☎ 0870 458 0022   `2 for 1`

e-mail: info@theneedles.co.uk

web: www.theneedles.co.uk

Overlooking the Needles on the western edge of the island, the park has attractions for all the family: included in the wide range of facilities is the spectacular chair lift to the beach to view the famous coloured sand cliffs, Needles Rocks and lighthouse. Other popular attractions are Alum

continued

Bay Glass and the Isle of Wight Sweet Manufactory. Kids will enjoy the Junior Driver roadway, and the Jurassic Golf course.

Times: Open Apr-30 Oct, daily 10-5. Hours extended in high season & on special event days **Fee:** No admission charged for entrance to Park. All day car park charge £3. Pay as you go attractions or Supersaver Attraction discount ticket. **Facilities:** P (charged) ⬛ ✕ licensed & (designated parking) toilets for disabled shop 🎴

ARRETON   Map 04 SZ58

ARRETON MANOR

Main Rd PO30 3AA

➲ (on main Sandown to Newport road)

☎ 01983 528134

e-mail: info@arretonmanor.co.uk

web: www.arretonmanor.co.uk

Set in five acres on the Arreton Downs, the manor was first mentioned in Alfred the Great's will in 885. Historical records in 1050 say it was owned by Edward the Confessor and the manor was mentioned thirty six years later in the Domesday Book. Although parts of the property are Jacobean, it still possesses many Tudor designs and features. Now a lived in family home.

Times: Open Etr hols & Jun-Sep, daily 10-5 (last tour 4.30pm). **Fee:** £4.50 (ch £2, pen £4) Garden only £3. **Facilities:** P ⬛ 🍴 & toilets for disabled shop 🎴

ROBIN HILL COUNTRY PARK

Downend PO30 2NU

➲ (0.5m from Arreton next to Hare & Hounds pub)

☎ 01983 527352

e-mail: dj@robin-hill.com

web: www.robin-hill.com

Set in 88 acres of woodland and countryside Robin Hill has a wide variety of activities and attractions including; Tree Top Trail, Mazes, Snake Slides, Troll Island, Squirrel Tower, Toboggan Run. A 5 year garden project is underway and the new Woodland Centre offers nature displays and wildlife cameras.

Times: Open 27 Mar-29 Oct, daily 10-5 (last admission 4). **Fee:** ✱ £7.50, pen £5.50, disabled £4. Saver ticket for 4 £27. **Facilities:** P ⬛ ✕ & (most areas are accessible, ramps access) toilets for disabled shop 🎴

BEMBRIDGE   Map 04 SZ68

BEMBRIDGE WINDMILL

PO35 5SQ

➲ (0.5m S of Bembridge on B3395)

☎ 01983 873945

e-mail: isleofwight@nationaltrust.org.uk

web: www.nationaltrust.org.uk

The only windmill on the island to survive, Bembridge mill was built about 1700 and was in use until 1913. The stone-built tower, with its wooden cap and machinery, has been restored for visitors to explore along with breathtaking views of glorious unspoilt countryside.

Times: Open 27 Mar-29 Oct, Sun-Fri, 10-4.30. Jul-Aug, daily. May be subject to change. **Fee:** £2.10 (ch £1.05) Family £6.30. Group £1.80 **Facilities:** P (200yds) in a lay-by ⬛ 🍴 hearing loop, pictorial guide, audio guide, Braille guide shop ✕ (ex guide dogs) 🐾 🎴

BLACKGANG — Map 04 SZ47

BLACKGANG CHINE FANTASY PARK
PO38 2HN
➲ (follow signs from Ventnor for Whitnell & Niton. From Niton follow signs for Blackgang)
☎ 01983 730330
e-mail: info@blackgangchine.com
web: www.blackgangchine.com

Opened as scenic gardens in 1843 covering some 40 acres, the park has imaginative play areas, water gardens, maze and coastal gardens. Set on the steep wooded slopes of the chine are the themed areas Smugglerland, Nurseryland, Dinosaurland, Fantasyland and Frontierland. St Catherine's Quay has a maritime exhibition showing the history of local and maritime affairs.
Times: Open mid Mar- end Oct daily, 10-5; late Jul-early Sep open until 10. **Fee:** ✱ Combined ticket (as from 15th May) to chine, sawmill & quay £8.50. Saver ticket (4 people) £31. **Facilities:** 🅿 (charged) ⬛ 🍴 ♿ toilets for disabled shop ▬

BRADING — Map 04 SZ68

BRADING THE EXPERIENCE
46 High St PO36 0DQ
➲ (on A3055, in Brading High St)
☎ 01983 407286
e-mail: info@bradingtheexperience.co.uk
web: www.bradingtheexperience.co.uk

Brading The Experience is more than just a waxworks! Comprising Great British Legends Gallery, 16th Century Rectory Mansion filled with famous and infamous characters from the past, Chamber of Horrors, award-winning Courtyards, Animal World and World of Wheels.
Times: Open all year, Summer 10-5.30, Winter 10.30-5 (last admission 1.5hrs before closing) **Fee:** £6.50 (ch 5-15, £4.50, under 5 free, pen £5.50). Family £20 (2ad+2ch), Family £23 (2ad+3ch). Party 20+.
Facilities: 🅿 ⬛ 🍴 ♿ (disabled route planner) toilets for disabled shop ▬

LILLIPUT ANTIQUE DOLL & TOY MUSEUM
High St PO36 0DJ
➲ (A3055 Ryde/Sandown road, in Brading High Street)
☎ 01983 407231
e-mail: lilliput.museum@btconnect.com
web: www.lilliputmuseum.com

This private museum contains one of the finest collections of antique dolls and toys in Britain. There are over 2000 exhibits, ranging in age from 2000BC to 1945 with examples of almost every seriously collectable doll, many with royal connections. Also dolls' houses, teddy bears and rare and unusual toys.
Times: Open all year, daily, 10-5. **Fee:** ✱ £1.95 (ch & pen £1.15, ch under 5 free). Party on request. **Facilities:** 🅿 (200 yds) 🍴 ♿ (ramps provided on request) shop collectables, wooden toys ▬

MORTON MANOR
PO36 0EP
➲ (off A3055 in Brading, well signed)
☎ 01983 406168

The manor dates back to 1249, but was rebuilt in 1680 with further changes during the Georgian period. The house contains furniture of both the 18th and 19th centuries, but its main attraction lies in the gardens and vineyard. The garden is landscaped into terraces, with ornamental ponds, a
continued

sunken garden and a traditional Elizabethan turf maze. There is also an established vineyard and winery.
Times: ✱ Open Apr-Oct, daily 10-5.30. Closed Sat. (Last admissions 4.30). **Facilities:** 🅿 ⬛ ✕ licensed 🍴 ♿ shop garden centre

NUNWELL HOUSE & GARDENS
Coach Ln PO36 0JQ
➲ (Off Ryde-Sandown Rd, A3055, follow brown tourist signs)
☎ 01983 407240   **2 for 1**

Set in beautiful gardens, Nunwell is an impressive, lived-in and much loved house where King Charles I spent his last night of freedom. It has fine furniture and interesting collections of family militaria. In summer, concerts are occasionally held in the music room.
Times: 28-29 May, early Jul-early Sep, Mon-Wed 1-5. Tours of House 1.30, 2.30 & 3.30 **Fee:** ✱ £4 inc guide book. (concessions £3.50, under 10's £1) **Facilities:** 🅿 shop 🐾 (ex guide dogs)

BRIGHSTONE — Map 04 SZ48

BRIGHSTONE SHOP AND MUSEUM
North St PO30 4AX
➲ (off B3399 in Brighstone onto North Street, next to Post Office)
☎ 01983 740689   **FREE**
e-mail: isleofwight@nationaltrust.org.uk
web: www.nationaltrust.org.uk/isleofwight

Within a row of pretty, thatched cottages you will find this museum which contains an evocative tableau and an interesting exhibition on village life in the 19th century.
Times: Open: 3 Jan-25 Mar, Mon-Sat 10-1; 27 Mar-27 May, Mon-Sat 10-4; 29 May-29 Oct, Mon-Sat 10-5, Sun 12-5; 30 Oct- 23 Dec, Mon-Sat 10-4. **Facilities:** 🅿 100m ♿ hearing loop shop 🐾 (ex guide dogs) 👜 ▬

CARISBROOKE — Map 04 SZ48

CARISBROOKE CASTLE
PO30 1XY
➲ (1.25m SW of Newport, off B3401)
☎ 01983 522107

A royal fortress and prison to King Charles I, Carisbrooke is set on a sweeping ridge at the heart of the Isle of Wight. Don't miss the donkeys that can be seen working a 16th-century wheel to draw water from the well.
Times: Open all year, Apr-Sep, daily 10-6; Oct-Mar, daily 10-4. Closed 24-26 Dec & 1 Jan. **Fee:** £5.30 (ch £2.70, concessions £4.00). Family £13.30. Opening times and prices are subject to change, for further details please phone 0870 333 1181 **Facilities:** 🅿 ⬛ ♿ shop 🎪

FRESHWATER — Map 04 SZ38

DIMBOLA LODGE
Terrace Ln, Freshwater Bay PO40 9QE
➲ (off A3054, visible from Freshwater Bay)
☎ 01983 756814   **2 for 1**
e-mail: administrator@dimbola.co.uk
web: www.dimbola.co.uk

Home of Julia Margaret Cameron, the pioneer Victorian portrait photographer. The house has the largest permanent collection of Cameron prints on display in the UK, as well as galleries exhibiting work by young, up and coming, and acclaimed modern photographers; and a large display of cameras and accessories.
Times: Open all year Tue-Sun. Closed 5 days at Xmas. **Fee:** £4 (ch 16 free) **Facilities:** 🅿 ✕ 🍴 ♿ (chairlifts) toilets for disabled shop 🐾 (ex guide dogs) ▬

MOTTISTONE Map 04 SZ48

Mottistone Manor Garden
PO30 4ED
➲ (2m W of Brighstone on B3399)
☎ 01983 741302
e-mail: isleofwight@nationaltrsut.org.uk
web: www.nationaltrust.org.uk/isleofwight
The garden of this 16th and 17th-century manor house, which is tenanted, is noted for its colourful herbaceous border, grassy terraces planted with fruit trees and lovely sea views. There are also some delightful walks between the Downs and the coast.

Mottistone Manor Garden

Times: Open 27 Mar-29 Oct, Sun-Thu 11-5.30 **Fee:** £3.10 (ch £1.55) Family £7.75. Group £2.65 each **Facilities:** 🅿 💻 🗊 🕹 (limited access, hearing loop, large print menu) toilets for disabled shop garden centre plant sales 🌿

NEWTOWN Map 04 SZ49

Old Town Hall
Town Ln PO30 4PA
➲ (1m N of A3054 between Yarmouth & Newport)
☎ 01983 531785
e-mail: isleofwight@nationaltrust.org.uk
web: www.nationaltrust.org.uk/isleofwight
The small, now tranquil, village of Newtown once sent two members to parliament and the Town Hall was the setting for, often, turbulent elections. Full of local history, mysterious benefactors and set in a wonderful nature reserve, the Town Hall is well worth a visit.

Times: Open 27 Apr-25 Oct, Mon, Wed & Sun, 2-5 (also open Good Fri & Etr Sat) **Fee:** £1.80 (ch 90p). Family £4.50. Group £1.50 each **Facilities:** 🅿 🗊 🕹 in car park toilets for disabled 🕷 (ex guide dogs) 🌿

OSBORNE HOUSE Map 04 SZ59

Osborne House
PO32 6JY
➲ (1m SE of East Cowes)
☎ 01983 200022
The beloved seaside retreat of Queen Victoria offers a glimpse into the private life of Britain's longest reigning monarch. The royal apartments are full of treasured mementos; and Queen Victoria's role as Empress of India is

continued

celebrated in the decoration of the Durbar Room. Visit the gardens and the charming Swiss Cottage.
Times: Open House: 24 Mar-Sep, 10-6, daily. Oct, 10-5, Sun-Thu. Nov-Mar, 10-4, Sun-Thu (guided tours only, pre-booking essential, last tour 2.30. Closed 24-26 Dec & 1 Jan **Fee:** House & Gardens: £8.95 (ch £4.50, concessions £6.70). Family £22.40. Garden only: £5.30 (ch £2.70, concessions £4.00). Family £13.30. Opening times and prices are subject to change, for further details please phone 0870 333 1181 **Facilities:** 🅿 💻 🕹 shop 🕷 🚼

PORCHFIELD Map 04 SZ49

Colemans Animal Farm
Colemans Ln PO30 4LX
➲ (A3054 Newport to Yarmouth road, follow brown tourist signs)
☎ 01983 522831
e-mail: info@colemansfarm.net
web: www.colemansfarm.com
Ideal for young children, this extensive petting farm has donkeys, goats, rabbits, guinea pigs, pigs, Highland cattle, Shetland ponies, chickens, ducks and geese. There is also a fun barn with slides and swings, an adventure playground, a Tractor Fun Park, and an Old Barn Café for adults who need to relax. Visitors can cuddle, stroke and feed the animals at special times throughout the day. Other special events run all day.
Times: Open mid Mar-end Oct, Tue-Sun. (Closed Mon, ex during school and BHs) **Fee:** ✱ £5.95 (ch £4.95), concessions £4.50, family ticket £18. **Facilities:** 🅿 💻 🕹 toilets for disabled shop 🛥

SANDOWN Map 04 SZ58

Dinosaur Isle
Culver Pde PO36 8QA
☎ 01983 404344
e-mail: dinosaur@iow.gov.uk
web: www.dinosaurisle.com

2 for 1

Britain's first purpose built dinosaur attraction where, in a building reminiscent of a Ptersaur flying across the Cretaceous skies, you can walk back through fossilised time. In recreated landscape meet life sized models of the island's famous five - Neovenator, Eotyrannus, Iguandon, Hypsilophodon and Polacanthus. Look out for the flying Pterodactyls and skeletons as they are found, watch volunteers preparing the latest finds or try the many hands-on activities.
Times: Open all year daily, Apr-Sep 10-6; Oct 10-5; Nov-Mar 10-4. Closed 24-26 Dec & 1 Jan, please phone to confirm opening Jan-10 Feb. Last admission 1hr before closing. **Fee:** £4.60 (ch 3-15 £2.60, concessions £3.50) Family £12.50 (2+2) **Facilities:** 🅿 🗊 🕹 (assist dogs) 🛥

SHANKLIN   Map 04 SZ58

SHANKLIN CHINE
12 Pomona Rd PO37 6PF
➲ (turn off A3055 at lights, left into Hope Rd &
continue onto Esplanade for entrance)
☎ 01983 866432
e-mail: jill@shanklinchine.co.uk
web: www.shanklinchine.co.uk

2 for 1

Part of Britain's national heritage, this scenic gorge at Shanklin
is a magical world of unique beauty and a haven for rare plants
and wildlife. A path winds through the ravine with overhanging
trees, ferns and other flora covering the steep sides. 'The
Island-Then and Now' is an exhibition detailing the history of
the Isle of Wight, including its military importance in WWII.
Times: Open daily, Apr-Oct (late May-late Sep illuminated after dusk)
Fee: ✱ £3.50 (ch under 16 £2, pen & students £2.50). Family ticket £9
(2ad+2ch), £11 (2ad +3ch). Group rates available.
Facilities: P (450yds) ♨ (access via lower entry only) shop on a lead

VENTNOR   Map 04 SZ57

VENTNOR BOTANIC GARDEN
Undercliff Dr PO38 1UL
➲ (on A3055 coastal road, 1.5m W of Ventnor)
☎ 01983 855397
e-mail: alison.ellsbury@iow.gov.uk
web: www.botanic.co.uk

Due to the unique microclimate of the 'Undercliff', plants
that can only survive in a Mediterranean climate thrive on
the Isle of Wight. Built on the site of a Victorian hospital for
TB sufferers, the garden was founded in 1970 by Sir Harold
Hillier, and opened in 1972 by Earl Mountbatten. The garden
has plants from Australasia, Africa, America, the
Mediterranean, and the Far East.
Times: Gardens: open all year; Visitor Centre & Green House: Mar-Oct,
daily 10-5 & Nov-Feb, wknds only 10-4 **Fee:** Free admission to Gardens
& Visitor Centre; Green House £1 **Facilities:** P (charged) ♨ ▦
♿ (lifts in garden, wheelchairs, 2 lifts) toilets for disabled shop garden
centre (guide dogs) ▰

WROXALL   Map 04 SZ57

APPULDURCOMBE HOUSE
PO38 3EW
➲ (off B3327, 0.5 miles W)
☎ 01983 852484

The shell of Appuldurcombe, once the grandest house on the
Isle of Wight, stands in its own grounds, designed by
'Capability' Brown. An exhibition of prints and photographs
depicts the house and its history.
Times: Open 19 Feb-Apr, daily 10-3; May-Sep, daily 10-5; 01-31 Oct,
daily 10-3 (last admission to property 1hr before closing). **Fee:** £2.50
(ch £1.50 & concessions £2.25). Family ticket £7. **Facilities:** P ♿ shop
✖ (ex dogs on leads) ▤

YARMOUTH   Map 04 SZ38

YARMOUTH CASTLE
Quay St PO4 1OP
➲ (adjacent to car ferry terminal)
☎ 01983 760678

The last addition to Henry VIII's coastal defences completed
in 1547, the Tudor castle is set in a beautiful old seaside
town. See the Isle of Wight paintings and memorable
photographs of Old Yarmouth.
Times: Open 24 Mar-Sep, Sun-Thu, 11-4. **Fee:** £2.60 (ch £1.30, concessions
£2.00). Opening times and prices are subject to change, for further details
please phone 0870 333 1181 **Facilities:** P (200yds) ♿ shop ▤

WILTSHIRE

EVENTS & FESTIVALS

April
29th Downton Cuckoo Fair, medieval fair in
    village centre

May
1st-3rd Swindon Festival of Literature, various
    venues
26th-11th Jun Salisbury Festival (various
    venues)
26th-29th Chippenham Folk Festival,
    Monkton Park

June
17th-24th Corsham Festival, various venues in
    and around Corsham

July
1st-2nd Calne Music & Arts Festival, various
    venues, Calne
7th-9th Marlborough International Jazz
    Festival, various venues
20th-23rd Southern Cathedrals Festival,
    Salisbury Cathedral
13th-16th Larmer Tree Festival of world
    music, Larmer Tree Victorian Pleasure
    Gardens, Cranbourne Chase

August
tbc Wiltshire Festival (music), Lydiard Park,
    Lydiard Tregoze, West Swindon

October
1st-9th Calne Music & Arts Festival
    (provisional)
tbc Cricklade Town Festival, arts events in
    various venues

Above: Stonehenge

AVEBURY   Map 04 SU06

ALEXANDER KEILLER MUSEUM
High St SN8 1RF
➲ (6m W of Marlborough. 1m N of Bath Rd (A4)
on A4361 and B4003)
☎ 01672 539250
e-mail: avebury@nationaltrust.org.uk
web: www.nationaltrust.org.uk
This is one of the most important megalithic monuments in
Europe, and was built before Stonehenge. The museum,
including an exhibition in the 17th-century threshing barn,
presents the full archaeological story of the stones using
finds from the site, along with inter-active and audio-visual
displays.
Times: Open Apr-Oct, daily 10-6; Nov-Mar 10-4 .Closed 24-26 Dec
Fee: £4.20 (ch £2.10) Family £10.50 (2ad+3ch) Family £7.50 (1ad+3ch).
Groups £3.60 (ch 1.80). **Facilities:** ▣ (charged) ▣ ✗ licensed ▯
& (Braille guide, large print guide, drop off point) toilets for disabled
shop ✗ (ex guide dogs) ✖ ▬

AVEBURY MANOR
SN8 1RF
➲ (from A4 take A4361/B4003)
☎ 01672 539250
e-mail: avebury@nationaltrust.org.uk
web: www.nationaltrust.org.uk
Avebury Manor has a monastic origin, and has been much
altered since then. The present buildings date from the early
16th century, with notable Queen Anne alterations and
Edwardian renovation. The flower gardens contain medieval
walls, and there are examples of topiary.
Times: Open: House end Mar-Oct, Sun-Tue, 2-4.40, BH Mon 2-5.30
(last admission 4.40). Garden end Mar-Oct daily (ex Wed & Thu)
11-5.30 (last admission 5 or dusk if earlier). Garden only open Good
Fri. **Fee:** ✱ Manor & Garden £3.90 (ch £2). Garden £3 (ch £1.50).
Facilities: ▣ (charged) ▣ ✗ & (audio visual, Braille/large print
guide, induction loop) toilets for disabled shop ✗ ✖ ▬

BRADFORD-ON-AVON   Map 03 ST86

BRADFORD-ON-AVON TITHE BARN   FREE
➲ (0.25m S of town centre, off B3109)
This impressive tithe barn, over 160ft long by 30ft wide, once
belonged to Shaftesbury Abbey. The roof is of stone slates,
supported outside by buttresses and inside by massive
beams and a network of rafters.
Times: Open all year, daily 10.30-4. Closed 25 Dec.
Facilities: ▣ (charged) & ✗ ▦

GREAT CHALFIELD MANOR
SN12 8NH
➲ (3m SW of Melksham off B3107 via Broughton
Gifford Common)
☎ 01225 782239
web: www.nationaltrust.org.uk
Built during the Wars of the Roses, the manor is a beautiful,
mellow, moated house restored in the 1920s. There is a
small 13th-century church next to the house.
Times: Open 22 Mar-30 Oct, Tue-Thu & Sun, guided tours only at
12.15, 2.15, 3, 3.45, 4.30. **Fee:** ✱ £4.60 (ch £2.30). Family ticket £11.80.
Groups £4.20 (ch £2.10) **Facilities:** ▣ ✗ ✖

THE PETO GARDEN AT IFORD MANOR
Iford Manor BA15 2BA
➲ (Brown tourist signs 0.5m S of Bradford-on-
Avon on B3109)
☎ 01225 863146
An award-winning garden in the romantic setting of the Frome
Valley. Designed by Harold Peto between 1899 and 1933, this
Italian style garden features terraces, statues and ponds.
Recitals and operas take place in the garden throughout the
summer season as part of the Iford Arts programme
Times: Open May-Sep. Apr & Oct open Sun only 2-5. Closed Mon &
Fri except BH Mons. **Fee:** £4.50 (concessions £4) **Facilities:** ▣ ▣
▯ & toilets for disabled ✗ (ex on leads)

CALNE   Map 03 ST97

BOWOOD HOUSE & GARDENS
SN11 0LZ
➲ (off A4 Chippenham to Calne road, in Derry Hill
village)
☎ 01249 812102   **2 for 1**
e-mail: houseandgardens@bowood.org
web: www.bowood.org
Built in 1624, the house was finished by the first Earl of
Shelburne, who employed celebrated architects, notably
Robert Adam, to complete the work. Adam's library is
particularly admired, and also in the house is the laboratory
where Dr Joseph Priestley discovered the existence of oxygen
in 1774. The house overlooks terraced gardens towards the
40-acre lake and some beautiful parkland. The gardens were
laid out by 'Capability' Brown in the 1760s, and are carpeted
with daffodils, narcissi and bluebells in spring. There is also
an adventure playground and new soft play area.
Times: Open mid Mar-Nov, daily 11-6, including BH. Rhododendron
Gardens (separate entrance off A342) open 6 weeks during mid
Apr-early Jun, 11-6. **Fee:** ✱ House & Gardens £6.60 (ch 2-4 £3.40; 5-15
£4.30; pen £5.50). Rhododendrons only £3.70 or £2.70 if combined
with a vist to Bowood House & Gardens on the same day. Children free.
Facilities: ▣ ▣ ✗ licensed & (parking by arrangement, DVD tour of
upstairs) toilets for disabled shop ✗ (assisstance dogs) ▬

CORSHAM   Map 03 ST87

CORSHAM COURT
SN13 0BZ
➲ (4m W of Chippenham off the A4)
☎ 01249 701610
web: www.corsham-court.co.uk

The Elizabethan manor was built in 1582, and then bought
by the Methuen family in the 18th century to house their
continued

collections of paintings and statues. 'Capability' Brown made additions to the house and laid out the park, and later John Nash made further changes. There is furniture by Chippendale, Adam, Cobb and Johnson inside, as well as the Methuen collection of Old Master paintings. The garden has flowering shrubs, herbaceous borders, a Georgian bath house and peacocks.

Times: ✱ Open Summer: 20 Mar-Sep daily (ex Mon & Fri), but incl BHs 2-5.30. Winter: Oct-19 Mar open wknds only 2-4.30. (Last admission 30 minutes before closing). Closed Dec. Open throughout year by appointment for groups 15+. **Facilities:** 🅿 💷 🔥 shop
See advertisement on opposite page

HOLT   Map 03 ST86

THE COURTS
BA14 6RR
➲ (3m SW of Melksham, 2.5m E of Bradford on Avon, on south side of B3107 follow signs to Holt)
☎ 01225 782875
e-mail: courtgarden@nationaltrust.org.uk
web: www.nationaltrust.org.uk

Weavers came to The Courts to have their disputes settled until the end of the 18th century. The house is not open, but it makes an attractive backdrop to the gardens - a network of stone paths, yew hedges, pools and borders with a strange, almost magical atmosphere.

Times: Open mid Mar-17 Oct, daily (ex Wed) 11-5.30; out of season by appointment only. **Fee:** ✱ £4.80 (ch £2.40).Family ticket £12.20. Groups £4.20 (ch £2.10) **Facilities:** 🅿 💷 📷 🔥 toilets for disabled shop ✹ (ex guide dogs) 🌿

LACOCK   Map 03 ST96

LACKHAM COUNTRY PARK
Wiltshire College, Lackham SN15 2NY
➲ (3m S of Chippenham, on A350. 6m S of M4 junct 17)
☎ 01249 466800   `2 for 1`
e-mail: daviaj@wiltscoll.ac.uk
web: www.lackhamcountrypark.co.uk

Various visitor attractions are situated within the 210-hectare estate of Wiltshire College - Lackham. Thatched and refurbished farm buildings accommodate the farm museum and the grounds feature a walled garden, glasshouses, and a farm park. Also grown in this garden was the largest citron (large lemon) which earned a place in the Guinness Book of Records. There is also a self-guided picturesque woodland walk available.

Times: Open Etr-Aug, Sun & BH Mon, Tue-Thu in Aug 10-5. (Last admission 4) **Fee:** £2 (concessions £1.50, up to 2 ch under 16 free). **Facilities:** 🅿 💷 📷 🔥 (wheelchair available, parking for disabled) toilets for disabled shop garden centre

LACOCK ABBEY, FOX TALBOT MUSEUM & VILLAGE
SN15 2LG
➲ (3m S of Chippenham, E of A350, car park signed)
☎ 01249 730227 (abbey) 01249 730459
web: www.nationaltrust.org.uk

Magnificent late Victorian country house with extensive servants quarters, gardens and wooded estate.

Times: Museum, Cloisters & Grounds, Mar-Oct, daily 11-5.30. Closed Good Fri. Abbey, 27 Mar- Oct daily, ex Tue, 1-5.30. Closed Good Fri. **Fee:** ✱ Museum, Abbey, Grounds & Cloisters £7.40 (ch £3.70) Family ticket £18.90 (2ad+2ch). Cloisters & Museum only £4.60 (ch £2.80) Family ticket £11.80. Abbey Cloisters & garden only £6 (ch £3) Family

ticket £15.30. Museum (Winter) £3.20 (ch £1.60). Family £8.70. **Facilities:** 🅿 🔥 (manual wheelchairs, Braille/large print & audio guides) toilets for disabled shop ✹ 🌿

LONGLEAT   Map 03 ST84

LONGLEAT
The Estate Office BA12 7NW
➲ (turn off A36 Bath-Salisbury road onto A362 Warminster-Frome road)
☎ 01985 844400
e-mail: enquiries@longleat.co.uk
web: www.longleat.co.uk

Nestling within magnificent 'Capability' Brown landscaped grounds in the heart of Wiltshire, Longleat House is widely regarded as one of the most beautiful stately homes open to the public. Longleat House was built by Sir John Thynne and completed in 1580. It has remained the home of the same family ever since. Many treasures are contained within the house: paintings by Tintoretto and Wooton, exquisite Flemish tapestries, fine French furniture and elaborate ceilings by John Dibblee Crace. The murals in the family apartments in the West Wing were painted by Alexander Thynne, the present Marquess, and are fascinating and remarkable additions to the collection. Apart from the ancestral home, Longleat is also renowned for its safari park, the first of its kind in the UK. Here, visitors have the rare opportunity to see hundreds of animals in natural woodland and parkland settings. Among the most magnificent sights are the famous pride of lions, wolves, rhesus monkeys and zebra. Other attractions which ensure a fun family day out include the 'Longleat Hedge Maze', the 'Adventure Castle', 'Longleat Railway', 'Pets' Corner' and the 'Safari Boats'.

Times: Open 11-19 Feb daily. 25 Feb-26 Mar wknds only. Daily 1 Apr-5 Nov. Telephone for opening times **Fee:** ✱ Longleat passport: £18 (ch 3-14 yrs & pen £14) **Facilities:** 🅿 💷 ✗ licensed 📷 🔥 (informative leaflet available or see website) toilets for disabled shop in grounds on leads 🔵

LUDGERSHALL   Map 04 SU25

LUDGERSHALL CASTLE AND CROSS
SP11 9QR
➲ (7m NW of Andover on A342)   `FREE`

Ruins of an early 12th-century royal hunting palace and medieval cross. The visitor can see large earthworks of the Norman motte-and-bailey castle and the flint walls of the later hunting palace. The stump of a medieval cross stands in the village street.

Times: Open at any reasonable time. **Facilities:** 🅿 🔥 🚻

LYDIARD PARK — Map 04 SU18

Lydiard Park

Lydiard Tregoze SN5 3PA
➲ (M4 junct 16, follow brown tourist signs to Lydiard Park)
☎ 01793 770401
e-mail: lydiardpark@swindon.gov.uk
web: www.swindon.gov.uk

Set in country parkland, Lydiard Park belonged to the St John family (the Bolingbrokes) for 500 years up until 1943 when the Swindon Corporation purchased it. Since then the house has been restored and many of the original furnishings returned, together with a family portrait collection dating from Elizabethan to Victorian times. Exceptional plasterwork, early wallpaper, a rare painted glass window, and a room devoted to the talented 18th-century amateur artist, Lady Diana Spencer (Beauclerk), can also be seen.

Times: Open all year, House: Mon-Sat 10-5, Sun 2-5. Winter closing 4 (Nov-Feb). Park: all year, daily closing at dusk each day. **Fee:** * £2.20 (ch £1) pen £2 **Facilities:** P ☕ ▤ ♿ (telephone 01793 770062 or see www.hts-centres.com) toilets for disabled shop ✈ (ex guide dogs in house)

MARLBOROUGH — Map 04 SU16

Crofton Beam Engines

Crofton Pumping Station, Crofton SN8 3DW
➲ (signed from A4/A338/A346 & B3087 at Burbage)
☎ 01672 870300
e-mail: enquiries@croftonbeamengines.org
web: www.croftonbeamengines.org

The oldest working beam engine in the world still in its original building and still doing its original job, the Boulton and Watt 1812, can be found in this rural spot. Its companion is a Harvey's of Hayle of 1845. Both are steam driven, from a hand-stoked, coal-fired boiler, and pump water into the summit level of the Kennet and Avon Canal with a lift of 40ft.

Times: * Open daily 9 Apr-26 Sep, 10.30-5 (last entry 4.30). 'In Steam' Etr, BH wknds & last wknd of Jun, Jul & Sep
Facilities: P (charged) ☕ ♿ (phone warden in advance, sighted guides provided) shop

MIDDLE WOODFORD — Map 04 SU13

Heale Gardens, Plant Centre & Shop

SP4 6NT
➲ (4m N of Salisbury, between A360 & A345)
☎ 01722 782504

Heale House and its eight acres of beautiful garden lie beside the River Avon at Middle Woodford. Much of the house is unchanged since King Charles II sheltered here after the Battle of Worcester in 1651. The garden provides a wonderfully varied collection of plants, shrubs, and musk and other roses, growing in the formal setting of clipped hedges and mellow stonework. Special Event: Snowdrop Sundays in Feb.

Times: Open: Plant centre daily, 10-5. Gardens daily (closed Mon ex BHs) **Fee:** £4 (ch 5-15 £1.50 under 5's free) **Facilities:** P ☕ ▤ ♿ (most parts accessible) shop garden centre good selection of plants, trees, shrubs ✈ (ex guide dogs) ▬

CORSHAM COURT

HOME OF THE METHUEN FAMILY

Corsham Court is one of England's finest Stately Homes. It was a Royal Manor in the days of the Saxon Kings, and the present building is based upon an Elizabethan Manor dating from 1582. Magnificent Georgian State Rooms were added in 1760. It houses one of the oldest and most distinguished collections of Old Masters and Furniture in the country, and with its 'Capability' Brown gardens and arboretum, and architecture by John Nash and Thomas Bellamy, Corsham Court provides the visitor with a wonderful opportunity to enjoy the many delights of the historic and beautiful Stately Home.

Tel/Fax: 01249 701610
www.corsham-court.co.uk
For opening times see gazetteer entry

SALISBURY — Map 04 SU12

The Medieval Hall (Secrets of Salisbury)

Cathedral Close SP1 2EY
➲ (look for signs within Salisbury Cathedral Close)
☎ 01722 412472 & 324731
e-mail: medieval.hall@ntworld.com
web: www.medieval-hall.co.uk

Visit the historic 13th-century Medieval Hall and watch the fascinating 40 minute sound and picture guide to the city and region. A witty and informative soundtrack, (sometimes available in other languages) specially composed music and some startling effects accompany hundreds of images to provide an insight into Salisbury's extraordinary past, the colourful city of today, and many of the attractions in the area. Enjoy refreshments 'while you watch'. Contact the Hall for full details of special events.

Times: * Open Apr-Sep, from 11-5. Also open throughout year for pre-booked groups. Occasionally closed for special events.
Facilities: P (charged) ☕ ♿ (ramp access) shop

Mompesson House

The Close SP1 2EL
➲ (on N side of Choristers Green in Cathedral Close, near High St Gate)
☎ 01722 335659
e-mail: mompessonhouse@nationaltrust.org.uk
web: www.nationaltrust.org.uk

With its high wrought-iron railings and perfect proportions, this Queen Anne house makes an impressive addition to the elegant Cathedral Close in Salisbury. Inside are stucco ceilings, a carved oak staircase and period furniture plus an

continued

important collection of 18th-century glasses, china and some outstanding paintings.
Times: Open 9 Apr-Oct, daily (ex Thu & Fri) 11-5. Open Good Friday. **Fee:** ✱ £4.20 (ch £2.10). Group rate £3.70. Garden only 90p. Family £10.40. **Facilities:** P (260 yds) (limited disabled parking available) ▆ ⅙ (ramps, Braille guide) toilets for disabled shop ✕ ⅍

OLD SARUM
Castle Rd SP1 3SD
➲ (2m N on A345)
☎ 01722 335398
The site of the original city of Salisbury. The 56-acre ruins of this once bustling town are rich in history and woodland. Founded in the Iron Age and occupied until the 16th-century. Romans, Saxons and Normans have all left their mark.
Times: Open 24-31 Mar, daily 10-5; Jul-Aug, daily 9-6. **Fee:** £2.90 (ch £1.50, concessions £2.20). Opening times and prices are subject to change, for further details please phone 0870 333 1181
Facilities: P ⅙ (assess to outer bailey and grounds only) shop ⌗

SALISBURY CATHEDRAL
33 The Close SP1 2EJ
➲ (S of city centre & Market Sq)
☎ 01722 555120
e-mail: visitors@salcath.co.uk
web: www.salisburycathedral.org.uk

Built in one phase between 1220 and 1258, the Cathedral is probably Britain's finest piece of medieval architecture. The spire is 123 metres tall, making it the tallest in England. The Chapter House displays a frieze depicting scenes from Genesis and Exodus, also the finest surviving Magna Carta. The Choir continues a tradition that began around 800 years ago, with performances at daily services. They are accompanied by Europe's finest romantic church organ. The surrounding Cathedral Close contains two museums, two small stately homes and acres of lawn.
Times: Open all year, daily 7.15am-6.15pm; Jun-Aug, Mon-Sat 7.15am-7.15pm. **Fee:** ✱ Suggested voluntary donations: £4 (ch 5-17 £2, pen & students £3.50). Family £8.50. **Facilities:** P (100yds) ▆ ✕ licensed ⌿ ⅙ (loop system, interpretative model for blind, wheelchairs) toilets for disabled shop (closed 25 Dec) ▆

SALISBURY & SOUTH WILTSHIRE MUSEUM
The King's House, 65 The Close SP1 2EN
➲ (in Cathedral Close)
☎ 01722 332151   **2 for 1**
e-mail: museum@salisburymuseum.org.uk
web: www.salisburymuseum.org.com
One of the most outstanding of the beautiful buildings in Cathedral Close houses this local museum. Galleries feature Stonehenge, History of Salisbury, the Pitt Rivers collection, ceramics and pictures and the Wedgwood room, a reconstruction of a pre-NHS surgery, and a costume, lace and embroidery gallery.
Times: Open all year Mon-Sat 10-5; also Suns Jul & Aug, 2-5. Closed Xmas. **Fee:** £4 (ch £1.50, concessions £3). Family ticket £9.50. Season saver tickets available. **Facilities:** P (100mtrs) (nearby parking charge) ✕ ▆ ⅙ (parking by prior arrangement, induction loop, wheelchair) toilets for disabled shop ✕ (ex guide dogs) ▆

STONEHENGE   Map 04 SU14
STONEHENGE
SP4 7DE
➲ (2m W of Amesbury on junct A303 and A344/A360)
☎ 01980 624715
Britain's greatest prehistoric monument and a World Heritage Site. What visitors see today are the substantial remains of the last in a series of monuments erected between c3000 and 1600BC.
Times: Open all year, 16 Mar-May, daily 9.30-6; Jun-Aug, daily 9-7; Sep-15 Oct, daily 9.30-6. 16 Oct-15 Mar, daily 9.30-4. Closed 24-26 Dec & 1 Jan. Note: Usual facilities may not apply around Summer Solstice 20-22 June, please check **Fee:** £5.50 (ch £2.80, concessions £4.10). Family ticket £13.80 **Facilities:** P ▆ ⅙ shop ✕ (ex guide & hearing dogs) ⌗

STOURHEAD   Map 03 ST73
STOURHEAD GARDEN & HOUSE
Stourhead Estate Office BA12 6QD
➲ (At Stourton off B3092, 3m NW Mere A303, follow brown tourist signs)
☎ 01747 841152
e-mail: stourhead@nationaltrust.org.uk
web: www.nationaltrust.org.uk
An outstanding example of the English landscape style, this splendid garden was designed by Henry Moore II and laid out between 1741 and 1780. Classical temples, including the Parthenon and Temple of Apollo, are set around the central lake at the end of a series of vistas, which change as the visitor moves around the paths and through the mature woodland with its extensive collection of exotic trees.
Times: ✱ Garden open all year 9-7 (or dusk if earlier). House open 19 Mar-Oct ,11-5 (closed Wed & Thu); King Alfred tower open 19 Mar-Oct, daily 12-5. **Fee:** Prices not confirmed for 2006 **Facilities:** P ▆ ✕ licensed ⅙ (wheelchairs, electric buggy, telephone in advance) toilets for disabled shop garden centre ✕ (ex in gardens Nov-Feb only) ⅍ ▆

STOURTON   Map 03 ST73
STOURTON HOUSE FLOWER GARDEN
Stourton House BA12 6QF
➲ (3m NW of Mere, on A303)
☎ 01747 840417
Set in the attractive village of Stourton, the house has more than four acres of beautifully maintained flower gardens.

continued

Many grass paths lead through varied and colourful shrubs and trees. Stourton House also specialises in unusual plants and dried flowers, many of which are for sale. It also has collections of daffodils, delphiniums and hydrangeas.

Stourton House Flower Garden

Times: Open last 2 Sun Feb & Apr-end Nov, Wed, Thu, Sun & BH Mon 11-6 (or dusk if earlier). Also open Dec-Mar, wkdays for plant/dried flower sales. **Fee:** ✱ £3.50 (ch 50p). **Facilities:** 🅿 💷 & (wheelchairs available) toilets for disabled shop garden centre ✖ (ex by arrangement)

SWINDON Map 04 SU18

STEAM - MUSEUM OF THE GREAT WESTERN RAILWAY

Kemble Dr SN2 2TA

➲ (from M4 junct 16 & A420 follow brown signs to 'Outlet Centre' & Museum)

☎ 01793 466646

e-mail: steampostbox@swindon.gov.uk

web: www.swindon.gov.uk/steam

This fascinating day out tells the story of the men and women who built, operated and travelled on the Great Western Railway. Hands-on displays, world-famous locomotives, archive film footage and the testimonies of ex-railway workers bring the story to life. A reconstructed station platform, posters and holiday memorabilia recreate the glamour and excitement of the golden age of steam. Located next door to the McArthurGlen Designer Outlet Great Western, STEAM offers a great day out for all. Good value group packages, special events and exhibitions and shop.

Times: Open daily 10-5. Closed 25-26 Dec & 1 Jan **Fee:** ✱ £5.95 (ch £3.80, pen £3.90) Family ticket £14.70 (2ad+2ch) **Facilities:** 🅿 (charged) 🍽 & (wheelchair or scooter can be pre-booked) toilets for disabled shop ✖ (ex guide dogs) 🎏

TEFFONT MAGNA Map 03 ST93

FARMER GILES FARMSTEAD

SP3 5QY

➲ (11m W of Stonehenge, off A303 to Teffont. Follow brown signs)

☎ 01722 716338

e-mail: tdeane6995@aol.com

web: www.farmergiles.co.uk

Forty acres of Wiltshire downland with farm animals to feed,

continued

ponds, inside and outside play areas, exhibitions, tractor rides, and giftshop.

Farmer Giles Farmstead

Times: ✱ Open 18 Mar-5 Nov, daily 10-6, wknds in winters, 10-dusk. Party bookings all year. **Facilities:** 🅿 ✖ licensed & (complete access for disabled/wheelchairs available for use) toilets for disabled shop 🎏

TISBURY Map 03 ST92

OLD WARDOUR CASTLE

SP3 6RR

➲ (2m SW)

☎ 01747 870487

This 14th-century castle stands in a romantic lakeside setting. Landscaped grounds and elaborate rockwork grotto surround the unusual hexagonal ruins. Scenes from *Robin Hood, Price of Thieves,* starring Kevin Costner were filmed here.

Times: Open all year, 24 Mar-Jun & Sep, daily 10-5; Jul-Aug, daily 10-6; Oct, daily 10-4; Nov-Mar, Sat-Sun 10-4. Closed 24-26 Dec & 1 Jan. **Fee:** £3.00 (ch £1.50, concessions £2.30). Opening times and prices are subject to change, for further details please phone 0870 333 1181 **Facilities:** 🅿 & ♯

TOLLARD ROYAL Map 03 ST91

LARMER TREE GARDENS

SP5 5PT

➲ (off A354 Blandford to Salisbury road, follow brown signs with flower) **2 for 1**

☎ 01725 516228

e-mail: events@larmertreegardens.co.uk

web: www.larmertreegardens.co.uk

Created by General Pitt Rivers in 1880 as a pleasure ground for 'public enlightenment and entertainment' the gardens are an extraordinary example of Victorian extravagance and vision. The garden contains a wonderful collection of ornate buildings, majestic trees and intimate arbours, retained in an enchanted and tranquil atmosphere.

Times: Garden open: Feb-Nov, Mon-Thu 11-5 (Sun from Etr-Oct). Tea Pavilion Sun & BHs Etr-Sep 11-5 **Fee:** ✱ £3.75 (ch over 5's £2.50, concessions/groups 15+ £3) Family £12.50 **Facilities:** 🅿 💷 ✖ licensed & toilets for disabled shop ✖ (ex guide dogs) 🎏

WESTBURY   Map 03 ST85

BROKERSWOOD COUNTRY PARK
Brokerswood BA13 4EH
➲ (off A36 at Bell Inn, Standerwick. Follow brown signs from A350)
☎ 01373 822238 & 823880
e-mail: woodland.park@virgin.net
web: www.brokerswood.co.uk

Brokerswood Country Park's nature walk leads through 80 acres of woodlands, with a lake and wildfowl. Facilities include a woodland visitor centre (covering wildlife and forestry), two children's adventure playgrounds (Etr-Oct school holidays & wknds only), guided walks and the woodland railway, over a third of a mile long.
Times: Open all year; Park open daily 10-5. Closed 24-26 Dec & 1 Jan. Ring for museum opening hours. **Fee:** £3.50 (ch 3-16yrs £2.50, pen £3) **Facilities:** 🅿 💷 ♿ (ramp access to cafe) toilets for disabled shop ➡

WESTWOOD   Map 03 ST85

WESTWOOD MANOR
BA15 2AF
➲ (1.5m SW of Bradford on Avon, off B3109)
☎ 01225 863374
web: www.nationaltrust.org.uk

This late 15th-century stone manor house was altered in the early 17th century and has late Gothic and Jacobean windows and fine plasterwork. There is a modern topiary garden.
Times: Open 3 Apr-28 Sep, Tue, Wed & Sun, 2-5. **Fee:** ✱ £4.60 (ch £2.30). Family ticket £11.80. **Facilities:** 🅿 ♿ ✈ 🚌 🐾

WILTON (NEAR SALISBURY) Map 04 SU03

WILTON HOUSE
SP2 0BJ
➲ (3m W of Salisbury, on A30, 10m from Stonehenge & A303)
☎ 01722 746720 & 746729(24 hr line) **2 for 1**
e-mail: tourism@wiltonhouse.com
web: www.wiltonhouse.com

This fabulous Palladian mansion amazes visitors with its treasures, including magnificent art, fine furniture and interiors by Inigo Jones. The traditional and modern gardens, some designed by the 17th Earl, are fabulous throughout the season and continue to delight visitors, whilst the adventure playground is a firm favourite with children.
Times: Open 2 Apr-Oct, daily, 10.30-5.30. (Last admission 4.30). House closed Mon, ex BHs. **Fee:** ✱ £9.75 (ch 5-15 £5.50, students & pen £8). Family ticket £24. **Facilities:** 🅿 💷 📷 ♿ (induction loop) toilets for disabled shop garden centre ✈ (ex service dogs) ➡

WOODHENGE   Map 04 SU14

WOODHENGE
➲ (1.5m N of Amesbury, off A345 just S of Durrington) **FREE**

A Neolithic ceremonial monument dating from about 2300 BC, consisting of six concentric rings of timber posts, now marked by concrete piles. The long axis of the rings, which are oval, points to the rising sun on Midsummer Day.
Times: ✱ Open all reasonable times. **Facilities:** 🅿 ♿ ♿

WORCESTERSHIRE

EVENTS & FESTIVALS

May
   11th-14th Spring Show, Three Counties Showground, Malvern
      Counties Show & the Autumn Show)
   30th-3rd Jun Elgar Festival, Malvern
   tbc Upton Folk Festival, various venues, Upton-upon-Severn

June
   12-15th Championship Dog Show, Three Counties Showground, Malvern
   16th-18th Three Counties Show, Three Counties Showground, Malvern
   23rd-25th Upton Jazz Festival (various venues), Upton-upon-Severn

July
   14th-16th Upton Blues Festival, Upton-upon-Severn (provisional)

September
   23rd-24th The Malvern Autumn Show, Three Counties Showground, Malvern

December
   tbc Victorian Christmas Fayre, Worcester

Above: All Saints Church in Evesham

BEWDLEY   Map 07 SO77

SEVERN VALLEY RAILWAY
Comberton Hill DY10 1QN
☎ 01299 403816
web: www.svr.co.uk
(For full entry see Kidderminster)

WEST MIDLAND SAFARI & LEISURE PARK
Spring Grove DY12 1LF
➲ (on A456 between Kidderminster & Bewdley)
☎ 01299 402114
e-mail: info@wmsp.co.uk
web: www.wmsp.co.uk
Located in the heart of rural Worcestershire, this 200-acre site is the home to a drive-through safari and White Tiger Ridge. There are a variety of rides, amusements and live shows suitable for all members of the family. Other features include Discovery Trail, Hippo Lakes, Twilight Cave Seaquarium, Creepy Crawlies exhibit, animal and reptile encounters and Sealion Theatre.
Times: Mid Feb-early Nov **Fee: ✱** £7.99 (ch 4 free). Multi ride wristband £8.75. Junior restricted £7 (restricted rides only). Ride tickets £3 for two tickets from machines (various no of tickets per ride).
Facilities: 🅿 💻 ✗ licensed 🛍 ♿ (most area accessible slopes/tarmac paths) shop ✖ (ex guide dogs) 🍴

BROADWAY   Map 04 SP03

BROADWAY TOWER & ANIMAL PARK
WR12 7LB
➲ (off A44, 1m SE of village)
☎ 01386 852390
e-mail: info@broadwaytower.co.uk
web: www.broadwaytower.co.uk
The 65ft tower was designed by James Wyatt for the 6th Earl of Coventry, and built in 1799. The unique building now houses exhibitions depicting its colourful past and various uses such as holiday retreat to artist and designer William Morris. The viewing platform is equipped with a telescope, giving wonderful views over 13 counties.
Times: Open Apr-Oct, daily 10.30-5. Nov-Mar (tower only) wknds weather permitting 11-3 or by prior booking. **Fee: ✱** Tower, £3.50 (ch 4-4 £2, concessions £3) Family £10 (2ad+3ch) **Facilities:** 🅿 💻 ✗ licensed shop 🍴

BROMSGROVE   Map 07 SO97

AVONCROFT MUSEUM OF HISTORIC BUILDINGS
Stoke Heath B60 4JR
➲ (2m S, off A38)
☎ 01527 831886   2 for 1
e-mail: avoncroft1@compuserve.com
web: www.avoncroft.org.uk
A visit to Avoncroft takes you through nearly 700 years of history. Here you can see 25 buildings rescued from destruction and authentically restored on a 15 acre rural site. There are 15th and 16th-century timber framed buildings, 18th-century agricultural buildings and a cockpit. There are industrial buildings and a working windmill from the 19th century, and from the 20th a fully furnished pre-fab.
Times: ✱ Open Jul-Aug, daily 10.30-5; Apr-Jun, Tue-Fri 10.30-4.30, Sat-Sun 10.30-5; Sep-Oct, Tue-Fri 10.30-4.30, Sat-Sun 10.30-5; Nov, wknds only; Mar, Tue-Thu, Sat & Sun, 10.30-4.**Fee:** £6 (ch £3, pen £5) Family £15. **Facilities:** 🅿 💻 🛍 ♿ (ramps, wheelchair available) toilets for disabled shop 🍴

EVESHAM   Map 04 SP04

THE ALMONRY HERITAGE CENTRE
Abbey Gate WR11 4BG
➲ (on A4184, opposite Merstow Green, main N/S route through Evesham)
☎ 01386 446944   2 for 1
e-mail: tic@almonry.ndo.co.uk
The 14th-century stone and timber building was the home of the Almoner of the Benedictine Abbey in Evesham. It now houses exhibitions relating to the history of Evesham Abbey, the Battle of Evesham, and the culture and trade of Evesham. Evesham Tourist Information Centre is also located here.
Times: Open all year, Mon-Sat & BHs, 10-5, Sun 2-5. Closed Xmas & Sun in Nov-Feb. **Fee: ✱** £2.50 (ch 16 free, pen & students £1.50)
Facilities: 🅿 (110yds) shop ✖

GREAT WITLEY   Map 03 SO76

WITLEY COURT
WR6 6JT
➲ (on A433)
☎ 01299 896636
Discover the spectacular ruins of this once-great house destroyed by fire in 1937. Explore the magnificent landscaped gardens which feature the stunning Perseus and Andromeda fountains and contemporary sculpture. Step back in time with the audio tour.
Times: Open all year, Mar-May, daily, 10-5; Jun-Aug, daily, 10-6; Sep-Oct, daily, 10-5; Nov-Feb, Thu-Mon, 10-4. Closed 24-26 Dec & 1 Jan. **Fee:** £4.95 (ch £2.50, concessions £3.70, family £12.40). Opening times and prices are subject to change, for further details please phone 0870 333 1181 **Facilities:** 🅿 💻 ♿ shop ✖ 🚻

HANBURY   Map 03 SO96

HANBURY HALL
School Rd WR9 7EA
➲ (4.5m E of Droitwich, 1m N of B4090 and 1.5m W of B4091)
☎ 01527 821214   2 for 1
e-mail: hanburyhall@nationaltrust.org.uk
web: www.nationaltrust.org.uk
This William and Mary style red-brick house, completed in 1701, was built by a prosperous local family. The house contains outstanding painted ceilings and staircase by Thornhill, and the Watney collection of porcelain. The 18th-century garden has recently been restored with many features including parterre, bowling green and working orangery.
Times: Open Mar-Oct, Sat-Wed 11-5.30. (Last entry 4.30)
Fee: ✱ House & Garden £5.70. Family ticket £13.50. Garden only £3.70. **Facilities:** 🅿 💻 ♿ (Braille guide, 2 wheelchairs) toilets for disabled shop ♻ 🍴

KIDDERMINSTER   Map 07 SO87

SEVERN VALLEY RAILWAY
Comberton Hill DY10 1QN
➲ (on A448, clearly signed)
☎ 01299 403816
web: www.svr.co.uk
The leading standard gauge steam railway, with one of the largest collections of locomotives and rolling stock in the country. Services operate from Kidderminster and Bewdley to Bridgnorth through 16 miles of picturesque scenery along the River Severn. Special steam galas and "Day out with

continued

Thomas" Weekends take place during the year along with Santa Specials.

Severn Valley Railway

Times: Trains operate wknds throughout year, daily, early May end of Sep, school hols & half terms, Santa Specials, phone for details. **Fee:** ✱ Subject to Review. (Train fares vary according to journey. Main through ticket £11.50 return, Family ticket £31) **Facilities:** 🅿 (charged) 🖴 📱 ☕ (some specially adapted trains, call for details) toilets for disabled shop (at Kidderminster/Bridgnorth) 🚩

See advertisement on opposite page

WORCESTERSHIRE COUNTY MUSEUM
Hartlebury Castle, Hartlebury DY11 7XZ
➲ (4m S of Kidderminster clearly signed from A449)
☎ 01299 250416   `2 for 1`
e-mail: museum@worcestershire.gov.uk
web: www.worcestershire.gov.uk/museum

Housed in the north wing of Hartlebury Castle, the County Museum contains a delightful display of crafts and industries. There are unique collections of toys and costume, displays on domestic life, period room settings and horse-drawn vehicles. Visitors can also see a reconstructed forge, a schoolroom, a wheelwright's and tailor's shop. 2006 sees the 40th anniversary of the museum's opening.

Times: Open Feb-Dec, Tue-Fri 10-5; Sat, Sun & BHs 11-5. Closed Good Fri. **Fee:** £3 (ch & pen £1.50). Family ticket £8. **Facilities:** 🅿 🖴 📱 ☕ (car parking spaces, close to main building) toilets for disabled shop ✱ (ex guide dogs & in grounds) 🚩

REDDITCH   Map 04 SP06

FORGE MILL NEEDLE MUSEUM & BORDESLEY ABBEY VISITOR CENTRE
Forge Mill, Needle Mill Ln, Riverside B98 8HY
➲ (N side of Redditch, off A441. M42 junct 2)
☎ 01527 62509
e-mail: museum@redditchbc.gov.uk
web: www.redditchbc.gov.uk

The Needle Museum tells the fascinating and sometimes gruesome story of how needles are made. Working, water-powered machinery can be seen in an original needle-scouring mill. The Visitor Centre is an archaeological museum showing finds from excavations at the nearby Bordesley

continued

Abbey. Children can become an archaeologist for the day and explore the ruins of this fascinating ancient monument.

Times: Open Etr-Sep, Mon-Fri 11-4.30, Sat-Sun 2-5; Feb-Etr & Oct-Nov, Mon-Thu 11-4 & Sun 2-5. Parties by arrangement. **Fee:** ✱ £3.70 (ch 60p, pen £2.70). Family ticket £8. Reduced admission charge for holders of a Reddicard. **Facilities:** 🅿 📱 ☕ (wheelchair, museum audio tour, Braille guide, hearing loop) toilets for disabled shop ✱ (ex guide dogs) 🚩

SEVERN STOKE   Map 03 SO84

CROOME PARK NEW
Builders Yard, High Green WR8 9JS   `2 for 1`
➲ (A38 signed from B4084 leaving Pershore)
☎ 01905 371006
e-mail: croomepark@nationaltrust.org.uk
web: www.nationaltrust.org.uk

'Capability' Brown's first complete landscape design. A decade restoration transforms the park to its 18th-century splendour.

Times: Open daily, 10-5.30, 29 May-3 Sep; Wed-Sun, 10-5.30, 3 Mar-28 May & 6 Sep-29 Oct; 10-4, Nov-17 Dec **Fee:** £3.70 (ch£1.80) Family £9 **Facilities:** 🅿 📱 ☕ (w/chair, Braille & large print guides, induction loop 🐾

SPETCHLEY   Map 03 SO85

SPETCHLEY PARK GARDENS
Spetchley Park WR5 1RS
➲ (2m E of Worcester on A44)
☎ 01905 345213 or 345224
e-mail: hb@spetchleygardens.co.uk
web: www.spetchleygardens.co.uk

The 110-acre deer park and the 30-acre gardens surround an early 19th-century mansion (not open), with sweeping lawns and herbaceous borders, a rose lawn and enclosed gardens with low box and yew hedges. There is a large collection of trees (including 17th-century Cedars of Lebanon), shrubs and plants, many of which are rare or unusual.

Times: Open Apr-Sep, Tue-Fri 11-6, Sun 2-6; BH Mons 11-6, (last admission 4). Other days by appointment. **Fee:** ✱ £5 (ch £2). Party 25+ £4.50. **Facilities:** 🅿 🖴 📱 ☕ (most of garden accessible) ✱ (ex guide dogs)

STONE — Map 07 SO87

Stone House Cottage Gardens

DY10 4BG
(2m SE of Kidderminster, on A448)
01562 69902
e-mail: louisa@shcn.co.uk
web: www.shcn.co.uk

A beautiful walled garden with towers provides a sheltered area of about one acre for rare shrubs, climbers and interesting herbaceous plants. Adjacent to the garden is a nursery with a large selection of unusual plants.

Times: Open Mar-mid Sept, Wed-Sat, 10-5. **Fee:** £3 (ch free).
Facilities: garden centre

WORCESTER — Map 03 SO85

City Museum & Art Gallery

Foregate St WR1 1DT
(in city centre, 150m from Foregate St Train Station)
01905 25371 FREE
e-mail: artgalleryandmuseum@cityofworcester.gov.uk
web: www.worcestercitymuseums.org.uk

The gallery has temporary art exhibitions from both local and national sources. Museum exhibits cover geology, local and natural history. Of particular interest is a complete 19th-century chemist's shop. There are collections relating to the Worcestershire Regiment and the Worcestershire Yeomanry Cavalry.

Times: Open all year, Mon-Fri 9.30-5.30, Sat 9.30-5. Closed Sun, 25-26 Dec, 1 Jan & Good Fri, Easter Mon and Whitsun BH Mon.
Facilities: (city centre) (lift, induction loop) toilets for disabled shop

Elgar's Birthplace Museum

Crown East Ln, Lower Broadheath WR2 6RH
(3m W of Worcester, signed off A44 to Leominster)
01905 333224 2 for 1
e-mail: birthplace@elgarmuseum.org
web: www.elgarmuseum.org

In 2000, the Elgar Centre was opened, to complement the historic Birthplace Cottage and to provide additional exhibition space for more treasures from this unique collection, telling the story of Elgar's musical development and inspirations. Listen to his music as the audio tour guides you round the easily accessible displays. Please telephone or visit website for details of events running throughout the year.

Times: Open daily, last admission 4.15. Closed 23 Dec-end Jan.
Fee: £5 (ch £2 & pen £4.50) concessions £3. **Facilities:** (large print guides, audio facilities, wheelchair) toilets for disabled shop (ex guide dogs)

Hawford Dovecote

(3 miles N of Worcester, half mile E of A449).
01527 821214
e-mail: hanburyhall@nationaltrust.org
web: www.nationaltrust.org.uk

An unusual square, half-timbered 16th-century dovecote. Access on foot only via the entrance drive to the adjoining house.

Times: Open Apr-Oct, daily 9-6 or sunset. (Closed Good Fri). Other times by prior appointment only. **Fee:** * £1 **Facilities:** 50yds (on street parking)

SEVERN VALLEY RAILWAY
the line for all seasons

The best way to see the beauty of the River Severn is from a steam-hauled train on the Severn Valley Railway.

Kidderminster-Bewdley-Bridgnorth

Open every weekend throughout the year, DAILY from early May to late September, plus local school holidays and half-terms.

THE RAILWAY STATION, BEWDLEY, WORCESTERSHIRE, DY12 1BG
Tel: 01299 403816
www.svr.co.uk

Museum of Worcester Porcelain

Severn St WR1 2NE
(M5 junct 7, follow signs to city centre, at 7th set of lights take 1st left into Edger St & bear left with road into Severn St. At T Junct bear right & after 700yds take 1st left. Museum on left)
01905 746000
e-mail: museum@royal-worcester.co.uk
web: www.worcesterporcelainmuseum.org

The Victorian buildings lead into the heart of a world famous porcelain industry and was founded in 1751. The guided tours and the Museum of Worcester Porcelain take visitors on a design journey through time. Exhibits include room settings, dining scenes and shop fronts in the Georgian, Victorian and 20th century galleries.

Times: * Open all year, Mon-Sat 9-5.30, Sun 11-5. Closed 25 Dec & Etr Sun. **Facilities:** (charged) (ex factory) toilets for disabled shop

Worcester Cathedral

WR1 2LH
(city centre, signed from M5 junct 7)
01905 28854 & 21004
e-mail: info@worcestercathedral.org.uk
web: www.cofe-worcester.org.uk

Worcester Cathedral is one of England's loveliest cathedrals, with Royal Tombs, medieval cloisters, an ancient crypt and Chapter House and magnificent Victorian stained glass. The tower is open in the summer. There are a number of different celebrations each year, including the Heart of England Food Fair and many concerts.

Times: Open all year, daily 7.30-6. **Facilities:** (500yds) (access from College Green) toilets for disabled shop (ex guide dogs)

EAST RIDING OF YORKSHIRE

EVENTS & FESTIVALS

May
18th-22nd Beverley & East Riding Early Music
Festival, Beverley Minster and various East
Riding churches (provisional)
tbc Bridlington Arts Festival, various venues
(provisional)

June
10th Lord Mayor's Gala, Hull
16th-18th Beverley Folk Festival, various
venues in Beverley
29th-1st Jul Hornsea Music Festival, various
venues
tbc Humber Mouth, Hull Literature Festival

July
19th Driffield Agricultural Show, Driffield
Showground
29th-6th Aug Hull Jazz Festival, various
venues

September
2nd-3rd Sea Fever Festival, international sea
shanty festival, Hull Marina, Hull
20th-23rd Beverley & East Riding Chamber
Music Festival (provisional)
tbc Hull Show, East Park, Hull

October
6th-14th Hull Fair, Walton Street Fairground,
Hull

Above: Skipsea Castle

BEMPTON   Map 08 TA17

RSPB NATURE RESERVE
YO15 1JD
➲ (take cliff road from B1229, Bempton Village
and follow brown tourist signs)
☎ 01262 851179

Part of the spectacular chalk cliffs that stretch from
Flamborough Head to Speeton. This is one of the best sites
in England to see thousands of nesting seabirds including
gannets and puffins at close quarters. Viewpoints overlook
the cliffs, which are best visited from April to July. Over 2
miles of chalk cliffs rising to 400ft with numerous cracks and
ledges. Enormous numbers of seabirds nest on these cliffs
including guillemots, razorbills, kittiwakes, fulmars, herring
gulls and several pairs of shag. This is the only gannetry in
England and is growing annually. Many migrants pass offshore including terns, skuas and shearwaters. Wheatears,
ring ouzels and merlins frequent the clifftop on migration.
Grey seal and porpoise are sometimes seen offshore.
Times: Visitor centre open daily, Mar-Nov 10-5. Dec-Feb 9.30-4.
Fee: ✱ £3.50 per car, £6 per minibus, £10 per coach.
Facilities: 🅿 (charged) 💻 ♿ large print guide toilets for disabled
shop on lead 🐾

BEVERLEY   Map 08 TA03

THE GUILDHALL
Register Sq HU17 9AU
➲ (in Register Sq, next to post office)
☎ 01482 392776
e-mail: stefan.ramsden@eastriding.gov.uk

A Guildhall has been on this site since 1500, although parts of
the building date back to a private dwelling of 1320. Largely
remodelled in the Palladian style in the 1760s, the Courtroom
features a magnificent stucco work ceiling, and the
Magistrate's Room houses rare 17th-century Civic furniture.
Times: Open every Fri, 10-4. Please phone for guide tours at other
times. **Fee:** ✱ Free on Fri. Charge for guided tours at other times.
Facilities: ♿ (disabled parking 100yds) 🐾 (ex guide dogs)

BURTON AGNES   Map 08 TA16

BURTON AGNES HALL
Estate Office YO25 0ND
➲ (on A614)
☎ 01262 490324
e-mail: burton.agnes@farmline.com
web: www.burton-agnes.com

Built in 1598, this is a magnificent Elizabethan house, with
continued

furniture, pictures and china amassed by the family owners over four centuries. There is a walled garden with maze, potager, herbaceous borders, clematis, campanula and geranium collections, and jungle garden, as well as woodland walks.

Times: Open Apr-Oct, daily 11-5. **Fee:** * Hall & grounds £5.20 (ch £2.60, pen £4.70). Grounds only £2.60 (ch £1.15, pen £2.35). Party 30+. **Facilities:** P (scented garden for the blind) toilets for disabled shop garden centre

Burton Agnes Manor House

(in Burton Agnes, 5m SW of Bridlington on A166) FREE

A rare and well-preserved example of a Norman house. Some interesting Norman architectural features can still be seen, but the building was encased in brick during the 17th and 18th centuries. The house is near Burton Agnes Hall and the gardens are privately owned and not managed by English Heritage.

Times: Open Apr-Oct, daily 11-5.

GOOLE Map 08 SE72

The Waterways Museum

Dutch River Side DN14 5TB

(M62 junct 36, enter Goole, turn right at next 3 sets of lights onto Dutch River Side. 0.75m and follow brown signs)

01405 768730

e-mail: waterwaysmuseum@btinternet.com

web: www.waterwaysmuseumandadventure centre.co.uk

Discover the story of the Aire & Calder Navigation and the growth of the 'company town' of Goole and its busy port. Find out how to sail and, in the interactive gallery, see how wooden boats were built. Enjoy the unique 'Tom Pudding' story, brought to life through the vessels on the canal and the boat hoist in South Dock. Rediscover the Humber keels and sloops, and Goole's shipbuilding history through the objects, photos and memories of Goole people.

Times: Open Mon-Fri 9-4.30 (Apr-Sep, Sun 12-5) **Fee:** £2.50 (concessions £1.50) Boat Trip £3. **Facilities:** P (disabled access on boats, nature trail, wheelchair) toilets for disabled shop (ex guide dogs)

HORNSEA Map 08 TA14

Hornsea Museum

11 Newbegin HU18 1AB

(turn off A165 onto B1244)

01964 533443 2 for 1

web: www.hornseamuseum.com

A former farmhouse whose outbuildings now illustrate local life and history. There are 19th-century period rooms and a dairy, plus craft tools and farming implements. Photographs, local personalities and industries are also featured along with a large display of Hornsea pottery.

Times: Open Etr-Sep & Oct half-term hols, Tue-Sat 11-5, Sun 2-5 (last admission 4). **Fee:** * £2.50 (concessions £2). Family ticket £7.50 **Facilities:** P (50yds) (audio interpretation for blind/partially sighted) toilets for disabled shop (ex guide dogs)

The Deep, Hull

The World's only Submarium telling the story of the oceans from the beginning of time and into the future.

Featuring 40 sharks and over 3000 fish. Voted Yorkshire's favourite family day out and the UK's Best Aquarium.

New! The Twilight Zone – the world's largest display of creatures from the deep sea including giant Japanese spider crabs, wolf eels and nautilus. Enjoy a hot meal or sandwich in one of our two cafes. On site parking.

Adults £7.50. Children £5.50. Seniors £6.00. Open daily from 10am.

Tel: 01482 381000 www.thedeep.co.uk

KINGSTON UPON HULL Map 08 TA02

Maister House

160 High St HU1 1NL

(Hull city centre)

01482 324114 FREE

web: www.nationaltrust.org.uk

The house is a mid-18th-century rebuilding, notable for its splendid stone and wrought-iron staircase, ornate stucco work and finely carved doors. Only the staircase and entrance hall are open as the house is now let as offices.

Times: Open all year, Mon-Fri 10-4 (Closed BH).
Facilities: P

Maritime Museum

Queen Victoria Square HU1 3DX

(from M62 follow A63 to town centre, museum is within pedestrian area of town centre)

01482 613902 FREE

e-mail: museums@hullcc.gov.uk

web: www.hullcc.gov.uk/museums

Hull's maritime history is illustrated here, with displays on whales and whaling, ships and shipping, and other aspects of this Humber port. There is also a Victorian court room which is used for temporary exhibitions. The restored dock area, with its fine Victorian and Georgian buildings, is well worth exploring too.

Times: * Open all year, Mon-Sat 10-5 & Sun 1.30-4.30. Closed 25 Dec-2 Jan & Good Fri) **Facilities:** P (100yds) shop (ex guide dogs)

'STREETLIFE' - HULL MUSEUM OF TRANSPORT

High St HU1 1PS

➲ (A63 from M62, follow signs for Old Town)

☎ 01482 613902   **FREE**

e-mail: museums@hullcc.gov.uk

web: www.hullcc.gov.uk/museums

This purpose built museum uses a 'hands-on' approach to trace 200 years of transport history. With a vehicle collection of national importance, state-of-the-art animatronic displays and authentic scenarios, you can see Hull's Old Town brought vividly to life.

Times: ✱ Open all year, Mon-Sat 10-5, Sun 1.30-4.30. Closed 24-25 Dec & Good Fri **Facilities:** P (500mtrs) 🍴 & toilets for disabled shop ✖ (ex guide dogs)

THE DEEP

HU1 4DP

➲ (follow signs from city centre)

☎ 01482 381000

e-mail: info@thedeep.co.uk

web: www.thedeep.co.uk

The Deep tells the story of the world's oceans using live animals and hands-on activities, with over 3000 fish and more than 40 sharks. New for 2005 is The Twilight Zone, an exhibition all about the weird and alien creatures from the deep sea like giant Pacific octopus, wolf eels and giant Japanese spider crabs.

Times: Open all year, daily 10-6. Closed 24-25 Dec **Fee:** ✱ £7.50 (ch under 16 £5.50, pen £6). Family ticket (2ad+2ch) £23, (2ad+3ch) £26 **Facilities:** P (charged) 💻 ✖ licensed 🍴 & (signing for the deaf if booked in advance, tactile guides) toilets for disabled shop ✖ (ex guide dogs) 🍴

See advertisement on page 263

WILBERFORCE HOUSE

23-25 High St HU1 1NE

➲ (A63 from M62 or A1079 from York, follow signs for Old Town)

☎ 01482 613902   **FREE**

e-mail: museums@hullcc.gov.uk

web: www.hullcc.gov.uk/museums

The early 17th-century Merchant's house was the birthplace of William Wilberforce, who became a leading campaigner against slavery. There are Jacobean and Georgian rooms and displays on Wilberforce and the anti-slavery campaign. The house also has secluded gardens. There are special exhibitions throughout the year.

Times: ✱ Open all year, Mon-Sat 10-5 & Sun 1.30-4.30. Closed 25-26 Dec, 1 Jan & Good Fri. **Facilities:** P (500mtrs) (meters on street) & (large print, video area & audio guides) shop ✖ (ex guide dogs)

POCKLINGTON   Map 08 SE84

BURNBY HALL GARDEN & STEWART COLLECTION

The Balk YO42 2QF

➲ (off A1079 at turning for Pocklington off B1247, follow brown signs)

☎ 01759 307125

e-mail: briah@briahprtrie.plus.com

web: www.burnbyhallgardens.com

The two lakes in this garden have an outstanding collection of 80 varieties of hardy water lilies, designated a National Collection. The lakes stand within nine acres of beautiful gardens including heather beds, a rock garden, a spring and summer bedding area, woodland walk and Victorian garden. The museum contains sporting trophies and ethnic material gathered on world-wide travels. There are band concerts every Sunday.

Times: Open 26 Mar-2 Oct, daily 10-6 (last admission 5pm).
Fee: ✱ £3.25 (ch 5-15 £1.50, pen £2.60). Party 20+.£2.25 each
Facilities: P 💻 & (free wheelchair hire, viewing platform for wheelchairs) toilets for disabled shop ✖ (ex guide dogs) 🍴

SEWERBY   Map 08 TA16

SEWERBY HALL & GARDENS

YO15 1EA

➲ (2m NE of Bridlington on B1255 towards Flamborough)

☎ 01262 673769

e-mail: sewerby.hall@eastring.gov.uk

web: www.eastriding.gov.uk/sewerby

Sewerby Hall and Gardens, set in 50 acres of parkland overlooking Bridlington Bay, dates back to 1715. The Georgian House, with its 19th-century Orangery, contains art galleries, archaeological displays and an Amy Johnson Room with a collection of her trophies and mementoes. The grounds include magnificent walled Old English and Rose gardens and host many events throughout the year. Activities for all the family include a Children's Zoo and play areas, golf, putting, bowls, plus woodland and clifftop walks. Phone for details of special events.

Times: Estate open all year, dawn-dusk. Hall open Etr-end Oct. Please contact for further details. **Facilities:** P 💻 🍴 & toilets for disabled shop 🍴

SPROATLEY   Map 08 TA13

BURTON CONSTABLE HALL

HU11 4LN

➲ (Follow signs for A165 Bridlington Road towards Sirlaugh, then right towards Hornsea and follow brown historic house signs to Buton Constable)

☎ 01964 562400   **2 for 1**

web: www.burtonconstable.com

This superb Elizabethan house was built in 1570, but much of the interior was remodelled in the 18th century. There are magnificent reception rooms and a Tudor long gallery with a pendant roof: the contents range from pictures and furniture to a unique collection of 18th-century scientific instruments. Outside are 200 acres of parkland landscaped by 'Capability' Brown, with oaks and chestnuts, and a lake with an island. Special Event: Country Fair 9 Jul 2006.

Times: Open, Hall & Grounds Etr Sat-end Oct. Grounds 12.30-5, Hall 1-5. (Last admission 4). Closed Fri. **Fee:** ✱ House £5.50 (ch £2.50, pen £5). Family ticket £12.50. Grounds only £1 (ch 50p)
Facilities: P 💻 🍴 & (stair lift to first foor, wheelchairs) toilets for disabled shop outside only (ex assist dogs)

NORTH YORKSHIRE

EVENTS & FESTIVALS

April
27th-30th Harrogate Spring Flower Show,
    Great Yorkshire Show Ground, Harrogate
28th-30th Moor & Coast Festival, Whitby,
    music, song, dance and arts
29th-1st May Ripon Spring Festival

June
18th North Yorkshire County Show,
    Otterington Hall, South Otterington
16th-1st Jul Grassington Festival of Arts &
    Music, various venues, Grassington

July
9th-16th York Early Music Festival
11th-13th Great Yorkshire Show, Great
    Yorkshire Showground, Harrogate
15th-16th Masham Steam Engine & Fair
    Organ Rally
20th-4th Aug Harrogate International Festival
    (various venues)
tbc Whitby Bay International Jazz Festival

August
12th Ripley Show, Ripley Castle Park, Ripley
tbc Feva, Knaresborough Festival of
    entertainment and visual arts, various
    venues

September
8th-17th Ripon International Festival of Music
    & the Arts, various venues
15th-17th Harrogate Autumn Flower Show,
    Great Yorkshire Show Ground, Harrogate
25th Nidderdale Show, Bewerley Park, Pately
    Bridge

*Above: The Middle Falls at Aysgarth Falls, Yorkshire
Dales National Park*

ALDBOROUGH   Map 08 SE46

ALDBOROUGH ROMAN SITE
YO5 9ES
➲ (0.75m SE of Boroughbridge, on minor road off
B6265 within 1m of junct of A1 & A6055)
☎ 01423 322768
View two spectacular mosaic pavements and discover the
remains of the once principal Roman town.
Times: Open 19 Mar-Jul, Thu-Mon, 10-5; Aug, daily, 10-5; Sep,
Thu-Mon, 10-5. **Fee:** £2.60 (ch £1.30, concessions £2.00). Opening
times and prices are subject to change, for further details please phone
0870 333 1181 **Facilities:** shop ♯

AYSGARTH   Map 07 SE08

NATIONAL PARK CENTRE
DL8 3TH
➲ (off A684, Leyburn to Hawes road at Falls junct,
Palmer Flatt Hotel & continue down hill over river,
centre 500yds on left)
☎ 01969 662910   `FREE`
e-mail: aysgarth@ytbtic.co.uk
web: www.yorkshiredales.org.uk
A visitor centre for the Yorkshire Dales National Park, with
maps, guides, walks and local information. Interactive
displays explain the history and natural history of the area.
Plan the day ahead with a light lunch in the coffee shop.
Various guided walks begin here throughout the year.
Times: Open Apr-Oct, daily 10-5; Winter open Fri-Sun, 10-4.
Facilities: 🅿 (charged) ▬ ♿ (viewing platform at Falls) toilets for
disabled shop ✖ (ex guide dogs) 🍴

BENINGBROUGH   Map 08 SE55

BENINGBROUGH HALL & GARDENS
YO6 1DD
➲ (off A19, 8m NW of York)
☎ 01904 470666
e-mail: beningbrough@nationaltrust.org.uk
web: www.nationaltrust.org.uk
Beningbrough was built around 1716. It houses 100 pictures
from the National Portrait Gallery in London. Ornately carved
wood panelling is a feature of several of the rooms. There is
also a fully equipped Victorian Laundry and walled garden.
Times: Open early Mar-end Oct daily (ex Thu & Fri) open Good Fri,
Jul-Aug daily (ex Thu) 12-5. Grounds 11-5.30. **Fee:** ✱ House, Garden
& Exhibition: £6.30 (ch £3.20) Family ticket £14.50 (2ad+3ch or
1ad+4ch). Garden & Exhibition: £5.30 (ch £2.40) Family £13. Reduced
when arriving by bicycle. **Facilities:** 🅿 ✖ licensed 🍴 ♿ (access to
Victorian laundry, shop & restaurant) toilets for disabled shop ✖ ♨

BRIMHAM Map 08 SE26

BRIMHAM ROCKS
Summerbridge HG3 4DW
➲ (10m NW of Harrogate, off B6265)
☎ 01423 780688
e-mail: brimhamrocks@nationaltrust.org.uk
web: www.nationaltrust.org.uk
The rocks stand on National Trust open moorland at a height of 987ft, enjoying spectacular views over the surrounding countryside. The area is filled with strange and fascinating rock formations and is rich in wildlife. Brinham House is now an information point and shop.
Times: Open 8-dusk, (facilities may close in bad weather): shop with exhibition room, kiosk mid Mar-end May & Oct, Sat & Sun 11-5, end May-end Sep daily 11-5, early Nov-mid Dec, Sun 11-5. Also open daily; local school hols, BHs, 26 Dec & 1 Jan (weather permitting).
Fee: ✱ Cars (up to 4hrs £3, over 4hrs £4). Minibuses £7. Coaches £12. Motorcycles free. **Facilities:** 🅿 (charged) 💻 📖 ♿ (adapted path steep in places, Braille/large print guide) toilets for disabled shop 🐾 🍴

CASTLE BOLTON Map 07 SE09

BOLTON CASTLE
DL8 4ET
➲ (off A684, 6m W of Leyburn)
☎ 01969 623981
e-mail: harry@boltoncastle.co.uk
web: www.boltoncastle.co.uk
Medieval castle completed in 1399, overlooking Wensleydale. Stronghold of the Scrope family. Mary Queen of Scots was imprisoned here for six months during 1568 and 1569. The castle was besieged and taken by Parliamentary forces in 1645. Tapestries, tableaux, arms and armour can be seen. Medieval gardens including maze. Events throughout the year, please telephone for details.
Times: Open Apr-Oct, 10-5; Nov-Mar, 10-4/dusk. Phone for winter opening times. **Fee:** ✱ £5 (ch, pen & students £3.50). Family ticket £12. **Facilities:** 🅿 💻 📖 shop 🍴 (ex guide dogs) 🍴

CASTLE HOWARD

See **Malton**

COXWOLD Map 08 SE57

BYLAND ABBEY
YO6 4BD
➲ (2m S of A170 between Thirsk & Helmsley, near Coxwold village)
☎ 01347 868614
A hauntingly beautiful monastic ruin set in peaceful meadows in the shadow of the Hambleton Hills. Marvel at the collection of medieval floor tiles still in their original setting.
Times: Open 19 Mar-Jul, Thu-Mon, 10-5; Aug, daily, 10-5; Sep, Thur-Mon, 10-5. **Fee:** £2.90 (ch £1.50, concessions £2.20). Opening times and prices are subject to change, for further details please phone 0870 333 1181 **Facilities:** 🅿 📖 ♿ (garden/grounds partly accessible) toilets for disabled 🚻 🍴

DANBY Map 08 NZ70

MOORS CENTRE
Lodge Ln YO21 2NB
➲ (turn S off A171, follow Moors Centre Danby signs . Left at crossroads in Danby and then 2m, Centre at bend on right)
☎ 01439 772737   `FREE`
e-mail: moorscentre@ytbtic.co.uk
web: www.moors.uk.net
The ideal place to start exploring the North York Moors National Park. There is an exhibition about the area as well as events, video, a shop and local walks. The Moorsbus service also operates from this site - phone for details.
Times: Open all year, Apr-Oct, daily 10-5. Nov-Feb wknds only 11-4, Mar daily 11-4. Closed 25-26 Dec **Facilities:** 🅿 (charged) 💻 📖 ♿ (woodland & garden trails, motorised & manual wheelchairs) toilets for disabled shop 🍴 (ex guide dogs & in grounds) 🍴

EASBY Map 08 NZ10

EASBY ABBEY
➲ (1m SE of Richmond off B6271)   `FREE`
Set beside the River Swale, this Premonstratensian Abbey was founded in 1155 and dedicated to St Agatha. Extensive remains of the monks' domestic buildings can be seen.
Times: Open Apr-Sep, daily, 10-6; Oct, daily, 10-5; Nov-Mar, daily, 10-4. Closed 24-25 Dec. & 1 Jan **Facilities:** 🅿 ⚏

ELVINGTON Map 08 SE74

YORKSHIRE AIR MUSEUM & ALLIED AIR FORCES MEMORIAL
Halifax Way YO41 4AU
➲ (from York take A1079 then immediate right onto B1228, museum is signposted on right)
☎ 01904 608595
e-mail: museum@yorkshireairmuseum.co.uk
web: www.yorkshireairmuseum.co.uk

This award-winning museum and memorial is based around the largest authentic former WWII Bomber Command Station open to the public. There is a restored tower, an air gunners museum, archives, an Airborne Forces display, Squadron memorial rooms, and much more. Among the exhibits are replicas of the pioneering Cayley Glider and Wright Flyer, along with the Halifax Bomber and modern jets like the Harrier GR3, Tornado GR1 and GR4.
Times: Open daily, 10-5 (summer), 10-3.30 (winter). Closed 25 & 26 Dec. **Fee:** ✱ £5 (ch £3 & pen £4). **Facilities:** 🅿 💻 ✗ licensed ♿ toilets for disabled shop 🍴

See advertisement on page 275

FAIRBURN Map 08 SE42

RSPB NATURE RESERVE

Fairburn Ings, The Visitor Centre, Newton Ln WF10 2BH
➲ (W of A1, N of Ferrybridge. Signed from Allerton Bywater off A656. Signed Fairburn Village off A1)
☎ 01977 603796
e-mail: chris.drake@rspb.org.uk

One-third of the 700-acre RSPB reserve is open water, and over 270 species of birds have been recorded. A visitor centre provides information, and there is an elevated boardwalk, suitable for disabled visitors.

Times: ✱ Access to the reserve via car park, open 9-dusk. Centre open 10-5 wknds and 11-4 wkdays. Closed 25-26 Dec.
Facilities: 🅿 ♿ (raised boardwalk for wheelchair) toilets for disabled shop ✖ (ex guide dogs)

GRASSINGTON Map 07 SE06

NATIONAL PARK CENTRE

Hebden Rd BD23 5LB
➲ (situated on B6265 in the main Grassington car park)
☎ 01756 752774 FREE
e-mail: grassington@ytbtic.co.uk
web: www.yorkshiredales.org.uk

The centre is a useful introduction to the Yorkshire Dales National Park. It has a video and a display on 'Wharfedale - Gateway to the Park', and maps, guides and local information are available. There is also a 24-hr public access information service through computer screens and a full tourist information service.

Times: Open Apr-Oct daily, 10-5; Nov-Mar, Fri, & Sat-Sun, 10-4 (also daily in school hols). **Facilities:** 🅿 (charged) ♿ toilets for disabled shop

GUISBOROUGH Map 08 NZ61

GISBOROUGH PRIORY

TS14 6HG
➲ (next to parish church)
☎ 01287 633801 2 for 1
web: www.redcar-cleveland.gov.uk

The remains of the east end of the 14th-century church make a dramatic sight here. The priory was founded in the 12th century for Augustinian canons.

Times: Open all year, Apr-Sep, Tue-Sun 9-6; Oct-Mar, Wed-Sun 9-5. Closed 24 Dec-1 Jan. **Fee:** £1.10 (ch 55p, concessions 75p). Opening times and prices are subject to change, for further details please phone 0870 333 1181 **Facilities:** 🅿 🗐 ♿ 🖾

HARROGATE Map 08 SE35

RHS GARDEN HARLOW CARR

Crag Ln, Otley Rd HG3 1QB
➲ (off B6162 Otley Rd, 1.5 miles from Harrogate centre)
☎ 01423 565418
e-mail: admin-harlowcarr@rhs.org.uk
web: www.rhs.org.uk

Established in1950, RHS Garden Harlow Carr provides a beautiful garden setting to assess the suitability of plants for growing in the North. The 58 acres includes; the new 'Gardens Through Time', streamside garden, contemporary herbaceous borders, scented and kitchen gardens, woodland and flower meadow, extensive plant centre and the new 'Betty's Café'. Events throughout the year include; outdoor

continued

---

theatre, festivals, workshops and children's activities. There is also a Museum of Gardening and a library on site.

Times: Open all year, daily 9.30-6, or 4 Nov-Mar. (Last admission 1hr before closing). **Fee: ✱** £5.50 (ch under 6 free, 6-16 £1.50)
Facilities: 🅿 💻 🗐 ♿ (electric and push wheelchairs available, scented garden) toilets for disabled shop books and gifts garden centre large selection of plants ✖ (ex guide dogs) 🖾

THE ROYAL PUMP ROOM MUSEUM

Crown Place HG1 2RY
➲ (A61 into town centre and follow brown heritage signs)
☎ 01423 556188
e-mail: museums@harrogate.gov.uk
web: www.harrogate.gov.uk/museums

Housed in an early Victorian pump room over the town's sulphur wells, the museum tells the story of Harrogate's heyday as England's European spa. Visitors discover some of the amazing spa treatments; taste the sulphur water; and explore stories of Russian royalty, communal ox-roasts and early bicycles, among many others. Changing exhibitions complement permanent displays

Times: Open all year, Apr-Oct, Mon-Sat 10-5, Sun 2-5, (Nov-Mar close at 4). Closed 24-26 Dec & 1 Jan. **Fee:** £2.80 (ch £1.50, concessions £1.70). Family rate £7 (2ad+2ch). Party. Combined seasonal tickets available for The Royal Pump Room Museum & Knaresborough Castle & Museum. **Facilities:** 🅿 (100yds) (restricted to 3hrs, need parking disc) 🗐 ♿ toilets for disabled shop ✖ (ex guide dogs) 🖾

HAWES Map 07 SD88

DALES COUNTRYSIDE MUSEUM CENTRE & TIC

Station Yard DL8 3NT
➲ (off A684 in Old Station Yard) East end of Hawse
☎ 01969 667450 & 667494 2 for 1
e-mail: hawes@ytbtic.co.uk
web: www.yorkshiredales.org.uk

Fascinating museum telling the story of the people and landscape of the Yorkshire Dales. Static steam loco and carriages with video and displays. Added features include hands-on interactive displays for children, temporary exhibitions & events. 2006 marks the 100th anniversary of the birth of Marie Hartley, local historian and founder of the Dales Countryside Museum.

Times: Open all year 10-5 daily. **Fee: ✱** Museum: £3 (ch free, concessions £2) . National park centre, temporary exhibitions free.
Facilities: 🅿 (charged) 🗐 ♿ (lifts, ramps and parking) toilets for disabled shop sells maps and books ✖ (ex guide dogs) 🖾

HELMSLEY Map 08 SE68

DUNCOMBE PARK

YO62 5EB
➲ (located within North York Moors National Park, off A170 Thirsk-Scarborough road, 1m from Helmsley market place)
☎ 01439 770213 2 for 1
e-mail: liz@duncombepark.com
web: www.duncombepark.com

Duncombe Park stands at the heart of a spectacular 30-acre early 18th-century landscape garden which is set in 300 acres of dramatic parkland around the River Rye. The house, originally built in 1713, was gutted by fire in 1879 and rebuilt in 1895. Its principal rooms are a fine example of the type of grand interior popular at the turn of the century. Home of the Duncombes for 300 years, for much of this century the house

continued

was a girls' school. In 1985 the present Lord and Lady Feversham decided to make it a family home again and after major restoration, opened the house to the public in 1990. Part of the garden and parkland were designated a 250-acre National Nature Reserve in 1994. Special events include a Country Fair (May), an Antiques Fair (June), Steam Fair (July), Antiques Fair (November). Please telephone for details.
Times: Open: May-end Oct, Sun-Thu; Gardens, Parkland Centre tea room & shop & Parkland walks 11-5.30. House by guided tour only every hour from 12.30-3.30. **Fee:** ✱ House & Gardens £6.50 (ch 10-16, £3, concessions £5) Gardens & Parkland £3.50 (ch £1.50, concessions £3) Parkland only £2 (ch £1). **Facilities:** 🅿 ✗ licensed ⏹ ♿ (portable ramp, lift, wheelchair for loan) toilets for disabled shop ✈ (ex park & guide dogs) ◼

HELMSLEY CASTLE
YO6 5AB
☎ 01439 770442
An atmospheric ruin with formidable double earthworks. Also, an exhibition of the history of the castle.
Times: Open all year, Apr-Sep, daily 10-6; Oct-Mar,Thu-Mon, 10-4. Closed 24-26 Dec & 1 Jan. **Fee:** £4 (ch £2, concessions £3, family £10). Opening times and prices are subject to change, for further details please phone 0870 333 1181 **Facilities:** 🅿 (charged) shop ⌗

KIRBY MISPERTON   Map 08 SE77
FLAMINGO LAND THEME PARK & ZOO
The Rectory YO17 6UX
➲ (turn off A64 onto A169, Pickering to Whitley road)
☎ 01653 668287
e-mail: info@flamingoland.co.uk
web: www.flamingoland.co.uk
Set in 375 acres of North Yorkshire countryside with over 100 rides and attractions there's something for everyone at Flamingo Land. Enjoy the thrills and spills of 12 white knuckle rides or enjoy a stroll through the extensive zoo where you'll find tigers, giraffes, hippos and rhinos. The theme park also boasts 6 great family shows.
Times: Open mid Mar-2 Nov from 10. Closing times vary depending upon season. **Fee:** ✱ £17.50 (ch 4-11 £16.50, ch under 4 free, pens £7.25). Family ticket (4 people) £64. **Facilities:** 🅿 🍴 ✗ licensed ⏹ ♿ (parking, wheelchair hire) toilets for disabled shop ◼

KIRKHAM   Map 08 SE76
KIRKHAM PRIORY
Whitwell-on-the-Hill YO6 7JS
➲ (5m SW of Malton on minor road off A64)
☎ 01653 618768
Discover the ruins of this Augustinian priory, which includes a magnificent carved gatehouse, set in a peaceful and secluded valley by the River Derwent.
Times: Open 19 Mar-Sep, daily 10-6; Oct, Thu-Mon 10-4. **Fee:** Prices not confirmed for 2006 **Facilities:** 🅿 ♿

An asterisk * indicates that opening times and prices are for 2005. Please contact the attraction for up-to-date information.

KNARESBOROUGH   Map 08 SE35
KNARESBOROUGH CASTLE & MUSEUM
Castle Yard HG5 8AS
➲ (off High St towards Market Square, right at police station into Castle Yard)
☎ 01423 556188
e-mail: museums@harrogate.gov.uk
web: www.harrogate.gov.uk/museums
High above the town of Knaresborough, the ruins of this 14th-century castle look down over the gorge of the River Nidd. This imposing fortress was once the hiding place of Thomas Becket's murderers and served as a prison for Richard II. Remains include the keep, the sally-port, parts of the curtain wall and the Old Court of Knaresborough. It now houses a local museum, and entrance is part of the combined ticket price.
Times: Open Good Fri-end Sep, daily 10.30-5. Guided tours regularly available **Fee:** ✱ £2.50 (ch £1.25, concessions £1.50). Family ticket (2ad+2ch) £6.50. Party 10+. Joint & season tickets available for Knaresborough Castle & Museum & The Royal Pump Room Museum. **Facilities:** 🅿 (charged) ⏹ ♿ toilets for disabled shop ✈ (ex guide dogs)

LAWKLAND   Map 07 SD76
YORKSHIRE DALES FALCONRY & WILDLIFE CONSERVATION CENTRE
Crows Nest LA2 8AS
➲ (on A65 follow brown signs)
☎ 01729 822832
web: www.falconryandwildlife.com   2 for 1
The first privately owned falconry centre in the north of England. The main aim of the centre is to educate and promote awareness that many of the world's birds of prey are threatened with extinction. Successful captive breeding and educational programmes will help to safeguard these creatures. Regular free flying demonstrations throughout the day with strong encouragement for audience participation.
Times: Open all year summer 10-6; winter 10-4. Closed 25 Dec **Fee:** £5.50 (ch & pen £3.50) Family ticket £16. Group 15+ £4.50 (ch£2.75) **Facilities:** 🅿 🍴 ♿ (ramp for w/chair into Tea Room) toilets for disabled shop ✈ (ex guide dogs) ◼

MALHAM   Map 07 SD96
MALHAM NATIONAL PARK CENTRE
BD23 4DA
➲ (off A65 at Gargrave opposite petrol station. Malham 7m)
☎ 01729 830363   FREE
e-mail: malham@ytbtic.co.uk
The national park centre has maps, guides and local information together with displays on the remarkable natural history of the area, local community and work of conservation bodies. Audio-visuals are provided for groups and a 24-hour teletext information service is available.
Times: Open Apr-Oct, daily 10-5; Winter, Sat-Sun, 10-4.
Facilities: 🅿 (charged) ⏹ ♿ (Radar key scheme for toilet) toilets for disabled shop ◼

MALTON   Map 08 SE77

CASTLE HOWARD
YO60 7DA
➲ (15m NE of York, off A64, follow brown heritage signs)
☎ 01653 648333
e-mail: house@castlehoward.co.uk
web: www.castlehoward.co.uk

Castle Howard is a magnificent 18th-century house with extensive collections and breathtaking grounds featuring temples, lakes and fountains. Attractions include historical character guides, outdoor tours, exhibitions, event programme plus lakeside adventure playground.
Times: Open March-Oct. House open from 11 (last admission 4).Grounds & Stable courtyard open from 10. **Fee:** ✱ £9.50 (ch £6.50, pen £8.50). Grounds only £6.50 (ch £4.50, pen £6). **Facilities:** P 💻 ✖ licensed ♿ (wheelchair lift, free adapted transport to house) toilets for disabled shop garden centre (ex guide dogs) 🍴

EDEN CAMP MODERN HISTORY THEME MUSEUM
Eden Camp YO17 6RT
➲ (junct of A64 & A169, between York & Scarborough)
☎ 01653 697777   **2 for 1**
e-mail: admin@edencamp.co.uk
web: www.edencamp.co.uk
The story of the people's war unfolds in this museum devoted to civilian life in World War II. The displays, covering the blackout, rationing, the Blitz, the Home Guard and others, are housed in a former prisoner-of-war camp built in 1942 for German and Italian soldiers. Hut 13, covers the conflicts that Britain has been involved with from 1945 to present day. Huts 24-29 cover the military and political events of the war, whilst Hut 11 is dedicated to telling the story of World War I. The Museum also houses an extensive collection of military vehicles and equipment. Special Events: Escapers and Evaders April, All Services Commemorative Day and Parade 2nd Sun after BH, Palestine Veterans Reunion Day 3rd Sat in Oct.
Times: Open 2nd Mon in Jan-23 Dec, daily 10-5. (Last admission 4) **Fee:** ✱ £4.50 (ch & pen £3.50) Party 10+.£3.50 (ch & pen £2.50) **Facilities:** P 💻 📷 ♿ (taped tours, Braille guides) toilets for disabled shop

MALTON MUSEUM
Old Town Hall, Market Place YO17 7LP
➲ (leave A64, follow signs for Malton town centre)
☎ 01653 695136
web: www.malton-pri.n.yorks.fch.uk/maltonmuseum
The extensive Roman settlements in the area are represented and illustrated in this museum, including collections from the Roman fort of Derventio. There are also displays of local prehistoric and medieval finds plus changing exhibitions of local interest. Special Event: Jul 2005-Oct 2006 'Wharram Percy, Life in a Medieval Village' exhibition.
Times: Open Etr Sat-Oct, Mon-Sat 10-4. **Fee:** ✱ £1.50 (ch, pen & students £1) Family ticket £4 (2ad+2ch) **Facilities:** P (adjacent) (pay & display-2hrs) 📷 ♿ shop ✖ (ex guide dogs)

MASHAM   Map 08 SE28

THEAKSTON WORKING BREWERY & VISITOR CENTRE
The Brewery HG4 4YD
➲ (on A6108)
☎ 01765 680000
e-mail: bookings@theakstons.co.uk
web: www.theakstons.co.uk

Visit the Theakston Brewery in Masham, home of the legendary 'Old Peculier' and witness the creation of real taste first-hand. Discover how traditional brewing techniques are still being applied to create today's award winning pint. As these tours are thirsty work, you'll be invited, to round off your visit in the bar with a glass of real British beer at its best.
Times: Open all year daily 10.30-4 Closed Xmas holidays **Fee:** Prices not confirmed for 2006 **Facilities:** P (400yds) ♿ (ex brewery tours) toilets for disabled shop ✖ (ex guide dogs) 🍴

MIDDLEHAM   Map 07 SE18

MIDDLEHAM CASTLE
DL8 4RJ
➲ (2m S of Leyburn on A6108)
☎ 01969 623899
Explore the maze of rooms and passageways at this impressive castle, once the boyhood home of the ill-fated Richard III. Oak viewing gallery of the magnificent views of the 12th-century keep and exhibition.
Times: Open all year, Apr-Sep, daily 10-6; Oct-Mar,Thu-Mon, 10-4. Closed 24-26 Dec & 1 Jan **Fee:** £3.30 (ch £1.70, concessions £2.50). Opening times and prices are subject to change, for further details please phone 0870 333 1181 **Facilities:** P ♿ (ex tower) shop ⌗

MIDDLESBROUGH   Map 08 NZ42

CAPTAIN COOK BIRTHPLACE MUSEUM
Stewart Park, Marton TS7 8AT
➲ (3m S on A172)
☎ 01642 311211
e-mail: captcookmuseum@
middlesbrough.gov.uk
web: www.middlesbrough.gov.uk
Opened to mark the 250th anniversary of the birth of the
voyager in 1728, this museum illustrates the early life of
James Cook and his discoveries with permanent and
temporary exhibitions. Located in spacious and rolling
parkland, the site also offers outside attractions for the
visitor. Recently refurbished, the museum has a special
resource centre which has fresh approaches to presentation
with computers, films, special effects, interactives and
educational aids.
Times: Open all year: Mar-Oct, Tue-Sun, 10-5.30. Nov-Feb 9-3.30.
(Last entry 45 mins before closure). Closed Mon except BH, 24-28 Dec
& 31 Dec-7 Jan. **Facilities:** 🅿 💷 ✕ 🛒 ৬ (lift to all floors, car
parking) toilets for disabled shop ✖ (ex guide dogs) ➡

NEWBY HALL & GARDENS   Map 08 SE36

NEWBY HALL & GARDENS
HG4 5AE
➲ (4m SE of Ripon & 2m W of A1M, off B6265,
between Boroughbridge and Ripon)
☎ 01423 322583
e-mail: info@newbyhall.com
web: www.newbyhall.com

A late 17th-century house with beautifully restored Robert
Adam interiors containing an important collection of
classical sculpture, Chippendale furniture and Gobelin
tapestries. 25 acres of award-winning gardens include a
miniature railway, an adventure garden for children and a
woodland discovery walk with contemporary sculpture park
(Jun-Sep).
Times: Open Apr-Sep, Tue-Sun & BHs, also Mon in Jul+Aug; Gardens
11-5.30; House 12-5. (Last admission 5 Gardens, 4.30 House)
Fee: ✱ House & Garden £8.20, (ch £5.70, pen £7.20). Gardens only
£6.70 (ch £5, pen £5.70). Party rates and family tickets on application.
Facilities: 🅿 💷 ✕ licensed ৬ (wheelchairs available, maps of
wheelchair routes) toilets for disabled shop garden centre
✖ (ex guide dogs) ➡

NORTH STAINLEY   Map 08 SE27

LIGHTWATER VALLEY THEME PARK
HG4 3HT
➲ (3m N of Ripon on A6108)
☎ 0870 458 0060 & 458 0040   **2 for 1**
e-mail: leisure@lightwatervalley.co.uk
web: www.lightwatervalley.net
The family sized theme park with thrills of all sizes, from
Europe's longest rollercoaster 'The Ultimate' and 'The
Grizzly Bear', to family favourites such as the 'ladybird'
rollercoaster and Grand Prix Go Karting along with spinning
teacups, vintage cars and much more for younger children.
You just pay once and enjoy the fun all day long!
Times: Open 23 Mar-7 Apr, wknds only; 13 Apr-26 May inc BH Mon;
daily from Jun-2 Sep, wknds only, 7 Sep-13 Oct, daily 19 Oct-27 Oct.
Fee: ✱ £15.50 over 1.2mtrs, £13.95 under 1.2mtrs, free under 1m; pen
£7.95. Family ticket £55.80 (2ad+2ch) or (1ad+3ch under 16)
Facilities: 🅿 💷 ✕ licensed ৬ (even pathways) toilets for disabled
shop garden centre ✖ (ex guide dogs) ➡

NUNNINGTON   Map 08 SE67

NUNNINGTON HALL
YO62 5UY
➲ (4.5m SE of Helmsley)
☎ 01439 748283
e-mail: nunningtonhall@nationaltrust.org.uk
web: www.nationaltrust.org
This large 16th to 17th-century house has panelled rooms
and a magnificent staircase. The Carlisle collection of
miniature rooms is on display. Changing programme of
temporary exhibitions.
Times: Mid Mar-May, Wed-Sun 1.30-5. Jun-Aug Tue-Sun 1.30-5.30. Sep,
Wed-Sun 1.30-5.30. **Fee:** ✱ House £5 (ch £2.50) Family ticket £12.50.
Gardens only £2.50 (ch free). Party £4.50. **Facilities:** 🅿 💷 🛒
৬ (wheelchairs, Braille guide, scented garden) toilets for disabled
shop ✖

ORMESBY   Map 08 NZ51

ORMESBY HALL
TS7 9AS
➲ (3m SE of Middlesborough, W of A19 take the
A174 to the A172 . Follow signs for Ormesby Hall.
Car entrance on Ladgate Lane B1380)
☎ 01642 324188
e-mail: ormesbyhall@ntrust.org.uk
web: www.nationaltrust.org.uk
An 18th-century mansion, Ormesby Hall has stables
attributed to John Carr of York. Plasterwork, furniture and
18th-century pictures are on view. Exhibiting a large model
railway.
Times: End Mar-end Oct, Fri-Mon 1.30-5 **Fee:** ✱ House & Gardens
£4.10 (ch £2) Family ticket £10.50 (2+3). Garden only £2.90 (ch £1.30).
Party £3.50. **Facilities:** 🅿 💷 🛒 ৬ (parking, Braille guide, special
tours, sensory list) toilets for disabled shop ✖ ✖

OSMOTHERLEY   Map 08 SE49

MOUNT GRACE PRIORY
DL6 3JG
➲ (1m NW)
☎ 01609 883494
The best preserved Carthusian monastery in the country, set
in breathtakingly beautiful woodland surroundings and
continued

gardens, including fully reconstructed Monks cells and herb garden, illustrating the solitary life of the monk.
Times: Open Apr-Sep, daily, 10-6; Oct-Mar, Thu-Mon, 10-4. Closed 24-26 Dec & 1 Jan. **Fee:** £3.60 (ch £1.80, concessions £2.70, family £9.00). National Trust members free except on event days.
Facilities: 🅿 shop ✖ 🐾

PARCEVALL HALL GARDENS Map 07 SE06

PARCEVALL HALL GARDENS
BD23 6DE
➲ (Off B6265 between Grassington and Pateley Bridge)
☎ 01756 720311
e-mail: info@parcevallhallgardens.co.uk
web: www.parcevallhallgardens.co.uk
Enjoying a hillside setting east of the main Wharfedale Valley, these beautiful gardens surround a Grade II listed house which is used as the Bradford Diocesan Retreat House (not open to the public).
Times: Open Apr-Oct, daily 10-6. Winter visitors by appointment.
Fee: £3.50 (ch up to 16, 50p). **Facilities:** 🅿 🍺 🍴 shop

PATELEY BRIDGE Map 07 SE16

STUMP CROSS CAVERNS
Greenhow HG3 5JL
➲ (on B6265 between Pateley Bridge & Grassington)
☎ 01756 752780
web: www.stumpcrosscaverns.co.uk
Discovered by the brothers Mark and William Newbould in 1860, Stump Cross Caverns have been an attraction for visitors since 1863 when one shilling was charged for entrance. Among the few limestone show caves in Britain, these require no special clothing, experience or equipment, as walkways are gravel and concrete and floodlighting is provided. Stalagmites, stalagtites and calcite precipitation make this an eerie day out.
Times: Open daily, mid Mar-2 Nov, then wknds (winter) 10-5.
Fee: ✱ £4.75 (ch £2.50, ch under 4 free) **Facilities:** 🅿 🍺 shop ✖ (ex guide dogs) 🍴

PICKERING Map 08 SE78

NORTH YORKSHIRE MOORS RAILWAY
Pickering Station YO18 7AJ
➲ (from A169 take road towards Kirkbymoorside, right at traffic lights, station 400yds on left)
☎ 01751 472508
e-mail: admin@nymr.pickering.fsnet.co.uk
web: www.northyorkshiremoorsrailway.com
Operating through the heart of the North York Moors National Park between Pickering and Grosmont, steam trains cover a distance of 18 miles. The locomotive sheds at Grosmont are open to the public. Events throughout the year include Day Out with Thomas, Steam Gala, Santa Specials.
Times: Open 29 Mar-Oct, daily; Dec, Santa specials and Christmas to New Year running. Further information available from Pickering Station.
Fee: ✱ Return: £13 (ch £6.50, pen £11). Family ticket £28 (2ad+3ch), others on request. Party 20+. **Facilities:** 🅿 (charged) 🍺 ✖ licensed 🍴 🕭 (ramp for trains) toilets for disabled shop (at Pickering, Goathland & Grosmont) 🍴

PICKERING CASTLE
YO6 5AB
☎ 01751 474989
Splendid 12th-century castle, on the edge of the Yorkshire Moors, originally built by William the Conqueror. Visit the exhibition on the castle's history and take in the views from the keep.
Times: Open 19 Mar-Sep, daily, 10-6; Oct, Thu-Mon, 10-4. **Fee:** £3 (ch £1.50, concessions £2.30, family £7.50). Opening times and prices are subject to change, for further details please phone 0870 333 1811
Facilities: 🅿 🕭 (ex motte) shop 🚻

REDCAR Map 08 NZ62

RNLI ZETLAND MUSEUM `FREE`
5 King St TS10 3AH
➲ (on corner of King St and The Promenade)
☎ 01642 485370 & 471813
The museum portrays the lifeboat, maritime, fishing and local history of the area, including its main exhibit 'The Zetland' - the oldest lifeboat in the world, dating from 1802. There is also a replica of a fisherman's cottage c1900 and almost 2000 other exhibits. The museum is housed in an early lifeboat station, now a listed building.
Times: May Wed 11-4, Sat-Sun 12-4. Jun-Sep Tue-Fri 11-4, Sat-Sun 12-4. Closed Mon. **Facilities:** 🅿 (20m) (60p per hour) 🕭 🕭 (ground floor accessible only) shop

RICHMOND Map 07 NZ10

GREEN HOWARDS MUSEUM
Trinity Church Square, Market Place DL10 4QN
➲ (take any turning on the A1, between Catterick & South Corner, signed to Richmond. Located in centre cobbled market square, in Holy Trinity Church)
☎ 01748 826561
e-mail: green.howardsmus@aol.com
web: www.greenhowards.org.uk
This award-winning museum traces the military history of the Green Howards from the late 17th century onwards. The exhibits include uniforms, weapons, medals and a special Victoria Cross exhibition. Regimental and civic plate is displayed, and there is CD ROM and touch screen video of the First World War Western Front and the Green Howards in the Second World War. Audio guide available.
Times: ✱ Open Feb, Mon-Fri 9-4.30; Mar, Mon-Fri 9-4.30; mid Apr-Oct, Mon-Sat 9-4.30 & Sun 2-4.30; Nov, Mon-Sat 9-4.30.
Facilities: 🅿 (in market place) (disk parking, 2hr max) 🕭 🕭 (stairlift for access to all floors, lightweight wheelchair) shop ✖ (ex guide dogs)

RICHMOND CASTLE
DL10 4QW
☎ 01748 822493
Overlooking the River Swale and market town of Richmond, the views from the keep are stunning. Built by William the Conqueror to subdue the rebellious North, the castle now houses an exciting interactive exhibition.
Times: Open all year, Apr-Sep, daily, 10-6; Oct-Mar, Thu-Mon, 10-4. Closed 24-26 Dec & 1 Jan. **Fee:** £3.60 (ch £1.80, concessions £2.70, family £9.00). Opening times and prices are subject to change, for further details please phone 0870 333 1181 **Facilities:** 🅿 (800 yds) 🕭 toilets for disabled shop 🚻

RIEVAULX Map 08 SE58

RIEVAULX ABBEY
➲ (2.25m W of Helmsley on minor road off B1257)
☎ 01439 798228

Explore the magnificent romantic ruin set in a tranquil wooded valley of the River Rye. Find out about monastic life with the help of our audio tour and exhibition.
Times: Open Apr-Sep, daily, 10-6; Oct-Mar, Thu-Mon, 10-4. Closed 24-26 Dec & 1 Jan **Fee:** £4 (ch £2, concessions £3). Opening times and prices are subject to change, for further details please phone 0870 333 1181 **Facilities:** 🅿 & shop 🚗 ♿

RIEVAULX TERRACE & TEMPLES
YO62 5LJ
➲ (2m NW of Helmsley on B1257)
☎ 01439 798340
e-mail: nunningtonhall@nationaltrust.org.uk
web: www.nationaltrust.org.uk

This curved terrace, half a mile long, overlooks the abbey, with views of Ryedale and the Hambleton Hills. It has two mock-Greek temples, one built for hunting parties, the other for quiet contemplation. There are also remarkable frescoes by Borgnis, and an exhibition on English landscape design.
Times: Mid Mar-end Sep, daily 10.30-6. Oct daily, 10.30-5.
Fee: ✸ £3.80 (ch £2). Family £9.60. Party £3.20 **Facilities:** 🅿 📶 & (w/chair/runaround vehicle/Braille guide/ramp) shop 🌿

RIPLEY Map 08 SE26

RIPLEY CASTLE
HG3 3AY
➲ (off A61, Harrogate to Ripon road)
☎ 01423 770152
e-mail: enquiries@ripleycastle.co.uk
web: www.ripleycastle.co.uk

Ripley Castle has been home to the Ingilby family since 1320, and stands at the heart of an estate with deer park, lake and Victorian walled gardens. The Castle has a rich history and a fine collection of Royalist armour housed in the 1555 tower. There are also walled gardens, tropical hot houses, woodland walks, pleasure grounds and the National Hyacinth collection in spring.
Times: Open Oct-Nov & Mar-May, Tue, Thu, Sat & Sun 10.30-3, Jul-Sep daily 10.30-3, Dec-Feb wkends only, also BH and school holidays. Groups all year by prior arrangement. Gardens open daily 9-5.30.
Fee: ✸ Castle & Gardens £6.50 (ch £4, pen £5.50). Gardens only £4
continued

(ch £2.50, pen £3.50). Party £3.50. **Facilities:** 🅿 🍽 ✗ licensed & (mobility buggy for hire, audio loop) toilets for disabled shop garden centre 🐕 (ex guide dogs) 🍴

RIPON Map 08 SE37

FOUNTAINS ABBEY & STUDLEY ROYAL
HG4 3DY
➲ (4m W of Ripon off B6265)
☎ 01765 608888
e-mail: fountainsenquiries@nationaltrust.org.uk
web: www.fountainsabbey.org.uk

A world heritage site comprising of; the ruin of a 12th-century Cistercian Abbey and monastic watermill, an Elizabethan mansion and one of the best surviving examples of a Georgian water garden. Elegant ornamental lakes, canals, temples and cascades provide eye-catching vistas. The site also contains a Victorian St. Mary's Church and medieval deer park.
Times: Open daily all year: Nov-Feb 10-4, Mar-Oct 10-5. Closed Fri Nov-Jan. **Fee:** ✸ £5.50 (ch £3). Family ticket £15 **Facilities:** 🅿 🍽 ✗ licensed 📶 & (pre-bk wheelchairs & batricars. Braille/large print guides) toilets for disabled shop on lead at all times 🌿 🍴

NORTON CONYERS HALL
HG4 5EQ
➲ (from Ripon take A61 to Thirsk. At top of hill just outside Ripon, turn sharp left onto Wath Road)
☎ 01765 640333
e-mail: norton.conyers@bronco.co.uk

This charming late medieval house has belonged to the Grahams since 1624, and its interior, pictures and furniture reflect nearly four hundred years of occupation by the same family. Famous visitors include Charles I in 1633, James II and his wife in 1679, and Charlotte Brontë in 1839. The last of these is said to have been inspired by a local legend of a mad woman in the attic to create mad Mrs Rochester in her novel *Jane Eyre*. The house is set in a fine park with an 18th-century walled garden.
Times: Open - House & Garden, Etr Sun & Mon, BH Sun & Mon; 23 Apr-2 Jul & 9 Jul-20 Aug Sun only; 3-8 Jul daily, House 2-5, Garden 12-4.30. Gardens open 10-4, throughought year (please check).
Fee: ✸ £4 (ch 10-16, pen, concessions £3). Garden entry is free, with donations welcome, although a charge is made at garden charity openings. Parties by arrangement. **Facilities:** 🅿 📶 & (ramp at entrance) toilets for disabled shop 🐕 (ex guide dogs)

SALTBURN-BY-THE-SEA Map 08 NZ62

SALTBURN SMUGGLERS HERITAGE CENTRE
Old Saltburn TS12 1HF
➲ (adjoining Ship Inn, on A174)
☎ 01287 625252 `2 for 1`
web: www.redcar-cleveland.gov.uk

Set in old fisherman's cottages, this centre skillfully blends costumed characters with authentic sounds and smells. Follow the story of John Andrew "King of Smugglers", who was at the heart of illicit local trade 200 years ago.
Times: Open Apr-Sep, daily 10-6: Winter open by arrangement only telephone 01642 471069. **Fee:** ✸ £1.95 (ch £1.45). Family ticket £5.80. Party. **Facilities:** 🅿 (200 mtrs) (charged) 📶 shop 🐕 assist dogs

SCARBOROUGH Map 08 TA08

SCARBOROUGH CASTLE

Castle Rd YO11 1HY
➲ (E of town centre)
☎ 01723 372451

This 12th-century fortress housed many important figures in history. Enjoy the spectacular coastal view and see the remains of the great keep still standing over three storeys high. Discover the castle's exciting history through the free audio tour.

Times: Open all year, Apr-Sep, daily 10-6; Oct-Mar, Thu-Mon, 10-4. Closed 24-26 Dec & 1 Jan. **Fee:** £3.30 (ch £1.70, concessions £2.50, family £8.30). Opening hours and prices are subject to change, for further details please phone 0870 333 1181 **Facilities:** P (100yds) ⅄ (ex in keep) ⚏

SEA LIFE & MARINE SANCTUARY

Scalby Mills Rd, North Bay YO12 6RP
➲ (follow brown tourist signs after entering Scarborough. Centre in North Bay Leisure Parks area of town)
☎ 01723 376125
web: www.sealife.co.uk

Made up of three large white pyramids, this impressive marine sanctuary overlooks the white sandy beaches of the North Bay, Scarborough's Castle, and Peasholm Park. The sanctuary features Jurassic seas, jellyfish, Otter River, penguins, and sea turtles.

Times: Open daily. Closed 25 Dec. **Facilities:** P (charged) ⬛ 🗊 ⅄ (lift to cafe) toilets for disabled shop ✖ (except guide dogs) 🛶

SKINNINGROVE Map 08 NZ71

CLEVELAND IRONSTONE MINING MUSEUM

Deepdale TS13 4AP
➲ (in Skinningrove Valley, just off A174 near coast between Middlesbrough and Whitby)
☎ 01287 642877
e-mail: visits@ironstonemuseum.co.uk
web: www.ironstonemuseum.co.uk

【2 for 1】

On the site of the old Loftus Mine, this museum offers visitors a glimpse into the underground world of Cleveland's ironstone mining past. Discover the special skills and customs of the miners who helped make Cleveland the most important ironstone mining district in Victorian and Edwardian England.

Times: Open Apr-Oct, Mon-Sat from 1 (last admission 4). Jul-Aug open daily. Nov-Mar, pre-booked parties can be arranged at any time **Fee:** ✱ £4 (ch £2). Family ticket (2ad+2ch) £10. **Facilities:** P 🗊 ⅄ (Please telephone to discuss) toilets for disabled shop ✖ (ex guide dogs)

SKIPTON Map 07 SD95

SKIPTON CASTLE

BD23 1AQ
➲ (in town centre at head of High Street)
☎ 01756 792442
e-mail: info@skiptoncastle.co.uk
web: www.skiptoncastle.co.uk

Skipton is one of the most complete and well-preserved medieval castles in England. Some of the castle dates from the 1650s when it was rebuilt after being partially damaged following the Civil War. However, the original castle was erected in Norman times and became the home of the Clifford family in 1310 and remained so until 1676. Illustrated

continued

tour sheets are available in a number of languages. Please see website for special events.

Skipton Castle

Times: Open daily from 10, (Sun noon). Last admission 6pm (4pm Oct-Feb). Closed 25 Dec. **Fee:** ✱ £5.20 (inc illustrated tour sheet) (ch under 18 £2.70, under 5 free, concessions £4.60). Family ticket £14.90. Party 15+. **Facilities:** P (200m) ⬛ 🗊 shop Good selection of books garden centre Specialist plant sales on a lead 🛶

SUTTON-ON-THE-FOREST Map 08 SE56

SUTTON PARK

YO61 1DP
➲ (off A1237 onto B1363 York to Helmsley road. 8m N of York city centre)
☎ 01347 810249 & 811239
e-mail: suttonpark@fsbdial.co.uk
web: www.statelyhome.co.uk

The early Georgian house contains fine furniture, paintings and porcelain. The grounds have superb, award-winning terraced gardens, a lily pond and a Georgian ice house. There are also delightful woodland walks as well as spaces for caravans.

Times: Open Gardens 2 Apr-end Sep, daily 11-5. House open 2 Apr-27 Sep, Wed & Sun, also Good Fri, Etr Mon and all BH Mons. **Fee:** ✱ Gardens only £3 (ch 50p, pen £2). House & Gardens £5.50 (ch £3, pen £4.50) **Facilities:** P ⬛ 🗊 ⅄ (wheelchair and lift in house, ramps in garden) toilets for disabled shop ✖ (ex guide dogs in garden)

WHITBY Map 08 NZ81

WHITBY ABBEY

YO22 4JT
➲ (on clifftop E of Whitby town centre)
☎ 01947 603568

Uncover the full story of these atmospheric ruins in their impressive clifftop location above the picturesque fishing town with associations ranging from Victorian jewellery and whaling, to Count Dracula.

Times: Open all year, Apr-Sep, daily, 10-6; Oct, daily 10-5; Nov-Mar, Thu-Mon, 10-4. Closed 24-26 Dec & 1 Jan. **Fee:** £4 (ch £2, concessions £3, family £10). Opening times and prices are subject to change, for further details please phone 0870 333 1181 **Facilities:** P (charged) ⬛ shop ⚏

WINTRINGHAM   Map 08 SE87

WOLDS WAY LAVENDER

Deer Farm Park, Sandy Ln, Wintringham YO17 8HW

➲ (off A64 between Malton & Scarborough, follow brown signs)

☎ 01944 758641   **2 for 1** **FREE**

e-mail: admin@deerparkfarm.com

web: www.deerparkfarm.com

The medicinal and therapeutic benefits of lavender are extolled at this 12-acre site close to the Yorkshire Wolds. Four acres are currently planted with lavender, and a wood-burning still for the extraction of lavender oil. Visitors can be calmed by the Sensory Areas, enjoy a cuppa at Lavender Lil's Tearoom, and purchase all manner of lavender items at the farm shop. 2-for-1 offer applies to tea/coffee and lavender scone.

Times: Open daily, wk before 21 Mar-Oct, 10-4. Jun-Aug 10-5
Facilities: P 🅿 🗐 & (sensory garden, raised flower beds) shop garden centre ✗ (ex guide dogs) ◀

YORK   Map 08 SE65

THE ARC

St Saviourgate YO1 8NN

➲ (follow A19 or A64 to York city centre then pedestrian signs for attraction)

☎ 01904 543403

e-mail: enquiries@vikingjorvik.com

web: www.jorvik-viking-centre.com

The ARC is the perfect place to visit to experience an unusual way to discover York's Viking history. Visitors have the opportunity to become an archaeologist and handle genuine 1000 year-old objects that once belonged to the Vikings themselves. With the help of a special detective guidebook, it is possible to deduce what life was really like at that time.

Times: ✱ Open: School term time Mon-Fri 10-3.30. School hols Mon-Sat 11-3 **Facilities:** P (50yds) 🗐 & (induction loop, sensory garden, hearing posts) toilets for disabled shop ✗ (ex guide dogs) ◀

CLIFFORD'S TOWER

Tower St YO1 1SA

☎ 01904 646940

Visit this proud symbol of the might of England's medieval kings - and enjoy magnificent views over York. The original wooden tower was built to help William the Conqueror subdue the North. It was burned down during the persecution of the Jewish community in 1190 and rebuilt in a rare design of interlocking circles by Henry III in the 13th-century.

Times: Open 13 Mar-Sep, daily 10-6; Oct, daily 10-5; Nov-Mar, daily 10-4. Closed 24-26 Dec & 1 Jan. **Fee:** £2.80 (ch £1.40, concessions £2.10, family £7.00). Opening times and prices are subject to change, for further details please phone 0870 333 1181 **Facilities:** P shop
✗ 🚗 ♯

FAIRFAX HOUSE

Castlegate YO1 9RN

➲ (city centre, close to Jorvik Centre and Cliffords Tower)

☎ 01904 655543

e-mail: peterbrown@fairfaxhouse.co.uk

web: www.fairfaxhouse.co.uk

An outstanding mid 18th-century house with a richly decorated interior, Fairfax House was acquired by the York Civic Trust in 1983 and restored. The house contains fine

continued

examples of Georgian furniture, porcelain, paintings and clocks which were donated by Mr Noel Terry, the great grandson of the founder of the York-based confectionery business. There is a special display of a recreated meal dating from 1763 in the dining room and kitchen.

Times: ✱ Open 7 Feb-5 Jan, Mon-Sat 11-5, (Fri guided tours only at 11& 2). Sun 1.30-5. (Last admission 4.30) **Facilities:** P (50yds) (3hr short stay) 🗐 & (with assistance, phone before visit) shop
✗ (ex guide dogs) ◀

GUILDHALL

Coney St YO1 9QN

➲ (5mins walk from rail station)

☎ 01904 613161   **FREE**

web: www.york.gov.uk

The present Hall dates from 1446 but in 1942 an air raid virtually destroyed the building. The present Guildhall was carefully restored as an exact replica and was re-opened in 1960. There is an interesting arch-braced roof decorated with colourful bosses and supported by 12 solid oak pillars. There are also some beautiful stained-glass windows.

Times: Open all year, May-Oct, Mon-Fri 9-5, Sat 10-5, Sun 2-5; Nov-Apr, Mon-Fri 9-5. **Facilities:** P (15-20 mins walk) & (electric chair lift & ramps) toilets for disabled ✗ (ex guide dogs) 🚋

JORVIK

Coppergate YO1 9WT

➲ (follow A19 or A64 to York. Jorvik in Coppergate shopping area (city centre) signed)

☎ 01904 543403

e-mail: enquiries@vikingjorvik.com   **2 for 1**

web: www.vikingjorvik.com

Explore York's Viking history on the very site where archaeologists discovered remains of the city of Jorvik. Encounter Viking residents, learn what life was like here 1000 years ago, and journey through a reconstruction of actual Viking streets. The 'Fearsome Craftsmen' exhibit reveals the skills and artistry of the Vikings, while 'Unearthed' tells how the people of ancient York lived and died, as revealed by real bone material. Special events throughout the year. Special Event: Jorvik Viking Festival 16-26 Feb 2006.

Times: Open all year, Apr-Oct daily 10-5; and Viking festival Nov-Mar daily 10-4. Closed 25 Dec. Opening times subject to change, please telephone for up to date details. **Fee:** ✱ £7.20 (ch 5-15 £5.10, under 5 free, student & pen £6.10) Family of 4 £21.95 & family of 5 £26.50. Telephone bookings on 01904 543403 (£1 booking fee per person at peak times). **Facilities:** P (400 yds) (limited to 3 hours) 🅿 🗐 & (lift & time car designed to take wheelchair, hearing loop) toilets for disabled shop ✗ (ex guide dogs) ◀

MERCHANT ADVENTURERS' HALL

Fossgate YO1 9XD

➲ (located in town centre, between Piccadilly and Fossgate)

☎ 01904 654818   `2 for 1`

e-mail: enquiries@theyorkcompany.co.uk

web: www.theyorkcompany.co.uk

The medieval guild hall of the powerful Merchant Adventurers' Company was built 1357-1361 and is one of the finest in Europe. The Hall contains early furniture, one piece dating from the 13th century, paintings, silver, and weights and measures. Special Events: 15-24 Feb 2006 York Art Society Exhibition. 1-13 May 2006 York and District Guild of Weavers, Spinners and Dyers Exhibition.

Times: Open early Jan-late Mar & early Oct-mid Dec, Mon-Sat 9-3.30 (closed Sun); late Mar- Oct, Mon-Thu 9-5, Fri-Sat 9-3.30, Sun 12-4. Closed over Xmas **Fee:** ✱ £2.50 (ch under 7 free, ch 7-17yrs £1, concessions £2). **Facilities:** P (500yds) 🍴 ♿ (access from Fossgate, lift) toilets for disabled ✖ (ex guide dogs)

NATIONAL RAILWAY MUSEUM

Leeman Rd YO26 4XJ

➲ (behind rail station. Signed from all major roads and city centre.

☎ 01904 621261   `FREE`

e-mail: nrm@nmsi.ac.uk

web: www.nrm.org.uk

The National Railway Museum is the world's largest railway museum. Housing: The Flying Scotsman, three enormous galleries, interactive exhibits and daily events, the National Railway Museum mixes education with fun. This attraction is also free.

Times: Open all year, Mon-Sun 10-6. Closed 24-26 Dec.

Facilities: P (charged) 💻 ✖ licensed ♿ ("Please Touch") evenings usually in June) toilets for disabled shop ✖ (ex guide/hearing dogs) 🍴

ST WILLIAMS COLLEGE

5 College St YO1 7JF

➲ (adjacent to York Minster at east end)

☎ 01904 557233

e-mail: conference@yorkminster.org

web: www.yorkminster.org

St Williams College, a 15th-century timber-framed building, housed chantry priests until 1549. It now contains York Minster's Conference & Banquet Centre, shop, restaurant and the medieval rooms are open to view when not being used for functions; an ideal venue for wedding receptions and medieval banquets. Craft Fairs most weekends.

Times: Open all year 10-5 for viewing of medieval rooms subject to private bookings - phone for details. Closed 24-26 Dec & Good Fri.

Fee: ✱ Medieval Rooms £1 (ch 50p) subject to functions.

Facilities: P 5min walk 💻 ✖ licensed 🍴 shop ✖ assisst dogs

TREASURER'S HOUSE

Minster Yard YO1 7JL

➲ (in Minster Yard, on N side of Minster, in the centre of York)

☎ 01904 624247

e-mail: treasurershouse@nationaltrust.org.uk

web: www.nationaltrust.org.uk

Named after the Treasurer of York Minster and built over a Roman Road, the house is not all it seems. Nestled behind the Minster, the size, splendour and contents of the house

continued

are a constant surprise to visitors - as are the famous ghost stories. Children's trails and access to the tea room free.

Times: Open mid Mar- end Oct, daily except Fri, 11-5. **Fee:** ✱ £4.80 (ch £2.40). Family ticket £12 (2+3). House and Ghost Cellar £6.80 (ch £3.60) **Facilities:** P (800 mtrs) 💻 ✖ 🍴 ♿ (Braille guide/tactile pictures/induction loop/scented path) ✖ (ex guide dogs) 🐾

THE YORK BREWERY CO LTD

12 Toft Green YO1 6JT 5 min walk from York train station. Turn right out of station, right at lights. Walk under Mickelgate Bar, then left into Toft Green. Brewery is 300yds on right.

☎ 01904 621162   `2 for 1`

e-mail: tony@yorkbrew.co.uk

web: www.yorkbrew.co.uk

One of the North's finest independent breweries now offers a tour of its premises inside the city walls. Visitors can observe all the processes that go into producing beers like Centurion's Ghost, Yorkshire Terrier, Guzzler, and Stonewall. Those made intolerably thirsty by the sight of all this brewing expertise will be glad to know that the adult ticket price includes one pint of beer.

Times: Open daily tours at 12.30, 2, 3.30 and 5 Mon-Sat (Sun, May-Sep) **Fee:** ✱ £4.50 (£4 pen & ch 14-17yrs £3).

Facilities: P (50yds) £1.40 p/hr shop ✖ (ex guide dogs) 🍴

YORK CASTLE MUSEUM
The Eye of York YO1 1RY
➲ (city centre, next to Clifford's Tower)
☎ 01904 653611
web: www.york.gov.uk

Fascinating exhibits that bring memories to life, imaginatively displayed through reconstructions of period rooms and two indoor streets, complete with cobbles, a Hansom cab and a park. The museum is housed in the city's former prison and is based on an extensive collection of 'bygones' acquired at the beginning of the twentieth century. It was one of the first folk museums to display a huge range of everyday objects in an authentic scene. The Victorian street includes a pawnbroker, a tallow candle factory and a haberdasher's. There is even a reconstruction of the original sweet shop of the York chocolate manufacturer, Joseph Terry. An extensive collection of many other items ranging from musical instruments to costumes and a gallery of domestic gadgets from Victorian times to the 1960s (entitled 'Every home should have one') are further attractions to this remarkable museum. The museum also has one of Britain's finest collections of Militaria; this includes a superb example of an Anglo-Saxon helmet - one of only three known. A special exhibition called 'Seeing it Through' explores the life of York citizens during the Second World War. The museum includes the cell where highwayman Dick Turpin was held. Please contact the museum for deatils of exhibition and events.

Times: ✱ Open all year, Apr-Oct Mon-Sat 9.30-5.30, Sun 10-5.30; Nov-Mar, Mon-Sat 9.30-4, Sun 10-4. Closed 25-26 Dec & 1 Jan.
Facilities: 🅿 & toilets for disabled shop ✖ 🛏

YORK CITY ART GALLERY
Exhibition Square YO1 7EW
➲ (3min walk from the minster in the centre of York).
☎ 01904 551861
e-mail: art.gallery@york.gov.uk
web: www.york.gov.uk/heritage/museums/art

The gallery is remarkable for the range and quality of its collections that provide a survey of most developments in Western European painting over the past six centuries. Works by Parmigianino, Bellotto, Lely, Reynolds, Frith, Boudin, Lowry and Nash and nudes by Etty are on permanent display. There are also fine collections of watercolours and pottery.

Times: ✱ Open all year, daily 10-5. (Closed 25 & 26 Dec & 1 Jan).
Facilities: 🅿 (500mtrs) & (chair lift) toilets for disabled shop ✖ (ex guide dogs) 🛏

THE YORK DUNGEON
12 Clifford St YO1 9RD
➲ (A64/A19/A59 to city centre)
☎ 01904 632599
e-mail: yorkdungeons@ merlinentertainments.biz
web: www.thedungeons.com

Deep in the heart of historic York, buried beneath its very paving stones, lies the York Dungeon bringing more than 2,000 years of gruesomely authentic history vividly back to life...and death. As you delve into the darkest chapters of our grim and bloody past, recreated in all its dreadful detail remember - everything you experience really happened. A warning - in the dungeon's dark catacombs it always pays to keep your wits about you. The 'exhibits' have an unnerving habit of coming back to life. The journey includes Dick

continued

Turpin, Guy Fawkes, Witch Trials, Clifford's Tower, Pit of Despair and Gorvik - the real Viking experience.
Times: ✱ Open all year, daily 10.30-5 (closes 4.30 Oct-Mar). Closed 25 Dec. **Facilities:** 🅿 (500yds) 🍴 & (wheelchair ramps, stairlifts, award winning access) toilets for disabled shop 🛏

YORK MINSTER
Deangate YO1 7EW
➲ (easy access via A19, A1 or A64)
☎ 01904 557216
e-mail: visitors@yorkminster.org
web: www.yorkminster.org

Enjoy the peaceful atmosphere of the largest Gothic cathedral in Northern Europe, a place of worship for over 1,000 years, and a treasure house of stained glass. Take an audio tour of the Undercroft to find out more about the Minster's fascinating history and climb the Tower for an amazing view.
Times: Open from 7 for services. Visitors Mon-Sat 9-4.45 (9.30 in winter), Sun noon-3.45. Phone for 2005 details. **Fee:** ✱ £5 (ch16 free, concessions £3.50). Small charge also for the Undercroft and Tower.
Facilities: 🅿 (440yds) & (tactile model, Braille & large print guide) toilets for disabled shop ✖ (ex assist dogs) 🛏

YORKSHIRE MUSEUM
Museum Gardens YO1 7FR
➲ (park & ride service from 4 sites near A64/A19/A1079 & A166, also 3 car parks within short walk)
☎ 01904 551800
e-mail: yorkshire.museum@york.gov.uk
web: www.york.gov.uk

The Yorkshire Museum is set in 10 acres of botanical gardens in the heart of the historic City of York, and displays some of the finest Roman, Anglo-Saxon, Viking and Medieval treasures ever discovered in Britain. The Middleham Jewel, a fine example of English Gothic jewellery, is on display, and in the Roman Gallery, visitors can see a marble head of Constantine the Great. The Anglo-Saxon Gallery houses the delicate silver-gilt Ormside bowl and the Gilling sword.
Times: ✱ Open all year, daily 10-5. **Facilities:** 🅿 (5 mins walk) 🍴 & (ramps & lift) toilets for disabled shop ✖ 🛏

SOUTH YORKSHIRE

e Griffin Wares

EVENTS & FESTIVALS

January
6th The Ancient Haxey Hood Game,
Doncaster

February
10th-19th Love2B programme of events,
various venues, Sheffield

May
tbc Highland Fling Country Fair, Graves Park,
Sheffield
tbc Sheffield Mayfest, Hillsborough Park, folk
festival with live music & dance
(provisional)

June
17th-22nd Jul Sheffield Children's Festival
25th-9th July Dore Festival & Gala, various
events and venues (Gala on 8th)

July
2nd Parson Cross Festival (provisional)
7th-9th Great Sheffield Art Show, Octagon
Centre, Sheffield
8th The Lord Mayor's Carnival Parade
8th Sharrow Festival & Fringe, multicultural
festival with stalls and performances
9th Abbeyfield Park Multicultural Festival
tbc Hillsborough Gala, Hillsborough Park,
Sheffield

August
11th-13th Bradfield Traditional Music Festival,
Edgemount Farm, High Bradfield
27th-28th Sheffield Fayre, horticultural show,
funfair, attractions, Norfolk Heritage Park,
Sheffield

October
27th-29th Sheffield Folk Festival, Kelham
Island Museum Great Hall
29th Fright Night, Britain's biggest Halloween
party, Sheffield city centre
tbc Sheffield International Documentary
Festival

Above: Rockingham Pottery

BARNSLEY Map 08 SE30

MONK BRETTON PRIORY
S71 5QD
➲ (1m E of town centre, off A633)
The priory was an important Cluniac house, founded in 1153.
The considerable remains of the gatehouse, church and
other buildings can be seen.
Times: Open all year, Apr-Sep, daily 10-6; Oct, daily 10-5; Nov-Mar,
daily 10-4 (managed by a key keeper). Closed 24-26 Dec & 1 Jan.
Facilities: 🅿 ⚏

CONISBROUGH Map 08 SK59

CONISBROUGH CASTLE
DN12 3HH
➲ (NE of town centre off A630)
☎ 01709 863329
The white, circular keep of this 12th-century castle is a
spectacular structure. Made of magnesian limestone, it is the
oldest of its kind in England. Recently restored, with two
new floors and a roof, it is a fine example of medieval
architecture and was the inspiration for Sir Walter Scott's
classic novel *Ivanhoe*.
Times: Open Apr-Sep, daily 10-5 (last admission 4.20); Oct-Mar, daily
10-4 (last admission 3.20). **Fee:** Prices not confirmed for 2006
Facilities: 🅿 ♨ ♿ (wheelchair access limited) shop ✖

DONCASTER Map 08 SE50

BRODSWORTH HALL & GARDENS
Brodsworth DN5 7XJ
➲ (between A635 & A638)
☎ 01302 722598
This Victorian country house has survived largely intact.
Imagine how the serving classes fared below stairs, then
experience, in contrast, the opulent 'upstairs' apartments.
Outside, visitors can enjoy a leisurely stroll around the
extensive newly restored gardens.
Times: House: open 19 Mar-2 Oct, Tue-Sun & BHs, 1-5; Oct, Sat-Sun,
12-4. Gardens: open 19 Mar-Oct, Daily 10-5.30. Garden, Tearoom, Shop
& Servants Wing: open Nov-Mar, Sat-Sun 10-4 **Fee:** House & Gardens;
£6.60 (ch £3.30, concessions £5.00). Gardens only; £4.60 (ch £2.30,
concessions £3.50). Opening times and prices are subject to change,
for further details please phone 0870 333 1181 **Facilities:** 🅿 ♨
♿ toilets for disabled shop ✖ ⚏ 🖼

DONCASTER MUSEUM & ART GALLERY
Chequer Rd DN1 2AE
➲ (off inner ring road)
☎ 01302 734293
e-mail: museum@doncaster.gov.uk
web: www.doncaster.gov.uk/museums
The wide-ranging collections include fine and decorative art
and sculpture. Also ceramics, glass, silver, and displays on
history, archaeology and natural history. The historical
collection of the Kings Own Yorkshire Light Infantry is
housed here. Temporary exhibitions are held.
Times: Open all year, Mon-Sat 10-5, Sun 2-5. Closed Good Fri, 25-26
Dec & 1 Jan. **Facilities:** 🅿 🗄 ♿ (lift, hearing loop in lecture room)
toilets for disabled shop ✖ (ex guide dogs)

MALTBY
Map 08 SK59

ROCHE ABBEY
S66 8NW
➲ (1.5m S off A634)
☎ 01709 812739

Visit the enchanting valley designed by 'Capability' Brown and discover the fascinating ruins of Roche Abbey, founded in 1147 by the Cistercians.
Times: Open Apr-Jul, Thu-Mon, 10-5; Aug, daily, 10-5; Sep, Thu-Mon, 10-5. **Fee:** £2.90 (ch £1.50, concessions £2.20). Opening times and prices are subject to change, for further details please phone 0870 333 1181 **Facilities:** 🅿 ㊅ shop ♯

ROTHERHAM
Map 08 SK49

MAGNA SCIENCE ADVENTURE CENTRE
Sheffield Rd, Templeborough S60 1DX
➲ (M1 junct 33/34, follow Templeborough sign off rdbt, then brown heritage signs)
☎ 01709 720002
e-mail: grodgers@magnatrust.co.uk
web: www.visitmagna.co.uk

2 for 1

Magna is the UK's first Science Adventure Centre, an exciting exploration of Earth, Air, Fire and Water. A chance for visitors to create their own adventure through hands-on interactive challenges. Visit the four Adventure Pavilions, two shows and Sci-Tec outdoor adventure playground and have fun unearthing the mysteries of our world.
Times: Please phone for 2005 details. Closed 24-27 Dec & 1 Jan.
Fee: ✱ £9 (ch & concessions £7). Family ticket (2ad+2ch) £28, (2ad+3ch) £35. **Facilities:** 🅿 ➟ ✕ licensed ㊅ (lifts, portable seating, wheelchair hire) toilets for disabled shop
✈ (ex guide dogs) ◗

SHEFFIELD
Map 08 SK38

KELHAM ISLAND MUSEUM
Alma St S3 8RY
➲ (0.5m NW of city centre, take A61 N to West Bar, follow signs)
☎ 0114 272 2106
e-mail: postmaster@simt.co.uk
web: www.simt.co.uk

The story of Sheffield, its industry and life, with the most powerful working steam engine in Europe, reconstructed workshops, and craftspeople demonstrating traditional 'made in Sheffield' skills - this is a 'living' museum. During the year Kelham Island stages events, displays and temporary exhibitions culminating in the annual Christmas Victorian Market.
Times: ✱ Open Mon-Thu 10-4, Sun 11-4.45. Closed Fri and Sat. Check opening days/times at Xmas & New Year before travelling.
Facilities: 🅿 ➟ ㊅ (wheelchair on request) toilets for disabled shop
✈

MILLENNIUM GALLERIES
Arundel Gate S1 2PP
☎ 0114 278 2600
e-mail: info@sheffieldgalleries.org.uk
web: www.sheffieldgalleries.org.uk

FREE

With four different galleries under one roof, the Millennium Galleries has something for everyone. Enjoy new blockbuster exhibitions drawn from the collections of Britain's national galleries and museums, including the Victoria & Albert Museum and Tate Gallery. See the best of contemporary craft and design in a range of exhibitions by established and up-and-coming makers. Be dazzled by Sheffield's magnificent and internationally important collection of decorative and domestic metalwork and silverware. Discover the Ruskin Gallery with its wonderful array of treasures by Victorian artist and writer John Ruskin.
Times: ✱ Open daily Mon-Sat 10-5, Sun 11-5. **Facilities:** 🅿 ➟ ✕ licensed ㊅ (hearing loop) toilets for disabled shop
✈ (ex guide dogs) ◗

The Temple of the Four Winds, built in 1726 as the summerhouse at Castle Howard

WEST YORKSHIRE

EVENTS & FESTIVALS

March
3rd-18th Bradford Film Festival, National Museum of Photography, Film & Television

April
17th World Coal Carrying Championship, Royal Oak Pub, Owl Lane, Ossett
29th-30th Complementary Medicine Festival, Kings Hall Winter Gardens, Ilkley
30th Unity Festival, Love Music Hate Racism, Millennium Square, Leeds

May
13th-20th Wharfedale Music Festival (100th anniversary), various venues in Ilkley (competitive festival of music, dance, poetry, speech and drama)

June
30th-2nd Jul Cleckheaton Folk Festival, various venues (provisional)
tbc Bradford Festival & Mela, Peel Park

July
23rd Arthington Show, Old Showfield, Pool Bank, Bramhope

August
26th-27th Saddlworth Rushcart Festival, morris dancing, wrestling and gurning
tbc Carling Leeds Festival

October
28th-29th Complementary Medicine Festival, Kings Hall Winter Gardens, Ilkley

November
17th-26th Huddersfield Contemporary Music Festival
tbc Leeds International Film Festival, Town Hall, Leeds (provisional)

Above: Shibden Hall

BRADFORD   Map 07 SE13

BOLLING HALL
Bowling Hall Rd BD4 7LP
➲ (1m from city centre off A650)
☎ 01274 431826   FREE
web: www.bradfordmuseums.org
A classic West Yorkshire manor house, complete with galleried 'housebody' (hall), Bolling Hall dates mainly from the 17th century but has medieval and 18th-century sections. It has panelled rooms, plasterwork in original colours, heraldic glass and a rare Chippendale bed.
Times: Open all year, Wed-Fri 11-4, Sat 10-5, Sun 12-5. Closed Mon ex BH, Good Fri, 25-26 Dec. **Facilities:** 🅿 🗐 ♿ shop
✖ (ex guide dogs)

BRADFORD INDUSTRIAL MUSEUM AND HORSES AT WORK
Moorside Mills, Moorside Rd, Eccleshill BD2 3HP
➲ (off A658)
☎ 01274 435900   FREE
web: www.bradfordmuseums.org
Moorside Mills is an original spinning mill, now part of a museum that brings vividly to life the story of Bradford's woollen industry. There is the machinery that once converted raw wool into cloth, and the mill yard rings with the sound of iron on stone as shire horses pull trams, haul buses and give rides. Daily demonstrations and changing exhibitions.
Times: Open all year, Tue-Sat 10-5, Sun 12-5. Closed Mon ex BH, Good Fri, 25-26 Dec **Facilities:** 🅿 🖭 🗐 ♿ (induction loop in lecture theatre, lift) toilets for disabled shop ✖ (ex guide dogs)

CARTWRIGHT HALL ART GALLERY
Lister Park BD9 4NS
➲ (1m from city centre on A650)
☎ 01274 431212   FREE
e-mail: cartwright.hall@bradford.gov.uk
web: www.bradfordmuseums.org
Built in dramatic Baroque style in 1904, the gallery has permanent collections of 19th and 20th-century British art, contemporary prints, and older works by British and European masters.
Times: Open all year, Tue-Sat 10-5, Sun 1-5. Closed Mon ex BH, Good Fri, 25-26 Dec. **Facilities:** 🅿 ♿ (wheelchair available, lift) toilets for disabled shop ✖ (ex guide dogs)

COLOUR MUSEUM
Perkin House, 1 Providence St BD1 2PW
➲ (from city centre follow signs B6144 (Haworth), then brown heritage signs)
☎ 01274 390955
e-mail: museum@sdc.org.uk
web: www.colour-experience.org
Europe's only Museum of Colour comprises two galleries packed with visitor-operated exhibits demonstrating the effects of light and colour, including optical illusions, and the story of dyeing and textile printing. There is a programme of special exhibitions and events. Please telephone for details.
Times: Open 2 Jan-18 Dec, Tue-Sat, 10-4. **Fee:** ✱ £2 (concessions £1.50). Family ticket £4 **Facilities:** 🅿 (200 yds) 🗐 ♿ (lifts, ramps at door) toilets for disabled shop ✖ (ex guide dogs) ▬

NATIONAL MUSEUM OF PHOTOGRAPHY, FILM & TELEVISION
BD1 1NQ
➲ (2m from end of M606, follow signs for city centre)
☎ 0870 7010200
2 for 1
e-mail: talk.nmpft@nmsi.ac.uk
web: www.nmpft.org.uk
Experience the past, present and future of photography, film and television with amazing interactive displays and spectacular 3D IMAX cinema.
Times: Open all year, Tue-Sun, BHs & main school hols 10-6. Closed Mon. **Fee:** ✱ Admission to permanent galleries free, IMAX Cinema £6.50 (concessions £4.30). Groups 20% discount.
Facilities: P (adjacent) 🍴 ✗ licensed 🛍 ⅇ (tailored tours,Braille signs,induction loop,cinema seating) toilets for disabled shop ✖ (ex guide dogs) ⬛

BRAMHAM   Map 08 SE44
BRAMHAM PARK
LS23 6ND
➲ (on A1, 4m S of Wetherby, take Bramham/Thorner slip road and follow signs)
☎ 01937 846000
e-mail: enquiries@bramhampark.co.uk
web: www.bramhampark.co.uk
This fine Queen Anne house was built by Robert Benson and is the home of his descendants. The garden has ornamental ponds, cascades, temples and avenues.
Times: ✱ Open Apr-Sep, daily 11.30-4.30. Closed 7-14 Jun & 16 Aug-4 Sep **Facilities:** P ⅇ toilets for disabled

GOMERSAL   Map 08 SE22
RED HOUSE
Oxford Rd BD19 4JP
➲ (M62 junct 26, take A58 towards Leeds then right onto A651 towards Gomersal. Red House is on right hand side)
☎ 01274 335100
FREE
web: www.kirkleesmc.gov.uk/community/museums.museum.shtml
Delightful redbrick house displayed as the 1830s home of a Yorkshire wool clothier and merchant. The house and family was frequently visited by Charlotte Brontë in the 1830s and featured in her novel *Shirley*. The gardens have been reconstructed in the style of the period and there are exhibitions on the Brontë connection and local history in restored barn and cartsheds.
Times: ✱ Open all year, Mon-Fri 11-5, Sat-Sun 12-5. Telephone for Xmas opening. Closed Good Fri & 1 Jan. **Facilities:** P 🛍 ⅇ (Braille & T-setting hearing aid available) toilets for disabled shop ✖ (ex guide dogs) ⬛

HALIFAX   Map 07 SE02
BANKFIELD MUSEUM
Boothtown Rd, Akroyd Park HX3 6HG
➲ (on A647 Bradford via Queensbury road, 0.5m from Halifax town centre)
☎ 01422 354823 & 352334
FREE
e-mail: bankfield-museum@calderdale.gov.uk
web: www.calderdale.gov.uk
Built by Edward Akroyd in the 1860s, this Renaissance-style building is set in parkland on a hill overlooking the town. It
continued

has an outstanding collection of costumes and textiles from many periods and parts of the world, including a new gallery featuring East European textiles. There is also a section on toys, and the museum of the Duke of Wellington's Regiment is housed here. Temporary exhibitions are held and there is a lively programme of events, workshops and activities. Please ring for details.
Times: Open all year, Tue-Sat 10-5, Sun 1-4, BH Mon 10-5.
Facilities: P 🛍 ⅇ (audio guide & tactile objects) toilets for disabled shop ✖ (ex guide dogs) ⬛

EUREKA! THE MUSEUM FOR CHILDREN
Discovery Rd HX1 2NE
➲ (M62 junct 24 follow brown heritage signs to Halifax centre - A629)
☎ 01422 330069
2 for 1
e-mail: info@eureka.org.uk
web: www.eureka.org.uk

With over 400 'must touch' exhibits, interactive activities and challenges, visitors are invited to embark upon a journey of discovery through four main gallery spaces: Me and My Body, Living and Working Together, Our Global Garden and SoundSpace, an interactive music gallery inviting children to explore the science behind sound, rhythm and technology. They can find out how their bodies and senses work, discover the realities of daily life, travel from the familiar 'backyard' to amazing and faraway places and experiment with creating their own sounds and music. Now with two new galleries designed especially for children under five: Sound Garden and Desert Discovery, which provide babies and small children with an introduction to the natural world. A brand new outdoor Maze of Illusions is due to open in 2005.
Times: Open all year, daily 10-5. Closed 24-26 Dec **Fee:** £6.50 (ch under 3 £1.95, ch under 1 free) Family Saver ticket admits 5 £27.50
Facilities: P (charged) 🍴 ⅇ (lift, staff trained in basic sign language, large print) toilets for disabled shop ✖ (ex guide dogs) ⬛

PIECE HALL
HX1 1RE
➲ (follow brown tourist signs, close to railway station)
☎ 01422 358087
FREE
e-mail: karen.belshaw@calderdale.gov.uk
web: www.calderdale.gov.uk
The merchants of Halifax built the elegant and unique hall in 1779, and it has over 300 merchant's rooms around a courtyard, now housing an industrial museum, art galleries and shops selling antiques, books etc. There is an open
continued

market on Friday and Saturday, and a flea market on Thursday. There is a lively programme of exhibitions, workshops, activities and events throughout the year, and a festival in the summer, please ring for details.
Times: ✱ Open all year daily. Closed 25-26 Dec. Art Gallery, Tue-Sun & BH Mon 10-5. **Facilities:** P (50 yds) ⬛ 🍴 ♿ (lifts, shopmobility on site & audio guide available) toilets for disabled shop ▬

SHIBDEN HALL
Lister's Rd HX3 6XG
➲ (2km E of Halifax on A58)
☎ 01422 352246 & 321455
e-mail: shibden.hall@calderdale.gov.uk
web: www.calderdale.gov.uk
The house dates back to the early 15th century, and its rooms have been laid out to illustrate life in different periods of its history. Craft weekends, featuring over 30 craftworkers demonstrating historic skills, are held, and there's a lively programme of craft events, workshops and family activities. Please apply for details.
Times: ✱ Open Mar-Nov, Mon-Sat 10-5, Sun 12-5. Dec-Feb, Mon-Sat 10-4, Sun 12-4. **Facilities:** P ⬛ 🍴 ♿ (garden only partially accessible) toilets for disabled shop ✖ (ex guide dogs) ▬

HAREWOOD   Map 08 SE34
HAREWOOD HOUSE & BIRD GARDEN
LS17 9LQ
➲ (junct A61/A659 Leeds to Harrogate road)
☎ 0113 218 1010
e-mail: business@harewood.org
web: www.harewood.org
Designed in 1759 by John Carr, Harewood House is the home of the Queen's cousin, the Earl of Harewood. His mother, HRH Princess Mary, Princess Royal lived at Harewood for 35 years and much of her memorabilia is still displayed. The House, renowned for its stunning architecture and exquisite Adam interiors, contains a rich collection of Chippendale furniture, fine porcelain and outstanding art collections from Italian Renaissance masterpieces and Turner watercolours to contemporary works. The old kitchen contains the best collection of noble household copperware in the country giving visitors a glimpse into below stairs life. The grounds include a restored parterre terrace, oriental rock garden, walled garden, lakeside and woodland walks, a bird garden and for youngsters, an adventure playground.
Times: Open 4 Feb-mid Nov, (grounds until mid Dec), Grounds (inc Bird Gardens) daily from 10, House from 11. **Facilities:** P ⬛ ✖ licensed 🍴 ♿ (electric ramp, lift, free audio tour) toilets for disabled shop ✖ (ex guide dogs or in gardens) ▬

HAWORTH   Map 07 SE03
BRONTË PARSONAGE MUSEUM
BD22 8DR
➲ (A629 & A6033 follow signs for Haworth, take Rawdon Rd, pass 2 car parks, next left, then right)
☎ 01535 642323   2 for 1
e-mail: bronte@bronte.org.uk
web: www.bronte.info
Haworth Parsonage was the lifelong family home of the Brontës. An intensely close-knit family, the Brontës saw the parsonage as the heart of their world and the moorland setting provided them with inspiration for their writing. The house contains much personal memorabilia, including the furniture Charlotte bought with the proceeds of her literary
continued

success, Branwell's portraits of local worthies, Emily's writing desk and Anne's books and drawings.
Times: Open Apr-Sep, daily 10-5.30; Oct-Mar daily 11-5 (final admission 30 min before closing). Closed 24-27 Dec & 3-31 Jan.
Fee: ✱ £4.90 (ch 5-16 £1.60, concessions £3.60). Family ticket £10.50.
Facilities: P (charged) 🍴 ♿ (Information in large type & Braille) shop ✖ (ex guide dogs) ▬

KEIGHLEY & WORTH VALLEY RAILWAY & MUSEUM
Keighley BD22 8NJ
➲ (1m from Keighley on A629 Halifax road, follow brown signs)
☎ 01535 645214 & 677777
e-mail: admin@kwvr.co.uk
web: www.kwvr.co.uk
The line was built mainly to serve the valley's mills, and passes through the heart of Brontë country. Beginning at Keighley (shared with Network Rail), it climbs up to Haworth, and terminates at Oxenhope, which has a storage and restoration building. At Haworth there are locomotive workshops and at Ingrow West, an award-winning museum.
Times: open every wknd, please phone for other times. **Fee:** ✱ All day fares: Family Day Rover £25, Adult Day Rover £12 (ch 5-16 £6 under 5's free, pen concessionary). Single and day returns, group rates available, phone for details. **Facilities:** P (charged) ⬛ ♿ (level access to all sites,ramps on trains and stations) toilets for disabled shop ▬

HUDDERSFIELD   Map 07 SE11
TOLSON MEMORIAL MUSEUM
Ravensknowle Park, Wakefield Rd HD5 8DJ
➲ (on A629, 1m from town centre)
☎ 01484 223830   FREE
e-mail: tolson.museum@kirkdees.gov.uk
web: tolson.museum.co.uk
Displays on the development of the cloth industry and a collection of horse-drawn vehicles, together with natural history, archaeology, toys and folk exhibits. There is a full programme of events and temporary exhibitions.
Times: Open all year. Mon-Fri 11-5, Sat & Sun noon-5. Closed Xmas.
Facilities: P ♿ (mini-com, partial stairlift, induction loop, parking) toilets for disabled shop ✖ (ex registered assist dogs) ▬

ILKLEY   Map 07 SE14
MANOR HOUSE GALLERY & MUSEUM
Castle Yard, Church St LS29 9DT
➲ (behind Ilkley Parish Church, on A65)
☎ 01943 600066   FREE
web: www.bradfordmuseums.org
This Elizabethan manor house, one of Ilkley's few buildings to pre-date the 19th century, was built on the site of a Roman fort. Part of the Roman wall can be seen, together with Roman objects and displays on archaeology. There is a collection of 17th and 18th-century farmhouse parlour and kitchen furniture, and the art gallery exhibits works by contemporary artists and craftspeople.
Times: Open all year, Tue-Sat 1-5, Sun 1-4. Open BH Mon. Closed Good Fri, 25-28 Dec. **Facilities:** P (5mins) ♿ shop ✖ (ex guide dogs)

KEIGHLEY Map 07 SE04

CLIFFE CASTLE MUSEUM & GALLERY
Spring Gardens Ln BD20 6LH
➪ (NW of town off A629)
☎ 01535 618231
FREE
web: www.bradfordmuseums.org
Built as a millionaires mansion, the house displays Victorian interiors, together with collections of local and natural history, ceramics, dolls, geological items and minerals. The grounds have a play area and an aviary. Temporary Exhibitions throughout the year.
Times: Open all year, Tue-Sat 10-5, Sun 12-5. Open BH Mon. Closed Good Fri & 25-28 Dec. **Facilities:** 🅿 💷 🔟 ᕼ toilets for disabled shop garden centre ✖ (ex guide dogs)

EAST RIDDLESDEN HALL
Bradford Rd BD20 5EL
➪ (1m NE of Keighley on S side of Bradford Rd)
☎ 01535 607075
e-mail: eastriddlesden@nationaltrust.org.uk
web: www.nationaltrust.org.uk
The interior of this 17th century manor house is furnished with textiles, Yorkshire oak and pewter, together with fine examples of 17th century embroidery. The honeysuckle and rose covered façade ruin of the Starke Wing, provides the backdrop to the garden. Wild flowers, perennials, and a fragrant herb border provide a transition of colour throughout the year.
Times: Open mid Mar-late Oct daily (ex Mon, Thu & Fri). Open Good Fri, BH Mons and Mons in Jul & Aug 12-5, Sat 1-5 **Fee:** ✱ £4 (ch £2). Family ticket £10. **Facilities:** 🅿 💷 🔟 ᕼ Braille and large print guides, sensory photo album shop ✖ 🍴

LEEDS Map 08 SE33

ABBEY HOUSE MUSEUM
Abbey Walk, Abbey Rd, Kirkstall LS5 3EH
➪ (3m W of city centre on A65)
☎ 0113 230 5492
e-mail: abbey.house@leeds.gov.uk
web: www.leeds.gov.uk
Displays at this museum include an interactive childhood gallery, a look at Kirkstall Abbey, and an exploration of life in Victorian Leeds. Three reconstructed streets allow the visitor to immerse themselves in the sights and sounds of the late 19th century, from the glamourous art furnishers shop to the impoverished widow washerwoman.
Times: Open all year Tue-Fri 10-5, Sat noon-5, Sun 10-5. Closed Mon ex BH Mon (open 10-5) **Fee:** £3.50 (ch £1.50 accompanied by an adult, concessions £2.50). Family ticket £5 **Facilities:** 🅿 💷 ✖ licensed ᕼ (Braille plaques on wall, tactile tours by request) toilets for disabled shop ✖ (ex guide dogs) 🍴

KIRKSTALL ABBEY
Abbey Rd, Kirkstall LS5 3EH
➪ (off A65, W of city centre)
☎ 0113 230 5492
e-mail: abbey.house@leeds.gov.uk
FREE
web: www.leeds.gov.uk
The most complete 12th-century Cistercian Abbey in the country stands on the banks of the River Aire. Many of the original buildings can still be seen, including the cloister, church and refectory. Regular tours take visitors to areas not normally accessible to the public. During the summer the Abbey hosts plays, fairs and musical events.
Times: ✱ Open all year. Abbey site open dawn to dusk.
Facilities: 🅿 ᕼ toilets for disabled shop

LEEDS CITY ART GALLERY
The Headrow LS1 3AA
➪ (in city centre, next to town hall and library)
☎ 0113 247 8248
FREE
e-mail: city.art.gallery@leeds.gov.uk
web: www.leeds.gov.uk/artgallery
Home to one of the best collections of 20th-century British art outside London, as well as Victorian and late 19th-century pictures, an outstanding collection of English watercolours, a display of modern sculpture and temporary exhibitions focusing on contemporary art. The gallery holds an active events programme with talks, demonstrations and workshops regularly planned.
Times: Open all year, Mon-Sat 10-5, Wed until 8, Sun 1-5. Closed BHs. **Facilities:** 🅿 street parking 💷 ✖ licensed 🔟 ᕼ (restricted access to upper floor, access ramp) toilets for disabled shop ✖ (ex guide dogs)

LEEDS INDUSTRIAL MUSEUM AT ARMLEY MILLS
Canal Rd, Armley LS12 2QF
➪ (2m W of city centre, off A65)
☎ 0113 263 7861
web: www.leeds.gov.uk
Once the world's largest woollen mill, Armley Mills evokes memories of the 18th-century woollen industry, showing the progress of wool from the sheep to knitted clothing. The museum has its own 1930s cinema illustrating the history of cinema projection, including the first moving pictures taken in Leeds. There are demonstrations of static engines and steam locomotives, a printing gallery and a journey through the working world of textiles and fashion.
Times: ✱ Open all year, Tue-Sat 10-5, Sun 1-5. (Last entry 1 hr before closing). Closed Mon ex BHs. **Facilities:** 🅿 ᕼ (chair-lifts between floors) toilets for disabled shop ✖ 🍴

MIDDLETON RAILWAY
Moor Rd, Hunslet LS10 2JQ
➪ (M621 junct 5 or follow signs from A61)
☎ 0113 271 0320 (ansaphone)
e-mail: info@middletonrailway.org.uk
web: www.middletonrailway.org.uk
This was the first railway authorised by an Act of Parliament (in 1758) and the first to succeed with steam locomotives (in 1812). Steam trains run each weekend in season from Tunstall Road roundabout to Middleton Park. There is a programme of special events. Undergoing some reconstruction but should re-open for 2006.
Times: ✱ Moor Road Station open for viewing every wknd. Trains run Apr-Dec, Sat-Sun & BH **Facilities:** 🅿 💷 🔟 ᕼ (ramped access to all areas) toilets for disabled shop 🍴

ROYAL ARMOURIES MUSEUM
Armouries Dr LS10 1LT
➪ (off A61 close to Leeds centre, follow brown heritage signs)
☎ 0113 220 1999 & 0990 106 666
FREE
e-mail: enquiries@armouries.org.uk
web: www.royalarmouries.org
The museum is an impressive contemporary home for the renowned national collection of arms and armour. The collection is divided between five galleries: War, Tournament, Self-Defence, Hunting and Oriental. The Hall of Steel features a 100ft-high mass of 3000 pieces of arms and armour. Visitors are encouraged to take part in and handle
continued

some of the collections. Live demonstrations and interpretations take place throughout the year.
Times: Open daily, from 10-5. Closed 24-25 Dec
Facilities: 🄿 (charged) 💻 ✕ licensed 🍴 ♿ (induction loops, wheelchairs, signers, low level counter) toilets for disabled shop 🐕 (ex guide & hearing dogs) 🍴

TEMPLE NEWSAM HOUSE & PARK
LS15 0AE
➲ (off A63)
☎ 0113 264 7321 (House) & 264 5535 (Park)
web: www.leeds.gov.uk

This Tudor and Jacobean mansion boasts extensive collections of decorative arts in their original room settings, including an incomparable Chippendale collection. Set in 1500 acres of parkland (landscaped by 'Capability' Brown), there is a Rare Breeds Centre, and the gardens have a magnificent display of rhododendrons. Free audio guides tour you around the house and tell you more about the people who lived there. On special days, visitors can join in with the laundry maids washing at the dolly tub, watch the blacksmith hammer out shoes and see logs cut at the saw-mill.
Times: ✱ Open all year. House: Tue-Sat 10-5, Sun 1-5; Nov-28 Dec & Mar, Tue-Sat 10-4, Sun 12-5. Open Bank Hols. Home Farm: Tue-Sun, 10-4 (3 in winter); Gardens: 10-dusk. Estate: daily, dawn-dusk. Closed Jan-Feb re-opens 28 Feb. **Facilities:** 🄿 (charged) 💻 ♿ (ramps for full access to parkland, electric wheelchairs) toilets for disabled shop 🐕 (ex guide dogs) 🍴

THACKRAY MUSEUM
Beckett St LS9 7LN
➲ (M1 junct 43, onto M621 junct 4. Follow signs for York & St James Hospital, then brown tourist signs)
☎ 0113 244 4343
e-mail: info@thackraymuseum.org
web: www.thackraymuseum.org

`2 for 1`

Housed in a large Victorian building, next to the famous St James's Hospital, the Thackray Museum offers a unique hands-on experience. A cow from Gloucester, green mould and smelly toilets - all these things have helped transform our lives. Find out how by walking back in time and exploring the sights, sounds and smells of Victorian slum life. Also the interactive Bodyworks Gallery offers the chance to explore the workings of the human body. Special Events:
continued

Body Parts: New for Old Exhibition until Dec 2006, How do you look? Exhibition 10th Dec 2005-Jun 2006.
Times: Open all year, daily 10-5. Closed 24-26 & 31 Dec & 1 Jan
Fee: ✱ £5.50 (ch 4-16 £4, pen, students & unemployed £4.50). Family ticket (2ad+3ch) £18. Group rates available. **Facilities:** 🄿 (charged) 💻 ♿ (wheelchairs, induction loop, texts) toilets for disabled shop 🐕 (ex guide dogs) 🍴

TROPICAL WORLD
Canal Gardens, Roundhay Park LS8 2ER
➲ (3m N of city centre off A58 at Oakwood)
☎ 0113 266 1850
web: www.leeds.gov.uk

The atmosphere of the tropics is recreated here as visitors walk on the beach among exotic trees. A waterfall cascades into a rock-pool and other pools contain terrapins and carp. There are reptiles, insects and more than 30 species of butterfly. Feel the dry heat of the desert and the darkness of the nocturnal zone, and watch out for the piranhas and other exotic fish in the depths of the aquarium.
Times: Open Winter (GMT), daily 10-4 (last admission 3.30); Summer (BST), 10-6 (last admission 5.30) **Fee:** ✱ £3 (ch 8-15 £2, under 8's & Leeds card holders free) **Facilities:** 🄿 💻 ♿ toilets for disabled shop 🐕 (ex guide dogs) 🍴

LOTHERTON HALL   Map 08 SE43
LOTHERTON HALL
Aberford LS25 3EB
➲ (off the A1, 0.75m E of junct with B1217)
☎ 0113 281 3259
web: www.leeds.gov.uk

Built in Edwardian times, the museum contains furniture, pictures, silver and ceramics from the Gascoigne collection, and works of art on loan from Leeds galleries. Outside, the Edwardian garden, bird garden and deer park are delightful places in which to stroll.
Times: ✱ Open Tue-Sat 10-5. Sun 1-5. BHs. Nov-Dec & Mar Tue-Sat 10-4, Sun 12-4. **Facilities:** 🄿 (charged) 💻 ✕ licensed ♿ shop 🐕 (ex in park) 🍴

MIDDLESTOWN   Map 08 SE21
NATIONAL COAL MINING MUSEUM FOR ENGLAND
Caphouse Colliery, New Rd WF4 4RH
➲ (on A642 between Wakefield & Huddersfield)
☎ 01924 848806
e-mail: info@ncm.org.uk `FREE`
web: www.ncm.org.uk

A unique opportunity to go 140 metres underground down one of Britain's oldest working mines. Take a step back in time with one of the museum's experienced local miners who will guide parties around the underground workings, where models and machinery depict methods and conditions of mining from the early 1800s to present day. Other attractions include the Hope Pit, pithead baths, Victorian steam winder, nature trail and adventure playground and meet the last ever working pit ponies. You are strongly advised to wear sensible footwear and warm clothing.
Times: Open all year, daily 10-5. Closed 24-26 Dec & 1 Jan.
Facilities: 🄿 💻 ✕ licensed 🍴 ♿ (nature trail not accessible) 2 w'chairs for underground toilets for disabled shop 🐕 (ex guide dogs) 🍴

NOSTELL PRIORY — Map 08 SE41

NOSTELL PRIORY
Doncaster Rd WF4 1QE
➲ (5m SE of Wakefield towards Doncaster, on A638)
☎ 01924 863892
e-mail: nostellpriory@nationaltrust.org.uk
web: www.nationaltrust.org.uk/nostellpriory/

Built by James Paine in the middle of the 18th century, the priory has an additional wing built by Robert Adam in 1766. It contains a notable saloon and tapestry room, and displays pictures and Chippendale furniture. There are lakeside walks within the grounds with rhododendrons and azaleas in bloom in late spring.

Times: Mid Mar-early Nov, Wed-Sun 1-5, Grounds 11-6.
Fee: ✱ House & Grounds £6 (ch £3). Family ticket £15. Gardens only £3.50 (ch £1.50). **Facilities:** P 🅿 📖 ⓺ & (lift, Braille guide/tactile books, wheelchair) toilets for disabled shop ⚄

OAKWELL HALL — Map 08 SE22

OAKWELL HALL
Nutter Ln, Birstall WF17 9LG
➲ (6m SE of Bradford, off M62 junct 26/27, follow brown heritage signs, turn off A652 onto Nutter Lane)
☎ 01924 326240   `2 for 1`
e-mail: oakwell.hall@kirklees.gov.uk
web: www.oakwellhallcountrypark.co.uk

A moated Elizabethan manor house, furnished as it might have looked in the 1690s. Extensive 110-acre country park with visitor information centre, period gardens, nature trails, arboretum and children's adventure playground.

Times: Open all year, daily Mon-Fri 11-5; Sat & Sun 12-5. Closed Good Fri & 24 Dec-1 Jan. **Fee:** Hall £1.50 (ch & wheelchair users 60p). Family ticket £3.30. Charges Mar-Oct. Free admission Nov-Feb. Vistor centre and park free all year. **Facilities:** P 🅿 ⓺ & (large print & Braille guide, induction loops) toilets for disabled shop ✂ (park only ex guide dogs) 🍴

WAKEFIELD — Map 08 SE32

WAKEFIELD ART GALLERY
Wentworth Ter WF1 3QW
➲ (N of city centre by Wakefield College and Clayton Hospital)   `FREE`
☎ 01924 305796
e-mail: museumsandarts@wakefield.gov.uk
web: www.wakefeild.gov.uk/cultureandleisure

Wakefield was home to two of Britain's greatest modern sculptors - Barbara Hepworth and Henry Moore. The art gallery, which has an important collection of 20th-century paintings and sculptures, has a special room devoted to these two local artists. There are frequent temporary exhibitions of both modern and earlier works.

Times: Open all year, Tue-Sat 10.30-4.30, Sun 2-4.30.
Facilities: P (on street) (on street parking restricted to 2hrs) & shop ✂ (ex guide dogs)

WEST BRETTON — Map 08 SE21

YORKSHIRE SCULPTURE PARK
WF4 4LG
➲ (M1 junct 38, follow brown heritage signs to A637. Left at rdbt, attraction signed)
☎ 01924 832631
e-mail: info@ysp.co.uk
web: www.ysp.co.uk

Set in the beautiful grounds and gardens of a 500 acre, 18th-century country estate, Yorkshire Sculpture Park is one of the world's leading open-air galleries and presents a changing programme of international sculpture exhibitions. The landscape provides a variety of magnificent scenic vistas of the valley, lakes, estate buildings and bridges. By organising a number of temporary exhibitions each year, the park ensures that there is always something new to see. The Visitor Centre provides all-weather facilities including a large restaurant, shop, coffee bar, audio-visual auditorium and meeting rooms. The Underground Gallery with links a 50 metre concourse to light-filled galleries.

Times: Open all year 10-6 (summer) 10-4 (winter). Please phone for details of Xmas closures **Fee:** Prices not confirmed for 2006
Facilities: P (charged) 🅿 ✂ licensed ⓺ & (free scooters, parking, trail accessible for wheelchairs) toilets for disabled shop ✂ (ex assist dogs)

HRH Queen Elizabeth II.

The British monarch was born in April 1926, and the year of her 80th birthday will see many national celebrations, as well as those that are to be staged in London.

GUERNSEY

EVENTS & FESTIVALS

April
15th-23rd Floral Guernsey Spring Festival
Week, events and open gardens

May
9th Liberation Day Celebrations, St Peter Port

June
3rd-11th Floral Guernsey Summer Festival
Week, featuring Floral Guernsey Show
(provisional)
8th-10th Floral Guernsey Show, Saumarez
Park (provisional)
18th Healthspan Half Marathon, Pleinmont to
Bulwer Avenue

July
3rd Le Viaer Marchi (the Old Market),
traditional arts, crafts, dance and music,
Saumarez Park

August
16th-17th West Show, agricultural show
(provisional)
23rd-24th North Show, agricultural show &
Battle of Flowers (provisional)

September
29th-30th Guernsey Jazz Festival, Duke of
Richmond Hotel, St Peter Port (provisional)

October
tbc Guernsey Lily International Amateur Film
Festival & Video Festival, La Villette Hotel,
St Martins

*Above: The 'Cup and Saucer', a 19th-century
Martello tower, and housing the Fort Grey Maritime
Museum*

FOREST   Map 16

GERMAN OCCUPATION MUSEUM
GY8 0BG
➲ (Behind Forest Church near the airport)
☎ 01481 238205
The museum has the Channel Islands' largest collection of
Occupation items, with tableaux of a kitchen, bunker rooms
and a street during the Occupation. Liberation Day 9th May
will be celebrated with special events and exhibitions.
Times: Open Apr-Oct 10-5, Nov-Mar 10-1 (Closed Mon). **Fee:** £3.75
(ch £2). **Facilities:** 🅿 🖳 ⅊ (ramps & handrails) ✈ (ex assist dogs)

ROCQUAINE BAY   Map 16

FORT GREY AND SHIPWRECK MUSEUM
GY7 9BY
➲ (on coast road at Rocquaine Bay)
☎ 01481 265036   **2 for 1**
e-mail: admin@museums.gov.gg
web: www.museum.guernsey.net
The fort is a Martello tower, built in 1804, as part of the
Channel Islands' extensive defences. It is nicknamed the 'cup
and saucer' because of its appearance, and houses a
museum devoted to ships wrecked on the treacherous
Hanois reefs nearby.
Times: Open Etr-Oct, 10-5 **Fee:** ✱ Fort Grey, £2.50 (pen £1.25),
3 Venue Ticket £9 (pen £5) **Facilities:** 🅿 (opposite fort) 🛍 shop
✈ (ex guide dogs) ◀

ST ANDREW   Map 16

**GERMAN MILITARY UNDERGROUND HOSPITAL
& AMMUNITION STORE**
La Vassalerie GY6 8XR
➲ (St Andrews Parish, centre of island)
☎ 01481 239100
The largest structure created during the German Occupation
of the Channel Islands, a concrete maze of about 75,000 sq.
ft, which took slave workers three-and-a-half years to
complete, at the cost of many lives. Most of the equipment
has been removed, but the central heating plant, hospital
beds and cooking facilities can still be seen.
Times: ✱ Open Jul-Aug, daily 10-noon & 2-4.30; May-Jun & Sep, daily
10-noon & 2-4; Apr & Oct, daily 2-4; Mar & Nov, Sun & Thu 2-3.
Facilities: 🅿 🛍 ⅊ shop

**Isambard Kingdom
Brunel (1806-1859).**
2006 is the 200th
anniversary of the birth of
one of Britain's most
important engineers. His
bicentenary will be
celebrated by many
attractions both directly
and indirectly connected
with Brunel.

ST MARTIN   Map 16

SAUSMAREZ MANOR
Sausmarez Rd GY4 6SG
➲ (halfway between airport & St Peter Port)
☎ 01481 235571
2 for 1
e-mail: sausmarezmanor@cwgsy
web: www.sausmarezmanor@cwgsy.net

The Manor has been owned and lived in by the same family for centuries. The style of each room is different, with collections of Oriental, French and English furniture and paintings. Outside the Formal Garden has herbaceous borders, and the Woodland Garden, set around two small lakes and a stream, is planted with colourful shrubs, bulbs and wild flowers from the subtropics. Also on view, a sculpture park which is now the most comprehensive in Britain.
Times: Open Etr-Oct 10.30 & 11.30, Mon-Thu; Jun-Aug 10.30, 11.30 & 2 Mon-Thu; or by appointment. **Fee:** ✱ House £5.90 (ch £2, pen £4.50). Woodland Garden £4 (accompanied ch & pen £3, disabled free). Dolls House Collection £2.50 (ch £1.50, stu & pen £2). Family ticket £7. Sculpture Park £4 (accompanied ch & pen £3, disabled free).
Facilities: 🅿 ➍ 🗊 ♿ (free admission, partial access to garden, wheelchair loan) shop (Specialises in dolls houses etc) ✈ (ex dogs for blind and deaf)

> ## Directions are provided by the attractions.

ST PETER PORT   Map 16

CASTLE CORNET
GY1 1AU 5 mins walk from St Peter Port bus terminus.
☎ 01481 721657
2 for 1
e-mail: admin@museums.gov.gg
web: www.museum.guernsey.net
The history of this magnificent castle spans eight centuries and its buildings now house several museums, the Refectory Cafe and a shop. Soldiers fire the noonday gun in a daily ceremony. Look for the Maritime Museum that charts Guernsey's nautical history, the 'Story of Castle Cornet' with its mystery skeleton, and special exhibitions in the Royal Guernsey Militia Museum and the 201 squadron RAF Museum.
Times: Open Mar-end Oct, daily 10-5. **Fee:** ✱ £6 (pen £4). 3 venue ticket £9 (pen £5) **Facilities:** 🅿 (100 yds) ➍ 🗊 shop ✈ (ex guide dogs) ➍

GUERNSEY MUSEUM & ART GALLERY
Candie Gardens GY1 1UG
➲ (On the outskirts of St Peter Port set in the Victorian 'Candie gardens')
☎ 01481 726518
2 for 1
e-mail: admin@museums.gov.gg
web: www.museum.guernsey.net
The museum, designed around a Victorian bandstand, tells the story of Guernsey and its people. There is an audio-visual theatre and an art gallery, and special exhibitions are arranged throughout the year. It is surrounded by beautiful gardens with superb views over St Peter Port harbour.
Times: Open Feb-Dec daily 10-5 (Winter 10-4) **Fee:** ✱ £3.50 (pen £2.50). 3 venue ticket £9 (pen £5) **Facilities:** 🅿 (outside museum) (2hr & 5hr) ➍ 🗊 ♿ toilets for disabled shop ✈ (ex guide dogs) ➍

VALE   Map 16

ROUSSE TOWER
Rousse Tower Headland
➲ (on Island's W coast, signed)
☎ 01481 726518 & 726965
FREE
e-mail: p.sarl@museums.gov.gg
web: www.museum.guernsey.net
One of the original fifteen towers built in 1778-9 in prime defensive positions around the coast of Guernsey. They were designed primarily to prevent the landing of troops on nearby beaches. Musket fire could be directed on invading forces through the loopholes. An interpretation centre displays replica guns.
Times: Open Apr-Oct 9-dusk, Nov-Mar Wed, Sat & Sun 9-4.
Facilities: 🅿 ✈ (ex guide dogs)

JERSEY

EVENTS & FESTIVALS

April
1st-2nd Spring Flower Show, Royal Jersey
  Horticultural Society, Royal Jersey
  Showground, La Route de la Trinite, Trinity
1st-23rd Colours of Spring, activities, arts and
  crafts, food fairs and flower shows around
  the island

May
9th Liberation Day,
  various activities & events
13th-20th Spring Walking Week, guided walks
  exploring Jersey's heritage and natural
  beauty
26th Jersey Air Rally, private aircraft from
  Europe and beyond

June
3rd Gorey Fete de la Mer, seafood and
  entertainment, Gorey Pier
17th-9th Jul Midsummer Jersey, history,
  heritage, gardens, walks, food fairs, music
  and film
24th Itex Walk, 48.1-mile walk raising money
  for Jersey charities

July
8th-9th West Show, country show in the
  parish of St Peter

August
10th-11th Jersey Battle of Flowers, a
  spectacular carnival
19th-20th Summer Flower Show, Royal Jersey
  Horticultural Society, Royal Jersey
  Showground, La Route de la Trinite, Trinity

September
16th-24th Autumn Walking Week, guided
  countryside, coastal and history walks

October
6th-8th Autumn Fruit & Flower Festival, Royal
  Jersey Showground, La Route de la Trinite,
  Trinity

November
25th-10th Dec Fête dé Noué (Christmas
  festival), various activities and events

Above: La Rocco Tower, St Ouen's Bay

GOREY   Map 16
MONT ORGUEIL CASTLE
JE3 6ET
➲ (A3 or coast road to Gorey)
☎ 01534 853292
e-mail: marketing@jerseyheritagetrust.org
web: www.jerseyheritagetrust.org

Standing on a rocky headland, on a site which has been
fortified since the Iron Age, this is one of the best-preserved
examples in Europe of a medieval concentric castle, and
dates from the 12th and 13th centuries.
Times: Closed until Apr 2006 - please phone for details. **Fee:** ✱ £5.25
(ch 10-16, pen & students £4.40, ch under 6 free). Family and discount
tickets **Facilities:** P (200yds) shop ✶ (ex guide dogs) ▰

LA GREVE DE LECQ   Map 16
GREVE DE LECQ BARRACKS
➲ (on right hand side of valley, overlooking
beach)   FREE
☎ 01534 483193 482238
e-mail: enquiries@nationaltrustjersey.org.je
web: www.nationaltrustjersey.org.je

Originally serving as an outpost of the British Empire, these
barracks, built in 1810, were used for civilian housing from
the end of WWI to 1972, when they were bought by the
National Trust and made into a museum that depicts the life
of soldiers who were stationed here in the 19th century. Also
includes a collection of old horse-drawn carriages. 2006 is
the 70th anniversary of the founding of the National Trust for
Jersey. Special Event: Heritage Open Day 9 Sep 2006.
Times: Open early May-late Sep, Tue-Sat 11-5 & Sun 2-5. (Closed
Mon). **Facilities:** P & (wheelchair ramps) toilets for disabled shop
✶ (ex guide dogs) ▰

GROUVILLE   Map 16
LA HOUGUE BIE
JE2 7UA
➲ (A6 or A7 to Five Oaks, at mini-rdbt take B28 to
site)
☎ 01534 853823
e-mail: marketing@jerseyheritagetrust.org
web: www.jerseyheritagetrust.org

This Neolithic burial mound stands 40ft high, and covers a
stone-built passage grave that is still intact and may be
entered. The passage is 50ft long, and built of huge stones,
the mound is made from earth, rubble and limpet shells. On
top of the mound are two medieval chapels, one of which
has a replica of the Holy Sepulchre in Jerusalem below. Also
on the site is an underground bunker built by the Germans
as a communications centre, now a memorial to the slave
workers of the Occupation.
Times: Open end Mar-end Oct, daily 10-5. **Fee:** ✱ £5.25 (ch under 6
free, student & concessions £4.40). Discount & family tickets.
Facilities: P & shop ✶ (ex guide dogs) ▰

ST BRELADE   Map 16

JERSEY LAVENDER FARM
Rue du Pont Marquet JE3 8DS
➲ (on B25 from St Aubin's Bay to Redhouses)
☎ 01534 742933
e-mail: admin@jerseylavender.co.uk
web: www.jerseylavender.co.uk

2 for 1

Jersey Lavender grows nine acres of lavender, distils out the essential oil and creates a range of fine toiletry products. Visitors are able to see the whole process from cultivating, through to harvesting, distillation and the production of the final product. There is a national collection of lavenders, extensive gardens, herb beds and walks among the lavender fields. There are also other herbs that are grown and distilled, namely eucalyptus, rosemary and tea tree.
Times: Open 10 May-18 Sep, Tue-Sun 10-5. **Fee:** ✱ £3.25 (ch under 14 free pen £3). **Facilities:** 🅿 💺 🍴 ♿ (free wheelchair loan) toilets for disabled shop garden centre Lavender plants ◀

ST CLEMENT   Map 16

SAMARÉS MANOR
JE2 6QW
➲ (2m E of St Helier on St Clements Inner Rd)
☎ 01534 870551
e-mail: barbara@samaresmanor.com
web: www.samaresmanor.com

2 for 1

The manor stands in 14 acres of beautiful gardens. The Japanese Garden occupies an artificial hill, and has a series of waterfalls cascading over Cumberland limestone. There are farm animals, a craft centre, a children's play area, tours of the manor house, a family Scavenger Hunt and medieval music.
Times: Open 8 Apr-14 Oct. **Fee:** £5.60 (ch under 16 £1.95, pen £5.20). **Facilities:** 🅿 💺 ✖ licensed 🍴 ♿ toilets for disabled shop garden centre ✈ (ex guide dogs) ◀

ST HELIER   Map 16

ELIZABETH CASTLE
JE2 3WU
➲ (access by causeway or amphibious vehicle)
☎ 01534 723971
e-mail: marketing@jerseyheritagetrust.org
web: www.jerseyheritagetrust.org

The original Elizabethan fortress was extended in the 17th and 18th centuries, and then refortified by the Germans during the Occupation. Please telephone for details of events.
Times: Open end Mar-Oct, daily 10-6. (Last admission 5). **Fee:** ✱ £5.25 (ch under 6 free, concessions & students £4.40). Discounts and family tickets **Facilities:** 🅿 (paycards required) 💺 ♿ toilets for disabled shop ✈ (ex guide dogs) ◀

JERSEY MUSEUM
The Weighbridge JE2 3NF
➲ (near bus station on weighbridge)
☎ 01534 633300
e-mail: marketing@jerseyheritagetrust.org
web: www.jerseyheritagetrust.org

Home to 'The Story of Jersey', Jersey's art gallery, an exhibition gallery which features a changing programme, a lecture theatre, and an audio-visual theatre. Special exhibitions take place throughout the year.
Times: Open all year, daily 10-5. Winter daily 10-4. Closed 24-26 Dec & 1 Jan. **Fee:** ✱ £5.25 (ch under 6 free, students & concessions £4.40). Discount and family tickets 🅿 (100yds) (paycard at most public parking) ✖ 🍴 (audio loop, car park) toilets for disabled shop ✈ (ex guide dogs) ◀

MARITIME MUSEUM & OCCUPATION TAPESTRY GALLERY
New North Quay JE2 3ND
➲ (alongside Marina, opposite Liberation Square)
☎ 01534 811043
e-mail: marketing@jerseyheritagetrust
web: www.jerseyheritagetrust.org

This converted 19th-century warehouse houses the tapestry consisting of 12 two-metre panels that tells the story of the occupation of Jersey during World War II. Each of the 12 parishes took responsibility for stitching a panel, making it the largest community arts project ever undertaken on the island. The Maritime Museum celebrates the relationship of islanders and the sea, including an award winning hands-on experience, especially enjoyed by children.
Times: Open all year, daily 10-5. Winter closing at 4. **Fee:** ✱ £5.95 (ch under 6 free, pen & students £5). Discount and family tickets **Facilities:** 🅿 (paycards in public car parks) ♿ (Braille books, audio guide etc) toilets for disabled shop ✈ (ex guide dogs) ◀

ST LAWRENCE   Map 16

GERMAN UNDERGROUND HOSPITAL
Les Charrieres Malorey JE3 1FU
➲ (bus route 8A from St Helier)
☎ 01534 860808
e-mail: info@jerseywartunnels.com
web: www.jerseywartunnels.com

On 1 July 1940 the Channel Islands were occupied by German forces, and this vast complex dug deep into a hillside is the most evocative reminder of that Occupation. A video presentation, along with a large collection of memorabilia, illustrates the lives of the islanders at war and a further exhibition records their impressions during 1945, the year of liberation.
Times: ✱ Open 14 Feb-19 Dec, daily 9.30-5.30 (last admission 4). **Facilities:** 🅿 💺 ✖ licensed 🍴 ♿ (ramp to restaurant & lift in Visitor Centre to restaurant) toilets for disabled shop ✈ (ex guide dogs) ◀

HAMPTONNE

La Rue de la Patente JE3 1HS

➲ (5m from St Helier on A1, A10 & follow signs)

☎ 01534 863955

e-mail: marketing@jerseyheritagetrust.org
web: www.jerseyheritagetrust.org

Here visitors will find a medieval 17th-century home, furnished in authentic style and surrounded by 19th-century farm buildings. Guided tours every weekday. Living history interpretation and daily demonstrations.

Times: Open end Mar-end Oct, daily 10-5. **Fee:** ✱ £5.25 (ch under 6 free, student & concessions £4.40). Discount and family tickets.

Facilities: 🅿 💷 ✿ (Sensory Garden) toilets for disabled shop ✖ (ex guide dogs) ▥

ST OUEN   Map 16

THE CHANNEL ISLANDS MILITARY MUSEUM

Five Mile Rd

➲ (N end of 5 Mile Rd, at rear of Jersey Woollen Mill & across rd from Jersey Pearl)

☎ 01534 723136

e-mail: damienhorn@jerseymail.co.uk

The museum is housed in a German coastal defence bunker, which formed part of Hitler's Atlantic Wall. It has been restored, as far as possible, to give the visitor an idea of how it looked. The visitor can also see German uniforms, motorcycles, weapons, documents, photographs and other items from the 1940-45 occupation.

Times: Open week before Etr-Oct **Fee:** ✱ £4 (ch £2) Groups by arrangement. **Facilities:** 🅿 💷 ✿ (all parts accessible ex 1 small room) toilets for disabled shop ✖ (ex guide dogs)

KEMPT TOWER VISITOR CENTRE

Five Mile Rd

☎ 01534 483651 & 483140   `FREE`

e-mail: marketing@jerseyheritagetrust.org
web: www.jerseyheritagetrust.org

The centre has displays on history and the wildlife of St Ouen's Bay, including Les Mielles, which is Jersey's miniature national park. Nature walks are held every Thursday (May to September). Check local press for details.

Times: ✱ Open BHs, Apr & Oct, Thu & Sun only 2-5; May-Sep, daily (ex Mon) 2-5. **Facilities:** 🅿 shop ✖

Directions are provided by the attractions.

The National Trust

For over a hundred years, the NT has been acquiring and protecting threatened coastline, countryside and buildings. To find about more about this organisation, its sites, and policies, click on their website:

www.nationaltrust.org.uk

ST PETER   Map 16

THE LIVING LEGEND

Rue de Petit Aleval JE3 7ET

➲ (from St Helier, along main esplanade & right to Bel Royal. Left and follow road to attraction, signed from German Underground Hospital)

☎ 01534 485496

e-mail: info@jerseyslivinglegend.co.je
web: www.jerseyslivinglegend.co.je

Pass through the granite archways into the landscaped gardens and the world of the Jersey Experience where Jersey's exciting past is recreated in a three dimensional spectacle. Learn of the heroes and villains, the folklore and the story of the island's links with the UK and its struggles with Europe. Other attractions include an adventure playground, street entertainment, the Jersey Craft and Shopping Village, a range of shops and the Jersey Kitchen Restaurant. Two 18 hole adventure golf courses are suitable for all ages. New for 2005 is Jersey Karting - a new formula one style experience. A unique track featuring adult and cadet karts.

Times: Open daily, Mar-Nov 9.30-5, Sat-Sun 10-5 **Fee:** ✱ £7.10 (ch 7-13 £4.85, pen £6.80, student £5.50, disabled £5.60).

Facilities: 🅿 💷 ✗ licensed ✿ (wheelchair available) toilets for disabled shop ✖ (ex guide dogs) ▥

LE MOULIN DE QUETIVEL

St Peters Valley, Le Mont Fallu

➲ (A11 through St Peter's Valley. Attraction located on left, with junct of Le Mont Fallu B58)

☎ 01534 483193 01534 745408

e-mail: enquiries@nationaltrustjersey.org.je
web: www.nationaltrustjersey.org.je

There has been a water mill on this site since 1309. The present granite-built mill was worked until the end of the 19th century, when it fell into disrepair; during the German Occupation it was reactivated for grinding locally grown corn, but after 1945 a fire destroyed the remaining machinery, roof and internal woodwork. In 1971 the National Trust for Jersey began restoration, and the mill is now producing stoneground flour again. 2006 sees the 70th anniversary of the founding of the National Trust for Jersey. Special Event: Heritage Open Day 9 Sep 2006, Open Mill Day 6 May 2006.

Times: Open mid May-mid Sep, Tue-Thu 10-4. **Fee:** £2 (ch under 16 free, pen & students £1.50). Free entry UK National Trust card.

Facilities: 🅿 ✿ shop ✖ (ex guide dogs) ▨

TRINITY   Map 16

DURRELL WILDLIFE CONSERVATION TRUST

Les Augres Manor, La Profunde Rue JE3 5BP

☎ 01534 860000

e-mail: info@durrell.org
web: www.durrell.org

Gerald Durrell's unique sanctuary and breeding centre for many of the world's rarest animals. Visitors can see these remarkable creatures, some so rare that they can only be found here, in modern, spacious enclosures in the gardens of the 16th-century manor house. Major attractions are the magical Aye-Ayes from Madagascar and the world-famous family of Lowland gorillas. There is a comprehensive programme of keeper talks, animal displays and activities.

Times: Open all year, daily 9.30-6 (summer); 9.30-5 (winter). Closed 25 Dec. **Fee:** ✱ £11.50 (ch 4-16 £7.40, pen £8.50). **Facilities:** 🅿 💷 ✗ ✿ toilets for disabled shop ✖ ▥

ISLE OF MAN

EVENTS & FESTIVALS

March
15th Manx Mountain Marathon, from Ramsey
to Port Erin over 12 peaks

May
27th-9th Jun Isle of Man TT Motorcycle
Festival, various venues

June
22nd-2nd Jul Mananan International Summer
Festival of Music & the Arts, various venues

July
5th Tynwald Day, Tynwald Hill &
Fair Field, St John's
tbc Manx International Car Rally, rallying on
closed roads throughout the island

August
11th-12th Royal Manx Agricultural Show,
Sulby
tbc Manx Traditional Boat Festival, Peel

September
11-13th & 15th Mananan International Opera
Festival, Erin Arts Centre, Port Erin

October
27th-29th Mananan International Autumn
Festival of Music & the Arts, various venues

Above: The triskelion of the Isle of Man

BALLASALLA   Map 06 SC27
RUSHEN ABBEY
IM9 3DB
⮑ (right at Whitestone Inn, left at next rdbt, then
1st right over bridge, car park on left)
☎ 01624 648000
e-mail: enquiries@mnh.gov.im
web: www.gov.im/mnh
The most substantial and important medieval religious site in
the Isle of Man. Remains of medieval buildings, exhibitions
and displays, set in beautifully landscaped gardens.
Times: ✱ Open Apr-late Oct, daily 10-5. **Facilities:** P ♿ toilets for
disabled shop ✕ (ex guide dogs) ◼

BALLAUGH   Map 06 SC39
CURRAGHS WILD LIFE PARK
IM7 5EA
⮑ (on main road halfway between Kirk Michael &
Ramsey)
☎ 01624 897323
e-mail: curraghswlp@gov.im
web: www.gov.im/wildlife
This park has been developed adjacent to the reserve area of
the Ballaugh Curraghs and a large variety of animals and
birds can be seen. A walk-through enclosure lets visitors
explore the world of wildlife, including local habitats along
the Curraghs nature trail. The miniature railway runs on
Sundays.
Times: Open all year Etr-Oct, daily 10-6. (Last admission 5). Oct-Etr,
Sat & Sun 10-4. **Fee:** ✱ £4.50 (ch £2.25, under 5's free, pen £3). Party.
Facilities: P ◼ ♿ (loan of wheelchair & electric wheelchair) toilets
for disabled shop ✕ (ex guide dogs by arrangement)

CASTLETOWN   Map 06 SC26
CASTLE RUSHEN
The Quay IM9 1LD
⮑ (centre of Castletown)
☎ 01624 648000
e-mail: enquiries@mnh.gov.im
web: www.storyofmann.com
One of Britain's most complete medieval castles, Castle
Rushen is a limestone fortress rising out of the heart of the
old capital of the island, Castletown. Once the fortress of the
Kings and Lords of Mann, Castle Rushen is bought alive with
rich decorations, and the sounds and smells of a bygone era.
Times: Open daily, Apr-late Oct, 10-5. **Fee:** ✱ £4.25 (ch £2.25) Family
£10.75. Group bookings available from £3.40. **Facilities:** P (100 yds)
(disc zone parking) ▦ ♿ shop ✕ (ex guide dogs) ◼

NAUTICAL MUSEUM
⮑ (From Castletown centre, cross footbridge over
harbour. Museum on right)
☎ 01624 648000
e-mail: enquiries@mnh.gov.im
web: www.storyofmann.com
Set at the mouth of Castletown harbour this museum is
home to an 18th-century armed yacht, *The Peggy*, built by a
Manxman in 1791. A replica sailmaker's loft, ship model and
photographs bring alive Manx maritime life and trade in the
days of sail.
Times: Open daily, Apr-Oct, 10-5. **Fee:** ✱ £3 (ch £1.50). Family £7.50.
Group bookings available **Facilities:** P ▦ ♿ shop
✕ (ex guide dogs) ◼

OLD GRAMMAR SCHOOL

IM9 1LE

➲ (centre of Castletown, opposite the castle)

☎ 01624 648000

e-mail: enquiries@mnh.gov.im

web: www.storyofmann.com

FREE

Built around 1200AD, the former capital's first church, St Mary's, has had a significant role in Manx education. It was a school from 1570 to 1930 and evokes memories of Victorian school life.

Times: Open daily, Apr-late Oct, 10-5. **Facilities:** 🅿 🗐 shop ✈ (ex guide dogs)

THE OLD HOUSE OF KEYS

IM9 1LA

➲ (opposite Castletown Rushen in centre of Castletown)

☎ 01624 648000

e-mail: enquiries@mnh.gov.im

web: www.storyofmann.com

The Old House of Keys is a portrayal of the long and often turbulent history of Manx politics. It has been restored to its appearance in 1866 and visitors are invited to participate in a lively debate with interactive Members of Tynwald, the Manx parliament.

Times: Open daily, Apr-late Oct, 10-5. **Fee:** ✱ £3 (ch £1.50) Family ticket £7.50. **Facilities:** 🅿 (30yds) (disc zone parking) � ✈ (ex guide dogs)

CREGNEASH
Map 06 SC16

CREGNEASH VILLAGE FOLK MUSEUM

➲ (2m from Port Erin/Port St Mary, signed)

☎ 01624 648000

e-mail: enquiries@mnh.gov.im

web: www.storyofmann.com

The Cregneash story begins in Cummal Beg - the village information centre where you can experience what life was really like in a Manx crofting village during the early 19th century. As you stroll around this attractive village, set in beautiful countryside, call into Harry Kelly's cottage, a Turner's shed, a Weaver's house, and the Smithy. The Manx Four-horned Loghtan Sheep can be seen grazing along with other animals from the village farm.

Times: Open Apr-Oct, daily, 10-5. **Fee:** ✱ £3 (ch £1.50) Family £7.50. Group rates from £2.40 **Facilities:** 🅿 ▣ 🗐 ⅙ toilets for disabled shop ✈ (ex guide dogs) ◼

DOUGLAS
Map 06 SC37

MANX MUSEUM

IM1 3LY

➲ (signed in Douglas)

☎ 01624 648000

e-mail: enquiries@mnh.gov.im

web: www.storyofmann.com

FREE

The Island's treasure house provides an exciting introduction to the "Story of Mann" where a specially produced film portrayal of Manx history complements the award winning displays. Galleries depict natural history, archaeology and the social development of the Island. There are also examples of famous Manx artists in the National Art Gallery together with the Island's National archive and reference library

Times: Open daily all year, Mon-Sat, 10-5. Closed 25-26 Dec & 1 Jan. **Facilities:** 🅿 ✕ licensed 🗐 ⅙ (lift) toilets for disabled shop ✈ (ex guide dogs) ◼

SNAEFELL MOUNTAIN RAILWAY

Banks Circus IM1 5PT

➲ (Manx Electric Railway from Douglas and change at Laxey)

☎ 01624 663366

e-mail: info@busandrail.dtl.gov.im

Snaefell is the Isle of Man's highest mountain. Running up it is Britain's oldest working mountain railway, which was laid in 1895. From the top of Snaefell, on a clear day, England, Ireland, Scotland and Wales are all visible.

Times: Open 25 Apr-25 Sep **Facilities:** 🅿 ▣ shop ◼

LAXEY
Map 06 SC48

GREAT LAXEY WHEEL & MINES TRAIL

➲ (signed in Laxey village)

☎ 01624 648000

e-mail: enquiries@mnh.gov.im

web: www.storyofmann.com

Built in 1854, the Great Laxey Wheel, 22 metres in diameter, is the largest working water wheel in the world. It was designed to pump water from the lead and zinc mines and is an acknowledged masterpiece of Victorian engineering. The wheel was christened by Lady Isabella, the wife of the Lieutenant Governor of the Isle of Man.

Times: Open Apr-Oct, daily, 10-5. **Fee:** ✱ £3 (ch £1.50) Family £7.50. Group rates available **Facilities:** 🅿 🗐 ⅙ shop ✈ (ex guide dogs) ◼

PEEL
Map 06 SC28

HOUSE OF MANANNAN

Mill Rd IM5 1TA

➲ (signed in Peel)

☎ 01624 648000

e-mail: enquiries@mnh.gov.im

web: www.storyofmann.com

This £6 million centre is an unforgettable experience. Reconstructions, interactive displays, audio visual presentations and original material explore the Celtic, Viking and maritime traditions of the Isle of Man. A visit will leave you in awe of the diversity of Manx heritage and eager to learn more.

Times: Open daily, 10-5. Closed 25-26 Dec & 1 Jan. **Fee:** ✱ £5 (ch £2.50) Family £12.50. Group rates available **Facilities:** 🅿 🗐 ⅙ toilets for disabled shop ✈ (ex guide dogs) ◼

PEEL CASTLE

IM5 1TB

➲ (on St Patrick's Isle, facing Peel Bay, signed)

☎ 01624 648000

e-mail: enquiries@mnh.gov.im

web: www.storyofmann.com

One of the Island's principle historic centres, this great natural fortress with its imposing curtain wall set majestically at the mouth of Peel Harbour is steeped in Viking heritage. The sandstone walls of Peel Castle enclose an 11th-century church and Round Tower, the 13th-century St German's Cathedral and the later apartments of the Lords of Mann.

Times: Open Apr-Oct, daily, 10-5. **Fee:** ✱ £3 (ch £1.50). Family £7.50. Group rates available **Facilities:** 🅿 (100yds) 🗐 shop ✈ (ex guide dogs)

PORT ST MARY
Map 06 SC26

SOUND VISITOR CENTRE
The Sound IM1 3LY

➲ (follow coastal road towards Port Erin/Port St Mary. Past Cregneash village towards most S point of Island)

☎ 01624 648000 01624 838123
e-mail: enquiries@mnh.gov.im
web: www.storyofmann.com

`FREE`

The Sound Visitor Centre is set in one of the Island's most scenic areas overlooking the natural wonders of the Sound and the Calf of Man. Along with information and audio presentations about the area, a new car park and high quality refreshments are provided for the enjoyment and convenience of visitors.

Times: Open daily, 10-5 incl BHs. For Winter schedule contact Manx Museum 01624 648000. **Facilities:** 🅿 💻 ✕ 🗑 ♿ toilets for disabled

RAMSEY
Map 06 SC49

THE GROVE HOUSE AND GARDENS
IM8 3UA

➲ (on W side of Andreas Rd. Signed in Ramsey)

☎ 01624 648000
e-mail: enquiries@mnh.gov.im
web: www.storyofmann.com

This Victorian time capsule was a country house built as a summer retreat for a Liverpool shipping merchant. Rooms are filled with period furnishings together with a costume exhibition. In the adjacent farmyard are buildings containing displays on farming and 19th century vehicles. Around the grounds you may see Loghtan sheep, ducks and perhaps a Manx cat.

Times: Open Apr-late Oct, daily, 10-5. **Fee:** ✱ £3 (ch £1.50). Family £7.50. Group rates available **Facilities:** 🅿 💻 🗑 ♿ shop ✈ (ex guide dogs) 🍴

Highland cow, Glencoe

SCOTLAND

EVENTS & FESTIVALS

January
31st Dec-1st Stonehaven Fireballing Festival, Stonehaven, various venues

1st Men's & Boy's 'Ba', mass football game, Kirkwall, Orkney Isles

11th-29th Celtic Connections Festival (International Celtic music festival), various venues, Glasgow

26th Up Helly Aa, Lerwick, Shetland Islands

March
9th-25th Glagow International Comedy Festival, various venues

24th-26th Reivers Festival, Hawick

tbc StAnza Poetry Festival, St Andrews

April
6th-15th Edinburgh International Science Festival, various venues

14th-16th Edinburgh Easter Festival, free events in Princes Street Gardens and Easter Sunday parade

27th-30th Shetland Folk Festival

30th Beltane Fire Festival, Carlton Hill, Edinburgh

May
6th-7th Big in Falkirk, Scotland's National Street Arts Festival

18th-28th Perth Festival of the Arts, various venues

tbc Scottish International Children's Festival

June
9th-25th West End Festival (10th anniversary), Glasgow, theatre, music, exhibitions, film, markets and Midsummer Carnival

16th-21st St Magnus Festival, Orkney (Kirkwall, Stromness & outlying parishes), music, drama, dance and visual art

22nd-25th Royal Highland Show, Ingliston, Edinburgh

tbc Glasgow International Jazz Festival

tbc Highland Festival, Inverness, music, theatre, art, comedy and street events

July
8th-9th Scottish Traditional Boat Festival, Portsoy, Banff

8th-9th T in the Park, Balado Airfield, near Kinross

14th-17th Bute Live Music & Arts Festival, Isle of Bute

15th-16th Glasgow River Festival, on land and water

28th-6th Aug Edinburgh International Jazz & Blues Festival (provisional)

August
2nd-12th Aberdeen International Youth Festival, various venues throughout the NE

4th-26th Edinburgh Military Tattoo

6th-28th Edinburgh Festival Fringe

13th-2nd Sep Edinburgh International Festival

16th-27th Edinburgh International Film Festival

19th-20th Motor Show Scotland, Royal Highland Showground, Ingleston, Edinburgh

26th Largs Viking Festival, various venues in Largs

September
2nd Braemar Gathering, Princess Royal & Duke of Fife Memorial Park

9th RAF Leuchars Airshow, Leuchars, Fife

12th-24th Techfest, Beach Ballroom & Beach Leisure Centre, Aberdeen

tbc Edinburgh Mela, Pilrig Park

tbc Merchant City Festival, multi-arts festival, Glasgow

October
tbc Scottish International Storytelling Festival, Edinburgh

October/November
tbc Glasgay, multi-arts festival, Glasgow

December
31st-1st Jan Edinburgh's Hogmanay Festival

Top: The Old Man of Hoy
Above: Rest and be Thankful, an old military road, passing through Argyll Forest Park

ABERDEEN CITY

ABERDEEN   Map 15 NJ90

ABERDEEN ART GALLERY
Schoolhill AB10 1FQ
➲ (located in city centre)
☎ 01224 523700
e-mail: info@aagm.co.uk
web: www.aagm.co.uk

One of the city's most popular tourist attractions Aberdeen's splendid art gallery houses an important fine art collection with many 19th and 20th century works.
Times: Open all year Mon-Sat 10-5, Sun 2-5. Closed Xmas & New Year **Facilities:** P (500yds) ▣ ᕕ (ramp, lift) toilets for disabled shop ✘ (ex guide dogs)

ABERDEEN MARITIME MUSEUM
Shiprow AB11 5BY
➲ (located in city centre)
☎ 01224 337700
e-mail: info@aagm.co.uk
web: www.aagm.co.uk

The museum is in Provost Ross's House, Aberdeen's oldest building (1593). It highlights the city's maritime history, its oil industry, and its shipbuilding.
Times: ✱ Open all year Mon-Sat 10-5, Sun 12-3. Closed Xmas & New Year. **Facilities:** P (250yds) ▣ ✘ licensed ▦ ᕕ (ramps, lifts) toilets for disabled shop ✘ ☕

CRUICKSHANK BOTANIC GARDEN
University of Aberdeen, St Machar Dr AB24 3UU
➲ (enter by gate in Chanonry, in Old Aberdeen)
☎ 01224 272704
e-mail: pss@abdn.ac.uk
web: www.abdn.ac.uk/pss/cruickshank

Developed at the end of the 19th century, the 11 acres include rock and water gardens, a rose garden, a fine herbaceous border, an arboretum and a patio garden. There are collections of spring bulbs, gentians and alpine plants, and a fine array of trees and shrubs.
Times: Open all year, Mon-Fri 9-4.30; also Sat & Sun, May-Sep 2-5.
Facilities: P (200mtrs) ▦ ᕕ ✘

THE GORDON HIGHLANDERS MUSEUM
St Lukes, Viewfield Rd AB15 7XH
☎ 01224 311200
e-mail: museum@gordonhighlanders.com
web: www.gordonhighlanders.com

Presenting a large collection of artefacts, paintings, films and reconstructions, the Gordon Highlanders Museum is the perfect day out for anyone interested in British military history. The grounds also contain a tea-room, shop, the home and paintings of Scottish artist, Sir George Reid, and gardens.
Times: Open Apr-Oct, Tue-Sat 10.30-4.30, Sun 1.30-4.30. (Closed Mon). Open by appointment only at other times. **Fee:** ✱ £2.50 (ch £1, con £1.50) **Facilities:** P ▣ ▦ ᕕ (low level cases, hearing loop) toilets for disabled shop ✘ (ex guide dogs) ☕

PROVOST SKENE'S HOUSE
Guestrow, off Broad St AB10 1AS
☎ 01224 641086
e-mail: info@aagm.co.uk
web: www.aagm.co.uk

Experience the epitome of style and elegance in this 16th-century townhouse, furnished and decorated in the styles of earlier times. See changing fashions in the Costume Gallery and view an important cycle of religious paintings in the gallery.
Times: Open all year Mon-Sat 10-5, Sun 1-4. Closed Xmas & New Year. Telephone for details. **Facilities:** P (200yds) ▣ ✘ (ex guide dogs)

SATROSPHERE ("HANDS-ON" SCIENCE & TECHNOLOGY CENTRE)
179 Constitution St AB24 5TU
➲ (located very close to Beach Esplanade. Follow signs to fun beach, then attraction)
☎ 01224 640340
e-mail: info@satrosphere.net
web: www.satrosphere.net

Satrosphere, the Discovery Place, is different from many museums or exhibition centres. It is an Interactive Centre where everything is 'hands-on'. Displays aren't locked in glass cases and there are certainly no 'Do Not Touch' signs. The emphasis is on doing and finding out, not just looking and standing back. Over 100 exhibits, interactive shows, workshops and special weekend events.
Times: Open all year, Mon-Sat 10-5, Sun 11.30-5. Closed 25-26 Dec & 1-2 Jan. **Facilities:** P ▣ ᕕ toilets for disabled shop ✘ (ex guide dogs) ☕

PETERCULTER   Map 15 NJ80

DRUM CASTLE
AB31 5EY
➲ (3m W, off A93)
☎ 01330 811204
e-mail: drum@nts.org.uk
web: www.nts.org.uk

The great 13th-century Square Tower is one of the three oldest tower houses in Scotland and has associations with Robert the Bruce. The handsome mansion, added in 1619, houses a collection of family memorabilia. The grounds contain the 100-acre Old Wood of Drum, a natural oak wood and an old rose garden.
Times: ✱ Open Apr-May & Sep, daily 12.30-5.30, Jun-Aug, daily 10-5.30. Grounds all year, daily 9.30-sunset. Times may change for 2006 please telephone or check on www.nts.org.uk **Facilities:** P ▣ ᕕ (wheelchair available) shop ✘ (ex guide dogs) ☃

ABERDEENSHIRE

ALFORD   Map 15 NJ51

ALFORD VALLEY RAILWAY
AB33 8AD
➲ (A944 Alford Village)
☎ 019755 62326 & 62811

Narrow-gauge passenger railway between Alford and Haughton Park, approx one mile. Diesel traction. Exhibitions.
Times: Open Apr, May & Sep wknds 1-5, Jun-Aug daily from 1pm (30 min service). Party bookings also available at other times. **Fee:** ✱ £2 (ch £1) return fare. **Facilities:** P ▦ ᕕ (ramps at station platforms) toilets for disabled shop

BALMORAL   Map 15 NO29

BALMORAL CASTLE GROUNDS & EXHIBITION
AB35 5TB
➲ (on A93 between Ballater & Braemar)
☎ 013397 42534
e-mail: info@balmoralcastle.com
web: www.balmoralcastle.com
Queen Victoria and Prince Albert first rented Balmoral Castle
in 1848, and Prince Albert bought the property four years
later. He commissioned William Smith to build a new castle,
which was completed by 1856 and is still the Royal Family's
Highland residence. Country walks and pony trekking can be
enjoyed, and an exhibition of paintings and other works of
art can be seen in the castle ballroom, together with a Travel
and Carriage exhibition and a wildlife exhibition.
Times: ✱ Open Apr-Jul, daily 10-5. **Facilities:** P (100yds) ⬛ ▦
& (wheelchairs & battricars available, reserved parking) toilets for
disabled shop ✖ (ex guide dogs/in grounds) ▰

BANCHORY   Map 15 NO69

BANCHORY MUSEUM
Bridge St AB31 5SX
➲ (in Bridge St beside tourist information centre)
☎ 01771 622906   FREE
e-mail: heritage@aberdeenshire.gov.uk
The museum has displays on Scott Skinner (The 'Strathspey
King'), natural history, royal commemorative china, local
silver artefacts and a variety of local history displays.
Times: ✱ Open May, Jun & Sep, Mon-Sat 11-1 & 2-4.30; Jul-Aug,
Mon-Sat 11-1, 2-4.30 & Sun 2-4.30. Telephone for Apr & Oct opening
times. **Facilities:** P (100yds) (limited) & toilets for disabled shop
✖ (ex guide dogs)

BANFF   Map 15 NJ66

BANFF MUSEUM
High St AB45 1AE
☎ 01771 622906   FREE
e-mail: heritage@aberdeenshire.gov.uk
Displays of geology, natural history, local history, Banff silver,
arms and armour, and displays relating to James Ferguson
(18th-century astronomer) and Thomas Edward (19th-
century Banff naturalist).
Times: Open Jun-Sep, Mon-Sat 2-4.30. **Facilities:** P (200yds)
& shop ✖ (ex guide dogs)

DUFF HOUSE
AB45 3SX
➲ (0.5m S, access south of town)
☎ 01261 818181
The house was designed by William Adam for William Duff,
later Earl of Fife. The main block was roofed in 1739, but the
planned wings were never built. Although it is incomplete,
the house is still considered one of Britain's finest Georgian
baroque buildings. Duff House is a Country House Gallery of
the National Galleries of Scotland.
Times: Telephone for details of opening dates and times.
Facilities: P ✖ & toilets for disabled shop ✖▮

CORGARFF   Map 15 NJ20

CORGARFF CASTLE
AB36 8YL
➲ (8m W of Strathdon village)
☎ 01975 651460
The 16th-century tower was besieged in 1571 and is
associated with the Jacobite risings of 1715 and 1745. It later
became a military barracks. Its last military use was to
control the smuggling of whisky between 1827 and 1831.
Times: Open all year, Apr-Sep, daily 9.30-6.30; Oct-Mar, wknds only.
Closed 25-26 Dec & 1-2 Jan. **Fee:** ✱ £3.30 (ch £1.30, concessions
£2.50). Group 11+ 10% discount. Prices valid until 31/12/05. Please
phone for further details. **Facilities:** P shop ▮

CRATHES   Map 15 NO79

CRATHES CASTLE & GARDEN
AB31 5QJ
➲ (On A93, 3m E of Banchory)
☎ 01330 844525
e-mail: crathes@nts.org.uk
web: www.nts.org.uk
This impressive 16th-century castle with magnificent
interiors has royal associations dating from 1323. There is a
large walled garden and a notable collection of unusual
plants, including yew hedges dating from 1702. The grounds
contain six nature trails, one suitable for disabled visitors,
and an adventure playground.
Times: ✱ Open: Castle & Visitor Centre: Apr-Sep, daily 10-5.30, Oct
daily 10-4.30. To help enjoy your visit & for safety reasons, admission to
the castle is by timed ticket (limited numbers: entry may be delayed).
Garden & grounds all year, daily 9-sunset. Times may change for 2006
please telephone or check on www.nts.org.uk
Facilities: P ✖ licensed & (tape for visually impaired) toilets for
disabled shop ✖ (ex guide dogs) ♨

HUNTLY   Map 15 NJ53

BRANDER MUSEUM
The Square AB54 8AE
➲ (in centre of Huntly, sharing building with
library, museum on ground floor)
☎ 01771 622906   FREE
e-mail: heritage@aberdeenshire.gov.uk
The museum has displays of local and church history, plus
the 19th-century Anderson Bey and the Sudanese
campaigns. Exhibits connected with George MacDonald,
author and playwright, can also be seen.
Times: Open all year, Tue-Sat 2-4.30. **Facilities:** P (25yds)
& (access difficult due to 3 large steps at entrance) shop
✖ (ex guide dogs)

HUNTLY CASTLE
AB54 4SH
☎ 01466 793191
The original medieval castle was rebuilt a number of times
and destroyed, once by Mary, Queen of Scots. It was rebuilt
for the last time in 1602, in palatial style, and is now an
impressive ruin, noted for its ornate heraldic decorations. It
stands in wooded parkland.
Times: Open all year, Apr-Sep, daily 9.30-6.30; Oct-Mar, daily
9.30-4.30. Closed Thu & Fri in winter, 25-26 Dec & 1-2 Jan.
Fee: ✱ £3.30 (ch £1.30, concessions £2.50) Groups 11+ 10% discount.
Prices valid until 31/12/05. Please telephone for details.
Facilities: P shop ▮

INVERURIE · Map 15 NJ72

CARNEGIE MUSEUM
Town House, The Square AB51 3SN
➲ (in centre of Inverurie, on left side of townhouse building, above library)
☎ 01771 622906
e-mail: heritage@aberdeenshire.gov.uk · **FREE**

This fine museum contains displays on local history and archaeology, including Pictish stones, Bronze Age material and the Great North of Scotland Railway.
Times: Open all year, Mon & Wed-Fri 2-4.30, Sat 10-1 & 2-4. Closed Tue & public hols. **Facilities:** P (50yds) shop ✗ (ex guide dogs)

KEMNAY · Map 15 NJ71

CASTLE FRASER
AB51 7LD
➲ (off A944, 4m N of Dunecht)
☎ 01330 833463
e-mail: castlefraser@nts.org.uk
web: www.nts.org.uk

The massive Z-plan castle was built between 1575 and 1636 and is one of the grandest of the Castles of Mar. The interior was remodelled in 1838 and decoration and furnishings of that period survive in some of the rooms. A formal garden inside the old walled garden, estate trails, a children's play area and a programme of concerts are among the attractions.
Times: ✱ Open Apr-Jun & Sep, Fri-Tue 12-5.30, Jul-Aug, daily 11-5.30. Times may change for 2006 please telephone or check on www.nts.org.uk **Facilities:** P ᗡ ᜌ shop garden centre ✗ (ex guide dogs, certain areas) ❦

KILDRUMMY · Map 15 NJ41

KILDRUMMY CASTLE
AB54 7XT
➲ (10m SW of Alford)
☎ 01975 571331

An important part of Scottish history, at least until it was dismantled in 1717, this fortress was the seat of the Earls of Mar. Now it is a ruined, but splendid, example of a 13th-century castle, with four round towers, hall and chapel all discernible. Some parts of the building, including the Great Gatehouse, are from the 15th and 16th centuries.
Times: Open Apr-Sep, daily 9.30-6.30. **Fees:** ✱ £2.50 (ch £1, concessions £1.90). Group 11+ 10% discount. Prices valid until 31/12/05. Please phone for further details. **Facilities:** P ᜌ toilets for disabled shop ▉

KILDRUMMY CASTLE GARDENS
AB33 8RA
➲ (on A97 off A944. 10m W of Alford)
☎ 019755 71277 & 71203
e-mail: information@
kildrummy-castle-gardens.co.uk
web: www.kildrummy-castle-gardens.co.uk

With the picturesque ruin as a backdrop, these beautiful gardens include an alpine garden in an ancient quarry and a water garden. There's a small museum and a children's play area.
Times: Open Apr-Oct, daily 10-5. **Fee:** £3.50 (ch free, pen £3)
Facilities: P ᗡ ᜌ toilets for disabled shop garden centre

MACDUFF · Map 15 NJ76

MACDUFF MARINE AQUARIUM
11 High Shore AB44 1SL
➲ (off A947 to Macduff, aquarium signed)
☎ 01261 833369
e-mail: macduff.aquarium@
aberdeenshire.gov.uk
web: www.marine-aquarium.com

Exciting displays feature local sealife. The central exhibit, unique in Britain, holds a living kelp reef. Divers feed the fish in this tank. Other displays include an estuary exhibit, splash tank, rock pools, deep reef tank and ray pool. Young visitors especially enjoy the touch pools. There are talks, video presentations and feeding shows throughout the week.
Times: Open 10-5 daily (last admission 4.15). Closed 25-26 Dec & 31 Dec-2 Jan **Fee:** ✱ £4.75 (ch £2.25, concessions £2.75). Family ticket (2ad+2ch) £12.75. Groups 10+ **Facilities:** P ᗡ ᜌ (audio tour for visually impaired) toilets for disabled shop ✗ (ex guide dogs) ◀

MARYCULTER · Map 15 NO89

STORYBOOK GLEN
AB12 5FT
➲ (5m W of Aberdeen on B9077)
☎ 01224 732941
web: www.storybookglenaberdeen.co.uk

This is a child's fantasy land, where favourite nursery rhyme and fairytale characters are brought to life. Grown-ups can enjoy the nostalgia and also the 20 acres of Deeside country, full of flowers, plants, trees and waterfalls.
Times: Open Mar-Oct, daily 10-6; Nov-Feb, daily 10-4. **Fee:** ✱ £4.85 (ch £3.50, pen £3.60). **Facilities:** P ᗡ ✗ licensed ᜌ toilets for disabled shop garden centre ✗ (ex guide dogs) ◀

METHLICK · Map 15 NJ83

HADDO HOUSE
AB41 7EQ
➲ (off B999, 4m N of Pitmedden)
☎ 01651 851440
e-mail: haddo@nts.org.uk
web: www.nts.org.uk

Haddo House is renowned for its association with the Haddo Choral Society and is the venue for international concerts. It is a splendid Palladian-style mansion built in the 1730s to designs by William Adam. Home to the Earls of Aberdeen, the house was refurbished in the 1880s in the 'Adam Revival' style. The adjoining country park offers beautiful woodland walks.
Times: ✱ Open, House: Jun, Fri-Mon 11-4.30; Jul-Aug, daily 11-4.30. Guided tours only, departing set times. Garden open all year, daily 9.30-6. Times may change for 2006 please telephone or check on www.nts.org.uk **Facilities:** P ✗ ᜌ (lift to first floor of house & wheelchair) toilets for disabled shop ✗ (ex in grounds & guide dogs) ❦

MINTLAW · Map 15 NJ94

ABERDEENSHIRE FARMING MUSEUM
Aden Country Park AB42 5FQ
➲ (1m W of Mintlaw on A950)
☎ 01771 622906
e-mail: heritage@aberdeenshire.gov.uk · **FREE**
web: www.aberdeenshire.gov.uk/heritage

Housed in 19th-century farm buildings, once part of the estate which now makes up the Aden Country Park. Two

continued

centuries of farming history and innovation are illustrated, and the story of the estate is also told. The reconstructed farm of Hareshowe shows how a family in the north-east farmed during the 1950s - access by guided tour only.
Times: Open May-Sep, daily 11-4.30; Apr & Oct, wknds only noon-4.30. (Last admission 30 mins before closing). Park open all year, Apr-Sep 7-10, winter 7-7. **Facilities:** 🅿 (charged) 💺 ᔕ (sensory garden) toilets for disabled 🐾 (ex guide dogs)

OLD DEER
Map 15 NJ94

DEER ABBEY
➲ (2m W of Mintlaw on A950)
☎ 01466 793191
FREE

The remains of the Cistercian Abbey, founded in 1218, include the infirmary, Abbot's House and the southern claustral range. The University Library at Cambridge now houses the famous Book of Deer.
Times: Open at all reasonable times. **Facilities:** 🅿 🐾 🎏

OYNE
Map 15 NJ62

ARCHAEOLINK
Berryhill AB52 6QP
➲ (1m off A96 on B9002)
☎ 01464 851500
e-mail: info@archaeolink.co.uk
web: www.archaeolink.co.uk

A stunning audio-visual show, a Myths and Legends Gallery and a whole range of interpretation techniques help visitors to explore what it was like to live 6000 years ago. In addition there are landscaped walkways, and outdoor activity areas including an Iron Age farm, Roman marching camp and Stone Age settlement in the 40-acre park. Enjoy daily hands-on activities for all ages, guided tours with costumed guides or relax in the coffee shop. Special weekend events held regularly.
Times: Open all year. Open daily, Apr-Oct 10-5, Nov-Mar 11-4.
Fee: Prices not confirmed for 2006 **Facilities:** 🅿 💺 ✗ licensed 🎁 ᔕ (induction loop in theatre, wheelchair) toilets for disabled shop 🐾 (ex guide dogs) 🍴

PETERHEAD
Map 15 NK14

ARBUTHNOT MUSEUM & ART GALLERY
St Peter St AB42 1QD
➲ (at St.Peter St & Queen St x-roads, above library)
☎ 01771 622906
e-mail: heritage@aberdeenshire.gov.uk
FREE

Specialising in local exhibits, particularly those relating to the fishing industry, this museum also displays Arctic and whaling specimens and a British coin collection. The regular programme of exhibitions changes approximately every six weeks.
Times: Open all year, Mon, Tue & Thu-Sat 11-1 & 2-4.30, Wed 11-1. Closed Sun and BHs. **Facilities:** 🅿 (150 yds) shop 🐾 (ex guide dogs)

PITMEDDEN
Map 15 NJ82

PITMEDDEN GARDEN
AB41 7PD
➲ (1m W of Pitmedden on A920)
☎ 01651 842352
e-mail: aclipson@nts.scot.demon.co.uk
web: www.nts.org.uk

The fine 17th-century walled garden, with sundials, pavilions and fountains dotted among the parterres, has been authentically restored, and there is a Museum of Farming Life and a woodland walk.
Times: ✱ Open May-Sep, daily 10-5.30. Grounds: all year, daily. Times may change for 2006 please telephone or check on www.nts.org.uk
Facilities: 🅿 💺 ᔕ (2 wheelchairs available) toilets for disabled shop 🍴

TOLQUHON CASTLE
AB41 7LP
➲ (2m NE off B999)
☎ 01651 851286

Now roofless, this late 16th-century quadrangular mansion encloses an early 15th-century tower. There is a fine gatehouse and a splendid courtyard.
Times: Open all year, Apr-Sep, daily 9.30-6.30; Oct-Mar, wknds only. Closed 25-26 Dec & 1-2 Jan. **Fee:** ✱ £2.20 (ch £1, concessions £1.90). Group 11+ 10% discount. Prices valid until 31/12/05. Please phone for further details. **Facilities:** 🅿 ᔕ toilets for disabled shop 🐾 🎏

RHYNIE
Map 15 NJ42

LEITH HALL & GARDEN
Kennethmont AB54 4NQ
➲ (on B9002, 1m W of Kennethmont)
☎ 01464 831216
e-mail: leithhall@nts.org.uk
web: www.nts.org.uk

Home of the Leith family for over 300 years, the house dates back to 1650, and has a number of Jacobite relics and fine examples of needlework. It is surrounded by charming gardens and extensive grounds.
Times: ✱ Open House: Good Fri-Etr Mon, daily 12-5; May-Sep, Fri-Tue 12-5. Garden & grounds all year, daily 9.30-sunset. Times may change for 2006 please telephone or check on www.nts.org.uk
Facilities: 🅿 💺 ᔕ (parking next to hall, scented garden for the blind) toilets for disabled 🐾 (ex guide dogs) 🍴

STONEHAVEN
Map 15 NO88

DUNNOTTAR CASTLE
AB39 2TL
➲ (2m S of Stonehaven on A92)
☎ 01569 762173

This once-impregnable fortress, now a spectacular ruin, was the site of the successful protection of the Scottish Crown Jewels from the might of Cromwell. A must for anyone who takes Scottish history seriously.
Times: Open all year, summer Mon-Sat 9-6, Sun 2-5; winter open Fri-Mon only. (Last entry 30mins before closing). Closed 25-26 Dec & New Year. **Facilities:** 🅿 🎁

TOLBOOTH MUSEUM
Old Pier AB39 2JU
➲ (on harbour front)
☎ 01771 622906
e-mail: heritage@aberdeenshire.gov.uk
FREE

Built in the late 16th century as a storehouse for the Earls Marischal at Dunnottar Castle, the building was the Kincardineshire County Tollbooth from 1600-1767. Displays feature local history and fishing.
Times: ✱ Open May-Oct, Wed-Mon, 1.30-4.30. Closed Tue.
Facilities: 🅿 (20yds) ᔕ shop 🐾 (ex guide dogs)

continued

TURRIFF   Map 15 NJ75

FYVIE CASTLE
Fyvie AB53 8JS
➲ (8m SE of Turriff on A947)
☎ 01651 891266
e-mail: aclipson@nts.scot.demon.co.uk
web: www.nts.org.uk

This superb castle, founded in the 13th century, has five towers, each built in a different century, and is one of the grandest examples of Scottish Baronial. It contains the finest wheel stair in Scotland, and a 17th-century morning room, lavishly furnished in Edwarian style. The collection of portraits is exceptional, and there are also displays of arms and armour and tapestries.

Times: ✱ Open Apr-Jun & Sep, Fri-Tue 12-5; Jul-Aug, daily 11-5. Grounds all year, daily, 9.30-sunset. Times may change for 2006 please telephone or check on www.nts.org.uk **Facilities:** 🅿 💷 ♿ (small lift, Braille sheets) toilets for disabled shop 🐕 (ex guide dogs) 🍽

ANGUS

ARBROATH   Map 12 NO64

ARBROATH ABBEY
DD11 1EG
☎ 01241 878756

The 'Declaration of Arbroath' - declaring Robert the Bruce as king - was signed at the 12th-century abbey on 6 April 1320. The abbot's house is well preserved, and the church remains are also interesting.

Times: Open all year, Apr-Sept, daily 9.30-6.30; Oct-Mar, daily 9.30-4.30. Closed 25-26 Dec & 1-2 Jan. **Fees:** ✱ £3.30 (ch £1.30, concessions £2.50). Group 11+ 10% discount. Prices valid until 31/12/05. Please phone for further details. **Facilities:** 🅿 ♿ 🐕 🍴

ARBROATH MUSEUM
Signal Tower, Ladyloan DD11 1PU
➲ (on A92 adjacent to harbour. 16m NE of Dundee)
☎ 01241 875598   **FREE**
e-mail: signal.tower@angus.gov.uk
web: www.angus.gov.uk

Fish and Arbroath Smokies, textiles and engineering feature at this local history museum housed in the 1813 shore station of Stevenson's Bell Rock lighthouse. Special Event: Sea Fest Aug 2006.

Times: Open all year, Mon-Sat 10-5; Jul-Aug, Sun 2-5. Closed 25-26 Dec & 1-2 Jan. **Facilities:** 🅿 📻 ♿ (induction loop) shop 🐕 (ex guide dogs)

BRECHIN   Map 15 NO66

BRECHIN TOWN HOUSE MUSEUM
28 High St DD9 7AA
➲ (off A90 at sign for Brechin, 2m into town centre)
☎ 01356 625536   **FREE**
e-mail: brechin.museum@angus.gov.uk
web: www.angus.gov.uk//localhistory

Within a former courtroom, debtor's prison and seat of local government, this museum covers the history of the little City of Brechin from the earliest settlement, through the market town to the industrialisation in the form of flax, jute mills, distilling, weaving and engineering. Brechin's fascinating history of development is portrayed in vivid displays.

Times: Open Mon-Tues & Thu-Sat 10-5, Wed 10-1
Facilities: 🅿 (150yds) (2hrs max in free car park) 📻 ♿ toilets for disabled shop 🐕 (ex guide dogs)

PICTAVIA VISITOR CENTRE
Brechin Castle Centre, Haughmuir DD9 6RL
➲ (off A90)
☎ 01356 626241
e-mail: stewarte@angus.gov.uk
web: www.pictavia.org.uk

Find about more about the ancient pagan nation of the Picts, who lived in Scotland nearly 2000 years ago. Visitors can learn about Pictish culture, art and religion through film, interactive displays and music. There are also nature and farm trails, a pets' corner, and an adventure playground.

Times: Open all year, mid Apr-mid Oct, Mon-Sat, 9.30-5.30, Sun 10-5.50; early Jan-mid Apr & mid Oct-Dec, close at 5. **Fee:** £3.25 (concessions £2.25, under 5's free). Family £10. **Facilities:** 🅿 💷 ✗ licensed 📻 ♿ toilets for disabled shop garden centre 🐕 (ex assist dogs) 🍽

CARNOUSTIE   Map 12 NO53

BARRY WATER MILL
Barry DD7 7RJ
➲ (N of Barry village between A92 & A930, 2m W of Carnoustie)
☎ 01241 856761
web: www.nts.org.uk

This restored 18th-century mill works on a demonstration basis. Records show that the site has been used for milling since the 16th century. Displays highlight the important place the mill held in the community. There is a waymarked walk and picnic area.

Times: ✱ Open Apr-Oct, Fri-Tue, 12-5. Times may change for 2006 please telephone or check on www.nts.org.uk **Facilities:** 🅿 ♿ (ramp from car park to mill) toilets for disabled 🍽

EDZELL   Map 15 NO56

EDZELL CASTLE
DD9 7UE
➲ (on B966)
☎ 01356 648631

The 16th-century castle has a remarkable walled garden built in 1604 by Sir David Lindsay. Flower-filled recesses in the walls are alternated with heraldic and symbolic sculptures of a sort not seen elsewhere in Scotland. There are ornamental and border gardens and a garden house.

Times: Open all year, Apr-Sep, daily 9.30-6.30; Oct-Mar, daily 9.30-4.30. Closed Thu & Fri in winter, 25-26 Dec & 1-2 Jan.
Fees: ✱ £3.30 (ch £1.30, concessions £2.50). Group 11+ 10% discount. Prices valid until 31/12/05. Please phone for further details.
Facilities: 🅿 ♿ shop 🍴

FORFAR   Map 15 NO45

THE MEFFAN ART GALLERY & MUSEUM
20 West High St DD8 1BB
➲ (off A90, 13m N of Dundee. Attraction in town centre)
☎ 01307 464123 467017   **FREE**
e-mail: the.meffan@angus.gov.uk
web: www.angus.gov

This lively, ever-changing contemporary art gallery and museum are full of surprises. Walk down a cobbled street full of shops, ending up at a witch-burning scene! Carved Pictish stones and a diorama of an archaeological dig complete the vibrant displays.

Times: Open all year. Closed 25-26 Dec & 1-2 Jan.
Facilities: 🅿 (150yds) (30 mins limit on street) 📻 ♿ (handrails, wide door, portable ramp) toilets for disabled shop 🐕 (ex guide dogs) 🍽

GLAMIS
Map 15 NO34

ANGUS FOLK MUSEUM
Kirkwynd Cottages DD8 1RT
➲ (off A94, in Glamis)
☎ 01307 840288
web: www.nts.org.uk

A row of stone-roofed, late 18th-century cottages now houses the splendid Angus Folk Collection of domestic equipment and cottage furniture. Across the wynd, an Angus stone steading houses 'The Life on the Land' exhibition.
Times: ✱ Open Apr-Jun & Sep, Fri-Tue 12-5; Jul & Aug 12-5. Times may change for 2006 please telephone or check on www.nts.org.uk
Facilities: 🅿 ♿ toilets for disabled ✖ (ex guide dogs) ♨

GLAMIS CASTLE
DD8 1RJ
➲ (5m W of Forfar on A94)
☎ 01307 840393   **2 for 1**
e-mail: enquires@glamis-castle.co.uk
web: www.glamis-castle.co.uk

Glamis Castle is the family home of the Earls of Strathmore and Kinghorne and has been a royal residence since 1372. It is the childhood home of the late Queen Mother, the birthplace of her daughter the late Princess Margaret and the setting for Shakespeare's play *Macbeth*. Though the Castle is open to visitors it remains the home of the Strathmore family.
Times: Open Mar-Oct, 10-6. Nov-Dec as advertised. (Last admission 4.30). **Fee:** ✱ Castle & grounds £7 (ch £3.80, pen & students £5.70). Family ticket £20. Grounds only £3.50 (ch, pen & students £2.50). Group 20+ **Facilities:** 🅿 ✖ licensed 🍽 ♿ (castle tour not suitable due to stairs) toilets for disabled shop ✖ (ex in grounds, guide dogs) ◀

KIRRIEMUIR
Map 15 NO35

J M BARRIE'S BIRTHPLACE
9 Brechin Rd DD8 4BX
➲ (on A90/A926, 6m NW of Forfar)
☎ 01575 572646
e-mail: aclipson@nts.scot.demon.co.uk
web: ww.nts.org.uk

The creator of Peter Pan, Sir James Barrie, was born in Kirriemuir in 1860. The upper floors of No 9 Brechin Road are furnished as they may have been when Barrie lived there, and the adjacent house, No 11, houses an exhibition about him. The wash-house outside was his first 'theatre' and gave him the idea for Wendy's house in *Peter Pan*.
Times: ✱ Open Apr-Jun & Sep, Fri-Tue 12-5; Jul-Aug, daily 12-5. Times may change for 2006 please telephone or check on www.nts.org.uk
Facilities: 🅿 (100yds) 🍽 ♿ (stairlift, audio programmes) shop ✖ (ex guide dogs) ♨

KIRRIEMUIR GATEWAY TO GLENS MUSEUM
The Town House, 32 High St DD8 4BB
➲ (in town centre square, 30mins from Dundee, N on A90)
☎ 01575 575479   **FREE**
e-mail: kirrie.gateway@angus.gov.uk
web: www.angus.gov.uk

Housed in the town house dating from 1604, this museum covers the history of Kirriemuir and the Angus Glens from prehistoric times. A realistic model of Kirriemuir on market day in 1604 can be seen and local voices can be heard telling their part in the area's history from sweet making to
continued

linen weaving. Animals and birds can be seen at close range in the Wildlife diorama. Special Events: Timothy Pont Maps exhibition summer 2006.
Times: Open Mon-Wed, Fri & Sat 10-5, Thu 2-5
Facilities: 🅿 (200yds) (free car park) ♿ toilets for disabled shop ✖ (ex guide dogs)

MONTROSE
Map 15 NO75

HOUSE OF DUN
DD10 9LQ
➲ (on A935, 3m W of Montrose)
☎ 01674 810264
e-mail: houseofdun@nts.org.uk
web: www.nts.org.uk

This Georgian house, overlooking the Montrose Basin, was built for Lord Dun in 1730 and is noted for the exuberant plasterwork of the interior. Family portraits, fine furniture and porcelain are on display, and royal mementos connected with a daughter of King William IV and the actress Mrs Jordan, who lived here in the 19th century. There is a walled garden and woodland walks.
Times: ✱ Open House: Apr-Jun, & Sep, Fri-Tue 12-5, Jul-Aug, daily 12-5. Garden & grounds all year daily 9.30-sunset. Times may change for 2006 please telephone or check on www.nts.org.uk
Facilities: 🅿 ✖ ♿ (Braille sheets, house wheelchair & stair lift) toilets for disabled shop ✖ (ex guide dogs) ♨

MONTROSE MUSEUM & ART GALLERY
Panmure Place DD10 8HE
➲ (opposite Montrose Academy in town centre, approach via A92 from Aberdeen or Dundee)
☎ 01674 673232   **FREE**
e-mail: montrose.museum@angus.gov.uk
web: www.angus.gov.uk

Extensive local collections cover the history of Montrose from prehistoric times, the maritime history of the port, the natural history of Angus, and local art.
Times: Open all year, Mon-Sat 10-5. Closed 25-26 Dec & 1-2 Jan.
Facilities: 🅿 20yds 🍽 ♿ shop ✖ (ex guide dogs)

ARGYLL & BUTE

ARDUAINE
Map 10 NM71

ARDUAINE GARDEN
PA34 4XQ
➲ (20m S of Oban, on A816)
☎ 01852 200366
web: www.nts.org.uk

An outstanding 18-acre garden on a promontory bounded by Loch Melfort and the Sound of Jura, climatically favoured by the North Atlantic Drift. It is famous for its rhododendrons and azalea species and other rare trees and shrubs.
Times: ✱ Open all year, daily 9.30-sunset. Reception Apr-Sep 9.30-4.30. Times may change for 2006 please telephone or check on www.nts.org.uk **Facilities:** 🅿 ♿ toilets for disabled ✖ (ex guide dogs) ♨

Directions are provided
by the attractions.

ARROCHAR   Map 10 NN20

ARGYLL FOREST PARK

Forest Enterprise, Ardgartan Visitor Centre G83 7AR
➲ (on A83 at foot of "The Rest and Be Thankful")
☎ 01301 702597   `FREE`
e-mail: robin.kennedy@forestry.gsl.gov.uk

This park extends over a large area of hill ground and forest, noted for its rugged beauty. Numerous forest walks and picnic sites allow exploration; the Arboretum walks and the route between Younger Botanic Gardens and Puck's Glen are particularly lovely.

Times: Open all year. **Facilities:** 🅿 🛈 shop ◾

AUCHINDRAIN   Map 10 NN00

AUCHINDRAIN TOWNSHIP OPEN AIR MUSEUM

PA32 8XN
➲ (6m SW of Inverarary on A83)
☎ 01499 500235   `2 for 1`
e-mail: joanne@auchindrain-museum.org.uk

Auchindrain is an original West Highland township of great antiquity, and the only communal tenancy township to have survived on its centuries-old site. The buildings are furnished and equipped to present a fascinating glimpse of Highland life in the last century.

Times: Open Apr-Sep, daily 10-5. **Fee:** ✱ £4.50 (ch £2.20, pen £3.50). Family ticket £12. **Facilities:** 🅿 🛈 shop

BARCALDINE   Map 10 NM94

SCOTTISH SEA LIFE SANCTUARY

PA37 1SE   `2 for 1`
➲ (10m N of Oban on A828 towards Fort William)
☎ 01631 720386
e-mail: obansealife@merlinentertainments.biz
web: www.sealsanctuary.co.uk

Set in one of Scotland's most picturesque locations, the Scottish Sea Life Sanctuary provides dramatic views of native undersea life including stingrays, seals, octopus and catfish. There are daily talks and feeding demonstrations and during the summer young seals can be viewed prior to their release back into the wild. Recent additions include Otter Creek - a large naturally landscaped enclosure with deep diving pool with underwater viewing and cascading streams through other pools and 'Into the Deep', a themed interactive area displaying living creatures from the deep. There is a restaurant, gift shop, children's play park and a nature trail.

continued

Times: Open all year, mid Feb-Nov, daily 10-5. Dec & Jan; Sat-Sun & school hols only **Fee:** ✱ £7.95 (ch £5.50, pen £6.50). Group 15+.
Facilities: 🅿 🛒 ✕ 🛈 ♿ (assistance available for wheelchairs) toilets for disabled shop ✖ (ex guide dogs) ◾

BENMORE   Map 10 NS18

BENMORE BOTANIC GARDEN

PA23 8QU
➲ (7m N of Dunoon on A815)
☎ 01369 706261
e-mail: benmore@rbge.org.uk
web: www.rbge.org.uk

From the formal gardens, through the hillside woodlands, follow the paths to a stunning viewpoint with a spectacular outlook across the garden and the Holy Loch to the Firth of Clyde and beyond. Amongst many highlights are the stately conifers, the magnificent avenue of giant redwoods, and an extensive magnolia and rhododendron collection.

Times: ✱ Open Mar & Oct daily 10-5, Apr-Sep daily 10-6
Facilities: 🅿 🛒 ✕ licensed 🛈 ♿ toilets for disabled shop garden centre ✖ (ex guide dogs) ◾

CARNASSERIE CASTLE   Map 10 NM80

CARNASSERIE CASTLE

PA31 8RQ
➲ (2m N of Kilmartin off A816)   `FREE`

A handsome combined tower house and hall, home of John Carswell, first Protestant Bishop of the Isles and translator of the first book printed in Gaelic. Very fine architectural details of the late 16th century.

Times: Open at all reasonable times. **Facilities:** ✖ ▉

HELENSBURGH   Map 10 NS28

THE HILL HOUSE

Upper Colquhoun St G84 9AJ
➲ (off B832, between A82 & A814)
☎ 01436 673900
web: www.nts.org.uk

The Hill House is a handsome example of Charles Rennie Mackintosh's work, modern but part-inspired by Scottish tower houses. It was commissioned by the publisher Walter Blackie. The gardens are being restored to Blackie's design, with features reflecting the suggestions of Mackintosh. There is also a special display about Mackintosh.

Times: ✱ Open Apr-Oct, daily 1.30-5.30. Morning visits available for pre-booked groups. Times may change for 2006 please telephone or check on www.nts.org.uk **Facilities:** 🅿 🛒 shop ✖ ♨

INVERARAY   Map 10 NN00

BELL TOWER OF ALL SAINTS' CHURCH

The Avenue PA32 8YX
➲ (through the arches on Front St, into Avenue car park)
☎ 01828 200293
e-mail: dean.sedati@virgin.net

The tower was built in the 1920s and stands at 126ft. It has the world's second heaviest ring of ten bells, installed as a Campbell War Memorial in 1931. An exhibition on campanology is mounted inside and visiting bell ringers give recitals, usually once a month. A splendid view rewards those who climb to the roof.

Times: Open Etr-Sep, daily 10-1 & 2-5. **Fee:** £2 (ch & pen 75p). Family ticket £4 **Facilities:** 🅿 (adjacent to church) ♿ Unsuitable as 176 step stone spiral staircase ✖ (ex guide dogs)

Inveraray Castle
PA32 8XE
➲ (on A83 Glasgow to Campbeltown road)
☎ 01499 302203
e-mail: enquiries@inveraray-castle.com
web: www.inveraray-castle.com

The third Duke of Argyll engaged Roger Morris to build the present castle in 1743; in the process the old Burgh of Inveraray was demolished and a new town built nearby. The 5th Duke commissioned the beautiful interior decoration. The great armoury hall and staterooms are of particular note.

Times: Open 1st Sat in Apr-last Sun in Oct. Apr-May, Oct, Mon-Thu & Sat 10-1 & 2-5.45. Sun 1-5.45; Jun-Sep, Mon-Sat 10-5.45, Sun 1-5.45. (Last admission 12.30 & 5). **Fee:** £6.30 (ch under 16 £4.10, concessions £5.20) Family ticket £17. School parties. Groups 20+. **Facilities:** P ☕ ♿ toilets for disabled shop ✗ (ex guide dogs)

Inveraray Jail
Church Square PA32 8TX
➲ (on A82/A83 Campbeltown road)
☎ 01499 302381
e-mail: Info@Inverarayjail.co.uk
web: www.inveraryjail.co.uk

Enter Inveraray Jail and step back in time. See furnished cells and experience prison sounds and smells. Ask the 'prisoner' how to pick oakum. Turn the heavy handle of an original crank machine, take 40 winks in a hammock or listen to Matron's tales of day-to-day prison life. Visit the magnificent 1820 courtroom and hear trials in progress. Imaginative exhibitions including 'Torture, Death and Damnation' and 'In Prison Today'. New at Inveraray Jail, a fully preserved "Black Maria", built in 1891.

Times: Open all year, Nov-Mar, daily 10-5 (last admisssion 4); Apr-Oct, daily 9.30-6 (last admission 5). Closed 25 Dec & 1 Jan. **Fee:** Prices not confirmed for 2006 **Facilities:** P (100 yds) ♿ (wheelchair ramp at rear, induction loop in courtroom) toilets for disabled shop

KILMARTIN — Map 10 NR89

Dunadd Fort
FREE
➲ (2m S of Kilmartin on A816)

Dunadd was one of the ancient capitals of Dalriada from which the Celtic kingdom of Scotland was formed. Near to this prehistoric hill fort (now little more than an isolated hillock) are carvings of a boar and a footprint; these probably marked the spot where early kings were invested with their royal power.

Times: Open at all reasonable times. **Facilities:** ✗

Kilmartin House Museum
PA31 8RQ
➲ (in centre of village, adjacent to church)
☎ 01546 510278
e-mail: museum@kilmartin.org
web: www.kilmartin.org

Kilmartin may seem to be a quiet Scottish village, but at least 150 prehistoric sites lie within six miles of it. There are mysterious carved rocks, enigmatic standing stones, fascinating burial cairns and the fortress of the earliest Scottish Kings. Thousands of years of history are traced in a museum that explores ancient peoples' struggles for survival, their attempts to understand the world around them, early agriculture, and social strife in the shape of aggression and conflict. There is also an audio-visual extravaganza that uses 12 projectors to project 600 slides in

continued

16 minutes. The presentation deals with the history and beauty of the landscape of Mid Argyll.

Times: Open Mar-Oct, daily, 10-5.30. Reduced days/hours Nov-Feb. **Fee:** * £4.90 (ch £1.70, concessions £3.90). Family ticket £6 or £10. **Facilities:** P ☕ ✕ licensed ♿ toilets for disabled shop ✗ (ex guide dogs) (small coaches, pre-booked)

LOCHAWE — Map 10 NN12

Cruachan Power Station
Visitor Centre, Dalmally PA33 1AN
➲ (A85 18m E of Oban)
☎ 01866 822618
e-mail: visit.cruachan@scottishpower.com
web: www.scottishpower.plc.uk

A vast cavern hidden 1km inside Ben Cruachan, which contains a 400,000-kilowatt hydro-electric power station, driven by water drawn from a high-level reservoir up the mountain. A guided tour takes you inside the mountain and reveals the generators in their underground cavern.

Times: Open Etr-Nov, daily 9.30-5 (last tour 4.15). **Fee:** * £4 (ch 6-16 £1.50, concessions £3.50) **Facilities:** P ☕ ♿ toilets for disabled shop ✗ (ex guide dogs)

MINARD — Map 10 NR99

Crarae Gardens
PA32 8YA
➲ (10m S of Inveraray on A83)
☎ 01546 886614

Set beside Loch Fyne, these gardens are among Scotland's loveliest, noted for their rhododendrons, azaleas, conifers and ornamental shrubs, which include a number of rare species.

Times: * Open all year, daily, 9-sunset. Visitor centre, Etr-Oct, daily 10-5. Times may change for 2006 please telephone or check on www.nts.org.uk **Facilities:** P ☕ ♿ toilets for disabled shop garden centre

OBAN — Map 10 NM83

Dunstaffnage Castle
PA37 1PZ
➲ (3m N on peninsula)
☎ 01631 562465

Now ruined, this four-sided stronghold has a gatehouse, two round towers and walls 10ft thick. It was once the prison of Flora MacDonald.

Times: Open all year, Apr-Sep, daily 9.30-6.30; Oct-Mar, daily 9.30-4.30. Closed Thu & Fri in winter, 25-26 Dec & 1-2 Jan. **Fee:** * £2.50 (ch £1, concessions £1.90). Group 11+ 10% discount. Prices valid until 31/12/05. Please phone for further details. **Facilities:** P shop

TAYNUILT — Map 10 NN03

Bonawe Iron Furnace
PA35 1JQ
➲ (0.75m NE off B845)
☎ 01866 822432

The furnace is a restored charcoal blast-furnace for iron-smelting and making cast-iron. It was established in 1753 and worked until 1876. The works exploited the Forest of Lorne to provide charcoal for fuel.

Times: Open Apr-Sep, daily 9.30-6.30. **Fee:** * £3 (ch £1.20, concessions £2.30). Group 11+ 10% discount. Prices valid until 31/12/05. Please phone for further details. **Facilities:** P ♿ toilets for disabled shop

CITY OF EDINBURGH

BALERNO   Map 11 NT16

MALLENY GARDEN
EH14 7AF
➲ (off A70 Lanark road)
☎ 0131 449 2283
web: www.nts.org.uk

The delightful gardens are set round a 17th-century house (not open to the public). Shrub roses, a woodland garden, and a group of four clipped yews, survivors of a group planted in 1603, are among its notable features. The National Bonsai Collection for Scotland is also at Malleny.
Times: ✱ Garden: all year daily 10-6 or dusk if earlier. House not open. Times may change for 2006 please telephone or check on www.nts.org.uk **Facilities:** 🅿 ♿ ✖ (ex guide dogs) 🐾

EDINBURGH   Map 11 NT27

BRASS RUBBING CENTRE
Trinity Apse, Chalmers Close, High St EH1 1SS
➲ (located on the Royal Mile)
☎ 0131 556 4364
web: www.cac.org.uk

Housed in the 15th-century remnant of Trinity Apse, the Centre offers the chance to make your own rubbing from a wide range of replica monumental brasses and Pictish stones. Tuition is available.
Times: Open Apr-Sep, Mon-Sat 10-5 (during Edinburgh Festival Sun 12-5). **Fee:** ✱ Free entry. Charge for brass rubbing.
Facilities: 🅿 (250mtrs) (parking meters, few spaces) shop ✖ (ex guide dogs)

CAMERA OBSCURA & WORLD OF ILLUSIONS
Castlehill, Royal Mile EH1 2ND
➲ (next to Edinburgh Castle)
☎ 0131 226 3709
e-mail: info@camera-obscura.co.uk

A unique view of Edinburgh - as the lights go down, a brilliant moving image of the surrounding city appears. The scene changes as a guide operates the camera's system of revolving lenses and mirrors.
Times: ✱ Open all year, daily, Apr-Oct 9.30-6; Nov-Mar 10-5. Closed 25 Dec. Open later Jul-Aug, phone for details. **Facilities:** 🅿 (300mtrs) shop ✖ (ex guide dogs) ◼

CITY ART CENTRE
2 Market St EH1 1DE
➲ (opposite rear of Waverley Stn)
☎ 0131 529 3993
e-mail: enquiries@city-art-centre.gov.uk
web: www.cac.org.uk

The City Art Centre houses the city's permanent fine art collection and stages a constantly changing programme of temporary exhibitions from all parts of the world. It has six floors of display galleries (linked by an escalator).
Times: Open Mon-Sat 10-5 & Sun 12-5 **Fee:** ✱ Free. Admission charged for some exhibitions. **Facilities:** 🅿 (500yds) (single yellow lines) 🔲 🔳 ♿ (induction loop, lifts, Braille signage, escalator) toilets for disabled shop ✖ (ex guide dogs) ◼

CRAIGMILLAR CASTLE
EH16 4SY
➲ (2.5m SE, off A68)
☎ 0131 661 4445

Mary, Queen of Scots retreated to this 14th-century stronghold after the murder of Rizzio. The plot to murder Darnley, her second husband, was also hatched here. There are 16th and 17th century apartments.
Times: Open all year, Apr-Sep, daily 9.30-6.30; Oct-Mar, daily 9.30-4.30. Closed Thu & Fri in winter, 25-26 Dec & 1-2 Jan. **Fee:** ✱ £3 (ch £1.20, concessions £2.25). Group 11+ 10% discount. Prices valid until 31/12/05. Please phone for further details. **Facilities:** 🅿 ♿ toilets for disabled shop ◼

DEAN GALLERY
73 Belford Rd EH4 3DS
➲ (20 min walk from Edinburgh Haymarket stn & Princes St)
☎ 0131 624 6200
e-mail: enquiries@nationalgalleries.org
web: www.nationalgalleries.org

Opened in March 1999, the Dean Gallery provides a home for the Eduardo Paolozzi gift of sculpture and graphic art, the Gallery of Modern Art's renowned Dada and Surrealist collections, a major library and archive centre, along with temporary exhibition space for modern and contemporary art.
Times: ✱ Open all year, daily 10-5. Extended opening during Edinburgh Festival. Closed 25-26 Dec. **Fee:** ✱ Admission to permanent collections free, charge may be made for special exhibitions.
Facilities: 🅿 🔲 ♿ (ramps & lift) toilets for disabled shop ✖ (ex guide dogs) ◼

DYNAMIC EARTH
Holyrood Rd EH8 8AS
➲ (on edge of Holyrood Park, opposite Palace of Holyrood House)
☎ 0131 550 7800   **2 for 1**
e-mail: enquiries@dynamicearth.co.uk
web: www.dynamicearth.co.uk

How the Earth works! Take a walk through Scotland's geological history. Travel back in time to follow the creation of planet earth. Be shaken by a volcano, feel the chill of polar ice and get caught in a tropical rainstorm. Before looking to the future. Please visit website for details of events running throughout the year.
Times: Open Apr-Oct daily & Nov-Mar Wed-Sat 10-5, (last entry 3.50); Jul-Aug daily, 10-5, (last entry 4.50). **Fee:** £9.45 (ch £5.95). Family ticket (2ad+2ch) £26.50. **Facilities:** 🅿 (charged) 🔲 ✖ licensed 🍴 ♿ (audio guides, large print gallery guides) toilets for disabled shop ✖ (ex guide dogs) ◼

EDINBURGH CASTLE
EH1 2NG
☎ 0131 225 9846

This historic stronghold stands on the precipitous crag of Castle Rock. One of the oldest parts is the 11th-century chapel of the saintly Queen Margaret, but most of the present castle evolved later, during its stormy history of sieges and wars, and was altered again in Victorian times. The Scottish crown and other royal regalia are displayed in the Crown Room. Also notable is the Scottish National War Memorial.
Times: Open all year, Apr-Sep daily 9.30-6.00; Oct-Mar 9.30-5.00. Closed 25-26 Dec. **Fee:** ✱ £9.80 (ch £3.50, concessions £7.50). Group 11+ 10% discount. Prices valid until 31/12/05. Please phone for further details. **Facilities:** 🅿 (charged) 🔲 ✖ licensed ♿ (free transport to top of Castle Hill lift) toilets for disabled shop ✖ ◼

THE EDINBURGH DUNGEON
31 Market St EH1 1QB
⊃ (close to Waverly Train Station)
☎ 0131 240 1000 & 240 1002
e-mail: edinburghdungeon@
merlinentertainments.biz
web: www.thedungeons.com

From the same team at The London Dungeon, there comes a Scottish "feast of fun with history's horrible bits". A mixture of live actors, rides, shows and special effects take the brave visitor back into a dark past that includes such delights as the 18th-century Judgement of Sinners, the 17th-century Plague, and the new attraction, Clan Wars, which attempts to recreate the horror of the Glencoe Massacre of 1692.
Times: Open all year ex Xmas. Please telephone for times.
Fee: ✱ £10.95 (ch 5-14 £6.95) concessions £8.95
Facilities: P (100mtrs) (metered bays limited to 1-2hrs) 🍴 & toilets for disabled shop ✖ (ex guide dogs) 🍽

EDINBURGH ZOO
Murrayfield EH12 6TS
⊃ (3m W of city centre on A8 towards Glasgow)
☎ 0131 334 9171
e-mail: marketing@rzss.org.uk
web: www.edinburghzoo.org.uk

Scotland's largest wildlife attraction, set in 80 acres of leafy hillside parkland, just ten minutes from the city centre. With over 1,000 animals ranging from the tiny poison arrow frog to massive white rhinos, including many threatened species. See the world's largest penguin pool with underwater viewing, and the Darwin Maze, based on the theme of evolution.
Times: ✱ Open all year, Apr-Sep, daily 9-6; Oct & Mar, daily 9-5; Nov-Feb, daily 9-4.30. **Facilities:** P (charged) 🍽 ✖ licensed 🍴 & (wheelchair loan free, 1 helper free - phone in advance) toilets for disabled shop ✖ (ex guide dogs) 🍽

GEORGIAN HOUSE
7 Charlotte Square EH2 4DR
⊃ (2 mins walk W end of Princes St)
☎ 0131 226 3318
e-mail: thegeorgianhouse@nts.org.uk
web: www.nts.org.uk

The house is part of Robert Adam's splendid north side of Charlotte Square, the epitome of Edinburgh New Town architecture. The lower floors of No 7 have been restored in the style of the early 1800s, when the house was new. There
continued

also videos of life in the New Town, and this house in particular.
Times: ✱ Open Apr-Oct, daily 10-5; Mar & Nov-24 Dec daily 11-3. Times may change for 2006 please telephone or check on www.nts.org.uk **Facilities:** P (100 yds) (meters, disabled directly outside) & (induction loop, Braille guide) shop ✖ (ex guide dogs) 🍽

GLADSTONE'S LAND
477b Lawnmarket EH1 2NT
⊃ (5 mins walk from Princes St via Mound)
☎ 0131 226 5856
web: www.nts.org.uk

Built in 1620, this six-storey tenement, once a merchant's house, still has its arcaded front - a rare feature now. Visitors can also see unusual tempera paintings on the walls and ceilings. It is furnished as a typical 17th-century merchant's home, complete with ground-floor shop front and goods of the period.
Times: ✱ Open Apr-Oct, Mon-Sat, 10-5, Sun 2-5. Times may change for 2006 please telephone or check on www.nts.org.uk
Facilities: P (440yds) (outside for disabled) & (tours for the blind can be arranged) shop ✖ (ex guide dogs) 🍽

JOHN KNOX HOUSE
The Netherbow, 43-45 High St EH1 1SR `2 for 1`
⊃ (between The Castle and Holyrood House)
☎ 0131 556 9579

John Knox the Reformer is said to have died in the house, which was built by the goldsmith to Mary, Queen of Scots. Renovation work has revealed the original floor in the Oak Room, and a magnificent painted ceiling.
Times: Open all year, Mon-Sat 10-6 & Sun 2-6. Closed Xmas.
Fee: ✱ £3 (ch £1, under 7's free, concessions £2). **Facilities:** P (5 min walk) (paying car park) 🍴 & (transcript of tapes, tours for blind, with notice) toilets for disabled shop ✖ (ex guide dogs) 🍽

LAURISTON CASTLE
Cramond Rd South, Davidson's Mains EH4 5QD
⊃ (NW outskirts of Edinburgh, 1m E of Cramond overlooking the Forth at Silverknowles)
☎ 0131 336 2060
web: www.cac.org.uk

The castle is a late 16th-century tower house with 19th-century additions but is most notable as a classic example of the Edwardian age. It has a beautifully preserved Edwardian interior and the feel of a country house, and the spacious grounds are very pleasant.
Times: Open all year by guided tour only; Apr-Oct, 11-1 & 2-5; Nov-Mar, wknds 2-4. (Closed Fri). **Fee:** Prices not confirmed for 2006
Facilities: P & toilets for disabled shop ✖ (ex guide dogs)

MUSEUM OF CHILDHOOD
42 High Street, Royal Mile, EH1 1TG
⊃ (On the Royal Mile)
☎ 0131 529 4142 `FREE`
web: www.cac.org.uk

One of the first museums of its kind, it was reopened after major expansion. It has a wonderful collection of toys, games and other belongings of children through the ages, to delight visitors both old and young. Ring for details of special events.
Times: Open all year, Mon-Sat 10-5, Sun 12-5. **Facilities:** P & (3 floors only) toilets for disabled shop ✖ (ex guide dogs)

MUSEUM OF EDINBURGH
142 Canongate, Royal Mile EH8 8DD
➲ (on the Royal Mile)
☎ 0131 529 4143   FREE
web: www.cac.org.uk
Housed in one of the best-preserved 16th-century buildings
in the Old Town. It was built in 1570 and later became the
headquarters of the Incorporation of Hammermen. Now a
museum of local history, it has collections of silver,
glassware, pottery, and other items such as street signs.
Times: Open all year, Mon-Sat 10-5. Sun in Aug noon-5.
Facilities: P (200yds) (parking meters, limited spaces) & shop
✖ (ex guide dogs)

MUSEUM OF SCOTLAND
Chambers St EH1 1JF
➲ (Situated in Chambers Street in the Old Town.
A few mins walk from Princes Street and The
Royal Mile)
☎ 0131 247 4422   FREE
e-mail: info@nms.ac.uk
web: www.nms.ac.uk

The museum is a striking new landmark in Edinburgh's
historic Old Town. It houses more than 10,000 of the nation's
most precious artefacts, as well as everyday objects which
throw light on life in Scotland through the ages. Admission
to the Royal Museum which is adjacent to the Museum of
Scotland is also free. Telephone for details of special events.
Times: Open all year, Mon-Sat 10-5, Tue 10-8 & Sun 12-5. Closed 25 Dec.
Please telephone for times on 26 Dec and 1 Jan. **Facilities:** P ▣
✖ licensed ▣ & toilets for disabled shop ✖ (ex assist dogs) ◀

NATIONAL GALLERY OF SCOTLAND
The Mound EH2 2EL
➲ (off Princes St)
☎ 0131 624 6200
e-mail: enquiries@nationalgalleries.org
web: www.nationalgalleries.org
Occupying a handsome neo-classical building designed by
William Playfair, the gallery is home to Scotland's greatest
collection of European paintings and sculpture from the
Renaissance to Post-Impressionism. It contains notable
collections of works by Old Masters, Impressionists and
Scottish artists.
Times: Open all year, daily 10-5, Thu until 7. New Year' Day noon-5.
Closed 25-26 Dec. **Fee:** Free. Admission charged to some major
exhibitions. **Facilities:** P (150yds) ▣ & (ramps & lift, room A1 not
accessible) toilets for disabled shop ✖ (ex guide dogs) ◀

NATIONAL WAR MUSEUM OF SCOTLAND
Edinburgh Castle EH1 2NG
➲ (At Edinburgh Castle, a few minutes walk up
the Royal Mile to Castlehill)
☎ 0131 247 4413
e-mail: info@nms.ac.uk
web: www.nms.ac.uk
Explore the Scottish experience of war and military service
over the last 400 years. A chance to experience the poignant
stories of the Scots who went to war, through their letters
and personal treasures.
Times: Open all year, daily, Apr-Oct, 9.45-5.45; Nov-Mar, daily,
9.45-4.45 Closed 25-26 Dec. **Fee:** ✳ Free admission after paying
entrance fee to Castle. **Facilities:** P & courtesy vehicle runs from the
Castle ticket kiosk toilets for disabled shop ✖ (ex assist dogs)

NELSON MONUMENT
Calton Hill EH7 5AA Calton Hill
➲ (Overlooking end of city)
☎ 0131 556 2716
web: www.cac.org.uk
Designed in 1807 the monument dominates the east end of
Princes Street. The views are superb, and every day except
Sunday the time ball drops at 1pm as the gun at the castle
goes off.
Times: Open all year, Apr-Sep, Mon 1-6 & Tue-Sat 10-6; Oct-Mar
Mon-Sat 10-3. **Fee:** ✳ £3 **Facilities:** P shop ✖ (ex guide dogs)

PALACE OF HOLYROODHOUSE
EH8 8DX
➲ (at east end of Royal Mile)
☎ 0131 556 5100
e-mail: holyrood@royalcollection.org.uk
web: www.royalcollection.org.uk
The Palace grew from the guest house of the Abbey of the
Holyrood, said to have been founded by David I after a
miraculous apparition. Mary, Queen of Scots had her court
here from 1561 to 1567, and 'Bonnie' Prince Charlie held
levees at the Palace during his occupation of Edinburgh. The
Palace is still used by the Royal Family, but can be visited
when they are not in residence. The picture gallery is notable
for its series of Scottish Monarchs.
Times: ✳ Open daily, Apr-Oct 9.30-6 (last admission 5); Nov-Mar
9.30-4.30 (last admission 3.30). Closed Good Fri, 25-26 Dec and when
The Queen is in residence. **Fee:** ✳ £5 (ch under 17 £3, concessions
£4). Family ticket (2ad + 3ch) £13. **Facilities:** P (charged) ▣
& (first floor by lift, wheelchair available) toilets for disabled shop
✖ (ex guide dogs) ◀

PARLIAMENT HOUSE
Supreme Courts, 2-11 Parliament Square EH1 1RQ
➲ (behind St Giles Cathedral)
☎ 0131 225 2595
Scotland's independent parliament last sat in 1707, in this
17th-century building hidden behind an 1829 façade, now
the seat of the Supreme Law Courts of Scotland. A large
stained glass window depicts the inauguration of the Court
of Session in 1540.
Times: ✳ Open all year, Mon-Fri 10-4. **Facilities:** P (400mtrs)
(metered parking in high street) ▣ ✖ & toilets for disabled
✖ (ex guide dogs)

THE PEOPLE'S STORY
Canongate Tolbooth, 163 Canongate, Royal Mile EH8 8BN
➲ (on the Royal Mile)
☎ 0131 529 4057
FREE
web: www.cac.org.uk

The museum, housed in the 16th-century tolbooth, tells the story of the ordinary people of Edinburgh from the late 18th century to the present day. Reconstructions include a prison cell, 1930s pub and 1940s kitchen supported by photographs, displays, sounds and smells.
Times: Open, Mon-Sat 10-5. Also open Sun during Edinburgh Festival 2-5. **Facilities:** P (100yds) (parking meters) ⬧ (lift, induction loop in video room, touch facilities) toilets for disabled shop ✈ (ex guide dogs)

THE REAL MARY KING'S CLOSE
2 Warriston's Close, High St EH1 1PG
➲ (off High St, opposite St. Giles Cathedral)
☎ 08702 430160
e-mail: info@realmarykingsclose.com
web: www.realmarykingsclose.com

Step back in time to walk through a warren of hidden streets, deep beneath The Royal Mile. Meet some of the real characters who used to inhabit these closes and hear tales of extraordinary apparitions as you are guided through dramatic episodes from Edinburgh's hidden past. Special Events: Mary Kings Ghost Fest. 2006. Please visit www.edinburghghostfest.co.uk for details.
Times: Open all year daily, tours run every 20mins from 10. (Last tour Apr-Oct 9pm, Nov-Mar 4pm Sun-Fri & 9pm Sat). Closed 25 Dec
Fee: £7.25 (ch £5, pen & student £6.25). Family ticket (2ad+2ch) £22.50 **Facilities:** P ⬧ hearing loop toilets for disabled shop ✈ (ex guide dogs)

ROYAL BOTANIC GARDEN EDINBURGH
20A Inverleith Row EH3 5LR
➲ (1m N of city centre, off A902)
☎ 0131 552 7171
e-mail: info@rbge.org.uk
web: www.rbge.org.uk

Established in 1670, on an area the size of a tennis court, the Garden is now over 70 acres of beautifully landscaped grounds. Spectacular features include the Rock Garden and the Chinese Hillside. The amazing glasshouses feature Britain's tallest palm house and the magnificent woodland gardens and arboretum.
Times: ✽ Open all year, daily; Apr-Sep, 10-7; Mar & Oct, 10-6; Nov-Feb, 10-4. Closed 25 Dec & 1 Jan. (Facilities close 30 mins before
continued

Garden) **Facilities:** P (restricted at certain times) ⬛ ✗ licensed ▤ ⬧ (wheelchairs available at east/west gates) toilets for disabled shop garden centre ✈ (ex guide dogs)

ROYAL MUSEUM
Chambers St EH1 1JF
➲ (Situated in Chambers Street, in the Old Town, a few mins walk from Princes Street and the Royal Mile)
☎ 0131 247 4422
FREE
e-mail: info@nms.ac.uk
web: www.nms.ac.uk

This magnificent museum houses extensive international collections covering the Decorative Arts, Natural History, Science, Technology and Working Life, and Geology. Temporary exhibitions, films, lectures and concerts take place throughout the year.
Times: Open all year, Mon-Sat 10-5, Sun 12-5 (Tue late opening till 8). Closed 25 Dec. Phone for times on 26 Dec/1 Jan. **Facilities:** P ⬛ ✗ licensed ⬧ (induction loops) toilets for disabled shop ✈ (ex assist dogs)

THE ROYAL YACHT BRITANNIA
Ocean Terminal, Leith EH6 6JJ
➲ (follow signs to North Edinburgh & Leith. Situated within Ocean Terminal)
☎ 0131 555 5566
e-mail: enquiries@tryb.co.uk
web: www.royalyachtbritannia.co.uk

Visit the Royal Yacht Britannia, now in Edinburgh's historic
continued

port of Leith. The experience starts in the Visitor Centre where you can discover Britannia's fascinating story. Then step aboard for a self-led audio tour which takes you around five decks giving you a unique insight into what life was like for the Royal Family, officers and yachtsmen. Highlights include the State Apartments, Admiral's Cabin, Engine Room, Laundry, Sick Bay and Royal Marine's Barracks. **Times:** Open Jan-Mar & Oct-Dec: 10-3.30 (last admission). Apr-Sep 9.30-4.30 (last admission). Closed 25 Dec & 1 Jan. **Fee:** £9 (ch 5-17 £5, pen £7). Family ticket (2ad+3ch) £25. **Facilities:** P & (lift to ship, all areas ramped, written scripts) toilets for disabled shop ✕ (ex guide dogs) ◼

SCOTCH WHISKY HERITAGE CENTRE
354 Castlehill, The Royal Mile EH1 2NE
➲ (next to Edinburgh Castle)
☎ 0131 220 0441
e-mail: enquiry@whisky-heritage.co.uk
web: www.whisky-heritage.co.uk
This fascinating heritage centre reveals the history of the Scottish Whisky industry. The tour has four main areas: The Making of Scotch Whisky, The Distillery, The Blender's Ghost, and Whisky Barrel Ride. The Whisky Bond Bar has over 280 different whiskies available.
Times: Open daily, 10-5.30 (extended in summer). Closed 25 Dec. **Fee:** £8.95 (ch 5-17 £4.95, concessions £6.95). **Facilities:** P (100m) (metered parking & NCP) ◼ ✕ licensed ◻ & (Braille script) toilets for disabled shop ✕ (ex guide dogs) ◼

SCOTTISH NATIONAL GALLERY OF MODERN ART
Belford Rd EH4 3DR
➲ (in West End, 20min walk from Haymarket station)
☎ 0131 624 6200
e-mail: enquiries@nationalgalleries.org
web: www.nationalgalleries.org
An outstanding collection of 20th-century painting, sculpture and graphic art. Includes major works by Matisse, Picasso, Bacon, Moore and Lichtenstein and an exceptional group of Scottish paintings. Set in leafy grounds with a sculpture garden.
Times: Open all year, daily 10-5. New Year's Day noon-5. Closed 25-26 Dec. **Fee:** Free. Admission charged to some major exhibitions. **Facilities:** P ◼ ◻ & (ramps & lift) toilets for disabled shop ✕ (ex guide dogs) ◼

SCOTTISH NATIONAL PORTRAIT GALLERY
1 Queen St EH2 1JD
➲ (parallel to Princes St, just behind St Andrew Square)
☎ 0131 624 6200
e-mail: enquiries@nationalgalleries.org
web: www.nationalgalleries.org
The collection provides a visual history of Scotland from the 16th century to the present day, told through the portraits of the people who shaped it. Among the most famous are Mary, Queen of Scots, Ramsay's portrait of David Hume and Raeburn's Sir Walter Scott. The building also houses the National Collection of Photography.
Times: Open all year, daily, 10-5. Thu until 7. New Year's Day noon-5. Closed 25-26 Dec. **Fee:** Free. Admission charged to some major exhibitions. **Facilities:** P (200yds) ◼ ◻ & (ramps & lift) toilets for disabled shop ✕ (ex guide dogs) ◼

THE WRITERS' MUSEUM
Lady Stair's House, Lady Stair's Close, Lawnmarket EH1 2PA
➲ (off the Royal Mile)
☎ 0131 529 4901 ▮FREE▮
e-mail: enquiries@writersmuseum.demon.co.uk
web: www.cac.org.uk
Situated in the historic Lady Stair's House which dates from 1622, the museum houses various objects associated with Robert Burns, Sir Walter Scott and Robert Louis Stevenson. Temporary exhibitions are planned throughout the year.
Times: Open all year, Mon-Sat 10-5. (During Festival period only, Sun 12-5). **Facilities:** P (500mtrs) (parking meters) ◻ shop ✕ (ex guide dogs)

GOGAR   Map 11 NT17

SUNTRAP GARDEN
43 Gogarbank EH12 9BY
➲ (between A8 & A71 W of city bypass)
☎ 0131 339 7283
e-mail: suntrap@btopenworld.com
web: www.suntrap-garden.org.uk
The three-acre garden comprises of many gardens within a single garden, including Italian, Rock, Peat and Woodland.
Times: Open all year Oct-Apr, 10-4; May-Sep, 10-6 **Fee:** £1 (accompanied ch and NT members free). **Facilities:** P ◻ & (limited access to toilet facilities at wknds) toilets for disabled garden centre (open Mon-Fri) ✕ (ex on lead)

SOUTH QUEENSFERRY   Map 11 NT17

DALMENY HOUSE
EH30 9TQ
☎ 0131 331 1888
e-mail: events@dalmeny.co.uk
web: www.dalmeny.co.uk
This is the home of the Earl and the Countess of Rosebery, whose family have lived here for over 300 years. The house, however, dates from 1815 when it was built in Tudor Gothic style. There is fine French furniture, tapestries and porcelain from the Rothschild Mentmore collection. Early Scottish furniture is also shown, with 18th-century portraits, Rosebery racing mementoes, a display of pictures and one of the world's most important Napoleonic collections.
Times: Open Jul-Aug, Sun-Tue 2-5.30. (Last admission 4.30). Open other times by arrangement for groups. **Fee:** ✱ £5 (ch 10-16 £3, pen & students £4). Party 20+. **Facilities:** P ◼ ◻ & toilets for disabled ✕ (ex guide dogs or in grounds)

HOPETOUN HOUSE
EH30 9SL
➲ (2m W of Forth Road Bridge, off A904)
☎ 0131 331 2451
e-mail: marketing@hopetounhouse.com
web: www.hopetounhouse.com
Hopetoun House at South Queensferry is just a short drive from Edinburgh and has all the ingredients for a great family day out. Whether it is a leisurely stroll, afternoon tea or a touch of nostalgia you crave, Hopetoun will fit the bill. Built some 300 years ago, it is a delight to wander the corridors and historical rooms of one of the most splendid examples of the work of Scottish architects Sir William Bruce and William Adam. It shows some of the finest examples in Scotland of carving, wainscoting and ceiling painting. With 100 acres of parkland including a deep park, the gardens are a colourful carpet of seasonal flowers. After a gentle walk,
continued

indulge yourself with a traditional tea and a browse through our shop.
Times: Open daily Etr-Sep **Facilities:** 🅿 ⏸ 🗊 & (ramps) toilets for disabled shop ⌦

INCHCOLM ABBEY
Inchcolm Island
➲ (1.5m S of Aberdour. Access by ferry Apr-Sep)
☎ 01383 823332
Situated on a green island on the Firth of Forth, the Augustinian abbey was founded in about 1192 by Alexander I. The well-preserved remains include a fine 13th-century octagonal chapter house and a 13th-century wall painting.
Times: Open Apr-Sep, daily 9.30-6.30. **Fee:** ✱ £3.30 (ch £1.30, concessions £2.50). Additional charge for ferry trip. Group 11+ 10% discount. Prices valid until 31/12/05. Please phone for further details.
Facilities: & toilets for disabled shop ✘ ◪

QUEENSFERRY MUSEUM
53 High St EH30 9HP
➲ (A90 from Edinburgh)
☎ 0131 331 5545 **FREE**
web: www.cac.org.uk
The museum commands magnificent views of the two great bridges spanning the Forth and traces the history of the people of Queensferry and Dalmeny, the historic passage to Fife, the construction of the rail and road bridges and the wildlife of the Forth estuary. An ancient annual custom, in August, is Burry Man, who is clad from head to toe in burrs, and parades through the town. See the full size model of the Burry Man in the museum.
Times: Open all year, Mon & Thu-Sat 10-1, 2.15-5, Sun noon-5. (Last admission 1/2 hour before closing). Closed 25-26 Dec & 1-2 Jan
Facilities: 🅿 (0.25m) (induction loop at reception) shop ✘ (ex guide dogs)

CITY OF GLASGOW

GLASGOW   Map 11 NS56
BURRELL COLLECTION
2060 Pollokshaws Rd G43 1AT
➲ (3.5m S of city centre)
☎ 0141 287 2550 **FREE**
e-mail: museums@cls.glasgow.gov.uk
web: www.glasgowmuseums.com
Set in Pollok Country Park, this award-winning building makes the priceless works of art on display seem almost part of the woodland setting. Shipping magnate Sir William Burrell's main interests were medieval Europe, Oriental art and European paintings. Colourful paintings and stained glass show the details of medieval life. Furniture, paintings, sculpture, armour and weapons help to complete the picture. Rugs, ceramics and metalwork represent the art of Islam. There is also a strong collection of Chinese and other Oriental ceramics. Paintings on display include works by Bellini, Rembrandt and the French Impressionists.
Times: Open all year, Mon-Thu & Sat 10-5, Fri & Sun 11-5. Closed 24-25 & 31 [pm] Dec & 1-2 Jan **Facilities:** 🅿 (charged) ⏸
✘ licensed 🗊 & (wheelchairs available, tape guides, lifts) toilets for disabled shop ✘

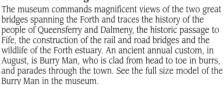

Directions are provided by the attractions.

CLYDEBUILT - SCOTTISH MARITIME MUSEUM AT BRAEHEAD
Braehead Shopping Centre, King Inch Rd G51 4BN
➲ (M8 junct 25A, 26, follow signs for Braehead Shopping Centre, then Green car park)
☎ 0141 886 1013 **2 for 1**
e-mail: clydebuilt@tinyworld.co.uk
web: www.scottishmaritimemuseum.org
On the banks of the River Clyde, home of the Scottish shipbuilding industry, visitors can discover how Glasgow's famous ships were built, from the design stages through to the launch. There are also displays on the textile and cotton industries, iron and steel, and tobacco. Hands-on activities allow you to operate a real ship's engine, become a ship's riveter, and steer a virtual ship up the Clyde.
Times: Open Mon-Sat 10-5.30; Sun 11-5. **Fee:** ✱ £4.25 (ch £2.50, concessions £3.00). Family ticket £10 **Facilities:** 🅿 🗊
& (lift/ramps/wheelchairs from shopping centre) toilets for disabled shop Maritime theme ✘ (ex guide dogs)

GALLERY OF MODERN ART
Royal Exchange Square G1 3AH
➲ (just off Buchanan St & close to Central Station & Queen St Stn)
☎ 0141 229 1996 **FREE**
e-mail: museums@cls.glasgow.gov.uk
web: www.glasgowmuseums.com
GoMA offers a thought-provoking programme of temporary exhibitions and workshops. It displays work by local and international artists, as well as addressing contemporary social issues through its major bi-annual projects.
Times: Open all year, Mon-Tue & Sat 10-5, Thu 10-8, Fri & Sun 11-5.
Facilities: 🅿 (200yds) ⏸ 🗊 & toilets for disabled shop
✘ (ex guide dogs)

GLASGOW CATHEDRAL
Castle St G4 0QZ
➲ (M8 junct 15, in centre of Glasgow)
☎ 0141 552 6891 **FREE**
The only Scottish mainland medieval cathedral to have survived the Reformation complete (apart from its western towers). Built during the 13th to 15th centuries over the supposed site of the tomb of St Kentigern. Notable features in this splendid building are the elaborately vaulted crypt, which included an introductory display and collection of carved stones, the stone screen of the early 15th century and the unfinished Blackadder Aisle.
Times: Open all year, Apr-Sep daily 9.30-6.00 Sunday 1pm-5pm; Oct-Mar daily 9.30-4.00 Sunday 1pm-4pm. Closed 25-26 Dec & 1-2 Jan.
Facilities: & (telephone for disabled access details) shop ✘ ◪

GLASGOW MUSEUMS RESOURCE CENTRE
200 Woodhead Rd, South Nitshill Ind Estate G53 7NN
➲ (on S side, close to Rail Stn)
☎ 0141 276 9300 **FREE**
web: www.glasgowmuseums.com
GMRC is the first publicly-accessible store for the city's museum service, offering a behind-the-scenes look at 200,000 treasures held in storage. Please note that access to the stores is by guided tour only. Viewings of a specific object can be arranged, with two weeks prior notice. Activities, tours and talks are held throughout the year - see website or phone for details.
Times: Open all year Mon-Thu & Sat 10-5, Fri-Sun 11-5. Guided tours for public at 2.30 Access is only by guided tours.
Facilities: 🅿 & toilets for disabled ✘ (ex guide dogs)

GLASGOW SCIENCE CENTRE

50 Pacific Quay G51 1EA

➲ (M8 junct 24 or M77 junct 21, follow brown signs, across Clyde from SECC)

☎ 0141 420 5000

e-mail: admin@glasgowsciencecentre.org

web: www.glasgowsciencecentre.org

The centre is home to many entertaining and exciting attractions and contains hundreds of interactive exhibits. Highlights include the Scottish Power Space Theatre, Scotland's only IMAX cinema and the 127m Glasgow Tower, a remarkable free-standing structure that gives breathtaking views of the city (check availability before visiting). GSC presents the world of science and technology in new and exciting ways.

Times: Open daily 10-6. **Fee:** Science Mall* or Imax: £6.95 (ch & concessions £4.95).Science Mall & Imax: £9.95 (ch & concessions £7.95). 10% off for groups 4+. * Scottish Power Space Theatre extra £2. **Facilities:** ☐ (charged) ☕ ♿ (induction loops) toilets for disabled shop ✕ (ex guide/hearing dogs) ◀

GREENBANK GARDEN

Flenders Rd, Clarkston G76 8RB

➲ (off A726 on southern outskirts of city)

☎ 0141 639 3281

web: www.nts.org.uk

The spacious, walled woodland gardens are attractively laid out in the grounds of an elegant Georgian house, and best seen between April and October. A wide range of flowers and shrubs are grown, with the idea of helping private gardeners to look at possibilities for their own gardens. A greenhouse and garden designed for the disabled gardener also displays specialised tools.

Times: ✱ Open daily 9.30-sunset. Times may change for 2006 please telephone or check on www.nts.org.uk **Facilities:** ☐ ☕ ♿ (wheelchairs available) toilets for disabled shop ✕ (ex guide dogs) ☙

HOLMWOOD HOUSE

61-63 Netherlee House, Cathcart G44 3YG

➲ (off Clarkston Rd)

☎ 0141 637 2129

web: www.nts.org.uk

Built in the mid 19th century, the architectural style of the house is an adaptation of classical Greek. Many rooms are richly ornamented in wood, plaster and marble.

Times: ✱ Open Apr-Oct, daily 12-5. Morning visits available for pre-booked groups. Times may change for 2006 please telephone or check on www.nts.org.uk

HOUSE FOR AN ART LOVER

10 Dumbreck Rd, Bellahouston Park G41 5BW

➲ (M8 W junct 23 signed B768, left at top of slip road onto Dumbreck Rd. Bellahouston Park on right)

☎ 0141 353 4770

e-mail: info@houseforanartlover.co.uk

web: www.houseforanartlover.co.uk

Originally designed by Glasgow's most celebrated architect, Charles Rennie Mackintosh, in 1901, this unusual cultural, corporate and academic resource began construction in 1989 and was completed in 1996. Contains art galleries and rooms to hire for conferences, private parties and weddings.

Times: Open Apr-Sep, Mon-Wed 10-4 & Thu-Sun 10-1; Oct-Mar, Sat-Sun 10-1, telephone for wkday opening details. **Fee:** £3.50 (ch under 10 free, concessions £2.50). **Facilities:** ☐ ☕ ▯ ♿ (lift to 2nd floor) toilets for disabled shop ✕ (ex guide dogs) ◀

HUNTERIAN ART GALLERY

82 Hillhead St, The University of Glasgow G12 8QQ

➲ (on University of Glasgow Campus in Hillhead District, 2m W of city centre)

☎ 0141 330 5431

e-mail: hunter@museum.gla.ac.uk

web: www.hunterian.gla.ac.uk

The founding collection is made up of paintings bequeathed in the 18th century by Dr William Hunter, including works by Rembrandt and Stubbs. The Gallery now has works by James McNeill Whistler, major displays of paintings by the Scottish Colourists, and a graphics collection holding some 300,000 prints. A popular feature of the Charles Rennie Mackintosh collection is the re-construction of the interiors of The Mackintosh House.

Times: Open Mon-Sat 9.30-5. Telephone for BH closures. **Facilities:** ☐ (500 yds) (pay & display) ☕ ♿ (lift, wheelchair available) toilets for disabled shop ✕ (ex guide dogs) ◀

HUNTERIAN MUSEUM

Gilbert Scott Building, The University of Glasgow G12 8QQ

➲ (on University of Glasgow campus in Hillhead District, 2m W of city centre)

☎ 0141 330 4221

e-mail: hunter@museum.gla.ac.uk

web: www.hunterian.gla.ac.uk

Named after the 18th-century physician, Dr William Hunter, who bequeathed his large and important collections of coins, medals, fossils, geological specimens and archaeological and ethnographic items to the university. The exhibits are shown in the main building of the university, and temporary exhibitions are held.

Times: Open all year, Mon-Sat 9.30-5. Closed certain BHs phone for details. **Facilities:** ☐ (100yds) (pay & display) ♿ (lift) toilets for disabled shop ✕ (ex guide dogs) ◀

HUTCHESONS' HALL

158 Ingram St G1 1EJ

➲ (near SE corner of George Square)

☎ 0141 552 8391

e-mail: hutchesonshall@nts.org.uk

web: www.nts.org.uk

This handsome early 19th-century building was designed by David Hamilton and houses a visitor centre and shop. There is a video about Glasgow's merchant city, and the Hall can be booked for functions. Telephone for details of concerts, recitals, etc.

Times: ✱ Gallery: open Mon-Sat, 10-5. Closed 24 Dec-mid Jan. Hall: open subject to functions. Times may change for 2006 please telephone or check on www.nts.org.uk **Facilities:** ☐ (on street) (meters)(outside for disabled) ▯ ♿ toilets for disabled shop ✕ ☙

McLELLAN GALLERIES

270 Sauchiehall St G2 3EH

➲ (N side of Sauchiehall St, close to Glasgow School of Art)

☎ 0141 565 4137

e-mail: museums@cls.glasgow.gov.uk

web: www.glasgowmuseums.com

The McLellan Galleries first opened in 1854 and featured the personal collection of Glasgow industrialist and coachbuilder Archibald McLellan. With over 1,200 sq metres of top gallery space, the McLellan Galleries provide Glasgow Museums with the opportunity to hold major exhibitions and establish

continued

Glasgow as Britain's second art city. With Kelvingrove Art Gallery closed for refurbishment until Spring 2006, the McLellan Galleries are showing 200 of Kelvingrove's famous paintings and objects in the exhibition 'Art Treasures of Kelvingrove' (closes Nov 2005).

Times: Open all year, Mon-Thu & Sat 10-5, Fri & Sun 11-5. Closed 24-25 & 31 Dec [pm] & 1-2 Jan **Facilities:** P (500mtrs) ☕ ▦ & (assistance available, lift) toilets for disabled shop ✈

MUSEUM OF TRANSPORT

1 Bunhouse Rd G3 8DP
➲ (1.5m W of city centre)
☎ 0141 287 2720
e-mail: museums@cls.glasgow.gov.uk
web: www.glasgowmuseums.com

Visit the Museum of Transport and the first impression is of gleaming metalwork and bright paint. All around you there are cars, caravans, carriages and carts, fire engines, buses, steam locomotives, prams and trams. The museum uses its collections of vehicles and models to tell the story of transport by land and sea, with a unique Glasgow flavour. Visitors can even go window shopping along the recreated Kelvin Street of 1938. Upstairs 250 ship models tell the story of the great days of Clyde shipbuilding. The Museum of Transport has something for everyone.

Times: Open all year, Mon-Thu & Sat 10-5, Fri & Sun 11-5. **Facilities:** P (charged) ☕ ▦ & (assistance available) toilets for disabled shop ✈ (ex guide dogs)

PEOPLE'S PALACE AND WINTER GARDENS

Glasgow Green G40 1AT
➲ (1m SE of city centre)
☎ 0141 271 2951
e-mail: museums@cls.glasgow.gov.uk
web: www.glasgowmuseums.com

Glasgow grew from a medieval town located by the Cathedral to the Second City of the British Empire. Trade with the Americas, and later industry, made the city rich. But not everyone shared in Glasgow's wealth. The People's Palace on historic Glasgow Green shows how ordinary Glaswegians worked, lived and played. Visitors can discover how a family lived in a typical one-room Glasgow 'single end' tenement flat, see Billy Connolly's amazing banana boots, learn to speak Glesga, take a trip 'doon the watter' and visit the Winter Gardens.

Times: Open all year, Mon-Thu & Sat 10-5, Fri & Sun 11-5. Closed 24-25 & 31 Dec [pm] & 1-2 Jan **Facilities:** P (50yds) ☕ & (lifts) toilets for disabled shop garden centre ✈

POLLOK HOUSE

Pollok Country Park, 2060 Pollokshaws Rd G43 1AT
➲ (3.5m S of city centre, off M77 junct 2, follow signs for Burrell Collection)
☎ 0141 616 6410
e-mail: pollokhouse@nts.org.uk
web: www.nts.org.uk

The house is one of Glasgow's most elegant, and was built by the Maxwell family in the 18th century and expanded between 1890 and 1901, including extensive servants' quarters. The rooms are decorated with 18th-century plasterwork, fine furniture and the Stirling Maxwell art collection, including works by El Greco, Goya and William Blake.

Times: House: open daily 10-5. Closed 25 & 26 Dec & 1 & 2 Jan. **Facilities:** P ✗ licensed & (lifts) toilets for disabled shop ✈

PROVAND'S LORDSHIP

3 Castle St G4 0RB
➲ (1m E of city centre)
☎ 0141 552 8819
e-mail: museums@cls.glsgow.gov.uk
web: www.glasgowmuseums.com

Provand's Lordship is the only house to survive from Medieval Glasgow. For over 500 years it has watched the changing fortunes of the city and the nearby Cathedral. Bishop Andrew Muirhead built the house as part of St Nicholas' Hospital in 1971. The prebendary of Barlanark later bought it for use as a manse. Inside, the displays recreate home life in the middle ages. Behind the house is the St Nicholas Garden, built in 1997. It is a medical herb garden, in keeping with the original purpose of the house.

Times: Open all year, Mon-Thu & Sat 10-5, Fri & Sun 11-5. **Facilities:** P (50 yds) ☕ ▦ & (please contact for details) shop ✈ (ex guide dogs)

ST MUNGO MUSEUM OF RELIGIOUS LIFE & ART

2 Castle St G4 0RH
➲ (1m NE of city centre)
☎ 0141 553 2557
e-mail: museums@cls.glasgow.gov.uk
web: www.glasgowmuseums.com

The award-winning St Mungo Museum explores the importance of religion in peoples' everyday lives and art. It aims to promote understanding and respect between people of different faiths and of none. Highlights of the collection include the Salvador Dali painting *Christ of St John of the Cross*. The museum also features stained glass, objects, statues and video footage. Within the grounds is Britain's first Japanese Zen garden.

Times: Open all year, Mon-Thu & Sat 10-5, Fri & Sun 11-5. **Facilities:** P (50yds) ☕ ▦ & (taped information & lift) toilets for disabled shop ✈ (ex guide dogs)

THE SCOTTISH FOOTBALL MUSEUM

The National Stadium, Hampden Park G42 9BA
➲ (3m S of city centre, follow brown tourist signs)
☎ 0141 616 6139
e-mail: info@scottishfootballmuseum.org.uk
web: www.scottishfootballmuseum.org.uk

Using 2500 pieces of footballing memorabilia, the Scottish Football Museum covers such themes as football's origins, women's football, fan culture, other games influenced by football, and even some social history. The exhibits include

continued

the world's oldest football, trophy and ticket, a reconstructed 1903 changing room and press box, and items of specific import, such as Kenny Dalglish's silver cap, Jimmy McGrory's boots, and the ball from Scotland's 5-1 win over England in 1928.

Times: Open Mon-Sat 10-5, Sun 11-5. Closed match days, special events and Xmas/New Year, please telephone in advance for confirmation **Fee:** Museum £5 (concessions & ch under 16 £2.50) Stadium £6 (concessions & ch under 16 £3) Combined Ticket £8 (concessions & ch under 16 £4) Children under 5 are free **Facilities:** 🅿 💷 📋 ♿ (ramps throughout) toilets for disabled shop ✖ (ex guide dogs) 🍴

THE TALL SHIP AT GLASGOW HARBOUR
100 Stobcross Rd G3 8QQ
➲ (from M8 junct 19 onto A814 follow signs for attraction)
☎ 0141 222 2513
e-mail: info@thetallship.com
web: www.thetallship.com

`2 for 1`

Visit The Tall Ship at Glasgow Harbour and step back in time to the days of sail. Experience Glasgow's maritime history at first hand and explore the UK's only remaining Clydebuilt sailing ship, the Glenlee. Exhibitions on board and in the visitor centre on the quayside tell the story of the ship and the Glasgow Harbour area. If you have ever wondered what it would have been like to be a sailor on a tall ship, this is your chance to find out! Children can have fun by joining in the hunt for Jock, the ship's cat. An unmissable experience, The Tall Ship offers guided tours, changing exhibitions, children's activities, a nautical gift shop and cafe.

Times: Open daily Mar-Oct 10-5, Nov-Feb 10-4. **Fee:** ✱ £4.95 (concessions £3.75, 1 ch free with paying adult/concession, additional ch £2.50). **Facilities:** 🅿 💷 ✖ licensed 📋 ♿ toilets for disabled shop 🍴

TENEMENT HOUSE
145 Buccleuch St, Garnethill G3 6QN
➲ (N of Charing Cross)
☎ 0141 333 0183
e-mail: tenementhouse@nts.org.uk
web: www.nts.org.uk

This shows an unsung but once-typical side of Glasgow life: it is a first-floor flat, built in 1892, with a parlour, bedroom, kitchen and bathroom, furnished with the original recess beds, kitchen range, sink, and coal bunker, among other articles. The home of Agnes Toward from 1911 to 1965, the flat was bought by an actress who preserved it as a 'time capsule'. The contents vividly portray the life of one section of Glasgow society.

Times: ✱ Open Mar-Oct, daily 2-5. Wkday morning visits available for pre-booked educational & other groups. Times may change for 2006 please telephone or check on www.nts.org.uk **Facilities:** 🅿 (100yds) (restricted, recommend parking in town) (Braille guide) ✖ (ex guide dogs) ♨

TRADES HALL
85 Glassford St G1 1UH
➲ (in city centre in Merchant City. Accessible from George Square & Argyle St)
☎ 0141 552 2418
e-mail: info@tradeshallglasgow.co.uk
web: www.tradeshallglasgow.co.uk

`2 for 1`

The Trades Hall is one of Glasgow's most historic buildings and was home to the 14 incorporated crafts who regulated

trade and played a vital role in shaping and making Glasgow the city it is today. Visitors can explore the impressive rooms of the building taking in the Grand Hall with its spectacular soaring windows, baroque chandeliers and striking dome, and the Saloon which features an original Adam fireplace and beautiful stained glass windows.

Times: Open Apr-Oct, by appointment Mon-Sat, 9-6, subject to availability **Fee:** £3.50 (ch £2, pen £2.50, ch under 5 free). Groups 10+ £3 each. **Facilities:** 🅿 (NCP 100yds) 💷 ♿ electronic ramps for rise in levels of 3 & 4 stairs toilets for disabled shop ✖ (ex guide dogs)

UNIVERSITY OF GLASGOW VISITOR CENTRE
University Av G12 8QQ
➲ (M8 junct 19 E or junct 18 W)
☎ 0141 330 5511
e-mail: visitorcentre@gla.ac.uk
web: www.gla.ac.uk/visitors

The Visitor Centre is spacious and pleasant, with leaflets, publications and video displays explaining how the university works and its history, plus what courses are available and which university events are open to the public. Historic attractions include the Memorial Chapel, Professors' Square and Lion and Unicorn Staircase. Hunterian Museum is not part of the tour but visitors are welcome to view the museum on their own.

Times: Open all year, Mon-Sat 9.30-5. Also May-Sep, Sun 2-5. **Facilities:** 🅿 (880yds) (few spaces available) 💷 📋 ♿ (designated seating) toilets for disabled shop ✖ (ex guide dogs) 🍴

CLACKMANNANSHIRE

ALLOA   Map 11 NS89
ALLOA TOWER
Alloa Park FK10 1PP
➲ (on A907)
☎ 01259 211701
web: www.nts.org.uk

Beautifully restored, the tower, completed in 1467, is the only remaining part of the ancestral home of the Earls of Mar. The structure retains rare medieval features, notably the complete timber roof structure and groin vaulting. A superb loan collection of portraits and chattels of the Erskine family includes paintings by Raeburn.

Times: ✱ Open Apr-Oct, daily 1-5. Wkday morning visits available for pre-booked groups. Times may change for 2006 please telephone or check on www.nts.org.uk **Facilities:** 🅿 ♿ toilets for disabled ✖ ♨

ALVA   Map 11 NS89
MILL TRAIL VISITOR CENTRE
Glentana Mill, West Stirling St FK12 5EN
➲ (on A91 approx 8m E of Stirling)
☎ 01259 769696

`FREE`

In the heart of Scotland's woollen mill country, the Centre recounts the history of Scotland's woollen and tweed traditions, and features machines from spinning wheels to large motorised looms of the type in use today. Hear 12 year-old Mary describe her working day as a mill girl 150 years ago, and then contrast her story with our modern working woollen mill. Factory bargains and local crafts, tourist information centre, café.

Times: ✱ Open all year, Jan-Jun 10-5; Jul-Aug 9-5; Sep-Dec 10-5. **Facilities:** 🅿 💷 ♿ toilets for disabled shop ✖ (ex guide dogs) 🍴

DOLLAR Map 11 NS99

CASTLE CAMPBELL
FK14 7PP
➲ (10m E of Stirling on A91)
☎ 01259 742408

Traditionally known as the 'Castle of Gloom', the 15th to 17th-century tower stands in the picturesque Ochil Hills, gives wonderful views, and can be reached by a walk through the magnificent Dollar Glen. Care must be taken in or after rain when the path may be dangerous.
Times: Open all year, Apr-Sep, daily 9.30-6.30; Oct-Mar, Mon-Wed & Sat-Sun 9.30-4.30. Closed Thu & Fri in winter, 25-26 Dec & 1-2 Jan.
Fee: ✱ £3.30 (ch £1.30, concessions £2.50). Group 11+ 10% discount. Prices valid until 31/12/05. Please phone for further details.
Facilities: 🅿 ✖ shop ◗ ♨

DUMFRIES & GALLOWAY

ARDWELL Map 10 NX14

ARDWELL HOUSE GARDENS
DG9 9LY
➲ (10m S of Stranraer, on A716)
☎ 01776 860227

Country house gardens and grounds with flowering shrubs and woodland walks. Plants for sale. House not open to the public.
Times: Open Mar-Oct, 10-5. Walled garden & greenhouses close at 5.
Fee: ✱ £3 (ch & pen £2). **Facilities:** 🅿 📷 garden centre

CAERLAVEROCK Map 11 NY06

CAERLAVEROCK CASTLE
Glencaple DG1 4RU
➲ (8m SE of Dumfries, on B725)
☎ 01387 770244

This ancient seat of the Maxwell family is a splendid medieval stronghold dating back to the 13th century. It has high walls and round towers, with machicolations added in the 15th century.
Times: Open all year, Apr-Sep, daily 9.30-6.30; Oct-Mar, daily 9.30-4.30. Closed 25-26 Dec & 1-2 Jan. **Fee:** ✱ £4 (ch £1.60, concessions £3). Group 11+ 10% discount. Prices valid until 31/12/05. Please phone for further details. **Facilities:** 🅿 ✖ & toilets for disabled shop ◗

WWT CAERLAVEROCK
Eastpark Farm DG1 4RS
➲ (9m SE of Dumfries, signed from A75)
☎ 01387 770200
e-mail: caerlaverock@wwt.org.uk
web: www.wwt.org.uk

This internationally important wetland is the winter habitat of the entire Svalbard population of Barnacle Geese which spends the winter on the Solway Firth. Observation facilities include 20 hides, 3 towers and a heated observatory. A wide variety of wildlife can be seen, notably the rare Natterjack Toad and a family of Barn Owls which can be observed via a CCTV system.
Times: Open daily 10-5. Closed 25 Dec. **Fee:** ✱ £4.40 (ch £2.70 & concessions £3.60). Family ticket £11.50 **Facilities:** 🅿 📷 & toilets for disabled shop ✖ (ex guide dogs)

CARDONESS CASTLE Map 11 NX55

CARDONESS CASTLE
DG7 2EH
➲ (1m SW of Gatehouse of Fleet, off A75)
☎ 01557 814427

A 15th-century stronghold overlooking the Water of Fleet. It was once the home of the McCullochs of Galloway. The architectural details inside the tower are of very high quality.
Times: Open Apr-Sep, daily 9.30-6.30; Oct closed Thu & Fri. Nov - Mar open weekends only. Closed 25-26 Dec & 1-2 Jan. **Fee:** ✱ £2.50 (ch £1, concessions £1.90). Group 11+ 10% discount. Prices valid until 31/12/05. Please phone for further details. **Facilities:** 🅿 shop ◗

CASTLE DOUGLAS Map 11 NX76

THREAVE CASTLE
DG7 1RX
➲ (3m W on A75)
☎ 0411 223101

Archibald the Grim built this lonely castle in the late 14th century. It stands on an islet in the River Dee, and is four storeys high with round towers guarding the outer wall. The island is reached by boat.
Times: Open Apr-Sep, daily 9.30-6.30. **Fee:** ✱ £3 (ch £1.20, concessions £2.25). Group 11+ 10% discount. Prices valid until 31/12/05. Please phone for further details. **Facilities:** 🅿 ✖ ◗

THREAVE GARDEN & ESTATE
DG7 1RX
➲ (1m W of Castle Douglas, off A75)
☎ 01556 502575
e-mail: threave@nts.org.uk
web: www.nts.org.uk

The best time to visit is in spring when there is a dazzling display of daffodils. The garden is a delight in all seasons, however, and is home to the National Trust for Scotland's School of Practical Gardening.
Times: ✱ Estate & Garden: all year, daily 9.30-sunset. Walled Garden & Glasshouse daily 9.30-5. Visitor Centre, Countryside Centre & exhibition Feb-Mar & Nov-23 Dec, daily 10-4; Apr-Oct, daily 9.30-5.30. House Mar-Oct, Wed-Fri & Sun, 11-4 (guided tours only, admission by timed ticket).Times may change for 2006 please telephone or check on www.nts.org.uk **Facilities:** 🅿 ✖ licensed & (wheelchairs available incl. electric wheelchair) toilets for disabled shop garden centre ✖ (ex guide dogs) ♨

CREETOWN Map 11 NX45

CREETOWN GEM ROCK MUSEUM
Chain Rd DG8 7HJ
➲ (follow signs from A75 at Creetown bypass)
☎ 01671 820357 & 820554
e-mail: gem.rock@btinternet.com
web: www.gemrock.net

2 for 1

The Gem Rock is the leading independent museum of its kind in the UK, and is renowned worldwide. Crystals, gemstones, minerals, jewellery and fossils, the Gem Rock displays some of the most breathtaking examples of nature's wonders. See the audio-visual 'Fire in the Stones', explore the Crystal Cave, and relax in the Prospector's Study.
Times: Open Etr-Sep, daily 9.30-5.30; Oct-Nov & Mar-Etr, daily 10-4; Dec-Feb, wknds 10-4 or by appointment wkdays. Closed 23 Dec-Jan. **Fee:** ✱ £3.50 (ch £2 under 5 free, concessions £3). Family ticket £9 (2ad+3ch). **Facilities:** 🅿 📷 📷 & (ideal attraction for wheelchair users) toilets for disabled shop ✖ (ex guide dogs) ▰

DRUMCOLTRAN TOWER   Map 11 NX86

DRUMCOLTRAN TOWER

➲ (7m NE of Dalbeattie, in farm buildings off A711)   `FREE`

A well-preserved tower of mid 16th-century date simply planned and built, sitting within a busy modern farmyard. **Times:** Open at any reasonable time. **Facilities:** 🅿 ✕ 🍴

DUMFRIES   Map 11 NX97

BURNS MAUSOLEUM

St Michael's Churchyard

➲ (at junct of Brooms Rd [ATS] and St Michael's St [B725])

☎ 01387 255297   `FREE`

e-mail: dumfriesmuseum@dumgal.gov.uk
web: www.dumgal.gov.uk/museums

The mausoleum is in the form of a Greek temple, and contains the tombs of Robert Burns, his wife Jean Armour, and their five sons. A sculptured group shows the Muse of Poetry flinging her cloak over Burns at the plough.
Times: Unrestricted access. **Facilities:** 🅿 (50yds) ♿ (visitors with mobility difficulties tel 01387 255297)

DUMFRIES MUSEUM & CAMERA OBSCURA

The Observatory, Rotchell Rd DG2 7SW

➲ (A75 from S Carlisle or SW from Castle Douglas, museum in Maxwelltown area of Dumfries)

☎ 01387 253374

e-mail: dumfriesmuseum@dumgal.gov.uk
web: www.dumgal.gov.uk/museums

Situated in and around the 18th-century windmill tower, the museum's collections were started over 150 years ago and exhibitions trace the history of the people and landscape of Dumfries & Galloway. The Camera Obscura is to be found on the top floor of the windmill tower.
Times: Open all year, Apr-Sep Mon-Sat 10-5, Sun, 2-5; Oct-Mar, Tue-Sat 10-1 & 2-5. **Fee:** Prices not confirmed for 2006 **Facilities:** 🅿 🍴 ♿ (camera obscura, parking available) toilets for disabled shop

OLD BRIDGE HOUSE MUSEUM

Mill Rd DG2 7BE

➲ (at W end of Devorgilla's Bridge)

☎ 01387 256904

e-mail: dumfriesmuseum@dumgal.gov.uk
web: www.dumgal.gov.uk/museums

The Old Bridge House was built in 1660, and is the oldest house in Dumfries. A museum of everyday life in the town, it has an early 20th-century dentist's surgery, a Victorian nursery and kitchens of the 1850s and 1900s.
Times: Open Apr-Sep, Mon-Sat 10-5 & Sun 2-5. **Fee:** ✱ Donations welcome **Facilities:** 🅿 🍴 shop

ROBERT BURNS CENTRE

Mill Rd DG2 7BE

➲ (on Westbank of River Nith)

☎ 01387 264808   `2 for 1`

e-mail: dumfriesmuseum@dumgal.gov.uk
web: www.dumgal.gov.uk/museums

This award-winning centre explores the connections between Robert Burns and the town of Dumfries. Situated in the town's 18th-century watermill, the centre tells the story of Burns' last years spent in the busy streets and lively atmosphere of Dumfries in the 1790s. In the evening the centre shows feature films in the Film Theatre.

continued

Times: Open all year, Apr-Sep, daily 10-8 (Sun 2-5); Oct-Mar, Tue-Sat 10-1 & 2-5. **Fee:** ✱ Free admission to museum, audio-visual theatre £1.55 (concessions 80p). **Facilities:** 🅿 💻 ✕ 🍴 ♿ (induction loop hearing system in auditorium, chairlift) toilets for disabled shop

ROBERT BURNS HOUSE

Burns St DG1 2PS

➲ (signed from Brooms Rd [ATS] car park)

☎ 01387 255297

e-mail: dumfriesmuseum@dumgal.gov.uk
web: www.dumgal.gov.uk/museums

It was in this house that Robert Burns spent the last three years of his short life; he died here in 1796. It retains much of its 18th-century character and contains many fascinating items connected with the poet. There is the chair in which he wrote his last poems, many original letters and manuscripts, and the famous Kilmarnock and Edinburgh editions of his work.
Times: Open all year, Apr-Sep, Mon-Sat 10-5, Sun 2-5; Oct-Mar Tue-Sat 10-1 & 2-5. **Fee:** ✱ Donations welcome **Facilities:** 🅿 (opposite) 🍴 shop

DUNDRENNAN   Map 11 NX74

DUNDRENNAN ABBEY

DG6 4QH

➲ (6.5m SE of Kirkcudbright, on A711)

☎ 01557 500262

The now ruined abbey was founded for the Cistercians. The east end of the church and the chapter house are of exceptional architectural quality. Mary, Queen of Scots is thought to have spent her last night in Scotland here on 15 May 1568, before seeking shelter in England, where she was imprisoned and eventually executed.
Times: Open, Apr-Sep, daily 9.30-6.30; Oct- closed Thu & Fri. Nov-Mar wknds only. Closed 25-26 Dec & 1-2 Jan. **Fee:** ✱ £2 (ch 80p, concessions £1.50). Group 11+ 10% discount. Prices valid until 31/12/05. Please phone for further details. **Facilities:** 🅿 ♿ ✕ 🍴

GLENLUCE   Map 10 NX15

GLENLUCE ABBEY

DG8 0AF

➲ (2m NW, off A75)

☎ 01581 300541

The abbey was founded for the Cistercians in 1192 by Roland, Earl of Galloway. The ruins include a vaulted chapter house, and stand in a beautiful setting.
Times: Open all year, Apr-Sep, daily 9.30-6.30; Oct- closed Thu & Fri. Nov-Mar, wknds only. Closed 25-26 Dec & 1-2 Jan. **Fee:** ✱ £2 (ch 80p, concessions £1.50). Prices valid until 31/12/05. Group 11 + 10% discount. Please phone for further details. **Facilities:** 🅿 💻 ♿ ✕ 🍴

KIRKCUDBRIGHT   Map 11 NX65

BROUGHTON HOUSE & GARDEN

12 High St DG6 4JX

➲ (off A711/A755)

☎ 01557 330437

e-mail: aclipson@nts.scot.demon.co.uk
web: www.nts.org.uk

An 18th-century house where Edward A Hornel, one of the 'Glasgow Boys' group of artists, lived and worked from 1901-1933. It features a collection of his work, an extensive library of local history, including rare editions of Burns' works, and a Japanese-style garden that he created.
Times: ✱ House may be closed part of 2004. Garden Feb-Mar & 1-20 Oct, Mon-Fri 11-4; Apr-Sep, Mon-Sat 11-5, Sun 1-5. Times may change for 2006 please telephone or check on www.nts.org.uk
Facilities: 🅿 (on street) (limited space) ✕ (ex guide dogs) ♿

MacLellan's Castle

➲ (in Kirkcudbright on A711)
☎ 01557 331856

This handsome structure has been a ruin since the mid 18th-century. It was once an imposing castellated mansion, elaborately planned with fine architectural detail. Something of its 16th-century grandeur still remains.
Times: Open Apr-Sep, daily 9.30-6.30. **Fee:** ✱ £2.50 (ch £1, concessions £1.90). Group 11+ 10% discount. Prices valid until 31/12/05. Please phone for further details. **Facilities:** P shop ✘ 🚌 🏮

Stewartry Museum

St Mary St DG6 4AQ
➲ (from A711 through town, pass parish church, museum approx 200mtrs on right)
☎ 01557 331643
e-mail: david@dumgal.gov.uk
web: www.dumgal.go.uk/museums

FREE

A large and varied collection of archaeological, social history and natural history exhibits relating to the Stewartry district.
Times: Open May, Jun & Sep, Mon-Sat 11-5 Sun 2-5; Jul-Aug, Mon-Sat 10-5 Sun 2-5; Oct Mon-Sat 11-4 Sun 2-5; Nov-Apr Mon-Sat 11-4
Facilities: P (outside) 📗 🚻 shop ✘ (ex guide dogs)

Tolbooth Art Centre

High St DG6 4JL
➲ (from A711, through town pass parish church & Stewartry Museum, 1st right into High St)
☎ 01557 331556
e-mail: DavidD@dumgal.gov.uk
web: www.dumgal.gov.uk/museums

FREE

Dating from 1629, the Tolbooth was converted into an art centre and provides an interpretive introduction to the Kirkcudbright artists's colony, which flourished in the town from the 1880s. It also provides studio and exhibition space for contemporary local and visiting artists. There is a programme of exhibitions from March to October.
Times: Open May, Jun & Sep, Mon-Sat 11-5 Sun 2-5; Jul & Aug, Mon-Sat 10-6 Sun 2-5; Oct, Mon-Sat 11-4 Sun 2-5; Nov-Apr, Mon-Sat 11-4 **Facilities:** P (on street parking) 🚻 🚻 (lift for access to upper floors) toilets for disabled shop ✘ (ex guide dogs)

NEW ABBEY   Map 11 NX96

New Abbey Corn Mill

DG2 8BX
➲ (7m S of Dumfries on A710)
☎ 01387 850260

Built in the late 18th century, this water-driven corn mill is still in working order, and regular demonstrations are held.
Times: Open all year, Apr-Sep, daily 9.30-6.30; Oct-Mar, daily 9.30-4.30. Closed Thu & Fri in winter, 25-26 Dec & 1-2 Jan. **Fee:** ✱ £3 (ch £1.20, concessions £2.30). Group 11+ 10% discount. Prices valid until 31/12/05. Please phone for further details. **Facilities:** P (100yds) shop ✘ 🏮

Shambellie House Museum of Costume

DG2 8HQ
➲ (7m S of Dumfries, on A710)
☎ 01387 850375
e-mail: info@nms.ac.uk
web: www.nms.ac.uk/costume

FREE

Shambellie House is a beautiful Victorian country house set in attractive wooded grounds. You are invited to step back in time and experience Victorian and Edwardian grace and
continued

refinement. See period costume from the 1850s to the 1950s displayed in appropriate room settings with accessories, furniture and decorative art. Telephone for details of special events.

Shambellie House Museum of Costume

Times: Open 25 Mar-Oct, daily, 10-5. **Facilities:** P 🚻 🚻 (house inaccessible for wheelchair users) shop ✘ (ex guide/hearing dogs) 🚌

Sweetheart Abbey

DG2 8BU
➲ (on A710)
☎ 01387 850397

Lady Devorgilla of Galloway founded Balliol College, Oxford in memory of her husband John Balliol; she also founded this abbey in his memory in 1273. When she died in 1289 she was buried in front of the high altar with the heart of her husband resting on her bosom; hence the name 'Sweetheart Abbey'. The abbey features an unusual precinct wall of enormous boulders.
Times: Open all year, Apr-Sep, daily 9.30-6.30; Oct-Mar, daily 9.30-4.30. Closed Thu & Fri in winter, 25-26 Dec & 1-2 Jan. **Fee:** ✱ £2 (ch 80p, concessions £1.50). Group 11+ 10% discount. Prices valid until 31/12/05. Please phone for further details. **Facilities:** P 🚻 (with assistance) ✘ 🏮

PALNACKIE   Map 11 NX85

Orchardton Tower

FREE

➲ (6m SE of Castle Douglas on A711)
A charming little tower house of mid-15th-century date. It is, uniquely, circular in plan.
Times: Open all reasonable times. Closed 25-26 Dec.
Facilities: P ✘ 🏮

PORT LOGAN   Map 10 NX04

Logan Botanic Garden

DG9 9ND
➲ (on B7065, 14m S of Stranraer)
☎ 01776 860231
e-mail: logan@rbge.org.uk
web: www.rgbe.org.uk

Logan's exceptionally mild climate allows a colourful array of tender plants to thrive out-of-doors. Amongst the many highlights are tree ferns, cabbage palms, unusual shrubs, climbers and tender perennials found within the setting of the walled, water, terrace and woodland gardens.
Times: ✱ Open Mar-Oct, Mar & Oct daily 10-5. Apr-Sep 10-6
Facilities: P ✘ licensed 📗 🚻 (access limited, wheelchairs available for loan) toilets for disabled shop garden centre
✘ (ex guide dogs) 🚌

RUTHWELL — Map 11 NY16

RUTHWELL CROSS `FREE`
➲ (sited within the parish church on B724)
Now in a specially built apse in the parish church, the carved cross dates from the 7th or 8th centuries. Two faces show scenes from the Life of Christ; the others show scroll work, and parts of an ancient poem in Runic characters. It was broken up in the 18th century, but pieced together by a 19th-century minister. **Times:** Open all reasonable times. Contact Key Keeper for access on 01387 870249. **Facilities:** 🅿 ✈ ♥

SAVINGS BANKS MUSEUM
DG1 4NN
➲ (off B724, 10m E of Dumfries & 7m W of Annan)
☎ 01387 870640
e-mail: tsbmuseum@btinternet.com `FREE`
web: www.lloydstsb.com/savingsbankmuseum
Housed in the building where Savings Banks first began, the museum traces their growth and development from 1810 up to the present day. The museum also traces the life of Dr Henry Duncan, father of savings banks, and restorer of the Ruthwell Cross. Multi-lingual leaflets available. **Times:** Open all year, Tue-Sat, 10-4; Open on BHs except Christmas Day & New Year **Facilities:** 🅿 📱 ♿ (touch facilities for blind, guide available) ✈ (ex guide dogs)

SANQUHAR — Map 11 NS70

SANQUHAR TOLBOOTH MUSEUM
High St DG4 6BN
➲ (on A76 Dumfries-Kilmarnock road)
☎ 01659 250186 `FREE`
e-mail: dumfriesmuseum@dumgal.gov.uk
web: www.dumgal.gov.uk/museums
Housed in the town's fine 18th-century tolbooth, the museum tells the story of the mines and miners of the area, its earliest inhabitants, native and Roman, the history and customs of the Royal Burgh of Sanquhar and local traditions. **Times:** Open Apr-Sep, Tue-Sat 10-1 & 2-5, Sun 2-5. **Facilities:** 🅿 📱 (museum up steps, phone for info) shop

STRANRAER — Map 10 NX06

CASTLE KENNEDY GARDENS
Stair Estates, Rephad DG9 8BX
➲ (5m E of Stranraer on A75, signed at Castle Kennedy Village)
☎ 01776 702024
e-mail: info@castlekennedygardens.co.uk
web: www.castlekennedygardens.co.uk
Situated on a peninsula between two lochs, the gardens around the Old Castle were first laid out in the early 18th century. Noted for their rhododendrons and azaleas (at their best May and early Jun) and walled kitchen garden with fine herbaceous borders (best in Aug and Sep). The gardens contain many avenues and walks amid beautiful scenery. **Times:** Open Etr-Sep, daily 10-5 **Facilities:** 🅿 📱 📱 ♿ (tearoom to enable access) toilets for disabled shop garden centre ☕

GLENWHAN GARDENS
Dunragit DG9 8PH
➲ (7m E of Stranraer, signed)
☎ 01581 400222
e-mail: tess@glenwhan.freeserve.co.uk
web: www.glenwhangardens.co.uk
Enjoying spectacular views over the Mull of Galloway and Luce Bay, Glenwhan is a beautiful 12-acre garden set on a hillside. There are two lakes filled with rare species, alpines, scree plants, heathers, conifers, roses, woodland walks and fascinating garden sculpture. **Times:** Open Apr-Sep, daily 10-5 **Fee:** £4.00 (ch £1.50, concessions £3) **Facilities:** 🅿 📱 ✕ licensed ♿ (wheelchairs provided) toilets for disabled shop garden centre On leads, not in tearooms

THORNHILL — Map 11 NX89

DRUMLANRIG CASTLE
DG3 4AQ
➲ (4m N of Thornhill off A76)
☎ 01848 331555
e-mail: bre@drumlanrigcastle.org.uk
web: www.drumlanrig.com
This unusual pink sandstone castle was built in the late 17th century in Renaissance style. It contains a outstanding collection of fine art. There is also French furniture, as well as silver and relics of Bonnie Prince Charlie. The old stable block has a craft centre with resident craft workers, and the grounds offer an extensive garden plant centre, working forge, mountain bike hire and woodland walks. For details of special events phone 01848 331555. **Times:** ✱ Open early May-late Aug, Castle open seven days a week. Guided tours and restricted route may operate at various times, please verify before visiting. **Facilities:** 🅿 ✕ licensed ♿ (lift for wheelchair users) toilets for disabled shop ✈ (ex in park on lead) ☕

WANLOCKHEAD — Map 11 NS81

MUSEUM OF SCOTTISH LEAD MINING
ML12 6UT
➲ (signed from M74 and A76)
☎ 01659 74387 `2 for 1`
e-mail: miningmuseum@hotmail.com
web: www.leadminingmuseum.co.uk

Wanlockhead is Scotland's highest village, set in the beautiful Lowther Hills. Visitors can see miners' cottages, the
continued

miners' library as well as the 18th-century lead mine. Visitors can also pan for gold.

Times: Open Apr-2 Nov, daily 10.30-4.30; Jul & Aug 10-5.
Fee: ✱ £5.00 (ch £3.50, concessions £3.75). Family ticket £13.50
Facilities: 🅿 💷 ✗ licensed 🏮 ♿ (induction loops) toilets for disabled shop ✖ (ex guide dogs) 🛏

WHITHORN   Map 10 NX44

WHITHORN-CRADLE OF CHRISTIANITY
45-47 George St DG8 8NS
➲ (follow directions S from junct at Newton Stewart & Glenluce A75. Centre on main street in centre of Whithorn)
☎ 01988 500508
e-mail: enquiries@whithorn.com
web: www.whithorn.com

The Whithorn Dig is the site of the first Christian settlement in Scotland - the Candida Casa of St Ninian. Friendly guides explain the excavation, and there's a museum of Early Christian stones.

Times: ✱ Open daily, Apr-Oct 10.30-5. **Facilities:** 🅿 💷 🏮 ♿ (one short staircase with 'stairmatic') toilets for disabled shop 🛏

WHITHORN PRIORY
DG8 8PY
➲ (on A746)
☎ 01988 500508

The first Christian church in Scotland was founded here by St Ninian in 397AD, but the present ruins date from the 12th century. These ruins are sparse but there is a notable Norman door, the Latinus stone of the 5th century and other early Christian monuments.

Times: Open Apr-Oct, daily 10.30-5.00. **Fee:** £2.70 (ch & concessions £1.50). Family ticket £7.50. Phone for further details.
Facilities: 🅿 ♿ ✖ 🏮

DUNDEE CITY

DUNDEE   Map 11 NO43

BROUGHTY CASTLE MUSEUM
Broughty Ferry DD5 2TF
➲ (turn S off A930 at traffic lights by Eastern Primary School in Broughty Ferry)
☎ 01382 436916   **FREE**
e-mail: broughty@dundeecity.gov.uk
web: www.dundeecity.gov.uk/broughtycastle

The 15th-century castle was rebuilt to defend the Tay estuary in the 19th century. It now houses fascinating displays on Dundee's whaling history, arms and armour, local history and seashore life. There are superb views across the Tay estuary from the observation room.

Times: Open all year Apr-Sep, Mon-Sat 10-4, Sun 12.30-4; Oct-Mar, Tue-Sat 10-4, Sun 12.30-4. Closed Mons, 25-26 Dec & 1-3 Jan. **Facilities:** 🅿 💷 🏮 (unsuitable for wheelchairs) shop ✖ (ex guide dogs)

CAMPERDOWN COUNTRY PARK
Coupar Angus Rd DD2 4TF
➲ (A90 to Dundee then onto A923 (Coupar-Angus road), left at 1st rdbt to attraction)
☎ 01382 431818
e-mail: camperdown@dundeecity.gov.uk
web: www.camperdownpark.com

The 19th-century mansion of Camperdown House was built for the son of Admiral Lord Duncan, who defeated the Dutch

at the Battle of Camperdown in 1797. The house is set in nearly 400 acres of fine parkland, which includes a wildlife centre, an adventure play area and an extensive network of footpaths and forest trails to follow.

Times: Open Park: all year. Wildlife Centre: Mar-Sep, daily 10-4.30(last admission 3.45), Oct-Mar 10-3.30(last admission 2.45). **Fee:** ✱ Park - free admission. Wildlife Centre charged. **Facilities:** 🅿 ♿ (ramps) toilets for disabled shop ✖ (ex guide dogs)

DISCOVERY POINT & RRS DISCOVERY
Discovery Quay DD1 4XA
➲ (follow brown heritage signs for Historic Ships)
☎ 01382 201245
e-mail: info@dundeeheritage.sol.co.uk
web: www.rrsdiscovery.com

Discovery Point is the home of *RRS Discovery*, Captain Scott's famous Antarctic ship. Spectacular lighting, graphics and special effects re-create key moments in the Discovery story. The restored bridge gives a captain's view over the ship and the River Tay. Learn what happened to the ship after the expedition, during the First World War and the Russian Revolution, and find out about her involvement in the first survey of whales' migratory patterns.

Times: Open Apr-Oct, Mon-Sat 10-6. Sun 11-6; Nov-Mar, Mon-Sat 10-5. Sun 11-5. **Fee:** ✱ £6.45 (ch £3.85, pen & concessions £4.90). Group £5.15 (ch £3.50, pen & concessions £4) **Facilities:** 🅿 (charged) ✗ ♿ (in-house wheelchairs & lifts, parking, ramps onto ship) toilets for disabled shop ✖ (ex guide & hearing dogs) 🛏

HM FRIGATE UNICORN
Victory Dock DD1 3JA
➲ (from W follow A85 from A90 at Invergowrie. From E follow A92. Near N end of Tay Road Bridge)
☎ 01382 200900 & 200893
e-mail: frigateunicorn@hotmail.com
web: www.frigateunicorn.org

The *Unicorn* is the oldest British-built warship afloat, and Scotland's only example of a wooden warship. Today she houses a museum of life in the Royal Navy during the days of sail, with guns, models and displays.

Times: Open all year Apr-Oct, daily 10-5; Nov-Mar, Wed-Fri 12-4, Sat & Sun 10-4.Closed Mon-Tue & 2 weeks at Xmas & New Year. **Fee:** £4.00 (concessions £3.00). Family ticket £9-£11. Groups 10+ £2.50 each.
Facilities: 🅿 💷 🏮 ♿ (audio visual presentations, introductory video) shop ✖ Guide dogs on deck area only 🛏

continued

MILLS OBSERVATORY

Balgay Park, Glamis Rd DD2 2UB
➲ (1m W of city centre, in Balgay Park, on Balgay Hill. Vehicle entrance at Glamis Rd gate to Balgay Park)
☎ 01382 435967
e-mail: mills.observatory@dundeecity.gov.uk
web: www.dundeecity.gov.uk/mills

The observatory was built in 1935, and has a Victorian 10in Cooke refracting telescope among its instruments. The gallery has displays on astronomy and space exploration; visitors can view a safe projection of the sun on bright days. There is a small planetarium for booked groups only. Open nights during the winter months, children's activities during the summer holidays.
Times: Open all year, Apr-Sep, Tue-Fri 11-5, Sat & Sun 12.30-4; Oct-Mar, Mon-Fri 4-10, Sat & Sun 12.30-4. Closed 25-26 Dec & 1-3 Jan.
Fee: ✱ Free except for planetarium shows extra, £1 (ch 50p) Groups £10. **Facilities:** 🅿 📺 ᕓ (portable telescopes available, images on screen) toilets for disabled shop 🐕 (ex guide dogs)

VERDANT WORKS

West Henderson's Wynd DD2 5BT
➲ (follow brown tourist signs)
☎ 01382 225282
e-mail: info@dundeeheritage.sol.co.uk
web: www.verdantworks.com

Dating from 1830, this old Jute Mill covers 50,000 sq ft and has been restored as a living museum of Dundee and Tayside's textile history and award-winning European Industrial Museum. Phase I explains what jute is, where it comes from and why Dundee became the centre of its production. Working machinery illustrates the production process from raw jute to woven cloth. Phase II deals with the uses of jute and its effects on Dundee's social history.
Times: Open Apr-Oct; Mon-Sat 10-5, Sun 11-5. Nov-Mar; Mon-Sat 10-4, Sun 11-4. Venue closes 1hr after last entry. Please check for winter opening times. Closed 25-26 Dec & 1-2 Jan) **Fee:** ✱ £5.95 (ch £3.85, pen & con £4.45). Family ticket (2ad+2ch) £17.
Facilities: 🅿 (charged) ᕓ (wheelchairs, induction loops) toilets for disabled shop 🐕 (ex guide & hearing dogs) 📢

EAST AYRSHIRE

GALSTON · Map 11 NS53

LOUDOUN CASTLE THEME PARK

KA4 8PE
➲ (signed from A74(M), from A77 and from A71)
☎ 01563 822296
e-mail: loudouncastle@btinternet.com
web: www.loudouncastle.co.uk

Loudoun Castle Theme Park is a great day out for the whole family. Theme park rides, live entertainment and McDougals Farm are just a taster of what's on offer.
Times: Open Etr-end of Sep. Please phone for further details.
Fee: £10.95 (under 4's free). For further details please phone or check website. **Facilities:** 🅿 📺 ✗ licensed 🍴 ᕓ toilets for disabled shop 🐕 (ex guide dogs) 📢

KILMARNOCK · Map 10 NS43

DICK INSTITUTE MUSEUM & ART GALLERIES

Elmbank Ave KA1 3BU
➲ (follow brown tourist signs from A77 S of Glasgow, into town centre)
☎ 01563 554343
web: www.east-ayrshire.gov.uk

Temporary and permanent exhibitions spread over two floors of this grand Victorian building. Fine art, social and natural history feature upstairs, whilst the downstairs galleries house temporary exhibitions of art and craft.
Times: Open all year, Tue-Sat 11-5 **Fee:** ✱ Free except for special exhibitions when a charge may be made. **Facilities:** 🅿 ᕓ (wheelchair available) toilets for disabled shop 🐕 (ex guide dogs)

EAST DUNBARTONSHIRE

BEARSDEN · Map 11 NS57

ANTONINE WALL: BEARSDEN BATH-HOUSE

Roman Rd G61 2SG · **FREE**
➲ (signed from Bearsden Cross on A810)

Considered to be the best surviving visible Roman building in Scotland, the bath-house was discovered in 1973 during excavations for a construction site. It was originally built for use by the Roman garrison at Bearsden Fort, which is part of the Antonine Wall defences. This building dates from the 2nd century AD. Visitors should wear sensible footwear.
Times: Open all reasonable times. **Facilities:** ᕓ 🐕 🚩

EAST LOTHIAN

ABERLADY · Map 12 NT47

MYRETON MOTOR MUSEUM

EH32 0PZ
➲ (1.5m from A198, 2m from A1) · **2 for 1**
☎ 01875 870288 & 07947 066666

The museum has on show a large collection, from 1899, of cars, bicycles, motor cycles and commercials. There is also a large collection of period advertising, posters and enamel signs etc.
Times: Open, Apr-Oct daily 11-4, Nov-Mar weekends only 11-3
Fee: £5 (ch £2). **Facilities:** 🅿 ᕓ 🐕 (ex guide dogs)

DIRLETON   Map 12 NT58

DIRLETON CASTLE
EH39 5ER
➲ (on A198)
☎ 01620 850330

The oldest part of this romantic castle dates from the 13th century. It was besieged by Edward I in 1298, rebuilt and expanded, and then destroyed in 1650. Now the sandstone ruins have a beautiful mellow quality. Within the castle grounds is a garden established in the 16th century, with ancient yews and hedges around a bowling green.
Times: Open all year, Apr-Sep daily 9.30-6.30; Oct-Mar daily 9.30-4.30. Closed 25-26 Dec & 1-2 Jan. **Fee:** ✱ £3.30 (ch £1.30, concessions £2.50). Group 11+ 10% discount. Prices valid until 31/12/05. Please phone for further details. **Facilities:** 🅿 shop ⚑

EAST FORTUNE   Map 12 NT57

MUSEUM OF FLIGHT
East Fortune Airfield EH39 5LF
➲ (signed from A1 near Haddington. Onto B1347, past Athelstaneford, 20m E of Edinburgh)
☎ 01620 880308
e-mail: info@nms.ac.uk   `2 for 1`
web: www.nms.ac.uk

The Museum of Flight is situated on 63 acres of one of Britain's best preserved wartime airfields, the museum has four hangars, with more than 50 aeroplanes, plus engines, rockets and memorabilia. Items on display include two Spitfires, a Vulcan bomber and Britain's oldest surviving aeroplane, built in 1896; recent exhibits also include a phantom jet fighter, harrier jump-jet and Scotland's Concorde G-BOAA.
Times: Open daily 16 Mar-30 Oct 10-5. 31 Oct-Mar wknds only by prior arrangement 10-4. **Fee:** ✱ £5, (ch under 12 free, concessions £4). NMS members free. To include Concorde Boarding Pass; +£3 ad, +£2 ch & concessions. **Facilities:** 🅿 🍽 ♿ toilets for disabled shop ✖ (ex assist dogs) 🍴

EAST LINTON   Map 12 NT57

HAILES CASTLE   `FREE`
➲ (1.5m SW of East Linton on A1)
A beautiful sited ruin incorporating a fortified manor of 13th-century date, extended in the 14th and 15th centuries. There are two vaulted pit-prisons.
Times: Open at all reasonable times. **Facilities:** 🅿 ✖ ⚑

PRESTON MILL & PHANTASSIE DOOCOT
EH40 3DS
➲ (signed from A1)
☎ 01620 860426
web: www.nts.org.uk

This attractive mill, with conical, pantiled roof, is the oldest working water-driven meal mill to survive in Scotland, and was last used commercially in 1957. Nearby is the charming Phantassie Doocot (dovecote), built for 500 birds.
Times: ✱ Open Apr-Sep, Thu-Mon 12-5, Sun 1-5. Times may change for 2006 please telephone or check on www.nts.org.uk
Facilities: 🅿 ♿ toilets for disabled shop ✖ (ex guide dogs) 🍸

INVERESK   Map 11 NT37

INVERESK LODGE GARDEN
EH21 7TE
➲ (A6124, S of Musselburgh)
☎ 01721 722502
web: www.nts.org.uk

This charming terraced garden, set in the historic village of Inveresk, specialises in plants, shrubs and roses suitable for growing on small plots. The 17th-century house makes an elegant backdrop.
Times: ✱ Open all year daily 10-6 or dusk if earlier. Times may change for 2006 please telephone or check on www.nts.org.uk
Facilities: 🅿 ♿ ✖ (ex guide dogs) 🍸

NORTH BERWICK   Map 12 NT58

SCOTTISH SEABIRD CENTRE
The Harbour EH39 4SS
➲ (A1 from Edinburgh, then A198 to North Berwick. Brown heritage signs clearly marked from A1)
☎ 01620 890202
e-mail: info@seabird.org
web: www.seabird.org

Get close to nature with a visit to this award-winning centre. With panoramic views over the islands of the Firth of Forth and sand-fringed bays of North Berwick, the area is a haven for wildlife. Use state-of-the-art 'Big Brother' cameras to see wide variety of wildlife action live - including gannet colony, hundreds of puffins seals and sometimes bottlenose dolphins. Wildlife boat safari with landings on the islands and passenger ferry to Fife (summer). New features include the Environmental Discovery Centre and Migration Tunnel.
Times: Open all year, Apr-Oct 10-6 (every day), Nov-Jan 10-4 (Mon-Fri) 10-5.30 (Sat & Sun), Feb-Mar 10-5 (Mon-Fri) 10-5.30 (Sat & Sun). Closed 25 Dec **Fee:** ✱ £5.95 (ch & concessions £3.95). Family ticket (4 persons) £16.50. Subject to change. **Facilities:** 🅿 🍽 ✖ 🎁 ♿ (1 w/chair, parking on site, walking frame available) toilets for disabled shop ✖ (ex guide dogs) 🍴

TANTALLON CASTLE
EH39 5PN
➲ (3m E, off A198)
☎ 01620 892727
A famous 14th-century stronghold of the Douglases facing towards the lonely Bass Rock from the rocky Firth of Forth shore. Nearby 16th and 17th century earthworks.
Times: Open all year, Apr-Sep, daily 9.30-6.30; Oct-Mar, daily 9.30-4.30. Closed Thu & Fri in winter, 25-26 Dec & 1-2 Jan.
Fee: ✱ £3.30 (ch £1.30, concessions £2.50). Group 11+ 10% discount. Prices valid until 31/12/05. Please phone for further details.
Facilities: 🅿 shop ✖ ⚑

PRESTONPANS Map 11 NT37
PRESTONGRANGE MUSEUM
Prestongrange
➲ (on B1348)
☎ 0131 653 2904 FREE
e-mail: elms@eastlothian.gov.uk
web: www.eastlothian.gov.uk/museums
The oldest documented coal mining site in Scotland, with 800 years of history, this museum shows a Cornish Beam Engine and on-site evidence of associated industries such as brickmaking and pottery. It is located next to a 16th-century customs port. Special Events - weekend events for families and children in July/August.
Times: Open end Mar-mid Oct, daily 11-4. **Facilities:** 🅿 💷 ॐ (grounds partly accessible) toilets for disabled shop ✖ (ex guide dogs or outside)

FALKIRK

BIRKHILL Map 11 NS97
THE BIRKHILL FIRECLAY MINE
EH51 9AQ
➲ (A706 from Linlithgow, A904 from Grangemouth, follow brown signs to Steam Railway & Fireclay Mine)
☎ 01506 825855
e-mail: mine@srps.org.uk
web: www.srps.org.uk
Tour guides will meet you at Birkhill Station and lead you down into the ancient woodland of the beautiful Avon Gorge, and then into the caverns of the Birkhill Fireclay mine. See how the clay was worked, what it was used for and find the 300-million-year-old fossils in the roof of the mine.
Times: Open Etr-Oct, wknds only; Jul-Aug, daily. **Fee:** ✱ Mine & Train £7.50 (ch £4, concessions £6) Family ticket (2ad+2ch) £19. Mine only £3 (ch £2, concessions £2.50) Family ticket £8. **Facilities:** 🅿 🖼

BO'NESS Map 11 NT08
BO'NESS & KINNEIL RAILWAY
Bo'ness Station, Union St EH51 9AQ
➲ (A904 from all directions, signed)
☎ 01506 825855 2 for 1
e-mail: railway@srps.org.uk
web: www.srps.org.uk
Historic railway buildings, including the station and train shed, have been relocated from sites all over Scotland. The Scottish Railway Exhibition tells the story of the development of railways and their impact on the people of Scotland. Take a seven mile return trip by steam train to the tranquil country station at Birkhill. Special events take place throughout the year. 2-for-1 voucher not valid on special event days.
Times: Open Apr-Jun & Sep-Oct, Sat-Sun; Jul-Aug, Tue-Sun. Steam trains daily, depart 11, 12.15, 1.45 & 3, diesel departs at 4.15. Ring for details of special events. **Fee:** ✱ Return fare £4.50 (ch 3-15 £2, concessions £3.50). Family ticket £11. Ticket for return train fare & tour of Birkhill Fireclay Mine £7.50 (ch £4, concessions £6), Family ticket £19. **Facilities:** 🅿 💷 ॐ (ramps to station & adapted carriage) toilets for disabled shop 🖼

KINNEIL MUSEUM & ROMAN FORTLET
Duchess Anne Cottages, Kinniel Estate EH51 0PR
➲ (follow tourist signs from Heritage Railway, off M9. Establishment at E end of town accessed via Dean Rd)
☎ 01506 778530 FREE
The museum is in a converted stable block of Kinneil House. The ground floor has displays on the industrial history of Bo'ness, while the upper floor looks at the history and environment of the Kinneil Estate. The remains of the Roman fortlet can be seen nearby. An audio visual presentation shows 2000 years of history.
Times: ✱ Open all year, Mon-Sat 12.30-4. **Facilities:** 🅿 ॐ shop ✖ (ex guide dogs)

FALKIRK Map 11 NS88
CALLENDAR HOUSE NEW
Callendar Park FK1 1YR
➲ (On southside of town centre, Callender House is signposted)
☎ 01324 503770
e-mail: callender.house@falkirk.gov.uk
web: www.callendarhouse.org
Mary, Queen of Scots, Oliver Cromwell, Bonnie Prince Charlie, noble earls and wealthy merchants all feature in the history of Callendar House. Costumed interpreters describe early 19th-century life in the kitchens and the 900-year history of the house is illustrated in the 'Story of Callendar House' exhibition. The house is set in parkland, offering boating and woodland walks. Regular temporary heritage, natural history and visual arts exhibitions in Callendar House's Large and Small Galleries.
Times: Open all year, Mon-Sat 10-5. Apr-Sep Sun also 2-5. **Fee:** ✱ £3 (ch £1 pen £1.50). Family ticket £7. **Facilities:** 🅿 💷 ॐ toilets for disabled shop 🖼 🖼

ROUGH CASTLE
➲ (1m E of Bonnybridge, signed from B816) FREE
The impressive earthworks of a large Roman fort on the Antonine Wall can be seen here. The buildings have disappeared, but the mounds and terraces are the sites of barracks, and granary and bath buildings. Running between them is the military road, which once linked all the forts on the wall and is still well defined.
Times: Open any reasonable time. **Facilities:** 🅿 ✖ ♫

FIFE

ABERDOUR Map 11 NT18
ABERDOUR CASTLE
KY3 0SL
➲ (in Aberdour, 5m E of Forth Bridge on A921)
☎ 01383 860519
The earliest surviving part of the castle is the 14th-century keep. There are also later buildings, and the remains of a terraced garden, a bowling green and a fine 16th-century doocot (dovecote).
Times: Open all year, Apr-Sep, daily 9.30-6.30; Oct-Mar, daily 9.30-4.30.Closed Thu & Fri in winter, 25-26 Dec & 1-2 Jan. **Fee:** ✱ £3 (ch £1.20, concessions £2.25). Group 11+ 10% discount. Prices valid until 31/12/05. Please phone for further details.
Facilities: 🅿 ✖ ॐ (wheelchairs) toilets for disabled shop ♫

ANSTRUTHER Map 12 NO50

Scottish Fisheries Museum

St Ayles, Harbour Head KY10 3AB

➲ (A917 through St Monans & Pittenweem to Anstruther)

☎ 01333 310628

e-mail: info@scotfishmuseum.org

web: www.scotfishmuseum.org

2 for 1

This award-winning national museum tells the story of Scottish fishing and its people from the earliest times to the present. With 10 galleries, 2 large boatyards, and a restored fisherman's cottage, which contain many fine paintings and photographs, boat models and actual boats, clothing and items of daily life to see, a visit to the museum makes for an exceptional day out. **Times:** Open all year, Apr-Sep, Mon-Sat 10-5.30, Sun 11-5; Oct-Mar, Mon-Sat 10-4.30, Sun 12-4.30. Closed 25-26 Dec & 1-2 Jan. (Last admission 1 hr before closing). **Fee:** £4.50 (concessions £3.50). Party 12+ £3 (primary ch £1, accompanied ch free, concessions £2) **Facilities:** P (20yds) (charge in summer) ⏺ & (ramps throughout to provide full access) toilets for disabled shop ✖ (ex guide dogs) ◀

BURNTISLAND Map 11 NT28

Burntisland Edwardian Fair Museum

102 High St KY3 9AS

➲ (in the centre of Burntisland)

☎ 01592 412860

web: kirkcaldy.museum@fife.gov.uk

FREE

Burntisland Museum has recreated a walk through the sights and sounds of the town's fair in 1910, based on a painting of the scene by local artist Andrew Young. See reconstructed rides, stalls and side shows of the time.

Times: Open all year, Mon, Wed, Fri & Sat 10-1 & 2-5; Tue & Thu 10-1 & 2-7. Closed PHs) **Facilities:** P (20m) (on street parking) ✖ (except guide dogs)

CULROSS Map 11 NS98

Culross Palace, Town House & The Study

West Green House KY12 8JH

➲ (off A985, 3m E of Kincardine Bridge)

☎ 01383 880359

A royal burgh, Culross dates from the 16th and 17th centuries and has remained virtually unchanged since. It prospered from the coal and salt trades, and when these declined in the 1700s, Culross stayed as it was. It owes its present appearance to the National Trust for Scotland, which has been gradually restoring it. In the Town House is a

continued

visitor centre and exhibition; in the building called The Study can be seen a drawing room with a Norwegian painted ceiling, and The Palace has painted rooms and terraced gardens.

Times: ✱ Open Palace, Study & Town House: Good Fri-Sep, daily 12-5. Garden all year 10-6 or sunset if earlier. Times may change for 2006 please telephone or check on www.nts.org.uk **Facilities:** P ⏺ & toilets for disabled shop ✖ (ex guide dogs) ◀

CUPAR Map 11 NO31

Hill of Tarvit Mansionhouse & Garden

KY15 5PB

➲ (2.5m S of Cupar, off A916)

☎ 01334 653127

web: www.nts.org.uk

Built in the first decade of the 20th century, the Mansionhouse is home to a notable collection of paintings, tapestries, furniture and Chinese porcelain. The grounds include formal gardens, and there is a regular programme of concerts and art exhibitions.

Times: ✱ Open Apr-Sep, daily 1-5; Oct wknds 1-5. Garden & grounds all year, daily 9.30-sunset. Times may change for 2006 please telephone or check on www.nts.org.uk **Facilities:** P ⏺ & toilets for disabled shop ✖ (ex guide dogs) ◀

The Scottish Deer Centre

Bow-of-Fife KY15 4NQ

➲ (3m W of Cupar on A91)

☎ 01337 810391

Guided tours take about 30 minutes and allow you to meet and stroke deer. There are indoor and outdoor adventure play areas. Other features include regular falconry displays, viewing platform and a tree top walkway.

Times: ✱ Open daily, Etr-Oct 10-6, Nov-Etr 10-5. **Facilities:** P ⏺ & (special parking bay, loan of wheelchairs) toilets for disabled shop ✖ (ex guide dogs) ◀

DUNFERMLINE Map 11 NT08

Abbot House Heritage Centre

Abbot House, Maygate KY12 7NE

➲ (in city centre)

☎ 01383 733266

e-mail: dht@abbothouse.fsnet.co.uk

web: www.abbothouse.co.uk

For the better part of a millennium, pilgrims have beaten a path to Dumfermline's door. Today visitors can still share the rich royal heritage of the capital of Fife's Magic Kingdom. The volunteer-run Abbot House Heritage Centre - dubbed 'The People's Tardis' - propels the traveller through time from the days of the Picts - a time warp peopled by a veritable Who's Who of characters from Dumfermline's past: Scotland's royal saint, Braveheart's Wallace and Bruce, Scotland's Chaucer, steel magnate Andrew Carnegie and a whole panoply of kings, ending with the birth of ill-starred Charles I.

Times: Open daily 10-5. Last entry to upper exhibitions 4.15. Closed 25 Dec & 1 Jan. **Fee:** ✱ £3 (accompanied ch under 16 free, concessions £2). Party 20+ **Facilities:** P (150yds) (disabled parking at establishment) ⏺ & (parking on site, videos of inaccesible areas) toilets for disabled shop ✖ (ex guide dogs) ◀

ANDREW CARNEGIE BIRTHPLACE MUSEUM

Moodie St KY12 7PL

➲ (400yds S from Abbey)

☎ 01383 724302

e-mail: carnegiebirthplace@hotmail.com

web: www.carnegiebirthplace.com

The museum tells the story of the handloom weaver's son, born here in 1835, who created the biggest steel works in the USA and then became a philanthropist on a huge scale. The present-day work of the philanthropic Carnegie Trust is also explained.

Times: Open Apr-Oct, Mon-Sat 11-5, Sun 2-5. **Fee:** ✱ £2 (ch under 16 free, concessions £1). **Facilities:** 🅿 📗 ዿ (photo album) toilets for disabled shop ✘ (ex guide dogs)

DUNFERMLINE ABBEY

Pittencrieff Park

☎ 01383 739026

The monastery was a powerful Benedictine house, founded by Queen Margaret in the 11th century. A modern brass in the choir marks the grave of King Robert the Bruce. The monastery guest house became a royal palace, and was the birthplace of Charles I.

Times: Open all year, Apr-Sep, daily 9.30-6.30; Oct-Mar, daily 9.30-4.30. Closed Thu (pm), Fri & Sun (am) in winter, 25-26 Dec & 1-2 Jan. **Fee:** ✱ £2.50 (ch £1, concessions £1.90). Group 11+ 10% discount. Prices valid until 31/12/05. Please phone for further details. **Facilities:** 🅿 shop ✘ 🍴

PITTENCRIEFF HOUSE MUSEUM

Pittencrieff Park KY12 8QH

➲ (off A994 on to Coal Rd, left into Pittencriefff Park Car Park. Attraction on W edge of town)

☎ 01383 722935 & 313838   FREE

e-mail: dunfermline.museum@fife.gov.uk

A fine 17th-century house standing in the beautiful park gifted to the town by Andrew Carnegie. Accessible displays tell the story of the park's animals and plants, with plenty of photographs of people enjoying the park over the last 100 years.

Times: Open daily Jan-Mar 11-4; Apr-Sep 11-5; Oct-Dec 11-4 **Facilities:** 🅿 (800yds) 📗 ዿ (ramp) toilets for disabled shop ✘ (ex guide dogs)

FALKLAND   Map 11 NO20

FALKLAND PALACE & GARDEN

KY15 7BU

➲ (off A912, 11m N of Kirkaldy)

☎ 01337 857397

web: www.nts.org.uk

The hunting palace of the Stuart monarchs, this fine building, with a French-Renaissance style south wing, stands in the shelter of the Lomond Hills. The beautiful Chapel Royal and King's Bedchamber are its most notable features, and it is also home to the oldest royal tennis court in Britain (1539). The garden has a spectacular delphinium border. Recorded sacred music is played hourly in the Chapel. Please telephone for details of concerts, recitals etc.

Times: ✱ Open Mar-Oct, Mon-Sat 10-6, Sun 1-5. Times may change for 2006 please telephone or check on www.nts.org.uk **Facilities:** 🅿 ዿ shop ✘ (ex guide dogs) 🍸

KELLIE CASTLE &   Map 12 NO50
GARDENS

KELLIE CASTLE & GARDENS

KY10 2RF

➲ (3m NW of Pittenweem on B9171)

☎ 01333 720271

e-mail: aclipson@nts-scot.demon.co.uk

web: www.nts.org.uk

The oldest part dates from about 1360, but it is for its 16th and 17th-century domestic architecture that Kellie is renowned. It has notable plasterwork and painted panelling, and there are also interesting Victorian gardens.

Times: ✱ Open Good Fri-Etr Mon & Jun-Sep, daily 1-5. Garden & grounds all year, daily 9.30-sunset. **Facilities:** 🅿 📗 ዿ (induction loop for hard of hearing) shop ✘ (ex guide dogs) 🍸

KIRKCALDY   Map 11 NT29

KIRKCALDY MUSEUM & ART GALLERY

War Memorial Gardens KY1 1YG

➲ (next to train station)

☎ 01592 412860   FREE

e-mail: kirkcaldy.museum@fife.gov.uk

web: www.fifedirect.org.uk/museums

Set in the town's lovely memorial gardens, the museum houses a collection of fine and decorative art, including 18th to 21st-century Scottish paintings, among them the works of William McTaggart and S J Peploe. An award-winning display 'Changing Places' tells the story of the social, industrial and natural heritage of the area.

Times: Open all year, Mon-Sat 10.30-5, Sun 2-5. Closed local hols **Facilities:** 🅿 📗 ዿ (ramp to main entrance & lift to 1st floor galleries) toilets for disabled shop ✘ (ex guide dogs)

NORTH QUEENSFERRY   Map 11 NT17

DEEP SEA WORLD

KY11 1JR

➲ (from N, M90 take exit for Inverkeithing. From S follow signs to Forth Rd Bridge, 1st exit left)

☎ 01383 411880

e-mail: info@deepseaworld.co.uk

web: www.deepseaworld.com/

The world's longest underwater tunnel gives you a diver's eye view of an underwater world. Come face to face with Sand Tiger sharks, and watch divers hand feed a wide array of sea life. Visit the Amazon Experience with ferocious piranhas and the amazing amphibian display featuring the world's most poisonous frog. Also featuring the newly opened Seal Sanctuary, dedicated to the rehabilitation and release of injured and orphaned seal pups. Please telephone or visit website for details of events running throughout the year.

Times: Open all year daily, Nov-Mar 10-5, Apr-Oct 10-6 wknds & school hols 10-6 **Fee:** £8.55 (ch 3-5 £6.30 under 3 free, concessions £6.75). Family ticket discount available. **Facilities:** 🅿 📗 ዿ (ramps & disabled parking, hearing loop) toilets for disabled shop ✘ (ex guide dogs) ◀

ST ANDREWS   Map 12 NO51

BRITISH GOLF MUSEUM
Bruce Embankment KY16 9AB
➲ (opposite Royal & Ancient Golf Club)
☎ 01334 460046 460053
e-mail: alisonwood@randa.org
web: www.britishgolfmuseum.co.uk
Where better to find out about golf than in St Andrews, the home of golf. Using diverse and exciting interactive displays, this museum explores the history of British golf from its origins to the personalities of today. The 18th Hole is fun for all the family, with dressing up, a mini-putting green and loads to do!
Times: Mar-Oct, Mon-Sat 9.30-5.30, Sun 10-5. Nov-Mar 2006, Mon-Sun 10-4. **Fee:** ✱ £5 (ch 6-15 £2.75) concessions £4, Family ticket £12.75. **Facilities:** P (charged) 🍴 ♿ toilets for disabled shop
✖ (ex guide dogs) ◼

CASTLE & VISITOR CENTRE
KY16 9AR
☎ 01334 477196
This 13th-century stronghold castle was the scene of the murder of Cardinal Beaton in 1546. The new visitor centre incorporates an exciting multi-media exhibition describing the history of the castle and nearby cathedral.
Times: Open all year, Apr-Sep, daily 9.30-6.30; Oct-Mar, daily 9.30-4.30. Closed 25-26 Dec & 1-2 Jan. **Fee:** ✱ £4 (ch £1.60, concessions £3). Joint ticket with St Andrews Cathedral £5 (ch £2, concessions £3.75). Group 11+ 10% discount. Prices valid until 31/12/05. Please phone for further details. **Facilities:** P ♿ toilets for disabled shop ✖ ▮

CATHEDRAL (& MUSEUM)
KY16 9QU
☎ 01334 472563
The cathedral was the largest in Scotland, and is now an extensive ruin. The remains date mainly from the 12th and 13th centuries, and large parts of the precinct walls have survived intact. Close by is St Rule's church, which the cathedral was built to replace. St Rule's probably dates from before the Norman Conquest, and is considered the most interesting Romanesque church in Scotland.
Times: Open all year, Apr-Sep, daily 9.30-6.30; Oct-Mar, daily 9.30-4.30. Closed 25-26 Dec & 1-2 Jan. **Fee:** ✱ £3 (ch £1.20, concessions £2.25). Joint ticket with St Andrews Castle £5 (ch £2, concessions £3.75). Group 11+ 10% discount. Prices valid until 31/12/05. Please phone for further details. **Facilities:** P shop ✖ ▮

ST ANDREWS AQUARIUM
The Scores KY16 9AS
➲ (signed in town centre)
☎ 01334 474786   **2 for 1**
web: www.standrewsaquarium.co.uk
This continually expanding aquarium is home to shrimps, sharks, eels, octopi, seals and much much more. Special features include the Seahorse Parade, and the Sea Mammal Research Unit, which is committed to the care of sea mammals and their environment.
Times: Open daily from 10. Please phone for winter opening
Fee: ✱ £5.95 (ch & student £3.95, pen £4.95). Family ticket (2ad+2ch) £17.50 **Facilities:** P (charged) 🍴 ✖ licensed ♿ toilets for disabled shop ✖ (ex guide dogs) ◼

AVIEMORE   Map 14 NH81

STRATHSPEY STEAM RAILWAY
Aviemore Station, Dalfaber Rd PH22 1PY
➲ (from A9 take B970 for Coylumbridge, on B9152, left after railway bridge, car park 0.25m on left. Other stations: Boat of Garten in village; Broomhill, off A95, 3.5m S of Grantown-on-Spey)
☎ 01479 810725
e-mail: information@strathspeyrailway.co.uk
web: www.strathspeyrailway.co.uk
This steam railway covers the ten miles from Aviemore via Boat of Garten to Broomhill. The journey takes about 40 minutes, but allow around two hours for the round trip. Shorter trips are possible and timetables are available from the station and the tourist information centre. Telephone, visit website or see local press for details of events running throughout the year.
Times: Open daily Etr, 23-29 Mar, 29 May-30 Sep; Apr, Wed & Sun; May & Oct, Wed-Thu, Sat-Sun & BH Mon, 9.30-4.30 **Fee:** Prices not confirmed for 2006 **Facilities:** P 🍴 ✖ ♿ (ramps) toilets for disabled shop ◼

BALMACARA   Map 14 NG82

BALMACARA ESTATE & LOCHALSH WOODLAND GARDEN
IV40 8DN
➲ (3m E of Kyle of Lochalsh, off A87)
☎ 01599 566325
e-mail: balmacara@nts.org.uk
web: www.nts.org.uk
The Balmacara Estate comprises some 5,600 acres and seven crofting villages, including Plockton, a conservation area. There are excellent views of Skye, Kintail and Applecross. The main attraction is the Lochalsh Woodland Garden, but the whole area is excellent for walking.
Times: ✱ Open Estate: all year. Woodland garden daily 9-sunset. Balmacara Square Visitor Centre, Apr-Sep, daily, 9-5 (Fri 9-4). Times may change for 2006 please telephone or check on www.nts.org.uk
Facilities: P ▾

BETTYHILL   Map 14 NC76

STRATHNAVER MUSEUM
KW14 7SS
➲ (By the A386 on outskirts of Bettyhill on the E of the village)
☎ 01641 521418
e-mail: strathnavermus@ukonline.co.uk
The museum has displays on the Clearances, with a fine collection of Strathnaver Clearances furnishings, domestic and farm implements, and local books. There is also a Clan Mackay room. The museum's setting is a former church, a handsome stone building with a magnificent canopied pulpit dated 1774. The churchyard contains a carved stone known as the Farr Stone, which dates back to the 9th century and is a fine example of Pictish art.
Times: Open Apr-Oct, Mon-Sat 10-1 & 2-5; Nov-Mar restricted opening. **Fee:** ✱ £1.90 (pen £1.20 ch 50p). **Facilities:** P ♿ shop ✖ (ex guide dogs)

BOAT OF GARTEN — Map 14 NH91

LOCH GARTEN OSPREY CENTRE
RSPB Reserve Abernethy Forest, Forest Lodge, Nethybridge PH25 3EF
➲ (signed from B970 & A9 at Aviemore, follow 'RSPB Ospreys' signs)
☎ 01479 821894

Home of the Loch Garten Osprey site, this reserve holds one of most important remnants of Scots Pine forest in the Highlands. Within its 30,760 acres are forest bogs, moorland, mountain top, lochs and crofting land. In addition to the regular pair of nesting ospreys, there are breeding Scottish crossbills, capercaillies, black grouse and many others. The ospreys can be viewed through telescopes and there is a live TV link to the nest. Please telephone for details of special events running throughout the year.
Times: Osprey Centre open daily, Apr-Aug 10-6. **Fee:** £3 (ch 50p) concessions £2. RSPB members free. **Facilities:** 🅿 🍴 ♿ (low level viewing slots & optics) toilets for disabled shop ✖ (ex guide dogs in centre) 🍽

CARRBRIDGE — Map 14 NH92

LANDMARK FOREST THEME PARK
PH23 3AJ
➲ (off A9 between Aviemore & Inverness)
☎ 01479 841613 & 0800 731 3446
e-mail: landmarkcentre@btconnect.com
web: www.landmark-centre.co.uk

This innovative centre is designed to provide a fun and educational visit for all ages. Microworld takes a close-up look at the incredible microscopic world around us. There is a 70ft forest viewing tower and a treetop trail. There are demonstrations of timber sawing, on a steam-powered sawmill and log hauling by a Clydesdale horse throughout the day. Attractions include a 3-track Watercoaster, a maze and a large covered adventure play area, mini electric cars and remote controlled truck arena. New features include; RopeworX, Freefall and The Plunge.
Times: Open all year, daily, Apr-mid Jul 10-6; mid Jul-mid Aug 10-7; Sep-Oct 10-5.30; Nov-Mar 10-5. **Fee:** Apr-Oct: £8.95 (ch £6.90); Multi-visit week, £12.95 (ch £10-90), Year £14.95 (ch £12.90)
Facilities: 🅿 🍽 ✖ licensed 🍴 ♿ (ramps) toilets for disabled shop 🍽

CAWDOR — Map 14 NH85

CAWDOR CASTLE
IV12 5RD
➲ (on B9090, off A96)
☎ 01667 404401
e-mail: info@cawdorcastle.com
web: www.cawdorcastle.com

Home of the Thanes of Cawdor since the 14th century, this lovely castle has a drawbridge, an ancient tower built round a tree, and a freshwater well inside the house. Gardens Weekend takes place in June - guided tours of gardens and Bluebell Walk in Cawdor Big Wood.
Times: Open May 1-8 Oct, daily 10-5.30. Last admission 5.
Fee: ✱ £6.80 (ch 5-15 £4, pen £5.80). Family ticket £19.50. Party 20+ £5.90 each. Gardens, grounds & nature trails only £3.50.
Facilities: 🅿 🍽 ✖ licensed 🍴 ♿ (ramps to restaurants, shops and gardens) toilets for disabled shop ✖ (ex guide dogs) 🍽

CLAVA CAIRNS — Map 14 NH74

CLAVA CAIRNS
➲ (6m E of Inverness, signed from B9091)
☎ 01667 460232   FREE

A well-preserved Bronze Age cemetery complex of passage graves, ring cairns, kerb cairn and standing stones in a beautiful setting. In addition, the remains of a chapel of unknown date can be seen at this site.
Times: Open at all reasonable times. **Facilities:** 🅿 ✖ 🛏

CROMARTY — Map 14 NH76

HUGH MILLER'S COTTAGE
Church St IV11 8XA
➲ (on A832)
☎ 01381 600245
web: www.nts.org.uk

The cottage houses an exhibition on the life and work of Hugh Miller, a stonemason born here in 1802 who became an eminent geologist and writer. It was built by his great-grandfather around 1698, and now has a charming cottage garden.
Times: ✱ Open Good Fri-Sep, daily 12-5; Oct, Sun-Wed 12-5. Times may change for 2006 please telephone or check on www.nts.org.uk
Facilities: 🅿 (5mins) (disabled is directly outside) ♿ ✖ (ex guide dogs) 🍽

CULLODEN MOOR — Map 14 NH74

CULLODEN BATTLEFIELD
IV2 5EU
➲ (B9006, 5m E of Inverness)
☎ 01463 790607
e-mail: culloden@nts.org.uk
web: www.nts.org.uk

A cairn recalls this last battle fought on mainland Britain, on 16 April 1746, when the Duke of Cumberland's forces routed 'Bonnie' Prince Charles Edward Stuart's army. The battlefield has been restored to its state on the day of the battle, and in summer there are 'living history' enactments. This is a most atmospheric evocation of tragic events. Telephone for details of guided tours.
Times: ✱ Open Site: all year, daily. Visitor Centre: Feb-Mar & Nov-Dec, daily 11-4; Apr-Jun & Sep-Oct, daily 9-6; Jul-Aug, daily 9-7. Times may change for 2006 please telephone or check on www.nts.org.uk
Facilities: 🅿 ✖ ♿ (wheelchair, induction loop, raised map) toilets for disabled shop ✖ (ex guide dogs) 🍽

DRUMNADROCHIT — Map 14 NH52

OFFICIAL LOCH NESS EXHIBITION CENTRE, LOCH NESS 2000
IV3 6TU
➲ (on A82, 12m S Inverness)
☎ 01456 450573 & 450218   2 for 1
e-mail: brem@loch-ness-scotland.com
web: www.loch-ness-scotland.com

A fascinating and popular multi-media presentation lasting 30 minutes. Seven themed areas cover the story of the Loch Ness monster, from the pre-history of Scotland, through the cultural roots of the legend in Highland folklore, and into the 50-year controversy which surrounds it. Using latest technology in computer animation, lasers and multi-media projection systems.
Times: Open all year; Etr-May 9.30-5.30; Jun-Sep 9.30-6 (9-8.30 Jul & Aug); Winter 10-4. (Last admission 30mins before closing). **Fee:** £5.95 (ch £3.50, pen & students £4.50, ch under 7 & disabled free). Family ticket £14.95. Group. **Facilities:** 🅿 🍽 ✖ licensed ♿ (parking) toilets for disabled shop ✖ (ex in grounds/guide dogs) 🍽

URQUHART CASTLE
IV63 6XJ
⮂ (on A82)
☎ 01456 450551
The castle was once Scotland's biggest and overlooks Loch Ness. It dates mainly from the 14th century, when it was built on the site of an earlier fort, and was destroyed before the 1715 Jacobite rebellion.
Times: Open all year, Apr-Sep, daily 9.30-6.30; Oct-Mar, daily 9.30-4.30. Closed 25-26 Dec & 1-2 Jan. **Fee:** ✱ £6 (ch £2.40, concessions £4.50). Group 11+ 10% discount. Prices valid until 31/12/05. Please phone for further details. **Facilities:** 🅿 shop ✖ 🎗

DUNBEATH   Map 15 ND12
LAIDHAY CROFT MUSEUM
KW6 6EH
⮂ (1m N of Dunbeath on A9)
☎ 01593 731244
The museum gives visitors a glimpse of a long-vanished way of life. The main building is a thatched Caithness longhouse, with the dwelling quarters, byre and stable all under one roof. It dates back some 200 years, and is furnished as it might have been 100 years ago. A collection of early farm tools and machinery is also shown. Near the house is a thatched winnowing barn with its roof supported on three 'Highland couples', or crucks.
Times: Open Etr-Oct, daily 10-6. **Fee:** £2 (ch 50p) **Facilities:** 🅿 ☕ 🎫 ♿ toilets for disabled

ELPHIN   Map 14 NC21
HIGHLAND & RARE BREEDS FARM
IV27 4HH
⮂ (on A835 in Elphin)
☎ 01854 666204
There are highland cattle, traditional 4-horned sheep with coloured fleeces, traditional Scottish ewes and lambs, rare breeds of pigs and goats. Many types of poultry, duck ponds, and a farm walk among the animals. Also on display are farm tools, crofting history, wool crafts and hand-spinning.
Times: ✱ Open Jul & Aug only **Facilities:** 🅿 🎫 ♿ (assistance available) toilets for disabled shop ✖ 🍴

FORT GEORGE   Map 14 NH75
FORT GEORGE
IV1 2TD
⮂ (11m NE of Inverness)
☎ 01667 462777
Built following the Battle of Culloden as a Highland fortress for the army of George II, this is one of the outstanding artillery fortifications in Europe and still an active army barracks.
Times: Open all year, Apr-Sep daily 9.30-6.30; Oct-Mar daily 9.30-4.30. Closed 25-26 Dec & 1-2 Jan. **Fee:** ✱ £6 (ch £2.40, concessions £4.50). Group 11+ 10% discount. Prices valid until 31/12/05. Please phone for further details. **Facilities:** 🅿 ✖ ♿ toilets for disabled ✖ 🎗

QUEEN'S OWN HIGHLANDERS REGIMENTAL MUSEUM COLLECTION
IV2 7TD
⮂ (off A96 5m from Inverness)
☎ 01463 224380
Fort George has been a military barracks since it was built in 1748-69, and was the Depot of the Seaforth Highlanders until 1961. The museum of the Queen's Own Highlanders (Seaforth and Camerons) is sited in the former Lieutenant Governor's house, where uniforms, medals and pictures are displayed.

continued

Times: Open Apr-Sep, daily 10-6; Oct-Mar, Mon-Fri 10-4. Closed Xmas, New Year & BH. **Fee:** Free. (Admission charged by Historic Scotland for entry to Fort George). **Facilities:** 🅿 ♿ (stair lift to 1st floor, wheelchair on 1st floor) toilets for disabled shop ✖ (ex guide dogs)

FORT WILLIAM   Map 14 NN17
INVERLOCHY CASTLE
PH33 6SN   FREE
⮂ (2m NE of Fort William, off A82)
A fine well-preserved 13th-century castle of the Comyn family; in the form of a square, with round towers at the corners. The largest tower was the donjon or keep. This is one of Scotland's earliest castles.
Times: Open at all reasonable times. **Facilities:** 🅿 ✖ 🎗

WEST HIGHLAND MUSEUM
Cameron Square PH33 6AJ
⮂ (museum next door to tourist office)
☎ 01397 702169
e-mail: info@westhighlandmuseum.org.uk
web: www.westhighlandmuseum.org.uk
The displays illustrate traditional Highland life and history, with numerous Jacobite relics. One of them is the 'secret portrait' of Bonnie Prince Charlie, which looks like meaningless daubs of paint but reveals a portrait when reflected in a metal cylinder.
Times: Open all year Jun-Sep, Mon-Sat 10-5 (also July-Aug, Sun 2-5); Oct-May, Mon-Sat 10-4. **Fee:** £3 (ch 50p, concessions £2) **Facilities:** 🅿 (100yds) (charge May-Oct, max. 2hrs stay) ♿ toilets for disabled shop ✖ (ex guide dogs)

GAIRLOCH   Map 14 NG87
GAIRLOCH HERITAGE MUSEUM
Achtercairn IV21 2BP
⮂ (on junct of A382 & B8021 near police station & public car park)   2 for 1
☎ 01445 712287
e-mail: info@gairlochheritagemuseum.org.uk
web: www.gairlochheritagemuseum.org.uk
A converted farmstead now houses the award-winning museum, which shows the way of life in this typical West Highland parish from early times to the 20th century. There are hands-on activities for children and reconstructions of a croft house room, a school room, a shop, and a smugglers' cave. You can also view Gairloch through one of the largest lenses assembled by the Northern Lighthouse Board. Special Events: The Big Draw 15 Oct. Please visit website for details.
Times: Open Apr-Sep, Mon-Sat 10-5; Oct, Mon-Fri 10-1.30 (last admission 4.30). Winter months by arrangement. **Fee:** ✱ £3 (ch 50p, students & pen £2). Group rates available **Facilities:** 🅿 ✖ 🎫 ♿ shop ✖ (ex guide dogs)

GLENCOE   Map 14 NN15
GLENCOE & NORTH LORN FOLK MUSEUM
PH49 4HS
⮂ (turn off A82 at Glencoe x-roads then immediately right into Glencoe village)
☎ 01855 811664
Two heather-thatched cottages in the main street of Glencoe now house items connected with the Macdonalds and the Jacobite risings. A variety of local domestic and farming exhibits, dairying and slate-working equipment, costumes and embroidery are also shown.
Times: Open 20 May-Sep, Mon-Sat 10-5.30. **Fee:** ✱ £2 (ch free, concessions £1.50). **Facilities:** 🅿 ♿ shop

GLENCOE VISITOR CENTRE

PA39 4HX

➲ (on A82, 17m S of Fort William)

☎ 01855 811307 & 811729

Glencoe has stunning scenery and some of the most challenging climbs and walks in the Highlands. Red deer, wildcats, eagles and ptarmigan are among the wildlife. It is also known as a place of treachery and infamy. The Macdonalds of Glencoe were hosts to a party of troops who, under government orders, fell upon the men, women and children, in a bloody massacre in 1692. The Visitor Centre tells the story.

Times: ✱ Open: Site all year, daily. Visitor Centre Apr-Aug, 9.30-5.30; Mar-Apr & Sep-Oct, daily 10-5; Nov-Feb, Fri-Mon 10-4 (last admission 30 mins before closing). Times may change for 2006 please telephone or check on www.nts.org.uk **Facilities:** P ⬛ & (induction loop in video programme room) toilets for disabled shop ✺ (ex guide dogs) ☙

GLENFINNAN · Map 14 NM98

GLENFINNAN MONUMENT

PH37 4LT

➲ (on A830, 18.5m W of Fort William)

☎ 01397 722250

e-mail: glenfinnan@nts.org.uk

web: www.nts.org.uk

The monument commemorates the Highlanders who fought for Bonnie Prince Charlie in 1745. It stands in an awe-inspiring setting at the head of Loch Shiel. There is a visitor centre with information (commentary in four languages) on the Prince's campaign.

Times: ✱ Site open all year, daily. Visitor centre: daily Apr-Jun & Sep-Oct 10-5; Jul-Aug 9.30-5.30. Times may change for 2006 please telephone or check on www.nts.org.uk **Facilities:** P ⬛ & (information centre only) shop ☙

GOLSPIE · Map 14 NH89

DUNROBIN CASTLE

KW10 6SF

➲ (1m NE on A9, from Golspie)

☎ 01408 633177 & 633268

e-mail: info@dunrobincastle.net

web: www.highlandescape.co.uk

The ancient seat of the Earls and Dukes of Sutherland is a splendid, gleaming, turreted structure, thanks largely to 19th-century rebuilding, and has a beautiful setting overlooking the sea. Paintings, furniture and family heirlooms are on display, and the gardens are on a grand scale to match the house. There are also falconry displays in the gardens.

Times: Open Apr-15 Oct, Mon-Sat 10.30-5.30, Sun 12-5.30. Closes 1 hr earlier Apr, May & Oct. (Last admission half hour before closing).

Fee: ✱ £6.80 (ch £4.70 & pen £5.80). Family ticket £18. Party.

Facilities: P ⬛ ▥ (access by arrangement only) shop ✺ ▤

HELMSDALE · Map 14 ND01

TIMESPAN

Dunrobin St KW8 6JX

➲ (off A9 in centre of village, by Telford Bridge)

☎ 01431 821327

e-mail: admin@timespan.org.uk

web: www.timespan.org.uk

Located in a historic fishing village, this museum relates to the social and natural history of the area, and the art gallery has changing exhibitions of contemporary art and works by *continued*

local artists. The garden has over 100 varieties of herbs and plants. There is a gift shop, and a café with beautiful views of the Telford Bridge.

Times: Open Apr- Oct, Mon-Sat 10-5, Sun 12-5. **Facilities:** P (150 mtrs) ⬛ & (lift) toilets for disabled shop garden centre ✺ (ex guide dogs) ▤

KINCRAIG · Map 14 NH80

HIGHLAND WILDLIFE PARK

PH21 1NL

➲ (on B9152, 7m S of Aviemore)

☎ 01540 651270

e-mail: info@highlandwildlifepark.org

web: www.highlandwildlifepark.org

As you drive through the main reserve, you can see awe-inspiring European bison grazing alongside wild horses, red deer and highland cattle plus a wide variety of other species. Then in the walk-round forest, woodland and moorland habitats prepare for close encounters with animals such as wolves, capercaillie, arctic foxes, wildcats, pine martens, otters and owls. Special events every weekend April to October.

Times: ✱ Open throughout the year, weather permitting. Apr-Oct, 10-6; Jun-Aug 10-7; Nov-Mar 10-4. (Last entry 2 hours before closing).

Facilities: P ⬛ & toilets for disabled shop ✺ ▤

KINGUSSIE · Map 14 NH70

HIGHLAND FOLK MUSEUM

Duke St PH21 1JG

➲ (12m SW of Aviemore off A9 at Kingussie)

☎ 01540 661307

e-mail: highland.folk@highland.gov.uk

web: www.highlandfolk.com

First established in 1935, this was Britain's first open-air museum. For a glimpse of life in a Blackhouse or a look at farming implements and domestic objects and furniture, this museum offers an internationally renowned collection of items. The Museum Store, not accessible to visitors in previous years, now displays in excess of 1,500 objects.

Times: Open Apr-Aug, Mon-Sat 9.30-5; Sep & Oct Mon-Fri, 9.30-4

Fee: ✱ £2.50 (ch & pen £1.50) **Facilities:** P & (ramp, door, rails) toilets for disabled shop ✺ (ex guide dogs) ▤

RUTHVEN BARRACKS

➲ (1m SE from Kingussie, signed from A9 and A86)

☎ 01667 460232 ▐FREE▌

An infantry barracks erected in 1719 following the Jacobite rising of 1715, with two ranges of quarters and a stable block. Captured and burnt by Prince Charles Edward Stuart's army in 1746.

Times: Open at any reasonable time. **Facilities:** P ✺ ▐

KIRKHILL · Map 14 NH54

MONIACK CASTLE (HIGHLAND WINERY)

IV5 7PQ

➲ (7m from Inverness on A862, near Beauly, on S side of Beauly Firth)

☎ 01463 831283

e-mail: jg@moniackcastle.co.uk

web: www.moniackcastle.co.uk

Commercial wine-making is not a typically Scottish industry, but nevertheless a wide range of country-style wines is produced, including elderflower and silver birch; mead and *continued*

sloe gin are also made here. A selection of related products and tours of the production area are available at this unique attraction, situated in a 16th-century castle.
Times: Open all year, Apr-Oct Mon-Sat 10-5. Nov-Mar, Mon-Fri 11-4.
Fee: ✱ £2 **Facilities:** 🅿 shop ✖ 🍴

NEWTONMORE   Map 14 NN79

CLAN MACPHERSON HOUSE & MUSEUM

Main St PH20 1DE
➲ (off A9 at junct of Newtonmore and Kingussie, museum on left after entering village)
☎ 01540 673332

Containing relics and memorials of the clan chiefs and other Macpherson families as well as those of Prince Charles Edward Stuart, this museum also displays the Prince's letters to the Clan Chief of 1745 and one to the Prince from his father, the Old Pretender, along with royal warrants and the green banner of the clan. Other interesting historic exhibits include James Macpherson's fiddle, swords, pictures, decorations and medals. Special Events: Special Exhibition marking the centenary of Ian Macpherson.
Times: Open Apr-Oct, Mon-Sat 10-5, Sun 2-5. Other times by appointment. **Fee:** ✱ Free. Donations welcome.
Facilities: 🅿 ♿ (ramp entrance from car park, subtitles on DVD) toilets for disabled shop ✖ (ex guide dogs) 🍴

HIGHLAND FOLK MUSEUM

Aultlarie Croft PH20 1AY
➲ (on A86, follow signs off A9)
☎ 01540 661307
e-mail: highland.folk@highland.gov.uk
web: www.highlandfolk.com

An early 18th-century farming township with turf houses has been reconstructed at this award-winning museum. A 1930s school houses old world maps, little wooden desks and a Coates library. Other attractions include a working croft with rare breed animals and tailor's workshop. Vintage buses run throughout the site.
Times: Open Apr-Aug, Mon-Sun 10.30-5.30; Sep Mon-Sun, 11-4.30; Oct Mon-Fri, 11-4.30 **Fee:** ✱ £5 (ch & pen £3) **Facilities:** 🅿 💻 ♿ (vintage bus with full disabled access) toilets for disabled shop ✖ (ex guide dogs) 🍴

POOLEWE   Map 14 NG88

INVEREWE GARDEN

IV22 2LG
➲ (6m NE of Gairloch, on A832)
☎ 01445 781200
e-mail: inverewe@nts.org.uk
web: www.nts.org.uk

The influence of the North Atlantic Drift enables this remarkable garden to grow rare and sub-tropical plants. At its best in early June, but full of beauty from March to October, Inverewe has a backdrop of magnificent mountains and stands to the north of Loch Maree.
Times: ✱ Open: Garden all year, Apr-Oct, daily 9.30-9 (or sunset if earlier). Nov-Mar, 9.30-4. Visitor Centre Apr-Sep, daily 9.30-5; Oct, daily 9.30-4. Times may change for 2006 please telephone or check on www.nts.org.uk **Facilities:** 🅿 ✖ licensed ♿ (some paths difficult) toilets for disabled shop ✖ (ex guide dogs) 🎭

ROSEMARKIE   Map 14 NH75

GROOM HOUSE MUSEUM

High St IV10 8UF
➲ (off A9 at Tore onto A832)
☎ 01381 620961 & 01381 621730   ▐FREE▌
e-mail: groamhouse@ecosse.net

Opened in 1980, this community-based museum explores the history, culture and crafts of the mysterious Picts, who faded from history over a thousand years ago. Visitors can see the Rosemarkie Stones, large slabs that show Pictish carvings; paintings, a replica Pictish harp, and a collection of photographs of Pictish stones all over the country and interactive computer programmes. Temporary exhibitions take place, often as loans from other major museums.
Times: Open Etr week, daily 2-4.30; May-Oct, Mon-Sat, 10-5, Sun 2-4.30; Apr, Sat-Sun 2-4.30. Other times by appointment. Closed 11 Dec-4 Mar. **Facilities:** 🅿 🍴 ♿ shop ✖ (ex guide dogs) 🍴

STRATHPEFFER   Map 14 NH45

HIGHLAND MUSEUM OF CHILDHOOD

The Old Station IV14 9DH
➲ (5m W of Dingwall on A834)
☎ 01997 421031
e-mail: info@
highlandmuseumofchildhood.org.uk
web: www.highlandmuseumofchildhood.org.uk

Located in a renovated Victorian railway station of 1885, the museum tells the story of childhood in the Highlands amongst the crofters and townsfolk; a way of life recorded in oral testimony, displays and evocative photographs. An award-winning video, A Century of Highland Childhood is shown. There are also doll and toy collections.
Times: Open Apr-Oct, daily 10-5, (Sun 2-5) also Jul & Aug evenings open to 7. Other times by arrangement. **Facilities:** 🅿 💻 🍴 ♿ (tape tour with induction loop for partially sighted) shop ✖ (ex guide dogs) 🍴

TORRIDON   Map 14 NG85

TORRIDON COUNTRYSIDE CENTRE

The Mains IV22 2EZ
➲ (N of A896)
☎ 01445 791221
e-mail: aclipson@nts.scot.demon.co.uk.
web: www.nts.org.uk

Set amid some of Scotland's finest mountain scenery, the centre offers audio-visual presentations on the local wildlife. At the Mains nearby visitors may see deer.
Times: ✱ Open Countryside Centre, Good Fri-Sep, daily 10-6. Estate and Deer Museum daily all year. **Facilities:** 🅿 ♿ toilets for disabled 🎭

WICK   Map 15 ND35

CASTLE OF OLD WICK

➲ (1m S on Shore Rd)
☎ 01667 460232   ▐FREE▌

The ruin of the best-preserved Norse castle in Scotland. Dating from the 12th-century this spectacular site is on a spine of rock projecting into the sea, between two deep, narrow gullies. Visitors must take great care and wear sensible shoes.
Times: Open at all reasonable times. **Facilities:** ✖ ▐

WICK HERITAGE MUSEUM
18-27 Bank Row KW1 5EY
➲ (close to the harbour)
☎ 01955 605393

The heritage centre is near the harbour in a complex of eight houses, yards and outbuildings. The centre illustrates local history from Neolithic times to the herring fishing industry. In addition, there is a complete working 19th-century lighthouse, and the famous Johnston collection of photographs.
Times: Open Apr-Oct, Mon-Sat 10-5, last admissions 3.45. (Closed Sun). **Fee:** ✱ £2 (ch 50p). **Facilities:** 🅿 ♿ toilets for disabled

INVERCLYDE

GREENOCK   Map 10 NS27

McLEAN MUSEUM & ART GALLERY
15 Kelly St PA16 8JX
➲ (close to Greenock West Railway Station and Greenock Bus Station)
☎ 01475 715624   FREE
e-mail: museum@inverclyde.gov.uk
web: www.inverclyde.gov.uk

James Watt was born in Greenock, and various exhibits connected with him are shown. The museum also has an art collection, and displays on shipping, local and natural history, Egyptology and ethnography.
Times: Open all year, Mon-Sat 10-5. Closed local & national PHs.
Facilities: 🅿 (200mtrs) 🍴 ♿ (induction loop) toilets for disabled shop ✖ (ex guide & service dogs)

PORT GLASGOW   Map 10 NS37

NEWARK CASTLE
PA14 5NH
➲ (on A8)
☎ 01475 741858

The one-time house of the Maxwells, dating from the 15th and 17th centuries. The courtyard and hall are preserved. Fine turrets and the remains of painted ceilings can be seen, and the hall carries an inscription of 1597.
Times: Open Apr-Sep, daily 9.30-6.30. **Fee:** ✱ £2.50 (ch £1, concessions £1.90). Group 11+ 10% discount. Prices valid until 31/12/05. Please phone for further details. **Facilities:** 🅿 shop ¶

MIDLOTHIAN

CRICHTON   Map 11 NT36

CRICHTON CASTLE
EH37 5QH
➲ (2.5m SW of Pathhead, off A68)
☎ 01875 320017

The castle dates back to the 14th century, but most of what remains today was built over the following 300 years. A notable feature is the 16th-century wing built by the Earl of Bothwell in Italian style, with an arcade below.
Times: Open Apr-Sep, daily 9.30-6.30. **Fee:** ✱ £2.50 (ch £1, concessions £1.90). Group 11+ 10% discount. Prices valid until 31/12/05. Please phone for further details. **Facilities:** 🅿 ¶

DALKEITH   Map 11 NT36

EDINBURGH BUTTERFLY & INSECT WORLD
Dobbies Garden World, Lasswade EH18 1AZ
➲ (0.5m S of Edinburgh city bypass at Gilmerton junct or Sherrifhall rdbt)
☎ 0131 663 4932
e-mail: info@edinburgh-butterfly-world.co.uk
web: www.edinburgh-butterfly-world.co.uk

Richly coloured butterflies from all over the world can be seen flying among exotic rainforest plants, trees and flowers. The tropical pools are filled with giant waterlilies and colourful fish, and are surrounded by lush vegetation. Also scorpions, leaf cutting ants, beetles, tarantulas and other remarkable creatures. There is a unique honeybee display and daily insect handling sessions.
Times: Open Summer daily 9.30-5.30; Winter daily 10-5. Closed 25-26 Dec & 1 Jan. **Fee:** ✱ £4.90 (ch, concessions & students £3.75). Family ticket £165 (2ad+2ch). Party 10+. **Facilities:** 🅿 🍴 🍴 ♿ toilets for disabled shop garden centre ✖ (ex guide dogs) 🍴

NEWTONGRANGE   Map 11 NT36

SCOTTISH MINING MUSEUM
Lady Victoria Colliery EH22 4QN
➲ (10m S of Edinburgh on A7, signed from bypass)
☎ 0131 663 7519   2 for 1
e-mail: visitorservices@
scottishminingmuseum.com
web: www.scottishminingmuseum.com

Based at Scotland's National Coalmining Museum offering an outstanding visit to Britains' finest Victorian colliery. Guided tours with miners, magic helmets, exhibitions, theatres, interactive displays and a visit to the coal face. Home to Scotland's largest steam engine.
Times: Open all year, daily Mar-Oct, 10-5. (Last entry 3.30). Nov-Feb, daily, 10-4. (Last entry 2.30) **Fee:** ✱ £4.95 (ch & concessions £3.30). Family ticket £15. Party 20+ (£4.25, ch £3) **Facilities:** 🅿 🍴 ✖ 🍴 ♿ (Tactile Opportunites, interactive, audio tours) toilets for disabled shop ✖ (ex guide dogs) 🍴

PENICUIK   Map 11 NT26

EDINBURGH CRYSTAL VISITOR CENTRE
Eastfield EH26 8HB
➲ (on A701Edinburgh to Peebles road)
☎ 01968 675128
e-mail: visitorcentre@edinburgh-crystal.co.uk
web: www.edinburgh-crystal.com

Watch skilled craftsmen as they take molten crystal and turn it into intricately decorated glassware. Not only can you talk

continued

to the craftsmen themselves but there is also video footage, story boards, artefacts and audio listening posts to help you understand the 300-year-old history of glassmaking. The shop includes the largest selection of Edinburgh crystal plus seconds at bargain prices.
Times: Open Mon-Sat 10-5, Sun 11-5. **Facilities:** 🅿 💷 ✕ licensed 📋 ⅃ (ramp to first floor) toilets for disabled shop ✖ (ex guide dogs) 📧

MORAY

BALLINDALLOCH   Map 15 NJ13
THE GLENLIVET DISTILLERY
Glenlivet AB55 5BS
➲ (10m N of Tomintoul, off B9008)
☎ 01340 821720   FREE
e-mail: betty.munro@chivas.com
web: www.theglenlivet.com
The visitor centre includes a guided tour of the whisky production facilities and a chance to see inside the vast bonded warehouses where the spirit matures. The multimedia exhibition and interactive presentations communicate the unique history, and traditions of Glenlivet Scotch Whisky.
Times: Open mid Mar- end Oct, Mon-Sat 10-4, Sun 12.30-4.
Facilities: 🅿 💷 📋 ⅃ (cafeteria, lift to exhibition) toilets for disabled shop ✖ (ex guide dogs) 📧

BRODIE CASTLE   Map 14 NH95
BRODIE CASTLE
IV36 2TE
➲ (4.5m W of Forres, off A96)
☎ 01309 641371
e-mail: brodiecastle@nts.org.uk
web: www.nts.org.uk
The Brodie family lived here for hundreds of years before passing the castle to the NTS in 1980. It contains many treasures, including furniture, porcelain and paintings. The extensive grounds include a woodland walk and an adventure playground. Wheelchairs for disabled visitors are available. Please telephone for details of recitals, concerts, open-air theatre etc.
Times: ✱ Open Apr & Jul-Aug, daily 12-4; May-Jun & Sep, Sun-Thu 12-4. Grounds all year, daily, 9.30-sunset. Times may change for 2006 please telephone or check on www.nts.org.uk **Facilities:** 🅿 💷 ⅃ (audio tape & information sheet in Braille) toilets for disabled shop ✖ (ex guide dogs) 🍼

CRAIGELLACHIE   Map 15 NJ24
SPEYSIDE COOPERAGE VISITOR CENTRE
Dufftown Rd AB38 9RS
➲ (1m S of Craigellachie, on A941)
☎ 01340 871108
e-mail: info@speyside-coopers.demon.co.uk
web: www.speysidecooperage.co.uk
A working cooperage with unique visitor centre, where skilled coopers and their apprentices practise this ancient craft. Each year they repair around 100,000 oak casks which will be used to mature many different whiskies. The 'Acorn to Cask' exhibition traces the history and development of the coopering industry.
Times: Open all year, Mon-Fri 9.30-4. Closed Xmas & New Year.
Fee: ✱ £3.10 (ch £1.80 & pen £2.50). Family ticket £8.50. Party 15+.
Facilities: 🅿 💷 ⅃ (Special picnic table, viewing point) toilets for disabled shop ✖ (ex guide dogs) 📧

DUFFTOWN   Map 15 NJ34
BALVENIE CASTLE
AB55 4DH
➲ (on A941)
☎ 01340 820121
The ruined castle was the ancient stronghold of the Comyns, and became a stylish house in the 16th century.
Times: Open Apr-Sep, daily 9.30-6.30. **Fee:** ✱ £2.50 (ch £1, concessions £1.90). Group 11+ 10% discount. Prices valid until 31/12/05. Please phone for further details. **Facilities:** 🅿 ⅃ toilets for disabled ▮

GLENFIDDICH DISTILLERY
AB55 4DH
➲ (N of town, off A941)
☎ 01340 820373   FREE
web: www.glenfiddich.com
Set close to Balvenie Castle, the distillery was founded in 1887 by William Grant and has stayed in the hands of the family ever since. Visitors can see the whisky-making process in its various stages, including bottling, and then sample the finished product.
Times: Open all year Mon-Fri 9.30-4.30, also Etr-mid Oct, Sat 9.30-4.30, Sun 12-4.30. Closed Xmas & New Year
Facilities: 🅿 ⅃ (ramp access to production area & warehouse gallery) toilets for disabled shop ✖ (ex guide dogs)

DUFFUS   Map 15 NJ16
DUFFUS CASTLE
➲ (5m NW of Elgin on B9012 to Burghead)   FREE
☎ 01667 460232
One of the finest examples of a motte and bailey castle in Scotland with a later, very fine, stone hall house and curtain wall. The original seat of the Moray family.
Times: Open at all reasonable times. **Facilities:** 🅿 ✖ ▮

ELGIN   Map 15 NJ26
ELGIN CATHEDRAL
North College St IV30 1EL
☎ 01343 547171
Founded in 1224, the cathedral was known as the Lantern of the North and the Glory of the Kingdom because of its beauty. In 1390 it was burnt, along with most of the town. Although it was rebuilt, it fell into ruin after the Reformation. The ruins are quite substantial, however, and there is still a good deal to admire, including the fine west towers and the octagonal chapter house.
Times: Open all year, Apr-Sep, daily 9.30-6.30; Oct-Mar, daily 9.30-4.30. Closed Thu & Fri in winter, 25-26 Dec & 1-2 Jan. **Fee:** ✱ £3.30 (ch £1.30, concessions £2.50). Group 11+ 10% discount. Prices valid until 31/12/05. Please phone for further details. **Facilities:** 🅿 ⅃ shop ▮

ELGIN MUSEUM
1 High St IV30 1EQ
➲ (E end of High St, follow brown heritage signs)
☎ 01343 543675
e-mail: curator@elginmuseum.org.uk
web: www.elginmuseum.org.uk
This award-winning museum is internationally famous for its fossil fish and fossil reptiles, and for its Pictish stones. The displays relate to the natural and human history of Moray.
Times: Open Apr-Oct, Mon-Fri 10-5, Sat 11-4. **Fee:** ✱ £2 (ch 50p, pen, students & UB40 £1). Family ticket £4.50. **Facilities:** 🅿 (charged) 📋 ⅃ (handrails, case displays at sitting level with large fonts) toilets for disabled shop ✖ (ex guide dogs)

PLUSCARDEN ABBEY

IV30 8UA

➲ (6m SW of Elgin on unclass road)

☎ 01343 890257 FREE

e-mail: monks@pluscardenabbey.org

web: www.pluscardenabbey.org

The original monastery was founded in 1230 by King Alexander II for monks of the Valliscaulian order from Burgundy, but it later became a Benedictine house. Monastic life was abandoned after the Reformation and the house passed through a succession of lay owners until it was bought by the third Marquess of Bute in 1898. His third son, Lord Colum Crichton Stuart gave the monastery to the Benedictines of Prinknash Abbey near Gloucester, and monastic life was recommenced n 1948. Today there are about two dozen monks who lead a life of prayer, study and manual work. The services in the Abbey church are sung in Latin with Gregorian chant and are all open to the public.

Times: Open all year, daily 4.45am-8.30pm **Facilities:** 🅿 🗄 ⚐ (induction loop, ramps to shop, garden partially accessible) toilets for disabled shop garden centre ✖ (ex guide dogs) 🔊

FOCHABERS   Map 15 NJ35

BAXTERS HIGHLAND VILLAGE

IV32 7LD

➲ (1m W of Fochabers on A96)

☎ 01343 820666 FREE

e-mail: highland.village@Baxters.co.uk

web: www.baxters.com

The Baxters food firm started here over 130 years ago and now sells its products in over 60 countries. Visitors can see the shop where the story began, watch an audio-visual display, and visit five shops. See the great hall, audio-visual theatre and cooking theatre. A food tasting area is open to visitors.

Times: ✱ Open all year, Jan-Mar 10-5; Apr-Dec 9-5.30.
Facilities: 🅿 ✗ licensed 🗄 ⚐ (parking facilities) toilets for disabled shop ✖ (ex guide dogs) 🔊

FORRES   Map 14 NJ05

DALLAS DHU DISTILLERY

IV36 2RR

➲ (1m S of Forres, off A940)

☎ 01309 676548

A perfectly preserved time capsule of the distiller's art. It was built in 1898 to supply malt whisky for Wright and Greig's 'Roderick Dhu' blend. Visitors are welcome to wander at will through this fine old Victorian distillery, or to take a guided tour, dram included.

Times: Open all year, Apr-Sep, daily 9.30-6.30; Oct-Mar, daily 9.30-4.30. Closed Thu & Fri in winter, 25-26 Dec & 1-2 Jan. **Fee:** ✱ £4 (ch £1.60, concessions £3). Group 11+ 10% discount. Prices valid until 31/12/05. Please phone for further details. **Facilities:** 🅿 ⚐ toilets for disabled shop ✖ 🔊

FALCONER MUSEUM

Tolbooth St IV36 1PH

➲ (11m W of Elgin, 26m E of Iverness)

☎ 01309 673701

e-mail: museums@moray.gov.uk

web: www.moray.gov.uk

Founded by bequests made by two brothers, Alexander and Hugh Falconer. Hugh was a distinguished scientist, friend of Darwin, recipient of many honours and Vice-President of the Royal Society. On display are fossil mammals collected by him, and items relating to his involvement in the study of

continued

anthropology. Other displays are on local wildlife, geology, archaeology and history. Also you can see the Forres Quincentennial Time Capsule. Special Events: Refurbishment and re-launch of museum due in Spring 2006.

Times: Open all year Apr-Oct, Mon-Sat 10-5; Nov-Mar, Mon-Thu 11-12.30 & 1-3.30. Closed Good Fri & May Day **Fee:** Donations welcome **Facilities:** 🅿 🗄 ⚐ (induction loop system) shop ✖ (ex guide dogs)

SUENO'S STONE

➲ (E end of Forres, off A96)

☎ 01667 460232 FREE

The most remarkable sculptured monument in Britain, probably a cenotaph, standing over 20 feet high and dating back to the end of the first millennium AD. Covered by a protective glass enclosure.

Times: Open at all reasonable times. **Facilities:** 🅿 ✖ 🏳

KEITH   Map 15 NJ45

STRATHISLA DISTILLERY

Seafield Av AB55 5BS

➲ (A96 Aberdeen to Inverness road, attraction signed midway through town)

☎ 01542 783104

e-mail: jeanett.grant@chivas.com

web: www.chivas.com

Tour the oldest distillery in the highlands, founded in 1786. A dram of Chivas Regal 12 year old malt is offered on arrival, before viewing the Chivas Brothers DVD and distillery tour.

Times: Open Apr-Oct, Mon-Sat 10-4, Sun 12.30-4 **Fee:** £5 per person (ch free, ch under 8 not admitted to production areas, but welcome in centre). Maybe subject to change. **Facilities:** 🅿 🗄 ⚐ (access is very limited) toilets for disabled shop ✖ (ex guide dogs) 🔊

MARYPARK   Map 15 NJ13

GLENFARCLAS DISTILLERY

AB37 9BD

➲ (4m W of Aberlour on A95 to Grantown-on-Spey)

☎ 01807 500245 & 500257

e-mail: J&GGrant@glenfarclas.demon.co.uk

web: www.glenfarclas.co.uk

Established in 1836, Glenfarclas Distillery is proud of its independence. There is a guided tour illustrating their whisky's history and production, followed by a dram in the splendour of the Ships Room or a chance to browse in the gift shop.

Times: ✱ Open Jan-Mar, Mon-Fri 10-4; Apr-Sep, Mon-Fri 10-5, Jul-Sep also open Sat 10-5; Oct-Dec, Mon-Fri 10-4. Closed Sun.
Facilities: 🅿 ⚐ (only visitor centre is accessible) toilets for disabled shop ✖ (ex guide dogs in centre) 🔊

ROTHES   Map 15 NJ24

GLEN GRANT DISTILLERY

AB55 5BS

➲ (on A941 Elgin-Rothes road)

☎ 01340 832118 FREE

e-mail: jennifer.robertson@chivas.com

Founded in 1840 in a sheltered glen by the two Grant brothers. Discover the secrets of the distillery, including the delightful Victorian garden originally created by Major Grant, and now restored to its former glory, where you can enjoy a dram.

Times: Open Mar-Oct, Mon-Sat 10-4, Sun 12.30-4. **Facilities:** 🅿 🗄 ⚐ (reception centre & still house) toilets for disabled shop ✖ (ex guide dogs) 🔊

SPEY BAY   Map 15 NJ36
THE WDCS WILDLIFE CENTRE
IV32 7PJ
➲ (off A96 onto B9014 at Fochabers, follow road approx 5m to village of Spey Bay. Turn left at Spey Bay Hotel and follow road for 500mtrs)
☎ 01343 829109   FREE
e-mail: enquiries@mfwc.co.uk
web: www.mfwc.co.uk

The centre, owned and operated by the Whale and Dolphin Conservation Society, lies at the mouth of the River Spey and is housed in a former salmon fishing station, built in 1768. There is a free exhibition about the Moray Firth dolphins and the wildlife of Spey Bay. Visitors can browse through a well-stocked gift shop and enjoy refreshments in the cosy tea room.
Times: Open Apr-Oct 10.30-5. Check for winter opening times
Facilities: P ⬛ 🗐 & toilets for disabled shop ✖ (ex guide dogs & outside) ◗

TOMINTOUL   Map 15 NJ11
TOMINTOUL MUSEUM
The Square AB37 9ET
➲ (on A939, 13m E of Grantown)
☎ 01309 673701   FREE
e-mail: museums@moray.gov.uk
web: www.moray.gov.uk

Situated in one of the highest villages in Britain, the museum features a reconstructed crofter's kitchen and smiddy, with other displays on the local wildlife, the story of Tomintoul, and the local skiing industry.
Times: Open 25 Mar-May, Mon-Fri 9.30-12 & 2-4; Jun-Aug, Mon-Sat, 9.30-12 & 2-4.30; Sep, Mon-Sat, 9.30-12 & 2-4; 30 Sep-25 Oct, Mon-Fri, 9.30-12 & 2-4. Closed May Day & Good Fri. **Facilities:** P 🗐 & (induction loop and sound commentaries) shop ✖ (ex guide dogs)

NORTH AYRSHIRE

IRVINE   Map 10 NS34
SCOTTISH MARITIME MUSEUM
Harbourside KA12 8QE
➲ (Follow AA signs from Irvine)
☎ 01294 278283   2 for 1
e-mail: smm@tildesley.fsbusiness.co.uk
web: www.scottishmaritimemuseum.org

The museum has displays that reflect all aspects of Scottish maritime history. Vessels can be seen afloat in the harbour and undercover. Experience life in a 1910 shipyard worker's tenement flat. Visit the Linthouse Engine Shop originally built in 1872, which is being developed and holds a substantial part of the museum's collection in open store.
Times: Open Apr-Oct, 10-5 **Fee:** £3 (ch & pen £2). Family ticket £7.
Facilities: P ⬛ & (audio tapes for blind) toilets for disabled shop ✖ (ex guide dogs)

If an attraction name appears in *italics*, details have not been confirmed for 2006.

VENNEL GALLERY
10 Glasgow Vennel KA12 0BD
☎ 01294 275059   FREE
e-mail: vennel@north-ayrshire.gov.uk
web: www.north-ayrshire.gov.uk/museums

The Vennel Gallery has a reputation for exciting and varied exhibitions, ranging from international to local artists. Behind the museum is the Heckling Shop where Robert Burns, Scotland's most famous poet, spent part of his youth learning the trade of flax dressing. In addition to the audio-visual programme on Burns, there is a reconstruction of his lodgings at No.4 Glasgow Vennel, Irvine.
Times: Open all year, Thu-Sun 10-1 & 2-5 **Facilities:** P (residential area) & toilets for disabled shop ✖ (ex guide dogs)

LARGS   Map 10 NS25
KELBURN CASTLE AND COUNTRY CENTRE
Fairlie KA29 0BE
➲ (2m S of Largs, on A78)
☎ 01475 568685   2 for 1
e-mail: admin@kelburncountrycentre.com
web: www.kelburncountrycentre.com

Historic home of the Earls of Glasgow, Kelburn is famous for its romantic Glen, family gardens, unique trees and spectacular views over the Firth of Clyde. Glen walks, riding and trekking centre, adventure course, activity workshop, Kelburn Story Cartoon Exhibition and a family museum. The "Secret Forest" at the centre, Scotland's most unusual attraction, is a chance to explore the Giant's Castle, maze of the Green Man and secret grotto. Also included is a Falconry Centre, pottery craft studio and an indoor Sawmill Adventure Playground.
Times: Open all year, Etr-end Oct, daily 10-6; Nov-Mar, 11-dusk. Grounds and Sawmill Adventure Playbarn, wknds only **Fee:** ✱ £6.50 (concessions £4.50). Family ticket £20. **Facilities:** P ⬛ ✖ licensed 🗐 & (Ranger service to assist disabled) toilets for disabled shop ◗

VIKINGAR!
Greenock Rd KA30 8QL
➲ (on A78, 0.5m into Largs, opposite RNLI lifeboat station)
☎ 01475 689777
e-mail: cmcnaught@naleisure.co.uk
web: www.naleisure.co.uk

A multi-media experience that takes you from the first Viking raids in Scotland to their defeat at the Battle of Largs.
Times: Open Apr-Sep, daily 10.30-5.30; Oct-Mar, daily 10.30-3.30; Nov & Feb, wknds only 10.30-3.30. Closed Dec & Jan. **Fee:** ✱ £4 (ch 4-15 £3). Family ticket £12.20 **Facilities:** P ⬛ & toilets for disabled shop ✖ (ex guide dogs) ◗

SALTCOATS   Map 10 NS24
NORTH AYRSHIRE MUSEUM
Manse St, Kirkgate KA21 5AA
☎ 01294 464174   FREE
e-mail: namuseum@north-ayrshire.gov.uk
web: www.north-ayrshire.gov.uk/museums

This museum is housed in an 18th-century church, and features a rich variety of artefacts from the North Ayrshire area, including archaeological and social history material. There is a continuing programme of temporary exhibitions.
Times: Open all year, Mon-Sat (ex Sun & Wed) 10-1 & 2-5.
Facilities: P (100mtrs) 🗐 & toilets for disabled shop ✖ (ex guide dogs)

NORTH LANARKSHIRE

COATBRIDGE   Map 11 NS76

SUMMERLEE HERITAGE TRUST
Heritage Way, West Canal St ML5 1QD
➲ (follow main routes towards town centre,
adjacent to Coatbridge central station)
☎ 01236 431261
e-mail: museums@northlan.gov.uk
web: www.nlcmuseums.bravehost.com

A 20-acre museum of social and industrial history centering
on the remains of the Summerlee Ironworks which were put
into blast in the 1830s. The exhibition hall features displays
of social and industrial history including working machinery
and recreated workshop interiors. Outside, Summerlee
operates the only working tram in Scotland, a coal mine and
reconstructed miners' rows with interiors dating from 1840.
Times: Open daily 10-5. Nov-Mar 10-4. Closed 25-26 Dec & 1-2 Jan.
Fee: ✱ Tram ride ticket valid all day 80p (ch 45p). **Facilities:** 🅿 💺
🗏 ♿ (wheelchair available & staff assistance) toilets for disabled shop
✖ (ex guide dogs)

MOTHERWELL   Map 11 NS75

MOTHERWELL HERITAGE CENTRE
High Rd ML1 3HU
➲ (A723 for town centre. Left at top of hill, after
pedestrian crossing and just before railway bridge)
☎ 01698 251000   **FREE**
e-mail: museums@northlan.gov.uk
web: www.nlcmuseums.bravehost.com

This award-winning audio-visual experince, 'Technopolis',
traces the history of the area from Roman times to the rise of
19th-century industry and the post-industrial era. There is
also a fine viewing tower, an exhibition gallery and family
history research facilities. A mixed programme of community
events and touring exhibitions occur throughout the year.
Times: Open Wed-Sat 10-5 (Thu 10-7), Sun 12-5. Closed Mon & Tue,
ex BHs. Local studies library closed Sun **Facilities:** 🅿 🗏 ♿ (lifts,
audio info & Braille buttons) toilets for disabled shop
✖ (ex guide dogs)

PERTH & KINROSS

ABERFELDY   Map 14 NN84

DEWAR'S WORLD OF WHISKY
Aberfeldy Distillery PH15 2EB
➲ (from A9 take A827 for Aberfeldy at Ballinluig)
☎ 01887 822010   **2 for 1**
e-mail: worldofwhisky@dewars.com
web: www.dewarswow.com

Tradition and the latest technology are combined here to tell
the story of Dewar's White Label Whisky. Visitors are able to
sample the product in the Nosing and Tasting Bar, and have
a guided tour of the Aberfeldy distillery, where they can see
traditional techniques being employed by skilled craftsmen.
Times: Open Apr-Oct, Mon-Sat 10-6, Sun noon-4; Nov-Mar, Mon-Sat
10-4. Closed Xmas & New Year. **Fee:** £5 (ch £2.50, concessions £3.50).
Family ticket £12. Party by arrangement. **Facilities:** 🅿 💺 ♿ (visitor
centre only accessible) toilets for disabled shop ✖ (ex guide dogs) 🍴

BLAIR ATHOLL   Map 14 NN86

BLAIR CASTLE
PH18 5TL
➲ (7m NW of Pitlochry, off A9 at Blair Atholl &
follow signs to attraction)
☎ 01796 481207
e-mail: office@blair-castle.co.uk
web: www.blair-castle.co.uk

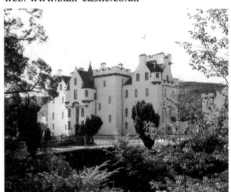

Ancient seat of the Dukes of Atholl and the Atholl
Highlanders, the Duke's unique private army. The castle
dates back to the 13th century but was altered in the 18th,
and later given a castellated exterior. The oldest part is
Cumming's Tower, built in about 1270. There are paintings,
furniture, porcelain, historic artefacts, Jacobite relics, lace,
tapestries, and Masonic regalia. The extensive grounds
include a deer park, and a restored 18th-century walled
garden. Audio-visual display available. Events are held
throughout the year, including the annual parade of the
Duke's Private Army (ring for details).
Times: Open Nov-end Mar, Tue & Sat 9.30-12.30 (last admission);
Apr-end Oct, daily 9.30-4.30 (last admission). **Fee:** ✱ £6.90 (ch £4.30,
pen £5.90). Family ticket £17.50. Party £5.55. Prices to be confirmed
Facilities: 🅿 💺 ✖ licensed 🗏 ♿ (scooter, parking) shop
✖ (ex guide dogs) 🍴

CRIEFF   Map 11 NN82

INNERPEFFRAY LIBRARY
PH7 3RF
➲ (4.5m SE on B8062)
☎ 01764 652819
e-mail: library@innerpeff.fsnet.co.uk
web: www.innerpeffraylibrary.co.uk

This is Scotland's oldest free lending library. It was founded
in 1680 and is still open every day except Thursdays. It is
housed in a late 18th-century building, and contains a
notable collection of bibles and rare books. Adjacent is St
Mary's Chapel, the original site for the library and the
Drummond family burial place.
Times: Open all year, Mon-Wed & Fri-Sat 10-12.45 & 2-4.45, Sun 2-4.
(Closed Thu). Nov-Feb by appointment only. **Fee:** ✱ £2.50 (ch under
15 50p) **Facilities:** 🅿 💺 ♿ ✖ (ex guide dogs)

THE FAMOUS GROUSE EXPERIENCE

The Hosh PH7 4HA

➲ (1.5m NW off A85)

☎ 01764 656565

e-mail: enquiries@famousgrouse.com

web: www.famousgrouse.com

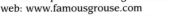

A trip to Crieff is incomplete without a visit to The Famous Grouse Experience, set in Scotland's oldest, most visited and award-winning distillery. Opened in July 2002, this attraction is a fun and interesting day out which combines the traditional distillery visit with a unique exciting sensory experience. Spend a relaxing few hours absorbing the history of the brand. Test your senses and see if you have what it takes to become a 'Whisky Nose'. Have lunch, a snack or even a barbecue at the family restaurant. Visit the well-stocked shop or enjoy a peaceful woodland walk over The Brig O' Dram.

Times: Open daily 9-6 (last tour 4.30). Closed 25-26 Dec. **Fee:** £6.95 (ch £2.50) VIP tour £9.95. **Facilities:** 🅿 💷 ✕ licensed 🎬 ♿ (lifts in all areas) toilets for disabled shop ✖ (ex guide dogs) 🖵

DUNKELD   Map 11 NO04

THE ELL SHOP & LITTLE HOUSES

The Cross PH8 0AN

➲ (off A9, 15m N of Perth)

☎ 01350 727460

e-mail: dunkfeld@nts.org.uk

web: www.nts.org.uk

The National Trust owns two rows of 20 houses in Dunkeld, and has preserved their 17th/18th-century character. They are not open to the public, but there is a display and audio-visual show in the Information Centre.

Times: ✱ Open Ell Shop mid Mar-Sep, Mon-Sat, 10-5.30, Sun 12.30-5.30. Oct-mid Dec, Mon-Sat 10-4.30, Sun 12.30-4.30.

Facilities: 🅿 (300yds) ♿ toilets for disabled shop ✖ 🌿

KILLIECRANKIE   Map 14 NN96

KILLIECRANKIE VISITOR CENTRE

NTS Visitor Centre PH16 5LG

➲ (3m N of Pitlochry on B8079)

☎ 01796 473233

e-mail: killiecrankie@nts.org.uk

web: www.nts.org.uk

The visitor centre features an exhibition on the battle of 1689, when the Jacobite army routed the English, although the Jacobite leader, 'Bonnie Dundee', was mortally wounded in the attack. The wooded gorge is a notable beauty spot, admired by Queen Victoria, and there are some splendid walks.

Times: ✱ Visitor Centre: Apr-Jun & Sep-Oct, daily 10-5.30, Jul & Aug, daily 9.30-6. Site: open all year daily. Times may change for 2006 please telephone or check on www.nts.org.uk **Facilities:** 🅿 💷 ♿ (visitor centre only) toilets for disabled shop 🌿

KINROSS   Map 11 NO10

KINROSS HOUSE GARDENS

KY13 8ET

➲ (M90 [Edinburgh to Perth] junct 6 to Kinross, signed in village)

☎ 01577 862900

e-mail: jm@kinrosshouse.com

web: www.kinrosshouse.com

Yew hedges, roses and herbaceous borders are the elegant attractions of these formal gardens. The 17th-century house

continued

---

was built by Sir William Bruce, but is not generally open to the public.

Times: Gardens only open Apr-Sep, daily 10-7. **Fee:** ✱ £2.50 (conc £1.50, accompanied ch free). **Facilities:** 🅿 ♿ ✖ (ex guide dogs)

LOCH LEVEN CASTLE

Castle Island KY13 7AR

➲ (on an island in Loch Leven accessible by boat from Kinross)

☎ 01786 450000

Mary, Queen of Scots was imprisoned here in this five-storey castle in 1567 - she escaped 11 months later and so gave the 14th-century castle its special place in history.

Times: Open Apr-Sep, daily 9.30-6.30. Last outward sailing at 5.15pm.

Fee: ✱ £3.50 (ch £1.30, concessions £2.50). Group 11+ 10% discount. Prices valid until 31/12/05. Please phone for further details.

Facilities: 🅿 shop ✖ 🏴

RSPB NATURE RESERVE VANE FARM

By Loch Leven KY13 9LX

➲ (2m E of M90 junct 5, on S shore of Loch Leven, entered off B9097 to Glenrothes)

☎ 01577 862355

e-mail: vane.farm@rspb.org.uk

web: www.rspb.org.uk

Well placed beside Loch Leven, with a nature trail and hides overlooking the Loch and a woodland trail with stunning panoramic views. Noted for its pink-footed geese. The area also attracts whooper swans, greylag geese and great spotted woodpeckers amongst others. Details of special events are available from the Visitors' Centre.

Times: Open daily, 10-5. Closed 25-26 Dec & 1-2 Jan.

Facilities: 🅿 💷 🎬 ♿ (wheelchair extensions, ramps, telescopes) toilets for disabled shop ✖ (ex guide dogs) 🖵

MILNATHORT   Map 11 NO10

BURLEIGH CASTLE

KY13 7XZ

➲ (0.5m E of Milnathort on A911)

The roofless but otherwise complete ruin of a tower house of about 1500, with a section of defensive barmkin wall and a remarkable corner tower with a square cap-house corbelled out. This castle was often visited by James IV.

Times: Open summer only. Keys available locally, telephone 01786 45000. **Facilities:** ✖ 🏴

MUTHILL   Map 11 NN81

DRUMMOND GARDENS

PH5 2AA

➲ (2m S of Crieff on A822)

☎ 01764 681433

e-mail: thegardens@drummondcastle.sol.co.uk

web: www.drummondcastlegardens.co.uk

The gardens of Drummond Castle were originally laid out in 1630 by John Drummond, 2nd Earl of Perth. In 1830, the parterre was changed to an Italian style. The multi-faceted sundial was designed by John Mylne, Master Mason to Charles I. These are Scotland's largest formal gardens and amongst the finest in Europe.

Times: Open Gardens May-Oct, daily 1-6 (last admission 5). Also Etr for 4 days. **Fee:** £4 (ch £1.50 & pen £3). **Facilities:** 🅿 ♿ toilets for disabled shop

PERTH   Map 11 NO12

BLACK WATCH REGIMENTAL MUSEUM
Balhousie Castle, Hay St PH1 5HR
➲ (follow signs to Perth & attraction, approach via Dunkeld Rd)
☎ 0131 310 8530
e-mail: rhq@theblackwatch.co.uk
web: www.theblackwatch.co.uk

The museum of Scotland's oldest highland regiment, which portrays the history of the Black Watch from 1725 to the present day. A memorial room remembers the soldiers of WWI with a lifelike figure in a trench, video footage and many artefacts from the period. Silver, uniforms, weapons and pictures are on display to give visitors an idea of what it was like to be in the regiment. **Times:** Open all year. May-Sep, Mon-Sat 10-4.30. Closed last Sat in Jun; Oct-Apr, Mon-Fri, 10-3.30. Closed 23 Dec-6 Jan. Other times & Parties 16+ by appointment. **Fee:** ✽ Donations. **Facilities:** 🅿 & (1 bay parking for disabled) toilets for disabled shop ✖ (ex guide dogs) ▰

BRANKLYN GARDEN
116 Dundee Rd PH2 7BB
➲ (on A85)
☎ 01738 625535
e-mail: aclipson@nts.scot.demon.co.uk
web: www.nts.org.uk

The gardens cover two acres and are noted for their collections of rhododendrons, shrubs and alpines. Garden tours and botanical painting courses are held. **Times:** ✽ Open Apr & Jul-Sep, Fri-Tue 10-5; May-Jun, daily, 10-5. Times may change for 2006 please telephone or check on www.nts.org.uk **Facilities:** 🅿 ✖ (ex guide dogs) ▯

HUNTINGTOWER CASTLE
PH1 3JL
➲ (2m W)
☎ 01738 627231

Formerly known as Ruthven Castle and famous as the scene of the so-called 'Raid of Ruthven' in 1582, this structure was built in the 15th and 16th centuries and features a painted ceiling. **Times:** Open all year, Apr-Sep, daily 9.30-6.30; Oct-Mar, daily 9.30-4.30. Closed Thu & Fri in winter, 25-26 Dec & 1-2 Jan. **Fee:** ✽ £3 (ch £1.20, concessions £2.25). Group 11+ 10% discount. Prices valid until 31/12/05. Please phone for further details. **Facilities:** 🅿 shop ✖▮

PERTH MUSEUM & ART GALLERY
78 George St PH1 5LB
➲ (in town centre)
☎ 01738 632488   FREE
e-mail: museum@pkc.gov.uk
web: www.pkc.gov.uk/ah/museums_galleries.htm

Visit Perth Museum and Art Gallery for a fascinating look into Perthshire throughout the ages. Collections cover silver, glass, art, natural history, archaeology and human history. **Times:** Open all year, Mon-Sat 10-5. Closed Xmas-New Year. **Facilities:** 🅿 (adjacent) & toilets for disabled shop ✖ (ex guide dogs)

PITLOCHRY   Map 14 NN95

EDRADOUR DISTILLERY
PH16 5JP
➲ (2.5m E of Pitlochry on A924)
☎ 01796 472095   FREE
web: www.edradour.co.uk

It was in 1825 that a group of local farmers founded Edradour, naming it after the bubbling burn that runs through it. It is Scotland's smallest distillery and is virtually unchanged since Victorian times. Have a dram of whisky while watching an audio-visual in the malt barn and then take a guided tour through the distillery itself. **Times:** Open Jan-Feb, Mon-Sat 10-5, Sun 12.4; Mar-Oct Mon-Sat 9.30-6, Sun 11.30-6; Nov-Dec, Mon-Sat 9.30-5, Sun 12-5. (Last tour 1hr before close, private tours arranged for a fee). **Facilities:** 🅿 & toilets for disabled shop ✖ (ex guide & hearing dogs)

SCOTTISH & SOUTHERN ENERGY VISITOR CENTRE, DAM & FISH PASS
PH16 5ND
➲ (off A9, 24m N of Perth)
☎ 01796 473152

The visitor centre features an exhibition showing how electricity is brought from the power station to the customer, and there is access to the turbine viewing gallery. The salmon ladder viewing chamber allows you to see the fish as they travel upstream to their spawning ground. **Times:** ✽ Open Apr-Sep, Mon-Fri 10-5.30. Wknd opening Jul, Aug & BHs **Facilities:** 🅿 ▯ & (monitor viewing of salmon fish pass) toilets for disabled shop ✖ (ex guide dogs) ▰

QUEEN'S VIEW   Map 14 NN85

QUEEN'S VIEW VISITOR CENTRE
PH16 5NR
➲ (7m W of Pitlochry on B8019)   FREE
☎ 01350 727284
e-mail: peter.fullarton@forestry.gsi.gov.uk
web: www.forestry.gov.uk

Queen Victoria admired the view on a visit here in 1866; it is possibly one of the most famous views in Scotland. The area, in the heart of the Tay Forest Park, has a variety of woodlands that visitors can walk or cycle in. **Times:** Open Apr-Nov, daily 10-6. **Facilities:** 🅿 (charged) 🚌 & toilets for disabled shop ▰

SCONE   Map 11 NO12

SCONE PALACE
PH2 6BD
➲ (2m NE of Perth on A93)
☎ 01738 552300   2 for 1
e-mail: visits@scone-palace.co.uk
web: www.scone-palace.co.uk

Scottish kings were crowned at Scone until 1651 and it was the site of the famous coronation Stone of Destiny from the 9th century until the English seized the Stone in 1296. The castellated edifice of the present palace dates from 1803 but incorporates the 16th-century and earlier buildings. The interior houses objets d'art, including French & Scottish furniture, an extensive porcelain collection and paintings. The grounds include a Pinetum, the original Douglas Fir, the

continued

unique Murray Star Maze, woodland walks and herbaceous plantings. Also David Douglas Trail.

Times: Open Apr-Oct **Fee:** ✱ Palace & Grounds £6.95 (ch £4, students & pen £5.95). Family ticket £22. Groups 20+ £5.80, (£3.80 & £5.10). Grounds only £3.50 (ch £2.20, students and pen £3).

Facilities: 🅿 💷 ✕ licensed 🍴 ᒼ (stairlift which gives access to all state rooms) toilets for disabled shop (ex assist dogs & in grounds) ◼

WEEM   Map 14 NN84

CASTLE MENZIES

PH15 2JD

⮑ (Follow signs from main roads)

☎ 01887 820982

e-mail: menziesclan@tesco.net

web: www.menzies.org

Restored seat of the Chiefs of Clan Menzies, and a fine example of a 16th-century Z-plan fortified tower house. Prince Charles Edward Stuart stayed here briefly on his way to Culloden in 1746. The whole of the 16th-century building can be explored, and there's a small clan museum.

Times: Open Apr-mid Oct, Mon-Sat 10.30-5, Sun 2-5. **Fee:** £4 (ch £2, concessions £3.50). **Facilities:** 🅿 🍴 ᒼ toilets for disabled shop ✖ (ex guide dogs)

RENFREWSHIRE

KILBARCHAN   Map 10 NS46

WEAVER'S COTTAGE

The Cross PA10 2JG

⮑ (off A737, 12m SW of Glasgow)

☎ 01505 705588

e-mail: aclipson@nts.scot.demon.co.uk

web: www.nts.org.uk

The weaving craft is regularly demonstrated at this delightful 18th-century cottage museum, and there is a collection of weaving equipment and other domestic utensils.

Times: ✱ Open Apr-Sep, Fri-Tue, 1-5; morning visits available for pre-booked groups. Times may change for 2006 please telephone or check on www.nts.org.uk **Facilities:** 🅿 ✖ (ex guide dogs) ♨

LANGBANK   Map 10 NS37

FINLAYSTONE COUNTRY ESTATE

PA14 6TJ

⮑ (on A8 W of Langbank, 10m W of Glasgow Airport, follow Thistle signs)

☎ 01475 540505   2 for 1

e-mail: info@finlaystone.co.uk

web: www.finlaystone.co.uk

A beautiful country estate, historic formal gardens which are renowned for thier natural beauty, woodland walks and play areas. The 'Dolly Mixture', an international collection of dolls, can be seen in the Visitor Centre.

Times: Open all year. Woodland & Gardens daily, 10-5.

Fee: ✱ Garden & Woods £3.50 (ch & pen £2.50). 'The Dolly Mixture' Doll Museum free. **Facilities:** 🅿 💷 🍴 ᒼ (lift to second floor pathways for wheelchairs) toilets for disabled shop ◼

LOCHWINNOCH   Map 10 NS35

RSPB LOCHWINNOCH NATURE RESERVE

Largs Rd PA12 4JF

⮑ (on A760, Largs road, opposite Lochwinnoch station, 16m SW of Glasgow)

☎ 01505 842663

e-mail: Lochwinnoch@rspb.org.uk

web: www.rspb.org.uk/reserves/lochwinnoch

The reserve, part of Clyde Muirshiel Regional Park and a Site of Special Scientific Interest, comprises two shallow lochs fringed by marsh which in turn is fringed by scrub and woodland. There are two trails with hides and a visitor centre with a viewing area. Please visit website for details of events running throughout the year.

Times: Open all year, daily 10-5. Closed 1-2 Jan & 25-26 Dec.

Fee: Trails £2 (concessions £1, ch 50p). Family ticket £4.

Facilities: 🅿 🍴 ᒼ (hides are all wheelchair accessible) toilets for disabled shop on lead only ◼

PAISLEY   Map 11 NS46

COATS OBSERVATORY

49 Oakshaw St West PA1 2DE

⮑ (M8 junct 27, follow signs to town centre until Gordon St (A761). Left onto Causeyside St, left onto New St then left onto High St)

☎ 0141 889 2013   FREE

e-mail: museums.els@renfrewshire.gov.uk

web: www.renfrewshire.gov.uk

The Observatory, funded by Thomas Coats and designed by John Honeyman, was opened in 1883. It houses a 5 inch telescope under the dome at the top. Weather recording activities have been carried out here continuously since 1884. There is also earthquake-measuring equipment and the Renfrewshire Astronomical Society holds regular meetings here.

Times: Open all year, Tue-Sat 10-5, Sun 2-5. Last entry 15 minutes before closing. **Facilities:** 🅿 (150yds) (meters/limited street parking) 🍴 shop ✖ (ex guide dogs)

PAISLEY MUSEUM & ART GALLERIES

High St PA1 2BA

⮑ (M8 junct 27 [A741], rdbt 2nd exit [A761-town centre]. At traffic lights take left lane towards Kilbride. Onto Gordon St, right onto Causeyside St, left onto New St, left onto High St)

☎ 0141 889 3151   FREE

e-mail: museums.els@renfrewshire

web: www.renfrewshire.gov.uk

Pride of place here is given to a world-famous collection of Paisley shawls. Other collections illustrate local industrial and natural history, while the emphasis of the art gallery is on 19th-century Scottish artists and an important studio ceramics collection.

Times: Open all year, Tue-Sat 10-5, Sun 2-5. BH 10-5.

Facilities: 🅿 (330yds) 🍴 ᒼ (parking on site) toilets for disabled shop ✖ (ex guide dogs)

SCOTTISH BORDERS

COLDSTREAM — Map 12 NT84

HIRSEL
Douglas & Angus Estates, Estate Office, The Hirsel
TD12 4LP
➲ (0.5m W on A697, on N outskirts of Coldstream)
☎ 01890 882834 & 882965
e-mail: rogerdodd@btconnect.com
web: www.hirselcountrypark.co.uk
The seat of the Home family, the grounds of which are open all year. The focal point is the Homestead Museum, craft centre and workshops. From there, nature trails lead around the lake, along the Leet Valley and into woodland noted for its rhododendrons and azaleas.
Times: Garden & Grounds open all year, daylight hours. Museum 10-5. Craft Centre Mon-Fri, 10-5, wknds noon-5. **Fee:** ✱ £2 per car
Facilities: 🅿 (charged) 💷 ✖ 🗐 ⚅ toilets for disabled shop on lead only

DRYBURGH — Map 12 NT53

DRYBURGH ABBEY
TD6 0RQ
➲ (5m SE of Melrose on B6404)
☎ 01835 822381
The abbey was one of the Border monasteries founded by David I, and stands in a lovely setting on the River Tweed. The ruins are equally beautiful, and the church has the graves of Sir Walter Scott and Earl Haig.
Times: Open all year, Apr-Sep daily 9.30-6.30; Oct-Mar daily 9.30-6.30. Closed 25-26 Dec & 1-2 Jan. **Fee:** ✱ £3.30 (ch £1.30, concessions £2.50). Group 11+ 10% discount. Prices valid until 31/12/05. Please phone for further details. **Facilities:** 🅿 ⚅ shop ✖ ▮

DUNS — Map 12 NT75

MANDERSTON
TD11 3PP
➲ (2m E of Duns on A6105)
☎ 01361 883450 & 882636   2 for 1
e-mail: palmer@manderston.co.uk
web: www.manderston.co.uk

This grandest of grand houses gives a fascinating picture of Edwardian life above and below stairs. Completely remodelled for the millionaire racehorse owner Sir James Miller, the architect was told to spare no expense, and so the house boasts the world's only silver staircase. The staterooms are magnificent, and there are fine formal

continued

gardens, with a woodland garden and lakeside walks. Manderston has been the setting for a number of films.
Times: Open mid May-end Sep, Thu & Sun (also late May & Aug English BH Mons). Gardens open, 11.30-dusk. House open, 1.30-4.15
Fee: ✱ House & Gardens £7 (ch £3.50); Gardens only free.
Facilities: 🅿 💷 🗐 shop ✖ (ex guide dogs & in gardens)

EYEMOUTH — Map 12 NT96

EYEMOUTH MUSEUM
Auld Kirk, Manse Rd TD14 5JE
➲ (off A1 onto A1107, follow signs to town centre, where museum located)
☎ 018907 50678
The museum was opened in 1981 as a memorial to the 129 local fishermen lost in the Great Fishing Disaster of 1881. Its main feature is the 15ft Eyemouth tapestry, which was made for the centenary. There are also displays on local history.
Times: Open Apr-Jun & Sep, Mon-Sat 10-5, Sun 12-3; Jul-Aug, Mon-Sat 10-5; Sun 12-4; Oct, Mon-Sat 10-4 (closed Sun) **Fee:** ✱ £2.50 (concessions £2). Accompanied ch free. Party. **Facilities:** 🅿 (250yds) (45min on street outside) 🗐 ⚅ shop ☞

GALASHIELS — Map 12 NT43

LOCHCARRON OF SCOTLAND VISITOR CENTRE
Waverley Mill, Huddersfield St TD1 3BA
➲ (32m S of Edinburgh on A7, follow signs to mill)
☎ 01896 752091 & 751100 2 for 1
e-mail: quality@lochcarron.com
web: www.quality@lochcarron.com
The museum brings the town's past to life and the focal point is a display on the woollen industry. Guided tours of the mill take about 40 minutes. Please note that disabled toilets are built for members of staff who are disabled but are not in wheelchairs.
Times: Open all year, Mon-Sat 9-5, Sun (Jun-Sep) 12-5. Mill tours Mon-Thu at 10.30, 11.30, 1.30 & 2.30, Fri am only. **Fee:** ✱ Museum free. Mill tour £2.50 (ch 14 free) group rate £2. **Facilities:** 🅿 ⚅ toilets for disabled shop ☞

GORDON — Map 12 NT64

MELLERSTAIN HOUSE
TD3 6LG
➲ (signed on A6089 [Kelso-Gordon road], 1m W)
☎ 01573 410225 2 for 1
e-mail: enquiries@mellerstain.com
web: www.mellerstain.com

One of Scotland's finest Georgian houses, begun by William Adam and completed by his son Robert in the 1770s. It has

continued

beautiful plasterwork, period furniture and pictures, terraced gardens and a lake.
Times: Open Etr & May-Sep, Sun, Mon & Wed-Fri 12.30-5 (last admission 4.30) & Sun only in Oct **Fee:** ✱ £5.50 (ch free) Party 20+ £5 (if normal opening times) Garden £3 **Facilities:** 🅿 💷 🍴 ♿ shop garden centre ✖ (ex guide dogs) 🍴

HERMITAGE — Map 12 NY59

HERMITAGE CASTLE
TD9 0LU
⮕ (5.5m NE of Newcastleton, on B6399)
☎ 01387 376222
A vast, eerie ruin of the 14th and 15th centuries, associated with the de Soulis, the Douglases and Mary, Queen of Scots. Much restored in the 19th century.
Times: Open Apr-Sep, daily 9.30-6.30. **Fee:** ✱ £2.50 (ch £1, concessions £1.90). Group 11+ 10% discount. Prices valid until 31/12/05. Please phone for further details. **Facilities:** 🅿 ♿ ♨

INNERLEITHEN — Map 11 NT33

ROBERT SMAIL'S PRINTING WORKS
7/9 High St EH44 6HA
☎ 01896 830206
e-mail: smails@nts.org.uk
web: www.nts.org.uk
These buildings contain a Victorian office, a paper store with reconstructed waterwheel, a composing room and a press room. The machinery is in full working order and visitors may view the printer at work and experience typesetting in the composing room.
Times: ✱ Open Good Fri-Etr Mon & Jun-Sep, Thu-Mon 12-5, Sun 1-5. Times may change for 2006 please telephone or check on www.nts.org.uk **Facilities:** 🅿 (300yds) ♿ shop ✖ (ex guide dogs) ♨

JEDBURGH — Map 12 NT62

JEDBURGH ABBEY
☎ 01835 863925
Standing as the most complete of the Border monasteries (although it has been sacked and rebuilt many times) Jedburgh Abbey has been described as 'the most perfect and beautiful example of the Saxon and early Gothic in Scotland'. David I founded it as a priory in the 12th century and remains of some of the domestic buildings have been uncovered during excavations.
Times: Open all year, Apr-Sep, daily 9.30-6.30; Oct-Mar, daily 9.30-4.30. Closed 25-26 Dec & 1-2 Jan. **Fee:** ✱ £4 (ch £1.60, concessions £3). Group 11+ 10% discount. Prices valid until 31/12/05. Please phone for further details. **Facilities:** 🅿 ♿ (limited access) toilets for disabled shop ✖ ♨

JEDBURGH CASTLE JAIL & MUSEUM
Castlegate TD8 6BD
⮕ (off A68 towards town centre, follow signs to top of Castlegate)
☎ 01835 864750
web: www.scotborders.gov.uk/museums
Relive the harsh realities of prison life in the 19th century with a visit to Jedburgh Castle Jail, built in the 1820s on the site of the Royal Burgh's medieval castle. Displays in the cell blocks recreate the lives of prisoners and staff, while the Jailer's House explores the history of the town.
Times: Open 26 Mar-Oct, Mon-Sat 10-4.30, Sun 1-4 **Fee:** ✱ £2 (ch free, concessions £1) **Facilities:** 🅿 🍴 ♿ (audio guide, touch screen tour, hearing loop) toilets for disabled shop ✖ (ex guide dogs)

KELSO — Map 12 NT73

FLOORS CASTLE
Roxburghe Estates Office TD5 7SF
⮕ (from town centre follow Roxburghe St to main gates)
☎ 01573 223333
e-mail: marketing@floorscastle.com
web: www.roxburghe.bordernet.co.uk
The home of the 10th Duke of Roxburghe, the Castle's lived-in atmosphere enhances the superb collection of French furniture, tapestries and paintings. The house was designed by William Adam in 1721 and enjoys a magnificent setting overlooking the River Tweed and the Cheviot Hills beyond.
Times: Open 25 Mar-30 Oct, daily 10-4.30 (last admission 4).
Facilities: 🅿 💷 ✖ licensed 🍴 ♿ (lift) toilets for disabled shop garden centre 🍴

KELSO ABBEY
☎ 0131 668 8800
Founded by David I in 1128 and probably the greatest of the four famous Border abbeys, Kelso became extremely wealthy and acquired extensive lands. In 1545 it served as a fortress when the town was attacked by the Earl of Hertford, but now only fragments of the once-imposing abbey church give any clue to its long history.
Times: Open at any reasonable time. **Facilities:** ♿ ♨

LAUDER — Map 12 NT54

THIRLESTANE CASTLE
TD2 6RU
⮕ (off A68, S of Lauder)
☎ 01578 722430
e-mail: admin@thirlestanecastle.co.uk
web: www.thirlestanecastle.co.uk
This fairy-tale castle has been the home of the Maitland family, the Earls of Lauderdale, since the 12th century. Some of the most splendid plasterwork ceilings in Britain may be seen in the 17th-century state rooms. The family nurseries house a sizeable collection of antique toys and dolls.The informal riverside grounds, with their views of the grouse moors, include a woodland walk, picnic tables and adventure playground. Please visit website for details of events running throughout the year.
Times: 1 May-19 Sep, Wed-Fri & Sun. Jul-Aug Sun-Fri. Open from 10.30, last admission 2.30. **Fee:** ✱ £5.50 (ch £3) Family ticket £15.00.
Facilities: 🅿 💷 🍴 shop ✖ (ex guide dogs) 🍴

MELROSE — Map 12 NT53

ABBOTSFORD
TD6 9BQ
⮕ (2m W off A6091, on B6360)
☎ 01896 752043
e-mail: enquiries@scottsabbotsford.co.uk
web: www.scottsabbotsford.co.uk
Set on the River Tweed, Sir Walter Scott's romantic mansion remains much the same as it was in his day. Inside there are many mementoes and relics of his remarkable life and also his historical collections, armouries and library, with some 9,000 volumes. Scott built the mansion between 1811 and 1822, and lived here until his death ten years after its completion.
Times: Open daily from 3rd Mon in Mar-Oct, Mon-Sat 9.30-5. Sun in Mar-May & Oct 2-5. Sun Jun-Sep 9.30-5. **Fee:** ✱ £4.75 (ch £2.40). Party £3.70 (ch £1.85) **Facilities:** 🅿 💷 ♿ (parking at private entrance, ramps at entrance) toilets for disabled shop ✖ (ex guide & hearing dogs) 🍴

HARMONY GARDEN

St Mary's Rd TD6 9LJ
➲ (opposite Melrose Abbey)
☎ 01721 722502
web: www.nts.org.uk

Set around the early 19th-century Harmony Hall (not open to visitors), this attractive walled garden has magnificent views of Melrose Abbey and the Eildon Hills. The garden comprises lawns, herbaceous and mixed borders, vegetable and fruit areas, and a rich display of spring bulbs.
Times: ✹ Open Good Fri-Etr Mon & Jun-Sep, Mon-Sat 10-5, Sun 1-5. Times may change for 2006 please telephone or check on www.nts.org.uk **Facilities:** 🅿 ♿ ✕ ❦

MELROSE ABBEY & ABBEY MUSEUM

TD6 9LG
☎ 01896 822562

The ruin of this Cistercian abbey is probably one of Scotland's finest, and has been given added glamour by its connection with Sir Walter Scott. The abbey was repeatedly wrecked during the Scottish wars of independence, but parts survive from the 14th century. The heart of Robert the Bruce is buried somewhere within the church.
Times: Open all year, Apr-Sep, daily 9.30-6.30; Oct-Mar daily 9.30-4.30. Closed 25-26 Dec & 1-2 Jan. **Fee:** ✹ £4 (ch £1.60, concessions £3). Group 11+ 10% discount. Prices valid until 31/12/05. Please phone for further details. **Facilities:** 🅿 ♿ shop ✕ ▮

PRIORWOOD GARDEN & DRIED FLOWER SHOP

TD6 9PX
➲ (off A6091, in Melrose, adjacent to Abbey. On National Cycle Route 1)
☎ 01896 822493
e-mail: priorwooddriedflowers@nts.org.uk
web: www.nts.org.uk

This small garden specialises in flowers suitable for drying. It is formally designed with herbaceous and everlasting annual borders, and the attractive orchard has a display of 'apples through the ages'. Dried flowers are on sale in the shop.
Times: ✹ Open Good Fri-Etr Mon, May-Jun & Sep-24 Dec, Mon-Sat 12-5, Sun 1-5; Jul-Aug, Mon-Sat 10-5, Sun 1-5. Times may change for 2006 please telephone or check on www.nts.org.uk
Facilities: 🅿 ♿ (ramps, paths) shop ❦

PEEBLES   Map 11 NT24

KAILZIE GARDENS

EH45 9HT
➲ (2.5m SE on B7062)
☎ 01721 720007
e-mail: info@kailziegardens.com
web: www.kailziegardens.com

These extensive grounds, with their fine old trees, provide a burnside walk flanked by bulbs, rhododendrons and azaleas. A walled garden contains herbaceous, shrub rose borders, greenhouses and a formal rose garden. A garden for all seasons - don't miss the snowdrops. A large stocked trout pond and rod hire available, and an 18-hole putting green, plus an open bait pond, ornamental duck pond and osprey viewing centre.
Times: Open 25 Mar-Oct, daily 11-5.30. Grounds close 5.30. Garden open all year. **Fee:** ✹ mid Mar-Jun £2.50, Jun-Oct £3.50, end Oct-mid Mar £2 honesty box (ch 5-12 80p) **Facilities:** 🅿 ▥ ✕ licensed ▤ ♿ (ramps in garden) toilets for disabled shop

NEIDPATH CASTLE

EH45 8NW
➲ (0.5m W of Peebles on A72)
☎ 01721 720333   **2 for 1**
e-mail: estateoffice@wemyssandmarch.co.uk
web: www.scotborders.org.uk

Occupying a spectacular position on the Tweed, this 14th-century stronghold was adapted to 17th-century living; it contains a rock-hewn well, a pit prison and a small museum. There are fine walks and a picnic area.
Times: Open Etr wknd, May-Sep Wed-Sat 10.30-5 Sun 12.30-5 (closed Mon & Tue except BHs) **Fee:** ✹ £3 (ch £1, concessions £2.50). Family ticket £7.50. Party 20+. **Facilities:** 🅿 ▤ shop

SELKIRK   Map 12 NT42

BOWHILL HOUSE AND COUNTRY PARK

TD7 5ET
➲ (3m W of Selkirk off A708)
☎ 01750 22204
e-mail: bht@buccleuch.com
web: www.heritageontheweb.co.uk

An outstanding collection of pictures, including works by Van Dyck, Canaletto, Reynolds, Gainsborough and Claude Lorraine are displayed here. Memorabilia and relics of people such as Queen Victoria and Sir Walter Scott, and a restored Victorian kitchen add further interest inside the house. Outside, the wooded grounds are perfect for walking. A small theatre provides a full programme of music and drama.
Times: Park open May-Jun 11-5 wknd and BHs only. Jul gardens daily 11-5, house daily 1-5. Aug Sat-Thu 11-5. **Fee:** ✹ House & grounds £6 (ch under 5 & wheelchair users free, pen & groups £4). Grounds only £2. **Facilities:** 🅿 ▥ ✕ licensed ♿ (guided tours for the blind by appointment) toilets for disabled shop (ex in park on leads) ▦

HALLIWELLS HOUSE MUSEUM

Halliwells Close, Market Place TD7 4BC
➲ (off A7 in town centre)
☎ 01750 20096   **FREE**
e-mail: museums@scotborders.gov.uk

A row of late 18th-century town cottages converted into a museum. Displays recreate the building's former use as an ironmonger's shop and home, and tell the story of the Royal Burgh of Selkirk. The Robson Gallery hosts a programme of contemporary art and craft exhibitions.
Times: Open Apr-Sep, Mon-Sat 10-5, Sun 10-12; Jul-Aug, Mon-Sat 10-5.30, Sun 10-12; Oct, Mon-Sat 10-4. **Facilities:** 🅿 (charged) ▤ ♿ (lift to first floor, large print, interpretation) toilets for disabled shop ✕ (ex guide dogs) ▦

SIR WALTER SCOTT'S COURTROOM

Market Place TD7 4BT
➲ (on A7 in town centre)
☎ 01750 20096   **FREE**
e-mail: museums@scotborders.gov.uk

Built in 1803-4 as a sheriff court and town hall this is where the famous novelist, Sir Walter Scott dispensed justice when he was Sheriff of Selkirkshire from 1804-1832. Displays tell of Scott's time as Sheriff, and of his place as a novelist as well as those of his contemporaries, writer, James Hogg and the explorer, Mungo Park.
Times: ✹ Open Apr-Sep, Mon-Fri 10-4, Sat 10-2; May-Aug also Sun 10-2; Oct, Mon-Sat 1-4. **Facilities:** 🅿 (100mtrs) (30min on street, car park 50p for 2hrs) ▤ shop ✕ (ex guide dogs) ▦

SMAILHOLM　　　　　Map 12 NT63

SMAILHOLM TOWER
TD5 7RT
⊃ (6m W of Kelso on B6937)
☎ 01573 460365

An outstanding example of a classic Border tower-house, probably erected in the 15th century. It is 57ft high and well preserved. The tower houses an exhibition of dolls and a display based on Sir Walter Scott's book *Minstrels of the Border*.
Times: Open Apr-Sep, daily 9.30-6.30; Oct- closed Thu & Fri. Nov-Mar, wknds only. Closed 25-26 Dec & 1-2 Jan. **Fee:** ✱ £2.50 (ch £1, concessions £1.90). Group 11+ 10% discount. Prices valid until 31/12/05. Please phone for further details. **Facilities:** 🅿 shop ✖ ◪

STOBO　　　　　Map 11 NT13

DAWYCK BOTANIC GARDEN
EH45 9JU
⊃ (8m SW of Peebles on B712)
☎ 01721 760254
e-mail: dawyck@rbge.org.uk
web: www.rbge.org.uk

From the landscaped walks of this historic arboretum an impressive collection of mature specimen trees can be seen - some over 40 metres tall and including the unique Dawyck beech-stand. Notable features include the Swiss Bridge, a fine estate chapel and stonework/terracing produced by Italian craftsmen in the 1820s.
Times: ✱ Open daily 14 Feb-14 Nov. Feb & Nov 10-4. Mar-Oct 10-5. Apr-Sep 10-6 **Facilities:** 🅿 💷 ▤ ♿ toilets for disabled shop garden centre ✖ (ex guide dogs) ◪

TRAQUAIR　　　　　Map 11 NT33

TRAQUAIR HOUSE
EH44 6PW
⊃ (at Innerleithen take B709, house in 1m)
☎ 01896 830323 & 830785　　　　**2 for 1**
e-mail: enquiries@traquair.co.uk
web: www.traquair.co.uk

Said to be Scotland's oldest inhabited house, dating back to the 12th century, 27 Scottish monarchs have stayed at Traquair House. William the Lion Heart held court here, and the house has associations with Mary, Queen of Scots and the Jacobite risings. The Bear Gates were closed in 1745, not to be reopened until the Stuarts should once again ascend the throne. There is croquet, a maze and woodland walks by the River Tweed, craft workshops and a children's mini adventure playground. Also a brewery museum and shop and antique shop.
Times: Open Etr-Oct **Fee:** ✱ Please telephone for admission costs. **Facilities:** 🅿 💷 ✖ licensed ♿ toilets for disabled shop on lead only ◪

SOUTH AYRSHIRE

ALLOWAY　　　　　Map 10 NS31

BURNS NATIONAL HERITAGE PARK
Murdoch's Lone KA7 4PQ
⊃ (2m S of Ayr)
☎ 01292 443700　　　　**2 for 1**
e-mail: info@burnsheritagepark.com
web: www.burnsheritagepark.com

The birthplace of Robert Burns, Scotland's National Poet set in the gardens and countryside of Alloway. An introduction
continued

to the life of Robert Burns, with an audio-visual presentation - a multi-screen 3D experience describing the Tale of Tam O'Shanter. This attraction consists of the museum, Burn's Cottage, visitor centre, tranquil landscaped gardens and historical monuments. Please telephone for further details.
Times: Open all year, Apr-Sep 9.30-5.30, Tam O'Shanter experience 10-5.30, Oct-Mar 10-5. Closed 25-26 Dec & 1-2 Jan. **Fee:** ✱ £3 (ch & pen £2) **Facilities:** 🅿 💷 ✖ licensed ▤ ♿ (wheelchair available) toilets for disabled shop ✖ (ex guide & hearing dogs) ◪

BARGANY

See **Old Dailly**

CULZEAN CASTLE　　　　Map 10 NS21

CULZEAN CASTLE & COUNTRY PARK
KA19 8LE
⊃ (4m W of Maybole, off A77)
☎ 01655 884455
e-mail: culzean@nts.org.uk
web: www.culzeancastle.net

This 18th-century castle stands on a cliff in spacious grounds and was designed by Robert Adam for the Earl of Cassillis. It is noted for its oval staircase, circular drawing room and plasterwork. The Eisenhower Room explores the American general's links with Culzean. The 563-acre country park has a wide range of attractions - shoreline, woodland walks, parkland, an adventure playground and gardens.
Times: ✱ Open Castle: Apr-Oct, daily 10.30-5 (last entry 4). Visitor centre: Apr-Oct, daily 9-5.30; Nov-Mar, wknds 11-4. Country Park: open all year 9.30-sunset. Times may change for 2006 please telephone or check on www.nts.org.uk **Facilities:** 🅿 💷 ✖ licensed ♿ (wheelchairs, lift in castle, Braille guides) toilets for disabled shop garden centre ✖ (ex castle, ex guide dogs) ◪

KIRKOSWALD　　　　　Map 10 NS20

SOUTER JOHNNIE'S COTTAGE
Main Rd KA19 8HY
⊃ (on A77, 4m SW of Maybole)
☎ 01655 760603
e-mail: aclipson@nts.scot.demon.co.uk
web: www.nts.org uk

'Souter' means cobbler and the village cobbler who lived in this 18th-century cottage was the inspiration for Burns' character Souter Johnnie, in his ballad *Tam O'Shanter*. The cottage is now a Burns museum and life-size stone figures of the poet's characters can be seen in the restored ale-house in the cottage garden.
Times: ✱ Open Apr-Sep, Fri-Tue 11.30-5. Times may change for 2006 please telephone or check on www.nts.org.uk **Facilities:** 🅿 (75yds) ♿ (only one small step into cottage) ✖ (ex guide dogs) ◪

MAYBOLE　　　　　Map 10 NS20

CROSSRAGUEL ABBEY
KA19 5HQ
⊃ (2m S)
☎ 01655 883113

The extensive remains of this 13th-century Cluniac monastery are impressive and architecturally important. The monastery was founded by Duncan, Earl of Carrick and the church, claustral buildings, abbot's house and an imposing castellated gatehouse can be seen.
Times: Open Apr-Sep, daily 9.30-6.30. **Fee:** ✱ £2.50 (ch £1, concessions £1.90). Group 11+ 10% discount. Prices valid until 31/12/05. Please phone for further details. **Facilities:** 🅿 ✖ ◪

OLD DAILLY   Map 10 NX29

BARGANY GARDENS
KA26 9PH
➲ (4m NE on B734 from Girvan)
☎ 01465 871249

Woodland walks with a fine show of azaleas and rhododendrons. Plants on sale from the gardens.
Times: Open Gardens, May 10-5. **Fee:** £2 (ch under 12 free).
Facilities: 🅿 ♿ (only rock garden not accessible)

TARBOLTON   Map 10 NS42

BACHELORS' CLUB
Sandgate St KA5 5RB
➲ (on B744, 7.5m NE of Ayr)
☎ 01292 541940
web: www.nts.org.uk

In this 17th-century thatched house, Robert Burns and his friends formed a debating club in 1780. Burns attended dancing lessons and was initiated into freemasonry here in 1781. The house is furnished in the style of the period.
Times: ✱ Open Apr-Sep, Fri-Tue 1-5. Morning visits available for pre-booked groups. Times may change for 2006 please telephone or check on www.nts.org.uk **Facilities:** 🅿 (in village)
♿ ✖ (ex guide dogs) ☕

SOUTH LANARKSHIRE

BIGGAR   Map 11 NT03

GLADSTONE COURT MUSEUM
ML12 6DT
➲ (On A702 40m from Glasgow, 30m from Edinburgh, entrance by 113 High St)
☎ 01899 221050   **2 for 1**
e-mail: margaret@bmtrust.freeserve.co.uk
web: www.biggar-net.co.uk

An old-fashioned village street is portrayed in this museum, which is set out in a century-old coach-house. On display are reconstructed shops, complete with old signs and advertisements - a bank, telephone exchange, photographer's booth and other interesting glimpses into the recent past.
Times: Open Etr-Oct, Mon-Sat 11-4.30, Sun 2-4.30. **Fee:** ✱ £2 (ch £1, pen £1.50). Family ticket £4. Party £1.25 each. **Facilities:** 🅿 ♿ shop ✖ (ex guide dogs)

GREENHILL COVENANTERS HOUSE
Burn Braes ML12 6DT
➲ (On A702, 30m from Edinburgh, 40m from Glasgow)
☎ 01899 221050   **2 for 1**
e-mail: margaret@bmtrust.freserve.co.uk
web: www.biggar-net.co.uk

This 17th-century farmhouse was brought, stone by stone, ten miles from Wiston and reconstructed at Biggar. It has relics of the turbulent 'Covenanting' period, when men and women defended the right to worship in Presbyterian style. Audio presentations.
Times: Open mid May-Sep, wknds only 2-4.30. **Fee:** ✱ £1 (ch 50p, pen 70p). Family ticket £2.50. Party 70p each. **Facilities:** 🅿 🗐
♿ ✖ (ex guide dogs)

MOAT PARK HERITAGE CENTRE
ML12 6DT
➲ (On A702, 30m from Edinburgh, 40m from Glasgow)
☎ 01899 221050   **2 for 1**
e-mail: margaret@bmtrust.co.uk
web: ww.biggar-net.co.uk

The centre illustrates the history, archaeology and geology of the Upper Clyde and Tweed valleys with interesting displays.
Times: Open all year, Apr-Oct, daily 11.30-4.30, Sun 2-4.30; Nov-Feb, wkdays during office hours. Other times by prior arrangement.
Fee: ✱ £2 (ch £1, pen £1.50). Family ticket £4. Party £1.25 each.
Facilities: 🅿 🗐 ♿ (upper floor with assistance on request) toilets for disabled shop ✖ (ex guide dogs)

BLANTYRE   Map 11 NS65

DAVID LIVINGSTONE CENTRE
165 Station Rd G72 9BT
➲ (M74 junct 5 onto A725, then A724, follow signs for Blantyre, right at lights. Centre is at foot of hill)
☎ 01698 823140
web: www.nts.org.uk

Share the adventurous life of Scotland's greatest explorer, from his childhood in the Blantyre Mills to his explorations in the heart of Africa, dramatically illustrated in the historic tenement where he was born. Various events are planned throughout the season.
Times: ✱ Open Apr-24 Dec, Mon-Sat 10-5, Sun 12.30-5. Times may change for 2006 please telephone or check on www.nts.org.uk
Facilities: 🅿 ♿ toilets for disabled shop ✖ (ex guide dogs/lead grounds) ☕ 🍴

BOTHWELL   Map 11 NS75

BOTHWELL CASTLE
G71 8BL
➲ (approach from Uddingston off B7071)
☎ 01698 816894

Besieged, captured and 'knocked about' several times in the Scottish-English wars, the castle is a splendid ruin. Archibald the Grim built the curtain wall; later, in 1786, the Duke of Buccleuch carved graffiti - a coronet and initials - beside a basement well.
Times: Open all year, Apr-Sep, daily 9.30-6.30; Oct-Mar, daily 9.30-4.30. Closed Thu & Fri in winter, 25-26 Dec & 1-2 Jan.
Fee: ✱ £2.50 (ch £1, concessions £1.90). Group 11+ 10% discount. Prices valid until 31/12/05. Please phone for further details.
Facilities: 🅿 shop 🚩

EAST KILBRIDE   Map 11 NS65

MUSEUM OF SCOTTISH COUNTRY LIFE
Wester Kittochside, Philipshill Rd, (off Stewartfield Way) G76 9HR
➲ (From Glasgow take A749 to East Kilbride. From Edinburgh follow M8 to Glasgow, turn off junct 6 onto A725 to East Kilbride. Kittochside is signed before East Kilbride)
☎ 0131 247 4377   **2 for 1**
e-mail: info@nms.ac.uk
web: www.nms.ac.uk

A fascinating museum built on a 170-acre farm and offering an insight into the working lives of people in rural Scotland. The museum runs a programme of events throughout the

continued

year, demonstrating its working collection and contrasting modern and traditional farming methods.

Museum of Scottish Country Life

Times: Open daily 10-5. Closed 25-26 Dec & 1-2 Jan **Fee:** ✱ £4 (ch under 18 free, concessions £3) NMS and NTS members free. Charge for some events. **Facilities:** 🅿 💻 ♿ (disabled parking, exhibition building is fully accessible) toilets for disabled shop ✖ (ex assist dogs) ◀

HAMILTON   Map 11 NS75

CHATELHERAULT COUNTRY PARK

Ferniegair ML3 7UE

➲ (2.5km SE of Hamilton on A72 Hamilton-Larkhall/Lanark Clyde Valley tourist route) **FREE**

☎ 01698 426213

e-mail: phyllis.crosbie@southlanarkshire.gov.uk

web: www.southlanarkshire.gov.uk

Designed as a hunting lodge by William Adam in 1732, Chatelherault, built of unusual pink sandstone, has been described as a gem of Scottish architecture. Situated close to the motorway, there is a visitor's centre, shop and adventure playground. Also a herd of white Cadzow cattle.

Times: Visitor Centre, open all year, Mon-Sat 10-5, Sun 12-5. House closed all day Fri & Sat. **Facilities:** 🅿 💻 ♿ (ramps, parking, large print guide) toilets for disabled shop garden centre ✖ (ex in grounds & guide dogs) ◀

LOW PARKS MUSEUM

129 Muir St ML3 6BJ

➲ (off M74 junct 6, by Asda Superstore) **FREE**

☎ 01698 328232

The museum tells the story of Hamilton and the Clyde Valley, created by linking the former District Museum and The Cameronians (Scottish Rifles) Museum. Housed in the town's oldest building, dating from 1696, the museum features a restored 18th-century assembly room and exhibitions on Hamilton Palace and The Covenanters.

Times: Open late Mar-mid Oct, Sun-Thu 10.30-5; House 11-4 (Sep-Oct 11-3). Gardens & tearoom open during winter, please contact for opening times. **Facilities:** 🅿 📱 ♿ shop ✖ (ex guide dogs) ◀

> Directions are provided
> by the attractions.

NEW LANARK   Map 11 NS84

NEW LANARK VISITOR CENTRE

New Lanark Visitor Centre, Mill 3, New Lanark Mills ML11 9DB

➲ (1m S of Lanark. Signed from all major routes. Less than 1hr from Glasgow (M741/A72) and Edinburgh (A70))

☎ 01555 661345

e-mail: trust@newlanark.org

web: www.newlanark.org

Founded in 1785, New Lanark became well known in the early 19th century as a model community managed by enlightened industrialist and educational reformer Robert Owen. Surrounded by woodland and situated close to the Falls of Clyde, this unique world heritage site explores the philosophies of Robert Owen, using theatre, interactive displays, and the 'Millennium Experience', a magical ride through history. Accommodation is also available at the New Lanark Mill Hotel. Please telephone for details of events running throughout the year.

Times: Open daily. Jun-Aug 10.30-5. Sep-May 11-5. Closed 25 Dec and 1 Jan. **Fee:** ✱ £5.95 (ch, concessions £3.95) family ticket (2ad+2ch) £16.95 family ticket (2ad+4ch) £19.95 **Facilities:** 🅿 💻 ✖ licensed 📱 ♿ (ramps, disabled parking, wheelchairs) toilets for disabled shop ✖ (ex guide dogs) ◀

STIRLING

BANNOCKBURN   Map 11 NS89

BANNOCKBURN HERITAGE CENTRE

Glasgow Rd FK7 0LJ

➲ (2m S of Stirling off M80/M9 junct 9)

☎ 01786 812664

web: www.nts.org.uk

The Heritage Centre stands close to what is traditionally believed to have been Robert the Bruce's command post before the 1314 Battle of Bannockburn, a famous victory for the Scots and a turning point in Scottish history.

Times: ✱ Site open all year, daily. Heritage Centre Apr-Oct, daily 10-5.30; Feb-Mar & Nov-24 Dec, daily 10.30-4. Last audio-visual show half-an-hour before closing. **Facilities:** 🅿 💻 ♿ (Induction loop for the hard of hearing) toilets for disabled shop ✖ (ex site only) ☕

BLAIR DRUMMOND   Map 11 NS79

BLAIR DRUMMOND SAFARI & LEISURE PARK

FK9 4UR

➲ (M9 junct 10, 4m on A84 towards Callander)

☎ 01786 841456 & 841396

e-mail: enquiries@blairdrummond.com

web: www.blairdrummond.com

Drive through the wild animal reserves where zebras, North American bison, antelope, lions, tigers, white rhino and camels can be seen at close range. Other attractions include the sea lion show, a ride on the boat safari through the waterfowl sanctuary and around Chimpanzee Island, an adventure playground, giant astraglide, and pedal boats. There are also African elephants, giraffes and ostriches.

Times: Open 19 Mar-3 Oct, daily 10-5.30. (Last admission 4.30)

Fee: £9.50 (ch 3-14 £5.50, ch under 3 free). Discount rates for party 15+. **Facilities:** 🅿 💻 ✖ licensed 📱 ♿ (special menus & waitress service if booked in advance) toilets for disabled shop ✖ (ex assist dogs) ◀

CALLANDER   Map 11 NN60

ROB ROY AND TROSSACHS VISITOR CENTRE
Ancaster Square FK17 8ED
➲ (on A84)
☎ 01877 330342
e-mail: robroy&t@aillst.ossian.net
web: robroyvisitorcentre.com
From Highland hero to Hollywood legend, follow the story of
Scotland's most famous Highlander, Rob Roy. Hear his
innermost thoughts and witness his exploits. Step back in
time and explore a reconstructed 18th-century farmhouse,
just as Rob Roy would have experienced it.
Times: ✱ Open Apr-May, daily 10-5; Jun-Sep, 10-6; Oct 10-5; Nov-Feb
11-4; Mar 10-5. (Winter openings may vary, please contact)
Facilities: P 🗊 ⅙ toilets for disabled shop ✖ 🖾

DOUNE   Map 11 NN70

DOUNE CASTLE
FK16 6EA
➲ (8m S of Callander on A84)
☎ 01786 841742
The 14th-century stronghold with its two fine towers has
been restored. It stands on the banks of the River Teith, and
is associated with 'Bonnie Prince Charlie' and Sir Walter
Scott.
Times: Open all year, Apr-Sep, daily 9.30-6.30; Oct-Mar, daily
9.30-4.30. Closed Thu & Fri in winter, 25-26 Dec & 1-2 Jan. **Fee:** ✱ £3
(ch £1.20, concessions £2.30). Group 11+ 10% discount. Prices valid
until 31/12/05. Please phone for further details. **Facilities:** P shop 🖪

KILLIN   Map 11 NN53

BREADALBANE FOLKLORE CENTRE
Falls of Dochart FK21 8XE
➲ (on A85)
☎ 01567 820254
e-mail: killin@aillst.ossian.net
web: www.breadalbanefolklorecentre.com
Overlooking the beautiful Falls of Dochart, the centre gives a
fascinating insight into the legends of Breadalbane -
Scotland's 'high country'. Learn of the magical deeds of St
Fillan and hear tales of mystical giants, ancient prophesies,
traditional folklore and clan history. Housed in historic St
Fillans Mill which features a restored waterwheel. Tourist
Information and gift shop.
Times: ✱ Open Mar-May & Oct, daily 10-5; Jun & Sep, daily 10-6;
Jul-Aug, daily 9.30-6.30. Closed Nov-Feb. **Facilities:** P (30mtrs)
⅙ shop ✖ 🖾

MILNGAVIE   Map 11 NS57

MUGDOCK COUNTRY PARK
Craigallian Rd G62 8EL
➲ (N of Glasgow on A81, signed)
☎ 0141 956 6100 956 6586   `FREE`
e-mail: lain@mcp.ndo.co.uk
web: www.mugdock-country-park.org.uk
This country park incorporates the remains of Mugdock and
Craigend castles, set in beautiful landscapes as well as an
exhibition centre, craft shops, orienteering course and many
walks.
Times: Open all year, daily. **Facilities:** P 🖳 ✖ licensed
⅙ (mobility equip., audio leaflet, lge print media) toilets for disabled
shop garden centre 🖾

PORT OF MENTEITH   Map 11 NN50

INCHMAHOME PRIORY
FK8 3RA
➲ (4m E of Aberfoyle, off A81)
☎ 01877 385294
Walter Comyn founded this Augustinian house in 1238, and
it became famous as the retreat of the infant Mary, Queen of
Scots in 1547. The ruins of the church and cloisters are
situated on an island in the Lake of Menteith.
Times: Open Apr-Sep, daily 9.30-6.30. Last outward sailing at 5.15pm.
Fee: ✱ £3.50 (ch £1.30, concessions £2.50). Admission charge
includes ferry trip. Group 11+ 10% discount. Prices valid until 31/12/05.
Please phone for further details. **Facilities:** P shop 🖪

STIRLING   Map 11 NS79

MAR'S WARK   `FREE`
Broad St FK8 1EE
A remarkable Renaissance mansion built by the Earl of Mar,
Regent for James VI in 1570 and later used as the town
workhouse. It was never completed and now the façade can
be seen.
Times: Open all reasonable times. **Facilities:** ✖ 🖪

MUSEUM OF ARGYLL & SUTHERLAND HIGHLANDERS
The Castle FK8 3PA
➲ (museum in Stirling Castle)
☎ 01786 475165
e-mail: museum@argylls.co.uk
web: www.argylls.co.uk
Situated in the King's Old Building in Stirling Castle, the
museum tells the history of the Regiment from 1794 to the
present day. Displays include uniforms, medals, silver,
paintings, colours, pipe banners, and commentaries.
Times: Open Etr-Sep, daily 9.30-5; Sep-Etr, daily 10-4.15. **Fee:** ✱ Entry
to museum free but entry fee to castle. **Facilities:** P (Castle
Esplanade) 🗊 shop ✖

NATIONAL WALLACE MONUMENT
Abbey Craig, Causewayhead FK8 2AD
➲ (from A907 [Stirling to Alloa road] follow
brown tourist signs)
☎ 01786 472140
e-mail: nationalwallacemonument@
aillst.ossian.net
web: www.nationalwallacemonument.com
Meet Scotland's national hero, William Wallace, and join his
epic struggle for a free Scotland. Step into Westminster Hall
and witness his trial. Climb the 220 foot tower and
experience one of the finest views in Scotland.
Times: ✱ Open all year Jan-Feb & Nov-Dec, daily 10.30-4; Mar-May &
Oct, daily 10-5; Jun, daily 10-6; Jul-Aug, daily 9.30-6.30; Sep, daily
9.30-5. **Facilities:** P 🖳 🗊 ⅙ (limited access) shop ✖ 🖾

An asterisk * indicates
that opening times and
prices are for 2005. Please
contact the attraction for
up-to-date information.

OLD TOWN JAIL

Saint John St FK8 1EA

⮑ (follow signs for castle up hill, jail on left at top of Saint John's St)

☎ 01786 450050

e-mail: otjva@aillst.ossian.net

web: www.oldtownjail.com

Experience life in a Victorian prison, where real history performances bring the past to life. Come face to face with Stirling's notorious hangman and you may even witness an attempted jailbreak. Stunning rooftop panorama and gift shop. Multi-lingual audio tour.

Times: ✱ Open Apr-Sep, daily 9.30-5.30; Oct & Mar, daily 9.30-4.30; Nov-Feb, daily 9.30-3.30 (last admission) **Facilities:** 🅿 🗐 ⅋ toilets for disabled shop ✈ 🍴

STIRLING CASTLE

Upper Castle Hill FK8 1EJ

☎ 01786 450000

Sitting on top of a 250ft rock, Stirling Castle has a strategic position on the Firth of Forth. As a result it has been the scene of many events in Scotland's history. James II was born at the castle in 1430. Mary, Queen of Scots spent some years there, and it was James IV's childhood home. Among its finest features are the splendid Renaissance palace built by James V, and the Chapel Royal, rebuilt by James VI.

Times: Open all year, Apr-Sep, daily 9.30-6; Oct-Mar, daily 9.30-5.00. Closed 25-26 Dec & 1-2 Jan. **Fee:** ✱ £8 (ch £3, concessions £6). Group 11+ 10% discount. Prices valid until 31/12/05. Please phone for further details. **Facilities:** 🅿 (charged) ✗ licensed ⅋ toilets for disabled shop ✈ 🍴

STIRLING SMITH ART GALLERY & MUSEUM

Dumbarton Rd FK8 2RQ

⮑ (M9 junct 10, follow Stirling Castle signs)

☎ 01786 471917

e-mail: museum@smithartgallery.demon.co.uk

web: www.smithartgallery.demon.co.uk

This award-winning museum and gallery presents a variety of exhibitions drawing on its own rich collections and works from elsewhere. Please telephone for details of events running throughout the year.

Times: Open all year, Tue-Sat 10.30-5, Sun 2-5. Closed Mon, 25-26 Dec & 1-2 Jan. **Fee:** ✱ Small charge for special events.

Facilities: 🅿 🍴 🗐 ⅋ (wheelchair lift, induction loop in theatre) toilets for disabled shop

WEST DUNBARTONSHIRE

DUMBARTON　　　　　　Map 10 NS37

DUMBARTON CASTLE

G82 1JJ

☎ 01389 732167

The castle, set on the 240ft Dumbarton Rock above the River Clyde, dominates the town (the capital of the Celtic kingdom of Strathclyde) and commands spectacular views. Most of what can be seen today dates from the 18th and 19th centuries, but there are a few earlier remains.

Times: Open all year, Apr-Sep, daily 9-6.30. Oct-Mar, daily 9-4.30. Closed Thu & Fri in winter, 25-26 Dec & 1-2 Jan. **Fee:** ✱ £3 (ch £1.20, concessions £2.25). Group 11+ 10% discount. Prices valid until 31/12/05. Please phone for further details. **Facilities:** 🅿 shop ✈ 🍴

WEST LOTHIAN

LINLITHGOW　　　　　　Map 11 NS97

BLACKNESS CASTLE

EH49 7AL

⮑ (4m NE)

☎ 01506 834807

This was once one of the most important fortresses in Scotland. Used as a state prison during covenanting time and in the late 19th-century as a powder magazine, it was one of four castles left fortified by the Articles of Union. Most impressive are the massive 17th-century artillery emplacements.

Times: Open all year, Apr-Sep, daily 9.30-6.30; Oct-Mar, daily 9.30-4.30. Closed Thu & Fri in winter, 25-26 Dec & 1-2 Jan. **Fee:** ✱ £3 (ch £1.20, concessions £2.25). Group 11+ 10% discount. Prices valid until 31/12/05. Please phone for further details. **Facilities:** 🅿 shop 🍴

HOUSE OF THE BINNS

EH49 7NA

⮑ (4m E of Linlithgow, off A904)

☎ 01506 834255

e-mail: houseofthebinns@nts.org.uk

web: www.nts.org.uk

An example of changing architectural tastes from 1612 onwards, this house reflects the transition from fortified stronghold to spacious mansion. The original three-storey building, with small windows and twin turrets, evolved into a fine crenellated house with beautiful moulded plaster ceilings - the ancestral home of the Dalyell family. There is a magnificent display of snowdrops and daffodils in spring.

Times: ✱ Open House: Jun-Sep, Sat-Mon 2-5. Parkland: Apr-Oct, daily 10-7, Nov-Mar, daily 10-4. Times may change for 2006 please telephone or check on www.nts.org.uk **Facilities:** 🅿 ⅋ (Braille sheets) 🍴 (ex guide dogs) 🍸

LINLITHGOW PALACE

EH49 7AL

⮑ (off M9)

☎ 01506 842896

The magnificent ruin of a great Royal Palace, set in its own park or 'peel'. All the Stuart kings lived here, and work commissioned by James I, III, IV, and VI can be seen. The great hall and the chapel are particularly fine. James V was born here in 1512 and Mary, Queen of Scots in 1542.

Times: Open all year, Apr-Sep, daily 9.30-6.30; Oct-Mar, daily 9.30-4.30. Closed 25-26 Dec & 1-2 Jan. **Fee:** ✱ £4 (ch £1.60, concessions £3). Group 11+ 10% discount. Prices valid until 31/12/05. Please phone for further details. **Facilities:** 🅿 shop 🍴 🍴

LIVINGSTON　　　　　　Map 11 NT06

ALMOND VALLEY HERITAGE CENTRE

Millfield EH54 7AR

⮑ (2m from M8 junct 3)

☎ 01506 414957

e-mail: info@almondvalley.co.uk

web: www.almondvalley.co.uk

A combination of fun and educational potential ideal for children, Almond Valley has a petting zoo of farm animals, an interactive museum on the shale oil industry, a narrow gauge railway, and tractor rides. Please telephone for details of events running throughout the year.

Times: Open all year, daily 10-5. Closed Dec 25-26, Jan 1-2 **Fee:** ✱ £3 (ch £2). Family (2ad+4ch) £10. **Facilities:** 🅿 🍴 🗐 ⅋ toilets for disabled shop 🍴

SCOTTISH ISLANDS

ARRAN, ISLE OF

BRODICK   Map 10 NS03

Brodick Castle, Garden & Country Park
KA27 8HY

⮡ (Ferry from Ardrossan-Brodick or Lochranza-Kintyre - frequent in summer, limited in winter)

☎ 01770 302202 & 302462

e-mail: brodick@nts.org.uk

web: www.nts.org.uk

The site has been fortified since Viking times, but the present castle dating from the 13th century was a stronghold of the Dukes of Hamilton. Splendid silver, fine porcelain and paintings acquired by generations of owners can be seen, including many sporting pictures and trophies. There is a magnificent woodland garden, started by the Duchess of Montrose in 1923, world famous for its rhododendrons and azaleas.

Times: ✱ Open Apr-Oct, daily 11-4.30 (closes 3.30 in Oct). Country Park: open all year, daily 9.30-sunset. Times may change for 2006 please telephone or check on www.nts.org.uk

Facilities: 🅿 ✗ ♿ (Braille, wheelchairs motorised buggy & stairlift) toilets for disabled shop ✗ (ex guide dogs) 🦮

ISLE OF ARRAN HERITAGE MUSEUM
Rosaburn KA27 8DP

⮡ (right at Brodick Pier, approx 1m)

☎ 01770 302636

e-mail: tom.macleod@arranmuseum.co.uk

web: www.arranmuseum.co.uk

The setting is an 18th-century croft farm, including a cottage restored to its pre-1920 state and a 'smiddy' where a blacksmith worked until the late 1960s. There are also several demonstrations of horse-shoeing, sheep-shearing and weaving and spinning throughout the season - please ring for details. There is a large archaeology and geology section with archive, where help with research is available.

Times: Open Apr-Oct, daily 10.30-4.30. **Fee:** ✱ £2.50 (ch £1.25, pen £175) Family £6.50. **Facilities:** 🅿 💺 🗐 ♿ toilets for disabled shop ✗ (ex guide dogs & in garden)

LOCHRANZA   Map 10 NR95

ISLE OF ARRAN DISTILLERY VISITOR CENTRE
KA27 8HJ

⮡ (from Brodick Ferry Terminal take coast road N for 14m. Distillery on edge of village)

☎ 01770 830264

e-mail: visitorcentre@arranwhisky.com

web: www.arranwhisky.com

Located amidst beautiful surroundings, the distillery was built to revive the dormant traditions of Arran single malt whisky production. After a guided tour of the distillery, visitors can now taste some of the first whiskies to be ready after production began in 1995.

Times: Open daily 10-6 **Fee:** ✱ £3.50 (ch under 12 free, pen/student £2.50). Party 20+. **Facilities:** 🅿 ✗ licensed ♿ (ex working distillery, chair lift in visitor centre) toilets for disabled shop ✗ (ex guide dogs) 🍽

BUTE, ISLE OF

ROTHESAY   Map 10 NS06

ARDENCRAIG
PA20 9HA

⮡ (1m off A844, S of Rothesay)

☎ 01700 504225

e-mail: allan.macdonald@argyll-bute.co.uk

web: www.argyll-bute.gov.uk

Particular attention has been paid to improving the layout of the garden and introducing rare plants. The greenhouse and walled garden produce plants for floral displays throughout the district. A variety of fish is kept in the ornamental ponds and the aviaries have some interesting birds.

Times: ✱ Open May-Sep. **Facilities:** 🅿 💺 ♿ ✗ (ex guide dogs)

BUTE MUSEUM
Stuart St PA20 0EP

⮡ (on road behind castle)

☎ 01700 505067

e-mail: Ivor@butemuseum.fsnet.co.uk

Local and natural history displays, including birds, mammals and seashore items; varied collections of recent bygones, a collection of early Christian crosses, and flints and pots from various Mesolithic and Neolithic burial cairns.

Times: Open all year, Apr-Sep, Mon-Sat 10.30-4.30, Sun 2.30-4.30; Oct-Mar, Tue-Sat 2.30-4.30. Closed Sun & Mon. **Fee:** ✱ £1.50 (ch 50p, pen £1) **Facilities:** 🅿 (3 mins walk) 🗐 ♿ (touch table for blind, ramps) shop

ROTHESAY CASTLE
PA20 0DA

☎ 01700 502691

The focal point of Rothesay is this 13th-century castle. It has lofty curtain walls defended by drum towers that enclose a circular courtyard.

Times: Open all year, Apr-Sep, daily 9.30-6.30; Oct-Mar, daily 9.30-4.30. Closed Thu & Fri in winter, 25-26 Dec & 1-2 Jan. **Fee:** ✱ £3 (ch £1.20, concessions £2.25). Group 11+ 10% discount. Prices valid until 31/12/05. Please phone for further details. **Facilities:** 🅿 shop ▮

GREAT CUMBRAE ISLAND

MILLPORT   Map 10 NS15

MUSEUM OF THE CUMBRAES
Garrison Grounds KA28 0DG

⮡ (Ferry to Millport, from Largs Cal-Mac Terminal. Bus meets each ferry) **FREE**

☎ 01475 531191

e-mail: namuseum@north-ayrshire.gov.uk

web: www.north-ayrshire.gov.uk/museums

A small museum which displays the history and life of the Cumbraes. There is also a fine collection of local photographs.

Times: Open Etr-Sep, Thu-Mon 10-1 & 2-5. **Facilities:** 🅿 ♿ shop ✗ (ex guide dogs)

Directions are provided
by the attractions.

LEWIS, ISLE OF

ARNOL   Map 13 NB34

BLACK HOUSE MUSEUM

PA86 9DB

➲ (11m NW of Stornoway on A858)

☎ 01851 710395

A traditional Hebridean dwelling, built without mortar and roofed with thatch on a timber framework. It has a central peat fire in the kitchen, no chimney and a byre under the same roof.

Times: Open all year, Apr-Sep, Mon-Sat 9.30-6.30; Oct-Mar, Mon-Sat 9.30-4.30. Closed 25-26 Dec & 1-2 Jan. **Fee:** ✱ £4 (ch £1.60, concessions £3). Group 11+ 10% discount. Prices valid until 31/12/05. Please phone for further details. **Facilities:** 🅿 ⟨ toilets for disabled shop ✕ ▮

CALLANISH   Map 13 NB23

CALLANISH STANDING STONES

PA86 9DY

➲ (12m W of Stornoway off A859)

☎ 01851 621422

An avenue of 19 monoliths leads north from a circle of 13 stones with rows of more stones fanning out to south, east and west. Probably constructed between 3000 and 1500BC, this is a unique cruciform of megaliths.

Times: Site accessible at all times. Visitor Centre open Apr-Sep, Mon-Sat 10-7; Oct-Mar, Mon-Sat 10-4. Site free but charge for visitor centre - call 01851 621422. **Facilities:** 🅿 ✕ ⟨ toilets for disabled shop ▮

CARLOWAY   Map 13 NB24

DUN CARLOWAY BROCH

➲ (1.5m S of Carloway on A858)   FREE

Brochs are late-prehistoric circular stone towers, and their origins are mysterious. One of the best examples can be seen at Dun Carloway, where the tower still stands about 30ft high.

Times: Open at all reasonable times. **Facilities:** 🅿 ▮

MULL, ISLE OF

CRAIGNURE   Map 10 NM73

MULL & WEST HIGHLAND NARROW GAUGE RAILWAY

Craignure (old pier) Station PA65 6AY

➲ (0.25m from Craignure Ferry Terminal, just off road to Iona)

☎ 01680 812494 (in season) or 01680 812567

e-mail: mullrail@dee-emm.co.uk

web: mullrail.co.uk

The first passenger railway on a Scottish island, opened in 1984. Both steam and diesel trains operate on the ten-and-a-quarter inch gauge line, which runs from Craignure to Torosay Castle. The 1.25 mile line offers dramatic woodland and mountain views taking in Ben Nevis, Glencoe and the Isle of Lismore.

Times: Open Etr-mid Oct **Fee:** ✱ Return £4.00 (ch £3.00); Single £3.00 (ch £2.00). Family ticket return £10.75, single £7.50 **Facilities:** 🅿 ⟨ (provision to carry person seated in wheelchair on trains) shop 🖃

TOROSAY CASTLE & GARDENS

PA65 6AY

➲ (1.5m S of Ferry Terminal at Craignure)

☎ 01680 812421

e-mail: info@torosay.com

web: www.holidaymull.org/members/torosay

The Scottish baronial architecture of this Victorian castle is complemented by the magnificent setting, and inside the house there are displays of portraits and wildlife pictures, family scrapbooks and a study of the Antarctic. The gardens include a statue walk and water garden, an avenue of Australian gum trees, and an Oriental garden. Within the grounds there is a narrow gauge steam and diesel railway.

Times: Open end Apr-Oct, daily 10.30-5. Gardens all year. **Fee:** House & Gardens: £5.50 (ch £2.25, student & pen £5) Family £14. Gardens only: £4.50 (ch £2.00, student & pen £3.50) Family £11.

Facilities: 🅿 🖳 🖃 shop ✕ guide/hearing dogs-garden only 🖃

ORKNEY

BIRSAY   Map 16 HY22

EARL'S PALACE

KW15 1PD

➲ (on A966)

☎ 01856 721205 & 841815   FREE

The gaunt remains of the residence of the 16th-century Earl of Orkney, constructed round a courtyard.

Times: Open at all reasonable times. **Facilities:** ✕ ▮

DOUNBY   Map 16 HY22

BROUGH OF BIRSAY

➲ (off A966)

☎ 01856 841815

This ruined Romanesque church stands next to the remains of a Norse village. The nave, chancel and semicircular apse can be seen, along with claustral buildings. Crossings must be made on foot at low-water - there is no boat.

Times: Open mid Jun-Sep (tides permitting), daily 9.30-6.30. **Fee:** ✱ £2 (ch 80p, concessions £1.50). Group 11+ 10% discount. Prices valid until 31/12/05. Please phone for further details. ▮

CLICK MILL

➲ (2.5m from Dounby on B905)

☎ 01856 841815   FREE

The last surviving horizontal water mill in Orkney, of a type well represented in Shetland and Lewis. The mill is in working condition and visitors should wear sensible footwear.

Times: Open at all reasonable times. ▮

SKARA BRAE

KW16 3LR

➲ (19m W of Kirkwall on B9056)

☎ 01856 841815

Engulfed in drift sand, this remarkable group of well-preserved Stone Age dwellings is the most outstanding survivor of its kind in Britain. Stone furniture and a fireplace can be seen.

Times: Open all year, Apr-Sep, daily 9.30-6.30; Oct-Mar, daily 9.30-4.30. Closed Sun am in winter, 25-26 Dec & 1-2 Jan. **Fee:** ✱ £6 (ch £2.40, concessions £4.50). Group 11+ 10% discount. Prices valid until 31/12/05. Please phone for further details.

Facilities: 🅿 ✕ ⟨ toilets for disabled shop ✕ ▮

FINSTOWN — Map 16 HY31

MAES HOWE CHAMBERED CAIRN
➲ (9m W of Kirkwall, on A965)
☎ 01856 761606

The masonry of Britain's finest megalithic tomb is in a remarkably good state of preservation. Dating from neolithic times, it contains Viking carvings and runes.

Times: Open all year, Apr-Sep, daily 9.30-6.30; Oct-Mar, daily 9.30-4.30. Closed Sun am in winter, 25-26 Dec & 1-2 Jan. **Fee:** ✱ £4 (ch £1.60, concessions £3). Group 11+ 10% discount. Prices valid until 31/12/05. Please phone for further details. **Facilities:** P ✗ shop ✖ ✿

STONES OF STENNESS CIRCLE AND HENGE
➲ (5m NE of Stromness on B9055) FREE
☎ 01856 841815

Dating back to the second millennium BC, the remains of this stone circle are near the Ring of Brogar - a splendid circle of upright stones surrounded by a ditch.

Times: Open at any reasonable time. **Facilities:** P ✿

HARRAY — Map 16 HY31

CORRIGALL FARM & KIRBUSTER MUSEUM
KW17 2JR
☎ 01856 771411 & 771268 FREE

The museum consists of two Orkney farmhouses with outbuildings. Kirbuster (Birsay) has the last surviving example of a 'Firehoose' with its central hearth; Corrigall (Harray) represents an improved farmhouse and steading of the late 1800s.

Times: Open Mar-Oct, Mon-Sat 10.30-1 & 2-5, Sun 2-7.
Facilities: P ▓ ♿ shop ✖ (ex guide dogs) ◥

KIRKWALL — Map 16 HY41

BISHOP'S & EARL'S PALACES
KW15 1PD
➲ (In Kirkwall on A960)
☎ 01856 875461

The Bishop's Palace is a hall-house of the 12th century, later much altered, with a round tower built by Bishop Reid in 1541-48. A later addition was made by the notorious Patrick Stewart, Earl of Orkney, who built the adjacent Earl's Palace between 1600 and 1607 in a splendid Renaissance style.

Times: Open Apr-Sep, daily 9.30-6.30. **Fee:** ✱ £2.50 (ch £1, concessions £1.90). Group 11+ 10% discount. Prices valid until 31/12/05. Please phone for further details. **Facilities:** shop ✿

SCAPA FLOW VISITOR CENTRE & MUSEUM
Hoy KW15 1DH
➲ (on A964 to Houton, ferry crossing takes 45 mins, visitors centre 2 mins from ferry terminal)
☎ 01856 791300 FREE
e-mail: museum@orkney.gov.uk
web: www.orkneyheritage.com

Also known as the Lyness Interpretation Centre, this fascinating museum is home to a large collection of military equipment used in the defence of the Orkneys during the First and Second World Wars. There are also guns salvaged from the German ships scuppered in WWII. Visitors arrive at the island after a short boat trip from the Orkney mainland.

Times: Open all year: Mon-Fri 9-4.30 (mid May-Oct also Sat, Sun 10.30-3.30) **Facilities:** P ▣ ▓ ♿ toilets for disabled shop ✖ (ex guide dogs) ◥

THE ORKNEY MUSEUM
Broad St KW15 1DH
➲ (town centre)
☎ 01856 873555 FREE
e-mail: museum@orkney.gov.uk

One of the finest vernacular town houses in Scotland, this 16th-century building now contains a museum of Orkney history, including the islands' fascinating archaeology.

Times: Open, Oct-Mar Mon-Sat, 10.30-12.30 & 1.30-5, Apr-Sep, 10.30-5 Mon-Sat. **Facilities:** P (50yds) ▓ ♿ shop ✖ (ex guide dogs) ◥

STROMNESS — Map 16 HY20

ORKNEY MARITIME & NATURAL HISTORY MUSEUM
52 Alfred St KW16 3DF
☎ 01856 850025

The museum focuses on Orkney's broad maritime connections, including fishing, whaling, the Hudson's Bay Company, the German Fleet in Scapa Flow, and the award-winning Pilot's House extension. The Natural History Gallery is fully restored, displaying a fine collection of curios and rare and interesting exhibits.

Times: Open Apr-Sep, Mon-Sun 10-5; Oct-Mar, Mon-Sat 11-3.30. Closed Xmas, New Year & 3 wks Feb-Mar. **Fee:** £2.50 (ch 50p con £2). Family ticket £5. **Facilities:** P (50yds) ♿ toilets for disabled shop ✖ (ex guide dogs)

WESTRAY — Map 16 HY44

NOLTLAND CASTLE
➲ (1m W of Pierowall village) FREE
☎ 01856 841815

A fine, ruined Z-plan tower, built between 1560 and 1573 but never completed. The tower is remarkable for its large number of gun loops and impressive staircase.

Times: Open 11 Jun-Sep, daily 9.30-6.30. **Facilities:** ✖ ✿

SHETLAND

LERWICK — Map 16 HU44

CLICKIMIN
ZE1 0QX
➲ (1m SW of Lerwick on A970) FREE
☎ 01466 793191

The remains of a prehistoric settlement that was fortified at the beginning of the Iron Age with a stone-built fort. The site was occupied for over 1000 years. The remains include a partially demolished broch (round tower) which still stands to a height of 17ft.

Times: Open at all reasonable times. ✿

FORT CHARLOTTE
ZE1 0JN
➲ (in centre of Lerwick) FREE
☎ 01466 793191

A five-sided artillery fort with bastions projecting from each corner. The walls are high and massive. It was built in 1665 to protect the Sound of Bressay from the Dutch, but taken by them and burned in 1673. It was rebuilt in 1781.

Times: Open at all reasonable times. Key available locally. ✿

SHETLAND MUSEUM

Lower Hillhead ZE1 0EL
☎ 01595 695057
e-mail: shetland.museum@sic.shetland.gov.uk
web: www.shetland-museum.gov.uk

The massive brass propeller blade outside the building is
from the 17,000-ton liner *Oceanic*, wrecked off Foula in 1914.
The archaeology gallery covers Neolithic burials, axe-
making, Bronze Age houses, Iron Age farming and domestic
life. There are also agricultural and social history displays,
including peat-working, corn harvest, local businesses,
medals, bootmaking and Shetland weddings. Changing
displays of local contemporary art. Please note the current
Museum is due to close on 31st March 2005. It will re-open
as the New Shetland Museum and Archives in August 2006.

Times: Re-launch of museum in Aug 2006. Please telephone for details
of opening times and admission prices. **Fee:** Prices not confirmed for
2006 **Facilities:** 🅿 💻 ✗ ♿ (lift, wheelchair available) toilets for
disabled shop ✖ (ex guide dogs) 🍴

MOUSA ISLAND   Map 16 HU42

MOUSA BROCH

⮩ (accessible by boat from Sandwick)
☎ 01466 793191   **FREE**

This broch is the best-preserved example of an Iron Age
drystone tower in Scotland. The tower is nearly complete
and rises to a height of 40ft. The outer and inner walls both
contain staircases that may be climbed to the parapet.

Times: Open at all reasonable time. �🏴

SCALLOWAY   Map 16 HU33

SCALLOWAY CASTLE

ZE1 0TP
⮩ (6m from Lerwick on A970)
☎ 01466 793191   **FREE**

The ruins of a castle designed on the medieval two-step
plan. The castle was actually built in 1600 by Patrick Stewart,
Earl of Orkney. When the Earl, who was renowned for his
cruelty, was executed in 1615, the castle fell into disuse.

Times: Open at all reasonable time. **Facilities:** 🅿 🏴

SUMBURGH   Map 16 HU30

JARLSHOF PREHISTORIC SITE

⮩ (at Sumburgh Head, approx 22m S of Lerwick)
☎ 01950 460112

One of the most remarkable archaeological sites in Europe.
There are remains of Bronze Age, Iron Age and Viking
settlements as well as a medieval farm. There is also a 16th-
century Laird's House, once the home of the Earls Robert
and Patrick Stewart, and the basis of 'Jarlshof' in Sir Walter
Scott's novel *The Pirate*.

Times: Open Apr-Sep, daily 9.30-6.30. **Fee:** ✱ £3.30 (ch £1.30,
concessions £2.50). Group 11+ 10% discount. Prices valid until
31/12/05. Please phone for further details. **Facilities:** 🅿 shop 🏴

> ## An asterisk * indicates that opening times and prices are for 2005. Please contact the attraction for up-to-date information.

ARMADALE   Map 13 NG60

ARMADALE CASTLE GARDENS & MUSEUM OF THE ISLES

IV45 8RS
⮩ (16m S of Broadford on A851. Follow Clan
Donald Centre or Armadale Castle Gardens &
Museum of the Isles signs. Easily reached by Skye
Bridge or the Mallaig A830 to Armdale Ferry)
☎ 01471 844305 & 844227
e-mail: office@clandonald.com
web: www.clandonald.com

Armadale Castle and Gardens were built in 1815 as the
home of Lord Macdonald. The warming effect of the Gulf
Stream allows exotic trees and plants to flourish. Within the
40 acres of gardens is the Museum of the Isles, where
visitors can discover the history of the Highlands.

Times: Open daily 9.30-5.30. Garden & Museum open Apr-Oct.
Fee: ✱ £4.80 (concessions & Group 8+ £3.80). **Facilities:** 🅿 💻
✗ licensed ♿ (wheelchairs available) toilets for disabled shop 🍴

DUNVEGAN   Map 13 NG24

DUNVEGAN CASTLE

IV55 8WF
⮩ (follow A87 over Skye Bridge. Turn onto A863
at Sligachan and continue to castle)
☎ 01470 521206
e-mail: info@dunvegancastle.com
web: www.dunvegancastle.com

This fortress stronghold set on the sea loch of Dunvegan has
been the home of the Chief of Macleod for 800 years. On
view are books, pictures, arms and treasured relics of the
clan. A pedigree Highland Cattle fold is also an attraction, as
is the boat trip to the nearby Seal Colony.

Times: ✱ Open 24 Mar-Oct, daily 10-5.30 (last entry 5). Castle &
Gardens, Nov-Mar, daily 11-4 (last entry 3.30). Closed 25-26 Dec & 1-2
Jan **Facilities:** 🅿 💻 ✗ licensed ♿ (restaurant has ramps for
wheelchair access) toilets for disabled shop garden centre
✖ (ex guide dogs & in grounds) 🍴

> # If an attraction name appears in *italics*, details have not been confirmed for 2006.

WALES

EVENTS & FESTIVALS

March
tbc Wrexham Science Festival, Wrexham

May
26th-4th Jun Hay Festival of Literature, Haye-on-Wye
27th-4th Jun St David's Cathedral Festival, St David's, Pembrokeshire
28th-29th Ales & Borders Game & Country Fair, Usk

June
tbc Llandudno Festival, week of events, concerts, crafts, parades and street festival

July
7th-9th North Wales Bluegrass Festival, Bodlondeb Field & Civic Hall, Conwy
22nd-29th Fishguard International Music Festival (various venues), Fishguard, Pembrokeshire

24th- 27th Royal Welsh Show, Royal Welsh Showground, Builth Wells
25th-28th Cardiff International Street Festival
tbc Llangollen Fringe Festival (provisional)
tbc Llangollen International Musical Eisteddfod, International Pavilion, Llangollen
tbc Welsh Proms, St David's Hall, The Hayes, Cardiff

August
5th-12th National Eisteddfod, Old Tin Works at Velindre
6th-13th Conwy River Festival, Harbour, Conwy
15th-16th Anglesey County Show, Anglesey Showground, Gwalchmai, Holyhead
26th-27th Talgarth Festival of the Black Mountains, all around the town
28th World Bog Snorkelling Championship (race through trench cut in peat bog with snorkel and flippers), Llanwrtyd Wells

September
15th-23rd North Wales International Music Festival, the Cathedral, St Asaph
tbc Tenby Arts Festival (various venues), Tenby, Pembrokeshire

October
27th-9th Nov Dylan Thomas Festival, Dylan Thomas Centre, Somerset Place Swansea

November
8th-18th Cardiff Screen Festival, various venues
27th-28th Royal Welsh Agricultural Winter Fair, Royal Welsh Showground, Builth Wells

Top: Mount Snowdon reflected in Llynnau Mymbyr   *Above: The Swallow waterfall in Snowdonia National Park*

BRIDGEND

BRIDGEND — Map 03 SS97

NEWCASTLE
☎ 01656 659515 **FREE**
The small castle dates back to the 12th century. It is ruined, but a rectangular tower, a richly carved Norman gateway and massive curtain walls enclosing a polygonal courtyard can still be seen.
Times: Open - accessible throughout the year. Key keeper arrangement. **Facilities:** 🅿 ✈ ☺

COITY — Map 03 SS98

COITY CASTLE
CF35 6BG
➲ (2m NE of Bridgend, off A4061)
☎ 01656 652021 **FREE**
A 12th to 16th-century stronghold, with a hall, chapel and the remains of a square keep.
Times: Open all year, at all times. Key keeper arrangement.
Facilities: 🅿 ✈ ☺

CAERPHILLY

CAERPHILLY — Map 03 ST18

CAERPHILLY CASTLE
CF8 1JL
➲ (on A469)
☎ 029 2088 3143
The concentrically planned castle was begun in 1268 by Gilbert de Clare and completed in 1326. It is the largest in Wales, and has extensive land and water defences. A unique feature is the ruined tower - the victim of subsidence - which manages to out-lean even Pisa! The south dam platform, once a tournament-field, now displays replica medieval siege-engines.
Times: Open 18 Mar-May & Oct, daily 9.30-5; Jun-Sep, daily 9.30-6; Nov-Mar, Mon-Sat 9.30-4, Sun 11-4. Telephone for Xmas opening times. **Fee:** £3 (ch 5-15, pen & students £2.50). Disabled & assisting companion free. Family ticket (2ad + 3 ch) £8.50. Prices quoted apply until 31/03/06. Party. **Facilities:** 🅿 ⅙ shop ✈ ☺ 🍴

LLANCAIACH FAWR MANOR
Gelligaer Rd, Nelson CF46 6ER
➲ (M4 junct 32, A470 to Merthyr Tydfil. Towards Ystrad Mynach A472, follow brown heritage signs)
☎ 01443 412248 **2 for 1**
e-mail: llancarchfowl@caerphilly.gov.uk
web: www.caerphilly.gov.uk/visiting
Step back in time to the Civil War period at this fascinating living history museum. The year is 1645 and visitors are invited into the Manor to meet the servants of 'Colonel' Edward Prichard - from the puritanical to the gossipy. Please telephone for details of events running throughout the year.
Times: Open Mon-Fri 10-3.30 (last admission), Sat & Sun 10-4.30. Closed Mon, Nov-Feb & 24 Dec-2 Jan. **Fee:** ✱ £4.95 (ch £3.50) concessions £3.75. Family ticket £14. **Facilities:** 🅿 ⅙ ✗ licensed 🍴 ⅙ (personal stereo, photo album & Braille map) toilets for disabled shop ✈ (ex guide dogs) 🍴

CWMCARN — Map 03 ST29

CWMCARN FOREST DRIVE
Nantcarn Rd NP11 7FA
➲ (8m N of Newport on A467, follow brown tourist signs)
☎ 01495 272001 **FREE**
e-mail: cwmcarn-vc@caerphilly.gov.uk
web: www.caerphilly.gov.uk/visiting
A seven-mile scenic drive with spectacular views over the Bristol Channel and surrounding countryside. Facilities include barbecues, picnic and play areas, and forest and mountain walks. Special events are held throughout the year, please ring for details.
Times: Open Forest Drive: Mar & Oct 11-5; Apr-Aug 11-7 (11-9 wknds during Jul & Aug); Sep, 11-6; Nov 11-4 (wknds only). Visitor Centre: all year except between Xmas & New Year. **Fee:** ✱ Cars & Motorcycles £3, Minibus £6, Coaches £20. Car season ticket £15. **Facilities:** 🅿 ⅙ toilets for disabled shop 🍴

CARDIFF

CARDIFF — Map 03 ST17

CARDIFF CASTLE
Castle St CF10 3RB
➲ (from M4, A48 & A470 follow signs to city centre)
☎ 029 2087 8100
e-mail: cardiffcastle@cardiff.gov.uk
web: www.cardiffcastle.com
Cardiff Castle is situated in the heart of the city. Contained within its mighty walls is a history spanning nearly 2000 years, dating from the coming of the Romans to the Norman Conquest. Discover spectacular interiors on your guided tour, and enjoy magnificent views of the city from the top of the 12th-century Norman keep.
Times: Open all year, daily (ex 25-26 Dec & 1 Jan) including guided tours, Mar-Oct, 9.30-6 (last tour 5); Nov-Feb, 9.30-5.30 (last tour 4). Royal Regiment of Wales Museum closed Tue. Queen's Dragoon Guards Museum closed Fri. **Facilities:** 🅿 (200 yds) ⅙ (access to Castle Green & Museum) toilets for disabled shop ✈ (ex in grounds & guide dogs) 🍴

DYFFRYN GARDENS
St Nicholas CF5 6SU
➲ (A4232 towards Barry, rdbt take 1st exit, exit at junct with A48/A4050. At Culverhouse Cross rdbt take 4th exit A48 signed Cowbridge. Left at lights in St Nicholas village, Dyffryn on right after 1.5m)
☎ 029 2059 3328
e-mail: jehopkins@valeofglamorgan.gov.uk
web: www.dyffryngardens.org.uk
One of Wales' finest Edwardian gardens, the beautiful grounds offer an endless variety of colour and form with many small garden rooms now restored with the aid of a Heritage Lottery fund grant. Additional works are still ongoing and some areas may be subject to closure. Dyffryn Gardens celebrates its centenary with a month long celebration in August 2006.
Times: Open Apr-Sep 10-6; Oct 10-5 **Fee:** ✱ £3.50 (ch & pen £2.50, disabled £2, carers free). Family ticket £7. **Facilities:** 🅿 ⅙ 🍴 ⅙ (wheelchairs for hire, parking, ramps) toilets for disabled shop garden centre 🍴

LLANDAFF CATHEDRAL

Llandaff CF5 2LA

⊃ (W on M4 junct 29 to A48(M), then onto A48 and follow brown signs. E on M4 junct 32 onto A470 towards Cardiff, leave A48 and follow brown signs)

☎ 029 2056 4554

e-mail: office@llandaffcathedral.org.uk

web: www.llandaffcathedral.org.uk

A medieval cathedral begun in the 12th century on the site of an early Christian place of worship. The cathedral was severely damaged during the bombing raids on Cardiff during World War II. The interior is dominated by a modernistic post-war 'Christ in Majesty' sculpture by Epstein. Please visit website for details of events running throughout the year.

Times: Open all year, daily 8-7 (Sun 7-7 & Mon 8.30-7).

Fee: Donations expected. No group bookings on Sun or Holy Days.

Facilities: P (100yds) (parking limited) 🍴 ♿ (wheelchair available) toilets for disabled shop ✕ (ex guide dogs)

MILLENNIUM STADIUM TOURS

Millennium Stadium, Westgate St, Gate 3 CF10 1JA

⊃ (A470 to city centre. Westgate St opposite Castle far end. Turn by Angel Hotel on corner of Westgate Street.)

☎ 029 2082 2228   **2 for 1**

e-mail: mg.bbons@weu.co.uk

In the late 1990s this massive stadium was completed as part of an effort to revitalise Welsh fortunes. It replaced Cardiff Arms Park, and now hosts major music events, exhibitions, and international rugby and soccer matches. Its capacity of around 75,000 and its retractable roof make it unique in Europe. The current home of five controlling bodies; Welsh Rugby, Welsh Football, English Football Association, Football league (English) & British Speedway.

Times: Open Mon-Sat, 10-5; Sun 10-4 **Fee:** £5.50 (ch up to 16 £3, ch under 5 free), concessions £3.50. Party 20+ 15% discount.

Facilities: P (opposite gate 3) 🍴 ♿ (lifts, escalators, disabled parking) toilets for disabled shop ✕ (ex guide dogs)

NATIONAL MUSEUM & GALLERY CARDIFF

Cathays Park CF10 3NP

⊃ (in Civic Centre, 5 mins walk from city centre & 20 mins walk from bus & train station)

☎ 029 2039 7951   **FREE**

e-mail: post@nmgw.ac.uk

web: www.nmgw.ac.uk

This establishment is unique amongst British museums and galleries in its range of art and science displays. 'The Evolution of Wales' exhibition takes visitors on a spectacular 4600-million year journey, tracing the world from beginning of time and the development of Wales. There are displays of Bronze Age gold, early Christian monuments, Celtic treasures, silver, coins and medals, ceramics, fossils and minerals. A significant collection of French Impressionist paintings sits alongside the work of Welsh artists, past and present in the elegant art galleries.

Times: Open all year, Tue-Sun 10-5. Closed Mon (ex BHs) & 24-26 Dec. **Facilities:** P (charged) 🍴 ✕ licensed ♿ (wheelchair available, Tel 029 2057 3509 for access guide) toilets for disabled shop ✕ (ex guide dogs)

TECHNIQUEST

Stuart St CF10 5BW

⊃ (A4232 to Cardiff Bay)

☎ 029 2047 5475   **2 for 1**

e-mail: info@techniquest.org

web: www.techniquest.org

Located in the heart of the Cardiff Bay, there's always something new to explore at this exciting science discovery centre. Journey into space in the planetarium, enjoy an interactive Science Theatre Show or experience one of the 150 hands-on exhibits. Please visit website for details of events running throughout the year.

Times: Open all year, Mon-Fri 9.30-4.30; Sat-Sun & BHs 10.30-5, school hols 9.30-5. Closed Xmas. **Fee:** ✱ £6.75 (ch 5-16 & concessions £4.65). Family ticket £18.50 (2ad+3ch). Friend season ticket £47. Groups 10+ **Facilities:** P (50mtrs) (limited parking for disabled visitors) 🍴 ♿ (lift, hearing loop) toilets for disabled shop ✕ (ex guide dogs)

ST FAGANS   Map 03 ST17

MUSEUM OF WELSH LIFE

CF5 6XB

⊃ (4m W of Cardiff on A4232. From M4 exit at junct 33 and follow brown signs)

☎ 029 2057 3500   **FREE**

e-mail: post@nmgw.ac.uk

web: www.nmgw.ac.uk

A stroll around the indoor galleries and 100 acres of beautiful grounds will give you a fascinating insight into how people in Wales have lived, worked and spent their leisure hours since Celtic times. You can see people practising the traditional means of earning a living, the animals they kept and at certain times of year, the ways in which they celebrated the seasons.

Times: Open all year daily, 10-5. Closed 24-26 Dec.

Facilities: P (charged) 🍴 ✕ licensed ♿ (wheelchairs, motorised buggy-must pre-book) toilets for disabled shop ✕ (ex in grounds if on lead)

TONGWYNLAIS   Map 03 ST18

CASTELL COCH

CF4 7YS

⊃ (A470 to Tongwynlais junct, then B4262 to castle on top of hill)

☎ 029 2081 0101

Castell Coch is Welsh for red castle, an appropriate name for this fairy-tale building with its red sandstone walls and conical towers. The castle was originally built in the 13th century but fell into ruins, and the present castle is a late-19th-century creation. Inside, the castle is decorated in fantasy style.

Times: Open 18 Mar-May & Oct, daily 9.30-5; Jun-Sep, daily 9.30-6; Nov-Mar, Mon-Sat 9.30-4, Sun 11-4. Telephone for Xmas opening times. **Fee:** £3 (ch 5-15, pen & students £2.50). Disabled visitors and assisting companion free. Family ticket (2ad + 3 ch) £8.50. Prices quoted apply until 31/03/06. Party. **Facilities:** P shop ✕ ☺

> Directions are provided by the attractions.

CARMARTHENSHIRE

ABERGWILI   Map 02 SN42

CARMARTHENSHIRE COUNTY MUSEUM
SA31 2JG
➲ (2m E of Carmarthen, just off A40, at Abergwili rdbt)
☎ 01267 228696   **FREE**
e-mail: museums@carmarthenshire.gov.uk
web: www.carmarthenshire.gov.uk/
Housed in the old palace of the Bishop of St David's and set in seven acres of grounds, the museum offers a wide range of local subjects to explore, from geology and prehistory to butter making, Welsh furniture and folk art. Temporary exhibitions are held.
Times: Open all year, Mon-Sat 10-4.30. Closed Xmas-New Year
Facilities: ⓟ 🖰 ㋡ (lift) toilets for disabled shop 🗙 (ex guide dogs)

CARREG CENNEN CASTLE   Map 03 SN61

CARREG CENNEN CASTLE
SA19 6UA
➲ (unclass road from A483 to Trapp village)
☎ 01558 822291
A steep path leads up to the castle, which is spectacularly sited on a limestone crag. It was first built as a stronghold of the native Welsh and then rebuilt in the late 13th century. Most remarkable among the impressive remains is a mysterious passage, cut into the side of the cliff and lit by loopholes. The farm at the site has a rare breeds centre.
Times: Open all year, Apr-Oct, daily 9.30-6.30; Nov-Mar, daily, 9.30-dusk. Telephone for Xmas opening times. **Fee:** £3 (ch 5-15, pen & students £2.50). Disabled visitors and assisting companion free. Family ticket (2ad + 3 ch) £8.50. Prices quoted apply until 31/03/06. Party.
Facilities: ⓟ 🖰 shop 🗙 ㋡ 🍴

DRE-FACH FELINDRE   Map 02 SN33

NATIONAL WOOLLEN MUSEUM
SA44 5UP
➲ (16m W of Carmarthen off A484, 4m E of Newcastle Emlyn)
☎ 01559 370929   **FREE**
web: www.nmgw.ac.uk
The museum is housed in the former Cambrian Mills and has a comprehensive display tracing the evolution of the industry from its beginnings to the present day. Demonstrations of the fleece to fabric process are given on 19th-century textile machinery.
Times: Open Apr-Sep, daily 10-5; Oct-Mar, Tue-Sat 10-5. Closed Xmas.
Facilities: ⓟ 🖰 ㋡ (wheelchair access to ground floor & ample seating) toilets for disabled shop 🗙 (ex guide dogs) 🍴

DRYSLWYN   Map 02 SN52

DRYSLWYN CASTLE
➲ (on B4279)
☎ 029 2050 0200   **FREE**
The ruined 13th-century castle was a stronghold of the native Welsh. It stands on a lofty mound, and was important in the struggles between English and Welsh. It is gradually being uncovered by excavation.
Times: Open - entrance by arrangement with Dryslwyn Farm.
Facilities: ⓟ 🗙 ㋡

KIDWELLY   Map 02 SN40

KIDWELLY CASTLE
SA17 5BQ
➲ (via A484)
☎ 01554 890104
This is an outstanding example of late 13th-century castle design, with its 'walls within walls' defensive system. There were later additions made to the building, the chapel dating from about 1400. Of particular interest are two vast circular ovens.
Times: Open 18 Mar-May & Oct, daily 9.30-5; Jun-Sep, daily 9.30-6; Nov-Mar, Mon-Sat 9.30-4, Sun 11-4. Telephone for Xmas opening times. **Fee:** £2.50 (ch 5-15, pen & students £2). Disabled visitors and assisting companion free. Family ticket (2ad + 3 ch) £7. Prices quoted apply until 31/03/06. Party. **Facilities:** ⓟ ㋡ toilets for disabled shop 🗙 ㋡ 🍴

KIDWELLY INDUSTRIAL MUSEUM
Broadford SA17 4LW
➲ (signed from Kidwelly by-pass & town, stack visible from by-pass)
☎ 01554 891078   **FREE**
Two of the great industries of Wales are represented in this museum: tinplate and coal mining. The original buildings and machinery of the Kidwelly tinplate works, where tinplate was hand made, are now on display to the public. There is also an exhibition of coal mining with pit-head gear and a winding engine, while the more general history of the area is shown in a separate exhibition.
Times: Open Etr, Jun-Sep, BH wknds, Mon-Fri 10-5, Sat-Sun 12-5. Last admission 4. Other times by arrangement for parties only.
Facilities: ⓟ 🖰 ㋡ (ramps on entrances) toilets for disabled shop

LAUGHARNE   Map 02 SN31

DYLAN THOMAS' BOAT HOUSE
Dylans Walk SA33 4SD
➲ (14m SW of Carmarthen)   **2 for 1**
☎ 01994 427420
e-mail: dylanthomas@carmarthenshire.gov.uk
web: www.dylanthomasboathouse.com

The home of Dylan Thomas and his family during the last four turbulent and creative years of his life. The house and its surrounding estuary, town and countryside feature considerably in the poet's work, including his famous 'Under Milk Wood'. The house contains interpretive display, original furniture, bookshop and tearoom. Please telephone for details of events running throughout the year.

continued

Times: Open all year, May-Oct & Etr wknd, daily 10-5.30 (last admission 5); Nov-Apr, daily 10.30-3.30 (last admission 3) **Fee:** ✳ £3 (ch under 7 free, ch over 7 £1, concessions £2). Family and group rates available. **Facilities:** P (200yds) ⬛ (not accessible for wheelchairs) shop ✖ (ex guide dogs) ◗

LAUGHARNE CASTLE
King St SA33 4SA
⮞ (on A4066)
☎ 01994 427906

Newly opened to the public, picturesque Laugharne Castle stands on a low ridge overlooking the wide Taff Estuary. A medieval fortress converted into an Elizabethan mansion, it suffered a civil war siege and later became the backdrop for elaborate Victorian gardens, now recreated. Laugharne Castle has also inspired two modern writers - Richard Hughes and Dylan Thomas.

Times: Open 18 Mar-Sep, daily 10-5. **Fee:** £2.75 (ch 5-15, pen & students £2.25). Disabled visitors and assisting companion free. Family ticket (2ad + 3 ch) £7.75. Prices quoted apply until 31/03/06. Party.
Facilities: P (150mtrs) & toilets for disabled shop ✖ ☺ ◗

LLANARTHNE   Map 02 SN52

MIDDLETON, THE NATIONAL BOTANIC GARDEN OF WALES
Middleton Hall SA32 8HG
⮞ (8m E of Carmarthen on A48, dedicated intersection - signed)
☎ 01558 668768
e-mail: info@gardenofwales.org.uk
web: www.middletongardens.com

Set amongst 568 acres of Parkland in the beautiful Towy Valley in West Wales, just 7 miles from Carmarthen. The Gardens centrepiece is the Great Glasshouse, an amazing tilted glass dome with a six-metre ravine. The Mediterranean landscape enables the visitor to experience the aftermath of an Australian bush fire, pause in an olive grove or wander through Fuchsia collections from Chile. A 220mtr herbaceous board walk forms the spine of the garden and leads to the children's play area and our 360°-surround screen cinema to the Old Stables Courtyard. Here the visitor can view art exhibitions, wander in the gift shop or enjoy a meal in the restaurant. Land train tours will take the visitor around the necklace of lakes, which surround the central garden.

Times: ✳ Open 30 Mar-25 Oct 10-6, 26 Oct-27 Mar 10-4.30
Facilities: P ⬛ ✖ licensed ▥ & (Braille interpretation wheelchairs/scooters shuttle svc) toilets for disabled shop garden centre ✖ (ex guide dogs) ◗

LLANDEILO   Map 03 SN62

DINEFWR PARK
SA19 6RT
⮞ (off A40 Carmarthenshire, on W outskirts of Llandeilo)
☎ 01558 823902
e-mail: dinefwr@nationaltrust.org.uk
web: www.ukindex.co.uk/nationaltrust

At the heart of Welsh history for a thousand years, the Park as we know it today took shape in the years after 1775 when the medieval castle, house, gardens, woods and deer park were integrated into one vast and breathtaking landscape. Access to Church Woods and Dinefwr Castle is through the landscaped park.

Times: Open Mar-Oct, daily (ex Tue & Wed) 11-4.30. (Last admission 30 mins before closing) **Facilities:** P (charged) ⬛ ▥ & toilets for disabled ✖ (ex outer park on lead) ♨ ◗

LLANELLI   Map 02 SN50

NATIONAL WETLAND CENTRE WALES
Penclacwydd, Llwynhendy SA14 9SH
⮞ (3m E of Llanelli, off A484)
☎ 01554 741087
e-mail: info.llanelli@wwt.org.uk
web: www.wwt.org.uk

2 for 1

A wide variety of wild birds, including oystercatchers, redshanks, curlews, little egrets and occasionally ospreys, can be seen here during the right season. The grounds are beautifully landscaped, and include CCTV transmitting pictures of wild birds on the reserve, a wetland craft area and a flock of colourful Caribbean Flamingos. There is also a Discovery Centre and outdoor activities for visitors to take part in. Facilities for the disabled include easy access on level paths, special viewing areas and wheelchair loan.

Times: Open summer 9.30-5; winter 9.30-4.30. Closed 24-25 Dec.
Fee: ✳ £5.50 (ch £3.50, pen £4.50). Family £14.50. **Facilities:** P ⬛ ✖ & toilets for disabled shop ✖ (ex guide/hearing dogs) ◗

LLANGATHEN   Map 02 SN52

ABERGLASNEY GARDENS
SA32 8QH
⮞ (4m W of Llandeilo, follow signs from A40)
☎ 01558 668998
e-mail: info@aberglasney.org.uk
web: www.aberglasney.org

Aberglasney is a 10-acre restoration project, containing a variety of rare and unusual plants, providing interest throughout the seasons. At its heart is a unique and fully

continued

restored Elizabethan/Jacobean cloister and parapet walk.
Special Events: Please telephone for details of events
running throughout the year.
Times: Open all year, Apr-Oct, daily 10-6 (last entry 5); Nov-Mar, daily
10.30-4. Closed 25 Dec **Fee:** ✱ £6 (ch £3, pen £5). Party 10+ £5.50
(ch £3, pen £4.50). **Facilities:** 🅿 ✗ licensed ♿ (most areas
accessible, wheelchairs available, parking) toilets for disabled shop
garden centre ✗ (ex guide dogs) 🖾

LLANSTEFFAN   Map 02 SN31

LLANSTEFFAN CASTLE
➲ (off B4312)
☎ 01267 241756   **FREE**
The ruins of this 11th to 13th-century stronghold stand
majestically on the west side of the Towy estuary.
Times: Open - access throughout the year. **Facilities:** ✗ ⊙

PUMSAINT   Map 03 SN64

DOLAUCOTHI GOLD MINES
SA19 8RR
➲ (on A482, signed both directions)
☎ 01558 650177
e-mail: dolaucothi@nationaltrust.org.uk
web: www.nationaltrust.org.uk
Here is an opportunity to spend a day exploring the gold
mines and to wear a miner's helmet and lamp while touring
the underground workings. The information centre and a
walk along the Miners' Way disclose the secrets of 2,000
years of gold mining. This is the only place in Britain where
the Romans mined gold.
Times: Open end Mar-end Oct, daily 10-5. **Facilities:** 🅿 ▆ 🗎
♿ toilets for disabled shop 🍴 🖾

ABERAERON   Map 02 SN46

LLANERCHAERON
Llanerchaeron, Ciliau Aeron SA48 8DG
➲ (2.5m E of Aberaeron off A482)
☎ 01545 570200
e-mail: llanerchaeron@nationaltrust.org.uk
web: www.nationaltrust.org.uk
Llanerchaeron, a few miles inland from Aberaeron on the
Cardigan Bay coast, is centred round a Regency Villa
designed by John Nash. The self sufficient country estate,
villa, service courtyard, grounds, working organic farm and
outbuildings remain virtually unaltered. The 18th century
estate features; The Walled Garden and farm complex,
mature woodland and ornamental lake, vast parkland and
farmland containing Llanwennog sheep and Welsh Black
Cattle. Produce and plants from the walled gardens are sold
in the visitor building. Please telephone for details of events
running throughout the year.
Times: Open early Apr-late Oct, Wed-Sun & BH Mons 11-5. (Last
admission 1hr before closing). Park open all year dawn to dusk.
Fee: ✱ £5.20 (ch £2.60). Family ticket £12.60 (2ad+2ch). Special group
rates available **Facilities:** 🅿 ▆ 🗎 ♿ (ramp access to villa,
wheelchair, braille guide) toilets for disabled ✗ (except guide dogs) 🍴

ABERYSTWYTH   Map 06 SN58

NATIONAL LIBRARY OF WALES
Penglais SY23 3BU
➲ (Off Penglais Hill, A487 in N area of
Aberystwyth)
☎ 01970 632800
e-mail: holi@llgc.org.uk
web: www.llgc.org.uk
This huge library is one of Britain's six copyright libraries,
and specialises in Welsh and Celtic literature. It has maps,
manuscripts, prints and drawings. There is a programme of
travelling exhibitions. Please telephone for details or check
the website.
Times: Open on selected BHs. Please check details by telephone or on
website before travelling. **Fee:** ✱ Free. Admission to reading rooms
available by readers ticket, two proofs of identity required, one
including address. Free admission to all exhibitions.
Facilities: 🅿 ✗ licensed ♿ (lift) toilets for disabled shop
✗ (ex guide dogs)

CENARTH   Map 02 SN24

THE NATIONAL CORACLE CENTRE
Cenarth Falls SA38 9JL   **2 for 1**
➲ (on A484 between Carmarthen and Cardigan,
centre of Cenarth village, beside bridge and river)
☎ 01239 710980
e-mail: martinfowler.coraclecentre@virgin.net
web: www.coracle-centre.co.uk
Situated by the beautiful Cenarth Falls, this fascinating
museum has a unique collection from all over the world,
including Tibet, India, Iraq, Vietnam, and North America.
Cenarth has long been a centre for coracle fishing, coracle
rides are often available in village during summer holiday.
Look out for the salmon leap by the flour mill.
Times: ✱ Open Etr-Oct, Daily 10.30-5.30. All other times by
appointment. **Fee:** £3 (ch £1, concessions £2.50). Party rates 12+.
Facilities: 🅿 ▆ 🗎 ♿ shop 🖾

EGLWYSFACH   Map 06 SN69

RSPB NATURE RESERVE
Visitor Centre, Cae'r Berllan SY20 8TA
➲ (6m S of Machynlleth on A487 in Eglwys-Fach.
Signed from main road)
☎ 01654 700222
e-mail: ynyshir@rspb.org.uk
web: www.rspb.co.uk
The mixture of different habitats is home to an abundance of
birds and wildlife. The saltmarshes in winter support the
only regular wintering flock of Greenland white-fronted
geese in England and Wales in addition to peregrines, hen
harriers and merlins. The sessile oak woodland is home to
pied flycatchers, wood warblers, redstarts in the summer but
woodpeckers, nut hatches, red kites, sparrow hawks and
buzzards are here all year round. Otters, polecats, 30
butterfly and 15 dragonfly species are also present. Guided
walks and children's activities. Please telephone for details of
events running throughout the year.
Times: Open daily, 9am-9pm (or sunset if earlier). Visitor Centre:
Apr-Oct 9-5 daily; Nov-Mar 10-4 (Wed-Sun) **Fee:** ✱ £3.50 (ch £1,
concessions £2.50) Family £7 RSPB members free. **Facilities:** 🅿 🗎
(Can take car to viewpoint) shop ✗ (ex guide dogs) 🖾

FELINWYNT   Map 02 SN25

FELINWYNT RAINFOREST CENTRE
Rhosmaen SA43 1RT
➲ (from A487 Blaenannerch Airfield turning, onto B4333. Signed 6m N of Cardigan)
☎ 01239 810882 & 810250   **2 for 1**
e-mail: dandjdevereux@btinternet.com
web: www.butterflycentre.co.uk
A chance to wander amongst free-flying exotic butterflies accompanied by the recorded wildlife sounds of the Peruvian Amazon. A waterfall, ponds and streams contribute to a humid tropical atmosphere and provide a habitat for fish and native amphibians. See the exhibition of rainforests of Peru and around the world. Free paper and crayons to borrow for children.
Times: 9 Apr-28 Oct **Fee:** ✱ £3.90 (ch 4-14 £1.75, pen £3.70)
Facilities: 🅿 ⬤ 🍴 ♿ toilets for disabled shop
✖ (ex guide dogs) ⬛

STRATA FLORIDA   Map 03 SN76

STRATA FLORIDA ABBEY
SY25 6BT
➲ (unclassified road from Pontrhydfendigaid, accessed from B4340)
☎ 01974 831261
Little remains of the Cistercian abbey founded in 1164, except the ruined church and cloister. Strata Florida was an important centre of learning in the Middle Ages, and it is believed that the 14th-century poet Dafyd ap Gwilym was buried here.
Times: Open 18 Mar-30 Sep, Wed-Sun & BH Mon 10-5. Monument will be opened and unstaffed with no admission charge at all other times between 10-4. **Fee:** £2.25 (ch 5-15, pen & students £1.75). Disabled visitors and assisting companion free. Family ticket (2ad + 3 ch) £6.25. Prices quoted apply until 31/03/06. Party. **Facilities:** 🅿 ♿ shop
✖ ☺ ⬛

CONWY

BETWS-Y-COED   Map 06 SH75

CONWY VALLEY RAILWAY MUSEUM
Old Goods Yard LL24 0AL
➲ (signed from A5 into Old Church Rd, adjacent to train station)
☎ 01690 710568
The two large museum buildings have displays on both the narrow and standard-gauge railways of North Wales, including railway stock and other memorabilia. There are working model railway layouts, a steam-hauled miniature railway in the grounds, which cover over four acres, and a 15inch-gauge tramway to the woods. The latest addition is the quarter-size steam 'Britannia' loco that is now on display. For children there are mini-dodgems, Postman Pat, school bus and Toby Tram.
Times: Open daily, 10-5.30. Closed Xmas **Fee:** ✱ £1.50 (ch & pen 80p). Family ticket £4.00. Steam train ride £1.50. Tram ride £1.00.
Facilities: 🅿 ⬤ ♿ (ramps & clearances for wheelchairs) toilets for disabled shop ⬛

> Directions are provided by the attractions.

CERRIGYDRUDION   Map 06 SH94

LLYN BRENIG VISITOR CENTRE
LL21 9TT
➲ (on B4501 between Denbigh & Cerrigydrudion)
☎ 01490 420463   **FREE**
e-mail: llyn.brenig@dwrcymru.com
The 1800-acre estate has a unique archaeological trail and round-the-lake walk of 10 miles. A hide is available and disabled anglers are catered for with a specially adapted fishing boat and an annual open day. The centre has an exhibition on archaeology, history and conservation and an audio-visual programme.
Times: Open mid Mar-Oct, daily 9-5. **Facilities:** 🅿 (charged) ⬤ ♿ (boats for disabled & fishing open days) toilets for disabled shop ✖ (ex guide dogs)

COLWYN BAY   Map 06 SH87

WELSH MOUNTAIN ZOO
Old Highway LL28 5UY
➲ (A55 junct 20 signed Rhos-on-Sea. Zoo signed)
☎ 01492 532938
e-mail: info@welshmountainzoo.org
web: www.welshmountainzoo.org
The zoo and gardens are set in a 37-acre estate overlooking Colwyn Bay, with magnificent panoramic views of the coast and mountains. The animals are housed in natural settings, interspersed with gardens and woodland. The traditional range of zoo animals can be seen, from lions and elephants to penguins and parrots, and the zoo also attracts a variety of local wildlife. There are falconry displays during the summer months, and Californian sealions can be seen performing tricks at feeding time. Visit the Chimpanzee World complex, featuring the unique Chimp Encounter, and a South American small monkey breeding centre.
Times: Open all year, Mar-Oct, daily 9.30-6; Nov-Feb, daily 9.30-5. Closed 25 Dec. **Fee:** £7.50 (ch & students £5.35, pen £6.50). Family ticket (2ad+2ch) £22.65. **Facilities:** 🅿 ⬤ ✖ licensed 🍴 ♿ toilets for disabled shop ✖ ⬛

CONWY   Map 06 SH77

ABERCONWY HOUSE
LL32 8AY
➲ (at junct of Castle St & High St)
☎ 01492 592246   **2 for 1**
e-mail: kenneth.grover@nationaltrust.org.uk
This house dates from the 14th century; it is the only medieval merchant's house in Conwy to have survived the centuries of turbulence, fire and pillage in this frontier town. Furnished rooms and an audio-visual presentation show daily life in the house at different periods in its history. The 2-for-1 is valid only during normal visiting hours and cannot be used for any ticketed events.
Times: Open 19 Mar-30 Oct, Wed-Mon 11-5. (Last admission 30 mins before closing). **Fee:** ✱ £2.60 Joint £3.30 Party adult £2.10 & ch £1 (ch £1.20). Family ticket £6. Party £6.50. **Facilities:** 🅿 (100yds & 0.5 mile) shop ✖ (ex guide dogs) ⬛

CONWY CASTLE
LL32 8AY
➲ (via A55 or B5106)
☎ 01492 592358
The castle is a magnificent fortress, built 1283-7 by Edward I. There is an exhibition on castle chapels on the ground floor of the Chapel Tower. The castle forms part of the same

continued

defensive system as the extensive town walls, which are among the most complete in Europe.
Times: Open 18 Mar-May & Oct, daily 9.30-5; Jun-Sep, daily 9.30-6; Nov-Mar, Mon-Sat 9.30-4, Sun 11-4. Telephone for Xmas opening times. **Fee:** £4 (ch 5-15, pen & students £3.50). Disabled visitors and assisting companion free. Family ticket £11.50. Joint ticket for both monuments £6.50 (concessions £5.50). Family ticket £18.50. Prices quoted apply until 31/03/06. Party. **Facilities:** 🅿 ♿ toilets for disabled shop ✈ ⊕ 🍴

CONWY SUSPENSION BRIDGE
LL32 8LD
➲ (adjacent to Conwy Castle)
☎ 01492 573282 **2 for 1**
e-mail: kenneth.grover@nationaltrust.org.uk
Designed by Thomas Telford, one of the greatest engineers of the late 18th and early 19th century, this was the first bridge to span the river at Conwy. The bridge has been restored and the toll house furnished as it would have been a century ago.
Times: Open daily 19 Mar-Oct 10 - 5 **Fee:** ✱ £1.40 (ch 70p) Joint £3.30 Family £3.50. **Facilities:** 🅿 100 yds 🍴 ♿ (except house) 🐾

PLAS MAWR
High St LL32 8DE
☎ 01492 580167
Plas Mawr is an excellent example of an Elizabethan townhouse. Built by Robert Wynn between 1576 and 1585, the interior remains almost unaltered and displays decorated plaster ceilings and wooden screens.
Times: Open 18 Mar-May 9:30 am - 5pm daily, Jun-Aug 9:30 - 6pm daily, Sept-Sept 9.30am - 5pm daily, Oct-Oct 9:30am - 4pm daily, site closed on Mondays (excl. bank holidays), site closed completely 1 Nov-31 Mar 2006 **Fee:** £4.50 (ch 5-15, pen & students £3.50). Disabled visitors and assisting companion free. Family ticket (2ad + 3 ch) £12.50. Joint ticket for both monuments £6.50 (ch 5-15, pen & students £5.50). Family (2ad + 3ch) £18.50. Prices quoted apply until 31/03/06. Party. **Facilities:** shop ⊕ 🍴

SMALLEST HOUSE
The Quay LL32 8BB
➲ (leave A55 at Conwy sign, through town, at bottom of High St for the quay, turn left)
☎ 01492 593484
The *Guinness Book of Records* lists this as the smallest house in Britain. Just 6ft wide by 10ft high, it is furnished in the style of a mid-Victorian Welsh cottage.
Times: Open Apr-May & Oct 10-5; Jun & Sep, 10-6, first half Jul 10-6 rest of Jul & Aug 10-9 **Fee:** ✱ 75p (ch under 16 50p, under 5 free). **Facilities:** 🅿 (100yds) 🍴 ♿ shop

DOLWYDDELAN CASTLE
LL25 0EJ
➲ (on A470 Blaenau Ffestiniog to Betws-y-Coed)
☎ 01690 750366
The castle is reputed to be the birthplace of Llywelyn the Great. It was captured in 1283 by Edward I, who immediately began strengthening it for his own purposes. A restored keep of around 1200, and a 13th-century curtain wall can be seen. An exhibition on the castles of the Welsh Princes is located in the keep.
Times: Open all year, Apr-Sep, Mon-Sat 10-6 & Sun 11-4; Oct-Mar, Mon-Sat 10-4, Sun 11-4. Telephone for Xmas opening times. **Fee:** £2 (ch 5-15, pen & students £1.50). Disabled visitors and assisting companion free. Family ticket (2ad + 3 ch) £5.50. Prices quoted apply until 31/03/06. Party. **Facilities:** 🅿 ✈ ⊕ 🍴

RSPB NATURE RESERVE
LL31 9XZ
➲ (off A55, signed)
☎ 01492 584091
e-mail: alan.davies@rspb.org.uk
web: www.rspb.org.uk
The visitor centre has a viewing area which overlooks the estuary and Conwy Castle, and there's a nature trail and four hides for viewing lapwings and shelduck amongst many others. Phone for details of events.
Times: Open all year, daily, 10-5(or dusk whichever is earlier). Closed 25 Dec **Fee:** £2.50 (ch £1, concessions £1.50), Family £5
Facilities: 🅿 🍴 ♿ (use of wheelchair) toilets for disabled shop ✈ (ex guide dogs) 🍴

GWYDYR UCHAF CHAPEL
➲ (0.5m SW off B5106) **FREE**
☎ 01492 640578
Built in the 17th century by Sir John Wynn of Gwydir Castle, the chapel is noted for its painted ceiling and wonderfully varied woodwork.
Times: Open any reasonable time. **Facilities:** 🅿 ✈ 🚌 ⊕

TY MAWR WYBRNANT
LL25 0HJ
➲ (From A5 3m S of Betws-y-Coed take B4406 to Penmachno. House is 2.5m NW of Penmachno by forest road)
☎ 01690 760213
Situated in the beautiful, secluded Wybrnant Valley, Ty Mawr was the birthplace of Bishop William Morgan (1545-1604), the first translator of the entire Bible into Welsh. The house has been restored to its probable 16th-17th century appearance. The Wybrnant Nature Trail, a short walk, covers approximately one mile.
Times: ✱ Open 30 Mar-Sep, Thu-Sun & BH Mon 12-5; Oct, Thu, Fri & Sun 12-4. (Last admission 30 mins before closing).
Facilities: 🅿 ✈ (ex in grounds) 🚌(33 seats minibus access only) 🐾

BODNANT GARDEN
LL28 5RE
➲ (8m S of Llandudno & Colwyn Bay off A470)
☎ 01492 650460
e-mail: office@bodnantgarden.co.uk
web: www.bodnantgarden.co.uk
Set above the River Conwy with beautiful views over Snowdonia, these gardens are a delight. Five Italian style terraces were constructed below the house - on the lowest terrace is a canal pool with an open-air yew hedge stage and a reconstructed Pin Mill. The garden is renowned for its collections of magnolias, camellias, rhododendrons and azaleas and the famous Laburnum Arch. Contact for details of open-air theatre.
Times: Open mid Mar-6 Nov, daily 10-5 (last admission half hour before closing) **Fee:** ✱ £5.50 (ch £2.75) Party of 20+ £5
Facilities: 🅿 💷 🍴 ♿ (ramps to gardens, wheelchairs & Braille guides) toilets for disabled shop garden centre large plantaria and sales point ✈ (ex guide dogs) 🐾 🍴

TREFRIW Map 06 SH76

TREFRIW WOOLLEN MILLS
LL27 0NQ
➲ (on B5106 in centre of Trefriw, 5m N of Betws-y-Coed)
☎ 01492 640462   **FREE**
e-mail: info@t-w-m.co.uk
web: www.t-w-m.co.uk

Established in 1859, the mill is situated beside the fast-flowing Afon Crafnant, which drives two hydro-electric turbines to power the looms. All the machinery of woollen manufacture can be seen here: blending, carding, spinning, dyeing, warping and weaving. In the Weaver's Garden, there are plants traditionally used in the textile industry, mainly for dyeing. Hand-spinning demonstrations.
Times: Mill Museum open Etr-Oct, Mon-Fri 10-1 & 2-5. Weaving demonstrations & turbine house: open all year, Mon-Fri 10-1 & 2-5. Handspinning & weaver's garden Jun-Sep Tue-Thu Jul-Aug Mon-Fri 10-5
Facilities: P (35yds) ⬛ 🍴 ♿ (access to shop, cafe, weaving & turbine house) shop 🐾 (ex in grounds on lead) 🎫

DENBIGHSHIRE

BODELWYDDAN Map 06 SJ07

BODELWYDDAN CASTLE
LL18 5YA
➲ (just off A55, near St Asaph, follow brown signs)
☎ 01745 584060
e-mail: enquiries@bodelwyddan-castle.co.uk
web: www.bodelwyddan-castle.co.uk

Bodelwyddan Castle houses over 100 portraits from the National Portrait Gallery's 19th-century collection. The portraits hang in beautifully refurbished rooms and are complemented by sculpture and period furnishings. Interactive displays show how portraits were produced and used in the Victorian era. The Castle Gallery hosts a programme of temporary exhibitions and events. The castle is set within 200 acres of woodland.
Times: ✳ Open Apr-Sep, daily 10.30-5. Oct-Apr, 10.30-4. Closed Mon & Fri **Facilities:** P ⬛ 🍴 ♿ (lift to first floor, Braille & audio guides) toilets for disabled shop 🐾 (ex guide dogs) 🎫

CORWEN Map 06 SJ04

EWE-PHORIA SHEEPDOG CENTRE
Glanrafon, Llangwm LL21 0PE
➲ (off A5 to Llangwm, follow signs)
☎ 01490 460369
e-mail: info@ewe-phoria.co.uk
web: www.ewe-phoria.co.uk

Ewe-Phoria is an Agri-Theatre and Sheepdog Centre that details the life and work of the shepherd on a traditional Welsh farm. The Agri-Theatre has unusual living displays of sheep with accompanying lectures on their history and breed, while outside sheepdog handlers put their dogs through their paces.
Times: ✳ Open Etr-end Oct, Tue-Fri & Sun. Closed Sat & Mon ex BHs
Fees: £4.50 (ch £3.20, concessions £4). **Facilities:** P ⬛ ✗ licensed ♿ toilets for disabled shop 🐾 (ex guide dogs) 🎫

PEN-Y-BRYN FARM PARK
LL21 9PB
➲ (off A5 onto B5105. 5m from Cerrigydrudion)
☎ 01490 420244 &
e-mail: islwynhawkeye@hotmail.co.uk
web: www.pybfarmpark.co.uk

Proudly catering to all ages, Pen-y-Bryn Park has a petting zoo, falconry, and 'Solo', its very own llama.
Times: Open Etr-Sep, Tue-Sun & BHs, 10-5 **Fee:** ✳ £3.25 (ch, pen £2.75) Family ticket £13.25 **Facilities:** P ⬛ ♿ toilets for disabled shop garden centre (on lead)

RUG CHAPEL
Rug LL21 9BT
☎ 01490 412025

Rug Chapel was built in 1637 for Colonel William Salusbury, famous Civil War defender of Denbigh Castle. A rare, little altered example of a 17th-century private chapel, it reflects the Colonel's High Church religious views. Prettily set in a wooded landscape, the chapel's modest exterior gives little hint of the interior where local artists and carvers were given a free reign, with some spectacular results.
Times: Open 18 Mar-30 Sep, daily 10-5. Access to Llangar is arranged daily at 2pm through Custodian at Rug Chapel, telephone 01490 412025 for details. Both monuments closed Mon & Tue (ex BH wknds).
Fee: ✳ £2.50 (ch 5-15, pen & students £2). Disabled visitors and assisting companion free. Family ticket (2ad + 3 ch) £7. Prices quoted apply until 31/03/06. Party. **Facilities:** P ♿ toilets for disabled shop 🐾 ♿ 🎫

DENBIGH Map 06 SJ06

DENBIGH CASTLE
➲ (via A525, A543 & B5382)
☎ 01745 813385

The castle was begun by Henry de Lacy in 1282 and has an inspiring and impressive gatehouse, with a trio of towers and a superb archway, which is surmounted by a figure believed to be that of Edward I.
Times: Open 25 Mar-Sep, Mon-Fri 10-5.30, Sat & Sun 9.30-5.30. (Monument open and unstaffed with no admission charge at all other times). Telephone for Xmas opening hours. **Fee:** £2.50 (ch 5-15, pen & students £2). Disabled visitors and assisting companion free. Family ticket (2ad + 3 ch) £7. Prices quoted apply until 31/03/06. Party.
Facilities: P ♿ shop 🐾 ♿ 🎫

LLANGOLLEN Map 07 SJ24

HORSE DRAWN BOATS CENTRE
The Wharf, Wharf Hill LL20 8TA
➲ (A5 onto Llangollen High St, across river bridge to T-junct. Wharf opposite)
☎ 01978 860702 & 01691 690322
e-mail: sue@horsedrawnboats.co.uk
web: www.horsedrawnboats.co.uk
Take a horsedrawn boat trip along the beautiful Vale of Llangollen. Visit the canal museum, inside the motor museum, approx 1m along the towpath from the wharf, which illustrates the heyday of canals in Britain. The displays include working and static models, photographs, murals and slides. There is also a narrowboat trip that crosses Pontcysyllte Aqueduct, the largest navigable aqueduct in the world. Full bar on board, commentary throughout.
Times: Open Etr-end Oct, daily 10-5. May be closed wkdays in Oct except school hols **Fee:** ✱ Horse Drawn Boat Trip from £4.50 (ch £2.50). Family ticket £12. Narrowboat Trip £8.50 (ch £6.50). **Facilities:** P (400yds) 💭 🗊 & (alighting/pick-up point available) toilets for disabled shop ⌗

LLANGOLLEN RAILWAY
Abbey Rd LL20 8SN
➲ (Llangollen Station - off A5 at Llangollen traffic lights onto A539, cross river bridge. Station on left at T-junct. Carrog Station - from A5 at Llidiart-y-Parc take B5437, station on right downhill after crossing railway bridge)
☎ 01978 860979 & 860951(timetable)
e-mail: office@llangollen-railway.co.uk
web: www.llangollen-railway.co.uk

Heritage Railway featuring steam and classic diesel services along the picturesque Dee Valley. The journey consists of a 15-mile roundtrip between Llangollen and Carrog. A special coach for the disabled is available on some services. Please contact for more information.
Times: Open Station wknds, reduced services off peak, daily services Apr-Oct. Principally steam hauled, diesel trains please refer to timetable for off peak services. **Facilities:** P (400yds) (free parking at Carrog Station) 💭 🗊 & (special coach for disabled on some trains, notice required) toilets for disabled shop (at Llangollen only) ⌗

PLAS NEWYDD
Hill St LL20 8AW
➲ (follow brown heritage signs from A5)
☎ 01978 861314
e-mail: rose.mcmahon@denbighshire.gov.uk
The 'Ladies of Llangollen', Lady Eleanor Butler and Sarah Ponsonby, lived here from 1780 to 1831. The original stained-glass windows, carved panels, and domestic miscellany of two lives are exhibited along with prints, pictures and letters.
Times: ✱ Open Apr-Oct, daily, 10-5. **Facilities:** P & toilets for disabled ✗ (ex guide dogs or in grounds)

VALLE CRUCIS ABBEY
LL29 8DD
➲ (on B5103, off A5 W of Llangollen)
☎ 01978 860326
Set in a deep, narrow valley, the abbey was founded for the Cistercians in 1201 by Madog ap Gruffydd. Substantial remains of the church can be seen, and some beautifully carved grave slabs have been found. There is a small exhibition on the Cistercian monks and the abbey.
Times: Open 18 Mar-30 Sep, daily 10-5. Monument open and unstaffed with no admission charge at all other times between 10-4. Telephone for Xmas opening times. **Fee:** £2 (ch 5-15, pen & students £1.50). Disabled visitors and assisting companion free. Family ticket (2ad + 3 ch) £5.50. Prices quoted apply until 31/03/06. Party. **Facilities:** P & shop ✗ ☺ ⌗

RHUDDLAN Map 06 SJ07

RHUDDLAN CASTLE
LL18 5AD
☎ 01745 590777
The castle was begun by Edward I in 1277, on a simple 'diamond' plan with round towers linked by sections of 9ft thick curtain wall. The moat was linked to a deep-water canal, allowing Edward's ships to sail from the sea right up to the castle.
Times: Open 18 Mar-30 Sept, daily 10-5. **Fee:** £2.75 (ch 5-15, pen & students £2). Disabled visitors and assisting companion free. Family ticket (2ad + 3 ch) £7.75. Prices quoted apply until 31/03/06. Party. **Facilities:** P & shop ✗ ☺ ⌗

FLINTSHIRE

EWLOE Map 07 SJ36

EWLOE CASTLE FREE
➲ (1m NW of village on B5125)
Standing in Ewloe Wood are the remains of Ewloe Castle. It was a native Welsh castle, and Henry II was defeated nearby in 1157. Part of the Welsh Tower in the upper ward still stands to its original height, and there is a well in the lower ward. Remnants of walls and another tower can also be seen.
Times: Open at all times. **Facilities:** ✗ ☺

> If an attraction name appears in *italics*, details have not been confirmed for 2006.

FLINT   Map 07 SJ27

FLINT CASTLE
CH6 5PH
➲ (NE side of Flint)
☎ 01352 733078   **FREE**

The castle was started by Edward I in 1277 and overlooks the River Dee. It is exceptional for its great tower, or Donjon, which is separated by a moat. Other buildings would have stood in the inner bailey, of which parts of the walls and corner towers remain.

Times: Open at all times. **Facilities:** 🅿 ✈ ♿

HOLYWELL   Map 07 SJ17

BASINGWERK ABBEY
Greenfield Valley Heritage Pk, Greenfield CH8 7GH
➲ (just S of A458)
☎ 01352 714172   **FREE**

The abbey was founded around 1131 by Ranulf de Gernon, Earl of Chester. The first stone church dates from the beginning of the 13th century. The last abbot surrendered the house to the crown in 1536. The Abbey is close to the Heritage Park Visitor Centre and access to the Museum and Farm Complex at Greenfield Valley.

Times: Open all year, daily 9-6. **Facilities:** 🅿 ✈ ♿ (disabled facilities in Heritage Park) toilets for disabled shop ✈ ♿

GREENFIELD VALLEY HERITAGE PARK
Greenfield Rd CH8 7GH
☎ 01352 714172
e-mail: info@greenfieldvalley.com
web: www.greenfieldvalley.com

This fascinating park covers one and a half miles of woodlands, reservoirs, ancient monuments and industrial history. Among the multitude of sights are a footpath that was once a railway line, the remnants of a number of mills relating to the copper industry, an environment centre, the shrine of St Winefride's Well, and Basingwerk Abbey.

Times: ✱ Park open all year. Museum & farm Apr-Oct, 10-4.30.
Facilities: 🅿 💻 📱 ♿ (ramps to enter buildings) toilets for disabled shop

GWYNEDD

BANGOR   Map 06 SH57

PENRHYN CASTLE
LL57 4HN
➲ (1m E of Bangor, off A5122 at Llandegai)
☎ 01248 353084
e-mail: penrhyncastle@nationaltrust.org.uk
web: www.nationaltrust.org.uk

A massive 19th-century castle built on the profits of Jamaican sugar and Welsh slate, crammed with fascinating artefacts such as a one-ton slate bed made for Queen Victoria and a grand staircase that took ten years to build. Also houses a doll museum, two railway museums and one of the finest collections of Old Master paintings in Wales. Regular programme of events throughout the season.

Times: Open 23 Mar-Oct, daily (ex Tue) Castle 12-5. Grounds and stableblock exhibitions 11-5 (Jul & Aug 10-5.30). (Last admission 4.30). Last audio tour 4. **Fee:** All inclusive ticket: £7 (ch £3.50). Family ticket £17.50. Party 15+ £5.50 each. Grounds & stableblock only £5 (ch £2.50). **Facilities:** 🅿 💻 ✈ licensed 📱 ♿ (wheelchairs & golf buggies pre bookable) toilets for disabled shop 🐕

BEDDGELERT   Map 06 SH54

THE RED DRAGON HERITAGE CENTRE
LL55 4NE
➲ (1m E of Beddgelert on A498. Turn off A5 from Llangollen left at Capel Curig onto A498)
☎ 01766 510100 & 510101
e-mail: sygunmine@hotmail.com
web: www.syguncoppermine.co.uk

Discover the very site where the Red Dragon of Wales conquered the White Dragon of England. Enter the ancient holy city of Dinas Emrys in the heart of Snowdonia, and uncover the mysteries and secrets of the legendary Merlin in this authentic Celtic village. Also learn about the history of the Celts, find out how they lived, see the blacksmith's forge, the potter's kiln, try the weaving loom, and search for metal.

Times: Open Apr-Oct & School Holidays, daily 10-5 **Fee:** ✱ £7.95 (ch £5.95, pen £6.95) Group rates available **Facilities:** 🅿 💻 📱 ♿ toilets for disabled shop 🐕

SYGUN COPPER MINE
LL55 4NE
➲ (1m E of Beddgelert on A498)
☎ 01766 510100 & 01766 510101
e-mail: sygunmine@aol.com   **2 for 1**
web: www.syguncoppermine.co.uk

Spectacular audio-visual underground experience where visitors can explore the workings of this 19th-century coppermine and see the magnificent stalactite and stalagmite formations. Other activities include archery, panning for gold, metal detecting and coin making. Marvel at the fantastic coin collection from Julius Caesar to Queen Elizabeth II, and visit the Time-Line Museum with Bronze Age and Roman artefacts.

Times: Open all year, 10-5 **Fee:** ✱ £7.95 (ch £5.95, pen £6.95)
Facilities: 🅿 💻 📱 ♿ (wide access) toilets for disabled shop 🐕

BLAENAU FFESTINIOG   Map 06 SH74

HYDRO CENTRE FFESTINIOG
Ffestiniog Hydro Centre, First Hydro Company, Tan-Y-Grisiau LL41 3TP
➲ (off A496)
☎ 01766 830465
e-mail: hydrocentre@edisonmission.com
web: www.fhc.co.uk

The scheme was the first hydroelectric pumped storage scheme, and was opened by Her Majesty the Queen in 1963. Water is released from an upper dam, through turbines, to

continued

generate electricity when needed, and then pumped back up when demand is low. Guided tours are available, and the Hydro Centre has a café, gift shop and picnic area.
Times: ✱ Open Etr-Oct 10-4.30. **Facilities:** 🅿 💻 📶 shop ✗ (ex guide dogs)

LLECHWEDD SLATE CAVERNS
LL41 3NB
➲ (beside A470, 1m from Blaenau Ffestiniog)
☎ 01766 830306
e-mail: **quarrytours@aol.com**
web: **www.llechwedd-slate-caverns.co.uk**

The Miners' Underground Tramway carries visitors into areas where early conditions have been recreated, while the Deep Mine is reached by an incline railway and has an unusual audio-visual presentation. Free surface attractions include several exhibitions and museums, slate mill and the Victorian village which has Victorian shops, bank, Miners Arms pub, lock-up and working smithy.
Times: Open all year, daily from 10. Last tour 5.15 (Oct-Feb 4.15). Closed 25-26 Dec & 1 Jan **Facilities:** 🅿 💻 ✗ licensed 📶 ♿ toilets for disabled shop (also Victorian shops in the Village) ✗ (ex on surface) 🟥

CAERNARFON   Map 06 SH46

CAERNARFON CASTLE
LL55 2AY
☎ 01286 677617
Edward I began building the castle and extensive town walls in 1283 after defeating the last independent ruler of Wales. Completed in 1328, it has unusual polygonal towers, notably the 10-sided Eagle Tower. There is a theory that these features were copied from the walls of Constantinople, to reflect a tradition that Constantine was born nearby. Edward I's son and heir was born and presented to the Welsh people here, setting a precedent that was followed in 1969, when Prince Charles was invested as Prince of Wales.
Times: Open 18 Mar-May & Oct, daily 9.30-5; Jun-Sep, daily 9.30-6; Nov-Mar, Mon-Sat 9.30-4, Sun 11-4. Telephone for Xmas opening times. **Fee:** £4.75 (ch 5-15, pen & students £3.75). Disabled visitors and assisting companion free. Family ticket (2ad + 3 ch) £13.25. Prices quoted apply until 31/03/06. Party. **Facilities:** 🅿 shop ✗ 💠 🟥

SEGONTIUM ROMAN MUSEUM
Beddgelert Rd LL55 2LN
➲ (on A4085 to Beddgelert approx 1m from Caernarfon)
☎ 01286 675625   [FREE]
e-mail: **info@segontium.org.uk**
web: **www.segontium.org.uk**
Segontium Roman Museum tells the story of the conquest and occupation of Wales by the Romans and displays the finds from the auxiliary fort of Segontium, one of the most famous in Britain. You can combine a visit to the museum with exploration of the site of the Roman Fort, which is in the care of Cadw: Welsh Historic Monuments. The exciting discoveries displayed at the museum vividly portray the daily life of the soldiers stationed in this remote outpost of the Roman Empire.
Times: ✱ Open Tue-Sun 12.30-4. Closed Mon except BH
Facilities: 🅿 ✗ (ex guide dogs) 🟥

WELSH HIGHLAND RAILWAY
St. Helen's Rd LL55 2YD
➲ (SW of Caernarfon Castle beside harbour. Follow brown signs)
☎ 01286 677018 & 01766 516000
e-mail: **enquiries@festrail.co.uk**
web: **www.festrail.co.uk**

A Millennium funded project to restore the old railway line from Caernarfon to Porthmadog. Experience the stunning scenery of Snowdonia National Park as the narrow gauge, steam and diesel trains travel between Caernarfon and Rhyd Ddu at the foot of Snowdon.
Times: Open Etr-Oct, daily except Mon & Fri in low season, limited service in Winter **Fee:** ✱ £16 adult return **Facilities:** 🅿 (charged) 💻 ♿ (prior booking advisable) toilets for disabled shop 🟥

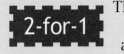

This symbol indicates attractions which have chosen to participate in our 2-for-1 voucher scheme

Directions are provided by the attractions.

CRICCIETH   Map 06 SH43
CRICCIETH CASTLE
LL52 0DP
➲ (off A497)
☎ 01766 522227
The castle dates from the 13th century and was taken and destroyed by Owain Glyndwr in 1404. Evidence of a fierce fire can still be seen. The gatehouse leading to the inner ward remains impressive, and parts of the walls are well preserved. **Times:** Open 18 Mar-May & Oct, daily 10-5; Jun-Sep, daily 10-6; Nov-Mar, Mon-Sat 9:30-4 Sun 11-4 (Monument open and unstaffed with no admission charge at all other times). Telephone for Xmas opening times. **Fee:** £2.90 (ch 5-15, pen & students £2.40). Disabled visitors and assisting companion free. Family ticket (2ad + 3 ch) £8.20. Prices quoted apply until 31/03/06. Party. **Facilities:** 🅿 shop ✖ ☺ 🍴

CYMER ABBEY   Map 06 SH71
CYMER ABBEY
➲ (2m NW of Dolgellau on A494)
☎ 01341 422854
The abbey was built for the Cistercians in the 13th century. It was never very large, and does not seem to have been finished. The church is the best-preserved building, with ranges of windows and arcades still to be seen. The other buildings have been plundered for stone, but low outlines remain. **Times:** Open all year, early Apr-Oct, daily 9.30-6; Nov-Mar, daily 9.30-4. Closed 24-26 Dec & 1 Jan **Facilities:** 🅿 ♿ ✖ ☺ 🍴

FAIRBOURNE   Map 06 SH61
FAIRBOURNE RAILWAY
Beach Rd LL38 2PZ
➲ (on A493 follow signs for Fairbourne, main terminus is just past level crossing on left)
☎ 01341 250362
e-mail: enquiries@fairbourne-railway.co.uk
web: www.fairbourne-railway.co.uk
One of the most unusual of Wales's 'little trains'; built in 1890 as a horse-drawn railway to carry building materials it was later converted to steam, and now covers two-and-a-half miles. Its route passes one of the loveliest beaches in Wales, with views of the beautiful Mawddach Estuary. **Times:** ✱ Open early/mid Apr-mid Sep, times vary according to season and events. Trains will run during Oct half term holiday and Santa Specials at Xmas. **Facilities:** 🅿 🍺 shop 🍴

GROESLON   Map 06 SH45
INIGO JONES SLATEWORKS
LL54 7UE
➲ (on A487, 6m S of Caernarfon towards Porthmadog)
☎ 01286 830242   2 for 1
e-mail: slate@inigojones.co.uk
web: www.inigojones.co.uk
Inigo Jones was established in 1861 primarily to make school writing slates. Today the company uses the same material to make architectural, monumental and craft products. A self-guided audio/video tour takes visitors round the slate workshops, and displays the various processes used in the extraction and working of Welsh slate. **Times:** Open all year, daily 9-5. Closed 25-26 Dec & 1 Jan. **Fee:** ✱ £4 (ch & pen £3.50) **Facilities:** 🅿 🍺 🍴 ♿ toilets for disabled shop ✖ (ex guide dogs) 🍴

HARLECH   Map 06 SH53
HARLECH CASTLE
LL46 2YH
➲ (from A496)
☎ 01766 780552
Harlech Castle was built in 1283-81 by Edward I, with a sheer drop to the sea on one side. Owain Glyndwr starved the castle into submission in 1404 and made it his court and campaigning base. Later, the defence of the castle in the Wars of the Roses inspired the song Men of Harlech. Today the sea has slipped away, and the castle's great walls and round towers stand above the dunes. **Times:** Open 18 Mar-May & Oct, daily 9.30-5; Jun-Sep, daily 9.30-6; Nov-Mar, Mon-Sat 9.30-4, Sun 11-4. Telephone for Xmas opening times. **Fee:** £3 (ch 5-15, pen & students £2). Disabled visitors and assisting companion free. Family ticket (2ad + 3 ch) £8.50. Prices quoted apply until 31/03/06. Party. **Facilities:** 🅿 (disabled spaces in car park) shop ✖ ☺ 🍴

LLANBERIS   Map 06 SH56
DOLBADARN CASTLE
LL55 4UD
➲ (A4086)   FREE
Built by Llywelyn the Great in the early 13th century, this Welsh castle overlooks Llyn Padarn in the Llanberis Pass. **Times:** Open any reasonable time. **Facilities:** 🅿 ✖ ☺ 🍴

LLANBERIS LAKE RAILWAY
Padarn Country Park LL55 4TY
➲ (off A4086 at Llanberis)
☎ 01286 870549
e-mail: info@lake-railway.co.uk
web: www.lake-railway.co.uk
Steam locomotives dating from 1889 to 1948 carry passengers on a five-mile return journey along the shore of Padarn Lake. The terminal station is adjacent to the Welsh Slate Museum, in the Padarn Country Park. The railway was formerly used to carry slate. **Times:** Open Etr-late Oct. Trains run frequently Sun-Fri (Sat in Jul & Aug), 11-4.30 in peak season. Send for free timetable. **Fee:** ✱ £6 (ch £4). Family ticket available. Reduced rate for groups. **Facilities:** 🅿 (charged) 🍺 🍴 ♿ (disabled carriage available) toilets for disabled shop (on trains, not in Cafe) 🍴

SNOWDON MOUNTAIN RAILWAY
LL55 4TY
➲ (on A4086, Caernarfon to Capel Curig road. 7.5m from Caernarfon)
☎ 0870 4580033
e-mail: info@snowdonrailway.co.uk
web: www.snowdonrailway.co.uk
The journey of just over four-and-a-half miles takes passengers more than 3,000ft up to the summit of Snowdon; breathtaking views include, on a clear day, the Isle of Man and the Wicklow Mountains in Ireland. The round trip to the summit and back takes two and a half hours including a half hour at the summit. **Times:** Open 15 Mar-5 Nov, daily from 9 (weather permitting). **Fee:** ✱ Return £20 (ch £14). Early bird discount on 9am train, pre-booking only **Facilities:** 🅿 (charged) 🍺 ♿ (some carriages suitable for wheelchairs - must notify) toilets for disabled shop ✖ (ex guide dogs) 🍴

WELSH SLATE MUSEUM
Gilfach Ddu, Padarn Country Park LL55 4TY
➲ (0.25m off A4086. Museum within Padarn
Country Park)
☎ 01286 870630   **FREE**
e-mail: slate@nmgw.ac.uk
web: www.nmgw.ac.uk
Set among the towering quarries at Llanberis, the Welsh
Slate Museum is a living, working site located in the original
workshops of Dinorwig Quarry, which once employed 15,000
men and boys. You can see the foundry, smithy, workshops
and mess room which make up the old quarry, and view
original machinery, much of which is still in working order.
Times: Open Etr-Oct, daily 10-5; Nov-Etr, Sun-Fri 10-4.
Facilities: 🅿 (charged) 🍽 ♿ (all parts accessible except patten loft)
toilets for disabled shop ✖ (ex guide dogs) ◀

LLANFIHANGEL-Y-PENNANT   Map 06
SH60

CASTELL-Y-BERE
➲ (off B4405)
☎ 029 2050 0200   **FREE**
The castle was begun around 1221 by Prince Llewelyn ap
Iorwerth of Gwynedd to guard the southern flank of his
principality. It is typically Welsh in design with its D-shaped
towers. Although a little off the beaten track, the castle lies
in a spectacular setting, overshadowed by the Cader Idris
range.
Times: Open all reasonable times. **Facilities:** ✖ ⊙

LLANGYBI   Map 06 SH44

ST CYBI'S WELL
➲ (off B4354)
☎ 01766 810047   **FREE**
Cybi was a sixth-century Cornish saint, known as a healer of
the sick, and St Cybi's Well (or Ffynnon Gybi) has been
famous for its curative properties through the centuries. The
corbelled beehive vaulting inside the roofless stone structure
is Irish in style and unique in Wales.
Times: Open at all times. **Facilities:** ♿ ✖ ⊙

LLANUWCHLLYN   Map 06 SH83

BALA LAKE RAILWAY
The Station LL23 7DD
➲ (off A494 Bala to Dolgellau road)
☎ 01678 540666
web: www.bala-lake-railway.co.uk
Steam locomotives which once worked in the slate quarries
of North Wales now haul passenger coaches for four-and-a-
half miles from Llanuwchllyn Station along the lake to Bala.
The railway has one of the few remaining double-twist lever-
locking framed GWR signal boxes, installed in 1896. Some of
the coaches are open and some closed, so passengers can
enjoy the beautiful views of the lake and mountains in all
weathers.
Times: Open Etr-last wknd in Sep, daily. (Closed certain Mon & Fri,
telephone for details). **Fee:** ✱ £7 return (pen £6.50). Family ticket
(2ad + 3 ch) £17. **Facilities:** 🅿 🍽 ♿ (wheelchairs can be taken on
train) shop

LLANYSTUMDWY   Map 06 SH43
LLOYD GEORGE MUSEUM & HIGHGATE
VICTORIAN COTTAGE
LL52 0SH
➲ (on A497 between Pwllheli & Criccieth)
☎ 01766 522071
e-mail: amgueddfeydd-museums@
gwynedd.gov.uk
web: www.gwynedd.gov.uk/museums
Explore the life and times of David Lloyd George in this
museum. His boyhood home is recreated as it would have
been when he lived there between 1864 and 1880, along
with his Uncle Lloyd's shoemaking workshop.
Times: Open Etr, daily 10.30-5; Apr-May, Mon-Fri 10.30-5 (open Sat in
Jun); Jul-Sep daily 10.30-5; Oct, Mon-Fri, 11-4. Open Bank Holidays;
Other times by appointment, telephone 01286 679098 for details.
Fee: ✱ £3 (ch & pen £2). Family ticket £7. **Facilities:** 🅿 🎞
♿ (induction loop in audio visual theatre, shop & cottage) toilets for
disabled shop ✖ (ex guide dogs) ◀

PENARTH FAWR   Map 06 SH43
PENARTH FAWR
➲ (3.5m NE of Pwllheli off A497)
☎ 01766 810880   **FREE**
The hall, buttery and screen are preserved in this house
which was probably built in the 15th century.
Times: Open at all times. **Facilities:** ♿ ✖ ⊙

PLAS-YN-RHIW   Map 06 SH22
PLAS-YN-RHIW
LL53 8AB
➲ (12m from Pwllheli signed from B4413 to
Aberdaron)
☎ 01758 780219
This is a small manor house, part medieval, with Tudor and
Georgian additions. The ornamental gardens have flowering
trees and shrubs including sub-tropical specimens, divided
by box hedges and grass paths. There is a stream and
waterfall, which descends from the snowdrop wood behind.
Times: ✱ Open Mar-14 May, Thu-Mon noon-5; mid May-Oct,
Wed-Mon noon-5. **Facilities:** 🅿 ♿ (Braille guides/scented plants)
toilets for disabled shop ✖ 🚌 ♨

PORTHMADOG   Map 06 SH53
FFESTINIOG RAILWAY
Harbour Station LL49 9NF
➲ (SE end of town beside the harbour, on A487)
☎ 01766 516000
e-mail: enquiries@festrail.co.uk
web: www.festrail.co.uk
A narrow gauge steam railway running for 13.5 miles
through Snowdonia National Park, with breathtaking views
and superb scenery. Buffet service on all trains including
licensed bar (in corridor carriages). Please telephone for
details of special events. The company also runs the Welsh
Highland Railway Caernarfon, which will eventually link up
with the Ffestiniog Railway.
Times: Open daily late Mar to end Oct. Limited Winter service mid
week trains Nov & early Dec. Santa specials in Dec. Open Feb half
term. **Fee:** ✱ Full distance return £16 (pen £12.80). Other fares
available. **Facilities:** 🅿 (charged) 🍽 ✖ licensed ♿ (Wheelchair
ramps, trains mostly accessible) toilets for disabled shop (open when
trains running) ◀

PORTMEIRION   Map 06 SH53

PORTMEIRION
LL48 6ET
➲ (off A487 at Minffordd)
☎ 01766 770000
2 for 1
e-mail: info@portmeirion-village.com
web: www.portmeirion-village.com
Welsh architect Sir Clough Williams Ellis built his fairy-tale, Italianate village on a rocky, tree-clad peninsula on the shores of Cardigan Bay. A bell-tower, castle and lighthouse mingle with a watch-tower, grottoes and cobbled squares among pastel-shaded picturesque cottages let as holiday accommodation. The 60-acre Gwyllt Gardens include miles of dense woodland paths and are famous for their fine displays of rhododendrons, azaleas, hydrangeas and sub-tropical flora. There is a mile of sandy beach and a playground for children. The village is probably best known as the major location for 1960s cult TV show, *The Prisoner*.
Times: Open all year, daily 9.30-5.30.   **Fee:** ✱ £6.50 (ch £4, pen £5)..
Facilities: 🅿 💷 ✗ licensed 🏮 ♿ toilets for disabled shop garden centre ✗ (ex guide dogs) 🍴

TYWYN   Map 06 SH50

TALYLLYN RAILWAY
Wharf Station LL36 9EY
➲ (A493 Machynlleth to Dolgellau for Tywyn station, B4405 for Abergynolwyn)
☎ 01654 710472
e-mail: enquiries@talyllyn.co.uk
web: www.talyllyn.co.uk
The oldest 27in-gauge railway in the world, built in 1865 to run from Tywyn on Cardigan Bay to Abergynolwyn slate mine some seven miles inland. The railway climbs the steep sides of the Fathew Valley and with stops on the way at Dolgoch Falls and the Nant Gwernol forest. The return trip takes 2.5 hours. All scheduled passenger trains are steam hauled.
Times: Open Sun mid Feb-Mar, daily; Apr-early Nov & 26 Dec-2 Jan. Ring for timetable.   **Fee:** ✱ £10 Day Rover (ch accompanied £2). Intermediate fares available.   **Facilities:** 🅿 (charged) 💷 🏮 ♿ (prior notice useful, wheelchair ramps into carriages) toilets for disabled shop 🍴

Y FELINHELI   Map 06 SH56

GREENWOOD FOREST PARK
LL56 4QN
➲ (A55 junct 11, follow Llanberis signs onto A4244, signed from next rdbt)
☎ 01248 670076
2 for 1
e-mail: info@greenwoodforestpark.co.uk
web: www.greenwoodforestpark.co.uk
This forest park provides a wide range of exciting activities for the whole family. Try the Great Green Run - the longest slide in Wales, shoot a real longbow, build dens in the woods and saw a log. Ride the Green Dragon, the world's first people-powered family rollercoaster. Try the Jungle Boat Adventure and explore the rainforest. There are large interactive exhibitions in the oak-framed great hall and the Forest Theatre stages events and shows during school holiday periods. The Toddlers Village is ideal for young children.
Times: Open daily mid Mar-end Oct 10-5.30 (Sep & Oct 10-5).
Fee: ✱ Seasonal. £4.95-£6.95 (ch £3.95-£5.95, pen £4.50-£6.30, disabled 20% discount). Family ticket (2ad + 2 ch) £15. 65-£22.70.
Facilities: 🅿 💷 ♿ (grounds partly accessible, parking) toilets for disabled shop 🍴

ISLE OF ANGLESEY

BEAUMARIS   Map 06 SH67

BEAUMARIS CASTLE
LL58 8AP
☎ 01248 810361
Beaumaris was built by Edward I and took from 1295 to 1312 to complete. In later centuries it was plundered for its lead, timber and stone. Despite this it remains one of the most impressive and complete castles built by Edward I. It has a perfectly symmetrical, concentric plan, with a square inner bailey and curtain walls, round corner towers and D-shaped towers in between. There are also two great gatehouses, but these were never finished.
Times: Open Apr-May & Oct, daily 9.30-5; Jun-Sep, daily, 9.30-6; Nov-Mar, Mon-Sat 9.30-4, Sun 11-4. Telephone for Xmas opening times.   **Fee:** £3 (ch 5-15, pen & students £2.50). Disabled visitors and assisting companion free. Family ticket (2ad + 3 ch) £8.50. Prices quoted apply until 31/03/06. Party.   **Facilities:** 🅿 ♿ shop ✗ ⊕ 🍴

MUSEUM OF CHILDHOOD
1 Castle St LL58 8AP
➲ (on A545 opposite Beaumaris Castle)
☎ 01248 712498
web: www.aboutbritain.com/museumofchildhoodmemories.htm
The museum illustrates the life and interests of children and families over 150 years. There are around 2,000 items in the museum's collection including money boxes, dolls, educational toys and games, early clockwork trains, cars and aeroplanes, push toys and cycles.
Times: Open daily 10.30-5.30, Sun 12-5. (Last admission 4.30, Sun 4). Closed Nov-2nd wk Mar   **Fee:** ✱ £4 (ch £2.25, pen & students £3.25). Family ticket £11. Free entry for wheelchair users.
Facilities: 🅿 (50yds) 🏮 ♿ shop ✗ (ex guide dogs)

BRYNCELLI DDU   Map 06 SH57

BRYN CELLI DDU BURIAL CHAMBER
➲ (3m W of Menai Bridge off A4080)
☎ 029 2050 0200
FREE
Excavated in 1865, and then again in 1925-9, this is a prehistoric circular cairn covering a passage grave with a polygonal chamber.
Times: Open at all times.   **Facilities:** 🅿 ✗ ⊕

BRYNSIENCYN   Map 06 SH46

ANGLESEY SEA ZOO
LL61 6TQ
➲ (1st turning off Britannia Bridge onto Anglesey then follow Lobster signs along A4080 to zoo)
☎ 01248 430411
2 for 1
e-mail: info@angleseyseazoo.co.uk
web: www.angleseyseazoo.co.uk
Nestling by the Menai Straits, this all-weather undercover attraction contains a shipwreck bristling with conger eels, a lobster hatchery, a seahorse nursery, crashing waves and the enchanting fish forest.
Times: Open 11 Feb 11-3. Apr8-Nov 5, 10-5   **Fee:** ✱ £5.95 (ch & student £4.95, pen & UB40 £5.50). Family ticket £14.95-£21.95. Party 10+. Please telephone to confirm 2005 prices.   **Facilities:** 🅿 💷 ✗ licensed 🏮 ♿ (2 wheelchairs available, Braile tour notes) toilets for disabled shop ✗ (ex guide dogs) 🍴

FOEL FARM PARK

Foel Farm LL61 6TQ

➲ (left off Britannia Bridge A55 onto A5/A4080 to Llanfairpwllgwyngyll, left on A4080 to Brynsiencyn & follow signs)

☎ 01248 430646

e-mail: foelfarm@btinternet.com

web: www.foelfarm.co.uk

Children will love this friendly farm experience, where they can meet animals big and small, and take tractor and trailer rides. The park also contains a luxury handmade chocolate business, a bistro and bar, as well as a tea room and gift shop. **Times:** ✱ Open daily Mar-Oct 10.30-5.30; Also wknds Nov-Feb 10.30-4.30. Also open half term Feb. **Facilities:** 🅿 ⬤ ✗ licensed 🏢 ♿ toilets for disabled shop ✖ (ex guide dogs) 🍴

HOLYHEAD Map 06 SH28

RSBP NATURE RESERVE SOUTH STACK CLIFFS

Plas Nico, South Stack LL65 1YH

➲ (A5 or A55 to Holyhead then follow brown heritage signs)

☎ 01407 764973   FREE

web: www.rspb.org.uk/reserves/southstack

High cliffs with caves and offshore stacks, backed by the maritime heathland of Holyhead Mountain, make this an ideal reserve to watch seabirds. Live video pictures of breeding seabirds are shown in the cliff-top information centre during the summer. Choughs, guillemots, razorbills, fulmars and puffins may be seen. **Times:** Open: Information Centre daily, Etr-Sep, 11-5. Reserve open daily at all times. **Facilities:** 🅿 🏢

LLANALLGO Map 06 SH58

DIN LLUGWY ANCIENT VILLAGE

➲ (0.75m NW off A5025)   FREE

The remains of a 4th-century village can be seen here. There are two circular and seven rectangular buildings, still standing up to head height and encircled by a pentagonal stone wall some 4 to 5ft thick. **Times:** Open at all times. **Facilities:** ✖ ☺

PLAS NEWYDD Map 06 SH56

PLAS NEWYDD

LL61 6DQ

➲ (2m S of Llanfairpwll, on A4080)

☎ 01248 714795

e-mail: plasnewydd@nationaltrust.org.uk

web: www.nationaltrust.org.uk

Set amidst breathtakingly beautiful scenery and with spectacular views of Snowdonia, this elegant 18th-century house was built by James Wyatt and is an interesting mixture of Classical and Gothic. The comfortable interior, restyled in the 1930s, is famous for its association with Rex Whistler, whose largest painting is here. There is also an exhibition about his work. A military museum contains campaign relics of the 1st Marquess of Anglesea, who commanded the cavalry at the Battle of Waterloo. There is a fine spring garden and Australasian arboretum with an understorey of shrubs and wild flowers, as well as a summer terrace and, later, massed hydrangeas and autumn colour. A woodland walk gives access to a marine walk on the Menai Strait. **Times:** Open Apr-Oct, Sat-Wed. House 12-5; Garden 11-5.30. (Last admission 4.30) **Fee:** £6 (ch £3). Family £15 (2ad+3ch). Parties 15+ £5.40 **Facilities:** 🅿 ⬤ 🏢 ♿ (close parking, wheelchairs, garden shuttle, Braille guide) toilets for disabled shop ✖ (ex assistance dogs) 🐾

MERTHYR TYDFIL Map 03 SO00

BRECON MOUNTAIN RAILWAY

Pant Station Dowlais CF48 2UP

➲ (follow Mountain Railway signs from A470 or A465 N of Merthyr Tydfil)

☎ 01685 722988

web: www.breconmountainrailway.co.uk

Opened in 1980, this narrow-gauge railway follows part of an old British Rail route which closed in 1964 when the iron industry in South Wales fell into decline. The present route starts at Pant Station and continues for 3.5 miles through the beautiful scenery of the Brecon Beacons National Park, as far as Taf Fechan reservoir. The train is pulled by a vintage steam locomotive and is one of the most popular railways in Wales. **Times:** Opening times on application to The Brecon Mountain Railway, Pant Station, Merthyr Tydfil. **Fee:** ✱ Fares are under review, please ring for details. **Facilities:** 🅿 ⬤ ✗ licensed ♿ (adapted carriage) toilets for disabled shop 🍴

CYFARTHFA CASTLE MUSEUM & ART GALLERY

Cyfarthfa Park CF47 8RE

➲ (off A470, N towards Brecon, follow brown heritage signs)

☎ 01685 723112   FREE

e-mail: museum@cyfarthfapark.freeserve.co.uk

web: www.museums.merthyr.gov.uk

Set in wooded parkland beside a beautiful lake, this imposing Gothic mansion now houses a superb museum and art gallery. Providing a fascinating glimpse into 3,000 years of history, the museum displays wonderful collections of fine art, social history and objects from around the world in a Regency setting. **Times:** Open Apr-Sep: Mon-Sun 10-5.30; Oct-Mar, Tue-Fri 10-4, Sat-Sun 12-4. Closed between Xmas & New Year **Facilities:** 🅿 ⬤ 🏢 ♿ (stair lift & wheelchair available) toilets for disabled shop ✖ (ex guide dogs)

CAERWENT Map 03 ST49

CAERWENT ROMAN TOWN

➲ (just off A48)

☎ 029 2050 0200   FREE

A complete circuit of the town wall of 'Venta Silurum', together with excavated areas of houses, shops and a temple. **Times:** Open - access throughout the year. **Facilities:** ✖ ☺

CALDICOT Map 03 ST48

CALDICOT CASTLE, MUSEUM & COUNTRYSIDE PARK

Church Rd NP26 4HU

➲ (M4 junct 23A onto B4245. From M48 junct 2 follow A48 & B4245. Signed from B4245)   2 for 1

☎ 01291 420241

e-mail: caldicotcastle@monmouthshire.gov.uk

web: www.caldicotcastle.co.uk

Caldicot Castle's well-preserved fortifications were founded by the Normans and fully developed by the late 14th century. Restored as a family home by a wealthy Victorian, the castle offers the chance to explore medieval walls and towers in a

continued

setting of tranquil gardens and wooded country parkland, plus the opportunity to play giant chess or draughts.
Times: Open Mar-Oct, daily 11-5; Nov-Feb, Sat & Sun 11-4. 19-23 Dec, 11-4 **Fee:** ✱ £3.50 (ch, pen, student & disabled £2.00). Family (2ad+3ch) £10.00 Party 10+. **Facilities:** 🅿 💻 🗑 ♿ (taped tour, level trails, induction loop, access guide) toilets for disabled shop 🍴

CHEPSTOW   Map 03 ST59

CHEPSTOW CASTLE
NP6 5EZ
☎ 01291 624065

Built by William FitzOsbern, Chepstow is the first recorded Norman stone castle. It stands in a strategic spot above the Wye. The castle was strengthened in the following centuries, but was not besieged (as far as is known) until the Civil War, when it was twice lost to the Parliamentarians. The remains of the domestic rooms and the massive gatehouse with its portcullis grooves and ancient gates are still impressive, as are the walls and towers.
Times: Open 18 Mar-May & Oct, daily 9.30-5; Jun-Sep, daily 9.30-6; Nov-Mar, Mon-Sat 9.30-4, Sun 11-4. Telephone for Xmas opening times. **Fee:** £3 (ch 5-15, pen & students £2.50). Disabled visitors and assisting companion free. Family ticket (2ad + 3 ch) £8.50. Prices quoted apply until 31/03/06. Party. **Facilities:** 🅿 ♿ shop 🍴 ⊕ 🍴

GROSMONT   Map 03 SO42

GROSMONT CASTLE
➲ (on B4347)
☎ 01981 240301   FREE

Grosmont is one of the 'trilateral' castles of Hubert de Burgh (see also Skenfrith and White Castle). It stands on a mound with a dry moat, and the considerable remains of its 13th-century great hall can be seen. Three towers once guarded the curtain wall, and the western one is well preserved.
Times: Open - access throughout the year. **Facilities:** ♿ 🍴 ⊕

LLANTHONY   Map 03 SO22

LLANTHONY PRIORY
☎ 029 2050 0200   FREE

William de Lacey discovered the remains of a hermitage dedicated to St David. By 1108 a church had been consecrated on the site and just over a decade later the priory was complete. After the priory was brought to a state of siege in an uprising, Hugh de Lacey provided the funds for a new church, and it is this that makes the picturesque ruin seen today. Visitors still make out the west towers, north nave arcade and south transept.
Times: Open - access throughout the year. **Facilities:** 🅿 ♿ toilets for disabled 🍴 ⊕

LLANTILIO CROSSENNY   Map 03 SO31

HEN GWRT
➲ (off B4233)
☎ 029 2050 0200   FREE

The rectangular enclosure of the former medieval house, still surrounded by a moat.
Times: Open - access throughout the year. **Facilities:** 🍴 🚌 ⊕

MONMOUTH   Map 03 SO51

NELSON MUSEUM & LOCAL HISTORY CENTRE
New Market Hall, Priory St NP25 3XA
➲ (in town centre)
☎ 01600 710630   FREE
e-mail: nelsonmuseum@monmouthshire.gov.uk

Commemorative glass, china, silver, medals, books, models, prints and Admiral Nelson's fighting sword feature here. The
continued

local history displays deal with Monmouth's past as a fortress market town, and include a section on the co-founder of the Rolls Royce company, Charles Stewart Rolls, who was also a pioneer balloonist, aviator and, of course, motorist.

Nelson Museum & History Centre

Times: ✱ Open all year, Mon-Sat 10-1 & 2-5; Sun 2-5. Closed Xmas & New Year. **Facilities:** 🅿 (200yds) (small daily charge) 🗑 ♿ toilets for disabled shop 🍴 (ex guide dogs) 🍴

RAGLAN   Map 03 SO40

RAGLAN CASTLE
NP5 2BT
➲ (signed off A40)
☎ 01291 690228

This magnificent 15th-century castle is noted for its 'Yellow Tower of Gwent'. It was built by Sir William ap Thomas and destroyed during the Civil War, after a long siege. The ruins are still impressive however, and the castle's history is illustrated in an exhibition situated in the closet tower and two rooms of the gate passage.
Times: Open 18 Mar-May & Oct, daily 9.30-5; Jun-Sep, daily 9.30-6; Nov-Mar, Mon-Sat 9.30-4, Sun 11-4. Telephone for Xmas opening times. **Fee:** £2.75 (ch 5-15, pen & students £2.25). Disabled visitors and assisting companion free. Family ticket (2ad + 3 ch) £7.75. Prices quoted apply until 31/03/06. Party. **Facilities:** 🅿 ♿ shop 🍴 ⊕ 🍴

SKENFRITH   Map 03 SO42

SKENFRITH CASTLE
➲ (on B4521)
☎ 029 2050 0200   FREE

This 13th-century castle has a round keep set inside an imposing towered curtain wall. Hubert de Burgh built it as one of three 'trilateral' castles to defend the Welsh Marches.
Times: Open - access throughout the year. Key keeper arrangement. **Facilities:** 🅿 🍴 ⊕ 🐄

TINTERN PARVA   Map 03 SO50

TINTERN ABBEY
NP6 6SE
➲ (via A466)
☎ 01291 689251

The ruins of this Cistercian monastery church are still surprisingly intact. The monastery was established in 1131 and became increasingly wealthy well into the 15th century. During the Dissolution, the monastery was closed and most of the buildings were completely destroyed. During the 18th
continued

century many poets and artists came to see the ruins and recorded their impressions.

Times: Open 18 Mar-May & Oct, daily 9.30-5; Jun-Sep, daily 9.30-6; Nov-Mar, Mon-Sat 9.30-4, Sun 11-4. Telephone for Xmas opening. **Fee:** £3.25 (ch 5-15, pen & students £2.75). Disabled visitors and assisting companion free. Family ticket (2ad + 3 ch) £9.25. Prices quoted apply until 31/03/06. Party. **Facilities:** 🅿 ৬ toilets for disabled shop ✖ ✿ ◼

WHITE CASTLE   Map 03 SO31

WHITE CASTLE
NP7 8UD
➲ (7m NE of Abergavenny, unclass road N of B4233)
☎ 01600 780380

The impressive 12th to 13th-century moated stronghold was built by Hubert de Burgh to defend the Welsh Marches. Substantial remains of walls, towers and a gatehouse can be seen. This is the finest of a trio of castles, the others being at Skenfrith and Grosmont.

Times: Open 18 Mar-Sep, Wed-Sun & BH Mon 10-5. Monument open and unstaffed on Mon & Tue between Apr-Sep. Monument open and unstaffed with no admission charge at all other times between 10-4. Telephone for Xmas opening times. **Fee:** £2 (ch 5-15, pen & students £1.50). Disabled visitors and assisting companion free. Family ticket (2ad + 3 ch) £5.50. Prices quoted apply until 31/03/06. Party.
Facilities: 🅿 ৬ ✖ ✿ ◼

NEATH PORT TALBOT

ABERDULAIS   Map 03 SS79

ABERDULAIS FALLS
SA10 8EU
➲ (from M4 junct 43, take A465 signed Vale of Neath. Onto A4109, Falls next to Dulais Rock Pub)
☎ 01639 636674
e-mail: aberdulais@nationaltrust.org.uk
web: www.ukindex.co.uk/nationaltrust

For over 300 years this famous waterfall has provided energy to drive the wheels of industry. The Turbine House allows visitors access to the top of the falls, with views of the power equipment, fish pass and displays. Please contact for details of special events.

Times: Open March, Sat & Sun 11-4 only. Apr-Oct Mon-Fri 10-5, Sat, Sun & BHs 11-6. **Fee:** ✱ £3.20 (ch £1.60). Family ticket £8. Parties 15+ £2.40 (ch £1.20). **Facilities:** 🅿 ◼ ▣ ৬ (lifts for disabled to view falls) toilets for disabled shop ✿ ◼

CRYNANT   Map 03 SN70

CEFN COED COLLIERY MUSEUM
SA10 8SN
➲ (1m S of Crynant, on A4109)
☎ 01639 750556   `FREE`

The museum is on the site of a former working colliery, and tells the story of mining in the Dulais Valley. A steam-winding engine has been kept and is now operated by electricity, and there is also a simulated underground mining gallery, boilerhouse, compressor house, and exhibition area. Outdoor exhibits include a stationary colliery locomotive. Exhibitions relating to the coal mining industry are held on a regular basis.

Times: Open daily, Apr-Oct 10.30-5; Nov-Mar, groups welcome by prior arrangement. **Facilities:** 🅿 shop ◼

CYNONVILLE   Map 03 SS89

SOUTH WALES MINERS MUSEUM
Afan Argoed Country Park SA13 3HG
➲ (M4 junct 40 onto A4107, 6m NE of Port Talbot)
☎ 01639 850564
e-mail: boastam@sagainternet.co.uk

The picturesquely placed museum gives a vivid picture of mining life, with coal faces, pit gear and miners' equipment. Guided tours of the museum on request. The country park has forest walks and picnic areas, and a visitor centre.

Times: ✱ Open all year daily, Apr-Sep 10.30-5 (Sat & Sun 10.30-6); Oct-Feb 10.30-4 (Sat & Sun 10.30-5). Closed Xmas week.
Facilities: 🅿 (charged) ◼ ✖ ▣ ৬ (mechanical & manual wheel chairs on request) toilets for disabled shop ✖ (ex guide dogs) ◼

NEATH   Map 03 SS79

GNOLL ESTATE COUNTRY PARK   `FREE`
SA11 3BS
➲ (follow brown heritage signs from town centre)
☎ 01639 635808
e-mail: e.ford@npt.gov.uk
web: www.neath-porttalbot.gov.uk

The extensively landscaped Gnoll Estate offers tranquil woodland walks, picnic areas, stunning views, children's play areas, adventure playground, 9-hole golf course, and coarse fishing. Varied programme of events and school holiday activities.

Times: Open all year - Vistor centre, daily from 10. Closed 24 Dec-2 Jan **Facilities:** 🅿 ◼ ৬ (wheelchair & scooter for hire, designated parking) toilets for disabled shop ✖ (ex guide dogs)

NEATH ABBEY
SA10 7DW
➲ (1m W off A465)
☎ 01639 812387   `FREE`

These ruins were originally a Cistercian abbey founded in 1130 by Richard de Grainville.

Times: Open at all times. Key keeper arrangement.
Facilities: 🅿 ৬ ✖ ✿

NEWPORT

CAERLEON   Map 03 ST39

CAERLEON ROMAN BATHS
NP6 1AE
➲ (on B4236)
☎ 01663 422518

Caerleon was an important Roman military base, with accommodation for thousands of men. The foundations of barrack lines and parts of the ramparts can be seen, with remains of the cookhouse, latrines and baths. The amphitheatre nearby is one of the best examples in Britain.

Times: Open 18 Mar-Oct, daily 9.30-5; Nov-Mar, Mon-Sat, 9.30-5, Sun 11-4pm. Telephone for Xmas opening times. **Fee:** £2.50 (ch 5-15, pen & students £2). Disabled visitors and assisting companion free. Family ticket (2ad + 3 ch) £7. Prices quoted apply until 31/03/06. Party.
Facilities: 🅿 ৬ shop ✖ ✿ ◼

ROMAN LEGIONARY MUSEUM

High St NP18 1AE

➲ (close to Newport, 20 min from M4, follow signs from Cardiff & Bristol)

☎ 01633 423134

FREE

e-mail: roman@nmgw.ac.uk

web: www.nmgw.ac.uk

The museum illustrates the history of Roman Caerleon and the daily life of its garrison. On display are arms, armour and equipment, with a collection of engraved gemstones, a labyrinth mosaic and finds from the legionary base at Usk. Please telephone for details of children's holiday activities.

Times: Open all year: Mon-Sat 10-5, Sun 2-5. **Facilities:** P (100yds) & toilets for disabled shop ✈ (ex guide dogs) ■

NEWPORT   Map 03 ST38

TREDEGAR HOUSE & PARK

NP10 8YW

➲ (2m W of Newport, signed from A48 and M4 junct 28)

☎ 01633 815880

e-mail: tredegar.house@newport.gov.uk

web: www.newport.gov.uk

Tredegar House is a fine example of restoration and reflects the rise and fall of the Morgan family through 5 centuries. The house and gardens are set in a 90 acre landscaped park and feature formal gardens, self guided trails, craft workshops and boating.

Times: Open Etr- end Sep, Wed-Sun 11.30-4. **Fee:** House tour £5.40 (ch free, concessions £3.95). **Facilities:** P 🛒 📶 & (wheelchairs for loan) toilets for disabled shop in park only ex. guide dogs ■

PEMBROKESHIRE

AMROTH   Map 02 SN10

COLBY WOODLAND GARDEN

SA67 8PP

➲ (1.5m inland from Amroth beside Carmarthen Bay, follow brown signs from A477 Tenby-Carmarthen road, or off coast road at Ambroth Castle)

☎ 01834 811885

web: www.nationaltrust.org.uk

From early spring to the end of June the garden is a blaze of colour, from the masses of daffodils to the rich hues of rhododendrons, azaleas and bluebells. Followed by hydrangeas in shaded walks through summer to glorious shades of autumn

Times: Open 25 Mar-30 Oct, daily 10-5. **Fee:** ✽ £3.60 (ch £1.80). Family ticket £9. Group £3 (ch £1.50) NT members free.

Facilities: P 🛒 📶 & (limited due to terrain) toilets for disabled shop ✈ (ex on leads) 🌺 ■

CAREW   Map 02 SN00

CAREW CASTLE & TIDAL MILL

SA70 8SL

➲ (on A4075, just off A477 Pembroke to Kilgetty road)

☎ 01646 651782

e-mail: enquiries@carewcastle.com

web: www.carewcastle.com

This magnificent Norman castle has royal links with Henry Tudor and was the setting for the Great Tournament of 1507. Nearby is the Carew Cross (Cadw), an impressive 13ft Celtic

continued

cross dating from the 11th century. Carew Mill is one of only four restored tidal mills in Britain, with records dating back to 1558.

Times: Open 25 Mar-5 Nov **Fee:** £3 (conc £2). Family ticket £8. **Facilities:** P & toilets for disabled shop ■

CILGERRAN   Map 02 SN14

CILGERRAN CASTLE

SA43 2SF

➲ (off A484 & A478)

☎ 01239 615007

Set above a gorge of the River Teifi - famed for its coracle fishermen - Cilgerran Castle dates from the 11th to 13th centuries. It decayed gradually after the Civil War, but its great round towers and high walls give a vivid impression of its former strength.

Times: Open Apr-Oct, daily 9.30-6.30; Nov-Mar, daily 9.30-dusk. Telephone for Xmas opening times. **Fee:** £2.50 (ch 5-15, pen & students £2). Disabled visitors and assisting companion free. Family ticket (2ad + 3 ch) £7. Prices quoted apply until 31/03/06. Party. **Facilities:** & shop ✈ ✢ ■

CRYMYCH   Map 02 SN13

CASTELL HENLLYS FORT

Pant-Glas, Meline SA41 3UT

➲ (off A487 between Cardigan and Newport)

☎ 01239 891319

e-mail: celts@castellhenllys.com

web: www.castellhenllys.com

This Iron Age hill fort is set in the beautiful Pembrokeshire Coast National Park. Excavations began in 1981 and three roundhouses have been reconstructed, another roundhouse has been completed and is the largest on the site. Celtic roundhouses have been constructed in the original way using hazel wattle walls, oak rafters and thatched conical roofs. A forge, smithy and looms can be seen, with other attractions such as trails and a herb garden. Please telephone for details of special events.

Times: Open Apr-early Nov, daily 10-5. Last entry 4.30 **Fee:** £3 (ch & pen £2) Family £8. **Facilities:** P & (ramp access to shop, hearing loop in shop) toilets for disabled shop ■

FISHGUARD   Map 02 SM93

OCEANLAB

The Parrog, Goodwick SA64 0DE

➲ (A40 to Fishguard, turn at by-pass, follow signs for Stenaline ferry terminal, pass 2 garages, turn right at rdbt & follow signs to attraction)

☎ 01348 874737

e-mail: fishguardharbour-tic@pembrokeshire.gov.uk

web: www.ocean-lab.co.uk

Overlooking the Pembrokeshire coastline, OceanLab is a multifunctional centre, which aims to provide a fun-filled experience for the family. There is also a hands on ocean quest exhibition, a soft play area and a cybercafé where visitors can surf the internet. New exhibition, 'Ollie the Octopus's Garden', with hands on displays and activities.

Times: Open Apr-Oct 10-5, Nov-Mar 10-4. **Fee:** Telephone for details **Facilities:** P 🛒 📶 & (lift, flat even ground, low counter) toilets for disabled shop ✈ (ex guide dogs) ■

LAMPHEY Map 02 SN00

Lamphey Bishop's Palace

SA71 5NT
➲ (off A4139)
☎ 01646 672224

This ruined 13th-century palace once belonged to the Bishops of St David's.

Times: Open Apr-Mar, daily 10-5 **Fee:** £2.50 (ch 5-15, pen & students £2). Disabled visitors and assisting companion free. Family ticket (2ad + 3 ch) £7.75. Prices quoted apply until 31/03/06. Party. **Facilities:** P ♿ toilets for disabled shop

LLAWHADEN Map 02 SN01

Llawhaden Castle

➲ (off A40, 3m NW of Narberth)
☎ 01437 541201

FREE

The castle was first built in the 12th century to protect the possessions of the Bishops of St David's. The 13th and 14th-century remains of the bishops' hall, kitchen, bakehouse and other buildings can be seen, all surrounded by a deep moat.

Times: Open at all times. Key keeper arrangement.
Facilities: ♿

NARBERTH Map 02 SN11

Oakwood Park

Canaston Bridge SA67 8DE
➲ (M4 W junct 49, take A48 to Carmarthen, signed)
☎ 01834 861889
e-mail: info@oakwoodthemepark.co.uk
web: www.oakwoodthemepark.co.uk

Wales' premier theme park, featuring the world's No. 1 wooden roller coaster Megafobia, the 50m-high sky coaster Vertigo, shot n' drop tower coaster The Bounce, and Snake River Falls. For young children there is KidzWorld featuring The Wacky Factory, The Lost Kingdom, Techniquest and Playtown. In summer there are firework displays and live shows at night.

Times: Open daily 24 Mar-25 Sep, from 10 (closing times vary)
Fee: * £13.75 (under 2's free, ch 3-9 £12.75, pen £8.85 & disabled £9.75). Family ticket (4) £49, family ticket (6) £70. Party 20+ tickets available £11.75 **Facilities:** P ♿ (wheelchair hire, special access to some rides) toilets for disabled shop (ex guide dogs)

NEWPORT Map 02 SN03

Pentre Ifan Burial Chamber

➲ (3m SE from B4329 or A487)
☎ 029 2050 0200

FREE

Found to be part of a vanished long barrow when excavated in 1936-37, the remains of this chamber include the capstone, three uprights and a circular forecourt.

Times: Open - access throughout the year. **Facilities:**

PEMBROKE Map 02 SM90

Pembroke Castle

SA71 4LA
➲ (W end of main street)
☎ 01646 681510 & 684585
e-mail: pembroke.castle@talk21.com
web: www.pembrokecastle.co.uk

This magnificent castle commands stunning views over the Milford estuary. Discover its rich medieval history, and that of Henry VII, the first Tudor king, through a variety of exhibitions. There are lively guided tours and events each Sunday in July and August. Before leaving, pop into the Brass Rubbing Centre and make your own special souvenir. To complete the day, wander round the tranquil millpond and medieval town walls, which surround other architectural gems from Tudor and Georgian times. Special Events: 1st week in Sep 'Pembroke Festival'. Please telephone for details.

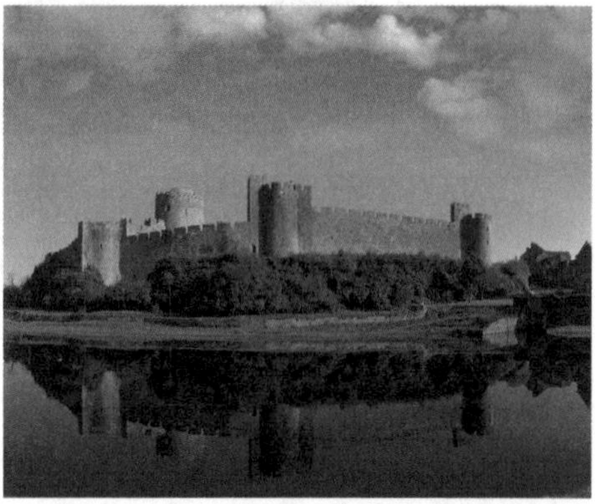

Pembroke Castle

Times: Open all year, daily, Apr-Sep 9.30-6; Mar & Oct 10-5; Nov-Feb, 10-4. Closed 24-26 Dec & 1 Jan. **Fee:** £3.50 (ch under 16 & pen £2.50, ch under 5 & wheelchairs users free). Family ticket £10.
Facilities: P (100yds) ♿ (induction loop, handrails, portable ramp) toilets for disabled shop on lead only

ST DAVID'S Map 02 SM72

St Davids Bishop's Palace

SA62 6PE
➲ (on A487)
☎ 01437 720517

These extensive and impressive ruins are all that remain of the principal residence of the Bishops of St David's. The palace shares a quiet valley with the cathedral, which was almost certainly built on the site of a monastery founded in the 6th century by St David. The Bishop's Palace houses an exhibition: 'Lords of the Palace'.

Times: Open 18 Mar-May & Oct daily 9.30-5; Jun-Sep, daily 9.30-6; Nov-Mar, Mon-Sat 9.30-4, Sun 11-4. Telephone for Xmas opening times. **Fee:** £2.50 (ch 5-15, pen & students £2). Disabled visitors and assisting companion free. Family ticket (2ad + 3 ch) £7. Prices quoted apply until 31/03/06. Party. **Facilities:** P ♿ toilets for disabled shop

St Davids Cathedral

The Close SA62 6PE
➲ (from Haverfordwest A487 into St Davids, pass Cross Sq, left into car park)
☎ 01437 720202
e-mail: info@stdavidscathedral.org.uk
web: www.stdavidscathedral.org.uk

Begun 1181 on the reputed site of St David's 6th-century monastic settlement. The present building was altered during the 12th to the 14th centuries and again in the 16th.

continued

The ceilings of oak, painted wood and stone vaulting are of considerable interest.

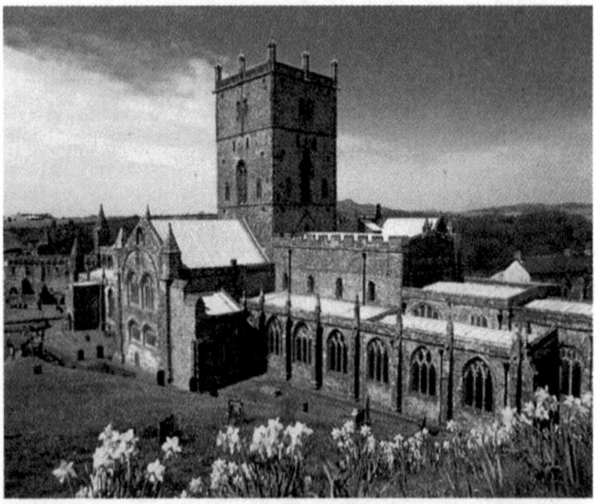

St Davids Cathedral

Times: Open all year 8.30-6. **Fee:** ✱ Free - Suggested donation of £2. **Facilities:** P (300yds) (no coach parking) ♿ (hearing loop) toilets for disabled shop (ex guide dogs)

ST FLORENCE — Map 02 SN00

MANOR HOUSE WILDLIFE & LEISURE PARK

Ivy Tower SA70 8RJ
(on B4318 between Tenby & St Florence)
☎ 01646 651201

The park is set in 35 acres of delightful wooded grounds and award-winning gardens. The wildlife includes exotic birds, reptiles and fish. Also here are a pets' corner, a children's playground with free rides on an astraglide slide, and roundabouts. Other attractions include a natural history museum, a go-kart track, model railway exhibition. Daily falconry displays. Telephone for details of displays and animal feeding times.

Times: ✱ Open Etr-end Sep, daily 10-6. Please telephone for late opening Jul & Aug. **Facilities:** P ♿ toilets for disabled shop

SCOLTON — Map 02 SM92

SCOLTON VISITOR CENTRE

SA62 5QL
(5m N of Haverfordwest, on B4329)
☎ 01437 731328 (Mus) & 731457 (Park)

Scolton Manor Museum is situated in Scolton Country Park. The early Victorian mansion, refurbished stables and the exhibition hall illustrate the history and natural history of Pembrokeshire. There are new displays in the house and stables, plus a 'Pembrokeshire Railways' exhibition. The 60-acre grounds, partly a nature reserve, have fine specimen trees and shrubs. Environmentally friendly Visitor Centre, alternative energy and woodland displays, guided walks and children's play areas.

Times: ✱ Open Museum Apr-Oct, Tue-Sun & BHs 10.30-1 & 1.30-5.30; Country Park all year, Etr-Sep 10-7, Oct-Etr 10-6. Closed 25-26 Dec. **Facilities:** P (charged) ♿ (disabled parking area near house) toilets for disabled shop (ex guide dogs & in grounds)

TENBY — Map 02 SN10

TENBY MUSEUM & ART GALLERY

Castle Hill SA70 7BP
(near town centre above Harbour)
☎ 01834 842809
e-mail: tenbymuseum@hotmail.com
web: www.tenbymuseum.free-online.co.uk

The museum is situated on Castle Hill. It covers the local heritage from prehistory to the present in galleries devoted to archaeology, geology, maritime history, natural history, militaria and bygones. The art galleries concentrate on local associations with an important collection of works by Augustus John, Gwen John and others.

Times: ✱ Open all year, Etr-7 Dec, daily 10-5; 8 Dec-Etr, Mon-Fri 10-5. (Last admission 4.30). **Facilities:** P (10 mins walk) ♿ (lifts, levelled floors, ramps) toilets for disabled shop (ex guide dogs)

TUDOR MERCHANT'S HOUSE

Quay Hill SA70 7BX
(turn left off lower end of High St, past Lifeboat PH and Caldey Shop)
☎ 01834 842279
e-mail: alysonbush@yahoo.co.uk
web: www.nationaltrust.org.uk

Recalling Tenby's history as a thriving and prosperous port, the Tudor Merchant's house is a fine example of gabled 15th-century architecture. There is a good Flemish chimney and on three walls the remains of seccoes can be seen. A small herb garden has been created.

Times: Open Apr-Oct, Sun-Fri, 11-5 (last admission 4.45) **Fee:** £2.20 (ch £1.10). Family £5.50. Group 15+ £1.80 (ch 90p). NT members free. **Facilities:** P (500yds) (no coaches nearby, no parking in town) ♿ (garden could be accessed, Braille guide, photo album) shop (ex guide dogs)

POWYS

ABERCRAF — Map 03 SN81

DAN-YR-OGOF THE NATIONAL SHOWCAVES CENTRE FOR WALES

SA9 1GJ
(M4 junct 45, midway between Swansea & Brecon on A4067, follow brown tourist signs for Dan-Yr-Ogof)
☎ 01639 730284 & 730801
e-mail: info@showcaves.co.uk
web: www.showcaves.co.uk

This award-winning attraction includes three separate caves, dinosaur park, Iron Age Farm, museum, shire horse centre and covered children's play area.

Times: Open Apr-Oct, daily from 10 (last admission 3). **Fee:** £9.50 (ch 4-16 £6). Group rates 15+. **Facilities:** P shop (ex assist dogs)

BERRIEW — Map 07 SJ10

GLANSEVERN HALL GARDENS

Glansevern SY21 8AH
(signed on A483 between Welshpool and Newtown)
☎ 01686 640200
web: www.glansevern@.co.uk

Built in the Greek Revival style for Arthur Davies Owen, who chose a romantically positioned site on the banks of the River Severn. The current owners have developed the gardens, respecting the plantings and features of the past, and added a vast collection of new and interesting species. There are many fine and unusual trees, a lakeside walk, walled garden, water gardens and a rock garden with lamp-lit grotto.

Times: Open May-Sep, BH Mon,Thurs-Sat 12-6. Parties other dates by arrangement. **Fee:** ✱ £3.50 (pen £3, ch under 15 free). **Facilities:** P ♿ (most areas accessible) toilets for disabled on lead only

continued

BRECON   Map 03 SO02

BRECKNOCK MUSEUM & ART GALLERY
Captain's Walk LD3 7DS
➲ (near town centre at junct of The Watton & Glamorgan St)
☎ 01874 624121
e-mail: brecknock.museum@powys.gov.uk

A wealth of local history is explored at the museum, which has archaeological and historical exhibits, with sections on folk life, decorative arts and natural history. Victorian Assize Court is interpreted with life-size figures, sound and light and there is one of the finest collections of Welsh Lovespoons. The museum also runs a lively programme of Welsh contemporary art exhibitions.
Times: Open all year, Mon-Fri 10-5, Sat 10-1 & 2-5; also open Sun 12-5 Apr-Sep. Closed Good Fri, 25-26 Dec & New Year's Day. 3 May, 4 Oct and 3 Jan (2006). **Fee:** £1 (ch & residents free, concessions 50p)
Facilities: 🅿 & (limited parking, must be accompanied by able-bodied) toilets for disabled shop ✖ (ex guide dogs) ◀

THE ROYAL REGIMENT OF WALES MUSEUM
The Barracks, The Watton LD3 7EB
➲ (close to town centre, well signed)
☎ 01874 613310
e-mail: swb@rrw.org.uk
web: www.rrw.org.uk

The museum of the South Wales Borderers and Monmouthshire Regiment, which was raised in 1689 and has been awarded 23 Victoria Crosses. Amongst the collections is the Zulu War Room, devoted to the war and in particular to the events at Rorke's Drift, 1879, when 121 men fought 4,500 Zulus.
Times: Open wkdays 9-5 throughout the year, wknds & BHs 10-4 Apr-Sep **Fee:** ✱ £3 (ch up to 16 free) **Facilities:** 🅿 (town centre) 🍴 & toilets for disabled shop ✖ (ex guide dogs) ◀

LLANFAIR CAEREINION   Map 06 SJ10

WELSHPOOL & LLANFAIR LIGHT RAILWAY
SY21 0SF
➲ (beside A458, Shrewsbury-Dolgellau road)
☎ 01938 810441   2 for 1
e-mail: info@wllr.org.uk
web: www.wllr.org.uk

The Llanfair Railway is one of the Great Little Trains of Wales. It offers a 16-mile round trip through glorious scenery by narrrow-gauge steam train. The line is home to a collection of engines and coaches from all round the world. Please ring for details of special events.
Times: Open wknds Etr-end Oct, daily during holiday periods, phone for timetable enquiries. **Fee:** ✱ £9.90 return (ch £1, pen £8.90). **Facilities:** 🅿 🍴 & (three coachs adapted for wheelchairs) toilets for disabled shop ◀

MACHYNLLETH   Map 06 SH70

CELTICA
Y Plas, Aberystwyth Rd SY20 8ER
➲ (well signed to south of town)
☎ 01654 702702
e-mail: celtica@celticawales.com
web: www.celticawales.com

Located in a restored mansion house, Celtica is an exciting heritage centre introducing the history and culture of the Celtic people. The sights and sounds of Celtic life are brought alive as you go on a journey portraying the Celtic spirit of the past, present and future. There's an interpretive centre dedicated to Welsh and Celtic history, a children's indoor
continued

play area, and conference rooms. Education resources are available and groups are welcome. Storytelling, lectures, music and craft events take place.
Times: ✱ Open daily 10-6. Closed Xmas, New Year & some dates in Jan. **Facilities:** 🅿 💻 ✖ licensed 🍴 & (lift & ramps to public areas, induction loop) toilets for disabled shop ✖ (ex guide dogs) ◀

CENTRE FOR ALTERNATIVE TECHNOLOGY
SY20 9AZ
➲ (3m N of Machynlleth, on A487)
☎ 01654 705950
e-mail: info@cat.org.uk
web: www.cat.org.uk

The Centre for Alternative Technology promotes practical ideas and information on sustainable technologies. The exhibition includes displays of wind, water and solar power, organic gardens, low-energy dwellings, and a unique water-powered railway which ascends a 200ft cliff from the car park. The Wave Tank and the underground 'Mole-Hole' are particularly popular with children.
Times: ✱ Open 7 Apr-Oct, daily 10-5; Nov-6 Apr, daily 10-4.
Facilities: 🅿 💻 (wheelchair available) shop ✖ (ex guide dogs) ◀

KING ARTHUR'S LABYRINTH
King Arthur's Labyrinth, Corris SY20 9RF
➲ (on A487 between Machynlleth and Dolgellau)
☎ 01654 761584
e-mail: king.arthurs.labyrinth@corris-wales.co.uk
web: www.kingarthurslabyrinth.com

A subterranean storybook, a boat ride through the great waterfall and into the Labyrinth of tunnels and caverns carved into the ancient rocks of Wales. Tales of King Arthur and other legends are re-told as you walk through this underground setting.
Times: Open 1 Apr-5 Nov, daily 10-5. **Fee:** ✱ £5.15 (ch £3.60, pen £4.60). **Facilities:** 🅿 💻 🍴 & toilets for disabled shop ✖ (ex guide dogs) ◀

MONTGOMERY   Map 07 SO29

MONTGOMERY CASTLE
☎ 029 2050 0200   FREE

Initially an earth and timber structure guarding an important ford in the River Severn, Montgomery was considered a 'suitable spot for the erection of an impregnable castle' in the 1220s. Building and modifications continued until 1251-53, but the final conquest of Wales by Edward I meant the castle lost much of its role.
Times: Open all year, any reasonable time. **Facilities:** & ✖ ☺

PRESTEIGNE   Map 03 SO36

THE JUDGE'S LODGING
Broad St LD8 2AD
➲ (in town centre, off B4362, signed from A44 & A49)
☎ 01544 260650   2 for 1
e-mail: info@judgeslodging.org.uk
web: www.judgeslodging.org.uk

A restored Victorian town house with integral courtroom, cells and service areas - step back into the 1860s, accompanied by an 'eavesdropping' audiotour of voices from the past. Explore the fascinating world of the Victorian judges, their servants and felonious guests at this award-winning, 'hands on', historic house. Special Events: Historical Dinners Jan 2006. The Big Draw Oct 2006.
Times: Open daily, Mar-Oct 10-6; Nov-Dec Wed-Sun 10-4. Closed Jan-Feb. **Fee:** £4.95 (ch £3.95), concessions £4.50. Family ticket £15. Party rates available. **Facilities:** 🅿 (200mtrs) 🍴 & (lift, disabled pack for inaccesible items, braille guides) shop ✖ (ex guide dogs)

RHAYADER   Map 06 SN96

GILFACH NATURE DISCOVERY CENTRE AND RESERVE

St Harmon LD6 5LF
➲ (off A470, 3m N of Rhayader)
☎ 01597 870301 &823298
e-mail: info@radnorshirewildlifetrust.org.uk
web: www.radnorshirewildlifetrust.org.uk

Situated in the Cambrian Mountains, Gilfach is locally unique due to its wide variety of habitats; high moorland to enclosed meadow, oak woodland to rocky upland river. The reserve therefore supports a tremendous abundance of plants and animals within a relatively small area. This richness of wildlife has adapted to living in the various habitats created over the centuries through the practice of traditional farming. Visitors can take a number of planned walks including the Nature Trail, the Monks Trod Trail, and the Oakwood Path. The Nature Discovery Centre offers the opportunity to learn about the various habitats and wildlife featuring footage from cameras in nestboxes, games and quizzes. Special Events: Childrens activities every Thu, Jul-Aug

Times: Open Reserve all year. Centre Apr-Jun, Sep-Oct-Fri-Mon 10-4.30; Jul-Aug all wk 10-4.30 **Fee:** Donations **Facilities:** P ⬤ 📖 ♿ wheelchair access path to viewpoint toilets for disabled shop dogs on lead only

TRETOWER   Map 03 SO12

TRETOWER COURT & CASTLE

NP8 2RF
➲ (3m NW of Crickhowell, off A479)
☎ 01874 730279

The castle is a substantial ruin of an 11th-century motte and bailey, with a three-storey tower and 9ft-thick walls. Nearby is the Court, a 14th-century fortified manor house which has been altered and extended over the years. The two buildings show the shift from medieval castle to more domestic accommodation over the centuries.

Times: Open 1-17 Mar & Oct, daily 10-4; 18 Mar-30 Sep, daily 10-5 **Fee:** £2.50 (ch 5-15, pen & students £2). Disabled visitors and assisting companion free. Family ticket (2ad + 3 ch) £7. Prices quoted apply until 31/03/06. Party. **Facilities:** P ♿ toilets for disabled shop ✕ 🔄 🍴

WELSHPOOL   Map 07 SJ20

POWIS CASTLE

SY21 8RF
➲ (1m S of Welshpool, signed off A483)
☎ 01938 551920
e-mail: ppcmsn@smtp.ntrust.org.uk
web: www.ukindex.co.uk/nationaltrust

Laid out in the Italian and French styles, the Garden retains its original lead statues, an Orangery and an aviary on the terraces. The medieval castle contains one of the finest collections of paintings and furniture in Wales and a beautiful collection of treasures from India. Please visit website for details of events running throughout the year.

Times: Open 21 Mar-30 Oct, Thu-Mon. Castle and museum 1-5, gardens, 11-6. **Fee:** ✱ Castle, Museum & Gardens £8.80, (ch under 17 £4.40) Family ticket £22. Group member £7.80. Garden only: £6.20 (ch £3.10) Family £15.20, Group member £5.20. NT members & ch under 5 free. **Facilities:** P ✕ licensed 📖 (photos of interior, braille guides) shop garden centre ✕ (ex guide dogs) 🌿 🍴

TREHAFOD   Map 03 ST09

RHONDDA HERITAGE PARK

Lewis Merthyr Colliery, Coed Cae Rd CF37 7NP
➲ (between Pontypridd & Porth, off A470, follow brown heritage signs from M4 junct 32) **2 for 1**
☎ 01443 682036
e-mail: reception@rhonddaheritagepark.com
web: www.rhonddaheritagepark.com

Based at the Lewis Merthyr Colliery, the Heritage Park is a fascinating 'living history' attraction. You can take the Cage Ride to 'Pit Bottom' and explore the underground workings of a 1950s pit, guided by men who were miners themselves. There are children's activities, an art gallery and a museum illustrating living conditions in the Rhondda Valley. Special events throughout the year, phone for details.

Times: Open all year, daily 10-6. Closed Mon from Oct-Etr. (Last admission 4). Closed 25 Dec-3 Jan. **Fee:** £5.60 (ch £4.30, pen £4.95). Family ticket from £16.50. **Facilities:** P ⬤ ✕ licensed 📖 ♿ (wheelchair available, accessible parking, lifts) toilets for disabled shop ✕ (ex guide dogs) 🍴

LLANRHIDIAN   Map 02 SS49

WEOBLEY CASTLE

SA3 1HB
➲ (from B4271 or B4295)
☎ 01792 390012

A 12th-to 14th-century fortified manor house with an exhibition on the history of Weobley and other historic sites on the Gower peninsula.

Times: Open all year, 1 Mar-31 Mar 9:30am-5pm daily, Apr-Oct 9:30am-6pm daily, Nov-Mar 9:30am-5pm daily **Fee:** £2 (ch 5-15, pen & students £1.50). Disabled visitors and assisting companion free. Family ticket (2ad + 3 ch) £5.50. Prices quoted apply until 31/03/06. Party. **Facilities:** P ♿ shop ✕ 🔄 🍴

> **If an attraction name appears in *italics*, details have not been confirmed for 2006.**

OXWICH   Map 02 SS48

OXWICH CASTLE
SA3 1NG
➲ (A4118 from Swansea)
☎ 01792 390359
Situated on the Gower peninsula, this Tudor mansion is a
striking testament in stone to the pride and ambitions of the
Mansel dynasty of Welsh gentry. The E-shaped wing houses
an exhibition on historical Gower and 'Chieftains and Princes
of Wales'.
Times: Open 18 Mar-Sept, daily 10-5. **Fee:** £2 (ch 5-15, pen &
students £1.50). Disabled visitors and assisting companion free. Family
ticket (2ad + 3 ch) £5.50. Prices quoted apply until 31/03/06. Party.
Facilities: 🅿 ♿ (Radar key toilet) toilets for disabled ✈ ⬦ 🍴

PARKMILL   Map 02 SS58

GOWER HERITAGE CENTRE
Y Felin Ddwr SA3 2EH
➲ (follow signs for South Gower on A4118 W
from Swansea. W side of Parkmill village)
☎ 01792 371206
e-mail: info@gowerheritagecentre.co.uk
web: www.gowerheritagecentre.co.uk

Based around a 12th-century water-powered cornmill, the site
also contains a number of craft workshops, two play areas,
animals, a museum and a miller's cottage, all set in attractive
countryside in an Area of Outstanding Natural Beauty.
Times: ✱ Open daily, Mar-Oct 10-5.30; Nov-Feb 10-4.30. Closed 25
Dec. **Facilities:** 🅿 ⬛ ✕ 📱 ♿ (ramp entrance access) toilets for
disabled shop 🍴

SWANSEA   Map 03 SS69

GLYNN VIVIAN ART GALLERY
Alexandra Rd SA1 5DZ
➲ (M4 junct 42 along Fabian Way A483 up Wind
St. Left at train station opposite library)
☎ 01792 516900
e-mail: glynn.vivian.gallery@swansea.gov.uk
web: www.swansea.gov.uk
A broad spectrum of visual arts form the original bequest of
Richard Glynn Vivian, including old masters and an international
collection of porcelain and Swansea china. The 20th century is
also well represented with modern painting and sculpture by
British and foreign artists, with the emphasis on Welsh artists.
Times: Open all year, Tue-Sun & BH Mon 10-5. Closed 25-26 Dec & 1
Jan. **Fee:** ✱ Donations welcome. **Facilities:** 🅿 (200 yds) ♿ toilets
for disabled shop ✈ (ex guide dogs & hearing dogs) 🍴

PLANTASIA
Parc Tawe SA1 2AL
➲ (M4 junct 42, follow A483 into Swansea, follow
car park signs for attraction)
☎ 01792 474555
e-mail: swansea.plantasia@swansea.gov.uk
web: www.plantasia.org
A unique, giant hot house garden located in the city centre,
Plantasia houses a huge variety of unusual and exotic plants of
great interest including several species that are extinct in the
wild. Also visit the Butterfly House and see a variety of species
fly freely and observe various stages of butterfly development.
Times: Open Tue-Sun 10-5 (BH Mons & all Mons Jun-Aug)
Facilities: 🅿 ⬛ 📱 ♿ toilets for disabled shop
✈ (ex guide dogs) 🍴

SWANSEA MUSEUM   `FREE`
Victoria Rd, Maritime Quarter SA1 1SN
➲ (M4 junct 42, on main road into city centre)
☎ 01792 653763
e-mail: swansea.museum@swansea.gov.uk
web: www.swanseaheritage.co.uk
This is the oldest museum in Wales, showing the history of
Swansea from the earliest times until today. The museum
has a Tramshed and floating boats to explore (summer only).
There is a continuous programme of temporary exhibitions
and events all year around.
Times: Open all year, Tue-Sun 10-5 (last admission 4.45). Closed Mon
except BH Mon, 25-26 Dec & 1 Jan. **Facilities:** 🅿 (50yds) (on street)
📱 ♿ toilets for disabled shop ✈ (ex guide dogs) 🍴

TORFAEN

BLAENAVON   Map 03 SO20

BIG PIT NATIONAL MINING MUSEUM OF WALES
NP4 9XP
➲ (M4 junct 25/26, follow signs on A4042 &
A4043 to Pontypool & Blaenavon. Signed off A465)
☎ 01495 790311   `FREE`
e-mail: bigpit@nmgw.ac.uk
web: www.nmgw.ac.uk/bigpit
The Real Underground Experience! Big Pit is the UK's leading
mining museum. It is a real colliery and was the place of
work for hundreds of men, woman and children for over 200
years. A daily struggle to extract the precious mineral that
stoked furnaces and lit household fires across the world.
Times: ✱ Open Mid Feb-End Nov, daily 9.30-5, telephone to confirm
Facilities: 🅿 ⬛ 📱 ♿ (underground tours by prior arrangement)
toilets for disabled shop

BLAENAVON IRONWORKS
North St
☎ 01495 792615
The Blaenavon Ironworks were a milestone in the history of
the Industrial Revolution. Constructed in 1788-99, they were
the first purpose-built, multi-furnace ironworks in Wales. By
1796, Blaenavon was the second largest ironworks in Wales,
eventually closing down in 1904.
Times: Open 18 Mar-Oct, Mon-Fri 9.30-4.30, Sat 10-5, Sun 10-4.30. For
details of opening outside this period, telephone Torfaen County
Borough Council on 01633 648081. **Fee:** £2 (ch 5-15, pen &
students £1.50). Disabled visitors and assisting companion free. Family
ticket (2ad + 3 ch) £5.50. Prices quoted apply until 31/03/06. Party.
Facilities: 🅿 ✈ ⬦ 🍴

CWMBRAN · Map 03 ST29

GREENMEADOW COMMUNITY FARM

Greenforge Way NP44 5AJ Junct 26 off m4. Follow signs for Cwmbran follow brown signs.

☎ 01633 862202

e-mail: greenmeadow_community_farm@compuserve.com

This is one of Wales' leading tourist attractions - a community farm that was built during the 1980s on land threatened by developers. There are milking demonstrations, tractor and trailer rides, a dragon adventure play area, a farm trail, a nature trail and lots more. Please telephone for details of special events running throughout the year.

Times: Open daily Summer 10-6, Winter 10-4. Closed 23 Dec-1 Feb. **Fee:** ✱ £4 (ch £3) Family (2ad+3ch) £14 **Facilities:** 🅿 💻 🗒 👌 (tractor & trailer rides for wheelchair users) toilets for disabled shop ◀

VALE OF GLAMORGAN

BARRY · Map 03 ST16

WELSH HAWKING CENTRE

Weycock Rd CF62 3AA

➲ (on A4226)

☎ 01446 734687 · **2 for 1**

There are over 200 birds of prey here, including eagles, hawks, owls, buzzards and falcons. They can be seen and photographed in the mews and some of the breeding aviaries. There are flying demonstrations at regular intervals during the day. A variety of tame, friendly animals, such as pigs, lambs and rabbits will delight younger visitors.

Times: Open end Mar-end Sep, daily 10.30-5, 1hr before dusk in winter. **Fee:** £5 (ch & pen £3). **Facilities:** 🅿 💻 🗒 👌 toilets for disabled shop 🖈 ◀

OGMORE · Map 03 SS87

OGMORE CASTLE

➲ (2.5m SW of Bridgend, on B4524) · **FREE**

☎ 01656 653435

Standing on the River Ogmore, the west wall of this castle is 40ft high. A hooded fireplace is preserved in the 12th-century, three-storey keep and a dry moat surrounds the inner ward.

Times: Open - access throughout the year. Key keeper arrangement. **Facilities:** 🅿 👌 🖈 ☺

PENARTH · Map 03 ST17

COSMESTON LAKES COUNTRY PARK & MEDIEVAL VILLAGE

Lavernock Rd CF64 5UY

➲ (on B4267 between Barry and Penarth)

☎ 029 2070 1678

e-mail: NColes@valeofglamorgan.gov.uk

web: www.valeofglamorgan.gov.uk

Deserted during the plagues and famines of the 14th century, the original village was rediscovered through archaeological excavations. The buildings have been faithfully reconstructed on the excavated remains, creating a living museum of medieval village life. Special events throughout the year include re-enactments and Living History.

Times: ✱ Open all year, daily 11-5 in Summer, 11-4 in Winter. Closed 25 Dec. Country park open at all times. **Facilities:** 🅿 💻 ✖ 🗒 👌 (access ramps & wheelchair hire) toilets for disabled shop

---

ST HILARY · Map 03 ST07

OLD BEAUPRE CASTLE

➲ (1m SW, off A48) · **FREE**

☎ 01446 773034

This ruined manor house was rebuilt during the 16th century. Its most notable features are an Italianate gatehouse and porch. The porch is an unusual three-storeyed structure.

Times: Open - access throughout the year. Key keeper arrangement. **Facilities:** 🅿 🖈 ☺

WREXHAM

CHIRK · Map 07 SJ23

CHIRK CASTLE

LL14 5AF

➲ (8m S of Wrexham, signed off A483) · **2 for 1**

☎ 01691 777701

e-mail: chirkcastle@nationaltrust.org.uk

Chirk Castle is one of a chain of late 13th-century Marcher castles. Its high walls and drum towers have hardly changed, but the inside shows the varied tastes of 700 years of occupation. One of the least altered parts is Adam's Tower. Many of the medieval-looking decorations were by Pugin in the 19th century. Varied furnishings include fine tapestries. The 2-for-1 voucher is valid only during normal visiting hours and cannot be used for any ticketed events.

Times: Open 29 Mar-30 Oct, Wed-Sun & BH Mon 12-5 (castle), 11-6 (gardens); Oct, Wed-Sun 12-4 (castle), 11-5 (gardens). (Last admission 30 mins before closing). **Fee:** ✱ £6.40 (ch £3.20). Family ticket £15.80. Party. Garden only £4 (ch £2) Family ticket £10. **Facilities:** 🅿 ✖ licensed 👌 (stairclimber, hearing loop) toilets for disabled shop 🖈 (ex guide dogs) 🐾 ◀

WREXHAM · Map 07 SJ35

ERDDIG

LL13 0YT

➲ (off A525, 2m S of Wrexham & A483/A5152)

☎ 01978 355314

web: www.nationaltrust.org

Built in 1680, the house was enlarged and improved by a wealthy London lawyer with a passion for gilt and silver furniture. Original furnishings remain, including a magnificent state bed in Chinese silk. The house is notable for the view it gives of both 'upstairs' and 'downstairs' life. The gardens, unusually, have been changed very little since the 18th century.

Times: ✱ Open 25 Mar-1 Nov, Sat-Wed (open Good Fri), house 12-5, garden 11-6 (Jul-Aug gardens 10-6); Oct-1 Nov, Sat-Wed, house 12-4, garden 11-5. **Facilities:** 🅿 ✖ licensed 👌 toilets for disabled shop garden centre 🖈 (ex guidance dogs) 🐾 ◀

NORTHERN IRELAND

EVENTS & FESTIVALS

March
17th St Patrick's Day Parade, Armagh

April
9th-16th World Dancing Championships, Waterfront Hall, Belfast

May
27th Lord Mayor's Show, Belfast (provisional)
tbc Balmoral Show, Balmoral Showgrounds, Belfast

June
23rd-25th Hookers Regatta, Portaferry
tbc Fleadh Amhrán agus Rince, traditional music and dancing, Castlewellan

July
13th The Sham Fight, Scarva, joust between William of Orange and James II
tbc Maritime Festival with tall ships and sailing vessels on the River Lagan, Belfast

August
6th-13th Maiden of the Mournes Festival, folk, country & western, Warrenpoint
   (provisional)
28th-29th Oul' Lammas Fair, Ballycastle (traditional fair from 1606)

September
tbc Hillsborough Oyster Festival, Hillsborough

October
tbc Belfast Festival at Queens, drama, comedy, ballet, music, film and art, Belfast
31st Halloween Celebrations, Belfast

Above: Murlough Bay near Fair Head

BELFAST

BELFAST   Map 01 D5

Belfast Zoological Gardens
Antrim Rd BT36 7PN
➲ (M2 junct 4 signed to Glengormley. Follow signs off rdbt to Zoo)
☎ 028 9077 6277
e-mail: blackrhonda@belfastcity.gov.uk
web: www.belfastzoo.co.uk

The 50-acre zoo has a dramatic setting on the face of Cave Hill, enjoying spectacular views. Attractions include the award-winning primate house (gorillas and chimpanzees), penguin enclosure, free-flight aviary, African enclosure, and underwater viewing of sealions and penguins. There are also red pandas, free-ranging lemurs and a group of very rare spectacled bears.
Times: Open all year, daily Apr-Sep 10-5; Oct-Mar 10-2.30. Closed 25 & 26 Dec. **Fee:** ✱ Summer: £7.00 (ch £3.20), Winter: £6.00 (ch £3.00, ch under 4, pen and disabled free) **Facilities:** 🅿 ➡ ✗ 🍴 ♿ (free admission & reserved parking) toilets for disabled shop ✕ (ex guide dogs) ◀

Botanic Gardens
3 College Park BT7 1LP
➲ (from City Hall, Bedford St then Dublin road for Botanic Avenue)
☎ 028 9032 4902
e-mail: maxwellr@belfastcity.gov.uk
web: www.belfastcity.gov.uk

One highlight of the park is the beautiful glass-domed Victorian Palm House, built between 1839-52. This palm house pre-dates the one in Kew Gardens and is one of the earliest curved glass and iron structures in the world. Another feature is the Tropical Ravine - stand on a balcony to get a wonderful view through a steamy ravine full of exotic plants.
Times: ✱ Open Palm House Tropical Ravine: Apr-Sep 10-12, 1-5; Oct-Mar 10-12, 1-4. Sat, Sun & BHs 1-5 (Summer), 1-4 (Winter).
Facilities: 🅿 (street) ♿

Giant's Ring
➲ (0.75m S of Shaws Bridge)
☎ 028 9023 5000   [FREE]

Circular, Bronze-age enclosure nearly 200ft in diameter similar in style to Stonehenge, with a stone chambered grave in the centre and bordered by banks 20ft wide and 12ft high. Very little is known for certain about this site, except that it was used for ritual burial.
Times: ✱ Open all times. **Facilities:** 🅿

Ulster Museum
National Museums of N.Ireland,
Botanic Gardens BT9 5AB
➲ (1m S of city centre on Stranmillis road)
☎ 028 9038 3000   [FREE]
e-mail: info@magni.org.uk
web: www.ulstermuseum.org.uk

The Ulster Museum is the perfect place to explore the arts, ancient and modern history, and the nature of Ireland. Art displays change regularly but always include a rich variety of Irish and international paintings, drawings and sculpture, along with ceramics, glass and costume. The history galleries tell the story of the north of Ireland from the Ice Age to the present day. The natural environment is explored in the Habitas galleries.

Ulster Museum

Times: Open all year, Mon-Fri 10-5, Sat 1-5, Sun 2-5. Closed 3 days Xmas **Facilities:** 🅿 (100yds on street) ➡ 🍴 ♿ (lifts, loop system) toilets for disabled shop ✕ (ex assist dogs) ◀

W5 at Odyssey
2 Queens Quay BT3 9QQ
☎ 028 9046 7700
web: www.w5online.co.uk

W5 investigates Who? What? Where? When? Why?... and that pretty much sums up the intent behind Ireland's first purpose built discovery centre. Visitors of any age will want to get their hands on interactive science and technology displays that include the laser harp, the fog knife, microscopes, robots and computers. W5 is part of a massive Millennium Landmark Project in the heart of Belfast.
Times: ✱ Open all year Mon-Sat 10-6, Sun 12-6. Closed 25-26 Dec & 12 Jul. **Facilities:** 🅿 (charged) ✗ licensed ♿ (hearing loop) toilets for disabled shop ✕ (ex guide dogs) ◀

CO ANTRIM

ANTRIM   Map 01 D5

Antrim Round Tower
BT41 1BJ
➲ (N of town)
☎ 028 9023 5000   [FREE]

Antrim round tower stands among lawns and trees but it was once surrounded by monastic buildings. Antrim was an

continued
continued

important early monastery, probably a 6th-century foundation, closely linked with Bangor.
Times: ✱ Open all year. **Facilities:** 🅿 ♿

BALLYCASTLE   Map 01 D6

BONAMARGY FRIARY
➲ (E of town, at golf course)
☎ 028 9023 5000   **FREE**
Founded by Rory MacQuillan around 1500 and later passed on to the MacDonnells, Earls of Antrim, there are still remains of the friary gatehouse, church and cloister for visitors to see.
Times: ✱ Open all year. **Facilities:** 🅿 ♿ 🚐

BALLYLUMFORD   Map 01 D5

BALLYLUMFORD DOLMEN
➲ (on B90 on NW tip of Island Magee)
☎ 028 9023 5000   **FREE**
Incorporated in the front garden of a house in Ballylumford Road are the remains of this huge 4-5,000-year-old single-chamber Neolithic tomb, also known as the Druid's Altar.
Times: ✱ Open all year. **Facilities:** ♿

BALLYMENA   Map 01 D5

ECOS MILLENNIUM ENVIRONMENTAL CENTRE
Ecos Centre, Kernohams Ln, Broughshane Rd BT43 7QA
➲ (follow signs from M2 bypass at Ballymena)
☎ 028 2566 4400
e-mail: info@ecoscentre.com
web: www.ecoscentre.com
At the Ecos Centre visitors can enjoy a fun day out on the Ecos Island free of charge where there is a wide range of fun activities for all including electric bikes, remote control boats, toy tractors and diggers sand pit, BBQ's and picnicking facilities, duck feeding, play park and much more. The visitor centre is packed with fun interactive hands with lots of information on the environment and renewable energy technologies and children's quizzes. This is all set in a 150-acre park and nature reserve where visitors can follow any of the picturesque walking trails along the riverside, and through developing woodlands.
Times: Open all year. Please phone for opening dates. Closed 24 Dec-1 Jan **Fee:** ✱ £4 (ch & concessions £3). Family ticket £12.50 **Facilities:** 🅿 🖭 ♿ toilets for disabled shop 🐾 (ex guide dogs) 🍴

HARRYVILLE MOTTE
➲ (N bank of River Braid)
☎ 028 9023 5000   **FREE**
On a ridge to the south of the town, this Norman fort, with its 40ft-high motte and rectangular bailey, is one of the finest examples of Norman earthworks left in Northern Ireland.
Times: ✱ Open all year. **Facilities:** 🅿 ♿ 🚐

BALLYMONEY   Map 01 C6

LESLIE HILL OPEN FARM
Leslie Hill BT53 6QL
➲ (1m NW of Ballymoney on MacFin Rd)
☎ 028 2766 6803
web: www.lesliehillopenfarm.co.uk
An 18th-century estate with a Georgian house, magnificent period farm buildings, and fine grounds with paths, lakes and trees. Attractions include an extensive collection of rare breeds, poultry, horsedrawn machinery and carriages,
continued

exhibition rooms, a museum, working forge, deer park, walled garden and an adventure playground.
Times: Open Jul-Aug, Mon-Sat 11-6, Sun 2-6; Jun, Sat-Sun & BHs 2-6; Etr-May, Sun & BHs 2-6, open all Etr wk 11-6. **Fee:** £3.20 (ch £2.20). Family ticket £9. **Facilities:** 🅿 🖭 ♿ (ramps) toilets for disabled shop garden centre 🐾 (ex on lead)

BUSHMILLS   Map 01 C6

OLD BUSHMILLS DISTILLERY
BT57 8XH
➲ (on Castlecatt Rd, in Bushmills Village)
☎ 028 2073 1521
e-mail: scroskery@idl.ie
web: www.whiskeytours.ie
Old Bushmills was granted its licence in 1608 and is the oldest licenced whiskey distillery in the world. There's a guided tour, and afterwards you can take part in a comparative tasting session and become a whiskey expert.
Times: Open Apr-Oct, Mon-Sat 9.30-5.30, Sun 12-5.30 (last tour 4); Nov-Mar, Mon-Fri 5 tours daily, 10.30, 11.30, 1.30, 2.30 & 3.30. Sat & Sun 3 tours, 1.30, 2.30, 3.30. Closed 12 July , Good Friday pm, Xmas & New Year **Fee:** ✱ £5 (accompanied ch £2.50, pen & student £4). Family ticket (2ad+2ch) £13 **Facilities:** 🅿 ✗ licensed 🍴 ♿ (audio visual theatre, shops & restaurant) toilets for disabled shop 🐾 (ex guide dogs) 🍴

CARRICK-A-REDE   Map 01 D6

CARRICK-A-REDE ROPE BRIDGE AND LARRYBANE VISITORS CENTRE
BT54 6LS
➲ (E of Ballintoy on B15)
☎ 028 2076 9839 & 2073 1582 (office)
e-mail: carrickarede@nationaltrust.org.uk
web: www.nationaltrust.org.uk
On the North Antrim Coastal Path is one of Northern Ireland's best-loved attractions: Carrick-a-Rede Rope Bridge and the disused limestone quarry of Larrybane. The island of Carrick is known as 'the rock in the road', as it is an obstacle on the path of migrating salmon, and fishermen have taken advantage of this to net the fish here for over 300 years.
Times: Open Bridge daily (weather permitting), 12 Mar-12 June, 10-6; 13-30 Jun 10-7, Jul & Aug 10-7; Sep 10-6. (Last admission 45 mins before closing). Coastal path open all year. **Facilities:** 🅿 🖭 ♿ (information centre, telescope at wheelchair height) toilets for disabled 🐾

CARRICKFERGUS   Map 01 D5

CARRICKFERGUS CASTLE
BT38 7BG
➲ (on N shore of Belfast Lough)
☎ 028 9335 1273
Imposingly placed on a rocky headland overlooking Belfast Lough, this is the best preserved and probably the most fought-over Norman castle in Ireland. Built by John de Courcy, Earl of Ulster, after 1180, it served a military purpose for more than eight centuries. Exhibits include a giant model of the castle, a short film, and a banqueting suite. The castle is often used as a venue for medieval banquets and fairs. There is a visitors' centre, shop and refreshment point.
Times: ✱ Open all year, Apr-Sep, wkdays 10-6, Sun 2-6; Oct-Mar closes at 4. **Facilities:** 🅿 🖭 ♿ toilets for disabled shop 🐾

TOWN WALLS
☎ 028 9023 5000   FREE

Lord Deputy Sir Arthur Chichester enclosed Carrickfergus with stone walls from 1611 onwards and more than half the circuit is still visible, often to its full height of 4 metres to the wall walk.
Times: ✱ Visible at all times. **Facilities:** 🅿 ♿

CHURCHTOWN   Map 01 D5

CRANFIELD CHURCH
➲ (3.75m SW of Randalstown)
☎ 028 9023 5000   FREE

This small medieval church is situated on the shores of Lough Neagh. Beside it is a famous holy well.
Times: ✱ Open all year. **Facilities:** 🅿 ♿ 🚌

GIANT'S CAUSEWAY   Map 01 C6

GIANT'S CAUSEWAY CENTRE
44 Causeway Rd BT57 8SU
➲ (2m N of Bushmills on B146)
☎ 028 2073 1855
e-mail: causewaytic@hotmail.com
web: www.northantrim.com

This dramatic rock formation is undoubtedly one of the wonders of the natural world. The Centre provides an exhibition and audio-visual show, and Ulsterbus provides a minibus service to the stones and there are guided walks, and special facilities for the disabled.
Times: ✱ Open all year, daily from 10am (closes 7pm Jul & Aug). Closed 1 wk Xmas. **Facilities:** 🅿 (charged) 🍴 ✗ ♿ (mini bus transport with wheelchair hoist, reserved parking) toilets for disabled shop ✈ (ex guide dogs) 🛏

LARNE   Map 01 D5

OLDERFLEET CASTLE
☎ 028 9023 5000   FREE

A 16th-century tower house, the last surviving of three which defended Larne.
Times: ✱ Open at all times.

LISBURN   Map 01 D5

DUNEIGHT MOTTE AND BAILEY
➲ (2.3m S beside Ravernet River)
☎ 028 9023 5000   FREE

Impressive Anglo-Norman earthwork castle with high mound-embanked enclosure, making use of the defences of an earlier pre-Norman fort.
Times: ✱ Open all year.

IRISH LINEN CENTRE & LISBURN MUSEUM
Market Square BT28 1AG
➲ (signed both in and outside town centre)
☎ 028 9266 3377   FREE
e-mail: irishlinencentre@lisburn.gov.uk
web: www.lisburncity.gov.uk

The centre tells the story of the Irish linen industry past and present. The recreation of individual factory scenes brings the past to life and a series of imaginative hands-on activities describe the linen manufacturing processes. The
continued

Museum has a range of temporary exhibitions of local interest.
Times: Open all year, Mon-Sat, 9.30-5. **Facilities:** 🅿 (200mtrs) (limited for disabled and coaches) 🍴 ♿ (lift, induction loop, staff trained in sign language) toilets for disabled shop ✈ (ex guide dogs) 🛏

PORTBALLINTRAE   Map 01 C6

DUNLUCE CASTLE
➲ (off A2)
☎ 028 2073 1938

Extensive and picturesque ruins of a 16th-century castle perched on a rocky crag high above the sea. Stronghold of the MacQuillans and MacDonnells, who significantly altered the original stonebuilt fortress. Randal MacDonnell built a house in the centre of the castle, of which parts of the Great Hall remain, as do the towers and early 17th-century gatehouse. The castle has new displays and there is an audio-visual show. The cave below the ruins provided a secret way into and out of the castle from the sea.
Times: ✱ Open all year, Apr-Sep, wkdays 10-7, Sun 2-7; Oct-Mar, Tue-Sat 10-4, Sun 2-4. **Facilities:** 🅿 ♿ toilets for disabled shop

TEMPLEPATRICK   Map 01 D5

PATTERSONS SPADE MILL
751 Antrim Rd BT39 0AP
➲ (2m SE of Templepatrick on A6)
☎ 028 9443 3619

This is the last surviving water-driven spade mill in Ireland. It has been completely restored by the National Trust and is now back in production.
Times: ✱ Open Mar, Sun 2-6; Apr-May, wknds, BHs, 2-6 ; Jun-Aug, daily 2-6; Sep, wknds & BHs 2-6. **Facilities:** 🅿 📷 ♿ (ramps, wheelchair available) toilets for disabled 🌿

TEMPLETOWN MAUSOLEUM   FREE
BT39
➲ (in Castle Upton graveyard on A6, Belfast-Antrim road)

Situated in the graveyard of Castle Upton, this family mausoleum is in the shape of a triumphal arch and was designed by Robert Adam.
Times: ✱ Open daily during daylight hours. **Facilities:** 🅿 🚌 🌿

CO ARMAGH

ARMAGH   Map 01 C5

ARMAGH COUNTY MUSEUM
The Mall East BT61 9BE
➲ (in city centre)
☎ 028 3752 3070
e-mail: acm.um@nics.gov.uk
web: www.magni.org.uk

EU Programme
for Peace and Reconciliation

Housed in a 19th-century schoolhouse, this museum contains an art gallery and library, as well as a collection of
continued

local folkcrafts and natural history. Special events are planned thoughout the year.

Armagh County Museum

Times: Open all year, Mon-Fri 10-5, Sat 10-1 & 2-5. **Facilities:** 🅿 📷 ♿ (entrance, ramp & lift for disabled) toilets for disabled shop ✺ (ex guide dogs) 🍴

ARMAGH FRIARY
➲ (SE edge of town)
☎ 028 9023 5000   `FREE`

Situated just inside the gates of the former Archbishop's Palace are the remains of the longest friary church in Ireland (163ft). The friary was established in 1263 by Archbishop O'Scanail and destroyed by Shane O'Neill in the middle of the 16th century to prevent it being garrisoned by Elizabethan soldiers.

Times: ✳ Open all year. **Facilities:** 🅿 ♿

ARMAGH PLANETARIUM
College Hill BT61 9DB
➲ (on Armagh-Belfast road close to mall, city centre)
☎ 028 3752 3689 & 3752 4725
e-mail: kate@armaghplanet.com
web: www.armaghplanet.com

The Planetarium is home to The Star Theatre, a multi-media environment equipped with the latest technology including a virtual reality digital system. Also featured are The Hall of Astronomy, the new Eartharium Building and surrounding the Planetarium is the Astropark, a 25-acre 'hands on' park.

Times: ✳ Open Mon-Fri 2-4.45. Presentations Mon-Fri 3pm. Closed Sat, Sun & BHs. **Facilities:** 🅿 ♿ (loop system in theatre) toilets for disabled shop ✺ (ex guide dogs) 🍴

NAVAN CENTRE & FORT
Killylea Rd BT60 4LD
➲ (2.5m W on A28)
☎ 028 3752 1801
e-mail: navan@armagh.gov.uk
web: www.visitarmagh.com

Navan was once known as Emain Macha, the ancient seat of kings and earliest capital of Ulster. Today it is an impressive archaeological site with its own museum and visitor centre located in a building that blends into the landscape. The Navan Centre uses audio-visuals and interactive devices to unravel history from myth. Travel into the 'Real World' of

continued

archaeology and the 'Other World' to hear the legends of the Ulster Cycle.

Times: Open Jun-Aug daily 10-5, Sun noon-5. Closed 12 Jul. Other times by arrangement for tour groups and educational visits.
Facilities: 🅿 📺 📷 ♿ (loop for hearing aids, parking) toilets for disabled shop ✺ (ex guide dogs) 🍴

PALACE STABLES HERITAGE CENTRE
The Palace Demesne BT60 4EL
➲ (off Friary Rd beside council offices)
☎ 028 3752 1801
e-mail: stables@armagh.gov.uk
web: www.visitarmagh.com

This picturesque Georgian building, set around a cobbled courtyard, has been lovingly restored and now houses a heritage centre. A daily Georgian interpretation is provided by authentic costumed characters.

Times: Open all year, Jul-Aug, Mon-Sat 10-5.30, Sun 1-5.30; Sep-Apr, Mon-Sat 10-5, Sun 2-5. (Last tour 1hr before closing) **Fee:** Prices not confirmed for 2006 **Facilities:** 🅿 ✖ licensed ♿ (ramps & lift in stables) toilets for disabled shop 🍴

SAINT PATRICK'S TRIAN VISITOR COMPLEX
40 English St BT61 7BA
➲ (in city centre)
☎ 028 3752 1801
e-mail: info@saintpatrickstrain.com
web: www.saintpatrickstrian.com

An exciting visitor complex in the heart of the city. Incorporating three major exhibitions - The Armagh story: traces Armagh's historic Pagan monuments through to the coming of St Patrick and Celtic Christianity to the modern day city. Patrick's Testament: takes a closer look at Ireland's patron saint through the writings found in ancient manuscript the Book of Armagh. The Land of Lilliput: Jonathan Swift's most famous book, Gulliver's Travels is narrated by a 20-foot giant.

Times: Open all year, Mon-Sat 10-5, Sun 2-5. Closed 12 Jul.
Fee: ✳ £4.50 (ch £2.75, concession £3.50). Family ticket £11
Facilities: 🅿 (charged) ✖ licensed ♿ (specially designed for disabled) toilets for disabled shop ✺ (ex guide dogs) 🍴

CAMLOUGH   Map 01 D5
KILLEVY CHURCHES
➲ (3m S lower eastern slopes of Slieve Gullion)
☎ 028 9023 5000   `FREE`

The ruins of the two churches (10th and 13th-century) stand back to back, at the foot of Slieve Gullion sharing a common wall, but with no way through from one to the other. The churches stand on the site of an important nunnery founded by St Monenna in the 5th century. A huge granite slab in the graveyard supposedly marks the founder's grave. A holy well can be reached by climbing the path north of the graveyard. The nunnery was in use until the Dissolution in 1542.

Times: ✳ Open all year. **Facilities:** ♿

JONESBOROUGH   Map 01 D5
KILNASAGGART INSCRIBED STONE
➲ (1.25m S)
☎ 028 9023 5000   `FREE`

A granite pillar stone dating back to 8th century, with numerous crosses and a long Irish inscription carved on it.
Times: ✳ Open all year. **Facilities:** 🅿

MOY   Map 01 C5

ARGORY
Derrycaw Rd BT71 6NA
⊃ (3m NE)
☎ 028 8778 4753
e-mail: argory@nationaltrust.org.uk
Originally the home of the McGeough family, this Regency house is situated on a hillside overlooking the Blackwater River. The house is full of period furniture and bric-a-brac. Of particular interest is the very unusual acetylene lighting, installed by the family in 1906.
Times: Grounds: Open Oct-Apr, daily 10-4; May-Sep, daily 10-7. House: Open 17 Mar 1-6; 19 Mar-May & Sep, wknds & BH/PH, 1-6; Jun-Aug, daily 1-6; Sep wknds 1-6; 1-9 Oct, wknds 1-5. **Facilities:** 🅿 (charged) 💻 🍴 ♿ (special parking facilities, wheelchair available, Braille) toilets for disabled shop ✖ (ex guide dogs) 🌂 🍴

NEWRY   Map 01 D5

MOYRY CASTLE
⊃ (7.5m S)
☎ 028 9023 5000   FREE
This tall, three-storey keep was built by Lord Mountjoy, Queen Elizabeth's deputy, in 1601, its purpose to secure the Gap of the North which was the main route into Ulster.
Times: ✷ Open all year **Facilities:**

OXFORD ISLAND   Map 01 D5

LOUGH NEAGH DISCOVERY CENTRE
Oxford Island National Nature, Reserve BT66 6NJ
⊃ (signed from M1 junct 10)
☎ 028 3832 2205
e-mail: oxford.island@craigavon.gov.uk
web: www.oxfordisland.com
In a spectacular setting on the water's edge, discover natural history, wildlife, family walks and much more.
Times: Open Apr-Sep, Mon-Sat 10-6; Sun 10-7, Oct-Mar, Mon-Sun 10-5. **Fee:** Free except for events. **Facilities:** 🅿 💻 ♿ (grounds accessible in part, bird watching hides) toilets for disabled shop ✖ (ex guide dogs) 🍴

PORTADOWN   Map 01 D5

ARDRESS HOUSE
64 Ardress Rd, Annaghmore BT62 1SQ
⊃ (on B28, 5m from Moy, 5m from Portadown, 3m from M1 junct 13)
☎ 028 3885 1236
e-mail: ardress@ntrust.org.uk
A plain 17th-century house, transformed around 1770 by its visionary architect-owner George Ensor, who added elegant wings and superb Adamesque plasterwork. The house has a fine picture gallery on loan from the Earl of Castlestewart. The grounds are beautifully unspoilt and there is a farmyard with livestock and a display of farm implements.
Times: Open 17 Mar, 2-6; 19 Mar-25 Sep, wknds, BHs & PHs 2-6
Facilities: 🅿 🍴 ♿ toilets for disabled shop ✖ (ex guide dogs) 🌂

TYNAN   Map 01 C5

VILLAGE CROSS
☎ 028 9023 5000   FREE
A carved High Cross, 11ft tall, which lay broken in two pieces for many years, but was skilfully mended in 1844.
Times: ✷ Open all year **Facilities:** 🅿 ♿

CO DOWN

ARDGLASS   Map 01 D5

JORDAN'S CASTLE
☎ 028 9054 6552   FREE
Although Ardglass is an important fishing port today, it was once the busiest seaport in Northern Ireland. Between the 14th and 15th centuries a ring of tower houses and fortified warehouses was built to protect the port. Jordan's Castle, a late 15th-century, four-storey tower house situated in the centre of town, is one of these. Besieged in the early 1600s and held for three years, the castle was bought, repaired and filled with bygones by a Belfast solicitor in the early part of the 20th century.
Times: ✷ Open Jul-Aug; Tue, Fri & Sat 10-1, Wed-Thu, 2-6. Other times on request. **Facilities:** ✖

BALLYWALTER   Map 01 D5

GREY ABBEY
⊃ (on E edge of village)
☎ 028 9054 6552   FREE
Founded in 1193 by Affreca, daughter of the King of the Isle of Man, these extensive ruins of a Cistercian abbey, sitting in lovely sheltered parkland, are among the best preserved in Northern Ireland. The chancel, with its tall lancet windows, magnificent west doorway and an effigy tomb - believed to be Affreca's - in the north wall, are particularly interesting. The abbey was burned down in 1572, and then re-used as a parish church. There are many 17th and 18th-century memorials to be seen in the church ruins, which occupy a pleasant garden setting. The abbey now has a beautiful medieval herb garden, with over 50 varieties of plants, and a visitors' centre.
Times: ✷ Open Apr-Sep; Tue-Sat 10-7, Sun 2-7; Oct-Mar, wknds, Sat 10-4, Sun 2-4. **Facilities:** 🅿 ♿ toilets for disabled

CASTLEWELLAN   Map 01 D5

DRUMENA CASHEL
⊃ (2.25m SW)
☎ 028 9023 5000   FREE
There are many stone ring forts in Northern Ireland, but few so well preserved as Drumena. Dating back to early Christian times, the fort is 30m in diameter and has an 11m accessible underground stone-built passage, probably used as a refuge and for storage.
Times: ✷ Open all times **Facilities:** 🅿

COMBER   Map 01 D5

WWT CASTLE ESPIE
Ballydrain Rd BT23 6EA
⊃ (12m SE of Belfast. A22 from Comber towards Killyleagh, 1st left into Ballydrain Rd)
☎ 028 9187 4146
e-mail: castleespie@wwt.org.uk
web: www.wwt.org.uk
Home to the largest collection of wildfowl in Ireland. Comfortable hides enable you to watch the splendour of migratory waders and wildfowl. Beautiful landscaped gardens, a taxidermy collection and fine paintings by wildlife artists can also be seen. Thousands of birds migrate to the reserve in winter and birdwatch mornings are held on the last Thursday of every month. The Centre's effluent is treated in a reed bed filtration system which can be seen on one walk.
Times: ✷ Open all year Mar-Oct, Mon-Sat 10.30-5, Sun 11.30-5.30; Nov-Feb Mon-Fri 11-4 Sat & Sun 11-4.30. **Facilities:** 🅿 💻 🍴 ♿ (hides have wheelchair platforms) toilets for disabled shop

DOWNPATRICK   Map 01 D5

DOWN COUNTY MUSEUM
The Mall BT30 6AH
➲ (on entry to town follow brown signs to museum)
☎ 028 4461 5218   **FREE**
e-mail: museum@downdc.gov.uk
web: www.downcountymuseum.com
The museum is located in the restored buildings of the 18th-century county gaol. In addition to restored cells that tell the stories of some of the prisoners, there are exhibitions on the history of County Down. Plus temporary exhibits, events, tea-room and shop.
Times: Open all year, Mon-Fri 10-5, wknds 1-5   **Facilities:** P (100yds) 🍴 🛈 ♿ (wheelchair available, handling boxes on application) toilets for disabled shop ✗ (ex guide dogs) ☕

INCH ABBEY
➲ (0.75m NW off A7)
☎ 028 9023 5000
Beautiful riverside ruins of a Cistercian abbey founded by John de Courcy around 1180. Of particular note is the tall, pointed, triple east window.
Times: ✱ Open Apr-Sep 10-7, Sun 2-7. Oct-Mar free access.
Facilities: P ♿

LOUGHINISLAND CHURCHES
➲ (4m W)
☎ 028 9023 5000   **FREE**
This remarkable group of three ancient churches stands on an island in the lough, accessible by a causeway. The middle church is the oldest, probably dating back to the 13th century, with a draw-bar hole to secure the door. The large North church was built in the 15th century, possibly to replace the middle church and continued in use until 1720. The smallest and most recent church is the South (MacCartan's) church.
Times: ✱ Open all times   **Facilities:** P ♿ ☕

MOUND OF DOWN   **FREE**
➲ (on Quoile Marshes, from Mount Crescent)
☎ 028 9023 5000
A hill fort from the Early Christian period, conquered by Anglo-Norman troops in 1177, who then built an earthwork castle on top. This mound in the marshes, beside the River Quoile, was the first town before the present Downpatrick.
Times: ✱ Open all times   **Facilities:** P

THE ST PATRICK CENTRE
St Patrick Visitor Centre, Market St BT30 6LZ
➲ (A7 from Belfast, follow brown heritage signs)
☎ 028 4461 9000   **2 for 1**
e-mail: director@saintpatrickcentre.com
web: www.saintpatrickcentre.com
This 21st-century multimedia, interactive, audio-visual feast is dedicated to the fascinating story of Ireland's Patron Saint Patrick, who brought Christianity to Ireland in the 5th century. The Centre is located beside the saint's grave, in the heart of St. Patrick's country, forty minutes from Belfast and two hours from Dublin.
Times: Open all year Oct-Mar, Mon-Sat, 10-5 & St Patricks Day 9.30-7; Apr-May & Sep, Mon-Sat 9.30-5.30, Sun 1-5.30 (morning opening on request), Jun-Aug Mon-Sat 9.30-6, Sun 10-6. (Last admission 1.5 hrs before closing). **Fee:** ✱ £4.90 (ch £2.50, concessions £3.30) family ticket (2ad+2ch) £11.70. Groups 25+, £3.25 (ch £2.20, concessions £2.65) **Facilities:** P 🍴 ✗ 🛈 ♿ (lifts & wheelchairs available) toilets for disabled shop garden centre ✗ (ex guide dogs) ☕

STRUELL WELLS
➲ (1.5m E)
☎ 028 9023 5000   **FREE**
Pilgrims come to collect the healing waters from these holy drinking and eye wells which are fed by a swift underground stream. Nearby are the ruins of an 18th-century church, and, even more interesting, single-sex bath-houses. The men's bath-house is roofed, has an anteroom and a sunken bath, while the ladies' is smaller and roofless.
Times: ✱ Open all times   **Facilities:** P ☕

DROMARA   Map 01 D5

LEGANANNY DOLMEN
➲ (4m S)
☎ 028 9023 5000   **FREE**
Theatrically situated on the slopes of Slieve Croob, this tripod dolmen with its three tall uprights and huge capstone is the most graceful of Northern Ireland's Stone Age monuments. There are views to the Mourne Mountains.
Times: ✱ Open at all times   **Facilities:** ♿ ☕

HILLSBOROUGH   Map 01 D5

HILLSBOROUGH FORT   **FREE**
☎ 028 9268 3285
On a site that dates back to early Christian times, the existing fort was built in 1650 by Colonel Arthur Hill to command a view of the road from Dublin to Carrickfergus. The building was ornamented in the 18th century. It is set in a forest park with a lake and pleasant walks.
Times: ✱ Open all year; Apr-Sep, Tue-Sat 10-7, Sun 2-7; Oct-Mar, Tue-Fri 10-4, Sat 10-4, Sun 2-4., **Facilities:** P ♿

HOLYWOOD

ULSTER FOLK AND TRANSPORT MUSEUM NEW
Cultra BT18 0EU

EU Programme for Peace and Reconciliation

➲ (12m outside Belfast on A2, past Holywood on main route to Bangor)
☎ 02890 428428
e-mail: uftmmarketing@magni.org.uk
web: www.uftm.org.uk

Voted Northern Ireland's Best Visitor Attraction and Irish Museum of the year, this attraction illustrates the way of life and traditions of Northern Ireland. The galleries of the Transport Museum display collections of horse drawn carts, cars, steam locomotives and the history of ship and aircraft

continued

building. Please telephone for details of special events running throughout the year.
Times: Open all year Mar-Jun, Mon-Fri 10-5, Sat 10-6, Sun 11-6; Jul-Sep, Mon-Sat 10-6, Sun 11-6; Oct-Feb, Mon-Fri 10-4, Sat 10-5, Sun 11-5. **Fee:** ✱ Folk Museum: £5 (ch 5-16 and concessions £3 under 5 free) Family ticket (2ad + 3ch) £14. Disabled visitors free. Transport Museum: as Folk Museum. combined ticket £6.50 (ch 5-16 and concessions £3.50) Family ticket £18. **Facilities:** 🅿 💷 🗐 & toilets for disabled shop on lead only 🖛

KILKEEL   Map 01 D4

GREENCASTLE
➲ (4m SW)
☎ 028 9023 5000
Looking very much like an English Norman castle with its massive keep, gatehouse and curtain wall, this 13th-century royal fortress stands on the shores of Carlingford Lough, with fine views of the Mourne Mountains. Greencastle has an eventful military history, it was beseiged and taken by Edward Bruce in 1316, attacked and spoiled by the Irish at least twice later in the 14th century, and maintained as a garrison for Elizabeth in the 1590s.
Times: ✱ Open Jul-Aug, Tue-Sat 10-7, Sun 2-7. **Facilities:** 🅿 &

KILLINCHY   Map 01 D5

SKETRICK CASTLE
➲ (3m E on W tip of Sketrick Islands)   **FREE**
☎ 028 9023 5000
A badly ruined tall tower house, probably 15th century. The ground floor rooms include a boat bay and prison. An underground passage leads from the north-east of the bawn to a freshwater spring.
Times: ✱ Open at all times. **Facilities:** 🅿 &

NEWCASTLE   Map 01 D5

DUNDRUM CASTLE
➲ (4m N)   **FREE**
☎ 028 9054 6518
This medieval castle, one of the finest in Ireland, was built in 1777 by John De Courcy in a strategic position overlooking Dundrum Bay, a position which offers visitors fine views over the sea and to the Mourne Mountains. The castle was captured by King John in 1210 and was badly damaged by Cromwellian troops in 1652. Still an impressive ruin, it shows a massive round keep with walls 16m high and 2m thick, surrounded by a curtain wall, and a gatehouse which dates from the 13th century.
Times: ✱ Open Apr-Sep, Tue-Sat 10-7, Sun 2-7; Oct-Mar, wknds, Sat 10-4, Sun 2-4. **Facilities:** 🅿 & toilets for disabled

MAGHERA CHURCH
➲ (2m NNW)   **FREE**
☎ 028 9023 5000
The stump of a round tower, blown down in a storm in the early 18th century, survives from the early monastery, with a ruined 13th-century church nearby.
Times: ✱ Open all year. **Facilities:** 🅿 &

NEWTOWNARDS   Map 01 D5

MOUNT STEWART HOUSE, GARDEN & TEMPLE OF THE WINDS
Greyabbey BT22 2AD
➲ (5m SE off A20)
☎ 028 4278 8387
e-mail: mountstewart@nationaltrust.org.uk
On the east shore of Strangford Lough, is a fascinating house which has survived for three centuries, famous for its many illustrious owners and guests and well renowned for its magnificent gardens created by Edith Lady Londonderry, wife of the 7th Marquess. In the inspired gardens, which are now a nominated world heritage site, many rare and subtropical trees thrive. Located by the shore is the Temple of the Winds, built by James 'Athenian' Stuart in 1782 for the first Marquess.
Times: Lakeside Gardens & Walks: Daily all year, 10-sunset;. Formal Gardens: Mar wknds & BHs 10-4; Apr & Oct, daily 10-6; May-Sep 10-8 (closed Nov-Feb). House: 12 Mar-end Apr wknds (including Etr) 12-6.; May, Jun & Sep, wknds 12-6, weekdays (ex Tue) 1-6; Oct, wknds 12-6 (Nov-Feb closed). Temple of Winds Apr-Oct, Sun & BH, 2-5.
Facilities: 🅿 💷 ✗ licensed 🗐 & (4 wheelchairs (2 electric) available) toilets for disabled shop 🖛

SCRABO TOWER
Scrabo Country Park, 203A Scrabo Rd BT23 4SJ
➲ (1m W)
☎ 028 9181 1491   **FREE**
The 135ft high Scrabo Tower, one of Northern Ireland's best-known landmarks, dominates the landscape of North Down and is also the centre of a country park around the slopes of Scrabo Hill. The Tower provides a fascinating series of interpretative displays about the surrounding countryside and the viewing platform boasts spectacular views over Strangford Lough and Co. Down. The park provides walks through fine beech and hazel woodlands and the unique sandstone quarries display evidence of volcanic activity as well as being breeding sites for peregrine falcons.
Times: ✱ Open end Mar-mid Sep, Sat-Thu 10.30-6.
Facilities: 🅿 shop ✖

PORTAFERRY   Map 01 D5

EXPLORIS AQUARIUM
The Rope Walk, Castle St BT22 1NZ
➲ (A20 or A2 or A25 to Strangford Ferry Service)
☎ 028 4272 8062
e-mail: info@ards-council.gov.uk
web: www.exploris.org.uk

Exploris Aquarium is Northern Ireland's only public aquarium

continued

and now includes a seal sanctuary. Situated in Portaferry on the shores of Strangford Lough it houses some of Europe's finest displays. The Open Sea Tank holds 250 tonnes of sea water. The complex includes a park with duck pond, picnic area, children's playground, caravan site, woodland and bowling green.
Times: Open all year, Mon-Fri 10-6, Sat 11-6, Sun 1-6. (Sep-Feb closing 1 hr earlier). **Fee:** £6.70 (concessions £3.80). Family £18.
Facilities: 🅿 🍴 ⬧ (2 lifts within complex) toilets for disabled shop ✈ (ex guide dogs) 🍴

SAINTFIELD   Map 01 D5

ROWALLANE GARDEN
BT24 7LH
⮑ (1m S of Saintfield on A7)
☎ 028 9751 0131
e-mail: rowallane@nationaltrust.org.uk
Beautiful and exotic 52-acre gardens, started by the Rev John Moore in 1860, containing exquisite plants from all over the world. They are particularly noted for their rhododendrons and azaleas and for the wonderful floral displays in spring and summer.
Times: ✱ Open Oct-Apr, 10-4; May-Sep, 10-8. Closed Dec 24-1 Jan.
Facilities: 🅿 🍴 ⬧ (parking facilities, manual wheelchairs, scented plants) toilets for disabled 😋

STRANGFORD   Map 01 D5

AUDLEY'S CASTLE
⮑ (1.5m W by shore of Strangford Lough)   FREE
☎ 028 9023 0560
15th-century tower house on Strangford Lough which offers lovely views from its top floor. The internal fittings are complete.
Times: ✱ Open Apr-Sep, daily 10-7. **Facilities:** 🅿 ✈

CASTLE WARD
BT30 7LS
⮑ (0.5m W of Strangford on A25)
☎ 028 4488 1204
e-mail: castleward@nationaltrust.org.uk
The curious diversity of styles in this house is due to the fact that its owner and his wife could never agree; so classical themes and a more elaborate Gothic look were both incorporated. The servants' living quarters are reached by an underground passage. Gardens, complete with a small lake and classical summerhouse, are richly planted and especially beautiful in spring.
Times: ✱ Ground daily 10-4 (8 May-Sep). House & Wildlife Centre; 15 Mar-Apr wknds, BH/PH 12-6; May wknds 12-6, Mon, Wed & Fri 1-6; Jun-Aug, daily noon-6 (Jun wkdays from 1); Sep-Oct wknds 12-6
Facilities: 🅿 (charged) 🍴 📷 ⬧ (wheelchair available, may be driven to house, Braille) toilets for disabled shop 😋 🍴

STRANGFORD CASTLE   FREE
☎ 028 9023 5000
A three-storey tower house built in the 16th century, overlooking the small double harbour of Strangford.
Times: ✱ Open all reasonable times. **Facilities:** ✈

BELLEEK   Map 01 B5

BELLEEK POTTERY
3 Main St BT93 3FY
⮑ (A46 from Ennisuilla to Belleek. Pottery at entrance to village)
☎ 028 6865 9300   2 for 1
e-mail: visitorcentre@belleek.ie
web: www.belleek.ie
Known worldwide for its fine Parian china, Ireland's oldest pottery was started in 1857 by the Caldwell family. Meet the craftspeople at work whilst touring the Pottery and visit the museum, which has exhibits dating back over 140 years.
Times: Open all year, Apr-Sep Mon-Fri 9-6, Sat & Sun 2-6; Jul & Aug Sun 11-6; Oct Mon-Fri 9-5.30. Closed wknds except Oct, Sat 10-5.30 & Sun 2-6,1 Jan, 17 Mar & Xmas. **Fee:** ✱ Guided tours £4 (ch under 12 free, pen £2). **Facilities:** 🅿 ✕ ⬧ (2 wheelchairs) toilets for disabled shop ✈ (ex guide dogs) 🍴

CASTLE ARCHDALE BAY   Map 01 C5

WHITE ISLAND CHURCH
⮑ (in Castle Archdale Bay; ferry from marina)
☎ 028 9023 5000
Lined up on the far wall of a small, roofless 12th-century church are eight uncanny carved-stone figures. Part Christian and part pagan in appearance, their significance has been the subject of great debate. The church ruins sit on an early monastic site.
Times: ✱ Open Jul-Aug, Tue-Sat 10-7, Sun 2-7. **Facilities:** 🅿 ✈ 🚌

DERRYGONNELLY   Map 01 C5

TULLY CASTLE
⮑ (3m N, on W shore of Lower Lough Erne)   FREE
☎ 028 9054 6552
Extensive ruins of a Scottish-style stronghouse with enclosing bawn overlooking Lough Erne. Built by Sir John Hume in the early 1600s, the castle was destroyed, and most of the occupants slaughtered, by the Maguires in the 1641 Rising. There is a replica of a 17th-century garden in the bawn.
Times: ✱ Open Jul & Aug, Wed-Sun, 10-6. **Facilities:** 🅿 ⬧ ✈

ENNISKILLEN   Map 01 C5

CASTLE COOLE
BT74 6JY
⮑ (on A4, 1.5m from Enniskillen towards Belfast)
☎ 028 6632 2690
e-mail: castlecoole@nationaltrust.org.uk
web: www.ntni.org.uk
No expense was spared in the building of this mansion. James Wyatt was the architect, the lovely plasterwork ceilings were by Joseph Rose, and the chimneypieces the work of Richard Westmacott. Vast amounts of Portland stone were specially imported, together with an Italian expert in stonework. The house is filled with beautiful Regency furniture.
Times: Open Grounds, Oct-Mar, daily 10-4; Apr-Sep, daily 10-8. House: 12 Mar-May, wknds & PHs/BHs 12-6; Jun, Wed-Mon 1-6; Jul-Aug daily 12-6; Sep wknds 12-6; 1-9 Oct wknds 1-5 **Facilities:** 🅿 🍴 ⬧ (may be driven to house, large print guide) toilets for disabled shop ✈ (ex in park & guide dogs) 😋 🍴

ENNISKILLEN CASTLE

BT74 7HL

☎ 028 6632 2711

Overlooking Lough Erne, this castle, a three-storey keep surrounded by massive stone-built barracks and with a turreted fairytale 17th-century water gate, now houses two museums and a heritage centre. In the castle keep is a small museum displaying Royal Enniskillen Fusiliers regimental exhibits, while the other rooms contain the Fermanagh County Museum's collection of local antiquities.

Times: ✱ Open all year Mon 2-5, Tue-Fri 10-5 (closed 1-2, Oct-Apr), Sat 2-5 May-Aug, Sun 2-5 Jul-Aug, all day BHs. **Facilities:** 🅿 & shop ✖

FLORENCE COURT

BT92 1DB

➲ (8m SW of Enniskillen via A4, then A32 to Swanlibar, well signed)

☎ 028 6634 8249

e-mail: florencecourt@nationaltrust.org.uk

web: www.ntni.org.uk

An 18th-century mansion overlooking wild and beautiful scenery towards the Mountains of Cuilcagh. The interior of the house, particularly noted for its flamboyant rococo plasterwork, was gutted by fire in 1955, but has been restored. There are pleasure grounds with an Ice House, Summer House, Water Powered Sawmill and also a walled garden.

Times: Open daily. Grounds, Oct-Mar 10-4; Apr-Sep 10-8. House: 12 Mar-May, wknds & BHs 12-6. Jun, Mon-Fri (ex Tue) 1-6, wknds 12-6; Jul-Aug, Daily 12-6. Sep, wknds 12-6; 1-9 Oct, wknds 1-5

Facilities: 🅿 (charged) ▰ ✖ 📱 & (electric wheelchair available & wheelchair path, Braille) toilets for disabled shop ✿ 🎏

MARBLE ARCH CAVES

Marlbank Scenic Loop BT92 1EW

➲ (off A4 Enniskillen to Sligo road. Left onto A32 and follow signs)

☎ 028 6634 8855

e-mail: mac@fermanagh.gov.uk

web: www.marblearchcaves.net

One of Europe's finest cave systems, under the Mountains of Cuilcagh. Visitors are given a tour of a wonderland of stalagmites, stalactites and underground rivers and lakes, starting with a boat trip on the lower lake. The streams, which feed the caves, flow down into the mountain then emerge at Marble Arch, a 30ft detached limestone bridge. The geological, historical and economic benefits of Marble Arch Caves and Cuilcagh Mountain Park were recognised on an international scale when they were jointly awarded the title of European Geopark.

Times: Open late Mar-Sep, daily, 10-4.30; Jul & Aug 10-5. **Fee:** ✱ £7 (ch £4, concessions £5). Family ticket £18. Group rates available.

Facilities: 🅿 ▰ 📱 & (induction loop in AV theatre) toilets for disabled shop ✖ (ex guide dogs) 🎏

MONEA CASTLE

➲ (6m NW)

☎ 028 9023 5000   FREE

A fine example of a plantation castle still with much of its enclosing bawn wall intact, built around 1618. Of particular interest is the castle's stone corbelling - the Scottish method of giving additional support to turrets.

Times: ✱ Open at any reasonable time. **Facilities:** 🅿 &

THE SHEELIN IRISH LACE MUSEUM

Ballanaleck BT92 2BA

➲ (from Enniskillen take A4 onto A509. Thatched Sheelin restaurant on left after 3m, museum in restaurant car park)

☎ 028 6634 8052

e-mail: infoirishlacemuseum.com

web: www.irishlacemuseum.com

The Irish Lace Museum has the largest and most comprehensive display of antique lace anywhere in Ireland. There are around 400 exhibits, representing the five main types of Irish lace: Inishmacsaint Needlelace, Crochet, Limerick, Carrickmacross, and Youghal Needlelace. The history of the Irish lace-making industry is described, and antique items can be bought in the museum shop.

Times: ✱ Open Mon-Sat 10-6. **Facilities:** 🅿 ✖ licensed 📱 & (toilets for disabled in restaurant) shop ✖ (ex guide dogs) 🎏

LISNASKEA   Map 01 C5

CASTLE BALFOUR

☎ 028 9023 5000

Dating from 1618 and refortified in 1652, this is a T-plan house with vaulted rooms. Badly burnt in the early 1800s, this house has remained in ruins.

Times: ✱ Open at all times. **Facilities:** 🅿 &

NEWTOWNBUTLER   Map 01 C5

CROM ESTATE

BT92 8AP

➲ (3m from A34, well signed from Newtownbutler)

☎ 028 6773 8118 6773 8174

e-mail: crom@nationaltrust.org.uk

web: www.ntni.org.uk

Featuring 2,000 acres of woodland, parkland and wetland, the Crom Estate is one of Northern Ireland's most important conservation areas. Nature trails are signposted through woodlands to the ruins of the old castle, and past the old boat house and picturesque summer house. Day tickets for pike fishing and boat hire are available from the Visitor Centre.

Times: Open Grounds: 12 Mar-Jun, daily 10-6; Jul-Aug, daily 10-8; Sep, daily 10-6; Oct, wknds 12-6. Visitor centre: 15 Mar-24 Apr, wknds & BH 10-6; May-Sep, daily 10-6; 1-9 Oct, wknds 1-5. **Facilities:** 🅿 (charged) ▰ 📱 & (adapted picnic bench & holiday cottage) toilets for disabled shop ✿ 🎏

CO LONDONDERRY

COLERAINE   Map 01 C6

HEZLETT HOUSE

107 Sea Rd, Castlerock BT51 4TW

➲ (5m W on Coleraine/Downhill coast road 1m from Castlerock)

☎ 028 7084 8728

e-mail: hezletthouse@nationaltrust.org.uk

web: www.ntni.org.uk

A low, thatched cottage built around 1690 with an interesting cruck truss roof, constructed by using pairs of curved timbers to form arches and infilling around this frame with clay, rubble and other locally available materials.

Times: Open Jun-Aug, please contact for opening times 028 7084 8728 **Facilities:** 🅿 & (parking) toilets for disabled ✖ (ex in gardens on lead) ✿

MOUNT SANDEL

➲ (1.25m SSE)
☎ 028 9023 0560   FREE

This 200ft oval mound overlooking the River Bann is believed to have been fortified in the Iron Age. Nearby is the earliest known inhabited place in Ireland, where post holes and hearths of wooden dwellings, and flint implements dating back to 6650BC have been found. The fort was a stronghold of de Courcy in the late 12th century and was refortified for artillery in the 17th century.

Times: ✷ Open at all times. **Facilities:** ▣ ♿

DOWNHILL   Map 01 C6

MUSSENDEN TEMPLE BISHOP'S GATE AND BLACK GLEN

Mussenden Rd BT51 4RP   FREE

➲ (1m W of Castlerock off A2, 6m from Coleraine)
☎ 028 7084 8728
e-mail: downhillcastle@nationaltrust.org.uk
web: www.ntni.org.uk

Spectacularly placed on a cliff edge overlooking the Atlantic, this perfect 18th-century rotunda was modelled on the Temple of Vesta at Tivoli. Visitors entering by the Bishop's Gate can enjoy a beautiful glen walk up to the headland where the temple stands. If you enjoy open windswept walks with views that stretch over the whole of the north coast of Ireland, then you must visit Downhill.

Times: Open Grounds, all year, dawn-dusk. Temple, 12 Mar-May wknds & BH 11-6; Jun, daily, 11-6; Jul-Aug, daily, 11-730; Sep wknds 11-6; Oct, wknds, 11-5. **Facilities:** ▣ (charged) 🅿 ♿ toilets for disabled ⛟

DUNGIVEN   Map 01 C5

BANAGHER CHURCH

➲ (2m SW)
☎ 028 9023 5000   FREE

This church was founded by St Muiredach O'Heney in 1100 and altered in later centuries. Today impressive ruins remain. The nave is the oldest part and the square-headed lintelled west door is particularly impressive. Just outside, the perfect miniature stone house, complete with pitched roof and the sculpted figures of a saint at the doorway, is believed to be the tomb of St Muiredach. The saint was said to have endowed his large family with the power of bringing good luck. All they had to do was to sprinkle whoever or whatever needed luck with sand taken from the base of the saint's tomb.

Times: ✷ Open at all times. **Facilities:** ▣ ♿

DUNGIVEN PRIORY

➲ (SE of town overlooking River Roe)
☎ 028 9023 5000   FREE

Up until the 17th century Dungiven was the stronghold of the O'Cahan chiefs, and the Augustinian priory, of which extensive ruins remain, was founded by the O'Cahans around 1150. The church, which was altered many times in later centuries, contains one of Northern Ireland's finest medieval tombs. It is the tomb of Cooey na Gall O'Cahan who died in 1385. His sculpted effigy, dressed in Irish armour, lies under a stone canopy. Below are six kilted warriors.

Times: ✷ Open Church at all times, chancel only when caretaker available. Check at house at end of lane. **Facilities:** ▣ ♿

LIMAVADY   Map 01 C6

ROUGH FORT

➲ (1m W off A2)
☎ 028 7084 8728   FREE
e-mail: downhillcastle@nationaltrust.org.uk
web: www.ntni.org.uk

Early Christian rath picturesquely surrounded by pine and beech trees, making it a significant landscape feature. The Rough Fort is one of the best examples of an earthwork ring fort in Ireland.

Times: ✷ Open at all times. **Facilities:** 🚌 ⛟

LONDONDERRY   Map 01 C5

CITY WALLS

☎ 028 9023 5000

The finest and most complete city walls to be found in Ireland. The walls, 20-25ft high, are mounted with ancient cannon, and date back to the 17th century. The walled city is a conservation area with many fine buildings. Visitors can walk round the city ramparts - a circuit of one mile.

Times: ✷ Open all times. **Facilities:** ▣ (charged) ♿

TOWER MUSEUM

Union Hall Place BT48 6LU
➲ (behind city wall, facing guildhall)
☎ 028 7137 2411
e-mail: museums@derrycity.gov.uk

This exhibition recounts the history of Londonderry from pre-historic times to the present day using real artefacts, theatrical displays and eleven audio-visual programmes showing the spread of Irish monasticism, the famous Siege of Derry and the road to the partition of Ireland.

Times: Open all year, Sep-Jun Tue-Sat 10-5. Jul-Aug, Mon-Sat 10-5, Sun 2-5. Also open BH Mons. **Fee:** ✷ £4.20 (pen, UB40s, students £1.60) Family ticket £8.50. **Facilities:** ℗ (300yds) ♿ toilets for disabled shop ✈ (ex guide dogs) 🍴

MAGHERA   Map 01 C5

MAGHERA CHURCH

➲ (E approach to the town)
☎ 028 9023 5000   FREE

Important 6th-century monastery founded by St Lurach, later a bishop's see and finally a parish church. This much-altered church has a magnificently decorated 12th-century west door. A cross-carved stone to the west of the church is supposed to be the grave of the founder.

Times: ✷ Key from Leisure Centre. **Facilities:** ▣ ♿

MONEYMORE   Map 01 C5

SPRINGHILL

BT45 7NQ
➲ (1m from Moneymore on B18 to Coagh)
☎ 028 8674 8210 & 8674 7927
e-mail: springhill@nationaltrust.org.uk

This pleasingly symmetrical manor house dates back to the 17th century. Today much of the family furniture, books and bric-a-brac have been retained. Outside, the laundry, stables, brewhouse, and old dovecote make interesting viewing, as does the excellent costume museum.

Times: ✷ Open 15 Mar-Jun, wknds & BH 2-6; Jul-Aug, daily 2-6; Sep, wknds only 2-6. **Facilities:** ▣ 🖵 🍴 ♿ (photograph album of 1st floor, wheelchair, scented plants) toilets for disabled shop ⛟

CO TYRONE

ARDBOE   Map 01 C5

ARDBOE CROSS
➲ (off B73)
☎ 028 9023 5000
Situated at Ardboe Point, on the western shore of Lough Neagh, is the best example of a high cross to be found in Northern Ireland. Marking the site of an ancient monastery, the cross has 22 sculpted panels, many recognisably biblical, including Adam and Eve and the Last Judgment. It stands over 18ft high and dates back to the 10th century. It is still the rallying place of the annual Lammas, but praying at the cross and washing in the lake has been replaced by traditional music-making, singing and selling of local produce. The tradition of 'cross reading' or interpreting the pictures on the cross, is an honour passed from generation to generation among the men of the village.
Times: ✱ Open at all times. **Facilities:** 🅿 &

BALLYGAWLEY   Map 01 C5

U S GRANT ANCESTRAL HOMESTEAD & VISITOR CENTRE
Dergenagh Rd BT70 1TW
➲ (off A4, 2m on Dergenagh road, signed)
☎ 028 8555 7133
e-mail: killymaddy@dstbc.org
web: www.dungannon.gov.uk
Ancestral homestead of Ulysses S Grant, 18th President of the United States of America. The homestead and farmyard have been restored to the style and appearance of a mid-19th-century Irish smallholding. There are many amenities including a children's play area, purpose built barbecue and picnic tables and butterfly garden.
Times: Open by appointment only **Fee:** ✱ £1.50 (ch & concessions 0.75p). **Facilities:** 🅿 & (wide doorway to audio-visual area/entrances/exits) ✕ (ex guide dogs)

BEAGHMORE   Map 01 C5

BEAGHMORE STONE CIRCLES AND ALIGNMENTS
☎ 028 9023 5000   FREE
Discovered in the 1930s, these impressive, ritualistic stones have been dated back to the early Bronze, and maybe even Neolithic Ages. There are three pairs of stone circles, one single circle, stone rows or alignments and cairns, which range in height from one to four feet. This is an area littered with historic monuments, many discovered by people cutting turf.
Times: ✱ Open at all times. **Facilities:** 🅿 &

BENBURB   Map 01 C5

BENBURB CASTLE
☎ 028 9023 5000   FREE
The castle ruins - three towers and massive walls - are dramatically placed on a cliff-edge 120ft above the River Blackwater. The northwest tower is now restored and has dizzy cliff-edge views. The castle, built by Sir Richard Wingfield around 1615, is actually situated in the grounds of the Servite Priory. There are attractive walks down to the river.
Times: ✱ Castle grounds open at all times. Special arrangements, made in advance, necessary for access to flanker tower.
Facilities: 🅿 & ✕

CASTLECAULFIELD   Map 01 C5

CASTLE CAULFIELD
☎ 028 9023 5000
Sir Toby Caulfield, an Oxfordshire knight and ancestor of the Earls of Charlemont, built this manor house in 1619 on the site of an ancient fort. It was badly burnt in 1641, repaired and lived in by the Caulfield/Charlemont family until 1670. It boasts the rare distinction of having had Saint Oliver Plunkett and John Wesley preach in its grounds. Some fragments of the castle are re-used in the fine, large 17th-century parish church.
Times: ✱ Open at all times. **Facilities:** 🅿 &

COOKSTOWN   Map 01 C5

TULLAGHOGE FORT
➲ (2m S)
☎ 028 9023 5000
This large hilltop earthwork, planted with trees, was once the headquarters of the O'Hagans, Chief Justices of the old kingdom of Tyrone. Between the 12th and 16th centuries the O'Neill Chiefs of Ulster were also crowned here - the King Elect was seated on a stone inauguration chair, new sandals were placed on his feet and he was then anointed and crowned. The last such ceremony was held here in the 1590s; in 1600 the stone throne was destroyed by order of Lord Mountjoy.
Times: ✱ Open at all times. **Facilities:** 🅿

WELLBROOK BEETLING MILL
20 Wellbrook Rd, Corkhill BT80 9RY
➲ (4m W, 0.5m off A505)
☎ 028 8674 8210 & 8675 1735
e-mail: wellbrookl@nationaltrust.org.uk
This 18th-century water-powered linen mill was used for bleaching and, until 1961, for finishing Irish linen. Beetling was the name given to the final process in linen making, when the material was beaten by 30 or so hammers (beetles) to achieve a smooth and slightly shiny finish.
Times: ✱ Open 15 Mar-Jun wknds & BHs, daily 12-6; Jul-Aug daily 12-6; Sep, wknds only 12-6. **Facilities:** 🅿 🗐 & toilets for disabled shop ♨

DUNGANNON   Map 01 C5

TYRONE CRYSTAL VISITOR CENTRE
Tyrone Crystal, Killybrackey BT71 6TT
➲ (M1 junct 14/A45 to T-junct, left towards Dungannon. Attraction 2.5m on left, signed)
☎ 028 8772 5335
e-mail: annamarie@tyronecrystal.com
web: www.tyronecrystal.com
Crystal making in Tyrone is a comparatively modern enterprise, dating its beginnings from the days of Benjamin Edwards in the 1770s. Tyrone Crystal is hand-cut, and visitors can see this craft in action on guided tours of the factory. The spacious visitor centre and facilities contribute to a fascinating insight of the history and heritage of this industry.
Times: Open Visitor Centre Mon-Sat 9-5, Sun 1-5 (seasonal); Tour times Mon-Fri 11, 12, 2, 3. Sat tours prior booking only **Fee:** ✱ £2 for tour. Visitor Centre free. **Facilities:** 🅿 ✕ 🗐 & (disabled parking spaces) toilets for disabled shop ✕ (ex guide dogs) ◼

NEWTOWNSTEWART   Map 01 C5

Harry Avery's Castle
➲ (0.75m SW)
☎ 028 9023 5000   **FREE**

The hilltop ruins of a Gaelic stone castle, built around the 14th century by one of the O'Neill chiefs, are the remains of the oldest surviving Irish-built castle in the north. Only the great twin towers of the gatehouse are left. A stairway enables the public to gain access to one of these.

Times: ✱ Open at all times. **Facilities:** ✕ 🚐

OMAGH   Map 01 C5

Ulster American Folk Park
BT78 5QY
➲ (5m NW Omagh on A5)
☎ 028 8224 3292
e-mail: info@uafp.co.uk
web: www.folkpark.com

EU Programme
for Peace and Reconciliation

An outdoor museum that traces the history of Ulster's links with America and the emigration of Ulster residents to the US during the 18th and 19th centuries. The 70-acre site is divided into two parts - Old World and New World. There are demonstrations of Old and New World crafts, and a visitor centre, with exhibitions and audio-visual presentations. The Centre for Emigration Studies is based here, with a research library and emigration database - please ring for details.

Times: Open Etr-Sep, daily 10.30-6, Sun & BH 11-6.30; Oct-Etr Mon-Fri 10.30-5. (Last admission 1hr 30mins before closing).
Facilities: 🅿 💻 ✕ 🗓 ♿ toilets for disabled shop ✕ (ex guide dogs) 🍴

ULSTER HISTORY PARK

Cullion BT79 7SU
➲ (7m on B48)
☎ 028 8164 8188
e-mail: uhp@omagh.gov.uk
web: www.omagh.gov.uk/historypark.htm

The story of settlement in Ireland, told with the aid of full-scale models of the houses and monuments built through the ages. Exhibitions and audio-visual presentations expand the theme.

Times: ✱ Open all year, Jul-Aug daily 10-6.30; Apr-Jun & Sep, daily 10-5.30; Oct-Mar, Mon-Fri 10-5. **Facilities:** 🅿 💻 🗓 ♿ toilets for disabled shop ✕ (ex guide dogs) 🍴

STEWARTSTOWN   Map 01 C5

Mountjoy Castle
Magheralamfield
➲ (3m SE, off B161)
☎ 028 9023 5000   **FREE**

Ruins of an early 17th-century brick and stone fort, with four rectangular towers, overlooking Lough Neagh. The fort was built for Lord Deputy Mountjoy during his campaign against Hugh O'Neill, Earl of Tyrone. It was captured and re-captured by the Irish and English during the 17th century and was also used by the armies of James II and William III.

Times: ✱ Open at all times. **Facilities:** 🅿

STRABANE   Map 01 C5

Gray's Printing Press
49 Main St BT82 8AU
➲ (in centre of Strabane)
☎ 028 7188 4094

Strabane was once an important printing and book-publishing centre, the only relic of this is a small shop in Main Street which now houses a museum illustrating the history of Strabane. The Print Museum, in a separate building, contains three 19th-century presses and shows the development of printing techniques over 150 years.

Times: ✱ Open Apr-Sep, Tue-Sat 2-5. **Facilities:** 🅿 (100yds) ♿ toilets for disabled ✕ (ex guide dogs) 🐾

We endeavour to be as accurate as possible, but changes to times and other information can occur after the guide has gone to press.

2-for-1 This symbol indicates attractions which have chosen to participate in our 2-for-1 voucher scheme

REPUBLIC OF IRELAND

EVENTS & FESTIVALS

January
1st Lord Mayor's New Year's Day Parade,
Dublin

February
17th-26th The Jameson Dublin International
Film Festival (provisional)

March
15th-20th St Patrick's Festival, Dublin
tbc Feis Ceoil (competitive classical music
festival), Dublin

April
18th-23rd Pan Celtic International Festival,
streets and various venues, Letterkenny
26th-30th Cork International Choral Festival,
various venues

May
22nd-29th Fleadh Nua, various venues Ennis
tbc Bantry International Mussel Fair, open air
concerts, street theatre, marching and pipe
bands, food events and fireworks
tbc Listowel Writers Week, St John's Arts &
Heritage Centre, Listowel

June
1st-5th The Smithwicks Cat Laughs,
international comedy festival, various
venues, Kilkenny
16th Bloomsday (James Joyce Festival), Dublin
tbc Enniscorthy Strawberry Festival,
Enniscorthy

July
tbc Galway International Arts Festival, various
venues

August
4th-7th Greystones Arts Festival, North
Wicklow
9th-13th Dublin Horse Show, Ballsbridge,
Dublin
10th-12th The Puck Fair, street fair – Ireland's
oldest – in Killorglin
11th-20th Kilkenny Arts Festival, various
venues Kilkenny city and county
18th-22nd Rose of Tralee Festival, Tralee
25th-27th Fleadh Cheoil na hEireann,
Letterkenny, biggest annual festival of Irish
traditional music in the world

September
18th-1st Oct Waterford International Festival
of Light Opera, Theatre Royal, Waterford
28th-1st Oct Galway International Oyster
Festival, Galway city
29th-14th Oct Dublin Theatre Festival, various
venues (provisional)

October
27th-30th Cork Jazz Festival, 75 venues
throughout the city
tbc Cork Film Festival,
various venues in the city
tbc Dublin City Marathon
tbc Wexford Festival Opera, Theatre Royal,
High Street, Wexford, Co Wexford

Top: The treaty stone of Limerick which celebrates the treaty of 1691   *Above: Blarney Castle on a misty day*

BALLYVAUGHAN   Map 01 B3

AILLWEE CAVE
➲ (3m S of Ballyvaughan. Signed from Galway and Ennis)
☎ 065 7077036
e-mail: theresa@aillweecave.ie
web: www.aillweecave.ie

2 for 1

An underground network of caves beneath the world famous Burren. Guided tours take you through large caverns, over bridged chasms and alongside thunderous waterfalls. There is a craftshop, a dairy where cheese is made, a speciality food shop and a tearoom. Santa uses the cave as a workshop around Christmas time, while Easter sees a massive egg hunt in the woods. In addition, a garden centre has opened here in the last year. Special Events: Santa's Workshop, appointments necessary, Dec 2005 & 2006. Ghost Evenings, summer months 2006.
Times: Open all year from 10 (mornings only in Dec) **Fee:** ✱ €10 (ch €5, pen €8). Family ticket €25-€30 **Facilities:** 🅿 ◢ ✗ licensed ▤ ♿ toilets for disabled shop garden centre ✈ (ex guide dogs) ◢

BUNRATTY   Map 01 B3

BUNRATTY CASTLE & FOLK PARK
➲ (8m from Limerick on N18 towards Ennis)
☎ 061 360788
e-mail: reservations@shannondev.ie
web: www.shannonheritage.com

Magnificent Bunratty Castle was built around 1425. The restored castle contains mainly 15th and 16th century furnishings and tapestries. Within its grounds is Bunratty Folk Park where 19th-century Irish life is tellingly recreated. Rural farmhouses, a village street and Bunratty House with its formal Regency gardens are recreated and furnished, as they would have appeared at the time.
Times: Open all year, daily 9-5.30, 9.30 Apr-May & Sep-Oct (last admission 4.15). Folk Park also open Jun-Aug 9-6 (last admission 5.15). (Last admission to Castle 4pm all year). Closed Good Fri & 24-26 Dec.
Fee: Castle & Folk Park €11.55 (ch€6.50, pen €7.30 & student €8.95). **Facilities:** 🅿 ◢ ✗ licensed ♿ toilets for disabled shop (on leads) ◢

KILLALOE   Map 01 B3

BRIAN BORU HERITAGE CENTRE NEW
➲ (N7 via Parkway Rdbt in Limerick city via Annacotty, Lisnagry and Birdhill. Turn left at Ballina R494)
☎ 061 360788
e-mail: reservations@shannondev.ie
web: www.shannonheritage.com

2 for 1

The 11th century High King of Ireland, Brian Boru one of the most influential and colourful figures in Irish history. The heritage centre reveals the story of Brian Boru through a series of colourful exhibits, graphic illustrations and interactive audio-visual presentation.
Times: Open daily, May-Sep 10-6 **Fee:** £3.15 (ch £1.55)
Facilities: 🅿 ♿ shop ◢

LISCANNOR   Map 01 B3

CLIFFS OF MOHER VISITORS CENTRE
➲ (6m NW of Lahinch)
☎ 065 7081 565
e-mail: reservations@shannondev.ie
web: www.shannonheritage.com

The Cliffs of Moher stand as a giant natural rampart against the aggressive might of the Atlantic Ocean, rising in places to 700ft, and stretch for almost 5 miles. O'Brien's Tower was built in the early 19th century as a viewing point for tourists on the highest point. There is a visitor centre with tourist information.
Times: Open Visitor Centre all year, 9.30-5.30; Jun-Aug 9-7. Visitor centre closed 21-27 Dec. O'Briens Tower open Mar-Oct 9.30-5.30 (weather permitting). **Fee:** O'Briens Tower €1.50 (ch €0.75).
Facilities: 🅿 (charged) ◢ ♿ toilets for disabled shop ✈ (ex in grounds) ◢

QUIN   Map 01 B3

CRAGGAUNOWEN THE LIVING PAST EXPERIENCE
➲ (signed from N18 Limerick to Galway road, off R462 from Cratloe and R469 from Ennis)
☎ 061 360788
e-mail: reservations@shannondev.ie
web: www.shannonheritage.com

The project includes a reconstructed ring fort and replicas of furniture, tools and utensils. Also on display is the 'Brendan', a replica of the leather canoe used by St Brendan the Navigator in the 6th century. The boat was sailed across the Atlantic Ocean in 1976 and 1977. A Bronze Age lake dwelling is currently under construction.
Times: Open mid Apr-Sep, daily 10-6 (last admission 5). **Fee:** €7.85 (ch €4.75, pen & students €5.85). **Facilities:** 🅿 ◢ ♿ toilets for disabled shop (on leads) ◢

KNAPPOGUE CASTLE & WALLED GARDEN NEW
➲ (off N18 3m from Quin)
☎ 061 360788
e-mail: reservations@shannondev.ie
web: www.shannonheritage.com

2 for 1

Built in 1467, Knappogue has a long and varied history. Occupied by Cromwell's troops in 1641 and completely restored in the mid-19th century, the castle fell into disrepair in the 1900's. In 1966 a careful restoration was completed and today the castle is famous for its medieval events. The attractive restored Victorian walled garden includes among many of its features a collection of plants from the Victorian era.
Times: Open May-mid Sep daily 9:30-5:30 **Fee:** ✱ €5.95 (ch €3, pen €2.95 **Facilities:** ♿ shop ◢

CO CORK

BLARNEY   Map 01 B2

BLARNEY CASTLE & ROCK CLOSE
➲ (5m from Cork on main road towards Limerick)
☎ 021 4385252
e-mail: info@blarneyc.iol.ie
web: www.blarneycastle.ie

The site of the famous Blarney Stone, known the world over for the eloquence it is said to impart to those who kiss it. The stone is in the upper tower of the castle, and, held by your feet, you must lean backwards down the inside of the battlements in order to receive the 'gift of the gab'. Special Events: Re-opening of Blarney House May 2006.
Times: Open Blarney Castle & Rock Close. Mon-Sat, May & Sep 9-6.30, Jun-Aug 9-7. Oct-Apr 9-Sundown or 6. Sun, Summer 9.30-5.30, Winter 9.30-sundown. Closed 24-25 Dec. **Fee:** Blarney Castle & Rock Close €8(ch 8-14 €2.50) concessions €6. Family ticket (2ad+2ch) € 18.00
Facilities: 🅿 🗐 & shop (ex guide dogs)

CARRIGTWOHILL (CARRIGTOHILL)   Map 01 B2

FOTA ARBORETUM & GARDENS
Fota Estate
➲ (14km from Cork on Cobh road)
☎ 021 4812728
web: www.heritageireland.ie   FREE

Fota Arboretum contains an extensive collection of trees and shrubs extending over an area of approx 27 acres and includes features such as an ornamental pond and Italian walled gardens. The collection includes many tender plants that could not be grown at inland locations, with many examples of exotic plants from the Southern Hemisphere.
Times: Arboretum - Apr-Oct Mon-Sat 9-6 Sun 11-6 Nov -Mar Mon-Sat 9-5 Sun 11-5 Walled Gardens - Apr-Oct Mon-Fri Selected Sunday openings please ring for times and dates. **Facilities:** 🅿 (charged) & toilets for disabled

FOTA WILDLIFE PARK
Fota Estate
➲ (16km E of Cork. From N25 (Cork to Waterford road) take Cobh road)
☎ 021 4812678
e-mail: info@fotawildlife.ie
web: www.fotawildlife.ie

Established with the primary aim of conservation, Fota has more than 90 species of exotic wildlife in open, natural

continued

surroundings. Many of the animals wander freely around the park. Giraffes, zebras, ostriches, antelope, cheetahs and a wide array of waterfowl are among the species here.
Times: Open 17 Mar-Oct, daily, 10-6 (Sun 11-6) (last admission 5); Nov-17 Mar 10-4.30 (Sun 11-4.30). (Last admission 3.30).
Fee: ✱ €10.50 (ch, pen & students €6.50, ch under 3 free). Family day ticket €42. **Facilities:** 🅿 (charged) ✗ 🗐 & (ramps where required) toilets for disabled shop ✈ 🍴

CLONAKILTY   Map 01 B2

WEST CORK MODEL VILLAGE RAILWAY
Inchydoney Rd
➲ (From Cork N71 West Cork left at junct for Inchydoney Island, signed at road junct. Village on bay side of Clonakilty)
☎ 023 33224   **2 for 1**
e-mail: modelvillage@eircom.net
web: www.modelvillage.ie

This miniature world depicts Irish towns as they were in the 1940s, with models of the West Cork Railway and various animated scenes. The tea room is set in authentic railway carriages that overlook picturesque Clonakilty Bay. Also take a guided tour of Clonakilty and the surrounding area on the road train.
Times: Open Feb-Oct daily 11-5; Jul-Aug, daily, extended hours 10-6.
Fee: ✱ €6 (concessions €4.50). Family ticket €19, Party 12+.
Facilities: 🅿 🍴 🗐 & toilets for disabled shop ✈ (ex guide dogs) 🍴

COBH   Map 01 B2

THE QUEENTOWN STORY
Cobh Railway Station
➲ (off N25, follow signs for Cobh. Attraction at Deepwater Quay, adjacent to train station)
☎ 021 4813591   **2 for 1**
e-mail: info@cobhheritage.com
web: www.cobhheritage.com

A dramatic exhibition of the origins, history and legends of Cobh. Between 1848 and 1950 over 3 million Irish people were deported from Cobh on convict ships. Visitors can explore the conditions onboard these vessels and learn about the harbour's connections with the *Lusitania* and the *Titanic*.
Times: Open May-Nov, 10-6 (last admission 5). Nov-May, 10-5 (last admission 4) **Fee:** ✱ €6 (ch & student u18 €3) pens €5). Family ticket €16.50 **Facilities:** 🅿 🍴 ✗ licensed 🗐 & (fully wheelchair accessible, wide access) toilets for disabled shop ✈ (ex guide dogs) 🍴

CORK   Map 01 B2

CORK CITY GAOL
Convent Av, Sundays Well
➲ (2km NW from Patrick St off Sundays Well Rd)
☎ 021 4305022   **2 for 1**
e-mail: corkgaol@indigo.ie
web: www.corkcitygaol.com

A restored 19th-century prison building. Furnished cells, lifelike characters and sound effects combine to allow visitors to experience day-to-day life for prisoners and gaoler. There is an audio-visual presentation of the social history of Cork City. Individual sound tours are available in a number of languages. A permanent exhibition, the Radio Museum Experience, is located in the restored 1920s broadcasting studio, home to Cork's first radio station, 6CK. Unfortunately the 1st and 2nd floors are not accessible to wheelchair users.

continued

Times: Open Mar-Oct, daily 9.30-6; Nov-Feb, daily 10-5. (Last admission 1hr before closing). Closed 23-28 Dec. **Fee:** ✻ €6 (ch €3.50, concessions €5) Family ticket €17 **Facilities:** 🅿 💷 🗐 ♿ (customer care policy - individual attention) toilets for disabled shop ✖ (ex guide dogs)

CORK PUBLIC MUSEUM
Fitzgerald Park, Mardyke
➲ (N of University College)
☎ 021 4270679
e-mail: museum@corkcity.ie

Displays illustrating the history of the city are housed in this museum. The collections cover the economic, social and municipal history from the Mesolithic period. There are fine collections of Cork Silver and Glass and Youghal Needlepoint Lace.
Times: ✻ Open all year, Jun-Aug Mon-Fri 11-1 & 2.15-6, Sun 3-5; Sep-May Mon-Fri 11-1 & 2.15-5, Sun 3-5. Closed Sat, BH wknds & PH **Facilities:** 🅿 (100yds) shop ✖ (ex guide dogs)

GARINISH ISLAND
➲ (1.5km boat trip from Glengarriff)
☎ 027 63040

Ilnacullin is a small island of 37 acres known to horticulturists and lovers of trees and shrubs all around the world as an island garden of rare beauty. The gardens of Ilnacullin owe their existence to the creative partnership, some 80 years ago, of Annan Bryce, then owner of the island and Harold Peto, architect and garden designer.
Times: Mar and Oct Mon-Sat 10.00-16.30 - Sun 13.00-17.00 Apr Mon-Sat 10.00-18.30 Sun 13.00 - 18.30 May and Sep Mon-Sat 10.00-18.30 Sun 12.00-18.30 Jun Mon-Sat 10.00-18.30 Sun 11.00-18.30 Jul and Aug - Mon-Sat 9.30-18.30 - Sun 11.00 18.30 - Last landing 1 hour before closing. **Fee:** ✻ €3.50 (ch & students €1.25, pen €2.50) Family ticket €8.25. Party. **Facilities:** 💷 🗐 ♿ (limited access) toilets for disabled

CHARLES FORT
➲ (3km from Kinsale)
☎ 021 4772263
e-mail: charlesfort@duchas.ie
web: www.heritageireland.ie

Built as part of the fortifications of the Irish coast in the late 17th century, Charles Fort was named after King Charles II. After the Battle of the Boyne in 1690, Williamite forces attacked and successfully besieged Charles Fort and the nearby James Fort, both of which held out for King James. The Fort also played a role in the Napoleonic Wars and was made a National Monument in 1973.
Times: Mid Mar - Oct Daily 10-6 Nov - Mid Mar - Daily 10 - 5 Last admission 45 minutes before closing. **Fee:** ✻ €3.50 (ch & students €1.25, pen €2.50) Family ticket €8.25. Party. **Facilities:** 🅿 💷 🗐 ♿ (lift) toilets for disabled ✖ (ex guide dogs)

DESMOND CASTLE
Cork St
➲ (R600 from Cork city to Kinsdale. From post office, 1st left then right, opposite Regional Museum then left and right again, castle on left)
☎ 021 4774855
e-mail: desmondcastle@duchas.ie
web: www.desmondcastle.ie

Built by the Earl of Desmond around the beginning of the 16th century, this tower was originally a custom house, but
continued

has also served as an ordnance office, prison, workhouse, stable and meeting place for the Local Defence Force during World War II. In 1938 it was declared a National Monument and restored. The Castle now houses the International Museum of Wine.
Times: Mid Apr - Oct Daily 10 - 6 - Last admission 45 mins. before closing. **Fee:** ✻ €2.75 (ch & students €1.25, pen €2) Family €7. **Facilities:** 🅿 (200mtrs) (parking discs required in town) 🗐 ✖ (ex guide dogs)

OLD MIDLETON DISTILLERY
➲ (E end of main street on left. Well signed)
☎ 021 4613594
e-mail: bookings@omd.ie
web: www.whiskeytours.ie

A tour of the Old Midleton Distillery consists of a 15-minute audio/visual presentation, then a 35-minute guided tour of the Old Distillery and then back to the Jameson Bar for a whiskey tasting - mineral water is available for children. The guided tour and audio-visual aids are available in seven languages.
Times: Open Nov-Feb daily, tours 11.30, 2.30 & 4. Mar-Oct daily 10-6 (last tour 5). Closed Good Fri & Xmas **Fee:** ✻ 8.50 (ch3.50) family ticket 22 **Facilities:** 🅿 💷 ✖ licensed 🗐 ♿ toilets for disabled shop ✖ (ex certain areas/guide dogs) ▤

THE WATER WHEELS
Abbey Assaroe
➲ (cross Abbey River on Rossnowlagh Rd, next turning left & follow signs)　　　**FREE**
☎ 071 9851580

Abbey Assaroe was founded by Cistercian Monks from Boyle Abbey in the late 12th century, who excelled in water engineering and canalised the river to turn water wheels for mechanical power. Two restored 12th-century mills, one is used as coffee shop and restaurant; the other houses a small museum related to the history of the Cistercians. Interesting walks in the vicinity.
Times: Open May-Oct, daily 10.30-6.30 **Facilities:** 🅿 💷 ✖ licensed 🗐 ♿ toilets for disabled shop garden centre

DONEGAL CASTLE
☎ 074 9722405

This restored 15th-century castle and adjoining 17th-century ruined English manor house contain exhibitions of Irish historical events. Guided tours are available.
Times: Mid Mar-End Oct Daily 10-6 1st Nov - 6 Mar (incl) Weekends, Fri, Sat, Sun 9.30-4.30 Last admission 45 mins. before closing. **Fee:** €6 (pen & students €3.50) Family €12. **Facilities:** 🅿 ✖ (ex guide dogs)

GLEBE HOUSE & GALLERY
Churchill
➲ (signed from Letterkenny on R251)
☎ 074 9137071

This Regency house, set in beautiful woodland gardens along the shore of Lough Gartan, was given to the nation along with his art collection by artist Derek Hill. The interior of the house is decorated with original wallpapers and textiles by William Morris.
Times: Easter 26-28 - Daily 11.00-6.30 Closed until Mid May - Mid May-End Sep Sat-Thur 11.00-6.30 (Closed Friday) Last tour 1 hour before closing. **Fee:** ✱ €2.75 (ch & students €1.25, pen €2) Family ticket €7. Group €2 each. **Facilities:** 🅿 💻 📱
🛆 ✖ (ex guide dogs)

GLENVEAGH NATIONAL PARK & CASTLE
Churchill
➲ (left off N56 onto L77)
☎ 074 9137090 & 9137262
e-mail: talchorn@duchas.ie
web: www.heritageireland.ie

Over 40,000 acres of mountains, glens, lakes and woods. A Scottish-style castle is surrounded by one of the finest gardens in Ireland, contrasting with the rugged surroundings.
Times: Open daily, St. Patrick's Day 17 Mar-1st Sun in Nov
Facilities: 🅿 💻 ✖ 📱 🛆 (visitor centre, gardens have paths) toilets for disabled shop

CAVANACOR HISTORIC HOUSE & ART GALLERY
Ballindrait
➲ (1.5m from town off N14 Strabane/Letterkenny road)
☎ 074 9141143
web: www.parsons.edu/~cokane/cavanacorgallery

Built in the early 1600s and commanding a view of the Clonleigh Valley and the River Deele, Cavanacor House is the ancestral home of James Knox Polk, 11th President of the USA (1845-1849). King James II dined under the sycamore tree in front of the house in 1689. There are over 10 acres of landscaped gardens and an old-fashioned walled garden. The Art Gallery will feature exhibitions of new work by national and international artists. Please ring for details.
Times: ✱ Open Etr & Jul-Aug Tue-Sat 12-6, Sun 2-6. Art gallery open all year **Facilities:** 🅿 💻 ✖ 📱 🛆 shop 🛒

ARDGILLAN CASTLE
➲ (R127 or M1 past Dublin Airport then follow signs)
☎ 01 8492212   **2 for 1**

A large and elegant country manor house built in 1738, set in 194 acres of parkland, overlooking the sea and coast as far as the Mourne Mountains. There is a permanent exhibition of the 17th century 'Down Survey' maps and various temporary exhibitions. Tours of the Gardens (June, July and August) begin at 3.30pm every Thursday. Guided tours of the house are conducted daily.
Times: Open Apr-Sep, Tue-Sun & BHs 11-6 (daily Jul-Aug); Oct-Mar, Wed-Sun & BHs 11-4.30. Closed 23 Dec-1 Jan. **Fee:** €6 (pen & students €3.50) Family €12. **Facilities:** 🅿 💻 📱 🛆 toilets for disabled shop ✖ (ex guide dogs)

NEWBRIDGE HOUSE AND TRADITIONAL FARM
Newbridge Demesne Take N1 and follow signs for Donabate.
☎ 01 8436534 & 8462184   **2 for 1**
e-mail: newbridgehouse@fingalcoco.ie

Newbridge House was designed by George Semple and built in 1737 for Charles Cobbe, Archbishop of Dublin. Set in 350 acres of parkland, the house contains many splendidly refurbished rooms featuring plasterwork, furniture and paintings. The house also features fully restored courtyard surrounded by; a dairy, estate workers house, carpenters shop and blacksmiths forge. The grounds contain a 29 acre traditional farm with many rare breeds and children's playground.
Times: Open Apr-Sep Tue-Sat 10-5, Sun & PH 2-6; Oct-Mar Sat-Sun & PH 2-5. Parties at other times by arrangement. **Fee:** ✱ House; €6.50 (ch €3.70, concessions €5.50). Family ticket €17.50. Farm; €3.50 (ch €2, concessions €2.50) family ticket (2ad + 2ch) €8, (2ad + 3-4ch) €10.50. **Facilities:** 🅿 💻 shop ✖ guide dogs 🛒

THE CASINO
off Malahide Rd, Marino DUBLIN 3
➲ (3m N of city, left off Fairview Strand up Malahide Rd, through junct with Griffith Ave. Left at Nazareth House, gates on left)
☎ 01 8331618
e-mail: casinomarino@duchias.ie
web: www.heritageireland.ie

Designed in 1757 by Sir William Chambers as a pleasure house for James Caulfield, 1st Earl of Charlemont, The Casino is possibly one of the finest 18th-century neo-Classical buildings in Europe. Its name means "small house", but The Casino surprisingly contains 16 finely-decorated rooms.
Times: Open Feb & Mar Sat & Sun only 12-4; Apr Sat & Sun only 12-5; May Daily 10-5; Jun-Sep Daily 10-6; Oct Daily 10-5; Nov & Dec Sat & Sun only 12-4 Last admission 45 mins. before closing. **Fee:** ✱ €2.75 (ch & students €1.25, pen €2) Family ticket €7. **Facilities:** 🅿 📱 🛆 ✖ (ex guide dogs)

THE CHESTER BEATTY LIBRARY

The Clock Tower Building, Dublin Castle
⮫ (10 mins walk from Trinity College, up Dame St towards Christ Church Cathedral)
☎ 01 4070750
e-mail: info@cbl.ie
web: www.cbl.ie

FREE

The contents of this fascinating gallery was bequeathed to Ireland by its first honorary citizen, American mining engineer and collector, Sir Alfred Chester Beatty (1875-1968). The collection includes manuscripts, prints, icons, miniatures, and objets d'art of great importance from 2700BC to the present day. See illuminated copies of the Qur'an and the Bible, Egyptian papyrus texts, and Buddhist paintings.
Times: ✱ Open all year, May-Sep, Mon-Fri 10-5; Oct-Apr, Tue-Fri 10-5, Sat 11-5, Sun 1-5. Closed BHs. **Facilities:** P (5mins walk) ⚇ ✗ ♿ toilets for disabled shop ✖ (ex guide dogs)

CHRIST CHURCH CATHEDRAL

Christchurch Place
⮫ (at top end of Dame St)
☎ 01 6778099
e-mail: welcome@cccdub.ie
web: www.cccdub.ie

2 for 1

Founded in 1030, the present building dates from 1180 with a major restoration in the 1870s. The crypt is the second largest medieval crypt in Britain or Ireland. There are daily services and choral services on Sundays and during the week.
Times: Open all year, Mon-Fri 9.45-5, Sat & Sun 10-5. Closed St Stephens Day 27 Dec. **Fee:** €5 (unwaged €2.50)
Facilities: P (100yds) ▤ ♿ (for access to crypt advance notice required) shop ✖ (ex guide dogs) ⚇

DRIMNAGH CASTLE

Long Mile Rd, Drimnagh DL12
⮫ (Dame St, left at Christchurch Cathedral into Patrick St, right into Cork St, through Dolphins Barn up to Crumlin Rd, past Halfway House. 500yds on right)
☎ 01 4502530 & 4508927
e-mail: drimnaghcastle@eircom.net

The last surviving medieval castle in Ireland with a flooded moat, Drimnagh dates back to the 13th century and was inhabited until 1954. The Castle consists of a restored Great Hall and medieval undercroft, a tall battlement tower and lookout posts, and other separate buildings including stables, an old coach house and a folly. One of the most attractive features of Drimnagh is the garden, a formal 17th-century layout with box hedges, yews and mop heads.
Times: Open Apr-Oct. Wed & Sun 12-5; Nov-Mar, Sun 2-5. (Last tour 4). Other times by appointment. Large groups advisable to book
Fee: ✱ €4 (ch €2, pen & students €3.50). Groups 20+ €3 each
Facilities: P ▤ ♿ (limited access gravel courtyard and gardens) ✖ (ex guide dogs)

DUBLIN CASTLE

Dame St
☎ 01 6777129

With two towers and a partial wall, this is the city's most outstanding legacy of the Middle Ages. Of interest are the Record Tower, state apartments, Church of the Most Holy Trinity and Heraldic Museum. The inauguration of the President of Ireland and related ceremonies are held in St. Patrick's Hall, an elegant state apartment.
Times: ✱ Open all year, Mon-Fri 10-5, Sat-Sun & BH 2-5. Closed 24-26 Dec & Good Fri. **Facilities:** P ✗ ♿ toilets for disabled

DUBLINIA & THE VIKING WORLD

St Michael's Hill, Christ Church
☎ 01 6794611
e-mail: info@dublinia.ie
web: www.dublinia.ie

The story of medieval Dublin. Housed in the former Synod Hall beside Christ Church Cathedral and developed by the Medieval Trust, Dublinia recreates the period from the arrival of Strongbow and the Anglo-Normans in 1170 to the closure of the monasteries by Henry VIII in 1540.
Times: Open Apr-Sep 10-5; Oct-Mar, Mon-Sat 11-4, Sun & BH 10-4.30. Closed 24-26 Dec. **Fee:** ✱ €6 (ch €3.75 concessions €5). Family ticket (2ad+3ch) €16 **Facilities:** P (100yds) ▤ ♿ (2 floors accessible, but bridge and tower are not) toilets for disabled shop ✖ (ex guide dogs) ⚇

DUBLIN WRITERS MUSEUM

18 Parnell Square
⮫ (on Parnell Sq, at North end of O'Connell St)
☎ 01 8722077
e-mail: writers@dublintourism.ie
web: www.visitdublin.com

The Dublin Writers Museum is housed in a restored 18th-century building and a modern annexe with lecture rooms and exhibition spaces. Dublin's rich literary heritage can be followed, through displays, tracing the written tradition in Ireland from the Book of Kells in the 8th century to the present day.
Times: Open all year, Mon-Sat 10-5, Sun & BH 11-5; Jun-Aug, Mon-Fri 10-6. **Fee:** €6.50 (ch €4, concessions €5.50). Family ticket €18. Group discounts & combined ticket for related attractions available.
Facilities: P (charged) ⚇ ✗ licensed shop ✖ (ex guide dogs) ⚇

DUBLIN ZOO

Phoenix Park
⮫ (10mins bus ride from city centre)
☎ 01 4748900
e-mail: info@dublinzoo.ie
web: www.dublinzoo.ie

Dublin Zoo first opened to the public in 1830, making it one of the oldest zoos in the world and has consistently been Ireland's favourite attraction. The new 'African Plains' is the biggest single development undertaken by the zoo. This 30-acre development has doubled the size of the zoo and provides spacious new areas for African species. Dublin Zoo is a modern zoo with conservation, education & study as its mission. The majority of the animals here have been born and bred in zoos and are part of global breeding programmes to ensure their continued survival.
Times: ✱ Open Mar-Oct, Mon-Sat 9.30-6, Sun 10.30-6; Nov-Feb, daily 10.30-dusk. **Facilities:** P ⚇ ✗ licensed ♿ (wheelchairs available) toilets for disabled shop ✖ ⚇

GUINNESS STOREHOUSE

St James's Gate
⮫ (next to James' St)
☎ 01 4084800 & 4538364
e-mail: guinness-storehouse@guinness.com
web: www.guinness-storehouse.com

Established in 1876, the Storehouse remained crammed with hopsacks until 1957, then it was converted and is now a high-tech, 21st-century mix of an art centre, conference facility, restaurant and bar. Find out about the drink's history and then sample a glass.
Times: ✱ Open daily 9.30-5 (last admission 5). Late summer Jul-Aug open until 8pm **Fee:** ✱ €14 (ch 6-12 €5, pen €9.50, students under 18 €7.50, over 18 €9.50). Family (2ad + 4 ch) €30. Group 15+ €13 each. **Facilities:** P ✗ ▤ ♿ toilets for disabled shop ✖ ⚇

HOWTH CASTLE RHODODENDRON GARDENS
Howth

➲ (9m NE of city centre, by coast road to Howth. Before Howth follow signs for Deer Park Hotel)
☎ 01 8322624 & 8322256   FREE
e-mail: sales@deerpark.iol.ie

Overlooking the sea on the north side of Dublin Bay, the rhododendron walks command spectacular views of the Castle and Irelands Eye. The flowers are at their best in May and June. Visitors should be aware that the gardens are in some disrepair and the paths somewhat rough and overgrown in parts.

Times: Open all year, daily 8am-dusk. Closed 25 Dec.
Facilities: 🅿 ㊉ (steep hills unsuitable, ramped entrance) toilets for disabled ✕ (ex guide dogs) 🛥

HUGH LANE MUNICIPAL GALLERY OF MODERN ART
Charlemont House, Parnell Square
☎ 01 8741903   FREE
e-mail: info@hughlane.ie
web: www.hughlane.ie

Situated in Charlemont House, a fine Georgian building, the gallery's collection includes one of the most extensive collections of 20th-century Irish art. A superb range of international and Irish paintings, sculpture, works on paper and stained glass is also on show. There are public lectures every Sunday and regular concerts (at noon on Sundays) throughout the year.

Times: ✱ Open all year, Tue-Thu 9.30-6, Fri-Sat 9.30-5, Sun 11-5. Late night opening Thu until 8, Apr-Aug only. Closed Mon, Good Fri & 24-25 Dec. **Facilities:** 🅿 (100mtrs) (meter parking) 🍴 ㊉ (ramp & reserved parking) toilets for disabled shop ✕ (ex guide dogs)

IRISH MUSEUM OF MODERN ART
Royal Hospital, Military Rd, Kilmainham
➲ (3.5km from city centre, just off N7 opposite Heuston Station)
☎ 01 6129900   FREE
e-mail: info@imma.ie
web: www.imma.ie

Housed in the Royal Hospital Kilmainham, an impressive 17th-century building, the Irish Museum of Modern Art is Ireland's leading national institution for the collection and presentation of modern and contemporary art. It presents a wide variety of art and artists' ideas in a dynamic programme of exhibitions, which regularly includes bodies of work from the museum's own collection, its award-winning Education and Community Department and the Studio and National Programmes.

Times: Open all year Tue-Sat 10-5.30, Sun & BHs 12-5.30. Closed Mon & 24-26 Dec. **Facilities:** 🅿 🍴 📓 ㊉ toilets for disabled shop ✕ (ex guide dogs)

JAMES JOYCE CENTRE
35 North Great George's St signed from N end of O'Connell Street and Parnell Square
☎ 01 8788547
e-mail: marketing@jamesjoyce.ie
web: www.jamesjoyce.ie

Situated in a beautifully restored 18th-century Georgian town house, the Centre is dedicated to the promotion of a greater interest in, and understanding of, the life and works of James Joyce. After an introductory film visitors follow a self-guided tour through the house, that includes the door to No.7 Eccles Street, home of Leopold Bloom, the hero of
continued

Ulysses; furniture from Joyce's Paris flat, and an extensive reference library.

Times: Open all year, Mon-Sat 9.30-5, Sun & BH 12.30-5. Closed Good Fri & 24-26 Dec. **Fee:** ✱ House Tour €5 (pen & students €4). Walking Tour €10 (pen & students €9) group rates 10+ available
Facilities: 🅿 📓 ㊉ toilets for disabled shop ✕ (ex guide dogs) 🛥

KILMAINHAM GAOL
Inchicore Rd
➲ (3.5km from city centre)
☎ 01 4535984

One of the largest unoccupied gaols in Europe, covering some of the most heroic and tragic events in Ireland's emergence as a modern nation from the 1720s. Attractions include a major exhibition detailing the political and penal history of the prison and its restoration.

Times: Open Apr-Sep, daily 9.30-6 (last admission 4.45); Oct-Mar, Mon-Sat 9.30-5.30 (last admission 4), Sun 10-6 (last admission 4.45). Access by guided tour only. **Fee:** ✱ €5 (ch & students €2, pen €3.50) Family ticket €11. **Facilities:** 🅿 (on street) 🍴 📓 ㊉ (tours available by prior appointment) toilets for disabled ✕

MARSH'S LIBRARY
St Patrick's Close
➲ (beside St Patrick Cathedral)
☎ 01 4543511
e-mail: keeper@marshlibrary.ie
web: www.marshlibrary.ie

The first public library in Ireland, dating from 1701. Designed by William Robinson, the interior has been unchanged for 300 years. The collection is of approximately 25,000 volumes of 16th, 17th and early 18th century books.

Times: Open Mon & Wed-Fri, 10-1 & 2-5; Sat 10.30-1. **Fee:** ✱ €2.50 (ch free, students & pen €1.50). maybe subject to change.
Facilities: 🅿 (100mtrs) 📓 ✕ (except guide dogs) 🚌

NATIONAL BOTANIC GARDENS
Glasnevin
➲ (on Botanic Road, between N1 and N2)   FREE
☎ 01 8374388 & 8377596

Ireland's premier Botanic Gardens, covers a total area of 19.5 hectares (48 acres), part of which is the natural flood plain of the River Tolka. The Gardens contain a large plant collection, which includes approximately 20,000 species and cultivated varieties. There are four ranges of glasshouses including the restored Curvilinear Range. Notable features include herbaceous borders, rose garden, rockery, alpine yard, arboretum, extensive shrub collections and wall plants.

Times: ✱ Open all year, Gardens: Summer Mon-Sat 9-6, Sun 11-6; Winter Mon-Sat 10-4.30, Sun 11-4.30. (Closed 25 Dec). Glasshouses: Summer Mon-Wed & Fri 9-5, Thu 9-3.15, Sat 9-5.45, Sun 2-5.45; Winter, Mon-Wed, Fri & Sat 10-4.15, Thu 10-3.15, Sun 2-4.15.
Facilities: 🅿 (charged) 🍴 📓 ㊉ toilets for disabled ✕ (ex guide dogs)

NATIONAL GALLERY OF IRELAND
Merrion Square
➲ (5 mins walk from Pearse Station)
☎ 01 6615133
e-mail: artgall@eircom.net
web: www.nationalgallery.ie

The gallery, founded in 1854 by an Act of Parliament, houses the national collections of Irish art and European Old
continued

Masters including Caravaggio, Poussin, El Greco, Roderic O'Conor, and the Yeats'.
Times: ✱ Open all year, Mon-Sat 10-5.30 (Thu 10-8.30), Sun 2-5. Closed 24-26 Dec & Good Fri. **Facilities:** P (5 mins walk) (meter parking, 2hrs max) ✖ licensed ▥ & (Braille/audio tours, lifts, ramps, parking bay) toilets for disabled shop ✖

NATIONAL LIBRARY OF IRELAND
Kildare St
☎ 01 6030200
web: www.nli.ie
Founded in 1877 and based on collections from The Royal Dublin Society. The National Library holds an estimated 5 million items. There are collections of printed books, manuscripts, prints and drawings, photos, maps, newspapers, mircofilms and ephemera. The library's research facilities are open to all those with genuine research needs. In addition to research facilities, services include a regular programme of exhibitions open to the public and Genealogy Service.
Times: Open all year, Mon-Wed 10-9, Thu-Fri 10-5 & Sat 10-1. Closed Sun, BHs, Good Fri & 23 Dec-2 Jan. **Facilities:** ▥ & toilets for disabled shop ✖ (ex guide dogs) ▦

NATIONAL PHOTOGRAPHIC ARCHIVE
Meeting House Square, Temple Bar
➲ (opposite The Gallery of Photography)
☎ 01 6030200
e-mail: photoarchive@nli.ie
web: www.nli.ie
The National Photographic Archive, which is part of the National Library of Ireland, was opened in 1998 in an award-winning building in the Temple Bar area of Dublin. The archive holds an unrivalled collection of photographic images relating to Irish history, topography and cultural and social life. The collection is especially rich in late 19th and early 20th century topographical views and studio portraits, but also includes photographs taken during the Rebellion of 1916 and the subsequent War of Independence and Civil War, as well as other historic events.
Times: Open all year, Mon-Fri 10-5. (Closed BH's, Good Fri & 23 Dec-2 Jan). **Facilities:** ▥ & toilets for disabled shop ✖ (ex guide dogs) ▬

NATURAL HISTORY MUSEUM
Merrion St
➲ (in city centre)
☎ 01 6777444
e-mail: education.nmi@indigo.ie
The Natural History Museum, which is part of The National Museum of Ireland, is a zoological museum containing diverse collections of world wildlife. The Irish Room, on the ground floor, is devoted largely to Irish mammals, sea creatures and insects. It includes the extinct giant Irish deer and the skeleton of a basking shark. The World Collection, has as its centre piece, the skeleton of a 60ft whale suspended from the roof. Other displays include the Giant Panda and a Pygmy Hippopotamus.
Times: Open all year, Tue-Sat 10-5, Sun 2-5. Closed Mon, Xmas day & Good Fri **Facilities:** P (parking meters wkdays) ✖

NEWMAN HOUSE
University College Dublin, 86 St Stephens Green
➲ (S side of St Stephens Green)
☎ 01 7067422 & 4757255
Newman House consists of two superb Georgian town houses, containing some of Ireland's finest 18th-century
continued

plasterwork and decoration. As the founding home of University College Dublin in 1854, the house has been associated with many famous literary and historical figures, including John Henry Newman, Gerard Manley Hopkins and James Joyce.
Times: ✱ Open Jun-Aug, Tue-Fri 12-5, Sat 2-5. Tours, Tue-Fri; 12,2,3 & 4; Sat 2,3 & 4. At other times tours by prior arrangement only.
Facilities: P (100yds) ✖ licensed ✖ (ex guide dogs)

NUMBER TWENTY NINE
29 Lower Fitzwilliam St on corner of Lower Fitzwilliam St & Mount Street Upper; adjacent to Merrion Sqare
☎ 01 7026165
e-mail: numbertwentynine@mail.esb.ie
Number Twenty-Nine is a lovingly restored middle class Dublin home from the late 18th and early 19th century, filled with a unique collection of original pieces, with excellent examples of Irish and international craftsmanship. Visitors are guided through the house from the basement kitchen to the attic nursery.
Times: Open all year, Tue-Sat 10-5, Sun 1-5. Closed Mon & 2 wks prior to Xmas. **Fee:** ✱ €4.50 (ch under 16 free) concessions €2).
Facilities: P (on street/meter) ▣ ▥ shop ✖ ▬

PHOENIX PARK VISITOR CENTRE
Phoenix Park
➲ (4km from Dublin)
☎ 01 677 0095
e-mail: phoenixparkvisitorcentre@duchas.ie
Situated in Phoenix Park, the Visitor Centre provides an historical interpretation of the park from 3500BC, through a series of attractive displays. Part of the building is devoted to nature and there is a colourful film of Phoenix Park. The castle, probably dating from the early 17th century has been restored to its former glory.
Times: Open all year, Jan-mid Mar, Sat & Sun 10-5; Mid-end Mar, daily 10-5.30; Apr-Sep, daily 10-6; Oct, daily 10-5.30; Nov & Dec, Sat & Sun 10-5. (Last admission 45 mins before closing) **Fee:** ✱ €2.75 (ch & students €1.25, pen €2) Family ticket €7. Group €2 each
Facilities: P ▣ ▥ & toilets for disabled ✖ (ex guide dogs)

DUN LAOGHAIRE   Map 01 D4

JAMES JOYCE TOWER
Joyce Tower, Sandycove
➲ (1m SE Dun Laoghaire by coast road to Sandycove Point or turn off main Dun Laoghaire-Dalkey road)
☎ 01 2809265 & 8722077
e-mail: joycetower@dublintourism.ie
web: www.visitdublin.com/museums
Built by the British as a defence against a possible invasion by Napoleon, the tower has walls approximately 8ft thick and an original entrance door 13ft above the ground. The tower was once the temporary home of James Joyce, who depicted this setting in the opening scene of *Ulysses*. The structure is now a museum devoted to the author. Bloomsday, the day in 1904 on which all the action of *Ulysses* is set, is celebrated annually on 16th June. On this day, the museum is open from 8-6 for visits, readings from *Ulysses* and performances of various kinds, Edwardian costume is encouraged.
Times: Open Feb-Oct, Mon-Sat 10-1 & 2-5, Sun & BHs 2-6; Nov-Jan by arrangement. **Fee:** €6.50 (ch 3-11 €4, pen, students & ch 12-17 €5.50). Family ticket €18. Parties 20+. **Facilities:** P (100yds) & shop ✖ (ex guide dogs) ▬

MALAHIDE Map 01 D4

FRY MODEL RAILWAY

Malahide Castle Demesne
⟲ (in grounds of Malahide Castle, 8m N of Dublin city centre, follow signs for Malahide)
☎ 01 8463779 & 8462184
e-mail: fryrailway@dublintourism.ie
web: www.visitdublin.com

The Fry Model Railway is a rare collection of '0' gauge trains and trams, depicting the history of Irish rail transport from the first train that ran in 1834. Cyril Fry began to build his model collection in his attic, in the late 1920s. All the models are built to scale, and they are now housed in a purpose-built setting adjacent to Malahide Castle.

Times: ✱ Open Apr-Sep, Mon-Sat 10-5, Sun & PH 2-6; Parties at other times by arrangement. Closed 1-2 & on Fri. **Facilities:** 🅿 🕭 shop ✖ ➡

MALAHIDE CASTLE

⟲ (from Dublin city centre follow signs for Malahide, then approaching village, main entrance to castle is signed to right off main road)
☎ 01 8462184
e-mail: malahidecastle@dublintourism.ie
web: www.visitdublin.com

One of Ireland's oldest castles, this romantic and beautiful structure, set in 250 acres of grounds, has changed very little in 800 years. Tours offer views of Irish period furniture and historical portrait collections. Additional paintings from the National Gallery depict figures from Irish life over the last few centuries.

Times: Open all year, Apr-Oct, daily 10-5 (Sun & BHs 11-6); Nov-Mar, daily 10-5 (Sun & BHs 11-5). Closed for tours 12.45-2. **Fee:** € 6.70 (ch € 4.20) concessions € 5.70. Family ticket € 19 (2ad + 3ch u12). Group rates available. Combined tickets for related attractions available.
Facilities: 🅿 🕭 ✖ 🗐 shop ✖ ➡

TALBOT BOTANIC GARDENS

Malahide Castle
⟲ (off R107 onto Back Rd, entrance 0.25m on left, well signed)
☎ 01 8462456

Malahide Castle has long been associated with ornamental gardening. Over seven hectares of shrubbery, and a Walled Garden of nearly two hectares are mainly the creation of Lord Milo Talbot de Malahide, whose family had lived at the estate for 800 years until his death in 1973. Lord Milo Talbot had travelled the world and brought home many exotic plants from Australia and Chile, among others. Visitors follow a path through the gardens, which gives them the best view of this impressive botanic garden.

Times: Open May-Sep 2-5. Groups by appointment only. Guided tour for general public on Wed at 2. **Fee:** ✱ € 4 (group rate € 3.50)
Facilities: 🅿 🕭 ✖ licensed 🗐 ৬ shop ✖ (ex in parkland)

SKERRIES Map 01 D4

SKERRIES MILLS

⟲ (signed off M1)
☎ 01 8495208
e-mail: skerriesmills@indigo.ie   `2 for 1` `FREE`

A collection of restored mills, including a watermill, a five-sail, and a four-sail windmill, all in working order. The site dates from the 16th century and was originally part of a monastic establishment. It came into private ownership in 1538, and a bakery has been there since 1840. Nature lovers
continued

will enjoy the millpond, nearby wetlands and town park, of which the mills are the focal landmark. 2-for-1 voucher can be used for paid guided tours.

Times: Open Apr-Sep, daily 10.30-5.30; 2 Jan-Mar & Oct-19 Dec, daily 10.30-4.30. Closed Good Fri **Facilities:** 🅿 🕭 ✖ licensed shop ✖

CO GALWAY

GALWAY Map 01 B3

GALWAY ATLANTAQUARIA

Salthill
⟲ (follow signs for Salthill. Next to Tourist Office at seafront rdbt)
☎ 091 585100   `2 for 1`
e-mail: atlantaquaria@eircom.net
web: www.nationalaquarium.ie

Concentrating on the native Irish marine ecosystem, the Galway Atlantiquaria contains some 170 species of fish and sealife, and features both fresh and saltwater exhibits.

Times: Open Apr, May, Jun & Sep daily 10-5; Jul & Aug daily 10-6; Oct-Dec, Jan-Mar Wed-Sun 10-5. Closed Mon & Tue. **Fee:** ✱ € 7.50 (ch 3-14 € 4, student, pen € 5). Family ticket (1ad+2ch) € 15, (2ad+3ch) € 21. **Facilities:** 🅿 🕭 ✖ licensed ৬ toilets for disabled shop ✖ (ex guide dogs) ➡

NORA BARNACLE HOUSE MUSEUM

Bowling Green
⟲ (close to St Nicholas Collegiate Church, in city centre)
☎ 091 564743

The smallest museum in Ireland, this tiny turn-of-century house was the home of Nora Barnacle, companion, wife and lifelong inspiration of James Joyce. It was here in 1909, sitting at the kitchen table that Joyce first met his darling's mother. Letters, photographs and other exhibits of the lives of James Joyce and Nora Barnacle make a visit here a unique experience.

Times: Open Jun-Aug, days may change during week, opening times posted on window. **Facilities:** 🅿 (100yds) (disc parking)

ROYAL TARA CHINA VISITOR CENTRE

Tara Hall, Mervue
⟲ (N6 from Tourist Office. At rdbt take 2nd left & at lights turn right)
☎ 091 705602   `FREE`
e-mail: mkilroy@royal-tara.com
web: www.royal-tara.com

Royal Tara China visitor centre, located minutes from Galway City Centre, operates from a 17th-century house situated on five acres.

Times: Open all year, Mon-Sat 9-6, Sun 10-5 **Facilities:** 🅿 ৬ (all facilities accessible for disabled) toilets for disabled shop ✖ (ex guide dogs) ➡

GORT Map 01 B3

THOOR BALLYLEE

⟲ (1km off N18 & N66)
☎ 091 631436 & 537733

This tower house is the former home of the poet William Butler Yeats and is where he completed most of his literary works. The tower, restored to appear exactly as it was when he lived there, houses an Interpretative Centre with audio-visual presentations and displays of his work.

Times: Open 27 May-Sep 9.30-5 Mon-Sat **Fee:** ✱ € 6 (pen & students € 5.50). Family ticket € 12. Party. **Facilities:** 🅿 ৬ (audio-visual presentation) toilets for disabled shop ✖ (ex guide dogs) ➡

KINVARRA · Map 01 B3

DUNGUAIRE CASTLE

➲ (off N18 Ennis to Galway road, through Gort. Left at Ardrahan & continue to Kinvara)

☎ 061 360768

e-mail: reservations@shannondev.ie

web: www.shannonheritage.com

`2 for 1`

The castle has stood for hundreds of years on the site of the 7th-century stronghold of Guaire, the King of Connaught. Today the restored castle gives an insight into the lifestyle of the people who lived there from 1520 to modern times.

Times: Open daily mid Apr-Sep, daily 9.30-5 (last admission 4.30). Medieval banquet, Apr-Oct 5.30 & 8.45 (reservations necessary). **Fee:** €4.75 (concessions €2.95). **Facilities:** 🅿 shop ✖ (ex guide dogs) 🍴

PORTUMNA · Map 01 B3

PORTUMNA CASTLE & GARDENS

☎ 090 9741658

e-mail: portumnacastle@duchas.ie

The great semi-fortified house at Portumna was built before 1618 by Richard Burke or de Burgo, 4th Earl of Clanricarde. This important Jacobean house, while influenced by Renaissance and English houses, remains distinctively Irish. It was the main seat of the de Burgo family for over 200 years, until it was gutted by fire in 1826. The ground floor of the house is now open to the public. To the north of the house is a formal, geometrically laid out garden, a feature often associated with large Jacobean mansions.

Times: Open 25 Mar - Mid Apr Daily 10-5; Mid Apr - Oct Daily 10-6 (Last admission 45mins before closing). **Fee:** ✱ €2 (ch & students €1, pen €1.25) Family ticket €5.50. Group €1.25 each **Facilities:** 🅿 🍴 ♿ (access limited) ✖ (ex guide dogs)

ROUNDSTONE · Map 01 A4

ROUNDSTONE MUSIC, CRAFTS & FASHION

Craft Centre

➲ (N59 from Galway to Clifden. After approx 50m turn left at Roundstone sign, 7m to village. Attraction at top of village)

☎ 095 35875

e-mail: bodhran@iol.ie

web: www.bodhran.com

`FREE`

The Roundstone Music Craft and Fashion shop is located within the walls of an old Franciscan Monastery. Here you can see Ireland's oldest craft: the Bodhran being made, and regular talks and demonstrations are given. The 1st RiverDance stage drums were made here and are still on display in the Craftsman's Craftshop. There is an outdoor picnic area in a beautiful location alongside the bell tower by the water where the dolphins swim up to the wall in summer.

Times: Open Apr-Oct 9.30-6, Jul-Sep 9-7, Winter 6 days 9.30-6.

Facilities: 🅿 🍽 🍴 ♿ toilets for disabled shop ✖ (ex guide dogs)

CO KERRY

CASTLEISLAND · Map 01 B2

CRAG CAVE

➲ (1m N, signed off N21)

☎ 066 7141244

e-mail: info@cragcave.com

web: www.cragcave.com

Crag Cave is one of the longest surveyed cave systems in Ireland, with a total length of 3.81km. It is a spectacular

world, where pale forests of stalagmites and stalactites, thousands of years old, throw eerie shadows around vast echoing caverns complemented by dramatic sound and lighting effects. Now features new indoor soft play area. Tours last about 30 minutes.

Times: Open daily, mid Mar-1 Nov 10-6 (Jul-Aug until 6.30). (Last tour 30 minutes before closing time). **Fee:** €7.50 (ch €5, pen & students €6.50). Family ticket €25 **Facilities:** 🅿 🍽 ✖ licensed 🍴 ♿ (ramp to visitor centre) toilets for disabled shop ✖ (ex guide dogs) 🍴

KILLARNEY · Map 01 B2

KILLARNEY TRANSPORT MUSEUM

Scotts Hotel Gardens

➲ (town centre, opposite railway station)

☎ 064 34677

A unique collection of Irish veteran, vintage and classic cars, motorcycles, bicycles, carriages and fire engines. Exhibits include the 1907 Silver Stream, reputed to be the rarest car in the world, it was designed and built by an Irishman and he only made one!

Times: Open Apr & Oct 11-4; May & Sep 11-5; Jun, Jul & Aug 10-6 **Fee:** €5 (pen & students €3.50). Family ticket €12-€14 **Facilities:** 🅿 ♿

MUCKROSS HOUSE, GARDENS & TRADITIONAL FARMS

Muckross

➲ (4m on Kenmare road)

☎ 066 31440 & 35571

e-mail: mucros@iol.ie

web: www.muckross-house.ie

The 19th-century mansion house of the formerly private Muckross Estate. It now houses a museum of Kerry folklife. In the basement craft centre, a weaver, blacksmith and potter demonstrate their trades. The grounds include Alpine and bog gardens, rhododendrons, azaleas and a rock garden.

Times: Open Jul-Aug, daily 9-7; Mid Mar-Jun & Sep-Oct, 9-6; Nov-16 Mar 9-5.30. **Fee:** ✱ €5.50 (ch €2.25, students & pen €4.25) Family €13.75. Group €4.25 each. **Facilities:** 🅿 ✖ licensed ♿ toilets for disabled shop ✖ (ex guide dogs) 🍴

TRALEE · Map 01 A2

KERRY THE KINGDOM MUSEUM

Ashe Memorial Hall, Denny St

➲ (in town centre, follow signs for museum & tourist information office)

☎ 066 7127777

e-mail: info@kerrymuseum.com

web: www.kerrymuseum.com

The museum tells the story of Kerry (and Ireland) from the Stone Age to the present day. Archaeological treasures are displayed in the Museum Gallery, while a stroll through the Medieval Experience reveals the streets of Tralee as they were in 1450, with all the sights, sounds and smells of a bustling community. Discover what people wore, what they ate and where they lived, and find out why the Earls of Desmond, who founded the town, also destroyed it.

Times: ✱ Open Jan-Mar, Tue-Fri 10-4.30; Apr-May, Tue-Sat 9.30-5.30; Jun-Aug, daily 9.30-5.30; Sep-Dec, Tue-Sat 9.30-5; BH wknds Sun & Mon 10-5. **Facilities:** 🅿 (charged) 🍽 ♿ (special time car through Medieval Experience) toilets for disabled shop ✖ (ex guide dogs) 🍴

continued

VALENTIA ISLAND — Map 01 A2

THE SKELLIG EXPERIENCE

⮑ (Ring of Kerry road, signed after Cahersiveen then Valentia bridge, or ferry from Rena Rd Point)
☎ 066 9476306
e-mail: info@skelligexperience.com
web: www.skelligexperience.com

The Skellig Rocks are renowned for their scenery, sea bird colonies, lighthouses, Early Christian monastic architecture and rich underwater life. The two islands - Skellig Michael and Small Skellig - stand like fairytale castles in the Atlantic Ocean, rising to 218 metres and their steep cliffs plunging 50 metres below the sea. The Heritage Centre, (on Valentia Island, reached from the mainland via a bridge), tells the story of the Skellig Islands in an exciting multimedia exhibition. Cruise around Valentia Habour.

Times: ✱ Open Mar-Jun 10-6; Jun-Aug 10-7; Sep-Oct 10-6.
Facilities: 🅿 💷 📱 ♿ toilets for disabled shop
🐕 (ex guide dogs) 🍴

See advertisement on opposite page

CO KILDARE

CELBRIDGE — Map 01 D4

CASTLETOWN

⮑ (13m from Dublin, follow signs to Celbridge from N4)
☎ 01 628 8252
e-mail: castletown@duchas.ie
web: www.heritageireland.ie

Ireland's largest and finest Palladian country house, begun c1722 for William Conolly, Speaker of the Irish House of Commons. The state rooms include the 'Pompeian' Long Gallery with its Venetian chandeliers, green silk drawing room and magnificent staircase hall with Lafranchini plasterwork. There is a fine collection of 18th-century Irish furniture and paintings.

Times: Easter Sun - Sep Mon-Fri 10-6 Sat, Sun and BH 1-5 October Mon-Fri 10-5 Sun and BH 1-5 **Fee:** ✱ €3.50 (ch & students €1.25, pen €2.50) Family ticket €8.25. Pre-booked groups 10+ €2.50.
Facilities: 🅿 💷 📱 ♿ (restricted access for disabled visitors) toilets for disabled 🐕 (ex guide dogs)

KILDARE — Map 01 C3

IRISH NATIONAL STUD & JAPANESE GARDENS ST FIACHRA'S GARDEN

Irish National Stud, Tully
⮑ (off N7, junct 11 then R415 towards Nurney & Kildare. Attraction well signed from rdbt)
☎ 045 521617
e-mail: stud@irish-national-stud.ie
web: www.irish-national-stud.ie

Situated in the grounds of the Irish National Stud, the gardens were established by Lord Wavertree between 1906 and 1910, and symbolise 'The Life of Man' in a Japanese-style landscape. You can also visit the Horse Museum which includes the skeleton of Arkle, an Irish racehorse that won a number of major races in the 1960s. The Commemorative Millennium Garden of St Fiachra has 4 acres of woodland and lakeside walks and features a Waterford Crystal garden and monastic cells of limestone.

Times: Open 12 Feb-1 Nov, daily 9.30-6 (last admission 5). **Fee:** €9 (ch €7, pen & students €7). Family ticket €20
Facilities: 🅿 ✗ licensed 📱 ♿ (all parts of stud accessible, only small part of gardens) toilets for disabled shop on lead only 🍴

CO KILKENNY

KILKENNY — Map 01 C3

KILKENNY CASTLE

☎ 056 7721450
Situated in a beautiful 50-acre park, the castle dates from 1172. The first stone castle was built 20 years later by William Marshall, Earl of Pembroke. It was home of the very powerful Butler family, Earls and Dukes of Ormonde from 1391 to 1935. Due to major restoration works, the central block now includes a library, drawing room, and bedrooms decorated in 1830s splendour, as well as the beautiful Long Gallery.

Times: Open all year, Apr-May, daily 10.30-5; Jun-Aug, daily 9.30-7; Sep, daily 10-6.30; Oct-Mar, daily 10.30-12.45 & 2-5. (Last tour 45mins before closing). Closed Xmas & Good Fri. **Fee:** ✱ €5 (ch & students €2, pen €3.50) Family ticket €11. Group €3.50 each.
Facilities: 🅿 (local authority restrictions) 💷 📱 ♿ (toilet close by) shop 🐕 (ex guide dogs)

CO LIMERICK

FOYNES
Map 01 B3

FOYNES FLYING BOAT MUSEUM
➲ (on N69 in Foynes)
☎ 069 65416
e-mail: famm@eircom.net
web: www.flyingboatmuseum.com

The museum recalls the era of the flying boats during the 1930s and early 1940s when Foynes was an important airport for air traffic between the United States and Europe. There is a comprehensive range of exhibits, graphic illustrations and a 1940s style cinema featuring a 17-minute film - all original footage from the 30s and 40s. Where Irish coffee was first invented by chef, Joe Sheridan, in 1942.

Times: Open Mar-Oct, daily 10-6. (Last admission 5.15)
Facilities: 🅿 🚊 ♿ toilets for disabled shop ✈ (ex guide dogs) 🍴

HOLYCROSS
Map 01 C3

LOUGH GUR STONE AGE CENTRE
Bruff Rd
➲ (17km S of Limerick, off R512 towards Kilmallock)
☎ 061 360788
e-mail: reservations@shannondev.ie
web: www.shannonheritage.com

2 for 1

Lough Gur introduces visitors to the habitat of Neolithic Man on one of Ireland's most important archaeological sites. The visitor centre interprets the history of the area which dates back to 3000BC.

Times: Open daily May-mid Sep, daily 10-6 (last admission 5.30)
Fee: €4.75 (concessions €2.95). **Facilities:** 🅿 ♿ toilets for disabled shop ✈ (ex guide dogs) 🍴

KILCORNAN
Map 01 B3

CELTIC PARK & GARDENS
➲ (N69 Limerick to Tralee road)
☎ 061 394243

Located on an original Celtic settlement in one of the most important Cromwellian plantations in the south-west of Ireland. As you walk through the park there's plenty to see, including a church built in 1250, a Mass rock, dolmen, a stone circle, lake dwellings, cooking site, Celtic tomb and a fine example of a ring fort. The gardens contain over 1,000 roses, flowering shrubs, a rockery, herbaceous borders, shrubbery, large pool and colonnades.

Times: Open mid Mar-Oct, daily 9.30-6. **Facilities:** 🅿 🚊 shop

LIMERICK
Map 01 B3

KING JOHN'S CASTLE
Nicholas St
➲ (on Kings Island in city)
☎ 061 360788
e-mail: reservations@shannondev.ie
web: www.shannonheritage.com

The Castle was built between 1200 and 1210 and was repaired and extended many times in the following centuries. The interpretative centre at the Castle has been completely redesigned and now contains an imaginative historical exhibition. The courtyard and the Castle display some of the trades and traditions of the 16th century.

Times: Open all year Mar, Apr, & Oct daily 9.30-5 (last admission 4); May-Sep 9.30-5.30 (last admission 4.30); Nov-Feb 10-4.30 (last admission 3.30). Closed Good Fri & 24-26 Dec. **Fee:** €8.35 (ch€4.95, pen & students €6.25). **Facilities:** 🅿 ♿ (lifts and ramps) toilets for disabled shop ✈ (ex guide dogs) 🍴

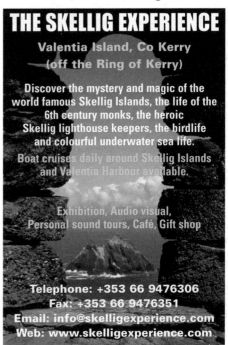
THE HUNT MUSEUM
The Custom House, Rutland St
➲ (a short walk from Arthur's Quay)
☎ 061 312833
e-mail: info@huntmuseum.com
web: www.huntmuseum.com

2 for 1

On show at the Hunt Museum is one of Ireland's finest private collections of art and antiquities. Reflecting Ireland's Celtic past as well as masterworks by da Vinci and Renoir. Set in an 18th-century customs house beside the broad majestic Shannon.

Times: Open daily Mon-Sat 10-5, Sun 2-5. **Fee:** ✱ €6.80 (ch €3.35, concessions €5.50). Family ticket €15.75. **Facilities:** 🅿 (50mtrs) (parking discs for street parking) 🚊 ✖ licensed 🍴 ♿ toilets for disabled shop ✈ (ex guide dogs) 🍴

CO LONGFORD

KEENAGH
Map 01 C4

CORLEA TRACKWAY VISITOR CENTRE
➲ (off R397, 3km from village)
☎ 043 22386

The centre interprets an Iron Age bog road which was built in the year 148BC across the boglands close to the River Shannon. The oak road is the largest of its kind to have been uncovered in Europe and was excavated over the years by Professor Barry Raferty of University College Dublin. Inside the building, an 18-metre stretch of preserved road is on permanent display in a specially designed hall with humidifiers to prevent the ancient wood from cracking in the heat.

Times: Apr - Sep Daily 10-6 **Facilities:** 🅿 🚊 ♿ toilets for disabled ✈ (ex guide dogs)

CO MAYO

BALLYCASTLE   Map 01 B5

CÉIDE FIELDS
➲ (5m W of Ballycastle on R314)
☎ 096 43325
e-mail: ceidefields@duchas.ie
web: www.heritageireland.ie

Beneath the wild boglands of North Mayo lies Céide Fields, the most extensive Stone-age monument in the world; field systems, dwelling areas and megalithic tombs of 5,000 years ago. In addition, the wild flora of the bog is of international importance and is bounded by some of the most spectacular rock formations and cliffs in Ireland.

Times: Mid Mar- May Daily 10-5 June-Sep Daily 10-6 Oct - Nov Daily 10 - 5 Rest of the year open to groups - Advance bookings only. Last tour 1 hr. before closing time. **Fee:** ✱ €3.50 (ch & students €1.25, pen €2.50). Family ticket €8.25. Group €2.50 each.
Facilities: 🅿 💻 📶 ♿ (parking) toilets for disabled ✖ (ex guide dogs)

CO MONAGHAN

INNISKEEN   Map 01 C4

PATRICK KAVANAGH RURAL & LITERARY RESOURCE CENTRE
Candlefort
➲ (from Dundalk take R178, ignore sign on right for Inniskeen. Continue to Conlon's Pub and turn right for Inniskeen)
☎ 042 78560
e-mail: infoatpkc@eircom.net
web: www.patrickkavanaghcountry.com

Birthplace of Patrick Kavanagh, one of Ireland's foremost 20th-century poets. The village grew around the ancient monastery of St Daig MacCairill, founded by 562, and its strong, 10th-century round tower still stands. The centre, housed in the former parish church, chronicles the ancient history of the region and its role in developing Kavanagh's work.

Times: Open all year, Tue-Fri 11-5, Sat 2-5. Jun-Sep Sun, 2-5. Closed Oct-May, wknds & BHs Dec-16 Mar. **Fee:** ✱ Euros 5 (ch 12 free when accompanied by an adult, concessions 3). Kavanagh trail guide map available €0.65. Kavanagh Country Tours - a guided tour with live performances lasting 90 mins, advance booking essential €7.50 including admission to centre. **Facilities:** 🅿 💻 ♿ toilets for disabled shop ⬛

MONAGHAN   Map 01 C5

MONAGHAN COUNTY MUSEUM
1-2 Hill St
➲ (near town centre, opposite market house exhibition galleries)
☎ 047 82928   FREE
e-mail: comuseum@monghancoco.ie
web: www.monaghan.ie

This is an award-winning museum of local archaeology, history, arts and crafts. Throughout the year various special exhibitions take place. Planned for 2006: 100 years of sporting history. Please telephone for details.
Times: Open Sep-May, Tue-Fri 10-1 & 2-5 Sat 11-1 & 2-5. Jun-Aug, Mon-Fri 11-5, Thu 11-7, Sat 11-1 & 2-5. **Facilities:** 🅿 (near town centre) (restricted on-street parking) 📶 ♿ ✖ (ex guide dogs)

CO OFFALY

BIRR   Map 01 C3

BIRR CASTLE DEMESNE
➲ (in town sq take exit beside Bank of Ireland and bear right. Turn left, entrance on right, car park on left)
☎ 0509 20336   2 for 1
e-mail: info@birrcastle.com
web: www.birrcastle.com

A large landscaped park with a lake, rivers and waterfalls, with important plant collections including magnolias, maples, limes and oaks. The Demesne is particularly colourful in the spring and autumn, and is noted for its formal gardens, containing the tallest box hedges in the world. It is also home to the Great Birr Telescope, built in 1844, and Ireland's Historic Science Centre, a series of galleries focusing on Ireland's scientific past.

Times: Open all year, Mar-Oct 9-6, Nov-Mar 10-5 **Fee:** ✱ €8.50 (ch €4.50, pen & students €6.50). Family ticket (2ad + 3ch) €24.
Facilities: 🅿 💻 ♿ toilets for disabled shop garden centre on lead only ⬛

CO ROSCOMMON

BOYLE   Map 01 B4

KING HOUSE INTERPRETIVE GALLERIES & MUSEUM
in town centre, 1km from N4 Dublin/Sligo and N61 Athlong/Boyle
☎ 071 9663242   2 for 1
e-mail: kinghouse@rascommoncoco.ie
web: www.roscommoncoco.ie/kinghouse.htm

King House is a magnificently restored Georgian mansion built around 1730 by Sir Henry King, whose family were one of the most powerful and wealthy in Ireland. After its first life as a home, King House became a military barracks to the famous Connaught Rangers from 1788-1922. In more recent years it has also been a barracks for the National Irish Army. Today visitors can explore and delve into its history with interactive presentations on: Gaelic Ireland, the lives of the King family, the architecture and restoration of the building and its military history.

Times: Open Apr-Sep, daily 10-6 (last admission 5). Pre-booked groups welcome all year round, telephone for details. **Fee:** ✱ €5 (ch €3, pen & students €4). Family ticket €15. Party rates available
Facilities: 🅿 ✖ licensed 📶 ♿ (lift to all areas, ramps, wide doors, parking) toilets for disabled shop ✖ (ex guide dogs)

STROKESTOWN   Map 01 C4

STROKESTOWN PARK HOUSE GARDEN & FAMINE MUSEUM
Strokestown Park
➲ (23km from Longford on N5)
☎ 071 9633013
e-mail: info@strokestownpark.ie
web: www.strokestownpark.ie

A fine example of an early 18th-century gentleman farmer's country estate. Built in Palladian style the house reflects perfectly the confidence of the newly emergent ruling class. The pleasure garden has also been restored, and the Famine

continued

Museum, located in the stable yard, commemorates the Great Irish Famine of the 1840s.

Times: Open 17 Mar-Oct, daily. **Fee:** ✱ €12.50 (ch €5.70, concessions €11). Family ticket €28. Group 20+ €9 each
Facilities: 🅿 ✖ licensed 📶 ♿ toilets for disabled shop garden centre ✖ (ex guide dogs & in grounds) 🔊

CO TIPPERARY

CASHEL   Map 01 C3

BRÚ BORÚ HERITAGE CENTRE
➲ (below Rock of Cashel in town)
☎ 062 61122
e-mail: bruboru@comhaltas.com
web: www.comhaltas.com

2 for 1

At the foot of the Rock of Cashel, a 4th-century stone fort, this Heritage Centre is dedicated to the study and celebration of native Irish music, song, dance, story telling, theatre and Celtic studies. There's a Folk Theatre where three performances are held daily in the summer, and in the evening, banquets evoke the Court of Brian Ború, 11th-century High King of Ireland with songs, poems and sagas. Promoted by Comhaltas Ceoltôiri ...ireann. There is also a Subterranean, "Sounds of History", experience.

Times: Open Jan-May & Oct-Dec, Mon-Fri 9-5; Jun-Sep Tue-Sat 9-11, Sun-Mon 9-5. **Fee:** Admission to centre free. Night show €16. Exhibition, 'Sounds of History' €5. Dinner Show/Option €45.
Facilities: 🅿 (charged) 💺 ✖ licensed ♿ (wheelchair bay in theatre) toilets for disabled shop ✖ (ex guide dogs) 🔊

CO WATERFORD

LISMORE   Map 01 C2

LISMORE CASTLE GARDENS
➲ (on N72 near town centre)
☎ 058 54424
e-mail: lismoreestates@eircom.net
web: www.lismorecastle.com

2 for 1

Lismore Castle is the Irish home of the Duke of Devonshire. The beautifully situated walled and woodland gardens contain a fine collection of camellias, magnolias and other shrubs and a remarkable Yew Walk. Several pieces of contemporary sculpture have been installed in the garden. The West Wing is being converted into a contemporary art space and is planned to host art exhibitions from around the world.

Times: Open 15 Apr-1 Oct, daily 1.45-4.45. Open at 11 during Jun-Aug. **Fee:** ✱ €6 (ch under 16: €3, party 20+ €2.50). Party 20+ €5.50.
Facilities: 🅿 📶 ♿ (some of grounds are accessible)

WATERFORD   Map 01 C2

WATERFORD CRYSTAL VISITOR CENTRE
➲ (on N25, 1m from city centre)
☎ 051 73311

There are factory tours to see mastercraftsmen mouth-blow and hand-cut this famous crystal. You can talk to the master engravers and see the crystal being sculpted. In the gallery there is the finest display of Waterford Crystal in the world.

Times: ✱ Tours of factory: Apr-Oct, daily 8.30-4, gallery daily 8.30-6; Nov-Feb, Mon-Fri 9-3.15, gallery 9-5. **Facilities:** 🅿 💺 ✖ ♿ (special tours on request) toilets for disabled shop ✖ 🔊

CO WEXFORD

FERRYCARRIG   Map 01 D3

IRISH NATIONAL HERITAGE PARK
➲ (3m from Wexford, on N11)
☎ 053 20733
e-mail: info@inhp.com
web: www.inhp.com

Sixteen historical sites set in a magnificent 35-acre mature forest explaining Ireland's history from the Stone and Bronze Ages, through the Celtic period and concluding with the Vikings and Normans. Among the exhibits are a reconstructed Mesolithic camp, a Viking boatyard with two full size ships and a Norman motte and bailey. Please visit website for details of events running throughout the year.

Times: Open daily 9.30-6.30 (last admission 5, times subject to seasonal variations) **Fee:** €7.50 (pen & students €6). Family (2 ad & upto 3 ch) €19. Group rates available on request. **Facilities:** 🅿 💺 ✖ licensed 📶 ♿ toilets for disabled shop ✖ (ex guide dogs) 🔊

NEW ROSS   Map 01 C3

DUNBRODY ABBEY VISITORS CENTRE
Dunbrody Abbey, Campile
➲ (10m from New Ross at base of Hook Peninsular)
☎ 051 88603
e-mail: patrickbelfast@aol.com
web: www.dunbrodyabbey.com

The visitor centre is based around the Abbey itself and Dunbrody Castle. There is an intriguing yew hedge maze with 1,550 yew trees and a museum. In addition there is a golf pitch-and-putt course, a local craft centre and Dunbrody Abbey Cookery School.

Times: Open May-Sep 10-6. **Fee:** ✱ Abbey €2, Family ticket €5. Maze/Golf €4, (ch €2). Family €10. **Facilities:** 🅿 💺 ✖ 📶 ♿ shop garden centre

JOHN F KENNEDY ARBORETUM

➲ (12km S of New Ross, off R733)
☎ 051 388171

The Arboretum covers 623 acres across the hill of Slievecoiltia which overlooks the Kennedy ancestral home at Dunganstown. There are 4,500 types of trees and shrubs representing the temperate regions of the world, and laid out in botanical sequence. There's a lake and a visitor centre.

Times: Open daily, May-Aug 10-8; Apr & Sep 10-6.30; Oct-Mar 10-5. (Last admission 45 mins before closing). Closed Good Fri & 25 Dec. **Facilities:** 🅿 💺 ♿ toilets for disabled shop

WEXFORD   Map 01 D3

JOHNSTOWN CASTLE GARDENS
Johnstown Castle
➲ (4m SW of town, signed off N25)
☎ 053 42888
e-mail: aosullivan@johnstown.teagase.ie

The 19th-century mansion is closed to the public but visitors can explore the 50 acres of grounds containing over 200 different varieties of trees and shrubs, ornamental lakes with wildfowl, and walled gardens and hothouses. The ruins of Rathlannon Castle, a medieval tower house, can also be seen.

Times: ✱ Open all year, daily 9-5.30. Closed 25 Dec.
Facilities: 🅿 💺 📶 ♿ toilets for disabled

WEXFORD WILDFOWL RESERVE

North Slob

➲ (8km NE from Wexford)

☎ 053 23129

The reserve is of international importance for Greenland white-fronted geese, Brent geese, Bewick's swans and wigeon. The reserve is a superb place for birdwatching and there are hides and a tower hide available as well as a visitor centre. **Times:** Open 16 Apr - End Sep Daily 9.00-18.00; Oct - 15th Apr Daily 10.00-17.00. Other hours by arrangement with the warden. Closed Christmas Day. Reserve may be closed temporarily for management operations - Notice on Gate. **Facilities:** 🅿 ♿ toilets for disabled ✖ (ex guide dogs)

CO WICKLOW

ENNISKERRY   Map 01 D4

POWERSCOURT GARDENS EXHIBITION

➲ (Powerscourt Estate From Dublin city centre; take N11 S, after 12m take exit left to Bray S, Enniskerry, Left at rdbt, over flyover, rejoin N11 N. Take 1st left for Enniskerry Village)

☎ 01 2046000

web: www.powerscourt.ie

Begun by Richard Wingfield in the 1740s, the gardens are a blend of formal plantings, sweeping terraces, statuary and ornamental lakes together with secret hollows, rambling walks and walled gardens. The house itself incorporates an exhibition which traces the history of the estate, and tells the story of the disastrous fire of 1974 which gutted the house. **Times:** Open Gardens & House Exhibition daily 9.30-5.30 (Winter time may vary). Waterfall open daily 9.30-7 (Summer), 10.30-dusk (Winter). **Fee:** Prices not confirmed for 2006 **Facilities:** 🅿 💷 ✖ licensed 🎁 ♿ (lift to first floor, 2 wheelchairs available) toilets for disabled shop garden centre only on lead on riverwalk 🍴

KILQUADE   Map 01 D3

NATIONAL GARDEN EXHIBITIONS CENTRE

Calumet Nurseries

➲ (7m S of Bray - turn off N11 at Kilpedder)

☎ 01 281 9890

e-mail: calumet@clubi.ie

web: www.clubi.ie/calumet

There are 20 different gardens designed by some of Ireland's leading landscapers and designers. There are lectures during the year and guided tours during summer. Ring for details and a calendar of events. The exhibitions are constantly changing and enjoy a high standard of maintenance. All plants are clearly labelled. **Times:** Open Mon-Sat 9-5.30; Sun 1-5.30. (Closed 24 Dec-1st Mon in Jan) **Fee:** ✱ €4.50 (ch under 16 free, pen €3.50). **Facilities:** 🅿 💷 🎁 ♿ shop garden centre ✖ (ex guide dogs) 🍴

RATHDRUM   Map 01 D3

AVONDALE HOUSE & FOREST PARK

➲ (S of Dublin on N11. At Rathnew on R752 to Glenealy and Rathdrum)

☎ 0404 46111   **2 for 1**

e-mail: costelloe_j@coillte.-ie

web: www.coillte.ie

It was here in 1846 that one of the greatest political leaders of modern Irish history, Charles Stewart Parnell, was born. Parnell spent much of his time at Avondale until his death in October 1891. The house is set in a magnificent forest park with miles of forest trails, plus a children's play area and picnic areas. **Times:** Open House 17 Mar-Oct, 11-6. Closed Mon (Mar, Apr, Sep & Oct). (Last admission 5). **Fee:** House €5.50 (pen €5). Family ticket (2ad+3ch) €16. Parking; car €5. **Facilities:** 🅿 (charged) ✖ licensed ♿ (special car park & one forest trail accessible) ✖ (ex on lead) 🍴

County Maps

The county map shown here will help you identify the counties within each country. You can look up each county in the guide using the county names at the top of each page. To find towns featured in the guide use the atlas and the index.

England

1. Bedfordshire
2. Berkshire
3. Bristol
4. Buckinghamshire
5. Cambridgeshire
6. Greater Manchester
7. Herefordshire
8. Hertfordshire
9. Leicestershire
10. Northamptonshire
11. Nottinghamshire
12. Rutland
13. Staffordshire
14. Warwickshire
15. West Midlands
16. Worcestershire

Scotland

17. City of Glasgow
18. Clackmannanshire
19. East Ayrshire
20. East Dunbartonshire
21. East Renfrewshire
22. Perth & Kinross
23. Renfrewshire
24. South Lanarkshire
25. West Dunbartonshire

Wales

26. Blaenau Gwent
27. Bridgend
28. Caerphilly
29. Denbighshire
30. Flintshire
31. Merthyr Tydfil
32. Monmouthshire
33. Neath Port Talbot
34. Newport
35. Rhondda Cynon Taff
36. Torfaen
37. Vale of Glamorgan
38. Wrexham

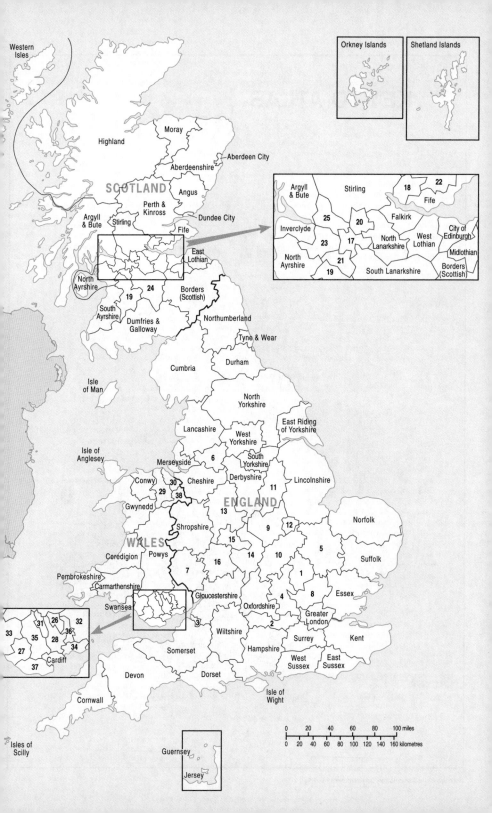

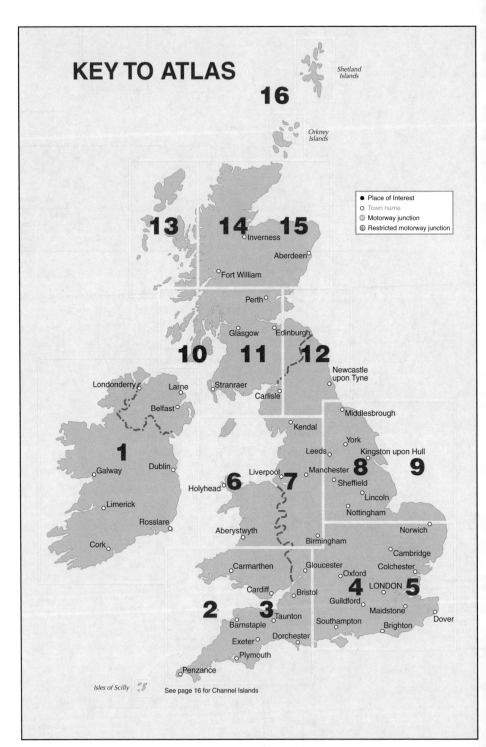

KEY TO ATLAS

Shetland Islands

16

Orkney Islands

- ● Place of Interest
- ○ Town name
- Motorway junction
- Restricted motorway junction

13 **14** ○Inverness **15**

○Aberdeen

○Fort William

Perth○

○Glasgow ○Edinburgh

10 **11** **12**

Newcastle upon Tyne

Londonderry○ Larne○ ○Stranraer

Belfast○ ○Carlisle

○Middlesbrough

○Kendal

○York

○Leeds Kingston upon Hull

1 Liverpool○ Manchester○ **8** **9**

Galway○ Dublin○ **6** **7** ○Sheffield

Holyhead○ ○Lincoln

Limerick○ Nottingham○

Rosslare○ Aberystwyth○ ○Norwich

Cork○ Birmingham○

○Cambridge

Carmarthen○ ○Gloucester ○Colchester

○Oxford

Cardiff○ **4** LONDON **5**

2 **3** ○Bristol Guildford○ ○Maidstone

Barnstaple○ ○Taunton Southampton○ ○Brighton ○Dover

Exeter○ ○Dorchester

○Plymouth

○Penzance

Isles of Scilly See page 16 for Channel Islands

© Automobile Association Developments Limited 2005

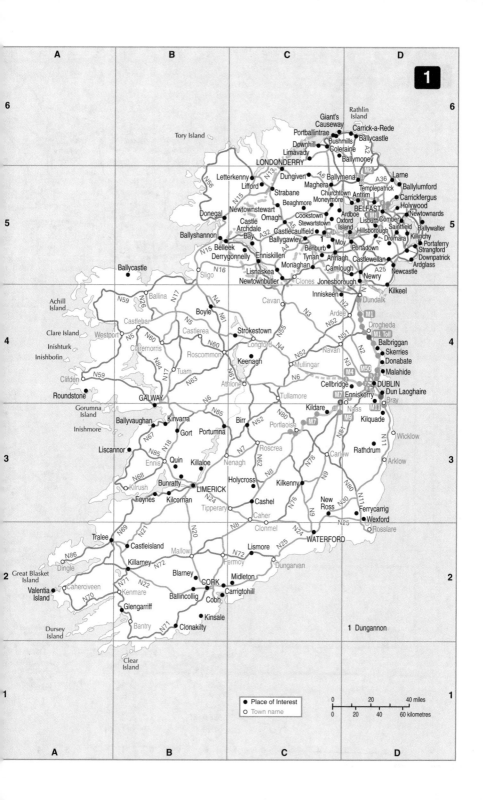

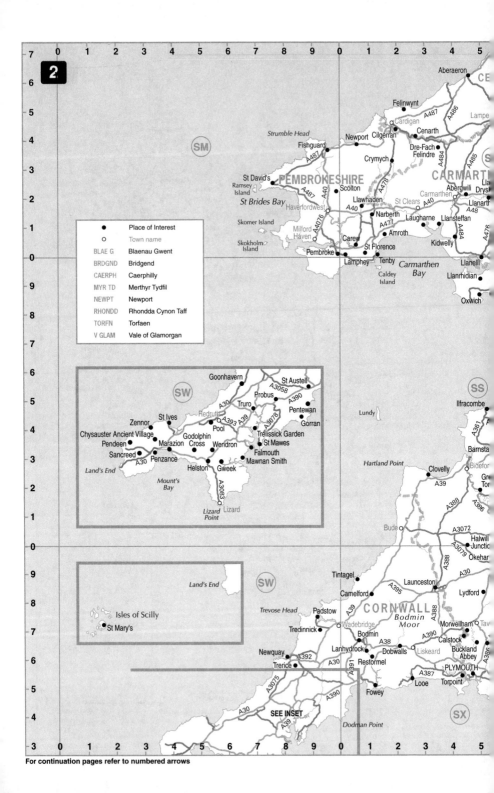

2

Aberaeron
CE

Felinwynt
A487 A486
Lampe
Cardigan Cenarth

Strumble Head
Newport Cilgerran
Fishguard
A487 Crymych Dre-Fach Felindre A484 A485
SM

St David's PEMBROKESHIRE S
CARMART
Ramsey Island Scolton A478 Abergwili Lla Drysl
St Brides Bay Haverfordwest Llawhaden Carmarthen Llanart
A40 A48
Skomer Island Narberth St Clears A40 Llansteffan Laugharne A484 A476
Milford Haven A4076 A477 Kidwelly
Skokholm Island Carew Amroth
Pembroke St Florence Llanelli
Lamphey Tenby Llanrhidian
Caldey Island Carmarthen Bay
Oxwich

Place of Interest
● Place of Interest
○ Town name
BLAE G Blaenau Gwent
BRDGND Bridgend
CAERPH Caerphilly
MYR TD Merthyr Tydfil
NEWPT Newport
RHONDD Rhondda Cynon Taff
TORFN Torfaen
V GLAM Vale of Glamorgan

Goonhavern St Austell
SS
A3058
Probus A390 Ilfracombe
Truro Pentewan A361
SW Redruth A393 A39 A3078 Gorran
Zennor St Ives Pool Lundy Barnsta
Chysauster Ancient Village Godolphin Trelissick Garden Bidefor
Pendeen Marazion Cross Wendron St Mawes Hartland Point Clovelly Gre
Sancreed Penzance Falmouth A39 Tor
A30 Helston Gweek Mawnan Smith A388 A386
Land's End Mount's Bay Bude A3072
A3083 Halwill Junctic
Lizard A3079 Okehar
Lizard Point A388

Tintagel A30
SW Launceston Lydford
Land's End Camelford A395
Isles of Scilly Trevose Head Padstow A39 CORNWALL A388 Morwellham Tav
St Mary's Bodmin Moor A390 Calstock
Tredinnick Wadebridge Bodmin Buckland Abbey
Newquay A392 Lanhydrock A38 Dobwalls Liskeard A387 PLYMOUTH
Trerice Restormel A30 A391 Looe Torpoint
A3075 SX
Fowey A387
SEE INSET A30
A39 Dodman Point
A390

For continuation pages refer to numbered arrows

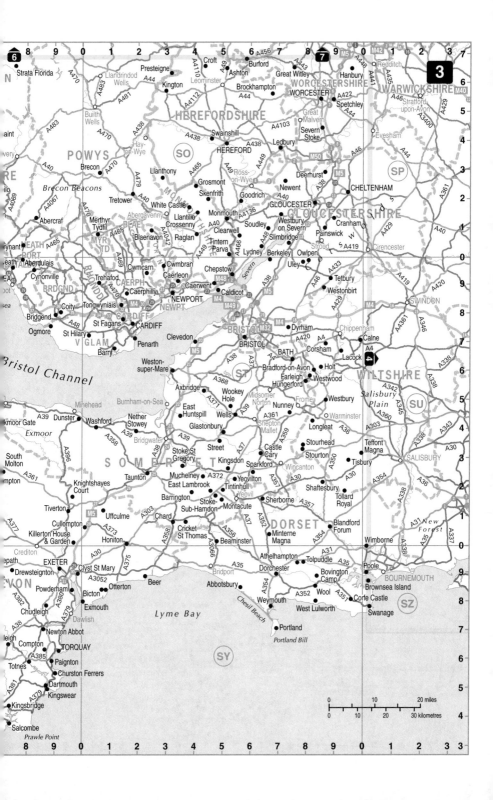

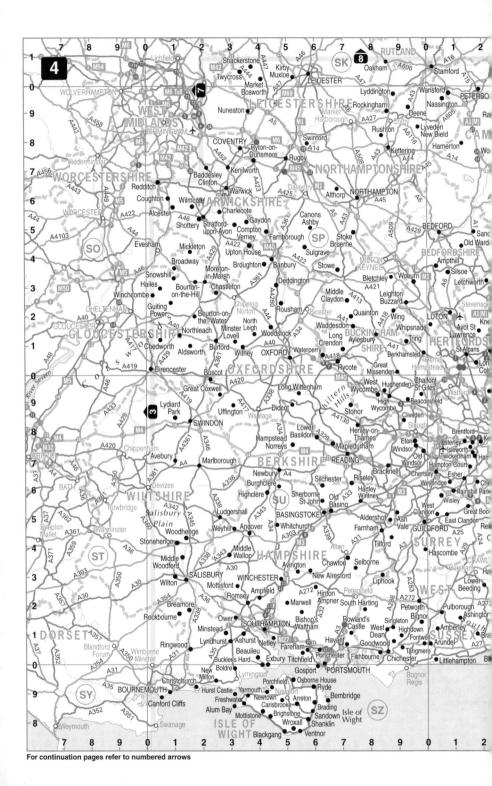

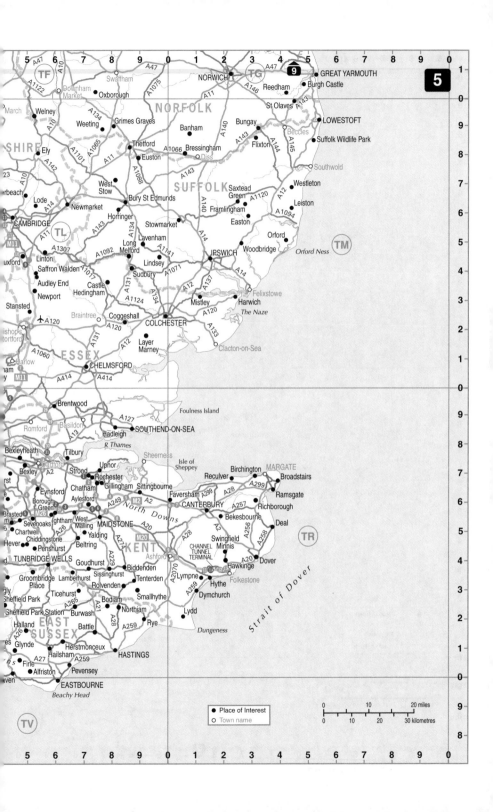

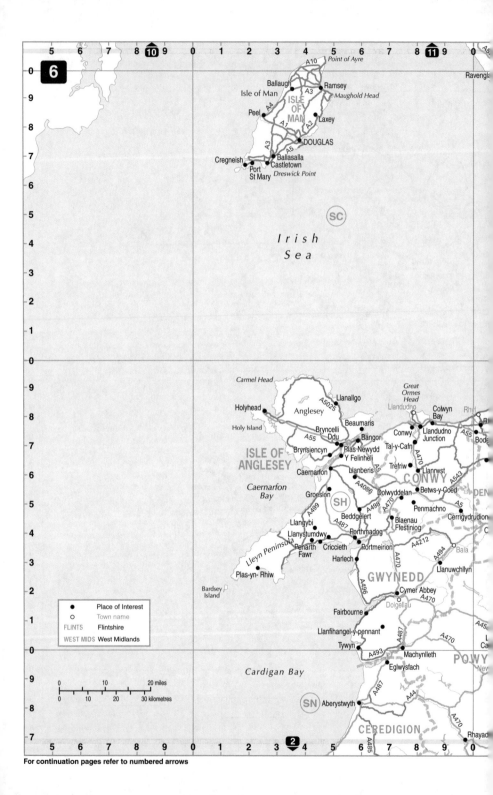

Point of Ayre
Ravengla

A10
Ballaugh · Ramsey
Isle of Man
A3 · Maughold Head
ISLE
OF
MAN
Peel · A4
A2 · Laxey
A1
A3 · DOUGLAS
A5
Cregneish · Ballasalla
Castletown
Port · Dreswick Point
St Mary

SC

*Irish
Sea*

Carmel Head
Llanallgo
Great
Ormes
Head
Holyhead · A5025 · Anglesey · Llandudno · Colwyn · Rhyl
Holy Island · Bryncelli · Beaumaris · Bay · Rl
Ddu · A55 · Conwy · Llandudno · Bode
ISLE OF · A55 · Junction
ANGLESEY · Brynsiencyn · Plas Newydd · Bangor · Tal-y-Cafn
Y Felinheli · A470 · Trefriw · Llanrwst
Caernarfon · Llanberis · CONWY · A543
Caernarfon · Groeslon · A4086 · Dolwyddelan · Betws-y-Coed · DEN
Bay · SH · A498 · A470 · Penmachno · A5 · C
Beddgelert · Blaenau · Cerrigydrudion
Llangybi · A499 · Ffestiniog
Llanystumdwy · A487 · Porthmadog · A4212 · A494 · Bala
Penarth · Criccieth · Portmeirion · A470 · A494 · Llanuwchllyn
Fawr · Harlech · GWYNEDD
Lleyn Peninsula · A496
Plas-yn-Rhiw · Cymer Abbey · A470
Bardsey · Dolgellau · A470
Island · Fairbourne · A487 · A45
· Llanfihangel-y-pennant · A470 · L
· Tywyn · Machynlleth · Ca
A493 · POWY
· Eglwysfach · Ney
Cardigan Bay · A487

SN · Aberystwyth · A44 · A470
CEREDIGION · A485 · Rhyad

●	Place of Interest
○	Town name
FLINTS	Flintshire
WEST MIDS	West Midlands

0 · 10 · 20 miles
0 · 10 · 20 · 30 kilometres

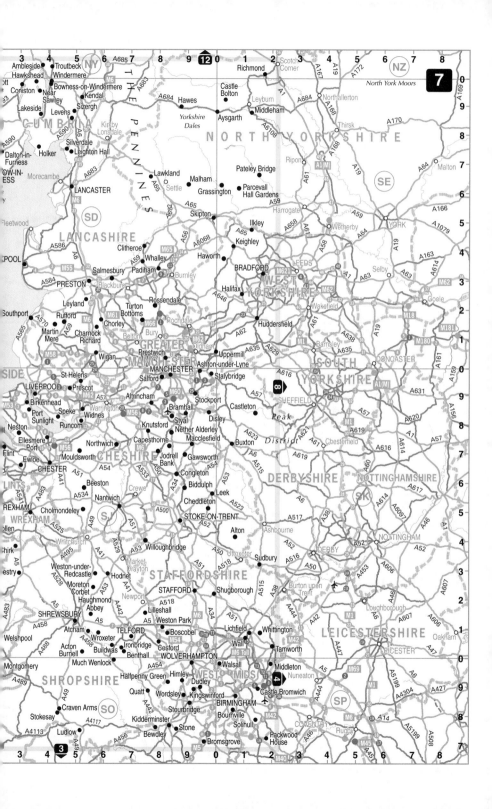

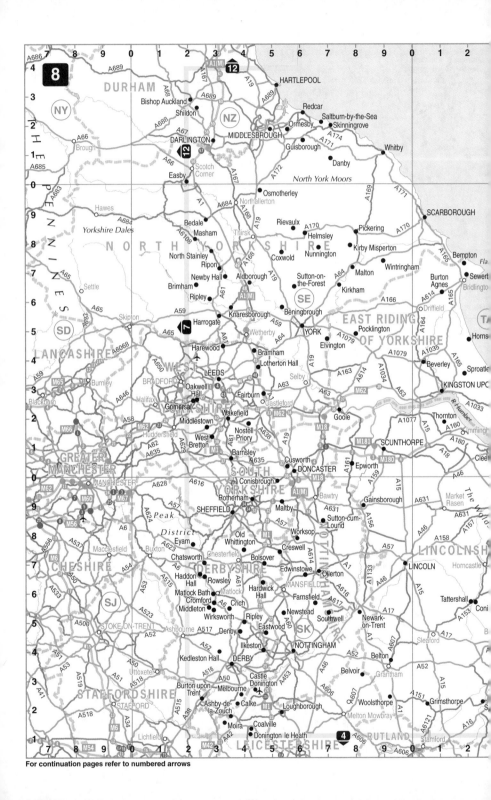

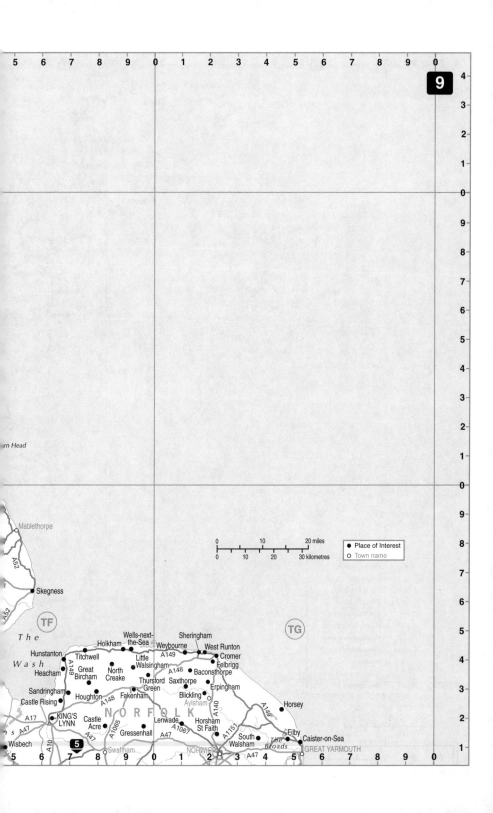

5   6   7   8   9   0   1   2   3   4   5   6   7   8   9   0

9

rn Head

Mablethorpe

Skegness

TF

The

Wash

Wells-next-the-Sea
Sheringham
Holkham
Weybourne
West Runton
Hunstanton
Titchwell
Cromer
Little
Walsingham
Felbrigg
A149
Heacham
Great
Bircham
North
Creake
Baconsthorpe
A148
Sandringham
Thursford
Green
Saxthorpe
Erpingham
Houghton
Fakenham
Blickling
Castle Rising
A148
Aylsham
Horsey
KING'S
LYNN
Castle
Acre
Lenwade
A140
Gressenhall
Horsham
St Faith
Filby
Wisbech
Swaffham
South
Walsham
The
Broads
Caister-on-Sea
NORWICH
GREAT YARMOUTH
A47

NORFOLK

5

● Place of Interest
○ Town name

0   10   20 miles
0   10   20   30 kilometres

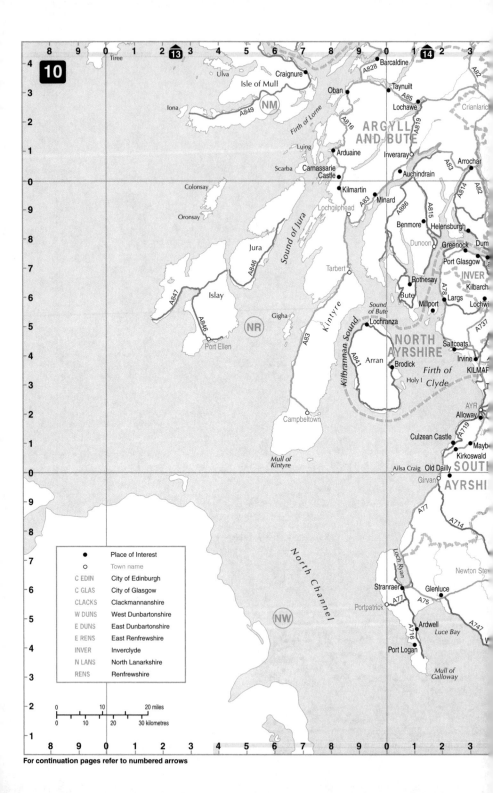

10

Tiree
Ulva
Isle of Mull
Iona
Craignure
A828 Barcaldine
Oban
Taynuilt
A85 Lochawe
Crianlaric
NM
A849
Firth of Lorne
A816
ARGYLL AND BUTE
Luing
Arduaine
Inveraray
Auchindrain
A819
Arrochar
A83
A814
A82
Scarba
Carnassarie Castle
Colonsay
Kilmartin
A83
Minard
Oronsay
Lochgilphead
A886
A815
Benmore
Helensburgh
Dunoon
Greenock
Dum
Port Glasgow
La
INVER
Jura
A846
Sound of Jura
Tarbert
Rothesay
Kilbarch
Bute
Millport
Largs
Lochwi
A78
A847
Islay
Kintyre
Sound of Bute
Lochranza
A737
Gigha
NR
Kilbrannan Sound
NORTH AYRSHIRE
Saltcoats
A806
Port Ellen
A83
Arran
Brodick
Irvine
KILMAF
A841
Holy I
Firth of Clyde
Campbeltown
AYR
Alloway
A719
Culzean Castle
Mayb
Kirkoswald
Mull of Kintyre
Ailsa Craig
Old Dailly
SOUT
Girvan
AYRSHI
A77
A714

Legend:
- ● Place of Interest
- ○ Town name
- C EDIN — City of Edinburgh
- C GLAS — City of Glasgow
- CLACKS — Clackmannanshire
- W DUNS — West Dunbartonshire
- E DUNS — East Dunbartonshire
- E RENS — East Renfrewshire
- INVER — Inverclyde
- N LANS — North Lanarkshire
- RENS — Renfrewshire

North Channel
NW
Newton Ste
Stranraer
Glenluce
Portpatrick
A77
A75
A747
Ardwell
Luce Bay
Port Logan
A716
Mull of Galloway
Loch Ryan

Scale:
0 — 10 — 20 miles
0 — 10 — 20 — 30 kilometres

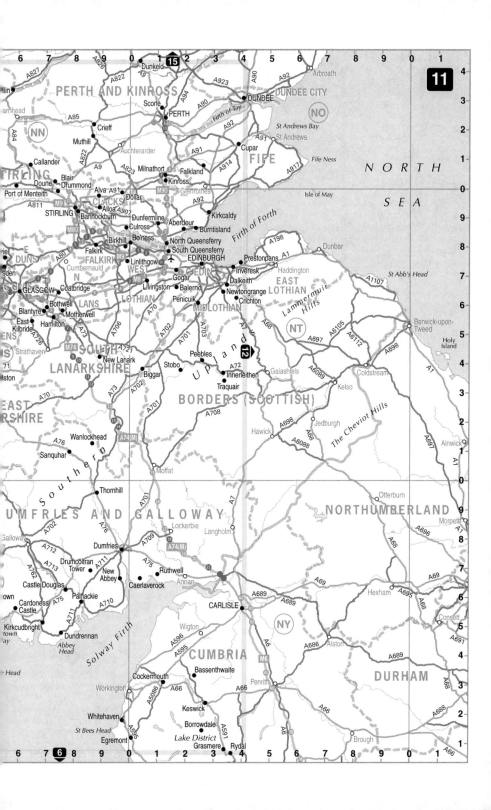

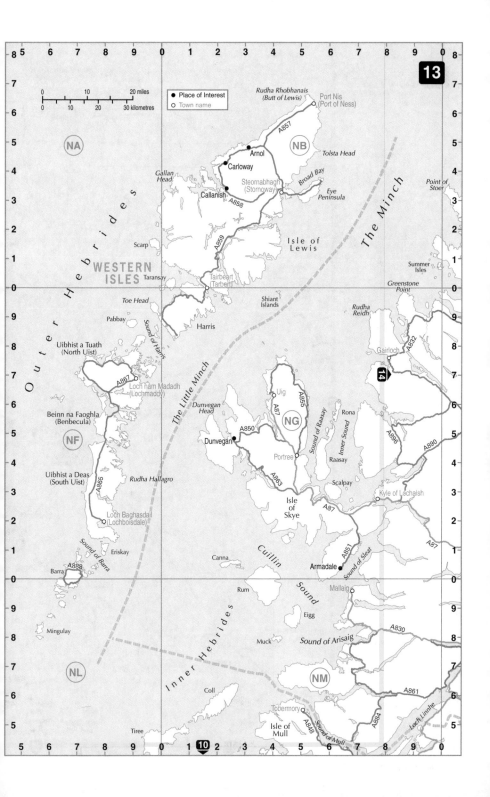

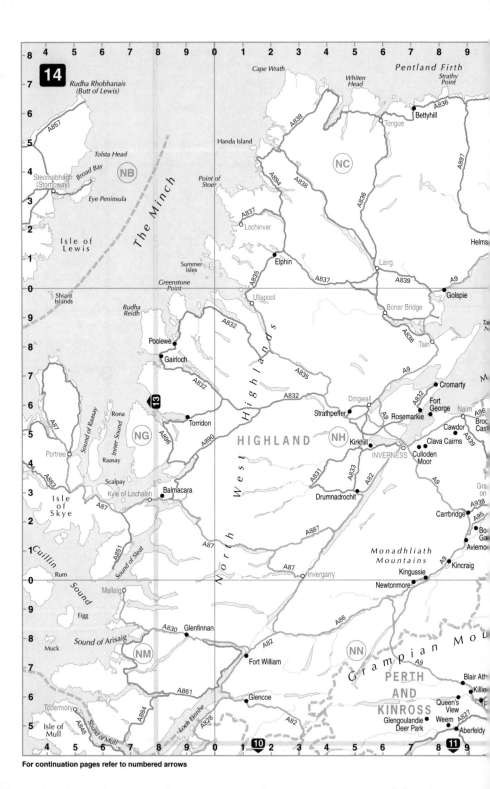

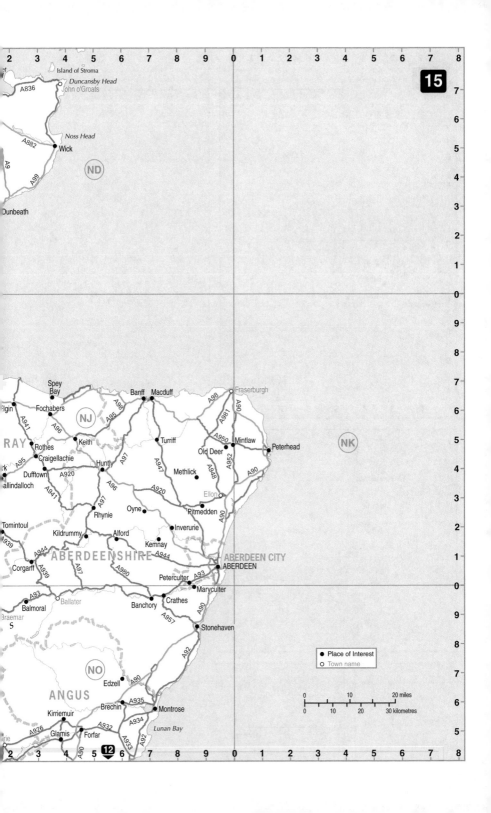

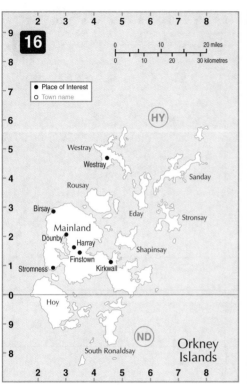

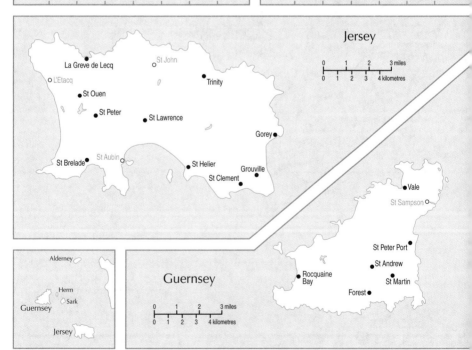

Index

0-9

1066 Battle of Hastings Abbey & Battlefield BATTLE 222
1066 Story in Hastings Castle HASTINGS 225
2 Willow Road LONDON NW3 143

A

Abbey House Museum LEEDS 282
Abbey Pumping Station LEICESTER 132
Abbot Hall Art Gallery KENDAL 45
Abbot House Heritage Centre DUNFERMLINE 319
Abbotsbury Swannery ABBOTSBURY 70
Abbotsford MELROSE 335
Aberconwy House CONWY 352
Aberdeen Art Gallery ABERDEEN 294
Aberdeen Maritime Museum ABERDEEN 294
Aberdeenshire Farming Museum MINTLAW 296
Aberdour Castle ABERDOUR 318
Aberdulais Falls ABERDULAIS 363
Aberglasney Gardens LLANGATHEN 350
Acorn Bank Garden and Watermill TEMPLE SOWERBY 48
Acton Burnell Castle ACTON BURNELL 194
African Violet Centre KING'S LYNN 170
Aillwee Cave BALLYVAUGHAN 385
Air Defence Radar Museum NORWICH 171
Airborne Forces Museum ALDERSHOT 97
Aldborough Roman Site ALDBOROUGH 265
Aldershot Military Museum ALDERSHOT 97
Alexander Keiller Museum AVEBURY 253
Alford Valley Railway ALFORD 294
Alfred East Gallery KETTERING 176
Alfriston Clergy House ALFRISTON 221
Allhallows Museum HONITON 63
Alloa Tower ALLOA 310
Almond Valley Heritage Centre LIVINGSTON 341
Almonry Heritage Centre EVESHAM 259
Alnwick Castle ALNWICK 178
Althorp ALTHORP 175
Alton Towers ALTON 207
Amberley Working Museum AMBERLEY 228
American Adventure Theme Park ILKESTON 54
American Museum BATH 198
Andrew Carnegie Birthplace Museum DUNFERMLINE 320
Anglesey Abbey LODE 22
Anglesey Sea Zoo BRYNSIENCYN 360
Angus Folk Museum GLAMIS 299
Anne Hathaway's Cottage SHOTTERY 240
Anne of Cleves House LEWES 225
Antonine Wall: Bearsden Bath-house BEARSDEN 316
Antony House TORPOINT 38
Antrim Round Tower ANTRIM 372
Appuldurcombe House WROXALL 252
Apsley House, The Wellington Museum LONDON W1 153
Aquarium of the Lakes LAKESIDE 46
Arbeia Roman Fort & Museum SOUTH SHIELDS 235
Arbroath Abbey ARBROATH 298
Arbroath Museum ARBROATH 298
Arbury Hall NUNEATON 239
Arbuthnot Museum & Art Gallery PETERHEAD 297
ARC YORK 274
Archaeolink OYNE 297
Ardboe Cross ARDBOE 382
Ardencraig ROTHESAY 342
Ardgillan Castle BALBRIGGAN 388
Address House PORTADOWN 376
Arduaine Garden ARDUAINE 299
Ardwell House Gardens ARDWELL 311
Argory MOY 376
Argyll Forest Park ARROCHAR 300
Arkwright's Cromford Mill CROMFORD 53

Arley Hall & Gardens NORTHWICH 29
Arlington Court ARLINGTON 57
Armadale Castle Gardens & Museum of the Isles ARMADALE 345
Armagh County Museum ARMAGH 374
Armagh Friary ARMAGH 375
Armagh Planetarium ARMAGH 375
Armitt AMBLESIDE 41
Army Medical Services Museum ASH VALE 217
Arreton Manor ARRETON 249
Arundel Castle ARUNDEL 228
Ascott WING 20
Ash End House Childrens Farm MIDDLETON 239
Ashby-de-la-Zouch Castle ASHBY-DE-LA-ZOUCH 131
Ashdown Forest Llama Park FOREST ROW 224
Ashmolean Museum of Art & Archaeology OXFORD 190
Ashridge Estate Visitor Centre BERKHAMSTED 111
Astley Cheetham Art Gallery STALYBRIDGE 95
Astley Hall Museum & Art Gallery CHORLEY 127
Aston Hall BIRMINGHAM 243
At-Bristol BRISTOL 14
Athelhampton House & Gardens ATHELHAMPTON 70
Atkinson Art Gallery SOUTHPORT 164
Attingham Park ATCHAM 194
Auchindrain Township Open Air Museum AUCHINDRAIN 300
Auckland Castle BISHOP AUCKLAND 77
Audley End House & Gardens AUDLEY END 81
Audley's Castle STRANGFORD 379
Avebury Manor AVEBURY 253
Avington Park AVINGTON 97
Avoncroft Museum of Historic Buildings BROMSGROVE 259
Avondale House & Forest Park RATHDRUM 398
Aylesford Priory AYLESFORD 115

B

Babbacombe Model Village TORQUAY 68
Bachelors' Club TARBOLTON 338
Baconsthorpe Castle BACONSTHORPE 166
Baddesley Clinton Hall BADDESLEY CLINTON 237
Bala Lake Railway LLANUWCHLLYN 359
Ballylumford Dolmen BALLYLUMFORD 373
Balmacara Estate & Lochalsh Woodland Garden BALMACARA 321
Balmoral Castle Grounds & Exhibition BALMORAL 295
Baltic Centre for Contemporary Art GATESHEAD 234
Balvenie Castle DUFFTOWN 327
Bamburgh Castle BAMBURGH 178
Banagher Church DUNGIVEN 381
Banbury Museum BANBURY 187
Banchory Museum BANCHORY 295
Banff Museum BANFF 295
Banham Zoo BANHAM 166
Bank of England Museum LONDON EC2 140
Bankfield Museum HALIFAX 280
Bankside Gallery LONDON SE1 144
Bannockburn Heritage Centre BANNOCKBURN 339
Banqueting House at Whitehall Palace LONDON SW1 149
Bantock House and Park WOLVERHAMPTON 247
Barbara Hepworth Museum & Sculpture Garden ST IVES 37
Bargany Gardens OLD DAILLY 338
Barnard Castle BARNARD CASTLE 77
Barrington Court Garden BARRINGTON 198
Barry Water Mill CARNOUSTIE 298

Basildon Park LOWER BASILDON 11
Basing House OLD BASING 103
Basingwerk Abbey HOLYWELL 356
Bass Museum BURTON-UPON-TRENT 207
Bateman's BURWASH 223
Bath Abbey BATH 198
Bath Postal Museum BATH 199
Batsford Arboretum MORETON-IN-MARSH 89
Battle Museum of Local History BATTLE 221
Battle of Britain Memorial Flight Visitor Centre CONINGSBY 135
Battlefield Line MARKET BOSWORTH 133
Battlefield Line Railway SHACKERSTONE 134
Baxters Highland Village FOCHABERS 328
Bayard's Cove Fort DARTMOUTH 60
Bayham Abbey LAMBERHURST 121
BBC Television Centre Tours LONDON W12 154
Beacon WHITEHAVEN 48
Beaghmore Stone Circles and Alignments BEAGHMORE 382
Beale Park LOWER BASILDON 12
Beamish, The North of England Open-Air Museum BEAMISH 77
Beatles Story LIVERPOOL 161
Beatrix Potter Gallery HAWKSHEAD 45
Beaulieu : National Motor Museum BEAULIEU 98
Beaumaris Castle BEAUMARIS 360
Bedes World & St Paul's Church JARROW 234
Bedford Museum BEDFORD 8
Beeston Castle BEESTON 25
Bekonscot Model Village and Railway BEACONSFIELD 17
Belfast Zoological Gardens BELFAST 372
Belgrave Hall & Gardens LEICESTER 132
Bell Tower of All Saints' Church INVERARAY 300
Belleek Pottery BELLEEK 379
Belsay Hall, Castle and Gardens BELSAY 179
Belton House Park & Gardens BELTON 135
Belvoir Castle BELVOIR 131
Bembridge Windmill BEMBRIDGE 249
Benburb Castle BENBURB 382
Beningbrough Hall & Gardens BENINGBROUGH 265
Benmore Botanic Garden BENMORE 300
Benthall Hall BENTHALL 194
Bentley Wildfowl & Motor Museum HALLAND 224
Berkeley Castle BERKELEY 85
Berkhamsted Castle BERKHAMSTED 111
Berney Arms Windmill BURGH CASTLE 167
Berrington Hall ASHTON 109
Berwick-Upon-Tweed Barracks BERWICK-UPON-TWEED 179
Beth Chatto Gardens COLCHESTER 82
Bicton Park Botanical Gardens BICTON 58
Biddenden Vineyards & Cider Works BIDDENDEN 115
Biddulph Grange Garden BIDDULPH 207
Big Pit National Mining Museum of Wales BLAENAVON 369
Bignor Roman Villa & Museum BIGNOR 229
Bircham Windmill GREAT BIRCHAM 168
Birdland BOURTON-ON-THE-WATER 85
Birdoswald Roman Fort BIRDOSWALD 42
Birdworld & Underwaterworld FARNHAM 218
Birkhill Fireclay Mine BIRKHILL 318
Birmingham Botanical Gardens & Glasshouses BIRMINGHAM 243
Birmingham Museum & Art Gallery BIRMINGHAM 244
Birr Castle Demesne BIRR 396
Bishop's & Earl's Palaces KIRKWALL 344
Bishop's Palace WELLS 205
Bishop's Waltham Palace BISHOP'S WALTHAM 98
Black Country Living Museum DUDLEY 246
Black House Museum ARNOL 343
Black Watch Regimental Museum PERTH 332

Index

Blackbrook Zoological Park LEEK 208
Blackgang Chine Fantasy Park
    BLACKGANG 250
Blackness Castle LINLITHGOW 341
Blackpool Zoo Park BLACKPOOL 126
Blackwell The Arts & Crafts House
    BOWNESS-ON-WINDERMERE 42
Blaenavon Ironworks BLAENAVON 369
Blair Castle BLAIR ATHOLL 330
Blair Drummond Safari & Leisure Park
    BLAIR DRUMMOND 339
Blaise Castle House Museum BRISTOL 14
Blakesley Hall BIRMINGHAM 244
Blarney Castle & Rock Close BLARNEY 386
Blenheim Palace WOODSTOCK 192
Bletchley Park BLETCHLEY 17
Blickling Hall BLICKLING 166
Blue Planet Aquarium ELLESMERE PORT 27
Blue Reef Aquarium NEWQUAY 35
Blue Reef Aquarium PORTSMOUTH 103
Blue Reef Aquarium TYNEMOUTH 236
Bluebell Railway
    SHEFFIELD PARK STATION 227
Blue-John Cavern & Mine CASTLETON 51
Bo'ness & Kinneil Railway BO'NESS 318
Boarstall Duck Decoy AYLESBURY 17
Boat Museum ELLESMERE PORT 27
Bodelwyddan Castle BODELWYDDAN 354
Bodiam Castle BODIAM 222
Bodnant Garden TAL-Y-CAFN 353
Bolling Hall BRADFORD 279
Bolsover Castle BOLSOVER 50
Bolton Castle CASTLE BOLTON 266
Bonamargy Friary BALLYCASTLE 373
Bonawe Iron Furnace TAYNUILT 301
Booth Museum of Natural History
    BRIGHTON 222
Borde Hill Garden HAYWARDS HEATH 230
Boscobel House and The Royal Oak
    BOSCOBEL 194
Bosworth Battlefield Visitor Centre & Country
    Park MARKET BOSWORTH 133
Botanic Gardens BELFAST 372
Bothwell Castle BOTHWELL 338
Bourton House Garden
    BOURTON-ON-THE-HILL 85
Bowes Castle BOWES 77
Bowes Museum BARNARD CASTLE 77
Bowhill House and Country Park SELKIRK 336
Bowood House & Gardens CALNE 253
Bradford Industrial Museum and Horses at
    Work BRADFORD 279
Bradford-on-Avon Tithe Barn
    BRADFORD-ON-AVON 253
Brading The Experience BRADING 250
Bradley Manor NEWTON ABBOT 65
Bramall Hall & Park BRAMHALL 93
Bramber Castle BRAMBER 229
Bramham Park BRAMHAM 280
Brander Museum HUNTLY 295
Branklyn Garden PERTH 332
Brantwood CONISTON 44
Brass Rubbing Centre EDINBURGH 302
Breadalbane Folklore Centre KILLIN 340
Breamore House & Countryside
    BREAMORE 98
Brechin Town House Museum BRECHIN 298
Brecknock Museum & Art Gallery
    BRECON 367
Brecon Mountain Railway
    MERTHYR TYDFIL 361
Bressingham Steam Museum & Gardens
    BRESSINGHAM 167
Brian Boru Heritage Centre KILLALOE 385
Bridewell Museum NORWICH 171
Brighstone Shop and Museum
    BRIGHSTONE 250
Brighton Museum & Art Gallery
    BRIGHTON 222
Brimham Rocks BRIMHAM 266
Brinkburn Priory LONGFRAMLINGTON 181

Bristol Industrial Museum BRISTOL 14
Bristol Zoo Gardens BRISTOL 15
Bristol's City Museum & Art Gallery
    BRISTOL 15
Bristol's Georgian House BRISTOL 15
Bristol's Red Lodge BRISTOL 15
British Airways London Eye LONDON SE1 144
British Commercial Vehicle Museum
    LEYLAND 128
British Cycling Museum CAMELFORD 32
British Empire & Commonwealth Museum
    BRISTOL 15
British Engineerium-Museum of Steam &
    Mechanical Antiquities HOVE 225
British Golf Museum ST ANDREWS 321
British Lawnmower Museum SOUTHPORT 165
British Museum LONDON WC1 155
Broadfield House Glass Museum
    KINGSWINFORD 247
Broadlands ROMSEY 105
Broadway Tower & Animal Park
    BROADWAY 259
Brockhampton Estate BROCKHAMPTON 109
Brodick Castle, Garden & Country Park
    BRODICK 342
Brodie Castle BRODIE CASTLE 327
Brodsworth Hall & Gardens DONCASTER 277
Brokerswood Country Park WESTBURY 258
Brontë Parsonage Museum HAWORTH 281
Brooklands Museum WEYBRIDGE 220
Brough Castle BROUGH 42
Brough of Birsay DOUNBY 343
Brougham Castle BROUGHAM 42
Broughton Castle BROUGHTON 187
Broughton House & Garden
    KIRKCUDBRIGHT 312
Broughty Castle Museum DUNDEE 315
Brownsea Island BROWNSEA ISLAND 71
Brú Ború Heritage Centre CASHEL 397
Bryn Celli Ddu Burial Chamber
    BRYNCELLI DDU 360
Buckfast Abbey BUCKFASTLEIGH 58
Buckfast Butterfly Farm & Dartmoor Otter
    Sanctuary BUCKFASTLEIGH 58
Buckingham Palace LONDON SW1 149
Buckinghamshire Railway Centre
    QUAINTON 19
Buckland Abbey BUCKLAND ABBEY 58
Buckler's Hard Village & Maritime Museum
    BUCKLER'S HARD 98
Building of Bath Museum BATH 199
Buildwas Abbey BUILDWAS 195
Bunratty Castle & Folk Park BUNRATTY 385
Burford House Gardens BURFORD 195
Burgh Castle BURGH CASTLE 167
Burghley House STAMFORD 137
Burleigh Castle MILNATHORT 331
Burnby Hall Garden & Stewart Collection
    POCKLINGTON 264
Burns Mausoleum DUMFRIES 312
Burns National Heritage Park ALLOWAY 337
Burntisland Edwardian Fair Museum
    BURNTISLAND 319
Burrell Collection GLASGOW 307
Burton Agnes Hall BURTON AGNES 262
Burton Agnes Manor House
    BURTON AGNES 263
Burton Constable Hall SPROATLEY 264
Buscot Park BUSCOT 188
Bute Museum ROTHESAY 342
Butterfly & Wildlife Park SPALDING 137
Butterfly Centre SWINGFIELD MINNIS 124
Bygones TORQUAY 68
Byland Abbey COXWOLD 266

C

C M Booth Collection of Historic Vehicles
    ROLVENDEN 123
Cadbury World BOURNVILLE 245
Caerhays Castle Gardens GORRAN 33
Caerlaverock Castle CAERLAVEROCK 311

Caerleon Roman Baths CAERLEON 363
Caernarfon Castle CAERNARFON 357
Caerphilly Castle CAERPHILLY 347
Caerwent Roman Town CAERWENT 361
Caister Roman Site CAISTER-ON-SEA 167
Caldicot Castle, Museum & Countryside Park
    CALDICOT 361
Calke Abbey CALKE 50
Callanish Standing Stones CALLANISH 343
Callendar House FALKIRK 318
Calleva Museum SILCHESTER 106
Cambridge & County Folk Museum
    CAMBRIDGE 21
Cambridge University Botanic Garden
    CAMBRIDGE 21
Camelot Theme Park
    CHARNOCK RICHARD 126
Camera Obscura & World of Illusions
    EDINBURGH 302
Camperdown Country Park DUNDEE 315
Canal Museum STOKE BRUERNE 177
Canons Ashby House CANONS ASHBY 175
Canonteign Falls CHUDLEIGH 59
Canterbury Roman Museum
    CANTERBURY 116
Canterbury Tales CANTERBURY 116
Canterbury West Gate Museum
    CANTERBURY 116
Capesthorne Hall CAPESTHORNE 25
Captain Cook Birthplace Museum
    MIDDLESBROUGH 270
Cardiff Castle CARDIFF 347
Cardoness Castle CARDONESS CASTLE 311
Carew Castle & Tidal Mill CAREW 364
Carisbrooke Castle CARISBROOKE 250
Carlisle Castle CARLISLE 42
Carlisle Cathedral CARLISLE 42
Carlyle's House LONDON SW3 151
Carmarthenshire County Museum
    ABERGWILI 349
Carn Euny Ancient Village SANCREED 38
Carnasserie Castle
    CARNASSERIE CASTLE 300
Carnegie Museum INVERURIE 296
Carreg Cennen Castle
    CARREG CENNEN CASTLE 349
Carrick-a-rede Rope Bridge and Larrybane
    Visitors Centre CARRICK-A-REDE 373
Carrickfergus Castle CARRICKFERGUS 373
Cartwright Hall Art Gallery BRADFORD 279
Casino DUBLIN 388
Castell Coch TONGWYNLAIS 348
Castell Henllys Fort CRYMYCH 364
Castell-y-Bere
    LLANFIHANGEL-Y-PENNANT 359
Castle & Visitor Centre ST ANDREWS 321
Castle Acre Priory and Castle
    CASTLE ACRE 167
Castle Balfour LISNASKEA 380
Castle Bromwich Hall Gardens
    CASTLE BROMWICH 245
Castle Campbell DOLLAR 311
Castle Caulfield CASTLECAULFIELD 382
Castle Coole ENNISKILLEN 379
Castle Cornet ST PETER PORT 286
Castle Drogo DREWSTEIGNTON 61
Castle Fraser KEMNAY 296
Castle Howard MALTON 269
Castle Kennedy Gardens STRANRAER 314
Castle Menzies WEEM 333
Castle of Old Wick WICK 325
Castle Rising Castle CASTLE RISING 167
Castle Rushen CASTLETOWN 290
Castle Ward STRANGFORD 379
Castletown CELBRIDGE 394
Catalyst Science Discovery Centre
    WIDNES 30
Cathedral (& Museum) ST ANDREWS 321
Cavanacor Historic House & Art Gallery
    LIFFORD 388
Cawdor Castle CAWDOR 322

Cecil Higgins Art Gallery & Museum BEDFORD 8
Cefn Coed Colliery Museum CRYNANT 363
Céide Fields BALLYCASTLE 396
Celtic Park & Gardens KILCORNAN 395
Celtica MACHYNLLETH 367
Central Art Gallery ASHTON-UNDER-LYNE 92
Central Library LIVERPOOL 161
Centre for Alternative Technology MACHYNLLETH 367
Ceramica STOKE-ON-TRENT 209
Channel Islands Military Museum ST OUEN 289
Charlecote Park CHARLECOTE 237
Charles Dickens Museum LONDON WC1 155
Charles Dickens' Birthplace Museum PORTSMOUTH 103
Charles Fort KINSALE 387
Charlestown Shipwreck & Heritage Centre ST AUSTELL 37
Chartwell CHARTWELL 117
Chastleton House CHASTLETON 188
Chatelherault Country Park HAMILTON 339
Chatsworth CHATSWORTH 52
Chavenage House TETBURY 91
Cheddleton Flint Mill CHEDDLETON 207
Chedworth Roman Villa CHEDWORTH 85
Chelsea Physic Garden LONDON SW3 152
Cheltenham Art Gallery & Museum CHELTENHAM 86
Chepstow Castle CHEPSTOW 362
Cheshire Military Museum CHESTER 25
Chessington World of Adventures CHESSINGTON 158
Chester Beatty Library DUBLIN 389
Chester Cathedral CHESTER 25
Chester Visitor Centre CHESTER 25
Chester Zoo CHESTER 26
Chesters Roman Fort & Museum WALWICK 181
Chichester Cathedral CHICHESTER 229
Chiddingstone Castle CHIDDINGSTONE 118
Chilford Hall Vineyard LINTON 22
Chillingham Castle CHILLINGHAM 179
Chillingham Wild Cattle Park CHILLINGHAM 179
Chiltern Open Air Museum CHALFONT ST GILES 17
China Clay Museum - Wheal Martyn ST AUSTELL 37
Chirk Castle CHIRK 370
Chislehurst Caves CHISLEHURST 158
Chiswick House LONDON W4 154
Cholmondeley Castle Gardens CHOLMONDELEY 26
Christ Church Cathedral DUBLIN 389
Christchurch Castle & Norman House CHRISTCHURCH 71
Christchurch Mansion IPSWICH 213
Church Farm Museum SKEGNESS 137
Churchill Museum & Cabinet War Rooms LONDON SW1 150
Churnet Valley Railway CHEDDLETON 207
Chysauster Ancient Village CHYSAUSTER ANCIENT VILLAGE 32
Cider Museum & King Offa Distillery HEREFORD 110
Cilgerran Castle CILGERRAN 364
City Arts Centre EDINBURGH 302
City Museum & Art Gallery PLYMOUTH 66
City Museum & Art Gallery WORCESTER 261
City Museum & Records Office PORTSMOUTH 103
City Museum (also 15 Castle Hill) LANCASTER 127
City of Norwich Aviation Museum HORSHAM ST FAITH 170
City Walls LONDONDERRY 381
Clan Macpherson House & Museum NEWTONMORE 325
Clandon Park WEST CLANDON 220

Claremont Landscape Garden ESHER 158
Clava Cairns CLAVA CAIRNS 322
Claydon House MIDDLE CLAYDON 19
Clearwell Caves Ancient Iron Mines CLEARWELL 86
Cleeve Abbey WASHFORD 204
Clevedon Court CLEVEDON 201
Cleveland Ironstone Mining Museum SKINNINGROVE 273
Click Mill DOUNBY 343
Clickimin LERWICK 344
Cliffe Castle Museum & Gallery KEIGHLEY 282
Clifford's Tower YORK 274
Cliffs of Moher Visitors Centre LISCANNOR 385
Clitheroe Castle Museum CLITHEROE 127
Cliveden CLIVEDEN 18
Clock Tower ST ALBANS 113
Clouds Hill BOVINGTON CAMP 71
Clumber Park WORKSOP 186
Clydebuilt - Scottish Maritime Museum at Braehead GLASGOW 307
Coats Observatory PAISLEY 333
Cobbaton Combat Collection CHITTLEHAMPTON 59
Cogges Manor Farm Museum WITNEY 192
Coity Castle COITY 347
Colby Woodland Garden AMROTH 364
Colchester Castle Museum COLCHESTER 82
Colchester Zoo COLCHESTER 82
Coldharbour Mill Working Wool Museum UFFCULME 69
Colemans Animal Farm PORCHFIELD 251
Coleridge Cottage NETHER STOWEY 203
Coleton Fishacre House & Garden KINGSWEAR 64
Collection: Art & Archaeology in Lincolnshire LINCOLN 136
Colne Valley Railway & Museum CASTLE HEDINGHAM 81
Colour Museum BRADFORD 279
Combe Martin Wildlife Park & Dinosaur Park COMBE MARTIN 60
Compton Acres Gardens CANFORD CLIFFS 71
Compton Castle COMPTON 60
Compton Verney COMPTON VERNEY 238
Conisbrough Castle CONISBROUGH 277
Conkers MOIRA 133
Conservation Centre LIVERPOOL 162
Conwy Castle CONWY 352
Conwy Suspension Bridge CONWY 353
Conwy Valley Railway Museum BETWS-Y-COED 352
Cookworthy Museum of Rural Life KINGSBRIDGE 64
Corbridge Roman Site and Museum CORBRIDGE 180
Corfe Castle CORFE CASTLE 72
Corfe Castle Museum CORFE CASTLE 72
Corgarff Castle CORGARFF 295
Corinium Museum CIRENCESTER 86
Cork City Gaol CORK 386
Cork Public Museum CORK 387
Corlea Trackway Visitor Centre KEENAGH 395
Cornish Mines & Engines POOL 36
Cornwall's Crealy Great Adventure Park TREDINNICK 38
Corrigall Farm & Kirbuster Museum HARRAY 344
Corsham Court CORSHAM 253
Cosmeston Lakes Country Park & Medieval Village PENARTH 370
Cotehele CALSTOCK 31
Cotswold Falconry Centre MORETON-IN-MARSH 89
Cotswold Farm Park GUITING POWER 88
Cotswold Wildlife Park BURFORD 187
Coughton Court COUGHTON 238
Courtauld Gallery LONDON WC2 155
Courthouse LONG CRENDON 18

Courts HOLT 254
Coventry Cathedral & Visitor Centre COVENTRY 245
Coventry Transport Museum COVENTRY 245
Crabble Corn Mill DOVER 118
Crag Cave CASTLEISLAND 393
Craggaunowen The Living Past Experience QUIN 385
Cragside ROTHBURY 181
Craigmillar Castle EDINBURGH 302
Cranfield Church CHURCHTOWN 374
Crarae Gardens MINARD 301
Crathes Castle & Garden CRATHES 295
Creake Abbey NORTH CREAKE 171
Crealy Adventure Park CLYST ST MARY 59
Creetown Gem Rock Museum CREETOWN 311
Cregneash Village Folk Museum CREGNEASH 291
Creswell Crags Museum and Education Centre CRESWELL 52
Criccieth Castle CRICCIETH 358
Crich Tramway Village CRICH 52
Crichton Castle CRICHTON 326
Croft Castle CROFT 109
Crofton Beam Engines MARLBOROUGH 255
Crom Estate NEWTOWNBUTLER 380
Croome Park SEVERN STOKE 260
Crossraguel Abbey MAYBOLE 337
Cruachan Power Station LOCHAWE 301
Cruickshank Botanic Garden ABERDEEN 294
Culloden Battlefield CULLODEN MOOR 322
Culross Palace, Town House & The Study CULROSS 319
Culzean Castle & Country Park CULZEAN CASTLE 337
Cumberland Pencil Museum KESWICK 46
Curraghs Wild Life Park BALLAUGH 290
Cutty Sark Clipper Ship LONDON SE10 147
Cwmcarn Forest Drive CWMCARN 347
Cyfarthfa Castle Museum & Art Gallery MERTHYR TYDFIL 361
Cymer Abbey CYMER ABBEY 358

D

D. H. Lawrence Heritage EASTWOOD 182
Dairy Land Farm World NEWQUAY 35
Dalemain DALEMAIN 44
Dales Countryside Museum Centre & TIC HAWES 267
Dali Universe LONDON SE1 144
Dallas Dhu Distillery FORRES 328
Dalmeny House SOUTH QUEENSFERRY 306
Dan-Yr-Ogof The National Showcaves Centre for Wales ABERCRAF 366
Dapdune Wharf GUILDFORD 218
Darlington Railway Centre & Museum DARLINGTON 78
Dartington Crystal GREAT TORRINGTON 62
Dartmouth Castle DARTMOUTH 61
David Livingstone Centre BLANTYRE 338
Dawyck Botanic Garden STOBO 337
D-Day Museum & Overlord Embroidery PORTSMOUTH 104
de Havilland Aircraft Heritage Centre LONDON COLNEY 112
Deal Castle DEAL 118
Dean Forest Railway LYDNEY 88
Dean Gallery EDINBURGH 302
Dean Heritage Centre SOUDLEY 91
Deddington Castle DEDDINGTON 188
Deene Park DEENE 175
Deep KINGSTON UPON HULL 264
Deep Sea Adventure & Sharky's Play & Party WEYMOUTH 75
Deep Sea World NORTH QUEENSFERRY 320
Deer Abbey OLD DEER 297
Denbigh Castle DENBIGH 354
Denby Pottery Visitor Centre DENBY 53
Denmans Garden FONTWELL 230
Derby Museum & Art Gallery DERBY 53

Index

Design Museum LONDON SE1 144
Desmond Castle KINSALE 387
Deva Roman Experience CHESTER 26
Dewar's World of Whisky ABERFELDY 330
Dick Institute Museum & Art Galleries
  KILMARNOCK 316
Dickens House Museum BROADSTAIRS 116
Didcot Railway Centre DIDCOT 188
Diggerland CULLOMPTON 60
Diggerland LANGLEY PARK 79
Diggerland STROOD 124
Dimbola Lodge FRESHWATER 250
Din Llugwy Ancient Village LLANALLGO 361
Dinefwr Park LLANDEILO 350
Dinosaur Adventure Park LENWADE 171
Dinosaur Isle SANDOWN 251
Dinosaur Museum DORCHESTER 72
Dirleton Castle DIRLETON 317
Discovery Point & RRS Discovery
  DUNDEE 315
Dobwalls Family Adventure Park
  DOBWALLS 32
Dock Museum BARROW-IN-FURNESS 41
Dolaucothi Gold Mines PUMSAINT 351
Dolbadarn Castle LLANBERIS 358
Dolphin Sailing Barge Museum
  SITTINGBOURNE 124
Dolwyddelan Castle DOLWYDDELAN 353
Doncaster Museum & Art Gallery
  DONCASTER 277
Donegal Castle DONEGAL 388
Donington Grand Prix Collection
  CASTLE DONINGTON 131
Donington-le-Heath Manor House
  DONINGTON-LE-HEATH 131
Dorney Court ETON 11
Dorothy Clive Garden WILLOUGHBRIDGE 211
Dorset County Museum DORCHESTER 72
Dorset Teddy Bear Museum DORCHESTER 72
Doune Castle DOUNE 340
Dove Cottage & The Wordsworth Museum
  GRASMERE 45
Dover Castle & Secret Wartime Tunnels
  DOVER 118
Down County Museum DOWNPATRICK 377
Down House - Home of Charles Darwin
  DOWNE 158
Dr Johnson's House LONDON EC4 141
Drayton Manor Theme Park TAMWORTH 210
Drimnagh Castle DUBLIN 389
Druidstone Park CANTERBURY 117
Drum Castle PETERCULTER 294
Drumcoltran Tower
  DRUMCOLTRAN TOWER 312
Drumena Cashel CASTLEWELLAN 376
Drumlanrig Castle THORNHILL 314
Drummond Gardens MUTHILL 331
Drusillas Park ALFRISTON 221
Dryburgh Abbey DRYBURGH 334
Dryslwyn Castle DRYSLWYN 349
Dublin Castle DUBLIN 389
Dublin Writers Museum DUBLIN 389
Dublin Zoo DUBLIN 389
Dublinia & The Viking World DUBLIN 389
Dudley Zoological Gardens DUDLEY 246
Dudmaston QUATT 197
Duff House BANFF 295
Duffus Castle DUFFUS 327
Dulwich Picture Gallery LONDON SE21 149
Dumbarton Castle DUMBARTON 341
Dumfries Museum & Camera Obscura
  DUMFRIES 312
Dun Carloway Broch CARLOWAY 343
Dunadd Fort KILMARTIN 301
Dunbrody Abbey Visitors Centre
  NEW ROSS 397
Duncombe Park HELMSLEY 267
Dundrennan Abbey DUNDRENNAN 312
Dundrum Castle NEWCASTLE 378
Duneight Motte and Bailey LISBURN 374
Dunfermline Abbey DUNFERMLINE 320

Dungiven Priory DUNGIVEN 381
Dunguaire Castle KINVARRA 393
Dunham Massey ALTRINCHAM 92
Dunluce Castle PORTBALLINTRAE 374
Dunnottar Castle STONEHAVEN 297
Dunrobin Castle GOLSPIE 324
Dunstaffnage Castle OBAN 301
Dunstanburgh Castle EMBLETON 180
Dunster Castle DUNSTER 201
Dunvegan Castle DUNVEGAN 345
Durham Cathedral DURHAM 78
Durham Light Infantry Museum & Durham Art
  Gallery DURHAM 78
Durrell Wildlife Conservation Trust
  TRINITY 289
Dyffryn Gardens CARDIFF 347
Dylan Thomas' Boat House LAUGHARNE 349
Dymchurch Martello Tower DYMCHURCH 118
Dynamic Earth EDINBURGH 302
Dyrham Park DYRHAM 87

E

Eagle Heights EYNSFORD 118
Earl's Palace BIRSAY 343
Easby Abbey EASBY 266
East Anglia Transport Museum
  LOWESTOFT 215
East Lambrook Manor Garden
  EAST LAMBROOK 202
East Riddlesden Hall KEIGHLEY 282
Eastney Beam Engine House
  PORTSMOUTH 104
Eastnor Castle LEDBURY 110
Easton Farm Park EASTON 212
Ecos Millennium Environmental Centre
  BALLYMENA 373
Eden Camp Modern History Theme Museum
  MALTON 269
Eden Project ST AUSTELL 37
Edinburgh Butterfly & Insect World
  DALKEITH 326
Edinburgh Castle EDINBURGH 302
Edinburgh Crystal Visitor Centre
  PENICUIK 326
Edinburgh Dungeon EDINBURGH 303
Edinburgh Zoo EDINBURGH 303
Edradour Distillery PITLOCHRY 332
Edzell Castle EDZELL 298
Egglestone Abbey BARNARD CASTLE 77
Elgar's Birthplace Museum WORCESTER 261
Elgin Cathedral ELGIN 327
Elgin Museum ELGIN 327
Elizabeth Castle ST HELIER 288
Elizabethan House Museum
  GREAT YARMOUTH 168
Ell Shop & Little Houses DUNKELD 331
Eltham Palace House & Gardens
  LONDON SE9 147
Ely Cathedral ELY 21
Emmetts Garden BRASTED 116
Enniskillen Castle ENNISKILLEN 380
Erasmus Darwin House LICHFIELD 208
Erddig WREXHAM 370
Eureka! The Museum for Children
  HALIFAX 280
Euston Hall EUSTON 213
Ewe-Phoria Sheepdog Centre CORWEN 354
Ewloe Castle EWLOE 355
Exbury Gardens & Railway EXBURY 99
Exeter Cathedral EXETER 62
Exmoor Zoological Park
  BLACKMOOR GATE 58
Exploris Aquarium PORTAFERRY 378
Explosion! Museum of Naval Firepower
  GOSPORT 99
Eyam Hall EYAM 54
Eyemouth Museum EYEMOUTH 334
Eynsford Castle EYNSFORD 119

F

Fairbourne Railway FAIRBOURNE 358
Fairfax House YORK 274
Fairhaven Woodland & Water Garden
  SOUTH WALSHAM 173
Falconer Museum FORRES 328
Falconry Centre STOURBRIDGE 247
Falkland Palace & Garden FALKLAND 320
Famous Grouse Experience CRIEFF 331
Farleigh Hungerford Castle FARLEIGH
  HUNGERFORD 202
Farmer Giles Farmstead
  TEFFONT MAGNA 257
Farmland Museum and Denny Abbey
  WATERBEACH 23
Farnborough Hall FARNBOROUGH 238
Farnham Castle Keep FARNHAM 218
Fashion & Textile Museum LONDON SE1 144
Felbrigg Hall FELBRIGG 168
Felinwynt Rainforest Centre FELINWYNT 352
Fenton House LONDON NW3 143
Ffestiniog Railway PORTHMADOG 359
Finch Foundry STICKLEPATH 68
Finchale Priory DURHAM 78
Finchcocks GOUDHURST 119
Finkley Down Farm Park ANDOVER 97
Finlaystone Country Estate LANGBANK 333
Firepower LONDON SE18 148
Firle Place FIRLE 223
Fishbourne Roman Palace FISHBOURNE 230
Fitzwilliam Museum CAMBRIDGE 21
Flag Fen Bronze Age Centre
  PETERBOROUGH 22
Flambards Experience HELSTON 33
Flamingo Land Theme Park & Zoo
  KIRBY MISPERTON 268
Fleet Air Arm Museum YEOVILTON 206
Fleur de Lis Heritage Centre FAVERSHAM 119
Flint Castle FLINT 356
Floors Castle KELSO 335
Florence Court ENNISKILLEN 380
Florence Mine Heritage Centre
  EGREMONT 45
Florence Nightingale Museum
  LONDON SE1 145
Foel Farm Park BRYNSIENCYN 361
Forde Abbey CHARD 201
Forge Mill Needle Museum & Bordesley
  Abbey Visitor Centre REDDITCH 260
Fort Amherst CHATHAM 117
Fort Charlotte LERWICK 344
Fort George FORT GEORGE 323
Fort Grey and Shipwreck Museum
  ROCQUAINE BAY 285
Fota Arboretum & Gardens CARRIGTOHILL
  (CARRIGTOHILL) 386
Fota Wildlife Park CARRIGTWOHILL
  (CARRIGTOHILL) 386
Fountains Abbey & Studley Royal RIPON 272
Foynes Flying Boat Museum FOYNES 395
Framlingham Castle FRAMLINGHAM 213
Freightliners City Farm LONDON N7 142
Freud Museum LONDON NW3 143
Frogmore House WINDSOR 13
Fry Model Railway MALAHIDE 392
Furness Abbey BARROW-IN-FURNESS 41
Furzey Gardens MINSTEAD 101
Fyvie Castle TURRIFF 298

G

Gainsborough Old Hall GAINSBOROUGH 135
Gainsborough's House SUDBURY 216
Gairloch Heritage Museum GAIRLOCH 323
Galleries of Justice NOTTINGHAM 184
Gallery of Costume MANCHESTER 93
Gallery of Modern Art GLASGOW 307
Galway Atlantaquaria GALWAY 392
Garinish Island GLENGARRIFF 387
Gawsworth Hall GAWSWORTH 27
Gawthorpe Hall PADIHAM 128

Geevor Tin Mine PENDEEN 36
Geffrye Museum LONDON E2 139
Georgian House EDINBURGH 303
German Military Underground Hospital &
  Ammunition Store ST ANDREW 285
German Occupation Museum FOREST 285
German Underground Hospital
  ST LAWRENCE 288
Giant's Causeway Centre
  GIANT'S CAUSEWAY 374
Giant's Ring BELFAST 372
Gibside ROWLANDS GILL 235
Gilbert Collection LONDON WC2 155
Gilbert White's House & The Oates Museum
  SELBORNE 106
Gilfach Nature Discovery Centre and Reserve
  RHAYADER 368
Gisborough Priory GUISBOROUGH 267
Gladstone Court Museum BIGGAR 338
Gladstone Working Pottery Museum
  STOKE-ON-TRENT 209
Gladstone's Land EDINBURGH 303
Glamis Castle GLAMIS 299
Glansevern Hall Gardens BERRIEW 366
Glasgow Cathedral GLASGOW 307
Glasgow Museums Resource Centre
  GLASGOW 307
Glasgow Science Centre GLASGOW 308
Glastonbury Abbey GLASTONBURY 202
Glebe House & Gallery LETTERKENNY 388
Glen Grant Distillery ROTHES 328
Glencoe & North Lorn Folk Museum
  GLENCOE 323
Glencoe Visitor Centre GLENCOE 324
Glendurgan MAWNAN SMITH 35
Glenfarclas Distillery MARYPARK 328
Glenfiddich Distillery DUFFTOWN 327
Glenfinnan Monument GLENFINNAN 324
Glenlivet Distillery BALLINDALLOCH 327
Glenluce Abbey GLENLUCE 312
Glenveagh National Park & Castle
  LETTERKENNY 388
Glenwhan Gardens STRANRAER 314
Gloucester City Museum & Art Gallery
  GLOUCESTER 87
Gloucester Folk Museum GLOUCESTER 87
Glynde Place GLYNDE 224
Glynn Vivian Art Gallery SWANSEA 369
Gnoll Estate Country Park NEATH 363
Godolphin House GODOLPHIN CROSS 32
Godstone Farm GODSTONE 218
Golden Hinde Educational Trust
  LONDON SE1 145
Goodrich Castle GOODRICH 110
Goodwood House GOODWOOD 230
Goonhilly Satellite Earth Station Experience
  HELSTON 34
Gordon Highlanders Museum ABERDEEN 294
Gorhambury ST ALBANS 113
Gower Heritage Centre PARKMILL 369
Grand National Experience LIVERPOOL 162
Gray's Printing Press STRABANE 383
Great Central Railway LOUGHBOROUGH 133
Great Chalfield Manor
  BRADFORD-ON-AVON 253
Great Comp Garden BOROUGH GREEN 116
Great Coxwell Barn GREAT COXWELL 188
Great Dixter House & Gardens
  NORTHIAM 226
Great Hall WINCHESTER 108
Great Laxey Wheel & Mines Trail LAXEY 291
Green House Visitor Centre PLYMOUTH 66
Green Howards Museum RICHMOND 271
Green's Windmill NOTTINGHAM 184
Greenbank Garden GLASGOW 308
Greencastle KILKEEL 378
Greenfield Valley Heritage Park
  HOLYWELL 356
Greenhill Covenanters House BIGGAR 338
Greenmeadow Community Farm
  CWMBRAN 370

Greenway Garden CHURSTON FERRERS 59
Greenwood Forest Park Y FELINHELI 360
Greve de Lecq Barracks
  LA GREVE DE LECQ 287
Grey Abbey BALLYWALTER 376
Greys Court HENLEY-ON-THAMES 188
Grimes Graves GRIMES GRAVES 169
Grimsthorpe Castle GRIMSTHORPE 135
Groam House Museum ROSEMARKIE 325
Groombridge Place Gardens & Enchanted
  Forest GROOMBRIDGE PLACE 119
Grosmont Castle GROSMONT 362
Grove House and Gardens RAMSEY 292
Guernsey Museum & Art Gallery
  ST PETER PORT 286
Guildford House Gallery GUILDFORD 218
Guildhall BEVERLEY 262
Guildhall EXETER 62
Guildhall LEICESTER 132
Guildhall LONDON EC2 140
Guildhall Museum CARLISLE 43
Guildhall Museum ROCHESTER 123
Guildhall TOTNES 69
Guildhall YORK 274
Guinness Storehouse DUBLIN 389
Gurkha Museum WINCHESTER 107
Gwydir Uchaf Chapel LLANRWST 353

H

Hack Green Secret Nuclear Bunker
  NANTWICH 29
Haddo House METHLICK 296
Haddon Hall HADDON HALL 54
Hadleigh Castle HADLEIGH 82
Hadspen Garden & Nursery
  CASTLE CARY 201
Hailes Abbey HAILES 88
Hailes Castle EAST LINTON 317
Halfpenny Green Vineyards
  HALFPENNY GREEN 208
Hall Place BEXLEY 157
Hall's Croft STRATFORD-UPON-AVON 240
Halliwells House Museum SELKIRK 336
Ham House HAM 158
Hamerton Zoo Park HAMERTON 22
Hampton Court Palace HAMPTON COURT 159
Hamptonne ST LAWRENCE 289
Hanbury Hall HANBURY 259
Hancock Museum
  NEWCASTLE UPON TYNE 235
Handel House Museum LONDON W1 153
Harcourt Arboretum OXFORD 190
Hardknott Castle Roman Fort
  HARDKNOTT CASTLE ROMAN FORT 45
Hardwick Hall HARDWICK HALL 54
Hardy's Cottage DORCHESTER 72
Hare Hill MACCLESFIELD 28
Harewood House & Bird Garden
  HAREWOOD 281
Harlech Castle HARLECH 358
Harmony Garden MELROSE 336
Harris Museum & Art Gallery PRESTON 128
Harry Avery's Castle
  NEWTOWNSTEWART 383
Harryville Motte BALLYMENA 373
Hartlepool's Maritime Experience
  HARTLEPOOL 79
Harwich Redoubt Fort HARWICH 82
Hat Works Museum STOCKPORT 96
Hatchlands Park EAST CLANDON 217
Hatfield House, Park and Gardens
  HATFIELD 112
Haughmond Abbey HAUGHMOND ABBEY 195
Hawford Dovecote WORCESTER 261
Hawk Conservancy and Country Park
  WEYHILL 107
Hawkstone Historic Park & Follies
  WESTON-UNDER-REDCASTLE 197
Haynes International Motor Museum
  SPARKFORD 203

Heale Gardens, Plant Centre & Shop
  MIDDLE WOODFORD 255
Heaton Hall PRESTWICH 95
Hedgehog Hospital at Prickly Ball Farm
  NEWTON ABBOT 65
Hedingham Castle CASTLE HEDINGHAM 81
Heights of Abraham Cable Cars, Caverns &
  Hilltop Park MATLOCK BATH 55
Helicopter Museum
  WESTON-SUPER-MARE 205
Hell-Fire Caves WEST WYCOMBE 19
Helmsley Castle HELMSLEY 268
Hen Gwrt LLANTILIO CROSSENNY 362
Henry Blogg Museum CROMER 167
Herbert Art Gallery & Museum
  COVENTRY 246
Hereford Cathedral HEREFORD 110
Hergest Croft Gardens KINGTON 110
Heritage Motor Centre GAYDON 238
Hermitage Castle HERMITAGE 335
Hestercombe Gardens TAUNTON 204
Hever Castle & Gardens HEVER 120
Hezlett House COLERAINE 380
Hidcote Manor Garden MICKLETON 89
Highclere Castle & Gardens HIGHCLERE 100
Highdown HIGHDOWN 231
Highgate Cemetery LONDON N6 142
Highland & Rare Breeds Farm ELPHIN 323
Highland Folk Museum KINGUSSIE 324
Highland Folk Museum NEWTONMORE 325
Highland Museum of Childhood
  STRATHPEFFER 325
Highland Wildlife Park KINCRAIG 324
Hill House HELENSBURGH 300
Hill of Tarvit Mansionhouse & Garden
  CUPAR 319
Hill Top NEAR SAWREY 47
Hillsborough Fort HILLSBOROUGH 377
Himley Hall & Park HIMLEY 208
Hinton Ampner Garden HINTON AMPNER 100
Hirsel COLDSTREAM 334
Historic Dockyard Chatham CHATHAM 117
Historic Warships BIRKENHEAD 161
HM Customs & Excise National Museum
  LIVERPOOL 162
HM Frigate Unicorn DUNDEE 315
HMS Belfast LONDON SE1 145
HMS Trincomalee HARTLEPOOL 79
Hodnet Hall Gardens HODNET 196
Hogarth House LONDON W4 154
Holburne Museum of Art BATH 199
Holker Hall & Gardens HOLKER 45
Holkham Hall & Bygones Museum
  HOLKHAM 169
Holly Gate Cactus Garden ASHINGTON 229
Hollycombe Steam Collection LIPHOOK 101
Holmwood House GLASGOW 308
Holst Birthplace Museum CHELTENHAM 86
Honister Slate Mine BORROWDALE 42
Hoo Farm Animal Kingdom TELFORD 197
Hop Farm & Country Park BELTRING 115
Hopetoun House SOUTH QUEENSFERRY 306
Horniman Museum & Gardens
  LONDON SE23 149
Hornsea Museum HORNSEA 263
Horse Drawn Boats Centre LLANGOLLEN 355
HorseWorld BRISTOL 15
Horsey Windpump HORSEY 169
Hospital of St Cross WINCHESTER 107
Houghton Hall HOUGHTON 170
Houghton House AMPTHILL 8
House for an Art Lover GLASGOW 308
House of Dun MONTROSE 299
House of Manannan PEEL 291
House of The Binns LINLITHGOW 341
Houses of Parliament LONDON SW1 150
Housesteads Roman Fort HOUSESTEADS 181
How We Lived Then - Museum of Shops &
  Social History EASTBOURNE 223

Howletts Wild Animal Park
    BEKESBOURNE   115
Howth Castle Rhododendron Gardens
    DUBLIN   390
Hugh Lane Municipal Gallery of Modern Art
    DUBLIN   390
Hugh Miller's Cottage CROMARTY   322
Hughenden Manor HUGHENDEN   18
Hunstanton Sea Life Sanctuary
    HUNSTANTON   170
Hunt Museum LIMERICK   395
Hunterian Art Gallery GLASGOW   308
Hunterian Museum GLASGOW   308
Hunterian Museum LONDON WC2   156
Huntingtower Castle PERTH   332
Huntly Castle HUNTLY   295
Hurst Castle HURST CASTLE   100
Hutchesons' Hall GLASGOW   308
Hutton-in-the-Forest SKELTON   48
Hydro Centre Ffestiniog
    BLAENAU FFESTINIOG   356

I

Ickworth House, Park & Gardens
    HORRINGER   213
Ightham Mote IGHTHAM   120
Ilfracombe Museum ILFRACOMBE   63
Imperial War Museum Duxford DUXFORD   21
Imperial War Museum LONDON SE1   145
Imperial War Museum North
    MANCHESTER   93
Inch Abbey DOWNPATRICK   377
Inchcolm Abbey SOUTH QUEENSFERRY   307
Inchmahome Priory PORT OF MENTEITH   340
Inigo Jones Slateworks GROESLON   358
Innerpeffray Library CRIEFF   330
INTECH - Family Science Centre
    WINCHESTER   107
Inveraray Castle INVERARAY   301
Inveraray Jail INVERARAY   301
Inveresk Lodge Garden INVERESK   317
Inverewe Garden POOLEWE   325
Inverlochy Castle FORT WILLIAM   323
Ipswich Museum IPSWICH   213
Irish Linen Centre & Lisburn Museum
    LISBURN   374
Irish Museum of Modern Art DUBLIN   390
Irish National Heritage Park
    FERRYCARRIG   397
Irish National Stud & Japanese Gardens St
    Fiachra's Garden KILDARE   394
Ironbridge Gorge Museums IRONBRIDGE   196
Isle of Arran Distillery Visitor Centre
    LOCHRANZA   342
Isle of Arran Heritage Museum BRODICK   342
Isles of Scilly Museum ST MARY'S   38

J

J M Barrie's Birthplace KIRRIEMUIR   299
Jaguar Daimler Heritage Centre
    COVENTRY   246
James Joyce Centre DUBLIN   390
James Joyce Tower DUN LAOGHAIRE   391
Jane Austen Centre BATH   199
Jane Austen's House CHAWTON   99
Jarlshof Prehistoric Site SUMBURGH   345
Jedburgh Abbey JEDBURGH   335
Jedburgh Castle Jail & Museum
    JEDBURGH   335
Jenner Museum BERKELEY   85
Jennings Brewery Tour and Shop
    COCKERMOUTH   43
Jersey Lavender Farm ST BRELADE   288
Jersey Museum ST HELIER   288
Jewish Museum LONDON N3   141
Jewish Museum LONDON NW1   142
Jewry Wall Museum & Site LEICESTER   132
Jodrell Bank Visitor Centre & Arboretum
    JODRELL BANK VISITOR CENTRE &
    ARBORETUM   27

John Dony Field Centre LUTON   9
John F Kennedy Arboretum NEW ROSS   397
John Knox House EDINBURGH   303
John Wesley's Chapel (The New Room)
    BRISTOL   15
Johnstown Castle Gardens WEXFORD   397
Jordan's Castle ARDGLASS   376
Jorvik YORK   274
Judge's Lodging PRESTEIGNE   367

K

Kailzie Gardens PEEBLES   336
Keats House LONDON NW3   143
Kedleston Hall KEDLESTON HALL   55
Keighley & Worth Valley Railway & Museum
    HAWORTH   281
Keith Harding's World of Mechanical Music
    NORTHLEACH   90
Kelburn Castle and Country Centre
    LARGS   329
Kelham Island Museum SHEFFIELD   278
Kellie Castle & Gardens
    KELLIE CASTLE & GARDENS   320
Kelso Abbey KELSO   335
Kelvedon Hatch Secret Nuclear Bunker
    BRENTWOOD   81
Kempt Tower Visitor Centre ST OUEN   289
Kendal Museum KENDAL   46
Kenilworth Castle KENILWORTH   239
Kensington Palace State Apartments & Royal
    Ceremonial Dress Collection
    LONDON W8   154
Kent & East Sussex Railway TENTERDEN   124
Kent Battle of Britain Museum
    HAWKINGE   120
Kents Cavern TORQUAY   68
Kentwell Hall LONG MELFORD   214
Kenwood House LONDON NW3   143
Kerry The Kingdom Museum TRALEE   393
Keswick Museum & Gallery KESWICK   46
Kew Bridge Steam Museum BRENTFORD   158
Kew Gardens (Royal Botanic Gardens)
    KEW   159
Kew Palace KEW   159
Kidwelly Castle KIDWELLY   349
Kidwelly Industrial Museum KIDWELLY   349
Kiftsgate Court Garden MICKLETON   89
Kildrummy Castle Gardens KILDRUMMY   296
Kildrummy Castle KILDRUMMY   296
Kilkenny Castle KILKENNY   394
Killarney Transport Museum KILLARNEY   393
Killerton House & Garden EXETER   62
Killerton House & Garden
    KILLERTON HOUSE & GARDEN   63
Killevy Churches CAMLOUGH   375
Killhope The North of England Lead Mining
    Museum COWSHILL   78
Killiecrankie Visitor Centre
    KILLIECRANKIE   331
Kilmainham Gaol DUBLIN   390
Kilmartin House Museum KILMARTIN   301
Kilnasaggart Inscribed Stone
    JONESBOROUGH   375
King Arthur's Labyrinth MACHYNLLETH   367
King House Interpretive Galleries & Museum
    BOYLE   396
King John's Castle LIMERICK   395
King John's Hunting Lodge AXBRIDGE   198
King's Head AYLESBURY   17
King's Lynn Arts Centre KING'S LYNN   170
King's Royal Hussars Regimental Museum
    WINCHESTER   108
Kingston Lacy House, Garden & Park
    WIMBORNE   75
Kinneil Museum & Roman Fortlet
    BO'NESS   318
Kinross House Gardens KINROSS   331
Kirby Hall DEENE   176
Kirkcaldy Museum & Art Gallery
    KIRKCALDY   320
Kirkham Priory KIRKHAM   268

Kirkstall Abbey LEEDS   282
Kirriemuir Gateway to Glens Museum
    KIRRIEMUIR   299
Knappogue Castle & Walled Garden
    QUIN   385
Knaresborough Castle & Museum
    KNARESBOROUGH   268
Knebworth House, Gardens & Country Park
    KNEBWORTH   112
Knightshayes Court
    KNIGHTSHAYES COURT   64
Knole SEVENOAKS   123
Knoll Gardens & Nursery WIMBORNE   75
Knowsley Safari Park PRESCOT   164

L

La Hougue Bie GROUVILLE   287
Lace Centre NOTTINGHAM   184
Lace Market Centre NOTTINGHAM   184
Lackham Country Park LACOCK   254
Lacock Abbey, Fox Talbot Museum & Village
    LACOCK   254
Lady Lever Art Gallery PORT SUNLIGHT   164
Laidhay Croft Museum DUNBEATH   323
Lake District Visitor Centre at Brockhole
    WINDERMERE   49
Lakeland Sheep & Wool Centre
    COCKERMOUTH   43
Lamb House RYE   226
Lamphey Bishop's Palace LAMPHEY   365
Lancaster Maritime Museum LANCASTER   127
Landmark Forest Theme Park
    CARRBRIDGE   322
Lanercost Priory BRAMPTON   42
Lanhydrock LANHYDROCK   34
Larmer Tree Gardens TOLLARD ROYAL   257
Laugharne Castle LAUGHARNE   350
Launceston Castle LAUNCESTON   34
Launceston Steam Railway LAUNCESTON   34
Lauriston Castle EDINBURGH   303
Lavenham Guildhall LAVENHAM   214
Layer Marney Tower LAYER MARNEY   82
Le Moulin de Quetivel ST PETER   289
Lee Valley Park Farms WALTHAM ABBEY   84
Leeds Castle MAIDSTONE   122
Leeds City Art Gallery LEEDS   282
Leeds Industrial Museum at Armley Mills
    LEEDS   282
Legananny Dolmen DROMARA   377
Legoland Windsor WINDSOR   13
Leicestershire Museum & Art Gallery
    LEICESTER   132
Leighton Buzzard Railway
    LEIGHTON BUZZARD   8
Leighton Hall LEIGHTON HALL   128
Leighton House Museum & Art Gallery
    LONDON W14   155
Leiston Abbey LEISTON   214
Leith Hall & Garden RHYNIE   297
Leonardslee Lakes & Gardens
    LOWER BEEDING   231
Leslie Hill Open Farm BALLYMONEY   373
Levens Hall LEVENS   46
Lewes Castle & Barbican House Museum
    LEWES   225
Lichfield Cathedral LICHFIELD   208
Lichfield Heritage Centre LICHFIELD   208
Life Science Centre
    NEWCASTLE UPON TYNE   235
Lightwater Valley Theme Park
    NORTH STAINLEY   270
Lilleshall Abbey LILLESHALL   196
Lilliput Antique Doll & Toy Museum
    BRADING   250
Lincoln Castle LINCOLN   136
Lindisfarne Castle (LINDISFARNE)   180
Lindisfarne Priory (LINDISFARNE)   181
Lindsey Chapel LINDSEY   214
Linley Sambourne House LONDON W8   154
Linlithgow Palace LINLITHGOW   341
Linton Zoological Gardens LINTON   22

Lismore Castle Gardens LISMORE 397
Little Moreton Hall CONGLETON 26
Liverpool Cathedral LIVERPOOL 162
Liverpool Football Club Visitors Centre Tour
   LIVERPOOL 162
Liverpool Museum LIVERPOOL 162
Liverpool University Botanic Gardens (Ness
   Gardens) NESTON 29
Living Coasts TORQUAY 69
Living Legend ST PETER 289
Living Rainforest HAMPSTEAD NORREYS 11
Llanberis Lake Railway LLANBERIS 358
Llancaiach Fawr Manor CAERPHILLY 347
Llandaff Cathedral CARDIFF 348
Llanerchaeron ABERAERON 351
Llangollen Railway LLANGOLLEN 355
Llansteffan Castle LLANSTEFFAN 351
Llanthony Priory LLANTHONY 362
Llawhaden Castle LLAWHADEN 365
Llechwedd Slate Caverns
   BLAENAU FFESTINIOG 357
Lloyd George Museum & Highgate Victorian
   Cottage LLANYSTUMDWY 359
Llyn Brenig Visitor Centre
   CERRIGYDRUDION 352
Loch Garten Osprey Centre
   BOAT OF GARTEN 322
Loch Leven Castle KINROSS 331
Lochcarron of Scotland Visitor Centre
   GALASHIELS 395
Locomotion: The National Railway Museum at
   Shildon SHILDON 79
Lodge Park & Sherborne Estate
   ALDSWORTH 85
Logan Botanic Garden PORT LOGAN 313
London Aquarium LONDON SE1 145
London Canal Museum LONDON N1 141
London Dungeon LONDON SE1 145
London Wetland Centre LONDON SW13 153
London Zoo LONDON NW1 142
Long Shop Museum LEISTON 214
Longdown Dairy Farm ASHURST 97
Longleat LONGLEAT 254
Longthorpe Tower PETERBOROUGH 23
Look & Sea! Visitor Centre
   LITTLEHAMPTON 231
Look Out Discovery Centre BRACKNELL 11
Lord's Tour & M.C.C. Museum
   LONDON NW8 143
Loseley Park GUILDFORD 219
Lost Gardens of Heligan PENTEWAN 36
Lotherton Hall LOTHERTON HALL 283
Loudoun Castle Theme Park GALSTON 316
Lough Gur Stone Age Centre HOLYCROSS 395
Lough Neagh Discovery Centre OXFORD
   ISLAND 376
Loughinisland Churches DOWNPATRICK 377
Low Parks Museum HAMILTON 339
Lowry SALFORD 95
Ludgershall Castle and Cross
   LUDGERSHALL 254
Ludlow Castle LUDLOW 196
Lullingstone Castle EYNSFORD 119
Lullingstone Roman Villa EYNSFORD 119
Lulworth Castle & Park WEST LULWORTH 75
Lunt Roman Fort COVENTRY 246
Lyddington Bede House LYDDINGTON 193
Lydford Castle and Saxon Town LYDFORD 64
Lydford Gorge LYDFORD 64
Lydiard Park LYDIARD PARK 255
Lyme Park DISLEY 26
Lytes Cary Manor KINGSDON 202
Lyveden New Bield LYVEDEN NEW BIELD 176

M

Macclesfield Silk Museum MACCLESFIELD 28
Macduff Marine Aquarium MACDUFF 296
MacLellan's Castle KIRKCUDBRIGHT 313
Madame Tussaud's & The London Planetarium
   LONDON NW1 142

Maes Howe Chambered Cairn
   FINSTOWN 344
Maghera Church MAGHERA 381
Maghera Church NEWCASTLE 378
Magna Science Adventure Centre
   ROTHERHAM 278
Maiden Castle DORCHESTER 73
Maidstone Museum & Bentlif Art Gallery
   MAIDSTONE 122
Maister House KINGSTON UPON HULL 263
Malahide Castle MALAHIDE 392
Malham National Park Centre MALHAM 268
Mall Galleries LONDON SW1 150
Malleny Garden BALERNO 302
Malton Museum MALTON 269
Manchester Art Gallery MANCHESTER 93
Manchester Museum MANCHESTER 93
Manchester United Museum & Tour Centre
   MANCHESTER 94
Manderston DUNS 334
Mannington Gardens & Countryside
   SAXTHORPE 172
Manor House Gallery & Museum ILKLEY 281
Manor House Museum
   BURY ST EDMUNDS 212
Manor House Wildlife & Leisure Park
   ST FLORENCE 366
Manx Museum DOUGLAS 291
Mapledurham House MAPLEDURHAM 189
Mapledurham Watermill MAPLEDURHAM 189
Mapperton BEAMINSTER 70
Mar's Wark STIRLING 340
Marble Arch Caves ENNISKILLEN 380
Marble Hill House TWICKENHAM 160
Maritime Heritage Centre BRISTOL 16
Maritime Museum & Occupation Tapestry
   Gallery ST HELIER 288
Maritime Museum
   KINGSTON UPON HULL 263
Maritime Museum LOWESTOFT 215
Marsh's Library DUBLIN 390
Marwell Zoological Park MARWELL 101
Marwood Hill Gardens BARNSTAPLE 57
Mary Arden's House and the Shakespeare
   Countryside Museum WILMCOTE 242
McLean Museum & Art Gallery
   GREENOCK 326
McLellan Galleries GLASGOW 308
Mechanical Music & Doll Collection
   CHICHESTER 229
Medieval Hall (Secrets of Salisbury)
   SALISBURY 255
Meffan Art Gallery & Museum FORFAR 298
Melbourne Hall & Gardens MELBOURNE 55
Melford Hall LONG MELFORD 214
Mellerstain House GORDON 334
Melrose Abbey & Abbey Museum
   MELROSE 336
Merchant Adventurers' Hall YORK 275
Merchant's House Museum PLYMOUTH 66
Merrivale Model Village
   GREAT YARMOUTH 168
Merseyside Maritime Museum
   LIVERPOOL 163
Metropolitan Cathedral of Christ the King
   LIVERPOOL 163
Michelham Priory HAILSHAM 224
Middle Temple Hall LONDON EC4 141
Middleham Castle MIDDLEHAM 269
Middleton Hall MIDDLETON 239
Middleton Railway LEEDS 282
Middleton Top Engine House
   MIDDLETON BY WIRKSWORTH 56
Middleton, The National Botanic Garden of
   Wales LLANARTHNE 350
Midland Railway Butterley RIPLEY 56
Milestones - Hampshire's Living History
   Museum BASINGSTOKE 98
Military Museum BODMIN 31
Military Museum of Devon & Dorset
   DORCHESTER 73

Milky Way Adventure Park CLOVELLY 59
Mill Trail Visitor Centre ALVA 310
Millennium Galleries SHEFFIELD 278
Millennium Stadium Tours CARDIFF 348
Millgate Museum NEWARK-ON-TRENT 183
Mills Observatory DUNDEE 316
Milton's Cottage CHALFONT ST GILES 18
Minster Lovell Hall & Dovecot
   MINSTER LOVELL 190
Minterne Gardens MINTERNE MAGNA 73
Mirehouse KESWICK 46
Mistley Towers MISTLEY 82
Moat Park Heritage Centre BIGGAR 338
Model Village BOURTON-ON-THE-WATER 85
Mole Hall Wildlife Park NEWPORT 82
Mompesson House SALISBURY 255
Monaghan County Museum MONAGHAN 396
Monea Castle ENNISKILLEN 380
Moniack Castle (Highland Winery)
   KIRKHILL 324
Monk Bretton Priory BARNSLEY 277
Monkey Sanctuary Trust LOOE 34
Monkey World WOOL 76
Mont Orgueil Castle GOREY 287
Montacute House MONTACUTE 202
Montgomery Castle MONTGOMERY 367
Montrose Museum & Art Gallery
   MONTROSE 299
Monument LONDON EC3 140
Moors Centre DANBY 266
Moors Valley Country Park RINGWOOD 105
Morden Hall Park MORDEN 160
Moreton Corbet Castle
   MORETON CORBET 196
Morpeth Chantry Bagpipe Museum
   MORPETH 181
Morton Manor BRADING 250
Morwellham Quay MORWELLHAM 64
Moseley Old Hall WOLVERHAMPTON 248
Motherwell Heritage Centre
   MOTHERWELL 330
Mottisfont Abbey Garden MOTTISFONT 102
Mottistone Manor Garden MOTTISTONE 251
Mouldsworth Motor Museum
   MOULDSWORTH 28
Mound of Down DOWNPATRICK 377
Mount Edgcumbe House & Country Park
   TORPOINT 38
Mount Grace Priory OSMOTHERLEY 270
Mount Sandel COLERAINE 381
Mount Stewart House, Garden & Temple of
   the Winds NEWTOWNARDS 378
Mountfitchet Castle & Norman Village
   STANSTED 83
Mountjoy Castle STEWARTSTOWN 383
Mousa Broch MOUSA ISLAND 345
Moyry Castle NEWRY 376
Moyse's Hall Museum
   BURY ST EDMUNDS 212
Much Wenlock Priory MUCH WENLOCK 196
Muchelney Abbey MUCHELNEY 203
Muckleburgh Collection WEYBOURNE 174
Muckross House, Gardens & Traditional Farms
   KILLARNEY 393
Mugdock Country Park MILNGAVIE 340
Mull & West Highland Narrow Gauge Railway
   CRAIGNURE 343
Museum & Art Gallery DUDLEY 247
Museum & Art Gallery LETCHWORTH 112
Museum in Docklands LONDON E14 139
Museum of Antiquities
   NEWCASTLE UPON TYNE 235
Museum of Archaeology SOUTHAMPTON 106
Museum of Argyll & Sutherland Highlanders
   STIRLING 340
Museum of Army Flying MIDDLE WALLOP 101
Museum of Bath at Work BATH 200
Museum of Canterbury CANTERBURY 117
Museum of Childhood BEAUMARIS 360
Museum of Childhood EDINBURGH 303
Museum of Costume BATH 200

Index

Museum of Dartmoor Life OKEHAMPTON 65
Museum of Domestic Design & Architecture BARNET 157
Museum of East Anglian Life STOWMARKET 215
Museum of Edinburgh EDINBURGH 304
Museum of English Rural Life READING 12
Museum of Flight EAST FORTUNE 317
Museum of Garden History LONDON SE1 146
Museum of Hartlepool HARTLEPOOL 79
Museum of Kent Life MAIDSTONE 122
Museum of Lakeland Life KENDAL 46
Museum of Lincolnshire Life LINCOLN 136
Museum of London LONDON EC2 140
Museum of Nottingham Life NOTTINGHAM 184
Museum of Oxford OXFORD 190
Museum of Rugby & Twickenham Stadium Tours TWICKENHAM 160
Museum of Science and Industry in Manchester MANCHESTER 94
Museum of Scotland EDINBURGH 304
Museum of Scottish Country Life EAST KILBRIDE 338
Museum of Scottish Lead Mining WANLOCKHEAD 314
Museum of St Albans ST ALBANS 113
Museum of the Cumbraes MILLPORT 342
Museum of the History of Science OXFORD 190
Museum of the Jewellery Quarter BIRMINGHAM 244
Museum of The Manchester Regiment ASHTON-UNDER-LYNE 92
Museum of The Order of St John LONDON EC1 139
Museum of Transport GLASGOW 309
Museum of Transport MANCHESTER 94
Museum of Welsh Life ST FAGANS 348
Museum of Worcester Porcelain WORCESTER 261
Musical Museum BRENTFORD 158
Mussenden Temple Bishop's Gate and Black Glen DOWNHILL 381
Myreton Motor Museum ABERLADY 316

N

National Archives KEW 159
National Army Museum LONDON SW3 152
National Birds of Prey Centre NEWENT 89
National Botanic Gardens DUBLIN 390
National Coal Mining Museum For England MIDDLESTOWN 283
National Coracle Centre CENARTH 351
National Fishing Heritage Centre GRIMSBY 135
National Football Museum PRESTON 128
National Gallery LONDON WC2 156
National Gallery of Ireland DUBLIN 390
National Gallery of Scotland EDINBURGH 304
National Garden Exhibitions Centre KILQUADE 398
National Glass Centre SUNDERLAND 235
National Horseracing Museum and Tours NEWMARKET 215
National Library of Ireland DUBLIN 391
National Library of Wales ABERYSTWYTH 351
National Marine Aquarium PLYMOUTH 67
National Maritime Museum Cornwall FALMOUTH 32
National Maritime Museum LONDON SE10 148
National Motorcycle Museum SOLIHULL 247
National Museum & Gallery Cardiff CARDIFF 348
National Museum of Photography, Film & Television BRADFORD 280
National Park Centre AYSGARTH 265
National Park Centre GRASSINGTON 267
National Photographic Archive DUBLIN 391

National Portrait Gallery LONDON WC2 156
National Railway Museum YORK 275
National Seal Sanctuary GWEEK 33
National Space Centre LEICESTER 132
National Wallace Monument STIRLING 340
National War Museum of Scotland EDINBURGH 304
National Waterways Museum GLOUCESTER 88
National Wetland Centre Wales LLANELLI 350
National Wildflower Centre LIVERPOOL 163
National Woollen Museum DRE-FACH FELINDRE 349
Natural History Museum & Butterfly House PORTSMOUTH 104
Natural History Museum DUBLIN 391
Natural History Museum LONDON SW7 152
Nature in Art GLOUCESTER 88
Nautical Museum CASTLETOWN 290
Navan Centre & Fort ARMAGH 375
Neath Abbey NEATH 363
Needles Old Battery ALUM BAY 249
Needles Park ALUM BAY 249
Neidpath Castle PEEBLES 336
Nelson Monument EDINBURGH 304
Nelson Museum & Local History Centre MONMOUTH 362
Nene Valley Railway WANSFORD 23
Nent Valley ALSTON 41
Nether Alderley Mill NETHER ALDERLEY 29
Netley Abbey NETLEY 102
New Abbey Corn Mill NEW ABBEY 313
New Art Gallery Walsall WALSALL 247
New Forest Museum & Visitor Centre LYNDHURST 101
New Lanark Visitor Centre NEW LANARK 339
New Place / Nash's House STRATFORD-UPON-AVON 240
New Pleasurewood Hills LOWESTOFT 215
Newark Air Museum NEWARK-ON-TRENT 183
Newark Castle PORT GLASGOW 326
Newarke Houses LEICESTER 132
Newbridge House and Traditional Farm DONABATE 388
Newby Hall & Gardens NEWBY HALL & GARDENS 270
Newcastle BRIDGEND 347
Newman House DUBLIN 391
Newquay Zoo NEWQUAY 35
Newstead Abbey NEWSTEAD 183
No 1 Royal Crescent BATH 200
Noltland Castle WESTRAY 344
Nora Barnacle House Museum GALWAY 392
Norfolk & Suffolk Aviation Museum FLIXTON 213
Norfolk Lavender HEACHAM 169
Norfolk Shire Horse Centre WEST RUNTON 174
Norham Castle NORHAM 181
Normanby Hall Country Park SCUNTHORPE 136
North Ayrshire Museum SALTCOATS 329
North Leigh Roman Villa NORTH LEIGH 190
North Norfolk Railway SHERINGHAM 172
North Somerset Museum WESTON-SUPER-MARE 205
North Yorkshire Moors Railway PICKERING 271
Northampton Museum & Art Gallery NORTHAMPTON 176
Norton Conyers Hall RIPON 272
Norton Priory Museum & Gardens RUNCORN 30
Norwich Castle Museum NORWICH 171
Norwich Cathedral NORWICH 171
Nostell Priory NOSTELL PRIORY 284
Nottingham Castle NOTTINGHAM 184
Nottingham Industrial Museum NOTTINGHAM 184
Number Twenty Nine DUBLIN 391

Nunney Castle NUNNEY 203
Nunnington Hall NUNNINGTON 270
Nunwell House & Gardens BRADING 250
Nymans Garden HANDCROSS 230

O

Oakham Castle OAKHAM 193
Oakwell Hall OAKWELL HALL 284
Oakwood Park NARBERTH 365
Observatory Science Centre HERSTMONCEUX 225
Oceanarium BOURNEMOUTH 71
OceanLab FISHGUARD 364
Odda's Chapel DEERHURST 87
Official Loch Ness Exhibition Centre, Loch Ness 2000 DRUMNADROCHIT 322
Ogmore Castle OGMORE 370
Okehampton Castle OKEHAMPTON 65
Old Beaupre Castle ST HILARY 370
Old Bridge House Museum DUMFRIES 312
Old Bushmills Distillery BUSHMILLS 373
Old Grammar School CASTLETOWN 291
Old House HEREFORD 110
Old House of Keys CASTLETOWN 291
Old Midleton Distillery MIDLETON 387
Old Oswestry Hill Fort OSWESTRY 196
Old Rectory EPWORTH 135
Old Royal Naval College LONDON SE10 148
Old Sarum SALISBURY 256
Old Town Hall Museum of Local History HASTINGS 224
Old Town Hall NEWTOWN 251
Old Town Jail STIRLING 341
Old Wardour Castle TISBURY 257
Olderfleet Castle LARNE 374
Oliver Cromwell's House ELY 22
Orchardton Tower PALNACKIE 313
Orford Castle ORFORD 215
Oriental Museum DURHAM 78
Orkney Maritime & Natural History Museum STROMNESS 344
Orkney Museum KIRKWALL 344
Orleans House Gallery TWICKENHAM 160
Ormesby Hall ORMESBY 270
Osborne House OSBORNE HOUSE 251
Osterley Park and House OSTERLEY 160
Otter Trust BUNGAY 212
Otter Trust's North Pennines Reserve BOWES 78
Otterton Mill Centre OTTERTON 65
Outwood Windmill OUTWOOD 219
Overbecks Museum & Garden SALCOMBE 67
Owlpen Manor OWLPEN 90
Oxburgh Hall OXBOROUGH 172
Oxford Story OXFORD 190
Oxford University Museum of Natural History OXFORD 190
Oxfordshire Museum WOODSTOCK 192
Oxwich Castle OXWICH 369

P

Packwood House PACKWOOD HOUSE 239
Paignton & Dartmouth Steam Railway PAIGNTON 66
Paignton Zoo Environmental Park PAIGNTON 66
Painshill Park PAINSHILL PARK 219
Painswick Rococo Garden PAINSWICK 90
Paisley Museum & Art Galleries PAISLEY 333
Palace of Holyroodhouse EDINBURGH 304
Palace Stables Heritage Centre ARMAGH 375
Pallant House Gallery CHICHESTER 229
Paradise Mill & Silk Industry Museum MACCLESFIELD 28
Paradise Park & Gardens NEWHAVEN 226
Parcevall Hall Gardens PARCEVALL HALL GARDENS 271
Parham House & Gardens PULBOROUGH 232
Parliament House EDINBURGH 304
Pashley Manor Gardens TICEHURST 227

Patrick Kavanagh Rural & Literary Resource
   Centre INNISKEEN 396
Pattersons Spade Mill TEMPLEPATRICK 374
Paultons Park OWER 103
Paxton House BERWICK-UPON-TWEED 179
Paycocke's COGGESHALL 81
Peak Cavern CASTLETON 51
Peak District Mining Museum
   MATLOCK BATH 55
Peckover House & Garden WISBECH 24
Pecorama Pleasure Gardens BEER 57
Peel Castle PEEL 291
Pembroke Castle PEMBROKE 365
Penarth Fawr PENARTH FAWR 359
Pencarrow BODMIN 31
Pendennis Castle FALMOUTH 32
Pendon Museum LONG WITTENHAM 189
Penrhyn Castle BANGOR 356
Penshurst Place & Gardens PENSHURST 122
Pensthorpe Waterfowl Park & Nature Reserve
   FAKENHAM 168
Pentre Ifan Burial Chamber NEWPORT 365
Pen-Y-Bryn Farm Park CORWEN 354
People's Palace and Winter Gardens
   GLASGOW 309
People's Story EDINBURGH 305
Perth Museum & Art Gallery PERTH 332
Peterborough Cathedral PETERBOROUGH 23
Peto Garden at Iford Manor
   BRADFORD-ON-AVON 253
Petrie Museum of Egyptian Archaeology
   LONDON WC1 155
Pettitts Animal Adventure Park REEDHAM 172
Petworth House & Park PETWORTH 231
Pevensey Castle PEVENSEY 226
Peveril Castle CASTLETON 51
Phoenix Park Visitor Centre DUBLIN 391
Pickering Castle PICKERING 271
Pickford's House Museum of Georgian Life &
   Costume DERBY 54
Pictavia Visitor Centre BRECHIN 298
Piece Hall HALIFAX 280
Pitmedden Garden PITMEDDEN 297
Pitt Rivers Museum OXFORD 191
Pittencrieff House Museum
   DUNFERMLINE 320
Plantasia SWANSEA 369
Plas Mawr CONWY 353
Plas Newydd LLANGOLLEN 355
Plas Newydd PLAS NEWYDD 361
Plas-yn-Rhiw PLAS-YN-RHIW 359
Pleasure Island Family Theme Park
   CLEETHORPES 135
Pleasureland SOUTHPORT 165
Pluscarden Abbey ELGIN 328
Plymouth Dome PLYMOUTH 67
Poldark Mine and Heritage Complex
   WENDRON 40
Polesden Lacey GREAT BOOKHAM 218
Pollock's Toy Museum LONDON W1 153
Pollok House GLASGOW 309
Poole's Cavern (Buxton Country Park)
   BUXTON 50
Port Lympne Wild Animal Park,Mansion &
   Garden LYMPNE 121
Portchester Castle PORTCHESTER 103
Portland Basin Museum
   ASHTON-UNDER-LYNE 93
Portland Castle PORTLAND 73
Portland Museum PORTLAND 73
Portmeirion PORTMEIRION 360
Portsmouth Historic Dockyard
   PORTSMOUTH 104
Portumna Castle & Gardens PORTUMNA 393
Potteries Museum & Art Gallery
   STOKE-ON-TRENT 210
Powderham Castle POWDERHAM 67
Powell-Cotton Museum, Quex House &
   Gardens BIRCHINGTON 115
Powerscourt Gardens Exhibition
   ENNISKERRY 398

Powis Castle WELSHPOOL 368
Prebendal Manor House NASSINGTON 176
Prescot Museum PRESCOT 164
Preston Manor BRIGHTON 222
Preston Mill & Phantassie Doocot
   EAST LINTON 317
Prestongrange Museum PRESTONPANS 318
Prideaux Place PADSTOW 36
Priest's House Museum and Garden
   WIMBORNE 75
Prinknash Abbey and Pottery CRANHAM 86
Prinknash Bird & Deer Park CRANHAM 87
Prior Park Landscape Garden BATH 200
Priorwood Garden & Dried Flower Shop
   MELROSE 336
Priory Visitor Centre COVENTRY 246
Provand's Lordship GLASGOW 309
Provost Skene's House ABERDEEN 294
Prudhoe Castle PRUDHOE 181

Q

Quarry Bank Mill & Styal Estate STYAL 30
Quay House Visitor Centre EXETER 62
Quebec House WESTERHAM 125
Queen Charlotte's Cottage KEW 160
Queen's Gallery LONDON SW1 150
Queen's Own Highlanders Regimental
   Museum Collection FORT GEORGE 323
Queen's View Visitor Centre
   QUEEN'S VIEW 332
Queens House LONDON SE10 148
Queensferry Museum
   SOUTH QUEENSFERRY 307
Queentown Story COBH 386
Quince Honey Farm SOUTH MOLTON 67

R

Raby Castle STAINDROP 80
Raglan Castle RAGLAN 362
Ragley Hall ALCESTER 237
Railworld PETERBOROUGH 23
Ramsey Abbey Gatehouse RAMSEY 23
Ramsgate Maritime Museum RAMSGATE 123
Raptor Foundation WOODHURST 24
Ravenglass & Eskdale Railway
   RAVENGLASS 47
Real Mary King's Close EDINBURGH 305
Record Office for Leicestershire & Rutland
   LEICESTER 133
Reculver Towers & Roman Fort RECULVER 123
Red Dragon Heritage Centre BEDDGELERT 356
Red House BEXLEYHEATH 157
Red House Glass Cone WORDSLEY 248
Red House GOMERSAL 280
Red House Museum & Gardens
   CHRISTCHURCH 71
Reigate Priory Museum REIGATE 219
Restormel Castle RESTORMEL 37
Revolution House OLD WHITTINGTON 56
Rheged - The Village in the Hill PENRITH 47
Rhondda Heritage Park TREHAFOD 368
RHS Garden Harlow Carr HARROGATE 267
RHS Garden Hyde Hall CHELMSFORD 81
RHS Garden Rosemoor
   GREAT TORRINGTON 62
RHS Garden Wisley WISLEY 220
Rhuddlan Castle RHUDDLAN 355
Richborough Castle RICHBOROUGH 123
Richmond Castle RICHMOND 271
Rievaulx Abbey RIEVAULX 272
Rievaulx Terrace & Temples RIEVAULX 272
Ripley Castle RIPLEY 272
River & Rowing Museum
   HENLEY-ON-THAMES 189
RNLI Zetland Museum REDCAR 271
Roald Dahl Museum & Story Centre
   GREAT MISSENDEN 18
Rob Roy and Trossachs Visitor Centre
   CALLANDER 340
Robert Burns Centre DUMFRIES 312

Robert Burns House DUMFRIES 312
Robert Smail's Printing Works
   INNERLEITHEN 335
Robin Hill Country Park ARRETON 249
Roche Abbey MALTBY 278
Rochester Castle ROCHESTER 123
Rockbourne Roman Villa ROCKBOURNE 105
Rockingham Castle ROCKINGHAM 176
Roman Army Museum GREENHEAD 180
Roman Baths & Pump Room BATH 200
Roman Legionary Museum CAERLEON 364
Roman Painted House DOVER 118
Roman Theatre of Verulamium
   ST ALBANS 113
Romney, Hythe & Dymchurch Railway
   HYTHE 120
Roots of Norfolk GRESSENHALL 169
Rothesay Castle ROTHESAY 342
Rough Castle FALKIRK 318
Rough Fort LIMAVADY 381
Roundstone Music, Crafts & Fashion
   ROUNDSTONE 393
Rousham House ROUSHAM 191
Rousse Tower VALE 286
Row 111 Houses/Old Merchant's House and
   Greyfriars Cloisters
   GREAT YARMOUTH 168
Rowallane Garden SAINTFIELD 379
Royal Academy Of Arts LONDON W1 153
Royal Air Force Museum COSFORD 195
Royal Air Force Museum LONDON NW9 144
Royal Albert Memorial Museum EXETER 62
Royal Armouries Fort Nelson FAREHAM 99
Royal Armouries Museum LEEDS 282
Royal Botanic Garden Edinburgh
   EDINBURGH 305
Royal Citadel PLYMOUTH 67
Royal Cornwall Museum TRURO 39
Royal Crown Derby Visitor Centre DERBY 54
Royal Doulton Visitor Centre
   STOKE-ON-TRENT 210
Royal Engineers Museum GILLINGHAM 119
Royal Gunpowder Mills WALTHAM ABBEY 84
Royal Hampshire Regiment Museum &
   Memorial Garden WINCHESTER 108
Royal Hospital Chelsea LONDON SW3 152
Royal Marines Museum PORTSMOUTH 104
Royal Mews LONDON SW1 150
Royal Museum & Art Gallery with Buffs
   Museum CANTERBURY 117
Royal Museum EDINBURGH 305
Royal Navy Submarine Museum & HMS
   Alliance GOSPORT 100
Royal Norfolk Regimental Museum
   NORWICH 172
Royal Observatory Greenwich
   LONDON SE10 148
Royal Pavilion BRIGHTON 223
Royal Pump Room Museum HARROGATE 267
Royal Regiment of Wales Museum
   BRECON 367
Royal Shakespeare Company Collection
   STRATFORD-UPON-AVON 240
Royal Signals Museum
   BLANDFORD FORUM 71
Royal Tara China Visitor Centre GALWAY 392
Royal Yacht Britannia EDINBURGH 305
RSBP Nature Reserve South Stack Cliffs
   HOLYHEAD 361
RSPB Lochwinnoch Nature Reserve
   LOCHWINNOCH 333
RSPB Nature Reserve BEMPTON 262
RSPB Nature Reserve EGLWYSFACH 351
RSPB Nature Reserve FAIRBURN 267
RSPB Nature Reserve
   LLANDUDNO JUNCTION 353
RSPB Nature Reserve LYDD 121
RSPB Nature Reserve Minsmere
   WESTLETON 216
RSPB Nature Reserve Radipole Lake
   WEYMOUTH 75

Index

RSPB Nature Reserve SANDY 9
RSPB Nature Reserve SILVERDALE 129
RSPB Nature Reserve TITCHWELL 174
RSPB Nature Reserve Vane Farm
KINROSS 331
RSPB Pulborough Brooks Nature Reserve
PULBOROUGH 232
RSPB Sandwell Valley Nature Reserve
BIRMINGHAM 244
Rufford Abbey and Country Park
OLLERTON 185
Rufford Old Hall RUFFORD 129
Rug Chapel CORWEN 354
Rum Story WHITEHAVEN 48
Runnymede OLD WINDSOR 12
Rural Life Centre TILFORD 220
Rushen Abbey BALLASALLA 290
Ruskin Museum CONISTON 44
Ruthven Barracks KINGUSSIE 324
Ruthwell Cross RUTHWELL 314
Rutland County Museum OAKHAM 193
Rycote Chapel RYCOTE 191
Rydal Mount and Gardens RYDAL 47
Rye Castle Museum RYE 226
Ryton Organic Gardens
RYTON-ON-DUNSMORE 240

S

Saddleworth Museum & Art Gallery
UPPERMILL 96
Saffron Walden Museum
SAFFRON WALDEN 83
St Albans Cathedral ST ALBANS 113
St Andrews Aquarium ST ANDREWS 321
St Augustine's Abbey CANTERBURY 117
St Catherine's Castle FOWEY 32
St Cybi's Well LLANGYBI 359
St Davids Bishop's Palace ST DAVID'S 365
St Davids Cathedral ST DAVID'S 365
St Edmund Hall OXFORD 191
St George's Chapel WINDSOR 13
St Leonard's Tower WEST MALLING 125
St Mary's Guildhall COVENTRY 246
St Mawes Castle ST MAWES 38
St Michael's Mount MARAZION 35
St Mungo Museum of Religious Life & Art
GLASGOW 309
St Olave's Priory ST OLAVES 172
St Patrick Centre DOWNPATRICK 377
Saint Patrick's Trian Visitor Complex
ARMAGH 375
St Paul's Cathedral LONDON EC4 141
St Williams College YORK 275
Salford Museum & Art Gallery SALFORD 95
Salisbury & South Wiltshire Museum
SALISBURY 256
Salisbury Cathedral SALISBURY 256
Sally Lunn's Refreshment House & Museum
BATH 201
Salt Museum NORTHWICH 30
Saltburn Smugglers Heritage Centre
SALTBURN-BY-THE-SEA 272
Saltram PLYMPTON 67
Samarés Manor ST CLEMENT 288
Samlesbury Hall SAMLESBURY 129
Sammy Miller Motorcycle Museum
NEW MILTON 102
Samuel Johnson Birthplace Museum
LICHFIELD 209
Sandham Memorial Chapel BURGHCLERE 99
Sandringham House, Grounds, Museum &
Country SANDRINGHAM 172
Sanquhar Tolbooth Museum SANQUHAR 314
Sarehole Mill BIRMINGHAM 244
Satrosphere ("Hands-On" Science &
Technology Centre) ABERDEEN 294
Sausmarez Manor ST MARTIN 286
Savill Garden (Windsor Great Park)
WINDSOR 13
Savings Banks Museum RUTHWELL 314

Saxtead Green Post Mill
SAXTEAD GREEN 215
Scalloway Castle SCALLOWAY 345
Scapa Flow Visitor Centre & Museum
KIRKWALL 344
Scarborough Castle SCARBOROUGH 273
Science Museum LONDON SW7 152
Scolton Visitor Centre SCOLTON 366
Scone Palace SCONE 332
Scotch Whisky Heritage Centre
EDINBURGH 306
Scotney Castle Garden LAMBERHURST 121
Scott Polar Research Institute Museum
CAMBRIDGE 21
Scott's Grotto WARE 114
Scottish & Southern Energy Visitor Centre,
Dam & Fish Pass PITLOCHRY 332
Scottish Deer Centre CUPAR 319
Scottish Fisheries Museum ANSTRUTHER 319
Scottish Football Museum GLASGOW 309
Scottish Maritime Museum IRVINE 329
Scottish Mining Museum
NEWTONGRANGE 326
Scottish National Gallery of Modern Art
EDINBURGH 306
Scottish National Portrait Gallery
EDINBURGH 306
Scottish Sea Life Sanctuary BARCALDINE 300
Scottish Seabird Centre NORTH BERWICK 317
Scrabo Tower NEWTOWNARDS 378
Sea Life & Marine Sanctuary
SCARBOROUGH 273
Sea Life Centre BRIGHTON 223
Sea Life Park & Marine Sanctuary
WEYMOUTH 75
Segedunum Roman Fort, Baths & Museum
WALLSEND 236
Segontium Roman Museum CAERNARFON 357
Selly Manor Museum BIRMINGHAM 244
Serpentine Gallery LONDON W2 154
Severn Valley Railway BEWDLEY 259
Severn Valley Railway KIDDERMINSTER 259
Sewerby Hall & Gardens SEWERBY 264
Sezincote MORETON-IN-MARSH 89
Shaftesbury Abbey Museum & Garden
SHAFTESBURY 74
Shakespeare's Birthplace
STRATFORD-UPON-AVON 241
Shakespeare's Globe Exhibition and Theatre
Tour LONDON SE1 146
Shambellie House Museum of Costume
NEW ABBEY 313
Shambles NEWENT 90
Shanklin Chine SHANKLIN 252
Shap Abbey SHAP 47
Shaw's Corner AYOT ST LAWRENCE 111
Sheelin Irish Lace Museum ENNISKILLEN 380
Sheffield Park Garden SHEFFIELD PARK 226
Sherborne Castle SHERBORNE 74
Sherborne Museum SHERBORNE 74
Sherborne Old Castle SHERBORNE 74
Sherwood Forest Country Park & Visitor Centre
EDWINSTOWE 182
Shetland Museum LERWICK 345
Shibden Hall HALIFAX 281
Shire Hall Gallery STAFFORD 209
Shire Hall LANCASTER 127
Shoe Museum STREET 204
Shrewsbury Castle and Shropshire Regimental
Museum SHREWSBURY 197
Shropshire Hills Discovery Centre
CRAVEN ARMS 195
Shugborough SHUGBOROUGH 209
Shuttleworth Collection OLD WARDEN 9
Silk Mill Derby's Museum of Industry and
History DERBY 53
Sir Harold Hillier Gardens AMPFIELD 97
Sir John Soane's Museum LONDON WC2 156
Sir Walter Scott's Courtroom SELKIRK 336
Sissinghurst Castle Garden
SISSINGHURST 124

Sizergh Castle & Garden SIZERGH 47
Skara Brae DOUNBY 343
Skegness Natureland Seal Sanctuary
SKEGNESS 137
Skellig Experience VALENTIA ISLAND 394
Skenfrith Castle SKENFRITH 362
Skerries Mills SKERRIES 392
Sketrick Castle KILLINCHY 378
Skipton Castle SKIPTON 273
Smailholm Tower SMAILHOLM 337
Smallest House CONWY 353
Smallhythe Place SMALLHYTHE 124
Smugglers Adventure HASTINGS 224
Snaefell Mountain Railway DOUGLAS 291
Snibston Discovery Park COALVILLE 131
Snowdon Mountain Railway LLANBERIS 358
Snowshill Manor SNOWSHILL 90
Soho House BIRMINGHAM 244
Sound Visitor Centre PORT ST MARY 292
Souter Johnnie's Cottage KIRKOSWALD 337
Souter Lighthouse WHITBURN 236
South Lakes Wild Animal Park
DALTON-IN-FURNESS 44
South London Gallery LONDON SE5 147
South Tynedale Railway ALSTON 41
South Wales Miners Museum
CYNONVILLE 363
Southampton City Art Gallery
SOUTHAMPTON 106
Southampton Maritime Museum
SOUTHAMPTON 107
Southend Museum, Planetarium & Discovery
Centre SOUTHEND-ON-SEA 83
Southend Pier Museum
SOUTHEND-ON-SEA 83
Southsea Castle PORTSMOUTH 104
Southwark Cathedral LONDON SE1 146
Speedwell Cavern CASTLETON 52
Speke Hall SPEKE 165
Spetchley Park Gardens SPETCHLEY 260
Speyside Cooperage Visitor Centre
CRAIGELLACHIE 327
Spinnaker Tower PORTSMOUTH 105
Spinners Garden and Nursery BOLDRE 98
Spitbank Fort PORTSMOUTH 105
Springhill MONEYMORE 381
Squerryes Court Manor House & Gardens
WESTERHAM 125
SS Great Britain BRISTOL 16
Staffordshire Regiment Museum
WHITTINGTON 211
Stained Glass Museum ELY 22
Stamford Museum STAMFORD 138
Standen EAST GRINSTEAD 230
Stanford Hall SWINFORD 134
Stansted Park ROWLAND'S CASTLE 105
Stapehill Abbey WIMBORNE 76
Stapeley Water Gardens NANTWICH 29
Staunton Country Park HAVANT 100
STEAM - Museum of the Great Western
Railway SWINDON 257
Steam Yacht Gondola CONISTON 44
Stewartry Museum KIRKCUDBRIGHT 313
Stirling Castle STIRLING 341
Stirling Smith Art Gallery & Museum
STIRLING 341
Stockwood Craft Museum & Gardens
LUTON 9
Stokesay Castle STOKESAY 197
Stoke-Sub-Hamdon Priory
STOKE-SUB-HAMDON 203
Stone House Cottage Gardens STONE 261
Stonehenge STONEHENGE 256
Stoneleigh Abbey KENILWORTH 239
Stones of Stenness Circle and Henge
FINSTOWN 344
Stonor House & Park STONOR 191
Storybook Glen MARYCULTER 296
Stourhead Garden & House STOURHEAD 256
Stourton House Flower Garden
STOURTON 256

Stowe House STOWE 19
Stowe Landscape Gardens STOWE 19
Strangford Castle STRANGFORD 379
Strata Florida Abbey STRATA FLORIDA 352
Stratford Butterfly Farm
    STRATFORD-UPON-AVON 241
Strathisla Distillery KEITH 328
Strathnaver Museum BETTYHILL 321
Strathspey Steam Railway AVIEMORE 321
Streetlife - Hull Museum of Transport
    KINGSTON UPON HULL 264
Strokestown Park House Garden & Famine
    Museum STROKESTOWN 396
Struell Wells DOWNPATRICK 377
Stump Cross Caverns PATELEY BRIDGE 271
Sudbury Hall SUDBURY 56
Sudeley Castle & Gardens WINCHCOMBE 91
Sudley House LIVERPOOL 163
Sueno's Stone FORRES 328
Suffolk Wildlife Park
    SUFFOLK WILDLIFE PARK 216
Sulgrave Manor SULGRAVE 177
Summerlee Heritage Trust COATBRIDGE 330
Sunderland Museum & Winter Gardens
    SUNDERLAND 235
Suntrap Garden GOGAR 306
Sutton Hoo WOODBRIDGE 216
Sutton House LONDON E9 139
Sutton Park SUTTON-ON-THE-FOREST 273
Swanage Railway SWANAGE 74
Swansea Museum SWANSEA 369
Sweetheart Abbey NEW ABBEY 313
Sygun Copper Mine BEDDGELERT 356
Syon House ISLEWORTH 159
Syon Park ISLEWORTH 159

T

Tabley House KNUTSFORD 27
Talbot Botanic Gardens MALAHIDE 392
Tales of Robin Hood NOTTINGHAM 185
Tall Ship at Glasgow Harbour GLASGOW 310
Talyllyn Railway TYWYN 360
Tamar Otter Sanctuary LAUNCESTON 34
Tamworth Castle TAMWORTH 211
Tanfield Railway TANFIELD 80
Tangmere Military Aviation Museum Trust
    TANGMERE 233
Tank Museum BOVINGTON CAMP 71
Tantallon Castle NORTH BERWICK 317
Tate Britain LONDON SW1 151
Tate Liverpool LIVERPOOL 163
Tate Modern LONDON SE1 146
Tate St Ives ST IVES 37
Tattershall Castle TATTERSHALL 138
Tatton Park KNUTSFORD 28
Techniquest CARDIFF 348
Teddy Bear Museum
    STRATFORD-UPON-AVON 242
Temple Mine MATLOCK BATH 55
Temple Newsam House & Park LEEDS 283
Temple of Mithras (Hadrian's Wall)
    CARRAWBROUGH 179
Templetown Mausoleum TEMPLEPATRICK 374
Tenby Museum & Art Gallery TENBY 366
Tenement House GLASGOW 310
Thackray Museum LEEDS 283
Thames Barrier Information & Learning Centre
    LONDON SE18 149
Theakston Working Brewery & Visitor Centre
    MASHAM 269
Theatre Museum LONDON WC2 156
Thetford Priory THETFORD 173
Thetford Warren Lodge THETFORD 173
Thinktank at Millennium Point
    BIRMINGHAM 244
Thirlestane Castle LAUDER 335
Thoor Ballylee GORT 392
Thornton Abbey and Gatehouse
    THORNTON 138
Thorpe Park CHERTSEY 217
Threave Castle CASTLE DOUGLAS 311

Threave Garden & Estate
    CASTLE DOUGLAS 311
Thrigby Hall Wildlife Gardens FILBY 168
Thursford Collection THURSFORD GREEN 174
Tilbury Fort TILBURY 84
Time and Tide Museum of Great Yarmouth Life
    GREAT YARMOUTH 169
Timespan HELMSDALE 324
Tintagel Castle TINTAGEL 38
Tintern Abbey TINTERN PARVA 362
Tintinhull Garden TINTINHULL 204
Titchfield Abbey TITCHFIELD 107
Tiverton Castle TIVERTON 68
Tiverton Museum of Mid Devon Life
    TIVERTON 68
Tolbooth Art Centre KIRKCUDBRIGHT 313
Tolbooth Museum STONEHAVEN 297
Tolhouse Museum GREAT YARMOUTH 169
Tolpuddle Martyrs Museum TOLPUDDLE 74
Tolquhon Castle PITMEDDEN 297
Tolson Memorial Museum HUDDERSFIELD 281
Tomintoul Museum TOMINTOUL 329
Torosay Castle & Gardens CRAIGNURE 343
Torridon Countryside Centre TORRIDON 325
Totnes Castle TOTNES 69
Totnes Museum TOTNES 69
Tower Bridge Exhibition LONDON SE1 146
Tower Museum LONDONDERRY 381
Tower of London LONDON EC3 140
Town House Museum KING'S LYNN 170
Town Walls CARRICKFERGUS 374
Townend TROUTBECK 48
Trades Hall GLASGOW 310
Traquair House TRAQUAIR 337
Treak Cliff Cavern CASTLETON 52
Treasurer's House YORK 275
Trebah Garden MAWNAN SMITH 35
Tredegar House & Park NEWPORT 364
Trefriw Woollen Mills TREFRIW 354
Trelissick Garden TRELISSICK GARDEN 39
Trengwainton Garden PENZANCE 36
Trerice TRERICE 39
Tretower Court & Castle TRETOWER 368
Trevarno Estate Garden & Museum of
    Gardening HELSTON 34
Trewithen Gardens PROBUS 36
Triangular Lodge RUSHTON 177
Tropical World LEEDS 283
Tropiquaria Animal and Adventure Park
    WASHFORD 204
Trotters World of Animals
    BASSENTHWAITE 41
Truggery HERSTMONCEUX 225
Tuckers Maltings NEWTON ABBOT 65
Tudor Merchant's House TENBY 366
Tullaghoge Fort COOKSTOWN 382
Tullie House Museum & Art Gallery
    CARLISLE 43
Tully Castle DERRYGONNELLY 379
Tunbridge Wells Museum and Art Gallery
    TUNBRIDGE WELLS (ROYAL) 125
Turton Tower TURTON BOTTOMS 130
Tutankhamun Exhibition DORCHESTER 73
Twycross Zoo Park TWYCROSS 134
Ty Mawr Wybrnant PENMACHNO 353
Tynemouth Priory and Castle
    TYNEMOUTH 236
Tyrone Crystal Visitor Centre
    DUNGANNON 382
Tyrwhitt Drake Museum of Carriages
    MAIDSTONE 122

U

U S Grant Ancestral Homestead & Visitor
    Centre BALLYGAWLEY 382
Uffington Castle, White Horse & Dragon Hill
    UFFINGTON 191
Uley Long Barrow (Hetty Pegler's Tump)
    ULEY 91
Ulster American Folk Park OMAGH 383

Ulster Folk and Transport Museum
    HOLYWOOD 377
Ulster History Park OMAGH 383
Ulster Museum BELFAST 372
University Museum of Archaeology &
    Anthropology CAMBRIDGE 21
University of Glasgow Visitor Centre
    GLASGOW 310
University of Leicester Harold Martin Botanic
    Garden LEICESTER 133
University of Oxford Botanic Garden
    OXFORD 191
Upnor Castle UPNOR 125
Uppark SOUTH HARTING 232
Upton House UPTON HOUSE 242
Urbis MANCHESTER 94
Urquhart Castle DRUMNADROCHIT 323
Usher Gallery LINCOLN 136

V

Valle Crucis Abbey LLANGOLLEN 355
Vennel Gallery IRVINE 329
Ventnor Botanic Garden VENTNOR 252
Verdant Works DUNDEE 316
Verulamium Museum ST ALBANS 113
Victoria and Albert Museum
    LONDON SW7 152
Vikingar! LARGS 329
Village Cross TYNAN 376
Vina Cooke Museum of Dolls & Bygone
    Childhood NEWARK-ON-TRENT 183
Vindolanda (Chesterholm) BARDON MILL 178
Vinopolis, City of Wine LONDON SE1 146
Vyne SHERBORNE ST JOHN 106

W

W5 at Odyssey BELFAST 372
Waddesdon Manor WADDESDON 19
Wakefield Art Gallery WAKEFIELD 284
Wakehurst Place & Millennium Seed Bank
    ARDINGLY 228
Walker Art Gallery LIVERPOOL 163
Wall Roman Site WALL 211
Wallace Collection LONDON W1 154
Wallington House Walled Garden & Grounds
    CAMBO 179
Walmer Castle DEAL 118
Walsall Leather Museum WALSALL 247
Walsingham Abbey Grounds & Shirehall
    Museum LITTLE WALSINGHAM 171
Walter Rothschild Zoological Museum
    TRING 114
Waltham Abbey Gatehouse, Bridge & Entrance
    to Cloisters WALTHAM ABBEY 84
Wardown Park Museum LUTON 9
Warkworth Castle & Hermitage
    WARKWORTH 181
Warwick Castle WARWICK 242
Warwickshire Yeomanry Museum
    WARWICK 242
Washington Old Hall WASHINGTON 236
Water Wheels BALLYSHANNON 387
Watercress Line NEW ALRESFORD 102
Waterford Crystal Visitor Centre
    WATERFORD 397
Waterfront Museum POOLE 73
Watermouth Castle & Family Theme Park
    ILFRACOMBE 63
Waterperry Gardens WATERPERRY 192
Waterslack Farm Shop, Cafe & Garden Centre
    SILVERDALE 129
Waterways Museum GOOLE 263
Wayside Folk Museum ZENNOR 40
WDCS Wildlife Centre SPEY BAY 329
Weald & Downland Open Air Museum
    SINGLETON 232
Weaver's Cottage KILBARCHAN 333
Webb Ellis Rugby Football Museum
    RUGBY 239

Wedgwood Visitor Centre STOKE-ON-TRENT 210
Weeting Castle WEETING 174
Weir Gardens SWAINSHILL 110
Wellbrook Beetling Mill COOKSTOWN 382
Wellington Country Park RISELEY 12
Wells & Walsingham Light Railway WELLS-NEXT-THE-SEA 174
Welsh Hawking Centre BARRY 370
Welsh Highland Railway CAERNARFON 357
Welsh Mountain Zoo COLWYN BAY 352
Welsh Slate Museum LLANBERIS 359
Welshpool & Llanfair Light Railway LLANFAIR CAEREINION 367
Weobley Castle LLANRHIDIAN 368
Wernher Collection at Ranger's House LONDON SE10 148
Wesley's Chapel, House & Museum Of Methodism LONDON EC1 140
West Berkshire Museum NEWBURY 12
West Cork Model Village Railway CLONAKILTY 386
West Dean Gardens WEST DEAN 233
West Green House Gardens HARTLEY WINTNEY 100
West Highland Museum FORT WILLIAM 323
West Midland Safari & Leisure Park BEWDLEY 259
West Stow Anglo Saxon Village WEST STOW 216
West Wycombe Park WEST WYCOMBE 20
Westbury Court Garden WESTBURY ON SEVERN 91
Westminster Abbey LONDON SW1 151
Westminster Cathedral LONDON SW1 151
Westminster Hall LONDON SW1 151
Weston Park WESTON PARK 211
Westonbirt The National Arboretum WESTONBIRT 91
Westwood Manor WESTWOOD 258
Wetheriggs Country Pottery PENRITH 47
Wetlands Waterfowl Reserve & Exotic Bird Park SUTTON-CUM-LOUND 186
Wexford Wildfowl Reserve WEXFORD 398
Whalley Abbey WHALLEY 130
Whipsnade Wild Animal Park WHIPSNADE 9
Whitaker Park & Rossendale Museum ROSSENDALE 128

Whitby Abbey WHITBY 273
Whitchurch Silk Mill WHITCHURCH 107
White Castle WHITE CASTLE 363
White Island Church CASTLE ARCHDALE BAY 379
White Post Farm Centre FARNSFIELD 183
Whiteladies Priory BOSCOBEL 195
Whithorn Priory WHITHORN 315
Whithorn-Cradle of Christianity WHITHORN 315
Whitworth Art Gallery MANCHESTER 95
Wick Heritage Museum WICK 326
Wigan Pier WIGAN 96
Wightwick Manor WOLVERHAMPTON 248
Wilberforce House KINGSTON UPON HULL 264
Wildlife Park at Cricket St Thomas CRICKET ST THOMAS 201
William Morris Gallery LONDON E17 139
Willow & Wetlands Visitor Centre STOKE ST GREGORY 203
Wilton House WILTON (NEAR SALISBURY) 258
Wimbledon Lawn Tennis Museum LONDON SW19 153
Wimpole Hall WIMPOLE 23
Wimpole Home Farm WIMPOLE 24
Winchester Cathedral WINCHESTER 108
Winchester City Mill WINCHESTER 108
Winchester College WINCHESTER 108
Windermere Steamboat Centre WINDERMERE 49
Windsor Castle WINDSOR 13
Winkworth Arboretum HASCOMBE 219
Winsford Walled Garden HALWILL JUNCTION 63
Winston Churchill's Britain at War Experience LONDON SE1 147
Wirksworth Heritage Centre WIRKSWORTH 56
Wish Tower Puppet Museum EASTBOURNE 223
Witley Court GREAT WITLEY 259
Woburn Abbey WOBURN 10
Woburn Safari Park WOBURN 10
Wolds Way Lavender WINTRINGHAM 274
Wollaton Hall & Park NOTTINGHAM 185
Wolterton Park ERPINGHAM 167

Woodbridge Tide Mill WOODBRIDGE 216
Woodhenge WOODHENGE 258
Woodlands Leisure Park DARTMOUTH 61
Wookey Hole Caves & Papermill WOOKEY HOLE 205
Woolsthorpe Manor WOOLSTHORPE 138
Worcester Cathedral WORCESTER 261
Worcestershire County Museum KIDDERMINSTER 260
Wordsworth House COCKERMOUTH 43
Workhouse SOUTHWELL 185
World in Miniature GOONHAVERN 33
World of Country Life EXMOUTH 62
World of Glass ST HELENS 164
Wrest Park Gardens SILSOE 9
Writers' Museum EDINBURGH 306
Wroxeter Roman City WROXETER 197
WWT Arundel ARUNDEL 229
WWT Caerlaverock CAERLAVEROCK 311
WWT Castle Espie COMBER 376
WWT Martin Mere MARTIN MERE 128
WWT Slimbridge SLIMBRIDGE 90
WWT Washington WASHINGTON 236
WWT Welney WELNEY 174
Wycombe Local History & Chair Museum HIGH WYCOMBE 18

Y
Yalding Organic Gardens YALDING 125
Yarmouth Castle YARMOUTH 252
Yelverton Paperweight Centre YELVERTON 69
Yesterday's World BATTLE 222
York Brewery Co Ltd YORK 275
York Castle Museum YORK 276
York City Art Gallery YORK 276
York Dungeon YORK 276
York Minster YORK 276
Yorkshire Air Museum & Allied Air Forces Memorial ELVINGTON 266
Yorkshire Dales Falconry & Wildlife Conservation Centre LAWKLAND 268
Yorkshire Museum YORK 276
Yorkshire Sculpture Park WEST BRETTON 284

The following photographs are held in the Automobile Association's own photo library (AA World Travel Library) and were taken by these photographers:

Stuart Abrahams 285, 287; Martyn Adelman 111, 262; Adrian Baker 166; Peter Baker 130; Jeff Beazley 5b, 178; 180; Pete Bennett 278; Malc Birkitt 8, 16b, 20, 80, 175, 184; E A Bowness 49; Steve Day 14, 84, 96, 161, 165; Michael Busselle 5t, 221; Chris Coe 3c; Ian Dawson 371; Kenya Doran 194; Derek Forss 10, 134, 177, 217, 227, 228, 248; Mike Haywood 194; Anthony Hopkins 50; Bob Johnson 293t; Caroline Jones 198, 346t, 346b; Max Jourdan 1; Cameron Lees 76; Tom Mackie 7, 40; S&O Mathews 160, 186, 265; Simon McBride 384b; Jenny McMillan 94; Eric Meacher 3t, 254; Hugh Palmer 109, 237; Ken Paterson 293b; Clive Sawyer 212; Michael Short 258; Tony Souter 16t; Rick Strange 114; Rupert Tenison 31; Martyn Trelawny 126, 138; Wyn Voysey 290; Jonathan Welsh 206, 243; Stephen Whitehorne 3b; Linda Whitwam 24; Harry Williams 70, 193; Peter Wilson 277, 279; Tim Woodcock 234; Peter Zoeller 384t.

Free Days Out

These attractions do not charge a fee for entry, although they may charge fo use of audio equipment, for example. We have not included attractions that expect a donation.

ENGLAND

BEDFORDSHIRE
Bedford Museum BEDFORD	8
Cecil Higgins Art Gallery BEDFORD	8
Houghton House AMPTHILL	8
John Dony Field Centre LUTON	9
Stockwood Park Museum LUTON	9
Wardown Park Museum LUTON	9

BERKSHIRE
Museum of English Rural Life READING	12
West Berkshire Museum NEWBURY	12

BRISTOL
Blaise Castle House Museum BRISTOL	14
Bristol Industrial Museum BRISTOL	14
Bristol's City Museum & Art Gallery BRISTOL	15
Bristol's Georgian House BRISTOL	15
Bristol's Red Lodge BRISTOL	15

BUCKINGHAMSHIRE
Wycombe Local History & Chair Museum HIGH WYCOMBE	18

CAMBRIDGESHIRE
Fitzwilliam Museum CAMBRIDGE	21
Ramsey Abbey Gatehouse RAMSEY	23
Scott Polar Research Institute Museum CAMBRIDGE	21
University Museum of Archaeology & Anthropology CAMBRIDGE	21

CHESHIRE
Chester Visitor Centre CHESTER	25

CORNWALL & ISLES OF SCILLY
Carn Euny Ancient Village SANCREED	38
Royal Cornwall Museum TRURO	39
St Catherine's Castle FOWEY	32

CUMBRIA
Brough Castle BROUGH	42
The Dock Museum BARROW-IN-FURNESS	41
The Guildhall Museum CARLISLE	43
Hardknott Castle Roman Fort HARDKNOTT CASTLE ROMAN FORT	45
Shap Abbey SHAP	47
Wetheriggs Country Pottery PENRITH	47

DERBYSHIRE
Derby Museum & Art Gallery DERBY	53
Pickford's House Museum of Georgian Life & Costume DERBY	54
Revolution House OLD WHITTINGTON	56
The Silk Mill, Derby's Museum DERBY	53

DEVON
Bayard's Cove Fort DARTMOUTH	60
Buckfast Abbey BUCKFASTLEIGH	58
City Museum & Art Gallery PLYMOUTH	66
Guildhall EXETER	62
Lydford Castle and Saxon Town LYDFORD	64
Otterton Mill OTTERTON	65
Quay House Visitor Centre EXETER	62
Royal Albert Memorial Museum EXETER	62
Yelverton Paperweight Centre YELVERTON	69

DORSET
Christchurch Castle & Norman House CHRISTCHURCH	71
Maiden Castle DORCHESTER	73
Tolpuddle Martyrs Museum TOLPUDDLE	74
Waterfront Museum POOLE	73

CO DURHAM
Bowes Castle BOWES	77
Egglestone Abbey BARNARD CASTLE	77
Locomotion: The National Railway Museum at SHILDON	79

ESSEX
Hadleigh Castle HADLEIGH	82
Mistley Towers MISTLEY	82
Waltham Abbey Gatehouse, Bridge & Entrance to Cloisters WALTHAM ABBEY	84

GLOUCESTERSHIRE
Gloucester City Museum & Art Gallery GLOUCESTER	87
Gloucester Folk Museum GLOUCESTER	87
Odda's Chapel DEERHURST	87
Uley Long Barrow (Hetty Pegler's Tump) ULEY	91

GREATER MANCHESTER
Astley Cheetham Art Gallery STALYBRIDGE	95
Central Art Gallery ASHTON-UNDER-LYNE	92
Gallery of Costume MANCHESTER	93
Heaton Hall PRESTWICH	95
Imperial War Museum North MANCHESTER	93
Manchester Art Gallery MANCHESTER	93
Manchester Museum MANCHESTER	93
Museum of The Manchester Regiment ASHTON-UNDER-LYNE	92
The Museum of Science and Industry in MANCHESTER	94
Portland Basin Museum ASHTON-UNDER-LYNE	93
Salford Museum & Art Gallery SALFORD	95
Urbis MANCHESTER	94
The Whitworth Art Gallery MANCHESTER	95

HAMPSHIRE
Calleva Museum SILCHESTER	106
City Museum & Records Office PORTSMOUTH	103
Eastney Beam Engine House PORTSMOUTH	104
The King's Royal Hussars Regimental Museum WINCHESTER	108
Museum of Archaeology SOUTHAMPTON	106
Natural History Museum & Butterfly House PORTSMOUTH	104
Netley Abbey NETLEY	102
Royal Armouries Fort Nelson FAREHAM	99
Royal Hampshire Regiment Museum & Memorial WINCHESTER	108
Southampton City Art Gallery SOUTHAMPTON	106
Southampton Maritime Museum SOUTHAMPTON	107

Titchfield Abbey TITCHFIELD	107

HEREFORDSHIRE
Berkhamsted Castle BERKHAMSTED	111
Museum & Art Gallery LETCHWORTH	112
Museum of St Albans ST ALBANS	113
Old House HEREFORD	110
The Walter Rothschild Zoological Museum TRING	114

ISLE OF MAN
Manx Museum DOUGLAS	291
Old Grammar School CASTLETOWN	291
Sound Visitor Centre PORT ST MARY	292

ISLE OF WIGHT
Brighstone Shop and Museum BRIGHSTONE	250

KENT
Eynsford Castle EYNSFORD	119
Guildhall Museum ROCHESTER	123
Maidstone Museum & Bentlif Art Gallery MAIDSTONE	122
Reculver Towers & Roman Fort RECULVER	123
Royal Museum & Art Gallery with Buffs Museum CANTERBURY	117
St Leonard's Tower WEST MALLING	125
Tunbridge Wells Museum and Art Gallery ROYAL TUNBRIDGE WELLS	125
Tyrwhitt Drake Museum of Carriages MAIDSTONE	122

LANCASHIRE
Astley Hall Museum & Art Gallery CHORLEY	127
Harris Museum & Art Gallery PRESTON	128
The National Football Museum PRESTON	128
Waterslack Farm Shop, Cafe & Garden Centre SILVERDALE	129
Whitaker Park & Rossendale Museum ROSSENDALE	128

LEICESTERSHIRE
Abbey Pumping Station LEICESTER	132
Donington-le-Heath Manor House DONINGTON LE HEATH	131
The Record Office for Leicestershire & Rutland LEICESTER	133

LINCOLNSHIRE
Stamford Museum STAMFORD	138
Thornton Abbey and Gatehouse THORNTON	138
Usher Gallery LINCOLN	136

LONDON POSTAL DISTRICTS
Bank of England Museum LONDON EC2	140
Bankside Gallery LONDON SE1	144
British Museum LONDON WC1	155
Freightliners City Farm LONDON N7	142
Geffrye Museum LONDON E2	139
The Guildhall LONDON EC2	140
Hogarth House LONDON W4	154
The Horniman Museum & Gardens LONDON SE23	149
Hunterian Museum LONDON WC2	156
Kenwood House LONDON NW3	143
Middle Temple Hall LONDON EC4	141

Museum of London LONDON EC2 140
National Army Museum
  LONDON SW3 152
National Maritime Museum
  LONDON SE10 148
Petrie Museum of Egyptian Archaeology
  LONDON WC1 155
Royal Air Force Museum
  LONDON NW9 144
Royal Hospital Chelsea
  LONDON SW3 152
Royal Observatory Greenwich
  LONDON SE10 148
Serpentine Gallery LONDON W2 154
South London Gallery LONDON SE5 147
The Wallace Collection LONDON W1 154
Wesley's Chapel, House & Museum
  LONDON EC1 140
Westminster Cathedral LONDON SW1 151

GREATER LONDON
Hall Place BEXLEY 157
Morden Hall Park MORDEN 160
The National Archives KEW 159
Orleans House Gallery TWICKENHAM 160

MERSEYSIDE
Atkinson Art Gallery SOUTHPORT 164
Central Library LIVERPOOL 161
Conservation Centre LIVERPOOL 162
HM Customs & Excise National Museum
  LIVERPOOL 162
Lady Lever Art Gallery
  PORT SUNLIGHT 164
Liverpool Museum LIVERPOOL 162
Merseyside Maritime Museum
  LIVERPOOL 163
Prescot Museum PRESCOT 164
Walker Art Gallery LIVERPOOL 163

NORFOLK
African Violet Centre KING'S LYNN 170
Baconsthorpe Castle
  BACONSTHORPE 166
Burgh Castle BURGH CASTLE 167
Caister Roman Site
  CAISTER-ON-SEA 167
Creake Abbey NORTH CREAKE 171
King's Lynn Arts Centre
  KING'S LYNN 170
RSPB Nature Reserve TITCHWELL 174
St Olave's Priory ST OLAVES 172
Thetford Priory THETFORD 173
Thetford Warren Lodge THETFORD 173
Weeting Castle WEETING 174

NORTHAMPTONSHIRE
Alfred East Gallery KETTERING 176
Northampton Museum & Art Gallery
  NORTHAMPTON 176

NORTHUMBERLAND
Morpeth Chantry Bagpipe Museum
  MORPETH 181
Temple of Mithras (Hadrian's Wall)
  CARRAWBROUGH 179

NOTTINGHAMSHIRE
Green's Windmill NOTTINGHAM 184
The Lace Centre NOTTINGHAM 184
The Lace Market Centre
  NOTTINGHAM 184
Millgate Museum NEWARK-ON-TRENT 183
Rufford Abbey and Country Park
  OLLERTON 185
Sherwood Forest Country Park & Visitor
  Centre EDWINSTOWE 182

OXFORDSHIRE
Banbury Museum BANBURY 187
Deddington Castle DEDDINGTON 188
Minster Lovell Hall & Dovecot
  MINSTER LOVELL 190
Museum of the History of Science
  OXFORD 190
North Leigh Roman Villa
  NORTH LEIGH 190
Oxford University Museum of Natural
  History OXFORD 190
Oxfordshire Museum WOODSTOCK 192
Pitt Rivers Museum OXFORD 191
St Edmund Hall OXFORD 191
Uffington Castle, White Horse & Dragon
  Hill UFFINGTON 191

RUTLAND
Oakham Castle OAKHAM 193
Rutland County Museum OAKHAM 193

SHROPSHIRE
Acton Burnell Castle ACTON BURNELL 194
Lilleshall Abbey LILLESHALL 196
Moreton Corbet Castle
  MORETON CORBET 196
Old Oswestry Hill Fort OSWESTRY 196
The Royal Air Force Museum
  COSFORD 195
Whiteladies Priory BOSCOBEL 195

SOMERSET
Nunney Castle NUNNEY 203
The Shoe Museum STREET 204
Stoke sub Hamdon Priory
  STOKE SUB HAMDON 203

STAFFORDSHIRE
Cheddleton Flint Mill CHEDDLETON 207
Halfpenny Green Vineyards
  HALFPENNY GREEN 208
The Potteries Museum & Art Gallery
  STOKE-ON-TRENT 210
Samuel Johnson Birthplace Museum
  LICHFIELD 209
Shire Hall Gallery STAFFORD 209

SUFFOLK
Christchurch Mansion IPSWICH 213
Ipswich Museum IPSWICH 213
Leiston Abbey LEISTON 214
Lindsey Chapel LINDSEY 214
Norfolk & Suffolk Aviation Museum
  FLIXTON 213

SURREY
Army Medical Services Museum
  ASH VALE 217
Guildford House Gallery GUILDFORD 218

EAST SUSSEX
Booth Museum of Natural History
  BRIGHTON 222
Brighton Museum & Art Gallery
  BRIGHTON 222
Old Town Hall Museum of Local History
  HASTINGS & ST LEONARDS 224
The Truggery HERSTMONCEUX 225

WEST SUSSEX
Bramber Castle BRAMBER 229
Chichester Cathedral CHICHESTER 229
Highdown Gardens HIGHDOWN 231

TYNE & WEAR
The Baltic Centre for Contemporary Art
  GATESHEAD 234

Museum of Antiquities
  NEWCASTLE UPON TYNE 235
Sunderland Museum & Winter Gardens
  SUNDERLAND 235

WARWICKSHIRE
The Webb Ellis Rugby Football Museum
  RUGBY 239

WEST MIDLANDS
Aston Hall BIRMINGHAM 243
Bantock House and Park
  WOLVERHAMPTON 247
Birmingham Museum & Art Gallery
  BIRMINGHAM 244
Blakesley Hall BIRMINGHAM 244
Broadfield House Glass Museum
  KINGSWINFORD 247
Coventry Transport Museum
  COVENTRY 245
Herbert Art Gallery & Museum
  COVENTRY 246
Jaguar Daimler Heritage Centre
  COVENTRY 246
Museum & Art Gallery DUDLEY 247
Museum of the Jewellery Quarter
  BIRMINGHAM 244
The New Art Gallery WALSALL 247
Priory Visitor Centre COVENTRY 246
RSPB Sandwell Valley Nature Reserve
  BIRMINGHAM 244
Sarehole Mill BIRMINGHAM 244
Soho House BIRMINGHAM 244
St Mary's Guildhall COVENTRY 246
Walsall Leather Museum WALSALL 247

WILTSHIRE
Bradford-on-Avon Tithe Barn
  BRADFORD-ON-AVON 253
Ludgershall Castle and Cross
  LUDGERSHALL 254
Woodhenge WOODHENGE 258

WORCESTERSHIRE
City Museum & Art Gallery
  WORCESTER 261

EAST RIDING OF YORKSHIRE
Burton Agnes Manor House
  BURTON AGNES 263
Maister House
  KINGSTON UPON HULL 263
Maritime Museum
  KINGSTON UPON HULL 263
Streetlife - Hull Museum of Transport
  KINGSTON UPON HULL 264
Wilberforce House
  KINGSTON UPON HULL 264

NORTH YORKSHIRE
Easby Abbey EASBY 266
Guildhall YORK 274
Malham National Park Centre
  MALHAM 268
The Moors Centre DANBY 266
National Park Centre AYSGARTH 265
National Park Centre GRASSINGTON 267
National Railway Museum YORK 275
RNLI Zetland Museum REDCAR 271
RSPB Nature Reserve FAIRBURN 267
Wolds Way Lavender WINTRINGHAM 274

SOUTH YORKSHIRE
Doncaster Museum & Art Gallery
  DONCASTER 277
Millennium Galleries SHEFFIELD 278
Monk Bretton Priory BARNSLEY 277

Free Days Out

WEST YORKSHIRE

Bankfield Museum HALIFAX	280
Bolling Hall BRADFORD	279
Bradford Industrial Museum and Horses at Work BRADFORD	279
Cartwright Hall Art Gallery BRADFORD	279
Cliffe Castle Museum & Gallery KEIGHLEY	282
Kirkstall Abbey LEEDS	282
Leeds City Art Gallery LEEDS	282
Manor House Gallery & Museum ILKLEY	281
National Coal Mining Museum For England WAKEFIELD	283
Piece Hall HALIFAX	280
Red House GOMERSAL	280
Royal Armouries Museum LEEDS	282
Tolson Memorial Museum HUDDERSFIELD	281
Wakefield Art Gallery WAKEFIELD	284

CHANNEL ISLANDS

GUERNSEY

Rousse Tower VALE	286

JERSEY

Greve de Lecq Barracks LA GREVE DE LECQ	287
Kempt Tower Visitor Centre ST OUEN	289

SCOTLAND

ABERDEEN CITY

Aberdeen Art Gallery ABERDEEN	294
Aberdeen Maritime Museum ABERDEEN	294
Cruickshank Botanic Garden ABERDEEN	294
Provost Skene's House ABERDEEN	294

ABERDEENSHIRE

Aberdeenshire Farming Museum MINTLAW	296
Arbuthnot Museum PETERHEAD	297
Banchory Museum BANCHORY	295
Banff Museum BANFF	295
Brander Museum HUNTLY	295
Carnegie Museum INVERURIE	296
Deer Abbey OLD DEER	297
Tolbooth Museum STONEHAVEN	297

ANGUS

Arbroath Museum ARBROATH	298
Brechin Town House Museum BRECHIN	298
Kirriemuir Gateway to Glens Museum KIRRIEMUIR	299
The Meffan Art Gallery & Museum FORFAR	298
Montrose Museum & Art Gallery MONTROSE	299

ARGYLL & BUTE

Argyll Forest Park ARROCHAR	300
Carnasserie Castle CARNASSERIE CASTLE	300
Dunadd Fort KILMARTIN	301

CITY OF EDINBURGH

Museum of Childhood EDINBURGH	303
Museum of Edinburgh EDINBURGH	304
Museum of Scotland EDINBURGH	304
The People's Story EDINBURGH	305

Queensferry Museum SOUTH QUEENSFERRY	307
Royal Museum EDINBURGH	305
The Writer's Museum EDINBURGH	306

CITY OF GLASGOW

Burrell Collection GLASGOW	307
Gallery of Modern Art GLASGOW	307
Glasgow Museums Resource Centre GLASGOW	307
Hunterian Art Gallery GLASGOW	308
Hunterian Museum GLASGOW	308
Hutchesons' Hall GLASGOW	308
McLellan Galleries GLASGOW	308
Museum of Transport GLASGOW	309
People's Palace & Winter Gardens GLASGOW	309
Provand's Lordship GLASGOW	309
St Mungo Museum of Religious Life & Art GLASGOW	309

CLACKMANNANSHIRE

Mill Trail Visitor Centre ALVA	310

DUMFRIES & GALLOWAY

Burns Mausoleum DUMFRIES	312
Drumcoltran Tower DRUMCOLTRAN TOWER	312
Orchardton Tower PALNACKIE	313
Ruthwell Cross RUTHWELL	314
Sanquhar Tolbooth Museum SANQUHAR	314
Savings Banks Museum RUTHWELL	314
Shambellie House Museum of Costume NEW ABBEY	313
Stewartry Museum KIRKCUDBRIGHT	313
Tolbooth Art Centre KIRKCUDBRIGHT	313

DUNDEE CITY

Broughty Castle Museum DUNDEE	315

EAST DUNBARTONSHIRE

Antonine Wall: Bearsden Bath-house BEARSDEN	316

EAST LOTHIAN

Hailes Castle EAST LINTON	317
Prestongrange Museum PRESTONPANS	318

FALKIRK

Kinneil Museum & Roman Fortlet BO'NESS	318
Rough Castle FALKIRK	318

FIFE

Burntisland Edwardian Fair Museum BURNTISLAND	319
Kirkcaldy Museum & Art Gallery KIRKCALDY	320
Pittencrieff House Museum DUNFERMLINE	320

HIGHLAND

Castle of Old Wick WICK	325
Clava Cairns CLAVA CAIRNS	322
Groam House Museum ROSEMARKIE	325
Inverlochy Castle FORT WILLIAM	323
Ruthven Barracks KINGUSSIE	324

INVERCLYDE

McLean Museum & Art Gallery GREENOCK	326

MORAY

Baxters Highland Village FOCHABERS	328

Duffus Castle DUFFUS	327
Glen Grant Distillery ROTHES	328
Glenfiddich Distillery DUFFTOWN	327
The Glenlivet Distillery BALLINDALLOCH	327
Pluscarden Abbey ELGIN	328
Sueno's Stone FORRES	328
Tomintoul Museum TOMINTOUL	329
The WDCS Wildlife Centre SPEY BAY	329

NORTH AYRSHIRE

Museum of the Cumbraes MILLPORT	342
North Ayrshire Museum SALTCOATS	329
Vennel Gallery IRVINE	329

NORTH LANARKSHIRE

Motherwell Heritage Centre MOTHERWELL	330

ORKNEY

Click Mill DOUNBY	343
Corrigall Farm & Kirbuster Museum HARRAY	344
Earl's Palace BIRSAY	343
Noltland Castle WESTRAY	344
The Orkney Museum KIRKWALL	344
Scapa Flow Visitor Centre & Museum KIRKWALL	344
Stones of Stenness Circle and Henge FINSTOWN	344

PERTH & KINROSS

Burleigh Castle MILNATHORT	331
Edradour Distillery PITLOCHRY	332
The Ell Shop & Little Houses DUNKELD	331
Killiecrankie Visitor Centre KILLIECRANKIE	331
Perth Museum & Art Gallery PERTH	332
Queen's View Visitor Centre QUEEN'S VIEW	332

RENFREWSHIRE

Coats Observatory PAISLEY	333
Paisley Museum & Art Galleries PAISLEY	333

SCOTTISH BORDERS

Halliwells House Museum SELKIRK	336
Kelso Abbey KELSO	335
Sir Walter Scott's Courtroom SELKIRK	336

SHETLAND

Clickimin LERWICK	344
Fort Charlotte LERWICK	344
Mousa Broch MOUSA ISLAND	345
Scalloway Castle SCALLOWAY	345

SOUTH LANARKSHIRE

Chatelherault Country Park HAMILTON	339
Low Parks Museum HAMILTON	339

STIRLING

Mugdock Country Park MILNGAVIE	340
Mar's Wark STIRLING	340

WESTERN ISLES

Dun Carloway Broch CARLOWAY	343

WALES

BRIDGEND

Coity Castle COITY	347
Newcastle BRIDGEND	347

Free Days Out

CARDIFF

Museum of Welsh Life ST FAGANS   348
National Museum & Gallery Cardiff
  CARDIFF   348

CARMARTHENSHIRE

Carmarthenshire County Museum
  ABERGWILI   349
Dryslwyn Castle DRYSLWYN   349
Kidwelly Industrial Museum
  KIDWELLY   349
Llansteffan Castle LLANSTEFFAN   351
National Woollen Museum
  DRE-FACH FELINDRE   349

CONWY

Gwydyr Uchaf Chapel LLANRWST   353
Llyn Brenig Visitor Centre
  CERRIGYDRUDION   352
Trefriw Woollen Mills Ltd TREFRIW   354

FLINTSHIRE

Basingwerk Abbey HOLYWELL   356
Ewloe Castle EWLOE   355
Flint Castle FLINT   356

GWYNEDD

Castell-y-Bere
  LLANFIHANGEL-Y-PENNANT   359
Cymer Abbey CYMER ABBEY   358
Dolbadarn Castle LLANBERIS   358
Penarth Fawr PENARTH FAWR   359
Segontium Roman Museum
  CAERNARFON   357
St Cybi's Well LLANGYBI   359
Welsh Slate Museum LLANBERIS   359

ISLE OF ANGLESEY

Bryn Celli Ddu Burial Chamber
  BRYNCELLI DDU   360
Din Llugwy Ancient Village
  LLANALLGO   361
RSPB Nature Reserve South Stack Cliffs
  HOLYHEAD   361

MERTHYR TYDFIL

Cyfarthfa Castle Museum & Art Gallery
  MERTHYR TYDFIL   361

MONMOUTHSHIRE

Caerwent Roman Town CAERWENT   361
Grosmont Castle GROSMONT   362
Hen Gwrt LLANTILIO CROSSENNY   362
Llanthony Priory LLANTHONY   362
The Nelson Museum & Local History
  Centre MONMOUTH   362
Skenfrith Castle SKENFRITH   362

NEATH PORT TALBOT

Cefn Coed Colliery Museum
  CRYNANT   363
Gnoll Estate Country Park NEATH   363
Neath Abbey NEATH   363

NEWPORT

Roman Legionary Museum
  CAERLEON   364

PEMBROKESHIRE

Llawhaden Castle LLAWHADEN   365
Pentre Ifan Burial Chamber NEWPORT 365

POWYS

Montgomery Castle MONTGOMERY   367

SWANSEA

Swansea Museum SWANSEA   369

TORFAEN

Big Pit National Mining Museum of Wales
  BLAENAVON   369

VALE OF GLAMORGAN

Ogmore Castle OGMORE   370
Old Beaupre Castle ST HILARY   370

NORTHERN IRELAND

ANTRIM

Antrim Round Tower ANTRIM   372
Ballylumford Dolmen
  BALLYLUMFORD   373
Bonamargy Friary BALLYCASTLE   373
Cranfield Church CHURCHTOWN   374
Duneight Motte and Bailey LISBURN   374
Harryville Motte BALLYMENA   373
Irish Linen Centre & Lisburn Museum
  LISBURN   374
Olderfleet Castle LARNE   374
Templetown Mausoleum
  TEMPLEPATRICK   374
Town Walls CARRICKFERGUS   374

ARMAGH

Armagh County Museum ARMAGH   374
Armagh Friary ARMAGH   375
Killevy Churches CAMLOUGH   375
Kilnasaggart Inscribed Stone
  JONESBOROUGH   375
Moyry Castle NEWRY   376
Village Cross TYNAN   376

BELFAST

Giant's Ring BELFAST   372
Ulster Museum BELFAST   372

DOWN

Audley's Castle STRANGFORD   379
Down County Museum
  DOWNPATRICK   377
Drumena Cashel CASTLEWELLAN   376
Dundrum Castle NEWCASTLE   378
Grey Abbey BALLYWALTER   376
Hillsborough Fort HILLSBOROUGH   377
Jordan's Castle ARDGLASS   376
Legananny Dolmen DROMARA   377
Loughinisland Churches
  DOWNPATRICK   377
Maghera Church NEWCASTLE   378
Mound of Down DOWNPATRICK   377
Scrabo Tower NEWTOWNARDS   378
Sketrick Castle KILLINCHY   378
Strangford Castle STRANGFORD   379
Struell Wells DOWNPATRICK   377

FERMANAGH

Castle Balfour LISNASKEA   380
Monea Castle ENNISKILLEN   380
Tully Castle DERRYGONNELLY   379

LONDONDERRY

Banagher Church DUNGIVEN   381
Dungiven Priory DUNGIVEN   381
Maghera Church MAGHERA   381
Mount Sandel COLERAINE   381
Mussenden Temple Bishop's Gate and
  Black Glen DOWNHILL   381
Rough Fort LIMAVADY   381

TYRONE

Ardboe Cross ARDBOE   382
Beaghmore Stone Circles and Alignments
  BEAGHMORE   382
Benburb Castle BENBURB   382
Castle Caulfield CASTLECAULFIELD   382

Harry Avery's Castle
  NEWTOWNSTEWART   383
Mountjoy Castle STEWARTSTOWN   383
Tullaghoge Fort COOKSTOWN   382

REPUBLIC OF IRELAND

CORK

Fota Arboretum & Gardens
  CARRIGTWOHILL   386

DONEGAL

The Water Wheels BALLYSHANNON   387

DUBLIN

The Chester Beatty Library DUBLIN   389
Howth Castle Rhododendron Gardens
  DUBLIN   390
Hugh Lane Municipal Gallery of Modern
  Art DUBLIN   390
Irish Museum of Modern Art DUBLIN   390
National Botanic Gardens DUBLIN   390
Natural History Museum DUBLIN   391
National Library of Ireland DUBLIN   390
National Photographic Archive
  DUBLIN   391
Skerries Mills SKERRIES   392

GALWAY

Royal Tara China Visitor Centre
  GALWAY   392
Roundstone Music, Crafts & Fashion
  ROUNDSTONE   393

LONGFORD

Corlea Trackway Visitor Centre
  KEENAGH   395

MONAGHAN

Monaghan County Museum
  MONAGHAN   396

WEXFORD

Wexford Wildfowl Reserve WEXFORD   398

Please send this form to:
Lifestyle Guides,
The Automobile Association
15th Floor
Fanum House
Basingstoke RG21 4EA

Readers' Report form

or fax: 01256 491647
or e-mail: lifestyleguides@theAA.com

Please use this form to recommend any visitor attraction you have been to, whether it is in the guide or not currently listed. Feedback from readers helps us to keep our guide accurate and up to date. Please note, however, that if you have a complaint to make during a visit, we strongly recommend that you discuss the matter with the establishment management there and then so that they have a chance to put things right before your visit is spoilt. The AA does not undertake to arbitrate between you and the attraction's management, or to obtain compensation or engage in correspondence.

Date:

Your name (block capitals)

Your address (block capitals)

....

....

....

e-mail address: ....

(Please *only* give us your e-mail address if you wish to hear from us about other products and services from the AA and partners by e-mail)

Comments (please include the name & address of the attraction)

....

....

....

....

....

....

....

....

(please attach a separate sheet if necessary)

PTO

Have you bought this guide before?   **YES**   **NO**

Have you bought any other Days Out guides recently? If yes, which ones?

....

....

Why did you buy this guide? (circle all that apply)

family holiday   short break   school holidays   special occasion

other...

How often do you have a Day Out? (circle one choice)

more than once a month   once a month   once in 2-3 months

once in six months   once a year   less than once a year

Please answer these questions to help us make improvements to the guide:

Which of these factors are most important when choosing a Day Out?

Price   Location   Previous experience   Recommendation   Type of attraction

Other (please state):..

Do you use the location atlas?   **YES**   **NO**

Which elements of the guide do you find the most useful when choosing somewhere to visit?

Description   Photo   Advertisement

Can you suggest any improvements to the guide?

....

....

....

....

....

Readers' Report form

Please send this form to:
Lifestyle Guides,
The Automobile Association
15th Floor
Fanum House
Basingstoke RG21 4EA

or fax: 01256 491647
or e-mail: lifestyleguides@theAA.com

Please use this form to recommend any visitor attraction you have been to, whether it is in the guide or not currently listed. Feedback from readers helps us to keep our guide accurate and up to date. Please note, however, that if you have a complaint to make during a visit, we strongly recommend that you discuss the matter with the establishment management there and then so that they have a chance to put things right before your visit is spoilt. The AA does not undertake to arbitrate between you and the attraction's management, or to obtain compensation or engage in correspondence.

Date:

Your name (block capitals)

Your address (block capitals)

....

....

....

e-mail address: ....

(Please *only* give us your e-mail address if you wish to hear from us about other products and services from the AA and partners by e-mail)

Comments (please include the name & address of the attraction)

....

....

....

....

....

....

....

....

(please attach a separate sheet if necessary)

PTO

Readers' Report Form

Have you bought this guide before?   **YES**   **NO**

Have you bought any other Days Out guides recently? If yes, which ones?

....

....

Why did you buy this guide? (circle all that apply)

family holiday   short break   school holidays   special occasion

other..

How often do you have a Day Out? (circle one choice)

more than once a month   once a month   once in 2-3 months

once in six months   once a year   less than once a year

Please answer these questions to help us make improvements to the guide:

Which of these factors are most important when choosing a Day Out?

Price   Location   Previous experience   Recommendation   Type of attraction

Other (please state):..

Do you use the location atlas?   **YES**   **NO**

Which elements of the guide do you find the most useful when choosing somewhere to visit?

Description   Photo   Advertisement

Can you suggest any improvements to the guide?

....

....

....

....

....

Please send this form to:
Lifestyle Guides,
The Automobile Association
15th Floor
Fanum House
Basingstoke RG21 4EA

Readers' Report form

or fax: 01256 491647
or e-mail: lifestyleguides@theAA.com

Please use this form to recommend any visitor attraction you have been to, whether it is in the guide or not currently listed. Feedback from readers helps us to keep our guide accurate and up to date. Please note, however, that if you have a complaint to make during a visit, we strongly recommend that you discuss the matter with the establishment management there and then so that they have a chance to put things right before your visit is spoilt. The AA does not undertake to arbitrate between you and the attraction's management, or to obtain compensation or engage in correspondence.

Date:

Your name (block capitals)

Your address (block capitals)

....

....

....

e-mail address: ....

(Please *only* give us your e-mail address if you wish to hear from us about other products and services from the AA and partners by e-mail)

Comments (please include the name & address of the attraction)

....

....

....

....

....

....

....

....

(please attach a separate sheet if necessary)

PTO

Readers' Report Form

Have you bought this guide before?   YES   NO

Have you bought any other Days Out guides recently? If yes, which ones?

....

....

Why did you buy this guide? (circle all that apply)

family holiday   short break   school holidays   special occasion

other...

How often do you have a Day Out? (circle one choice)

more than once a month   once a month   once in 2-3 months

once in six months   once a year   less than once a year

Please answer these questions to help us make improvements to the guide:

Which of these factors are most important when choosing a Day Out?

Price   Location   Previous experience   Recommendation   Type of attraction

Other (please state):..

Do you use the location atlas?   YES   NO

Which elements of the guide do you find the most useful when choosing somewhere to visit?

          Description   Photo   Advertisement

Can you suggest any improvements to the guide?

....

....

....

....

Days Out Guide 2006

Please send this form to:
Lifestyle Guides,
The Automobile Association
15th Floor
Fanum House
Basingstoke RG21 4EA

Readers' Report form

or fax: 01256 491647
or e-mail: lifestyleguides@theAA.com

Please use this form to recommend any visitor attraction you have been to, whether it is in the guide or not currently listed. Feedback from readers helps us to keep our guide accurate and up to date. Please note, however, that if you have a complaint to make during a visit, we strongly recommend that you discuss the matter with the establishment management there and then so that they have a chance to put things right before your visit is spoilt. The AA does not undertake to arbitrate between you and the attraction's management, or to obtain compensation or engage in correspondence.

Date:

Your name (block capitals)

Your address (block capitals)

....

....

....

e-mail address: ....

(Please *only* give us your e-mail address if you wish to hear from us about other products and services from the AA and partners by e-mail)

Comments (please include the name & address of the attraction)

....

....

....

....

....

....

....

....

(please attach a separate sheet if necessary)

PTO

Readers' Report Form

Have you bought this guide before?   YES   NO

Have you bought any other Days Out guides recently? If yes, which ones?

....

....

Why did you buy this guide? (circle all that apply)

family holiday   short break   school holidays   special occasion

other...

How often do you have a Day Out? (circle one choice)

more than once a month   once a month   once in 2-3 months

once in six months   once a year   less than once a year

Please answer these questions to help us make improvements to the guide:

Which of these factors are most important when choosing a Day Out?

Price   Location   Previous experience   Recommendation   Type of attraction

Other (please state):...

Do you use the location atlas?   YES   NO

Which elements of the guide do you find the most useful when choosing somewhere to visit?

          Description   Photo   Advertisement

Can you suggest any improvements to the guide?

....

....

....

....

Days Out Guide 2006

Readers'
Report form

Please send this form to:
Lifestyle Guides,
The Automobile Association
15th Floor
Fanum House
Basingstoke RG21 4EA

or fax: 01256 491647
or e-mail: lifestyleguides@theAA.com

Please use this form to recommend any visitor attraction you have been to, whether it is in the guide or not currently listed. Feedback from readers helps us to keep our guide accurate and up to date. Please note, however, that if you have a complaint to make during a visit, we strongly recommend that you discuss the matter with the establishment management there and then so that they have a chance to put things right before your visit is spoilt. The AA does not undertake to arbitrate between you and the attraction's management, or to obtain compensation or engage in correspondence.

Date:

Your name (block capitals)

Your address (block capitals)

....

....

....

e-mail address: ....

(Please *only* give us your e-mail address if you wish to hear from us about other products and services from the AA and partners by e-mail)

Comments (please include the name & address of the attraction)

....

....

....

....

....

....

....

....

(please attach a separate sheet if necessary)

PTO

Readers' Report Form

Have you bought this guide before? YES   NO

Have you bought any other Days Out guides recently? If yes, which ones?

....

....

Why did you buy this guide? (circle all that apply)

family holiday   short break   school holidays   special occasion

other...

How often do you have a Day Out? (circle one choice)

more than once a month   once a month   once in 2-3 months

once in six months   once a year   less than once a year

Please answer these questions to help us make improvements to the guide:

Which of these factors are most important when choosing a Day Out?

Price   Location   Previous experience   Recommendation   Type of attraction

Other (please state):...

Do you use the location atlas?   YES   NO

Which elements of the guide do you find the most useful when choosing somewhere to visit?

Description   Photo   Advertisement

Can you suggest any improvements to the guide?

....

....

....

....

Terms: This voucher is valid at any venue specified as accepting vouchers within the AA 'The Days Out Guide 2006'. This voucher admits one adult or child free when presented at the time of purchase of one fully priced adult ticket. Valid until 31 Oct 2006. Subject to availability at the venue when presented. Photocopies will <u>not</u> be accepted.

 Lifestyle Guides

Terms: This voucher is valid at any venue specified as accepting vouchers within the AA 'The Days Out Guide 2006'. This voucher admits one adult or child free when presented at the time of purchase of one fully priced adult ticket. Valid until 31 Oct 2006. Subject to availability at the venue when presented. Photocopies will <u>not</u> be accepted.

Lifestyle Guides

Terms: This voucher is valid at any venue specified as accepting vouchers within the AA 'The Days Out Guide 2006'. This voucher admits one adult or child free when presented at the time of purchase of one fully priced adult ticket. Valid until 31 Oct 2006. Subject to availability at the venue when presented. Photocopies will <u>not</u> be accepted.

Lifestyle Guides

Terms: This voucher is valid at any venue specified as accepting vouchers within the AA 'The Days Out Guide 2006'. This voucher admits one adult or child free when presented at the time of purchase of one fully priced adult ticket. Valid until 31 Oct 2006. Subject to availability at the venue when presented. Photocopies will <u>not</u> be accepted.

 Lifestyle Guides

Terms: This voucher is valid at any venue specified as accepting vouchers within the AA 'The Days Out Guide 2006'. This voucher admits one adult or child free when presented at the time of purchase of one fully priced adult ticket. Valid until 31 Oct 2006. Subject to availability at the venue when presented. Photocopies will <u>not</u> be accepted.

Lifestyle Guides

Terms: This voucher is valid at any venue specified as accepting vouchers within the AA 'The Days Out Guide 2006'. This voucher admits one adult or child free when presented at the time of purchase of one fully priced adult ticket. Valid until 31 Oct 2006. Subject to availability at the venue when presented. Photocopies will <u>not</u> be accepted.

 Lifestyle Guides

Terms: This voucher is valid at any venue specified as accepting vouchers within the AA 'The Days Out Guide 2006'. This voucher admits one adult or child free when presented at the time of purchase of one fully priced adult ticket. Valid until 31 Oct 2006. Subject to availability at the venue when presented. Photocopies will <u>not</u> be accepted.

Lifestyle Guides

Terms: This voucher is valid at any venue specified as accepting vouchers within the AA 'The Days Out Guide 2006'. This voucher admits one adult or child free when presented at the time of purchase of one fully priced adult ticket. Valid until 31 Oct 2006. Subject to availability at the venue when presented. Photocopies will <u>not</u> be accepted.

Lifestyle Guides

Terms: This voucher is valid at any venue specified as accepting vouchers within the AA 'The Days Out Guide 2006'. This voucher admits one adult or child free when presented at the time of purchase of one fully priced adult ticket. Valid until 31 Oct 2006. Subject to availability at the venue when presented. Photocopies will <u>not</u> be accepted.

Lifestyle Guides

Terms: This voucher is valid at any venue specified as accepting vouchers within the AA 'The Days Out Guide 2006'. This voucher admits one adult or child free when presented at the time of purchase of one fully priced adult ticket. Valid until 31 Oct 2006. Subject to availability at the venue when presented. Photocopies will <u>not</u> be accepted.

 Lifestyle Guides

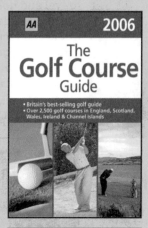